PHILIP'S

STREET ATLAS
Greater
Manchester

D0191375

NOT TO BE TAKEN AWAY

www.philips-maps.co.uk
First published in 1995 by Philip's
a division of Octopus Publishing Group Ltd
www.octopusbooks.co.uk
Endeavour House 189 Shaftesbury Avenue
London WC2H 8JY
An Hachette UK Company
www.hachette.co.uk

Fifth edition 2011
First impression 2011
GMAEA

ISBN 978-1-84907-139-0 (pocket)

© Philip's 2011

 Ordnance Survey®

This product includes mapping data licensed from
Ordnance Survey® with the permission of the
Controller of Her Majesty's Stationery Office.
© Crown copyright 2011. All rights reserved.
Licence number 100011710.

Contents

II	Mobile safety cameras
III	**Key to map symbols**
IV	**Key to map pages**
VI	**Route planning**
VIII	Major administrative and Postcode boundaries
1	**Street maps** at 2⅔ inches to 1 mile
138	**Street maps** of selected areas at 5⅓ inches to 1 mile
172	**Index** of towns, villages, streets, hospitals, industrial estates, railway stations, schools, shopping centres, universities and places of interest

CHEADLE & MARPLE
SIXTH FORM COLLEGE
CHEADLE CAMPUS LIBRARY
CHEADLE HULME SK8 5HA

Digital Data

The exceptionally high-quality mapping found in this atlas is available as digital data in TIFF format,
which is easily convertible to other bitmapped (raster) image formats.

The index is also available in digital form as a standard database table. It contains all the details
found in the printed index together with the National Grid reference for the map square in which each
entry is named.

For further information and to discuss your requirements, please contact
philips@mapsinternational.co.uk

Cheadle & Marple - Cheadle Site

00028946

Mobile safety cameras

For locations of mobile safety camera sites, please check the safety camera partnership websites for the latest 'located' mobile sites on your route prior to every journey.

Some safety camera partnerships post a weekly list of the locations in which they will be operating mobile speed cameras. Others have a general list of those places where mobile cameras will be used.

Please note, however, that local authorities can now place mobile cameras at different locations which may not be listed on the partnership website. Always drive within the speed limit.

Mike Harrington / Alamy

Useful websites

The Greater Manchester Casualty Reduction Partnership
www.drivesafe.org.uk

Cheshire Safer Roads Partnership
www.mysaferroads.org.uk

Derby & Derbyshire Road Safety Partnership
www.slowitdown.co.uk

Lancashire Partnership for Road Safety
www.safe2travel.co.uk

Merseyside Road Safety Partnership
www.no-excuses.org.uk

West Yorkshire Casualty Reduction Partnership
www.safetycameraswestyorkshire.co.uk

Further information
www.dvla.gov.uk

www.thinkroadsafety.gov.uk

www.dft.gov.uk

www.road-safe.org

Key to map symbols

(22)	Motorway with junction number
	Primary route – dual/single carriageway
	A road – dual/single carriageway
	B road – dual/single carriageway
	Minor road – dual/single carriageway
	Other minor road – dual/single carriageway
	Road under construction
	Tunnel, covered road
30 30	Speed cameras – single, multiple
	Rural track, private road or narrow road in urban area
	Gate or obstruction to traffic – may not apply at all times or to all vehicles
	Path, bridleway, byway open to all traffic, restricted byway
	Pedestrianised area
BS22	Postcode boundaries
	County and unitary authority boundaries
	Railway with station
	Tunnel
	Railway under construction
	Metro station
	Private railway station
	Miniature railway
	Tramway, tramway under construction
	Tram stop, tram stop under construction
	Bus, coach station

	Ambulance station
	Coastguard station
	Fire station
	Police station
	Accident and Emergency entrance to hospital
H	Hospital
+	Place of worship
i	Information centre – open all year
	Shopping centre
P	Parking
P&R	Park and Ride
PO	Post Office
	Camping site
	Caravan site
	Golf course
	Picnic site
Church	Non-Roman antiquity
ROMAN FORT	Roman antiquity
Univ	Important buildings, schools, colleges, universities and hospitals
	Built-up area
	Woods
River Medway	Water name
	River, weir
	Stream
	Canal, lock, tunnel
	Water
	Tidal water

112	Adjoining page indicators
58 87	The small numbers around the edges of the maps identify the 1-kilometre National Grid lines

The dark grey border on the inside edge of some pages indicates that the mapping does not continue onto the adjacent page

Enlarged maps only

	Railway or bus station building
	Place of interest
	Parkland

Abbreviations

Acad	Academy	Meml	Memorial
Allot Gdns	Allotments	Mon	Monument
Cemy	Cemetery	Mus	Museum
C Ctr	Civic centre	Obsy	Observatory
CH	Club house	Pal	Royal palace
Coll	College	PH	Public house
Crem	Crematorium	Recn Gd	Recreation ground
Ent	Enterprise		
Ex H	Exhibition hall	Resr	Reservoir
Ind Est	Industrial Estate	Ret Pk	Retail park
IRB Sta	Inshore rescue boat station	Sch	School
		Sh Ctr	Shopping centre
Inst	Institute	TH	Town hall / house
Ct	Law court	Trad Est	Trading estate
L Ctr	Leisure centre	Univ	University
LC	Level crossing	W Twr	Water tower
Liby	Library	Wks	Works
Mkt	Market	YH	Youth hostel

The map scale on the pages numbered in blue is 2⅔ inches to 1 mile
4.2 cm to 1 km • 1:23 810

0	¼ mile	½ mile	¾ mile	1 mile
0	250m	500m	750m	1km

The map scale on the pages numbered in red is 5⅓ inches to 1 mile
8.4 cm to 1 km • 1:11 900

0	220yds	440yds	660yds	½ mile
0	125m	250m	375m	500m

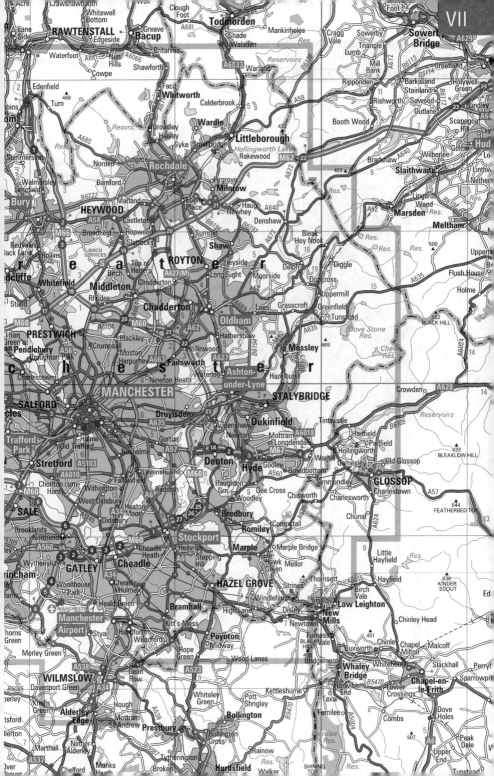

Major administrative and Postcode boundaries

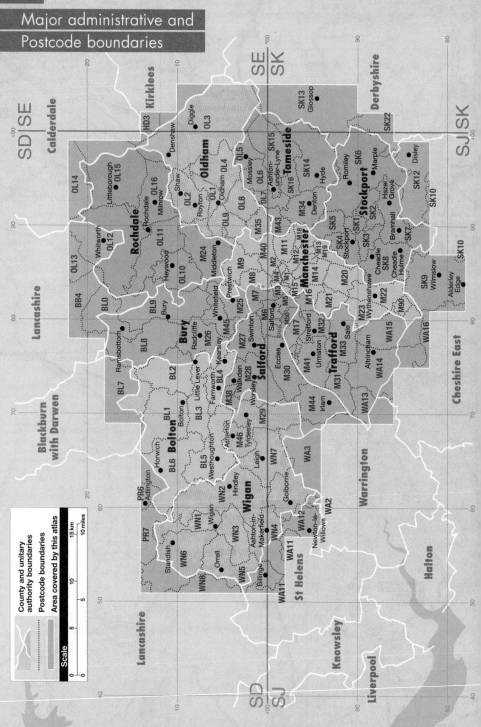

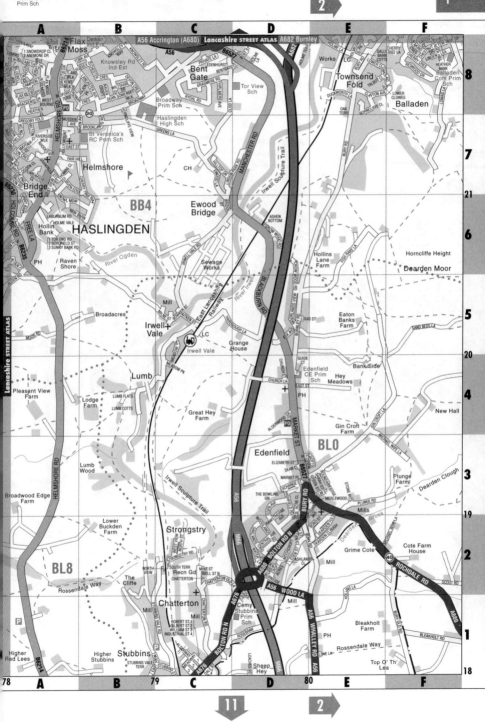

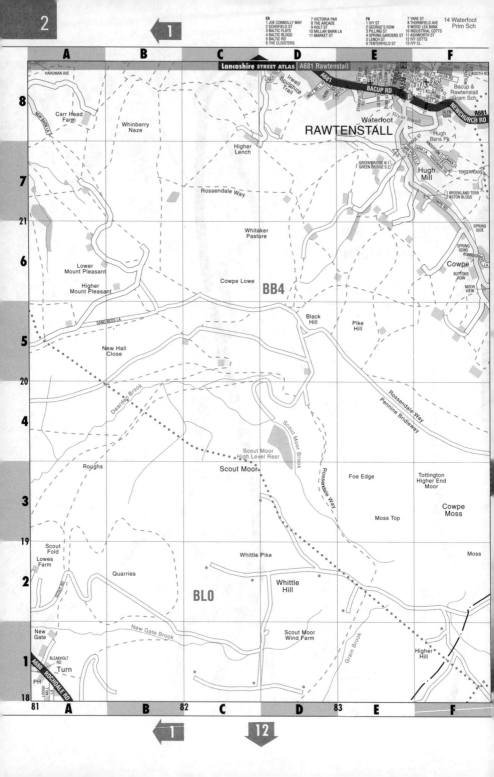

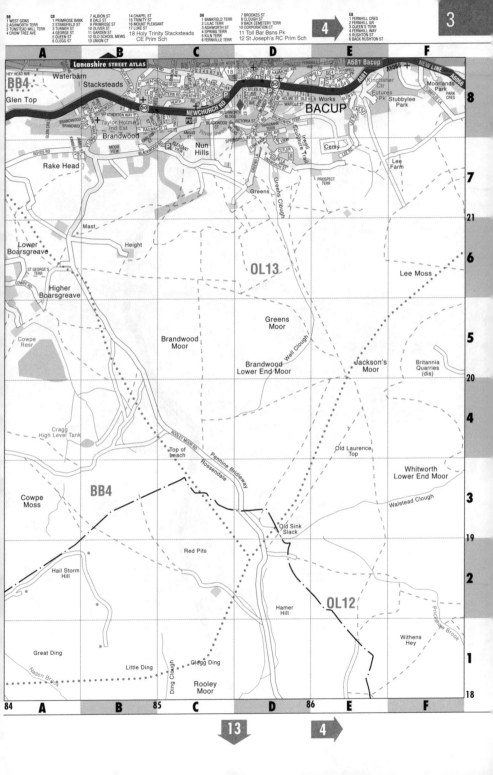

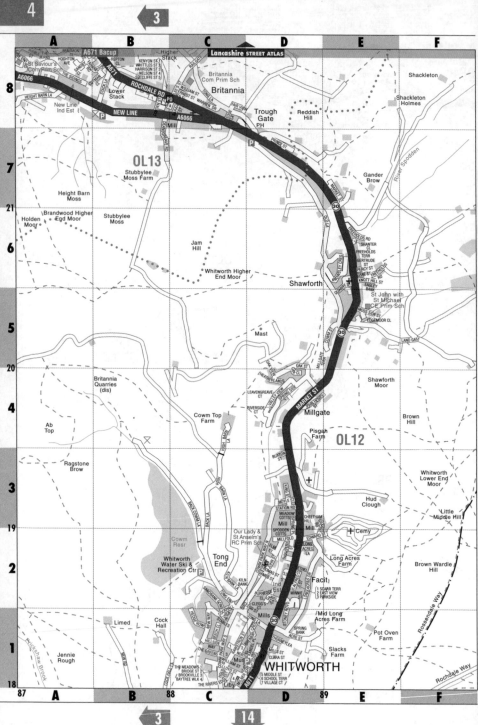

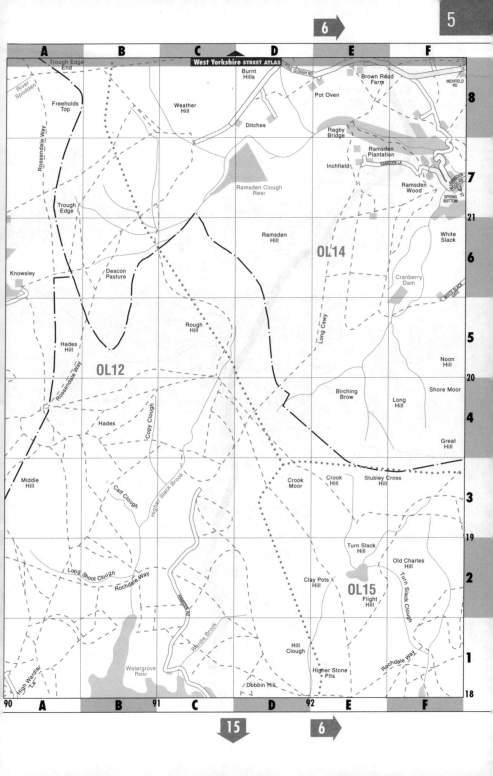

West Yorkshire **STREET ATLAS**

A **B** **C** **D** **E** **F**

Trough Edge
End

River
Spodden

Freeholds
Top

Burnt
Hills

FOUL CLOUGH RD

Brown Road
Farm

INCHFIELD
RD

8

Weather
Hill

Ditches

Pot Oven

Rossendale Way

Ragby
Bridge

Ramsden
Plantation

RAMSDEN LA

Inchfield

Ramsden
Wood

7

Trough
Edge

Ramsden Clough
Resr

SPRING
BOTTOM

21

Ramsden
Hill

OL14

White
Slack

Knowsley

Deacon
Pasture

Cranberry
Dam

WHITE SLACK GATE

6

Rossendale Way

Rough
Hill

Long Cawy

Hades
Hill

OL12

Noon
Hill

5

20

Shore Moor

Hades

Copy Clough

Birching
Brow

Long
Hill

4

Middle
Hill

Calf Clough

Higher Slack Brook

Crook
Moor

Crook
Hill

Stubley Cross
Hill

Great
Hill

3

Turn Slack
Hill

19

Long Shoot Clough

Rochdale Way

RAMSDEN RD

Clay Pots
Hill

Old Charles
Hill

2

OL15

Flight
Hill

Turn Slack Clough

High Wardle La

Wardle Brook

Hill
Clough

Rochdale Way

1

Watergrove
Resr

Dobbin Hill

Higher Stone
Pits

18

90 **A** **B** 91 **C** **D** 92 **E** **F**

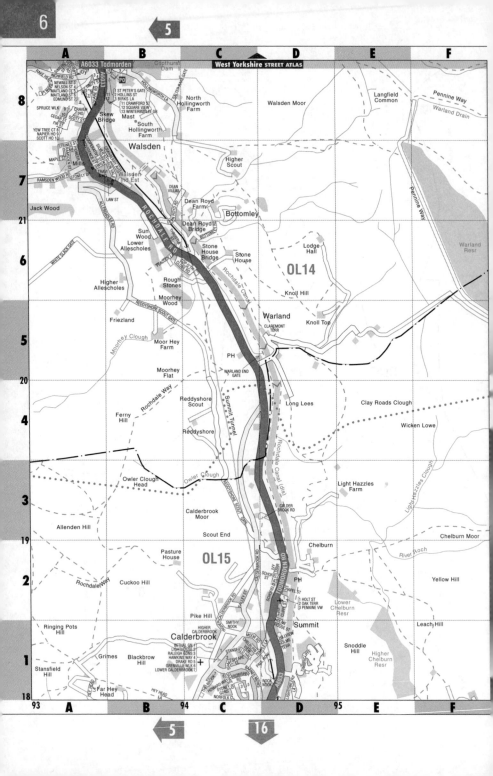

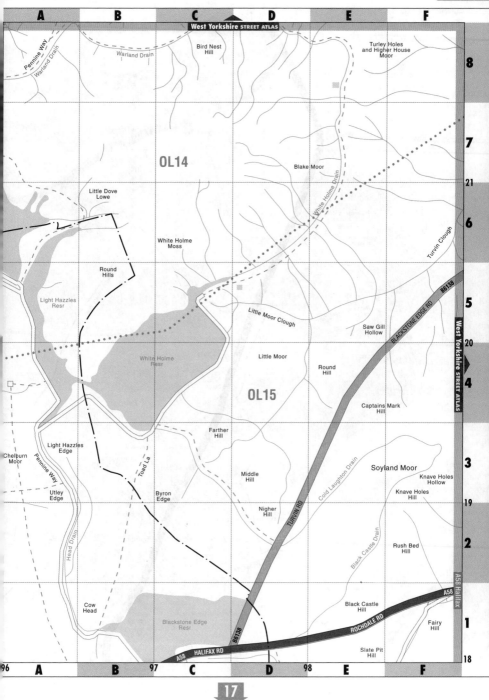

Pennine Way
Warland Drain
Warland Drain

Bird Nest Hill

Turley Holes and Higher House Moor

8

OL14

Blake Moor

White Holme Drain

7

Little Dove Lowe

21

White Holme Moss

Turvin Clough

6

Round Hills

Light Hazzles Resr

Little Moor Clough

Saw Gill Hollow

BLACKSTONE EDGE RD

B6138

West Yorkshire STREET ATLAS

5

White Holme Resr

Little Moor

Round Hill

20

OL15

Captains Mark Hill

4

Farther Hill

Light Hazzles Edge

Toad La

Middle Hill

Cold Laughton Drain

Soyland Moor

Knave Holes Hollow

Knave Holes Hill

3

Chelburn Moor

Pennine Way

Utley Edge

Byron Edge

Nigher Hill

TURVIN RD

Black Castle Drain

Rush Bed Hill

19

Head Drain

Cow Head

Blackstone Edge Resr

B6138

A58 HALIFAX RD

Black Castle Hill

ROCHDALE RD

A58

A58 Halifax

Fairy Hill

Slate Pit Hill

2

1

18

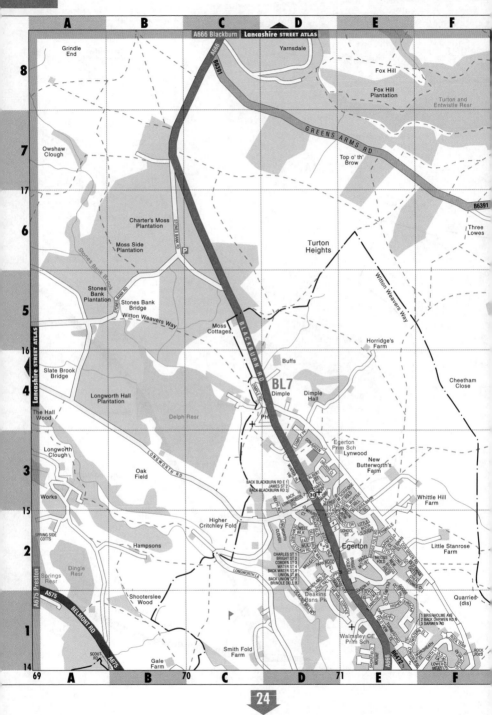

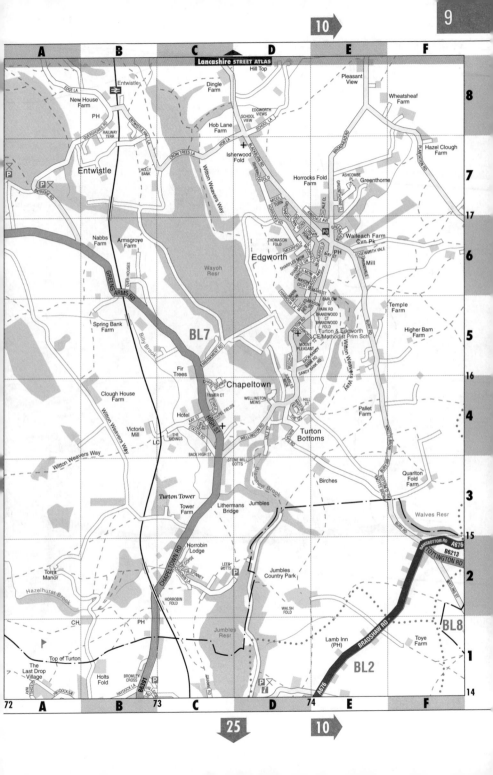

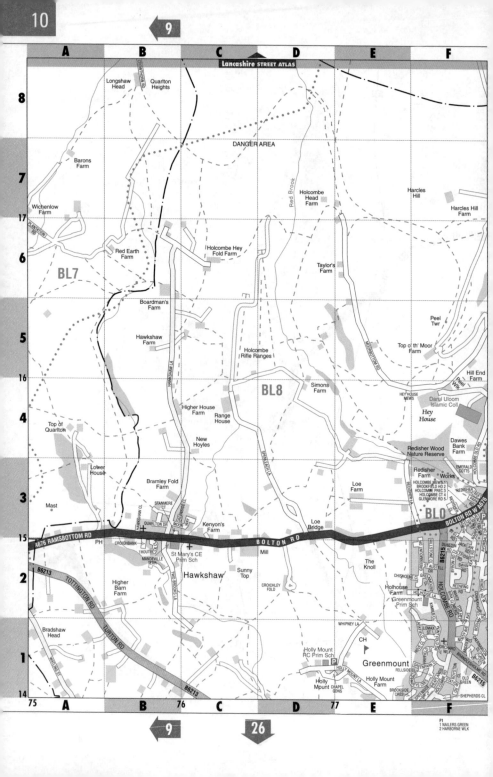

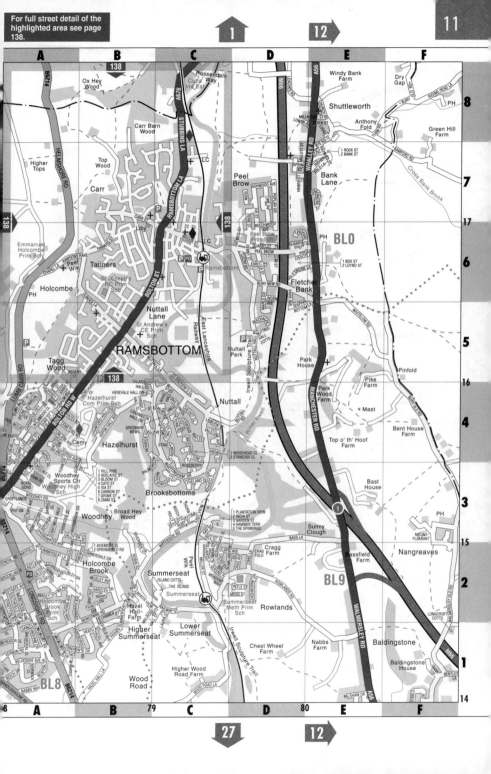

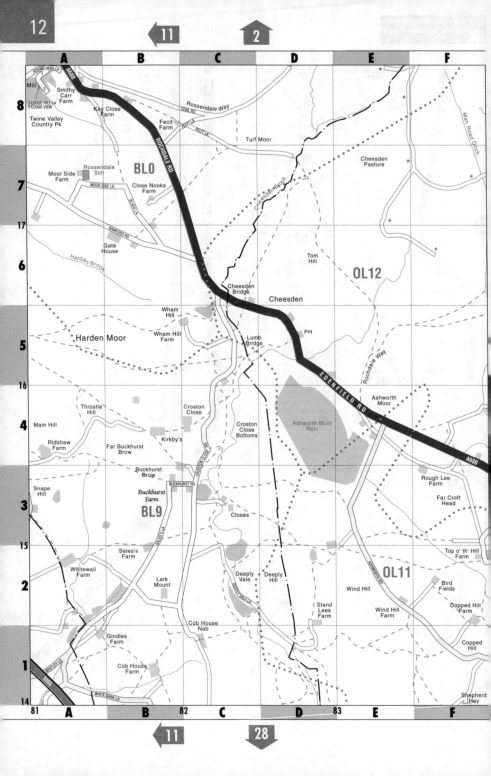

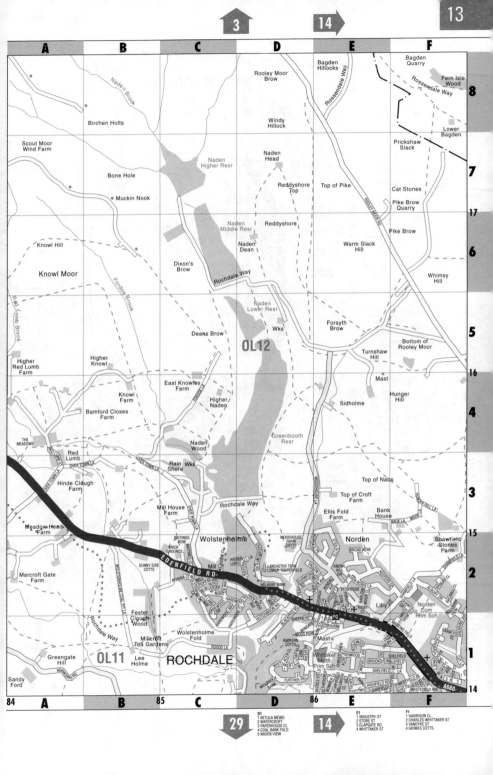

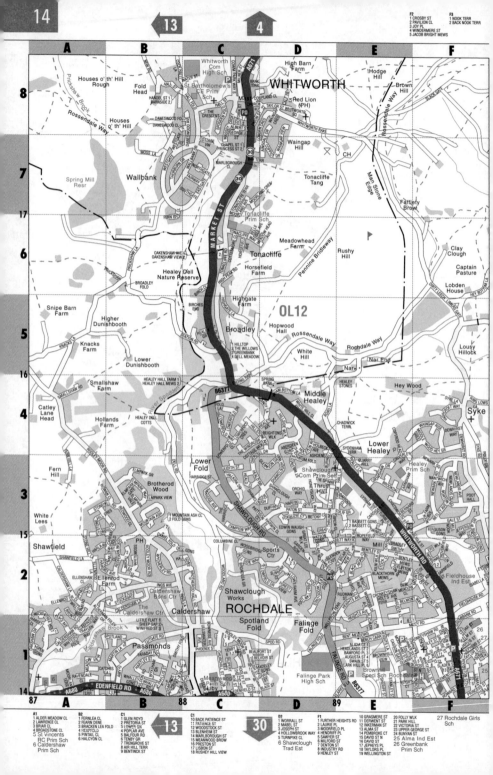

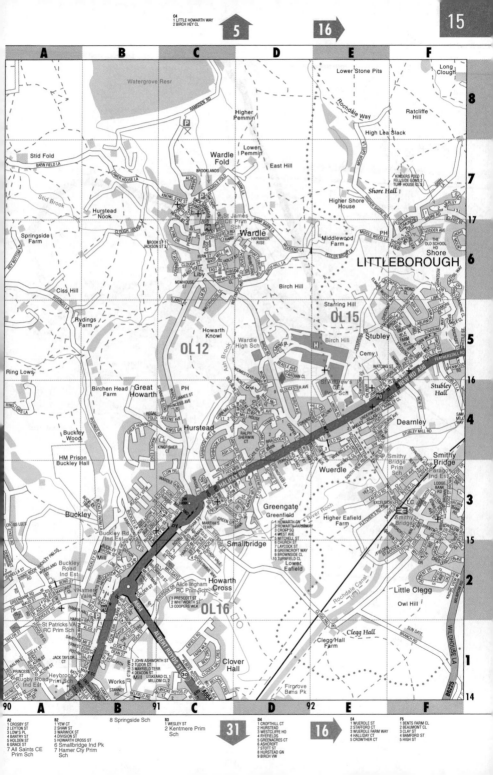

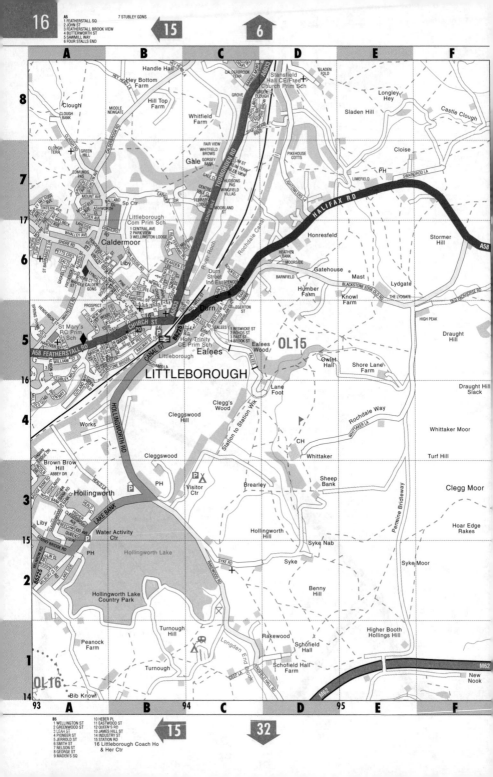

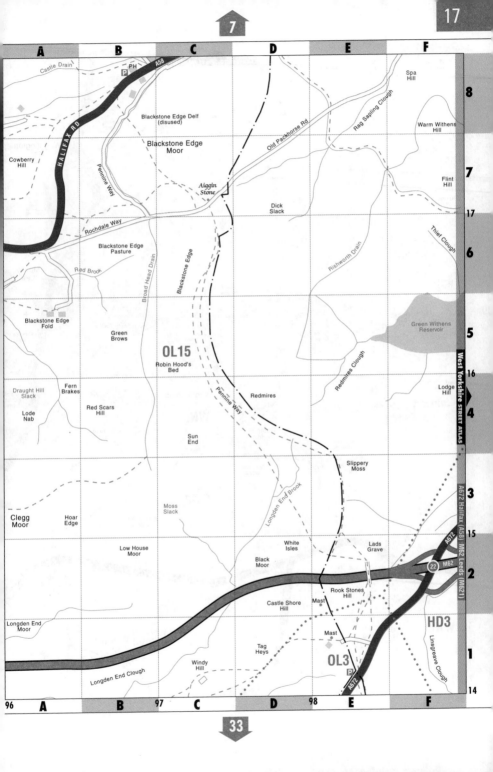

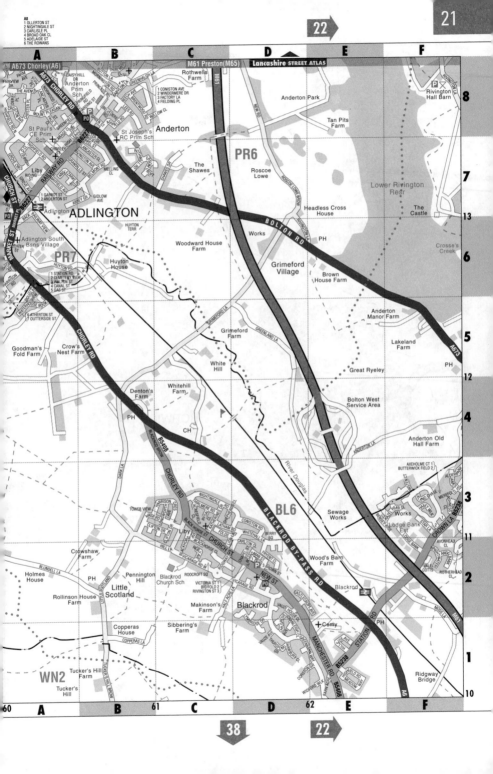

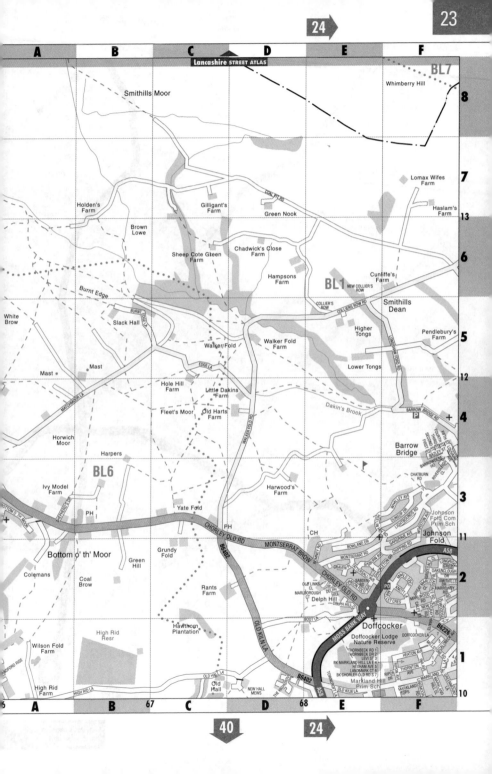

Lancashire STREET ATLAS

BL7

Smithills Moor

Whimberry Hill

8

Lomax Wifes Farm

7

Holden's Farm

Gilligant's Farm

COAL PIT RD

Green Nook

Haslam's Farm

13

Brown Lowe

Sheep Cote Green Farm

Chadwick's Close Farm

Hampsons Farm

BL1

Cunliffe's Farm

NEW COLLIER'S ROW

6

White Brow

Burnt Edge

COLLIER'S ROW

COLLIERS ROW RD

Smithills Dean

Slack Hall

BURNT EDGE LA

Walker Fold

Walker Fold Farm

Higher Tongs

Pendlebury's Farm

5

Mast

Mast

EDGE LA

Lower Tongs

LONGSHAW ROAD RD

12

Hole Hill Farm

Little Dakins Farm

Dakin's Brook

BARROW BRIDGE RD

4

MATCHMOOR LA

Fleet's Moor

Old Harts Farm

WALKER FOLD RD

Barrow Bridge

CHATBURN RD

Horwich Moor

Harpers

Harwood's Farm

Johnson Fold Com Prim Sch

3

BL6

Ivy Model Farm

Yate Fold

PH

Johnson Fold

A58

BOTTOM O' TH' MOOR RD

SHEPHERDS RD

PH

CHORLEY OLD RD

CH

MONTSERRAT BROW

11

Bottom o' th' Moor

Grundy Fold

Green Hill

B6402

Delph Hill

2

Colemans

Coal Brow

Rants Farm

OLD LINKS MARLBOROUGH

Doffcocker

B6226

Hawthorn Plantation

High Rid Resr

OLD KILN LA

MOSS BANK WAY

Doffcocker Lodge Nature Reserve

DOFFCOCKER

1

Wilson Fold Farm

THORNBECK RD 1
THORNBECK DR 2
LEVI ST 3
BK MARKLAND HILL LA 4
HEXHAM AVE 5
LANDMARK CT 6
BK CHORLEY OLD RD 5 7

HEATON AVE

High Rid Farm

HIGH RID LA

OLD HALL LA

Old Hall

NEW HALL MEWS

B6402

A58

TONGE MOOR LA OLD KILN LA

Markland Hill Prim Sch

MARKLAND TOPS

10

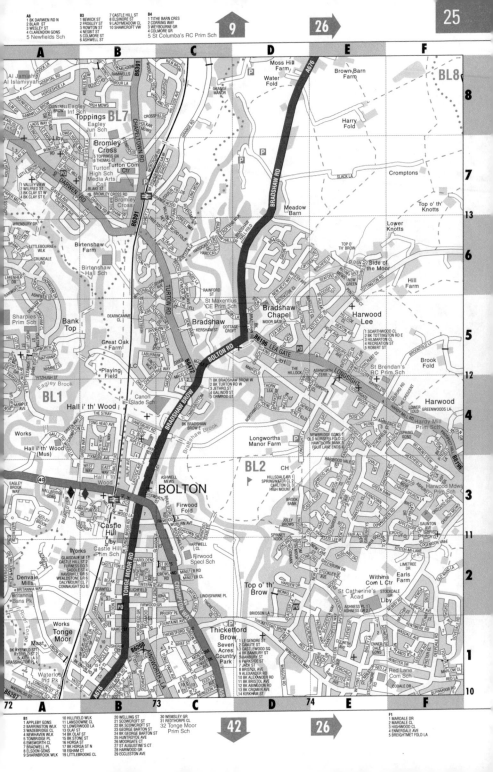

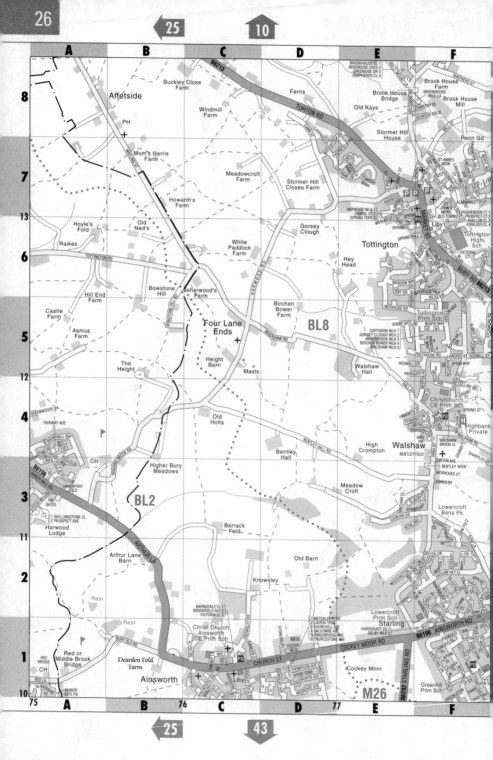

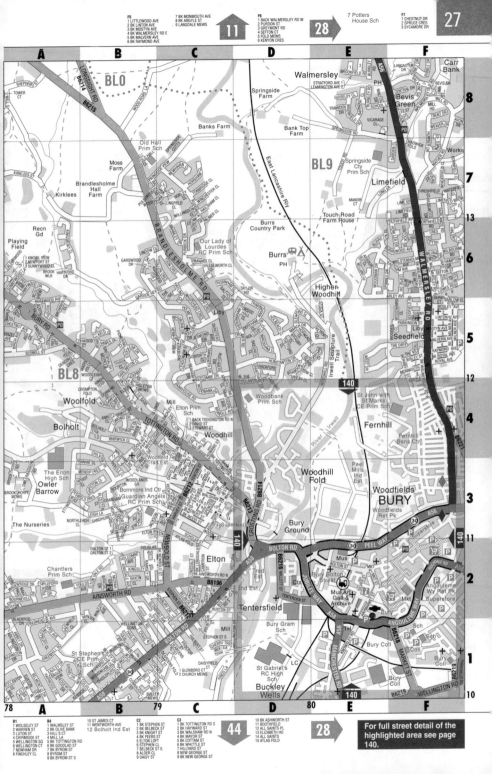

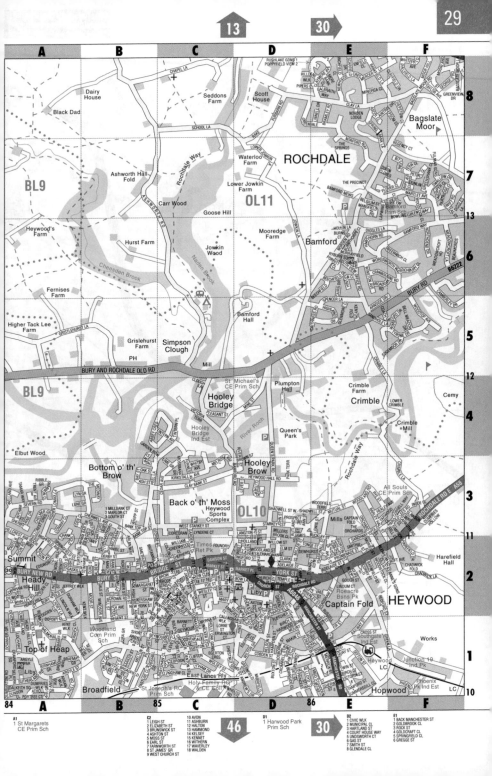

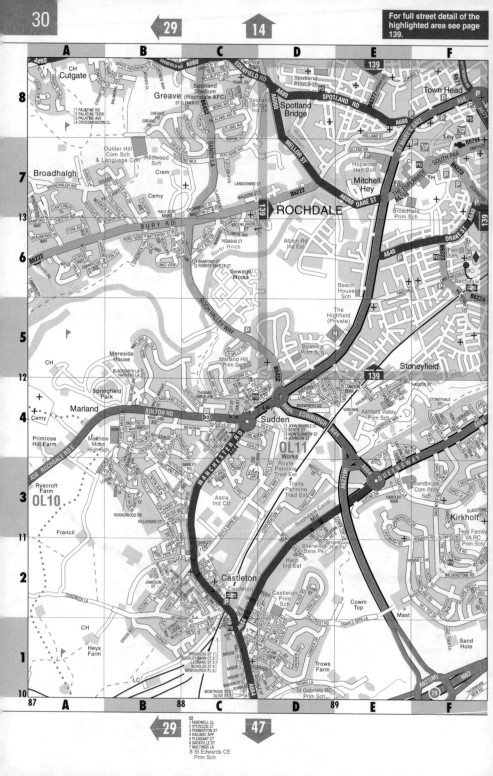

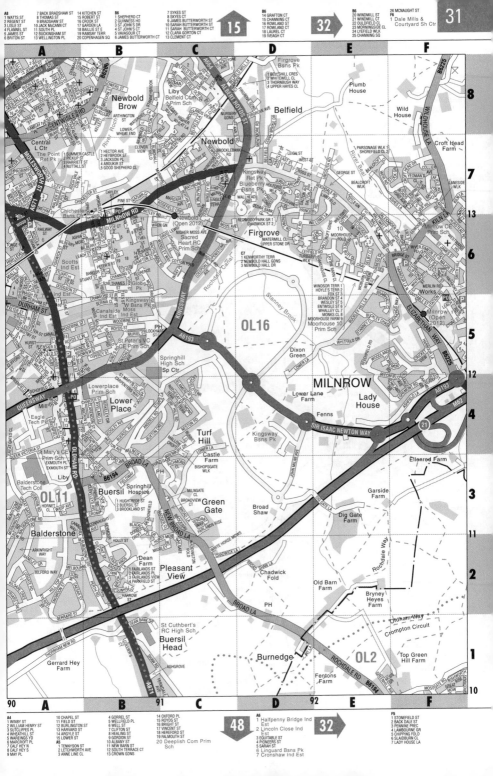

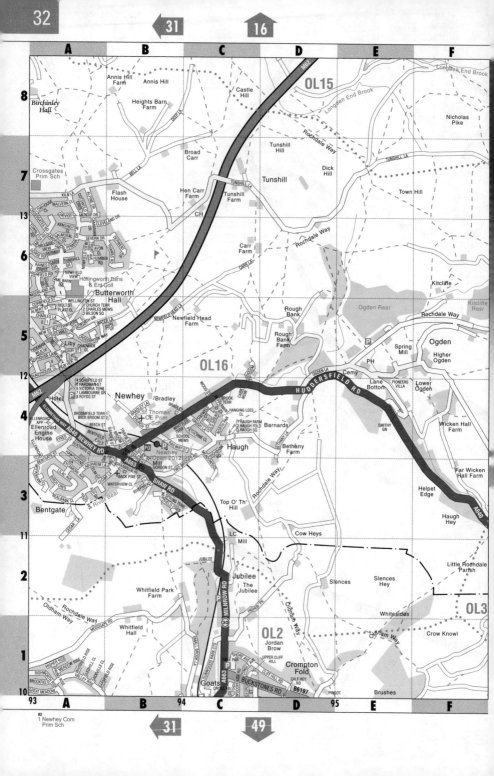

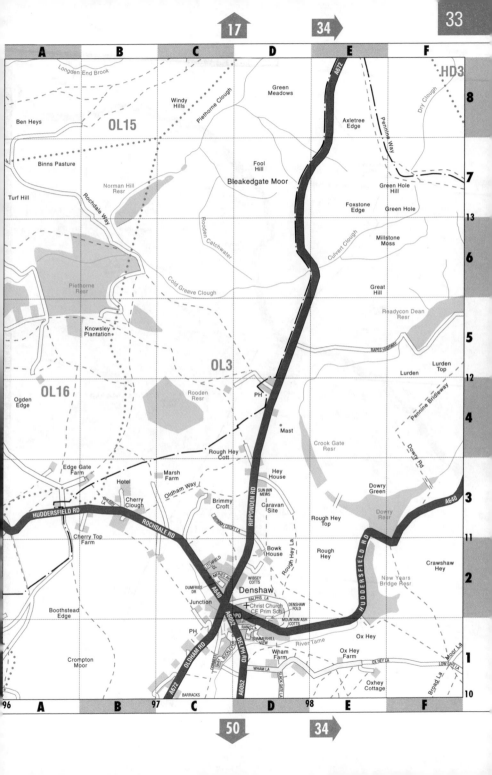

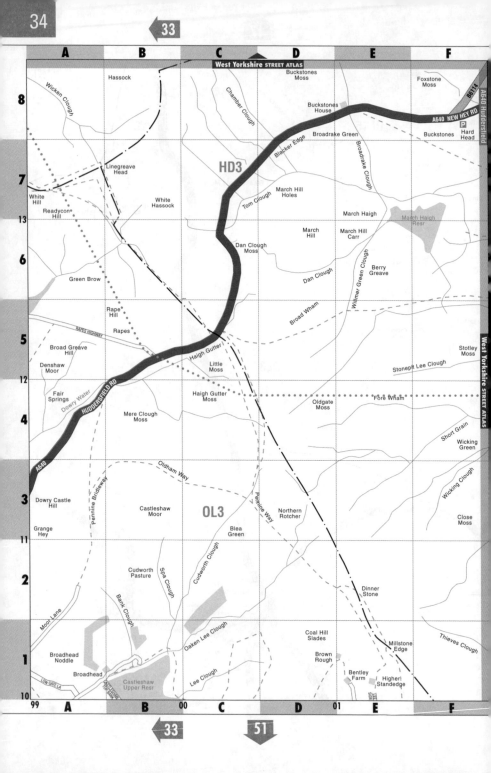

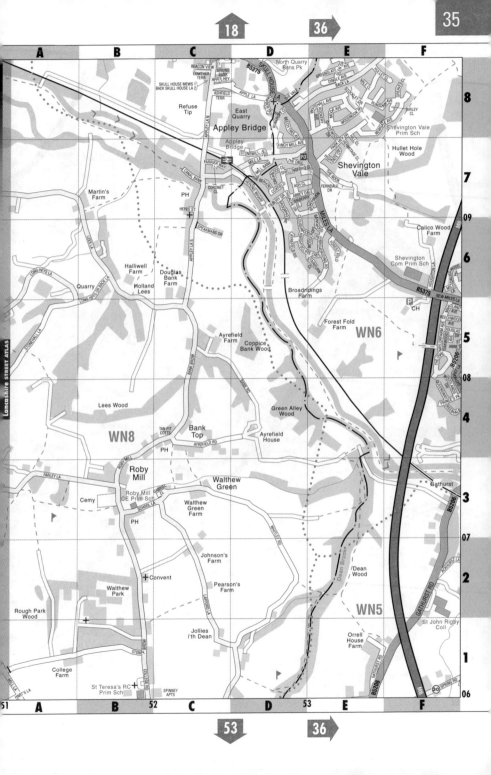

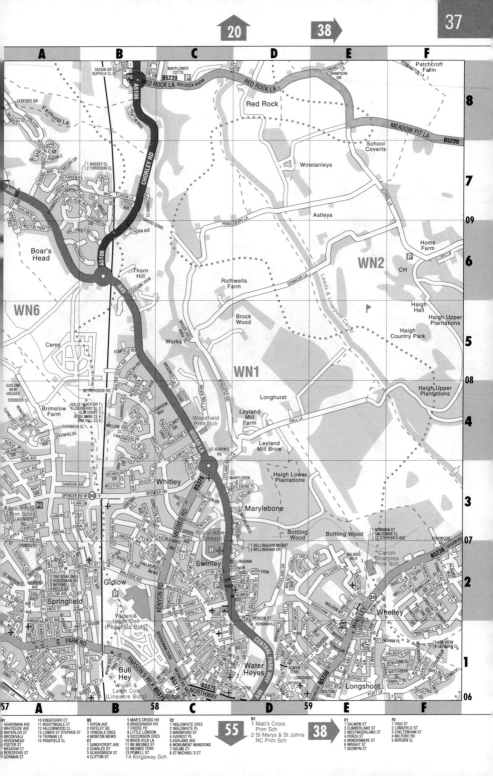

A   B   C   D   E   F

8

7

09

6

5

08

4

3

07

2

07

1

06

Red Rock

School Coverts

Patchcroft Farm

PENNINGTON LA

MEADOW PIT LA

B5239

Winstanleys

Astleys

WN2

CH

Home Farm

Haigh Hall

Haigh Upper Plantations

Haigh Country Park

Haigh Upper Plantations

Rothwells Farm

Brock Wood

WN1

Works

Longhurst

Leyland Mill Farm

Leyland Mill Brow

Woodfield Prim Sch

Haigh Lower Plantations

Whitley

Marylebone

Bottling Wood

Bottling Wood

Balniel Wk

Canon Sharples Prim Sch

B5238

Swinley

Royal Albert Edward

Whelley

WN6

Boar's Head

Cemy

Gidlow New Houses

Brimelow Farm

Greenfields

Beech Hill Prim Sch

Liby

Springfield

Gidlow

Park Rd

Bull Hey

Wigan & Leigh Coll (Lineacre Bldg)

Water Heyes

Longshoot

Wigan & Leigh Coll (Pagefield Bldg)

Thorn Hill

Fairhurst La

Chorley Rd

A5106

A49

Red Rock La

B5239

Leeds & Liverpool Canal

Sennicar La

Wigan La

Hall La

Central Park Way

B5376

B5375

Wigan Rd

B5238

A1
1 HEARDMAN AVE
2 WHITESIDE AVE
3 WATERLOO ST
4 BROOKVALE
5 HEDGEMEAD
6 FOSTER ST
7 MEADOW CT
8 BERESFORD ST
9 GORMAN ST

10 KINGFISHER CT
11 NIGHTINGALE CT
12 FALCONWOOD CL
13 LOWER ST STEPHEN ST
14 TIERNAN LO
15 PAGEFIELD CL

B3
1 RIPON AVE
2 PATELEY SQ
3 YEWDALE CRES
4 MONTON MEWS

C1
1 SANDYCROFT AVE
2 CHARLES ST
3 SCARSBRICK ST
4 CLIFTON ST

5 MAB'S CROSS HO
6 BRADSHAIGH HO
7 CROSS YD
8 LITTLE LONDON
9 DICOONSON CRES
10 BRICK KILN LA
11 BK MESNES ST
12 MESNES TERR
13 POWELL ST
14 Kingsway Sch

C2
1 INGLEWHITE CRES
2 INGLEWHITE PL
3 WARNFORD ST
4 EVERIEST PL
5 ASHLAND AVE
6 MONUMENT MANSIONS
7 HOLME CT
8 ST MICHAEL'S CT

D1
1 Mab's Cross Prim Sch
2 St Marys & St Johns RC Prim Sch

E1
1 SALMON ST
2 CUMBERLAND ST
3 WESTMOORLAND ST
4 PERCH ST
5 WINDERMERE ST
6 WRIGHT ST
7 SEDWYN ST

F2
1 VIGO ST
2 LONGFIELD ST
3 CHELTENHAM ST
4 MILFORD ST
5 BORDEN CL

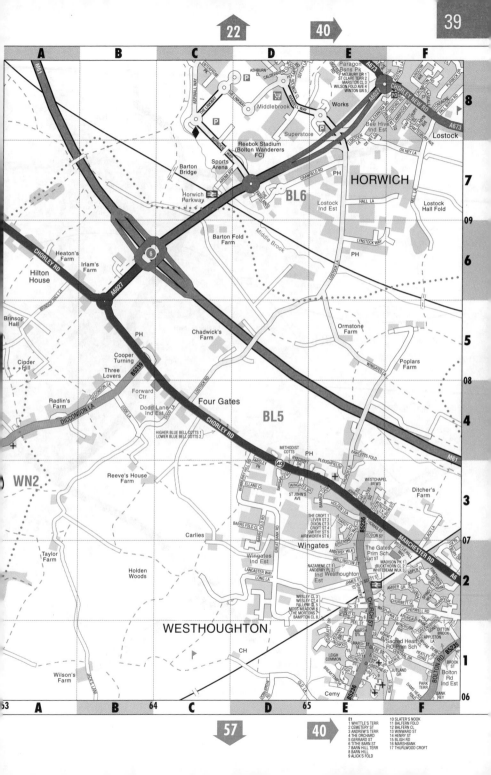

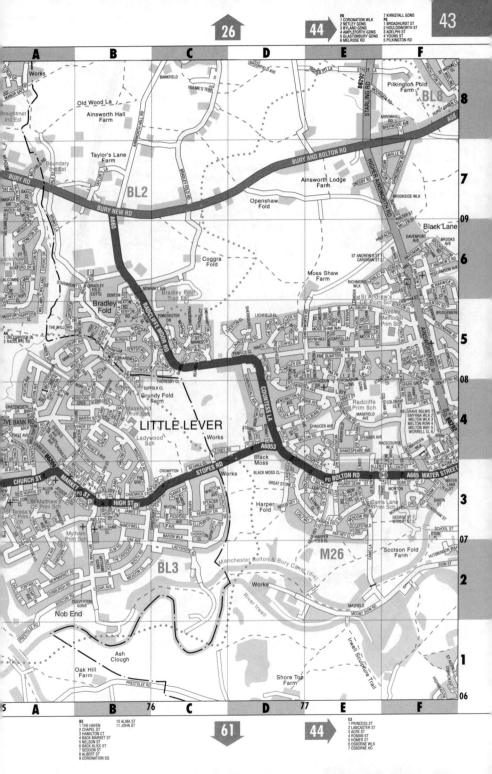

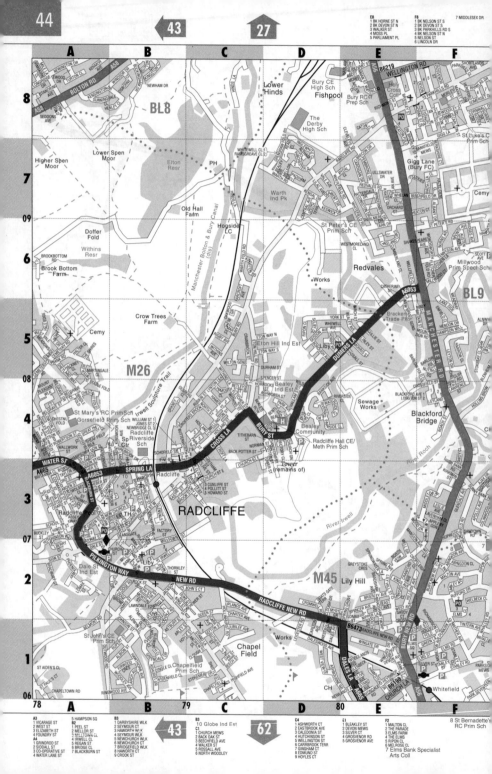

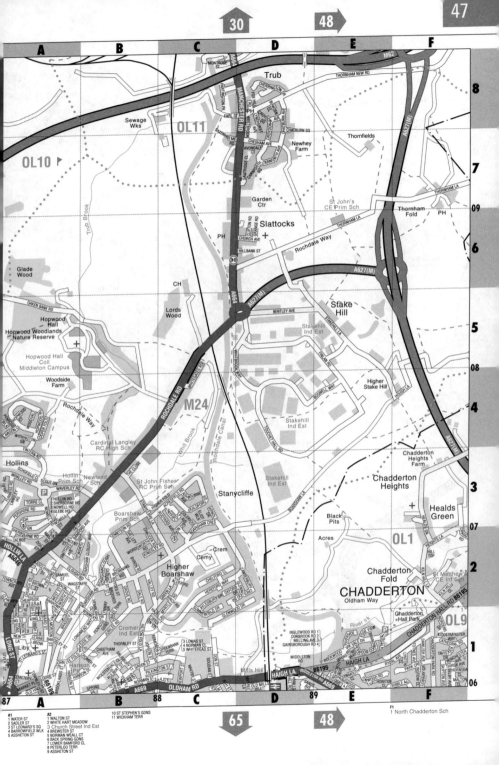

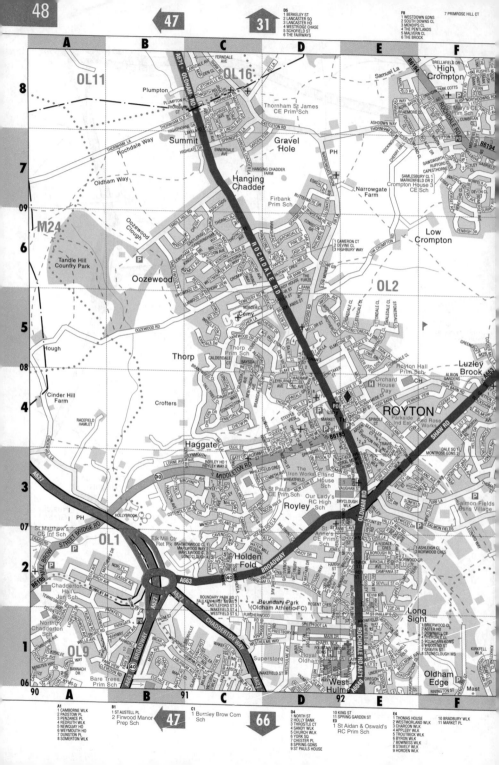

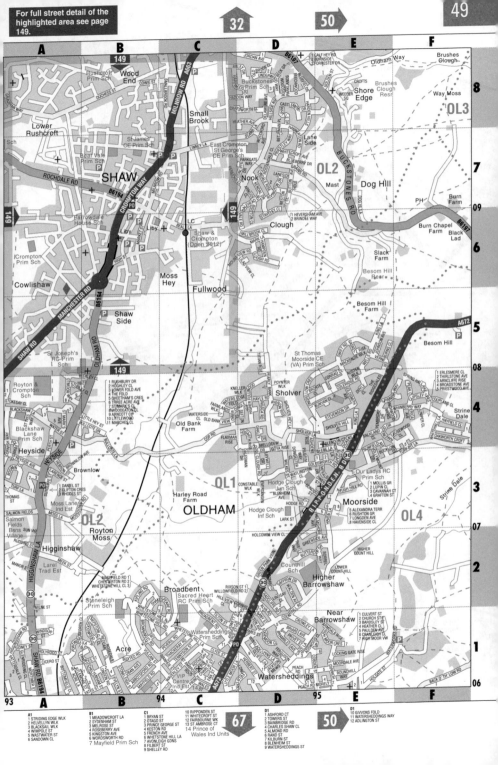

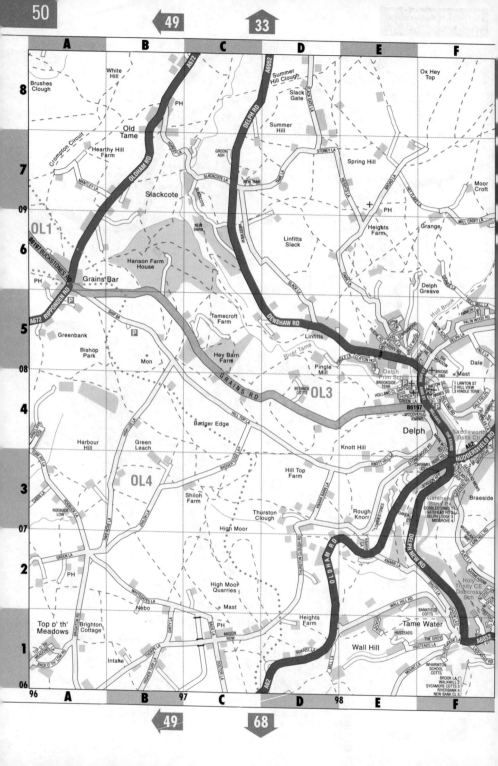

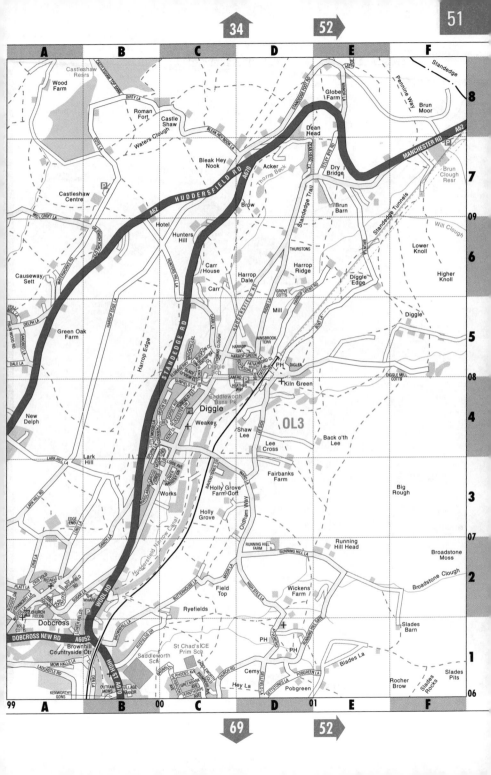

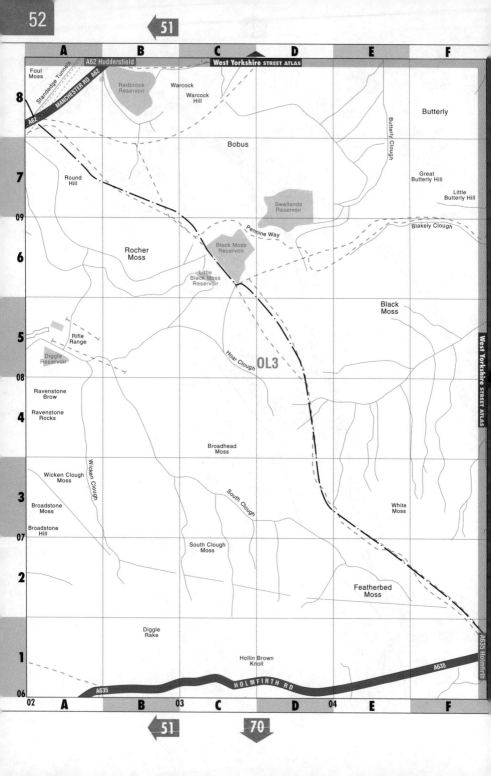

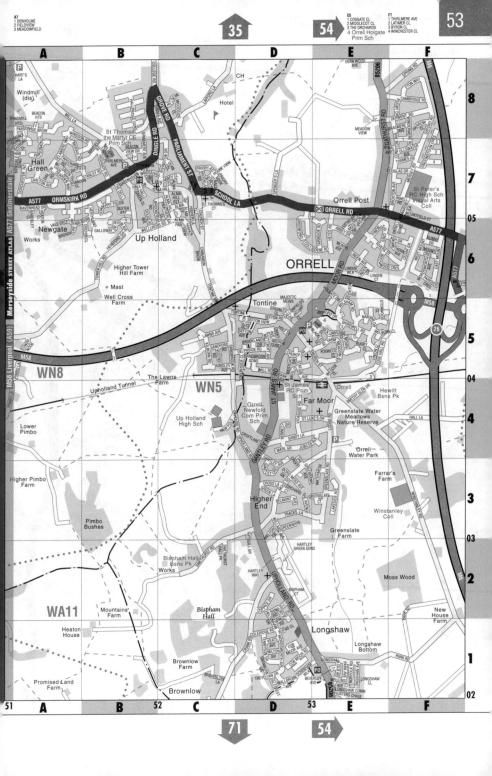

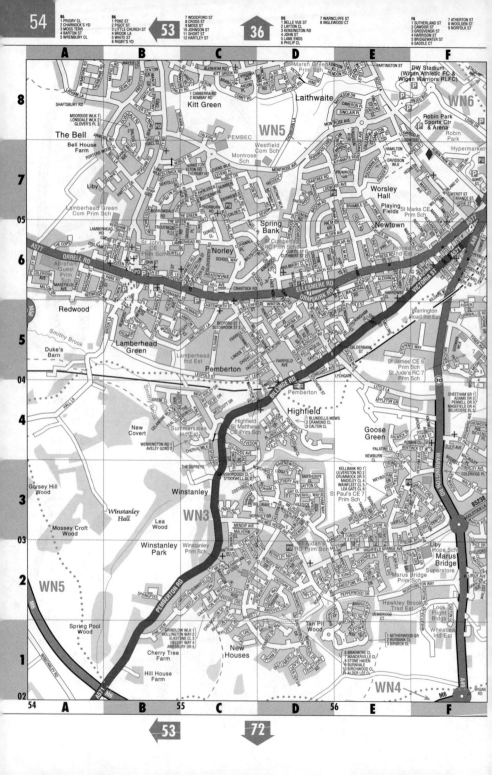

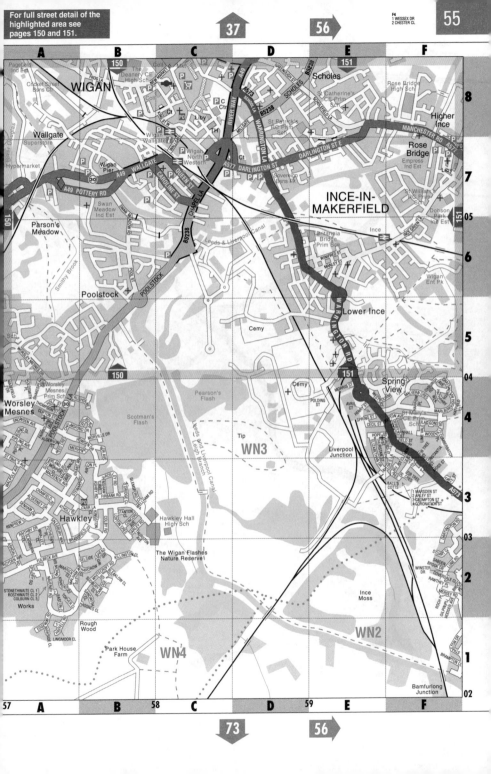

For full street detail of the highlighted area see pages 150 and 151.

37

56

F4
1 WESSEX DR
2 CHESTER CL

55

WIGAN

Wallgate
Superstore

Hypermarket

Wigan Pier

Parson's
Meadow

Poolstock

Worsley
Mesnes

Hawkley

Works

Rough
Wood

Park House
Farm

WN4

Scholes

Higher
Ince

Rose
Bridge

INCE-IN-
MAKERFIELD

Lower Ince

Spring
View

Liverpool
Junction

Ince
Moss

WN3

WN2

Bamfurlong
Junction

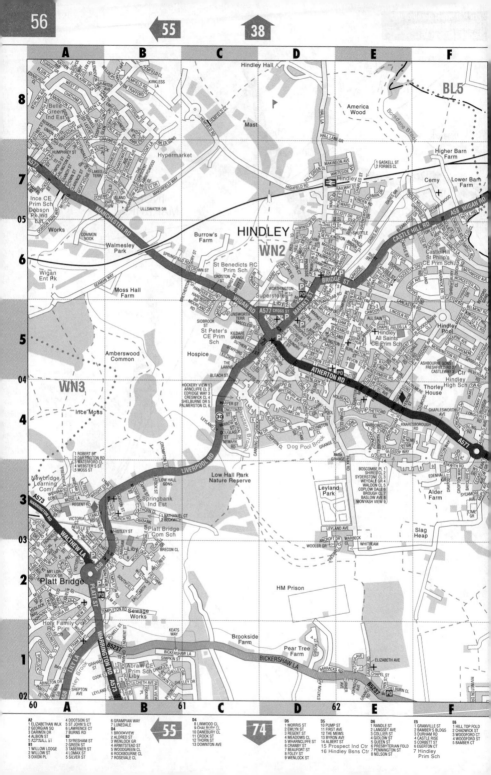

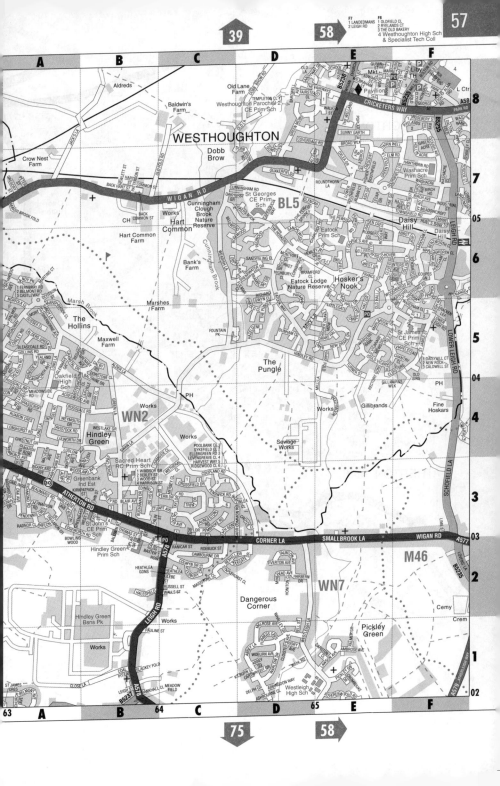

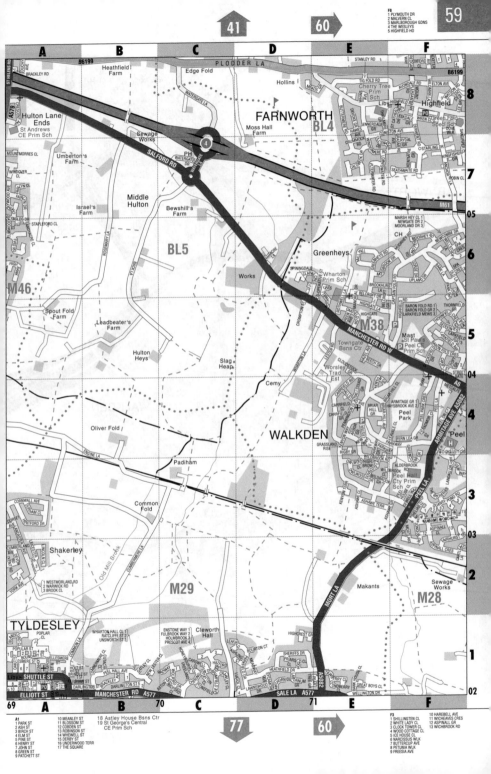

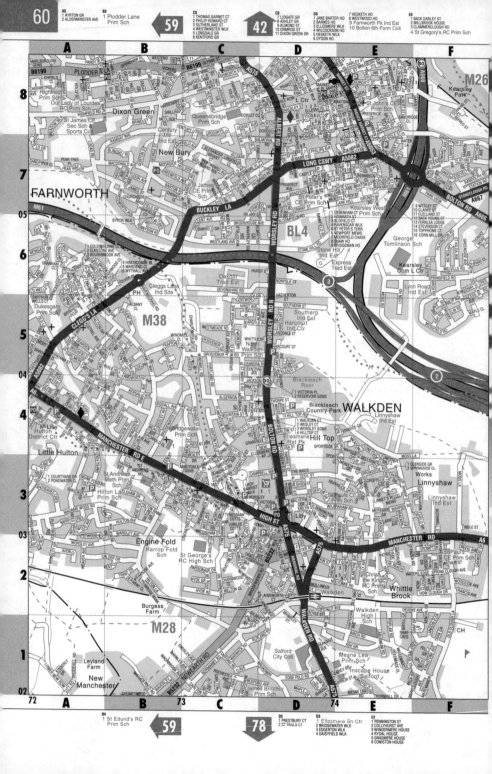

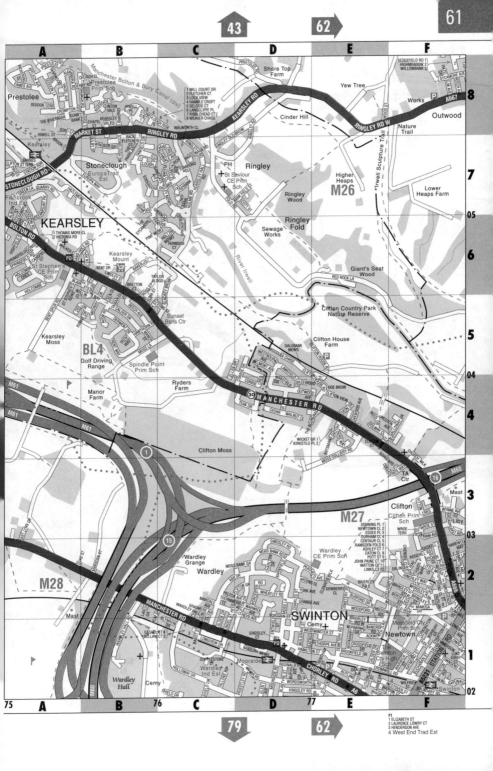

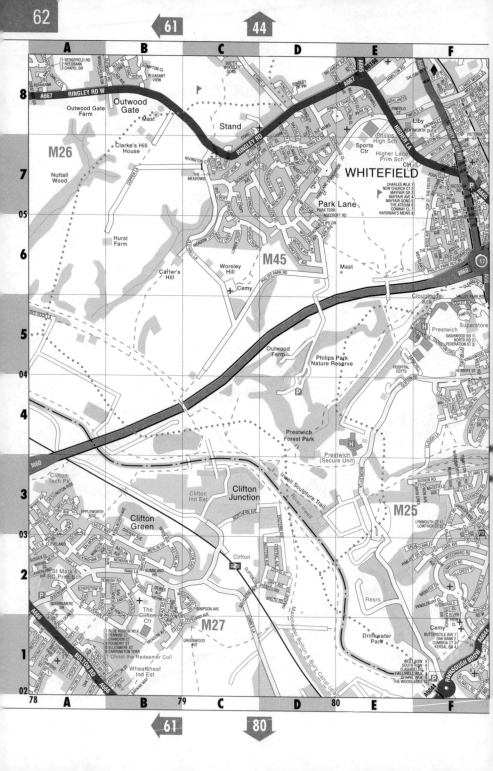

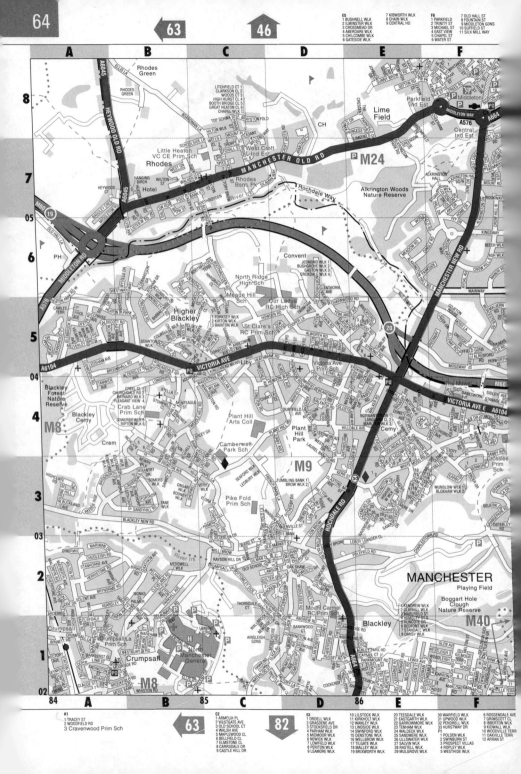

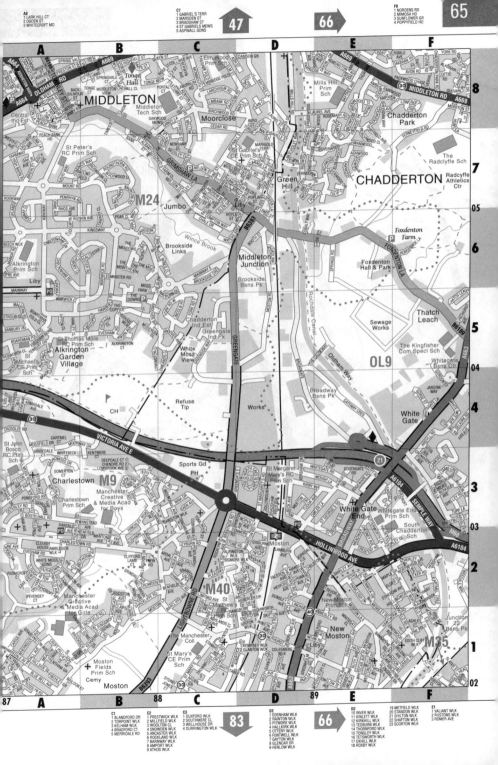

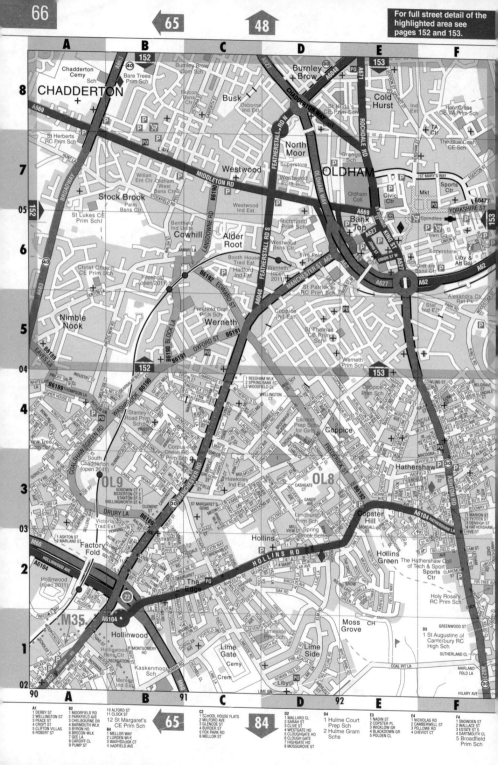

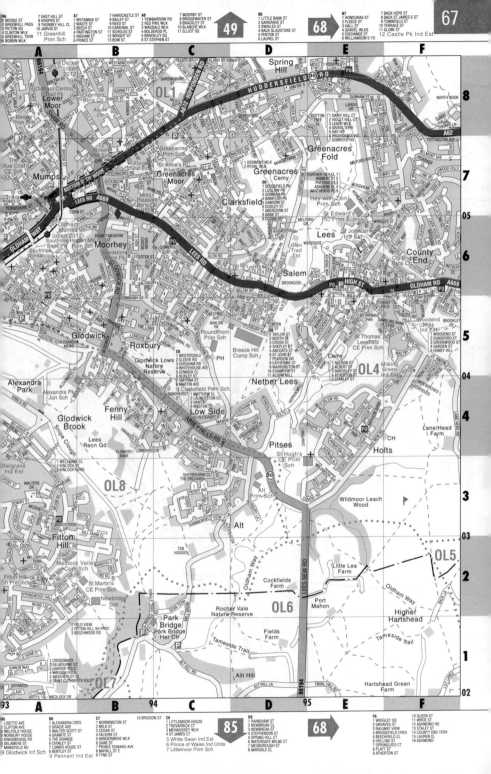

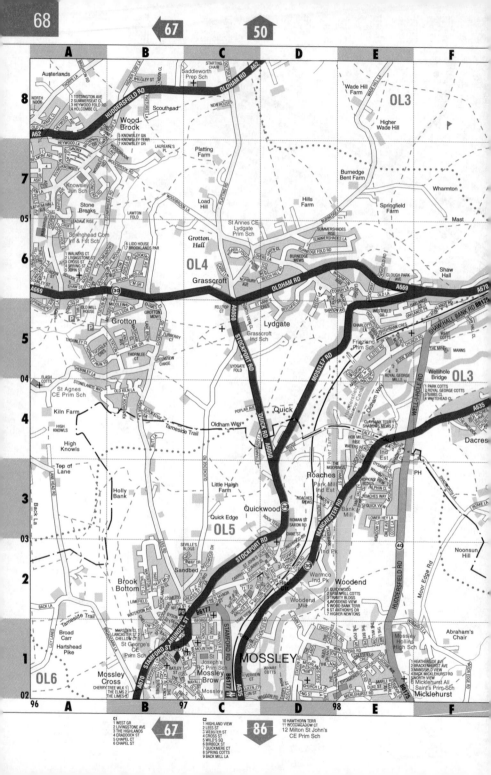

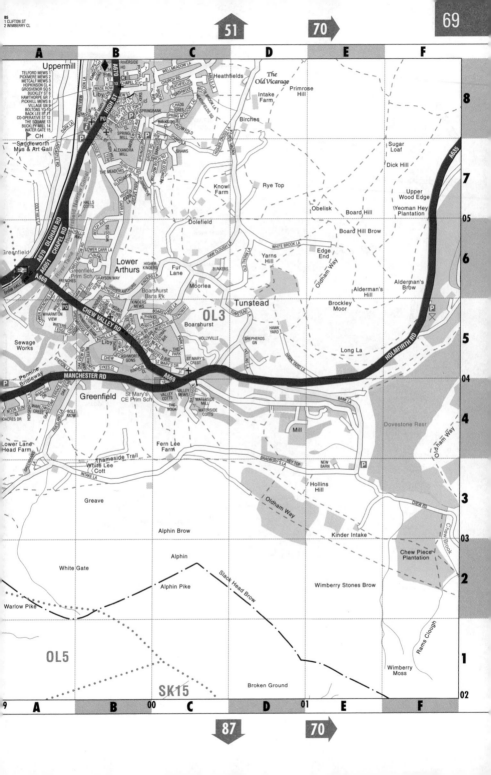

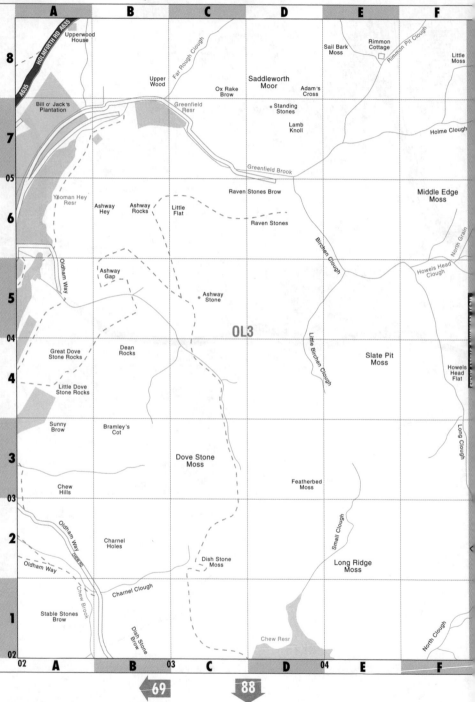

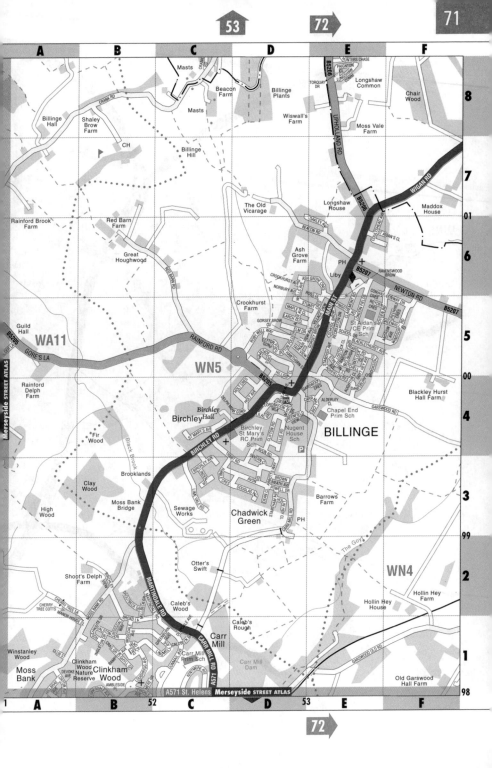

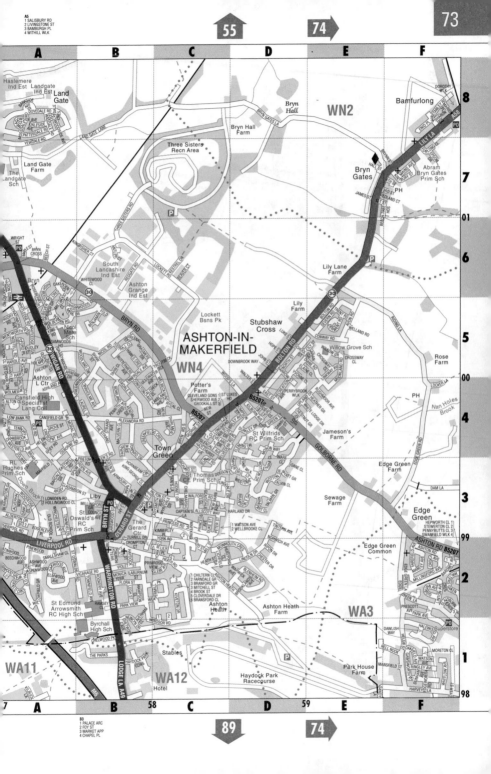

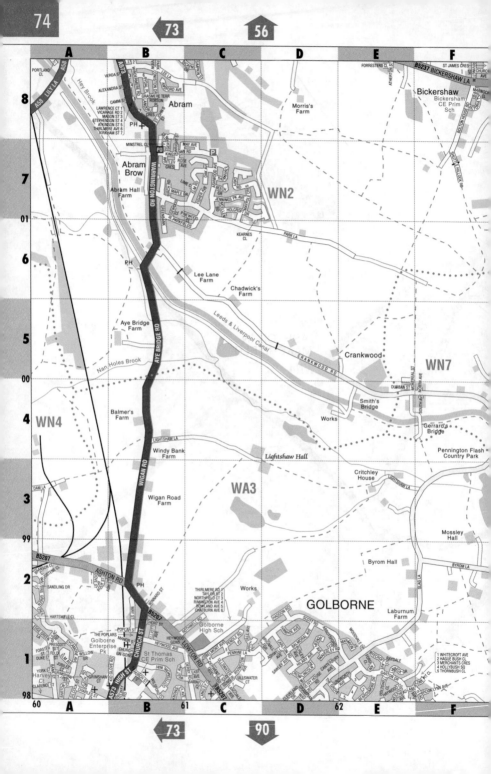

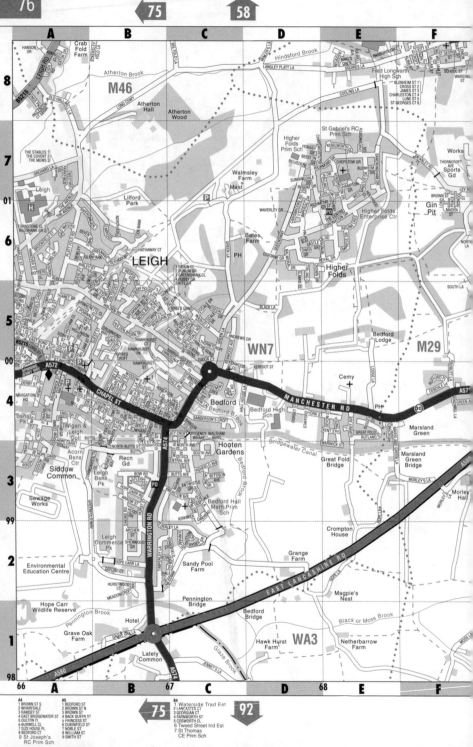

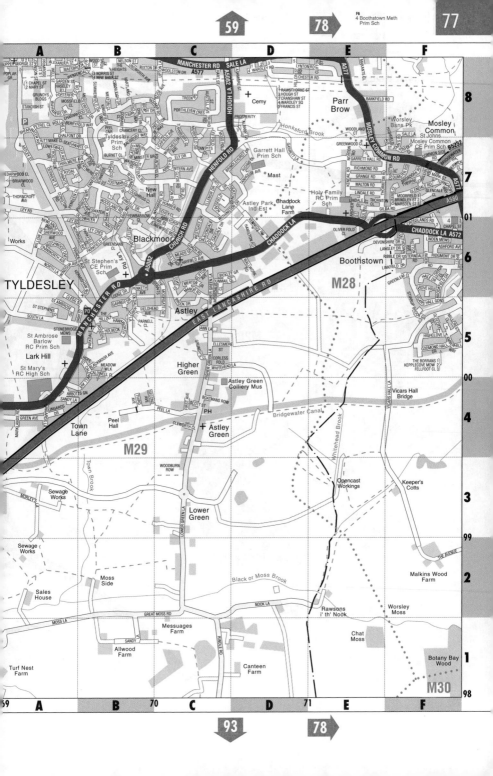

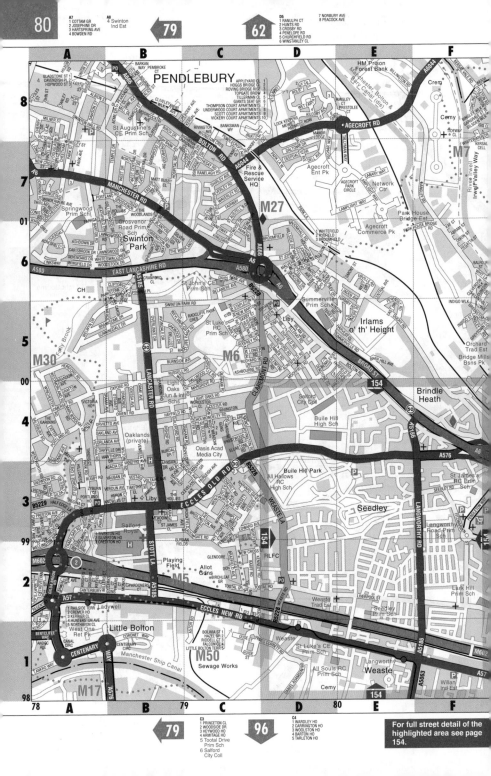

For full street detail of the highlighted area see page 154.

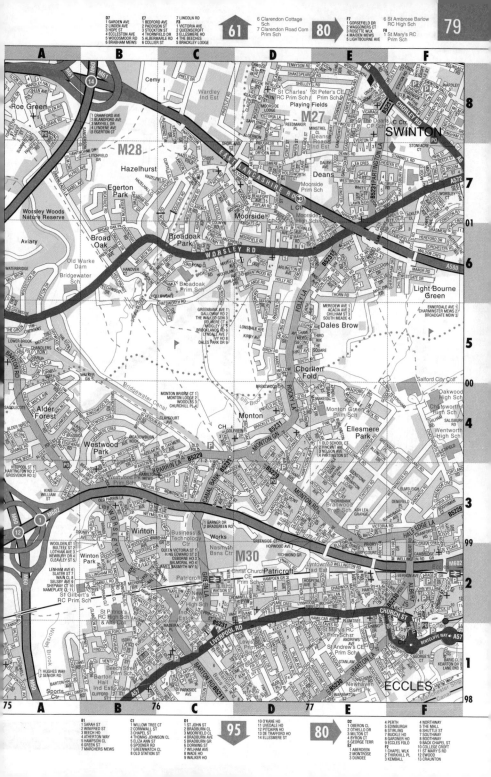

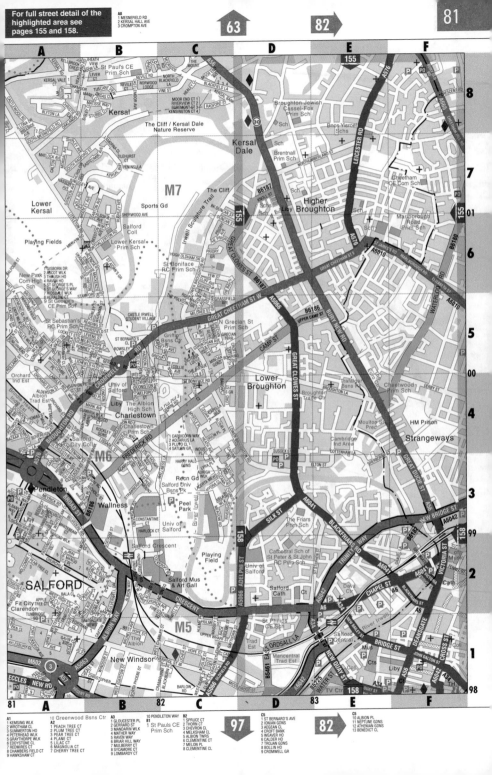

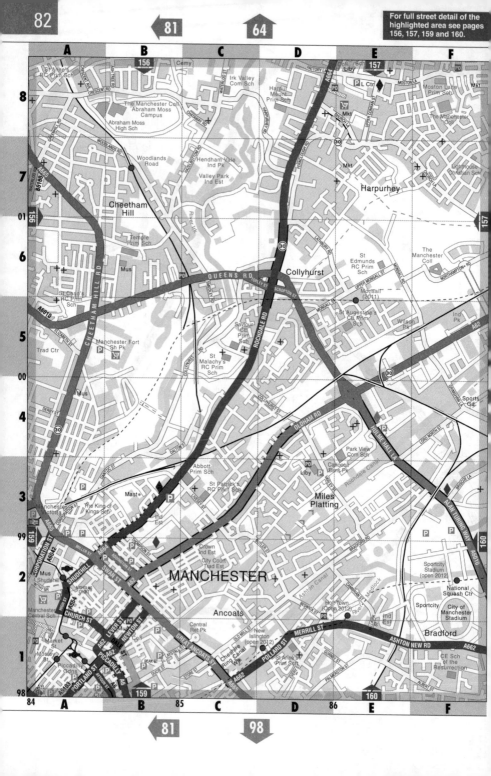

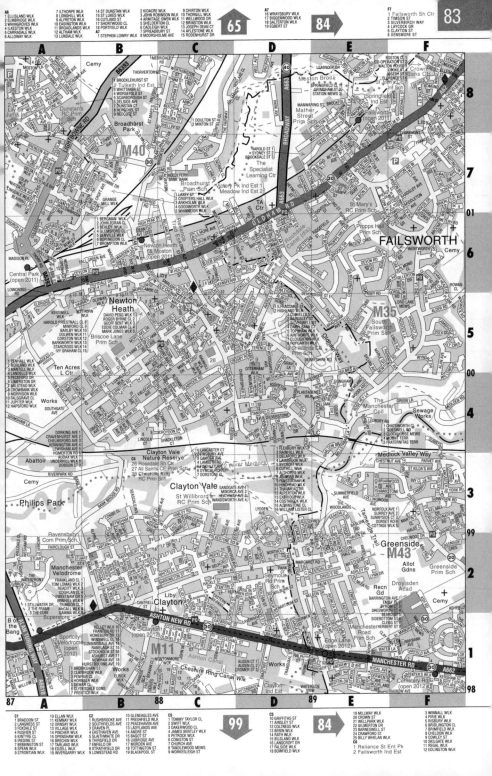

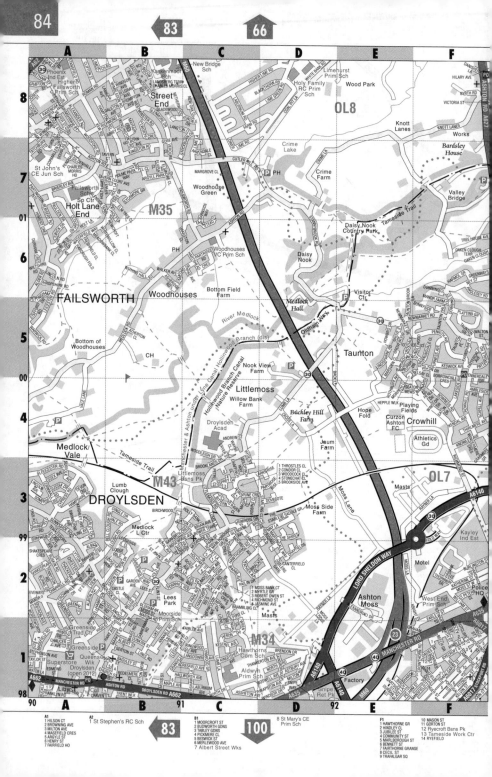

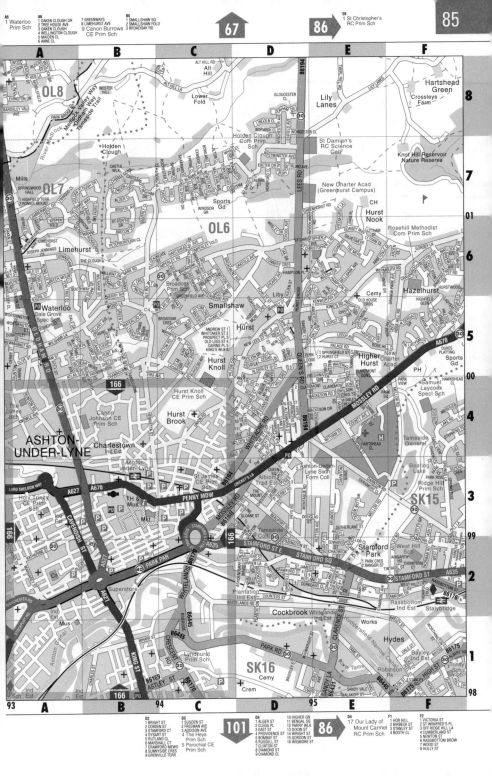

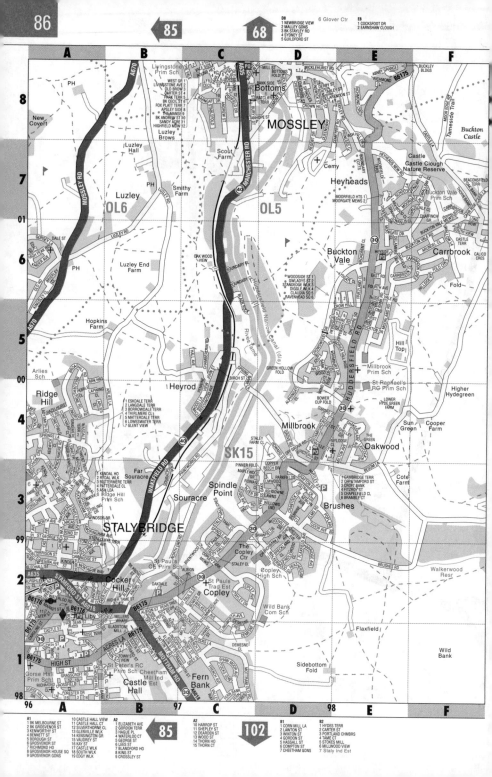

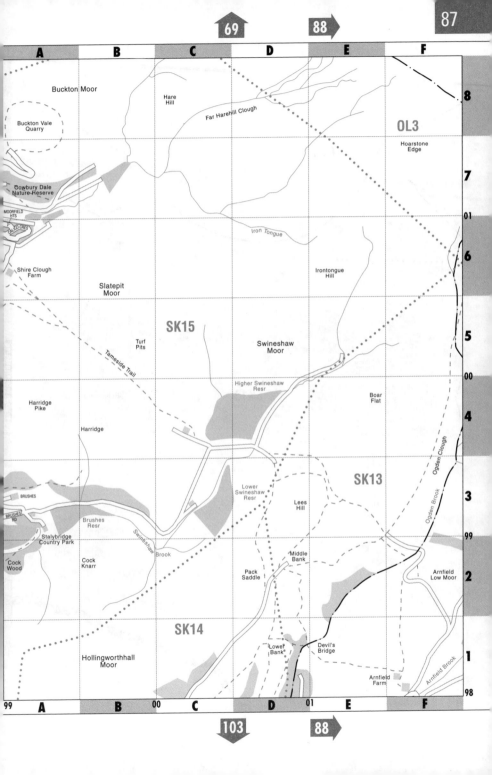

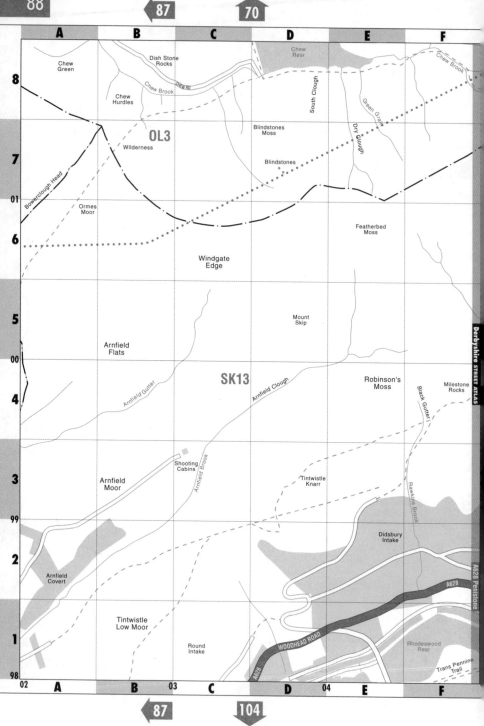

Derbyshire STREET ATLAS

Chew Green

Dish Stone Rocks

Chew Brook

CHEW RD

Chew Resr

Chew Brook

Chew Hurdles

South Clough

Green Grain

OL3

Wilderness

Blindstones Moss

Dry Clough

Bowerclough Head

Ormes Moor

Blindstones

Featherbed Moss

Windgate Edge

Mount Skip

Arnfield Flats

SK13

Arnfield Gutter

Arnfield Clough

Robinson's Moss

Black Gutter

Milestone Rocks

Shooting Cabins

Arnfield Brook

Arnfield Moor

Tintwistle Knarr

Rawkins Brook

Didsbury Intake

A628 Penistone

Arnfield Covert

A628

Tintwistle Low Moor

Round Intake

WOODHEAD ROAD

A628

Rhodeswood Resr

Trans Pennine Trail

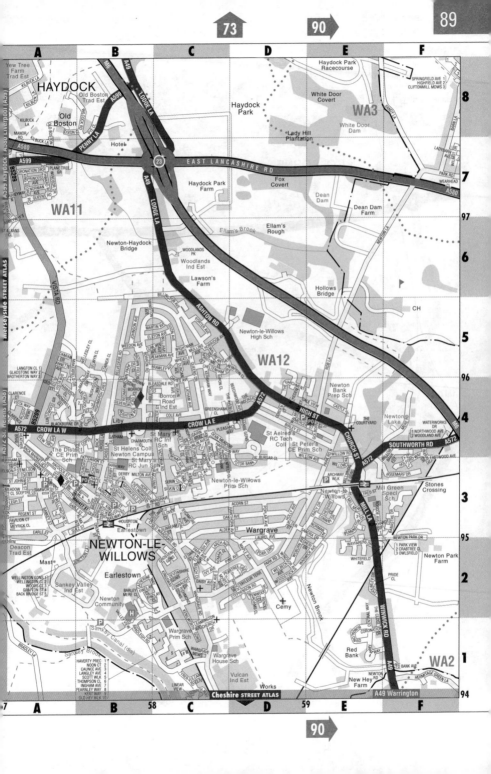

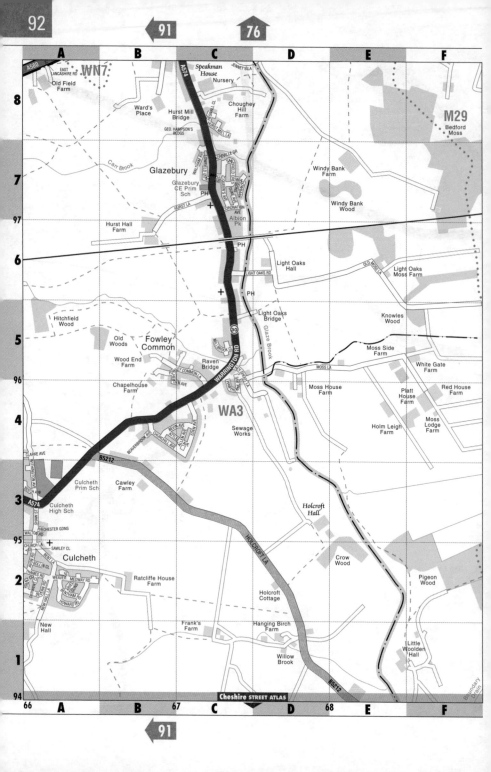

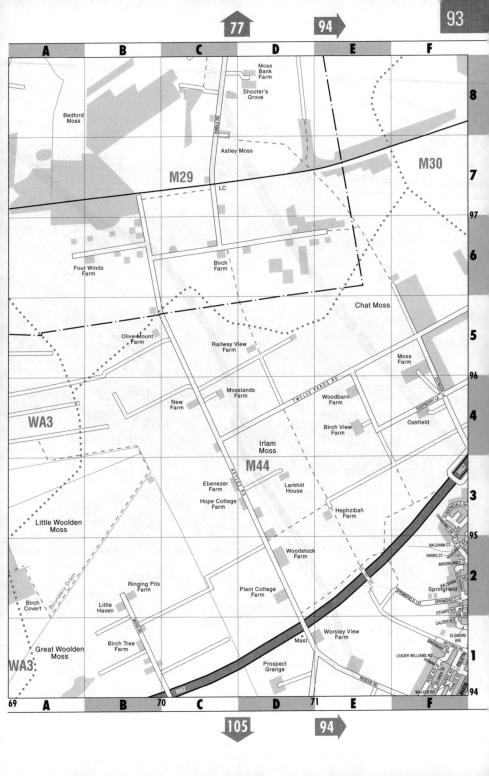

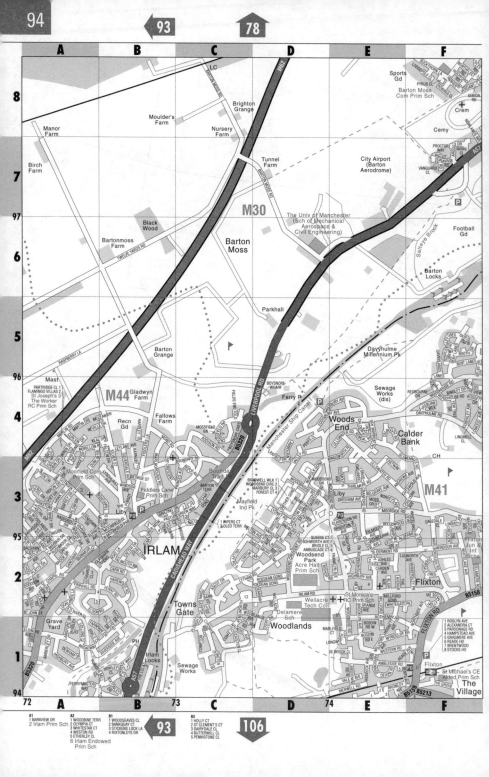

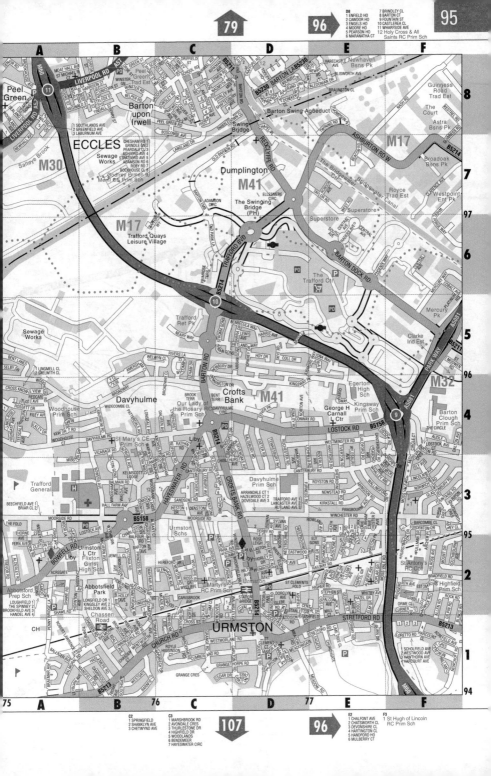

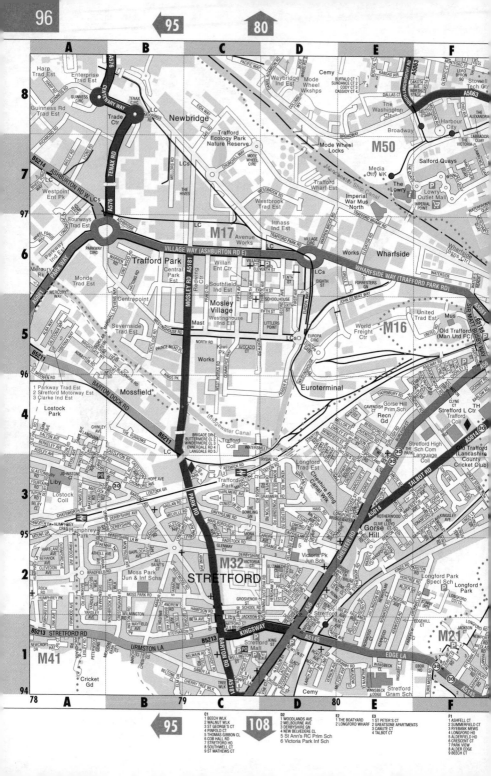

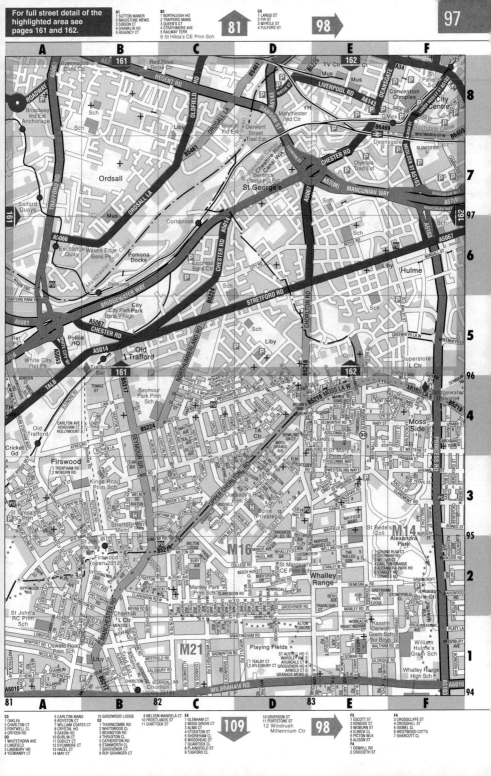

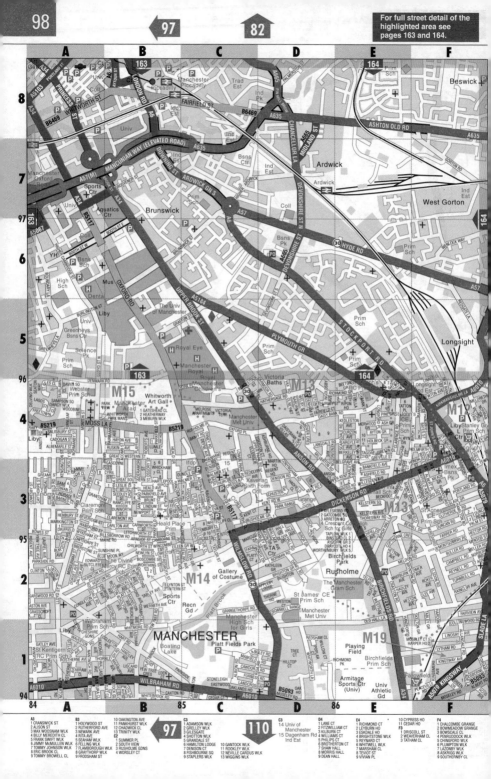

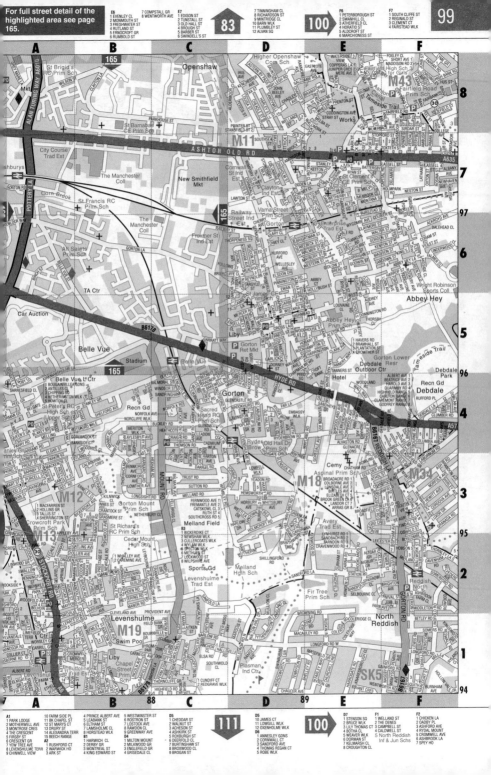

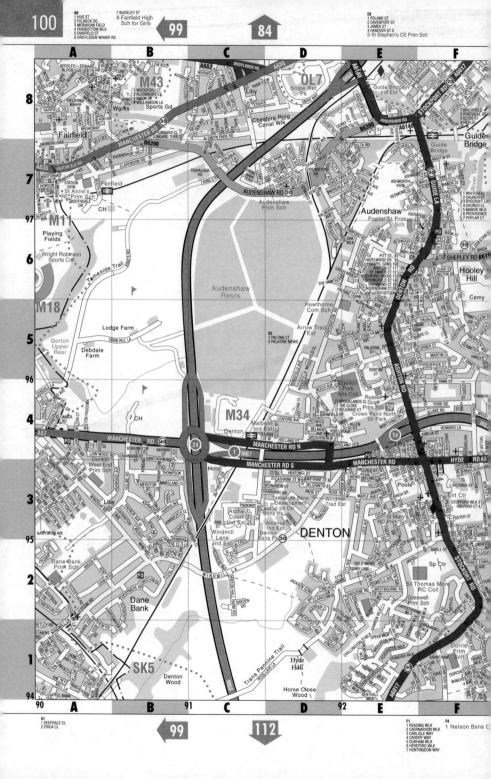

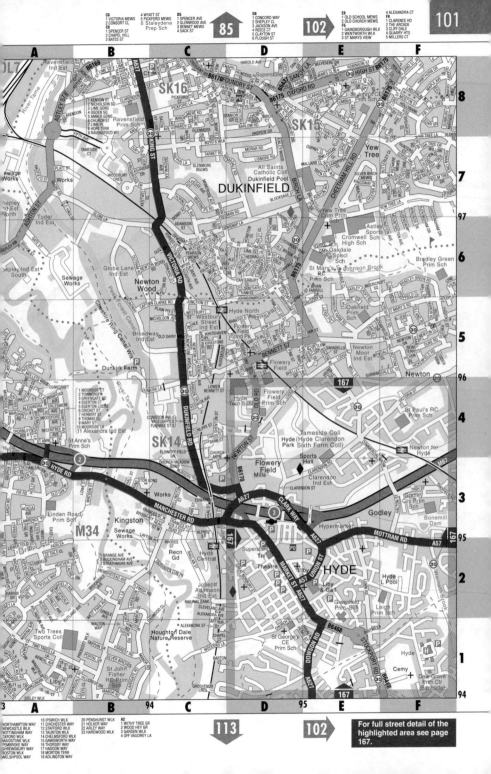

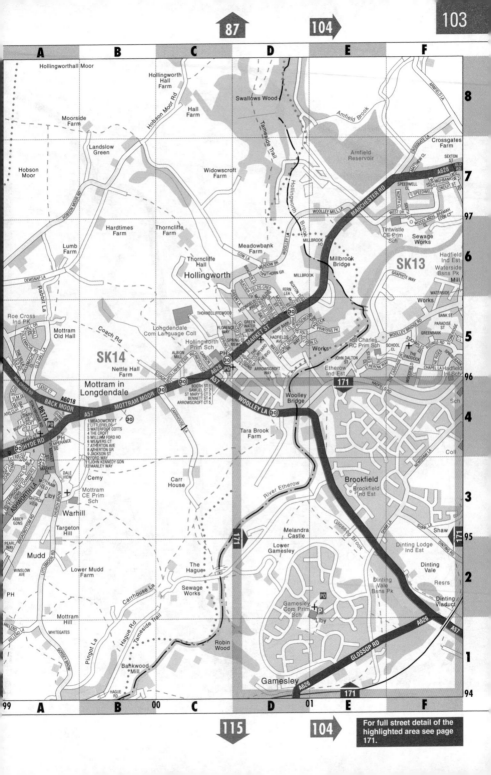

104

A5
1 THE CROSS
2 WARHURST FOLD
3 OLD HALL SQ
4 BLENHEIM CL
5 MARLOW ST

103

88

Derbyshire STREET ATLAS

A57 Sheffield

C1
1 HAYDEN CT
2 MARKET ARC
3 NORFOLK SQ
4 THE YARD
5 VICTORIA ST
6 CENTRAL STORE

D1
1 BOOTH'S CT
2 HOLLY MOUNT
3 DROVERS WLK
4 REGENCY CL

F1
1 DOVEDALE CT
2 PARTINGTON CT
3 MILLERSDALE CT
4 HILLWOOD DR
5 HATHERSAGE DR
6 Hurst Mills Ind Est

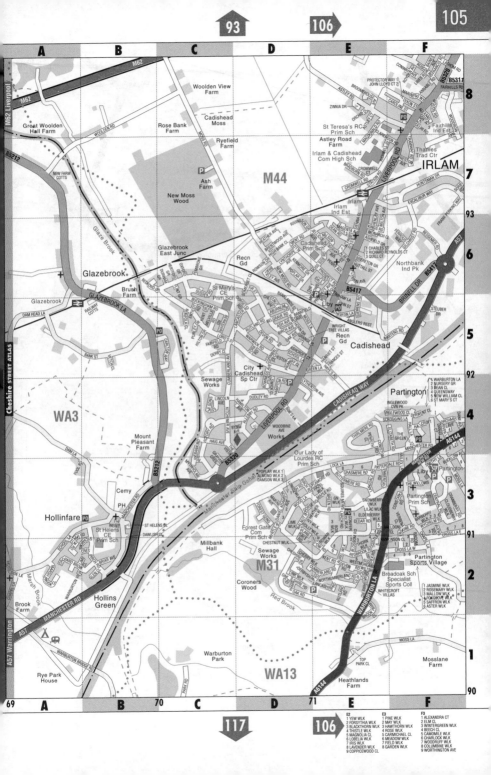

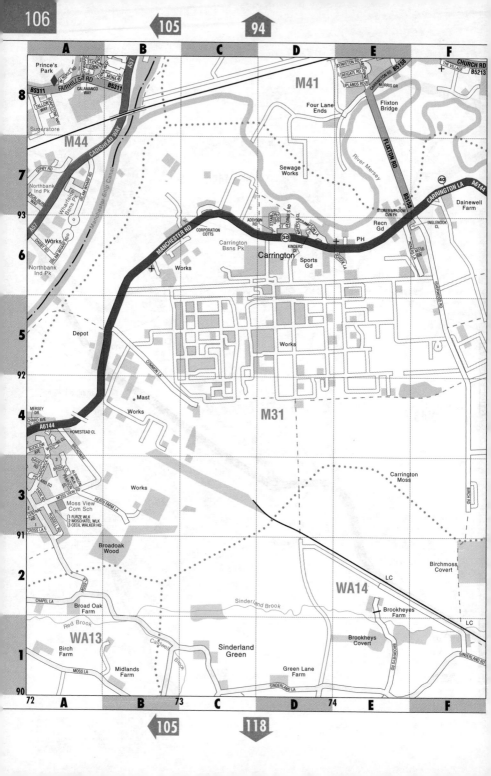

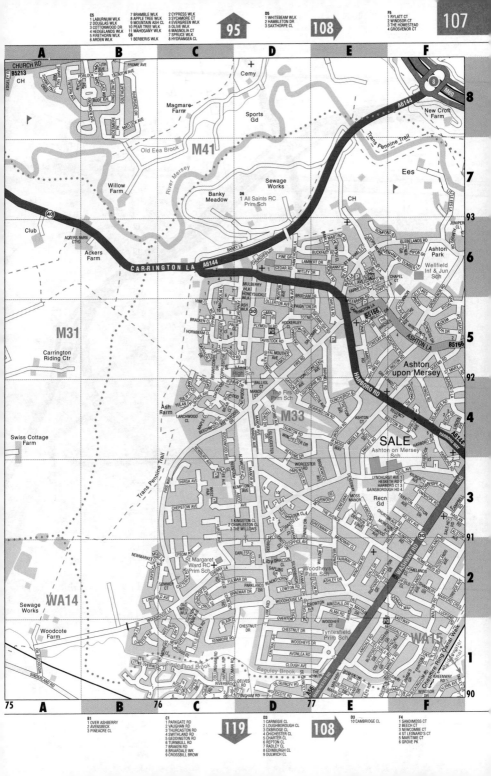

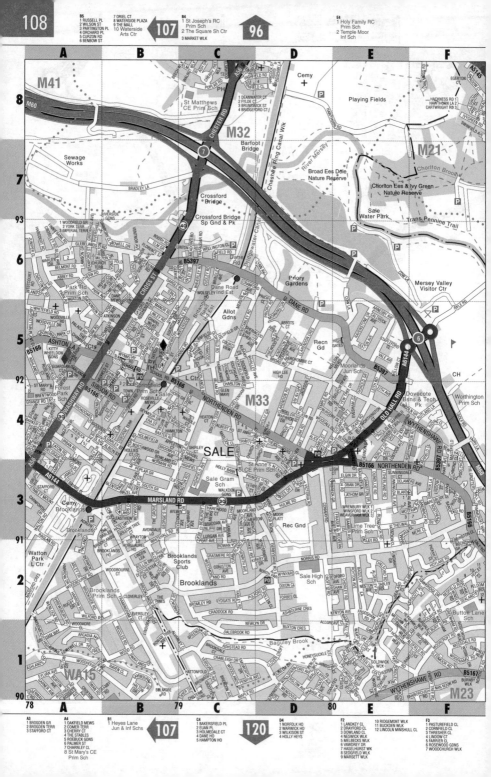

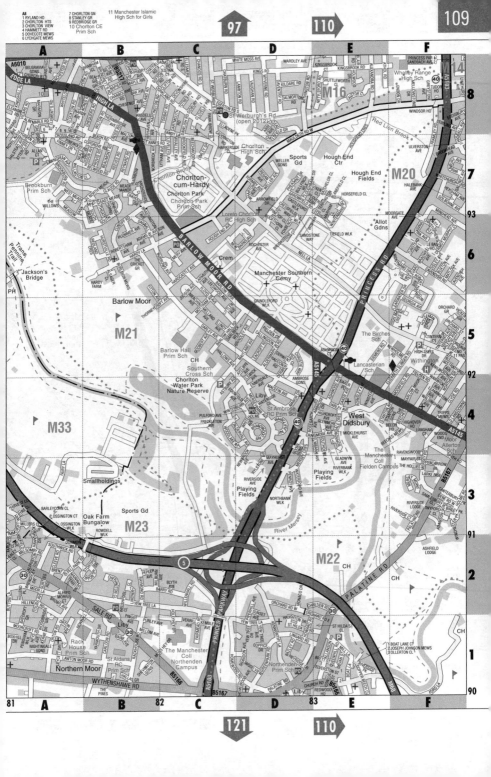

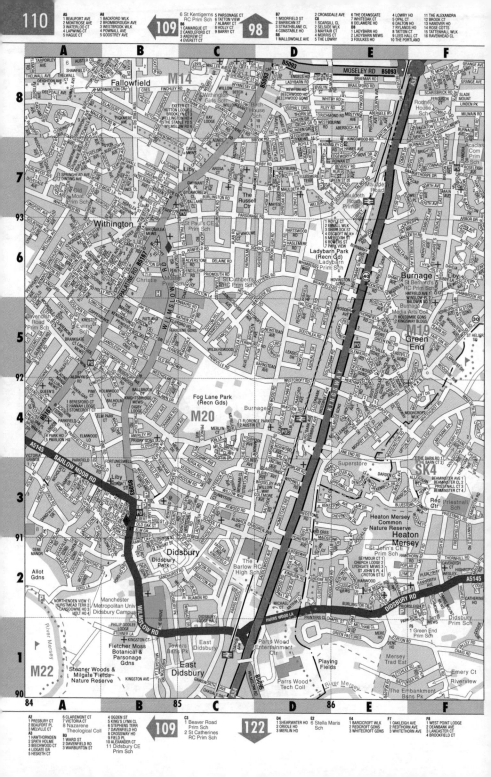

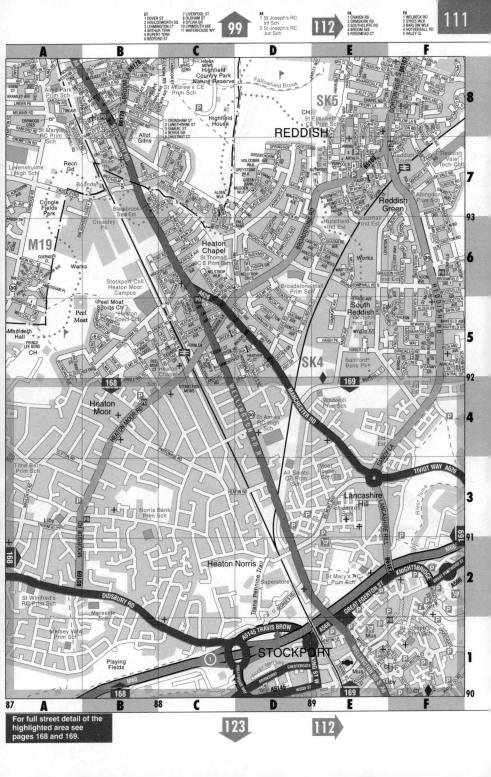

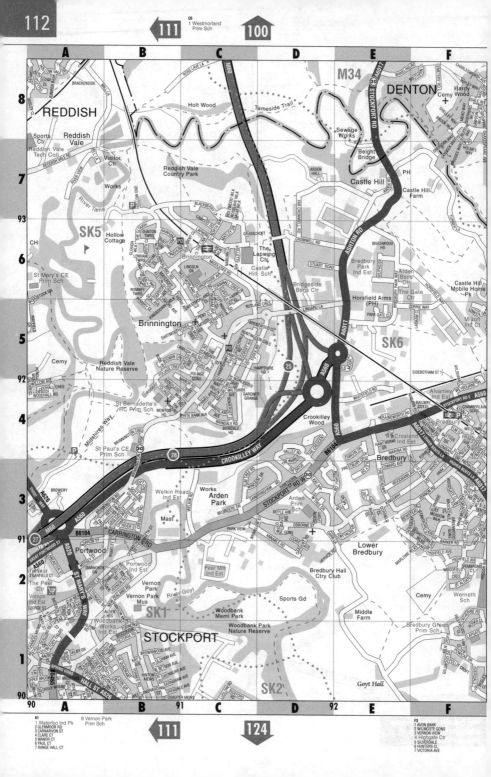

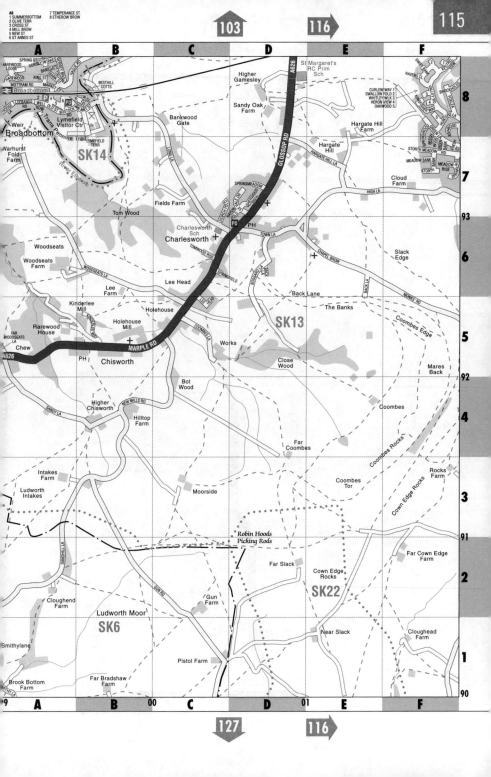

B8
1 PRIMROSE CRES
2 PRIMROSE TERR
3 SUNNY BANKS
4 BRIDGEFIELD
5 EARLS WAY
6 St James CE Sch
7 St Philip Howard
  RC Sports Coll

115

C8
1 HADFIELD SQ
2 VICTORIA MEWS
3 LITTLEMOOR CT
4 NURSERY CL
5 KINGS CT
6 VICTORIA CT

C7
7 JAMES ST
1 ASHTON GDNS
2 RIVERVIEW COTTS
3 THOMAS CHAMBERS
4 ACRE ST
5 ACRE CT

104

F8
1 PEVERIL CT
2 FURNESS CL
3 ASHBOURNE CT
4 GLOUCESTER WAY
5 LINCOLN WAY
6 STAFFORD CL

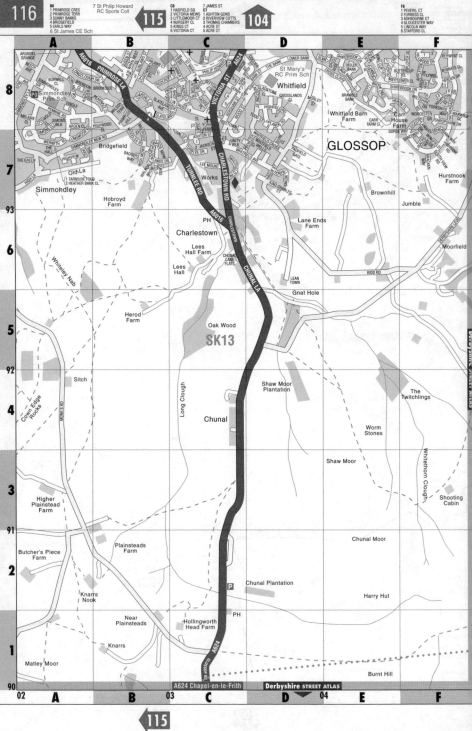

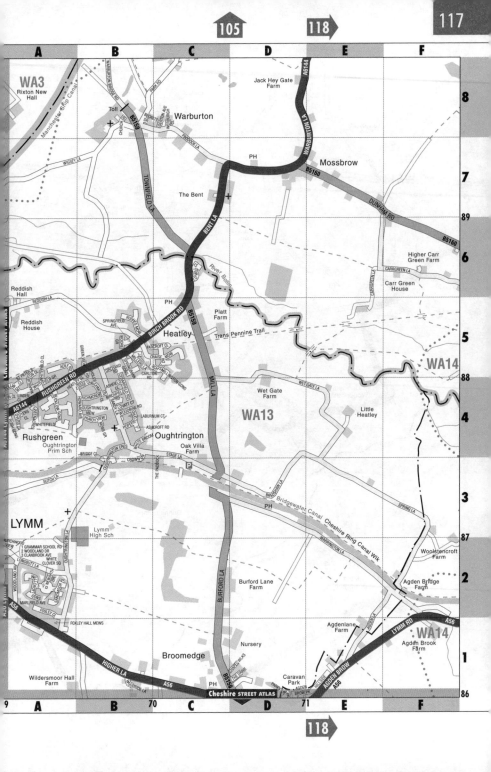

117

106

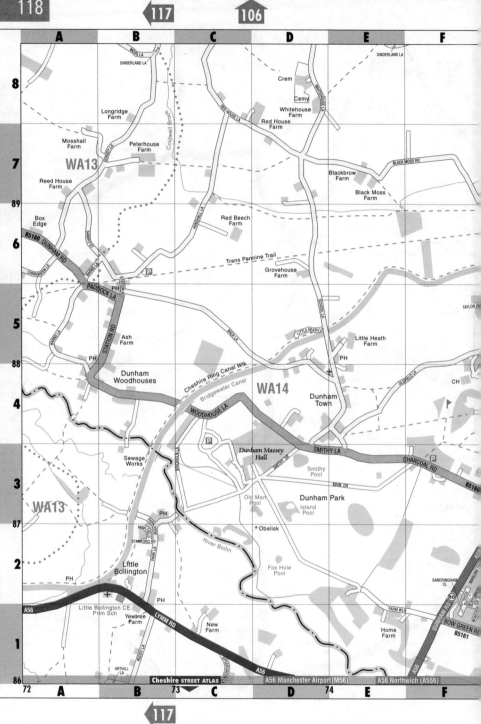

117

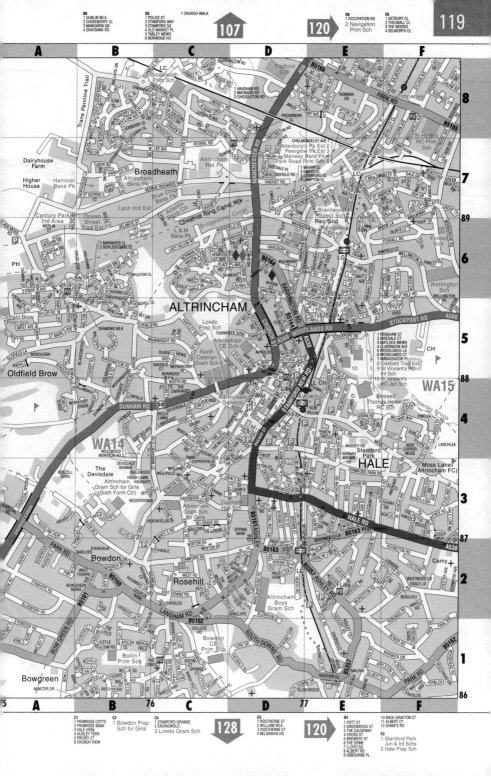

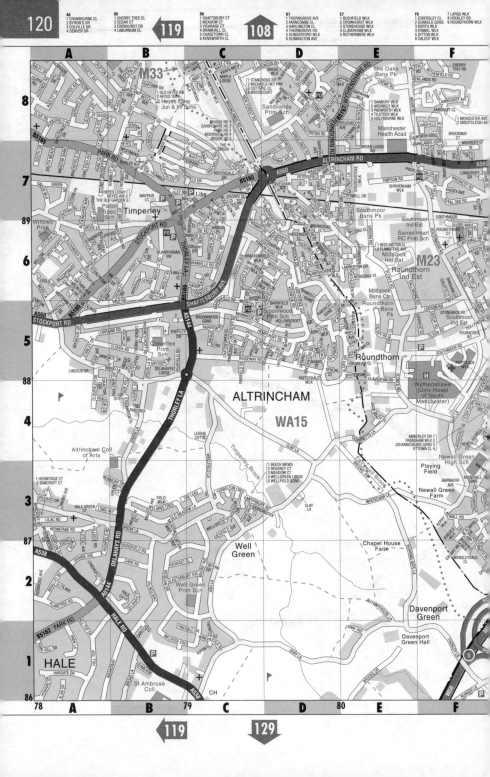

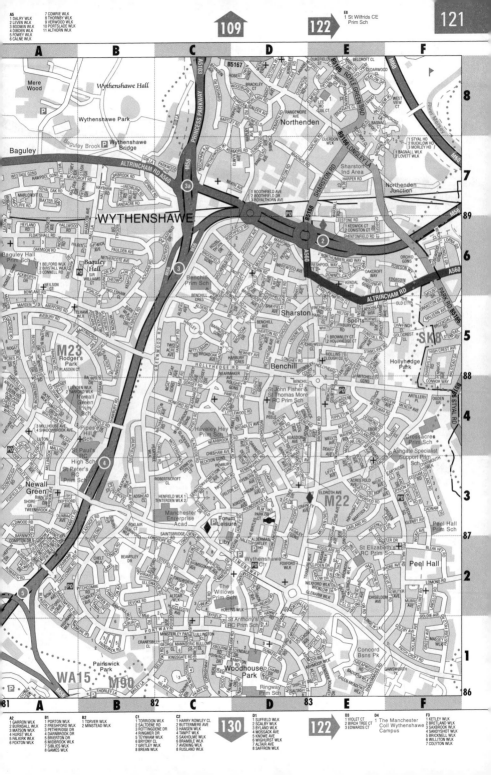

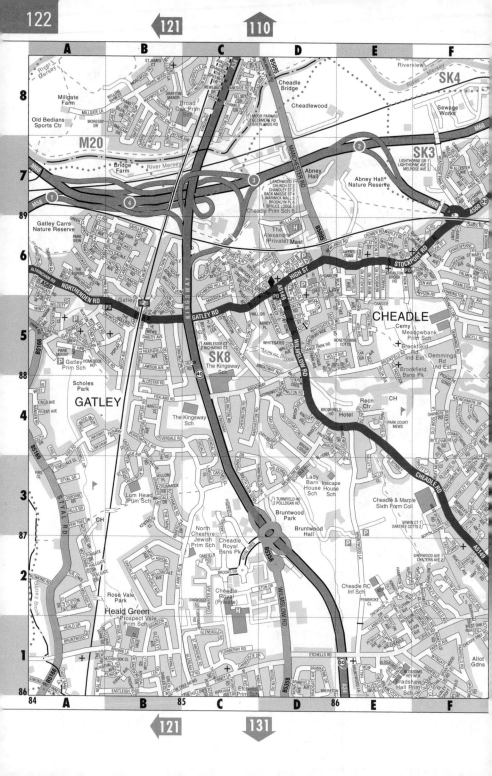

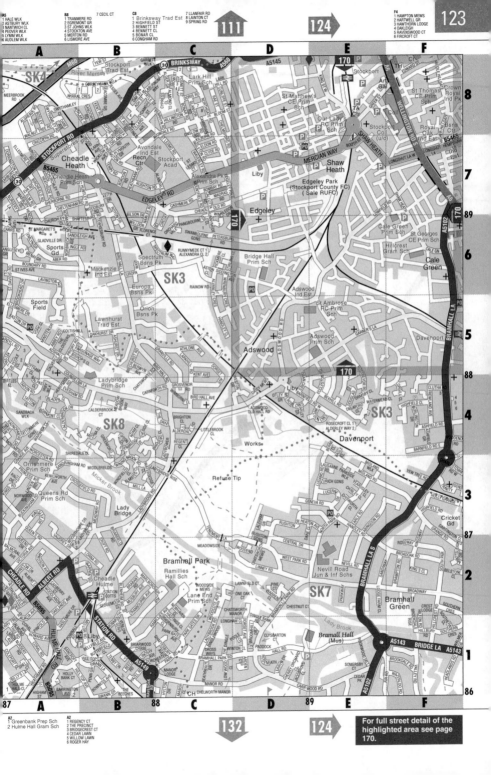

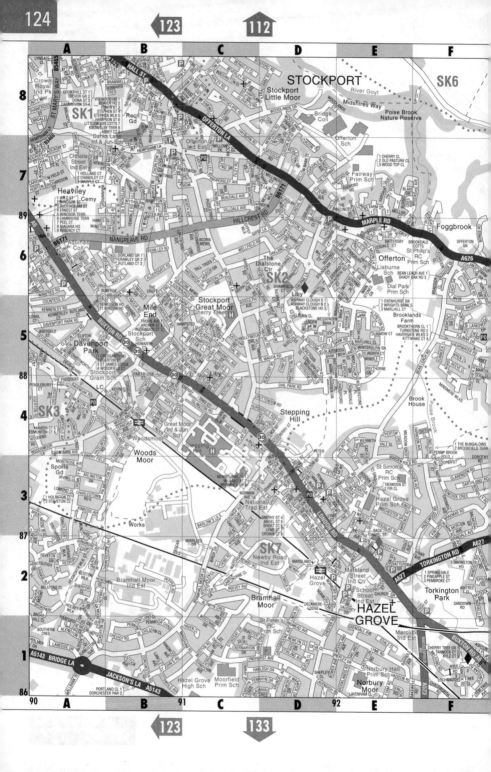

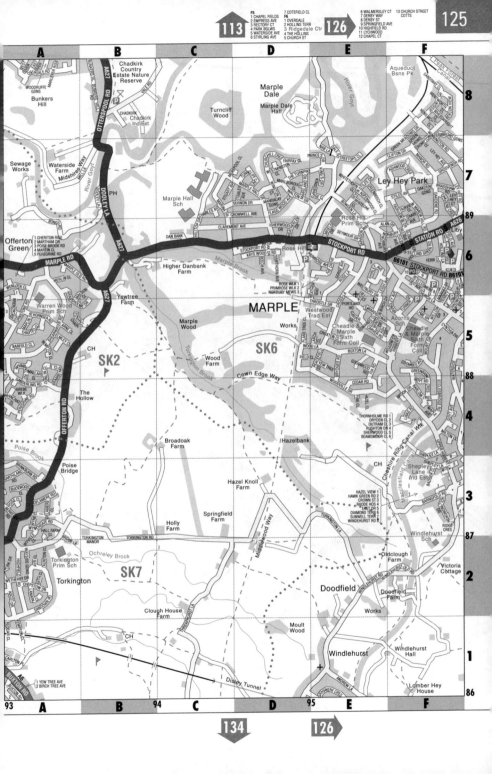

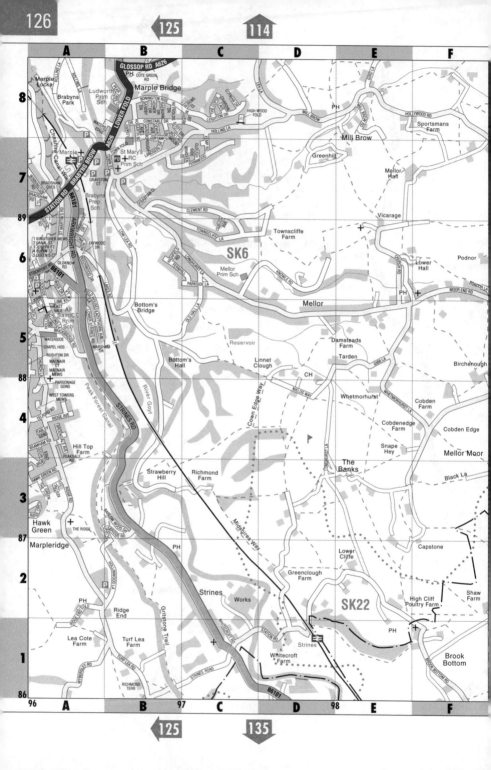

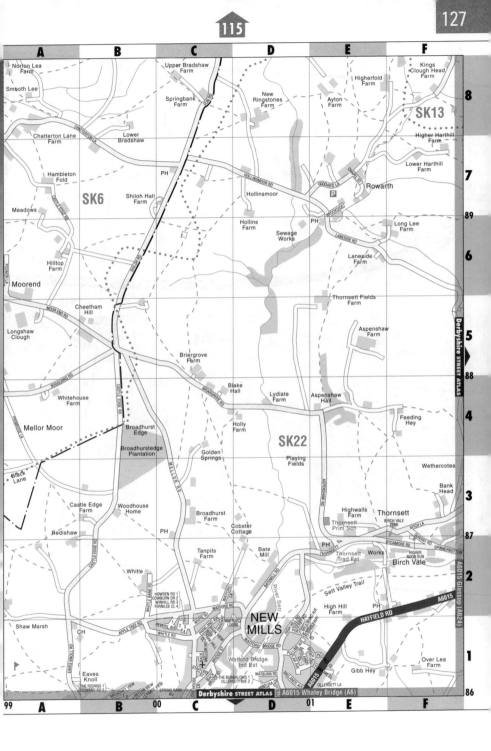

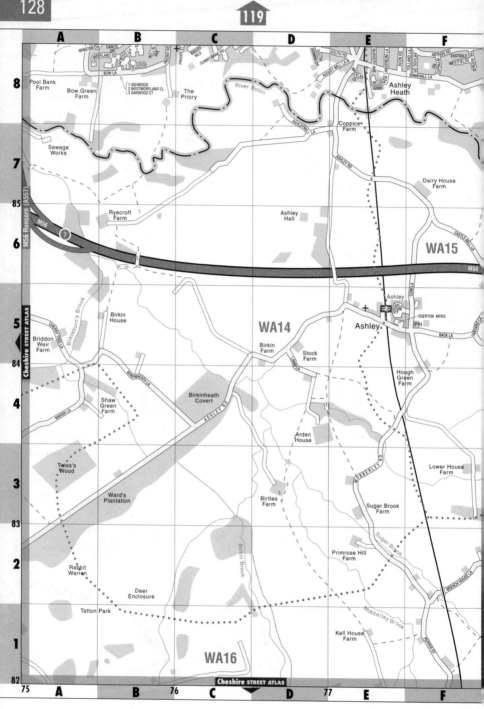

WA15

WA14

WA16

Pool Bank Farm

Bow Green Farm

1 ASHWOOD
2 WESTMORELAND CL
3 OAKWOOD CT

The Priory

River Bollin

Ashley Heath

Coppice Farm

Dairy House Farm

Sewage Works

Ryecroft Farm

Ashley Hall

M56 Runcorn (A557)

M56

M56

Birkin House

Blackburn's Brook

Briddon Weir Farm

Ashley

Ashley

PH

Egerton Moss

Back La

Birkin Farm

Stock Farm

Hough Green Farm

Shaw Green Farm

Birkinheath Covert

Arden House

Lower House Farm

Twiss's Wood

Ward's Plantation

Birtles Farm

Sugar Brook Farm

Sugar Brook

Mobberley Rd

Rabbit Warren

Primrose Hill Farm

Deer Enclosure

Birkin Brook

Mobberley Brook

Tatton Park

Kell House Farm

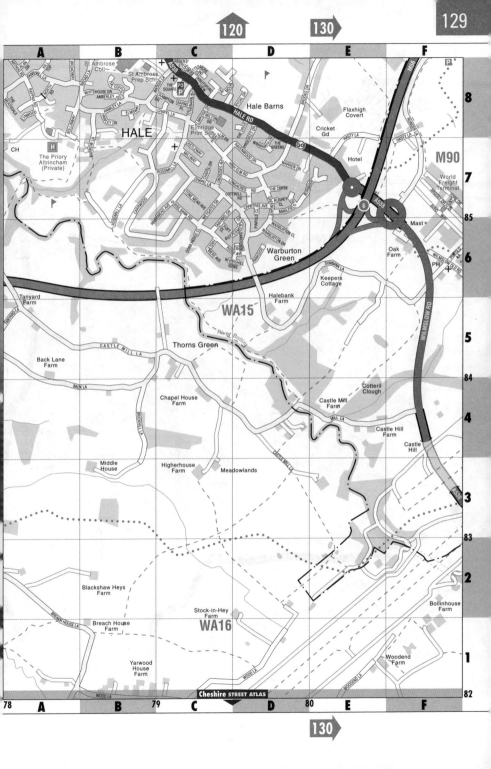

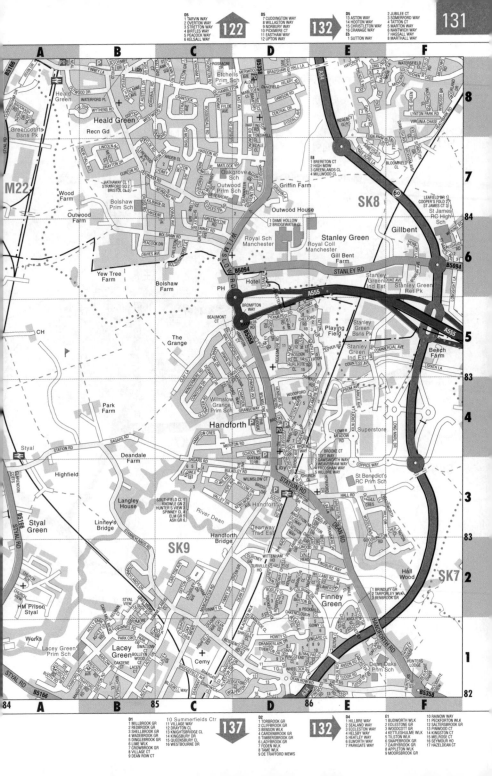

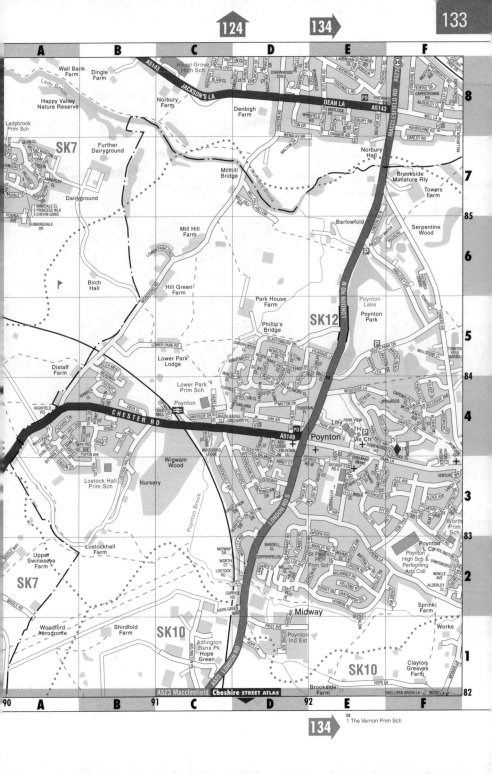

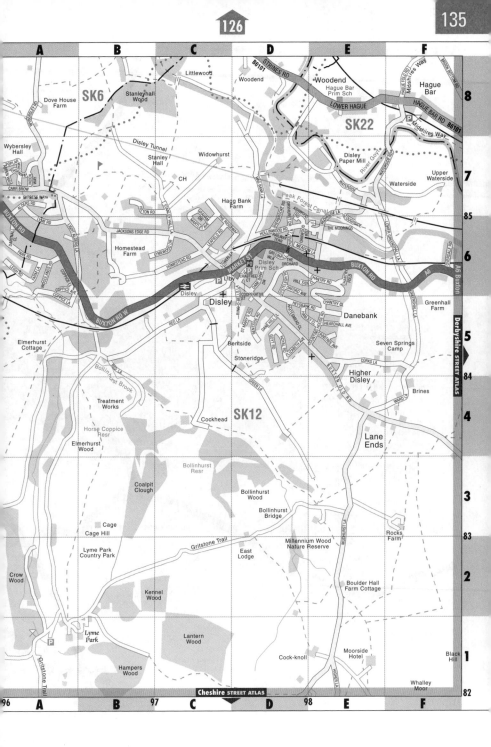

SK6

SK22

SK12

Dove House Farm
Stanleyhall Wood
Littlewood
Woodend
Woodend
Hague Bar Prim Sch
Hague Bar
LOWER HAGUE
STRINES RD
B6101
B6101
HAGUE BAR RD
Midshires Way
BROOK BOTTOM RD
Midshires Way
Wybersley Hall
Disley Tunnel
Stanley Hall
Widowhurst
Disley Paper Mill
Upper Waterside
Waterside
River Goyt
CH
Hagg Bank Farm
Peak Forest Canal
Homestead Farm
Jacksons Edge Rd
THE RIDGEWAY
Disley Prim Sch
THE ORCHARD
THE MOORINGS
RAILWAY TERR
BUXTON RD
A6 Buxton
A6
Greenhall Farm
Disley
Disley
MARKET ST
Lib
PO
CRABTREE CT
HILL SIDE CL
ORFORD AVE
CHANTRY RD
CHANTRY CL
CHANTRY RD
Danebank
SHEARDHALL AVE
Bentside
Stoneridge
GREEN LA
RED LA
ST MARY'S RD
DANE HEY CL
HEYBANK RD
WHITE SMITH CL
HINDLEY CL
ELIZABETH AVE
ROYAL AVE
CORKS LA
Seven Springs Camp
Higher Disley
Brines
WARD'S LA
Elmerhurst Cottage
Bollinhurst Brook
RED LA
Treatment Works
Cockhead
Horse Coppice Resr
Elmerhurst Wood
Lane Ends
Coalpit Clough
Bollinhurst Resr
Bollinhurst Wood
Bollinhurst Bridge
MUCHURST LA
Rocks Farm
Cage
Cage Hill
Lyme Park Country Park
Gritstone Trail
East Lodge
Millennium Wood Nature Reserve
Boulder Hall Farm Cottage
Crow Wood
Kennel Wood
Lantern Wood
Cock-knoll
Moorside Hotel
Black Hill
Lyme Park
Gritstone Trail
Hampers Wood
Whalley Moor

Derbyshire STREET ATLAS

8
7
85
6
5
84
4
3
83
2
1
82

130

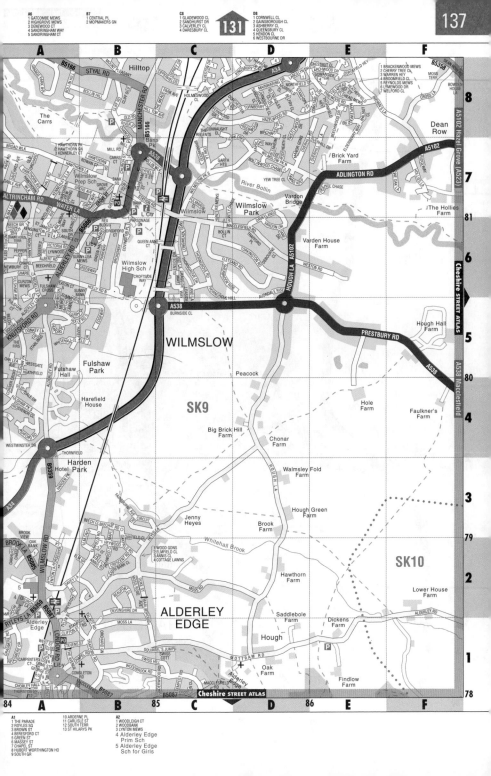

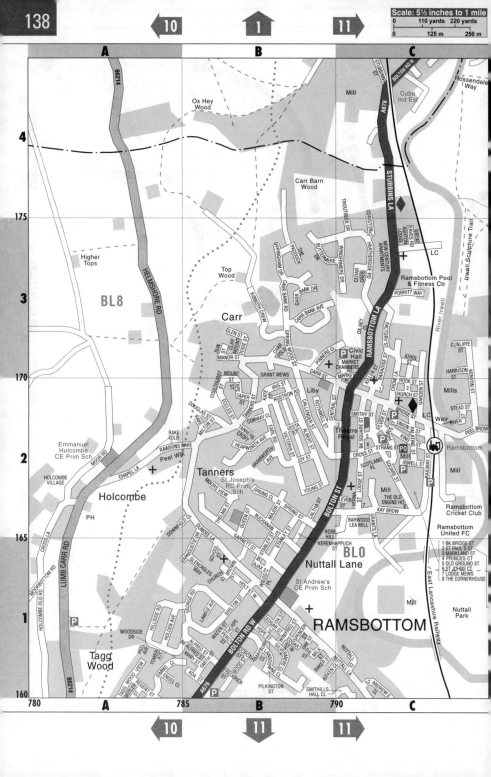

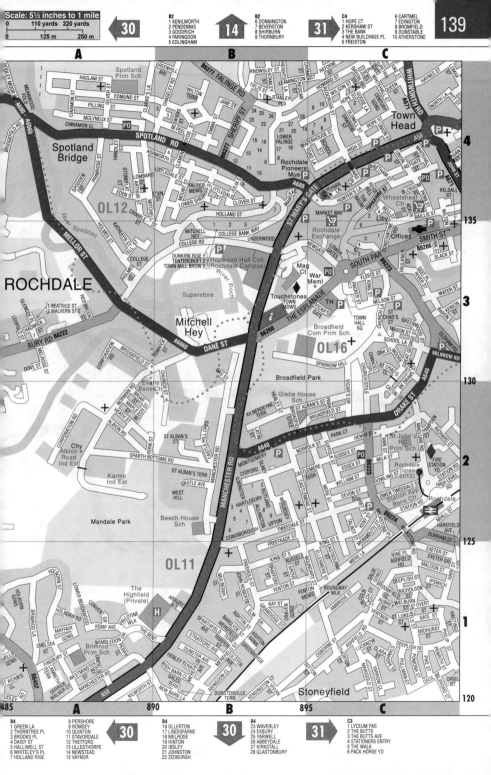

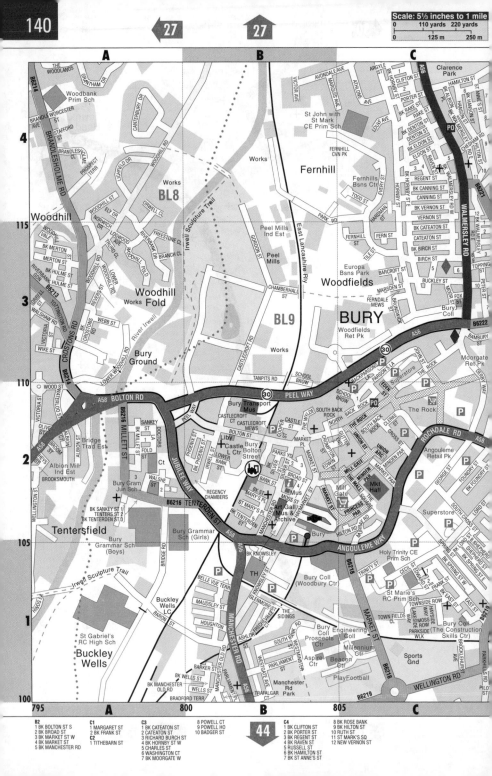

Scale: 5⅓ inches to 1 mile

| 0 | 110 yards | 220 yards |
| 0 | 125 m | 250 m |

B2
1 BK BOLTON ST S
2 BK BROAD ST
3 BK MARKET ST W
4 BK MARKET ST
5 BK MANCHESTER RD

C1
1 MARGARET ST
2 BK FRANK ST
C2
1 TITHEBARN ST

C3
1 BK CATEATON ST
2 CATEATON ST
3 RICHARD BURCH ST
4 BK HORNBY ST W
5 CHARLES ST
6 WASHINGTON CT
7 BK MOORGATE W

8 POWELL CT
9 POWELL HO
10 BADGER ST

C4
1 BK CLIFTON ST
2 BK PORTER ST
3 BK REGENT ST
4 BK RAVEN ST
5 RUSSELL ST
6 BK HAMILTON ST
7 BK ST ANNE'S ST

8 BK ROSE BANK
9 BK HILTON ST
10 RUTH ST
11 ST MARK'S SQ
12 NEW VERNON ST

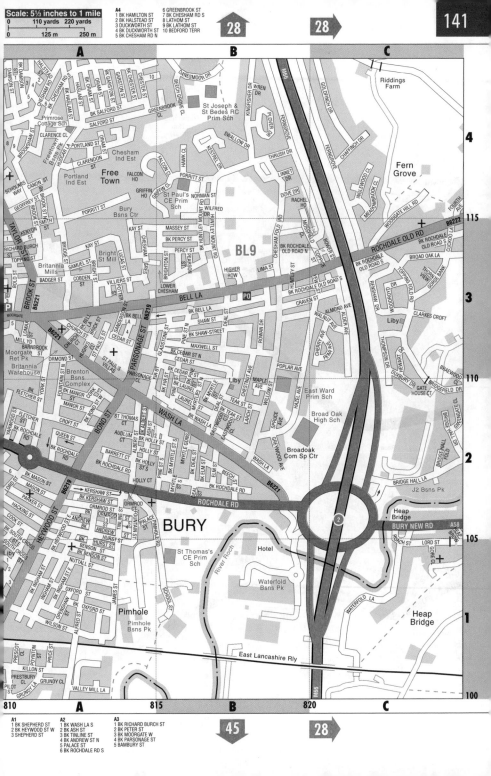

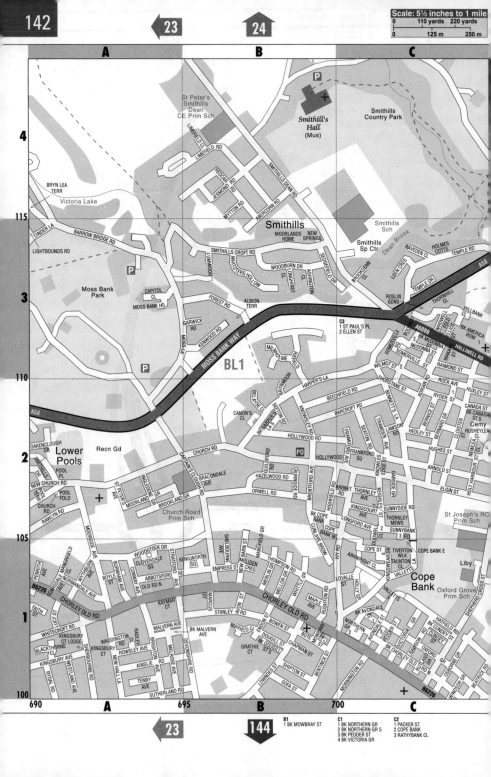

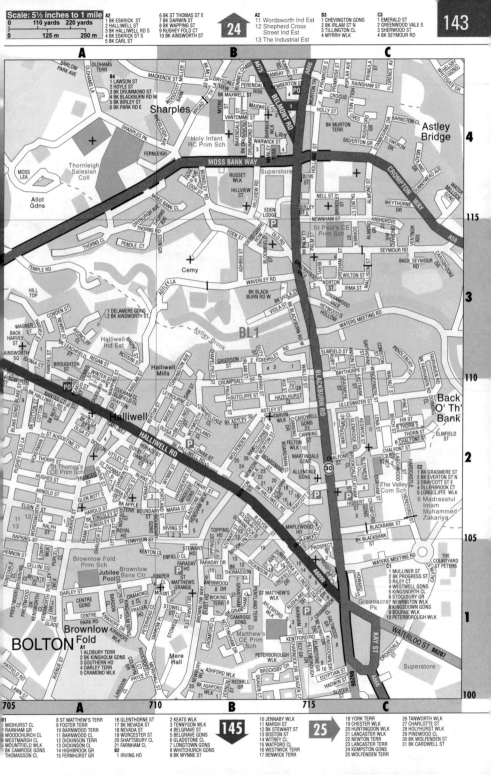

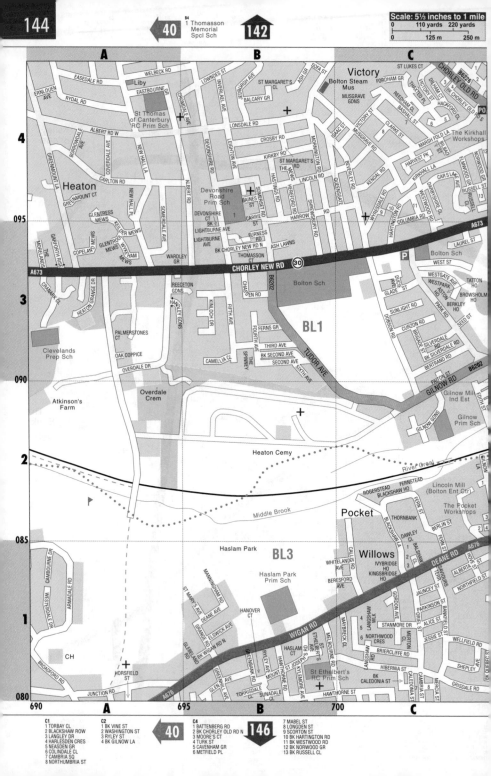

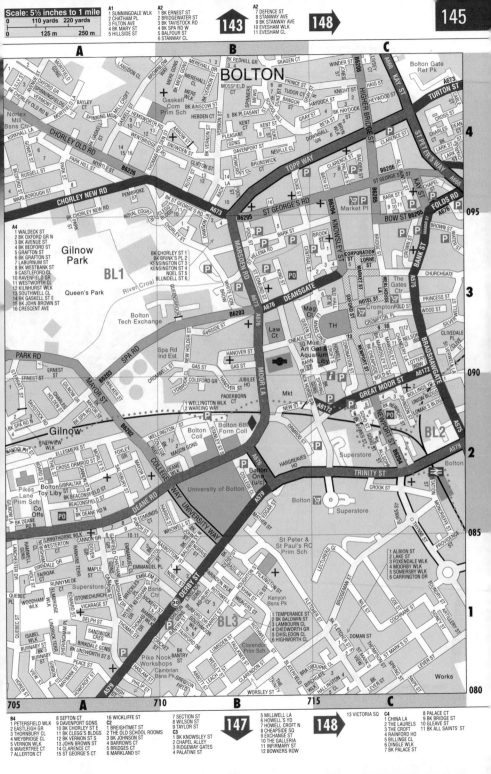

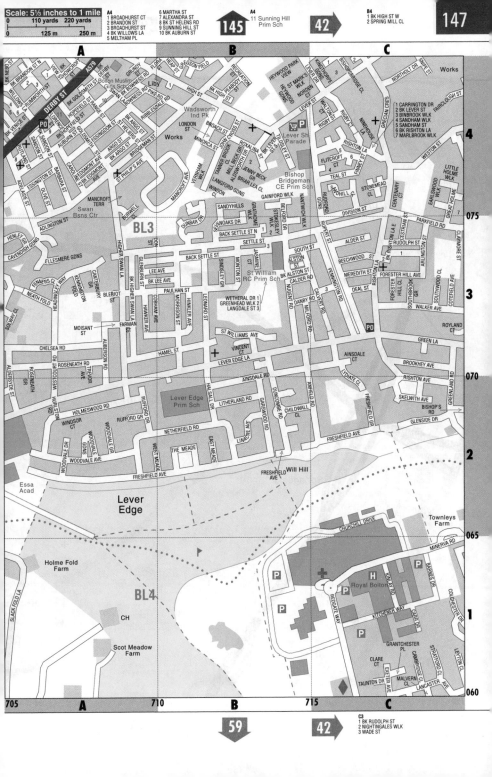

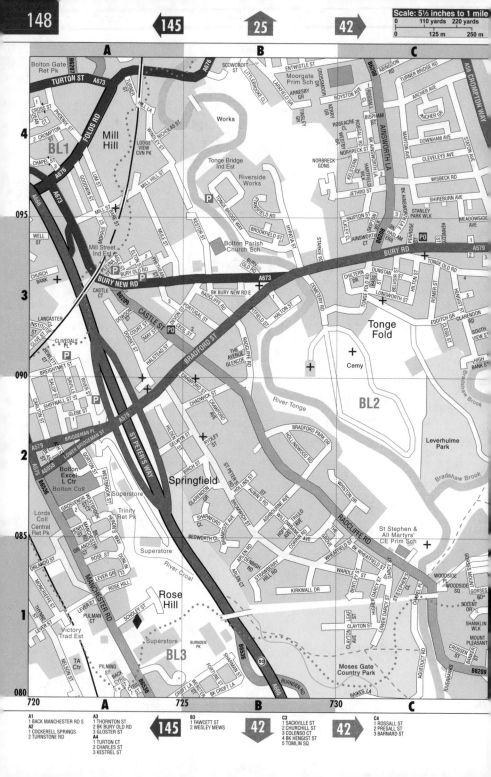

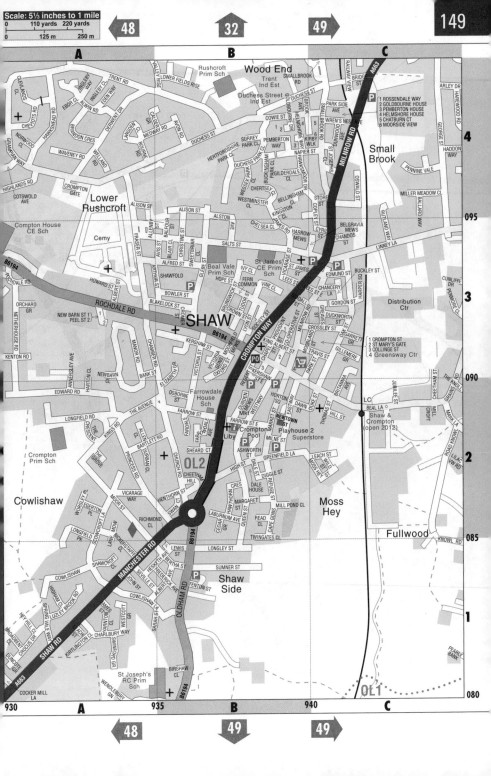

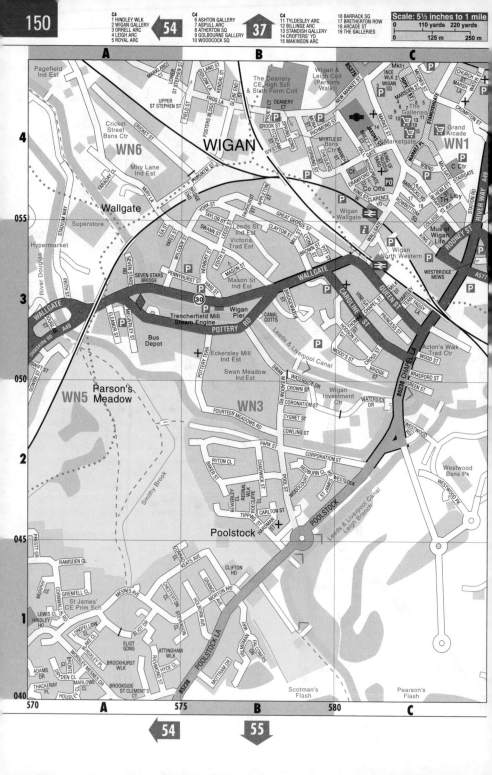

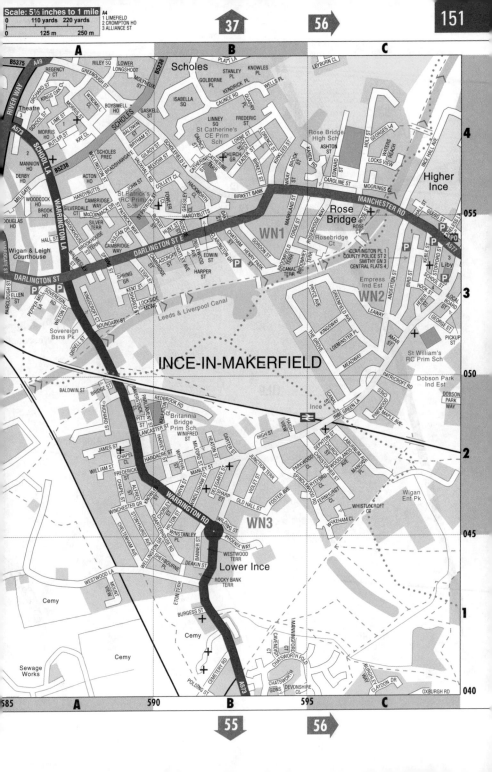

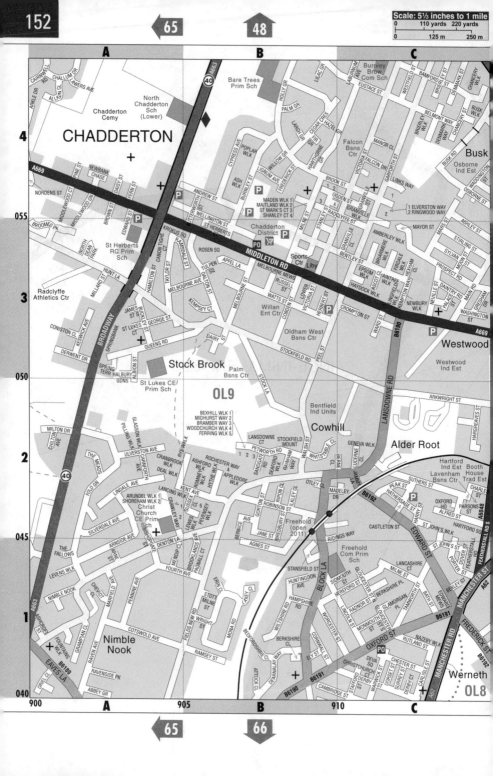

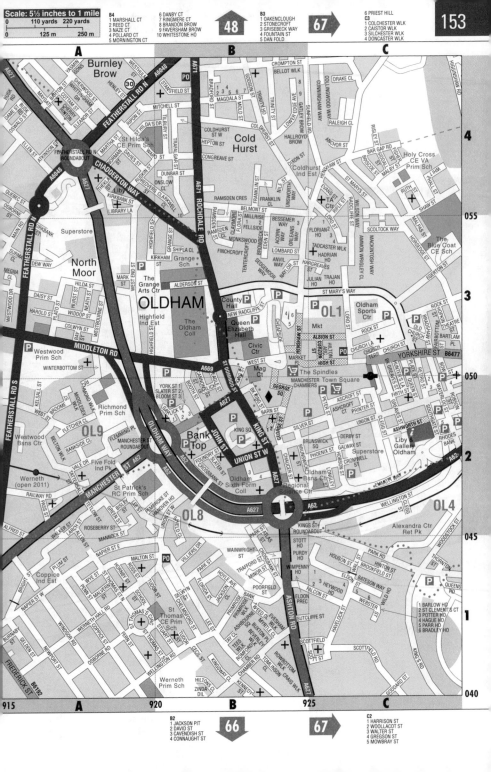

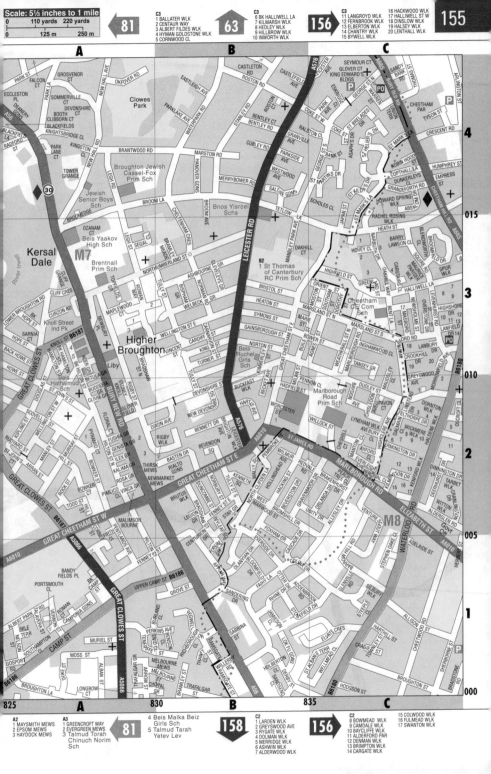

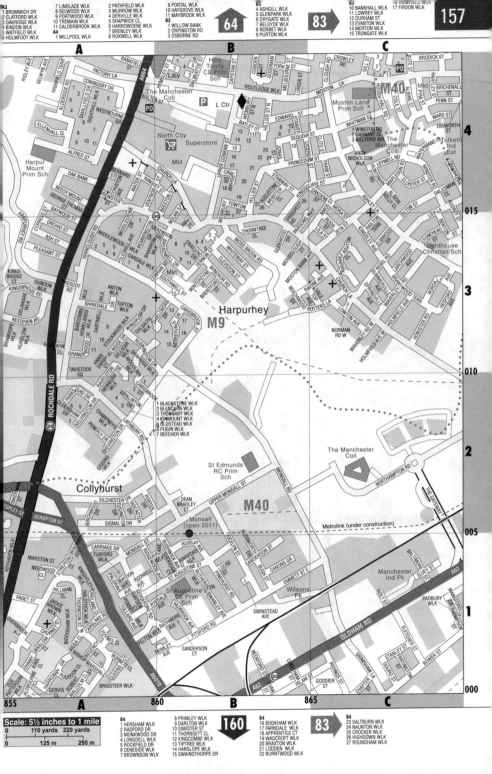

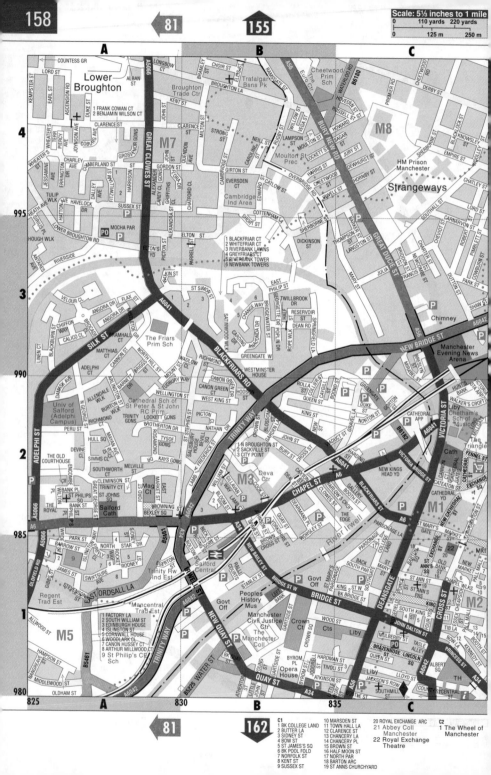

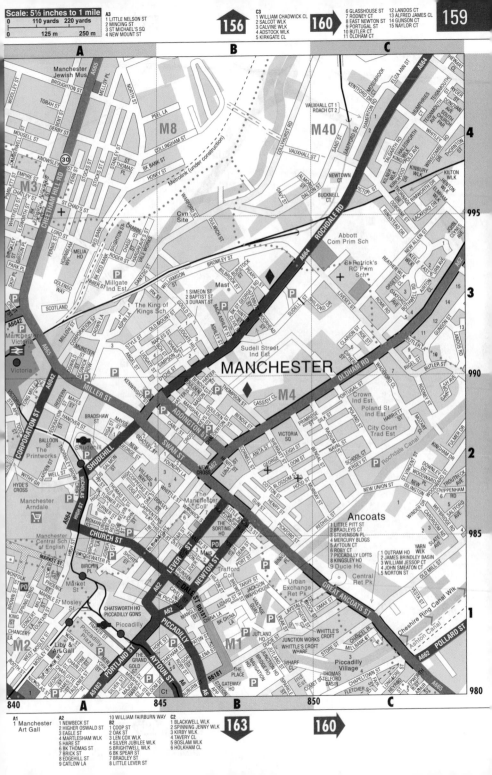

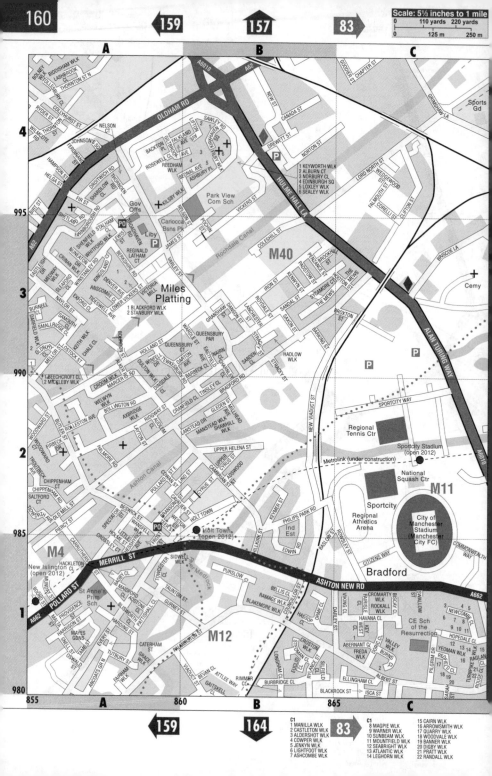

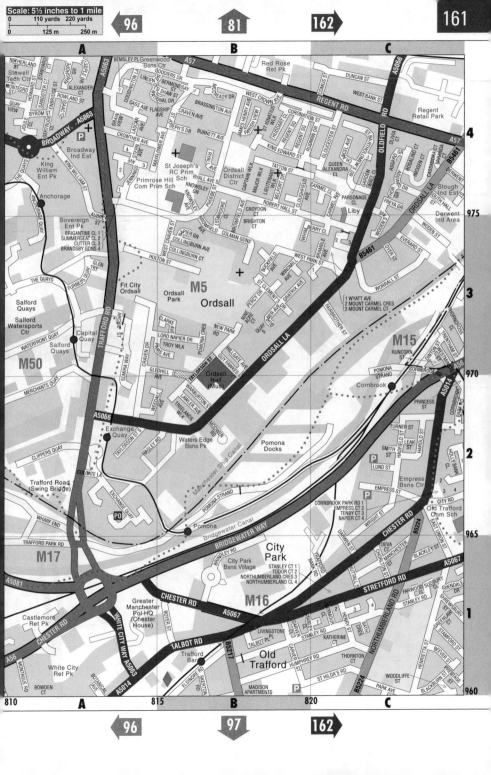

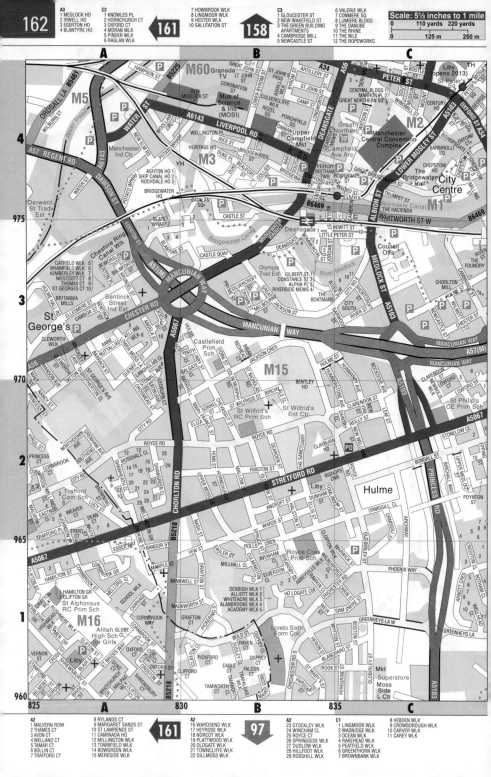

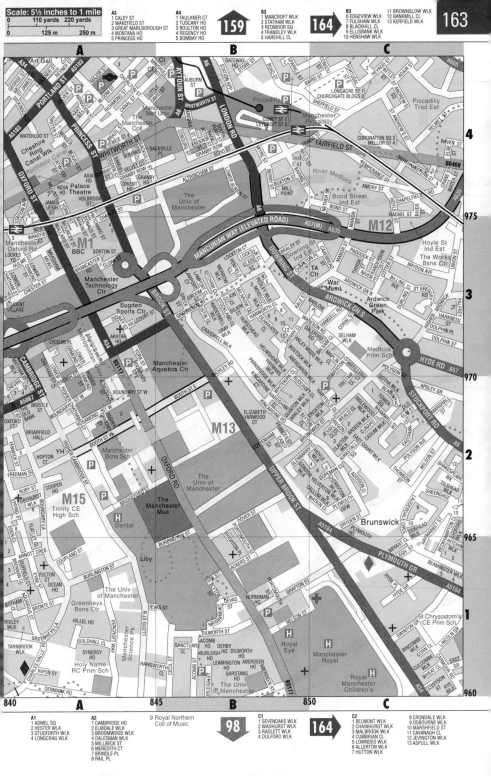

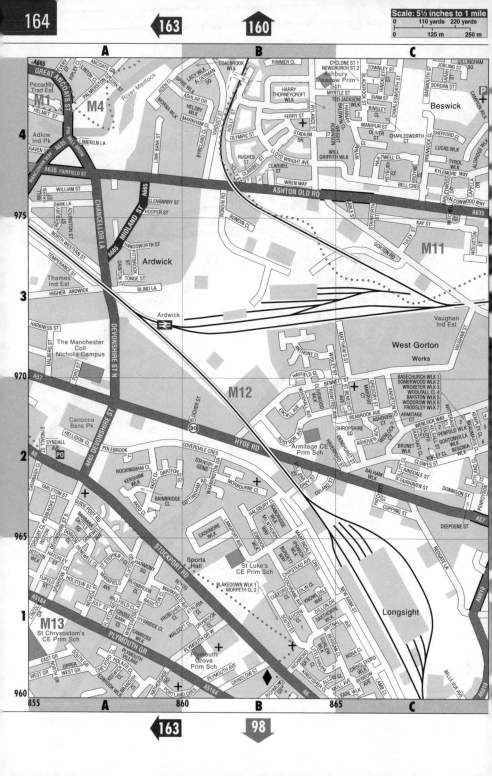

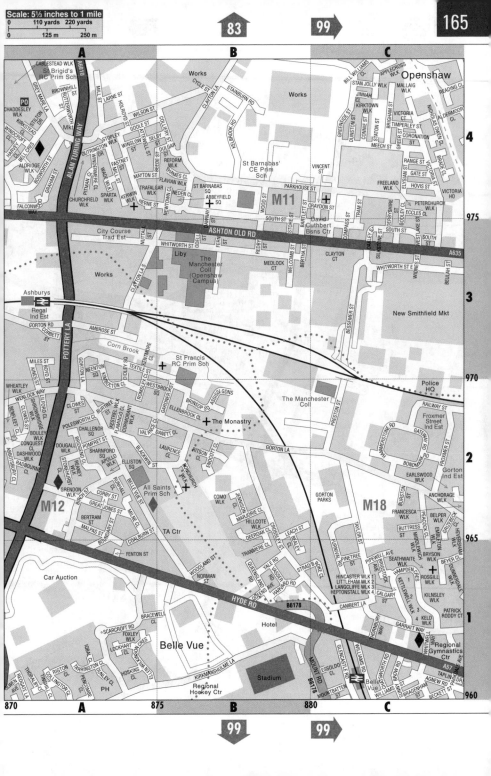

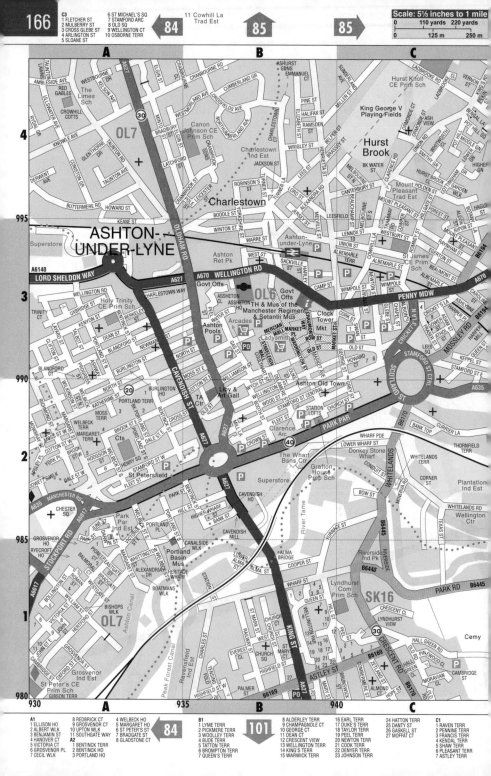

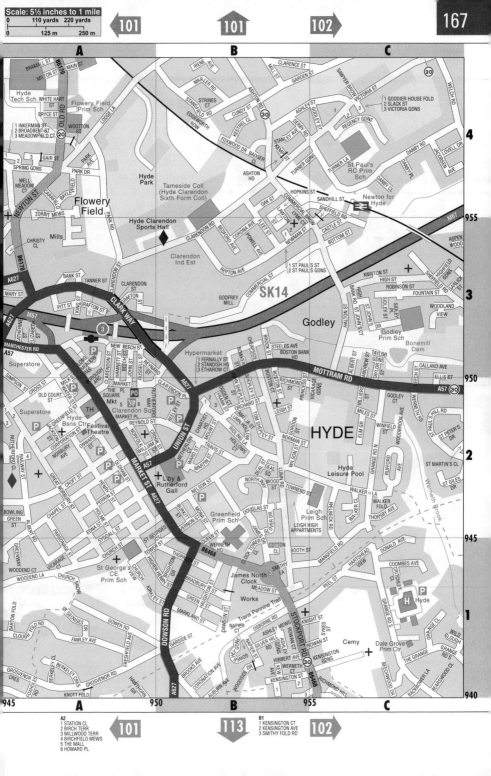

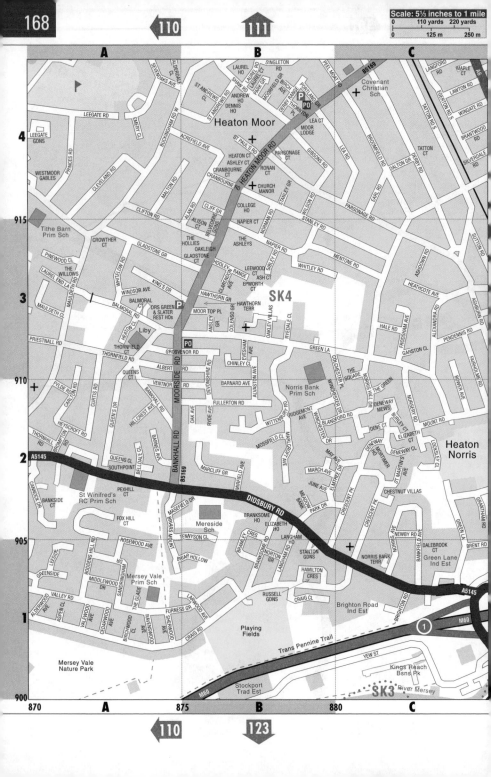

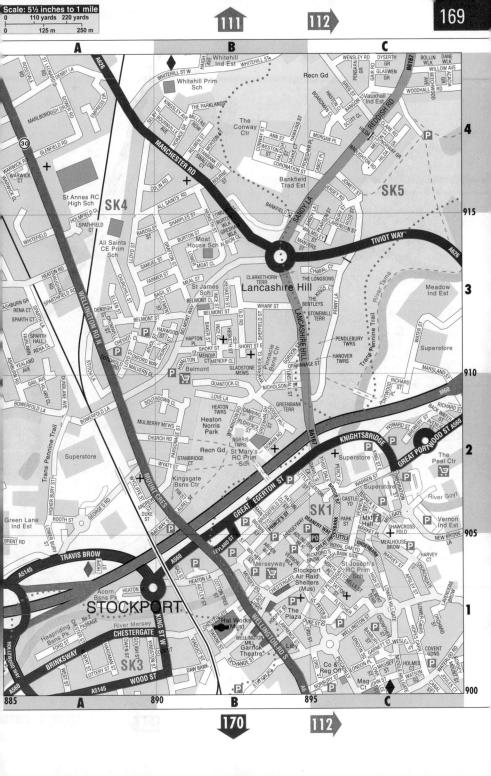

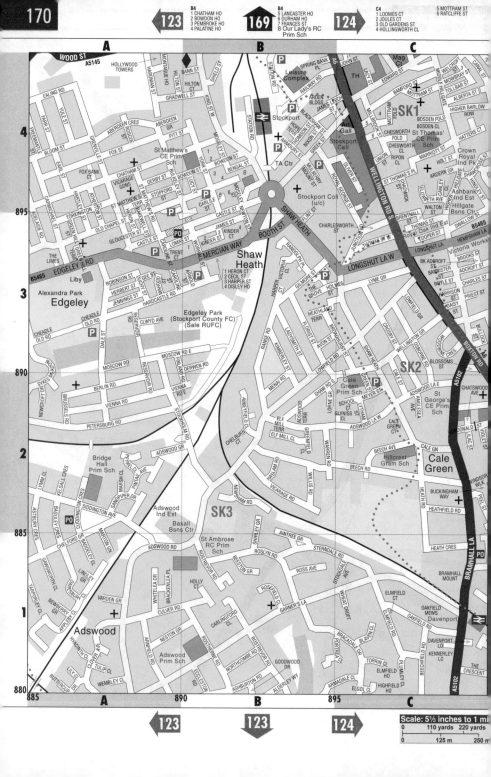

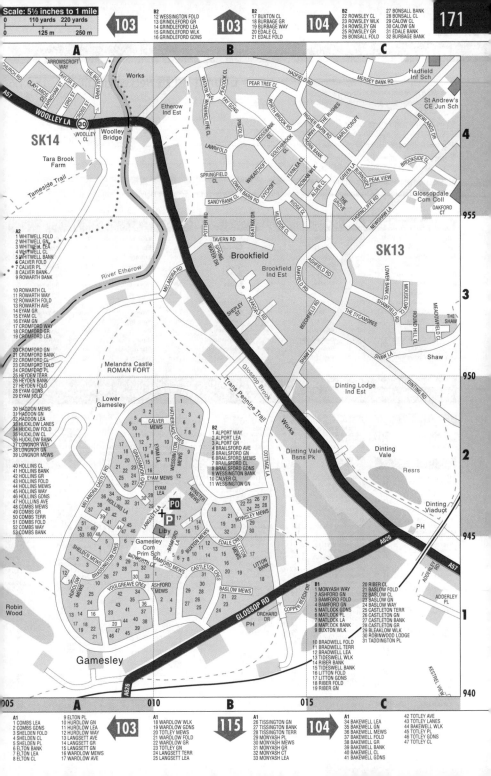

B2
12 WESSINGTON FOLD
13 GRINDLEFORD GR
14 GRINDLEFORD LEA
15 GRINDLEFORD WLK
16 GRINDLEFORD GDNS

B2
17 BUXTON CL
18 BURBAGE GR
19 BURBAGE WAY
20 EDALE CL
21 EDALE FOLD

B2
22 ROWSLEY CL
23 ROWSLEY WLK
24 ROWSLEY GN
25 ROWSLEY GR
26 ROWSLEY FOLD

27 BONSALL BANK
28 BONSALL CL
29 CALOW CL
30 CALOW GN
31 EDALE BANK
32 BURBAGE BANK

A2
1 WHITWELL FOLD
2 WHITWELL GN
3 WHITWELL LEA
4 WHITWELL CL
5 WHITWELL BANK
6 CALVER FOLD
7 CALVER PL
8 CALVER BANK
9 ROWARTH BANK

10 ROWARTH CL
11 ROWARTH WAY
12 ROWARTH FOLD
13 ROWARTH AVE
14 EYAM GR
15 EYAM CL
16 EYAM GN
17 CROMFORD WAY
18 CROMFORD GR
19 CROMFORD LEA

20 CROMFORD GN
21 CROMFORD BANK
22 CROMFORD CL
23 CROMFORD FOLD
24 CROMFORD PL
25 HEYDEN TERR
26 HEYDEN BANK
27 HEYDEN FOLD
28 EYAM GDNS
29 EYAM FOLD

30 HADDON MEWS
31 HADDON GN
32 HADDON LEA
33 HUCKLOW LANES
34 HUCKLOW FOLD
35 HUCKLOW CL
36 HUCKLOW BANK
37 LONGNOR WAY
38 LONGNOR GN
39 LONGNOR MEWS

40 HOLLINS CL
41 HOLLINS BANK
42 HOLLINS GN
43 HOLLINS FOLD
44 HOLLINS MEWS
45 HOLLINS WAY
46 HOLLINS GDNS
47 HOLLLINS AVE
48 COMBS MEWS
49 COMBS GR
50 COMBS TERR
51 COMBS FOLD
52 COMBS WAY
53 COMBS BANK

B2
1 ALPORT WAY
2 ALPORT LEA
3 ALPORT GR
4 BRAILSFORD AVE
5 BRAILSFORD GR
6 BRAILSFORD MEWS
7 BRAILSFORD CL
8 BRAILSFORD GDNS
9 WESSINGTON BANK
10 CALVER CL
11 WESSINGTON GN

B1
1 MONYASH WAY
2 ASHFORD GN
3 BAMFORD FOLD
4 BAMFORD GN
5 MATLOCK GDNS
6 MATLOCK PL
7 MATLOCK LEA
8 MATLOCK BANK
9 BUXTON WLK

10 BRADWELL FOLD
11 BRADWELL TERR
12 BRADWELL LEA
13 TIDESWELL WLK
14 RIBER BANK
15 TIDESWELL BANK
16 LITTON FOLD
17 LITTON GDNS
18 RIBER FOLD
19 RIBER GN

20 RIBER CL
21 BASLOW FOLD
22 BASLOW CL
23 BASLOW GN
24 BASLOW WAY
25 CASTLETON TERR
26 CASTLETON BANK
27 CASTLETON GR
28 CASTLETON GR
29 BLEAKLOW WLK
30 ROBINWOOD LODGE
31 TADDINGTON PL

A1
1 COMBS LEA
2 COMBS GDNS
3 SHELDEN FOLD
4 SHELDEN CL
5 SHELDEN FOLD
6 SHELDEN PL
7 ELTON LEA
8 ELTON CL

9 ELTON PL
10 HURDLOW GN
11 HURDLOW LEA
12 HURDLOW WAY
13 LANGSETT AVE
14 LANGSETT GR
15 WARDLOW MEWS
16 WARDLOW MEWS
17 WARDLOW AVE

A1
18 WARDLOW WLK
19 WARDLOW GDNS
20 TOTLEY MEWS
21 WARDLOW FOLD
22 WARDLOW GR
23 TOTLEY GN
24 LANGSETT TERR
25 LANGSETT LEA

A1
26 TISSINGTON GN
27 TISSINGTON BANK
28 TISSINGTON TERR
29 MONYASH PL
30 MONYASH WAY
31 MONYASH GR
32 MONYASH CT
33 MONYASH LEA

A1
34 BAKEWELL LEA
35 BAKEWELL GN
36 BAKEWELL MEWS
37 BAKEWELL FOLD
38 BAKEWELL GR
39 BAKEWELL BANK
40 BAKEWELL CL
41 BAKEWELL GDNS

42 TOTLEY AVE
43 TOTLEY LANES
44 BAKEWELL WLK
45 TOTLEY PL
46 TOTLEY GDNS
47 TOTLEY CL

Index

Place name May be abbreviated on the map

Location number Present when a number indicates the place's position in a crowded area of mapping

Locality, town or village Shown when more than one place has the same name

Postcode district District for the indexed place

Page and grid square Page number and grid reference for the standard mapping

Church Rd **6** Beckenham BR2..........**53** C6

Cities, towns and villages are listed in CAPITAL LETTERS

Public and commercial buildings are highlighted in magenta   **Places of interest** are highlighted in blue with a star★

Abbreviations used in the index

Acad	Academy	Comm	Common	Gd	Ground	L	Leisure	Prom	Promenade
App	Approach	Cott	Cottage	Gdn	Garden	La	Lane	Rd	Road
Arc	Arcade	Cres	Crescent	Gn	Green	Liby	Library	Recn	Recreation
Ave	Avenue	Cswy	Causeway	Gr	Grove	Mdw	Meadow	Ret	Retail
Bglw	Bungalow	Ct	Court	H	Hall	Meml	Memorial	Sh	Shopping
Bldg	Building	Ctr	Centre	Ho	House	Mkt	Market	Sq	Square
Bsns, Bus	Business	Ctry	Country	Hospl	Hospital	Mus	Museum	St	Street
Bvd	Boulevard	Cty	County	HQ	Headquarters	Orch	Orchard	Sta	Station
Cath	Cathedral	Dr	Drive	Hts	Heights	Pal	Palace	Terr	Terrace
Cir	Circus	Dro	Drove	Ind	Industrial	Par	Parade	TH	Town Hall
Cl	Close	Ed	Education	Inst	Institute	Pas	Passage	Univ	University
Cnr	Corner	Emb	Embankment	Int	International	Pk	Park	Wk, Wlk	Walk
Coll	College	Est	Estate	Intc	Interchange	Pl	Place	Wr	Water
Com	Community	Ex	Exhibition	Junc	Junction	Prec	Precinct	Yd	Yard

Index of towns, villages, streets, hospitals, industrial estates, railway stations, schools, shopping centres, universities and places of interest

1st–Acr

1st St WN2 . . . . 73 E7
3rd St WN2 . . . . 73 E7
4th St WN2 . . . . 73 F7

A

Abberley Dr M40 . . . . . . 65 D2
Abberley Way WN3 . . . 54 B4
Abberton Rd M20 . . . . . 110 A6
Abbey Cl
Altrincham WA14 . . . . 119 B1
Bolton BL3 . . . . 146 B2
Radcliffe M26 . . . . . . 43 E5
Up Holland WN8 . . . . 53 C7
Urmston M32 . . . . . . 95 F3
Abbey Coll Manchester **21**
M2 . . . . 158 C1
Abbeycourt M30 . . . . . 79 E2
Abbey Cres OL10 . . . . 29 B4
Abbeycroft Cl M29 . . . . 77 C6
Abbey Ct
Manchester M18 . . . . . 99 E6
Poynton SK12 . . . . . . 133 D3
Radcliffe M26 . . . . . . 43 E4
Stockport SK1 . . . . . . 124 B8
Wigan WN5 . . . . 36 E2
Abbeydale **26** OL12 . . . 139 B4
Abbey Dale M36 . . . . . 35 D7
Abbeydale Cl
Ashton-u-l OL6 . . . . . 85 E6
Cheadle SK8 . . . . . . 131 E7
Abbeydale Gdns M28 . . 60 C3
Abbeydale Rd M40 . . . . 83 C8
Abbey Dr
Bury BL8 . . . . 27 A1
Littleborough OL15 . . . 15 F3
Orrell WN5 . . . . 53 E6
Swinton M27 . . . . . . 61 E1
Abbeyfield Cl SK3 . . . 170 B2
Abbeyfields WN6 . . . . 36 E2
Abbeyfield Sq M11 . . . 165 B4
Abbey Gdns SK14 . . . 103 A3
Abbey Gr
Adlington PR6 . . . . . 21 B7
Chadderton OL9 . . . . 152 A1
Eccles M30 . . . . 79 E2
Mottram-in-L SK14 . . . 102 F3
Stockport SK1 . . . . . 124 B8
ABBEY HEY 99 F5

Abbey Hey La M11, M18 . . . 99 F6
Abbey Hey Prim Sch M18 . 99 E5
Abbey Hills Rd OL4, OL8 . . 67 C4
Abden La WN7 . . . . . . 57 D1
Abbey Lawn M16 . . . . 97 B3
Abbeylea Cres BL5 . . . 40 A2
Abbeylea Dr BL5 . . . . 40 A2
Abbey Rd
Cheadle SK8 . . . . . . 123 A5
Delph OL3 . . . . 50 E5
Droylsden M43 . . . . . 83 F3
Failsworth M35 . . . . . 84 B8
Golborne WA3 . . . . . 91 C8
Middleton M24 . . . . . 46 F4
Sale M33 . . . . 108 A6
Tyldesley M29 . . . . . 77 C7
Abbey Sq WN7 . . . . . 57 D1
Abbey St WN7 . . . . . 75 F6
Abbeystead M21 . . . . 109 D8
Abbeyville Wlk M15 . . 162 B1
Abbey Way M16 . . . . 44 A3
Abbeyway N WA11 . . . 89 A7
Abbeyway S WA11 . . . 89 A7
Abbeywood Ave M18 . . 99 E4
Abbingdon Way WN7 . . 57 D1
Abbot Croft BL5 . . . . 57 F6
Abbotsbury Cl
Manchester M12 . . . . 165 A2
Poynton SK12 . . . . . 133 D5
Abbots Cl M33 . . . . . 108 D5
Abbots Cl M33 . . . . . 108 D5
Abbotsfield Cl M41 . . . 94 D3
Abbotsfield Cl WA3 . . . 74 D1
Abbot's Fold Rd M28 . . 78 B7
Abbotsford Cl WA3 . . . 74 D1
Abbotsford Dr M24 . . . 46 D4
Abbotsford Gr WA14 . . 119 E8
Abbotsford Prep Sch M41 . 95 A2
Abbotsford Rd
Bolton BL1 . . . . 142 A1
Chadderton OL9 . . . . 65 E8
Manchester M21 . . . . 97 B1
Oldham OL1 . . . . . . 49 B1
Abbotside Cl M16 . . . . 97 D3
Abbotsleigh Ave M23 . . 120 F8
Abbington Dr WN2 . . . 56 A3
Abbington Rd M33 . . . 108 C3
Abbott Com Prim Sch
M40 . . . . 159 C3
Abbotts Gn M29 . . . . 77 A4
Abbott St
Bolton BL3 . . . . 145 B1
Horwich BL6 . . . . . . 22 B4

Abbott St *continued*
Rochdale OL11 . . . . . . 30 B3
Abbotts Way WN5 . . . . 71 D3
Abden St M26 . . . . . . 44 A3
Abel Ho BL8 . . . . 26 A4
Abels La OL3 . . . . 69 C8
Aber Ave SK2 . . . . . . 124 C4
Abercorn Cl M8 . . . . . 156 A3
Abercorn Rd BL1 . . . . 142 B4
Abercorn St **7** OL4 . . . 67 D6
Abercrombie Ct M33 . . 108 D5
Aberdare Wlk **4** M9 . . . 64 E5
Aberdaron Wlk M13 . . 163 B3
Aberdeen **1** M30 . . . . . 79 E2
Aberdeen Cres SK3 . . . 170 A4
Aberdeen Gdns OL12 . . 14 D4
Aberdeen Gr SK3 . . . . 170 A4
Aberdeen Ho M13 . . . 163 B1
Aberdeen St M13, M15 . 163 B1
Aberford Rd M23 . . . . 121 A5
Abergele Rd M14 . . . . 110 E8
Abergele St SK2 . . . . 124 A5
Aberley Fold OL15 . . . 15 F7
Abernant Cl M11 . . . . 160 C1
Abernethy Ct BL6 . . . . 22 D2
Abernethy St BL6 . . . . 22 D2
Aber Rd SK8 . . . . 123 A6
Abersoch Ave M14 . . . 110 E8
Abingdon Ave M45 . . . 44 F2
Abingdon Cl
Oldham OL9 . . . . 66 B4
Rochdale OL11 . . . . . 139 B1
Whitefield M45 . . . . . 44 F2
Abingdon Prim Sch SK5 . 111 F7
Abingdon Rd
Bolton BL2 . . . . 25 E6
Reddish SK5 . . . . . . 111 F7
Stockport SK7 . . . . . 123 E3
Urmston M41 . . . . . . 95 E3
Abingdon St
Ashton-u-l OL6 . . . . . 85 D2
Manchester M1 . . . . . 163 A4
Abinger Rd WN4 . . . . 73 D4
Abinger Wlk M40 . . . . 83 D4
Abington Dr WN2 . . . . 56 A3
Abington Rd M33 . . . . 108 C3
Abney Grange OL5 . . . 86 E8
Abney Hall Nature Reserve★
SK8 . . . . 122 E7
Abney Pl SK8 . . . . . . 122 D5
Abney Rd
Mossley OL5 . . . . . . 86 C8
Reddish SK4 . . . . . . 111 C5

Acomb St
Manchester M14 . . . . 98 B4
Manchester M15 . . . . 163 B1
Acorn Ave
Cheadle SK8 . . . . . . 122 E5
Hyde SK14 . . . . 113 E8
Acorn Bsns Ctr
Leigh WN7 . . . . 76 B4
Stockport SK4 . . . . . 169 A1
Acorn Cl
Leigh WN7 . . . . 75 F3
Manchester M19 . . . . 110 F8
Whitefield M45 . . . . . 62 F6
Acorn Ctr WN7 . . . . . 76 B3
Acorn Ctr OL1 . . . . . 67 B8
Acorn Mews SK2 . . . . 124 C6
Acorn Mill **11** OL4 . . . 67 E6
Acorns Sch SK6 . . . . 125 F5
Acorn St
Newton-le-W WA12 . . 89 D3
Oldham OL4 . . . . . . 67 E6
Acorn Way OL11 . . . . 153 B3
ACRE 49 B1
Acre Ave OL13 . . . . . 3 D8
Acre Barn OL2 . . . . . 48 E8
Acre Cl BL0 . . . . 1 D3
Acre Ct **5** SK13 . . . . 116 C7
Acrefield M33 . . . . . . 108 A3
Acre Field BL2 . . . . . 25 D4
Acrefield Ave
Stockport SK4 . . . . . 168 B4
Urmston M41 . . . . . 95 F1
Acre Hall Prim Sch M41 . 94 D2
Acregate M41 . . . . . 95 A2
Acre La
Cheadle SK8 . . . . . . 132 C6
Oldham OL1 . . . . . . 49 A1
Acre Mill Rd OL13 . . . 3 D8
Acresbrook SK15 . . . . 102 C7
Acresbrook Wlk BL8 . . 26 F5
Acresdale BL6 . . . . . 40 C7
Acresfield
Adlington PR7 . . . . . 20 F5
Tyldesley M29 . . . . . 77 C7
Manchester M34 . . . . 84 C1
Acresfield Cl
Blackrod BL6 . . . . . . 21 C3
Pendlebury M27 . . . . 80 A6
Acresfield Rd
Dukinfield SK14 . . . . 101 F5
Middleton M24 . . . . . 47 C3
Sale WA15 . . . . 120 A8
Salford M6 . . . . 80 D5

Acresfield Rd *continued*
Walkden M38 . . . . 60 B4
Acres Fold Ave M22 . . . 121 E3
Acres La SK15 . . . . 86 B1
Acres Rd
  Gatley SK8 . . . . 122 A5
  Manchester M21 . . . . . 109 B8
Acres St BL8 . . . . 26 F5
Acre St
  Denton M34 . . . . 100 E3
  4 Glossop SK13 . . . . . 116 C7
  Oldham OL9 . . . . 66 B2
  3 Radcliffe M26 . . . . . 43 E3
  Whitworth OL12 . . . . . . 4 D1
Acreswood Ave WN2 . . . 57 A4
Acreswood Cl PR7 . . . . . 19 E8
Acre Top Rd M9 . . . . 64 B5
Acre View OL13 . . . . 3 D7
Acreville Gr WA3 . . . . . . 92 C7
Acre Wood BL6 . . . . 40 B3
A' Ct WN4 . . . . 73 B2
Acton Ave M40 . . . . 83 B4
Acton Ho WN1 . . . . 151 A4
Acton Sq M5 . . . . 81 B2
Acton St
  Oldham OL1 . . . . 67 B8
  Rochdale OL12 . . . . 15 A1
  Wigan WN1 . . . . 37 C1
Acton's Walk Trad Ctr
  WN3 . . . . 150 C3
Acton Terr WN1 . . . . 37 C1
Actonville Ave M22 . . . 121 D3
Adair St
  Manchester M1 . . . . . . 163 C4
  Rochdale OL11 . . . . 30 B2
Adam Cl SK8 . . . . 123 B4
Adams Ave M21 . . . . . . 109 B6
Adams Cl
  Newton-le-W WA12 . . . 89 D2
  Poynton SK12 . . . . 133 E2
Adams Dr WN3 . . . . 150 A1
Adamson Cir M17 . . . . . 95 F3
Adamson Gdns M20 . . . 109 F3
Adamson Rd M30 . . . . . 95 C8
Adamson St
  Ashton-in-M WN4 . . . . 73 A3
  Dukinfield SK16 . . . . . 101 C6
Adamson Wlk 1 M14 . . . 98 C3
Adam St
  Ashton-u-L OL6 . . . . . 166 C3
  Oldham OL8 . . . . 66 F2
Ada St
  Manchester M9 . . . . . . 64 D1
  Ramsbottom BL0 . . . . 138 B1
  Rochdale OL12 . . . . 15 A2
Adastral Ho M21 . . . . . 109 C8
Adbaston Rd M32 . . . . . 96 A5
Adcroft St SK1 . . . . 170 C3
Addenbrook Rd M8 . . . 155 B1
Adderley Pl SK13 . . . . . 171 C1
Adderley Rd SK13 . . . . 171 C1
Addingham Cl M9 . . . . . 64 B5
Addington Rd BL3 . . . . . 40 F3
Addington St M4 . . . . . 159 B2
Addison Ave 3 OL6 . . . . 85 D3
Addison Cl M13 . . . . . . 163 C2
Addison Cres M16 . . . . . 97 B4
Addison Dr M24 . . . . . . 47 C3
Addison Rd
  Altrincham WA15 . . . . 119 E2
  Carrington M31 . . . . . 106 D6
  Irlam M44 . . . . 94 C4
  Stretford M32 . . . . 96 B3
  Urmston M41 . . . . 95 C1
Adelaide Rd
  Bramhall SK7 . . . . 132 F5
  Stockport SK3 . . . . 170 A3
Adelaide St
  5 Adlington PR6 . . . . 21 A8
  Bolton BL3 . . . . 147 A4
  Eccles M30 . . . . 79 D1
  Heywood OL10 . . . . . . 29 D2
  Middleton M24 . . . . . . 65 A8
  Ramsbottom BL0 . . . . . 11 A4
  Salford M8 . . . . 155 C1
  Swinton M27 . . . . 79 D7
Adelaide Street E OL10 . 29 E2
Adelphi Dr M38 . . . . . . 158 A3
Adelphi Gr M38 . . . . 60 B5
Adelphi Gr M38 . . . . 60 B5
Adelphi St
  3 Radcliffe M26 . . . . . 43 F5
  Salford M3 . . . . 158 A2
  Standish WN6 . . . . 19 E2
Aden Cl M12 . . . . 164 A4
Aden St
  Oldham OL4 . . . . 67 D5
  Rochdale OL12 . . . . 15 A1
Adey Rd WA13 . . . . 117 A5
Adisham Dr BL1 . . . . . . 143 C1
ADLINGTON 21 B7
Adlington Cl
  Altrincham WA15 . . . . 120 D6
  Bolton BL8 . . . . 27 A1
  Poynton SK12 . . . . 133 F2
Adlington Dr M32 . . . . . 96 F4
Adlington Pk SK10 . . . . 133 C1
Adlington Prim Sch PR7 . 20 F7
Adlington South Bsns Village
  PR7 . . . . 21 A6
Adlington St
  Bolton BL3 . . . . 147 A3
  Manchester M12 . . . . 164 A4
  12 Oldham OL4 . . . . . . 49 D1
Adlington Sta PR6 . . . . 21 A7

Adlington Way 19 M34 . 101 A1
Adlington Wlk SK1 . . . . 169 B1
Adlow Ind Pk M12 . . . . 164 A4
Admel Sq 1 M15 . . . . . 163 A1
Adrian Rd BL1 . . . . 142 C2
Adrian St M40 . . . . 83 A7
Adrian Terr OL16 . . . . . 31 C7
Adria Rd M20 . . . . 110 C3
Adscombe St M16 . . . . . 97 E4
Adshall Rd SK8 . . . . . . 123 A5
Adshead Cl M22 . . . . . . 121 B3
Adstock Wlk 4 M40 . . . 159 C3
Adstone Cl M4 . . . . 160 A1
ADSWOOD 170 A1
Adswood Cl OL4 . . . . . . 49 D1
Adswood Gr SK3 . . . . . 170 A2
Adswood Ind Est SK3 . . 170 A2
Adswood Lane E SK2 . . 170 C2
Adswood Lane W SK2,
  SK3 . . . . 170 C2
Adswood Old Hall Rd
  SK8 . . . . 122 C6
Adswood Prim Sch SK3 . 170 B1
Adswood Rd SK3, SK8 . . 170 A1
Adswood St M40 . . . . . 160 B2
Adswood Terr SK3 . . . . 170 B2
Adwell Cl WA3 . . . . 91 A8
Aegean Cl 3 M7 . . . . . . 81 C5
Aegean Rd WA14 . . . . . 119 A6
AFFETSIDE 26 B8
Affetside Dr BL8 . . . . . . 26 E2
Affleck Ave M26 . . . . . . 61 A8
Afghan St OL1 . . . . 67 B8
Afifah High Sch for Girls
  M16 . . . . 162 A1
Agden Brow M13 . . . . . 117 E1
Agden Brow Pk WA13 . . 117 D1
Agden La WA13 . . . . . . 117 E1
Age Croft OL8 . . . . 67 C2
Agecroft Commerce Pk
  M6 . . . . 80 E6
Agecroft Ent Pk M27 . . 80 E7
Agecroft Park Circle M27 80 E7
Agecroft Rd
  Manchester M27 . . . . . 80 E8
  Prestwich M25 . . . . . . 62 D7
  Romiley SK6 . . . . 113 A1
Agecroft Road E M25 . . 63 A2
Agecroft Road W M25 . 63 A2
Ager St OL13 . . . . 3 C8
Agincourt St OL10 . . . . . 29 B2
Agnes Cl OL9 . . . . 66 C4
Agnes Ct M14 . . . . 110 C7
Agnes St
  Chadderton OL9 . . . . . 152 B2
  Manchester M19 . . . . . 99 A2
  Salford M7 . . . . 155 C3
Agnew Pl M6 . . . . 81 A4
Agnew Rd M18 . . . . 165 C1
Aigburth Gr SK5 . . . . . . 99 E2
Ailsa Cl M40 . . . . 157 A1
Ailsa Ho M6 . . . . 154 F3
Aimson Pl WA15 . . . . . 120 C6
Aimson Road E WA15 . 120 C6
Aimson Road W WA15 . 120 C7
Aines St M12 . . . . 165 A3
Aingarth Ho SK15 . . . . . 85 F2
Ainley Rd M22 . . . . 121 D3
Ainley Wood
  Delph OL3 . . . . 50 E5
  Dukinfield SK16 . . . . . 101 D7
Ainsbrook Ave
  Delph OL3 . . . . 50 F4
  Manchester M9 . . . . . . 65 B2
Ainsbrook Terr OL3 . . . . 51 D5
Ainscoughs Ct WN7 . . . . 75 F4
Ainscow Ave BL6 . . . . . . 39 F8
Ainsdale Ave
  Atherton M46 . . . . 58 C4
  Bury BL8 . . . . 27 B2
  Edgworth BL7 . . . . 9 E6
  Manchester M7 . . . . . . 63 D1
Ainsdale Cl
  Bramhall SK7 . . . . 133 A4
  Oldham OL8 . . . . 66 D4
Ainsdale Cres OL2 . . . . . 48 E2
Ainsdale Ct BL3 . . . . . . 147 C3
Ainsdale Dr
  Gatley SK8 . . . . 122 B1
  Sale M33 . . . . 107 E2
  Whitworth OL12 . . . . . . 14 D7
Ainsdale Gr SK5 . . . . . . 111 F8
Ainsdale Rd BL3 . . . . . . 147 B3
Ainsdale St M12 . . . . . . 164 D8
Ainse Rd BL6 . . . . 21 B3
Ainsford Rd M20 . . . . . 110 D5
Ainsleigh Gdns M9 . . . . 64 D1
Ainsley Gr M28 . . . . 60 D2
Ainsley St 11 M40 . . . . 83 C5
Ainslie Rd BL1 . . . . 142 A1
Ainsty Rd M14 . . . . 98 B4
AINSWORTH 26 B1
Ainsworth Ave BL6 . . . . 22 E2
Ainsworth Cl M34 . . . . 100 B3
Ainsworth Ct
  Bolton BL3 . . . . 148 C3
  Walkden M28 . . . . 60 E2
Ainsworth Hall Rd BL2 . 43 B8
Ainsworth La BL2 . . . . 148 C4
Ainsworth Rd
  Bury BL8 . . . . 27 B2
  Little Lever BL3 . . . . . . 43 B4
  Radcliffe M26 . . . . 43 F5
Ainsworth Sq BL1 . . . . 143 A3
Ainsworth St
  Bolton BL1 . . . . 142 C2
  Rochdale OL16 . . . . 31 A6

Ainthorpe Wlk M40 . . . . 83 D5
Aintree Ave M33 . . . . . 107 C3
Aintree Cl SK7 . . . . 124 F2
Aintree Dr OL11 . . . . . . 29 E8
Aintree Gr SK3 . . . . 170 B1
Aintree Rd BL3 . . . . 43 A3
Aintree St M11 . . . . 83 B1
Aintree Wlk OL9 . . . . . 152 C3
Airedale Cl SK8 . . . . . . 122 C6
Airedale Ct WA14 . . . . 119 E5
Aire St BL2 . . . . 25 B5
Aireworth St BL5 . . . . . . 39 F3
Air Hill Terr 8 OL12 . . . 14 C1
Airton Cl M40 . . . . 159 C3
Airton Pl WN3 . . . . 55 B3
Aitken Cl BL0 . . . . 138 B1
Aitken St
  Haslingden BL0 . . . . 1 C5
  Reddish M19 . . . . 99 C1
Ajax Dr BL9 . . . . 45 A4
Ajax St
  Ramsbottom BL0 . . . . 138 B1
  Rochdale OL11 . . . . 30 B3
Aked Cl M12 . . . . 164 A2
Akesmoor Dr SK2 . . . . 124 C6
Akhtar Ho M1 . . . . 163 A3
Alamein Dr SK6 . . . . . . 113 F2
Alan Ave M35 . . . . 83 B1
Alanbrooke Wlk M15 . . 162 B1
Alandale Ave M34 . . . . 100 E7
Alandale Dr OL2 . . . . . . 48 E5
Alandale Rd SK3 . . . . . 123 C7
Alan Dr
  Altrincham WA15 . . . . 120 A1
  Marple SK6 . . . . 125 F6
Alan Rd
  Manchester, Withington
  M20 . . . . 110 C6
  Stockport, Heaton Moor
  SK4 . . . . 168 B4
Alan St BL1 . . . . 143 A3
Alan Turing Way
  Droylsden M11 . . . . . . 83 A1
  Manchester M11, M40 . 160 C3
Alasdair Cl OL9 . . . . 65 F8
Alba Cl M30 . . . . 79 D1
Alban Ct
  Ashton-u-L OL6 . . . . . . 85 D7
  Westhoughton BL5 . . . . 57 E7
Alban St M7 . . . . 155 A1
Albany Ave M11 . . . . . . 99 F1
Albany Cl M38 . . . . 60 B5
Albany Ct
  7 Manchester M20 . . 110 B6
  Sale M33 . . . . 108 C5
  Urmston M41 . . . . 95 B3
Albany Dr BL9 . . . . 44 F7
Albany Gr M29 . . . . 77 D8
Albany Rd
  Bramhall SK7 . . . . 132 F4
  Eccles M30 . . . . 79 B3
  Manchester M21 . . . . . 97 B1
  Wilmslow SK9 . . . . 136 F5
Albany St
  Middleton M24 . . . . . . 65 B7
  Oldham OL4 . . . . 49 D1
  10 Rochdale OL11 . . . 31 A5
Albany Trad Est M21 . . 97 B1
Albany Way
  Hattersley SK14 . . . . . 102 E2
  Salford M6 . . . . 81 A3
Alba Way M32 . . . . 96 A5
Albemarle Ave M20 . . . 110 A6
Albemarle Pl BL8 . . . . . 26 F7
Albemarle Rd M21 . . . . 109 A8
Albemarle St
  Ashton-u-L OL6 . . . . . 166 C3
  Manchester M14 . . . . . 98 A4
Albemarle Terr OL6 . . . 166 C3
Alberbury Ave M23 . . . 120 D7
Alberta St
  Bolton BL3 . . . . 144 C1
  Stockport SK1 . . . . 170 C4
Albert Ave
  Dukinfield SK16 . . . . . 101 C6
  Manchester M25 . . . . . 63 D1
  Reddish M18 . . . . 99 F4
  Shaw OL2 . . . . 149 B1
  Urmston M41 . . . . 95 E2
  Walkden M28 . . . . 60 C5
Albert Cl
  Cheadle SK8 . . . . 123 A2
  Whitefield M45 . . . . . . 63 A8
Albert Close Trad Est
  M45 . . . . 63 A8
Albert Ct 11 WA14 . . . 119 D4
Albert Dr M45 . . . . 45 B1
Albert Fildes Wlk 3 M8 . 155 C3
Albert Gdns M40 . . . . . 83 D5
Albert Gr
  Farnworth BL4 . . . . 60 D8
  Manchester M12 . . . . . 99 A4
Albert Hill St M20 . . . . 110 B3
Alberton Cl WN2 . . . . . . 38 C6
Albert Park Rd M7 . . . . 155 A1
Albert Pl
  Altrincham WA14 . . . . 119 D5
  Manchester M13 . . . . . 98 F3
  Whitefield M45 . . . . . . 45 B3
Albert Rd
  8 Altrincham WA14 . . 119 D4
  Bolton BL1 . . . . 144 B4
  Cheadle SK8 . . . . 123 A2
  Eccles M30 . . . . 79 D1
  Farnworth BL4 . . . . 60 D8
  Hale WA15 . . . . 119 E3
  Hyde SK14 . . . . 167 A2

Albert Rd *continued*
  Manchester M19 . . . . . 99 A1
  Sale M33 . . . . 108 C4
  Stockport SK4 . . . . 168 A3
  Whitefield M45 . . . . . . 63 A8
  Wilmslow SK9 . . . . 137 A6
Albert Road E WA15 . . 119 E3
Albert Road W BL1 . . . . 40 F8
Albert Royds St OL12,
  OL16 . . . . 15 B2
Albert Sq
  Altrincham WA14 . . . . 119 D3
  Manchester M2 . . . . . 158 C1
  Stalybridge SK15 . . . . . 85 F1
Albert St
  Ashton-in-M WN4 . . . . 73 B3
  Bolton BL7 . . . . 8 D3
  Bury BL9 . . . . 141 A2
  Denton M34 . . . . 100 F3
  Droylsden M43 . . . . . . 84 A8
  Farnworth BL4 . . . . 60 D7
  Glossop SK13 . . . . 104 A5
  Hazel Grove SK7 . . . . . 124 D3
  Heywood OL10 . . . . . . 29 B2
  Horwich BL6 . . . . 22 B4
  Hyde SK14 . . . . 167 D2
  Irlam M44 . . . . 105 E6
  Littleborough OL15 . . . 16 B5
  8 Little Lever BL3 . . . 43 B3
  Manchester M11 . . . . 160 C1
  Middleton M24 . . . . . . 65 A8
  Milnrow OL16 . . . . 32 A5
  Oldham, Factory Fold OL9 . 66 B3
  Oldham, Hollinwood OL8 . 66 B1
  Oldham, Werneth Low OL4 . 67 E5
  Prestwich M25 . . . . . . 63 C4
  Ramsbottom BL0 . . . . 138 B2
  Royton OL2 . . . . 48 D4
  Shaw OL2 . . . . 149 A3
  Stockport SK4 . . . . 169 A1
  Whitworth OL12 . . . . . . 14 C8
  Wigan WN5 . . . . 54 F6
Albert Street W M35 . . 83 D5
Albert Street Works 7
  M34 . . . . 84 B1
Albert Terr SK1 . . . . . . 170 C4
Albert Webb Ho 6 M5 . 154 B1
Albert Wlk 2 OL7 . . . . . 166 A1
Albine St M38 . . . . 157 C4
Albinson Wlk M31 . . . . 106 A3
Albion Cl
  Manchester M46 . . . . . 58 A2
  Stockport SK4 . . . . 169 B3
  Wigan WN2 . . . . 38 B2
Albion Ct BL8 . . . . 140 A2
Albion Fold M43 . . . . . . 84 A2
Albion Gardens Cl OL2 . 48 D4
Albion Gdns SK15 . . . . . 86 B1
Albion Gr M33 . . . . 108 A4
Albion High Sch The M6 . 81 B4
Albion Ho SK15 . . . . 86 C2
Albion Mill SK14 . . . . . 103 C5
Albion Mill Ind Est BL8 . 140 A2
Albion Pl WA3 . . . . 92 C7
Albion Rd
  Prestwich M25 . . . . . . 63 A4
  10 Salford M7 . . . . . . 81 C5
Albion St
  Ashton-u-L OL6 . . . . . 166 C3
  3 Bacup OL13 . . . . 3 C8
  Bolton BL3 . . . . 145 C1
  Bury BL8 . . . . 140 A2
  Chadderton OL9 . . . . . 152 A3
  Failsworth M35 . . . . . . 83 E7
  Kearsley BL4 . . . . 61 A7
  6 Leigh WN7 . . . . 75 C5
  Littleborough OL15 . . . 16 A5
  Manchester, City Centre
  M1 . . . . 162 C4
  Manchester, Old Trafford
  M16 . . . . 97 D4
  Oldham OL1 . . . . 153 C3
  Pendlebury M27 . . . . . . 80 A8
  4 Platt Bridge WN2 . . 56 A3
  Radcliffe M26 . . . . 44 B1
  Rochdale OL11 . . . . 30 D1
  Sale M33 . . . . 108 A4
  Stalybridge SK15 . . . . . 86 B2
  Westhoughton BL5 . . . . 39 F3
  Wigan WN2 . . . . 38 B2
Albion Terr BL1 . . . . . . 142 B3
Albion The M35 . . . . 81 B1
Albion Trad Est
  Ashton-u-L OL6 . . . . . . 85 D3
  Salford M6 . . . . 81 A4
Albion Twrs 5 M5 . . . . . 81 B2
Albion Way M5 . . . . 81 B1
Alburn Ct M40 . . . . 160 B4
Albury Dr
  Manchester M19 . . . . . 110 D2
  Rochdale OL12 . . . . 13 F2
Albury Way WN2 . . . . . . 37 F2
Albyns Ave M8 . . . . 156 A3
Alcester Ave SK3 . . . . . 122 F7
Alcester Cl
  Bury BL8 . . . . 27 B3
  Middleton M24 . . . . . . 65 B6
Alcester Rd
  Gatley SK8 . . . . 122 B4

Alcester Rd *continued*
  Sale M33 . . . . 108 B2
Alcester St OL9 . . . . 66 A3
Alconbury Ct M43 . . . . 100 B8
Alconbury Wlk M9 . . . . 64 B6
Aldborough Cl M20 . . . 110 B4
Aldbourne Cl M40 . . . . 157 A1
Aldbury Terr 1 BL1 . . . 143 A1
Aldcliffe WN3 . . . . 90 F8
Aldcroft St M18 . . . . . . 99 F6
Alden Cl
  Haslingden BB4 . . . . 1 A6
  Standish WN1 . . . . 20 B1
  Whitefield M45 . . . . . . 63 A8
Alden Rd BB4 . . . . 1 A5
Alden Rise BB4 . . . . 1 A6
Alden Wlk SK4 . . . . 111 D7
Alder Ave
  Ashton-in-M WN4 . . . . 72 F5
  Billinge WN5 . . . . 71 D5
  Bury BL9 . . . . 141 C3
  Poynton SK12 . . . . 133 F3
  Wigan WN5 . . . . 54 D6
Alderbank
  Horwich BL6 . . . . 21 F3
  Wardle OL12 . . . . 15 C7
Alderbank Cl BL4 . . . . . 60 F6
Alderbrook Rd M38 . . . . 59 F3
Alder Cl
  Ashton-u-L OL6 . . . . . . 85 B7
  8 Bury BL8 . . . . 27 C2
  Dukinfield SK16 . . . . . 102 A7
  Glossop SK13 . . . . 171 C4
  Leigh WN7 . . . . 75 F2
Alder Com High Sch
  SK14 . . . . 114 A8
Aldercroft Ave
  Bolton BL2 . . . . 25 D1
  Wythenshawe M22 . . . 121 C2
Alder Ct M8 . . . . 63 F1
Alderdale Cl SK4 . . . . . 168 A4
Alderdale Dr
  Droylsden M43 . . . . . . 83 E2
  High Lane SK6 . . . . 134 E7
  Manchester SK4 . . . . . 111 A5
Alderdale Gr SK9 . . . . . 136 E5
Alderdale Rd SK8 . . . . . 123 C4
Alder Dr
  Altrincham WA15 . . . . 120 E5
  Stalybridge SK15 . . . . . 86 C3
  Swinton M27 . . . . 61 C1
Alder Edge 8 M21 . . . . 96 F1
Alderfield Ho SK14 . . . . 96 F1
Alderfield Rd M21 . . . . . 96 F1
Alderfold St M46 . . . . . . 58 B3
Alderford Par M8 . . . . . 155 C2
ALDER FOREST 79 A4
Alder Forest Ave M30 . 79 A4
Aldergate Gr OL6 . . . . . 85 F5
Alderglen Rd M8 . . . . . 156 A1
Alder Gr
  Bolton BL7 . . . . 25 C6
  Denton M34 . . . . 101 A3
  Stockport SK3 . . . . 123 C8
  Stretford M32 . . . . 96 E2
Alder Hts SK1 . . . . 112 B2
Alder La
  Hindley WN2 . . . . 57 B5
  Oldham OL8 . . . . 66 B1
Alder Lee Cl WN3 . . . . . 54 D1
Alderley Ave
  Bolton BL1 . . . . 24 E5
  Golborne WA3 . . . . 90 D7
Alderley Cl
  Billinge WN5 . . . . 71 E5
  Hazel Grove SK7 . . . . . 133 F8
  Poynton SK12 . . . . 133 F2
Alderley Dr SK6 . . . . . . 112 E3
Alderley Ho 6 SK9 . . . . 137 D1
ALDERLEY EDGE 137 C2
Alderley Edge* SK9 . . . 137 D1
Alderley Edge Prim Sch 6
  SK9 . . . . 137 A2
Alderley Edge Sch for Girls
  5 SK9 . . . . 137 A2
Alderley Edge Sta SK9 . 137 A2
Alderley La WN7 . . . . . . 76 B2
Alderley Lo SK9 . . . . . . 137 A2
Alderley Rd
  Hindley WN2 . . . . 57 A5
  Reddish SK5 . . . . 111 F5
  Stockport SK3 . . . . 170 B1
  Urmston M41 . . . . 95 A2
  Wilmslow SK9 . . . . 137 A6
Alderley St
  Ashton-u-L OL6 . . . . . . 85 D5
Alderley Terr 8 SK16 . . 166 B1
Alderman Foley Dr OL12 . 14 A2
Alderman Gatley Ho
  M22 . . . . 121 D2
Alderman Sq M12 . . . . 164 B4
Aldermary Rd M21 . . . 109 D5
Aldermaston Gr M9 . . . . 64 B6
Alder Meadow Cl OL12 . 14 A1
Aldermere Cres M41 . . . 94 D1
Alderminster Ave 2 M38 . 60 A5
Aldermoor Cl M11 . . . . . 99 D8
Alderney Dr WN3 . . . . . 55 A3
Alder Rd
  Cheadle SK8 . . . . 122 E5
  Failsworth M35 . . . . . . 83 F5
  Golborne WA3 . . . . 90 F8

Alder Rd continued
Middleton M24.....47 C2
Rochdale OL11.....30 D2
ALDER ROOT.....152 C2
Alders SK9.....136 F6
Alders Ave M22.....121 C5
Alders Ct OL8.....85 A8
Aldersgate Rd
Cheadle SK8.....132 C5
Stockport SK2.....124 B6
Alders Green Ave SK6...134 F7
Alders Green Rd WN2...57 A5
Aldershot Wlk 3 M11...160 C1
Alderside Rd M9.....157 A4
Aldersley Ave M9.....64 B5
Alderson St
Oldham OL9.....153 B3
Salford M6.....81 A4
Alders Rd
High Lane SK12.....135 A7
Wythenshawe M22.....121 C5
Alder St
Atherton M46.....58 D3
Bolton BL3.....147 C3
Eccles M30.....79 A4
Newton-le-W WA12.....89 C3
Salford M6.....152 C2
Alders The WN6.....36 D4
Aldersyde St BL3.....147 A3
Alderton Dr BL5.....57 E6
Alderue Ave M22.....121 D6
Alderway BL0.....1 C1
Alderwood Ave M8...168 A1
Alderwood Fold OL4...67 F5
Alderwood Gr BL0.....1 D4
Alderwood Wlk 7 M8...155 C2
Aldfield Rd M23.....108 F1
Aldford Cl M20.....110 C3
Aldford Dr M46.....58 E5
Aldford Gr BL2.....43 B5
Aldford Pl SK9.....136 F2
Aldford Way M16.....36 E8
Aldham Ave M40.....83 C4
Aldon St OL6.....166 C3
Aldred Cl M8.....156 B2
Aldred St
Bolton BL3.....146 B3
Eccles M30.....79 C1
Failsworth M35.....83 E7
2 Hindley WN2.....56 D4
Leigh WN7.....75 E8
Salford M5.....81 B2
Aldridge Cl WN3.....55 B3
Aldridge Wlk M11.....164 C4
Aldsworth Dr
Bolton BL3.....147 B4
Manchester M40.....157 B1
Aldwick Ave M20.....110 C3
Aldwinians Cl M34....100 E5
Aldworth Gr M33.....107 D3
Aldwych OL11.....30 F3
Aldwych Ave M14.....98 B2
Aldwyn Cl
Denton M34.....100 E5
Radcliffe M26.....44 B1
Aldwyn Cres SK7.....124 C2
Aldwyn Park Rd M44...100 C8
Aldwyn Prim Sch M34...84 C1
Alexander Ave M35.....84 A8
Alexander Briant Ct BL4...60 C7
Alexander Ct
10 Manchester, Didsbury
M20.....110 B3
Manchester, Ordsall M5...161 A4
Alexander Dr
Altrincham WA15.....120 A6
Milnrow OL16.....31 F6
Whitefield BL9.....44 A2
Alexander Gdns M7...158 A4
Alexander Rd BL2.....25 C1
Alexander St
Rochdale OL11.....30 B2
Salford M6.....154 B2
Tyldesley M29.....77 A8
Alexandra Ave
Hyde SK14.....101 C2
Manchester M14.....97 F2
Whitefield M45.....63 A8
Alexandra Cl SK3.....123 C6
Alexandra Cres
4 Oldham OL1.....67 B8
Wigan WN5.....54 E6
Alexandra Ct
4 Dukinfield SK14...101 F5
1 Partington M31.....105 F3
Urmston M41.....94 E1
Alexandra Ctr Ret Pk
OL4.....153 C2
Alexandra Dr M19.....110 F7
Alexandra Gr M44.....105 F8
Alexandra Hospl (private)
The SK8.....122 D6
Alexandra Mews OL4....67 A5
Alexandra Mill OL3.....69 B8
ALEXANDRA PARK.....67 A4
Alexandra Park Ho M16...97 E2
Alexandra Park Jun Sch
OL8.....67 A4
Alexandra Park Prim Sch
SK3.....123 C2
Alexandra Rd
Ashton-in-M WN4.....73 B4
Ashton-u-L OL6.....166 B4
Denton M34.....101 A4

Alexandra Rd continued
Eccles M30.....95 C8
Horwich BL6.....39 E8
Kearsley BL4.....61 A7
Kearsley, Prestolee M26...61 A8
Manchester, Moss Side M16 97 E4
Oldham OL8.....67 A4
Sale M33.....108 D3
Stockport, Heaton Norris
SK4.....168 C3
Walkden M28.....60 C5
Alexandra Road S M16 ... 97 E2
Alexandra St
Abram WN2.....74 B8
Ashton-u-L OL6.....85 D4
8 Bolton BL3.....147 A4
Farnworth BL4.....60 D7
Heywood OL10.....46 E8
Hyde SK14.....101 C1
Oldham OL8.....67 A5
Bury M7.....158 A3
Wigan WN5.....54 F6
Alexandra Terr
14 Manchester M19.....99 A1
Oldham OL4.....49 E3
Alexandra The
11 Manchester M14.....110 D8
Stretford M50.....96 A8
Alexandria Dr
Ashton-u-L OL7.....84 E2
Ashton under Lyne OL7 ...166 A1
Westhoughton BL5.....58 B8
Alford Ave M20.....110 A8
Alford Cl BL2.....42 F6
Alford Rd SK4.....111 C6
Alford St 10 OL9.....66 B2
Alfred Ave M28.....79 A7
Alfred James Cl 15 M40 159 C3
Alfred Morris Ct M23...109 A2
Alfred Rd WA3.....91 A8
Alfred St
Ashton-u-L OL6.....85 D4
Bolton, Burnden BL3.....42 B4
Bolton, Egerton BL7.....8 D3
Bury BL9.....141 A1
Dukinfield SK14.....101 C3
Eccles M30.....79 D3
Farnworth BL4.....42 D2
Ince-in-M WN3.....151 A2
Irlam M44.....105 E6
Kearsley BL4.....60 F8
Littleborough OL15.....16 A6
Manchester M7.....157 A4
Newton-le-W WA12.....89 E3
Oldham OL9.....152 C2
Platt Bridge WN2.....56 A3
Ramsbottom BL0.....138 B1
Shaw OL2.....149 B3
9 Tyldesley M29.....58 F1
Walkden M28.....60 D3
Whitworth OL12.....4 D2
Wigan WN1.....37 B2
Alfreton Ave M34.....113 A8
Alfreton Rd SK2.....124 E5
Alfreton Wlk 9 M40.....83 A6
Alfriston Dr M23.....109 A2
Alger Mews OL6.....85 D4
Algernon Rd M28.....60 C4
Algernon St
Eccles M30.....79 D3
Hindley WN2.....56 D5
Swinton M27.....79 D8
Wigan WN3.....55 A4
Alger St 1 OL6.....85 D4
Algreave Rd SK3.....123 A8
Alice Ingham RC Prim Sch
OL16.....15 C2
Alice St
Bolton BL3.....144 C1
Hyde SK14.....113 E7
Pendlebury M27.....80 B8
Rochdale OL12.....15 B1
Sale M33.....108 D4
Alicia Ct OL12.....14 E1
Alicia Dr OL12.....14 E1
Alick's Fold 7 BL5.....39 E1
Alison Ct SK4.....168 B3
Alison Kelly Cl M9.....157 C4
Alison St
6 Manchester M14.....97 F3
Shaw OL2.....149 B4
Al Jamiah Al Islamiyyah
3 Bolton BL7.....146 B4
Bolton BL7.....25 A8
Alker Rd M40.....160 A3
Alker St WN5.....54 F6
Alkrington Cl BL9.....45 A2
Alkrington Ct M24.....65 B5
ALKRINGTON GARDEN
VILLAGE.....65 A5
Alkrington Gn M24.....64 F7
Alkrington Hall M24...64 F7
Alkrington Hall Road
M24.....64 F7
Alkrington Hall Road S
M24.....64 E6
Alkrington Park Rd M24...58 C1
Alkrington Prim Sch M24 65 A6
Alkrington Woods Nature
Reserve* M24.....64 E7
Allama Iqbal Rd OL4...67 C5
Allandale Ct 12 M7.....63 E1
Allan Ct M21.....109 A7
Allandale WA14.....119 B4
Allandale Rd M19.....98 F1
Allan Roberts Cl M9.....64 D1
Allanson Rd M22.....109 E1
Allan St M29.....76 F8

Alldis Cl M12.....164 B1
Alldis St SK2.....124 B5
Allen Ave
Fowley Common WA3 ... 92 C4
Hyde SK14.....113 F8
Allenby Gr BL5.....57 D7
Allenby Rd
Irlam M44.....105 D4
Swinton M27.....79 C6
Allenby St
Atherton M46.....58 B2
Shaw OL2.....149 C3
Allenby Wlk 4 M40.....156 C1
Allen Cl OL2.....149 A2
Allen Ct M34.....100 E4
Allendale Dr BL9.....45 A3
Allendale Gdns BL1.....143 B2
Allendale Wlk M3.....158 A2
Allen Rd M41.....95 F2
Allen St
Bury M8.....27 C3
Little Lever BL3.....43 A3
Oldham OL8.....153 A2
Radcliffe M26.....44 E1
Allerby Way WA3.....90 E8
Allerdean Wlk SK4.....110 F3
Allerford St M16.....97 E4
Allerton Cl BL5.....40 A1
Allerton Ct 7 BL1.....145 B4
Allerton Wlk 6 M13....163 C2
Allescholes Rd OL14.....6 B7
Allesley Cl BL5.....40 A1
Allesley Dr M7.....155 C2
Allgreave Cl M33.....108 E1
All Hallows RC High Sch
M5.....154 A3
Alliance Ind Est M34...100 D3
Alliance St 1 M11.....151 A4
Alligin Cl OL9.....152 A4
Allingham St M13.....98 E4
Allington Cl OL11.....139 B2
Allington Dr M30.....79 E4
Alliott Wlk M15.....162 B1
Allison Gr M30.....79 B1
Allison St M8.....155 C1
Allonby Wlk M24.....46 C2
Allotment Rd M44.....105 D6
Alloway Wlk 6 M40.....83 A6
All Saints BL8.....27 C3
All Saints CE Prim Sch
27 Failsworth M40.....83 C5
Marple SK6.....126 A5
7 Rochdale OL12.....15 A2
Stockport SK4.....169 A3
Whitefield M45.....45 A2
All Saints' CE Prim Sch
BL4.....42 D2
All Saint's Cl OL2.....48 D5
All Saints St M32.....96 B2
All Saints Pl 12 BL8 .... 27 C3
All Saints RC Coll SK16 .. 101 D7
All Saints RC Prim Sch
Glossop SK13.....104 D2
1 Golborne WA3.....90 B8
7 Sale M33.....107 D6
All Saints' Rd SK4.....169 B4
All Saints' St
Failsworth M40.....83 C5
15 Failsworth M40.....83 C5
Allscott Way WN4.....73 C3
Allsopp St BL3.....145 C2
All Souls CE Prim Sch
OL10.....29 F3
All Souls RC Prim Sch
M5.....154 A1
Allwood St M5.....158 A1
Alma Bridge OL6.....166 B1
Alma Cl WN8.....53 C7
Alma Ct
3 Manchester M15.....97 E4
Up Holland WN8.....53 C7
Alma Gr WN3.....54 E2
Alma Hill WN8.....53 C7
Alma Hill Est WN8.....53 C7
Alma Ind Est 10 OL12...14 F1
Alma La SK9.....137 A7
Alma Par WN8.....53 C7
Alma Park Prim Sch
M19.....111 A8
Alma Rd
Hazel Grove SK7.....134 A8
Manchester, Heaton Moor
SK4.....111 B5
Manchester, Levenshulme
M19.....111 A8
Sale M33.....107 E2
Up Holland WN8.....53 C7
Westhoughton BL5.....57 D7
Alma St
Ashton under Lyne OL6...166 B1
Atherton M46.....58 B2
Bolton BL3.....146 C4
Eccles M30.....79 F1
Kearsley BL4.....61 B5
Leigh WN7.....75 E8
10 Little Lever BL3.....43 B3
Newton-le-W WA12.....89 B3
Radcliffe M26.....43 F5
13 Rochdale OL12.....14 F1
Stalybridge SK15.....86 B2
Tyldesley M29.....76 F8
Alminstone Cl M40.....83 A6
Almond Ave BL9.....141 C3
Almond Brook Rd WN6...19 C1

Almond Cl
Failsworth M35.....83 F6
Littleborough OL15.....15 F6
Salford M6.....81 B2
Stockport SK3.....123 C8
Almond Cres
Rawtenstall BB4.....1 F8
Standish WN6.....36 F7
Almond Ct SK16.....166 C1
Almond Dr M33.....107 F6
Almond Gr
Bolton BL1.....143 C3
Wigan WN5.....54 E6
Almond Rd 5 OL4.....49 D1
Almond St
Bolton BL1.....143 C4
9 Farnworth BL4.....60 C8
Manchester M40.....159 B4
Almond Tree Rd SK8...123 A1
Almond Way SK14.....102 A2
Almond Wlk M31.....105 D3
Alms Hill Rd M8.....156 A3
Alness Rd M16.....97 D2
Alnwick Cl WN2.....38 D5
Alnwick Dr BL9.....45 A5
Alnwick Rd M9.....64 D5
Alperton Wlk M40.....83 D4
Alpha Court Ind Est M34 100 C3
Alpha Ct M34.....100 C3
Alphagate Dr M34.....100 C3
Alpha Hospl BL8.....27 C1
Alpha Pl M15.....162 B3
Alpha M32.....96 C1
Alpha St
Manchester M11.....99 E7
Salford M6.....154 C3
Alpha Street W M6....154 B3
Alpin Cl
Mossley OL5.....68 E3
Uppermill OL3.....69 B5
Alphingate Cl SK15.....86 D4
Alphin Sq OL5.....68 D1
Alphonsus St M16.....97 C4
Alpine St
Leigh WN7.....75 C8
Milnrow OL16.....32 A7
Royton OL2.....48 C3
Wardle OL12.....15 C6
Alpine Rd SK1.....112 A1
Alpine St
Droylsden M11.....83 B2
Newton-le-W WA12.....89 A3
Alpington Wlk M40.....65 C2
Alport Ave M16.....97 C2
Alport Gr 8 SK13.....171 B2
Alport Lea 2 SK13.....171 B2
Alport Way 1 SK13.....171 B2
Alresford Rd
Middleton M9.....64 F5
Salford M6.....80 D5
Alric Wlk M22.....130 E8
Alsager Cl M21.....109 B6
Alsham Wlk M8.....156 A6
Alsop Ave M7.....81 B7
Alstead Ave WA15.....120 A3
Alston Ave
Sale M33.....107 F3
Shaw OL2.....149 B4
Stretford M32.....96 B3
Alston Cl SK7.....124 A1
Alstone Dr WA14.....119 B4
Alstone Rd SK4.....111 C6
Alston Gdns M19.....110 F5
Alston Lea M46.....58 E4
Alston Rd
Manchester M18.....99 E5
Wigan WN2.....37 F2
Alston St
Bolton BL3.....147 B3
Bury BL8.....27 C4
Alston Wlk M24.....46 C2
ALT.....67 D3
Altair Ave 7 M22.....121 D1
Altair Pl M7.....81 C4
Altcar Gr SK5.....99 E2
Altcar Wlk M22.....121 C2
Alt Cl WN7.....75 C6
Alt Fold Dr OL8.....67 C6
Alt Gr OL6.....85 B6
Altham Cl BL9.....44 D7
Altham Wlk 12 M40....83 A6
Alt Hill La OL6, OL7.....85 C8
Althorn Wlk 11 M23...121 A5
Althorpe Wlk M40.....83 D4
Alt La OL8.....67 C3
Alton Ave M41.....94 D2
Alton Cl
Ashton-in-M WN4.....73 A4
Ashton-u-L OL6.....85 C7
Whitefield BL9.....45 A5
Alton Rd SK9.....136 F7
Alton Sq M11.....99 E7
Alton St OL8.....153 A5
Alton Towers M16.....97 D1
Alt Prim Sch OL8.....67 D3
Alt Rd OL6.....85 B6
ALTRINCHAM.....119 C5
Altrincham Boys Gram Sch
WA14.....119 D2
Altrincham Bsns Pk
WA14.....119 D2
Altrincham CE Sch
WA14.....119 D5
Altrincham Coll of Arts
WA15.....120 B3
Altrincham General Hospl
WA14.....119 D4

Altrincham Gram Sch for
Girls WA14.....119 C3
Altrincham Gram Sch for
Girls (Sixth Form Ctr)
WA14.....119 B3
Altrincham L Ctr WA15 .. 119 E4
Altrincham Prep Sch
WA14.....119 D2
Altrincham Rd
Styal SK9.....130 C4
Wilmslow SK9.....130 C2
Wythenshawe M23.....120 E7
Wythenshawe, Sharston
M22.....121 E5
Altrincham Ret Pk WA14 119 C7
Altrincham St M1.....163 B4
Altrincham Sta & Metro Sta
WA15.....119 D2
Alt Wlk M45.....45 C2
Alum Cres BL9.....45 A3
Alvanley Cl
Sale M33.....108 C1
Wigan WN5.....36 C1
Alvanley Cres SK3.....123 C6
Alvanley Ind Est SK6...112 F4
Alvan Sq 12 M11.....99 E7
Alva Rd OL4.....49 D2
Alvaston Ave SK4.....168 B2
Alvaston Rd M18.....99 E4
Alveley Ave M20.....110 C3
Alverstone Rd M20.....110 C6
Alveston Dr SK9.....137 C8
Alvington Gr SK7.....124 A1
Alvon Ct SK14.....102 A2
Alwin Rd OL2.....149 A4
Alwinton Ave M20.....110 E3
Alworth Rd M9.....64 D5
Alwyn Cl WN7.....75 F1
Alwyn Dr M13.....98 E4
Alwyn St WN1.....37 D1
Alwyn Terr WN1.....37 D1
Amar St WN2.....151 C3
Ambassador Pl WA15 ...119 E5
Ambergate M46.....58 D2
Amber Gdns
Dukinfield SK16.....101 B8
Hindley WN2.....56 E4
Amber Gr BL5.....39 F2
Amberhill Way
Boothstown M28.....77 F5
Worsley M28.....78 A5
Amberley Cl
Bolton BL3.....40 F5
Wigan WN2.....37 F2
Amberley Dr
Altrincham WA15.....129 B8
Irlam M44.....94 A1
Sale M33.....107 E5
Wythenshawe M23.....121 A4
Amberley Rd M33.....107 E5
Amberley Wlk OL9.....152 C3
Amberswood Cl WN2...56 B7
Amberswood E M38.....60 A6
Amberwood Dr M23...120 D6
Amblecote Drive E M38 .. 60 A6
Amblecote Drive W M38.. 60 A6
Ambleside
Ince-in-M WN2.....56 B7
Stalybridge SK15.....86 A3
Wigan WN5.....54 C7
Ambleside Ave
Altrincham WA15.....120 C5
Ashton-u-L OL7.....84 F4
Ambleside Cl
Bolton BL2.....25 F4
Middleton M24.....46 E1
Ambleside Ct
Cheadle SK8.....122 C5
Stalybridge SK15.....86 A3
Ambleside Pl WA11.....71 B1
Ambleside Rd
Reddish SK5.....111 F6
Urmston M41.....94 E1
Ambleside Wlk M9.....65 A3
Amblethorn Dr BL1.....24 D5
Ambrose Ave WN7.....57 D1
Ambrose Cres OL3.....51 B3
Ambrose Dr M20.....109 E4
Ambrose Gdns M20....109 E4
Ambrose St
Hyde SK14.....113 E7
Manchester M12.....165 A3
Rochdale OL12.....139 C1
Ambuscade Ct M41.....94 F2
Ambush St M11.....99 F7
Amelia St
Denton M34.....100 F4
Hyde SK14.....167 B2
Amersham Cl M41.....95 B5
Amersham Pl M19.....111 A6
Amersham St M5.....154 C1
Amesbury Dr WN3.....54 C2
Amesbury Gr SK5.....111 F5
Amesbury Rd M9.....64 E4
Amethyst Cl WN2.....38 A2
Amherst Rd M14, M20 ...110 D2
Amis Gr WA3.....90 E8
Amlwch Ave SK2.....124 D6
Ammon's Way OL3.....50 F5
Ammon Wrigley Cl OL1...153 C3
Amory St M12.....163 C4
Amos Ave M40.....83 C4
Amos St
Manchester M9.....157 C4
Salford M6.....80 C5
Ampleforth Gdns 4 M26...43 E5
Ampney Cl M30.....79 B1
Amport Wlk 8 M40.....65 C2

Amwell St M8 156 C3
Amy St
Middleton M24 47 B1
Rochdale OL12 14 B1
Anaconda Dr M3 158 B3
Ancaster Wlk 5 M40 65 C2
Anchorage Metro Sta M5 161 A4
Anchorage Quay M50 161 A4
Anchorage Rd M41 96 A1
Anchorage Wlk M18 165 C2
Anchor Cl M19 99 C1
Anchor Ct M8 63 F1
Anchor La BL4, M38 59 F7
Anchorside Cl M21 109 B7
Anchor St OL1 153 C4
ANCOATS 159 C2
Ancoats Gr M4 164 A4
Ancoats Grove N M4 160 A1
Ancoats St 5 OL4 67 E6
Ancroft Dr WN2 56 D3
Ancroft Gdns BL3 146 C2
Ancroft St M15 162 B2
Anderby Pl BL5 39 E2
Anderby Wlk BL5 39 E2
ANDERTON 21 C8
Anderton Cl
Bury BL8 26 F1
Rawtenstall BB4 2 F7
Anderton Gr OL6 85 E5
Anderton La BL6 21 E4
Anderton Prim Sch PR6 21 B8
Anderton St
Adlington PR7 21 A7
Ince-in-M WN2 151 C3
Anderton Way
Handforth SK9 131 D3
Wigan WN2 38 B2
Andoc Ave M30 80 A1
Andover Ave M24 65 C5
Andover Cres WN3 54 D2
Andover Rd WA11 72 E1
Andover St M30 79 C1
Andover Wlk M8 156 A4
Andre St 14 M11 83 C2
Andrew Ave WN5 71 F5
Andrew Cl
Radcliffe M26 44 C1
Ramsbottom BL8 10 F1
Andrew Ct 3 M20 110 B6
Andrew Gr SK16 101 D8
Andrew Ho SK4 168 B4
Andrew La
Bolton BL1 24 F6
High Lane SK6 134 F8
Andrew Rd M9 64 D1
Andrews Ave M41 94 E3
Andrew St
Ashton-u-L OL6 85 D5
Bury BL9 141 A2
Chadderton OL9 152 B4
Compstall SK6 114 A2
Droylsden M43 84 C4
Failsworth M35 83 E8
Hyde SK14 167 C3
Middleton M24 65 C7
Mossley OL5 86 C8
Stockport SK4 169 A2
Andrew's Terr 3 BL5 39 E1
Andy Nicholson Wlk M9 157 C4
Anemone Dr BB4 1 A8
Anerley Rd M20 110 B4
Anfield Cl BL9 45 B3
Anfield Rd
Bolton BL3 147 C2
Cheadle SK8 122 F3
Failsworth M40 65 D1
Sale M33 108 C5
Angela Ave OL1, OL2 48 E2
Angela St M15 162 A3
Angelbank BL6 21 F2
Angel Cl SK16 101 B8
Angelo St BL1 143 A2
Angel St
Denton M34 101 A4
Hazel Grove SK7 124 D3
Manchester M4 159 A3
Angier Gr M34 100 F3
Anglers Rest M44 105 E5
Anglesea Ave SK2 170 C2
Anglesey Cl OL7 85 A6
Anglesey Dr SK12 133 F6
Anglesey Gr SK8 123 A6
Anglesey Rd OL7 84 F6
Anglesey Water SK12 133 E6
Angleside Ave M19 110 E4
Angle St BL2 25 B1
Anglezarke Rd PR6 21 A7
Anglia Gr BL3 146 C4
Angora Dr M3 158 A3
Angouleme Way BL9 140 C1
Angouleme Way Ret Pk BL9 140 C2
Angus Ave
Heywood OL10 29 A1
Leigh WN7 75 C7
Angus St OL13 3 C8
Aniline St
Droylsden M11 83 B1
Manchester M43 99 F8
Anita St M4 159 B2
Anjou Bvd WN5 54 F8
Annable Rd
Droylsden M43 84 B1
Irlam M44 105 F8
Manchester M18 99 E6
Romiley SK6 112 D3
Annald Sq M43 100 A8
Annandale Gdns WN8 53 A7
Annan Gr WN4 73 E5
Annan St M34 100 F4
Anne Cl 6 OL7 85 A6
Annecy Cl BL8 27 B4
Anne Line Cl 3 OL11 31 A5
Anne Nuttall Rd M15 162 A3
Annersley Ave OL2 149 A2
Annesley Cres WN3 54 F3
Annesley Gdns 1 M18 99 D6
Annesley Rd M40 65 E1
Anne St SK16 101 D8
Annette Ave WA12 89 A5
Annie Darby Ct M9 157 A3
Annie St
Ramsbottom BL0 11 A4
Salford M6 154 B2
Annis Cl SK9 137 B2
Annisdale Cl M30 79 B2
Annisfield Ave OL3 69 C5
Annis Rd
Alderley Edge SK9 137 B2
Bolton BL3 146 B4
Annis St M9 157 B3
Ann La M29 77 C5
Ann Sq OL4 67 D8
Ann St
Ashton-u-L OL7 100 F8
Denton M34 100 E3
Dukinfield SK14 101 C3
Farnworth BL4 60 E7
Heywood OL10 29 D3
Leigh WN7 75 E8
Reddish SK5 169 B4
Rochdale OL11 139 C2
Anscombe Cl M40 160 A3
Ansdell Ave M21 109 C8
Ansdell Dr M43 83 E2
Ansdell Rd
Horwich BL6 22 C4
Reddish SK5 100 A1
Rochdale OL16 31 B4
Wigan WN5 54 D5
Ansdell St M8 156 A3
Ansell Cl M18 99 D6
Anselms Ct OL8 66 C4
Ansford Ave WN2 74 B8
Ansford Wlk M9 156 C2
Ansleigh Ave M8 64 A1
Ansley Gr SK4 168 B3
Anslow Cl M40 157 A1
Anson Ave M27 79 E6
Anson Cl SK7 132 F5
Anson Ct M14 98 D3
Anson Engine Mus The★ SK12 134 C4
Anson Pl WN5 54 C8
Anson Rd
Handforth SK9 131 E1
Manchester M14 98 D3
Poynton SK12 134 B3
Reddish M34, SK5 100 A2
Swinton M27 79 E6
Anson St
Bolton BL1 143 C3
Eccles M30 79 B4
Wigan WN5 54 F7
Answell Ave M8 64 A2
Antares Ave M7 158 A3
Anthistle Ct M5 154 A2
Anthony Cl M12 164 B3
Anthony St OL5 68 B1
Anthorn Rd WN3 54 E3
Antilles Cl M12 99 A4
Antler Ct WN4 73 B6
Anton Wlk M9 157 A3
Antrim Cl
Manchester M19 110 D2
Wigan WN3 54 C2
Anvil Cl WN5 53 D5
Anvil St OL13 3 E8
Anvil Way OL1 153 B3
Apethorn La SK14 113 D7
Apfel La OL9 152 B3
Apollo Ave BL9 44 F3
Apollo Wlk M12 165 A2
Apperley Grange M30 79 E4
Appian Way M7 155 B1
Appleby Ave
Altrincham WA15 120 C5
Dukinfield SK14 101 C5
Manchester M12 99 A3
Appleby Cl
Bury BL8 26 F2
Stockport SK3 170 A1
Appleby Gdns
1 Bolton BL2 25 B1
Whitefield BL9 44 F3
Appleby Lo M14 98 D2
Appleby Rd SK8 122 B4
Appleby Wlk 4 OL2 48 E4
Apple Cl OL8 67 C3
Applecross Wlk M11 165 C4
Apple Dell Ave WA3 74 C1
Appledore Dr
Bolton BL2 25 F3
Wythenshawe M23 120 D7
Appledore Wlk OL9 152 B2
Appleford Ave M23 121 A4
Appleford Dr M8 156 B2
Apple Hey WN6 35 C8
Apple La WN6 35 D8
Apple St SK14 114 C7
Applethwaite WN2 56 B8
Appleton Ct M33 108 B4
Appleton Dr SK13 116 F8
Appleton Gr
Sale M33 107 E2
Appleton Gr *continued*
Wigan WN3 54 E4
Appleton La BL5 39 F1
Appleton Rd
Altrincham WA15 119 F1
Reddish SK4 111 D6
Appleton St WN3 150 B4
Appleton Wlk 8 SK9 131 E1
Apple Tree Ct M5 81 A2
Apple Tree Rd SK22 127 B1
Apple Tree Wlk 8 M33 107 C5
Apple Way M24 65 B6
Applewood OL9 65 E7
Appleyard Cl M27 80 D8
APPLEY BRIDGE 35 D8
Appley Bridge All Saints CE Prim Sch WN6 18 C1
Appley Bridge Sta WN6 35 C7
Appley Cl WN6 18 C2
Appley Lane N WN6 18 C1
Appley Lane S WN6, WN8 35 C6
Apprentice Ct 18 M9 157 B4
April Cl OL8 67 C4
Apsley Cl WA14 119 B1
Apsley Gr
Altrincham WA14 119 B1
Manchester M12 163 C2
Apsley Pl OL6 166 A2
Apsley Rd M34 100 F4
Apsley Side OL5 86 C8
Apsley St SK1 169 C1
Aquarius La M6 81 C4
Aquarius St M15 163 A1
Aqueduct Bsns Pk SK6 125 F8
Aqueduct Rd BL3 148 C1
Aquinas Coll SK2 124 A6
Aragon Dr OL10 29 C2
Aragon Way SK6 125 E6
Arbor Ave M19 110 F6
Arbor Dr M19 110 F7
Arbor Gr
Droylsden M43 83 F3
Walkden M38 59 E4
Arbory Ave M40 83 B7
Arbory Cl WN7 76 C5
Arbour Cl
Bury BL9 27 E6
Salford M6 154 C3
Arbour La WN6 19 B1
Arbour Rd OL4 67 E4
Arbroath St M43 83 E1
Arbury Ave
Cheadle SK3 123 A7
Rochdale OL11 139 B1
Arcades Sh Ctr OL6 166 B3
Arcade St 18 WN1 150 C4
Arcade The
Brinnington SK5 112 C5
8 Rawtenstall BB4 2 E8
2 Stalybridge SK15 101 F8
Arcadia Ave M33 108 A1
Arcadia L Ctr M19 99 A1
Archer Ave BL2 148 C4
Archer Gr BL2 148 C4
Archer Pk M24 64 E8
Archer Pl M32 95 F3
Archer St
Boothstown M28 77 E7
Droylsden M11 83 A2
Leigh WN7 76 B2
Mossley OL5 68 C2
Stockport SK2 124 C5
Archie St M5 161 A3
Arch La WN4 72 B3
Arch St BL1 25 A1
Archway M15 162 C2
Archway Wlk WA12 89 E3
Arclid Cl SK9 131 E1
Arcon Cl OL16 31 E6
Arcon Dr M16 97 E3
Arcon Pl WA14 119 A6
Ardale Ave M40 65 C2
Ardcombe Ave M9 64 C5
Ardeen Wlk M13 163 C2
Arden Ave M24 65 B5
Arden Bldgs SK3 170 B4
Arden Bsns Ctr SK6 112 E6
Arden Cl
Ashton-u-L OL6 85 F6
Bury BL9 44 E8
Gatley SK8 131 C7
Glossop SK13 116 A8
Arden Ct SK7 123 D1
Ardenfield M34 113 A7
Ardenfield Cl M26 44 B1
Ardenfield Dr M22 121 E3
Arden Gr M40 65 C1
Arden Hall SK6 112 D7
Arden Ho OL2 48 E4
Arden Lodge Rd M23 120 E7
ARDEN PARK 112 C3
Arden Prim Sch SK6 112 D3
Arden Rd SK6 112 E7
Ardens Cl M27 61 D2
Arden St OL9 66 A3
Ardent Way M25 63 B1
Arden Wlk
6 Sale M33 107 C5
Stockport SK1 169 B1
Arderne Pl 10 SK9 137 A1
Arderne Rd WA15 120 A8
Ardern Gr SK1 170 C4
Ardern Rd M8 63 F2
Ardingly Wlk M23 120 D8
Ardley Rd BL6 22 C4
Ardmore Wlk M22 121 E2
ARDWICK 164 A3
Ardwick Green N M12 163 C3
Ardwick Green S M12, M13 163 C3
Ardwick L Ctr M12 98 F4
Ardwick Sta M12 164 A3
Arena App BL6 39 C7
Argo St BL3 147 A4
Argosy Dr
Eccles M30 94 F7
Wythenshawe M90 129 F7
Argus St OL8 66 C2
Argyle Ave
Manchester M14 98 E4
Walkden M28 60 C5
Whitefield M45 63 A8
Argyle Cres OL10 29 B1
Argyle Par OL10 29 A1
Argyle St
Atherton M46 58 C2
Bury BL9 140 C4
5 Droylsden M43 84 A1
Hazel Grove SK7 124 E2
Heywood OL10 29 A1
Hindley WN2 56 E5
Manchester M18 99 D5
Mossley OL5 68 C1
Oldham OL1 67 B8
14 Rochdale OL16 31 A4
Swinton M27 79 E7
Wigan WN5 54 F6
Argyll Ave M32 96 B2
Argyll Cl
Failsworth M35 84 B7
Garswood WN4 72 C4
Argyll Park Rd M35 84 B7
Argyll Rd
Cheadle SK8 122 F5
Oldham OL9 65 F4
Argyll St OL6 85 E3
Ariel Gdns WA3 92 A2
Ariel Wlk 4 WA3 90 E8
Arkendale Cl M35 84 C7
Arkholme M28 78 A8
Arkholme Wlk M40 83 B7
Arkle Ave SK8, SK9 131 E4
Arkle Dr OL9 65 F8
Arkley Wlk M13 163 B2
Ark St 3 M19 99 A2
Arkwright Dr SK6 126 A6
Arkwright Rd SK6 126 A6
Arkwright St
Horwich BL6 22 C2
Oldham OL9 152 C2
Arkwright Way OL11 31 A2
Arlen Ct BL2 148 B1
Arlen Rd BL2 148 B1
Arlen Way OL10 29 B2
Arley Ave
Bury BL9 27 F6
Manchester M20 109 F5
Arley Cl
Altrincham WA14 119 D8
Dukinfield SK16 101 D6
Wigan WN2 38 B2
Arley Dr
Sale M33 108 A2
Shaw OL2 49 D8
Arley Gr SK3 123 D4
Arley Ho M23 121 A4
Arley La WN1, WN2 20 D2
Arley Mere Cl SK8 122 F3
Arley Moss Wlk M13 163 B3
Arley St
Ince-in-M WN3 55 F4
Radcliffe M26 44 B1
Arley Way
Atherton M46 58 E2
22 Denton M34 101 A1
Arlies Cl SK15 86 A4
Arlies La SK15 86 B4
Arlies Sch SK15 86 A4
Arlies St OL6 85 D4
Arlington Ave
Denton M34 101 A2
Manchester M25 63 B2
Swinton M27 79 D6
Arlington Cl
Ramsbottom BL9 11 C2
Royton OL2 48 E2
Arlington Cres SK9 136 E5
Arlington Dr
Golborne WN7 91 C8
Poynton SK12 133 D3
Stockport SK2 124 A3
Arlington Rd
Cheadle SK8 122 C4
Stretford M32 96 B1
Arlington St
4 Ashton-u-L OL6 166 C3
Bolton BL3 147 C3
Salford, Broughton Park M8 155 C4
Salford M3 158 A2
Arlington Way SK9 136 E5
Arliss Ave M19 111 A8
Armadale Ave M9 65 A4
Armadale Cl SK3 170 C1
Armadale Ct BL1 40 E5
Armadale Rd
Bolton BL3 40 E5
Dukinfield SK16 101 D7
Armdale Rise OL4 49 E1
Armitage Ave M38 59 F4
Armitage CE Prim Sch M12 164 B2
Armitage Cl
Hyde SK14 113 E8
Middleton M24 64 D7
Oldham OL8 66 C3
Armitage Ct M12 164 C2
Armitage Gr M38 59 F4
Armitage Ho 4 M6 80 C3
Armitage Owen Wlk 4 M40 83 A7
Armitage Rd WA14 119 D3
Armitage Sports Ctr (Univ of Manchester) M14 98 E1
Armitage St M30 79 D1
Armit Rd OL3 68 E5
Armitstead St 4 WN2 56 D4
Armour Pl 1 M9 64 C2
Armoury Bank WN4 73 B3
Armoury St SK3 170 B4
Arm Rd OL15 15 E4
Armstrong Hurst Cl OL12 15 B2
Armstrong St
Horwich BL6 22 C2
Wigan WN2 38 A3
Arncliffe WA14 119 D2
Arncliffe Cl
5 Farnworth BL4 42 D1
Hindley WN2 56 C4
Arncliffe Dr M23 121 A3
Arncliffe Rise OL4 50 A4
Arncot Rd BL1 24 F5
Arncott Cl OL2 49 A4
Arndale Ctr M4 159 A2
Arne Cl SK2 125 A5
Arnesby Ave M33 108 E5
Arnesby Gr BL2 148 B4
Arne St OL9 152 A1
Arnfield Dr 1 M28 78 B6
Arnfield La SK13 103 F8
Arnfield Rd
Manchester M20 110 C6
Stockport SK3 170 A1
Arnold Ave
Heywood OL10 46 E7
Hyde SK14 113 F7
Arnold Cl SK16 102 A7
Arnold Ct M16 97 E1
Arnold Dr
Droylsden M43 84 A1
Middleton M24 47 C3
Arnold Rd
Bolton BL7 24 F8
Hyde SK14 113 F7
Manchester M16 97 E1
Arnold St
Bolton BL1 142 C2
Oldham OL1 67 A8
Stockport SK3 170 B3
Arnolds Yd WA14 119 D5
Arnold Wlk 9 M34 113 A7
Arnott Cres M15 162 C1
Arnside Ave
Chadderton OL9 152 A1
Hazel Grove SK7 124 C2
Ince-in-M WN2 56 A7
Reddish SK4 111 E6
Arnside Cl
Gatley SK8 122 B4
High Lane SK6 134 E8
Shaw OL2 49 D7
Arnside Dr
Dukinfield SK14 101 C4
Rochdale OL11 29 E5
Salford M6 80 B3
Arnside Gr
Bolton BL2 42 E8
Sale M33 108 B6
Arnside Rd
Hindley WN2 57 A5
Wigan WN5 54 B8
Arnside St M14 98 B2
Arosa Ct M20 110 C7
Arran Ave
Oldham OL8 66 F3
Sale M33 108 C3
Stretford M32 96 A2
Arran Cl BL3 40 E6
Arrandale Ct M41 95 D3
Arran Gdns M41 95 C5
Arran Gr M26 43 E5
Arran Rd SK16 101 C7
Arran St
12 Manchester M40 64 F1
Salford M7 155 A2
Arran Wlk OL10 29 A1
Arras Gr M34 99 F3
Arreton Sq M14 98 D3
Arrivals Way M90 130 B7
Arrowfield Dr M21 109 D7
Arrowfield Rd M21 109 D7
Arrowhill Rd M26 43 F8
Arrowscroft Ct SK14 103 D5
Arrowscroft Way SK14 171 A4
Arrowsmith Ct 7 BL6 22 E1
Arrowsmith Wlk 16 M11 160 C1
Arrow St
Bolton BL1 145 B4
Leigh WN7 76 B3
Salford M7 155 A1
Arrow Trad Est M34 100 D5
Arthill La WA14 118 B1
Arthington St OL16 31 B8
Arthog Dr WA15 128 F8
Arthog Rd
Altrincham WA15 128 F8
Manchester M20 110 C3
Arthur Ave M28 60 C5
Arthur La BL2 26 B2
Arthur Millwood Ct M3 158 A1
Arthur Rd M16 97 C3

Arthurs La OL3 69 B6
Arthur St
Bury BL8 27 C2
Eccles M30 79 C1
Farnworth BL4 60 D8
Heywood OL10 29 D2
Hindley WN2 56 E5
Hyde SK14 101 C1
Leigh WN7 75 E4
Little Lever BL3 43 B3
Prestwich M25 62 F4
Reddish SK5 111 E7
Rochdale OL12 139 A4
Shaw OL2 149 B3
Swinton M27 79 D7
Walkden M28 60 E1
Arthur Terr 4 SK5 111 E7
Artillery Ct M13 163 C3
Artillery Pl M22 121 F4
Artillery St
Bolton BL3 145 C1
Manchester M3 162 B4
Artwright Cl BL1 142 C1
Arundale BL5 39 F2
Arundale Ave M16 97 E1
Arundale Cl SK14 102 F3
Arundale Ct M16 97 E1
Arundale Gr SK14 102 F3
Arundale Prim Sch SK14 102 F3
Arundel Ave
Hazel Grove SK7 133 D8
Prestwich M45 63 B7
Rochdale OL11 30 E4
Urmston M41 94 C1
Arundel Cl
Altrincham WA15 120 C1
Bury BL8 27 C6
Mossley SK15 86 F6
Arundel Dr WN7 75 F6
Arundel Gr SK2 124 B4
Arundel Grange SK13 116 A8
Arundel Rd SK8 132 A6
Arundel St
Ashton-u-L OL6 85 E3
Bolton BL1 24 E5
Glossop SK13 104 C1
Hindley WN2 56 E5
Manchester M15 162 A3
Mossley OL5 68 B1
Oldham OL4 67 C7
Rochdale OL11 30 E4
Swinton M27 61 C1
Wigan WN5 54 F6
Arundel Wlk OL9 152 A2
Asby Cl M24 46 D2
Ascension Rd M7 158 A4
Ascot Ave
Sale M33 107 D3
Stretford M32 96 F3
Ascot Cl
Chadderton OL9 152 C3
Rochdale OL11 29 E8
Ascot Dr
Atherton M46 58 E4
Hazel Grove SK7 125 A2
Urmston M41 94 C2
Ascot Mdws BL9 44 E8
Ascot Par M19 110 F6
Ascot Rd
Failsworth M40 83 B4
Little Lever BL3 42 F3
Ascot Wlk M6 81 A5
Ascroft Ave WN6 36 F3
Ascroft St
Oldham OL1 153 C2
Wigan WN1 151 B3
Asgard Dr M5 161 C4
Asgard Gr M5 161 C4
Ash Ave
Altrincham WA14 119 A5
Cheadle SK8 122 E5
Irlam M44 105 D5
Newton-le-W WA12 89 C2
Ashawe Cl M38 59 E3
Ashawe Gr M38 59 F3
Ashawe Terr M38 59 E3
Ashbank Ave BL3 40 E6
Ashbank Ind Est SK1 170 C4
Ashbee St BL1 143 B3
Ashberry Cl 3 SK9 137 D8
Ashborne Dr BL9 11 D2
Ashbourne Ave
Bolton BL2 148 B2
Cheadle SK8 122 F6
Hindley WN2 56 F5
Middleton M24 47 C3
Urmston M41 94 E2
Wigan WN2 38 A2
Ashbourne Cl
Leigh WN7 57 D1
Wardle OL12 15 D6
Ashbourne Cres M33 108 D2
Ashbourne Ct 3 SK13 116 F8
Ashbourne Dr
Ashton-u-L OL6 85 F6
High Lane SK6 134 F6
Ashbourne Gdns WN2 56 F5
Ashbourne Gr
Salford M7 155 B3
Whitefield M45 44 D1
Worsley M28 78 E8
Ashbourne Rd
Denton M34 100 E2
Eccles M30 79 E1
Hazel Grove SK7 133 F8
Ashbourne Rd *continued*
Salford M6 80 C5
Stretford M32 96 A3
Ashbourne Sq OL8 153 B1
Ashbourne St OL11 13 E1
Ashbridge M17 96 B6
Ashbridge Rd M35 84 B6
Ashbrook Ave M34 100 B3
Ashbrook Cl
Gatley SK8 122 B1
Reddish M34 100 B3
Whitefield M45 63 B8
Ashbrook Cres OL12 15 C4
Ashbrook Farm Cl SK5 99 F2
Ashbrook Hey La OL12 15 C4
Ashbrook La 6 SK5 99 F2
Ashbrook Rd OL4 67 F5
Ashbrook St M11 100 A7
Ashburn 11 OL10 29 C2
Ashburn Ave M19 110 F5
Ashburn Cl 7 BL6 22 D1
Ashburne Ho M14 98 D4
Ashburn Gr SK4 169 A3
Ashburn Rd SK4 169 A3
Ashburton Cl SK14 102 E2
Ashburton Rd SK3 170 B1
Ashburton Road W M17, M41 95 E7
Ashbury Cl BL3 145 B1
Ashbury Meadow Prim Sch M11 164 B4
Ashbury Pl M40 160 B4
Ashburys Sta M12 165 A3
Ashby Ave M19 110 E4
Ashby Cl BL3 42 C2
Ashby Gr
Leigh WN7 75 C8
Whitefield M45 63 B7
Ashby Rd WN3 55 B3
Ash Cl
Appley Bridge WN6 35 D7
Ashton-u-L OL6 85 D5
Mottram in L SK14 103 A4
Rochdale OL12 15 C4
Stockport SK2 124 C5
Ashcombe Dr
Bolton BL2 43 A6
Radcliffe M26 43 D5
Ashcombe Pl BL7 9 E7
Ashcombe Wlk 7 M11 160 C1
Ashcott Ave M22 121 D4
Ashcott Cl BL6 40 E5
Ashcroft
6 Rochdale OL12 15 D4
Wilmslow SK9 136 F5
Ashcroft Ave M6 154 B4
Ashcroft Ct
Irlam M44 105 D5
Oldham OL1 153 C2
Ashcroft Rd WA13 117 B4
Ashcroft St
Chadderton OL9 152 A1
Hindley WN2 56 E4
Ash Ct
Manchester, Whalley Range M16 97 E2
Romiley SK6 113 A5
Stockport, Heaton Moor SK4 168 B3
Ashdale Ave BL3 40 E5
Ashdale Cl
Coppull PR7 19 D8
Reddish SK5 111 F5
Ashdale Cres M43 83 F1
Ashdale Dr
Gatley SK8 122 B2
Manchester M20 110 D5
Ashdale Rd
Hindley WN2 57 A5
Wigan WN3 55 A2
Ashdene
Ashton-u-L OL6 85 D2
Rochdale OL12 14 D4
Ashdene Cl
Chadderton OL1, OL9 48 C1
Oldham OL4 67 F7
Ashdene Cres BL2 25 D4
Ashdene Prim Sch SK9 136 F5
Ashdene Rd
Manchester, Heaton Mersey SK4 110 D2
Manchester, Withington M20 110 D6
Wilmslow SK9 136 F5
Ashdene Rise OL1 49 D4
Ashdown Ave
Manchester M9 64 D4
Romiley SK6 113 C5
Ashdown Cl SK8 132 A6
Ashdown Dr
Bolton BL2 25 C3
Pendlebury M27 80 A6
Walkden M28 78 A7
Ashdowne Lawns SK15 86 D3
Ashdown Gr M9 64 D4
Ashdown Rd SK4 168 C3
Ashdown Terr M9 64 D4
Ashdown Way OL2 48 E8
Ash Dr M27 61 C2
Ashen Bottom BB4 1 D6
Asher St BL3 146 C2
Ashes Cl SK15 102 C8
Ashes Dr BL2 42 F8
Ashes La
Glossop SK13 104 B2
Milnrow OL16 31 F7
Oldham OL4 67 F6
Stalybridge SK15 102 C8
Ashes The SK13 104 B2
Ashfell Ct 1 M21 96 F1
Ashfield M34 101 A5
Ashfield Ave
Atherton M46 58 C4
Hindley WN2 56 F4
Ashfield Cl
Lymm WA13 117 B4
Salford M6 154 B3
Ashfield Cres
Billinge WN5 71 E4
Cheadle SK8 122 D6
Oldham OL4 67 F6
Ashfield Ct M41 95 D1
Ashfield Dr
Aspull WN2 38 C5
Failsworth M40 83 D4
Ashfield Gr
Bolton BL1 25 A6
Irlam M44 105 E6
Marple SK6 114 B1
Reddish M18 99 F4
Stockport SK3 123 F4
Ashfield Ho OL11 139 C1
Ashfield House Gdns WN6 36 F8
Ashfield La OL16 31 F4
Ashfield Lo M20 109 F2
Ashfield Park Dr WN6 36 F8
Ashfield Rd
Adlington PR6 21 B8
Altrincham WA15 119 E3
Cheadle SK8 122 D5
Glossop SK13 171 C3
Manchester M13 98 E3
Rochdale OL11 139 C1
Sale M33 108 B5
Stockport SK3 123 F4
Urmston M41 95 D2
Ashfield Sq M43 83 F2
Ashfield St OL8 66 C3
Ashfield Terr WN6 35 C8
Ashfield Valley Prim Sch OL11 30 E4
Ashford M33 107 C4
Ashford Ave
Boothstown M28 77 F6
Eccles M30 95 C8
3 Reddish SK5 99 F2
Swinton M27 79 C7
Ashford Cl
Bolton BL2 25 E4
Bury BL8 27 B1
Handforth SK9 131 C4
Ashford Ct 1 OL4 49 D1
Ashford Gn 2 SK13 171 B1
Ashford Gr M28 78 F8
Ashford Mews SK13 171 B1
Ashford Rd
Manchester M20 110 B7
Reddish SK4 111 D6
Wilmslow SK9 137 A4
Ashford Rise WN1 37 B4
Ashford St OL10 28 F2
Ashford Wlk
Bolton BL1 143 B1
Chadderton OL9 152 B2
Ashgate Ave M22 121 E4
Ashgate Specialist Support Prim Sch M22 121 F4
Ashgill Wlk 4 M9 157 B3
Ash Gr
Altrincham, Rosehill WA14 119 C1
Altrincham WA15 119 F7
Bolton, Harwood BL2 25 F3
Bolton, Victory BL1 144 B4
Bury BL8 27 A5
Droylsden M43 100 A8
Gatley SK8 131 B8
Golborne WA3 90 B8
Handforth SK9 131 C3
8 Horwich BL6 22 E1
Littleborough OL15 15 F5
Manchester M14 98 E4
Marple SK6 125 E5
Newhey OL16 32 A3
Oldham OL4 68 A7
Orrell WN5 53 F6
Prestwich M25 63 A6
Ramsbottom BL0 10 F3
Reddish SK4 111 D5
Royton OL2 48 D6
Stalybridge SK15 85 F3
Standish WN6 36 F8
Stretford M32 108 C8
Swinton M27 79 D5
Walkden M28 60 E1
Westhoughton BL5 57 E7
Ashgrove OL16 31 B1
Ash Grove Cres WN5 71 E6
Ash Hill Dr OL5 86 E8
Ashia Cl OL16 31 B6
Ashill Wlk M3 162 B4
Ashington Cl
Bolton BL1 142 B3
Wigan WN5 36 B1
Ashington Dr BL8 26 F2
Ashkirk St 4 M18 99 D5
Ash La
Altrincham WA15 120 C2
Wigan WN2 38 A2
Ashland Ave
Ashton-in-M WN4 73 A4
5 Wigan WN1 37 C2
Ashlands M33 108 A5
Ashlands Ave
Failsworth M40 65 C1
Ashlands Ave *continued*
Swinton M27 79 D6
Walkden M28 78 A7
Ashlands Cl BL0 1 D2
Ashlands Dr M34 100 E6
Ashlands Rd WA15 108 A1
Ashlar Dr M12 164 B4
Ash Lawns BL1 144 B3
Ash Lea SK15 86 A3
Ashlea Gr OL4 68 B6
Ash Lea Grange M30 79 E3
Ashleigh Ave SK13 104 B2
Ashleigh Cl OL2 48 E2
Ashleigh Dr BL1 40 E8
Ashleigh Rd WA15 120 B8
ASHLEY 128 E5
Ashley Ave
Bolton BL2 42 D8
Manchester M16 97 D4
Swinton M27 79 D6
Urmston M41 94 E2
Ashley Cl OL11 30 C4
Ashley Court Dr M40, OL9 65 F1
Ashley Cres M27 79 D7
Ashley Ct
Altrincham WA15 119 E1
Failsworth M40 65 F1
Stockport SK4 168 B4
Swinton M27 61 F2
Ashley Dr
Bramhall SK7 132 C6
Leigh WN7 75 C8
Sale M33 107 E2
Swinton M27 79 D6
Ashley Gdns
High Lane SK6 134 D8
Hyde SK14 167 B1
Ashley Gr 8 BL4 60 C8
ASHLEY HEATH 128 E8
Ashley La M9 157 C4
Ashley Mews
Hyde SK14 167 B1
Whitefield M45 63 B7
Ashleymill La WA14 128 D7
Ashley Mill Lane N WA14 128 E8
Ashley Rd
Altrincham WA14, WA15 119 E2
Ashley, Ashley Heath WA14, WA15 128 E7
Ashley WA14, WA15, WA16 128 C4
Droylsden M43 83 E2
Handforth SK9 131 B1
Hindley WN2 57 B3
Stockport SK2 124 C8
Ashley St
Hyde SK14 167 B4
Manchester M4 159 B3
Oldham OL9 152 C3
Salford M6 154 B2
Ashley Sta WA14 128 E5
Ashleys The SK4 168 B3
Ashling Ct M29 59 D1
Ash Lo SK12 133 D4
Ashlor St BL9 140 B1
Ashlyn Gr M14 110 D8
Ashlynne OL6 166 C3
Ashmeade WA15 120 B1
Ashmill Wlk M9 156 C2
Ashmond 16 OL4 67 F6
Ashmond Rd 12 OL4 67 F6
Ashmoor Rd M22 121 E1
Ashmoor Wlk M22 121 E1
Ashmore Ave SK3 122 F7
Ashmore St M29 77 D8
Ashmount Dr OL12 14 F2
Ashness Cl BL6 21 F3
Ashness Dr
Bolton BL2 25 E1
Bramhall SK7 132 E8
Middleton M24 46 D3
Ashness Gr BL2 25 E1
Ashness Pl BL2 25 E1
Ashover Ave M12 164 C2
Ashover Cl 8 BL1 24 F6
Ashover Ct M12 164 C2
Ashover St M32 96 E3
Ash Rd
Coppull PR7 19 E8
Droylsden M43 83 F2
Hollinfare WA3 105 A2
Kearsley BL4 60 F5
Partington M31 105 D3
Poynton SK12 133 F3
Reddish M34 99 F3
Ashridge Cl BL6 40 C6
Ashridge Dr
Dukinfield SK16 101 B7
Eccles M30 95 C8
Ashridge Way WN5 36 B1
Ash Sq OL4 67 D8
Ash St
Bolton BL2 148 A2
Bury BL9 141 A2
Denton M34 100 D7
Failsworth M35 83 E8
Golborne WA3 74 B2
Hazel Grove SK7 124 D3
Heywood OL10 29 B3
Manchester M9 157 A3
Middleton M24 65 C8
Oldham OL4 67 B6
Rochdale OL11 30 C2
Salford M6 154 C2
Stockport SK3 123 B8
2 Tyldesley M29 59 A1
Ashstead Rd M33 108 C1
Ashton Ave WA14 119 E6
Ashton Cres OL9 66 A2
ASHTON CROSS 72 D2
Ashton Ct
Denton M34 100 F6
Sale M33 107 E4
Ashton Field Dr M28 60 C4
Ashton Gallery 6 WN1 150 C4
Ashton Gdns
1 Glossop SK13 116 C7
Rochdale OL11 139 B1
Ashton Grange Ind Est WN4 73 B6
Ashton Heath WN4 73 C2
Ashton Hill La M43 100 A8
Ashton Ho
Hyde SK14 167 B4
Manchester M15 162 B4
ASHTON-IN-MAKERFIELD 73 C5
Ashton La
Middleton M24 65 A8
Sale M33 107 F5
Ashton L Ctr WN4 73 A4
Ashton Lodge BL0 138 C3
ASHTON MOSS 84 E2
Ashton New Rd
Droylsden M11, M43 83 C1
Manchester M12 160 C1
Ashton Old Rd
Manchester, Beswick M11, M12 164 B4
Manchester, Openshaw M11 99 D7
ASHTON OLD TOWN 166 B2
Ashton on Mersey Sch M33 107 F3
Ashton Pl SK7 124 F1
Ashton Pools OL6 166 B3
Ashton Rd
Brinnington SK6 112 E6
Denton M34 100 E5
Droylsden M43 84 B1
Dukinfield SK14 101 E5
Failsworth M35 84 C7
Golborne WA3 74 A2
Manchester M9 64 D5
Newton-le-W WA12 89 C5
Oldham OL8, OL7 66 F3
Windy Arbour WN5 72 B8
Ashton Ret Pk OL6 166 B3
Ashton Road E M35 84 A7
Ashton Road W M35 83 F7
Ashton St
Bolton BL3 146 B4
Chadderton OL9 66 A3
Dukinfield SK16 101 A7
Glossop SK13 116 C7
4 Heywood OL10 29 C2
Little Lever BL3 43 B3
Rochdale OL11 139 B1
Romiley SK6 113 C6
Wigan WN1 151 C4
ASHTON-UNDER-LYNE 166 A3
Ashton-under-Lyne Sixth Form Coll OL6 85 E3
Ashton-under-Lyne Sta OL6 166 B3
ASHTON UPON MERSEY 107 F5
Ash Tree Ave M43 83 F2
Ash Tree Dr SK16 101 F7
Ash Tree Rd
Dukinfield SK14 102 B5
Manchester M8 64 A1
Ashurst Ave M11 83 B2
Ashurst Cl
Bolton BL2 25 F3
Hyde SK14 102 A1
Ashurst Dr SK3, SK8 123 B5
Ashurst Gdns OL6 166 B4
Ashurst Gr M26 44 B1
Ashurst Rd
Shevington Moor WN6 19 B2
Wythenshawe M22 121 F3
Ash View OL6 166 C4
Ashville Terr M40 64 F1
Ashway OL6 166 A3
Ashway Clough N SK2 124 D5
Ashway Clough S SK2 124 D5
Ashwell Ave WA3 74 D1
Ashwell Mews BL2 25 C3
Ashwell Rd M23 121 B7
Ashwell St 6 BL2 25 B3
Ashwin Wlk 6 M8 155 C2
Ash Wlk
Chadderton OL9 152 B4
Middleton M24 64 F6
Sale M33 107 D5
Ashwood
Altrincham WA14 128 B8
Chadderton OL9 65 E7
Glossop SK13 115 F8
Kearsley M26 61 B7
Ashwood Ave
Abram Brow WN2 74 C7
Ashton-in-M WN4 73 A2
Golborne WA3 90 D8
Manchester M20 109 E4
Ramsbottom BL0 11 D7
Reddish M34 100 B3
Sale M33 107 E3
Walkden M28 60 C5
Ashwood Cres SK6 125 F7
Ashwood Ct M20 109 E5
Ashwood Dr
Bury BL8 27 B6
Littleborough OL15 15 F5

Ashwood Dr *continued*
Royton OL2 . . . . 48 C5
Ashwood Rd SK12 . . . . 135 D6
Ashworth Ave
Denton M34 . . . . 100 F7
Little Lever BL3 . . . . 43 C3
Urmston M41 . . . . 94 E2
Ashworth Cl
Altrincham WA14 . . . . 119 B1
Littleborough OL15 . . . . 16 A7
Oldham OL9 . . . . 66 C4
Royton OL2 . . . . 48 F4
Ashworth Ct
1 Radcliffe M26 . . . . 44 C4
Shaw OL2 . . . . 149 B2
Ashworth Gdns OL3 . . . . 69 B5
Ashworth La
Bolton BL1 . . . . 25 A5
Mottram in L SK14 . . . . 103 A3
Ashworth Rd OL10, OL11 . . 13 A1
Ashworth St
Aspull WN2 . . . . 38 E4
3 Bacup OL13 . . . . 3 D8
Bury BL8 . . . . 27 C3
Denton M34 . . . . 100 E4
Failsworth M35 . . . . 83 D6
Farnworth BL4 . . . . 60 C8
Heywood OL10 . . . . 46 E8
Oldham OL1 . . . . 153 C2
Radcliffe M26 . . . . 44 C4
11 Rawtenstall BB4 . . . . 2 F8
Rochdale OL12 . . . . 139 B4
Ashworth Terr
2 Bacup OL13 . . . . 3 B8
Bolton BL2 . . . . 25 E4
Ashworth View M34 . . . . 100 F7
Ashworth Way 8 SK14 . . 102 F2
Asia Ho M1 . . . . 163 A4
Asia St 1 BL3 . . . . 42 A3
Askern Ave M22 . . . . 121 D3
Askett Cl M40 . . . . 83 D6
Askrigg Cl M46 . . . . 76 A8
Askrigg Wlk 8 M13 . . . . 98 F4
Askwith Rd WN2 . . . . 56 F3
Aspell Cl M24 . . . . 64 F8
Aspen Cl
Altrincham WA15 . . . . 120 E5
Stockport SK4 . . . . 168 A1
Westhoughton BL5 . . . . 39 F2
Aspen Gdns OL12 . . . . 14 A1
Aspen Gn M34 . . . . 101 A2
Aspenshaw Rd SK22 . . . . 127 E3
Aspens The SK8 . . . . 122 A6
Aspen Way SK6 . . . . 135 A7
Aspenwood WN4 . . . . 73 A2
Aspen Wood SK14 . . . . 167 C3
Aspenwood Cl SK6 . . . . 125 E7
Aspenwood Dr
Chadderton OL9 . . . . 65 E7
Manchester M9 . . . . 64 D2
Sale M33 . . . . 107 C4
Aspinall Cl
Horwich BL6 . . . . 22 D1
Walkden M28 . . . . 59 F3
Aspinall Cres M28 . . . . 59 F2
Aspinall Gdns M24 . . . . 65 C7
Aspinall Gr 12 M28 . . . . 59 F3
Aspinall Rd WN6 . . . . 19 B1
Aspinall St
Heywood OL10 . . . . 29 E2
Manchester M14 . . . . 98 C3
5 Middleton M24 . . . . 65 C7
5 Platt Bridge WN2 . . . . 56 A2
Aspinall Way BL6 . . . . 22 C1
Aspinal Prim Sch M18 . . . . 99 E3
Aspin La M4 . . . . 159 A3
Aspland Rd SK14 . . . . 113 F8
ASPULL 38 D6
Aspull Arc 7 WN1 . . . . 150 C4
Aspull Church Prim Sch
WN2 . . . . 38 C4
Aspull Comm WN7 . . . . 75 C1
ASPULL COMMON 75 C1
Aspull Ct WN7 . . . . 75 C1
Aspull St OL4 . . . . 67 C5
Aspull Wlk 13 M13 . . . . 163 C2
Asquith Ave SK16 . . . . 101 C6
Asquith Rd M19 . . . . 110 F6
Asquith St SK5 . . . . 99 F1
Assheton Ave M34 . . . . 84 C1
Assheton Cl
Ashton-u-L OL6 . . . . 166 C3
Newton-le-W WA12 . . . . 89 B4
Assheton Cres M40 . . . . 83 D4
Assheton Ho OL6 . . . . 166 B3
Assheton Rd
Failsworth M40 . . . . 83 D4
Shaw OL2 . . . . 48 F7
Assheton St 5 M24 . . . . 47 A1
Assheton Way M24 . . . . 65 A8
Assissi Gdns M12 . . . . 165 B2
Assumption Rd M24 . . . . 46 D3
Astan Ave M43 . . . . 83 D2
Astbury Ave
Droylsden M34 . . . . 84 D1
Manchester M21 . . . . 109 C4
Astbury Cl
1 Altrincham WA15 . . . . 119 E6
Bury BL9 . . . . 45 A8
Golborne WA3 . . . . 91 B8
Oldham OL4 . . . . 67 F6
Astbury Cres SK3 . . . . 170 A2
Astbury St M26 . . . . 44 B1
Astbury Wlk 2 SK8 . . . . 123 A5
Aster Ave BL4 . . . . 42 A1
Aster Ho OL1 . . . . 48 E1
Aster St OL1 . . . . 48 E1
Aster Wlk M31 . . . . 105 F2
ASTLEY 77 C5
ASTLEY BRIDGE 143 C4
Astley Brook Cl BL1 . . . . 25 A3
Astley Cl OL2 . . . . 48 F7
Astley Ct M44 . . . . 105 E8
Astley Gdns SK16 . . . . 101 B8
Astley Gr SK15 . . . . 85 F3
ASTLEY GREEN 77 C4
Astley Green Colliery Mus★
M29 . . . . 77 C4
Astley Hall Dr
Ramsbottom BL0 . . . . 11 C4
Tyldesley M29 . . . . 77 B6
Astley House Bsns Ctr 18
M29 . . . . 59 A1
Astley La BL1 . . . . 143 B3
Astley Park Ind Est M29 . . 77 D7
Astley Rd
Bolton BL2 . . . . 25 E5
Irlam M44 . . . . 93 C3
Stalybridge SK15 . . . . 85 F2
Astley Sports Sch SK16 . . 101 E6
Astley St
Bolton BL1 . . . . 143 B2
Droylsden M11 . . . . 83 C1
Dukinfield SK16 . . . . 101 A8
Leigh WN7 . . . . 76 B4
Stalybridge SK15 . . . . 102 A8
Stockport SK4 . . . . 169 B1
Tyldesley M29 . . . . 77 A7
Astley Terr 7 SK16 . . . . 166 C1
Aston Ave M14 . . . . 98 A2
Aston Bldgs BB4 . . . . 2 F7
Aston Cl SK3 . . . . 123 C6
Aston Gdns 4 BL4 . . . . 42 D1
Aston Gr M29 . . . . 59 C1
Aston Ho BL1 . . . . 144 C3
Aston Way 13 SK9 . . . . 131 D5
Astor Rd
Manchester M19 . . . . 110 E7
Salford M50 . . . . 80 C1
Astra Bsns Pk M17 . . . . 95 F8
Astra Ind Ctr OL11 . . . . 30 C3
Atcham Gr M9 . . . . 64 B6
Athenian Gdns 12 M7 . . . . 81 C5
Athens Dr M28 . . . . 60 C2
Athens St SK1 . . . . 124 A8
Athens Way OL4 . . . . 67 E6
Atherfield BL2 . . . . 25 E4
Atherfield Cl 3 M18 . . . . 99 F6
Atherleigh Gr WN7 . . . . 75 F7
Atherleigh Way WN7 . . . . 75 D4
Atherley Gr OL9 . . . . 65 F2
Atherstone 10 OL12 . . . . 139 C4
Atherstone Ave M8 . . . . 64 A2
Atherstone Cl BL8 . . . . 27 C4
ATHERTON 58 A3
Atherton Ave SK14 . . . . 103 A4
Atherton Bsns Ctr M46 . . . . 58 C4
Atherton Cl M35 . . . . 84 B5
Atherton Gr SK14 . . . . 103 A4
Atherton Ho M46 . . . . 58 D4
Atherton Ind Ctr M46 . . . . 58 D4
Atherton La M44 . . . . 105 E5
Atherton Rd WN2 . . . . 56 D5
Atherton Sq 8 WN1 . . . . 150 C4
Atherton St
Adlington PR7 . . . . 21 A6
Bacup OL13 . . . . 3 C8
Bickershaw WN2 . . . . 74 E8
Eccles M30 . . . . 79 B1
Manchester M3 . . . . 158 B1
Oldham, County End OL4 . . 67 F5
9 Oldham, County End OL4 67 F6
Oldham, Salem OL4 . . . . 67 E5
Stockport SK3 . . . . 170 A4
7 Wigan WN5 . . . . 54 F6
Atherton Sta M46 . . . . 58 E4
Atherton Way
Bacup OL13 . . . . 3 B8
4 Eccles M30 . . . . 79 B1
Athlone Ave
Bolton BL1 . . . . 24 D5
Bury BL9 . . . . 140 C4
Cheadle SK8 . . . . 123 C5
Manchester M40 . . . . 83 A8
Athol Cres WN2 . . . . 57 B3
Athole St M5, M6 . . . . 154 C1
Atholl Ave M32 . . . . 96 A2
Atholl Cl BL3 . . . . 40 F6
Atholl Dr OL10 . . . . 46 A8
Atholl Gr WN3 . . . . 55 A3
Athol Rd
Bramhall SK7 . . . . 132 D5
Manchester M16 . . . . 109 E8
Athol St
Ashton-u-L OL6 . . . . 166 C3
Eccles M30 . . . . 79 C1
Ramsbottom BL0 . . . . 138 C3
Reddish M18 . . . . 99 E3
Rochdale OL12 . . . . 15 B1
Stockport SK4 . . . . 169 A3
Athos Wlk 9 M40 . . . . 65 C2
Atkinson Ave BL3 . . . . 42 B3
Atkinson Ho M33 . . . . 108 B5
Atkinson Rd
Sale M33 . . . . 108 A5
Urmston M41 . . . . 95 D2
Atkinson St
Abram WN2 . . . . 74 B8
Manchester M3 . . . . 158 B1
Oldham OL9 . . . . 153 A4
2 Rochdale OL11 . . . . 30 C2
Stockport SK1 . . . . 124 A7
Atkin St M28 . . . . 60 D2
Atlanta Ave M90 . . . . 130 A8
Atlantic Bsns Ctr WA14 . . 119 C7
Atlantic St WA14 . . . . 119 B6
Atlantic Wlk 13 M11 . . . . 160 C1
Atlas Fold 15 BL8 . . . . 27 C3
Atlas St
Ashton-u-L OL7 . . . . 85 A5
Dukinfield SK16 . . . . 101 D8
Oldham OL8 . . . . 153 B2
Atlow Dr M23 . . . . 121 B5
Atrium The M45 . . . . 62 F7
Attenbury's La WA14 . . . . 119 E8
Attenbury's Pk Est WA14 119 E8
Attercliffe Rd M21 . . . . 109 A7
Attewell St M11 . . . . 165 A4
Attingham Wlk
Denton M34 . . . . 100 E1
Wigan WN3 . . . . 150 A1
Attleboro Rd M40 . . . . 83 A7
Attlee Ave WA3 . . . . 92 B4
Attlee Way M12 . . . . 160 B1
Attock Cl OL9 . . . . 152 B1
Attwood Rd WA15 . . . . 120 B5
Attwood St M12 . . . . 99 A3
Atwood Rd M20 . . . . 110 C3
Atwood St M1 . . . . 163 A4
Auberge Ho SK2 . . . . 124 A6
Auberson Rd BL3 . . . . 147 A3
Aubrey Rd M14 . . . . 110 E7
Aubrey St
Rochdale OL11 . . . . 139 C1
Salford M5 . . . . 161 A3
Auburn Ave
Hyde SK14 . . . . 167 B1
Romiley SK6 . . . . 112 F4
Auburn Dr M41 . . . . 95 E1
Auburn Rd
Denton M34 . . . . 100 E2
Manchester M16 . . . . 97 B4
Auburn St
Bolton BL3 . . . . 147 A4
Manchester M1 . . . . 159 B1
Manchester M1 . . . . 163 B4
Auckland Dr M6 . . . . 81 A5
Auckland Rd M19 . . . . 110 F8
Audax Wlk M40 . . . . 83 B4
Auden Cl M11 . . . . 83 D1
Auden Ct M11 . . . . 83 D1
AUDENSHAW 100 E7
Audenshaw Ct M34 . . . . 100 E6
Audenshaw Hall Gr M34 . 100 B7
Audenshaw Prim Sch
M34 . . . . 100 D7
Audenshaw Rd
Ashton-u-L M34 . . . . 100 E8
Denton M34 . . . . 100 D7
Audenshaw Sch M34 . . . . 100 E6
Audlem Cl M40 . . . . 160 A2
Audlem Wlk 6 SK8 . . . . 123 A5
Audley Ave M32 . . . . 95 F4
Audley Rd M19 . . . . 99 B2
Audley St
Ashton-u-L OL6 . . . . 85 E2
Mossley, Bottoms OL5 . . . . 86 D8
Mossley OL5 . . . . 68 D1
Audlum Ct BL9 . . . . 141 A2
Audrey Ave M18 . . . . 99 E5
Audrey St M9 . . . . 157 C3
Aughton Cl WN5 . . . . 71 E4
Aughton St WN2 . . . . 56 D4
Augusta Cl OL12 . . . . 14 E2
Augusta St OL12 . . . . 14 E1
Augustine Webster Cl
M9 . . . . 157 B4
Augustus St
1 Bolton BL3 . . . . 42 A4
Manchester M3, M8 . . . . 159 A4
Augustus Way M15 . . . . 97 E4
Auriga Wlk M7 . . . . 81 C3
Austell Rd M22 . . . . 121 D1
Austen Ave BL9 . . . . 44 F6
Austen Rd M30 . . . . 79 D1
Austen Wlk OL1 . . . . 49 E4
Auster Cl M14 . . . . 110 A8
Austin Ave WN4 . . . . 72 E4
Austin Ct M20 . . . . 110 C4
Austin Dr M20 . . . . 110 C4
Austin Gr M19 . . . . 110 F8
Austin's La BL6 . . . . 22 F1
Austin St WN7 . . . . 75 D5
Autumn St M13 . . . . 98 C4
Avallon Cl BL8 . . . . 26 F7
Avalon Dr M20 . . . . 122 C8
Avalon Pk OL4 . . . . 67 D6
Avebury Cl
Golborne WA3 . . . . 90 E8
Horwich BL6 . . . . 22 F1
Salford M7 . . . . 155 C2
Avebury Rd M23 . . . . 121 A5
Aveley Gdns WN3 . . . . 54 C4
Avenham Cl M15 . . . . 162 B1
Avening Wlk 7 M22 . . . . 121 C2
Avensbeck 2 M33 . . . . 107 B1
Avens Rd M31 . . . . 105 F3
Avenue St
Bolton BL1 . . . . 143 A1
Stockport SK1 . . . . 169 C2
Avenue The
Adlington PR6 . . . . 21 A8
Alderley Edge SK9 . . . . 137 A1
Altrincham WA15 . . . . 128 F8
Bolton BL2 . . . . 148 B3
Bury BL9 . . . . 27 F5
Eccles M30 . . . . 79 D1
Gatley SK8 . . . . 122 A1
Glossop SK13 . . . . 104 A4
Leigh WN7 . . . . 76 A6
Newton-le-W WA12 . . . . 89 D4
Orrell WN5 . . . . 53 D3
Romiley SK6 . . . . 112 D4
Sale M33 . . . . 107 E3
Avenue The *continued*
Salford M7 . . . . 81 C5
Shaw OL2 . . . . 149 A2
Urmston M41 . . . . 94 E2
Westhoughton BL5 . . . . 39 F1
Wigan, Standish Lower Ground
WN6 . . . . 36 E4
Wigan, Swinley WN1 . . . . 37 D2
Worsley M28 . . . . 78 B3
Avenue Works M17 . . . . 96 C6
Averham Cl WN4 . . . . 73 B2
Averhill M28 . . . . 78 B8
Averill St M40 . . . . 83 D5
Averon Rise OL1 . . . . 49 D4
Avery Trad Est SK5 . . . . 99 E3
Aveson Ave M21 . . . . 109 B6
Avian Cl M30 . . . . 94 F7
Avian Dr M14 . . . . 110 B8
Aviary★ M28 . . . . 79 A6
Aviary Rd M28 . . . . 78 F6
Aviation Rd BL9 . . . . 45 B6
Aviemore Cl
Garswood WN4 . . . . 72 D4
Ramsbottom BL0 . . . . 11 A2
Avis St OL2 . . . . 149 B3
Avocado Ct M17 . . . . 96 C5
Avocet Cl
Leigh WN7 . . . . 76 A6
Newton-le-W WA12 . . . . 89 C4
Avocet Dr
Altrincham WA14 . . . . 119 B8
Irlam M44 . . . . 94 A4
Avon 10 OL10 . . . . 29 C2
Avon Bank 1 SK6 . . . . 112 F3
Avonbrook Dr OL9 . . . . 65 F2
Avon Cl
Marple SK6 . . . . 125 E5
Milnrow OL16 . . . . 32 A6
Walkden M28 . . . . 60 A2
Avoncliff Cl BL1 . . . . 143 A3
Avoncourt Dr M20 . . . . 110 A4
Avon Ct 3 M15 . . . . 162 A2
Avondale M27 . . . . 62 A2
Avondale Ave
Bury BL9 . . . . 140 C4
Hazel Grove SK7 . . . . 124 F3
Avondale Cres 2 M41 . . . . 95 C3
Avondale Ct OL11 . . . . 47 D7
Avondale Dr
Ramsbottom BL0 . . . . 10 F2
Salford M6 . . . . 80 B5
Tyldesley M29 . . . . 77 C6
Avondale Ind Est SK3 . . . 123 B7
Avondale Lo M33 . . . . 108 B3
Avondale Rd
Farnworth BL4 . . . . 59 F8
Hazel Grove SK7 . . . . 124 F2
Stockport SK3 . . . . 123 C8
Stretford M32 . . . . 96 F4
Whitefield M45 . . . . 44 E1
Wigan WN1 . . . . 37 C1
Avondale Rise SK9 . . . . 137 D6
Avondale St
Bolton BL1 . . . . 142 C1
Manchester M8 . . . . 156 A3
Oldham OL8 . . . . 66 F4
Standish WN6 . . . . 19 E2
Avon Dr BL9 . . . . 28 A8
Avon Gdns M19 . . . . 111 A6
Avonhead Cl BL6 . . . . 21 F3
Avonlea Dr M19 . . . . 110 E6
Avonlea Rd
Droylsden M43 . . . . 83 E2
Sale M33 . . . . 107 D1
Avonleigh Gdns 7 OL1 . . . 49 C1
Avon Rd
Altrincham WA15 . . . . 128 E8
Ashton-in-M WN4 . . . . 73 E5
Billinge WN5 . . . . 71 D3
Chadderton OL9 . . . . 65 F8
Culcheth WA3 . . . . 92 A2
Gatley SK8 . . . . 131 C7
Heywood OL10 . . . . 29 A2
Kearsley BL4 . . . . 61 B5
Manchester M19 . . . . 111 A6
Shaw OL2 . . . . 149 B4
Tyldesley M29 . . . . 77 C7
Wigan WN5 . . . . 54 C7
Avon St
Bolton BL1 . . . . 142 B1
Leigh WN7 . . . . 76 B4
Oldham OL8 . . . . 66 F4
Stockport SK3 . . . . 170 B3
Avril Cl SK5 . . . . 111 F8
Avril Ct WN3 . . . . 55 E4
Avro Cl M14 . . . . 98 B1
Avro Ct M24 . . . . 65 D8
Avroe Rd M30 . . . . 94 F7
Avro Way M90 . . . . 129 F7
Awburn Rd SK14 . . . . 102 E1
Axbridge Wlk M40 . . . . 160 A2
Axeholme Ct BL6 . . . . 21 F3
Axford Cl M7 . . . . 155 C2
Axminster Wlk SK7 . . . . 132 E7
Axon Sq M16 . . . . 97 F4
Aycliffe Ave M21 . . . . 109 D5
Aycliffe Gr M13 . . . . 98 E3
Aye Bridge Rd WA3 . . . . 74 B5
Aylesbury Ave
Denton M34 . . . . 100 F1
Urmston M41 . . . . 95 E3
Aylesbury Cl
Salford M5 . . . . 81 A1
14 Salford M5 . . . . 154 C1
Aylesbury Cres WN2 . . . . 57 C2
Aylesbury Ct M21 . . . . 97 C1
Aylesbury Gr M24 . . . . 47 C2
Aylesby Ave M18 . . . . 99 B4
Aylesford Rd M14 . . . . 98 D3
Aylesford Wlk BL1 . . . . 143 B1
Aylestone Wlk 14 M40 . . . . 83 A7
Aylsham Cl SK6 . . . . 112 F4
Aylsham Mews M27 . . . . 79 D5
Aylwin Dr M33 . . . . 108 C3
Ayr Ave OL8 . . . . 66 F3
Ayr Cl SK7 . . . . 125 A2
Ayrefield Gr WN6 . . . . 35 D6
Ayrefield Rd WN8 . . . . 35 C4
Ayres Rd M16 . . . . 97 C4
Ayr Gr OL10 . . . . 29 A1
Ayrshire Rd M7 . . . . 81 B6
Ayr St BL2 . . . . 25 C3
Ayrton Gr 1 M38 . . . . 60 A5
Aysgarth OL16 . . . . 15 B1
Aysgarth Ave
Cheadle SK8 . . . . 122 C6
Droylsden M18 . . . . 99 E5
Romiley SK6 . . . . 113 D4
Aysgarth Cl M33 . . . . 107 D3
Ayshford Cl WA14 . . . . 119 B6
Ayton Gr M14 . . . . 98 E4
Aytoun Ct M1 . . . . 159 B1
Aytoun St M1 . . . . 159 B1
Azalea Ave M18 . . . . 99 D6

B

Babbacombe Gr M9 . . . . 64 B5
Babbacombe Rd SK2 . . . . 124 C6
Babylon La PR6 . . . . 21 B8
Back Abingdon Rd BL2 . . . 25 C1
Back Acton St M1 . . . . 163 B4
Back Adcroft St SK1 . . . . 170 C3
Back Ainscow St BL1 . . . . 145 B4
Back Ainsworth Rd N BL8 27 C2
Back Ainsworth St 10
BL1 . . . . 143 A2
Back Albert St BL9 . . . . 141 A2
Back Albion Pl BL9 . . . . 140 C4
Back Alexander Rd BL2 . . 25 C1
Back Alexandra St BL3 . . 146 C4
Back Alfred St BL0 . . . . 138 B1
Back Alice St 6 BL3 . . . . 43 B3
Back Alicia St BL3 . . . . 42 D5
Back All Saints' St 11
BL1 . . . . 145 C4
Back Alston St BL3 . . . . 147 B3
Back America Row BL1 . . 142 C3
Back Andrew St N 4
BL9 . . . . 141 A2
Back Andrew St
Bury BL9 . . . . 141 A2
Mossley OL5 . . . . 86 C8
Back Apple Terr BL1 . . . . 143 A2
Back Argo St BL3 . . . . 147 A4
Back Argyle St 8 BL9 . . . . 27 F5
Back Ashford Wlk BL1 . . . 143 B1
Back Ashley St M4 . . . . 159 B3
Back Ash St
Bolton BL2 . . . . 148 A2
2 Bury BL9 . . . . 141 A2
Back Ashworth St 10 BL8 . 27 C3
Back Astley St BL1 . . . . 143 B2
Back Auburn St 10 BL3 . . 147 A4
Back Avenue St 3 BL1 . . . 145 A4
Back Avondale St BL1 . . . 142 C1
Back Baldwin St BL3 . . . . 145 B1
Back Baldwin Street N
BL3 . . . . 145 B1
Back Banbury St BL2 . . . . 25 C1
Back Bank St M8 . . . . 159 A4
Back Bantry St BL3 . . . . 145 B1
Back Bark St BL1 . . . . 145 B3
Back Bayley St BL1 . . . . 145 A4
Back Beaconsfield St
BL3 . . . . 145 A2
Back Bedford St 4 BL1 . . 145 A4
Back Belbeck St 2 BL8 . . 27 C2
Back Bell La BL9 . . . . 141 A3
Back Benson St BL9 . . . . 141 A1
Back Birch St BL9 . . . . 140 C3
Back Birley St 5 BL1 . . . 143 B4
Back Blackbank St BL1 . . 143 C2
Back Blackburn Rd BL7 . . . 8 D3
Back Blackburn Road E
BL7 . . . . 8 D3
Back Blackburn Road W 4
BL1 . . . . 143 B4
Back Bolton Road S BL8 . . 27 C2
Back Bolton Street S 1
BL9 . . . . 140 B2
Back Bond Street W BL9 141 A2
BACKBOWER 113 E8
Back Bower La SK14 . . . . 113 F8
Back Bowness Rd BL3 . . . 147 A4
Back Bradshaw Brow E
BL2 . . . . 25 C4
Back Bradshaw Brow W
BL2 . . . . 25 C4
Back Bradshawgate 1
BL1 . . . . 145 C2
Back Bradshaw Road E
BL2 . . . . 25 D5
Back Bradshaw St 7
OL16 . . . . 31 A8
Back Brandon Street N
BL3 . . . . 147 A4
Back Bridge St
9 Bolton BL1 . . . . 145 C4
Manchester M3 . . . . 158 C1
New Mills SK22 . . . . 127 C1
Newton-le-W WA12 . . . . 89 B3

Back Bridge La *continued*
Ramsbottom BL0 . . . .**138** C2
Back Brierley Street S
BL9 . . . .**44** E8
Back Brink's Pl BL1 . . . . . .**145** B3
Back Bristol Ave BL2 . . . . . .**25** C1
Back Bristol St BL3 . . . .**145** A1
Back Broad St 2 BL9 . . . . .**140** B2
Back Brook Street N
BL9 . . . .**141** A4
Back Broom St OL16 . . . .**32** B4
Back Brow WN8 . . . .**53** C7
Back Burnaby St BL3 . . . . . .**145** A1
Back Bury New Road E
BL2 . . . .**148** B3
Back Bury Old Rd 2
BL2 . . . .**148** A3
Back Byrom St 7 BL8 . . . . . .**27** B4
Back Byrom Street S 9
BL8 . . . .**27** B4
Back Cambridge St OL7 . . . . .**84** F1
Back Camp St M7 . . . .**155** A1
Back Camrose Gdns 6
BL1 . . . .**143** B1
Back Canada St BL8 . . . .**22** B3
Back Canada Street S
BL1 . . . .**142** C2
Back Canning St BL9 . . . . . .**140** C4
Back Cardwell St 31 BL1 . . .**143** B2
Back Carl St 9 BL1 . . . .**143** A2
Back Cateaton St BL1 . . . . .**140** C3
Back Cecil St OL5 . . . .**86** C8
Back Cedar St 3 BL1 . . . . . .**141** B3
Back Cedar Street N
BL1 . . . .**141** B3
Back Cemetery Terr 9
OL13 . . . .**3** D8
Back Chalfont St BL1 . . . . . .**143** C2
Back Chapel St
Bury BL8 . . . .**26** F7
9 Eccles M30 . . . .**79** F2
Hazel Grove SK7 . . . .**124** E3
Horwich BL6 . . . .**22** C3
11 Manchester M19 . . . .**99** A1
Wardle OL12 . . . .**15** C7
Back Cheapside BL1 . . . .**145** A3
Back Chesham Road N 6
BL9 . . . .**141** A4
Back Chesham Road S 7
BL9 . . . .**141** A4
Back Cheshire St OL5 . . . .**86** D8
Back Chester St BL1 . . . .**141** A4
Back China La M1 . . . .**159** B1
Back Chorley New Rd
BL1 . . . .**145** A3
Back Chorley New Road N
BL1 . . . .**145** A3
Back Chorley Old Road N
Bolton, Cope Bank BL1 . . . . .**142** C1
2 Bolton, Victory BL1 . . . . . .**144** C4
Back Chorley Old Road S
Bolton, Victory BL1 . . . .**144** C4
Doffcocker BL1 . . . .**23** F1
Back Chorley St BL1 . . . .**145** B3
Back Chorley Street E 16
BL1 . . . .**145** B4
Back Clay Street E BL7 . . . . .**25** A7
Back Clay Street W BL7 . . . . .**25** A7
Back Clegg's Bldgs 11
BL1 . . . .**145** B4
Back Clifton St 1 BL9 . . . . .**140** C4
Back Clyde St BL1 . . . .**143** B2
Back Colenso Rd BL2 . . . .**42** D7
Back College Land 1
M3 . . . .**158** C1
Back College Way BL3 . . . . .**145** B2
Back Collings St BL1 . . . .**143** B2
Back Common St BL5 . . . .**57** B7
Back Coop St BL3 . . . .**143** B4
Back Cope Bank BL1 . . . .**142** B2
Back Cornall St BL8 . . . .**27** C3
Back Cottam St 8 BL3 . . . . . .**145** B1
Back Cotton St BL1 . . . .**143** A2
Back Cowm La OL12 . . . .**4** C3
Back Cox Green Road N 3
BL7 . . . .**24** F8
Back Cox Green Road S 1
BL7 . . . .**24** F8
Back Crescent Ave BL1 . . . . .**145** A4
Back Croft La BL3 . . . .**148** B1
Back Cromer Ave BL2 . . . .**25** C1
Back Cross La WA12 . . . .**89** B4
Back Crostons Rd BL8 . . . . . .**140** A3
Back Croston St BL3 . . . .**146** C4
Back Crown St BL6 . . . .**22** A4
Back Cundey St BL1 . . . .**142** C1
Back Cyril St BL3 . . . .**148** A1
Back Daisy St BL3 . . . .**146** C4
Back Dale St 2 OL16 . . . .**31** F5
Back Darley St 1 BL1 . . . .**60** E8
Back Darwen Road N
Bolton, Bromley Cross BL7 . . . .**25** B7
Bolton, Cox Green BL7 . . . .**8** E1
1 Bolton, Toppings BL7 . . . . .**25** A8
Back Darwin St 7 BL1 . . . . .**143** A2
Back Dawes St BL3 . . . .**145** C2
Back Deal St BL9 . . . .**140** C4
Back Deane Church Lane W
BL3 . . . .**146** B4
Back Deane Road N BL3 . . . .**145** A2
Back Delamere Street N
BL9 . . . .**140** C4
Back Delamere Street S
BL9 . . . .**28** A5
Back Denton St BL9 . . . .**140** C4

Back Derby St
Bolton BL3 . . . .**145** B1
Bolton BL3 . . . .**147** A4
Back Devon Street N 2
BL9 . . . .**44** E8
Back Devon Street S 2
BL9 . . . .**44** E8
Back Dijon St BL3 . . . .**146** C4
Back Dougill Street S
BL1 . . . .**142** B1
Back Drake St OL16 . . . .**139** C3
Back Drummond St 3
BL1 . . . .**143** B4
Back Duckworth St 3
BL9 . . . .**141** A4
Back Duncan St M7 . . . .**81** C7
Back Durham St OL11 . . . .**31** A5
Back Earnshaw St BL3 . . . . .**146** B3
Back East St BL9 . . . .**140** C1
Back Edgmont Ave BL3 . . . . .**147** A4
Back Eldon St BL9 . . . .**140** C4
Back Elgin St BL3 . . . .**143** A2
Back Ellesmere Rd BL3 . . . . .**146** C3
Back Elm St BL9 . . . .**140** C2
Back Elsworth St M3, M4 . . .**159** A4
Back Emmett St BL6 . . . .**22** B3
Back Ernest St 1 BL1 . . . . . .**145** A4
Back Eskrick St 1 BL1 . . . . .**143** A4
Back Eskrick Street S 4
BL1 . . . .**143** A2
Back Everton Street N 2
BL1 . . . .**143** C2
Back Ewart St 3 BL1 . . . .**143** B2
Back Fairhaven Rd BL1 . . . . .**143** C3
Back Fenton St BL8 . . . .**27** C3
Back Fir St BL9 . . . .**141** A4
Back Fletcher St
Bury BL9 . . . .**141** A2
Kearsley M26 . . . .**61** B8
Back Fletcher Street S
BL3 . . . .**145** C1
Backford Wlk 1 M20 . . . . . .**110** A8
Back Fortune St BL3 . . . .**148** B1
Back Foundry St BL9 . . . . . .**140** C2
Back Frank St 8 BL9 . . . . . .**140** C1
Back Garston St BL1 . . . .**143** A4
Back Gaskell St BL1 . . . .**145** A4
Back Gaskell Street E 14
BL1 . . . .**145** A4
Back George Barton St 24
BL2 . . . .**25** B1
Back George St
Horwich BL6 . . . .**22** C3
Manchester M1 . . . .**159** A1
Back Gilmour St M24 . . . .**65** A8
Back Gilnow La 4 BL3 . . . . .**144** C2
Back Gladstone St 4 OL4 . . .**67** B6
Back Glen Ave BL3 . . . .**144** B1
Back Goldsmith St BL1 . . . . .**147** A4
Back Goodlad St BL8 . . . .**27** C3
Back Grafton St
6 Altrincham WA14 . . . .**119** D4
6 Bolton BL1 . . . .**145** A4
Back Grantham Cl BL1 . . . . .**143** B1
Back Grasmere St 1
BL1 . . . .**143** C2
Back Greaves St OL1 . . . .**153** C2
Back Greenhalgh St BL3 . . . . .**43** A3
Back Green La BL3 . . . .**42** B3
Back Grosvenor St 2
SK15 . . . .**86** A1
Back Halliwell La 6 M8 . . . .**155** C3
Back Halliwell Rd BL1 . . . . . .**143** B2
Back Halliwell Road S 3
BL1 . . . .**143** A2
Back Halstead St 2 BL9 . . . .**141** A4
Back Hamilton St
8 Bury BL9 . . . .**140** C4
Salford M7 . . . .**155** A3
Back Hanson St BL9 . . . .**140** C4
Back Harper's Lane S
BL1 . . . .**142** B2
Back Hartington Rd 10
BL1 . . . .**144** C4
Back Hart St BL5 . . . .**57** B7
Back Harvey St
Bolton BL3 . . . .**143** A3
Bury BL8 . . . .**27** C3
Back Haslam St BL9 . . . .**141** A4
Back Haslam Terr BL2 . . . . . .**148** C3
Back Hatfield Rd BL3 . . . . . .**143** A1
Back Haydock St BL1 . . . . . .**145** C4
Back Hayward St 2 BL8 . . . . .**27** C3
Back Hengist St 8 BL2 . . . . .**148** C3
Back Heywood Street E
BL9 . . . .**141** A2
Back Heywood Street W 2
BL9 . . . .**141** A1
Back Higher Shady Lane W
BL7 . . . .**25** B7
Back Higher Swan La
BL3 . . . .**147** A3
Back High St
Bolton BL3 . . . .**147** B4
Chapeltown BL7 . . . .**9** C4
Heywood OL10 . . . .**29** B2
Back High Street W 1
BL3 . . . .**147** B4
Back Hilton St
1 Bury BL9 . . . .**140** C4
Salford M7 . . . .**155** A3
Back Holly St BL3 . . . .**141** A2
Back Holly Street S BL3 . . . .**141** A2
Back Hopefield St BL3 . . . . .**147** A4
Back Hope St
7 Oldham OL1 . . . .**67** B7
Salford M7 . . . .**155** A3
Back Hornby St BL9 . . . .**140** C4

Back Hornby Street E
BL9 . . . .**140** C4
Back Hornby Street W 4
BL9 . . . .**140** C3
Back Horne Street N 1
BL9 . . . .**44** E8
Back Horsa Street N 17
BL2 . . . .**25** B1
Back Howcroft St BL3 . . . . . .**147** A4
Back Howe St M7 . . . .**155** A3
Back Hulbert St BL8 . . . .**27** C1
Back Hulme St
Bury BL8 . . . .**140** A3
Salford M5 . . . .**81** C1
Back Huntley Mount Rd
BL9 . . . .**141** B3
Back Hurst St BL9 . . . .**141** A1
Back Ingham St BL9 . . . .**141** A1
Back Ingham Street E
BL9 . . . .**141** A1
Back Irlam Street N 2
BL1 . . . .**143** B3
Back Ivanhoe St 2 BL3 . . . . .**42** C2
Back Ivy Bank Rd BL1 . . . . . .**24** E5
Back John Brown St 19
BL1 . . . .**145** A4
Back Johnson St 3 BL1 . . . .**145** A4
Back John St BL3 . . . .**145** B3
Back Jubilee St BL3 . . . .**146** C3
Back Kershaw St BL9 . . . . . .**141** A2
Back Kingholm Gdns 2
BL1 . . . .**143** A1
Back Kingsley St BL1 . . . . . .**143** A2
Back King St OL1 . . . .**153** B2
Back King Street N 4
BL7 . . . .**24** F8
Back Knight St 3 BL8 . . . . . .**27** C2
Back Knowl St SK15 . . . .**86** B2
Back Knowsley St BL9 . . . . .**140** B2
Back La
Altrincham WA15 . . . .**129** B4
Appley Bridge WN6 . . . .**35** E8
Ashton-u-L OL7 . . . .**84** D5
Bolton BL1 . . . .**145** B4
Glossop SK13 . . . .**115** D6
Mossley OL5, OL6 . . . .**68** A2
Mottram in L SK14 . . . .**103** A4
Oldham OL4 . . . .**50** C1
Over Hulton BL5 . . . .**59** B6
Partington WA14 . . . .**118** C3
Rochdale OL12 . . . .**13** F3
Whitworth OL12 . . . .**4** C3
Back Lark St BL1 . . . .**145** A4
Back Lathom St 8 BL9 . . . . .**141** A4
Back Laurel St BL9 . . . .**141** B2
Back Leachfield St BL3 . . . . .**143** A3
Back Lee Ave BL3 . . . .**147** A3
Back Lee St OL3 . . . .**69** B8
Back Lever Street S BL3 . . . .**147** A4
Back Lightburne Ave
BL1 . . . .**144** B3
Back Lilly St BL1 . . . .**145** A4
Back Linton Ave 2 BL7 . . . . .**27** F5
Back Longfellow Ave
BL3 . . . .**146** B3
Back Longfield St BL3 . . . . .**146** B3
Back Longworth Rd BL7 . . . . . .**8** D3
Back Lonsdale St BL8 . . . . . .**27** C2
Back Lord St
Bury BL9 . . . .**140** C2
Little Lever BL3 . . . .**43** B3
Back Luton St BL3 . . . .**42** A4
Back Malvern Ave
Bolton BL1 . . . .**142** A1
3 Bury BL9 . . . .**27** F5
Back Manchester Old Rd
BL9 . . . .**140** B1
Back Manchester Rd
Bolton BL2 . . . .**148** A2
5 Bury BL9 . . . .**140** B2
1 Farnworth BL2 . . . .**42** C2
Back Manchester Road E
BL2 . . . .**148** A1
Back Manchester Road S 3
BL3 . . . .**42** A4
Back Manchester St 1
OL10 . . . .**29** E1
Back Manor St BL9 . . . .**141** A2
Back Marion Street S 3
BL3 . . . .**42** C2
Back Market St
4 Bury BL9 . . . .**140** B2
Hindley WN2 . . . .**56** D5
Leigh WN7 . . . .**75** F5
4 Little Lever BL3 . . . .**43** B3
Newton-le-W WA12 . . . .**89** A3
Back Market Street W 3
BL9 . . . .**140** B2
Back Markland Hill Lane E
BL1 . . . .**23** F1
Back Mary St 4 BL3 . . . .**145** A1
Back Mason St BL3 . . . .**141** A2
Back Massie St SK8 . . . .**122** D6
Back Mawdsley St BL1 . . . . .**145** C3
Back Maxwell St BL1 . . . . . .**143** B4
Back Mayor St 4 BL3 . . . .**27** C3
Back Mayor Street N
BL1 . . . .**27** C3
Back Melbourne St 1
SK15 . . . .**86** A1
Back Mellor Rd SK22 . . . . . .**127** C1
Back Mere Gdns BL1 . . . .**145** B4
Back Merton St BL8 . . . .**27** A4
Back Mesnes St 11 WN1 . . . .**37** C1
Back Methwold St BL3 . . . . .**146** C4
Back Micklehurst Rd OL5 . . . .**68** E1
Back Miller St BL1 . . . .**143** B4
Back Millett St BL9 . . . .**140** A2

Back Mill La 9 OL5 . . . .**68** C2
Back Mill Street N 6 BL7 . . . .**24** F8
Back Mill Street S 7 BL7 . . . .**24** F8
Back Milner Ave BL9 . . . .**27** F5
Back Mirey La BL6 . . . .**40** B4
Back Monmouth Ave 7
BL9 . . . .**27** F5
Back Moor SK14 . . . .**103** A4
Back Moorgate W 7
BL9 . . . .**140** C3
Back Mostyn Ave 3 BL9 . . . .**27** F5
Back Mowbray St BL1 . . . . . .**142** B1
Back Murton Terr BL1 . . . . . .**143** C4
Back Myrtle St BL9 . . . .**141** B2
Back Myrtle Street S
BL9 . . . .**141** B2
Back Nebo St BL3 . . . .**147** A4
Back Nelson St BL6 . . . .**22** D3
Back Nelson Street N 4
BL9 . . . .**44** F8
Back Nelson Street S 4
BL9 . . . .**44** F8
Back Nevada St 17 BL1 . . . .**143** B1
Back Newbold St BL8 . . . .**27** C2
Back New George St 9
BL8 . . . .**27** C3
Back Newport St BL1 . . . . . .**145** C2
Back Newton St BL1 . . . .**143** B2
Back Nixon Rd BL3 . . . .**146** C3
Back Nook Terr 2 OL12 . . . .**14** F3
Back Northern Gr 1
BL1 . . . .**142** C1
Back Northern Grove S 2
BL1 . . . .**142** C1
Back Norwood Gr 12
BL1 . . . .**144** C4
Back Nut St BL1 . . . .**143** A2
Back Oak St 2 M26 . . . .**44** C1
Back Olaf St 14 BL2 . . . .**25** B1
Back Oldham Rd OL16 . . . .**31** A6
Back Olga St BL1 . . . .**143** A2
Back Olga Street N BL1 . . . .**143** A2
Back Olive Bank 2 BL8 . . . . .**27** B4
Back Oram St BL9 . . . .**141** A4
Back Ormrod St BL3 . . . .**141** A2
BACK O' TH' BANK
BACK o' th' Low Rd OL4 . . . .**49** F1
BACK O' TH' MOSS
Back Owen's Row 2 BL6 . . . . .**22** C3
Back Oxford Grove N 1
BL1 . . . .**145** A4
Back Oxford St BL1 . . . .**145** A1
Back Palace St 7 BL1 . . . . . .**145** C4
Back Parkhills Road S
BL9 . . . .**44** F8
Back Park Road E 6
BL1 . . . .**143** B4
Back Park St BL1 . . . .**145** A4
Back Park View BL1 . . . .**24** F6
Back Park View Rd BL3 . . . . .**146** C4
Back Parsonage St 4
BL9 . . . .**141** A3
Back Patience St 14 OL12 . . .**14** C1
Back Pedder St 3 BL1 . . . . . .**142** C1
Back Peers St 4 BL8 . . . .**27** C2
Back Percy St BL1 . . . .**141** B3
Back Peter St 2 BL9 . . . .**141** A3
Back Phoenix St BL9 . . . .**140** B2
Back Piccadilly M1 . . . .**159** B1
Back Pine St
Bury BL9 . . . .**141** B2
Newhey OL16 . . . .**32** B4
Back Pleasant St BL1 . . . . . .**145** B4
Back Pool Fold 6 M2 . . . . . .**158** C1
Back Porter St 2 BL9 . . . . . .**140** C4
Back Portland St OL10 . . . . .**166** A2
Back Potter St M26 . . . .**44** D4
Back Preston St BL3 . . . .**42** B4
Back Primrose St BL1 . . . . . .**143** C4
Back Proctor St BL8 . . . .**27** C1
Back Progress St 2 BL3 . . . . .**143** C1
Back Quay St M3 . . . .**158** B1
Back Quebec St BL3 . . . .**144** C1
Back Queen St 4 WN7 . . . . . .**76** A5
Back Railway View PR7 . . . . .**21** A7
Back Rake St BL9 . . . .**140** C4
Back Ramsden Rd OL12 . . . . .**13** C7
Back Rathbone St WA12 . . . . .**89** A3
Back Raven St 4 BL9 . . . . . .**140** C4
Back Rawlinson St 18 BL6 . . .**22** B4
Back Raymond Ave
BL9 . . . .**27** F5
Back Red Bank M4 . . . .**159** A3
Back Redhill Gr BL1 . . . .**145** B4
Back Regent St 8 BL9 . . . . . .**140** C4
Back Richard Burch St 1
BL9 . . . .**141** A3
Back Rishton La BL3 . . . .**147** C4
Back Rochdale Old Road N
BL9 . . . .**141** C3
Back Rochdale Old Road S
BL9 . . . .**141** B3
Back Rochdale Old South Rd
BL9 . . . .**28** D3
Back Rochdale Rd BL3 . . . . . .**141** B3
Back Rochdale Road S 6
BL3 . . . .**146** C4
Back Roland Rd 3 BL3 . . . . .**146** C4
Back Rose Bank 8 BL9 . . . . .**140** C4
Back Roseberry St 6
BL3 . . . .**146** C4
Back Rowena St BL3 . . . .**42** C2
Back Royal Ave BL9 . . . .**27** F5
Back Rudolph St 3 BL3 . . . . .**147** C3
Back Rushton St 6 OL13 . . . . .**3** E8
Back Russell Cl 13 BL1 . . . . .**144** C4

Back Ryefield St BL1 . . . .**25** A1
Back St Anne's St 7
BL9 . . . .**140** C4
Back St George's Rd
Bolton BL1 . . . .**145** B4
Manchester M4 . . . .**159** B3
Back St Helens Rd 8
BL3 . . . .**147** A4
Back St Helens Road S
BL3 . . . .**146** C2
Back St James's St 8
OL1 . . . .**67** B7
Back St Mark's La M8 . . . . . .**155** C4
Back St Mary's Pl BL9 . . . . .**140** B2
Back St Philip's Ave BL3 . . . .**147** A4
Back St Thomas Street E 6
BL1 . . . .**143** A2
Back Salford WN7 . . . .**75** F5
Back Salford St BL9 . . . .**141** A4
Back Sandon St BL3 . . . .**147** A4
Back Sandy Bank Rd BL7 . . . . .**9** D5
Back Sankey St BL9 . . . .**140** A2
Back Sapling Rd BL3 . . . .**146** C4
Back School La WN8 . . . .**53** C7
Back Scowcroft St 22 BL2 . . .**25** B1
Back Second Ave BL1 . . . . . .**144** B3
Back Seymour Rd 2
BL1 . . . .**143** C3
Back Shakerley Rd 6
M29 . . . .**58** F1
Back Sharman St 3 BL3 . . . .**148** B1
Back Shaw-Street BL9 . . . . .**141** B3
Back Shepherd St 1
BL9 . . . .**141** A1
Back Short St 4 M46 . . . .**58** F1
Back Silverdale St BL1 . . . . .**144** C3
Back Silver St BL9 . . . .**140** C2
Back Skull House La WN6 . . . .**35** C8
Back Smethurst La BL3 . . . . .**146** C2
Back Smethurst Lane W
BL3 . . . .**146** B2
Back Soho St BL3 . . . .**145** C2
Back South Cross Street E
BL9 . . . .**140** C4
Back South Par M3 . . . .**158** C1
Back Spa Rd BL1 . . . .**145** A2
Back Spa Road N BL1 . . . . . .**145** A2
Back Spa Road W
BL1 . . . .**145** A2
Back Spear St 6 M1, M4 . . .**159** B2
Back Springfield St 6
BL3 . . . .**42** A4
Back Spring Gdns
Bolton BL1 . . . .**145** C2
6 Middleton M24 . . . .**47** A2
Back Spring Street E
BL9 . . . .**140** C1
Back Spring Street W
BL9 . . . .**140** C1
Back Square St BL0 . . . .**138** C2
Back Stanley St BL0 . . . .**138** B1
Back Stanway Ave 9
BL3 . . . .**145** A2
Back Stayley Rd 3 BL9 . . . . .**140** C3
Back Stephen St 3 OL8 . . . . .**66** D8
Back Stewart St 8 BL8 . . . . .**27** C2
Back Stewart St 1 BL3 . . . . .**145** B1
Back Stone St 8 BL2 . . . .**25** B1
Back Tavistock Rd 3
BL1 . . . .**145** A2
Back Teak St 6 BL9 . . . .**141** B2
Back Tenterden St
Bury BL9 . . . .**140** A2
Bury BL9 . . . .**140** B2
Back Thomasson Cl BL1 . . . .**143** B1
Back Thomas St 6 M4 . . . . .**159** A2
Back Thorn St BL1 . . . .**143** A2
Back Tinline St 3 BL9 . . . . . .**141** A2
Back Tonge Moor Rd BL2 . . . .**25** B2
Back Tonge Moor Road E
BL2 . . . .**25** B2
Backton Pl M40 . . . .**160** A4
Back Tottington Rd 8
BL8 . . . .**27** B4
Back Tottington Road N
BL2 . . . .**25** E5
Back Tottington Road S 1
BL8 . . . .**27** C3
Back Tudor St 3 BL3 . . . . . .**146** C4
Back Turner St M4 . . . .**159** A2
Back Union Rd BL2 . . . .**25** B1
Back Union St BL7 . . . .**8** D2
Back Unsworth Street S
BL1 . . . .**145** A1
Back Vernice St BL3 . . . .**144** C4
Back Vernon St
Bolton BL1 . . . .**145** B4
Bury BL9 . . . .**140** C4
Back Vernon Street S 13
BL1 . . . .**145** B4
Back Victoria Gr 4 BL1 . . . .**142** C1
Back Viking Street N 4
BL3 . . . .**42** A4
Back Vine St 1 BL3 . . . .**144** C2
Back Viola St BL1 . . . .**143** B3
Back Walmersley Road E
Bury, Fernhill BL9 . . . .**140** C4
4 Bury, Seedfield BL9 . . . . .**27** F5
Back Walmersley Road W 1
BL9 . . . .**27** F6
Back Walshaw Road N 3
BL8 . . . .**27** C3
Back Walshaw Road S
BL8 . . . .**27** C3
Back Wapping St 8 BL1 . . . .**143** A2
Back Wash La BL9 . . . .**141** B2

Back Wash Lane S [1] BL9 141 A2
Back Water St
Ashton-u-L OL6 166 C4
Bolton BL7 8 D2
Stockport SK1 169 C2
Back Webster St BL3 148 B1
Back Wells St BL9 140 B1
Back Westbank St [8] BL1 145 A4
Back Weston Street N BL3 42 A4
Back Westwood Rd [11] BL1 144 C4
Back Wheatfield St BL2 148 C1
Back Whittle St [6] BL8 27 C3
Back Wigan Road N
Bolton BL3 144 B1
Bolton BL3 146 A4
Back Wigan Road S BL3 144 B1
Back Willows La [4] BL3 147 A4
Back Wolfenden St [30] BL1 143 B2
Back Woodbine Road N [1] BL3 146 C3
Back Wright St BL6 22 B4
Back Young St BL4 60 E7
Baclaw Cl WN1 37 F1
Bacon Ave M34 113 A7
BACUP 3 E8
Bacup & Rawtenstall Gram Sch BB4 2 F8
Bacup Rd BB4, OL13 2 E8
Bacup St M40 83 A8
Badby Cl M4 160 A1
Baddeley Cl SK3 170 A1
Badder St BL1 145 C4
Bader Dr OL10 46 D7
Badger Cl
Hyde SK14 167 B4
Marple SK6 125 F3
Rochdale OL16 31 C3
Badger Edge La OL3, OL4 50 C3
Badger La OL16 31 B2
Badger Rd WA14 119 C8
Badger St [10] BL9 140 C3
Badgers Way SK13 116 B7
Badgers Wlk M22 121 E1
Badminton Rd M21 97 C1
Bag La M46 58 C4
Bagnall Cl
Rochdale OL12 13 F2
Uppermill OL3 51 C1
Bagnall Ct M22 121 E8
Bagnall Wlk M22 121 E8
Bagot St
[15] Droylsden M11 83 C2
Swinton M27 61 C1
Bagshaw La WN2 38 E2
Bagshaw St SK14 101 E5
BAGSLATE MOOR 29 F8
Bagslate Moor La OL11 29 F8
Bagslate Moor Rd OL11 29 F8
Bagstock Ave SK12 133 E2
BAGULEY 121 A7
Baguley Cres
Middleton M25 64 A7
Stockport SK3 170 A2
Baguley Dr BL9 45 A2
Baguley Hall Prim Sch M23 121 A6
Baguley La M33 108 E2
Baguley Rd M33 108 E4
Baguley St M43 84 B1
Baildon Rd OL12 14 B1
Baildon St M40 65 A1
Bailey Fold BL5 58 B8
Bailey La
Bolton BL2 25 E1
Partington M31 105 F3
Wythenshawe M90 121 B1
Bailey Rd M17 96 A7
Bailey's Ct WN1 150 C4
Bailey St
Droylsden M43 83 E1
[8] Oldham OL1 67 A7
Prestwich M25 63 C4
Bailey Wlk WA14 128 C8
Baillie St
Radcliffe M26 44 E5
Rochdale OL16 139 C4
Baillie Street E [18] OL16 31 A8
Bails The
Salford M7 81 C6
Walkden M28 60 D3
Bainbridge Ave WA3 90 F8
Bainbridge Cl M12 164 A2
Bainbridge Rd [3] OL4 49 D1
Bainburgh Clough OL8 67 C4
Baines Ave M44 93 F1
Baines St BL1 144 B4
Bain St M27 79 F7
Bainton Wlk M9 64 C5
Baird St M1 163 C4
Baitings Cl OL12 13 C2
Baitings Row OL12 13 C2
Bakersfield Pl [1] M33 108 C4
Baker St
[6] Heywood OL10 46 E8
Kearsley BL4 61 B6
Middleton M24 65 B8
Ramsbottom BL0 138 B1
Sale WA15 120 C7
Stalybridge SK15 86 B1
Stockport SK4 169 B3
Wigan WN3 150 B2
Bakery Ct OL6 85 D5
Bakewell Ave
Ashton-u-L OL6 85 F6
Denton M34 113 A8
Bakewell Bank [39] SK13 171 A1
Bakewell Cl [40] SK13 171 A1
Bakewell Dr WN6 37 A4
Bakewell Fold [37] SK13 171 A1
Bakewell Gdns [41] SK13 171 A1
Bakewell Gn [35] SK13 171 A1
Bakewell Gr [38] SK13 171 A1
Bakewell Lea [34] SK13 171 A1
Bakewell Mews [36] SK13 171 A1
Bakewell Rd
Droylsden M43 83 E2
Eccles M30 95 C8
Hazel Grove SK7 133 E8
Stretford M32 96 A3
Bakewell St
Manchester M18 99 C4
Stockport SK3 170 A3
Bakewell Wlk [44] SK13 171 A1
Bala Cl M5 81 A2
Balcarres Ave WN1 37 E2
Balcarres Rd WN2 38 C5
Balcary Gr BL1 144 B4
Balcombe Cl BL8 27 C7
BALDERSTONE 31 A3
Balderstone Rd OL11 31 A3
Balderstone Tech Coll OL11 31 A3
BALDINGSTONE 11 F1
Baldock Rd M20 110 D3
Baldrine Dr WN2 57 B5
Baldwin Rd M19 110 F6
Baldwins Cl OL2 48 D2
Baldwin St
Bacup OL13 3 B8
Hindley WN2 57 B3
Ince-in-M WN3 151 A2
Wigan, Redwood WN5 54 B6
Wigan, Scholes WN1 151 A4
Bale St M2 162 C4
Balfern Cl [12] BL5 39 E1
Balfern Fold [11] BL5 39 E1
Balfour Gr SK5 111 F8
Balfour Rd
Altrincham WA14 119 D7
[5] Rochdale OL12 14 C1
Urmston M41 95 B3
Balfour St
[5] Bolton BL3 145 A2
Manchester M8 156 A4
Oldham OL4 67 C7
Salford M6 81 A6
Shaw OL2 149 B3
Balham Wlk M12 164 C2
Balholm Ct M20 110 B4
BALLADEN 1 F8
Balladen Com Prim Sch BB4 1 F8
Ballantine St M40 83 C4
Ballantyne Way [5] WA3 90 E8
Ballard Cl OL15 16 B7
Ballard Way OL2 149 C4
Ballater Ave M41 95 A1
Ballater Cl OL10 29 B1
Ballater Wlk [1] M8 155 C3
Ballbrook Ave M20 110 B5
Ballbrook Ct M20 110 B4
Balleratt St M19 99 A1
Balliol Cl SK6 113 C4
Balliol Ct M33 107 D4
Balliol St
Manchester M8 156 A4
Swinton M27 79 E8
Balliol Way WN4 72 F4
Balloon St M4 159 A2
Ball's Cotts WN3 55 F3
Ball St
Rochdale OL16 31 A8
Wigan WN6 36 E2
Ball Wlk SK14 102 F1
Balmain Ave M18 99 C3
Balmain Rd M41 95 B3
Balmer Dr M23 121 B4
Balmfield St M8 156 A1
Balmforth St M15 162 A3
Balmoral PR7 20 E6
Balmoral Ave
Cheadle SK8 123 A2
Denton M34 100 D7
Golborne WA3 74 D1
Hyde SK14 113 E8
Little Lever BL3 43 A3
Rochdale OL11 30 B8
Royton OL2 48 F4
Stretford M32 96 D3
Urmston M41 95 B1
Whitefield M45 63 A7
Balmoral Cl
Horwich BL6 22 E2
Milnrow OL16 32 A6
Ramsbottom BL8 11 A1
Whitefield BL9 45 A5
Balmoral Ct
Ashton-u-L OL7 166 A1
Stockport SK4 168 A3
Balmoral Dr
Altrincham WA14 119 F8
Heywood, Top of Heap OL10 29 A1
High Lane SK6 134 E7
Hindley WN2 56 C4
Leigh WN7 76 D6
Poynton SK12 133 D3
Reddish M34 100 A3
Stalybridge SK15 86 A3
Balmoral Gr SK7 124 F3
Balmoral Grange M25 63 E3
Balmoral Ho M30 79 C2
Balmoral Rd
Altrincham WA15 119 E4
Ashton-in-M WN4 73 A4
Farnworth BL4 60 D7
Manchester, Burnage M14 110 D8
Stockport, Heaton Mersey SK4 168 A3
Swinton M27 62 A2
Urmston M41 95 A1
Wigan WN5 54 E6
Balmoral St M18 99 C4
Balmoral Way SK9 137 A6
Balmore Cl BL3 146 A3
Balm St BL0 11 A4
Balniel Wlk WN1 37 E2
Balsam Cl M13 163 C3
Balshaw Ave M44 93 F2
Balshaw Cl BL3 144 C1
Balshaw Ct M44 94 A2
Baltic Bldgs [4] BB4 2 E8
Baltic Flats [3] BB4 2 E8
Baltic Rd
Altrincham WA14 119 A6
[5] Rawtenstall BB4 2 E8
Baltic St M5 154 B2
Baltimore St M40 157 C1
Bamber Ave M33 108 E3
Bamber Croft BL5 39 E3
Bamber Ct [5] WN2 56 E6
Bamber's Bldgs [2] WN2 56 E5
Bamber St M9 64 D5
Bamber Wlk BL3 145 A1
Bamburgh Cl M26 43 C5
Bamburgh Dr OL7 84 E5
Bamburgh Pl [3] WN4 73 A5
Bambury St [5] BL9 141 A3
BAMFORD 29 E6
Bamford Ave
Denton M34 112 F8
Middleton M24 47 A2
Bamford Bsns Pk SK4 111 E5
Bamford Cl
Bury BL9 28 E4
Gatley SK8 131 D8
Bamford Ct OL11 30 C6
Bamford Dr WN2 37 F2
Bamford Fold [3] SK13 171 B1
Bamford Gdns WA15 120 D6
Bamford Gn [4] SK13 171 B1
Bamford Gr
Ashton-u-L OL6 85 F6
Manchester M20 110 A3
Bamford La SK13 171 B1
Bamford Mews
Gamesley SK13 171 B1
Rochdale OL11 29 E7
Bamford Pl OL12 14 E1
Bamford Prim Sch OL11 29 F7
Bamford Rd
Heywood OL10 29 D3
Manchester M20 110 A3
Ramsbottom BL0 12 B6
Bamford St
Chadderton OL9 152 C4
Droylsden M11 83 B2
[4] Littleborough OL15 15 F5
Royton OL2 48 E3
Stockport SK1 170 C4
Bamford Way OL11 29 F6
BAMFURLONG 73 F8
Bampton Ave WA11 71 B1
Bampton Cl
Stockport SK2 124 B7
Westhoughton BL5 39 E2
Bampton Rd M22 121 D1
Bampton Wlk M24 46 E2
Banastre Dr WA12 89 F3
Banbury Cl WN7 75 E1
Banbury Dr WA14 119 E8
Banbury Mews M27 61 D1
Banbury Rd
Failsworth M35, M40 83 E4
Longshaw WN5 53 D2
Middleton M24 65 A5
Wythenshawe M23 120 F5
Banbury St
Bolton BL2 25 C1
Stockport SK1 169 C1
Bancroft Ave SK8 123 A1
Bancroft Cl SK6 112 E3
Bancroft Ct WA15 120 A3
Bancroft Fold SK14 102 B5
Bancroft Rd
Altrincham WA15 120 A3
Swinton M27 61 E1
Bandy Fields Pl M7 155 A1
Banff Gr OL10 29 A1
Banff Rd M14 98 C4
Bangor Fold WN7 76 C4
Bangor Rd SK8 122 F6
Bangor St
Ashton-u-L OL6 85 E2
Bolton BL1 145 B4
Manchester M15 162 A1
Reddish SK5 169 C4
Rochdale OL16 31 B6
Banham Ave WN3 54 C3
Bank Ave WN5 53 D5
Bank Barn La OL12 15 D6
Bankbottom SK13 104 A5
Bank Bridge Rd M11, M40 83 B3
Bankbrook WN6 36 D4
Bank Brow WN8 35 C5
Bank Cl OL15 16 A3
Banker St BL3 148 C1
Bankes Ave WN5 54 A6
Bankfield
Ainsworth BL2 43 C8
Dukinfield SK14 101 D5
Bank Field BL5 58 A7
Bankfield Ave
Droylsden M43 84 A2
Irlam M44 105 D5
Manchester M13 98 E3
Stockport SK4 168 C1
Bankfield Cl BL2 26 C1
Bankfield Cotts OL3 50 F2
Bankfield Dr
Oldham OL8 67 B2
Worsley M28 78 B7
Bankfield La OL11 29 E8
Bankfield Mews BL9 44 F7
Bankfield Rd
Cheadle SK8 122 F1
Farnworth BL4 60 D6
Romiley SK6 113 B5
Sale M33 107 E6
Tyldesley M29 77 E8
Bankfield St
Bacup OL13 3 D8
Bolton BL3 144 C1
Bolton BL3 146 C4
Manchester M9 157 A4
Reddish SK4 169 B3
Bank Field St M26 61 D7
Bankfield Terr [1] OL13 3 D8
Bankfield Trad Est SK5 169 B4
Bankfoot Wlk M8 156 A1
Bankgate SK14 115 A8
Bank Gr M38 59 F6
Bank Hall BL8 27 A2
Bankhall Cl WN2 57 B1
Bankhall La WA14, WA15 128 F8
Bankhall Rd SK4 168 A2
Bankhall Wlk [10] M9 157 B3
BANK HEATH 90 A8
Bank Hey BL5 39 F1
Bank Hill St OL4 67 C7
Bankhirst Cl M8 64 A1
Bank Hos WN2 75 B8
Bank House Cl M29 59 E1
Bankhouse Rd BL8 27 C4
Bank House Rd M9 64 C4
Bank La
Glossop SK13 104 A7
Pendlebury M6, M27 80 D6
Uppermill OL3 69 E4
Walkden M38 59 F6
Wardle OL12 15 D7
Banklands Cl M44 105 D5
BANK LANE 11 E7
Bankley St M19 99 A1
Bank Mdw BL6 22 C4
Bank Mill OL5 68 E3
Bankmill Cl [12] M13 163 B3
Bank Pl
Bury BL8 27 C3
Salford M3 158 A2
Wilmslow SK9 137 B7
Bankquay Ct [2] M44 94 B1
Bank Rd
Manchester M8 64 A1
Mossley SK15 86 E6
Romiley SK6 113 A3
Up Holland WN8 35 D4
Bank Row SK13 104 A7
Banks Croft OL10 46 D7
Banks Croft Sch OL10 46 D7
Banks Ct
Altrincham WA15 120 D5
[8] Leigh WN7 75 D5
Bankside
Altrincham WA15 129 D6
Hattersley SK14 102 D1
Bank Side
Mossley OL5 86 C8
Westhoughton BL5 58 A7
Bankside Ave
Ashton-in-M WN4 73 A8
Radcliffe M26 44 D4
Uppermill OL3 69 C7
Bankside Cl
Handforth SK9 131 D1
Marple SK6 114 C1
Oldham OL9 153 A2
Uppermill OL3 69 C8
Bankside Ct
Manchester M12 99 A4
Stockport SK4 168 A2
Bankside Rd M20 122 B7
Banks La SK1 124 B8
Banks Lane Inf Sch SK1 124 B8
Banks Lane Jun Sch SK1 124 B8
Banksman Way M27 80 D8
Bank Sq SK9 137 B7
Bank St
Adlington PR7 21 A7
Ashton-u-L OL6 166 B2
Bolton BL1 145 C3
Broadbottom SK14 115 A8
Bury BL9 140 B2
Bury, Walshaw BL8 26 F4
Chapeltown BL7 9 C4
Cheadle SK8 122 E6
Denton, Haughton Green M34 113 B8
Denton, Hooley Hill M34 100 F6
Droylsden, Clayton M11 83 B2
Droylsden, Fairfield M43 99 F8
Failsworth M40 83 A3
Farnworth BL4 60 D8
Glossop SK13 116 D8
Golborne WA3 74 A1
Hadfield SK13 104 A5
Bank St *continued*
Heywood OL10 29 B2
Hollinfare WA3 105 B5
Hyde SK14 167 A3
[8] Oldham OL4 67 D6
Platt Bridge WN2 56 A3
Radcliffe M26 44 B2
Ramsbottom BL0 11 E7
Rochdale OL11 31 A4
Romiley SK6 113 B5
Sale M33 108 C5
Salford, Broughton Park M7 155 C4
Salford M3 158 A2
Shaw OL2 149 A3
Whitefield M45 44 E1
Wigan WN5 54 E6
BANKS THE 126 E3
Bankswood Cl SK13 104 A4
Bank Terr
Glossop SK13 104 A5
Whitworth OL12 14 C8
Bank The
Glossop SK13 116 D8
[3] Rochdale OL16 139 C4
BANK TOP
Bolton 25 A5
Oldham 153 B2
Skelmersdale 35 C4
Bank Top
Ashton-u-L OL6 166 C2
Bury BL9 11 F1
Heywood OL10 29 B3
Bank Top Gr BL1 25 A5
Bank Top Pk [4] OL4 67 D6
Bank Top St OL10 29 B3
Bankwell St M15 162 B1
Bankwood WN6 35 E6
Bank Wood BL1 40 F7
Bankwood Ct M9 64 D1
Banky La M33 107 D6
Bannach Dr OL9 48 A1
Bannatyne Cl M40 65 E1
Banner Dale Cl M13 98 F4
Bannerman Ave M25 63 C3
Bannerman Rd M43 84 B1
Banner St
Hindley WN2 56 E5
Ince-in-M WN3 151 B1
Banner Wlk [19] M11 160 C1
Bannister Dr SK8 122 F2
Bannister St
Bolton BL2 42 E8
Stockport SK1 170 C3
Bannister Way WN3 54 E2
Bann St SK3 170 B4
Banstead Ave M22 121 D7
Bantry Dr M9 64 B3
Bantry St
Bolton BL3 145 B1
[4] Rochdale OL12 15 A2
Baptist St M4 159 B3
Barathea Cl OL11 30 B3
Barbara Castle Sq M13 164 A2
Barbara Rd BL3 146 A2
Barbara St BL3 147 A4
Barbeck Cl M40 160 B3
Barberry Bank BL7 8 E2
Barberry Cl WA14 119 B7
Barberry Wlk M31 105 F3
Barber St
[5] Droylsden M11 99 E7
Glossop SK13 104 B5
Barber Wlk BL1 143 B4
Barbican St [2] M20 110 B7
Barbirolli Sq M2 162 C4
Barbrook Cl WN6 19 B2
Barbury Cl WN7 75 F7
Barchester Ave BL2 25 E1
Barcheston Rd SK8 122 C4
Barcicroft Rd M19, SK4 110 E4
Barcicroft Wlk [1] M19 110 E4
Barclay Dr M30 79 E3
Barclay Rd SK12 133 E2
Barclays Ave M6 80 D6
Barcliffe Ave M40 65 C2
Barclyde St OL11 139 B1
Barcombe Cl
Oldham OL4 49 D2
Urmston M32 95 F3
Barcombe Wlk M9 157 A3
Barcroft Rd BL1 142 C2
Barcroft St BL9 140 C3
Bardale Gr WN4 73 A3
Bardell Cl SK12 133 D2
Bardney Ave WA3 73 F2
Bardon Cl BL1 143 A1
Bardon Rd M23 120 F6
Bardsea Ave M22 121 D1
Bardsley Ave M35 83 F7
Bardsley Cl
Bolton BL2 25 D5
[1] Hattersley SK14 102 E2
Up Holland WN8 53 A7
Bardsley Gate Ave SK15 102 E6
Bardsley St
Failsworth M40 83 D5
Middleton M24 47 A1
Oldham, Salem OL4 67 E5
Oldham, Watersheddings OL4 49 E1
Oldham, White Gate OL9 65 F3
Stockport SK4 169 A3
Bardsley Vale Ave OL8 85 A8
Bardwell Ave BL5 57 D8

Barehill St OL15 . . . . 16 B6
Bare St BL1 . . . . 148 A4
Bare Trees Prim Sch
OL9 . . . . 152 B4
Barff Rd M5 . . . . 80 C2
Barfold Cl SK2 . . . . 125 A5
Barford Cl WN8 . . . . 53 A7
Barford Dr
Golborne WA3 . . . . 91 A8
Handforth SK9 . . . . 131 C1
Barford Gr BL6 . . . . 22 F1
Barford Wlk M23 . . . . 121 A4
Bar Gap Rd OL1 . . . . 153 C4
Baric Cl M30 . . . . 79 F1
Baring St M1, M12 . . . . . . 163 B4
Baring Street Ind Est
M1 . . . . 163 B4
Barkan Way M27 . . . . 80 B8
Barker Rd SK6 . . . . 112 F2
Barker's La M33 . . . . 107 F4
Barker St
Bury BL9 . . . . 140 B1
Heywood OL10 . . . . 29 B1
Leigh WN7 . . . . 75 C5
Manchester M3 . . . . 158 C3
Barke St OL15 . . . . 15 F3
Barking St M40 . . . . 160 B3
Bark St
Bolton BL1 . . . . 145 B3
Kearsley BL4 . . . . 61 B5
Bark Street E BL1 . . . . . . 145 C4
Barkway Rd M32 . . . . 96 A2
Barkwell La OL5 . . . . 68 B1
Barkworth Wlk M40 . . . . . . 83 B6
Bar La BL1 . . . . 24 E5
Barlborough Rd WN5 . . . . . 54 D5
Barlby St M40 . . . . 83 B6
Barlea Ave M40 . . . . 65 D1
Barley Brook Mdw BL1 . . . . 24 F6
Barley Brook St WN6 . . . . . 37 B1
Barleycorn Cl M33 . . . . . . 109 A3
Barleycroft SK13 . . . . 171 C4
Barley Croft SK8 . . . . 122 F1
Barley Croft Rd SK14 . . . . 101 E6
Barleycroft St M16 . . . . 97 F4
Barley Dr SK7 . . . . 132 E7
Barleyfield Wlk M24 . . . . . . 46 F1
Barley Hall St OL10 . . . . . . 29 E3
Barley Mere Cl WA12 . . . . . 89 C2
Barleywood Dr M11 . . . . . 164 C4
Barleywood Wlk SK15 . . . . 102 F5
Barlow Cl BL9 . . . . 27 F5
Barlow Cres SK6 . . . . 125 F4
Barlow Ct
Edgworth BL7 . . . . 9 E5
Walkden M28 . . . . 60 E3
Barlow Fold
Bury BL9 . . . . 44 F5
Romiley SK6 . . . . 113 D3
Barlow Fold Cl BL9 . . . . . . 44 F5
Barlow Fold Rd
Reddish SK5 . . . . 111 F8
Romiley SK6 . . . . 113 D3
Barlow Hall Prim Sch
M21 . . . . 109 C5
Barlow Hall Rd M21 . . . . . 109 C5
Barlow Ho OL8 . . . . 153 C1
Barlow La M30 . . . . 79 C2
Barlow Lane N SK5 . . . . . . 111 F8
BARLOW MOOR 109 B5
Barlow Moor Cl OL12 . . . . . 13 E2
Barlow Moor Ct M20 . . . . . 109 F4
Barlow Moor Rd M21 . . . . 109 C6
Barlow Park Ave BL1 . . . . . 24 D5
Barlow Pl M13 . . . . 163 C7
Barlow RC High Sch &
Specialist Science Coll The
M20 . . . . 110 C2
Barlow Rd
Altrincham WA14 . . . . 119 B7
Dukinfield SK16 . . . . 101 D8
Handforth SK9 . . . . 131 B1
Reddish M19 . . . . 99 C1
Salford M5 . . . . 81 C1
Stretford M16, M32 . . . . . . 96 F4
Barlow's Croft M3 . . . . . . 158 B2
Barlow's Lane S SK7 . . . . 124 C3
Barlow St
Bacup OL13 . . . . 3 B7
Eccles M30 . . . . 79 C1
⬛ Heywood OL10 . . . . . . 46 E8
Horwich BL6 . . . . 22 B4
Oldham OL4 . . . . 67 A6
Radcliffe M26 . . . . 44 B3
Rochdale OL16 . . . . 31 A7
Walkden M28 . . . . 60 D4
Barlow Terr M21 . . . . 109 C6
Barlow Wlk 3 SK5 . . . . . . 111 F8
Barlow Wood Dr SK6 . . . . 126 B3
Barmeadow OL3 . . . . 50 F2
Barmhouse Cl SK14 . . . . . 102 A3
Barmhouse La SK14 . . . . . 102 B3
Barmhouse Mews SK14 . 102 A3
Barmouth St M11 . . . . 164 C4
Barmouth Wlk 4 OL8 . . . . 66 B2
Barmskin La WN6 . . . . 18 C8
Barnaby Rd SK12 . . . . . . 133 D2
Barnabys Rd BL5 . . . . 39 D3
Barn Acre BL6 . . . . 21 E1
Barnacre Ave
Bolton BL2 . . . . 42 F7
Wythenshawe M23 . . . . . 120 F3
Barnard Ave
Prestwich M45 . . . . 63 B7
Stockport SK4 . . . . 168 B2

Barnard Cl OL7 . . . . 84 F4
Barnard Rd M18 . . . . 99 B3
Barnard St 3 BL2 . . . . . . 148 C4
Barnbrook St BL9 . . . . . . 141 A3
Barnby St M12 . . . . 99 A3
Barn Cl
Glossop SK13 . . . . 116 D7
Urmston M41 . . . . 94 C2
Barnclose Rd M22 . . . . . . 121 D1
Barncroft Gdns M22 . . . . 121 C5
Barncroft Rd BL4 . . . . 60 D8
Barnes Ave SK4 . . . . 168 A2
Barnes Cl
Farnworth BL4 . . . . 60 D8
Ramsbottom BL0 . . . . 11 A3
Barnes Ho 3 BL4 . . . . 60 D8
Barnes Mdws OL15 . . . . . . 6 C1
Barnes St BL4 . . . . 60 B8
Barnes Terr 3 BL4 . . . . . . 61 A7
Barneswell St 3 M40 . . . . 83 C5
Barnet Rd BL1 . . . . 142 C2
Barnett Ave M20 . . . . 110 B6
Barnett Cl OL10 . . . . 29 C1
Barnett Dr M3 . . . . 158 A2
Barnfield
Littleborough OL15 . . . . . . 16 D6
Urmston M41 . . . . 95 B1
Barnfield Ave SK6 . . . . . . 113 D3
Barnfield Cl
Bolton BL7 . . . . 8 E2
Radcliffe M26 . . . . 43 E3
⬛ Salford M5 . . . . 154 C1
Tyldesley M29 . . . . 58 F1
Barnfield Cres M33 . . . . . 107 F6
Barnfield Dr
Westhoughton BL5 . . . . . . 40 A1
Worsley M28 . . . . 78 B6
Barn Field La OL12 . . . . . . 15 A7
Barnfield Rd
Dukinfield SK14 . . . . 102 B5
Manchester M19 . . . . 110 E4
Swinton M27 . . . . 61 D2
Barnfield Rise OL2 . . . . . . 32 A1
Barnfield Road E SK3 . . . . 123 F4
Barnfield Road W SK3 . . 123 D4
Barnfield St
Denton M34 . . . . 100 D4
Heywood OL10 . . . . 29 E2
Rochdale OL12 . . . . 14 F2
Barnfield Wlk WA15 . . . . 120 C5
Barn Fold OL4 . . . . 67 E5
Barngate Dr OL5 . . . . 86 C8
Barngate Rd SK8 . . . . 122 A6
Barngill Gr WN3 . . . . 54 E3
Barn Gr M34 . . . . 100 E7
Barnham Cl WA3 . . . . 90 A8
Barnham Wlk M23 . . . . . . 120 E8
Barn Hill 3 BL5 . . . . 39 E1
Barnhill Ave M25 . . . . 63 B2
Barnhill Dr M25 . . . . 63 B2
Barnhill Rd M25 . . . . 63 B2
Barnhill St M14 . . . . 97 F4
Barn Hill Terr 7 BL5 . . . . . 39 E1
Barn La WA3 . . . . 89 F8
Barnley Cl M44 . . . . 94 B3
Barn Mdw BL7 . . . . 9 D5
Barnsdale Cl BL2 . . . . 26 C1
Barnsdale Dr M8 . . . . 156 A2
Barnsfold Ave M14 . . . . . 110 C8
Barnsfold Rd SK6 . . . . . . 125 F3
Barnside OL12 . . . . 14 B8
Barnside Ave M28 . . . . 60 E3
Barnside Cl BL9 . . . . 27 E8
Barnside Way M35 . . . . . . 84 C6
Barns La WA14 . . . . 118 A5
Barnsley St
Stockport SK1 . . . . 124 B8
Wigan WN6 . . . . 37 B2
Barns Pl WA15 . . . . 129 C8
Barn St
Bolton BL1 . . . . 145 B3
Oldham OL1 . . . . 153 B2
Whitefield M45 . . . . 62 F7
Barnstable Dr M40 . . . . . 156 C2
Barnstead Ave M20 . . . . . 110 D5
Barnston Ave M14 . . . . 98 B2
Barnston Cl BL1 . . . . 143 C4
Barnton Cl WA3 . . . . 90 D7
Barn View PR6 . . . . 20 F8
Barnview Dr 1 M44 . . . . . . 94 A1
Barn Way WA12 . . . . 89 B3
Barnway Wlk 7 M40 . . . . . 65 C2
Barnwell Ave WA3 . . . . 91 D4
Barnwell Cl M34 . . . . 100 E5
Barn Wlk 10 M11 . . . . 99 E7
Barnwood Cl 11 BL1 . . . . 143 B1
Barnwood Dr BL1 . . . . . . 143 B1
Barnwood Rd M23 . . . . . . 121 A3
Barnwood Terr 10 BL1 . . . 143 B1
Baroness Gr M7 . . . . 81 C4
Baron Fold M38 . . . . 60 A5
Baron Fold Cres M38 . . . . 59 F5
Baron Fold Gr M38 . . . . . . 59 F5
Baron Fold Rd M38 . . . . . . 59 F5
Baron Gn SK8 . . . . 131 D7
Baron Rd SK14 . . . . 113 F7
Barons Ct M35 . . . . 83 D6
Baron St
Bury BL9 . . . . 140 A1
Rochdale OL16 . . . . 139 C3
Baron Wlk BL3 . . . . 43 C3
BARRACK HILL 113 B2
Barrack Hill SK6 . . . . 113 A2
Barrack Hill Cl SK6 . . . . . 113 A3
Barracks OL3 . . . . 33 C1
Barrack Sq 10 WN1 . . . . . 150 C4

Barracks Rd WN2 . . . . 56 D1
Barrack St M15 . . . . 162 A3
Barracks Yd WN1 . . . . . . 150 C4
Barra Dr M41 . . . . 95 D5
Barrass St M11 . . . . 99 D7
Barratt Gdns M24 . . . . 46 D4
Barrett Ave BL4 . . . . 60 F7
Barrett Ct BL9 . . . . 141 A2
Barrett St OL4 . . . . 67 B5
Barrfield Rd M6 . . . . 154 B4
Barr Hill Ave M6 . . . . 80 E5
Barrhill Cl M15 . . . . 162 B2
Barrie St WN7 . . . . 75 D8
Barrie Way BL1 . . . . 25 B4
Barrington Ave
Cheadle SK8 . . . . 123 A1
Droylsden M43 . . . . 83 F1
Barrington Cl
Altrincham WA14 . . . . 119 D6
Wigan WN3 . . . . 54 D2
Barrington Rd WA14 . . . . 119 D5
Barrington St M11 . . . . 83 C2
Barrington Wlk 8 BL2 . . . . 25 B1
Barrisdale Cl BL3 . . . . 40 F5
Barron Mdw WN7 . . . . 75 D7
Barrowdale Rd WA3 . . . . . . 90 B8
Barrowdene Ho BL1 . . . . . 23 F4
Barrowfield Rd M22 . . . . . 121 A2
Barrowfields M24 . . . . 47 A2
Barrowfield Wlk 4 M24 . . . 47 A1
Barrow Hill Rd M8 . . . . . . 155 C1
Barrow La
Altrincham WA15 . . . . 129 B7
Golborne WA2, WA3 . . . . . 90 C2
Barrow Mdw SK8 . . . . 131 E8
Barrows Ct 4 BL1 . . . . . . 145 C2
Barrowshaw Cl M28 . . . . . 60 C2
Barrow St
Ashton-in-M WN4 . . . . 73 D5
Salford M3, M5 . . . . 158 A1
Barrule Ave SK7 . . . . 124 E1
Barry Cres M28 . . . . 60 A3
Barry Ct 3 M20 . . . . 110 B6
Barry Lawson Cl M8 . . . . 155 C3
Barry Rd
Reddish SK5 . . . . 111 F5
Wythenshawe M23 . . . . . 109 C2
Barry Rise WA14 . . . . 119 A2
Barry St OL1 . . . . 67 B8
Barsham Dr BL3 . . . . 145 A1
Bar St WN2 . . . . 56 A1
Bar Terr OL12 . . . . 14 C7
Bartlam Pl OL1 . . . . 153 C3
Bartlemore St OL1 . . . . . . 49 B1
Bartlett Rd OL2 . . . . 149 A2
Bartlett St M11 . . . . 165 B4
Bartley Rd M22 . . . . 121 C8
Barton Arc 18 M2 . . . . . . 158 C1
Barton Ave
Urmston M41 . . . . 95 B2
Wigan WN1 . . . . 37 B2
Barton Bsns Pk M30 . . . . . 79 C1
Barton Cl SK9 . . . . 131 D2
Barton Clough WN5 . . . . . . 71 E5
Barton Clough Prim Sch
M32 . . . . 95 F4
Barton Ct
8 Eccles M30 . . . . 95 D8
Hyde SK14 . . . . 101 C1
Barton Dock Rd
Stretford M32 . . . . 96 B4
Urmston M41 . . . . 95 E6
Barton Emb M17 . . . . 95 C7
Barton Fold SK14 . . . . . . 102 A1
Barton Hall Ent Est M30 . . 79 B1
Barton Ho 4 M6 . . . . 80 C4
Barton La M30 . . . . 79 E1
Barton Moss Com Prim Sch
M30 . . . . 94 F8
Barton Moss Rd M30 . . . . 94 D7
Barton Rd
Dukinfield SK14, SK16 . . . 101 C6
Eccles, Alder Forest M30 . . 78 F5
Eccles M30 . . . . 79 C1
Farnworth BL4 . . . . 60 B7
Manchester SK4 . . . . 110 E1
Middleton M24 . . . . 64 F8
Pendlebury M27 . . . . 80 A6
Stretford M32 . . . . 96 C1
Urmston M41 . . . . 95 C5
Barton Sq M2 . . . . 158 C1
Barton St
Farnworth BL4 . . . . 60 B7
Golborne WA3 . . . . 74 A1
Manchester M3 . . . . 162 B4
Oldham OL1 . . . . 153 A4
Platt Bridge WN2 . . . . 56 B3
Tyldesley M29 . . . . 58 F1
4 Wigan WN5 . . . . 54 B5
Barton Swing Aqueduct *
M41 . . . . 95 D8
Barton Terr M44 . . . . 94 C3
BARTON UPON IRWELL . . 95 B8
Barway Rd M21 . . . . 96 F1
Barwell Cl
Altrincham WA15 . . . . 119 A2
Golborne WA3 . . . . 74 C1
Reddish SK5 . . . . 112 A8
Barwell Rd M33 . . . . 107 E5
Barwell Sq 1 BL4 . . . . 42 B2
Barwick Pl M33 . . . . 108 A4
Barwood Lea Mill BL0 . . . 138 C2
Basechurch Wlk M12 . . . . 164 C2

Basford Rd M16 . . . . 97 B3
Bashall St BL1 . . . . 144 C4
Basil Cl OL16 . . . . 31 B6
Basildon Cl M13 . . . . 164 A1
Basil St
Bolton BL3 . . . . 145 B1
Manchester M14 . . . . 98 C3
Rochdale OL16 . . . . 31 B6
Stockport SK4 . . . . 169 B3
Basle Cl SK7 . . . . 123 E4
Baslow Ave
Hindley WN2 . . . . 56 F3
Manchester M19 . . . . 99 C2
Baslow Cl 22 SK13 . . . . . . 171 E1
Baslow Dr
Gatley SK8 . . . . 131 C8
Hazel Grove SK7 . . . . 133 F8
Baslow Fold 21 SK13 . . . . 171 E1
Baslow Gn 21 SK13 . . . . . 171 E1
Baslow Gr SK5 . . . . 111 F5
Baslow Mews SK13 . . . . . 171 E1
Baslow Rd
Denton M34 . . . . 112 F8
Droylsden M43 . . . . 83 E3
Stretford M32 . . . . 96 A3
Baslow St M11 . . . . 160 B2
Baslow Way 24 SK13 . . . . 171 B1
Bassenthwaite Cl M24 . . . . 46 D3
Basset Ave M6 . . . . 81 C5
Bassett Cl OL12 . . . . 14 E3
Bassett Gdns OL12 . . . . . . 14 E3
Bassett Gr WN5 . . . . 54 A7
Bassett Way OL12 . . . . 14 E2
Bass La BL9 . . . . 11 D3
Bass St
Bolton BL2 . . . . 148 C3
Dukinfield SK16 . . . . 101 B8
Basswood Gn WN2 . . . . . . 57 A3
Basten Rd M7 . . . . 155 B2
Bateman St BL6 . . . . 22 D2
Batemill Rd SK22 . . . . . . 127 D2
Bates Cl OL11 . . . . 30 D1
Bateson Dr OL4 . . . . 67 F6
Bateson St SK1 . . . . 112 A2
Bateson Way OL8 . . . . . . 153 C1
Bates St
8 Dukinfield SK16 . . . . . 101 C8
Manchester M13 . . . . 98 F4
Bath Cl SK7 . . . . 125 A2
Bath Cres
Cheadle SK8 . . . . 132 B6
Manchester M16 . . . . 161 C1
Batheaston Gr WN7 . . . . . . 75 D8
Bath Pl WA14 . . . . 119 D2
Bath St
Altrincham WA14 . . . . 119 D2
Atherton M46 . . . . 58 A3
Bolton BL1 . . . . 145 C4
Oldham OL9 . . . . 152 C1
Rochdale OL12 . . . . 15 B1
Wigan WN2 . . . . 37 F2
Batley St
Manchester M9 . . . . 157 B4
Mossley OL5 . . . . 68 B1
Batridge Rd BL7 . . . . 9 A7
Batsmans Dr M27 . . . . 61 E4
Battenberg Rd 1 BL1 . . . . 144 C4
Battersbay Gr SK7 . . . . . . 124 E2
Battersby Ct SK2 . . . . 124 E6
Battersby St
Bury BL9 . . . . 28 D3
Droylsden M11 . . . . 99 E7
Ince-in-M WN2 . . . . 56 B8
Leigh WN7 . . . . 76 B4
Rochdale OL11 . . . . 30 B6
Battersea Rd SK4 . . . . . . 110 F1
Battery La WN6 . . . . 136 D6
Batty St M8 . . . . 156 C1
Baucher Rd WN3 . . . . 54 F5
Baum The OL16 . . . . 139 C4
Baverstock Cl WN3 . . . . . 151 A2
Baxall Bsns Ctr SK3 . . . . 170 B2
Baxendale St BL1 . . . . . . 143 B4
Baxter Gdns M23 . . . . . . 121 A7
Baxter Rd M33 . . . . 108 B4
Baxter's Row WN2 . . . . 57 C2
Baxter St
Oldham OL8 . . . . 66 B2
Standish WN6 . . . . 19 F1
Baybutt St M26 . . . . 44 C3
Baycliffe Cl WN7 . . . . 56 F3
Baycliffe Wlk 10 M8 . . . . . 155 C2
Baycroft Gr M23 . . . . 109 A1
Baydon Ave M7 . . . . 155 C2
Bayfield Gr M40 . . . . 65 A1
Bayley Cl SK14 . . . . 101 E5
Bayley Ct BL1 . . . . 143 A4
Bayleyfield SK14 . . . . 167 A4
Bayley St SK15 . . . . 85 F1
Baynard Wlk M9 . . . . 64 B4
Baysdale Ave BL3 . . . . 40 F4
Baysdale Dr OL2 . . . . 48 C5
Bay St
Heywood OL10 . . . . 29 B3
Oldham OL9 . . . . 153 A3
Rochdale OL12 . . . . 15 A1
Bayston Wlk M12 . . . . . . 164 C2
Bayswater Ave M40 . . . . . . 83 C4
Bayswater St BL3 . . . . . . 146 C2
Baythorpe St BL1 . . . . . . 143 C3
Baytree Ave
Chadderton OL9 . . . . 65 E8
Denton M34 . . . . 101 A4
Bay Tree Ave M28 . . . . 79 A5
Baytree Dr SK6 . . . . 112 F4
Baytree Gr BL0 . . . . 11 B2

Baytree La M24 . . . . 65 D8
Baytree Rd WN6 . . . . 36 F2
Baytree Wlk OL12 . . . . 4 C1
Baywood St M9 . . . . 157 A4
Bazaar St M6 . . . . 81 A4
Bazley Rd M22 . . . . 109 D1
Bazley St BL2 . . . . 42 A3
BBC Manchester M1 . . . . 163 A3
Beacomfold SK6 . . . . 114 B3
Beacon Cl M46 . . . . 58 B2
Beacon Dr M23 . . . . 121 A2
Beacon Gr OL8 . . . . 67 C4
Beacon Hts WN8 . . . . 53 A8
Beacon Rd
Billinge WN5 . . . . 71 E6
Leigh WN2 . . . . 75 A8
Romiley SK6 . . . . 113 A1
Shevington Moor WN6 . . . . 19 B2
Urmston M41 . . . . 95 E7
Beaconsfield M14 . . . . . . 110 C7
Beaconsfield Rd WA14 . . . 119 D7
Beaconsfield St BL3 . . . . 145 A2
Beaconsfield Terr SK15 . . 86 F7
Beacon View
Appley Bridge WN6 . . . . . . 35 C8
Marple SK6 . . . . 125 F8
Standish WN6 . . . . 19 D1
Beacon View Dr WN8 . . . . . 53 B7
Beadham Dr M9 . . . . 64 A5
Beadle Ave OL12 . . . . 15 D5
Beaford Cl WN5 . . . . 54 B5
Beagle Wlk M22 . . . . 130 E8
Bealbank Cl OL16 . . . . 32 A3
Beal Cl SK4 . . . . 110 D3
Beal Cres OL16 . . . . 15 C1
Bealcroft Cl OL16 . . . . 31 E7
Bealcroft Wlk OL16 . . . . . . 31 E7
Beal Dr WN2 . . . . 56 A2
Beale Gr M21 . . . . 109 B8
Bealey Ave M26 . . . . 44 E5
Bealey Cl
Manchester M18 . . . . 165 B1
Radcliffe M26 . . . . 44 D4
Bealey Com Hospl M26 . . . 44 D4
Bealey Dr BL9 . . . . 44 D7
Bealey Ind Est M26 . . . . . . 44 D4
Bealey Row M26 . . . . 44 D4
Beal La OL2 . . . . 149 C2
Beal Vale Prim Sch OL2 . 149 B3
Beaminster Ave SK4 . . . . 110 F3
Beaminster Cl SK4 . . . . . 110 F3
Beaminster Ct SK4 . . . . . 110 F3
Beaminster Rd SK4 . . . . . 110 F3
Beaminster Wlk M13 . . . . 163 C1
Beamish Cl M12, M13 . . . . 163 C2
Beamsley Dr M22 . . . . . . 121 B2
Beamsmoor Cl SK6 . . . . . 125 F4
Beanfields M28 . . . . 78 F5
Bean Leach Ave SK2 . . . . 124 E6
Bean Leach Dr SK2 . . . . . 124 F6
Bean Leach Rd SK2, SK7 . 124 F5
Beard Rd M18 . . . . 99 C4
Beardsmore Dr WA3 . . . . . 74 C1
Beard St
Droylsden M43 . . . . 83 F1
Royton OL2 . . . . 48 E3
Beardwood Rd M9 . . . . 64 D4
Bearswood Cl SK14 . . . . . 167 C1
Beathwaite Dr SK7 . . . . . . 123 C1
Beatrice Ave
Cheadle SK8 . . . . 122 F2
Reddish M18 . . . . 99 F4
Beatrice Mews 9 BL6 . . . . 22 B4
Beatrice Rd
Bolton BL1 . . . . 142 C1
Swinton M28 . . . . 79 B7
Beatrice St
Denton M34 . . . . 100 E3
Farnworth BL4 . . . . 60 C8
9 Horwich BL6 . . . . 22 B4
Rochdale OL13 . . . . 139 A3
Swinton M27 . . . . 61 D1
Beatrice Wignall St M43 . 100 A8
Beatrix Dr SK13 . . . . 171 B3
Beattock St M15 . . . . 162 A3
Beatty Dr BL5 . . . . 39 E1
Beauchamp St BL6 . . . . . 166 C4
Beaufort Dr OL4 . . . . 67 C5
Beaufort Ave
1 Manchester M20 . . . . . 110 A5
Sale M33 . . . . 108 C2
Swinton M27 . . . . 79 D7
Beaufort Chase SK9 . . . . 131 F1
Beaufort Cl
Alderley Edge SK9 . . . . . . 137 B2
Hattersley SK14 . . . . 102 E2
Beaufort Pl 2 M20 . . . . . . 110 A2
Beaufort Rd
Ashton-u-L OL6 . . . . 85 D3
Hattersley SK14 . . . . 102 E2
Sale M33 . . . . 108 C2
Stockport SK3 . . . . 124 D5
Beaufort St
Eccles M30 . . . . 79 B3
7 Hindley WN2 . . . . 56 D5
Manchester M3 . . . . 162 B4
Prestwich M25 . . . . 63 C4
Rochdale OL12 . . . . 14 C1
Wigan WN5 . . . . 54 E6
Beaufort Way SK14 . . . . . 102 E2
Beaulieu WA15 . . . . 119 F2
Beauly Cl BL0 . . . . 11 A2
Beaumaris Cl
Leigh WN7 . . . . 75 C5
Manchester M12 . . . . 164 C2
Beaumaris Cres SK7 . . . . 124 C1

Beaumaris Rd WN2 ..... 57 A3
Beaumonds OL11 ..... 29 F6
Beaumonds Way OL11 ..... 30 A6
Beaumont Ave BL6 ..... 22 C4
Beaumont Chase BL3 ..... 40 F3
Beaumont Cl
  Bacup OL13 ..... 4 A8
  2 Littleborough OL15 ..... 15 F5
Beaumont Ct
  Bolton BL1 ..... 40 D8
  Handforth SK9 ..... 131 C5
Beaumont Dr BL3 ..... 40 E5
Beaumont Gr WN5 ..... 54 B8
Beaumont Hospl (Private)
  The BL6 ..... 40 C8
Beaumont Prim Sch BL3 ..... 40 E5
Beaumont Rd
  Bolton BL1, BL3, BL6 ..... 40 E5
  Horwich BL6 ..... 22 C4
  Manchester M21 ..... 109 B7
Beaumont St OL6 ..... 166 C3
Beaupre WA3 ..... 119 C3
Beauvale Ave SK2 ..... 124 C7
Beaverbrook Ave WA3 ..... 92 B4
Beaver Ct WN4 ..... 73 C6
Beaver Dr BL9 ..... 45 B4
Beaver Ho SK1 ..... 124 B8
Beaver Rd M20 ..... 110 B3
Beaver Road Prim Sch 1
  M20 ..... 110 C3
Beaver St M1 ..... 163 A4
Bebbington Cl M33 ..... 108 F3
Bebbington St 7 M11 ..... 83 C1
Beccles Rd M33 ..... 108 B1
Beckenham Cl BL8 ..... 27 B7
Beckenham Rd M8 ..... 156 A3
Becket Ave M7 ..... 155 B2
Becket Mdws OL4 ..... 67 B6
Becket Meadow St OL4 ..... 67 B6
Beckett Dr WA13 ..... 117 B8
Beck Gr
  Shaw OL2 ..... 49 D8
  Walkden M28 ..... 60 F1
Beckhampton Cl M13 ..... 163 C2
Beck Ho SK14 ..... 102 D1
Beckley Ave M25 ..... 63 A2
Beckley Cl OL2 ..... 49 B4
Beckside
  Reddish SK5 ..... 100 A1
  Tyldesley M29 ..... 76 E8
Beck St
  Droylsden M11 ..... 99 E7
  Manchester M18 ..... 158 B1
Beckton Gdns M22 ..... 121 C3
Beckwith WN2 ..... 56 B3
Beccontree Ave M34 ..... 101 A4
Beccontree Dr M23 ..... 120 E7
Bedells La SK9 ..... 137 A6
Bedfont Wlk M9 ..... 64 E1
BEDFORD 76 C4
Bedford Ave
  Hyde SK14 ..... 167 B3
  Manchester M16 ..... 97 D2
  Sale M33 ..... 108 D2
  Shaw OL2 ..... 48 F7
  1 Swinton M27 ..... 79 E7
  Walkden M28 ..... 60 C1
Bedford Ct
  Altrincham WA15 ..... 120 C6
  6 Leigh WN7 ..... 76 A4
Bedford Dr
  Altrincham WA15 ..... 120 C6
  Atherton M46 ..... 58 A1
Bedford Gdns WN2 ..... 56 F6
Bedford Gn M44 ..... 105 B6
Bedford Hall Meth Prim Sch
  WN7 ..... 76 C3
Bedford High Sch WN7 ..... 76 D4
Bedford Pl WN4 ..... 73 A5
Bedford Rd
  Eccles M30 ..... 79 E3
  Manchester M16 ..... 97 A3
  Urmston M41 ..... 95 C4
Bedfordshire Cl OL9 ..... 152 B1
Bedford St
  Bolton BL1 ..... 145 A4
  Bolton, Egerton BL7 ..... 8 D2
  Heywood OL10 ..... 29 E2
  1 Leigh WN7 ..... 76 A5
  Prestwich M25 ..... 63 C5
  6 Reddish SK5 ..... 111 E7
  Reddish SK5 ..... 111 E8
  Wigan, Longshoot WN1 ..... 37 E1
  Wigan, Norley WN5 ..... 54 C5
Bedford Terr
  10 Bury BL9 ..... 141 A4
  Haslingden BB4 ..... 1 A8
Bedlington Cl M23 ..... 120 E6
Bednal Ave M40 ..... 160 B4
Bedwell St BL6 ..... 97 F3
Bedworth Cl BL2 ..... 148 B1
Beechacre BL0 ..... 11 D5
Beech Ave
  Adlington PR6 ..... 21 B8
  Atherton M46 ..... 58 E3
  Chadderton OL1, OL9 ..... 48 A2
  Culcheth WA3 ..... 92 A3
  Denton M34 ..... 100 D4
  Droylsden M43 ..... 83 F1
  Farnworth BL4 ..... 60 A8
  Gatley SK8 ..... 122 B5
  Glossop SK13 ..... 116 A8

Beech Ave continued
  Golborne WA3 ..... 90 F7
  Hazel Grove SK7 ..... 124 E2
  Horwich BL6 ..... 22 A4
  Irlam M44 ..... 94 C3
  Kearsley BL4 ..... 61 B5
  Little Lever BL3 ..... 43 B2
  Marple SK6 ..... 125 D6
  New Mills SK22 ..... 127 D1
  Oldham OL4 ..... 67 D8
  Radcliffe M26 ..... 61 F8
  Sale WA15 ..... 120 B8
  Salford M6 ..... 154 B4
  Stockport SK2, SK3 ..... 170 C2
  Uppermill OL3 ..... 69 B6
  Urmston M41 ..... 95 C2
  Whitefield M45 ..... 62 F6
  Worsley M28 ..... 78 A6
  Wythenshawe M22 ..... 121 D8
Beech Cl
  Manchester, Crumpsall
    M8 ..... 63 F1
  Manchester, Fallowfield
    M14 ..... 110 C8
  9 Manchester M21 ..... 96 F1
  2 Sale M33 ..... 107 F4
  Salford M6 ..... 81 A3
Beechdale Cl M40 ..... 83 C8
Beech Dr WN7 ..... 75 F2
Beecher Wlk M9 ..... 157 A2
Beeches SK9 ..... 136 F6
Beeches End SK14 ..... 102 A6
Beeches Mews M20 ..... 109 F4
Beeches The
  Altrincham WA14 ..... 119 C2
  4 Atherton M46 ..... 58 D3
  Bolton BL1 ..... 24 D2
  Cheadle SK8 ..... 123 B1
  4 Eccles M30 ..... 79 F3
  Manchester M20 ..... 109 F4
  Mossley OL5 ..... 68 E1
  Romiley SK6 ..... 113 B2
Beechfield
  Altrincham WA14 ..... 119 C3
  Rochdale OL11 ..... 29 E6
  Sale M33 ..... 107 F2
  Uppermill OL3 ..... 68 D5
  Wilmslow SK9 ..... 137 A6
Beechfield Ave
  Hindley WN2 ..... 57 A4
  3 Radcliffe M26 ..... 44 C1
  Urmston M41 ..... 95 A3
  Walkden M38 ..... 60 A5
  Wilmslow SK9 ..... 136 E5
Beechfield Cl
  6 Oldham OL4 ..... 67 F6
  Rochdale OL11 ..... 29 E6
Beechfield Dr
  Bury BL9 ..... 44 F7
  Leigh WN7 ..... 75 F3
Beechfield Mews SK14 ..... 102 A3
Beechfield Rd
  Bolton BL1 ..... 142 C2
  Cheadle SK8 ..... 132 B8
  Glossop SK13 ..... 171 C3
  Milnrow OL16 ..... 31 F4
  Stockport SK3 ..... 170 C1
  Swinton M27 ..... 79 D5
Beechfield St M8 ..... 156 A2
Beech Gr
  Abram Brow WN2 ..... 74 C7
  Ashton-u-L OL7 ..... 84 F1
  Leigh WN7 ..... 75 E2
  Manchester M14 ..... 110 D7
  Ramsbottom BL8 ..... 11 A1
  Sale M33 ..... 108 A4
  Salford M6 ..... 154 B4
  Stalybridge SK15 ..... 101 F8
  Walkden M38 ..... 59 E5
  Wigan WN6 ..... 36 E3
  Wilmslow SK9 ..... 137 A6
Beech Grove Sch 1 ..... 141 B4
Beech Hall St WN6 ..... 37 A2
BEECH HILL 36 F3
Beech Hill Ave WN6 ..... 36 E3
Beech Hill La WN6 ..... 36 E3
Beech Hill Prim Sch WN6 ..... 37 A3
Beech Hill Rd OL4 ..... 68 D6
Beecho Ho M20 ..... 110 B4
Beech Holme Gr SK2 ..... 124 C8
Beech House 3 M30 ..... 79 B1
Beech House La OL11 ..... 139 B2
Beech Hurst Cl M16 ..... 97 D2
Beech La
  Romiley SK6 ..... 113 C2
  Uppermill OL4 ..... 68 D5
  Wilmslow SK9 ..... 137 A6
Beech Lawn WA14 ..... 119 C4
Beech Mews
  Altrincham WA15 ..... 120 C3
  Manchester M21 ..... 109 A8
  Stockport SK2 ..... 124 A5
Beechmill Dr WA3 ..... 91 E3

Beech Mount
  Altrincham WA14 ..... 119 D2
  Ashton-u-L OL7 ..... 85 A6
  Manchester M9 ..... 157 A4
Beechpark Ave M22 ..... 121 C7
Beech Range 15 M19 ..... 99 A1
Beech Rd
  Alderley Edge SK9 ..... 137 B3
  Altrincham WA15 ..... 119 E3
  Cheadle SK8 ..... 123 B1
  Golborne WA3 ..... 74 A1
  High Lane SK6 ..... 134 F7
  Manchester M21 ..... 109 B7
  Paddockhill WA16 ..... 136 B5
  Sale M33 ..... 108 D4
  Stockport SK2, SK3 ..... 170 C2
Beech St
  Ashton-in-M WN4 ..... 73 A6
  Atherton M46 ..... 58 E3
  Bolton BL1 ..... 143 C2
  Bury BL9 ..... 141 B2
  Eccles M30 ..... 79 B1
  Edgworth BL7 ..... 9 D5
  Failsworth M35 ..... 83 B8
  Hyde SK14 ..... 167 A3
  Middleton M24 ..... 64 F8
  Newhey OL16 ..... 32 B4
  8 Oldham OL1 ..... 67 A7
  Radcliffe M26 ..... 44 C1
  Ramsbottom BL9 ..... 11 C3
  Rochdale OL11 ..... 139 A2
  Swinton M27 ..... 79 F7
Beech Street Prim Sch
  M30 ..... 79 B1
Beech Tree Ave WN6 ..... 35 D8
Beech Tree Hos WN2 ..... 73 F7
Beechurst Rd SK8 ..... 123 B5
Beech View SK14 ..... 102 A2
Beechway
  High Lane SK6 ..... 134 F7
  Wilmslow SK9 ..... 136 F5
Beech Wlk
  Leigh WN7 ..... 75 E2
  Middleton M24 ..... 65 A6
  Standish WN6 ..... 36 D8
  1 Stretford M32 ..... 96 C1
Beech Wlks WN3 ..... 54 C2
Beechwood
  Altrincham WA14 ..... 119 B1
  Glossop SK13 ..... 115 F7
  Shaw OL2 ..... 49 D8
  Whitefield BL9 ..... 45 A6
Beechwood Ave
  Ashton-in-M WN4 ..... 73 A2
  Littleborough OL15 ..... 16 A3
  Manchester M21 ..... 109 C7
  Newton-le-W WA12 ..... 89 D4
  Ramsbottom BL0 ..... 11 D6
  Reddish SK5 ..... 169 C4
  Romiley SK6 ..... 113 D2
  Shevington WN6 ..... 35 F5
  Stalybridge SK15 ..... 86 C4
  Urmston M41 ..... 94 E3
Beechwood Cres
  Orrell WN5 ..... 53 E6
  Tyldesley M29 ..... 77 A6
Beechwood Ct
  Bury BL8 ..... 27 A5
  Coppull PR7 ..... 19 F8
  3 Manchester M20 ..... 110 A3
Beechwood Dr
  Hyde SK14 ..... 167 C1
  Marple SK6 ..... 126 A6
  Mossley OL5 ..... 68 C2
  Royton OL2 ..... 48 D5
  Sale M33 ..... 107 C4
  Swinton M28 ..... 79 B6
  Wilmslow SK9 ..... 137 E8
Beechwood Gdns M14 ..... 110 D8
Beechwood Gr
  Cheadle SK8 ..... 132 A8
  Manchester M9 ..... 157 B3
Beechwood Ho
  Brinnington SK6 ..... 112 E6
  Manchester M14 ..... 110 D8
Beechwood La
  Culcheth WA3 ..... 91 D4
  Stalybridge SK15 ..... 86 C4
Beechwood Rd
  Manchester M25 ..... 63 D3
  Oldham OL8 ..... 66 F2
Beechwood St BL3 ..... 147 C3
Beechwood Sq OL1 ..... 67 A7
Beede St M11 ..... 165 B4
Beedon Ave BL3 ..... 43 A4
Bee Fold La M46 ..... 58 C1
Beeford Dr WN5 ..... 53 E5
Beehive Gn BL5 ..... 40 B1
Bee Hive Ind Est BL6 ..... 39 E8
Beehive St OL8 ..... 66 F3
Beeley St
  Hyde SK14 ..... 167 B2
  Salford M6 ..... 81 B5
Beenham Cl M33 ..... 107 C3
Beeston Ave
  Altrincham WA15 ..... 119 F6
  Salford M7 ..... 81 B6
Beeston Cl BL1 ..... 23 A3
Beeston Gr
  Leigh WN7 ..... 76 D7
  Prestwich M45 ..... 63 B7
  Stockport SK3 ..... 170 B1
Beeston Rd
  Handforth SK9 ..... 131 D5
  Sale M33 ..... 107 F4
Beeston St M9 ..... 157 B4
Beetham Twr M3 ..... 162 B4
Beeth St M11 ..... 99 D7

Beeton Gr M13 ..... 98 E4
Beever Prim Sch OL1 ..... 67 A8
Beever St
  Manchester M16 ..... 161 C1
  Oldham OL1 ..... 67 A7
Begley Cl SK6 ..... 112 F1
Begonia Ave BL4 ..... 42 B1
Begonia Wlk M12 ..... 164 C2
Beightons Wlk M7 ..... 155 A3
Beis Hathaimud Sch M7 ..... 155 A3
Beis Malka Beiz Girls Sch 1
  M7 ..... 155 A3
Beis Ruchel Girls' Sch
  2 Manchester M8 ..... 63 F1
  Salford M7 ..... 155 B3
Beis Yaakov High Sch
  M7 ..... 155 A3
Belayse Cl BL1 ..... 142 B2
Belbeck St S 7 BL8 ..... 27 C2
Belbeck St BL8 ..... 27 C2
Belcroft Cl M22 ..... 121 E8
Belcroft Dr M38 ..... 59 E6
Belcroft Gr M38 ..... 59 E5
Belding Ave M40 ..... 65 F1
Beldon Rd M9 ..... 64 B4
Belfairs Cl OL7 ..... 85 B7
BELFIELD 31 D8
Belfield Cl OL16 ..... 31 C8
Belfield Com Prim Sch
  OL16 ..... 31 C8
Belfield La
  Milnrow OL16 ..... 31 D7
  Rochdale OL16 ..... 31 C8
  Rochdale, Mill La OL16 ..... 31 C8
Belfield Old Rd OL16 ..... 31 C8
Belfield Rd
  Manchester, Didsbury
    M20 ..... 110 B3
  Manchester, Sedgley Park
    M25 ..... 63 E2
  Reddish SK5 ..... 99 F3
  Rochdale OL16 ..... 31 C8
Belford Ave M34 ..... 100 A3
Belford Rd M32 ..... 96 D3
Belford Wlk M23 ..... 121 A6
Belfort Dr M5 ..... 161 B4
Belfry Cl SK9 ..... 137 D8
Belfry Cres WN6 ..... 19 F2
Belgate Cl M12 ..... 99 A4
Belgium St OL16 ..... 29 E7
Belgrave Ave
  Failsworth M35 ..... 84 B8
  Manchester M14 ..... 98 E3
  Marple SK6 ..... 125 F6
  Oldham OL8 ..... 67 A4
  Urmston M41 ..... 94 E3
Belgrave Bglws M26 ..... 43 F4
Belgrave Cl
  Golborne WN7 ..... 91 C8
  Radcliffe M26 ..... 44 A4
  Wigan WN3 ..... 54 D3
Belgrave Cres
  Eccles M30 ..... 79 F2
  Horwich BL6 ..... 22 D3
  Stockport SK2 ..... 124 B4
Belgrave Ct
  Denton M34 ..... 100 A4
  Oldham OL8 ..... 66 F4
Belgrave Dr M26 ..... 44 A4
Belgrave Gdns 5 BL1 ..... 143 B2
Belgrave Ind Est OL8 ..... 67 A3
Belgrave Rd
  Altrincham WA15 ..... 119 C3
  Failsworth M40 ..... 105 D5
  Irlam M44 ..... 105 D5
  Oldham OL8 ..... 66 F4
  Sale M33 ..... 108 A4
Belgrave St S BL1 ..... 143 B1
Belgrave St
  Atherton M46 ..... 58 A2
  4 Bolton BL1 ..... 143 B2
  Denton M34 ..... 100 D4
  Heywood OL10 ..... 29 C1
  Radcliffe M26 ..... 44 A4
  Rochdale OL12 ..... 14 D1
Belgrave Gdns
  Altrincham WA15 ..... 128 E8
  Manchester M21 ..... 109 A8
Belgravia Ho 4 WA14 ..... 119 D3
Belgravia Mews OL2 ..... 149 C3
Belhaven Rd M8 ..... 63 F2
Belhill Gdns M6 ..... 154 C3
Bellam Ct M27 ..... 61 C1
Bellamy Dr WN7 ..... 76 B5
Bella St BL3 ..... 146 C4
Bell Clough Rd M43 ..... 84 B3
Bell Cres M11 ..... 164 C4
Belldale Cl SK4 ..... 168 A2
Belldean WN2 ..... 56 A2
Belle Green Ind Est WN2 ..... 56 A8
Belle Green La WN2 ..... 56 A8
Belle Isle Ave OL12 ..... 14 C6
Bellerby Cl M45 ..... 62 E8
Belleville Ave M22 ..... 130 E8
BELLE VUE 165 B1
Belle Vue Ave M12 ..... 164 C1
Belle Vue L Ctr M12 ..... 99 A4
Belle Vue St
  Manchester M12 ..... 165 A2
  1 Wigan WN5 ..... 54 D5
Belle Vue Sta M18 ..... 165 C1
Belle Vue Terr BL7 ..... 140 B1
Bellfield Ave
  Cheadle SK8 ..... 123 B1
  Oldham OL8 ..... 67 A4
Bellfield Cl 6 M9 ..... 64 C2
Bellfield View BL1 ..... 25 A3

Bellingham Cl WN1 ..... 37 C2
Bellingham Cl
  Bury BL8 ..... 26 F2
  Shaw OL2 ..... 149 B4
Bellingham Dr WN1 ..... 37 D2
Bellingham Mount WN1 ..... 37 D2
Bellis Cl M12 ..... 160 B1
Bell La
  Bury BL9 ..... 141 B3
  Milnrow OL16 ..... 32 B7
  Wigan WN5 ..... 54 B7
Bell Meadow Dr OL11 ..... 29 F5
Bellott St M8 ..... 156 B2
Bellot Wlk OL1 ..... 153 B4
Belpit Cl M78 ..... 78 C7
Bells Croft Ave M40 ..... 83 B7
Bellshill Cres OL16 ..... 15 C1
Bell St
  Droylsden M43 ..... 84 B2
  Hindley WN2 ..... 56 E6
  Leigh WN7 ..... 57 D1
  Oldham OL1 ..... 67 A7
  Rochdale OL16 ..... 139 C4
Bell Terr M30 ..... 95 C8
Bellwood BL5 ..... 57 C6
Belmont Ave
  Atherton M46 ..... 58 F4
  Denton M34 ..... 100 D4
  Golborne WA3 ..... 74 C1
  Leigh WN2 ..... 57 A1
  Orrell WN5 ..... 53 D3
  Salford M6 ..... 80 A2
  Swinton M27 ..... 61 D5
Belmont Cl SK4 ..... 169 B3
Belmont Dr
  Assull WN2 ..... 38 D5
  Bury BL8 ..... 27 A1
  Marple SK6 ..... 114 B1
Belmont Pl PR7 ..... 19 D6
Belmont Rd
  Adlington PR6 ..... 21 B7
  Altrincham WA15 ..... 119 E2
  Bolton BL1 & BL7 ..... 24 D6
  Bramhall SK7 ..... 132 F5
  Gatley SK8 ..... 122 B6
  Hindley WN2 ..... 56 F5
  Horwich BL6 ..... 22 C7
  Radcliffe M26 ..... 44 A1
  Sale M33 ..... 108 A6
Belmont St
  Eccles M30 ..... 79 D3
  Manchester M16 ..... 162 A1
  Oldham, Cold Hurst OL1 ..... 153 B4
  Oldham, Nether Lees OL4 ..... 67 E5
  Salford M5 ..... 154 A1
  Stockport SK4 ..... 169 A3
Belmont View BL2 ..... 25 F4
Belmont Way
  Chadderton OL9 ..... 152 C4
  Rochdale OL12 ..... 14 E2
  Stockport SK4 ..... 169 B3
Belmont Wlk 1 M13 ..... 163 C2
Belmore Ave M8 ..... 63 F1
Belmore Rd M33 ..... 108 B1
Belper Rd
  Eccles M30 ..... 95 B8
  Manchester SK4 ..... 110 F1
Belper St OL6 ..... 166 B4
Belper Way M14 ..... 113 A8
Belper Wlk M18 ..... 165 C2
Belroy Ct M25 ..... 63 B3
Belsay Cl OL7 ..... 84 F5
Belsay Dr M23 ..... 121 A4
Belstone Ave M23 ..... 121 A3
Belstone Cl SK7 ..... 123 F2
Belsyde Wlk 9 M9 ..... 157 B8
Belthorne Ave M45 ..... 65 B2
Belton Ave OL16 ..... 15 C1
Belton Cl WA3 ..... 90 A7
Belton Wlk
  10 Manchester M8 ..... 156 A2
  Oldham OL9 ..... 153 A2
Belvedere Ave
  Atherton M46 ..... 58 F4
  Ramsbottom BL8 ..... 11 A1
  Reddish SK5 ..... 99 F2
Belvedere Ct WN7 ..... 76 D7
Belvedere Ct M25 ..... 63 A3
Belvedere Dr
  Dukinfield SK15, SK16 ..... 101 E8
  Romiley SK6 ..... 112 C3
Belvedere Gdns SK4 ..... 168 B3
Belvedere Hts BL1 ..... 40 E8
Belvedere Pl WN3 ..... 54 F5
Belvedere Rd
  Adlington PR6 ..... 21 B8
  Ashton-in-M WN4 ..... 73 C4
  Manchester M14 ..... 110 E8
  Newton-le-W WA12 ..... 89 B5
  Salford M6 ..... 81 A3
Belvedere Sq M22 ..... 121 F3
Belvoir Ave
  Hazel Grove SK7 ..... 133 E8
  Manchester M19 ..... 99 A2
Belvoir Mdws OL16 ..... 15 C4
Belvoir St
  Bolton BL2 ..... 148 C3
  Rochdale OL12 ..... 14 C1
  Wigan WN1 ..... 151 B4
Belvor Ave M34 ..... 100 E7
Belwood Rd M21 ..... 109 B7
Bembridge Cl M14 ..... 98 C3

Bembridge Ct WN3 . . . . . . 54 E2
Bembridge Dr BL3 . . . . . . 42 D5
Bembridge Rd M34 . . . . . 113 B8
Bempton Cl SK2 . . . . . . 125 A5
Bemrose Ave WA14 . . . . 119 C6
Bemsley Pl M5 . . . . 161 A4
Benbecula Way M41 . . . . 95 D5
Benbow Ave M12 . . . . . 164 C1
Benbow St **5** M33 . . . 108 B5
Ben Brierley Way OL1 . . 153 C3
Benbrook Gr SK9 . . . . . 131 E2
Bench Carr OL12 . . . . . . 14 E1
Benches La SK6 . . . . . . 114 E3
BENCHILL 121 D5
Benchill Ave M22 . . . . . 121 C5
Benchill Court Rd M22 121 E4
Benchill Cres M22 . . . . . 121 C5
Benchill Ct M22 . . . . . . 121 E4
Benchill Dr M22 . . . . . . 121 C5
Benchill Prim Sch M22. 121 C5
Benchill Rd M22 . . . . . . 121 D5
Bendall St M11 . . . . 99 E8
Bendemeer **5** M41 . . . 95 D3
Bendix St M4 . . . . 159 B2
Benedict Ct **3** M7 . . . 81 C5
Benedict Dr SK16 . . . . . 101 D6
Benfield Ave M40 . . . . . 65 C2
Benfield St OL10 . . . . . . 29 D1
Benfleet Cl M12 . . . . . . 165 A2
Benfold Wlk M24 . . . . . 46 D3
Bengairn Cl WN1 . . . . . 37 F1
Bengal La OL6 . . . . 166 C4
Bengal Sq **1** OL6 . . . . 85 D4
Bengal St
  Leigh WN7 . . . . 75 F5
  Manchester M4 . . . . . 159 C2
  Stockport SK3 . . . . . . 170 B4
Benhale Wlk **3** M8 . . 156 A2
Benham Cl M20 . . . . . 110 C3
Benin Wlk **3** M40 . . . 83 C5
Benjamin Fold WN4 . . . 73 B5
Benjamin St **3** OL7 . . 166 A1
Benjamin Wilson Ct M7. 158 A4
Benmore Cl OL10 . . . . 29 A1
Benmore Rd M9 . . . . . 64 F3
Bennet Mews **8** SK14. 101 D5
Bennett St M26 . . . . . . 43 D4
Bennett Cl **2** SK3 . . . 123 C8
Bennett Dr
  Orrell WN5 . . . . 53 D4
  Salford M7 . . . . 155 B2
Bennett Rd M8 . . . . . . 63 F1
Bennett's La BL1 . . . . 142 C2
Bennett St
  6 Ashton-u-L OL7. . . 84 F1
  Dukinfield SK14 . . . . 101 D5
  Hollingworth SK14 . . . 103 D5
  Manchester M12 . . . . 164 B2
  4 Stalybridge SK15. . 86 A1
  3 Stockport SK3. . . . 123 C8
  Stretford M32 . . . . . . 96 C1
Benny La M43 . . . . 84 D3
Benney Rise BL6 . . . . . 21 E3
Benson Cl M7 . . . . 155 B1
Benson St
  Bury BL9 . . . . 141 A1
  Edgworth BL7 . . . . . . 9 E5
Benson Wlk **3** SK9 . . 131 D2
Ben St M11 . . . . 83 B2
Bentcliffe Way M30 . . 80 A1
Bentfield Cres OL16 . . 32 A4
Bentfield Ind Units OL9 152 B2
Bent Fold Dr BL9 . . . . 45 A1
BENTGATE 32 A3
BENT GATE 1 C8
Bentgate Cl
  Haslingden BB4 . . . . . 1 D8
  Newhey OL16 . . . . . . 32 A4
Bentgate St OL16 . . . . 32 A3
Benthall Wlk M34 . . . . 100 E1
Bentham Cl
  Bury BL8 . . . . 26 E3
  6 Farnworth BL4 . . . 42 D1
Bentham Pl WN6 . . . . 19 F2
Bentham Rd
  Culcheth WA3 . . . . . . 92 A2
  Standish WN6 . . . . . . 19 F2
Bent Hill St BL3 . . . . . 146 A4
Bentinck Bsns Ctr OL6. 166 A2
Bentinck Cl WA14 . . . . 119 C4
Bentinck Ho **2** OL6 . . 166 A2
Bentinck Rd WA14 . . . 119 C4
Bentinck St
  Ashton-u-L OL6 . . . . . 166 A2
  Bolton BL1 . . . . 142 B1
  Farnworth BL4 . . . . . 42 C1
  Manchester M15 . . . . 162 A3
  Oldham OL8 . . . . 66 F4
  9 Rochdale OL12 . . . 14 C1
  Wigan WN3 . . . . 54 F4
Bentinck Street Ind Est
  M15 . . . . 162 A3
Bentinck Terr **1** OL6. 166 A2
Bent La
  Culcheth WA3 . . . . . . 92 A2
  Lymm WA13 . . . . 117 C6
  Prestwich M25 . . . . . 63 C4
  Salford M8 . . . . 155 C3
Bent Lanes M41 . . . . . 94 F5
Bentley Ave M24 . . . . 47 D5
Bentley Brook Cl BL6. 22 E4
Bentley Cl M26 . . . . . 44 D4
Bentley Ct
  Farnworth BL4 . . . . . 42 D1
  Salford M7 . . . . 155 B4

Bentley Fold BL8 . . . . . 26 F4
Bentley Hall Rd BL2, BL8.. 26 D4
Bentley Ho M15 . . . . . 162 B2
Bentley La BL9 . . . . . . 12 A1
Bentley Mdw BL2 . . . . 26 F3
Bentley Mews OL12 . . 14 E2
Bentley Rd
  Denton M34 . . . . 100 F3
  Manchester M21 . . . . 97 A1
  Salford M7 . . . . 155 B4
Bentley St
  Bolton BL2 . . . . 148 C1
  Chadderton OL9 . . . . 152 C8
  Farnworth BL4 . . . . . 42 D1
  8 Oldham OL4 . . . . 67 E6
  Rochdale OL12 . . . . . 14 E2
Bentleys The SK5 . . . . 169 C3
Bentmeadows OL12 . . 14 E1
Benton Dr SK6 . . . . . . 126 C8
Benton St M9 . . . . . . 157 C3
Bents Ave
  Romiley SK6 . . . . 112 F3
  Urmston M41 . . . . . . 94 F1
Bents Farm Cl **1** OL12.. 15 F5
Bentside Rd SK12 . . . 135 D5
Bent Spur Rd BL4 . . . 61 A5
Bent St
  Farnworth BL4 . . . . . 60 E7
  Haslingden BB4 . . . . . 1 D8
  Manchester M3, M8 . . 159 A4
Bent Terr M41 . . . . . . 95 C4
Bent The OL11 . . . . . 139 A1
Bentworth Cl BL5 . . . . 57 F6
Benville Wlk M40 . . . . 83 B6
Benwick Terr **1** BL1 . 143 B2
Benyon St OL4 . . . . . 67 E6
Berberis Wlk **1** M33. 107 C6
Beresford Ave BL3 . . . 144 C1
Beresford Cres
  Oldham OL4 . . . . 67 D8
  Reddish SK5 . . . . 99 E3
Beresford Ct
  4 Alderley Edge SK9 137 A1
  Manchester M20 . . . . 110 A4
Beresford Rd
  Manchester M13 . . . . 98 F3
  Stretford M32 . . . . . . 96 E4
Beresford St
  Failsworth M35 . . . . . 83 E7
  Manchester M14 . . . . 97 F3
  Newhey OL16 . . . . . . 32 B4
  8 Oldham OL4 . . . . 67 D8
  8 Wigan WN6 . . . . 37 A1
Bergman Wlk M40 . . . 83 B6
Berigan Cl M12 . . . . . 164 B1
Berisford Cl WA15 . . . 119 E7
Berkeley Ave
  Manchester M14 . . . . 98 E4
  Oldham OL9 . . . . 65 F3
  Stretford M32 . . . . . . 96 A4
  Wigan WN3 . . . . 54 D2
Berkeley Cl
  Golborne WN7 . . . . . 91 C8
  Hyde SK14 . . . . 167 A1
  Stockport SK2 . . . . . 124 C8
Berkeley Cres
  Hyde SK14 . . . . 167 A1
  Little Lever M26 . . . . 43 C5
Berkeley Ct **1** M7 . . 63 E1
Berkeley Dr
  Rochdale OL16 . . . . . 31 B4
  Royton OL2 . . . . 48 D2
Berkeley Rd
  Bolton BL1 . . . . 143 B4
  Hazel Grove SK7 . . . 124 F3
Berkeley St
  Ashton-u-L OL6 . . . . 166 A3
  1 Royton OL2 . . . . 48 D5
Berkley Ave M19 . . . . 99 A1
Berkley Ho BL1 . . . . . 144 C3
Berkshire Cl OL9 . . . . 152 B1
Berkshire Dr BL9 . . . . 44 F7
Berkshire Dr M44 . . . . 105 C5
Berkshire Pl OL9 . . . . 152 C1
Berkshire Rd M40 . . . 160 A3
Berlin Rd SK3 . . . . . . 170 A2
Berlin St BL3 . . . . . . 144 C2
Bermondsay St M5 . . . 161 B4
Bernard Gr BL1 . . . . . 142 C2
Bernard St
  Glossop SK13 . . . . . . 104 C1
  Manchester M9 . . . . . 157 A4
  Rochdale OL12 . . . . . 14 E3
Bernard Walker Ct SK6. 114 B2
Berne Ave BL6 . . . . . . 22 A3
Berne Cl
  Chadderton OL9 . . . . 152 C2
  Stockport SK7 . . . . . 123 E4
Bernice Ave OL9 . . . . 152 B2
Bernice St BL1 . . . . . . 142 C2
Berriedale Cl M16 . . . 97 D2
Berrie Gr M19 . . . . . . 111 B8
Berrington Gr WN4 . . 73 A3
Berry Brow
  Failsworth M40 . . . . 83 D4
  Uppermill OL3 . . . . . 69 B5
Berry Cl SK9 . . . . 137 A5
Berrycroft La SK6 . . . 113 A3
Berryfold Way M29 . . 77 B8
Berry Sq BL6 . . . . 21 D3
Berry St
  Eccles M30 . . . . 95 B8
  Manchester M1 . . . . . 163 B4
  Stalybridge SK15 . . . 102 C8
  Swinton M27 . . . . . . 61 F2
  Uppermill OL3 . . . . . 69 B5
Bertha Rd OL16 . . . . . 31 C7

Bertha St
  Bolton BL1 . . . . 143 A2
  Manchester M11 . . . . 165 B3
  Shaw OL2 . . . . 149 B1
Bertie St OL11 . . . . . 30 D4
Bertram St
  Manchester M12 . . . . 165 A2
  Newton-le-W WA12 . . 89 A4
  Sale M33 . . . . 108 E4
Bertrand Rd BL1 . . . . 144 C3
Berwick Ave
  Manchester SK4 . . . . 110 E2
  Stretford M41 . . . . . 96 A2
  Whitefield M45 . . . . 63 A7
Berwick Cl
  Boothstown M28 . . . 77 F7
  Heywood OL10 . . . . 29 A1
Berwick Pl WN1 . . . . 37 E1
Berwick St OL16 . . . . 31 B6
Berwyn Ave
  Cheadle SK8 . . . . . . 123 B5
  Manchester M9 . . . . 64 C5
  Middleton M24 . . . . 65 C8
Berwyn Cl
  Horwich BL6 . . . . . . 22 C5
  Oldham OL8 . . . . 66 E3
Beryl Ave BL8 . . . . . . 26 F7
Beryl St BL1 . . . . 143 C3
Besom La SK15 . . . . . 86 E3
Bessemer Rd M44 . . . 105 E6
Bessemer St M11, M18.. 165 C3
Bessemer Way OL1 . . 153 B3
BESSES O' TH' BARN.. 63 A7
Besses o' th' Barn Metro Sta
  M45 . . . . 63 A7
Bessie's Well Pl WN6. 36 F8
Bessybrook Cl BL6 . . 40 C6
Besthill Cotts SK14 . . 115 B8
BESWICK 164 C4
Beswick Cotts OL3 . . 50 D4
Beswick Dr M35 . . . . 84 A6
Beswicke Royds St OL16. 15 C1
Beswick St
  Littleborough OL15 . . 16 C5
  Rochdale OL12 . . . . 139 B4
  Beswick Row M4 . . 159 A3
Beswicks La SK9 . . . . 136 C3
Beswick St
  5 Droylsden M43 . . 84 B1
  Manchester M4 . . . . 160 A2
  Royton OL2 . . . . 48 E2
  Walsden OL14 . . . . . 6 A7
Beta Ave M32 . . . . . . 96 C1
Beta Ct M22 . . . . 121 E7
Beta St BL1 . . . . 145 C4
Bethal Gn OL15 . . . . 6 C1
Bethany La OL16 . . . 32 D4
Bethel Ave M35 . . . . 83 E7
Bethel Gr WN3 . . . . . 150 C1
Bethersden Rd WN1.. 37 B4
Bethesda St OL8 . . . 66 F4
Bethnal Dr M14 . . . . 110 B8
Betjeman Pl OL12 . . 49 D8
Betleymere Rd SK8 . 122 F4
Betley Rd SK5 . . . . . 99 F1
Betley St
  Heywood OL10 . . . . 29 C1
  Manchester M1 . . . . 163 C4
  Radcliffe M26 . . . . 44 C4
Betnor Ave SK1 . . . . 112 B1
Betony Cl OL12 . . . . 14 D3
Bettison Ave WN7 . . 76 C3
Bettwood Dr M8 . . . . 63 F2
Betty Nuppy's La OL16. 31 C5
Betula Gr M7 . . . . . . 155 A3
Betula Mews **1** OL11. 13 D1
Beulah Ave WN5 . . . 71 D4
Beulah St M18 . . . . . 165 C3
Bevan Cl M12 . . . . . . 160 B1
Bevendon Sq M7 . . . 155 B2
Beveridge St M14 . . . 98 A3
Beverley Ave
  Denton M34 . . . . 101 A2
  Leigh WN7 . . . . 76 A6
  Longshaw WN5 . . . . 53 E1
  Urmston M41 . . . . . . 95 E3
Beverley Cl M45 . . . . 45 B1
Beverley Pl OL16 . . . 31 A8
Beverley Rd
  Bolton BL1 . . . . 144 C4
  Little Lever BL3 . . . . 60 C7
  Pendlebury M27 . . . . 80 C7
  Stockport SK2 . . . . . 124 C8
  Wigan WN5 . . . . 54 B8
Beverley St M9 . . . . . 64 E1
Beverley Wlk
  Oldham OL8 . . . . 153 B1
  Romiley SK6 . . . . 113 A1
Beverly Cl OL6 . . . . . 85 B8
Beverly Rd M14 . . . . 110 E7
Beverston **7** OL11.. 139 B2
Beverston Dr M7 . . . 155 B2
Bevill Sq M3 . . . . . . 158 B2
Bevin Ave WA3 . . . . 92 B4
Bevis Gn BL9 . . . . . . 27 F8
Bevis St BL9 . . . . 27 F8
BEVIS GREEN 27 F8
Bewerley Cl WN3 . . . 150 B2
Bewick St **1** BL2 . . 25 B3
Bewley Gr WN7 . . . . 76 A6
Bewley St OL8 . . . . . 66 D2
Bewley Wlk M40 . . 83 A6
Bexhill Ave WA15 . . 119 F6
Bexhill Cl BL3 . . . . . . 43 C3
Bexhill Dr
  Hindley WN7 . . . . . . 57 C2
  Manchester M13 . . . . 98 F3

Bexhill Rd SK3 . . . . . 123 E4
Bexhill Wlk OL9 . . . . 152 B2
Bexington Rd **3** M16.. 97 E3
Bexley Cl
  Glossop SK13 . . . . . 104 C3
  Urmston M41 . . . . . . 95 B4
Bexley Dr
  Bury BL8 . . . . 27 B1
  Walkden M38 . . . . . 60 C4
Bexley Sq M3 . . . . . . 158 A2
Bexley St
  Hindley WN2 . . . . . . 57 B3
  Oldham OL9 . . . . 152 C1
Bexley Wlk M40 . . . . 83 B6
Beyer Cl M18 . . . . . . 165 C1
Bibby La M19 . . . . . . 110 F6
Bibby St
  Bury BL9 . . . . 44 F5
  Dukinfield SK14 . . . . 101 D5
Bibury Ave M22 . . . . 121 B2
Bickerdike Ave M12 . 99 B3
Bickerdike Ct **1** M12. 99 B3
BICKERSHAW 74 F8
Bickershaw CE Prim Sch
  WN2 . . . . 74 F8
Bickershaw Dr M28 . 60 C2
Bickershaw La
  Abram WN2 . . . . 74 F8
  Leigh WN2 . . . . 56 D1
Bickerstaffe Cl OL2 . 149 A1
Bickerton Ct OL9 . . . . 66 B3
Bickerton Dr SK7 . . . 124 A1
Bickerton Rd WA14 . 119 B6
Bickley Gr M29 . . . . 77 C6
Biddall Dr M23 . . . . 121 B6
Biddisham Wlk
  Manchester M40 . . . . 157 A1
  Manchester M40 . . . . 160 A4
Biddulph Ave SK2 . . 124 C5
Bideford Dr
  Bolton BL2 . . . . 43 A6
  Wythenshawe M23 . 120 F8
Bideford Rd
  Rochdale OL11 . . . . 30 B3
  Stockport SK2 . . . . . 124 C8
Bidford Cl M29 . . . . 59 C1
Bidston Ave M14 . . . 98 B2
Bidston Cl
  Bury BL8 . . . . 27 A2
  Shaw OL2 . . . . 49 D6
Bidston Dr SK9 . . . . 131 E2
Bidworth La SK13 . . 171 A1
Big Fold BL6 . . . . 40 B4
Biggenwood Wlk **7** M40. 83 A7
Biggin Gdns OL10 . . 46 E7
Bignor St M8 . . . . . . 156 A2
Bilbao St BL1 . . . . . . 144 C4
Bilberry St OL16 . . . 31 A6
Bilbrook St M4 . . . . 159 B3
Billberry St M45 . . . 63 B8
Billing Ave M12 . . . . 163 C3
Billinge St BL3 . . . . . 147 E4
BILLINGE 71 E4
Billinge Arc **8** WN1. 150 C4
Billinge Cl **5** BL1 . . 145 C4
Billinge Rd
  Garswood WN4 . . . . 72 C5
  Wigan, Pemberton WN3,
  WN5 . . . . 54 D4
  Wigan, Worsley Hall WN5. 54 E6
Billington Ave WA12. 89 C5
Billington Rd M27 . . 80 E8
Bill La M45 . . . . 62 F8
Billsborrow Rd M14 . 98 A3
Bill Williams Cl M11. 165 C4
Billy La M42 . . . . . . 62 A2
Billy Meredith Cl **4** M14. 98 A2
Billy's La SK6 . . . . . . 123 A1
Billy Whelan Wlk **2** M40. 83 C5
Bilsland Wlk **1** M40. 83 C5
Bilson Dr SK3 . . . . . 123 B7
Bilson Sq OL16 . . . . 32 A5
Bilton Wlk M8 . . . . . 156 C4
Binbrook Wlk BL3 . . 147 C4
Bincombe Wlk M13 . 163 C1
Binfield Rd M5 . . . . 80 A3
Bindon Wlk **8** M9 . 157 A3
Bingham Dr M23 . . . 120 F6
Bingham St M27 . . . 79 F8
Bingley Cl M11 . . . . 164 C4
Bingley Dr M41 . . . . 94 F4
Bingley Rd OL16 . . . 31 C7
Bingley Sq OL16 . . . 31 C7
Bingley Terr OL16 . . 31 C7
Bingley Wlk
  Farnworth BL4 . . . . 60 D7
  Manchester M7 . . . . 80 F8
Binns Nook Rd OL12. 14 A4
Binns Pl M4 . . . . . . 159 B1
Binns St SK15 . . . . . 85 E1
Binsley Cl M44 . . . . 94 A1
Birbeck Cl WN3 . . . 54 E1
Birbeck St
  5 Mossley OL5 . . 68 C2
  2 Stalybridge SK15. 85 F1
BIRCH 46 C4
Birchacre Gr M14 . . 110 D7
Birchall Ave WA3 . . 91 E4
Birchall Cl SK16 . . . 101 D6
Birchall Gn SK6 . . . 113 A5
Birchall Way M15 . . 162 C2
Birch Ave
  Bury BL9 . . . . 27 A5
  Chadderton OL1, OL9.. 48 A2
  Failsworth M35 . . . . 83 F5
  Irlam M44 . . . . 105 D3

Birch Ave *continued*
  Middleton M24 . . . . 65 A7
  Oldham OL8 . . . . . . 66 D2
  Rochdale OL12 . . . . 15 D4
  Romiley SK6 . . . . . . 113 D2
  Sale M33 . . . . 108 B3
  Salford M6 . . . . 154 B4
  Standish WN6 . . . . . 36 F8
  Stockport, Heaton Moor
  SK4 . . . . 168 B4
  Westhoughton BL5 . 57 F7
  Whitefield M45 . . . . 62 F6
  Wilmslow SK9 . . . . . 136 F6
Birch Brook Rd WA13. 117 C5
Birch Cl OL12 . . . . . . 14 C6
Birch Cres OL16 . . . 32 A3
Birch Ct
  Dukinfield SK16 . . 101 D8
  Heywood OL10 . . . . 29 E1
  Manchester M13 . . 98 E3
  Marple SK6 . . . . 125 E5
  Birchdale WA14 . . . 119 C2
  Birchdale Ave SK8 . 122 B2
Birch Dr
  Hazel Grove SK7 . . 124 C2
  Oldham OL4 . . . . 67 F5
  Pendlebury M27 . . . 80 B8
Birchenall St M40 . . 157 C4
Birchen Bower Wlk BL8. 26 F5
Birchenlea St OL9 . . 66 A3
Birches End OL12 . . 14 C5
Birches Sch The M20. 109 F5
Birches The
  Mossley OL5 . . . . . . 68 B1
  Sale M33 . . . . 107 C5
Birchfield
  Ashton-u-L OL7 . . . 100 F8
  Bolton BL2 . . . . 25 E6
Birchfield Ave
  Atherton M46 . . . . . 58 B4
  Heywood BL9 . . . . . 28 E1
Birchfield Dr
  Rochdale OL11 . . . . 30 C4
  Worsley M28 . . . . . . 78 A7
Birchfield Gr BL3 . . . 40 E4
Birchfield Mews **4**
  SK14 . . . . 167 A2
Birchfield Rd
  Cheadle SK3 . . . . . . 123 A7
  Lymm WA13 . . . . . . 117 B4
Birchfields
  Altrincham WA15 . 119 F1
  Oldham OL4 . . . . 67 F4
Birchfields Ave M13 . 98 E3
Birchfields Prim Sch M14,
  M19 . . . . 98 E1
Birchfields Rd M13, M14.. 98 E2
Birchfold Cl M38 . . . 60 B4
Birchgate Wlk BL3 . . 145 C1
Birch Gn SK13 . . . . . 104 E1
Birch Gr
  Altrincham WA15 . . 120 E5
  Denton, Hooley Hill M34.. 100 E4
  Denton M34 . . . . 100 E3
  Downall Green WN4 . 72 D5
  Manchester M14 . . . 98 D3
  Prestwich M25 . . . . 63 A6
  Ramsbottom BL0 . . . 11 A3
Birchgrove Cl BL3 . . 146 A3
Birch Hall Cl OL4 . . 67 F4
Birch Hall La M13 . . 98 E3
Birch Hey Cl **2** OL12. 15 C4
Birch Hill Bsns Ctr OL10. 46 C5
Birch Hill Cres OL10. 46 C5
Birch Hill Hospl OL12. 15 C1
Birch Hill La OL12 . . 15 D6
Birch Hill Wlk OL15 . 15 F5
Birch Ho BL5 . . . . . . 57 F7
Birch House Sch M14. 110 D4
Birch Ind Est OL10 . . 46 A5
Birchington Rd M14,
  M20 . . . . 110 A8
Birchin La M4 . . . . . 159 A1
Birchinlee Ave OL2 . 48 C3
Birchin Pl M4 . . . . . 159 A1
Birch La
  Dukinfield SK16 . . 101 D7
  Manchester M13 . . 98 F4
Birchlea WA15 . . . . 119 F4
Birch-Lea Cl BL9 . . . 44 F7
Birchleaf Gr M5 . . . 80 C2
BIRCHLEY 71 C4
Birchley Ave WN5 . . 71 C3
Birchley Rd WN5 . . . 71 C3
Birchley St Mary's RC Prim
  Sch WN5 . . . . 71 D4
Birchley View WA11. 71 B2
Birch Mount OL12 . . 15 E4
Birch Polygon M14 . 98 D3
Birch Rd
  Abram Brow WN2 . . 74 B7
  Atherton M46 . . . . . 58 C3
  Carrington M31, WA14. 106 F3
  Coppull PR7 . . . . . . 19 E8
  Gatley SK8 . . . . 122 A5
  Hollinfare WA3 . . . . 105 B2
  Kearsley BL4 . . . . . 60 F6
  Leigh WN7 . . . . 75 F7
  Manchester M8 . . . . 64 B1
  Middleton M24 . . . . 47 C2
  Partington M31 . . . 105 D3
  Poynton SK12 . . . . 133 F2
  Rochdale OL12 . . . . 15 D3
  Swinton M27 . . . . . . 79 D5
  Uppermill OL3 . . . . 69 C7
  Walkden M28 . . . . . 60 E1
Birchside Ave SK13 . 104 B2

Birch St
Ashton-u-L OL7 ....84 E1
Bolton BL2 ....148 B2
Bury BL9 ....140 C3
Droylsden M43. ....100 B8
Heywood OL10. ....29 D1
Hindley WN2 ....56 D5
Manchester M12 ....165 A2
Radcliffe M26 ....44 E5
Stalybridge SK15. ......86 C5
3 Tyldesley M29. ....59 A1
Wardle OL12 ....15 C6
Wigan WN6 ....15 C5
Birch Terr **2** SK14 ......167 A2
Birch Tree Ave SK7 .....134 A8
Birch Tree Cl WA14 .....119 C1
Birch Tree Cl **2** M22...121 D3
Birch Tree Dr OL12 .....121 C3
Birch Tree Rd **6** WA3...90 F8
Birch Tree Way **4** BL6...22 E1
BIRCH VALE 127 F2
Birchvale Cl
Manchester M15 ....162 B2
Poynton SK12. ....133 E3
Birchvale Dr SK6 ....113 D3
Birch Vale Terr SK22 ....127 F3
Birch View **9** OL12 .....15 D4
Birchway
Bramhall SK7 ....132 D7
High Lane SK6. ....134 F7
Birchwood
Chadderton OL9. ....65 E7
Droylsden M43. ....84 B3
Birchwood Cl
Leigh WN7 ....75 F3
Stockport SK4 ....168 A1
Wigan WN3 ....54 D1
Birchwood Cres SK14 ...102 A6
Birchwood Dr
Manchester M40 ....157 A2
Wilmslow SK9 ....137 D8
Birchwood Rd M24.......65 C8
Birchwood Way SK16....101 D6
Bird Hall Ave SK8 ....123 C4
Birdhall Gr M19. ....111 A8
Bird Hall La SK8 ....123 B6
Bird Hall Rd SK8 ....123 C5
Birdlip Dr M23. ....151 C3
Bird St WN2 ....151 C3
Birkby Dr M24 ....46 E2
Birkdale Ave
Atherton M46. ....58 C5
Royton OL2 ....48 E2
Whitefield M45 ....62 D6
Birkdale Cl
Bramhall SK7 ....133 A7
Dukinfield SK14 ....101 F5
Heywood OL10. ....46 D8
Birkdale Dr
Bury BL8 ....27 B2
Sale M33 ....107 E2
Birkdale Gr
Eccles M30 ....79 F2
Reddish SK5. ....111 F5
Birkdale Rd
Reddish SK5. ....111 F5
Rochdale OL16. ....31 C4
Birkdale St M8 ....156 A3
Birkenhills Dr BL3 ....40 E5
Birkett Bank WN1. ......151 B4
Birkett Cl BL1. ....24 D6
Birkett Dr BL1. ....24 D6
Birkett St WN1. ....151 B4
Birkinbrook Cl M45 .....45 A1
Birkinheath La WA14....128 B4
Birleigh Wlk BL2. ......42 E6
Birks Ave OL4. ....67 F8
Birkside Cl WN3 ....55 A1
Birks La OL14... ....6 B8
Birkworth Ct SK2 ....124 D6
Birley Cl
Altrincham WA14. ......119 F7
Appley Bridge WN6 ....35 F8
Birley Pk M20. ....109 F3
Birley St
Bolton BL1. ....143 B4
Bury BL9 ....27 F5
Leigh WN7 ....76 A6
Newton-le-W WA12.....89 D4
Rochdale OL12. ....15 A1
Birling Dr M23. ....121 B4
Birnham Gr OL10 ....29 A1
Birshaw Cl OL2 ....78 F1
Birstall Wlk M23........121 A6
Birtenshaw Cres BL7....25 B7
Birtenshaw Hall Sch BL7..25 B6
Birtle Dr M29 ....77 C7
Birtle Rd BL9 ....28 E6
Birtles Ave SK5 ....99 F3
Birtles Cl
Cheadle SK8 ....123 A5
Dukinfield SK16. ....101 D6
Birtlespool Rd SK8 .....122 F4
Birtles The M22. ....121 D3
Birtles Way **4** SK9 .....131 D5
Birt M40 ....160 A4
Birwood Rd M8 ....64 B2
Biscay Cl M11 ....160 C1
Bishopbridge Cl BL3 ....147 C4
Bishop Bridgeman CE Prim
  Sch BL3 ....147 B4
Bishop Cl M16 ....97 E4
Bishopdale Cl OL2 ......48 D5
Bishopgate WN1. ......150 C4
Bishopgate St OL9 .....152 A1
Bishop Marshall Cl M40..157 A1

Bishop Marshall Way
  M24 ....46 D4
Bishop Rd
Salford M6. ....80 B4
Urmston M41. ....94 D2
Bishops Cl
Altrincham WA14. ......119 B1
Ashton-u-L OL7 ....85 A5
Bishop's Ct
Bolton BL3. ....42 A2
Cheadle SK8 ....123 A5
Bishops Cnr M15. ......162 C2
Bishopsgate M2 ....162 C4
Bishopsgate Wlk OL16 ..31 C4
Bishops Mdw M24 .....46 D3
Bishops Mews M33 .....107 E6
Bishops Rd M25 ....63 C2
Bishop's Rd BL3 ....42 A2
Bishop St
Middleton M24. ....65 D7
Rochdale OL16. ....15 B1
Stockport SK1 ....112 A1
Bishops Wlk OL7. ......166 A1
Bishopton Cl M19. ......99 C1
Bisley Ave M33 ....120 F6
Bisley St OL8 ....153 A2
Bismarck St OL4 ....67 A5
Bispham Ave
Bolton BL2. ....42 F7
Reddish SK5. ....99 F3
Bispham Cl BL8. ....26 F1
Bispham Ct WN5. ......53 D2
Bispham Dr WN4 ....72 F5
Bispham Gr M7 ....155 B3
Bispham Hall Bsns Pk
  WN5 ....53 C2
Bispham St BL2. ....148 C4
Bittern Cl
Poynton SK12. ....133 A4
Rochdale OL11. ....29 F7
Bittern Dr M43. ....84 C3
Blackbank St BL1. ......143 C2
Blackberry Cl WA14 ....119 B8
Blackberry Dr WN2 .....56 C4
Blackberry La SK5 ......112 C7
Black Brook Rd SK4 ....111 D7
Blackbrook Trad Est
  M19. ....111 B7
Blackburn Cl WA3 ......90 E8
Blackburne Dr M12. ....89 A4
Blackburn Gdns M20....110 A4
Blackburn Pl M5. ....81 C1
Blackburn Rd
Bolton, Back O' Th' Bank
  BL1. ....143 C2
Bolton, Egerton BL7 ....8 C4
Edenfield BL0, BB4 .....1 D5
Edgworth BL7 ....9 D7
Blackburn St
Manchester M16 ....161 C1
Prestwich M25 ....63 C4
Radcliffe M26 ....44 A3
7 Radcliffe M26.......44 B2
Backcap Cl M28 ....78 B7
Blackcarr Rd M23 ......121 B6
Blackchapel Dr OL16....31 B3
Blackden Wlk SK9 ......131 D1
Blackdown Gr **4** OL8 ..66 E3
Blackfield La M7. ....81 C8
Blackfields M7 ....155 A4
Blackford Ave BL0 .....44 F4
BLACKFORD BRIDGE ...44 F4
Blackford Rd M19. ......111 B7
Blackford Wlk M40.....160 A3
Blackfriar Ct M3. ....158 A3
Blackfriars Rd M3 ......158 B2
Blackfriars St M3 ....158 C2
Blackhill Cl **6** M13.....163 B3
Blackhorse Ave BL6....21 C2
Blackhorse Cl BL6 ......21 C3
Black Horse St
Blackrod BL6. ....21 C3
Bolton BL3. ....145 B2
Farnworth BL4. ....60 E7
Black La
Leigh WN7 ....76 D5
Ramsbottom BL0 ......12 B7
BLACK LANE 43 F6
Blackleach Ctry Pk* M28 60 D4
Blackleach Dr M28. .....60 D5
Blackledge Cl WN5 .....53 E5
Blackledge St M3 ......146 C4
BLACKLEY 64 E1
Blackley Cl **2** M9 ......45 A2
Blackley Forest Nature
  Reserve* M8. ....64 A4
Blackleyhurst Ave WN5..71 E5
Blackley New Rd M9, M25 64 D1
Blackley Park Rd M9 ....64 D1
Blackley St
Manchester M16 ....161 C1
Middleton M24. ....64 B7
Blacklock St M8. ....158 C4
BLACKMOOR. 77 B5
Blackmoor Ave M29. ....77 B5
Black Moss Cl M28. .....43 D3
Black Moss Rd WA14....118 F7
Blackpits Rd OL15. ......13 D1
Blackpool St **10** M11...83 C2
Blackrock OL5. ....86 C6
Blackrock St M11. ......160 C1
BLACKROD 21 D2
Blackrod Brow BL6 .....21 B4
Blackrod By-Pass BL6 ..21 D2
Blackrod Church Sch BL6..21 C2
Blackrod Dr BL1. ....26 F1
Blackrod Ind Est BL6....38 E7

Blackrod Prim Sch BL6...38 E8
Blackrod Sta BL6. ....21 E2
Blacksail Wlk **3** OL1 ...49 A1
Blackshaw Clough SK13..104 E3
Blackshaw Ho BL3 ......144 C2
Blackshaw La
Alderley Edge SK9 .....136 F1
Bolton BL3. ....144 C2
Royton OL2 ....49 A4
Blackshaw Lane Prim Sch
  OL2 ....49 A4
Blackshaw Prim Sch BL2..43 A6
Blackshaw Rd SK13 .....104 C2
Blackshaw Row **2** BL3..144 C1
Blacksmith La OL11 ....30 B3
Blacksmiths Fold M46...58 E3
Blackstock St M13 .....98 C4
Blackstone Ave OL16....31 C8
Blackstone Edge Old Rd
  OL15 ....16 E6
Blackstone Edge Rd HX7 ..7 F5
Blackstone Ho SK2 .....124 D5
Blackstone Wlk M9 .....157 A2
Blackthorn Ave
Manchester M19 ....111 A7
Wigan WN6 ....36 F3
Blackthorn Cl OL12 .....14 E2
Blackthorne Dr M33.....107 D2
Blackthorne Rd SK14....113 E7
Blackthorn Mews OL12..14 E2
Blackthorn Rd OL8. .....84 C8
Blackthorn Wlk **3** M31..105 E2
Blackwell Wlk **1** M4 ...159 C2
Blackwin St M12. ....165 A2
Blackwood Ct OL13 .....3 C8
Blackwood Dr M23. .....120 D8
Blackwood Rd OL13. ....3 B7
Blackwood St BL3. .....42 A4
Bladen Cl SK8 ....123 A4
Blainscough Rd PR7 ....19 E8
Blair Ave
Hindley WN2 ....57 B3
Urmston M41. ....94 B3
Walkden M38. ....60 B4
Blair Cl
Hazel Grove SK7. ......133 C8
Sale M33 ....107 C1
Shaw OL2. ....149 B3
Blairhall Ave M40. ......43 A2
Blair La BL2 ....25 D1
Blairmore Dr BL3. ......43 A4
Blair Rd M16 ....97 E1
Blair St
2 Bolton BL7. ....25 A8
Kearsley BL4. ....61 B6
Rochdale OL12. ....14 D1
Blake Ave M46. ....58 B4
Blakeborough Ho **7** M46..58 D3
Blake Cl WN3. ....150 A1
Blakedown Wlk M12....164 B1
Blake Dr SK2 ....133 C8
Blakefield Dr M28. ......60 C1
Blake Gdns BL1. ....143 A2
Blakelock St OL2 ....149 E3
Blakemere Ave M33.....108 C3
Blakemore Pk **1** M46...58 B4
Blakemore Wlk M12 ....160 B1
Blake St
Bolton, Bromley Cross
  BL7. ....25 A7
Bolton, Halliwell BL1....143 A2
Rochdale OL16. ....31 A8
Blakeswell Cl M41 ......94 D3
Blakeswood WA14 .....119 B5
Blakey Cl BL3. ....40 F4
Blakey St M12 ....99 A4
Blanche St M13 ....165 B3
Blanche St OL12 ....15 A2
Blanche Wlk **10** OL1 ...67 A8
Bland Cl M35 ....42 E3
Blandford Ave M28. ....79 A8
Blandford Cl
Bury BL8 ....27 D5
Tyldesley M29. ....59 A1
Blandford Ct
Ashton-u-L OL6 ....166 A3
Stalybridge SK15. ......86 A2
Blandford Dr **1** M40 ...65 C1
Blandford Ho **2** SK15..86 A2
Blandford Rd
Eccles M30 ....79 A3
Salford M6. ....81 B4
Stockport SK4 ....168 C3
Blandford Rise BL6 .....22 F1
Blandford St
Ashton-u-L OL6 ....166 A3
Stalybridge SK15. ......86 A2
Bland Rd M25 ....63 C1
Bland St M16 ....97 E4
Blanefield Cl M21. ......109 E7
Blantyre Ave M28. .....60 E2
Blantyre Ho **4** M27....162 A3
Blantyre Rd M27 ....80 B6
Blantyre St
Eccles M30 ....79 A3
Hindley WN2 ....56 D5
Manchester M15 ....162 A3
Swinton M27 ....61 D1
Blanwood Dr M8. ......156 B3
Blaven Cl SK3. ....170 C1
Blaydon Cl M40 ....38 D5
Blazemoss Bank SK2....124 D5
Bleach St WN2. ....56 C4
Bleackley St BL8. ......27 C4

Bleadale Cl SK9. ....131 D1
Bleak Hey Nook La OL3..51 C8
Bleak Hey Rd M22 ......121 F2
Bleakholt Rd BL0 ......1 F1
Bleakledge Gr WN2 ....56 F7
Bleakley St **1** M45.....44 E1
Bleaklow Cl WN3 ....55 B2
Bleaklow Wlk **24** SK13..171 B1
Bleak St BL2. ....25 B2
Bleasby St OL4. ....67 C7
Bleasdale Cl
Horwich BL6. ....39 F8
Whitefield M45 ....45 A3
Bleasdale Rd
Bolton BL1. ....23 F2
Newton-le-W WA12.....89 C4
Wythenshawe M22 .....121 A2
Bleasdale St OL2. ......48 E5
Bleasedale Rd WN2 ....57 A5
Bleasefell Chase M28...78 A5
Bleatarn Rd SK1 ....124 B7
Bledlow Cl M30. ....79 E3
Blencarn Wlk M9. ......157 A2
Blendworth Cl M8 .....155 C3
Blenheim Cl
Altrincham WA14. ......119 D2
4 Glossop SK13. ......104 A5
Heywood OL10. ....29 E2
Poynton SK12. ....133 F4
Whitefield M45 ....45 A5
Wilmslow SK9 ....137 D7
Blenheim Dr WN7. ......76 E7
Blenheim Rd
Ashton-in-M WN4 ......73 D2
Bolton BL2. ....42 E6
Cheadle SK8 ....123 B2
Wigan WN5 ....54 C8
Blenheim St
6 Oldham OL4 ....49 D1
8 Rochdale OL12. ....14 C1
Tyldesley M29. ....76 F8
Blenheim Ave OL1 .....49 D3
Blenmar Cl M26 ....44 C5
Bleriot St BL3. ....147 A3
Blessed Thomas Holford RC
  Sch WA15 ....119 E4
Bletchley Rd SK4 ....110 E1
Blethyn St BL3. ....146 B2
Blewberry Cl WN7 .....75 F7
Bligh Rd **5** BL5. ....39 E1
Blinco Rd M41. ....95 F1
Blind La M12 ....164 A3
Blindsill Rd BL4. ....60 B7
Bliss worth Cl M4 ....160 A1
Blisworth Ave M30 .....95 E8
Blisworth Cl M4 ....160 A1
Blithfield Wlk M34 .....100 E2
Block La OL9 ....152 B1
Blocksage St SK16 .....101 D7
Blodwell St M5, M6......154 C2
Blofield Ct BL4 ....60 D7
Blomley St OL11 ....30 C2
Bloomfield Cl SK8 ......131 E7
Bloomfield Dr
Bury BL9 ....45 B3
Worsley M28 ....78 A7
Bloomfield Rd BL4. .....60 D6
Bloomfield St BL1. .....143 B3
Bloomsbury Gr WA15...120 A6
Bloomsbury La WA15...120 A6
Bloom St
Manchester M1 ....163 A4
Oldham OL9 ....153 B2
Ramsbottom BL0 ......11 A4
Salford M3. ....158 B2
Stockport SK3 ....170 A4
Blossom Pl **1** OL16 ...139 C4
Blossom Rd M31. ....105 E2
Blossoms Hey SK8 .....122 A3
Blossoms Hey Wlk SK8..122 E1
Blossoms La SK7. ......132 B2
Blossoms St SK2 ....170 C3
Blossom St
Manchester M4 ....159 B2
Salford M3. ....158 B2
11 Tyldesley M29. ....59 A1
Blucher St
Ashton-u-L OL6 ....85 A6
Manchester M12 ....164 B2
Salford M5. ....81 C1
Blueball La M5, M25.....46 A1
Bluebell Ave BB4 ......1 A8
Blue Bell Ave
Manchester M40 ....65 C3
Wigan WN6 ....36 F4
Bluebell Cl OL14 ....101 F5
Bluebell Dr OL11. ......30 B3
Bluebell Gr SK8. ....122 D4
Bluebell Way SK9. .....131 C1
Blueberry Ave M40. ....65 C3
Blueberry Bsns Pk OL16..31 D7
Blueberry Dr OL2 ......49 D7
Blueberry Rd WA15.....119 D2
Blue Chip Bsns Pk WA14 119 C2
Blue Coat CE Sch The
  OL1 ....153 C3
Bluefields OL2. ....49 D8
Blue Moon Way M14....98 A2
Blue Ribbon Wlk M27 ..62 A1
Bluestone Dr SK4 ......110 E3
Bluestone Rd
Manchester M40 ....83 A8
Reddish M34 ....100 A2
Blundell Cl BL9 ....45 B3

Blundell La BL6. ....21 A2
Blundells Ct WN3 ......54 D4
Blundells Mews WN3....54 D4
Blundell St BL1. ....145 B3
Blundering La SK15 ....102 D6
Blunn St OL8 ....66 F4
Blyborough Cl M6 ......154 B4
Blyth Ave
Littleborough OL15 ....15 F3
Wythenshawe M23 .....109 C2
Blythe Ave BL7 ....132 C6
Blyton La M7 ....81 A8
Blyton St M15 ....163 B1
Blyton Way M34 ....112 B7
Bnos Yisroel Schs M7...155 B4
Boad St M1. ....163 B4
Boardale Dr M24. ......46 E1
Boardman Cl
Bolton BL1. ....143 B2
Reddish SK5. ....169 C4
Boardman Fold Cl M24..65 A5
Boardman Fold Rd M24..65 A5
Boardman La M24 .....64 C8
Boardman M8 ....63 F2
Boardman St
Blackrod BL6. ....21 D2
Bolton BL1. ....143 B2
Eccles M30 ....79 E1
Hyde SK14. ....167 A2
Board St
Ashton-u-L OL6 ....85 D4
Bolton BL3. ....145 A2
Boarfold La SK13, SK14..114 E5
Boar Green Cl M40. ....83 C7
Boarsgreave La BB4.....2 F6
Boarshaw Clough M24..47 B2
Boarshaw Clough Way
  M24 ....47 B2
Boarshaw Cres M24 ....47 C3
Boarshaw La M24 ......47 D3
Boarshaw Prim Sch M24..47 B3
Boarshaw Rd M24. .....47 B2
BOAR'S HEAD. 37 A6
Boars Head Ave WN6....37 A7
Boarshurst Bsns Pk OL3..69 B6
Boarslurst La OL3 ......69 C5
Boat La
Diggle OL3. ....51 E5
Irlam M44 ....94 B2
Wythenshawe M22 .....109 E1
Boat Lane Ct M22 ......109 E1
Boatmans Row M29 ....77 C4
Boatmans The M15 .....162 B3
Boatmans Wlk OL7. ....166 A1
Boatyard The **1** M32 ..96 E2
Bobbin Wlk **8** OL1.....67 A6
Bob Massey Cl M11 ....83 C1
Bob's La M44 ....105 D4
Boddens Hill Rd SK4 ...168 A1
Bodden St WA3 ....73 A1
Boddington Rd M30. ...79 A1
Bodiam Rd BL8 ....27 B1
Bodley St M11 ....83 C2
Bodmin Cl OL2. ....49 A3
Bodmin Cres SK5. ......112 B5
Bodmin Dr
Bramhall SK7. ....132 E7
Platt Bridge WN2. .....56 A1
Bodmin Rd
Sale M33 ....107 D5
Tyldesley M29. ....77 C8
Bodmin Wlk **3** M23 ...121 A5
Bodney Wlk M9 ....64 B3
Bogburn La PR7 ....19 D6
Boggard St WN7 ....75 F5
Boggart Hole Clough Nature
  Reserve* M40. ....64 F2
Bogguard Rd SK6. ......127 A4
Bognor Rd SK3. ....123 E4
BOLD. 27 A4
Bolam Cl M23 ....108 F1
Boland Dr M14. ....99 A2
Bolbury Cres M27. ......80 D8
Bolderod Pl **4** OL1 ....28 A4
Bolderstone Pl SK2 ....124 E4
Bolderwood Dr WN2....56 D4
Bold St
Altrincham WA14. ......119 D3
Bolton BL3. ....145 C2
Bury BL9 ....141 A3
Leigh WN7 ....75 F5
Manchester, Moss Side M16 97 D3
Manchester, Old Trafford
  M15. ....162 B1
Swinton M27 ....61 F2
Wigan WN5 ....54 D5
Bolesworth Cl M21. ....108 F3
Boleyn Ct OL10 ....29 C1
BOLHOLT. 27 A4
Bolholt Ind Est **12** BL8..27 B4
Bolholt Terr BL8. ....27 B4
Bolivia St M5. ....80 C2
Bollwyn Wood Ct SK9...131 B1
Bollin Ave WA14 ....119 B1
Bollin Cl
Culcheth WA3 ....92 A2
Kearsley BL4. ....61 B6
Lymm WA13 ....117 A4
Bollin Ct
Altrincham WA14. ......119 B1
8 Manchester M15 ...162 A2
Wilmslow SK9 ....137 C6
Bollin Dr
Altrincham WA14. ......119 E8

Bollin Dr continued
Lymm WA13. . . . . .117 A4
Sale M33 . . . . .108 B2
Bollings Yd BL1. . . . . . . .145 C2
Bollington Rd
Manchester M40 . . . . . . .160 A2
Reddish SK4. . . . . .111 D5
Bollington St OL7 . . . . . .166 A1
Bollin Hill SK9 . . . . .137 B8
Bollin Ho 8 M7. . . . . . . .81 C5
Bollin Prim Sch WA14. . . .119 B1
Bollin Sq WA14 . . . . .119 B1
Bollinway WA15 . . . . . . .129 A8
Bollin Way M45. . . . . . . .45 C2
Bollin Wlk
Reddish SK5. . . . . .169 C4
Whitefield M45 . . . . .45 C2
Wilmslow SK9 . . . . .137 C7
Bollinwood Chase SK9 . . .137 C7
Bolney St WN2. . . . . .38 A3
Bolney Wlk M40. . . . . . . .160 D4
Bolshaw Farm La SK8. . . .131 C6
Bolshaw Prim Sch SK8. . . .131 B7
Bolshaw Rd SK8 . . . . .131 C6
Bolt Mdw OL3 . . . . .169 A3
BOLTON 145 B4
Bolton 6th Form Coll
  (Farnworth Campus) **10**
  BL4 . . . . .60 D8
Bolton 6th Form Coll (Town
  Ctr Campus) BL3 . . . . .145 B2
Bolton Cl
  Cheadle SK8 . . . . .132 B6
  Manchester M19 . . . . . . .110 D2
Bolton Cl
  Golborne WA3 . . . . .91 B8
  Poynton SK12. . . . . .133 D4
  Prestwich M25. . . . . .62 F2
Bolton Coll (Farnworth
  Campus) BL3 . . . . . . .145 B2
Bolton Coll (Horwich
  Campus) BL6. . . . . . . .22 D2
Bolton Coll (Manchester
  Campus) BL2 . . . . .148 B2
Bolton Excel L Ctr BL2 . . .148 A2
Bolton Gate Ret Pk BL1 . .145 C4
Bolton House Rd WN2. . . .74 F8
Bolton Mus, Art Gal &
  Aquarium ✶ BL1 . . . . . .145 C3
Bolton Muslim Girls Sch
  BL3 . . . . .147 A4
Bolton Old Rd M46. . . . . . .58 E3
Bolton Parish Church Sch
  BL2 . . . . .148 B3
Bolton Rd
  Adlington BL6, PR6. . . . . .21 D6
  Ashton-in-M WN2, WN4. . .73 D5
  Aspull WN2 . . . . .38 D4
  Atherton M46. . . . . .58 E4
  Bolton, Bradshaw BL2 . . . .25 C5
  Bolton, Hunger Hill BL3. . .40 D2
  Bury BL8, BL9 . . . . .27 C1
  Edgworth BL7 . . . . .9 D5
  Farnworth BL4. . . . . .42 D2
  Kearsley BL4 . . . . .60 F7
  Pendlebury M27 . . . . .80 C7
  Radcliffe M26 . . . . .43 E3
  Ramsbottom BL8 . . . . . . .10 D2
  Rochdale OL11 . . . . .30 B4
  Salford M6. . . . . .80 E5
  Swinton M27 . . . . .62 A1
  Walkden M28 . . . . .60 D4
  Westhoughton BL5 . . . . . .39 F1
Bolton Road N BL5 . . . . . .39 F1
Bolton Road N BL0 . . . . . .1 D2
Bolton Road W BL0 . . . . . .11 A4
Bolton Sch
  Bolton BL1 . . . . .144 B3
  Bolton BL1 . . . . .144 C3
Bolton Sh Pk BL3 . . . . . . .145 B2
Bolton Sq WN1 . . . . .37 E1
Bolton St
  Bury BL9 . . . . .140 B2
  Downall Green WN4 . . . . . .72 D5
  Manchester M3 . . . . .158 B1
  Oldham OL4 . . . . .67 B6
  Radcliffe M26 . . . . .43 F3
  Ramsbottom BL0 . . . . . . .138 B2
  Rochdale OL5. . . . . .111 E7
  Swinton M27 . . . . .62 A1
Bolton Sta BL2. . . . . .145 C2
Bolton Steam Mus ✶ BL1. .144 B4
Boltons Yd OL3 . . . . .69 B8
Bolton Tech Exchange
  BL1. . . . . .145 A3
Bombay Ho 5 M1 . . . . . . .163 A4
Bombay Rd
  Stockport SK3 . . . . .123 C7
  Wigan WN5 . . . . .36 C1
Bombay St
  5 Ashton-u-L OL6. . . . . .85 D4
  Manchester M1. . . . . .163 A4
Bonar Cl 5 SK3. . . . . . . .123 C8
Bonar Rd SK3 . . . . .123 C8
Boncarn Dr M23 . . . . .121 A4
Bonchurch Wlk M18 . . . . .165 B2
Bond's La PR7 . . . . .20 F7
Bond St
  Bury BL8 . . . . .141 A2
  Denton M34. . . . . .100 F3
  Edenfield BL0. . . . . .1 E2
  Leigh WN7 . . . . .75 F5
  Manchester M12. . . . . . . .163 C4
  Rochdale OL12. . . . . .15 A2

Bond St continued
  Stalybridge SK15. . . . . . . .86 A3
  Tyldesley M29. . . . . .58 F1
Bond Street Ind Est M12 .163 C4
Bongs Rd SK2 . . . . .124 F6
Bonhill Wlk M11. . . . . . . .83 B2
Bonington Rise SK6. . . . . .126 B8
Bonis Cres SK2. . . . . .124 C4
Bonny Brow St M24 . . . . . .64 B7
Bonnyfields SK6 . . . . .113 B2
Bonnywell Rd WN7. . . . . . .75 F3
Bonsall Bank 27 SK13 . . .171 B2
Bonsall Cl 20 SK3 . . . . . .171 B2
Bonsall Fold 20 SK13 . . . .171 B2
Bonsall St M15 . . . . .162 C2
Bonscale Cres M24 . . . . . .46 E3
Bonville Chase WA14. . . . .119 A4
Bonville Rd WA14 . . . . . . .119 A4
Boodle St OL6. . . . . .166 B4
Bookham Wlk 16 M9 . . . . .157 B4
Bond St
  Manchester M4 . . . . .160 A1
  Salford M3. . . . . .158 B2
Boonfields BL7 . . . . .25 A8
Booth Ave M14 . . . . .110 D7
Booth Bridge Cl M24. . . . .64 C7
Boothby Rd M27 . . . . .61 E1
Boothby St SK2. . . . . .124 C4
Booth Cl
  Bury BL8 . . . . .27 A5
  4 Stalybridge SK15. . . . .85 F1
Booth Clibborn Ct M7. . . .155 A4
Boothcote M34 . . . . .100 D6
Boothdale Dr M34 . . . . . .100 A7
Booth Dr M41. . . . . .94 F5
Boothfield
  8 Bury BL8 . . . . .27 C3
  Eccles M30 . . . . .79 A3
Boothfield Ave M22 . . . . .121 D6
Boothfield Dr M22 . . . . . .121 D6
Boothfield Rd M22 . . . . . .121 D6
Booth Hall Dr BL8. . . . . . .26 F5
Booth Hall La OL4 . . . . . . .48 E1
Booth Hill La OL1 . . . . .48 E1
Booth House Trad Est
  OL9 . . . . .152 C2
Boothman Ct M30. . . . . . .79 F3
Booth Rd
  Altrincham WA14. . . . . . .119 C4
  Bacup OL13 . . . . .3 B8
  Droylsden M43. . . . . .100 A7
  Handforth SK9 . . . . .131 A1
  Little Lever BL3 . . . . .43 B2
  Manchester M16. . . . . . . .97 C3
  Sale M33 . . . . .108 B6
Boothroyden Cl M24. . . . .64 C7
Boothroyden Rd
  Manchester M24, M9. . . . .64 C6
  Middleton M24. . . . . .64 C6
Boothroyden Terr M9 . . . . .64 C6
Boothsbank Ave M28. . . . .78 B6
Booth's Brow Rd WN4 . . . .72 D6
Booth's Hall 1 SK13. . . . .104 D1
Booth's Hall M28. . . . . . . .78 B5
Booth's Hall Gr 2 M28. . . .78 B6
Boothshall Paddock M28 . .78 B5
Booth's Hall Rd M28 . . . . .78 B6
Boothshall Way M28 . . . . .78 A5
Booth's Hall Way M28 . . . .78 B6
Booth St
  Ashton-u-L OL6. . . . . . . .166 B2
  Bolton BL1 . . . . .142 C3
  Bury BL8 . . . . .26 F5
  Denton M34. . . . . .100 F5
  Hollingworth SK14. . . . . .103 C5
  Hyde SK14 . . . . .167 B1
  Manchester M3 . . . . .158 C2
  Middleton M24. . . . . .65 D6
  Oldham, Bank Top OL9 . . .153 B2
  2 Oldham, Lees OL4 . . . .67 E6
  Rawtenstall BB4 . . . . .2 B7
  Stalybridge SK15. . . . . . .101 F8
  Stockport SK3 . . . . .170 E8
BOOTHSTOWN 78 A5
Boothstown Dr M28. . . . . .78 A5
Boothstown Meth Prim Sch
  4 M28 . . . . .77 F6
Booth Street E M13 . . . . .163 B2
Boothway 8 M30. . . . . . . .79 F2
Booth Way BL8 . . . . .26 F5
Boot La BL1 . . . . .23 E1
Bootle St M2 . . . . .162 C4
Bor Ave WN3 . . . . .55 B4
Bordale Ave M9. . . . . . . .157 C3
Bordan St M11. . . . . .164 C4
Borough St 5 SK15 . . . . . .86 A1
Borrans 5 M28 . . . . .77 F5
Borron Ct WA12 . . . . .89 B4
Borron Rd WA12 . . . . .89 B5

Borron Rd Ind Est WA12. . .89 C4
Borron St SK1 . . . . .112 A2
Borrowdale Ave
  Bolton BL1 . . . . .144 A4
  Gatley SK8. . . . . .122 B4
Borrowdale Cl OL2 . . . . . . .48 D6
Borrowdale Cres
  Ashton-u-L OL7 . . . . .84 F4
  Manchester M20 . . . . . . .109 E4
Borrowdale Dr
  Rochdale OL11. . . . . .30 C4
  Whitefield BL9 . . . . .45 A3
Borrowdale Rd
  Middleton M24. . . . . .46 E2
  Stockport SK2 . . . . .124 B6
  Wigan WN5 . . . . .54 B7
Borrowdale Terr SK15. . . . .86 A4
Borsdane Ave WN2 . . . . . .56 F5
Borsdane Wood Nature
  Reserve ✶ WN2 . . . . . . .38 F1
Borsden St M27. . . . . .61 D2
Borth Ave SK2 . . . . .124 C7
Borth Wlk 3 M23 . . . . . .120 F6
Borwell St M18 . . . . .99 D5
Boscobel Rd BL3. . . . . . . .42 B2
Boscombe Ave M30. . . . . . .95 C8
Boscombe Dr SK7 . . . . . . .124 C1
Boscombe Pl WN2 . . . . . . .56 E4
Boscombe St
  Manchester M14 . . . . .98 B2
  Reddish SK5. . . . . .99 F2
Boscow Rd BL3 . . . . .43 A2
Bosden Ave SK7 . . . . .124 F3
Bosden Cl
  Handforth SK9 . . . . .131 D5
  Stockport SK1. . . . . .170 C4
Bosden Fold SK1 . . . . . . .170 C4
Bosden Fold Rd SK7 . . . . .124 E3
Bosden Hall Rd SK7 . . . . .124 E3
Bosdin Road E M41. . . . . . .94 E1
Bosdin Road W M41. . . . . .94 E1
Boslam Wlk 8 M4 . . . . . . .159 C2
Bosley Ave M20. . . . . .110 A8
Bosley Cl SK9. . . . . .131 D2
Bosley Dr SK12 . . . . .134 A3
Bosley Rd SK3 . . . . .123 A8
Bossall Ave M9 . . . . .64 E4
Bossington Cl SK2 . . . . . .124 C8
Bostock Rd SK14 . . . . . . .115 A8
Bostock Wlk M13 . . . . . . .163 B3
Boston Bank Ho SK14 . . . .167 B3
Boston Cl
  Bramhall SK7. . . . . .132 D7
  Culcheth WA3 . . . . .91 F4
  Failsworth M35 . . . . .83 F8
Boston Ct
  Hyde SK14 . . . . .167 B3
  Salford M50. . . . . .96 E8
Boston Gr WN7 . . . . .75 E8
Boston St
  15 Bolton BL1 . . . . .143 B2
  Hyde SK14 . . . . .167 B2
  Manchester M15 . . . . . . .162 C1
  Oldham OL8 . . . . .66 F4
Boston Wlk 8 M34 . . . . . .101 A1
Boswell Ave M34. . . . . . . .84 D1
Boswell Pl WN3. . . . . .54 F4
Boswell Way M24. . . . . . . .47 E4
Bosworth Cl M45 . . . . .63 C8
Bosworth Sq OL11 . . . . . . .30 C4
Bosworth St
  Horwich BL6 . . . . .22 B4
  Manchester M11. . . . . . . .165 A4
  Rochdale OL11. . . . . .30 D4
Botanical Ave M16 . . . . . .161 A1
Botany Cl
  Heywood OL10. . . . . .29 B2
  Wigan WN2 . . . . .38 B2
Botany La OL6 . . . . .166 C3
Botany Rd
  Eccles M30 . . . . .79 A4
  Romiley SK6. . . . . .113 A6
Botesworth Cl WN2 . . . . . .57 A4
Botesworth Gn OL16 . . . . .32 A5
Botha Cl 4 M11 . . . . .99 D7
Botham Cl M15 . . . . .162 C1
Bothwell Rd M40 . . . . . . .159 C3
Bottesford Ave M20 . . . . .109 F5
Bottomfield Cl OL11 . . . . . .49 A1
BOTTOMLEY 6 C7
Bottomley Rd OL14 . . . . . . .6 C6
Bottomley Side M9 . . . . . .64 C2
BOTTOM O' TH' BROW 29 B3
Bottom o' th' Knotts Brow
  BL7. . . . . .9 E3
BOTTOM O' TH' MOOR 23 A2
Bottom o' th Moor BL2. . . .25 D2
Bottom o' th' Moor
  Horwich BL6 . . . . .23 A3
  Oldham OL1, OL4 . . . . . . .67 B7
BOTTOMS 86 D8
Bottoms Fold OL5. . . . . . . .86 D8
Bottom St SK14 . . . . .167 C3
Bougainvillea Gdns M12. . .99 A4
Boughey St WN7. . . . . .75 E5
Boulden Dr BL8. . . . . .27 C5
Boulder Dr M23. . . . . .121 A2
Boulderstone Rd SK15 . . . .86 A4
Boulevard The
  Hazel Grove SK7 . . . . . . .124 E2
  Hollingworth SK14. . . . . .171 A4
  Hyde SK14 . . . . .103 D5
  Manchester M20 . . . . . . .109 F6
Bouley Wlk M12 . . . . .165 A2
Boulton Ho 8 M1. . . . . . .163 A4
Boundary Cl
  Mossley OL5 . . . . .86 C6
  Romiley SK6. . . . . .113 C5

Boundary Cotts SK15. . . . .86 E7
Boundary Ct SK8. . . . . . . .122 C5
Boundary Ct SK8. . . . . . . .111 A7
Boundary Ct M28 . . . . .78 B8
Boundary Dr BL2. . . . . . . .43 A5
Boundary Edge BL0 . . . . . . .1 E3
Boundary Gdns
  Bolton BL1 . . . . .143 B2
  Oldham OL1. . . . . .48 E1
Boundary Gn M34 . . . . . . .100 E4
Boundary Gn M33 . . . . . . .108 F2
Boundary Ind Est BL2. . . . .43 A7
Boundary La
  Manchester M15 . . . . . . .163 A2
  Shevington Moor WN6. . . .19 A3
Boundary Park Rd OL1 . . . .48 C1
Boundary Pk (Oldham
  Athletic AFC) OL1. . . . . .48 D2
Boundary Rd
  Cheadle SK8 . . . . .123 A6
  Irlam M44. . . . . .94 C3
  Swinton M27 . . . . .61 F1
Boundary St
  Bolton BL1 . . . . .143 A2
  Leigh WN7 . . . . .76 B4
  Littleborough OL15 . . . . . .16 B6
  Manchester M12 . . . . . . .165 A2
  Rochdale OL11. . . . . .139 C1
  Tyldesley M29. . . . . .59 A1
  Wigan WN3 . . . . .151 A3
Boundary Street E M1,
  M13 . . . . .163 A3
Boundary Street W M15 . .163 A2
Boundary Terr SK9. . . . . .130 F6
Boundary The M27 . . . . . . .61 E4
Boundary Trad Pk M44 . . . .94 C3
Boundary St M40 . . . . . . .160 A3
Bourdon St M40 . . . . .160 A3
Bournbrook Ave M38. . . . . .60 A6
Bourne Ave
  Golborne WA3 . . . . .90 D8
  Swinton M27 . . . . .79 F7
Bourne Dr M40. . . . . .65 B1
Bourne Ho 1 M6. . . . . . . .154 C2
Bournelea Ave M19 . . . . . .110 F6
Bourne Rd OL2 . . . . .149 A4
Bourne St
  Oldham OL9. . . . . .66 B2
  Stockport SK4 . . . . .169 D2
  Wilmslow SK9 . . . . .136 F6
Bourneville Dr BL8. . . . . . .27 A2
Bourne Wlk 9 BL1. . . . . . .143 C1
Bournville Ave SK4 . . . . . .169 B4
Bourton Cl BL8 . . . . .27 B3
Bourton Ct M29. . . . . .59 D1
Bourton Dr M18 . . . . .99 B4
Bowden Cl
  Culcheth WA3 . . . . .91 F4
  Hattersley SK14. . . . . . . .102 E1
  Leigh WN7 . . . . .76 C2
  Trub OL11. . . . . .47 D8
Bowden St M16. . . . . .97 A4
Bowden House La SK9. . . .137 F8
Bowden La SK6 . . . . .125 E7
Bowden Rd
  Glossop SK13. . . . . .104 C3
  4 Pendlebury M27 . . . . . .80 A7
Bowden St
  Denton M34. . . . . .100 E3
  Hazel Grove SK7 . . . . . . .124 E3
BOWDON. 119 B2
Bowdon Ave M14 . . . . .97 F1
Bowdon CE Prim Sch
  WA14 . . . . .119 C1
Bowdon Ho 2 SK3 . . . . . .170 B4
Bowdon Prep Sch for Girls
  1 WA14. . . . . .119 C2
Bowdon Rd WA14 . . . . . . .119 C3
Bowdon Rise WA14 . . . . . .119 D2
Bowdon St SK3 . . . . .170 B4
Bowen Cl SK7 . . . . .132 F5
Bowen St BL1. . . . . .142 B1
Bower Ave
  Hazel Grove SK7 . . . . . . .124 D1
  Rochdale OL12. . . . . .15 D4
  Stockport SK4 . . . . .168 C2
Bower Ct SK14. . . . . .102 A5
Bower Cup Fold SK15. . . . .86 E4
Bowerfield Ave SK7 . . . . .133 D8
Bowerfield Cres SK7 . . . . .133 E8
Bower Fold SK15. . . . . . . .102 C8
Bowerfold La SK4 . . . . . . .169 A2
Bower Gdns SK15. . . . . . .102 D8
Bower Gr SK15. . . . . .86 C2
Bower Rd WA15. . . . . .119 F1
Bowers Ave M41. . . . . .95 B3
Bowers St M14 . . . . .110 E7
Bower St
  Bury BL9 . . . . .141 C3
  Failsworth M40 . . . . .83 A5
  Oldham OL1. . . . . .67 B8
  Reddish SK5. . . . . .99 F2
  Salford M7 . . . . .155 C3
Bower Terr M43 . . . . .84 C3
Bowery Ave SK8 . . . . .131 B6
Bowes Cl BL8 . . . . .27 B5
Bowes St M14 . . . . .97 F3
Bowfell Cl SK6 . . . . .134 E8
Bowfell Gr M9 . . . . .64 B4
Bowfell Rd M41. . . . . .95 B2
Bowfield Wlk 18 M40. . . . .83 C5
Bowgreave Ave BL2. . . . . .42 F7
BOWGREEN 119 B1
Bow Green Mews WA14 . . .119 B2
Bow Green Rd WA14. . . . .119 A1
Bowgreen Wlk 14 M15 . . .162 A2
Bowker Ave M34 . . . . .113 B8

Bowker Bank Ave M8 . . . . .63 F2
Bowker Cl OL11. . . . . .13 E1
Bowker Ct M7. . . . . .155 A2
Bowkers Row 12 BL1 . . . .145 C3
Bowker St
  Haslingden BL0 . . . . .1 C5
  Hyde SK14 . . . . .167 B3
  Radcliffe M26 . . . . .44 A3
  Salford M7 . . . . .155 A2
  Walkden M28 . . . . .60 B3
Bowker Vale Gdns M9 . . . . .63 F3
Bowker Vale Metro Sta
  M8 . . . . .63 F3
Bowker Vale Prim Sch
  M8 . . . . .63 F4
Bow La
  Altrincham WA14 . . . . . . .128 B8
  Heywood OL10. . . . . .29 D2
  Manchester M2. . . . . .158 C1
Bowlacre Rd SK14 . . . . . .113 D7
Bowland Ave
  Ashton-in-M WN3 . . . . . . .73 B4
  Golborne WA3 . . . . .74 C1
  Reddish M18 . . . . .100 A4
Bowland Cl
  Ashton-u-L OL6. . . . . .85 C7
  Bury BL8 . . . . .26 F3
  Shaw OL2. . . . . .48 E7
  Stockport SK2 . . . . .124 E5
Bowland Ct M33 . . . . .108 B4
Bowland Dr BL1. . . . . .23 E2
Bowland Gr OL16 . . . . .31 F4
Bowland Rd
  Glossop SK13. . . . . .116 A8
  Reddish M34 . . . . .100 B3
  Romiley SK6. . . . . .113 B5
  Wythenshawe M23 . . . . . .121 A6
BOWLEE 46 B1
Bowlee Cl BL9 . . . . .45 A2
Bowlee Com Sch M24. . . . .46 D2
Bowler St
  Manchester M19 . . . . . . .111 B8
  Shaw OL2. . . . . .149 B3
Bowlers Wlk OL12. . . . . . . .14 F2
Bowley Ave M22 . . . . .121 A2
Bowling Ct BL1 . . . . .24 E5
Bowling Gn The
  Edenfield BL0. . . . . .1 D3
  Manchester M32 . . . . .96 C3
Bowling Green Cl OL9 . . . .66 A4
Bowling Green Ct M16 . . . .97 D4
Bowling Green Row M46 . . .58 B2
Bowling Green St
  Heywood OL10. . . . . .29 D2
  Hyde SK14 . . . . .167 A2
Bowling Green Way OL11 . .29 F7
Bowling Rd M18 . . . . .99 C5
Bowling St OL9 . . . . .66 B2
Bowlings The WN6 . . . . . . .37 A2
Bowling Wood WN2. . . . . . .57 A3
Bowman Cres OL6 . . . . . . .85 D3
Bowmeadow Grange 2
  M12 . . . . .98 F4
Bowmead Wlk 8 M8. . . . .155 F2
Bowmont Cl SK8. . . . . . . .123 A4
Bowness Ave
  Cheadle SK8 . . . . .123 B1
  Irlam M44. . . . . .105 D4
  Reddish SK4. . . . . .111 E6
  Rochdale OL12. . . . . .14 C1
Bowness Ct 5 M24 . . . . . .46 D2
Bowness Dr M33. . . . . . . .107 F5
Bowness Pl WN2 . . . . .56 B8
Bowness Prim Sch BL3. . . .42 F3
Bowness Rd
  Altrincham WA15. . . . . . .120 C5
  Ashton-u-L OL7 . . . . .84 F4
  Bolton BL3 . . . . .147 A4
  Little Lever BL3 . . . . .42 F4
  Middleton M24. . . . . .46 D1
Bowness St
  Droylsden M11. . . . . .99 F7
  Stretford M32. . . . . .96 C3
Bowness Wlk 7 OL2 . . . . .48 E4
Bow Rd WN7 . . . . .76 B3
Bowring St M7 . . . . .81 C5
Bowscale Cl 3 M13. . . . . . .98 F4
Bow St
  Ashton-u-L OL6. . . . . . . .166 B3
  Bolton BL1 . . . . .145 C2
  Dukinfield OL6, SK16 . . . .166 C2
  4 Manchester M2. . . . . .158 C1
  Oldham OL1. . . . . .153 C3
  Rochdale OL11. . . . . .30 D3
  Stockport SK3 . . . . .170 E4
Bowstone Hill Rd BL2, BL8 .26 B5
Bowtree Park Com Prim Sch
  M24. . . . . .46 D2
Bowyer Gdns BL3 . . . . . . .40 F3
Boxgrove Rd M33 . . . . . . .107 F5
Boxgrove Wlk 3 M8 . . . . .156 A2
Boxhill Dr M23. . . . . .109 A1
Box St
  Littleborough OL15 . . . . . .16 A5
  Ramsbottom BL0 . . . . . . .11 D6
Boxtree Ave M18. . . . . . . .99 D4
Box Wlk M31 . . . . .105 E3
Boyd Cl WN6 . . . . .19 F1
Boydell's Hos WN3 . . . . . . .75 B8
Boydell St M12 . . . . .165 A3
Boyd St M12 . . . . .165 A3
Boyd's Wlk SK16 . . . . .101 C7
Boyer St M16 . . . . .161 B1
Boyle St
  Bolton BL1 . . . . .142 A1
  Manchester M8 . . . . .156 B4
Boysnope Cres M30. . . . . . .94 C4
Boysnope Wharf M30 . . . . .94 D4

Boyswell Ho WN1........ 151 A4
Brabant Rd SK8........ 123 B2
Brabazon PI WN6........ 54 C8
Brabham Cl M21........ 109 B8
Brabham Mews 6 M27... 79 D7
Brabyns Ave SK6........ 113 D3
Brabyns Brow SK6...... 126 A7
Brabyns Prep Sch SK6.. 126 A7
Brabyns Rd SK14....... 113 E7
Bracadale Dr SK3...... 170 C1
Bracewell Cl M12...... 165 B1
Bracken Ave M28........ 60 E3
Bracken Cl
  Bolton BL1........... 24 D6
  Droylsden M43........ 84 D2
  Heywood OL10......... 46 D8
  Hollingworth SK14.... 103 D6
  Marple SK6.......... 126 C7
  Oldham OL4.......... 67 C5
  Sale M33............ 107 C5
Bracken Dr M23........ 121 B5
Brackenfield Way WA15. 120 D8
Bracken Gr BB4......... 1 A8
Bracken Hill Terr 14
  M34................ 113 A7
Brackenhurst Ave OL5.. 68 C1
Bracken Lea BL5....... 57 F5
Brackenlea Dr M9...... 64 C2
Bracken Lea Fold 3 OL12 14 B2
Brackenlea PI SK3..... 170 A1
Bracken Rd
  Atherton M46........ 58 D2
  Leigh WN7........... 75 B5
Brackenside SK5...... 112 A8
Bracken Trade Pk M44.. 44 E5
Bracken Way SK13..... 116 F7
Brackenwood Cl OL2... 48 C2
Brackenwood Dr SK8... 122 E4
Brackenwood Mews SK9 137 E8
Brackley Ave
  Irlam M44........... 105 D6
  Manchester M15...... 162 A3
  Tyldesley M29........ 59 B1
Brackley Ct M22....... 121 D8
Brackley Dr M24....... 65 A5
Brackley Lodge 5 M30. 79 F3
Brackley Rd
  Eccles M30.......... 79 D4
  Over Hulton BL5..... 59 A8
  Reddish SK4......... 111 D5
Brackley Sq 5 OL1.... 67 A8
Brackley St
  Farnworth BL4....... 60 D8
  9 Oldham OL1....... 67 A8
  Walkden M28......... 60 C4
Bracondale Ave BL1... 142 B2
Bradbourne Cl BL3.... 145 C1
Bradburn Ave 4 M30.. 79 D1
Bradburn Cl 2 M30... 79 D1
Bradburn Gr M30..... 79 D1
Bradburn Rd M44..... 105 E7
Bradburn St M30..... 79 D1
Bradburn Wlk 8 M8... 156 B2
Bradbury Ave WA14... 119 A5
Bradbury's La OL3.... 69 B3
Bradbury St
  Ashton-u-L OL7...... 166 A4
  Hyde SK14.......... 167 B1
  Radcliffe M26........ 44 A2
Bradbury Wlk 10 OL2.. 48 D4
Bradda Mount SK7.... 124 A2
Braddan Ave M8...... 108 C3
Bradden Cl M5....... 81 A1
Braddocks Cl OL12... 15 D4
Braddon Ave M41..... 95 D2
Braddon St 8 M11.... 83 C1
Braddyll Rd BL5...... 58 F8
Brade Cl M11........ 165 C4
Bradfield Ave M6.... 80 C2
Bradfield Cl SK5..... 99 E2
Bradfield Rd M32, M41. 96 A2
BRADFORD........... 160 C1
Bradford Ave BL3.... 42 B3
Bradford Ct 4 M40... 65 C1
Bradford Park Dr BL2. 148 B2
Bradford Rd
  Bolton BL3, BL4..... 42 A2
  Eccles M30.......... 79 E4
  Manchester M40...... 160 B2
Bradford St
  Bolton BL2.......... 148 B3
  Farnworth BL4....... 60 D7
  Oldham OL1......... 153 B4
  Wigan WN3.......... 150 C3
Bradford Terr BL9.... 140 B1
Bradgate Ave SK8.... 122 D1
Bradgate Cl M22..... 121 E8
Bradgate Rd
  Altrincham WA14..... 119 A5
  Sale M33............ 108 B2
Bradgate St 9 OL7... 166 A2
Bradgreen Rd M30.... 79 C3
Bradleigh Ave WA12.. 89 B1
Bradley Ave M7...... 81 B7
Bradley Cl WA15..... 119 E7
Bradley Dr BL9...... 45 B2
BRADLEY FOLD....... 43 B5
Bradley Fold OL4.... 67 E6
Bradley Fold Cotts 2.. 43 C7
Bradley Fold BL2.... 43 C7
Bradley Fold Trad Est
  BL2............... 43 C6
Bradley Green Prim Sch
  SK14.............. 101 F6
Bradley Green Rd SK14. 101 F6

Bradley Hall Trad Est
  WN6............... 20 A2
Bradley Ho OL8...... 153 C1
Bradley La
  Little Lever BL2, M26.. 43 B5
  Newhey OL16........ 32 B4
  Newton-le-W WA5, WA12. 89 A1
  Standish WN6....... 19 F2
Bradleys Ct M1...... 159 B1
Bradley Smithy Cl OL12. 14 E2
Bradley St
  7 Manchester M1.... 159 B2
  Newhey OL16........ 32 B4
Bradney Cl M9...... 64 B4
Bradnor Rd M22..... 121 D7
Bradshaigh Ho 6 WN1. 37 C1
BRADSHAW.......... 25 C5
Bradshaw Ave
  Failsworth M35...... 83 E5
  Manchester M20..... 110 B7
  Whitefield M45..... 44 E2
Bradshaw Brow BL2... 25 C4
BRADSHAW CHAPEL.... 25 D5
Bradshaw Cres SK6... 125 E8
Bradshaw Fold Ave M40. 65 D3
Bradshawgate
  Bolton BL1, BL3..... 145 C3
  Leigh WN7.......... 75 F5
  Wigan WN1......... 151 A4
Bradshaw Hall Dr BL2. 25 C6
Bradshaw Hall Fold BL2. 25 C6
Bradshaw Hall La SK8.. 131 D8
Bradshaw Hall Prim Sch
  SK8.............. 122 E1
Bradshaw La
  Lymm WA13......... 117 D3
  Stretford M32....... 108 D8
Bradshaw Mdws BL2.. 25 D6
Bradshaw Rd
  Bolton BL2.......... 25 D7
  Bury BL8........... 26 D5
  Marple SK6......... 125 F7
Bradshaw St
  Atherton M46....... 58 D3
  Farnworth BL4....... 60 D7
  Heywood OL10...... 29 E2
  Manchester M4..... 159 A2
  3 Middleton M24... 65 C2
  Oldham OL1......... 153 C3
  6 Rochdale OL16... 31 A8
  Salford M7......... 155 B2
  Wigan, Redwood WN5. 54 A6
  Wigan, Whelley WN1. 37 E2
Bradshaw Street N M7. 155 A3
Bradstock Rd M8..... 156 A1
Bradwell Ave
  Manchester M20..... 109 F6
  Stretford M32....... 96 A3
Bradwell Dr SK8..... 131 C7
Bradwell Fold 10 SK13. 171 B1
Bradwell Lea 12 SK13. 171 B1
Bradwell PI 7 BL2... 25 B1
Bradwell Rd
  Golborne WA3....... 90 E7
  Hazel Grove SK7.... 133 E8
Bradwell Wlk 11 SK13. 171 B1
Bradwen Ave M8..... 64 A1
Bradwen Cl M34..... 101 A1
Brady St WN7....... 75 D5
Braeburn Ct WN7... 75 D5
Braemar Ave
  Stretford M32....... 96 A2
  Urmston M41........ 95 A1
Braemar Dr M33..... 107 C2
Braemar Gdns BL3... 40 E5
Braemar Gr OL10.... 29 A1
Braemar La M28..... 78 B6
Braemar Wlk WN2... 38 D5
Braemore Cl
  Shaw OL2........... 48 E8
  Wigan WN3......... 54 D2
Braemore Dr
  Broadbottom SK14... 102 F1
  Bury BL9........... 28 D2
Brae Side OL6...... 85 D4
Braeside SK2........ 124 F6
Braeside Cres WN5.. 71 D5
Braeside Gr BL3..... 40 F5
Braewood Cl BL9.... 28 D2
Bragenham St M18... 165 C1
Braidhaven WN6..... 35 E7
Brailsford Ave 4 SK13. 171 B2
Brailsford Cl 7 SK13. 171 B2
Brailsford Gdns 8 SK13. 171 B2
Brailsford Gn 5 SK13. 171 B2
Brailsford Mews 6
  SK13............. 171 B2
Brailsford Rd
  Bolton BL2......... 25 C3
  Manchester M14..... 110 E8
Braintree Rd M22.... 130 E8
Braithwaite WN6.... 36 A6
Braithwaite Rd
  Golborne WA3....... 90 D8
  Manchester M18..... 99 D2
  Middleton M24...... 46 D4
Brakehouse Cl OL16.. 31 E6
Brakenhurst Dr M7... 155 C2
Braken Rd 7 WA14.. 107 C1
Brakesmere Gr M28.. 60 A4

Braley St M12....... 163 B3
Bramah Edge Ct SK13. 103 F7
Bramall Cl BL9...... 45 B2
Bramall Hall (Mus)*
  SK7.............. 123 E1
Bramall St SK14..... 167 A4
Bramber Way OL9.... 152 B2
Bramble Ave
  Oldham OL4......... 49 D1
  Salford M5......... 161 C3
Bramble Bank SK13.. 116 E8
Bramble Cl OL15.... 15 F5
Bramble Croft BL6.. 40 A3
Bramble Ct SK15.... 86 D4
Bramble Gr WN5.... 54 E7
Brambles The WN4.. 72 D5
Bramble Wlk
  5 Sale M33........ 107 C5
  6 Wythenshawe M22. 121 C2
Bramblewood
  Chadderton OL9.... 65 E8
  Hindley WN2....... 56 F7
Brambling Cl
  Droylsden M34..... 84 C2
  Hazel Grove SK7... 125 A5
Brambling Dr BL5... 57 D2
Brambling Way WA3. 90 E7
Bramcote Ave
  Bolton BL2......... 148 B2
  Wythenshawe M23... 121 B6
Bramdean Ave BL2.. 25 E5
Bramfield Wlk M15.. 162 A3
Bramford Cl BL5.... 57 E6
BRAMHALL.......... 132 D8
Bramhall Ave BL2... 26 A4
Bramhall Cl
  8 Altrincham WA15. 120 D6
  Dukinfield SK16.... 101 D6
  Milnrow OL16....... 31 E5
  Sale M33........... 108 E3
Bramhall Ct M3..... 158 A3
Bramhall Ctr The SK7. 132 E8
Bramhall High Sch SK7. 132 E8
Bramhall La S SK7... 132 E6
Bramhall Lane S
  Bramhall SK7....... 132 E7
  Stockport SK3, SK7.. 123 E2
BRAMHALL MOOR..... 124 D2
Bramhall Moor Ind Est
  SK7.............. 124 E2
Bramhall Moor La SK7. 124 C2
Bramhall Mount SK2.. 170 C1
BRAMHALL PARK..... 123 C2
Bramhall Park Rd SK7,
  SK8.............. 123 D2
Bramhall St
  Bolton BL3......... 42 B3
  Manchester M18..... 99 E5
  7 Bury SK14....... 132 E6
Bramhall Wlk M34... 100 F1
Bramham Rd SK6.... 126 A4
Bramhope Wlk M9... 157 A3
Bramley Ave
  Manchester M19..... 111 A8
  Stretford M32....... 96 B1
Bramley Cl
  Bramhall SK7....... 132 E6
  Swinton M27........ 79 C6
  Wilmslow SK9....... 136 D4
Bramley Cres SK4... 168 B1
Bramley Ct WN6.... 19 E1
Bramley Dr
  Bramhall SK7....... 132 E6
  Bury BL8........... 27 C6
Bramley Meade M7.. 155 B3
Bramley Rd
  Bolton BL1......... 25 A6
  Bramhall SK7....... 132 E6
  Rochdale OL11...... 29 E8
Bramley St M7...... 155 B1
Brammay Dr BL8.... 26 E6
Brampton Cl WN2... 55 F1
Brampton Rd
  Bolton BL3......... 146 A2
  Stockport SK7...... 123 F2
Brampton St 9 M46. 58 D3
Brampton Wlk M40.. 83 B6
Bramway
  Bramhall SK7....... 132 C7
  High Lane SK6...... 134 F7
Bramwell Dr M13.... 163 C2
Bramwell St SK1.... 124 B8
Bramwood Cl SK7... 132 E6
Bramworth Ave BL0. 138 B2
Brancaster Dr WA3. 91 A7
Brancaster Rd M1... 163 A3
Branch Cl BL8...... 140 A3
Branch Rd OL15.... 15 F1
Branch St
  Bacup OL13........ 3 D8
  Ince-in-M WN2..... 56 A7
Brancker St BL5.... 40 C1
Brandforth Gdns BL5. 40 A2
Brandforth Rd M8... 156 C3
Brandish Cl M13.... 164 A1
Brandle Ave BL8.... 27 C4
Brandlehow Dr M40. 64 C2
Brandlesholme Cl BL8. 140 A4
Brandlesholme Rd BL8. 27 C4
Brandon Ave
  Gatley SK8......... 122 B5
  Reddish M34........ 99 F3
  Salford M30........ 80 A5
  Wythenshawe M22... 121 C4
Brandon Brow 8 OL1. 153 B4
Brandon Cl
  Bury BL8........... 27 D5

Brandon Cl continued
  Handforth SK9...... 131 D2
  Up Holland WN8.... 53 A7
Brandon Cres OL2... 149 A4
Brandon Rd M6..... 80 B5
Brandon St
  2 Bolton BL3...... 147 A4
  Milnrow OL16....... 31 E6
Brandram Rd M25... 63 C4
Brandreth PI WN6... 19 F1
Brandsby Gdns M5.. 161 A4
BRANDWOOD......... 3 B8
Brandwood Cl....... 47 E1
Brandwood Ave M21. 109 C4
Brandwood Cl M28.. 78 A8
Brandwood Cl BL7.. 9 E5
Brandwood Fold BL7. 9 E5
Brandwood Pk OL13. 3 B8
Brandwood Prim Sch
  BL3.............. 146 C4
Brandwood Rd OL13. 3 B8
Brandwood St BL3... 146 C4
Branfield Ave SK8... 122 D1
Branford St WN4... 73 C2
Brankgate Ct M20.. 110 A5
Branksome Ave M25. 63 B4
Branksome Dr
  Cheadle SK8........ 122 D1
  Manchester M9..... 64 B6
  Salford M6......... 80 B5
Branksome Ho SK4.. 168 B2
Branksome Rd SK4.. 168 B1
Bransby Ave M9.... 64 E4
Branscombe Dr M33. 107 C5
Branscombe Gdns BL3. 42 D5
Bransdale Ave OL2.. 48 C4
Bransdale Cl BL3... 40 F4
Bransdale Wlk M24. 73 D3
Bransford Cl WN4.. 73 C2
Bransford Rd
  Droylsden M11..... 99 E8
  Urmston M41....... 95 C3
Branson St M4, M40. 160 A2
Branson Wlk WA15.. 120 C6
Branston Rd M40... 65 D2
Brantfell Gr BL2... 42 F8
Branthwaite WN2... 38 B1
Brantingham Ct M16. 97 E1
Brantingham Rd M16,
  M21.............. 97 D1
Brantwood Cl OL2.. 48 C4
Brantwood Dr BL2.. 42 F8
Brantwood Rd
  Cheadle SK8........ 122 F1
  Salford M7......... 155 A4
  Stockport SK4...... 168 C4
Branwood Terr M9.. 157 C3
Brassey St
  Ashton-u-L OL6..... 166 B4
  Middleton M24..... 47 A1
Brassica Cl M30.... 79 A4
Brassington Ave
  Manchester M21.... 109 B7
  Salford M5......... 161 B4
Brassington Cres SK13. 171 A1
Brassington Rd SK4.. 110 E4
Brathay Cl
  Bolton BL2......... 25 F2
  Prestwich M45..... 63 C8
Brattice Dr M27.... 80 C8
Bratton Cl WN3.... 54 C2
Brattray Dr M24... 46 E3
Braunston Cl M30.. 95 E8
Braxton Wlk 20 M9. 157 B4
Bray Ave M9........ 79 B3
Braybrook Dr BL1.. 40 D7
Bray Cl SK8........ 122 E2
Brayford Dr WN2... 38 C5
Brayford Rd M22... 121 D1
Brayshaw Cl OL10.. 29 C1
Brayside Rd M19, M20. 110 D4
Braystan Gdns SK8.. 122 B6
Brayton Fold M24.. 64 C2
Brayton Ave
  Manchester M20.... 110 C2
  Sale M33........... 107 D5
Brayton Ct WN2.... 56 D6
Brazennose St M2.. 158 C1
Brazil St M1........ 163 A4
Brazley Ave
  Bolton BL3......... 42 B3
  Horwich BL6........ 22 E1
Breach House La WA16. 129 A1
Bread St M18....... 99 E6
Breaktemper BL5... 39 E1
Bream Wlk 8 M22... 121 C1
Brearley St OL13... 3 D8
Breaston Ave WN7.. 76 C3
Brechin Way OL10.. 29 A1
Brechin Wlk 16 M11. 83 C1
Breckland Cl SK15.. 86 D2
Breckland Dr BL1.. 40 D8
Breckles PI BL3.... 145 A1
Breck Rd M30...... 79 B2
Brecon Ave
  Cheadle SK8........ 122 E1
  Denton M34........ 100 F1
  Manchester M19.... 110 F7
  Urmston M41....... 94 D3

Brecon Dr
  Bury BL9........... 44 E7
  Hindley WN2....... 57 A3
Brecon Wlk 6 OL8.. 66 B2
BREDBURY.......... 112 E4
Bredbury Dr BL4.... 60 E8
Bredbury Gn SK6... 113 A1
BREDBURY GREEN.... 113 A1
Bredbury Green Prim Sch
  SK6.............. 112 F1
Bredbury Park Ind Est
  SK6.............. 112 E6
Bredbury Park Way SK6. 112 E6
Bredbury Rd M14... 98 B2
Bredbury St
  Chadderton OL9.... 152 B2
  Dukinfield SK14.... 101 D5
Bredbury Sta SK6... 112 F4
Brede Wlk M23..... 120 D8
Bredon Way OL8.... 66 E3
Breeze Hill Wlg..... 37 B7
Breeze Hill Comp Sch
  OL4.............. 67 D5
Breeze Hill Rd
  Oldham OL4........ 67 D5
  Over Hulton M46... 58 F5
Breeze Mount M25.. 63 C3
BREIGHTMET........ 42 F8
Breightmet Dr BL2.. 42 E7
Breightmet Fold La 5
  BL2.............. 25 F1
Breightmet Ind Est BL2. 43 A8
Breightmet St
  1 Bolton BL1...... 145 C3
  Bolton BL2......... 148 A3
Brellafield Dr OL2... 48 F8
Brenbar Cres OL12.. 4 D1
Brenchley Dr M23... 109 A2
Brencon Ave M23... 108 C1
Brendall Cl SK2.... 125 A5
Brendon Ave
  Manchester M40.... 83 A7
  Reddish SK5....... 111 F6
Brendon Cl SK13... 116 A8
Brendon Dr M34... 84 D1
Brendon Hills OL2.. 48 D3
Brenley Wlk 7 M9.. 157 A4
Brennan Cl M15.... 163 A1
Brennan Ct OL8.... 66 C2
Brennock Cl M11... 164 C4
Brentbridge Rd M14. 110 B8
Brent Cl
  Little Lever BL2.... 43 B5
  Poynton SK12...... 133 B4
Brentfield Ave M8.. 156 A2
Brentford Ave BL1.. 142 B2
Brentford Rd SK5... 111 F6
Brentford St M9.... 157 B3
Brent Moor Rd SK7. 124 A3
Brentnall Prim Sch M7. 155 A3
Brentnall St SK1... 170 C3
Brentnor Rd M40.. 65 C3
Brenton Ave M33... 108 A4
Brenton Bsns Complex
  BL9.............. 141 A2
Brent Rd
  Stockport SK4...... 168 C3
  Wythenshawe M23... 109 A2
Brentwood
  Sale M33........... 108 A4
  Salford M6......... 154 B3
  Urmston M41....... 94 F1
Brentwood Ave
  Altrincham WA14.... 119 E7
  Irlam M44.......... 105 D6
  Swinton M28........ 79 B6
  Urmston M41....... 95 D2
Brentwood Cl
  Brinnington SK5.... 112 D5
  Littleborough OL15.. 15 F3
  Stalybridge SK15... 86 C2
Brentwood Cres WA14. 119 E6
Brentwood Ct M25.. 62 F3
Brentwood Dr
  Eccles M30......... 79 D4
  Farnworth BL3, BL4.. 42 C2
  Gatley SK8......... 122 B5
Brentwood Gr WN7. 75 F7
Brentwood Rd
  Adlington PR6...... 21 B8
  Swinton M27........ 79 D6
Brentwood Specl Sch
  WA14............ 119 F3
Brentwood St M16.. 97 F3
Brereton Cl WA14.. 119 C1
Brereton Ct SK8... 122 E1
Brereton Dr M28... 78 F7
Brereton Gr M44... 105 E6
Brereton Rd
  Eccles M30......... 78 F1
  Handforth SK9..... 131 E3
Breslyn St M3...... 158 C3
Bretherton Row 11 WN1. 150 C4
Bretherton St WN7. 76 C3
Brethren's Ct M43.. 100 A8
Bretland Gdns SK14. 102 E1
Bretland Wlk 8 M22. 121 F3
Breton Ho SK2..... 124 A6
Brettargh St M6.... 81 A4
Bretton Ct BL4.... 61 B6
Bretton Wlk M28... 120 D8
Brett St M28....... 77 F6
Brett St M22....... 109 E1
Brewer's Gn SK7... 124 D3

Brewer St M1 159 B1
Brewerton Rd OL4 67 C6
Brewery La WN7 76 A5
Brewery St
 5 Altrincham WA14 119 D4
 Stockport SK1 112 A3
Brewery Yd M3 158 B2
Brewster St
 Manchester M9 157 A4
 4 Middleton M24 47 A2
Brian Ave M43 84 C3
Brian Farrell Dr SK16 101 D6
Brian Rd BL4 42 A1
Brian Redhead Ct M15 162 B3
Brian St OL11 30 B2
Brian Statham Way M16 97 A4
Briar Ave
 Hazel Grove SK7 124 F2
 Hollinfare WA3 105 B2
 Oldham OL4 49 D1
Briar Cl
 Ashton-in-M WN4 73 A4
 Hindley WN2 57 B4
 3 Rochdale OL12 14 A1
 Sale M33 107 C4
 Urmston M41 95 A3
Briar Cres M22 121 E5
Briarcroft Dr M46 58 A1
Briardale Wlk 8 WA14 107 C1
Briardene M34 101 A4
Briardene Gdns M22 121 E4
Briarfield BL7 8 D2
Briarfield Hall M1 163 A2
Briarfield Rd
 Altrincham WA15 120 C6
 Cheadle SK8 123 B3
 Farnworth BL4 42 A1
 Manchester M19, M20 110 D6
 Reddish SK4 111 E6
 Uppermill OL3 51 A2
 Worsley M28 78 F7
Briar Gr
 Chadderton OL9 48 B1
 Leigh WN7 75 E8
 Romiley SK6 113 A5
Briargrove Rd SK22 127 C4
Briar Hill Ave M38 59 E4
Briar Hill Cl M38 59 E4
Briar Hill Gr M38 59 E4
Briar Hill Way 6 M6 81 A3
Briar Hollow SK4 168 B1
Briarlands Ave M33 107 F2
Briarlands Cl SK7 132 D6
Briar Lea Cl BL3 147 B4
Briarlea Gdns M19 110 E5
Briarley Gdns SK6 113 C6
Briarly WN6 37 A7
Briarmere Wlk OL9 152 C3
Briar Rd
 Golborne WA3 90 B8
 Wigan WN5 54 E7
Briars Mount SK4 168 A2
Briars Pk SK7 123 C1
Briar St OL11 139 A2
Briarstead Cl SK7 132 D7
Briar Wlk WA3 90 B8
Briarwood
 Bolton BL2 25 B1
 Wilmslow SK9 137 C7
Briarwood Ave
 Droylsden M43 83 F3
 Wythenshawe M23 120 E8
Briarwood Chase SK8 123 B1
Briarwood Cl M29 77 A7
Briarwood Cres SK6 126 A3
Briary Dr M29 77 B8
Brice St SK16 101 B8
Brickbridge Rd SK6 126 A5
Brickfield St
 Glossop SK13 104 B5
 Rochdale OL16 15 B2
Brick Ground OL12 13 C2
Brickhill La WA15 129 B4
Brickkiln La WA14 118 C3
Brick Kiln La 10 WN1 37 C1
Brickkiln Row WA14 119 C1
Brickley St M3, M4 159 A3
Bricknell Wlk 5 M22 121 F3
Brick St
 Bury BL9 141 A3
 7 Manchester M4 159 A2
Bridcam St M8 156 A1
Briddon St M3 158 C3
Brideoak Ct M8 156 A2
Brideoake St WN7 76 B4
Brideoak St
 Manchester M8 156 A2
 Oldham OL4 67 E8
Bride St BL1 143 B2
Bridestowe Ave SK14 102 C3
Bridestowe Wlk SK14 102 C3
Bridge Ave SK6 113 A5
Bridge Bank Cl WA3 90 B7
Bridge Bank Rd OL15 16 A3
Bridge Cl
 Lymm WA13 117 B4
 Partington M31 106 A3
 6 Radcliffe M26 44 B2
Bridge Coll SK2 124 D8
Bridgecrest Ct 3 SK8 123 A2
Bridge Dr
 Cheadle SK8 122 D4
 Handforth SK9 131 D3
BRIDGE END 1 A7
Bridge End
 Delph OL3 50 F4
 Wigan WN3 150 B4
Bridge End Cl BB4 1 A7
Bridgefield 4 SK13 116 B8
Bridgefield Ave SK9 131 C1
Bridgefield Cl SK6 134 E7
Bridgefield Cres 4 OL4 67 F6
Bridgefield Dr BL9 28 D2
Bridgefield St
 Radcliffe M26 44 B3
 Rochdale OL11 139 A3
 Stockport SK1 169 B2
Bridgefield Wlk 7 M26 44 B3
Bridgefold Rd OL11 139 A4
Bridgefoot Cl M28 78 A5
Bridgeford Ct M32 108 D8
Bridgeford St M13, M15 163 A2
Bridge Gr WA15 119 F7
Bridgehall Dr WN8 53 B7
Bridge Hall Dr BL9 141 C2
Bridge Hall Fold BL9 141 C2
Bridge Hall La BL9 28 D2
Bridge Hall Prim Sch SK3 170 A2
Bridge Ho M1 159 B1
Bridge La SK7 123 F1
Bridgelea Mews M20 110 B6
Bridgelea Rd M20 110 B6
Bridgeman Ho BL4 60 D7
Bridgeman Pl BL2 148 A2
Bridgeman St
 Bolton BL3 145 C1
 Farnworth BL4 42 D1
Bridgeman Terr WN1 37 C1
Bridgemere Cl M26 43 F5
Bridge Mill 1 BL7 24 F7
Bridge Mills Bsns Pk M6 80 F5
Bridgend Cl
 Cheadle SK8 123 C4
 Manchester M12 165 A2
Bridgenorth Ave M41 95 F2
Bridgenorth Dr OL15 15 F3
Bridge Rd
 Bury BL9 140 A1
 Sale M23 120 C7
Bridges Ave BL9 44 F6
Bridges Ct 5 BL3 145 C2
Bridgeside Bsns Ctr SK6 112 D6
Bridge's St M46 58 B2
Bridge St
 Bolton BL1 145 C3
 Bury BL9 141 A3
 Denton, Guide Bridge M34 100 F7
 Droylsden M43 99 E8
 Dukinfield SK16 101 A6
 Farnworth BL4 42 E1
 Golborne WA3 90 A7
 Haslingden BB4 1 C6
 Heywood OL10 29 C2
 Hindley WN2 56 E6
 Horwich BL6 22 C4
 Ince-in-M WN3 151 A2
 Kearsley M26 61 B8
 Manchester M3 158 B1
 Middleton M24 65 A8
 Milnrow OL16 31 F6
 New Mills SK22 127 C1
 Newton-le-W WA12 89 B3
 Oldham, County End OL4 67 F6
 1 Oldham, Lower Moor OL1 67 A6
 Oldham, West Hulme OL1 48 D1
 Pendlebury M27 80 A8
 Ramsbottom BL0 138 C2
 Rawtenstall BB4 2 E7
 Rochdale, Castleton OL11 30 C1
 Rochdale, Hurstead OL12 15 C3
 Shaw OL2 149 C4
 Stalybridge SK15 85 F1
 Stockport SK1 169 C2
 Uppermill OL3 69 B7
 Whitworth OL12 4 C1
 Wigan WN3 150 C3
Bridge Street W M3 158 B1
Bridges Way M34 112 F7
Bridge Trad Est BL8 140 A2
Bridgewater Bsns Pk WN7 75 F4
Bridgewater Cl SK8 131 D7
Bridgewater Ct M32 96 E3
Bridgewater Ctr The M41 95 E7
Bridgewater Hall The* M2 162 C4
Bridgewater Ho M15 162 A4
Bridgewater Hospl (private) M15 97 F4
Bridgewater Pl M4 159 A1
Bridgewater Prim Sch M38 60 B4
Bridgewater Rd
 Altrincham WA14 119 D7
 Pendlebury M27 80 B7
 Walkden, Ellenbrook M28 78 A8
 Walkden, Engine Fold M28 60 D2
Bridgewater Sch M28 79 A6
Bridgewater St
 2 Bolton BL1 145 A2
 Eccles M30 79 B2
 Farnworth BL4 60 E8
 Hindley WN2 56 E6
 Manchester M3 162 B4
 8 Oldham OL1 67 A8
 Sale M33 108 B5
 Salford M3 158 B3
 Stretford M32 96 E2
 Walkden M38 60 B4
 Wigan WN3 150 B3
Bridgewater St *continued*
 5 Wigan, Worsley Hall WN5 54 F6
Bridgewater Viaduct M15, M3 162 B3
Bridgewater Way M15, M16 161 B1
Bridgewater Wlk 2 M28 60 D3
Bridgnorth Rd M9 64 A3
Bridle Cl
 Droylsden M43 84 C3
 Urmston M41 94 E2
Bridle Ct SK7 132 F2
Bridle Fold M26 44 A4
Bridle Rd
 Prestwich M25 63 E7
 Woodford SK7 132 F2
Bridleway SK22 127 D1
Bridle Way SK7 133 A2
Bridlington Ave M6 80 C3
Bridlington Cl 6 M40 83 C6
Bridport Ave M40 83 D8
Bridson La BL2 25 D2
Bridson St
 10 Oldham OL4 67 C7
 Salford M5 154 B1
Brief St BL2 25 C1
Brien Ave WA14 119 E7
Briercliffe Cl M18 99 D6
Briercliffe Rd BL3 144 C1
Brierfield Ave M46 58 C4
Brierfield Dr BL9 27 E8
Brierholme Ave BL7 8 E1
Brierley Ave
 Failsworth M35 84 A7
 Whitefield M45 44 E2
Brierley Cl
 Ashton-u-L OL6 86 A6
 Denton M34 100 E1
Brierley Dr M24 65 A7
Brierley Road E M27 61 E1
Brierley Road W M27 61 E1
Brierley St
 Bury BL9 44 E8
 Chadderton OL9 152 C4
 Heywood OL10 29 D2
 Oldham OL8 66 F3
 Stalybridge SK16 85 D1
Brierley Wlk OL9 152 C4
Brierton Dr 5 M22 121 B1
Brierwood Cl OL1 48 E1
Briery Ave BL2 25 D6
Brigade Dr M32 96 C3
Brigade St BL1 144 C3
Brigadier Cl M20 110 B6
Brigantine Cl M5 161 A4
Briggs Cl M33 107 C1
Briggs Fold BL7 8 E2
Briggs Fold Cl BL7 8 E2
Briggs Fold Rd BL7 8 E2
Briggs Rd M32 96 F4
Briggs St
 Leigh WN7 75 E7
 Salford M3 158 A3
Brigham St M11 165 C4
Brightgate Way M32 96 A5
Brightman St M18 99 E6
Brighton Ave
 Bolton BL1 142 A1
 Manchester M19 110 F7
 Reddish SK5 99 F2
 Salford M7 155 B2
 Urmston M41 94 E3
Brighton Cl SK8 123 C4
Brighton Ct
 Manchester M14 98 D2
 Salford M5 161 B3
Brighton Gr
 Hyde SK14 167 B1
 Manchester M14 98 D2
 Sale M33 108 B5
 Urmston M41 94 E3
Brighton Pl M13 163 B2
Brighton Range M18 99 F4
Brighton Rd
 Oldham OL4 50 A1
 Stockport SK4 168 C1
Brighton Road Ind Est SK4 168 C1
Brighton St
 Bury BL9 141 B3
 Manchester M4 159 A3
Bright Rd M30 79 E2
Bright St Mill BL9 141 A3
Bright St
 1 Ashton-u-L OL6 85 D2
 Bolton BL7 8 D2
 Bury BL9 141 A3
 Chadderton OL9 66 A4
 Droylsden M43 84 B1
 Leigh WN7 75 E7
 Oldham OL8 153 A1
 Radcliffe M26 44 C4
 16 Rochdale OL16 31 A5
Brightstone Wlk 4 M13 98 E4
Brightwater BL6 21 F2
Brightwater Cl M45 63 A8
Brightwell Wlk 5 M4 159 B2
Brignall Gr WA3 74 D1
Brigsteer Wlk M40 157 A1
Brigstock Ave M18 165 C1
Briksdal Way BL6 40 C7
Brimelow St SK6 112 D3
Brimfield Ave M29 59 C1
Brimfield Wlk 7 M40 83 C6
Brimmy Croft La OL3 33 C3
Brimpton Wlk 13 M8 155 C2
Brimrod La OL11 139 A1
Brimrod Prim Sch OL11 139 A1
Brimscombe Ave M22 121 C2
Brindale Ho SK5 112 C4
Brindale Rd SK5 112 C4
Brindle Cl M6 154 C4
Brindle Dell BL7 8 D2
BRINDLE HEATH 154 C4
Brindle Heath Ind Est M6 81 A4
Brindle Heath Rd M6 154 C4
Brindlehurst Dr M29 77 D7
Brindle Pl 7 M15 163 A2
Brindle St
 Hindley WN2 56 F6
 Tyldesley M29 59 A1
Brindle Way OL2 49 D7
Brindley Ave
 Manchester M9 64 B5
 Marple SK6 125 F5
 Sale M33 108 C6
Brindley Cl
 Atherton M46 58 A2
 7 Eccles M30 95 D8
 Farnworth BL4 60 B8
Brindley Gr SK9 131 E2
Brindley Rd
 Manchester M16 161 B1
 7 Worsley M28 78 A6
Brindley St
 Bolton BL1 143 C4
 Boothstown M28 77 F6
 Eccles M30 79 B3
 Horwich BL6 22 C2
 Swinton M27 61 F2
 Walkden M28 60 D2
 Wigan WN5 54 C5
Brinell Dr M44 105 F6
Brinkburn Rd SK7 125 A3
Brinklow Cl M11 99 E7
Brinkshaw Ave M22 121 E2
Brinks La BL2 43 A6
Brink's Row BL6 22 D5
Brinksway
 Bolton BL1 40 D7
 Stockport SK3 123 C8
Brinksway Trad Est 1 SK3 123 C8
Brinksworth Cl BL2 43 A8
BRINNINGTON 112 B5
Brinnington Cres SK5 112 B4
Brinnington Rd
 Brinnington SK5 112 C4
 Stockport SK1 112 A3
Brinnington Rise SK1, SK5 112 B4
Brinnington Sta SK5 112 C6
Brinsop Hall La BL5 39 A6
Brinsop Sq M12 165 B2
Brinston Wlk 12 M40 83 A7
Brinsworth Dr M8 156 A2
Briony Ave WA15 120 C2
Briony Cl OL2 48 E2
Brisbane Cl SK7 132 F5
Brisbane St M13, M15 163 B1
Briscoe La M40 83 B4
Briscoe Lane Prim Sch M40 83 B5
Briscoe Mews 8 BL3 42 A4
Briscoe St OL1 153 C4
Brisco Wlk M24 46 C2
Bristle Hall Way BL5 39 F2
Bristle St M1 163 A2
Bristol Ave
 Ashton-u-L OL6 85 B7
 Bolton BL2 25 C1
 Manchester M19 111 B8
Bristol Cl SK8 131 C7
Bristol Ct 2 M7 63 E1
Bristol St M7 155 B3
Bristowe St M11, M43 83 D3
Britain St BL9 44 F5
BRITANNIA 4 C8
Britannia Ave OL2 149 C2
Britannia Bridge Prim Sch WN3 151 B2
Britannia Bsns Pk BL2 25 A2
Britannia Cl M26 44 A3
Britannia Com Prim Sch OL13 4 C8
Britannia Mill Ind Est OL10 29 C2
Britannia Mills BL9 141 A3
Britannia Mills M15 162 A3
Britannia Rd
 Sale M33 108 C5
 Wigan WN5 54 B8
Britannia Road Ind Est M33 108 C5
Britannia St
 Ashton-u-L OL7 100 F8
 Heywood OL10 29 B2
 1 Oldham OL1 67 A7
 Salford M6 81 A5
Britannia Warehouse BL9 141 A3
Britannia Way
 Bolton BL1 25 A2
 Haslingden BB4 1 A8
Britnall Ave M12 164 C1
Briton St
 6 Rochdale OL16 31 A8
 Royton OL2 48 E2
Britwell Wlk M8 156 C4
Brixham Ave SK8 131 F7
Brixham Dr M33 107 D6
Brixham Rd M16 97 B4
Brixham Wlk SK7 132 E7
Brixton Ave M20 110 A6
Brixworth Wlk 19 M9 64 E3
Broach St BL3 147 B4
Broadacre
 Shevington Moor WN6 19 B2
 Stalybridge SK15 102 E6
 Up Holland WN8 53 A6
Broad Acre OL12 13 E2
Broadacre Pl SK9 136 D3
Broadacre Rd M18 99 E3
BROADBENT 49 C2
Broadbent Ave
 Ashton-u-L OL6 85 C6
 Dukinfield SK16 101 D8
Broadbent Cl
 Mossley SK15 86 E6
 Royton OL2 149 A1
Broadbent Dr BL9 28 E4
Broadbent Fold Prim Sch SK16 102 A7
Broadbent Gr SK14 102 E1
Broadbent Rd OL1 49 C1
Broadbent St
 Hyde SK14 167 A4
 Swinton M27 79 D7
BROADBOTTOM 115 A8
Broadbottom Prim Sch SK14 114 F8
Broadbottom Rd SK14 103 A3
Broadbottom Sta SK14 115 A8
Broadcarr La OL5 68 B1
Broad Ees Dole Nature Reserve* M32 108 D7
BROADFIELD 29 B1
Broadfield Cl M34 101 A2
Broadfield Com Prim Sch OL16 139 B3
Broadfield Distribution Ctr OL10 46 B8
Broadfield Dr OL15 15 F3
Broadfield Gr SK5 99 E3
Broadfield Prim Sch 5 OL8 66 F4
Broadfield Rd
 Manchester M14 98 A3
 Reddish SK5 99 E3
Broadfield St
 Heywood OL10 29 B1
 Rochdale OL16 139 C2
Broadfield Stile OL16 139 B2
Broadford Rd BL3 40 F5
Broadgate
 Bolton BL3 40 F5
 Middleton M24, OL9 65 D5
 Uppermill OL3 50 E1
Broadgate Ho BL3 40 F5
Broadgate Mdw M27 79 F6
Broadgreen Gdns 4 BL4 42 D2
BROADHALGH 30 A7
Broadhalgh Ave OL11 30 A7
Broadhalgh Rd OL11 30 A6
Broadhaven Rd M40 160 A3
Broadhead Rd BL7 9 E7
Broadhead Wlk M45 45 B1
BROADHEATH 119 C7
Broadheath Cl BL5 40 A1
Broadheath Prim Sch WA14 119 C8
Broad Hey SK6 113 D3
Broadhey View SK22 127 B1
Broad Hill Cl SK7 124 A2
Broadhill Rd
 Manchester M19 110 E6
 Stalybridge SK15 86 A5
Broadhurst M34 101 A5
Broadhurst Ave
 Chadderton OL1 48 C1
 Culcheth WA3 91 F2
 Swinton M27 61 F3
Broadhurst Ct 1 BL3 147 A4
Broadhurst Gr OL6 85 C6
Broadhurst La WN6 18 F7
Broadhurst Prim Sch M40 83 C7
Broadhurst St
 3 Bolton BL3 147 A4
 1 Radcliffe M26 43 F5
 Stockport SK3 170 C3
Broad Ing OL12 14 C1
Broad La
 Altrincham WA15 120 B1
 Billinge WA11 71 B1
 Delph OL3 50 E7
 Rochdale, Buersil OL16 31 B3
 Rochdale, Burnedge OL16 31 D2
Broadlands WN6 36 B6
Broadlands Rd M28 79 C6
Broadlands Wlk 11 M40 83 A6
Broad Lea M41 95 C3
Broadlea Gr OL12 14 C2
Broadlea Rd M19 110 E5
BROADLEY 14 C5
Broadley Ave
 Golborne WA3 90 C7
 Wythenshawe M22 121 D4
Broadley Fold OL12 14 B6
Broadlink M24 65 D6
Broadmeadow BL7 25 B8
Broadmeadow Ave M16 97 F1
Broadmoss Dr M9 65 A3
Broadmoss Rd M9 65 A3
BROAD OAK 79 B6
Broadoak Ave
 Boothstown M28 77 F7
 Wythenshawe M22 121 C5
Broadoak Bsns Pk M17 95 F7
Broad Oak Cl 4 PR6 21 A8
Broadoak Com Sports Ctr BL9 141 B2
Broadoak Cres OL6 85 B5

Broad Oak Cres OL8 . . . . 67 A2
Broadoak Ct M8 . . . . 156 B2
Broadoak Dr M7 . . . . 121 D5
Broad Oak High Sch BL9 141 B2
Broad Oak La
　Bury BL9 . . . . 28 D3
　Manchester M20 . . . . . . 122 B8
BROADOAK PARK 79 C6
Broad Oak Pk
　Eccles M30 . . . . 79 D4
　Swinton M28 . . . . 79 B6
Broadoak Prim Sch
　Ashton-u-L OL6 . . . . 85 C6
　Swinton M27 . . . . 79 A6
Broad Oak Prim Sch
　M20 . . . . 122 C8
Broadoak Rd
　🔳 Ashton under Lyne OL6 . 85 B5
　Rochdale OL11 . . . . 29 E6
　Stockport SK7 . . . . 123 F2
　Wythenshawe M22 . . . . . 121 C5
Broad Oak Rd BL3 . . . . . . 42 A2
Broadoak Sch Specialist
　Sports Coll BL1 . . . . 105 F2
Broadoaks Rd
　Sale M33 . . . . 108 A4
　Urmston M41 . . . . 95 B1
Broad Oak Terr BL9 . . . . . 28 E3
Broad o' th' La
　Bolton BL1 . . . . 143 B4
　Shevington Wn M6 . . . . . 36 A6
Broad Rd M33 . . . . 108 D5
Broadriding Rd WN6 . . . . 35 E6
Broad Shaw La OL16 . . . 31 D2
Broad St
　Bury BL9 . . . . 140 B2
　Middleton M24 . . . . 64 C7
　Salford M6 . . . . 154 C4
Broadstone Ave OL4 . . . . 49 F4
Broadstone Cl
　Prestwich M25 . . . . 63 A3
　🔳 Rochdale OL12 . . . . . 14 A1
Broadstone Hall Prim Sch
　SK4 . . . . 111 D6
Broadstone Hall Rd N
　SK4 . . . . 111 D6
Broadstone Hall Rd S SK4,
　SK5 . . . . 111 E6
Broadstone Rd
　Bolton BL2 . . . . 25 D5
　Reddish SK4, SK5 . . . . . 111 D5
Broadview Ct OL16 . . . . . 31 C3
Broadway
　Altrincham WA15 . . . . . 120 B1
　Chadderton, Stock Brook
　OL9 . . . . 152 A3
　Chadderton, White Gate End M40,
　OL9 . . . . 65 E2
　Cheadle SK8 . . . . 122 C4
　Droylsden M43 . . . . 100 A8
　Dukinfield SK14, SK16 . . 101 B5
　Failsworth M35, M40 . . . 83 D8
　Irlam M44 . . . . 42 A1
　Haslingden BB4 . . . . 1 B8
　Hindley WN2 . . . . 57 A5
　Horwich BL6 . . . . 22 D3
　Irlam M44 . . . . 94 A1
　Over Hulton M46 . . . . . . 58 F5
　Partington M31 . . . . 106 A4
　Royton OL1, OL2 . . . . . . 48 D2
　Sale M33 . . . . 108 A5
　Salford M50 . . . . 96 E8
　Stockport, Bramhall Green
　SK7 . . . . 123 F2
　Stockport SK2 . . . . 124 C7
　Urmston M41 . . . . 95 B4
　Walkden M28 . . . . 60 D1
　Wilmslow SK9 . . . . 136 F8
Broadway Ave SK8 . . . . . 122 D5
Broadway Bsns Pk OL9 . . 65 E4
Broadway Cl M41 . . . . 95 C5
Broadway Cres BB4 . . . . . 1 A8
Broadway Ind Est
　Dukinfield SK16 . . . . 101 B5
　Salford M50 . . . . 161 A4
Broadway Metro Sta M50. 96 F8
Broadway N M43 . . . . . . 100 A8
Broadway Prim Sch BB4 . . 1 C8
Broadway St OL8 . . . . 66 F4
Broadway The SK6 . . . . . 112 E3
Broadwell Dr
　Leigh WN7 . . . . 75 E1
　Manchester M9 . . . . 157 B3
Broad Wlk
　Salford M6 . . . . 81 A3
　Westhoughton BL5 . . . . . 57 E7
　Wilmslow SK9 . . . . 136 F8
Broadwood BL6 . . . . 40 C7
Broadwood Cl SK6 . . . . . 134 F7
Brocade Cl M3 . . . . 158 A3
Broche Cl OL11 . . . . 30 B3
Brock Ave BL2 . . . . 42 F7
Brock Cl M11 . . . . 99 D7
Brock Dr SK8 . . . . 132 B8
Brockenhurst Dr BL2 . . . . 25 F3
Brockford Dr M9 . . . . 64 E5
Brockholes SK13 . . . . . . 115 B8
Brockhurst Wlk WN3 . . . . 150 A1
Brocklebank Rd
　Manchester M14 . . . . . . 110 C8
　Rochdale OL16 . . . . 31 D7
Brocklehurst Ave BL9 . . . 140 C1
Brocklehurst St M9, M40 . . 83 A8
Brockley Ave M14 . . . . 98 B2
Brock Mill La WN1 . . . . . . 37 C4
Brock Pl WN2 . . . . 55 F2
Brocksby Chase BL1 . . . . 143 B1

Brock St
　Manchester M1 . . . . 159 B1
　Wigan WN1 . . . . 151 B4
Brockstedes Ave WN4 . . . 72 E6
Brock The 🔳 OL2 . . . . 48 F8
Brockton Wlk M8 . . . . . . 156 A4
Brockway OL16 . . . . 31 C3
Brocstedes Rd WN4 . . . . . 72 D7
Brocton Ct M7 . . . . 63 D1
Brodick Dr BL2 . . . . 42 F6
Brodick St M40 . . . . 157 C4
Brodie Cl M30 . . . . 79 B2
Brogan St 🔳 M18 . . . . 99 D5
Brogden Ave WA3 . . . . 91 E4
Brogden Dr SK8 . . . . 122 B5
Brogden Gr 🔳 M33 . . . . . 108 A3
Brogden Terr 🔳 M33 . . . . 108 A3
Bromborough Ave 🔳
　M20 . . . . 110 A8
Bromfield 🔳 OL12 . . . . . 139 C4
Bromfield Ave M19 . . . . . . 64 D1
Bromleigh Ave SK8 . . . . . 122 B6
Bromley Ave
　Golborne WA3 . . . . 90 D7
　Royton OL2 . . . . 48 C6
　Urmston M41 . . . . 94 E1
Bromley Cl WN2 . . . . 38 A2
Bromley Cres OL6 . . . . 85 B6
Bromley Cross Rd BL7 . . . . 9 B1
Bromley Cross Rd BL7 . . . 25 B7
Bromley Dr WN7 . . . . 75 D8
Bromley Rd M33 . . . . 108 C2
Bromley St
　Chadderton OL9 . . . . 66 A3
　Denton M34 . . . . 100 F3
　Manchester M4, M40 . . . 159 B3
　Newton-le-W M11 . . . . . . 83 C1
Brompton Ave M35 . . . . . 84 B8
Brompton Rd
　Manchester M14 . . . . 98 B2
　Stockport SK4 . . . . 168 A2
　Urmston M32 . . . . 95 F3
Brompton Terr 🔳 SK16 . . 166 B1
Bromsgrove Ave M30 . . . . 79 B2
Bromshill Dr M7 . . . . 155 B2
Bromwich Dr 🔳 M9 . . . . . 157 A3
Bromwich St BL2 . . . . . . 148 B2
Bronington Cl M22 . . . . . 121 E7
Bronington Cl BL9 . . . . . . 44 F6
Bronte Cl
　Bolton BL1 . . . . 143 A1
　Oldham OL1 . . . . 49 D4
　Rochdale OL12 . . . . 14 A1
　Wigan WN3 . . . . 150 A1
Bronte St M15 . . . . 163 A1
Bronville Cl OL1 . . . . 48 C1
Brookash Rd M22 . . . . . . 131 A8
Brook Ave
　Altrincham WA15 . . . . . . 119 E6
　Droylsden M43 . . . . 83 E1
　Handforth SK9 . . . . 131 D4
　Manchester M19 . . . . 99 B2
　Reddish SK4 . . . . 111 D5
　Shaw OL2 . . . . 149 B4
　Swinton M27 . . . . 79 F7
　Uppermill OL3 . . . . 69 C8
Brook Bank
　Bolton BL2 . . . . 25 D3
　Poynton SK12 . . . . 134 C2
Brookbank Cl M24 . . . . . . 65 B7
BROOK BOTTOM
　Mossley 68 B2
　New Mills 126 F1
Brookbottom Rd M26 . . . . 43 F6
Brook Bottom Rd SK6 . . . 126 F1
BROOKBOTTOMS 11 C3
Brookburn Com Sch
　M21 . . . . 109 A7
Brookburn Rd M21 . . . . . 109 A7
Brook Cl
　Altrincham WA15 . . . . . . 119 E6
　Tyldesley M29 . . . . 59 A2
　Whitefield M45 . . . . 63 B8
Brookcot Rd BL2 . . . . 120 F7
Brookcroft Ave M22 . . . . 121 D5
Brookcroft Rd M22 . . . . . 121 D5
Brook Ct
　🔳 Manchester M14 . . . . 110 D8
　Prestwich M7 . . . . 63 C1
Brookdale
　Over Hulton M46 . . . . 58 F6
　Rochdale OL12 . . . . 14 E3
Brookdale Ave
　Denton, Audenshaw M34. 100 E7
　Denton M34 . . . . 101 B2
　Failsworth M40 . . . . 83 D4
　Marple SK6 . . . . 125 F5
Brookdale Cl
　Bolton BL1 . . . . 143 C2
　Romiley SK6 . . . . 112 F3
Brookdale Cotts SK2 . . . . 124 F6
Brookdale Ct M33 . . . . . . 108 C1
Brookdale Rd
　Bramhall SK7 . . . . 123 F1
　Hindley WN2 . . . . 56 F5
　Wythenshawe SK8 . . . . . 121 F5
Brookdale Rise SK7 . . . . 123 F1
Brookdean Cl BL1 . . . . . . 83 E7
Brookdene Rd
　Manchester M19 . . . . . . 110 E6
　Whitefield BL9 . . . . 45 A2
Brook Dr
　Marple SK6 . . . . 125 F4

Brook Dr continued
　Tyldesley M29 . . . . 77 C5
　Whitefield M45 . . . . 63 B8
Brooke Ct SK9 . . . . 131 E4
Brooke Dr SK9 . . . . 131 D4
Brookes St
　🔳 Bacup OL13 . . . . 3 D8
　Middleton M24 . . . . 47 B2
Brooke Way SK9 . . . . 131 D4
Brook Farm Cl M31 . . . . . 105 E2
BROOKFIELD 171 B3
Brookfield
　Prestwich M25 . . . . 63 B4
　Shaw OL2 . . . . 32 A1
Brookfield Ave
　Ainsworth BL2 . . . . 26 C1
　Altrincham WA15 . . . . . . 119 F8
　Manchester M21 . . . . . . 109 C7
　Poynton SK12 . . . . 133 C3
　Romiley SK6 . . . . 113 A4
　Royton OL2 . . . . 48 D3
　Salford M6 . . . . 80 C3
　Stockport SK1 . . . . 124 A7
　Urmston M41 . . . . 95 A2
Brookfield Bsns Pk SK8 . 122 E5
Brookfield Cl
　Prestwich M25 . . . . 63 B4
　Stockport SK1 . . . . 124 A7
Brookfield Cres SK8 . . . . 122 D4
Brookfield Cl 🔳 M19 . . . . 110 F8
Brookfield Dr
　Altrincham WA15 . . . . . . 120 A7
　Boothstown M28 . . . . 77 F6
　Littleborough OL15 . . . . . 15 F6
　Swinton M27 . . . . 61 F8
Brookfield Gdns M22 . . . . 121 C6
Brookfield Gr OL6 . . . . 85 D2
Brookfield Ho
　Cheadle SK8 . . . . 122 D4
　Ramsbottom BL0 . . . . 10 F3
Brookfield Ind Est SK13 . 171 B3
Brookfield Rd
　Bury BL9 . . . . 27 E8
　Cheadle SK8 . . . . 122 E5
　Culcheth WA3 . . . . 91 D3
　Eccles M30 . . . . 79 B4
　Manchester M8 . . . . 64 A1
　Shevington Moor WN6 . . . 19 B2
　Up Holland WN8 . . . . 53 B7
Brookfield Road Ind Est
　SK8 . . . . 122 F5
Brookfield St
　Bolton BL2 . . . . 148 B3
　Leigh WN7 . . . . 76 A6
　Newton-le-W WA12 . . . . . 89 B3
　Oldham OL8 . . . . 153 C1
Brookfield Terr SK7 . . . . . 124 F4
Brookfold M35 . . . . 83 E8
Brookfold La BL2 . . . . 25 F5
Brook Fold La SK14 . . . . 102 B2
Brookfold Rd SK4 . . . . . . 111 D6
Brook Gdns
　Bolton BL2 . . . . 25 E4
　Heywood OL10 . . . . 29 C2
Brook Gr M44 . . . . 94 A2
Brook Green La M34 . . . . . 99 F3
Brookhead Ave M20 . . . . 109 F7
Brookhead Dr SK8 . . . . . 123 A6
Brookhey SK14 . . . . 101 B3
Brookhey Ave BL3 . . . . . . 147 C3
Brook Hey Cl OL12 . . . . . . 15 D4
Brookheys Rd WA14 . . . . 106 E1
Brookhill Cl OL3 . . . . 51 C5
Brookhill St M40 . . . . 160 B3
Brook Ho
　Sale WA15 . . . . 120 C7
　Wigan WN1 . . . . 151 A4
Brookhouse Ave
　Eccles M30 . . . . 95 A8
　Farnworth BL4 . . . . 60 C6
Brookhouse Cl BL8 . . . . . 26 E8
Brook House Cl BL2 . . . . . 25 E3
Brookhouse Mill La BL8 . . 26 F8
Brookhouse St WN1 . . . . 151 A3
Brookhurst La M38 . . . . . . 59 E6
Brookhurst Rd M18 . . . . . . 99 D4
Brook La
　Alderley Edge SK9 . . . . . 136 F3
　Altrincham WA15 . . . . . . 119 F6
　Oldham, Alexandra Park
　OL8 . . . . 67 B4
　Oldham, Salem OL4 . . . . 67 E6
　Rochdale OL16 . . . . 31 B3
　Uppermill OL3 . . . . 50 F2
　Whitefield BL9 . . . . 45 A4
　Wigan WN5 . . . . 54 B5
Brookland Ave
　Denton M34 . . . . 100 D4
　Farnworth BL4 . . . . 60 C7
　Hindley WN2 . . . . 56 D5
Brookland Gr BL1 . . . . . . 142 A2
Brookland Rd WN1 . . . . . . 37 B3
BROOKLANDS 108 C2
Brooklands
　Horwich BL6 . . . . 22 C3
　Wardle OL12 . . . . 15 C7
Brooklands Ave
　Ashton-in-M WN4 . . . . . . 73 D2
　Atherton M46 . . . . 58 D4
　Chadderton OL9 . . . . . . 152 B1
　Haslingden BB4 . . . . 1 B7
　Leigh WN7 . . . . 75 E3
　Manchester M20 . . . . . . 110 A6
Brooklands Cl
　Denton M34 . . . . 100 D4
　Irlam M44 . . . . 93 F2

Brooklands Cl continued
　Mossley OL5 . . . . 68 B2
　Reddish SK4 . . . . 111 D5
Brooklands Cres M33 . . . 108 B3
Brooklands Ct
　Manchester M8 . . . . 63 F2
　Rochdale OL11 . . . . 30 C6
　Sale M33 . . . . 108 B3
Brooklands Dr
　Droylsden M43 . . . . 84 C3
　Glossop SK13 . . . . 116 B7
　Oldham OL4 . . . . 68 B6
　Orrell WN5 . . . . 53 D5
Brooklands Ho M33 . . . . 108 B2
Brooklands Metro Sta
　M33 . . . . 108 A3
Brooklands Par OL4 . . . . . 68 B6
Brooklands Pl M33 . . . . . 108 A3
Brooklands Prim Sch
　M33 . . . . 108 A2
Brooklands Rd
　Hazel Grove SK7 . . . . . . 124 E1
　Manchester M8 . . . . 63 E2
　Ramsbottom BL0 . . . . 11 A2
　Reddish SK5 . . . . 99 E2
　Sale M23, M33 . . . . 108 B2
　Swinton M27 . . . . 79 D6
　Up Holland WN8 . . . . 53 C7
Brooklands Sports Club
　M33 . . . . 108 B2
Brooklands St
　Middleton M24 . . . . 47 A1
　Royton OL2 . . . . 48 D5
Brooklands Station App
　M33 . . . . 108 A3
Brooklawn Dr
　Manchester M20 . . . . . . 110 B4
　Prestwich M25 . . . . 63 C6
Brookleigh Rd M20 . . . . . 110 D6
Brooklet Cl OL4 . . . . 67 F5
Brook Lo SK8 . . . . 122 D4
Brooklyn Ave
　Littleborough OL15 . . . . . 16 A7
　Manchester M16 . . . . 97 C2
　Rochdale OL16 . . . . 15 E2
　Urmston M41 . . . . 95 A2
Brooklyn Cres SK8 . . . . . 122 D5
Brooklyn Ct M20 . . . . 110 C7
Brook Lynn Ave WA3 . . . . 74 F1
Brooklyn Pl SK8 . . . . 122 D6
Brooklyn Rd
　Cheadle SK8 . . . . 122 D5
　Stockport SK2 . . . . 124 C6
Brooklyn St BL1 . . . . 143 B1
Brook Mdw
　Glossop SK13 . . . . 104 E1
　Westhoughton BL5 . . . . . 40 A1
Brook Mill 🔳 BL7 . . . . 24 F7
Brook Rd
　Cheadle SK8 . . . . 122 D6
　Manchester M14 . . . . . . 110 D7
　Sale M33 . . . . 111 C5
　Urmston M41 . . . . 95 A2
Brooks Ave
　Hazel Grove SK7 . . . . . . 124 D3
　Hyde SK14 . . . . 167 B1
　Radcliffe M26 . . . . 43 F6
Brook's Bar M16 . . . . 97 D4
Brooksbottom Cl BL0 . . . . 11 C4
Brooks Dr
　Altrincham, Halebarns
　WA15 . . . . 129 D8
　Altrincham M23, WA15 . . 120 D6
　Failsworth M35 . . . . 83 E6
　Gatley SK8 . . . . 122 C2
Brooks End OL11 . . . . 13 E1
Brookshaw St
　Bury BL9 . . . . 141 A4
　Manchester M11 . . . . 83 A1
Brooks Hos 🔳 WN7 . . . . . 75 E8
Brookside
　Glossop SK13 . . . . 116 B8
　Mossley OL5 . . . . 68 B2
　New Mills SK22 . . . . 127 E2
　Oldham OL4 . . . . 67 D6
　Wigan WN3 . . . . 150 A1
Brookside Ave
　Ashton-in-M WN4 . . . . . . 72 F8
　Droylsden M43 . . . . 84 C3
　Farnworth BL4 . . . . 60 C7
　Poynton SK12 . . . . 133 E3
　Stockport SK2 . . . . 124 F7
Brookside Cl
　Atherton M46 . . . . 58 E4
　Billinge WN5 . . . . 71 E5
　Bolton BL2 . . . . 25 D5
　Cheadle SK8 . . . . 122 D4
　Glossop SK13 . . . . 171 C4
　Hyde SK14 . . . . 102 A3
　Ramsbottom BL0 . . . . 11 A3
Brookside Cres
　Bury BL8 . . . . 26 E8
　Middleton M24 . . . . 65 C6
　Ramsbottom BL8 . . . . 10 E1
　Walkden M28 . . . . 60 E3
Brookside Ct M19 . . . . 99 A2
Brookside Dr
　Hyde SK14 . . . . 102 A3
　Manchester M7 . . . . 63 D1
Brookside La SK6 . . . . . . 134 E7
Brookside Miniature Rly*
　SK12 . . . . 134 E6
Brookside Prim Sch 134 E6

Brookside Rd
　Bolton BL2 . . . . 42 D8
　Gatley SK8 . . . . 122 A6
　Manchester M40 . . . . 65 A1
　Sale M33 . . . . 108 A2
　Standish WN1 . . . . 20 B1
Brookside Terr
　Delph OL3 . . . . 50 E4
　Wilmslow SK9 . . . . 136 E3
Brookside Wlk M26 . . . . . 43 F7
Brooksmouth BL8 . . . . . . 140 A2
Brook's Pl 🔳 OL12 . . . . . 139 B4
Brook's Rd M16 . . . . 97 C3
Brooks St SK1 . . . . 170 C3
Brook St
　Ashton-in-M WN4 . . . . . . 73 C2
　Atherton M46 . . . . 58 B3
　Bank Heath WA3 . . . . 90 A8
　Bolton BL1 . . . . 145 C3
　Bury BL9 . . . . 141 A3
　Chadderton OL9 . . . . . . 152 B4
　Cheadle SK8 . . . . 122 F6
　Failsworth M35 . . . . 83 D6
　Farnworth BL4 . . . . 42 E1
　Glossop SK13 . . . . 104 C1
　Golborne, Aspull Common
　WA3 . . . . 75 A1
　Hazel Grove SK7 . . . . . . 124 E2
　Hyde SK14 . . . . 167 B3
　Ince-in-M WN2 . . . . 56 A7
　Kearsley M26 . . . . 61 A7
　Littleborough OL15 . . . . . 16 C5
　Manchester M1 . . . . 163 A3
　Oldham OL1 . . . . 67 A7
　Radcliffe M26 . . . . 44 B3
　Royton OL2 . . . . 48 D3
　Sale M33 . . . . 108 C5
　Swinton M27 . . . . 79 D8
　Wardle OL12 . . . . 15 C6
　Westhoughton BL5 . . . . . 39 F1
　Wigan WN3 . . . . 54 F4
Brookstone Cl M21 . . . . . 109 D6
Brook Street E
　Ashton-u-L OL6 . . . . 166 A2
　Ashton-u-L OL6 . . . . 166 A2
　Ashton-u-L OL6 . . . . 166 B2
　Ashton-u-L OL6 . . . . 166 C3
　🔳 Bolton BL1 . . . . 143 C2
　Bolton BL1 . . . . 145 B4
Brook Street E BL1 . . . . . 145 C3
Brook Street E
　Bury BL8 . . . . 27 C5
　Cheadle SK3 . . . . 123 A7
Brook Street E
　Cheadle SK8 . . . . 122 F3
　Diggle SK15 . . . . 51 C5
Brook Street E
　Failsworth M35 . . . . 83 E5
　Glossop SK13 . . . . 104 E2
　Manchester M4, SK13 . . 115 B8
Brook Street E
　Horwich BL6 . . . . 22 A4
　Horwich BL6 . . . . 20 B1
　Horwich BL6 . . . . 22 D2
　Horwich BL6 . . . . 22 D2
　Newton-le-W WA12 . . . . . 89 C4
Brook Street E OL15 . . . . 16 C6
Brook Street E
　Manchester, Chorlton-cum-
　Hardy M21 . . . . 109 C8
　Manchester, Heaton Chapel
　SK4 . . . . 111 C5
Brook Street E M8 . . . . . 156 B4
Brook Street E
　Manchester M11, M12 . . 165 A3
　Manchester M13 . . . . . . 164 A3
　Manchester M13 . . . . . . 164 A1
　Manchester M13 . . . . . . 164 A1
　Manchester M13 . . . . . . 162 B1
　Manchester M16 . . . . . . 161 B1
Brook Street E
　Manchester M16, M21 . . 97 C1
　Manchester M21 . . . . . . 109 F3
　Manchester M21 . . . . 97 B2
　Manchester M21 . . . . . . 109 C8
Brook Street E M38 . . . . . 60 B6
Brook Street E M40 . . . . . 157 B1
Brook Street E M43 . . . . . 83 E1
Brook Street E SK4 . . . . . 111 C5
Brook Street E
　Marple SK6 . . . . 125 F5
　Marple SK6 . . . . 125 F5
Brook Street E
　Newton-le-W WA12 . . . . . 89 A4
　Newton-le-W WA12 . . . . . 89 C4
　Oldham OL1 . . . . 153 B4
　Oldham OL4 . . . . 67 A6
　Oldham OL4 . . . . 67 E8
　🔳 Oldham OL8 . . . . 66 F4
　Partington M31 . . . . 105 F2
　Partington M31 . . . . 105 F3
　Radcliffe M26 . . . . 43 F4
　Radcliffe M26 . . . . 44 B3
　Ramsbottom BL0 . . . . . . 138 B1
　🔳 Rochdale OL12 . . . . . 14 F1
Brook Street E* M21 . . . 108 E7
Brook Street E
　Sale M33 . . . . 108 D2
　Sale M33 . . . . 108 D4
　Sale M33 . . . . 108 D4

Brook Street E *continued*
Salford M7 . . . . 155 C4
Stockport, Heaton Moor SK4 . . . . 168 C4
Stockport SK2 . . . . 124 A3
Stockport SK3 . . . . 123 F3
Brook Street E SK3 . . . . 170 B3
Brook Street E
Stretford M32 . . . . 96 B2
Stretford M32 . . . . 96 D3
Tyldesley M29 . . . . 59 B1
Warrington WA3 . . . . 74 B1
Wigan WN1 . . . . 151 B3
Brook Street E M23 . . . . 120 F5
Brook Street E* M23 . . . . 121 B8
Brook Street Ind Est SK1 . . . . 170 C3
Brook Street W OL6 . . . . 166 A2
Brook Terr
Manchester M13 . . . . 98 F3
Newhey OL16 . . . . 32 C4
Urmston M41 . . . . 95 C4
Brook The OL15 . . . . 6 C1
Brookthorn Cl SK2 . . . . 124 F5
Brookthorpe Ave M19 . . . . 110 E6
Brookthorpe Mdws BL8 . . . . 27 A3
Brookthorpe Rd BL8 . . . . 27 A3
Brookvale 4 WN6 . . . . 37 A1
Brookview 1 WN2 . . . . 56 D4
Brook View SK9 . . . . 137 A3
Brookville OL12 . . . . 4 C1
Brookwater Cl BL8 . . . . 26 F6
Brookway
Altrincham WA15 . . . . 119 F7
Littleborough OL15 . . . . 16 A4
Oldham OL4 . . . . 67 E5
Uppermill OL4 . . . . 68 E6
Brookway Cl M19 . . . . 110 E4
Brookway Ct M23 . . . . 120 F7
Brook Wlk
Bury BL8 . . . . 27 A6
Denton M34 . . . . 112 F8
Brookwood Ave
Manchester M8 . . . . 156 C4
Sale M33 . . . . 107 E3
Brookwood Cl M34 . . . . 113 A7
Broom Ave
Leigh WN7 . . . . 75 E7
Manchester M19 . . . . 111 B8
4 Reddish SK5 . . . . 111 F6
Salford M7 . . . . 155 B4
BROOMEDGE 117 C1
Broomedge M7 . . . . 155 A4
Broome Gr M35 . . . . 83 F6
Broomehouse Ave M44 . . 105 E8
Broome St OL9 . . . . 153 A2
Broomfield M6 . . . . 80 D6
Broomfield Cl
Ainsworth BL2 . . . . 26 C1
Reddish SK5 . . . . 111 F6
Wilmslow SK9 . . . . 137 E8
Broomfield Cres
Middleton M24 . . . . 46 D1
Stockport SK2 . . . . 124 A4
Broomfield Dr
Reddish SK5 . . . . 111 F6
Salford M8 . . . . 155 C3
Broomfield La WA15 . . . . 119 E3
Broomfield Pk M24 . . . . 64 E8
Broomfield Pl WN6 . . . . 19 E1
Broomfield Rd
4 Bolton BL3 . . . . 146 C4
Standish WN6 . . . . 19 E2
Stockport SK4 . . . . 168 C4
Broomfields M34 . . . . 101 A5
Broomfield Sq OL11 . . . . 139 C1
Broomfield Terr
Newhey OL16 . . . . 32 B4
Wigan WN1 . . . . 151 B3
Broomflat Cl WN6 . . . . 19 E1
Broomgrove La M34 . . . . 101 A4
Broomhall Rd
Manchester M9 . . . . 64 B5
Pendlebury M27 . . . . 80 D6
Broomhey Ave WN1 . . . . 37 C4
Broomhey Terr WN1 . . . . 151 B3
Broomhill Dr SK7 . . . . 123 D1
Broomholme WN6 . . . . 35 D7
Broomhurst Ave OL8 . . . . 66 D4
Broom La
Manchester M19 . . . . 111 B8
Salford M7 . . . . 155 A4
Broom Rd
Altrincham WA15 . . . . 119 E3
Partington M31 . . . . 105 F2
Wigan WN5 . . . . 54 D7
Broom St
Bury BL8 . . . . 140 A2
Newhey OL16 . . . . 32 B4
Swinton M27 . . . . 79 F7
Broomstair Rd M34 . . . . 100 F6
Broomville Ave M33 . . . . 108 B4
Broom Way BL5 . . . . 40 A2
Broomwood Gdns WA15 . 120 C5
Broomwood Prim Sch WA15 . . . . 120 D5
Broomwood Rd WA15 . . . . 120 C5
Broomwood Wlk 3 M15 . 163 A2
Broseley Ave
Culcheth WA3 . . . . 91 D4
Manchester M20 . . . . 110 D3
Broseley La WA3 . . . . 91 D5
Broseley Rd M16 . . . . 97 A2
Brosscroft SK13 . . . . 104 A6
Brosscroft Cl SK13 . . . . 104 A6
Brosscroft Village SK13 . 104 A6
Brotherdale Cl OL2 . . . . 48 D5
Brotherod Hall Rd OL12 . . 14 C2
Brotherton Cl M15 . . . . 162 A2
Brotherton Ct 6 M14 . . . . 98 D4
Brotherton Dr M3 . . . . 158 A2
Brotherton Way WA12 . . . . 89 B4
Brougham St M28 . . . . 60 C3
Brough Cl WN2 . . . . 56 E3
Brough St 4 M11 . . . . 99 E7
Broughton Ave
Golborne WA3 . . . . 90 D7
Walkden M38 . . . . 60 B4
Broughton Cl M24 . . . . 46 D2
Broughton Jewish Cassel-Fox Prim Sch M7 . . . . 155 A4
Broughton La
Salford M7 . . . . 155 A1
Salford M7, M8 . . . . 158 B4
BROUGHTON PARK 63 D1
Broughton Rd
Reddish SK5 . . . . 169 C4
Salford M6 . . . . 81 A4
Broughton Rd E M6 . . . . 81 B4
Broughton St
Bolton BL1 . . . . 143 A2
Manchester M8 . . . . 159 A4
Salford M8 . . . . 155 C1
Broughton Trade Ctr M7 . 158 B4
Broughville Dr M20 . . . . 122 C8
Brow Ave M24 . . . . 65 C6
Browbeck OL1 . . . . 153 B3
Browfield Ave
Manchester M5 . . . . 161 B4
Salford M5 . . . . 161 B3
Browfield Way OL1 . . . . 48 E1
Browmere Dr M20 . . . . 110 A4
Brownacre St M20 . . . . 110 B6
Brown Bank Rd OL15 . . . . 15 F3
Brownbank Wlk 7 M15 . 162 C1
Browncross St M3 . . . . 158 B1
Brown Edge Rd OL4 . . . . 67 E4
Brown Heath Ave WN5 . . . 71 D3
Brownhill Countryside Ctr* OL3 . . . . 51 B1
Brownhill Dr OL4 . . . . 68 A7
Brownhill La OL3 . . . . 51 B1
Brownhills Cl BL8 . . . . 27 A5
Brownhill Specl Sch OL12 14 E1
Brownhill St M11 . . . . 165 A4
Brownhill View OL12 . . . . 14 E1
Browning Ave
Atherton M46 . . . . 58 D5
2 Droylsden M43 . . . . 84 A1
Wigan WN3 . . . . 54 F4
Browning Cl BL1 . . . . 143 A1
Browning Gr WN6 . . . . 36 E3
Browning Rd
Middleton M24 . . . . 47 B2
Oldham OL1 . . . . 49 B1
Reddish SK5 . . . . 99 E2
Swinton M27 . . . . 79 E8
Browning St
Leigh WN7 . . . . 75 D6
Manchester M15 . . . . 162 A2
Salford M3 . . . . 158 A2
Browning Wlk M46 . . . . 58 D5
Brown La SK8 . . . . 122 B1
Brownlea Ave SK16 . . . . 101 C7
Brownley Court Rd M22 . 121 D5
Brownley Ct M22 . . . . 121 E5
Brownley Rd M22 . . . . 121 E4
Brown Lodge Dr OL15 . . . . 15 F3
Brown Lodge St OL15 . . . . 15 F3
BROWNLOW 53 C1
Brownlow Ave
Ince-in-M WN2 . . . . 56 B7
Royton OL2 . . . . 49 A3
Brownlow Bsns Ctr BL1 . 143 A1
Brownlow Cl SK12 . . . . 133 E2
BROWNLOW FOLD 143 A1
Brownlow Fold Prim Sch BL1 . . . . 143 A1
Brownlow La WN5 . . . . 53 C1
Brownlow Rd BL6 . . . . 22 C5
Brownlow Way BL1 . . . . 143 B1
Brownmere WN6 . . . . 36 F2
Brownrigg Cl M24 . . . . 46 C1
Brownside Cl OL16 . . . . 15 C3
Brown's La SK9 . . . . 137 E8
Brownslow Wlk 11 M13 . 163 B3
Brownson Wlk 7 M9 . . . . 157 B4
Browns Rd BL2 . . . . 43 B6
Brown St
3 Alderley Edge SK9 . . . . 137 A1
Altrincham WA14 . . . . 119 D3
Bickershaw WN2 . . . . 56 E1
Blackrod BL6 . . . . 21 D2
Bolton BL1 . . . . 145 C3
Chadderton OL9 . . . . 152 A4
Failsworth M35 . . . . 83 E7
Heywood OL10 . . . . 29 D3
Ince-in-M WN2 . . . . 56 A7
3 Leigh WN7 . . . . 76 A5
Littleborough OL15 . . . . 16 B5
Manchester M2 . . . . 159 A1
Middleton M24 . . . . 47 A2
Oldham OL1 . . . . 67 A7
Radcliffe M26 . . . . 43 F6
Ramsbottom BL0 . . . . 138 B1
Salford M6 . . . . 154 C1
Stockport SK1 . . . . 169 B2
Tyldesley M29 . . . . 76 F7
Wigan WN3 . . . . 150 B3
Brown Street N 2 WN7 . . 76 A5
Brown Street S 1 WN7 . . 76 A4
Brownsville Rd SK4 . . . . 111 C5
Brownville Gr SK16 . . . . 101 E7
Brownwood Ave SK1 . . . . 112 B1
Brownwood Cl M33 . . . . 108 C1
Brows Ave M23 . . . . 109 A2
Browsholm Ho BL1 . . . . 144 C3
Brow St OL11 . . . . 31 A4
Brow Wlk M9 . . . . 64 D3
Broxton Ave
Bolton BL3 . . . . 146 B3
Orrell WN5 . . . . 53 F7
Broxton St M40 . . . . 160 C3
Broxwood Cl 8 M18 . . . . 99 D5
Broyne Cl M11 . . . . 164 C4
Bruce St OL11 . . . . 30 C4
Bruce Wlk 2 M11 . . . . 99 D7
Brundage Rd M22 . . . . 121 D2
Brundrett's Rd M21 . . . . 109 B8
Brundrett St SK1 . . . . 124 A8
Brunel Ave M5 . . . . 81 B1
Brunel Cl M32 . . . . 96 E2
Brunel St
Bolton BL1 . . . . 143 A3
Horwich BL6 . . . . 22 C2
Brunet Wlk M12 . . . . 164 C2
Brun La OL3 . . . . 51 E6
Brunstead Cl M23 . . . . 120 D6
BRUNSWICK 163 C2
Brunswick Ave BL6 . . . . 22 E2
Brunswick Ct BL1 . . . . 145 B4
Brunswick Rd
Altrincham WA14 . . . . 119 D7
Manchester M20 . . . . 110 C7
Brunswick Sq OL1 . . . . 153 C2
Brunswick St
Bury BL9 . . . . 140 C3
Dukinfield SK16 . . . . 101 C8
Heywood OL10 . . . . 29 C2
3 Heywood OL10 . . . . 29 C2
Leigh WN7 . . . . 76 A4
Manchester M13 . . . . 163 B2
Mossley OL5 . . . . 86 D8
Oldham OL1 . . . . 153 B2
Rochdale OL16 . . . . 31 A8
Shaw OL2 . . . . 149 B3
Stretford M32 . . . . 108 D8
Brunswick Terr OL13 . . . . 3 D8
Brunton Rd SK5 . . . . 111 F6
Brunt St M14 . . . . 98 B3
Bruntwood Ave SK8 . . . . 122 A1
Bruntwood La
Cheadle Hulme SK8 . . . . 122 E2
Cheadle SK8 . . . . 122 E1
BRUSHES 86 D3
Brushes SK15 . . . . 87 A3
Brushes Ave SK15 . . . . 86 D3
Brushes Rd
Hollingworth SK15 . . . . 87 A3
Stalybridge SK15 . . . . 86 E2
Brussels Rd SK3 . . . . 170 A2
Bruton Ave M32 . . . . 96 B1
Brutus Wlk M7 . . . . 155 B2
Bryan Rd M21 . . . . 97 B2
Bryan St 1 OL4 . . . . 49 C1
Bryant Cl M13 . . . . 163 C1
Bryant's Acre BL1 . . . . 40 D7
Bryantsfield BL1 . . . . 40 D6
Bryce St SK14 . . . . 167 A4
Brydges Rd SK6 . . . . 125 E5
Brydon Ave M12 . . . . 163 C3
Brydon Cl M6 . . . . 154 C2
Bryham St WN1 . . . . 151 A4
BRYN 72 F6
Bryn Cross WN4 . . . . 73 A6
Bryndale Gr M33 . . . . 107 F1
Brynden Ave M20 . . . . 110 C5
Bryn Dr SK5 . . . . 111 F5
Brynford Ave M9 . . . . 64 A5
BRYN GATES 73 E7
Bryn Gates La WN2 . . . . 73 D8
Bryngs Dr BL2 . . . . 25 F4
Brynhall Cl M26 . . . . 43 E5
Brynheys Cl M38 . . . . 60 A5
Bryn Lea Terr BL1 . . . . 142 A4
Brynmoor BL1 . . . . 142 B2
Brynn St WN2 . . . . 73 F7
Brynorme Rd M8 . . . . 64 A2
Bryn Rd WN4 . . . . 73 B5
Bryn Road S WN4 . . . . 73 C4
Bryn St
Ashton-in-M WN4 . . . . 73 B3
Ince-in-M WN3 . . . . 151 B2
Bryn Sta WN4 . . . . 73 A6
Brynton Rd M13 . . . . 98 E2
Bryn Wlk BL1 . . . . 145 C4
Bryone Dr SK2 . . . . 124 B5
Bryony Cl
Orrell WN5 . . . . 53 D5
Walkden M28 . . . . 60 D5
6 Wythenshawe M22 . . . . 121 C1
Bryson Wlk M18 . . . . 165 C1
Buchanan Dr WN2 . . . . 57 B3
Buchanan Rd WN5 . . . . 54 E7
Buchanan St
Leigh WN7 . . . . 75 E5
Ramsbottom BL0 . . . . 138 B1
Swinton M27 . . . . 61 F1
Buchan St M11 . . . . 83 B2
Buckden Rd SK4 . . . . 111 D7
Buckden Wlk 11 M23 . . . . 108 F2
Buckfast Ave
Haydock WA11 . . . . 89 A7
Oldham OL8 . . . . 67 D3
Buckfast Cl
Altrincham WA15 . . . . 120 B2
Cheadle SK8 . . . . 132 B6
Manchester M21 . . . . 97 B1
Poynton SK12 . . . . 133 D5
Buckfast Rd
Middleton M24 . . . . 46 F3
Buckfast Rd *continued*
Sale M33 . . . . 107 E6
Buckfast Wlk M7 . . . . 155 B2
Buckfield Ave M5 . . . . 161 B3
Buckhurst Rd
Manchester M19 . . . . 99 A1
Ramsbottom BL9 . . . . 12 C3
Buckingham Ave
Denton M34 . . . . 101 B2
Horwich BL6 . . . . 22 E2
Salford M6 . . . . 154 A2
Whitefield M45 . . . . 63 A7
Buckingham Cl WN5 . . . . 54 E5
Buckingham Dr
Bury BL8 . . . . 44 B8
Dukinfield SK16 . . . . 101 F7
Buckingham Park Cl OL2 . . . . 149 B4
Buckingham Pl
Manchester M21 . . . . 97 B1
Tyldesley M29 . . . . 58 F3
Buckingham Rd
Cheadle SK8 . . . . 123 A3
Droylsden M43 . . . . 83 E1
Irlam M44 . . . . 105 C6
Manchester, Heaton Chapel SK4 . . . . 111 C6
Manchester, Heaton Moor SK4 . . . . 111 B5
Manchester, Hilton Park M25 . . . . 63 C2
Manchester M21 . . . . 97 B1
Poynton SK12 . . . . 133 D3
Sale WA14 . . . . 107 F1
Stalybridge SK15 . . . . 86 A3
Stretford M32 . . . . 96 F4
Swinton M27 . . . . 62 A2
Wilmslow SK9 . . . . 136 F6
Buckingham Road W SK4 . . . . 168 A4
Buckingham St
12 Rochdale OL16 . . . . 31 A8
Salford M5 . . . . 154 C1
Stockport SK2 . . . . 124 A6
Buckingham Way
Altrincham WA15 . . . . 120 A7
Stockport SK2 . . . . 170 C2
Buck La M33 . . . . 107 E6
Buckland Ave M9 . . . . 64 A3
Buckland Dr WN5 . . . . 36 B1
Buckland Gr SK14 . . . . 114 A8
Buckland Rd M6 . . . . 154 A4
Buckle Ho 7 M30 . . . . 79 E2
BUCKLEY 15 A3
Buckley Ave M18 . . . . 99 C4
Buckley Barn Ct OL11 . . . . 30 C1
Buckley Bldgs OL5 . . . . 86 E8
Buckley Brook St OL12 . . . 15 B2
Buckley Chase OL16 . . . . 31 E5
Buckley Cl SK14 . . . . 113 E7
Buckley Dr
Denshaw OL3 . . . . 33 C1
Romiley SK6 . . . . 113 A1
Buckley Farm La OL12 . . . . 15 B3
Buckley Fields OL12 . . . . 15 A2
Buckley Hall Ind Est OL12 15 B3
Buckley Hill La OL16 . . . . 31 E5
Buckley Ho M46 . . . . 58 D3
Buckley La
Farnworth BL4 . . . . 60 C7
Prestwich M25 . . . . 62 E3
Rochdale OL12 . . . . 15 B3
Buckley Mill OL3 . . . . 69 B8
Buckley Rd
Manchester M18 . . . . 99 C4
Oldham OL4 . . . . 67 D8
Rochdale OL12 . . . . 15 B2
Buckley Road Ind Est OL12 . . . . 15 A2
Buckley Sq BL4 . . . . 60 C6
Buckley St
Bury BL9 . . . . 140 C3
Chadderton OL9 . . . . 152 A3
Denton M34 . . . . 100 D7
Droylsden M43 . . . . 84 A1
Heywood OL10 . . . . 29 E3
Oldham OL4 . . . . 67 E5
Radcliffe M26 . . . . 44 A3
Reddish SK5 . . . . 99 E2
Rochdale OL16 . . . . 31 A8
Shaw OL2 . . . . 149 C3
Stalybridge SK15 . . . . 101 F8
Uppermill OL3 . . . . 69 B8
Wigan WN6 . . . . 37 B2
Buckley Street W WN6 . . . 37 A2
Buckley Terr OL12 . . . . 15 B3
Buckley View OL12 . . . . 15 B3
BUCKLEY WELLS 140 A1
Bucklow Ave
Manchester M14 . . . . 98 B1
Partington M31 . . . . 105 F3
Bucklow Cl
Broadbottom SK14 . . . . 102 F1
Oldham OL4 . . . . 49 E4
Bucklow Dr M22 . . . . 121 E8
Bucklow Gdns WA13 . . . . 117 A4
Bucklow Ho M22 . . . . 121 F7
Bucklow View WA14 . . . . 119 A3
Bucknell Ct M40 . . . . 159 C4
Buck St WN7 . . . . 75 F4
Buckstones Prim Sch OL2 . . . . 49 D8
Buckstones Rd OL1, OL2 . . 49 E7
Buckthorn Cl
Altrincham WA15 . . . . 120 E5
Manchester M21 . . . . 109 D6
Westhoughton BL5 . . . . 39 F2
Buckthorn La M30 . . . . 94 F8
Buckton Cl OL3 . . . . 51 C5
Buckton Dr SK15 . . . . 86 E5
BUCKTON VALE 86 E6
Buckton Vale Mews SK15. 86 F7
Buckton Vale Prim Sch SK15 . . . . 86 F7
Buckton Vale Rd SK15 . . . . 86 F6
Buckwood Cl SK7 . . . . 125 A3
Buddleia Gr M7 . . . . 155 A2
Bude Ave
Brinnington SK5 . . . . 112 B5
Tyldesley M29 . . . . 77 C8
Urmston M41 . . . . 107 B8
Bude Cl SK7 . . . . 132 F7
Bude Terr 4 SK16 . . . . 166 B1
Bude Wlk M23 . . . . 121 B5
Budsworth Ave M20 . . . . 110 B7
Budworth Gdns 2 M43 . . . 84 B1
Budworth Rd M33 . . . . 108 E3
Budworth Wlk 1 SK9 . . . . 131 E1
Buer Ave WN3 . . . . 54 F4
BUERSIL 31 B3
Buersil Ave OL16 . . . . 31 B4
BUERSIL HEAD 31 C1
Buersil St OL16 . . . . 31 B3
Buerton Ave M9 . . . . 64 A5
Buffalo Ct M50 . . . . 96 E8
Buffoline Trad Est M19 . . . 99 B1
Bugle St M1 . . . . 162 B4
Buile Dr M9 . . . . 64 F4
Buile Hill Ave M38 . . . . 60 B5
Buile Hill Dr M5 . . . . 154 A3
Buile Hill Gr M38 . . . . 60 B5
Buile Hill High Sch M6 . . 154 A4
Buile St M7 . . . . 155 B3
Buille Ho M6 . . . . 154 B3
Bulford Ave M22 . . . . 121 B2
Bulkeley Rd
Cheadle SK8 . . . . 122 E6
Handforth SK9 . . . . 131 D3
Poynton SK12 . . . . 133 E3
Bulkeley St SK3 . . . . 170 A4
Bullcote Gn OL2 . . . . 49 B4
Bullcote La OL1, OL2 . . . . 49 B4
Bullcroft Dr M29 . . . . 77 C6
Buller Mews BL8 . . . . 27 B1
Buller Rd M13 . . . . 98 F2
Buller St
Bury BL8 . . . . 27 C1
Droylsden M43 . . . . 100 B8
Farnworth BL3 . . . . 42 C2
Oldham OL4 . . . . 67 D8
Bullfinch Dr BL9 . . . . 28 B5
Bullfinch Wlk M21 . . . . 109 D7
BULL HEY 37 B1
Bull Hill Cres M26 . . . . 62 B8
Bullock St SK1 . . . . 170 C3
Bullough St M46 . . . . 58 C2
Bullows Rd M38 . . . . 59 F6
Bullrush Cl M28 . . . . 60 D5
Bulteel St
Bolton BL3 . . . . 146 C2
Boothstown M28 . . . . 77 E7
Eccles M30 . . . . 79 B3
Wigan WN5 . . . . 54 D6
Bulwer St OL16 . . . . 31 A8
Bungalow Rd WA12 . . . . 89 E1
Bungalows The
Ashton-in-M WN4 . . . . 72 F7
Hazel Grove SK7 . . . . 124 F4
New Mills SK22 . . . . 127 D1
Bunkers OL3 . . . . 69 C6
Bunkers Hill SK6 . . . . 113 B1
Bunkershill Rd SK6 . . . . 125 B8
Bunkers Hill Rd SK14 . . . . 102 E1
Bunsen St M1 . . . . 159 B1
Bunting Cl 6 WA3 . . . . 90 E8
Bunting Mews M28 . . . . 78 B8
Bunyan Cl OL1 . . . . 49 E4
Bunyan St 24 OL12 . . . . 14 F1
Bunyard St M8 . . . . 156 B2
Burbage Bank 32 SK13 . . . 171 B2
Burbage Gr 18 SK13 . . . . 171 B2
Burbage Rd M23 . . . . 121 A2
Burbage Way 19 SK13 . . . 171 B2
Burbank Cl WN3 . . . . 54 E1
Burbridge Cl M11 . . . . 160 B1
Burchall Field OL16 . . . . 31 B7
Burdale Dr M6 . . . . 80 B4
Burdale Wlk M23 . . . . 108 F1
Burder St 4 OL8 . . . . 66 C2
Burdett Ave OL12 . . . . 13 F1
Burdett Way M12 . . . . 164 B1
Burdith Ave M14 . . . . 98 A2
Burdon Ave M22 . . . . 121 E3
Burford Ave
Bramhall SK7 . . . . 132 D5
Manchester M16 . . . . 97 D2
Urmston M41 . . . . 95 E4
Burford Cl SK9 . . . . 136 E5
Burford Cres SK9 . . . . 136 E5
Burford Dr
Bolton BL3 . . . . 145 B1
Manchester M16 . . . . 97 D2
Swinton M27 . . . . 61 E2
Burford Gr M33 . . . . 107 E1
Burford La WA13 . . . . 117 C2
Burford Rd M16 . . . . 97 D2
Burford Wlk M16 . . . . 97 D2
Burgess Ave OL6 . . . . 85 C5
Burgess Dr M35 . . . . 83 F7
Burgess St WN3 . . . . 151 B1
Burghley Ave OL4 . . . . 67 D6
Burghley Cl
Little Lever M26 . . . . 43 B5
Stalybridge SK15 . . . . 86 A2
Burghley Dr M26 . . . . 43 B5
Burghley Way WN3 . . . . 151 C1

Burgin Wlk M40 .... 156 C1
Burgundy Dr BL8 .... 26 F7
Burke St BL1 .... 143 A2
Burkhardt Dr WA12 .... 89 E3
Burkitt St SK14 .... 167 B2
Burland Cl M7 .... 155 A1
Burland St WN5 .... 54 F7
Burleigh Cl SK7 .... 124 A1
Burleigh Ct M32 .... 96 E4
Burleigh Ho M13 .... 163 B1
Burleigh Mews M21 .... 109 B6
Burleigh Rd M32 .... 96 E4
Burleigh St WN5 .... 54 C1
Burlescombe Cl WA14 .... 119 B6
Burley Ave WA3 .... 74 D1
Burley Cres WN3 .... 54 C2
Burley Ct SK4 .... 168 C2
Burleyhurst La SK9, WA16 .... 136 B7
Burlin Cl 10 M16 .... 97 D3
Burlington Ave OL8 .... 66 E4
Burlington Cl SK4 .... 110 C2
Burlington Cl WA14 .... 119 D5
Burlington Dr SK3 .... 123 F4
Burlington Gdns SK3 .... 123 F4
Burlington Ho OL6 .... 166 A3
Burlington Rd Altrincham WA14 .... 119 C5
Eccles M30 .... 79 E4
Manchester M20 .... 110 C7
Burlington St Ashton-u-L OL6, OL7 .... 166 A3
Hindley WN2 .... 56 D5
Hindley WN2 .... 56 E5
Manchester M13, M15 .... 163 B1
12 Rochdale OL11 .... 31 A4
Burlton Gr WN3 .... 38 A2
Burman St M11, M43 .... 99 F7
Burnaby St Bolton BL3 .... 145 A1
Oldham OL8 .... 153 A1
Manchester OL11 .... 30 C4
BURNAGE 110 F6
Burnage Ave M19 .... 110 F8
Burnage Hall Rd M19 .... 110 F7
Burnage La M19 .... 110 F4
Burnage Media Arts Coll M19 .... 110 E5
Burnage Range M19 .... 99 A1
Burnage Sta M20 .... 110 D5
Burnaston Gr WN5 .... 54 D5
Burn Bank OL3 .... 68 F5
Burnbray Ave M19 .... 110 E6
Burnby Wlk M23 .... 108 F1
Burndale Dr BL9 .... 45 A3
BURNDEN 42 B4
Burden Ind Est BL3 .... 42 B4
Burnden Pk BL3 .... 148 B1
Burnden Rd BL3 .... 148 B1
Burnden Way BL6 .... 39 C7
BURNEDGE 31 D1
Burnedge Cl OL12 .... 4 D2
Burnedge Fold Rd OL4 .... 68 D6
Burnedge La OL4 .... 68 D7
Burnedge Mews OL4 .... 68 D6
Burnell Cl M40 .... 160 A3
Burnell Cl OL10 .... 46 D2
Burnedge Cres M24 .... 46 E3
Burnet Cl Rochdale OL16 .... 31 C4
Tyldesley M29 .... 77 B7
Burnett Ave M5 .... 161 B4
Burnett Cl M40 .... 157 A1
Burnfell WA3 .... 90 E7
Burnfield Rd Manchester M18 .... 99 D3
Reddish SK5 .... 99 F3
Burnham Ave Bolton BL1 .... 142 A1
Reddish SK5 .... 99 F1
Burnham Cl Cheadle SK8 .... 122 F2
Culcheth WA3 .... 91 E4
Burnham Dr Manchester M19 .... 110 F8
Urmston M41 .... 95 C3
Burnham Gr WN2 .... 37 F2
Burnham Rd M34 .... 100 A3
Burnhill Ct WN6 .... 36 E8
Burnleigh Ct BL5 .... 58 F8
BURNLEY BROW 153 A4
Burnley Brow Com Sch OL9 .... 152 C4
Burnley La Chadderton, Busk OL9 .... 48 C1
Chadderton OL1, OL9 .... 48 A2
Burnley Rd Bury BL9 .... 27 E8
Edenfield BL0 .... 1 D5
Burnley Road E BB4 .... 2 E8
Burnley St Chadderton OL9 .... 152 B4
Failsworth M35 .... 84 A8
Burnmoor Rd BL2 .... 42 F8
Burnsall Ave Golborne WA3 .... 90 F8
Whitefield M45 .... 62 D8
Burnsall Gr OL2 .... 48 D4
Burnsall Wlk 2 M22 .... 121 A2
Burns Ave Atherton M46 .... 58 D5
Bury BL9 .... 44 F6
Cheadle SK8 .... 122 F6
Leigh WN7 .... 75 C8
Swinton M27 .... 61 D1
Burns Cl Ashton-in-M WN4 .... 72 F6

Burns Cl continued
Longshaw WN5 .... 53 D1
Manchester M11 .... 160 C1
Oldham OL1 .... 49 E5
Wigan WN3 .... 55 A4
Burns Cres SK2 .... 124 E7
Burns Fold SK16 .... 102 A7
Burns Gdns M25 .... 62 F3
Burns Gr M43 .... 84 A2
Burnside Altrincham WA15 .... 129 D7
Edenfield BL0 .... 1 D2
Glossop SK13 .... 171 C4
Shaw OL2 .... 49 D8
Stalybridge SK15 .... 102 D7
Burnside Ave Reddish SK4 .... 111 E6
Salford M6 .... 80 B5
Burnside Cl Heywood OL10 .... 29 D1
Radcliffe M26 .... 43 F7
Romiley SK6 .... 112 F3
Stalybridge SK15 .... 102 D7
Tyldesley M29 .... 77 B7
Wilmslow SK9 .... 137 C6
Burnside Dr M19 .... 110 F7
Burnside Rd Bolton BL1 .... 142 B2
Gatley SK8 .... 122 B5
Rochdale OL16 .... 31 C6
Burns Rd 7 Abram WN2 .... 56 B1
Denton M34 .... 113 A7
Walkden M38 .... 60 B5
Burns St Bolton BL3 .... 145 C2
Heywood OL10 .... 29 E1
Oldham OL8 .... 153 D6
Radcliffe M26 .... 44 D4
Reddish SK5 .... 169 C3
Sale M33 .... 108 C1
Burnt Edge La BL6 .... 23 B5
Burnthorpe Ave M9 .... 64 B3
Burnthorpe Cl OL11 .... 29 E6
Burntwood Wlk 2 M9 .... 157 B4
Burnvale WN3 .... 54 D2
Burran Rd M22 .... 130 D8
Burrington Dr M7 .... 75 D7
Burrows Ave M21 .... 109 C6
BURRS 27 D6
Burrs Cl BL8 .... 27 C6
Burrs Ctry Pk BL8 .... 27 E6
Burrs Lea Cl BL9 .... 27 E6
Burrswood Ave BL9 .... 27 F6
Bursar Cl WA12 .... 89 D4
Burslem Ave M20 .... 110 A8
Burstead St M18 .... 99 F7
Burstock St M4 .... 159 B3
Burston St M18 .... 165 C2
Burtinshaw St 7 M18 .... 99 D5
Burton Ave Bury BL8 .... 26 F4
Manchester M20 .... 110 B6
Sale WA15 .... 108 A1
Burton Cl WA3 .... 91 F3
Burton Dr SK12 .... 133 D4
Burton Gr M28 .... 79 C8
Burton Pl M15 .... 162 A3
Burton Rd M20 .... 110 A6
Burton St Middleton M24 .... 64 F8
Oldham OL4 .... 67 E5
Stockport SK4 .... 169 B3
Burton Wlk Salford M3 .... 158 A2
Stockport SK4 .... 169 B3
Burtonwood Ct M24 .... 46 F1
Burtree St M12 .... 165 A2
Burwell Ave PR7 .... 19 D8
Burwell Cl Bolton BL3 .... 147 A5
Glossop SK13 .... 116 A8
Rochdale OL12 .... 14 D4
Burwell Gr M23 .... 120 F7
BURY 140 C3
Bury Art Gall, Mus & Archives ★ BL9 .... 140 B2
Bury Ave M16 .... 97 C2
Bury & Bolton Rd M26 .... 43 E7
Bury Bolton Street Sta ★ BL9 .... 140 B2
Bury Bsns Ctr BL9 .... 141 A4
Bury CE High Sch BL9 .... 44 D8
Bury Coll (Aspire Ctr) BL9 .... 140 B1
Bury Coll (Beacon Ctr) BL9 .... 140 B1
Bury Coll (Business Solutions Link Ho) BL9 .... 140 C3
Bury Coll (Engineering Coll) BL9 .... 140 C1
Bury Coll (Millennium Ctr) BL9 .... 140 C1
Bury Coll (PlayFootball) BL9 .... 140 C1
Bury Coll (Prospect Ctr) BL9 .... 140 B1
Bury Coll (The Construction Skills Centre) BL9 .... 140 C1
Bury Coll (Woodbury Ctr) BL9 .... 140 B1
Bury Gram Jun Sch (Boys) BL9 .... 140 A2
Bury Gram Sch (Boys) BL9 .... 140 A2
Bury Gram Sch (Girls) BL9 .... 140 B2
BURY GROUND 140 A3
Bury Ind Est BL2 .... 42 F8
Bury Intc BL9 .... 140 B1

Bury Metro Sta BL9 .... 140 B2
BURYMEWICK 113 B1
Bury Mkt Hall ★ BL9 .... 140 C2
Bury New Rd
Ainsworth BL2, M26 .... 43 B7
Bolton BL1, BL2 .... 148 A3
Bury BL9 .... 141 C2
Heywood BL9, OL10 .... 28 E2
Prestwich M25 .... 63 B3
Ramsbottom BL0 .... 11 D6
Salford M7, M8, M25 .... 155 B1
Whitefield M45 .... 62 F7
Bury Old Rd
Ainsworth BL2 .... 26 B1
Bolton BL2 .... 148 A3
Edenfield BL0 .... 1 F1
Heywood BL9, OL10 .... 28 E1
Prestwich M25, M45, M7, M8 .... 63 C4
Ramsbottom BL9 .... 11 F4
Salford M8 .... 155 C4
Bury Pl M11 .... 83 C2
Bury RC Prep Sch BL9 .... 44 E8
Bury Rd
Bolton BL8 .... 42 D7
Bury BL8 .... 27 A5
Edenfield BL0 .... 1 D3
Edgworth BL7 .... 9 E5
Radcliffe BL9, M26 .... 44 C5
Rawtenstall BB4 .... 1 E7
Rochdale OL11 .... 30 B6
Bury & Rochdale Old Rd BL9, OL10 .... 29 B5
Bury St
Heywood OL10 .... 29 D1
Mossley OL5 .... 86 C8
Radcliffe M26 .... 44 D4
Reddish SK5 .... 169 C3
Salford M3 .... 158 B2
Bury Transport Mus ★ BL9 .... 140 B2
Bury & Whitefield Jewish Prim Sch BL9 .... 45 B3
Bushell St BL3 .... 146 B4
Bushey Dr M23 .... 121 A5
Bushfield Cl SK14 .... 101 D5
Bushfield Wlk 1 M23 .... 120 E7
Bushgrove Wlk M9 .... 64 D5
Bushnay Wlk 3 M8 .... 156 B2
Bushnell Wlk 1 M9 .... 64 E5
Bush St M40 .... 157 B1
Bushton Wlk 9 M40 .... 156 C1
Business & Technology Ctr M30 .... 79 C2
BUSK 152 C4
Busk Rd OL9 .... 152 C4
Busk Wlk OL9 .... 152 C4
Butcherfield Row WN2 .... 38 B7
Butcher La Royton OL2 .... 48 C5
Wythenshawe M23 .... 120 D7
Butchers La WN4 .... 73 B3
Bute Ave OL8 .... 66 F3
Bute St
Bolton BL1 .... 142 B1
Glossop SK13 .... 104 E3
Manchester M40 .... 157 C4
Salford M5, M50 .... 154 A1
Butler Ct 10 M40 .... 159 C3
Butler Gn 7 OL9 .... 66 A4
Butler La M44, M43 .... 159 C3
Butler St
Manchester M4, M40 .... 160 A2
Ramsbottom BL0 .... 138 A1
Wigan WN1 .... 151 A4
Butley St SK7 .... 124 E4
Butman St M18 .... 99 F6
Buttercup Ave 7 M28 .... 59 F3
Buttercup Cl
Atherton M46 .... 58 D5
Glossop SK13 .... 116 E8
Buttercup Dr
Oldham OL4 .... 49 D2
Rochdale OL11 .... 30 B3
Stockport SK3 .... 170 A1
Butterfield Cl SK8 .... 123 B1
Butterfield Rd BL5 .... 58 F5
Butterhouse La OL3 .... 51 C2
Butter La 3 M3 .... 158 C1
Butterley Cl SK16 .... 101 F7
Buttermere Ave
Ashton-u-L OL7 .... 166 A4
Heywood OL10 .... 46 D8
Swinton M27 .... 79 F6
2 Wythenshawe M22 .... 121 C2
Buttermere Cl
Little Lever BL3 .... 42 F4
Stretford M32 .... 96 C3
Buttermere Dr
Altrincham WA15 .... 129 D6
Middleton M24 .... 46 E2
Ramsbottom BL0 .... 138 B3
Buttermere Gr OL2 .... 48 D7
Buttermere Rd
Ashton-u-L OL7 .... 166 A4
Farnworth BL4 .... 59 E8
Gatley SK8 .... 122 B3
Oldham OL4 .... 67 D8
Partington M31 .... 105 E3
Wigan WN5 .... 54 C7
Buttermere Terr SK15 .... 86 A3
Butterstile Ave M25 .... 94 B3
Butterstile La M25 .... 62 F1
Butterstile Cl M25 .... 62 F1
Butterstile Prim Sch M25 .... 63 A2
Butterwick Cl M12 .... 99 B3

Butterwick Field BL6 .... 21 F3
BUTTERWORTH HALL 32 B6
Butterworth Hall OL16 .... 32 A5
Butterworth La M40, OL9 .... 65 E2
Butterworth St
Chadderton OL9 .... 152 B4
4 Littleborough OL15 .... 16 A5
Manchester M11 .... 165 A4
Middleton M24 .... 65 C7
Radcliffe M26 .... 44 B4
Butterworth Way OL3 .... 69 B5
Butteryhouse La WA15 .... 120 E2
Butt Hill Ave M25 .... 63 B3
Butt Hill Ct M25 .... 63 B3
Butt Hill Dr M25 .... 63 B3
Butt Hill Rd M25 .... 63 B3
Butt La OL4 .... 68 B4
Button Hole OL2 .... 49 D7
Button La M23 .... 109 A2
Button Lane Sch M23 .... 108 F2
Buttons Row BB4 .... 2 F6
Buttress St M11 .... 99 D8
Butts Ave The 3 OL16 .... 139 C3
Butts La SK13 .... 104 D4
Butts La OL3 .... 50 D4
Butts St WN7 .... 76 B3
Butts The 2 OL16 .... 139 C3
Buxted Rd OL1 .... 49 B1
Buxton Ave
Ashton-u-L OL6 .... 85 F6
Manchester M20 .... 109 F6
Buxton Cl
Atherton M46 .... 58 E4
17 Gamesley SK13 .... 171 B2
Buxton Cres
Rochdale OL16 .... 31 B4
Sale M33 .... 108 D1
Buxton La
Droylsden M43 .... 83 E1
Marple SK6 .... 125 E5
Buxton Mews SK13 .... 171 B2
Buxton Old Rd SK12 .... 135 E4
Buxton Pl OL8 .... 153 B1
Buxton Rd
High Lane SK6, SK7, SK12 .... 134 D8
Stockport SK2 .... 124 B5
Stretford M32 .... 96 A3
Buxton Road W SK12 .... 135 B5
Buxton St
Bury BL8 .... 27 C2
Gatley SK8 .... 122 A5
Hazel Grove SK7 .... 124 D3
Heywood OL10 .... 29 D1
Manchester M1 .... 163 B4
Whitworth OL12 .... 4 D3
Buxton Terr SK14 .... 103 D5
Buxton Way M34 .... 113 A8
Buxton Wlk 9 SK13 .... 171 B1
Bycroft Wlk M40 .... 83 D4
Bye Rd BL0 .... 11 E4
Bye St M34 .... 100 F7
Byfield Rd M22 .... 121 C4
Byfleet Cl WN3 .... 54 C1
Byland Ave
Cheadle SK8 .... 132 B6
Oldham OL4 .... 67 D4
Byland Cl BL1 .... 143 B2
Byland Gdns 3 BL3 .... 152 C3
Bylands Cl SK12 .... 133 D4
Bylands Fold SK16 .... 101 D6
Byland Wlk 3 M22 .... 121 D1
Byley Rise WN6 .... 36 E8
Byng Ave M44 .... 105 D4
Byng St
Farnworth BL4 .... 60 D8
Heywood OL10 .... 46 D8
Byrchall High Sch WN4 .... 73 B1
Byrcland Cl M12 .... 164 A4
Byre Cl M23 .... 109 A3
Byre View PR6 .... 20 F8
Byrness Cl M46 .... 58 E4
Byrom Ave M19 .... 99 C1
Byrom Ct M43 .... 83 F1
Byrom La WA3 .... 74 F2
Byrom Par M19 .... 99 C1
Byrom Pl M3 .... 158 B1
Byrom St
Altrincham WA14 .... 119 D3
8 Bury BL8 .... 27 B4
Manchester M3 .... 158 B1
Manchester M16 .... 97 C4
Salford M5 .... 161 A4
Byron Ave
Droylsden M43 .... 84 A2
13 Hindley WN2 .... 56 D5
Prestwich M25 .... 63 A4
Radcliffe M26 .... 43 E4
Swinton M27 .... 79 E8
Byron Cl
Abram WN2 .... 56 B1
3 Gretel WN5 .... 53 F7
Wigan WN6 .... 36 E3
Byron Cres PR7 .... 19 F8
Byron Ct
Altrincham WA14 .... 119 D6
4 Eccles M30 .... 79 D2
Byron Dr SK8 .... 122 F6
Byron Gr
Atherton M46 .... 58 D5
Leigh WN7 .... 75 F7
Reddish SK5 .... 99 E1
Byron Ho 6 OL8 .... 66 B2
Byron Rd
Denton M34 .... 112 F4

Byron Rd continued
Middleton M24 .... 47 B2
Ramsbottom BL8 .... 10 F2
Stretford M32 .... 96 F3
Byron's Dr 2 WA15 .... 120 A6
Byron St
Eccles M30 .... 79 D2
Leigh WN7 .... 75 F7
Oldham OL8 .... 48 E4
Royton OL2 .... 48 E4
Byrom Wlk
Farnworth BL4 .... 60 B6
6 Royton OL2 .... 48 E4
Byrth Rd OL8 .... 84 F8
Bywell Wlk 15 M8 .... 155 C3

C

Cabin La OL4 .... 50 A3
Cable St
Bolton BL1 .... 145 C4
Manchester M4 .... 159 B2
Cablestead Wlk M11 .... 165 A4
Cabot Pl SK5 .... 169 C4
Cabot St M13 .... 163 B2
Caddington Rd M21 .... 109 C8
CADISHEAD 105 E5
Cadishead Prim Sch M44 .... 105 E6
Cadishead Way M41, M44 .... 94 C2
Cadleigh Wlk 6 M40 .... 83 A7
Cadman Gr WN2 .... 56 D6
Cadmium Wlk M18 .... 99 C4
Cadman Dr M22 .... 121 F3
Cadogan Dr WN3 .... 54 D2
Cadogan Pl 7 M7 .... 63 E1
Cadogan St M14 .... 98 A4
Cadum Wlk M13 .... 163 C2
Caen Ave M40 .... 65 C3
Caernarvon Cl BL8 .... 10 F1
Caernarvon Dr SK7 .... 124 C1
Caernarvon Rd WN2 .... 57 A3
Caernarvon Way 2 M34 .... 100 F1
Caesar St OL11 .... 31 A2
Cairn Brae WA12 .... 89 C4
Cairn Dr
Rochdale OL11 .... 29 E6
Salford M6 .... 81 C5
Cairngorm Dr BL3 .... 40 E5
Cairns Pl OL6 .... 85 D5
Cairnwell Rd OL9 .... 65 F8
Cairn Wlk 18 M11 .... 160 C1
Caister Ave M45 .... 63 A7
Caister Cl M41 .... 94 C1
Caister Cl SK16 .... 109 E8
Caistor St SK1 .... 112 B3
Caistor Wlk 2 OL1 .... 153 C3
Caithness Cl M23 .... 121 A4
Caithness Dr BL3 .... 40 E6
Caithness Rd OL11 .... 29 E5
Cakebread St M12 .... 163 C3
Calamanco Way M44 .... 106 A8
Calbourne Cres 2 .... 99 B3
Calcot Wlk 6 M23 .... 120 F6
Calcutta Rd SK3 .... 123 C7
Caldbeck Ave
Bolton BL1 .... 23 F1
Sale M33 .... 108 E5
Caldbeck Cl WN4 .... 73 B4
Caldbeck Dr
Farnworth BL4 .... 59 E7
Middleton M24 .... 46 E2
Caldbeck Gr WA11 .... 71 C1
Caldecott Rd M9 .... 64 A5
Calder Ave
Hindley WN2 .... 57 C3
Irlam M44 .... 93 F1
Littleborough OL15 .... 16 A7
Wythenshawe M22 .... 121 D8
CALDER BANK 94 F4
Calderbank Ave M41 .... 94 E4
Calderbank St WN5 .... 54 E5
Calderbeck Way M22 .... 121 E6
CALDERBROOK 6 C1
Calderbrook Ct SK8 .... 123 B4
Calderbrook Dr SK8 .... 123 A4
Calderbrook Rd
Calderbrook OL15 .... 6 C2
Littleborough OL15 .... 6 D3
Calderbrook Terr OL15 .... 16 C8
Calderbrook Wlk OL4 .... 67 B5
Calderbrook Wlk 11 M9 .... 157 A3
Calderburn Cl BL8 .... 39 D8
Calder Cl
Bury BL9 .... 28 A8
Poynton SK12 .... 133 D2
Reddish SK5 .... 112 A4
Caldercourt M41 .... 94 E4
Calder Cres M45 .... 45 B2
Calderdale Ct OL2 .... 48 C5
Calder Dr
Kearsley BL4 .... 61 B5
Platt Bridge WN2 .... 56 A2
Swinton M27 .... 61 E1
Walkden M28 .... 60 B2
Calder Gdns OL15 .... 16 B6
Calder Gr OL2 .... 149 B4
Calder Ho 6 M7 .... 81 C5
CALDERMOOR 16 B6
Calder Pl WN5 .... 54 C7
Calder Rd BL3 .... 147 B3
CALDERSHAW 14 C2
Caldershaw Bsns Ctr OL12 .... 14 B2

Caldershaw Ctr The OL12 . 14 B2
Caldershaw La OL12 . . . . . . 14 A2
Caldershaw Prim Sch 6
  OL12 . . . . 14 A1
Caldershaw Rd OL11 &
  OL12 . . . . 14 A1
Calder St OL16 . . . . 15 B2
Caldervale Ave M21 . . . . . 109 C4
Calder Way M45 . . . . 45 B2
Calder Wlk
  Middleton M24 . . . . 46 C2
  Whitefield M45 . . . . 45 B2
Calderwood Cl BL8 . . . . . . 27 A6
Caldew Cl WN2 . . . . 56 C4
Caldey Rd M23 . . . . 120 E5
Caldford Cl WN2 . . . . 38 C6
Caldon Cl M30 . . . . 95 D8
Caldwell Ave M29 . . . . 77 B4
Caldwell Cl M29 . . . . 77 B5
Caldwell St
  4 Reddish SK5 . . . . 99 F1
  Westhoughton BL5 . . . . . . 57 F5
Caldy Dr BL0 . . . . 11 A3
Caldy Rd
  Handforth SK9 . . . . 131 D3
  Salford M6 . . . . 154 A4
Caleb Cl M29 . . . . 58 F1
Caledon Ave M40 . . . . 83 A8
Caledonian Dr M30 . . . . . . 95 E8
Caledonia St
  Bolton BL3 . . . . 144 C1
  3 Radcliffe M26 . . . . 44 C4
Caledonia Way M32 . . . . . 96 A5
CALE GREEN 170 C2
Cale Gn SK2 . . . . 170 C2
Cale Green Prim Sch
  SK3 . . . . 170 C2
Cale La WN2 . . . . 38 B2
Cale St SK2 . . . . 170 C2
Caley St
  Bolton BL1 . . . . 23 F2
  1 Manchester M1 . . . . . . 163 A3
Calf Hey OL15 . . . . 15 F6
Calf Hey Cl M26 . . . . 43 D3
Calf Hey La OL12 . . . . 14 D8
Calf Hey N 7 OL11 . . . . . . 31 A4
Calf Hey Rd OL2 . . . . 49 D8
Calf Hey S 8 OL11 . . . . . . 31 A4
Calf La OL3, OL5 . . . . 68 E4
Calgar Dr M24 . . . . 46 D3
Calgarth Dr M24 . . . . 46 D3
Calgary St M18 . . . . 165 C1
Calico Cl M3 . . . . 158 A3
Calico Cres
  Hollingworth SK15 . . . . . . 87 A6
  Mossley SK15 . . . . 86 F6
Calico Wood Ave WN6 . . . 35 F6
Callaghan Wlk OL10 . . . . . 29 C1
Calland Ave SK14 . . . . . . 167 C3
Callander Ct WN5 . . . . . . 54 E8
Callander Sq OL10 . . . . . . 28 F1
Callander St BL0 . . . . 138 B2
Callards Rd OL16 . . . . 15 E4
Callington Rd M21 . . . . . . 109 D5
Callington Cl 4 SK14 . . . . 102 E2
Callington Dr SK14 . . . . . . 102 E2
Callington Wlk 3 SK14 . . . 102 E2
Callis Rd BL3 . . . . 144 C1
Callum Wlk M13 . . . . 163 C2
Calluna Mews M20 . . . . . 110 A4
Calne Wlk 4 M23 . . . . 121 A5
Calow Cl SK13 . . . . 171 B2
Calow Dr WN7 . . . . 76 C3
Calow Gn 30 SK13 . . . . . . 171 B2
Caltha St BL0 . . . . 138 B2
Calthorpe Ave M9 . . . . . . 156 C3
Calton Ave M7 . . . . 81 A7
Calve Croft Rd M22 . . . . . 121 F2
Calveley Wlk WN6 . . . . . . 36 E8
Calver Ave M30 . . . . 95 C8
Calver Bank 8 SK13 . . . . . 171 A2
Calver Cl
  10 Gamesley SK13 . . . . . 171 B2
  Urmston M41 . . . . 94 D3
Calver Fold 6 SK13 . . . . . 171 A2
Calverhall Way WN4 . . . . 73 A3
Calver Hey BL5 . . . . 40 C2
Calverleigh Cl BL3 . . . . . . 146 A2
Calverley Ave M19 . . . . . . 110 F7
Calverley Cl 3 SK9 . . . . . 137 C8
Calverley Way OL12 . . . . . 14 E4
Calverly Rd SK8 . . . . 123 A5
Calver Mews SK13 . . . . . 171 B2
Calver Pl 7 SK13 . . . . 171 A2
Calverton Dr M40 . . . . . . 83 C7
Calvert Rd BL3 . . . . 147 C3
Calvert St M5 . . . . 154 A2
Calver Wlk
  Cheadle SK8 . . . . 122 E1
  Denton M34 . . . . 113 A8
Calvine Wlk 3 M40 . . . . . 159 C3
Calvin St BL1 . . . . 143 C1
Camargue Cl 1 M20 . . . . . 110 B6
Cambeck Cl M45 . . . . 45 B1
Cambeck Wlk M45 . . . . . . 45 A1
Cambell Rd M30 . . . . 79 B2
Camberley Cl
  Bramhall SK7 . . . . 133 A7
  Bury BL8 . . . . 27 A5
Camberley Dr OL11 . . . . . 29 F5
Cambert La
  Manchester, Belle Vue
  M18 . . . . 165 C1
  Manchester M18 . . . . 99 D5

Camberwell Cres WN2 . . . 37 F1
Camberwell Dr OL7 . . . . . 85 A7
Camberwell Park Sch M9 64 C4
Camberwell St
  Manchester M3, M8 . . . . . 159 A4
  2 Oldham OL8 . . . . 66 E4
Camberwell Way OL2 . . . . 48 C4
Camborne Rd SK14 . . . . . 102 E3
Camborne St M14 . . . . . . 98 B3
Camborne Wlk 1 OL9 . . . . 48 A1
Cambourne Dr
  Bolton BL3 . . . . 144 A1
  Hindley WN2 . . . . 57 C2
Cambo Wlk SK4 . . . . 110 F3
Cambrai Cres M30 . . . . . . 79 A4
Cambrian Bsns Pk BL3 . . 145 B1
Cambrian Cres WN3 . . . . 54 C2
Cambrian Dr
  Milnrow OL16 . . . . 32 A6
  Royton OL2 . . . . 48 C3
Cambrian Rd SK3 . . . . . . 123 C8
Cambrian St M11, M40 . . . 160 B2
Cambria Sq 7 BL3 . . . . . 144 C1
Cambria St
  Bolton BL3 . . . . 144 C1
  Oldham OL4 . . . . 67 D7
Cambridge Ave
  Manchester M16 . . . . 97 C2
  Rochdale OL11 . . . . 30 A6
  Wilmslow SK9 . . . . 136 F7
Cambridge Cl
  Farnworth BL4 . . . . 147 C1
  10 Sale M33 . . . . 107 D3
Cambridge Dr
  Little Lever BL3 . . . . 43 B4
  Reddish M34 . . . . 100 A3
  Romiley SK6 . . . . 113 C5
Cambridge Gr
  Eccles M30 . . . . 79 F2
  Whitefield M45 . . . . 63 A7
Cambridge Ho 1 M1 . . . . 163 A2
Cambridge Ind Area M7 . 158 B4
Cambridge Mill 4 M1 . . . . 162 C3
Cambridge Rd
  Altrincham WA15 . . . . . . 119 E2
  Droylsden M43 . . . . 83 F3
  Failsworth M35 . . . . 83 F5
  Gatley SK8 . . . . 122 B5
  Horwich BL6 . . . . 39 F8
  Manchester M9 . . . . 64 D1
  Orrell WN5 . . . . 53 F8
  Reddish M34 . . . . 111 C5
  Urmston M41 . . . . 95 B1
Cambridge St
  Ashton-u-L OL7 . . . . 84 F1
  Atherton M46 . . . . 58 C2
  Dukinfield SK16 . . . . 166 C1
  Manchester M1, M15 . . . . 162 C2
  Oldham OL9 . . . . 66 C4
  Salford M7 . . . . 158 B4
  Stalybridge SK15 . . . . . . 86 A2
  Stockport SK2 . . . . 124 A6
  Wigan WN1 . . . . 151 A3
Cambridge Terr
  Stalybridge SK15 . . . . . . 86 D4
  Stockport SK2 . . . . 124 A6
Cambridge Way WN1 . . . 151 A4
Camdale Wlk 6 M8 . . . . . 155 C2
Camden Ave M40 . . . . . . 83 C4
Camden Cl BL2 . . . . 26 C1
Camden St OL5 . . . . 68 D3
Camelia Rd M9 . . . . 156 C3
Camellia Cl BL1 . . . . 144 B3
Cameron Cl OL2 . . . . 48 D6
Cameron Pl WN5 . . . . 54 E8
Cameron St
  Bolton BL1 . . . . 143 A4
  Bury BL8 . . . . 27 C2
  Leigh WN7 . . . . 75 D7
  Manchester M1 . . . . 162 C4
Caminada Ho 11 M15 . . . . 162 A2
Camley Wlk 1 M8 . . . . . . 156 B2
Camm St WN2 . . . . 74 B8
Camms View BB4 . . . . . . 1 A8
Camomile Wlk 8 M31 . . . 105 F3
Campania St OL2 . . . . 48 E2
Campbell Cl BL8 . . . . 26 F4
Campbell Ct BL4 . . . . 42 C2
Campbell Rd
  Bolton BL3 . . . . 146 A2
  Manchester M13 . . . . 98 F2
  Sale M33 . . . . 107 F3
  Swinton M27 . . . . 79 E6
Campbell St
  Farnworth BL4 . . . . 42 B1
  3 Reddish SK5 . . . . 99 F1
  Rochdale OL12 . . . . 14 E2
  Wigan WN5 . . . . 54 D5
Campbell Way 6 M28 . . . . 60 D3
Campbell Wlk 4 BL4 . . . . 42 C2
Campden Way SK9 . . . . . 131 D4
Campfield Ave Arc M3 . . 162 B4
Campion Dr BB4 . . . . 1 A8
Campion Gr WN4 . . . . . . 72 F4
Campion Way
  8 Denton M34 . . . . 113 A8
  Rochdale OL12 . . . . 14 C3
Campion Wlk M11 . . . . . 164 C4
Camponia Gdns M7 . . . . 155 A1
Camp Rd WN4 . . . . 72 E4
Camp St
  Ashton-u-L OL6 . . . . . . 166 B3
  Bury BL8 . . . . 27 C3
  Manchester M3 . . . . 162 B4
  Salford M7 . . . . 155 A1
Camrose Gdns BL1 . . . . . 143 B1
Camrose Wlk M13 . . . . . 164 A1

Cams La M26 . . . . 43 E2
Cams Lane Prim Sch M26 43 F3
Canaan WA3 . . . . 91 C8
Canada St
  Bolton BL1 . . . . 142 C2
  Horwich BL6 . . . . 22 B3
  Manchester M40 . . . . . . 160 B4
  Stockport SK2 . . . . 124 A6
Canal Bank
  Appley Bridge WN6 . . . . . 35 C7
  Eccles M30 . . . . 79 C3
Canal Circ M50 . . . . 80 A1
Canal Cotts WN3 . . . . . . 150 B3
Canal Rd WA14 . . . . 119 E8
Canal Row WN2 . . . . 20 D1
Canal Side M30 . . . . 79 C3
Canalside Ind Est OL16 . . . 31 B5
Canalside Wlk OL7 . . . . . 166 B1
Canal St
  Adlington PR7 . . . . 21 A6
  Droylsden M43 . . . . 84 A1
  Dukinfield SK14 . . . . 101 C3
  Heywood OL10 . . . . 46 F8
  Ince-in-M WN2 . . . . 151 C2
  Leigh WN7 . . . . 75 F4
  Littleborough OL15 . . . . . 16 B5
  Manchester M1 . . . . 163 A4
  Marple SK6 . . . . 126 A6
  Oldham OL9 . . . . 66 B3
  Rochdale OL16 . . . . 31 A5
  Salford M5 . . . . 81 C1
  Stalybridge SK15 . . . . . . 86 A1
  Stockport SK1 . . . . 170 C4
  Wigan WN6 . . . . 37 F2
Canal Terr WN1 . . . . 151 B3
Canary Way M27 . . . . 80 E7
Canberra Rd
  Bramhall SK7 . . . . 132 F5
  Wigan WN5 . . . . 36 C1
Canberra St M11 . . . . . . 83 C2
Canberra Way OL11 . . . . 31 A3
Candahar St BL3 . . . . . . 42 A3
Candleford Cl 2 M20 . . . 110 B6
Candleford Pl SK2 . . . . . 124 E4
Candleford Rd M20 . . . . 110 B6
Candlestick Pk BL9 . . . . . 28 D4
Canisp Cl OL9 . . . . 48 A1
Canley Cl SK1 . . . . 170 C4
Canmore Cl BL3 . . . . . . 146 A3
Cannel Fold M28 . . . . . . 78 B7
Canning Cl WN2 . . . . 56 C4
Canning Dr BL1 . . . . 143 B2
Canning St
  Bolton BL1 . . . . 143 C2
  Bury BL9 . . . . 140 C4
  Stockport SK4 . . . . 169 B2
Cannock Dr SK4 . . . . 168 A2
Cannon Ct M4 . . . . 158 C2
Cannon Gr BL3 . . . . 145 A1
Cannon St
  Atherton M46 . . . . 58 D3
  Bolton BL3 . . . . 145 A1
  Eccles M30 . . . . 79 E1
  Hollingworth SK14 . . . . . 103 C5
  Oldham OL9 . . . . 153 B3
  Radcliffe M26 . . . . 43 F5
Cannon Street N BL3 . . . 145 A2
Cannon Wlk BL4 . . . . 60 D3
Cann St BL8 . . . . 26 D8
Canon Burrows CE Prim Sch
  9 OL7 . . . . 85 A6
Canon Cl WN6 . . . . 19 F2
Canon Dr WA14 . . . . 119 B1
Canon Flynn Ct OL16 . . . 31 C7
Canon Green Ct M3 . . . . 158 B2
Canon Green Dr M3 . . . . 158 B2
Canon Hussey Ct M3 . . . 158 A1
Canon Johnson CE Prim Sch
  OL7 . . . . 166 B4
Canon's Cl BL1 . . . . 142 B2
Canons Gr M40 . . . . 157 B1
Canon Sharples Prim Sch
  WN1 . . . . 37 A2
Canon Slade Sch BL2 . . . 25 C4
Canon St
  Bury BL9 . . . . 141 A4
  Rochdale OL16 . . . . 15 B2
Canonsway M27 . . . . . . 79 E8
Canon Tighe Ct OL9 . . . . 152 A3
Cansfield Cl BL4 . . . . 61 A6
Cansfield Gr WN4 . . . . . . 73 A4
Cansfield High Specialist
  Language Coll WN4 . . . 73 A4
Canterbury Ave WA3 . . . . 74 D1
Canterbury Cl
  Atherton M46 . . . . 58 E4
  Dukinfield SK16 . . . . 101 D6
  Rochdale OL11 . . . . 30 A7
Canterbury Cres M24 . . . 47 D2
Canterbury Dr
  Bury BL8 . . . . 140 A4
  Manchester M25 . . . . . . 63 C2
Canterbury Gdns M5 . . . 80 A2
Canterbury Gr BL3 . . . . . 147 A3
Canterbury Pk M20 . . . . 109 F3
Canterbury Rd
  Altrincham WA15 . . . . . . 120 C3
  Stockport SK1 . . . . 112 B1
  Urmston M41 . . . . 95 D3
Canterbury St OL6 . . . . . 166 C4
Canterfield Cl M43 . . . . . 84 D2
Cantley Wlk 4 M8 . . . . . 156 A2
Cantrell St M11 . . . . 83 B2
Canute Ct 3 M32 . . . . . . 96 E3
Canute Rd M32 . . . . 96 E3

Canute St
  Bolton BL2 . . . . 25 C1
  Radcliffe M26 . . . . 43 E3
Cape Gdns OL2 . . . . 149 B2
Capella Dr M11 . . . . 164 C4
Capella Wlk M7 . . . . 81 C4
Capenhurst Cl
  Poynton SK12 . . . . 133 F4
  Wythenshawe M23 . . . . . 120 F4
Cape St M20 . . . . 110 C7
Capesthorne Cl SK7 . . . . 133 F8
Capesthorne Dr OL2 . . . . 48 F7
Capesthorne Rd
  Altrincham WA15 . . . . . . 120 D6
  Dukinfield SK16 . . . . 101 D6
  Hazel Grove SK7 . . . . . . 133 F8
  High Lane SK6 . . . . 134 E7
  Wilmslow SK9 . . . . 136 E5
Capesthorne Wlk M34 . . 100 E2
Capital Quay M50 . . . . . 161 A3
Capital Rd M11 . . . . 99 F7
Capitol Cl BL1 . . . . 142 A3
Cappadocia Way BL5 . . . 57 D7
Capps St WN2 . . . . 56 B3
Capricorn Rd M9 . . . . . . 65 B3
Capricorn Way M6 . . . . . 81 C4
Capstan St M9 . . . . 157 B4
Captain Dr SK6 . . . . 125 B5
Captain Clarke Rd SK14 . 101 C1
CAPTAIN FOLD 29 E2
Captain Fold OL10 . . . . . 29 E2
Captain Fold Rd M38 . . . . 59 F6
Captain Lees Gdns BL5 . . 58 A8
Captain Lees Rd BL5 . . . . 40 A1
Captain's Clough Rd BL1 142 B2
Captain's La WN4 . . . . . . 73 C3
Captain St
  Bolton BL6 . . . . 22 B4
  Horwich BL6 . . . . 22 B4
Capton Cl SK7 . . . . 124 A2
Caradoc Ave 12 M8 . . . . 156 B2
Carawood Cl WN6 . . . . . 35 D7
Car Bank Ave M46 . . . . . 58 D4
Car Bank Cres M46 . . . . . 58 D4
Car Bank Sq M46 . . . . . . 58 D4
Car Bank St M46 . . . . . . 58 D4
Carberry Ct SK8 . . . . . . 123 A2
Carberry Rd M18 . . . . . . 99 D5
Cardale Wlk M9 . . . . 157 A3
Carden Ave M41 . . . . . . 94 E4
Cardenbrook Gr 4 SK9 . . 131 D2
Carder Cl M27 . . . . 79 F7
Carders Cl WN7 . . . . 75 E4
Cardew Ave M22 . . . . . . 121 F4
Cardiff Cl 11 OL8 . . . . . . 66 B2
Cardiff St M7 . . . . 155 B3
Cardiff Wlk 4 M34 . . . . . 100 F1
Cardigan Dr BL9 . . . . 44 E7
Cardigan Rd OL8 . . . . . . 66 B2
Cardigan St
  Radcliffe M26 . . . . 43 F6
  Rochdale OL12 . . . . 14 E3
  Royton OL2 . . . . 48 E4
  2 Salford M6 . . . . 154 B1
Cardigan Terr M14 . . . . . 97 F4
Cardinal Langley RC High
  Sch M24 . . . . 47 B4
Cardinal Mews M24 . . . . 46 D2
Cardinal St
  Manchester M8 . . . . 156 B3
  10 Oldham OL1 . . . . 67 A7
Carding Gr M3 . . . . 158 B3
Cardrona St M18 . . . . . . 99 D3
Cardroom Rd M4 . . . . . . 159 C2
Cardus St M19 . . . . 99 A1
Cardwell Gdns BL1 . . . . 143 B2
Cardwell Rd M30 . . . . . . 79 A1
Cardwell St OL8 . . . . 66 F3
Careless La WN2 . . . . . . 151 C3
Caremine Ave M19 . . . . . 99 B2
Carey Cl
  Salford M7 . . . . 158 A4
  Wigan WN3 . . . . 54 C2
Carey Wlk 11 M15 . . . . . 162 C1
Carfax Fold OL12 . . . . . . 14 B2
Carfax St M18 . . . . 99 D5
Cargate Wlk 8 M8 . . . . . 155 C2
Carib St M15 . . . . 162 C1
Carill Ave M40 . . . . 65 A1
Carill Dr M14 . . . . 110 D8
Carina Pl M7 . . . . 81 C4
Cariocca Bsns Pk
  Manchester, Ardwick
  M12 . . . . 164 A2
  Manchester, Miles Platting
  M40 . . . . 160 A3
Carisbrook Ave
  Prestwich M25, M45 . . . . 63 A6
  Urmston M41 . . . . 95 C2
Carisbrook Dr M27 . . . . . 80 A6
Carisbrooke Ave SK7 . . . 124 D1
Carisbrooke Dr BL1 . . . . 143 D3
Carisbrooke Rd WN7 . . . 76 D6
Carisbrook St M9 . . . . . 157 B3
Cariburn St M11 . . . . . . 83 D2
Carleton Rd SK12 . . . . . 134 C4
Carley Gr M9 . . . . 64 B4
Carlford Gr M25 . . . . 62 F3
Carlile St SK3 . . . . 170 B4
Carlin Gate WA15 . . . . . 120 A6
Carling Dr M22 . . . . 121 E2
Carlingford Cl SK3 . . . . . 170 B1
Carlisle Cl
  Little Lever BL3 . . . . 43 A2
  Prestwich M45 . . . . 63 B7
  Romiley SK6 . . . . 113 A1
Carlisle Cres OL6 . . . . . . 85 C7
Carlisle Dr
  Altrincham WA14 . . . . . . 119 E8

Carlisle Dr *continued*
  Irlam M44 . . . . 94 A2
Carlisle Pl 3 PR6 . . . . . . 21 A8
Carlisle St
  11 Alderley Edge SK9 . . . 137 A1
  Bolton BL7 . . . . 25 A8
  Hindley WN2 . . . . 56 E6
  Oldham OL9 . . . . 152 C1
  Rochdale OL12 . . . . 14 E3
  Swinton M27 . . . . 61 F2
  Wigan WN5 . . . . 54 D6
Carlisle Way
  Aspull WN2 . . . . 38 D5
  3 Denton M34 . . . . 100 F1
Carloon Rd M23 . . . . . . 109 B1
Carlow Dr M22 . . . . 121 E2
Carl St BL1 . . . . 143 A2
Carlton Ave
  Bolton BL3 . . . . 146 A4
  Bramhall SK7 . . . . 132 D5
  Cheadle SK8 . . . . 122 F3
  Handforth SK9 . . . . 131 C2
  Manchester M14 . . . . 98 B3
  Manchester, Old Trafford
  M16 . . . . 97 B4
  Oldham OL4 . . . . 49 D1
  Prestwich M25 . . . . 63 E2
  Romiley SK6 . . . . 113 D2
  Up Holland WN8 . . . . 53 A7
  Whitefield M45 . . . . 44 D1
Carlton Cl
  Blackrod BL6 . . . . 21 C2
  Bolton BL2 . . . . 25 E3
  Walkden M28 . . . . 60 C1
Carlton Cres
  Stockport SK1 . . . . 112 A2
  Urmston M41 . . . . 95 D1
Carlton Ct
  Altrincham WA15 . . . . . . 120 B1
  Manchester M25 . . . . 63 A1
Carlton Dr
  Gatley SK8 . . . . 122 A6
  Manchester M25 . . . . 63 E2
Carlton Gdns BL4 . . . . . . 42 D1
Carlton Gr
  Hindley WN2 . . . . 56 F4
  6 Horwich BL6 . . . . 22 D1
Carlton Grange M16 . . . . 97 E2
Carlton Mans 5 M16 . . . . 97 D3
Carlton Pl
  Farnworth BL4 . . . . 42 D1
  Hazel Grove SK7 . . . . . . 125 A1
Carlton Rd
  Altrincham WA15 . . . . . . 120 B2
  Ashton-u-L OL7 . . . . 85 C5
  Bolton BL1 . . . . 144 A4
  Golborne WA3 . . . . 74 D1
  Hyde SK14 . . . . 102 A3
  Lymm WA13 . . . . 117 B5
  Manchester, Whalley Range
  M16 . . . . 97 D3
  Sale M33 . . . . 108 A6
  Salford M6 . . . . 154 E4
  Stockport, Heaton Moor
  SK4 . . . . 168 A2
  Urmston M41 . . . . 95 D1
  Walkden M28 . . . . 60 C1
Carlton St
  Bolton BL2 . . . . 148 A2
  Bury BL9 . . . . 44 F8
  Eccles M30 . . . . 79 D3
  Farnworth BL4 . . . . 42 D1
  Manchester M16 . . . . 97 C4
  Wigan WN3 . . . . 150 B2
Carlton Way
  Irlam M44 . . . . 105 C5
  Royton OL1, OL2 . . . . . . 48 D2
Carlyle Cl M8 . . . . 156 A2
Carlyle St WN7 . . . . 75 C8
Carlyn Ave M33 . . . . 108 D4
Carmel Ave M5 . . . . 161 C4
Carmel Cl M5 . . . . 161 C4
Carmel Ct M9 . . . . 64 E1
Carmenna Dr SK7 . . . . . 132 F7
Carmichael Cl 8 M31 . . . 105 E3
Carmichael St SK3 . . . . . 170 A4
Carmine Fold M24 . . . . . 47 A2
Carmona Dr M25 . . . . . . 63 A4
Carmona Gdns M7 . . . . . 63 C1
Carmoor Rd M13 . . . . . . 163 C1
Carnaby St M9 . . . . 64 F1
Carna Rd SK5 . . . . 99 E2
Carnarvon St
  Manchester M3 . . . . 158 C3
  Oldham OL8 . . . . 66 B2
  Salford M7 . . . . 155 B3
  3 Stockport SK1 . . . . . . 112 A1
Carnation Rd
  Farnworth BL4 . . . . 42 A1
  Oldham OL4 . . . . 67 E4
Carnegie Ave M19 . . . . . 99 B1
Carnegie Cl 1 M33 . . . . 107 D3
Carnegie Dr WN4 . . . . . . 73 A5
Carnforth Ave
  Chadderton OL9 . . . . . . 152 A2
  Hindley WN2 . . . . 57 A5
  Trub OL11 . . . . 47 C4
Carnforth Dr
  Ramsbottom BL0, BL9 . . . 11 A2
  Sale M33 . . . . 108 A1
Carnforth Rd
  Cheadle SK8 . . . . 123 C4
  Reddish SK4 . . . . 111 D7
Carnforth Sq OL11 . . . . . 47 D7
Carnforth St M14 . . . . . . 98 B3
Carnoustie BL3 . . . . 146 A3

Carnoustie Cl
Failsworth M40 . . . . 83 C7
Wilmslow SK9 . . . . 137 D8
Carnoustie Dr
Gatley SK8 . . . . 122 C1
Ramsbottom BL0 . . . . . 138 B1
Carnwood Cl M40 . . . . . 83 D4
Carolina Way M50 . . . . 154 B1
Caroline St
Ashton-u-L OL6 . . . . . . 166 C3
Bolton BL3 . . . . 147 A4
Irlam M44 . . . . 105 F8
Salford M7 . . . . 158 B4
Stalybridge SK15 . . . . . . 86 A1
Stockport SK3 . . . . 170 A3
Wigan, Rose Bridge WN1 . 151 C4
Wigan WN3 . . . . 150 C3
Carpenters Ct SK9 . . . . 137 A1
Carpenters La M4 . . . . 159 A2
Carpenters Way OL16 . . 31 B4
Carpenter's Wlk M43 . . . 83 F1
CARR 138 B3
Carradale Dr M33 . . . . . 107 C5
Carradale Wlk ⑤ M40 . . . 83 A6
Carradon Dr WN6 . . . . . 19 E1
Carr Ave M25 . . . . 62 F2
CARR BANK 27 F8
Carr Bank Ave
Manchester M9 . . . . 63 F3
Ramsbottom BL0 . . . . . 138 B3
Carr Bank Dr BL0 . . . . . 138 B3
Carr Bank Rd BL0 . . . . . 138 B3
CARRBROOK 86 F6
Carrbrook Cl SK15 . . . . 86 F6
Carrbrook Cres SK15 . . 86 F6
Carrbrook Dr OL1 . . . . . 48 E1
Carr Brook Dr M46 . . . . 58 E4
Carrbrook Rd SK15 . . . . 86 F7
Carrbrook Terr ⑥ M26 . . 44 C4
Carr Brow SK6 . . . . . . 135 A7
Carr Cl SK1 . . . . 124 B8
Carr Common Rd WN2 . . 57 D3
Carr Dr L4 . . . . 147 C1
Carr Farm Cl SK13 . . . 116 E8
Carrfield SK14 . . . . . . 167 A4
Carrfield Ave
Altrincham WA15 . . . . . 120 D6
Stockport SK3 . . . . 124 A4
Walkden M38 . . . . 59 E4
Carrfield Cl M38 . . . . . . 59 E4
Carrfield Gr M38 . . . . . . 59 E4
Carr Fold BL0 . . . . . . 138 B3
Carrgate Rd M34 . . . . . 101 B1
Carr Gr OL16 . . . . 32 A6
Carrgreen Cl M19 . . . . 110 F5
Carrgreen La WA3 . . . . 117 F6
Carrhill Quarry Cl OL5 . . 68 C2
Carrhill Rd OL5 . . . . . . 68 C2
Carrhouse La SK14 . . . 103 C4
Carr House La WN6 . . . 18 F8
Carr House Rd OL4 . . . 67 F6
Carriage Dr
Littleborough OL15 . . . . 16 B7
Manchester M40 . . . . . 157 A1
Carriage Dr The SK13 . 103 F5
Carriage St M16 . . . . . 162 C5
Carriages The WA14 . . 119 C4
Carrick Cl WN1 . . . . . . 37 C2
Carrick Gdns
Middleton M24 . . . . 46 F4
Wythenshawe M22 . . . . 121 D4
Carrie St BL1 . . . . 144 B4
Carrigart M25 . . . . 63 B3
Carrill Gr M19 . . . . 99 A1
Carrill Grove E M19 . . . 99 A1
CARRINGTON 106 D6
Carrington Cl OL16 . . . . 15 D3
Carrington Dr BL3 . . . . 145 C1
Carrington Field St SK1 . 124 A7
Carrington Gr WN7 . . . . 75 F7
Carrington Ho ② M6 . . . 80 C4
Carrington La
Carrington M31 & M33 . . 107 C2
Sale M33 . . . . 107 E5
Carrington Rd
Adlington PR7 . . . . 20 F7
Flixton M41 . . . . 106 E8
Manchester M14 . . . . . 98 C1
Stockport SK1 . . . . 112 B3
Carrington St
Leigh WN7 . . . . 75 F7
Oldham OL9 . . . . 66 B3
Swinton M27 . . . . 62 B1
Carrington Terr M27 . . . 62 A1
Carr La
Alderley Edge SK9 . . . . 136 D2
Diggle OL3 . . . . 51 C5
Golborne WA3 . . . . 91 A7
Leigh WN7 . . . . 91 E8
Milnrow OL16 . . . . 32 C4
Mossley SK15 . . . . 86 F7
Rawtenstall BL0 . . . . 2 F7
Uppermill OL3 . . . . 69 B7
Wigan WN3 . . . . 55 B3
Carr Lea OL4 . . . . 68 C6
Carr Mdw OL16 . . . . . . 32 C4
Carrmel Ct OL3 . . . . . . 50 F3
Carr Mill Cres WN5 . . . 71 E4
Carr Mill Mews SK9 . . . 131 B1
Carr Mill Prim Sch WA11 . 71 C1
Carr Mill Rd WA11, WN5 . 71 D3
Carrock Wlk M24 . . . . . 46 B1
Carron Ave M9 . . . . . . 64 F1
Carron Gr BL2 . . . . 42 F7
Carr Rd
Altrincham WA15 . . . . . 120 B2

Carr Rd continued
Horwich BL6 . . . . 22 B5
Irlam M44 . . . . 94 B2
Carr Rise SK5 . . . . 86 F7
Carrs Ave SK3, SK8 . . . 123 A6
Carrs Ct SK9 . . . . 137 B7
Carrsdale Dr ⑧ M9 . . . 64 C2
Carrsfield Rd M22 . . . . 121 E6
Carrslea Cl M26 . . . . . . 43 E5
Carrs St SK8 . . . . 122 F6
Carr St
Ashton-u-L OL6 . . . . 85 D5
Hindley WN2 . . . . 56 D6
Leigh WN7 . . . . 75 C5
Ramsbottom BL0 . . . . . 138 B3
Swinton M27 . . . . 79 D7
Carrsvale Ave M41 . . . . 95 B3
Carrswood Rd M23 . . . 120 D8
Carruthers Cl OL10 . . . . 29 F3
Carruthers St M4 . . . . 160 A1
Carrwood WA15 . . . . . 129 B7
Carr Wood Ave SK7 . . . 132 E8
Carrwood Hey BL0 . . . . 11 A4
Carr Wood Rd SK7 . . . 123 E1
Carsdale Rd M23 . . . . 121 A6
Carslake Ave BL1 . . . . 144 C4
Carslake Rd M40 . . . . 157 A1
Carson Rd M19 . . . . . 111 A8
Car St WN2 . . . . 56 A2
Carstairs Ave SK2 . . . 124 A4
Carstairs Cl M8 . . . . . 155 C3
Carswell Cl M29 . . . . . 59 C1
Carter St M34 . . . . . . 100 F2
Carter Pl SK14 . . . . . . 101 D5
Carter St
Bolton BL3 . . . . 42 A4
Dukinfield SK14 . . . . . . 101 D5
Farnworth BL4 . . . . 60 E7
Ince-in-M WN3 . . . . . . 151 B2
Mossley OL5 . . . . 86 C8
Salford, Weaste M50 . . . 80 C1
Stalybridge SK15 . . . . . . 85 F1
Carthage St OL8 . . . . . 66 F4
Carthorpe Arch M5 . . . 154 C1
Cartleach Gr M28 . . . . . 60 A2
Cartleach La M28 . . . . . 60 A2
Cartmel ⑥ OL12 . . . . . 139 C4
Cartmel Ave
Milnrow OL16 . . . . 31 F4
Reddish SK4 . . . . 111 E6
Wigan WN1 . . . . 37 B3
Cartmel Cl
Bolton BL3 . . . . 40 D2
Gatley SK8 . . . . 122 C3
Hazel Grove SK7 . . . . . 124 C3
Oldham OL8 . . . . 66 D3
Whitefield BL9 . . . . 45 A3
Cartmel Cres
Bolton BL2 . . . . 25 C2
Failsworth OL9 . . . . 65 F2
Cartmel Ct M9 . . . . 65 A4
Cartmel Dr WA15 . . . . 120 D6
Cartmel Gr M28 . . . . . . 79 B7
Cartmel Wlk
Manchester M9 . . . . . . 157 A3
Middleton M24 . . . . 46 F2
Cartridge Cl M22 . . . . 121 F3
Cartridge St OL10 . . . . 29 C2
Cartwright St WN1 . . . . 57 D1
Cartwright Rd M21 . . . 108 F8
Cartwright St
Denton M34 . . . . 100 F6
Dukinfield SK14 . . . . . . 102 A5
Carver Ave M25 . . . . . . 63 C5
Carver Cl M16 . . . . . . 161 B1
Carver Dr SK6 . . . . . . 125 E5
Carver Rd
Altrincham WA15 . . . . . 119 E2
Marple SK6 . . . . 125 E5
Carver St M16 . . . . . . 161 B1
Carver Wlk ⑩ M15 . . . . 162 C1
Carville Gr WN2 . . . . . . 57 B4
Carville Rd M9 . . . . 65 B3
Carwood Gr BL6 . . . . . . 22 D1
Cascade Dr M7 . . . . . . 155 B1
Cashel Ct M27 . . . . 61 C1
Cashgate Ct OL8 . . . . . 66 D3
Cashmere Rd SK3 . . . . 123 C2
Cashmore Dr WN2 . . . . 56 D4
Cashmore Wlk M12 . . . 164 B2
Caspian Rd
Altrincham WA14 . . . . . 119 A6
Manchester M9 . . . . . . 65 B3
Cassandra Ct M5 . . . . 161 C4
Cass Ave M5 . . . . 161 A4
Cassidy Cl M4 . . . . . . 159 B2
Cassidy Cl M50 . . . . . . 96 E8
Cassidy Gdns M24 . . . . 46 D4
Casson Gate OL12 . . . . 14 E1
Casson St M35 . . . . . . 83 F7
Casterton Way M28 . . . 78 A5
Castle Ave
Denton M34 . . . . 100 E2
Rochdale OL11 . . . . . . 139 B2
Castlebrook Cl BL9 . . . . 45 B4
Castlebrook High Sch
BL9 . . . . 45 C3
Castle Cl M43 . . . . 84 B2
Castle Clough Nature
Reserve* SK15 . . . . . . 86 F7
Castle Cres BL6 . . . . . . 22 C5
Castle Croft BL2 . . . . . . 25 E3
Castlecroft Ave BL6 . . . 21 D2
Castlecroft Ct M30 . . . 140 E2
Castlecroft Mews M30 . 140 B2
Castlecroft Rd BL9 . . . . 44 E1

Castle Ct
Ashton-u-L OL6 . . . . 85 B7
Bolton BL2 . . . . 148 A3
Glossop SK13 . . . . 104 A4
Castledene Ave M6 . . . 154 B3
Castle Dr PR7 . . . . 20 E6
Castle Edge Rd SK22 . . 127 B2
Castle Farm Dr SK2 . . . 124 B5
Castle Farm La SK2 . . . 124 C5
Castlefield Ave M7 . . . 155 B4
Castlefield Prim Sch
M15 . . . . 162 B3
Castleford Cl ⑨ BL1 . . . 145 A4
Castleford St OL1 . . . . . 48 C1
Castleford Wlk M21 . . . 109 D7
Castle Gr
Leigh WN7 . . . . 76 D6
Ramsbottom BL0 . . . . . 11 A2
CASTLE HALL 86 B1
Castle Hall Cl SK15 . . . 86 B1
Castle Hall Ct ⑪ SK15 . . 86 A1
Castle Hall View ⑩ SK15 . 86 A1
Castle Hey Gr BL9 . . . . 45 C3
CASTLE HILL
Bolton 25 B3
Romiley 112 E7
Castle Hill
Glossop SK13 . . . . 104 E2
Newton-le-W WA12 . . . . 89 E4
Castle Hill Cres OL11 . . 139 B2
Castle Hill Dr ⑨ M9 . . . 64 C3
Castle Hill Mobile Home Pk
SK14 . . . . 113 A6
Castle Hill Pk WN2 . . . . 56 F7
Castle Hill Sch SK2 . . . 25 B2
Castle Hill Rd
Bury BL9 . . . . 28 D5
Hindley WN2 . . . . 56 E6
Manchester M25 . . . . . 63 D2
Castle Hill St Philip's CE
Prim Sch WN2 . . . . . . 56 F6
Castle Hill St SK15 . . . 112 C6
Castle Hill St
⑦ Bolton BL2 . . . . 25 B3
Bolton, Castle Hill BL2 . . 25 B3
Castle House La PR7 . . . 20 E6
Castle Irwell Student Village
M6 . . . . 81 B5
Castle La SK5, SK15 . . . 86 F8
Castle L Ctr BL9 . . . . . 140 B2
Castlemere Ct M9 . . . . 64 C3
Castlemere Dr OL2 . . . . 49 D8
Castlemere Rd M9 . . . . 64 C3
Castlemere Terr OL11 . . 139 C2
Castle Mews BL4 . . . . . 60 D7
Castle Mill La WA15 . . . 129 B5
Castlemill St OL1 . . . . . 67 B7
Castlemoor Ave M7 . . . 81 B8
Castlemore Ret Pk M16 . 161 A1
Castle Park Ind Est ⑫
OL1 . . . . 67 B7
Castle Quay M15 . . . . 162 B3
Castle Rd BL9 . . . . 45 C4
Castlerea Cl ⑩ M30 . . . 95 D8
Castlerigg Cl SK4 . . . . 111 D7
Castlerigg Dr
Middleton M24 . . . . 46 C2
Royton OL2 . . . . 48 C6
Castle Rise ④ M2 . . . . . 56 E5
Castle Shaw Rd SK2 . . . 124 E5
Castleshaw Top Bank
Delph OL3 . . . . 51 B8
Denshaw OL3 . . . . 34 B1
Castle St
Bolton BL2 . . . . 148 A3
Bury BL9 . . . . 140 C1
Eccles M30 . . . . 79 F2
Farnworth BL4 . . . . 60 D7
Glossop SK13 . . . . 104 A4
Hindley WN2 . . . . 56 E6
Hyde SK14 . . . . 167 C3
Manchester M3 . . . . . . 162 B4
Middleton M24 . . . . 65 D7
Ramsbottom BL9 . . . . . 11 D2
Stalybridge SK15 . . . . . . 86 A1
Stockport SK3 . . . . 170 B4
Tyldesley M29 . . . . 58 F1
Castle Terr SK15 . . . . . 86 F6
CASTLETON 30 C7
Castleton Ave M32 . . . . 96 B3
Castleton Bank ⑳ SK13 . 171 B1
Castleton Cres SK13 . . 171 B1
Castleton Ct
⑮ Denton M34 . . . . . . 113 A8
⑬ Tyldesley M29 . . . . . 58 F1
Castleton Dr SK6 . . . . 134 F6
Castleton Gn ㉒ SK13 . . 171 B1
Castleton Gr
Ashton-u-L OL6 . . . . 85 F6
㉓ Gamesley SK13 . . . . 171 B1
Castleton Prim Sch OL11 . 30 D2
Castleton Rd
Hazel Grove SK7 . . . . . 124 E1
⑬ Manchester M7 . . . . . 63 E1
Royton OL2, OL16 . . . . 48 D8
Salford M7 . . . . 155 B4
Stretford M32 . . . . 96 B4
Castleton Road S OL11 . 30 D3
Castleton St
Altrincham WA14 . . . . . 119 C7
Bolton BL2 . . . . 25 B3
Oldham OL9 . . . . 152 C2
Castleton Sta OL11 . . . 30 C2
Castleton Way
⑯ Denton M34 . . . . . . 113 A8
Wigan WN3 . . . . 54 C2

Castleton Wlk ② M11 . . 160 C1
Castleway
Altrincham WA15 . . . . . 129 C7
Hindley WN2 . . . . 57 A5
Rochdale OL11 . . . . . . 30 B1
Salford M6 . . . . 154 B4
Castle Way M27 . . . . . . 62 A3
Castle Wlk
Ashton-u-L OL6 . . . . 85 B7
⑰ Stalybridge SK15 . . . 86 A1
Castlewood Gdns SK2 . . 124 C5
Castlewood Rd M7 . . . . 81 A8
Castlewood Sq BL2 . . . 25 C1
Castle Yd SK1 . . . . . . 169 C2
Catalan Sq M15 . . . . . 162 B4
Catchdale Cl M9 . . . . . 64 C5
Catches Cl OL11 . . . . . 30 B8
Catches La OL11 . . . . . 14 B1
Cateaton St
② Bury BL9 . . . . 140 C3
Manchester M3 . . . . . . 158 C2
Caterham Ave BL3 . . . . 146 A2
Caterham St M4 . . . . . 160 A1
Catesby Rd M16 . . . . . 97 D3
Catford Rd M23 . . . . . 120 F5
Catford Wlk M15 . . . . . 162 A3
Cathedral App M3 . . . . 158 C2
Cathedral Cl SK16 . . . . 101 D6
Cathedral Gates M3 . . . 158 C2
Cathedral Rd OL9 . . . . . 48 A1
Cathedral St M3 . . . . . 158 C2
Cathedral Sch of St Peter &
St John RC Prim M3 . . 158 A2
Catherine Ho SK14 . . . . 110 F2
Catherine St
Altrincham WA14 . . . . . 119 C3
Manchester M7, M8 . . . . 63 E1
Romiley SK6 . . . . 112 F2
Swinton M27 . . . . 79 C7
Catherine St E BL6 . . . . 22 B4
Catherine Street W BL6 . 22 B5
Catherine Terr WN1 . . . 151 B4
Catherine Way WA12 . . . 89 B2
Catherston Rd ⑤ M16 . . 97 E3
Cathrine Street E M34 . . 100 D3
Cathrine Street W M34 . 100 D3
Catlow La M4 . . . . 159 A1
Catlow St M7 . . . . 158 B4
Caton Cl BL9 . . . . 44 E8
Caton Dr M46 . . . . 76 A8
Cato St BL0 . . . . 11 A4
Catskow Cl M18 . . . . . . 99 D3
Catterick Ave
⑧ Ashton-u-L OL7 . . . . . 84 F1
Bolton BL2 . . . . 148 B3
Bury BL9 . . . . 140 C1
Dukinfield SK16 . . . . . . 101 C8
Ince-in-M WN3 . . . . . . 55 E4
Leigh WN7 . . . . 75 F7
Littleborough OL15 . . . . 15 F5
Manchester M15 . . . . . 163 B1
Mossley OL5 . . . . 86 C8
Oldham OL8 . . . . 153 B1
Rochdale OL11 . . . . . . 139 C1
Royton OL2 . . . . 48 C4
Stalybridge SK15 . . . . . . 86 B1
Stockport SK3 . . . . 170 B3
Walkden M28 . . . . 60 D3
Wigan WN1 . . . . 151 B4
Cecil Walker Ho M31 . . . 106 A3
Cecil Wlk ⑦ OL7 . . . . 166 A1
Cedar Ave
Altrincham WA14 . . . . . 119 C4
Ashton-u-L OL6 . . . . 85 D5
Atherton M46 . . . . 58 B3
Hazel Grove SK7 . . . . . 124 E2
Heywood OL10 . . . . 29 C3
Hindley WN2 . . . . 56 F3
Horwich BL6 . . . . 22 E1
Little Lever BL3 . . . . . . 43 B2
Stalybridge SK15 . . . . . . 86 C3
Standish WN6 . . . . 36 F8
Whitefield M45 . . . . 62 F6
Cedar Bank Cl OL16 . . . 31 D7
Cedar Cl
Glossop SK13 . . . . 104 B2
Poynton SK12 . . . . 133 E3
Cedar Cres
Chadderton OL9 . . . . . . 152 B4
Newton-le-W WA12 . . . . 89 D2
Ramsbottom BL0 . . . . . 138 C3
Cedar Ct
② Altrincham WA15 . . . 120 B5
Culcheth WA3 . . . . 91 F1
Manchester M14 . . . . . 98 C1
Cedar Dr
Swinton M27 . . . . 61 D4
Urmston M41 . . . . 95 C1
Wigan WN1 . . . . 37 D2
Cedarfield Rd WA13 . . . 117 B4
Cedar Gr
Denton M34 . . . . 100 E3
Downall Green WN4 . . . 72 D5
Farnworth BL4 . . . . 60 B8

Cavendish Rd continued
Rochdale OL11 . . . . 30 E3
Stretford M32 . . . . 96 E4
Swinton M28 . . . . 79 B6
Urmston M41 . . . . 95 C2
Cavendish Road Prim Sch
M20 . . . . 110 A5
Cavendish St
Ashton-u-L OL6 . . . . . . 166 A2
Leigh WN7 . . . . 75 F7
Manchester M15 . . . . . 163 A2
③ Oldham OL8 . . . . . . 153 B2
Cavendish Way OL12 . . . 48 C2
Cavenham Gr ⑥ BL1 . . 144 C4
Cavenham Wlk M9 . . . . 156 C3
Caversham Dr M9 . . . . 157 B4
Cawdor Ave BL4 . . . . . . 42 B2
Cawdor Ct BL4 . . . . 42 C2
Cawdor Ho ② M30 . . . . 95 D8
Cawdor Pl WA15 . . . . . 120 C6
Cawdor Rd M14 . . . . . . 98 C1
Cawdor St
Eccles M30 . . . . 79 C1
Farnworth BL4 . . . . 42 C2
Hindley WN2 . . . . 56 E5
Leigh WN7 . . . . 75 F7
Manchester M15 . . . . . 162 A3
Swinton M27 . . . . 79 D8
Walkden M28 . . . . 60 E2
② Wigan WN5 . . . . 54 F6
Cawdor Wlk ⑤ BL4 . . . 42 C2
Cawley Ave
Culcheth WA3 . . . . 91 E4
Prestwich M25 . . . . 62 F2
Cawley Terr M9 . . . . . . 64 A5
Cawood Sq SK5 . . . . . 112 C6
Cawston Wlk ⑧ M8 . . . 156 A2
Caxton Cl WN3 . . . . . . 54 F2
Caxton Rd M14 . . . . . . 110 B8
Caxton St
Heywood OL10 . . . . 29 D2
Rochdale OL11 . . . . 30 C1
Salford M3 . . . . 158 B2
Caxton Way M5 . . . . . . 81 B1
Caygill St M3 . . . . 158 B2
Cayley St OL16 . . . . . . 31 B7
Caythorpe St M14 . . . . 98 A3
Cayton St M12 . . . . . . 99 A3
C' Ct WN4 . . . . 73 B2
Ceal The SK6 . . . . 114 B2
Cecil Ave
Sale M33 . . . . 107 F3
Wigan WN6 . . . . 37 A2
Cecil Ct ⑦ SK3 . . . . . . 123 B8
Cecil Dr M41 . . . . 94 E2
Cecil Gr M18 . . . . 99 D5
Cecilia St BL3 . . . . 42 A4
Cecil Rd
Altrincham WA15 . . . . . 119 E2
Eccles M30 . . . . 79 E1
Manchester M9 . . . . . . 64 D5
Stretford M32 . . . . 96 C1
Cecil St
⑧ Ashton-u-L OL7 . . . . . 84 F1
Bolton BL2 . . . . 148 B3
Bury BL9 . . . . 140 C1
Dukinfield SK16 . . . . . . 101 C8
Ince-in-M WN3 . . . . . . 55 E4
Leigh WN7 . . . . 75 F7
Littleborough OL15 . . . . 15 F5
Manchester M15 . . . . . 163 B1
Mossley OL5 . . . . 86 C8
Oldham OL8 . . . . 153 B1
Rochdale OL11 . . . . . . 139 C1
Royton OL2 . . . . 48 C4
Stalybridge SK15 . . . . . . 86 B1
Stockport SK3 . . . . 170 B3
Walkden M28 . . . . 60 D3
Wigan WN1 . . . . 151 B4

Cedar Gr continued
Manchester, Heaton Chapel
SK4 . . . . .111 C5
Manchester M14 . . . . . . .110 D8
Orrell WN5 . . . . 53 F6
Prestwich M25 . . . . 63 A6
Royton OL2 . . . . 48 D6
Shaw OL2 . . . . .149 B2
Stalybridge SK16 . . . . . . .101 F8
Westhoughton BL5 . . . . . . 57 E7
Cedar Ho [11] M14 . . . . . 98 E4
Cedar La
Newhey OL16 . . . . 32 A3
Uppermill OL4 . . . . 68 D6
Cedar Lawn [4] SK8 . . .123 A2
Cedar Lo SK7 . . . . .132 F7
Cedar Mews SK7 . . . . . . 85 B5
Cedar Mount High Sch
M18 . . . . 99 C3
Cedar Pk SK7 . . . . .123 E1
Cedar Pl M7 . . . . 81 C4
Cedar Rd
Altrincham WA15 . . . . . . .119 E3
Failsworth M35 . . . . 83 F6
Gatley SK8 . . . . .122 A5
Leigh WN7 . . . . 75 E8
Marple SK6 . . . . .125 E4
Middleton M24 . . . . 65 C8
Partington M31 . . . . .105 E3
Sale M33 . . . . .107 D6
Stockport SK2 . . . . .124 B4
Cedars SK9 . . . . .136 F6
Cedars Rd M22 . . . . . . .121 D3
Cedar St
Ashton-u-L OL6 . . . . 85 D4
Bury BL9 . . . . .141 A3
Dukinfield SK14 . . . . .101 E5
Newton-le-W WA12 . . . . . . 89 C2
[3] Oldham OL4 . . . . 67 C7
Rochdale OL12 . . . . 14 F1
Walsden OL14 . . . . 6 48
Cedars The
Bolton BL1 . . . . 24 F6
Manchester SK4 . . . . .111 C5
Cedarway SK9 . . . . .136 F5
Cedarwood Ave SK4 . . .168 A1
Cedarwood Cl
Manchester M9 . . . . 77 A7
Wythenshawe M22 . . . . . .121 E8
Cedric Rd
Manchester M8 . . . . 63 E2
Oldham OL4 . . . . 67 C7
Cedric St M5 . . . . .154 B2
Celandine Cl OL15 . . . . . 15 F6
Celandine Wlk WN3 . . . . 54 B4
Celia St M8 . . . . .156 C4
Cellini Sq BL1 . . . . .143 A1
Celtic St SK1 . . . . .124 A8
Cemetery La BL9 . . . . . . 45 A7
Cemetery Rd
Bolton, Clammerclough
BL4 . . . . 42 F1
Bolton, Tonge Fold BL2 . . .148 B3
Denton, Hooley Hill M34 . .100 F6
Denton M34 . . . . .100 F1
Droylsden M43 . . . . 83 F1
Failsworth M35 . . . . 83 F6
Glossop SK13 . . . . .104 C4
Ince-in-M WN3 . . . . .151 B1
Mossley OL5 . . . . 86 E8
Radcliffe M26 . . . . 43 F4
Ramsbottom BL0 . . . . 11 A4
Royton OL2 . . . . 48 C5
Salford M5 . . . . .154 B1
Cemetery Road N M27 . . 61 E2
Cemetery Road S M27 . . 61 E1
Cemetery Sta M43 . . . . . 83 F1
Cemetery St
Middleton M24 . . . . 47 A1
[2] Westhoughton BL5 . . 39 E1
Cemetery View PR7 . . . . 21 A6
Cenacle Ho M16 . . . . 97 E2
Cennick Cl [5] OL4 . . . . . 67 C6
Centaur Cl M27 . . . . 61 F2
Centaur Way [2] M8 . . .155 C3
Centenary [3] BL3 . . . . .147 C4
Centenary Ave
Eccles M17 . . . . 96 B8
Salford M17, M50 . . . . 80 A1
Central Art Gall* OL6 . .166 B2
Central Ave
Atherton M46 . . . . 58 E4
Bury BL9 . . . . 44 D7
Edenfield BL0 . . . . 1 D2
Farnworth BL4 . . . . 60 B8
Leigh WN7 . . . . 76 C3
Littleborough OL15 . . . . . . 16 B6
Manchester M19 . . . . 99 A1
Manchester M41 . . . . 95 E6
Pendlebury M6 . . . . 80 E6
Sale M33 . . . . .107 D1
Swinton M27 . . . . 62 D2
Uppermill OL3 . . . . 69 B5
Walkden M28 . . . . 60 C5
Central Bldgs M2 . . . . . .162 C4
Central Dr
Bury BL9 . . . . 27 F8
Gatley SK8 . . . . .131 D8
Manchester M8 . . . . 64 B1
Pendlebury M27 . . . . 80 B7
Reddish SK5 . . . . .111 F5
Romiley SK6 . . . . .113 C3
Shevington WN6 . . . . 36 B6
Stockport SK7 . . . . .123 D2

Central Dr continued
Urmston M41 . . . . 95 E2
Westhoughton BL5 . . . . . . 39 F1
Central Flats WN2 . . . . .151 C3
Central Ho [1] M9 . . . . . 64 E5
Central Park Est M24 . . . 64 F8
Central L Ctr OL16 . . . . . 31 A7
Central Park Est M17 . . . 96 B6
Central Park Sta M40 . . . 83 A6
Central Park Way WN1 . . 37 D1
Central Pl [1] SK9 . . . . .137 B7
Central Rd
Manchester M20 . . . . .110 A5
Partington M31 . . . . .105 F3
Central Ret Pk
Bolton BL2 . . . . .148 A2
Manchester M4 . . . . .159 C1
Central St
Bolton BL1 . . . . .145 B3
Manchester M2 . . . . .158 C1
Ramsbottom BL0 . . . . . . .138 C2
Central Store [5] SK13 . .104 C1
Central Way
Altrincham WA14 . . . . . . .119 D4
Newton-le-W WA12 . . . . . . 89 E2
Centre Ct WN7 . . . . 75 B1
Centre Gdns BL1 . . . . . .143 A1
Centre Park Rd BL1 . . . .143 A1
Centrepoint M17 . . . . 96 B5
Centre The WN7 . . . . 76 E6
Centre Vale OL15 . . . . . . 16 C7
Centre Vale Cl OL15 . . . . 16 C7
Centurion Gr M7 . . . . . . .155 B2
Century Gdns OL12 . . . . .139 C4
Century Ho M2 . . . . .162 C4
Century Lo BL4 . . . . 60 C8
Century Mill Ind Est BL4 . 60 B7
Century Park Ind Area
WA14 . . . . .119 A6
Century St M3 . . . . .162 B4
CE Sch of the Resurrection
M11 . . . . .160 C1
Cestrian St BL3 . . . . . . .147 C3
Ceylon St
Failsworth M40 . . . . 83 A6
Oldham OL4 . . . . 67 D5
Chadbury Cl BL6 . . . . 40 C3
CHADDERTON 152 A4
Chadderton District Sch
OL9 . . . . .152 B3
Chadderton Dr BL9 . . . . . 45 A2
CHADDERTON FOLD 47 F2
Chadderton Hall Jun Sch
OL9 . . . . 48 A2
Chadderton Hall Rd OL1,
OL9 . . . . 47 F1
CHADDERTON HEIGHTS . . 47 F3
Chadderton Ind Est M24 . . 65 C5
CHADDERTON PARK 65 F8
Chadderton Rd OL9 . . . . . 47 F1
Chadderton St M4 . . . . .159 B2
Chadderton Way
Oldham, Burnley Brow OL1,
OL9 . . . . .153 A4
Oldham, Holden Fold OL1,
OL9 . . . . 48 C1
Chaddesley Wlk M11 . . . .165 A4
Chaddock La
Boothstown M28 . . . . 77 F6
Tyldesley M29, M29 . . . . . 77 F7
Chaddock Level The M28 . 78 A5
Chadkirk SK6 . . . . .125 B8
Chadkirk Chapel* SK6 . . .113 C1
Chadkirk Ctry Est Nature
Reserve* SK6 . . . . .125 B8
Chadkirk Est SK6 . . . . . .125 B8
Chadkirk Rd SK6 . . . . . . .113 C2
Chadvil Rd SK8 . . . . .122 C5
Chadwell Rd SK2 . . . . . .124 E7
Chadwick Cl
Handforth SK9 . . . . .131 C1
[12] Manchester M14 . . . 98 B3
Milnrow OL16 . . . . 32 A5
Stalybridge SK15 . . . . 85 F3
Chadwick Fold
Bury BL9 . . . . 27 F7
Heywood OL10 . . . . 29 F2
CHADWICK GREEN 71 D3
Chadwick Hall Rd OL11 . . 30 B6
Chadwick La
Rochdale, Castleton OL10,
OL11 . . . . 30 A2
Rochdale, Pleasant View
OL16 . . . . 31 C2
Chadwick Rd
Eccles M30 . . . . 79 E2
Urmston M41 . . . . 95 F2
Chadwick St
Ashton-u-L OL6 . . . . 85 E2
Bolton BL2 . . . . .148 B2
Bury BL9 . . . . 28 E4
Glossop SK13 . . . . .116 B8
[2] Hindley WN2 . . . . . . 56 E6
Leigh WN7 . . . . 75 F6
Little Lever BL3 . . . . 43 B3
Marple SK6 . . . . .125 F5
Milnrow OL16 . . . . 31 D7
Rochdale OL11 . . . . .139 A3
Swinton M27 . . . . .170 C4
Swinton M27 . . . . 79 F8
Wigan WN3 . . . . .150 B2
Chadwick Terr OL12 . . . . 14 D4
Chadwick Wlk M27 . . . . . 79 F8
Chaffinch Cl
Droylsden M43 . . . . 84 C3
Oldham OL4 . . . . 67 D4
Wythenshawe M22 . . . . . .121 F5
Chaffinch Dr BL9 . . . . . .141 C4

Chaffinch Gr SK15 . . . . . 86 E7
Chain Bar La SK14 . . . . .102 F2
Chain Bar La SK14 . . . . .102 F2
Chainhurst Wlk [2] M13 . .163 C2
Chain Rd M9 . . . . 64 D5
Chain St M1 . . . . .159 A1
Chain Wlk [8] M9 . . . . . . 64 E5
Chaise Mdw WA13 . . . . .117 C5
Chalbury Cl [9] M40,Q . . . 56 D4
Chalcombe Grange [1]
M12 . . . . 98 F4
Chale Cl M40 . . . . .160 A3
Chale Dr M24 . . . . 65 C6
Chale Gn BL2 . . . . 25 E3
Chalfont Ave [1] M41 . . . 95 E2
Chalfont Cl OL8 . . . . 67 B4
Chalfont Dr
Manchester M8 . . . . .156 A3
Tyldesley M29 . . . . 77 A8
Walkden M28 . . . . 78 E8
Chalfont Ho [2] M6 . . . .154 C2
Chalfont St BL1 . . . . . . .143 C2
Chalford Rd M23 . . . . . . .121 A4
Challenge Way WN5 . . . . 36 D1
Challenor Sq M12 . . . . . .165 A2
Challum Dr OL9 . . . . .152 A4
Chamber Hall Cl OL8 . . . . 66 D4
Chamberhall St BL9 . . . .140 B3
Chamber House Dr OL11 . 30 B3
Chamberlain Dr SK9 . . . .131 D1
Chamberlain Gdns SK6 . .112 F4
Chamberlain Rd SK15 . . . 86 C5
Chamber Rd
Oldham OL8 . . . . 66 D4
Shaw OL2 . . . . .149 A3
Chambers Cl SK14 . . . . .103 A3
Chambers Field Ct [8] M5 . 81 A1
Chambers The M33 . . . . .108 A5
Champagnole Ct [3]
SK16 . . . . .166 B1
Champneys Wlk M9 . . . . .157 A2
Chancel Ave M5 . . . . . . .161 C4
Chancel Cl SK16 . . . . . . .101 C6
Chancel La SK9 . . . . .137 B8
Chancellor La M12 . . . . . .164 A3
Chancel Mews M11 . . . . .112 A1
Chancel Pl
Manchester M1 . . . . .159 C1
Rochdale OL16 . . . . .139 C3
Chancery Cl M29 . . . . 77 B8
Chancery La
Bolton BL1 . . . . .145 C3
[1] Manchester M3 . . . . .158 C1
Shaw OL2 . . . . .149 C3
Uppermill OL3 . . . . 51 A2
Chancery Pl [14] M2 . . . .158 C1
Chancery St
Chadderton OL9 . . . . .152 C4
Oldham OL4 . . . . 67 C6
Chancery Wlk OL9 . . . . . .152 C4
Chanders Mews M22 . . .109 E1
Chandlers Row M28 . . . . 79 A5
Chandler Way WA3 . . . . . 90 E8
Chandley St SK14 . . . . . .124 A7
Chandley St SK8 . . . . . . .122 D6
Chandos Gr M5 . . . . .154 A2
Chandos Rd
Manchester, Heaton Chapel
SK4 . . . . .111 C6
Manchester, Hilton Park
M25 . . . . 63 B2
Manchester M21 . . . . 97 C1
Chandos St OL2 . . . . . . .149 C3
Change Way M3 . . . . . . .158 B3
Channing Ct [1] SK16 . . . 31 B6
Channing Sq [2] OL16 . . . 31 B6
Channing St OL16 . . . . . . 31 B6
Chanters Ave M46 . . . . . 58 E3
Chanters Cl M9 . . . . 64 C4
Chanters Ind Est M46 . . . 58 E2
Chanters The M28 . . . . . 78 C7
Chantlers Ave BL8 . . . . . 27 A2
Chantlers Prim Sch BL8 . . 27 A2
Chantry Cl
Disley SK12 . . . . .135 E5
Reddish SK5 . . . . .111 E7
Westhoughton BL5 . . . . . . 57 F5
Chantry Fold SK12 . . . . .135 E6
Chantry Rd SK12 . . . . . . .135 E6
Chantry Wlk
Ashton-in-M WN4 . . . . 72 F5
[4] Salford M6 . . . . .155 C3
Chapel Alley [2] BL1 . . . .145 C3
Chapel Brow
Broadbottom SK13 . . . . . .115 E6
Glossop SK13 . . . . .104 A7
Chapel Cl
Dukinfield SK16 . . . . .101 D8
Ince-in-M WN3 . . . . .151 A2
Whitefield BL9 . . . . 45 B4
Chapel Croft OL2 . . . . . . 48 D4
Chapel Ct
Altrincham WA14 . . . . . . .119 D4
Bury BL8 . . . . 26 E7
Hyde SK14 . . . . .101 C1
[6] Marple SK6 . . . . . . .125 F6
[5] Mossley OL5 . . . . . . 68 C1
Sale M33 . . . . .107 E6
Wilmslow SK9 . . . . .137 A6
Chapel Dr
Altrincham WA15 . . . . . . .129 C7
Ashton-u-L OL6 . . . . 85 E5
Chapel End Prim Sch
WN5 . . . . 71 E4
CHAPEL FIELD 44 C1
Chapelfield M26 . . . . 44 C1
Chapelfield Cl SK15 . . . . . 86 D4

Chapelfield Dr M28 . . . . . 60 B3
Chapelfield Prim Sch
M26 . . . . 44 C1
Chapelfield Rd M12 . . . . .163 C4
Chapel Field Rd M34 . . . .100 F3
Chapel Fields
Chapeltown BL7 . . . . 9 C4
[1] Marple SK6 . . . . . . .125 F5
Chapel Fields La WN2 . . . 56 E5
Chapelfield St BL1 . . . . . .143 B3
Chapel Gate OL16 . . . . . . 31 F6
Chapel Gdns
Denton M34 . . . . .100 F6
Ramsbottom BL8 . . . . 10 E1
Chapel Gn M34 . . . . .100 F3
Chapel Gr
Radcliffe M26 . . . . 62 A8
Urmston M41 . . . . 95 E2
Chapel Grange BL7 . . . . . 9 C4
Chapel Green Rd WN2 . . . 56 E5
Chapel Hill
[2] Dukinfield SK16 . . . .101 C8
Littleborough OL15 . . . . . . 16 B5
Chapelhill Dr M9 . . . . 64 C3
Chapel Ho SK5 . . . . .111 E8
Chapel House Mews [5]
WA3 . . . . 90 D8
Chapel Houses SK6 . . . .126 A5
Chapel La
Altrincham WA15 . . . . . . .129 C7
Coppull PR7 . . . . 19 F8
Glossop SK13 . . . . .103 F5
Hollinfare WA3 . . . . .105 A2
Manchester M9 . . . . 64 C3
Partington M31 . . . . .105 F2
Ramsbottom BL8 . . . . . . .138 A2
Rochdale OL11 . . . . 29 C8
Royton OL2 . . . . 48 D4
Sale M33 . . . . .107 E6
Stretford M32 . . . . 96 C1
Wigan WN1 & WN3 . . . . . .150 C3
Wilmslow SK9 . . . . .137 A6
Chapel Lofts SK13 . . . . .104 B5
Chapel Mdw M28 . . . . . . 78 B7
Chapel Pl
[4] Ashton-in-M WN4 . . . 73 B3
Bolton BL2, BL3 . . . . .148 C1
Urmston M41 . . . . 95 D8
Chapel Rd
Alderley Edge SK9 . . . . . .137 A1
Irlam M44 . . . . 94 A2
Manchester M25 . . . . 63 A1
Oldham OL8 . . . . 66 C2
Swinton M27 . . . . 79 C7
Uppermill OL3 . . . . 69 A6
Wythenshawe M22 . . . . . .121 D8
Chapel St
Adlington PR7 . . . . 20 F6
[7] Alderley Edge SK9 . .137 A1
Ashton-in-M WN4 . . . . 73 B3
Atherton M46 . . . . 58 D3
Bickershaw WN2 . . . . 56 E1
Blackrod BL6 . . . . 21 D2
Bolton BL1 . . . . .145 C4
Bolton, Egerton BL7 . . . . . . 8 D3
Boothstown M28 . . . . 77 F6
Bury, Tottington BL8 . . . . . . 8 D3
Calderbrook OL15 . . . . 6 D2
Cheadle SK8 . . . . .122 D5
Denton M34 . . . . .100 F6
Droylsden M43 . . . . 84 B1
Dukinfield SK16 . . . . .101 B8
[3] Eccles M30 . . . . 79 C1
Farnworth BL4 . . . . 60 E8
Glossop SK13 . . . . .104 C1
Hazel Grove SK7 . . . . .124 E3
Heywood OL10 . . . . 29 D2
Hindley WN2 . . . . 56 D5
Horwich BL6 . . . . 22 C3
Hyde SK14 . . . . .167 A2
Ince-in-M WN3 . . . . .151 A2
Kearsley M26 . . . . 61 B8
Leigh WN7 . . . . 76 B4
[2] Little Lever BL3 . . . . 43 B3
Manchester, Heaton Mersey
SK4 . . . . .110 C1
Manchester, Levenshulme
M19 . . . . 99 B1
[6] Middleton M24 . . . . . 46 F1
[5] Mossley OL5 . . . . . . 68 C1
New Mills, Rowarth SK22 . .127 E7
Newton-le-W WA12 . . . . . . 89 B3
Oldham OL4 . . . . 67 B6
Platt Bridge WN2 . . . . 56 B2
Prestwich M25 . . . . 63 A4
[10] Rochdale OL11 . . . . 31 A4
Romiley SK6 . . . . .113 B5
Royton OL2 . . . . 48 D4
Salford M3 . . . . .158 B2
Shaw OL2 . . . . .149 B3
Stalybridge SK15 . . . . 86 A2
Swinton M27 . . . . 62 A1
Tyldesley M29 . . . . 77 A8
Uppermill OL3 . . . . 69 B8
Wardle OL12 . . . . 15 C7
Whitworth OL12 . . . . 14 C8
Wigan, Lamberhead Green
WN5 . . . . 54 B5
Wigan, Lamberhead Green
WN5 . . . . 54 B6
Wigan, Whelley WN2 . . . . . 38 A2
Wigan WN3 . . . . .150 C3
Chapelstead BL5 . . . . 57 F5
Chapel Street Prim Sch
M19 . . . . 99 B1
Chapel Terr WA3 . . . . 91 B8

CHAPELTOWN 9 D4
Chapeltown Rd
Chapeltown BL7 . . . . 9 C2
Radcliffe M26 . . . . 62 A8
Chapeltown St M1 . . . . . .159 C1
Chapel View Cl SK14 . . . .113 C7
Chapel Way PR7 . . . . 19 F8
Chapelway Gdns OL2 . . . 48 D6
Chapel Wlk
[1] Eccles M30 . . . . 79 F2
Golborne WA3 . . . . 91 B8
Middleton M24 . . . . 64 C7
Oldham OL1 . . . . 48 D1
Prestwich M25 . . . . 62 F1
Whitefield M45 . . . . 45 B1
Chapel Wlks
Broomedge WA13 . . . . . . .117 D1
Cheadle SK8 . . . . .132 B6
Manchester M2 . . . . .158 C1
Sale M33 . . . . .108 B5
Chaplin Cl M6 . . . . .154 B4
Chapman Mews M18 . . . . 99 D5
Chapman Rd SK14 . . . . . .102 E1
Chapman St
Bolton BL1 . . . . .142 B1
Manchester M18 . . . . 99 D5
Chappell Rd M43 . . . . 84 A2
Chapter St M40 . . . . .160 C4
Chapter Ho OL11 . . . . . . .118 F3
Charcoal Woods WA14 . . .119 A3
Charcon Wlk [3] OL2 . . . . 48 E4
Chard Dr M22 . . . . .121 D1
Chardin Ave SK6 . . . . . . .126 C8
Chard St M26 . . . . 44 A3
Charges St OL7 . . . . 84 F1
Chariot St M11 . . . . 99 D8
Charlbury Ave
Manchester M25 . . . . 63 E3
Reddish SK5 . . . . .111 F6
Charlbury Way OL2 . . . . . 48 E4
Charlecote Rd SK12 . . . . .133 F4
Charles Ave
Droylsden M34 . . . . .100 A7
Marple SK6 . . . . .125 C7
Charles Ct
Altrincham WA15 . . . . . . .120 B6
Bolton BL1 . . . . .145 C4
Charles Halle Rd M15 . . .163 A1
Charles Holden St BL1 . . .145 A2
Charles La
Glossop SK13 . . . . .104 E3
Milnrow OL16 . . . . 32 A5
Charles Mews OL16 . . . . . 32 A5
Charles Morris Ho M35 . . 84 B8
Charles Morris Ho M35 . . 84 A7
Charles Shaw Cl [4] OL4 . . 49 D1
Charles St
Ashton-u-L OL7 . . . . .166 B2
Bolton BL1 . . . . .145 C4
Bolton, Egerton BL7 . . . . . . 8 D2
[2] Bolton, Mill Hill BL1 . .148 A4
[6] Bury BL9 . . . . .140 C3
Denton M34 . . . . .100 F5
Droylsden M43 . . . . 83 E1
Dukinfield SK16 . . . . .166 B1
[3] Farnworth BL4 . . . . . 42 E1
Farnworth BL4 . . . . 60 E7
Glossop SK13 . . . . .104 C1
Golborne WA3 . . . . 74 A1
Hazel Grove SK7 . . . . .124 D3
Heywood OL10 . . . . 46 E8
Hindley WN2 . . . . 56 E7
Ince-in-M WN2 . . . . 56 A7
Irlam M44 . . . . .105 E6
Leigh WN7 . . . . 75 F7
Leigh WN7 . . . . 76 A5
Littleborough OL15 . . . . . . 16 A5
Manchester M1 . . . . .163 A4
Oldham OL9 . . . . .152 C2
Royton OL2 . . . . 48 D4
Salford M6 . . . . .154 C4
Stockport SK1 . . . . .124 A2
Swinton M27 . . . . 61 D2
Tyldesley M29 . . . . 58 F1
Whitefield M45 . . . . 62 F7
[2] Wigan WN1 . . . . 37 C1
Charleston Cl M33 . . . . . .107 D2
Charleston Ct M29 . . . . . . 76 F8
Charleston Sq M41 . . . . . 95 B3
Charleston St OL8 . . . . . . 66 F4
CHARLESTOWN
Ashton-under-Lyne 166 B4
Glossop 116 C6
Manchester 65 A3
Salford 81 B4
Charlestown SK13 . . . . . .116 C6
Charlestown Cl OL6 . . . . .166 B4
Charlestown Ind Est OL6 . .166 B4
Charlestown Prim Sch
Manchester M9 . . . . 65 B3
Salford M6 . . . . 81 B4
Charlestown Rd
Glossop SK13 . . . . .116 C7
Manchester M9 . . . . 65 A3
Charlestown Way OL6 . . .166 A3
Charles Whittaker St [2]
OL12 . . . . 13 F1
Charles Wlk M45 . . . . 62 F7
CHARLESWORTH 115 C6
Charlesworth Ave
Bolton BL3 . . . . 42 B3
Denton M34 . . . . .112 F8
Hindley WN2 . . . . 56 C7
Charlesworth Ct M11 . . . .164 C4
Charlesworth St
Manchester M11 . . . . .164 C4

Charlesworth St *continued*
Stockport SK1, SK3 . . . . **170** C3
Charley Ave M7 . . . . **158** A4
Charlock Ave BL5 . . . . **57** E6
Charlock Cl WN7 . . . . **75** F3
Charlock Sq WA14 . . . . **119** B8
Charlock Wlk 6 M31 . . . . **105** F3
Charlotte La OL4 . . . . **68** E5
Charlotte Pl WA15 . . . . . . **119** F3
Charlotte St
27 Bolton BL1 . . . . **143** B2
Cheadle SK8 . . . . **122** D5
Manchester M1, M2 . . . . **159** A1
Rochdale OL16 . . . . **31** B3
Stockport SK1 . . . . **112** B3
Charlton Ave
Dukinfield SK14 . . . . **102** A4
Eccles M30 . . . . **79** D1
Prestwich M25 . . . . **63** B3
Charlton Ct WN4 . . . . **73** A5
Charlton Ct M25 . . . . **63** B3
Charlton Dr
Sale M33 . . . . **108** C4
Swinton M27 . . . . **61** D2
Charlton Fold M28 . . . . . . **60** C5
Charlton Pl M12 . . . . **163** B3
Charlton Rd M19 . . . . **99** B1
Charminster Dr M8 . . . . **156** B4
Charminster Mews M27 . . **79** F6
Charmouth Cl WA12 . . . . **89** B4
Charmouth Wlk M22 . . . . **121** F3
Charnley Cl
Manchester M40 . . . . **160** B3
7 Sale M33 . . . . **108** A4
Charnley Grange BL6 . . . . **40** B7
Charnley St M45 . . . . **62** F8
Charnock Dr BL1 . . . . **143** B1
Charnock Rd WA3 . . . . **91** F3
Charnock St WN2 . . . . **56** B1
Charnock's Yd 2 WN5 . . . **54** B5
Charnville Rd SK8 . . . . . **121** F5
Charnwood SK6 . . . . **134** F7
Charnwood Ave M34 . . . . **100** B3
Charnwood Cl
Ashton-u-L OL6 . . . . **85** C7
Shaw OL2 . . . . **48** E8
Tyldesley M29 . . . . **77** B8
Walkden M28 . . . . **60** C2
Charnwood Cres SK7 . . . . **133** D8
Charnwood Rd
Manchester M9 . . . . **64** D5
Romiley SK6 . . . . **113** C5
Charter M26 . . . . **44** C2
Charter Cl 3 M33 . . . . . . **107** D3
Charter Ho M30 . . . . **79** F1
Charterhouse Rd WN3 . . **151** A2
Charter Rd WA15 . . . . **119** E4
Charter St
Manchester M3 . . . . **158** C3
Oldham OL1 . . . . **67** A8
Rochdale OL16 . . . . **31** B4
Chartist Ho SK14 . . . . . . **167** B2
Chartwell Cl M5, M6 . . . . **154** C2
Chartwell Dr M23 . . . . . . **120** E7
Chasefield WA14 . . . . **119** A2
Chaseley Rd
Rochdale OL12 . . . . **139** B4
Salford M6 . . . . **154** C2
Chase St M4 . . . . **159** A3
Chase The M28 . . . . **79** A5
Chasetown Cl 5 M23 . . . **120** D6
Chassen Ave M41 . . . . **95** B1
Chassen Ct M41 . . . . **95** B1
Chassen Rd
Bolton BL1 . . . . **144** B3
Urmston M41 . . . . **95** B1
Chassen Road Sta M41 . . **95** B1
Chataway Rd M8 . . . . **156** C4
Chatburn Ave
Golborne WA3 . . . . **74** C1
Trub OL11 . . . . **47** D8
Chatburn Ct
Culcheth WA3 . . . . **91** F2
Shaw OL2 . . . . **149** C4
Chatburn Gdns OL10 . . . . **28** F2
Chatburn Rd
Bolton BL1 . . . . **23** F3
Manchester M21 . . . . **109** C8
Chatburn Sq OL11 . . . . **47** D8
Chatcombe Rd M22 . . . . . **121** A2
Chatfield Rd M21 . . . . **109** B8
Chatford Cl M7 . . . . **158** B4
Chatham Ct M20 . . . . **110** A6
Chatham Gdns BL3 . . . . . **145** A1
Chatham Gr M20 . . . . **110** A6
Chatham Ho 1 SK3 . . . . . **170** B4
Chatham Pl 2 BL3 . . . . . **145** A1
Chatham Rd
Manchester M16 . . . . **97** C3
Reddish M18 . . . . **99** E3
Chatham St
Hyde SK14 . . . . **113** E7
Ince-in-M WN2 . . . . **56** A8
Leigh WN7 . . . . **75** F7
Manchester M1 . . . . **159** B1
Stockport SK3 . . . . **170** A4
Wigan WN1 . . . . **151** B3
Chatley Rd M30 . . . . **78** F1
Chatley St M3, M4 . . . . . **159** A4
Chatswood Ave SK2 . . . . **170** C2
Chatsworth Ave
Culcheth WA3 . . . . **91** F4
Ince-in-M WN3 . . . . **55** F4
Prestwich M25 . . . . **63** B4
Chatsworth Cl
Altrincham WA15 . . . . **120** C5
Ashton-in-M WN4 . . . . **72** F4
Droylsden M43 . . . . **83** E3

Chatsworth Cl *continued*
Shaw OL2 . . . . **49** D8
2 Urmston M41 . . . . **95** E2
Whitefield BL9 . . . . **45** A5
Chatsworth Cres M32 . . . . **95** F3
Chatsworth Ct
Adlington PR6 . . . . **20** F8
Stockport SK2 . . . . **124** A5
Chatsworth Dr WN7 . . . . . **76** D7
Chatsworth Fold WN3 . . **151** B1
Chatsworth Gdns WN3 . . **151** B1
Chatsworth Gr
Little Lever BL3 . . . . **43** A4
Manchester M16 . . . . **97** D2
Chatsworth High Sch M30 **79** F4
Chatsworth Ho M1 . . . . . . **159** A1
Chatsworth Manor SK7 . . **123** C2
Chatsworth Mews SK7 . . **123** D2
Chatsworth Rd
Cheadle SK8 . . . . **123** B5
Droylsden M43 . . . . **83** E2
Eccles M30 . . . . **79** F4
Hazel Grove SK7 . . . . **133** F8
High Lane SK6 . . . . **134** F6
Manchester M18 . . . . **165** C1
Radcliffe M26 . . . . **43** D5
Stretford M32 . . . . **96** A3
Swinton M28 . . . . **79** C5
Wilmslow SK9 . . . . **136** E4
Chatsworth St
Oldham OL4 . . . . **67** C5
Rochdale OL12 . . . . **14** E3
Wigan WN5 . . . . **54** C5
Chatteris Cl WN2 . . . . **56** E4
CHATTERTON **1** C1
Chatterton BL0 . . . . **1** C1
Chatterton Cl M20 . . . . . **110** C6
Chatterton La SK6 . . . . . **127** B8
Chatterton Old La BL0 . . . . **1** C1
Chattock St 11 M16 . . . . . **97** E3
Chatton Cl BL8 . . . . **26** F2
Chatwell Ct OL16 . . . . **32** C4
Chatwood Rd M40 . . . . **65** D2
Chaucer Ave
Denton M34 . . . . **113** A7
Droylsden M43 . . . . **84** A1
Radcliffe M26 . . . . **43** E4
Reddish SK5 . . . . **99** D1
Chaucer Gr
Atherton M46 . . . . **58** D5
Leigh WN7 . . . . **75** D8
Chaucer Mews SK1 . . . . . **112** B1
Chaucer Pl
Abram WN2 . . . . **56** B1
Wigan WN1 . . . . **37** C3
Chaucer Rd M24 . . . . **47** B2
Chaucer Rise SK16 . . . . . **102** A7
Chaucer St
Bolton BL1 . . . . **143** A2
Oldham OL1 . . . . **153** B2
Rochdale OL11 . . . . **30** C2
Royton OL2 . . . . **48** E5
Chaumont Way OL6 . . . . **166** B3
Chauncy Rd M40 . . . . **83** E8
Chaytor Ave M40 . . . . **83** B7
CHEADLE **122** E5
Cheadle Ave M7 . . . . **81** A7
Cheadle Ct SK4 . . . . **168** B4
CHEADLE HEATH **123** A7
Cheadle Heath Prim Sch
SK3 . . . . **123** A7
CHEADLE HULME **132** A8
Cheadle Hulme High Sch
SK8 . . . . **132** B7
Cheadle Hulme Sch SK8 . **132** A8
Cheadle Hulme Sta SK8 . **123** B2
Cheadle Old Rd SK3 . . . . . **123** C7
Cheadle Point SK8 . . . . . . **122** E6
Cheadle Prim Sch SK8 . . **122** D6
Cheadle RC Inf Sch SK8 . **122** E2
Cheadle RC Jun Sch
SK8 . . . . **122** E2
Cheadle Rd SK8 . . . . **122** F3
Cheadle Royal Bsns Pk
SK8 . . . . **122** C2
Cheadle Royal Hospl
(private) SK8 . . . . **122** C2
Cheadle Sq BL1 . . . . **145** B3
Cheadle St M11 . . . . **99** D8
Cheadle Wood SK8 . . . . . **131** E8
Cheam Rd WA15 . . . . **119** F8
Cheapside
Hyde SK14 . . . . **167** B3
Manchester M2 . . . . **158** C1
Middleton M24 . . . . **47** A2
Oldham OL1 . . . . **153** B3
Cheapside Sq 8 BL1 . . . **145** C3
Cheddar St 1 M18 . . . . . . **99** D5
Cheddington Cl SK8 . . . . **132** A7
Cheddleton Rd WA14 . . . **119** C8
Chedlee Dr SK8 . . . . **131** E8
Chedlin Dr M23 . . . . **121** A4
Chedworth Cres M38 . . . . **60** A6
Chedworth Dr M23 . . . . . **121** B6
Chedworth Gr 4 BL3 . . . **147** B1
Cheeryble St M11, M43 . . . **99** F7
CHEESDEN **12** D6
Cheesden Wlk M45 . . . . . . **45** C1
Cheetham CE Com Sch
M8 . . . . **155** C3
Cheetham Fold Sch SK14 **113** B8
Cheetham Gdns 7 SK15 . . **86** B1
Cheetham Gr WN3 . . . . **54** F5
Cheetham Hill **156** B3
Cheetham Hill
Shaw OL2 . . . . **149** B2

Cheetham Hill *continued*
Whitworth OL12 . . . . **4** D3
Cheetham Hill Rd
Dukinfield SK15, SK16 . . . **101** E7
Manchester, Cheetham Hill
M8 . . . . **156** A2
Cheetham Mill Ind Est
SK15 . . . . **86** B1
Cheetham Par M8 . . . . **155** C4
Cheetham Pl SK6 . . . . **112** D3
Cheetham Rd M27 . . . . **80** A7
Cheetham's Cres OL2 . . . . **49** A4
Cheetham St
Failsworth M35 . . . . **84** A8
Manchester M40 . . . . **157** B1
Middleton M24 . . . . **64** F8
Oldham OL1 . . . . **67** B7
Radcliffe M26 . . . . **44** C4
Rochdale OL16 . . . . **139** C4
Shaw OL2 . . . . **149** C2
Cheethams The BL6 . . . . . . **38** E7
Cheetwood Prim Sch
M8 . . . . **158** B4
Cheetwood Rd M8 . . . . . . **155** C1
Cheetwood St M8 . . . . . . **158** B4
Chelbourne Dr 3 OL8 . . . **66** B2
Chelburn Cl
Leigh WN2 . . . . **56** E1
Stockport SK2 . . . . **124** D5
Chelburn Ct SK3 . . . . **170** B2
Chelburn View OL15 . . . . . . **6** C1
Cheldon Wlk 8 M40 . . . . . **83** C6
Chelford Ave
Bolton BL1 . . . . **24** E5
Golborne WA3 . . . . **90** D8
Chelford Cl
Altrincham WA15 . . . . **119** E6
Manchester M13 . . . . **164** A1
Middleton M24 . . . . **47** C2
Wigan WN3 . . . . **54** F2
Chelford Dr
Swinton M27 . . . . **61** E2
Tyldesley M29 . . . . **77** C6
Chelford Gr 3 SK3 . . . . . **170** A1
Chelford Rd
Alderley Edge SK9 . . . . . . **136** E1
Handforth SK9 . . . . **131** D5
Manchester M16 . . . . **97** C3
Sale M33 . . . . **108** C2
Chellow Ct OL5 . . . . **68** B1
Chellow Dene OL5 . . . . **68** B1
Chell St M13 . . . . **98** F4
Chelmarsh Ave WN4 . . . . . **73** C3
Chelmer Cl BL5 . . . . **40** A1
Chelmer Gr OL10 . . . . **29** A3
Chelmorton Gr WN3 . . . . . . **54** C2
Chelmsford Ave M40 . . . . **83** B4
Chelmsford Dr WN3 . . . . . . **55** A4
Chelmsford Mews WN1 . . **37** C2
Chelmsford Rd SK3 . . . . . **123** C8
Chelmsford St OL8 . . . . . **153** B1
Chelmsford Wlk 4 M34 . **101** A1
Chelsea Ave M26 . . . . **43** D4
Chelsea Cl OL2 . . . . **149** B3
Chelsea Rd
Bolton BL3 . . . . **147** A3
Failsworth M40 . . . . **83** C5
Urmston M41 . . . . **94** C1
Chelsea St
Bury BL9 . . . . **44** F4
Rochdale OL11 . . . . **139** A1
Chelsfield Gr M21 . . . . . . **109** D8
Chelston Ave M40 . . . . **65** D2
Chelston Dr
Gatley SK8 . . . . **131** C6
Haslingden BB4 . . . . **1** A7
Cheltenham Ave WN3 . . . **151** A1
Cheltenham Cres M7 . . . **155** B3
Cheltenham Dr
Longshaw WN5 . . . . **53** D2
Newton-le-W WA12 . . . . **89** C3
Sale M33 . . . . **108** C4
Cheltenham Gn M24 . . . . . **65** A6
Cheltenham Rd
Cheadle SK3 . . . . **123** A7
Manchester M21 . . . . **97** B2
Middleton M24 . . . . **65** A6
Cheltenham St
Oldham OL1 . . . . **49** B1
Rochdale OL11 . . . . **30** D4
Salford M6 . . . . **81** A4
1 Wigan WN2 . . . . **37** F2
Chelt Wlk M22 . . . . **121** B2
Chelwood Cl BL1 . . . . **24** D7
Chelwood Dr M43 . . . . **83** F2
Chelwood Mews BL6 . . . . **40** B7
Chelwood Pk WA12 . . . . . . **73** B1
Chelworth Manor SK7 . . . **123** C1
Chemical St WA12 . . . . **89** B3
Chendre Cl M27 . . . . **61** F2
Chendre Rd M9 . . . . **65** B3
Cheney Cl M11 . . . . **99** D7
Chenies The 5 M7 . . . . . . **63** C1
Chepstow Ave M33 . . . . . **107** C3
Chepstow Cl OL11 . . . . **29** F8
Chepstow Dr
Hazel Grove SK7 . . . . **125** A2
Oldham OL1 . . . . **49** B1
Chepstow Gr WN7 . . . . **76** E7
Chepstow Ho M1 . . . . **162** C4
Chepstow Rd
Manchester M21 . . . . **97** A1
Swinton M27 . . . . **62** A2
Chepstow St M1, M2 . . . . **162** C4
Chepstow St N M1 . . . . . . **162** C4
CHEQUERBENT **40** D1
Chequers Rd M21 . . . . . . **109** B8
Chequers St WN1 . . . . . . **150** B4

Cherington Cl
Handforth SK9 . . . . **131** F3
Wythenshawe M23 . . . . . . **109** B2
Cherington Rd SK8 . . . . . . **59** C1
Cherington Rd SK8 . . . . . . **122** C4
Cheriton Ave M33 . . . . . . **108** C5
Cheriton Cl SK14 . . . . **102** D2
Cheriton Dr BL2 . . . . **42** E6
Cheriton Gdns BL6 . . . . . . **22** B5
Cheriton Rd M41 . . . . **94** D3
Cheriton Rise SK2 . . . . . . **125** A6
Cherry Ave
Ashton-u-L OL6 . . . . **85** B6
Bury BL9 . . . . **141** C3
Oldham OL8 . . . . **67** C3
Cherrybrook Dr WN3 . . . . **54** D1
Cherry Cl
Bury BL9 . . . . **45** A7
Stockport SK2 . . . . **124** E7
Cherry Cres BB4 . . . . **1** F8
Cherry Croft SK6 . . . . **113** E1
Cherry Ct
3 Sale, Ashton u M
M33 . . . . **108** A4
Sale, Timperley WA15 . . . **120** C7
Cherry Dr M27 . . . . **80** A8
Cherry Gdns BL1 . . . . **40** F8
Cherry Gr
Leigh WN7 . . . . **75** F8
Rochdale OL11 . . . . **30** A8
Royton OL2 . . . . **48** C6
Stalybridge SK15 . . . . **102** A8
Urmston M41 . . . . **95** E3
Whitefield M45 . . . . **63** A7
Cherry Hall Dr OL2 . . . . . . **48** E7
Cherry Hinton OL1 . . . . . . **153** A4
Cherry Holt Ave SK4 . . . **110** F4
Cherry La
Denshaw OL16, OL3 . . . . . . **33** B3
Sale M33 . . . . **107** D3
Wigan WN6 . . . . **36** F3
Cherry Orchard Cl SK7 . **123** D1
Cherry St M25 . . . . **63** C5
Cherryton Wlk M13 . . . . . **163** C2
CHERRY TREE **113** F2
Cherry Tree Ave
Farnworth BL4 . . . . **60** A8
Poynton SK12 . . . . **133** F3
Cherry Tree Cl
1 Altrincham WA15 . . . . **120** B5
Romiley SK6 . . . . **113** E2
Wilmslow SK9 . . . . **137** E8
Cherry Tree Cotts WA11 . **71** A2
Cherry Tree Ct
7 Salford M6 . . . . **81** A2
Standish WN6 . . . . **19** D2
Stockport SK2 . . . . **124** C4
Cherry Tree Dr SK7 . . . . . **134** A8
Cherry Tree Gr
Atherton M46 . . . . **58** C4
Leigh WN7 . . . . **75** D6
Cherry Tree Hospl SK2 . **124** C5
Cherry Tree La
Ashley WA14 . . . . **128** A5
Billinge WA11 . . . . **71** A2
Bury BL8 . . . . **27** C1
Rawtenstall BB4 . . . . **1** F8
Romiley SK6 . . . . **113** E2
Stockport SK2 . . . . **124** C5
Cherry Tree Prim Sch
SK6 . . . . **59** E8
Cherry Tree Rd
Cheadle SK8 . . . . **123** A1
Golborne WA3 . . . . **90** F8
Wythenshawe M23 . . . . . . **108** F1
Cherry Tree Way
Bolton BL2 . . . . **25** C5
Haslingden BB4 . . . . **1** B7
5 Horwich BL6 . . . . **22** E1
Cherry Tree Wlk
Mossley OL5 . . . . **68** B1
Stretford M32 . . . . **96** C1
Cherry Wlk
Cheadle SK8 . . . . **132** C8
Partington M31 . . . . **105** D2
Cherrywood Ave OL9 . . . . . **65** D7
Cherrywood Ave BL5 . . . . . **59** A7
Cherrywood Cl M28 . . . . . . **60** B1
Chertsey Cl
Droylsden M18 . . . . **99** E5
Shaw OL2 . . . . **149** B4
Chervil Cl M14 . . . . **110** C8
Chervil Wlk WN3 . . . . **54** C4
Cherwell Ave OL10 . . . . . . **29** B3
Cherwell Cl
Aspull WN2 . . . . **38** C6
Cheadle SK8 . . . . **132** A7
Oldham OL8 . . . . **66** C1
Whitefield M45 . . . . **63** A8
Cherwell Rd BL5 . . . . **39** F2
CHESHAM **28** B5
Chesham Ave
Bolton BL1 . . . . **143** B2
Trub OL11 . . . . **47** D7
Urmston M41 . . . . **94** E3
Wythenshawe M22 . . . . . . **121** C4
Chesham Cl
Hadfield SK13 . . . . **104** A5
Wilmslow SK9 . . . . **136** F4
Chesham Cres BL9 . . . . . . **141** A3
Chesham Fold Rd BL9 . . . **141** B4
Chesham Ho 2 M5 . . . . . **154** C1
Chesham Ind Est BL9 . . . **141** A4
Chesham Pl WA14 . . . . . . **119** C2
Chesham Prim Sch BL9 . . **28** A5
Chesham Rd
Bury BL9 . . . . **28** A5
Eccles M30 . . . . **95** C8
3 Oldham OL4 . . . . **67** C6

Chesham Rd *continued*
Wilmslow SK9 . . . . **136** F4
Chesham St BL3 . . . . **146** B2
**Chesham Woods Nature
Reserve ★** BL9 . . . . **28** A5
Cheshill Ct M7 . . . . **155** C2
Cheshire Cl
Newton-le-W WA12 . . . . **89** E3
Stretford M32 . . . . **96** B1
Cheshire Ct BL0 . . . . **11** D6
Cheshire Gdns M14 . . . . . . **98** A1
Cheshire Rd
Mossley SK15 . . . . **86** E5
Partington M31 . . . . **105** D2
Cheshire Sq SK15 . . . . **86** E5
Cheshire St OL5 . . . . **68** D8
Cheshires The OL5 . . . . . . **68** D1
Chesney Ave OL9 . . . . **65** C2
Chesshyre Ave M4 . . . . . . **160** A1
Chessington Rise M27 . . . **62** A3
Chester Ave
Altrincham WA15 . . . . **119** F2
Dukinfield SK16 . . . . **101** E7
Golborne WA3 . . . . **90** D8
Little Lever BL3 . . . . **43** B4
Rochdale OL11 . . . . **30** A6
Sale M33 . . . . **107** B1
Stalybridge SK15 . . . . **102** A8
Urmston M41 . . . . **95** E3
Whitefield M45 . . . . **63** A7
Chester Cl
Handforth SK9 . . . . **131** E2
Irlam M44 . . . . **105** D5
Little Lever BL3 . . . . **43** B4
2 Wigan WN3 . . . . **55** F4
Chester Cres BB4 . . . . **1** B8
Chester Dr
Ashton-in-M WN4 . . . . **73** D2
Ramsbottom BL0 . . . . **11** A4
Chesterfield Gr OL6 . . . . . **85** D3
Chesterfield St OL4 . . . . . . **67** B6
Chesterfield Way 4
M34 . . . . **113** A8
Chestergate SK1, SK3,
SK4 . . . . **169** B1
Chester Pl
Adlington PR6 . . . . **21** A8
7 Royton OL2 . . . . **48** D4
Chester Rd
Hazel Grove SK7 . . . . **124** D1
Manchester, City Park M15,
M16 . . . . **161** B1
Manchester, St George's
M15 . . . . **162** A3
Poynton SK12 . . . . **133** D4
Stretford M16, M32 . . . . . . **96** E3
Tyldesley M29 . . . . **77** D8
Woodford SK7 . . . . **132** E2
Chester's Croft Pk SK8 . **132** A5
Chester Sq OL7 . . . . **166** A2
Chester St
Bury BL9 . . . . **141** A4
Denton M34 . . . . **100** F2
Leigh WN7 . . . . **75** F5
Manchester M1 . . . . **163** A3
Oldham OL9 . . . . **152** C1
Prestwich M25 . . . . **63** A5
Stockport SK3 . . . . **169** A1
Swinton M27 . . . . **79** F7
Tyldesley M46 . . . . **58** E1
Chesterton Cl WN3 . . . . . **150** A1
Chesterton Dr BL3 . . . . **40** E5
Chesterton Gr M43 . . . . . . **84** A2
Chesterton Rd
Oldham OL1 . . . . **49** B2
Wythenshawe M23 . . . . . . **120** D8
Chester Wlk 19 BL1 . . . . **143** B2
Chester Wlks SK6 . . . . . . **113** A1
Chestnut Ave
Atherton M46 . . . . **58** C4
Bury BL9 . . . . **141** B2
Bury, Tottington BL8 . . . . . . **27** A5
Cheadle SK8 . . . . **122** E5
Droylsden M43 . . . . **83** E3
Irlam M44 . . . . **105** D5
Leigh WN7 . . . . **109** B8
Walkden M28 . . . . **60** D2
Whitefield M45 . . . . **63** A7
Chestnut Cl
Bolton BL3 . . . . **146** B4
New Mills SK22 . . . . **127** E1
Oldham OL4 . . . . **67** D8
Stalybridge SK15 . . . . **101** F8
Wilmslow SK9 . . . . **137** E8
Chestnut Cres OL8 . . . . . . **67** A7
Chestnut Dr
1 Bury BL9 . . . . **27** F7
Leigh WN7 . . . . **75** F2
Poynton SK12 . . . . **133** F3
Rawtenstall BB4 . . . . **1** F8
Sale M33 . . . . **107** D1
Westhoughton BL5 . . . . **57** F7
Chestnut Fold M26 . . . . . . **44** A4
Chestnut Gdns
Denton M34 . . . . **100** C4
Heywood OL10 . . . . **29** C1
Chestnut Gr
Ashton-in-M WN4 . . . . **73** D4
Failsworth M35 . . . . **83** F6
Golborne WA3 . . . . **90** F8
Hindley WN2 . . . . **57** A4

Chestnut Gr continued
Hyde SK14 . . . . 102 A6
Radcliffe M26 . . . . 62 A8
Chestnut La WN7 . . . . . 75 F2
Chestnut Rd
Eccles M30 . . . . 79 A4
Wigan WN1 . . . . 37 E2
Chestnut St OL9 . . . . 66 A3
Chestnut Villas SK4 . . 168 C2
Chestnut Way OL15 . . . 15 F6
Chestnut Wlk M31 . . . . 105 D2
Chesworth Ct SK1 . . . 170 C4
Chesworth Ct M43 . . . . . 83 F1
Chesworth Fold SK1 . . 170 C4
Chetham's Sch of Music
M3 . . . . 158 C2
Chetwode Ave WN4 . . . 73 B1
Chetwyn Ave
Bolton BL7 . . . . 25 A7
Royton OL2 . . . . 48 C4
Chetwynd Ave 3 M41 . . 95 C2
Chetwynd Cl M33 . . . . 107 E6
Chevassut St M15 . . . . 162 B2
Chevin Gdns SK7 . . . . 133 A7
Chevington Dr
Manchester, Collyhurst
M9 . . . . 157 A2
Manchester, Heaton Mersey
SK4 . . . . 110 E3
Chevington Gdns 1 BL1 143 B3
Cheviot Ave
Cheadle SK8 . . . . 122 F2
Oldham OL8 . . . . 66 E3
Royton OL2 . . . . 48 C3
Cheviot Cl
Bolton BL1 . . . . 24 D5
Bury BL8 . . . . 27 A3
Chadderton OL9 . . . . 152 A1
Horwich BL6 . . . . 22 C5
Middleton M24 . . . . 65 D8
Ramsbottom BL0 . . . . 11 C4
Salford M6 . . . . 154 B3
Stockport SK4 . . . . 169 A3
Wigan WN3 . . . . 54 C2
Cheviot Ct 4 OL8 . . . . . 66 E4
Cheviot Ho OL11 . . . . . . 30 B8
Cheviot Rd SK7 . . . . . . 124 B1
Cheviots Rd OL2 . . . . . 149 A4
Cheviot St M1 . . . . 158 C3
Chevithorne Cl WA14 . . 119 B5
Chevril Cl M15 . . . . 163 A2
Chevron Cl
Rochdale OL11 . . . . 30 B3
3 Salford M6 . . . . 81 B2
Chevron Pl WA14 . . . . . 119 D7
Chew Brook Dr OL3 . . . . 69 B5
CHEW MOOR 40 B3
Chew Moor La BL5, BL6 . 40 A2
Chew Rd
Glossop OL3 . . . . 88 C8
Oldham OL3 . . . . 70 A2
Chew Vale
Dukinfield SK16 . . . . 101 F7
Uppermill OL3 . . . . 69 B5
Chew Valley Rd OL3 . . . . 69 B5
Chicago Ave M90 . . . . . 130 B7
Chichester Ave M46 . . . . 58 A2
Chichester Bsns Ctr OL16 31 A7
Chichester Cl
Littleborough OL15 . . . . . 15 F3
4 Sale M33 . . . . 107 D3
Chichester Rd
Manchester M15 . . . . 162 C1
Romiley SK6 . . . . 113 C2
Chichester St OL16 . . . . . 31 B7
Chichester Way 11 M34 101 A1
Chicken La 1 SK5 . . . . . 99 F2
Chidlow Ave M20 . . . . . 110 A7
Chidwall Rd M22 . . . . . 121 B2
Chief St OL4 . . . . 67 A6
Chiffon Way M3 . . . . . . 158 A3
Chigwell Cl M22 . . . . . . 121 E5
Chilcombe Wlk 5 M9 . . . 64 E5
Chilcote Ave M33 . . . . . 107 E4
Childwall Cl BL3 . . . . . . 147 B2
Chilgrove Ave BL6 . . . . . 21 D1
Chilham Rd
Eccles M30 . . . . 79 F4
Walkden M28 . . . . 60 E2
Chilham St
Bolton BL3 . . . . 146 B2
Swinton M27 . . . . 79 E6
Wigan WN5 . . . . 54 B6
Chillingham Dr WN7 . . . . 76 C4
Chillington Wlk M34 . . . 100 E1
Chilmark Dr M23 . . . . . 121 A6
Chiltern Ave
Atherton M46 . . . . 58 F5
Cheadle SK8 . . . . 122 F2
Urmston M41 . . . . 94 F3
Chiltern Cl
Ashton-in-M WN4 . . . . . . 73 C2
Horwich BL6 . . . . 22 C5
Ramsbottom BL0 . . . . 11 C4
Shaw OL2 . . . . 48 F8
Stockport SK7 . . . . 124 B1
Walkden M28 . . . . 78 E8
Chiltern Dr
Altrincham WA15 . . . . . . 119 F2
Bolton BL3 . . . . 148 C3
Bury BL8 . . . . 27 B4
Royton OL2 . . . . 48 C4
Stockport SK2 . . . . 124 B4

Chiltern Dr continued
Swinton M27 . . . . 79 F6
Wigan WN3 . . . . 54 D2
Chiltern Gdns M33 . . . . 108 C1
Chiltern Rd
Culcheth WA3 . . . . 91 E4
Ramsbottom BL0 . . . . 11 C4
Chiltern Way M29 . . . . . 77 B8
Chilton Ave OL9 . . . . . . 152 A2
Chilton Cl WN7 . . . . 75 F7
Chilton Dr M24 . . . . 65 C7
Chilton St M14 . . . . 98 B2
Chime Bank M8 . . . . . . 156 B2
Chimes Ct OL4 . . . . 68 B5
Chimes Rd WN4 . . . . 72 F6
China La
1 Bolton BL1 . . . . 145 C4
Manchester M1 . . . . 159 B1
Chingford Wlk 5 M13. . . 98 F4
Chinley Ave
Manchester M40 . . . . 83 A8
Stretford M32 . . . . 96 A4
Chinley Cl
Sale M33 . . . . 108 D3
Stockport, Davenport SK7 123 E3
Stockport, Heaton Norris
SK4 . . . . 168 B3
Chinley St
6 Oldham OL1 . . . . 67 B8
Salford M6 . . . . 81 B5
Chinnor Cl WN7 . . . . 75 F7
Chinwell View 9 M19. . . 99 A1
Chip Hill Rd BL3 . . . . . . 146 A4
Chippendale Pl OL6 . . . . 85 E5
Chippenham Ave SK2 . . 124 D7
Chippenham Cl M4 . . . . 160 A2
Chippenham Rd M4 . . . . 160 A2
Chipping Fold 5 OL16 . . 31 F5
Chipping Rd M12 . . . . . 164 B1
Chipping Sq M12 . . . . . . 99 A4
Chipstead Ave M12 . . . 164 B1
Chirmside St 4 BL8. . . . . 27 B1
Chirton Wlk 7 M40 . . . . . 83 A7
Chisacre Dr WN6 . . . . . . 35 D7
Chiseldon Ave M22 . . . 121 E2
Chiselhurst St M8 . . . . 156 A3
Chisholm Cl WN6 . . . . . . 19 B2
Chisholm Ct 9 M24 . . . . 46 F1
Chisholme Cl BL8 . . . . . . 10 F2
Chisholm St M11 . . . . . . 99 D7
Chisledon Ave M7 . . . . 155 C2
Chisledon Cl BL3 . . . . . 145 B1
Chislehurst Ave M41 . . . 95 D3
Chislehurst Cl BL8 . . . . . 27 B1
Chisnall Ave WN6 . . . . . 18 F6
Chisnall La
Coppull PR7 . . . . 19 C6
Wrightington Bar WN6 . . . 19 A5
Chiswell St WN5 . . . . . . 54 C5
Chiswick Dr M26 . . . . . . 43 B5
Chiswick Rd M20 . . . . . 110 C3
CHISWORTH 115 B5
Chisworth Cl
Leigh WN7 . . . . 75 E7
Stockport SK7 . . . . 123 E3
Chisworth St BL2 . . . . . . 25 B3
Chisworth Wlk 3 M34 . . 113 A8
Choir St M7 . . . . 158 B4
Chokeberry Cl 2 WA14 . 119 B8
Cholmley Dr M12 . . . . . . 89 E2
Cholmondeley Ave
WA14 . . . . 119 E8
Cholmondeley Rd M6 . . . 80 C4
Chomlea WA14 . . . . 119 B4
Choral Gr M7 . . . . 155 A1
Chorley Cl BL8 . . . . 26 F1
Chorley Hall Cl SK9 . . . 136 F1
Chorley Hall La SK9 . . . 137 A1
Chorley New Rd
Bolton BL1, BL6 . . . . 40 C7
Horwich BL6 . . . . 22 D2
Chorley New Road Prim Sch
BL6 . . . . 22 D2
Chorley Old Rd
Bolton, Cope Bank BL1 . . 142 B1
Doffcocker BL1, BL6 . . . . . 23 C3
Chorley Rd
Adlington PR6 . . . . 21 A8
Blackrod BL6, PR7 . . . . . . 21 B5
Four Gates BL5, BL6 . . . . 39 C4
Sale M33 . . . . 108 E2
Standish WN1 . . . . 20 C3
Swinton M27 . . . . 79 F8
Chorley St
Adlington PR6 . . . . 21 B8
Bolton BL1 . . . . 145 B3
Ince-in-M WN3 . . . . 151 B2
Stretford M32 . . . . 96 F5
Chorley Wood Ave M19 . 110 F6
Chorlton Brook Ho SK8. 122 E6
Chorlton CE Prim Sch 10
M21 . . . . 109 A8
Chorlton Cl 2 M46 . . . . . 97 C3
CHORLTON-CUM-
HARDY 109 C7
Chorlton Dr SK8 . . . . . . 122 E6
CHORLTON FOLD 79 D5
Chorlton Fold
Eccles M30 . . . . 79 D4
Romiley SK6 . . . . 113 C5
Chorlton Gn 7 M21 . . . . 109 A8
Chorlton Gn 1 M21 . . . . 124 B7
Chorlton High Sch M21 . 109 D7
Chorlton Hts 2 M21 . . . 109 A8
Chorlton L Ctr M21 . . . . . 97 B2
Chorlton Mill M1 . . . . . 162 C3
Chorlton Park Prim Sch
M21 . . . . 109 C6

Chorlton Pl M21 . . . . 97 B1
Chorlton Rd M15, M16 . . 162 A2
Chorlton St
Manchester M1 . . . . 163 A4
Manchester, Old Trafford
M16 . . . . 161 C1
Chorlton Sta M21 . . . . . . 97 B1
Chorlton View 5 M21 . . 109 A8
Chorlton Water Park Nature
Reserve* M21 . . . . 109 C4
Chowbent Cl M46 . . . . . . 58 E3
Chretien Rd M22 . . . . . 121 D5
Christ Church Ainsworth CE
Prim Sch BL2 . . . . 26 C1
Christchurch Ave M5 . . . 81 B2
Christ Church CE Prim Sch
Bury BL8 . . . . 26 F4
Chadderton OL9 . . . . 152 A2
Denshaw OL3 . . . . 33 D1
Eccles M30 . . . . 79 D2
Christ Church Cl BL2 . . . . 25 F2
Christchurch Ct OL9 . . . 152 C1
Christ Church La BL2 . . . 25 F3
Christ Church Pennington CE
Prim Sch WN7 . . . . 75 F4
Christchurch Rd M33 . . 107 C5
Christie (Hospl) The
M20 . . . . 110 B6
Christie La M7 . . . . 81 A8
Christie Rd M32 . . . . 96 E2
Christie St SK1 . . . . . . 124 A7
Christie Street Ind Est
SK1 . . . . 124 A7
Christie Way M21 . . . . . 109 D5
Christleton Ave SK4 . . . 168 C3
Christleton Dr SK6 . . . . . 36 B6
Christleton Way 14 SK9 . 131 D5
Christopher Acre OL11 . . 13 E1
Christopher St
Failsworth M40 . . . . 83 D4
Ince-in-M WN3 . . . . 151 C2
Salford M5 . . . . 81 B1
Christ the King RC Prim Sch
28 Failsworth M40 . . . . . 83 C5
Walkden M28 . . . . 60 E2
Christ the Redeemer Coll
M27 . . . . 62 A1
Chronnell Dr BL2 . . . . . . 42 E8
Chudleigh Cl
Altrincham WA14 . . . . . . 119 B6
Stockport SK7 . . . . 124 A3
Chudleigh Rd M8 . . . . . . 64 A2
Chulsey Gate La BL6 . . . 40 A4
Chulsey St BL3 . . . . 146 B4
CHUNAL 116 C4
Chunal La SK13 . . . . . . 116 D6
Chunal Lane Flats SK13 . 116 C6
Church Ave
Bickershaw WN2 . . . . 74 F8
Denton M34 . . . . 113 A8
7 Failsworth M40 . . . . . 83 C5
Handforth SK9 . . . . 131 A2
Hyde SK14 . . . . 113 F8
Leigh WN2 . . . . 75 A8
Salford M6 . . . . 154 B1
Slattocks OL16 . . . . 47 D6
Churchbank SK15 . . . . . . 86 D2
Church Bank
Altrincham WA14 . . . . . . 119 B2
Bolton BL1 . . . . 148 A3
Church Brow
Altrincham WA14 . . . . . . 119 D2
Hyde SK14 . . . . 167 A1
Mottram in L SK14 . . . . . 103 A3
Church Cl
Denton M34 . . . . 100 F7
Glossop SK13 . . . . 104 E2
Handforth SK9 . . . . 131 D3
Kearsley M26 . . . . 61 B8
Ramsbottom BL0 . . . . . . 138 B1
Church Croft BL9 . . . . . . 45 C4
Church Ct
Altrincham WA15 . . . . . . 119 E1
Bury BL9 . . . . 141 A3
Dukinfield SK16 . . . . 166 B1
Edenfield BL0 . . . . 1 D4
Tyldesley M46 . . . . 58 E2
Churchdale Rd M9 . . . . . 64 B4
Church Dr
Newton-le-W WA12 . . . . . 89 C1
Orrell M45 . . . . 53 D5
Prestwich M25 . . . . 63 A4
Churchfield
Manchester M21 . . . . 109 A8
Shevington WN6 . . . . 36 A5
Church Field Cl M26 . . . . 43 F1
Churchfield Rd 6 M6 . . . 80 D5
Churchfields
Altrincham WA14 . . . . . . 119 B1
Denton M34 . . . . 100 E7
Sale M33 . . . . 107 D6
Church Fields OL3 . . . . . . 51 A2
Churchfield Wlk M11 . . . 165 A4
Church Fold
Broadbottom SK13 . . . . . 115 C7
Coppull PR7 . . . . 19 F8
Churchgate
Bolton BL1 . . . . 145 C3
Stockport SK1 . . . . 169 C1
Urmston M41 . . . . 95 B3
Churchgate Bldgs M1 . . 163 C4
Church Gn
Lymm WA13 . . . . 117 B8
Radcliffe M26 . . . . 44 D4
Salford M6 . . . . 154 D1

Church Gr
Hazel Grove SK7 . . . . 124 E2
Wigan WN1 . . . . 151 B4
Churchill Ave
Ainsworth BL2 . . . . 26 D1
Fowley Common WA3 . . . . 92 B4
Manchester M16 . . . . 97 D2
Churchill Cl 4 OL10 . . . . 46 E8
Churchill Cres
Marple SK6 . . . . 125 D7
Reddish SK5 . . . . 99 E1
Stretford M16, M32 . . . . . 154 C2
Churchill Dr
Bolton BL4 . . . . 147 C2
Little Lever BL3 . . . . 43 C3
Churchill Pl M30 . . . . 79 C4
Churchill Rd WA14 . . . . . 119 D7
Churchill St
Bolton BL2 . . . . 148 C3
2 Oldham OL4 . . . . 67 A6
Rochdale, Greave OL11 . . . 30 C8
Rochdale, Spotland Fold OL11 &
OL12 . . . . 14 C1
Stockport SK4 . . . . 169 A3
Churchill Way
Salford M5, M6 . . . . 81 A2
Stretford M17 . . . . 96 C7
Church La
Alderley Edge SK9 . . . . . 137 A2
Bramhall SK7 . . . . 132 C2
Culcheth WA3 . . . . 91 F3
Edenfield BL0 . . . . 1 D4
Golborne WA3 . . . . 90 D7
Manchester, Broughton Park
M7 . . . . 63 C1
Manchester, Burnage M19. 110 F6
Manchester, Harpurhey
M9 . . . . 157 B4
Manchester, Harpurhey M40,
M9 . . . . 157 C3
Marple SK6 . . . . 125 F5
Mossley OL5 . . . . 68 D1
Oldham OL1 . . . . 153 C3
Prestwich M25 . . . . 63 A4
Rochdale OL16 . . . . 139 C3
Romiley SK6 . . . . 113 C2
Sale M33 . . . . 107 E6
Shevington WN6 . . . . 36 A6
Uppermill OL3 . . . . 51 D1
Westhoughton BL5 . . . . . . 39 E3
Whitefield M45 . . . . 44 E1
Wrightington Bar WN6 . . . 18 D8
Churchlands La WN6 . . . 19 F2
Churchley Cl SK3 . . . . . 123 A6
Churchley Rd SK3 . . . . . 123 A7
Church Lodge SK4 . . . . 110 E2
Church Manor SK4 . . . . 168 B4
Church Mdw
Dukinfield SK14 . . . . 101 C3
Whitefield BL9 . . . . 45 C4
Church Mdws
Bolton BL2 . . . . 25 F3
Uppermill OL3 . . . . 68 E5
Church Meadow Gdns
SK14 . . . . 101 C3
Church Mews
Bury BL8 . . . . 27 C1
Denton M34 . . . . 100 E3
1 Radcliffe M26 . . . . 44 C1
Church Pl OL10 . . . . 29 D2
Church Rd
Bolton BL1 . . . . 142 B2
Cheadle SK8 . . . . 132 B8
Eccles M30 . . . . 79 F2
Farnworth BL4 . . . . 60 E8
Gatley SK8 . . . . 122 A5
Handforth SK9 . . . . 131 D3
Hollingworth SK14 . . . . . 171 A4
Kearsley M26 . . . . 61 A8
Marple SK6 . . . . 126 E6
Middleton M24 . . . . 65 D7
Platt Bridge WN2 . . . . 56 B3
Ramsbottom BL0 . . . . 11 E8
Rochdale OL16 . . . . 31 B6
Sale M33 . . . . 108 D4
Shaw OL2 . . . . 149 B2
Stockport SK4 . . . . 169 B2
Tyldesley M29 . . . . 77 C6
Uppermill, Lydgate OL3 . . 68 E5
Uppermill OL3 . . . . 69 C8
Urmston M41 . . . . 95 C1
Walkden M28 . . . . 60 D3
Wilmslow SK9 . . . . 136 E4
Wythenshawe M22 . . . . . 121 E5
Church Road Prim Sch
BL1 . . . . 142 B2
Church Sq
Adlington PR7 . . . . 21 A7
Ainsworth BL2 . . . . 26 D1
Altrincham WA14 . . . . . . 119 D5
Ashton-u-L OL6 . . . . 166 B2
Aspull WN2 . . . . 38 B6
Atherton M46 . . . . 58 D3
Bacup OL13 . . . . 3 C8
Blackrod BL6 . . . . 21 C2
Bolton BL2 . . . . 25 B6
Bury BL9 . . . . 141 A3
Bury, Walshaw BL8 . . . . . 26 F5
Cheadle SK8 . . . . 122 D6
Delph OL3 . . . . 50 E4
Denton M34 . . . . 100 F7
Droylsden M43 . . . . 84 B1
Dukinfield SK16 . . . . 166 B1
Eccles M30 . . . . 79 F2
Failsworth M35 . . . . 83 F8

Church St continued
Farnworth BL4 . . . . 60 E7
Glossop SK13 . . . . 104 D2
Golborne WA3 . . . . 74 B1
Hadfield SK13 . . . . 103 A4
Heywood OL10 . . . . 29 D2
Hindley WN2 . . . . 56 D5
Horwich BL6 . . . . 22 C3
Hyde SK14 . . . . 167 A1
Ince-in-M WN3 . . . . 151 C2
Leigh WN7 . . . . 75 F5
Littleborough OL15 . . . . . 16 B5
Little Lever BL3 . . . . 42 F3
Manchester M4 . . . . 159 A2
Marple SK6 . . . . 125 F6
Marple SK6 . . . . 126 A5
Middleton M24 . . . . 47 A2
Newhey OL16 . . . . 32 B4
Newton-le-W WA12 . . . . . 89 E4
Oldham OL1 . . . . 153 C3
Oldham, Salem OL4 . . . . . 67 E5
Orrell WN5 . . . . 53 E5
Pendlebury M27 . . . . 80 B8
Radcliffe M26 . . . . 44 B2
Rawtenstall BB4 . . . . 2 E8
Rochdale, Greengate OL16 . 15 D3
Rochdale, Mitchell Hey
OL12 . . . . 139 B3
Romiley SK6 . . . . 113 A5
Royton OL2 . . . . 48 D4
Stalybridge SK15 . . . . 86 A2
Standish WN6 . . . . 19 E1
Stockport SK4 . . . . 169 B3
Stretford M32 . . . . 96 C1
Swinton M27 . . . . 79 E8
Tintwistle SK13 . . . . 104 A7
Up Holland WN8 . . . . 53 C7
Westhoughton BL5 . . . . . . 39 E2
Whitworth OL12 . . . . 14 C8
Wigan, Norley WN5 . . . . . 54 B6
Wigan WN1 . . . . 150 C4
Wilmslow SK9 . . . . 137 B7
Church Stile OL16 . . . . . 139 C3
Churchstoke Wlk M23 . . 120 E7
Churchston Ave SK7 . . . 124 A2
Church Street Cotts 13
SK6 . . . . 125 F6
Church Street Ind Est 3
M24 . . . . 47 A2
Church Terr
Ashton-in-M WN4 . . . . . . 73 B2
Glossop SK13 . . . . 104 D2
Handforth SK9 . . . . 131 D4
Milnrow OL16 . . . . 32 A5
Oldham OL1 . . . . 153 C3
Sale M33 . . . . 108 A2
Churchtown Ave BL2 . . . 42 F7
Church View
6 Altrincham WA14 . . . 119 C1
Handforth SK9 . . . . 131 A2
Hyde SK14 . . . . 167 A1
Irlam M44 . . . . 94 A2
Lymm WA13 . . . . 117 B4
Mottram in L SK14 . . . . . 103 A3
Rochdale OL12 . . . . 15 A2
Churchward Sq BL6 . . . . 22 C2
Church Wlk
7 Farnworth BL4 . . . . . 119 D5
Farnworth BL4 . . . . 60 C8
Glossop SK13 . . . . 104 E2
5 Royton OL2 . . . . 48 D4
Stalybridge SK15 . . . . 86 A3
Swinton M27 . . . . 61 F4
Wilmslow SK9 . . . . 136 F6
Churchwood Rd M20 . . . 110 B3
Churchwood View WA13 117 A2
Churnet St M40 . . . . 157 A1
Churnett Cl BL5 . . . . 39 F2
Churning Terr M44 . . . . . 94 B3
Churston Ave M9 . . . . . . 64 E4
Churton Ave
Manchester M14 . . . . 98 B2
Sale M33 . . . . 107 F3
Churton Gr WN6 . . . . 19 B2
Churton Rd M18 . . . . 99 C3
Churwell Ave SK4 . . . . . 110 F4
Cicero St
Manchester M9 . . . . 157 C4
Oldham OL1 . . . . 49 A1
Cinamon St OL12 . . . . . . 14 C3
Cinder Hill La M24, OL1,
OL2 . . . . 48 A3
Cinder La BL1 . . . . 142 A3
Cinder St M4 . . . . 159 C2
Cinnabar Dr M24 . . . . . . 46 F2
Cinnamon Ave WN2 . . . . 57 A4
Cinnamon Brow WN8 . . . 53 C6
Cinnamon Cl
Rochdale OL12 . . . . 139 A4
Wythenshawe M22 . . . . . 121 E8
Cipher St M4 . . . . 159 C3
Circle Ct M32 . . . . 95 F4
Circle S M17 . . . . 96 E6
Circle The M32 . . . . 95 F4
Circuit The
Alderley Edge SK9 . . . . . 137 B3
Cheadle SK8 . . . . 132 A7
Manchester M20 . . . . 110 B5
Stockport SK3 . . . . 123 C6
Wilmslow SK9 . . . . 136 D5
Circular Rd
Denton M34 . . . . 100 E1
Manchester, Hilton Park
M25. . . . . 63 B2
Manchester, Withington
M20. . . . . 110 B5
Cirencester Cl M38 . . . . . 60 A6
Ciss La M41 . . . . 95 E2

Citizens Way M11 160 C1
Citrus Way M6 81 A2
City Airport (Barton Aerodrome) M30 94 E7
City Ave M34 100 E2
City Course Trad Est M11 165 A3
City Court Trad Est M4 159 C2
City Gdns M34 100 D2
City of Manchester Stadium (Manchester City FC) M11 160 C2
CITY PARK 161 B1
City Point M3 158 B2
City Rd
Manchester M15 162 A2
Walkden M28 78 A8
Wigan WN5 54 B7
City South M15 162 C3
City Wlk M27 80 B8
Civic Wlk 1 OL10 29 D2
Clacton Wlk M13 163 C2
Claife Ave M40 65 B2
Clammcclough Rd BL4 60 F8
CLAMMERCLOUGH 42 F1
Clanbrook Ave WA13 117 A2
Clandon Ave M30 79 B1
Clanwood Cl WN3 54 E2
Clapgate SK6 112 F1
Clap Gate La WN3 54 E3
Clapgate Rd 3 OL11 13 E1
Clapham St M40 83 C8
Clara Gorton Ct 12 OL16 31 B6
Clara St
Oldham OL9 66 C4
Rochdale OL11 139 C1
Whitworth OL12 4 D1
Clare Ave SK9 131 C3
Clarebank BL1 40 F7
Clare Cl BL8 27 D5
Clare Ct
Farnworth BL4 147 C1
4 Stockport SK1 112 A1
Claremont Ave
Altrincham WA14 119 E8
Hindley WN2 56 F5
Manchester, Heaton Chapel SK4 111 C5
Manchester, Withington M20 110 A5
Marple SK6 125 C6
Claremont Ct 6 M20 110 A3
Claremont Dr
Altrincham WA14 119 E8
Walkden M38 60 B5
Claremont Gdns OL6 85 E4
Claremont Gr
Altrincham WA15 119 E3
Manchester M20 110 A3
Claremont Prim Sch M14 98 A3
Claremont Range M18 99 F4
Claremont Rd
Billinge WN5 71 E5
Cheadle SK8 132 A8
Culcheth WA3 91 D4
Manchester M14 98 B3
Manchester M16 97 F3
Milnrow OL16 31 F5
Rochdale OL11 30 C7
Sale M33 108 B5
Salford M6 80 C4
Stockport SK2 124 B4
Claremont St
Ashton-u-L OL6 85 D4
Chadderton OL9 48 C1
Failsworth M35 83 F8
Oldham OL8 66 F2
Claremont Terr OL14 6 D5
Clarence Arc OL6 166 B2
Clarence Ave
Oldham OL8 66 D4
Urmston M17 95 F7
Whitefield M45 63 A7
Clarence Cl BL9 141 A4
Clarence Ct
14 Bolton BL1 145 B4
Newton-le-W WA12 89 A4
Wilmslow SK9 137 A6
Clarence Ho 1 SK15 101 F8
Clarence Rd
Altrincham WA15 119 F3
Ashton-u-L OL6 166 C4
Manchester, Heaton Chapel SK4 111 C5
Manchester, Longsight M13 98 E4
Swinton M27 79 C7
Clarence St
6 Ashton-in-M WN4 72 F5
Bolton BL1 145 C4
Farnworth BL4 42 E1
Golborne WA3 74 A1
Hyde SK14 167 B4
Ince-in-M WN2 56 A7
Leigh WN7 76 B4
12 Manchester M3 158 C1
Rochdale OL12 14 D2
Royton OL2 49 A3
Salford M7 158 A4
Stalybridge SK15, SK16 85 E1
Tyldesley M46 58 E2
Clarence Yd WN1 150 C4
Clarendon Ave
Altrincham WA15 119 E5
Stockport SK4 168 B3
Clarendon Cottage Sch 6 M30 79 F3
Clarendon Cotts SK9 131 A3
Clarendon Cres
Eccles M30 79 F3
Sale M33 108 D5
Clarendon Gdns 4 BL7 25 A8
Clarendon Gr BL2 148 B2
Clarendon Ind Est SK14 167 B3
Clarendon Pl SK14 167 B2
Clarendon Prim Sch BL3 145 B1
Clarendon Rd
Bolton BL2 148 C3
Denton M34 101 B2
Droylsden M34 100 B7
Eccles M30 79 F3
Hazel Grove SK7 124 F3
Hyde SK14 167 B3
Irlam M44 105 F7
Manchester M16 97 D2
Sale M33 108 D4
Swinton M27 79 F8
Urmston M41 94 E3
Clarendon Recn Ctr M5 81 A2
Clarendon Road Com Prim Sch 7 M30 79 F3
Clarendon St
Bolton BL3 145 B1
Bury BL9 141 A4
Dukinfield SK16 101 A8
Hyde SK14 167 A3
Manchester M15 162 C3
Mossley OL5 86 D8
Reddish SK5 169 C3
Rochdale OL16 31 B4
Whitefield M45 62 F8
Clare Rd
Manchester M19 111 A8
Reddish SK5 169 C4
Clare St
Denton M34 100 E4
Manchester M1 163 B3
Salford M5 81 C1
Claribel St M11 164 B4
Claridge Rd M21 97 A1
Clarington Gr WN1 151 B3
Clarington Pl WN2 151 C3
Clarion St M4 159 C3
Clark Ave M18 99 E5
Clarke Ave
Culcheth WA3 92 A4
Salford M5 161 B3
Clarke Brow M24 47 A1
Clarke Cres
Altrincham WA15 120 B3
Walkden M38 59 E6
Clarke Ind Est M32 96 A5
Clarkes Croft BL9 141 C3
Clarke's La OL12 139 A4
Clarke St
Altrincham WA14 119 D7
Ashton-u-L OL7 100 F8
Bolton BL1 144 C4
Farnworth BL4 60 E7
Heywood OL10 29 D2
Leigh WN7 75 E4
Rochdale OL16 15 B2
Clarkethorn Terr SK5 169 B3
Clark's Cross M25 63 D8
CLARKSFIELD 67 D7
Clarksfield Prim Sch 9 OL4 67 C6
Clarksfield Rd OL4 67 C6
Clarksfield St OL4 67 C6
Clark's Hill M25 63 A4
Clarkson Cl
Denton M34 100 D2
Middleton M24 64 C7
Clark Way SK14 167 A3
Clarkwell Cl OL1 153 B4
Clatford Wlk 2 M9 157 A3
Claude Ave M27 79 D8
Claude Rd M21 109 B7
Claude St
Eccles M30 79 B3
Manchester M8 64 A1
Swinton M27 79 D8
Wigan WN5 54 D6
Claudia Sq SK15 86 E5
Claughton Ave
Bolton BL2 42 F7
Walkden M28 78 C8
Claughton Rd BL8 26 F5
Claverham Wlk 4 M23 120 E7
Claverton Rd M23 120 E5
Claxton Ave M9 64 D3
Clay Bank M43 83 F1
Claybank Dr BL8 26 E7
Clay Bank St OL10 29 C3
Claybank Terr OL5 68 E4
Claybar Dr M30 79 E3
Claybarn Mews M44 94 B2
Claybridge Cl WN5 36 B1
Claybrook Cl M46 58 A2
Claybrook Wlk M11 83 A1
Clayburn Rd M15 162 B2
Claycourt Ave M30 79 B4
Claydon Dr
Ince-in-M WN3 151 C1
Little Lever M26 43 C5
Clayfield Dr OL11 29 F8
Claygate Dr M9 64 D5
Clayhill Gr WA3 91 B8
Clayhill Wlk M9 64 E1
Clay La
Altrincham WA15 120 D4
Handforth SK9 131 C5
Rochdale OL11 29 E8
Wilmslow SK9 136 C4
Wythenshawe M23 120 F4
Claylands Cl SK14 171 A4
Claymere Ave OL11 29 E8
Claymore OL1 153 B3
Claymore St
Bolton BL3 147 C3
Droylsden M18 99 E6
Claypool Prim Sch BL6 22 F1
Claypool Rd BL6 22 E1
Clay St
Bolton BL7 25 A7
3 Littleborough OL15 15 F5
Oldham OL8 66 E4
Claythorpe Wlk 2 M8 63 E2
CLAYTON 83 C2
Clayton Ave
Bolton BL3 148 C1
Golborne WA3 90 E8
Manchester M20 110 B4
Rawtenstall BB4 1 E8
Claytonbrook Rd M11 83 D1
Clayton Cl
Bury BL8 26 F1
Manchester M15 162 B1
Clayton Ct M11 165 C3
Clayton Hall Rd M11 83 C2
Clayton Ho WN7 75 C5
Clayton Ind Est M11 83 D1
Clayton La M11 83 B1
Claytons Cl OL4 67 F7
Clayton St
Bolton BL3 148 C1
Chadderton OL9 66 A3
Denton M34 100 F2
Droylsden M11 83 B2
5 Dukinfield SK16 101 D8
5 Failsworth M35 83 F7
Rochdale OL12 15 B2
Wigan WN3 150 B3
Clayton Sta M11 83 B1
CLAYTON VALE 83 C3
Clayton Vale Nature Reserve★ M40 83 B4
Cleabarrow Dr M28 78 A5
Cleadon Ave M18 99 C4
Clearwater Dr M20 109 F5
Cleavley St M30 79 B2
Clee Ave M13 98 F2
Cleethorpes Ave M9 64 B3
Cleeve Rd
2 Oldham OL4 67 C6
Wythenshawe M23 109 A2
Cleeve Way SK8 132 B6
Clegg Hall Rd OL15, OL16 15 E1
Clegg Pl 2 OL6 85 D4
Clegg's Bldgs BL1 145 B4
Clegg's Ct OL12 4 C2
Clegg's La M38 60 A5
Clegg St
6 Bacup OL13 3 C8
Bolton BL2 148 C3
Droylsden M43 83 F1
Littleborough OL15 15 F7
Milnrow OL16 32 A5
Oldham, Grotton OL4 68 A6
Oldham OL4 153 C2
Romiley SK6 112 F3
Tyldesley M29 77 A5
Whitefield M45 62 F7
Whitworth OL12 4 C2
Cleggswood Ave OL15 16 A3
Clelland St BL4 60 E7
Clematis Wlk M27 61 E2
Clement Ave M46 58 A2
Clement Ct
3 Droylsden M11 99 F7
13 Rochdale OL16 31 B6
Clementina St OL12 14 F1
Clementine Cl 8 M6 81 B2
Clementine Ct 6 M6 81 B2
Clement Rd SK6 126 C7
Clement Royds St OL12 139 B4
Clement St
Oldham OL9 66 B3
Stockport SK4 169 B3
Clement Stott Cl M9 64 F4
Cleminson St M3 158 A2
Clemshaw Cl OL10 29 C1
Clerewood Ave SK8 131 B7
Clerke St BL9 140 C2
Clerks Ct M5 80 B2
Clevedon Ave M41 96 A2
Clevedon Dr WN3 54 D4
Clevedon Rd OL9 48 B1
Clevedon St M9 157 B3
Cleveland Ave
Hyde SK14 101 C2
Manchester M19 99 B2
Salford M6 80 C3
Wigan WN3 54 C3
Cleveland Cl
Ramsbottom BL0 11 C3
Swinton M27 62 A2
Cleveland Dr
Ashton-in-M WN4 73 C4
Golborne WA3 74 D1
Milnrow OL16 32 A6
Cleveland Gdns
Ashton-in-M WN4 73 C4
Bolton BL3 146 B4
Cleveland Gr OL2 48 C3
Cleveland Rd
Altrincham WA15 119 F3
Manchester, Crumpsall M8 64 B2
Stockport SK4 168 A4
Clevelands Prep Sch BL1 144 A3
Cleveland St 2 BL3 146 B4
Cleveleys Ave
Bolton BL2 148 C4
Cleveleys Ave continued
Bury BL9 44 E7
Gatley SK8 122 B1
Manchester M21 109 C7
Rochdale OL16 31 B3
Cleveleys Gr M7 155 B3
Cleves Ct OL10 29 C1
Clevlands Cl OL2 149 A4
Cleworth Cl M29 77 C4
Cleworth Rd M24 46 F2
Cleworth St M15 162 A3
Cleworth Wlk M15 162 A3
Clibran St M8 156 B2
Clifden Dr M22 121 E2
Cliff Ave
Ramsbottom BL9 11 C2
Salford M7 81 C6
Cliffbrook Gr 2 SK9 131 D2
Cliff Cres M7 155 A3
Cliff Dale 3 SK15 101 F8
Cliffdale Dr M8 64 A1
Cliffe Rd SK13 116 D8
Cliffe St OL15 6 D2
Cliff Gr SK4 168 B4
Cliff Grange M7 155 A3
Cliff Hill Rd OL2 32 D1
Cliff / Kersal Dale Nature Reserve The★ M7 81 C8
Cliffmere Cl SK8 122 F3
Cliff Mount BL0 138 B3
Clifford Ave
Altrincham WA15 120 B6
Denton M34 100 E5
Clifford Ct M15 162 B1
Clifford Ho M20 110 B5
Clifford Lamb Ct M9 65 B2
Clifford Rd
Bolton BL3 146 A2
Poynton SK12 133 D3
Wilmslow SK9 136 F6
Clifford St
Eccles M30 95 B8
Leigh WN7 76 B4
Pendlebury M27 80 B8
Rochdale OL11 139 C1
Cliff Rd
Bury BL9 44 F5
Wilmslow SK9 137 B8
Cliff Side
Wilmslow/Alderley Edge SK9 136 D5
Wilmslow SK9 137 B8
Cliff St OL16 15 B1
CLIFTON 61 F3
Clifton Ave
Altrincham WA15 119 E5
Culcheth WA3 91 D3
Eccles M30 79 D3
Gatley SK8 122 A2
Manchester M14 110 D8
2 Oldham OL4 67 B5
Tyldesley M29 77 C6
Clifton Cl
Heywood OL10 29 C1
Manchester M16 97 D4
Oldham OL4 67 B5
Clifton Cres
Royton OL2 49 A3
Wigan WN1 37 C2
Clifton Ct
5 Farnworth BL4 42 B2
Swinton M27 61 F3
Clifton Ctr The M27 62 B1
Clifton Ctry Pk Nature Reserve★ M26&M27 61 E5
Clifton Dr
Blackrod BL6 21 C3
Gatley, Heald Green SK8 122 A2
Gatley SK8 122 A6
Marple SK6 125 F7
Swinton, Clifton Junction M27 62 C2
Swinton M27 61 D2
Wilmslow SK9 136 E4
Clifton Gr
Manchester M16 162 A1
Swinton M27 61 D2
CLIFTON GREEN 62 B3
Clifton Ho WN3 150 B1
Clifton Holmes OL3 50 E5
Clifton House Rd M27 61 E4
Clifton Ind Est M27 62 C3
CLIFTON JUNCTION 62 C3
Clifton Lo SK2 124 A5
Cliftonmill Mdw WA3 89 F8
Clifton Park Rd SK2 124 A5
Clifton Pl M25 63 A5
Clifton Prim Sch M27 61 F3
Clifton Rd
Ashton-in-M WN4 72 F6
Billinge WN5 71 D4
Eccles M30 79 D3
Leigh WN7 75 E2
Manchester, Chorlton-cum-Hardy M21 109 C8
Prestwich M25 62 E4
Sale M33 108 B3
Slattocks OL11 47 D6
Stockport, Heaton Moor SK4 168 A4
Urmston M41 95 A2
Clifton St
Alderley Edge SK9 137 A1
Ashton-u-L OL6 166 A3
Bolton BL1 145 B4
Bury BL9 140 C4
Failsworth M35 66 A1
Farnworth BL4 42 B2
Clifton St continued
Kearsley BL4 60 F7
Leigh WN7 75 D5
Manchester, Old Trafford M16 162 A1
Manchester, Philips Park M40 160 C4
Milnrow OL16 31 F6
7 Rochdale OL11 31 A5
Tyldesley M29 77 E8
1 Uppermill OL3 69 B5
4 Wigan, Water Heyes WN1 37 C1
Wigan, Worsley Mesnes WN3 55 A4
Clifton Sta M27 62 C2
Clifton Tech Pk M27 62 A3
Clifton View M27 61 E4
Clifton Villas 5 M35 66 A1
Cliftonville Dr M6, M27 80 B6
Cliftonville Rd OL16 48 C8
Clifton Wlk M24 46 D3
Clinkham Wood Nature Reserve★ WA11 71 B1
Clinton Ave M14 98 A2
Clinton Gdns M14 98 A2
Clinton Ho 3 M5 154 C1
Clinton St 7 OL6 85 D4
Clinton Wlk 4 OL4 67 A6
Clippers Quay M50 161 A2
Clipsley Cres OL4 49 F4
Cliston Wlk SK7 124 A2
Clitheroe Cl OL10 29 D3
Clitheroe Dr BL8 26 F2
Clitheroe Rd M13 98 F3
Clito St M9 157 C4
Clive Ave M45 44 E1
Clivedale Pl BL1 145 C3
Cliveley Wlk M27 80 B8
Clive Lloyd Ct M32 96 E3
Clively Ave M27 62 C1
Clive Rd
Failsworth M35 83 E6
Westhoughton BL5 57 E6
Clive St
Ashton-u-L OL7 85 A5
Bolton BL2 148 A3
Manchester M4 159 B3
3 Oldham OL8 66 D2
Clivewood Wlk M12 164 B2
Clivia Gr M7 155 A2
Cloak St M1 163 A3
Clock House Ave M43 83 E3
Clockhouse Mews M43 83 E3
Clock St 11 OL9 66 B2
Clock Tower Cl
Hyde SK14 167 B1
3 Walkden M28 59 F3
Clod La BB4 1 C8
Cloister Ave WN7 57 D1
Cloister Cl SK16 101 C6
Cloister Rd SK4 110 D2
Cloister St
Bolton BL1 142 C2
Manchester M9 157 C4
Cloisters The
Cheadle SK8 123 A5
6 Rawtenstall BB4 2 E8
Rochdale OL16 15 B1
Sale M33 108 D4
Westhoughton BL5 57 E5
Clondberry Cl M29 59 E1
Clopton Wlk M15 162 B1
Closebrook Rd WN5 54 D6
Close La
Hindley WN2 56 E4
Leigh WN2 57 B1
Closes Farm BL3 146 B2
Close St WN2 56 F6
Close The
Altrincham WA14 119 C5
Bolton BL2 25 B3
Bury BL8 27 C5
Denton M34 100 D4
Marple SK6 114 B1
Middleton M24 47 B3
Newton-le-W WA12 89 E1
Over Hulton M46 58 F5
Stalybridge SK15 85 F4
Clothorn Rd M20 110 B4
Cloudberry Wlk M31 105 F3
Cloudstock Gr M38 59 E5
CLOUGH 49 D6
Clough Ave
Handforth SK9 131 B2
Marple SK6 126 C6
Sale M33 107 D1
Westhoughton BL5 57 F7
Cloughbank M26 61 C7
Clough Bank
Littleborough OL15 16 A8
Manchester M9 64 D2
Clough Cl OL4 68 E6
Clough Dr M25 62 F4
Clough End Rd SK14 102 F1
Cloughfield Ave M5 161 B4
Clough Fold
Kearsley M26 61 B7
Westhoughton BL5 57 F8
Clough Fold Rd SK14 167 A1
Clough Gate
Hyde SK14 113 F8
6 Oldham OL8 66 D2
Cloughgate Ho 5 OL8 66 D2

Clough Gr
Ashton-in-M WN4 . . . . . . 72 F5
Whitefield M45 . . . . 44 D2
Clough Ho M9 . . . . 65 A2
Clough House Dr WN7 . . 76 B5
Clough House La OL12 . . 15 B6
Clough La
Heywood OL10. . . . . 29 C4
Prestwich M25. . . . . 62 F4
Uppermill OL4 . . . . 68 E6
Clough Mdw
Bolton BL1. . . . . 40 D6
Romiley SK6. . . . . 113 C5
Clough Meadow Rd M26 . 43 E3
Clough Park Ave OL4. . . 68 E6
Clough Rd
Droylsden M43. . . . . 84 B2
Failsworth M35 . . . . 84 A6
Littleborough OL15 . . . . 16 A7
Manchester M9 . . . . 64 F1
Middleton M24. . . . . 47 A2
Shaw OL2. . . . . 49 D6
Cloughs OL9. . . . . 65 D8
Cloughside SK12. . . . . . 135 E6
Clough Side
Manchester M9 . . . . 64 F1
Marple SK6 . . . . 126 C7
Cloughside Sch M25 . . . 62 F5
Clough St
8 Bacup OL13 . . . . 3 D8
Failsworth M40 . . . . 83 C4
Kearsley BL4 . . . . 60 F7
Middleton M24. . . . . 47 B2
Radcliffe M26 . . . . 44 C1
Wardle OL12 . . . . 15 C6
Clough Terr OL15 . . . . . 16 A7
Clough The
Ashton-u-L OL7 . . . . 85 B6
Brinnington SK5. . . . . . 112 B6
Garswood WN4 . . . . 72 D4
Cloughton Wlk M40 . . . . 83 D5
Clough Top Rd M9 . . . . . 65 A2
Clough Wlk SK5 . . . . . . 112 B6
Cloughwood Cres WN6. . 35 D6
Clove Ave M18. . . . . 99 E6
Clovelly Ave
Leigh WN7 . . . . 75 F8
Oldham OL8. . . . . 66 C2
Clovelly Rd
Manchester M21 . . . . . 109 C8
Stockport SK2 . . . . 124 A2
Swinton M27 . . . . 79 C6
Clovelly St
Failsworth M40 . . . . 83 D5
Rochdale OL11. . . . . 30 B3
Clover Ave SK3 . . . . . . 170 A1
Cloverbank Ave M19 . . 110 D4
Clover Cres OL8 . . . . . . 67 C3
Clover Croft M33 . . . . . 108 D1
Cloverdale Dr WN4 . . . . 73 C2
Cloverdale Sq BL1 . . . . 142 A1
CLOVER HALL 15 C1
Clover Hall Cres OL16 . . 15 C1
Cloverlea Prim Sch
WA15. . . . . 120 B5
Cloverley M33 . . . . 108 B2
Cloverley Dr WA15 . . . . 120 A4
Clover Rd
Altrincham WA15. . . . . 120 B5
Romiley SK6. . . . . 113 E3
Clover St
Rochdale OL12. . . . . . . 139 D4
Wigan WN6 . . . . 37 B2
Clover View OL16 . . . . . 31 C7
Clowes St
Manchester M12 . . . . . 164 C2
Oldham OL9 . . . . 66 B2
Salford M3. . . . . 158 B2
Club St
Billinge WA11 . . . . 71 A1
Droylsden M11. . . . . 99 F7
Clumber Cl SK12. . . . . . 133 E3
Clumber Rd
Poynton SK12. . . . . 133 E3
Reddish M18 . . . . 99 F4
Clunton Ave BL3 . . . . . 146 B4
Clutha Rd SK3 . . . . 123 F4
Clwyd Ave SK3. . . . . . . 170 A3
Clyde Ave M45. . . . . 62 F4
Clyde Ct OL16. . . . . 31 B6
Clyde Rd
Manchester M20 . . . . . 110 A5
Radcliffe M26 . . . . 43 F5
Stockport SK3 . . . . 123 C7
Tyldesley M29 . . . . 77 C7
Clydesdale Gdns M11 . . 83 A1
Clydesdale Rise OL3 . . . 51 D5
Clydesdale St OL8. . . . . 66 E4
Clyde St
Ashton-u-L OL7 . . . . . . 100 F8
Bolton BL1. . . . . 143 B2
Leigh WN7 . . . . 76 B4
Oldham OL1 . . . . 49 C1
Clyde Terr M26 . . . . 43 F5
Clyne St M32 . . . . 96 F4
Clyne St M32 . . . . 96 F5
Clysbarton Ct SK12. . . 123 D1
Coach House Dr WN6 . . 36 B6
Coach La OL11. . . . . 29 E5
Coach St
Hollingworth SK14. . . . 103 C5
Tyldesley M29 . . . . 77 C6
Coach St M46. . . . . 58 D3
Coal Bank Fold 4 OL11 . 13 D1
Coalbrook Wlk M40. . . . 164 B4

Coalburn St M12. . . . . . 165 A2
Coal Pit La
Atherton M46. . . . . 58 B3
Leigh, Tamer Lane End WN2 57 B1
6 Leigh, Westleigh WN7 . 75 E4
Oldham OL8. . . . . 66 E1
Coal Pit Rd BL1 . . . . 23 D7
Coal Pit Rd 2 BL0 . . . . . 12 C8
Coalshaw Green Rd OL9. 66 A3
Coatbridge St M11. . . . . 83 C1
Cobal Ct SK2 . . . . 124 A5
Cobalt Ave M41. . . . . . . 95 F6
Cobalt Way M24 . . . . . . 65 D6
Cobb Cl M6. . . . . 63 E3
Cobbett's Way SK9. . . . 136 F4
Cobble Bank M9 . . . . . . 64 D3
Cobblestones OL3 . . . . . 50 F3
Cobden Ctr The M50 . . 154 C1
Cobden Mill Ind Est BL4. . 42 C1
Cobden St
2 Ashton-u-L OL6. . . . . 85 C2
Bolton, Egerton BL7 . . . . 8 D2
Bolton, Halliwell BL1 . . 143 A3
Britannia OL13. . . . . 4 B8
Bury BL9 . . . . 141 A3
Chadderton OL9. . . . . . 152 B3
Heywood OL10. . . . . 29 D1
Manchester M9 . . . . 64 E1
Newton-le-W WA12. . . . 89 D4
Oldham OL4 . . . . 68 B6
Radcliffe M26 . . . . 43 F6
Salford M6. . . . . 81 A4
12 Tyldesley M29 . . . . . 59 A1
Cob Hall Rd 6 M32 . . . . 96 C1
Cobham Ave
Bolton BL3 . . . . 147 A3
Manchester M40 . . . . . . 65 C2
Coblers Hill OL3 . . . . . . 50 F5
Cob Moor Ave WN5 . . . 53 D1
Cob Moor Rd WN5 . . . . . 53 D1
Cobourg St M1 . . . . 163 B4
Coburg Ave M7 . . . . . . 158 A4
Cochrane Ave M41. . . . 164 B1
Cochrane St BL3 . . . . . 145 C1
COCKBROOK. 85 D2
Cock Brow SK14 . . . . . 114 C7
Cock Clod St M26. . . . . . 44 C3
Cockcroft Rd M5. . . . . . . 81 B2
Cockcroft St M9 . . . . . . 64 D1
Cockerell Springs 1
BL2. . . . . 148 A2
COCKER HILL 86 B2
Cocker Hill SK15. . . . . . 86 B2
Cocker Mill La OL2. . . . . 48 F5
Cockerham Ave M13 . . . 98 F3
Cockhall La OL12 . . . . . . 4 C1
Cockshott Dr 7 OL5 . . . 86 E8
Coconut Gr M6. . . . . 81 B2
Codale Dr BL2 . . . . 25 F4
Coddington Ave M11. . . 99 E8
Codale La BL5 . . . . 39 B4
Cody Ct M50. . . . . 96 E8
Coe St BL3 . . . . 145 C1
Coghlan Cl M11. . . . . 83 B2
Coin St OL2. . . . . 48 E4
Cojeton Ho M9 . . . . 64 F5
Coke St M7. . . . . 155 C4
Colborne Ave
Eccles M30 . . . . 79 B2
Reddish SK5. . . . . 99 F3
Romiley SK6. . . . . 113 C2
Colbourne Ave M8. . . . . 63 F1
Colbourne Gr SK14. . . 102 E3
Colbourne Way SK14. . 102 E3
Colburn Cl WN3 . . . . 55 B2
Colby Rd WN3 . . . . 55 B3
Colby Wlk M40 . . . . 83 A7
Colchester Ave
Bolton BL2. . . . . 42 E8
Manchester M25 . . . . . . 63 C2
Colchester Cl M23 . . . . 108 E1
Colchester Dr BL4 . . . . . 42 A1
Colchester PI SK4. . . . . 168 C3
Colchester Wlk 1 OL1 . . 153 C3
Colclough Cl M40. . . . . . 83 B6
Coldalhurst La M29 . . . . 77 B5
Coldfield Dr M23 . . . . . 120 F6
Cold Greave Cl OL16 . . . 32 C4
COLD HURST 153 B4
Coldhurst Ind Est OL1 . . 153 B4
Coldhurst St OL1 . . . . . 153 B4
Coldstone Dr WN4 . . . . . 72 D4
Coldstream Ave M9 . . . . 64 D4
Cole Ave WA12 . . . . 89 C4
Colebrook Dr M40 . . . . . 83 A6
Colebrook Rd WA15. . . 120 A6
Coleby Ave
Manchester M16 . . . . . . 97 C4
Wigan WN5 . . . . 54 A6
Cleclough PI WA3 . . . . . 91 F4
Coledale Dr M24. . . . . . . 46 C2
Coleford Gr 1 BL1 . . . . 145 B2
Colemore Ave M20. . . . 110 D3
Colenso Ct 3 BL2. . . . . 148 C3
Colenso Gr SK4 . . . . . . 168 B3
Colenso Rd BL2. . . . . . . 42 D7
Colenso St OL8 . . . . 66 D3
Colenso Way M4. . . . . . 159 A3
Coleport Cl SK8. . . . . . . 123 A1
Coleridge Ave
Middleton M24. . . . . 47 C3
Radcliffe M26 . . . . 43 E4
Wigan WN5 . . . . 54 A6
Coleridge Cl SK5 . . . . . . 99 E1
Coleridge PI WN3. . . . . . 54 F3

Coleridge Rd
Littleborough OL15 . . . . 15 F2
Longshaw WN5 . . . . 53 D1
Manchester M16 . . . . . . 97 C4
Oldham OL1. . . . . 49 E4
Ramsbottom BL8 . . . . . . 10 F2
Reddish SK5. . . . . 99 E1
Coleridge Way SK5 . . . . 99 E1
Colerne Way WN3 . . . . . 54 D2
Colesbourne Cl M38 . . . 60 A6
Coleshill Rise M40 . . . . 54 C2
Colesshaw St M40 . . . . 160 B3
Colesmere Wlk M40. . . . 65 D1
Coleshill St M40 . . . . . . 157 C4
Colgate Cres M14. . . . . 110 B8
Colgate La M5. . . . . 161 A2
Colgrove Ave M40 . . . . . 65 C2
Colina Dr M7. . . . . 155 B1
Colindale Ave M9 . . . . . . 64 E4
Colindale 6 BL3 . . . . . 144 F1
Colin Murphy Rd M15 . . 162 B2
Colin Rd SK4 . . . . 169 B4
Colin St WN1. . . . . 37 D1
Colinton Cl BL1. . . . . . . 143 A1
Colinwood Cl BL9 . . . . . 44 F3
Collard St M46. . . . . 58 B4
Coll Dr M41 . . . . 95 D5
College Ave
Droylsden M43. . . . . 99 F8
Oldham OL8. . . . . 66 D3
Wigan WN1 . . . . 37 C1
College Bank Way OL12 . 139 B4
College Cl
Bolton BL3. . . . . 145 B2
Stockport SK2 . . . . 124 A6
Wilmslow SK9 . . . . 136 F8
College Croft 1 M30 . . . 79 F2
College Dr M16 . . . . 97 C2
College Farm WN3 . . . . . 35 A1
College Ho
Altrincham WA14. . . . . 119 C1
Stockport SK4 . . . . 168 B4
College Land M3. . . . . . 158 C1
College Rd
Manchester M16 . . . . . . 97 D2
Oldham OL8. . . . . 66 E4
Rochdale OL12. . . . . . . 139 B3
Salford M30. . . . . 80 A2
Up Holland WN8 . . . . . . 53 B8
College St WN7 . . . . 76 A5
College Way BL3. . . . . . 145 B2
College Way M27 . . . . . . 62 F1
Collen Cres BL8. . . . . . . 27 C6
Collett Cl WN1. . . . . 151 B4
Collett St OL1 . . . . 67 C8
Colley St
Rochdale OL16. . . . . 15 B1
Stretford M32 . . . . 96 F5
Collie Ave M6 . . . . 81 C5
Collier Ave OL16 . . . . . . 31 F7
Collier Brook Ind Est M46 58 C3
Collier Cl SK14. . . . . . . 102 E1
Collier Ct M19 . . . . 99 B1
Collier Hill OL8 . . . . 66 D3
Collier Hill Ave OL8 . . . 66 C3
Colliers Cl WN7 . . . . 75 E2
Collier's Ct OL11. . . . . . 31 B1
Collier's Rd M46. . . . . . . 58 B2
Collier's Row Rd BL1 . . 23 E5
Collier St
Glossop SK13. . . . . 116 D8
3 Hindley WN2. . . . . . . 56 D6
Manchester, City Centre
M3. . . . . 162 B4
Salford M3 . . . . 158 B2
6 Swinton M27 . . . . 79 E7
Collier Wlk 4 SK14 . . . 102 E1
Colliery La M46 . . . . 58 A4
Colliery St
Droylsden M11. . . . . 83 A1
Manchester M11 . . . . . 165 B4
Collin Ave M18 . . . . 99 C4
Collingburn Ave M5. . . 161 B3
Collingburn Ct M5. . . . . 161 B3
Colling Cl M44 . . . . 94 A1
Collinge Ave M24 . . . . . 65 C8
Collinge St
Bury BL8 . . . . 27 B4
Heywood OL10. . . . . 29 C2
Middleton M24. . . . . 56 A2
Platt Bridge WN2. . . . . . 56 A2
Shaw OL2. . . . . 149 B3
Collingham St M8. . . . . 159 B4
Collingwood Ave M43 . . 83 E3
Collingwood Cl SK12. . 134 A3
Collingwood Dr M27. . . . 80 B7
Collingwood Rd
Manchester M19 . . . . . . 98 F1
Newton-le-W WA12. . . . 89 B3
Collingwood St
Standish WN6 . . . . 19 E1
Trub OL11. . . . . 47 D8
Collingwood Way
Oldham OL1. . . . . 153 C4
Westhoughton BL5 . . . . 39 E1
Collins La M23 . . . . 121 A7
Collins St BL8 . . . . 26 F4
Collisdene Rd WN5 . . . . 53 B4
Collop Dr OL10 . . . . 46 E7
COLLYHURST 157 A2
Collyhurst Ave 2 M28. . 60 E2
Collyhurst Rd M40 . . . . 156 C1
Collyhurst St M40. . . . . 160 A4

Colman Gdns M5 . . . . . 161 B3
Colmore Dr M9 . . . . 65 A4
Colmore Gr 5 BL2. . . . . 25 B4
Colmore St 8 BL2 . . . . . 25 B4
Colnbrook WN6. . . . . . . 19 B1
Colne St OL11 . . . . 30 D1
Colonial Rd SK2 . . . . . . 124 A6
Colshaw Dr SK9. . . . . . 131 D2
Colshaw Rd M23 . . . . . 121 A4
Colson Dr M24. . . . . 64 F7
Colsterdale Cl OL2 . . . . 48 E5
Colt Hill La OL13. . . . . . 68 F8
Coltishall Ho SK8 . . . . 123 A5
Coltness Wlk 12 M40. . . 83 C5
Coltsfoot Cl WN7. . . . . . 76 B5
Coltsfoot Dr WA14 . . . . 119 B8
Columbia Ave M18. . . . . 99 F4
Columbia Rd BL1 . . . . . 144 C4
Columbia St OL8. . . . . . 66 F4
Columbine Cl OL12. . . . . 14 C3
Columbine St M11 . . . . . 99 D7
Columbine Wlk 8 M31. . 105 F3
Columbus St 2 WN4. . . . 72 F5
Columbus Way M50. . . . 96 D8
Colville Dr BL8. . . . . 27 B1
Colville Gr
3 Altrincham WA15. . . 120 A6
Sale M33 . . . . 107 E1
Colville Rd OL1. . . . . . . 48 E8
Colwell Ave M32 . . . . . . 96 B1
Colwell Wlk M9. . . . . . . 64 B5
Colwick Ave WA14 . . . 119 E6
Colwith Ave BL2 . . . . . . 25 E1
Colwood Wlk 19 M8. . . 155 C2
Colwyn Ave
Manchester M14 . . . . . 110 E8
Manchester M24. . . . . . 65 A6
Colwyn Cres SK5. . . . . 111 F5
Colwyn Dr WN2. . . . . . . 57 C2
Colwyn Gr
Atherton M46. . . . . 58 C5
Bolton BL1. . . . . 143 A1
Colwyn Rd
Bramhall SK7. . . . . 132 F8
Cheadle SK8 . . . . 122 E1
Swinton M27 . . . . 79 C6
Colwyn St
Ashton-u-L OL7 . . . . 85 A6
Oldham OL9. . . . . 153 A3
Rochdale OL11. . . . . 30 B2
Salford M6 . . . . 154 C3
Colyton Wlk 7 M22. . . . 121 F3
Combe Cl M11. . . . . 83 B3
Combermere Ave M20. . 110 A7
Combermere Cl
Cheadle SK8 . . . . 122 F4
Combermere St SK16 . . 166 C1
Combs Bank 53 SK13. . 171 A2
Combs Fold 51 SK13 . . 171 A2
Combs Gdns 52 SK13 . . 171 A2
Combs Lea 54 SK13 . . . 171 A1
Combs Mews 48 SK13 . 171 A1
Combs Terr 50 SK13. . . 171 A1
Combs Way 52 SK13. . . 171 A1
Comer Terr 2 M33 . . . . 108 A4
Comet Rd WN5 . . . . 54 C8
Comet St M1. . . . . 159 B1
Commerce Way M17 . . . 96 C5
Commercial Ave SK8. . 131 F5
Commercial Brow SK14 . 167 B4
Commercial Rd SK7. . . 124 E3
Commercial St
Bacup OL13 . . . . 3 D8
Hyde SK14. . . . . 167 B3
Manchester M15 . . . . . 162 B3
5 Swinton M27 . . . . 36 E1
Whitefield M45. . . . . 63 A7
Common End PR7. . . . . 20 E5
Common La
Culcheth WA3 . . . . 91 E4
Leigh WN7 . . . . 75 B4
Partington M31. . . . . . . 106 B5
Tyldesley M29 . . . . 59 A1
Common Nook WN2 . . . 56 A6
Common Side Rd M28. . 77 F7
Common St BL5 . . . . 57 B7
Common The PR7. . . . . . 20 E5
Commonwealth WN7. . . 76 B3
Commonwealth Way
M11. . . . . 160 C1
Community St 4 OL7 . . . 84 F1
Como St 9 BL5. . . . . 57 A6
Como Wlk M18 . . . . 165 B2
Compass St M11 . . . . . 165 C3
COMPSTALL 114 A3
Compstall Ave M14 . . . . 98 B1
Compstall Gr 7 M18 . . . 99 E6
Compstall Mills Est SK6 . 114 B2
Compstall Rd
Compstall SK6 . . . . 114 A3
Marple SK6. . . . . 114 A2
Romiley SK6. . . . . 113 E2
Compton Cl
Hindley WN2 . . . . 56 D4
Urmston M41 . . . . 94 C1
Compton Dr M23 . . . . . 121 A2
Compton St 6 SK15. . . . 86 B1
Compton Way M24. . . . . 65 C6
Comus St 5 M5. . . . . . . 161 C4
Concert La M2 . . . . 159 A1
Concord Ave WN3 . . . . . 55 A3
Concord Bsns Pk M22. . 121 E1
Concord PI M6 . . . . 81 A5
Concord Way 4 SK16. . 101 D3
Condor Cl M43. . . . . 84 C3
Condor PI M6 . . . . 81 A5

Condor Wlk M13. . . . . . 163 B2
Conduit St
Ashton-u-L OL6 . . . . . . 166 C2
Oldham OL1 . . . . 49 E3
Tintwistle SK13 . . . . . . 103 F7
Coney Gr M23 . . . . 121 A7
Coney Green Sports Ctr
M26. . . . . 44 B4
Coneymead SK15 . . . . . 86 A4
Congham Rd 6 SK3. . . 123 C8
Congleton Ave M14 . . . . 98 A2
Congleton Rd SK9 . . . . 137 A3
Congou St M1. . . . . 163 C4
Congreave St OL1. . . . . 153 B4
Congresbury Rd WN7 . . 75 D7
Conifer Wlk
Leigh WN7 . . . . 75 B5
Partington M31. . . . . . . 105 E3
Coningsby Dr M9 . . . . . 157 A4
Coningsby Gdns 13 WA3. . 90 E8
Conisber Cl 2 BL7 . . . . . E1
Conisborough OL11. . . 139 B2
Conisborough Pl M45. . 63 B7
Coniston Ave
Adlington PR6. . . . . 21 B8
Ashton-in-M WN4 . . . . . 73 B4
Atherton M46. . . . . 58 D5
Dukinfield SK14. . . . . . 101 C4
Farnworth BL4 . . . . 59 F8
Ince-in-M WN2 . . . . 56 B7
Manchester M9 . . . . . . 157 A4
Oldham OL8. . . . . 66 D4
Orrell WN5. . . . . 53 F7
Sale M33 . . . . 108 C3
Walkden M38. . . . . 60 A4
Whitefield M45 . . . . 62 F8
Wigan WN1 . . . . 37 C3
Coniston Cl
Chadderton OL9. . . . . . 152 A3
Little Lever BL3 . . . . . . 43 A4
Ramsbottom BL0 . . . . . 138 C3
Reddish M34 . . . . 100 B2
Coniston Ct M22. . . . . . 121 E6
Coniston Dr
Abram WN2. . . . . 74 B8
Bury BL9 . . . . 44 E7
Handforth SK9. . . . . . . 131 C4
Middleton M24. . . . . 46 F2
Stalybridge SK15. . . . . . 86 A3
Coniston Gr
Ashton-u-L OL7 . . . . . . 166 A4
Heywood OL10. . . . . 46 D8
Royton OL2 . . . . 46 D6
Walkden M38. . . . . 60 A4
Coniston Ho 6 M28. . . . 60 E2
Coniston Park Dr WN6 . . 37 A6
Coniston Rd
Blackrod BL6 . . . . 21 D3
Flixton M41 . . . . 106 E8
Gatley SK8 . . . . 122 B5
High Lane SK6 . . . . 134 D8
Hindley WN2 . . . . 56 E4
Partington M31. . . . . . . 105 E4
Reddish SK5. . . . . 111 F6
Stretford M32 . . . . 96 F7
Swinton M27 . . . . 79 F7
Tyldesley M29 . . . . 77 A7
Coniston St
Bolton BL1. . . . . 143 C3
6 Failsworth M40 . . . . . 83 C5
Leigh WN7 . . . . 75 E5
Salford M6. . . . . 81 A4
Coniston Wlk WA15 . . . 120 D5
Conival Way OL9. . . . . . 48 A1
Conmere Sq 7 M15. . . . 162 C3
Connaught Ave
Manchester M19 . . . . . 110 F7
Rochdale OL16. . . . . 31 B3
Whitefield M45. . . . . 63 A7
Connaught Cl SK9 . . . . 137 C8
Connaught Dr WA12 . . . 89 C2
Connaught Sq BL2 . . . . 25 B2
Connaught St
Bury BL8. . . . . 27 B1
Oldham OL8 . . . . 153 B2
Connel Cl BL2 . . . . 42 F6
Connell Rd M23. . . . . . . 121 A6
Connell Way OL10. . . . . 29 F3
Connery Cres OL6. . . . . 85 D6
Connie St M11 . . . . 165 C4
Conningsby Cl 10 BL7. . 24 F8
Connington Ave M9. . . . 64 D1
Connington Cl OL2 . . . . 48 C4
Conran Way SK8 . . . . . 122 E1
Conquest Cl M12. . . . . . 165 A2
Conrad Cl
Oldham OL1. . . . . 49 E4
Wigan WN3 . . . . 150 A1
Conran St M9 . . . . 157 E8
Consett Ave M23 . . . . . 121 A6
Consort Ave OL2 . . . . . . 48 C6
Consort Cl 2 SK16. . . . 101 C6
Consort Pl WA14. . . . . . 119 B3
Constable Cl BL1 . . . . . 143 A1
Constable Dr
Marple SK6 . . . . 125 F5
Wilmslow SK9 . . . . 137 E8
Constable Ho 4 M20. . 110 B7
Constable St M18 . . . . . 99 E6
Constable Wlk
12 Denton M34 . . . . . . 113 A7
Oldham OL1. . . . . 49 D3
Constance Gdns M5. . . 154 C1
Constance Rd
Bolton BL3. . . . . 146 C4
Partington M31. . . . . . . 105 F3
Constance St M15 . . . . 162 B3
Constantia St WN3. . . . . 55 F3

Constantine Ct M6 ... 81 B3
Constantine Rd OL16 ... 139 C3
Constantine St OL4 ... 67 D7
Consul St M22 ... 109 E1
Convamore Rd SK7 ... 132 D7
Convent Gr OL11 ... 139 A1
Convent St SK14 ... 67 C4
Conway Ave
　Bolton BL1 ... 142 A1
　Irlam M44 ... 105 F8
　Swinton M27 ... 62 B3
　Whitefield M45 ... 62 F7
Conway Cl
　Heywood OL10 ... 29 A3
　Leigh WN7 ... 76 E7
　Manchester M16 ... 97 A3
　Middleton M24 ... 65 A7
　Ramsbottom BL0 ... 138 B2
　Whitefield M45 ... 62 F7
Conway Cres
　Billinge WN5 ... 71 E6
　Ramsbottom BL8 ... 10 F2
Conway Ctr The SK5 ... 169 B4
Conway Dr
　Altrincham WA15 ... 120 C6
　Aspull WN2 ... 38 D5
　Billinge WN5 ... 71 F5
　Bury BL9 ... 28 D2
　Hazel Grove SK7 ... 124 C1
　Newton-le-W WA12 ... 89 E3
　Stalybridge SK15 ... 86 A3
Conway Gr OL9 ... 47 F1
Conway Rd
　Ashton-in-M WN4 ... 73 E5
　Cheadle SK8 ... 122 E2
　Hindley WN2 ... 56 F4
　Sale M33 ... 108 D3
　Urmston M41 ... 95 D4
Conway St
　Farnworth BL4 ... 60 D7
　Reddish SK5 ... 169 B4
　Wigan WN5 ... 54 C5
Conyngham Rd M14 ... 98 D3
Cooke St
　Ashton-in-M WN4 ... 72 F6
　Denton M34 ... 100 F3
　Dukinfield SK14 ... 101 F5
　Farnworth M35 ... 83 F8
　Farnworth BL4 ... 60 E7
　Hazel Grove SK7 ... 124 C3
　Horwich BL6 ... 22 D4
Cook St
　Abram WN2 ... 56 B1
　Bury BL9 ... 141 D4
　Denton M34 ... 100 F6
　Eccles M30 ... 79 C2
　Leigh WN7 ... 75 F5
　Oldham OL4 ... 67 C7
　Rochdale OL16 ... 15 B1
　Salford M3 ... 158 B2
　Stockport SK3 ... 169 B1
Cook Terr
　[21] Dukinfield SK16 ... 166 B1
　Rochdale OL16 ... 15 B1
Cooling La M29, WN7 ... 76 E8
Coomassie St
　Heywood OL10 ... 29 C1
　Radcliffe M26 ... 44 A3
　Salford M6 ... 154 C3
Coombe Cl M29 ... 77 B8
Coombes Ave
　Hyde SK14 ... 167 C1
　Marple SK6 ... 125 F5
Coombes La SK13 ... 115 C5
Coombes St SK2 ... 124 B5
Coombes View SK14 ... 114 F8
Co-operation St M35 ... 83 F8
Co-operative St
　Disley SK12 ... 135 D6
　Hazel Grove SK7 ... 124 E3
　[5] Leigh WN7 ... 75 D5
　Oldham OL4 ... 67 F5
　[3] Radcliffe M26 ... 44 A4
　Salford M6 ... 154 C2
　Shaw OL2 ... 149 B3
　Uppermill OL3 ... 69 B8
　Walkden M38 ... 59 E5
Cooper Fold M24 ... 47 A4
Cooper Ho M15 ... 163 A2
Cooper La
　Manchester M9 ... 64 D5
　Middleton M24 ... 46 F3
Cooper's Fold SK8 ... 131 F6
Coopers Glen WN2 ... 56 A8
Cooper's La PR7 ... 18 B8
Cooper St
　Bury BL9 ... 140 B2
　Dukinfield SK16 ... 166 B1
　Glossop SK13 ... 104 B1
　Hazel Grove SK7 ... 124 F3
　Horwich BL6 ... 22 B4
　Manchester M2 ... 158 C1
　Oldham OL4 ... 68 A7
　Rochdale OL16 ... 15 C4
　Stockport SK1 ... 170 C3
　Stretford M32 ... 96 D1
Coopers Wlk OL16 ... 15 C2
Coops Foyer & Coops Bsns
　Ctr WN1 ... 150 B4
Coop St
　Bolton BL1 ... 143 B4
　[1] Manchester M4 ... 159 B2
　Wigan WN1 ... 37 D1
Copage Dr SK6 ... 113 A4
COPE BANK ... 142 C1
Cope Bank [2] BL1 ... 142 C2
Cope Bank E BL1 ... 142 C1

Cope Bank W BL1 ... 142 B2
Cope Cl M11 ... 99 E7
Copeland Ave M27 ... 62 C1
Copeland Cl M24 ... 46 C1
Copeland Dr WN6 ... 19 F2
Copeland Mews BL1 ... 144 A3
Copeland St SK14 ... 101 D5
Copeman Cl M13 ... 163 C7
Copenhagen Sq [20] OL16 ... 31 A8
Copenhagen St
　Failsworth M40 ... 83 A6
　Rochdale OL16 ... 31 A8
Cope St BL1 ... 144 A3
Copesthorne Cl WN2 ... 38 C6
Copgrove Rd M21 ... 109 B7
Copgrove Wlk M22 ... 130 E7
COPLEY ... 86 C2
Copley Ave SK15 ... 86 C2
Copley Ctr The SK15 ... 86 C2
Copley High Sch SK15 ... 86 D2
Copley Park Mews SK15 ... 86 C2
Copley Rd M21 ... 109 B7
Copley St OL2 ... 149 C4
Coplow Dale ... 56 E3
Copperas Cl WN6 ... 36 B7
Copperas St
　Aspull WN2 ... 38 A6
　Blackrod BL6 ... 21 B1
　Droylsden M43 ... 99 E8
Copperas St M4 ... 159 A2
Copper Beech Cl M22 ... 109 E1
Copperbeech Dr WN6 ... 37 B7
Copper Beech Dr
　Gamesley SK13 ... 171 B1
　Stalybridge SK15 ... 86 D3
Copperfield Cl WA14 ... 119 C3
Copperfield Rd
　Cheadle SK8 ... 132 B5
　Poynton SK12 ... 133 D2
Copperfields
　Bolton BL6 ... 40 B3
　Poynton SK12 ... 133 D2
　Wilmslow SK9 ... 137 C8
Coppice Ave
　High Lane SK12 ... 135 A6
　Sale M33 ... 107 D2
Coppice Cl
　High Lane SK12 ... 135 A6
　Romiley SK6 ... 113 B4
Coppice Ct SK8 ... 131 B8
Coppice Dr
　Longshaw WN5 ... 53 D2
　Whitworth OL12 ... 14 D7
　Wigan WN3 ... 54 F2
　Wythenshawe M22 ... 109 D1
Coppice Ho SK13 ... 133 D2
Coppice Ind Est OL8 ... 153 A1
Coppice La SK12 ... 135 A5
Coppice Prim Sch OL8 ... 66 E4
Coppice Rd SK12 ... 134 B3
Coppice St
　Bury BL9 ... 141 C3
　Oldham OL8 ... 66 E4
Coppice The
　Altrincham WA15 ... 129 B8
　Bolton BL2 ... 25 D5
　Manchester M9 ... 65 A2
　Middleton M24 ... 65 B5
　Prestwich M25 ... 63 A4
　Ramsbottom BL0 ... 11 A4
　Swinton M28 ... 79 C5
　Worsley M28 ... 78 F8
Coppice Way SK9 ... 131 E3
Coppice Wlk M34 ... 100 D2
Coppicewood Cl [9] M31 ... 105 E2
Copping St M12 ... 164 C2
Coppins The SK9 ... 136 E4
Coppleridge Dr M8 ... 64 A2
Copplestone Ct M27 ... 61 C1
Copplestone Dr M33 ... 107 B1
Coppull Cross Rds PR7 ... 19 F7
Coppull Hall La PR7 ... 20 B8
Coppull La WN1 ... 37 D2
COPPULL MOOR ... 19 D6
Coppull Moor La PR7 ... 19 E6
Coppy Bridge Dr OL16 ... 31 D8
Cop Rd OL1 ... 49 C4
Copse Ave M22 ... 121 E3
Copse Dr BL9 ... 27 F6
Copse The
　Altrincham WA15 ... 129 D7
　Chapeltown BL7 ... 9 C2
　High Lane SK6 ... 134 E7
　Marple SK6 ... 126 C8
　Newton-le-W WA12 ... 89 B4
　Wigan WN5 ... 53 C6
Copse Wlk OL15 ... 15 F5
Copson St M20 ... 110 B7
Copster Ave OL8 ... 66 E3
Copster Hill Rd OL8 ... 66 E4
Copster Pl [2] OL8 ... 66 E3
Copthall La M8 ... 155 C4
Copthorne Cres WN3 ... 98 E3
Copthorne Dr BL2 ... 42 E6
Copthorn Wlk BL8 ... 26 F5
Coptic Rd OL9 ... 65 F8
Coptrod Head Cl OL12 ... 14 E4
Coral Ave SK8 ... 123 A1
Coral Gr WN7 ... 75 E4

Coralin Way WN4 ... 72 F7
Coral Mews OL2 ... 48 E3
Coral Rd SK8 ... 123 A1
Coral St
　Manchester M13 ... 163 C3
　Wigan WN6 ... 37 A3
Coram St M18 ... 99 F6
Corbar Rd SK2 ... 124 B5
Corbel Way M30 ... 79 D3
Corbett St [5] WN2 ... 56 E5
Corbett St
　Droylsden M11 ... 83 A1
　Manchester M12 ... 165 A3
　Rochdale OL16 ... 31 B8
Corbett Way OL3 ... 33 C1
Corbridge Wlk [7] M8 ... 156 B2
Corby St M12 ... 165 A2
Corcoran Cl OL10 ... 29 C3
Corcoran Dr SK6 ... 113 F2
Corda Ave M22 ... 121 D8
Corday La M5 ... 63 D8
Cordingley Ave M43 ... 99 F8
Cordova Ave M34 ... 99 F3
Corelli St M40 ... 160 C4
Corfe Cl
　Aspull WN2 ... 38 D5
　Urmston M41 ... 94 C1
Corfe Cres SK7 ... 124 D1
Corhampton Cres M46 ... 58 E5
Corinthian Ave M7 ... 81 C5
Corinth Wlk M20 ... 60 D2
Corkland Cl OL6 ... 85 E2
Corkland Rd M21 ... 109 C8
Corkland St OL6 ... 85 E2
Corks La SK12 ... 135 E5
Cork St
　Ashton-u-L OL6 ... 166 C3
　Bury BL9 ... 141 A2
　Manchester M12 ... 164 A4
Corless Fold M29 ... 77 C5
Corley Ave SK3 ... 122 F7
Cormallen Gr M35 ... 84 A7
Cormorant Cl M28 ... 60 C3
Cormorant Wlk M12 ... 165 A2
Cornall St SK2 ... 27 C3
Cornbrook Cl
　Wardle OL12 ... 15 C6
　Westhoughton BL5 ... 57 D6
Cornbrook St M15 ... 161 A2
Cornbrook Gr M16 ... 162 A1
Cornbrook Metro Sta
　M15 ... 161 C2
Cornbrook Park Rd M15 ... 161 C2
Cornbrook Rd M15 ... 161 C2
Cornbrook St M16 ... 162 A1
Cornbrook Way M16 ... 162 A1
Corn Cl M13 ... 163 C1
Cornelian Gr WN4 ... 72 F5
Cornell St M4 ... 159 B2
Corner Brook BL6 ... 40 A3
Corner Croft SK9 ... 137 A4
Corn Hey Rd M33 ... 107 C2
Cornhill Ave M41 ... 95 B3
Corn Hill La M34 ... 100 B5
Cornhill St OL1 ... 49 D2
Cornhill St M11 ... 99 D7
Cornishway M22 ... 130 D8
Cornishway M22 ... 130 D8
Cornish Way OL2 ... 49 A4
Cornishway Ind Est [3]
　M22 ... 130 D8
Corn Mill Cl
　Garswood WN4 ... 72 D4
　Rochdale OL12 ... 15 C4
Corn Mill Dr BL4 ... 60 E7
Cornmill Ho SK13 ... 104 D1
Corn Mill La [1] SK15 ... 86 B1
Corn St
　Failsworth M35 ... 83 C6
　Glossop SK13 ... 104 D1
　Leigh WN7 ... 75 D5
　Oldham OL4 ... 67 A7
Cornwall Ave
　Manchester M19 ... 111 B8
　Over Hulton BL5 ... 58 F8
　Tyldesley M29 ... 59 A3
Cornwall Cl SK14 ... 134 E7
Cornwall Cres
　Brinnington SK5 ... 112 C6
　Diggle OL3 ... 51 B4
　Standish WN1 ... 20 B1
Cornwall Ct [2] M18 ... 99 D6
Cornwall Dr
　Bury BL9 ... 45 A8
　Hindley WN2 ... 56 F6
Cornwall Ho M3 ... 158 A1
Cornwallis Rd WN3 ... 150 A1
Cornwall Pl WN5 ... 54 C6
Cornwall Rd
　Droylsden M43 ... 84 A3
　Gatley SK8 ... 131 B8
　Irlam M44 ... 105 D5
Cornwall St Ind Est M11 ... 99 A7

Cornwall St
　[2] Eccles M30 ... 79 C1
　Manchester M11, M18 ... 99 D7
　Oldham OL9 ... 152 B1
Cornwell Cl [1] SK9 ... 137 D8
Cornwood Cl [8] M8 ... 155 C3
Corona Ave
　Hyde SK14 ... 167 B3
　Oldham OL8 ... 66 E3
Coronation Ave
　Atherton M46 ... 58 C5
　Dukinfield SK16 ... 101 F6
　Glazebury WA3 ... 92 C7
　Heywood OL10 ... 46 E8
　Hyde SK14 ... 167 B1
Coronation Dr
　Haydock WA11 ... 89 A7
　Leigh WN7 ... 76 E6
　Newton-le-W WA12 ... 89 E1
Coronation Gdns M26 ... 43 E4
Coronation Rd
　Ashton-u-L OL6 ... 85 C6
　Droylsden M43 ... 83 F3
　Failsworth M35 ... 83 E6
　Radcliffe M26 ... 43 E4
　Wigan WN6 ... 36 D3
Coronation Sq
　Denton M34 ... 100 D7
　[3] Little Lever BL3 ... 43 B3
　Manchester M1, M12 ... 163 C4
Coronation St
　Bolton BL1 ... 145 C3
　Denton M34 ... 100 D3
　Downall Green WN4 ... 72 D6
　Ince-in-M WN3 ... 55 F3
　Manchester M11 ... 165 C4
　Oldham, Mumps OL4 ... 67 A7
　Reddish SK5 ... 169 B4
　Salford M5 ... 161 B4
　Swinton M27 ... 62 A1
　Wigan WN3 ... 150 B2
Coronation Wlk
　Billinge WN5 ... 71 D4
　[8] Radcliffe M26 ... 43 E5
Coronet Cl WN6 ... 35 C7
Coronet Way M50 ... 80 B1
Corporation Cotts BL3 ... 106 C6
Corporation St
　[10] OL13 ... 3 D8
Corporation Rd
　Denton M34 ... 100 D5
　Eccles M30 ... 79 F1
　Rochdale OL11 ... 139 A2
Corporation St
　Bolton BL1 ... 145 C3
　Hyde SK14 ... 167 A2
　Manchester M4 ... 159 A2
　Middleton M24 ... 65 A8
　Stalybridge SK15 ... 86 A1
　Stockport SK1 ... 169 C2
　Wigan WN3 ... 150 B2
Corpus Christi RC Prim Sch
　OL9 ... 66 B4
Corran Cl M30 ... 79 B2
Corranstone Cl BL6 ... 22 B3
Correction Brow SK12 ... 134 C6
Corrie Cl M34 ... 100 F1
Corrie Cres BL4 ... 61 D4
Corrie Dr BL4 ... 61 D5
Corrie Prim Sch M34 ... 100 F1
Corrie Rd M27 ... 62 A3
Corrie St M38 ... 60 A4
Corrie Way SK6 ... 112 F5
Corrigan St M18 ... 99 E6
Corringham Rd M19 ... 111 C7
Corring Way [2] BL1 ... 25 B4
Corrin Rd BL2 ... 148 B1
Corris Ave WN4 ... 64 A5
Corry St OL10 ... 29 E2
Corsey Rd WN2 ... 56 E4
Corsock Dr WN1 ... 37 E1
Corson St BL4 ... 42 D2
Corston Gr BL6 ... 21 D1
Corston Wlk M40 ... 83 B6
Corwen Cl OL8 ... 66 E4
Cosgate Cl [1] WN5 ... 53 E5
Cosgrove Cres M35 ... 83 E5
Cosgrove Rd M35 ... 83 E5
Cosham Rd M22 ... 121 F3
Costabeck Wlk M40 ... 83 D4
Costessey Way WN3 ... 54 C3
Costa St
　Manchester M18 ... 99 E6
Costobadie Cl SK14 ... 102 F3
Costobadie Way [4] SK14 ... 102 F3
Cosworth Cl [3] WN7 ... 76 B4
Cotaline Cl OL4 ... 30 B3
Cotefield Ave BL3 ... 147 C3
Cotefield Cl [7] SK6 ... 125 F5
Cotefield Rd M22 ... 121 C2
COTE GREEN ... 114 C1
Cote Green La SK6 ... 114 B1
Cote Green Rd SK6 ... 114 C1
Cote La
　Delph OL3 ... 51 B7
　Littleborough OL15 ... 15 F6
　Mossley OL5 ... 68 E3
Cotford Rd BL1 ... 24 F5
Cotman Cl OL13 ... 4 B8
Cotman Dr SK6 ... 126 C8
Cotswold Ave
　Chadderton OL9 ... 152 A1
　Golborne WA3 ... 90 D6
　Hazel Grove SK7 ... 124 E1
　Shaw, High Crompton OL2 ... 48 F8
　Shaw, Lower Rushcroft
　OL2 ... 149 A4
　Urmston M41 ... 94 F3
　Wigan WN5 ... 54 B5
Cotswold Cl
　Glossop SK14 ... 116 A8

Cotswold Cl continued
　Prestwich M25 ... 63 C5
　Ramsbottom BL0 ... 11 C4
Cotswold Cres
　Bury BL8 ... 27 B3
　Milnrow OL16 ... 32 A7
Cotswold Dr
　Horwich BL6 ... 22 C5
　Royton OL2 ... 48 B3
　Salford M6 ... 154 C3
Cotswold Gdns WA3 ... 90 E6
Cotswold Rd SK4 ... 169 A3
Cottage Croft BL2 ... 25 D5
Cottage Gdns SK6 ... 112 D3
Cottage Gr
　Leigh WN7 ... 136 F5
　Wilmslow SK13 ... 171 B2
Cottage Lawns SK9 ... 137 B2
Cottage View OL12 ... 14 C7
Cottage Wlk
　Droylsden M43 ... 83 F3
　Rochdale OL12 ... 14 C4
Cottam Cres SK6 ... 126 B7
Cottam Gr [1] M27 ... 80 A7
Cottam St
　Bury BL8 ... 27 C3
　Oldham OL1 ... 153 A4
Cottenham La M7 ... 158 B4
Cottenham St M13 ... 163 B2
Cotterdale Cl M16 ... 97 D2
Cotterill Cl M12 ... 120 C8
Cotterill St M6 ... 81 B2
Cottesmore Cl SK13 ... 163 C3
Cottesmore Dr OL12 ... 14 C6
Cottesmore Dr M8 ... 156 C4
Cottesmore Gdns WA15 ... 129 C8
Cottesmore Way WA3 ... 74 B1
Cottingham Dr OL6 ... 166 C4
Cottingham Rd M12 ... 164 B2
Cottingley [1] BL1 ... 2
Cotton Cl SK14 ... 167 B1
Cottonfield Rd M20 ... 110 C6
Cottonfields BL7 ... 24 F7
Cotton Fold OL16 ... 31 C6
Cotton Hill M20 ... 110 C5
Cotton La M20 ... 110 C6
Cotton Lodge Cl [4] BL3 ... 42 A3
Cotton Mill Cres OL9 ... 66 B4
Cotton St
　Bolton BL1 ... 143 A2
　Leigh WN7 ... 75 D5
　Manchester M4 ... 159 B2
Cotton Tree Cl OL4 ... 67 D8
Cotton Tree St SK4 ... 169 B1
Cottonwood Dr [3] M33 ... 107 C5
Cottrell Rd WA15 ... 129 D7
Coucill Sq BL4 ... 60 E8
Coudhurst Ct BL6 ... 22 E4
Coulsden Dr M9 ... 64 D3
Coulthart St OL6 ... 166 B3
Coulthurst St BL0 ... 138 B2
Coulton Cl OL1 ... 67 A8
Coulton Wlk M5 ... 154 C2
Coultshade Ave WN5 ... 71 E6
Council Ave WN4 ... 73 B3
Councillor La SK8 ... 123 A4
Councillor St M12 ... 160 B1
Countess Ave SK8 ... 131 E5
Countess Gr M7 ... 158 A4
Countess La M26 ... 43 D4
Countess Pl M25 ... 63 C4
Countess Rd M20 ... 110 B3
Countess St
　Ashton-u-L OL6 ... 85 C2
　Stockport SK2 ... 124 A5
Counthill Dr M8 ... 63 E2
Counthill Rd OL4 ... 49 D1
Counthill Sch OL4 ... 49 D2
Counting House Rd
　SK12 ... 135 E5
Count St OL16 ... 31 A5
County Ave OL6 ... 85 E4
County End Bsns Ctr OL4 ... 67 F6
County End Terr [14] OL4 ... 67 F6
County Police St WN2 ... 151 C3
County Rd M28 ... 60 A4
County St
　Manchester M2 ... 158 C1
　Oldham OL3 ... 66 C2
Coupes Gn BL5 ... 57 F6
Coupland Cl
　Oldham OL4 ... 49 A4
　Whitworth OL12 ... 14 C8
Coupland Rd WN2 ... 57 C3
Coupland St M15 ... 163 A1
Courage Low La WN6 ... 18 D5
Courier Pl WN5 ... 36 E1
Courier St M18 ... 99 F6
Course View OL4 ... 67 E3
Court Dr M40 ... 83 E4
Courtfield Ave M9 ... 64 D4
Courthill St SK1 ... 124 A8
Court House Way [4] OL10 ... 29 D2
Courtney Gn SK9 ... 131 D2
Courtney Pl WA14 ... 119 A1
Court St
　Bolton BL2 ... 148 A3
　Uppermill OL3 ... 69 B8
Courts View M33 ... 108 C5
Court The M17 ... 95 F8
Courtyard Dr M28 ... 60 A3
Courtyard St Peters The
　BL1 ... 143 C1
Courtyard The
　Hollingworth SK14 ... 103 D5

Courtyard The continued
Newton-le-W WA12..... 89 E4
Cousin Fields BL7..... 25 C7
Covall Wlk 4 M8..... 156 B2
Covell Rd SK12..... 133 D5
Covenant Christian Sch
SK4..... 168 C4
Covent Gdns SK1..... 169 C1
Coventry Ave SK3..... 122 F7
Coventry Gr O9..... 48 A1
Coventry Rd M26..... 43 F5
Covent The WN7..... 76 A7
Coverdale Ave
Bolton BL1..... 144 A4
Royton OL2..... 48 C5
Coverdale Cl
Heywood OL10..... 29 C1
Platt Bridge WN2..... 55 F2
Coverdale Cres M12..... 164 B2
Coverdale Rd BL5..... 57 D8
Cover Dr OL11..... 30 B2
Coverham Ave OL4..... 67 D4
Coverhill Rd OL4..... 68 B5
Covert Rd
Oldham OL4..... 67 D3
Wythenshawe M22..... 121 E5
Coverts The WN6..... 36 F2
Cove The WA15..... 119 F3
Covington Pl SK9..... 137 B6
Cowan St M40..... 160 A2
Cowbrook Ave SK13..... 104 F1
Cowbrook Cl SK13..... 104 F1
Cowburn Dr SK22..... 127 C1
Cowburn St
Heywood OL10..... 29 E1
Hindley WN2..... 56 F6
1 Leigh WN7..... 75 D5
Manchester M3..... 158 C3
Cowbury Dale Nature
Reserve SK15..... 87 A7
Cowdals Rd BL6..... 40 B4
Cowesby St M14..... 98 A3
COWHILL..... 152 B2
Cowhill La OL6..... 166 C3
Cowhill Lane Trad Est 11
OL6..... 166 C3
Cowie St OL2..... 149 B4
Cow La
Ashley WA15..... 128 F6
Bolton BL3..... 146 B2
Failsworth M35..... 83 E7
Hyde SK14..... 103 D6
Oldham OL4..... 67 C7
Sale M33..... 108 E5
Salford M5..... 81 C1
Wilmslow SK9..... 137 C7
Cow Lees BL5..... 40 A1
Cowley Rd BL1..... 24 F5
Cowley St 9 M40..... 83 C6
Cowling St
Manchester M7..... 80 F8
Oldham OL8..... 66 F4
Wigan WN3..... 150 B2
COWLISHAW..... 149 A2
Cowlishaw OL2..... 149 A1
Cowlishaw La OL2..... 149 A1
Cowlishaw La SK14..... 113 F4
Cowm Park Way N OL12..... 4 D2
Cowm Park Way S OL12..... 4 C1
Cowm St OL12..... 4 E3
Cowm Top La OL11..... 30 E3
COWPE..... 2 F6
Cowper Ave M46..... 58 D5
Cowpe Rd BB4..... 2 F7
Cowper St
Ashton-u-L OL6..... 166 C3
Leigh WN7..... 75 D5
Middleton M24..... 65 D8
Cowper Wlk 4 M11..... 160 C1
Coxfield WN6..... 35 D7
COX GREEN..... 24 F8
Cox Green Cl BL7..... 8 D3
Cox Green Rd
2 Bolton, Cox Green BL7.. 24 F8
Bolton, Egerton BL7..... 8 E2
Coxton Rd M22..... 121 E1
Cox Way M46..... 58 D3
Coxwold Gr BL3..... 146 C2
Crabbe St M4..... 159 A3
Crab Brow M46..... 58 B3
Crab La M9..... 64 B4
Crab Lane Prim Sch M9.. 64 B4
Crabtree Ave
Altrincham WA15..... 129 D7
Disley SK12..... 135 E5
Crabtree Cl WA12..... 89 E3
Crabtree Ct SK12..... 135 D6
Crabtree La M11..... 83 D1
Crab Tree La M46..... 58 D2
Crabtree Rd
Oldham OL1..... 67 B8
Wigan WN5..... 54 D7
Craddock Rd M33..... 108 C2
Craddock St 2 OL5..... 68 C1
Cradley Ave M11..... 99 D8
Crag Ave BL9..... 11 D2
Crag Fold BL9..... 11 D2
Crag Gr WA11..... 71 B1
Cragg Rd OL1..... 48 A2
Cragie St M8..... 155 C1
Crag La BL9..... 11 D2
Cragside Way SK9..... 137 C6
Craig Ave
Bury BL8..... 27 B1
Urmston M41..... 95 A3

Craig Cl SK4..... 168 B1
Craigend Dr M9..... 157 B3
Craighall Ave M19..... 110 F8
Craighall Rd BL1..... 24 E6
Craiglands OL16..... 31 B2
Craigmore Ave M40..... 109 E4
Craignair Ct M27..... 80 C7
Craig Rd
Manchester M18..... 99 C4
Stockport SK4..... 168 B1
Craigslands Ave M40..... 83 A6
Craigweil Ave M20..... 110 D3
Craigwell Rd M25..... 63 D1
Craigwell Wlk M13..... 163 B3
Craigwood Dr WA..... 153 B1
Crail Pl OL10..... 28 F1
Cramer St M40..... 157 C1
Crammond Cl M40..... 83 D6
Cramond Cl BL1..... 143 A1
Cramond Wlk 8 BL1..... 143 A1
Crampton Dr WA15..... 129 C8
Crampton La M31..... 106 D6
Cranage Rd M19..... 111 B8
Cranage Way 16 SK9..... 131 D5
Cranark Cl BL1..... 144 A3
Cranberry Ave
Walsden OL14..... 6 B7
Wigan WN6..... 36 F3
Cranberry Cl WA14..... 119 B8
Cranberry Dr
Bolton BL3..... 40 F4
Denton M34..... 100 D3
Cranberry Rd M31..... 105 F3
Cranberry St OL4..... 67 B6
Cranborne Cl
Horwich BL6..... 22 F1
Standish WN6..... 19 D1
Cranbourne Ave SK8..... 123 B2
Cranbourne Cl
1 Altrincham WA15..... 120 A6
Ashton-u-L OL7..... 166 A4
Cranbourne Ct SK4..... 168 B4
Cranbourne Rd
Ashton-u-L OL7..... 166 B4
Manchester, Chorlton-cum-Hardy
M21..... 109 B8
Manchester, Old Trafford
M16..... 97 C4
Rochdale OL11..... 29 E6
Stockport, Heaton Moor
SK4..... 168 B4
Cranbourne St M5..... 81 C1
Cranbourne Terr OL6..... 85 B5
Cranbrook Ave M44..... 73 A4
Cranbrook Cl BL1..... 143 C1
Cranbrook Dr M25..... 63 C2
Cranbrook Gdns OL7.. 166 B4
Cranbrook Pl OL4..... 67 C6
Cranbrook Rd
Eccles M30..... 79 E4
Reddish M18..... 99 F3
Cranbrook St
Ashton-u-L OL7..... 166 B4
Oldham OL4..... 67 C6
Radcliffe M26..... 44 C5
Cranbrook Way WN1..... 37 B4
Cranbrook Wlk OL9..... 152 A2
Cranby St 8 WN2..... 56 D5
Crandon Ct M27..... 62 A1
Crandon Dr M20..... 122 C8
Cranesbill Cl M22..... 121 C2
Crane St
Bolton BL3..... 146 B3
Coppull PR7..... 19 D6
Manchester M12..... 163 C4
Cranfield Rd
Horwich BL6..... 39 E7
Wigan WN3..... 55 A3
Cranford Ave
Manchester M20..... 110 D4
Sale M33..... 108 C6
Stretford M32..... 96 F3
Whitefield M45..... 44 E2
Cranford Cl
Salford M27..... 80 B6
Whitefield M45..... 44 E2
Cranford Dr M44..... 93 F3
Cranford Gdns
Marple SK6..... 125 F8
Urmston M41..... 94 E3
Cranford Ho M30..... 79 F3
Cranford Rd
Handforth SK9..... 131 A1
Urmston M41..... 94 E3
Cranford St BL3..... 146 C2
Cranham Ave WA3..... 90 E7
Cranham Cl
Bury BL8..... 27 B3
Walkden M38..... 60 A6
Cranham Rd M22..... 121 C2
Crank Rd WA11, WN5.. 71 B8
CRANKWOOD..... 74 E5
Crankwood Rd WN2 &
WN7..... 74 D5
Cranleigh M16..... 37 A8
Cranleigh Ave SK4..... 110 F4
Cranleigh Cl
Blackrod BL6..... 21 D1
Oldham OL4..... 49 E1
Cranleigh Dr
Cheadle SK8..... 122 F6
Hazel Grove SK7..... 134 A8
Sale M33..... 108 A5
Tyldesley M29..... 77 B8
Walkden M28..... 78 E8
Wythenshawe M23, M33.. 108 C1
Cranlington Dr M8..... 155 C2

Cranmer Ct OL10..... 29 C1
Cranmere Ave M19..... 99 C2
Cranmere Dr M33..... 107 D2
Cranmer Rd M20..... 110 B4
Cranshaw St M29..... 77 D8
Cranstal Dr WN2..... 57 A5
Cranston Dr
Manchester M20..... 122 B8
Sale M33..... 108 E3
Cranston Gr SK8..... 121 F5
Cranswick St 1 M14..... 98 A3
Crantock Dr
Gatley SK8..... 131 C8
Stalybridge SK15..... 86 D3
Crantock Rd WN5..... 54 C6
Crantock St M19..... 99 B3
Cranwell Ave WA3..... 91 F4
Cranwell Dr M19..... 110 E4
Cranworth Ave M29..... 77 A6
Cranworth St SK15..... 86 B1
Craston Rd M13..... 98 E2
Craunton 18 M30..... 79 F2
Craven Ave
Golborne WA3..... 90 E7
Salford M5..... 161 B4
Craven Ct BL6..... 22 D2
Craven Dr
Altrincham WA14..... 119 C8
Salford M5..... 161 A3
Craven Gdns OL11..... 139 B1
Craven Ho OL4..... 6 A8
Cravenhurst Ave M40.. 83 B4
Craven Pl
Bolton BL1..... 23 E2
3 Droylsden M11..... 83 C2
Craven Rd
Altrincham WA14..... 119 C7
1 Reddish SK5..... 111 F6
Craven St
Ashton-u-L OL6..... 85 D5
Bury BL9..... 141 C3
Droylsden M43..... 84 A1
Oldham OL1..... 48 E1
Salford M5..... 81 C1
Craven Terr M33..... 108 C4
Cravenwood OL6..... 85 F6
Cravenwood Prim Sch 3
M8..... 64 A1
Cravenwood Rd
Manchester M8..... 156 A4
Stockport SK8..... 99 E2
Crawford Ave
Adlington PR7..... 20 E5
Aspull WN2..... 38 C5
Bolton BL2..... 148 B2
Tyldesley M29..... 58 F2
Worsley M28..... 79 A8
Crawford Cl WN2..... 38 C5
Crawford Sq OL10..... 29 A4
Crawford St
Ashton-u-L OL6..... 85 D2
Aspull WN2..... 38 C5
Bolton BL2..... 148 B2
Eccles M30..... 79 D3
24 Failsworth M40..... 83 C5
Rochdale OL16..... 31 B6
Walsden OL14..... 6 B8
Wigan WN1..... 150 C4
Crawley Ave
Salford M30..... 80 A3
Wythenshawe M22..... 121 E3
Crawley Cl M29..... 59 C1
Crawley Gr SK2..... 124 B6
Crawley Way M9..... 152 A2
Craydon St M11..... 165 C4
Crayfield Rd M19..... 111 B3
Crayford Rd M40..... 83 B4
Cray The OL16..... 31 E6
Cray Wlk M13..... 163 B3
Creaton Way M24..... 46 D4
Creden Ave M22..... 121 F3
Crediton Cl
Altrincham WA14..... 119 B6
Manchester M15..... 162 C1
Crediton Dr
Bolton BL2..... 43 A7
Platt Bridge WN2..... 56 A1
Crediton Ho M6..... 80 A3
Creel Cl M9..... 64 B4
Cremer Ho M30..... 80 A2
Cresbury St M12..... 164 A4
Crescent M5..... 81 C2
Crescent Ave
Ashton-u-M WN4..... 73 A4
16 Bolton BL1..... 145 A4
Farnworth BL4..... 60 C6
Manchester, Crumpsall
M8..... 156 A4
Manchester, Hilton Park
M25..... 63 B2

Crescent Gr continued
6 Manchester, Levenshulme
M19..... 99 A1
Crescent Pk SK4..... 168 C2
Crescent Range M14..... 98 C3
Crescent Rd
Alderley Edge SK9..... 137 B2
Altrincham, Ashley Heath
WA15..... 119 C1
Altrincham, Oldfield Brow
WA14..... 119 A6
Bolton BL3..... 42 B3
Cheadle SK8..... 122 C6
Dukinfield SK16..... 166 C1
Failsworth OL9..... 65 G3
Horwich BL6..... 39 F8
Kearsley BL4..... 60 F6
Manchester M8..... 156 A4
Rochdale OL11..... 30 B4
Stockport SK1..... 112 B3
Urmston M41..... 94 F3
Crescent St M8..... 156 C4
Crescent The
Altrincham, Oldfield Brow
WA14..... 119 A5
Bolton, Bromley Cross BL7 .. 25 A7
Bolton, Harwood BL2..... 25 F4
Cheadle SK8..... 122 D6
Droylsden M43..... 83 F1
Horwich BL6..... 22 E1
Ince-in-M WN2..... 56 A4
Irlam M44..... 94 B3
Little Lever BL3..... 43 B2
4 Manchester M19..... 99 A1
Middleton M24..... 64 E8
Mossley OL5..... 68 B1
Prestwich M25..... 63 B4
Radcliffe M26..... 43 D5
Romiley SK6..... 112 D4
Shaw OL2..... 149 A2
Stalybridge SK15..... 102 D6
Stockport SK3..... 124 A4
Urmston M41..... 94 F3
Westhoughton BL5..... 57 E7
Whitworth OL12..... 14 C8
Wigan WN5..... 54 D6
Worsley M28..... 79 A5
Crescent View 12 SK16.. 166 B1
Crescent Way SK3..... 124 A5
Cresgarth Ho SK3..... 124 A4
Cressell Pk WN6..... 19 B1
Cressfield Way M21..... 109 D7
Cressingham Rd
Bolton BL3..... 146 A4
Stretford M32..... 96 B2
Cressington Cl 4 M5.. 154 B2
Cresswell Gr M20..... 110 A5
Crestfield Gr WN6..... 36 F2
Crestfold M38..... 60 A4
Crest Lo SK7..... 123 F2
Crest St M4..... 159 A3
Crest The M43..... 100 A7
Crestwood Ave WA3.... 54 C2
Crestwood Wlk M40.... 54 C2
Creswick Cl WN2..... 56 C4
Crete OL8..... 66 F4
Crewe Rd M23..... 120 E8
Crib Fold OL3..... 51 A2
Crib La OL3..... 51 A2
Criccieth Ave WN2..... 38 D5
Criccieth Rd SK3..... 123 A7
Criccieth St 2 M16..... 97 F4
Cricketers Way BL5..... 57 F8
Cricketfield La BL8..... 60 C3
Cricket Gr The M21..... 109 B6
Cricket's La OL6..... 85 D3
Cricket St
Bolton BL3..... 145 A1
Denton M34..... 101 A4
Wigan WN6..... 150 A4
Cricket Street Bsns Ctr
WN6..... 150 A4
Cricket View OL16..... 31 F5
Cricklewood Rd M22..... 121 C2
CRIMBLE..... 29 E4
Crimble La OL10, OL11.. 29 F3
Crimble St OL12..... 139 A4
Crime La OL8..... 84 D7
Crimsworth Ave M16.. 97 B2
Crinan Sq OL10..... 28 F1
Crinan Way BL2..... 42 F6
Crinan Wlk M40..... 160 A3
Cringle Barrow Cl M28.. 78 A5
Cringle Cl BL3..... 40 F4
Cringle Dr SK8..... 122 C6
Cringleford Wlk M12.. 164 C1
Cringle Hall Rd M19..... 110 F8
Cringle Rd M19..... 111 C7
Crippen St M46..... 58 A1
Cripple Gate La OL11..... 30 E1
Cripple Gate La OL11..... 30 E1
Crispin Rd M22..... 130 E8
Critchley Cl SK14..... 167 C1
Criterion St SK5..... 99 F2
Croal Ave WN2..... 56 A2
Croal Wlk M45..... 45 B1
Croasdale Ave 2 M14.. 110 B8
Croasdale Cl OL2..... 48 E5
Croasdale St BL1..... 143 C1
Crocker Wlk 25 M9..... 157 B4
Crocus Dr OL2..... 149 A1
Crocus St BL1..... 143 C4
Crocus Wlk M7..... 155 A2
Croft Acres BL0..... 1 D2
Croft Ave
Atherton M46..... 58 D2
Golborne WA3..... 73 F2
Middleton M25..... 63 F8

Croft Ave continued
Orrell WN5..... 53 D5
Croft Bank
Manchester M18..... 99 E5
4 Salford M7..... 81 C5
Stalybridge SK15..... 86 D4
Croft Brow OL8..... 66 E2
Croft Cl WA15..... 129 C6
Croft Ct WN7..... 75 C1
Croft Dr BL1..... 26 E6
Croft Edge OL3..... 69 A5
Crofters Brook M26..... 44 C4
Crofters Gn SK9..... 136 F6
Crofters Hall Wlk M40.. 83 B7
Crofters The M23..... 108 F3
Crofters Wlk BL2..... 25 D6
Crofters' Yd 11 WN1..... 150 C4
Croft Gate BL2..... 25 E4
Croft Gates Rd M24..... 64 E7
Croft Gr M38..... 59 F5
Croft Head OL2..... 48 D6
Croft Head Dr OL16..... 31 F7
Croft Hill Rd M40..... 65 A1
Croft Ind Est BL9..... 45 A5
Croft La
Bolton BL3..... 148 B1
Radcliffe M26..... 44 C4
Whitefield BL9..... 45 A5
Croftlands
Orrell WN5..... 53 D4
Ramsbottom BL0..... 11 A3
Croftlands Rd M22..... 121 E4
Croftleigh Cl M45..... 44 E2
Croft Manor SK13..... 104 E1
Crofton Ave WA15..... 120 A8
Crofton Gdns WA3..... 91 E3
Crofton St
Manchester M14..... 98 B3
Manchester, Old Trafford
M16..... 97 D4
Oldham OL8..... 66 F3
Croft Pl M29..... 76 F8
Croft Rd
Cheadle SK8..... 123 B2
Sale M33..... 108 D2
Wilmslow SK9..... 136 E4
Croft Row OL5..... 68 D1
Crofts OL2..... 49 E8
CROFTS BANK..... 95 D4
Crofts Bank Rd M41..... 95 D3
Croft Side BL3..... 42 E5
Croftside Ave M28..... 60 E3
Croftside Cl M28..... 60 E3
Croftside Gr M28..... 60 E3
Croftside Way SK9..... 137 C6
Croft Sq OL12..... 15 C3
Croft St
Bolton BL3..... 42 B4
Bury BL9..... 141 A2
Droylsden M11..... 83 B1
4 Failsworth M35..... 66 A1
Golborne WA3..... 90 A8
Hyde SK14..... 167 A2
Rochdale OL12..... 15 C3
Salford M7..... 81 C5
Stalybridge SK15..... 86 B3
Walkden M38..... 59 F5
Westhoughton BL5..... 39 E3
Croft The
3 Bolton BL1..... 145 C4
Glossop SK13..... 104 A6
Mottram-in-L SK14..... 103 A4
Oldham OL8..... 66 E2
Orrell WN5..... 53 D3
Stockport SK2..... 124 B6
Westhoughton BL5..... 39 E3
Whitefield BL9..... 45 A6
Croftwood Sq WN5..... 36 C2
Croichbank BL8..... 12 B2
Croichley Fold BL8..... 10 D2
Cromar Rd SK7..... 124 B3
Cromarty Ave OL9..... 65 F3
Cromarty Sq OL10..... 28 F1
Cromarty Wlk M11..... 160 C1
Crombie Ave M22..... 121 D7
Crombouke Dr WN7..... 57 E1
Crombouke Fold M28.. 78 B7
Cromdale Ave
Bolton BL1..... 144 B4
Hazel Grove SK7..... 124 F3
Cromedale Cres WN6.. 37 A7
Cromer Ave
Bolton BL2..... 25 C1
Manchester M20..... 110 B6
Reddish M34..... 100 A3
Cromer Dr M46..... 58 A2
Cromer Ind Est M24..... 47 B1
Cromer Rd
Bury BL8..... 27 D5
Cheadle SK8..... 122 E6
Sale M33..... 108 C3
Wigan WN3..... 54 E3
Cromer St
Droylsden M11..... 83 D1
Middleton M24..... 47 B1
Rochdale OL12..... 139 B4
Shaw OL2..... 149 B3
Stockport SK1..... 112 A2
Cromford Ave M32..... 96 B3
Cromford Bank 21 SK13.. 171 A2
Cromford Bsns Ctr OL1... 67 B8
Cromford Cl
Bolton BL1..... 143 B1
22 Gamesley SK13..... 171 A2
Cromford Dr WN5..... 54 B5
Cromford Fold 23 SK13.. 171 A2
Cromford Gdns BL1..... 143 C2

Cromford Gn **20** SK13 . . . 171 A2
Cromford Ct **18** SK13 . . . 171 A2
Cromford Lea **19** SK13 . . 171 A2
Cromford PI **21** SK13 . . . 171 A2
Cromford St OL1 . . . . 67 A8
Cromford Way **17** SK13 . . 171 A2
Cromhurst St M8 . . . . 156 A4
Cromley Rd
High Lane SK6 . . . . 134 E6
Stockport SK2 . . . . 124 A3
Crompton Ave
Bolton BL1 . . . . 42 E8
Rochdale OL16 . . . . 31 B3
3 Salford M7 . . . . 81 A8
Crompton Cl
Bolton BL1 . . . . 25 A4
Marple SK6 . . . . 125 F7
Radcliffe M26 . . . . 62 B8
Crompton Ct
Ashton-in-M WN4 . . . . 73 B2
Little Lever BL3 . . . . 43 C3
CROMPTON FOLD 32 D1
Crompton Fold BL8 . . . . . . 27 B4
Crompton Gate OL2 . . . . . 149 A4
Crompton Ho **2** WN1 . . . 151 A4
Crompton House CE Sch
OL2 . . . . 48 F7
Crompton Pl
Bolton BL1 . . . . 145 C3
Radcliffe M26 . . . . 44 B3
Crompton Pool OL2 . . . . . 149 A4
Crompton Prim Sch OL2 149 A2
Crompton Rd
Horwich BL6 . . . . 39 F8
Kearsley M26 . . . . 61 A8
Manchester M19 . . . . 111 A7
Crompton St
Ashton-u-L OL6 . . . . 85 E4
Bolton BL1 . . . . 148 A4
Bury BL9 . . . . 140 B2
Chadderton OL9 . . . . 152 C3
Farnworth BL4 . . . . 60 F7
Ince-in-M WN3 . . . . 55 F3
Oldham OL1 . . . . 153 B4
Platt Bridge WN2 . . . . 56 A3
Royton OL2 . . . . 48 E3
Shaw OL2 . . . . 149 B3
Swinton M27 . . . . 79 E8
Walkden, Greenheys M38 . 59 D5
Walkden, Whittle Brook
M28 . . . . 60 F2
Wigan WN1 . . . . 150 C4
Crompton Vale BL2 . . . . . . 42 D8
Crompton Way
Bolton BL2 . . . . 25 C2
Golborne WA3 . . . . 91 B8
Shaw OL2 . . . . 149 B3
Cromwell Ave
Gatley SK8 . . . . 122 A6
Manchester M16 . . . . 97 C2
Marple SK6 . . . . 125 D7
Reddish SK5 . . . . 100 A2
Cromwell Cl WA12 . . . . 89 A4
Cromwell Ct M44 . . . . 105 E7
Cromwell Gr
Manchester M19 . . . . 99 B1
3 Salford M7 . . . . 81 C5
Cromwell High Sch
SK16 . . . . 101 E6
Cromwell Range M14 . . . . 98 D2
Cromwell Rd
Bramhall SK7 . . . . 132 D6
Brinnington SK6 . . . . 112 D6
Eccles M30 . . . . 79 D2
Irlam M44 . . . . 63 C4
Prestwich M25 . . . . 63 C4
Royton OL2 . . . . 48 C6
Salford M6 . . . . 81 B5
Stretford M32 . . . . 96 F2
Swinton M27 . . . . 61 E1
Whitefield M45 . . . . 44 D2
Cromwell St
Bolton BL1 . . . . 145 B3
Heywood OL10 . . . . 29 D1
Oldham OL1 . . . . 153 C2
Stockport SK4 . . . . 169 A3
Crondale Wlk **8** M13 . . 163 C2
Crondall St M14 . . . . 98 A3
Cronkeyshaw Ave OL12 . . 14 F1
Cronkeyshaw Rd OL12. . . 14 F1
Cronshaw Ind Est **8** OL11 31 A6
Cronshaw St M19 . . . . 111 B8
Crookall St WN4 . . . . 73 C4
CROOKE 36 C3
Crooke Rd WN6 . . . . 36 C3
Crookhill Dr M8 . . . . 155 C3
Crookhurst Ave WN5 . . . . 71 D6
Crookilley Way SK1, SK6 . 112 C4
Crook St
Adlington PR7 . . . . 20 F7
Bolton BL3 . . . . 145 C2
1 Hindley WN2 . . . . 56 D4
Hyde SK14 . . . . 167 B2
9 Radcliffe M26 . . . . 44 B3
16 Rochdale OL16 . . . . . . 31 A8
Wigan WN1 . . . . 150 B4
Croom Wlk M40 . . . . 160 A2
Cropton Way WN2 . . . . . . 56 F3
Crosby Ave M28 . . . . 60 F2
Crosby Gr M46 . . . . 58 E4
Crosby Rd
Bolton BL1 . . . . 144 B4
Failsworth M40 . . . . 83 D5
Radcliffe M26 . . . . 43 E7
3 Salford M6 . . . . 80 D5
Crosby St
Atherton M46 . . . . 58 E4
1 Rochdale OL12 . . . . 15 A2

Crosby St continued
Stockport SK2 . . . . 170 C3
Crosfield Ave BL9 . . . . 11 C2
Crosfield Gr M18 . . . . 99 D4
Crosland Ind Est SK6 . . . 112 E4
Crossacres Prim Sch
M22 . . . . 121 F4
Crossacres Rd M22 . . . . . 121 E3
Crossbank Ave M25 . . . . . 63 A6
Crossbank Ave OL4 . . . . . . 67 F7
Crossbank St M13 . . . . . . 164 A1
Crossbank St
Oldham, Bank Top OL8 . . 153 B2
Oldham OL8 . . . . 67 A8
Crossbank Way M46 . . . . . 46 F1
Crossbill Brow **9** WA14 . 107 C1
Crossbridge Rd SK14 . . . . 102 A2
Crossbrook Way OL16 . . . . 32 A5
Crosby Cl M9 . . . . 64 F5
Cross Cliffe
Glossop SK13 . . . . 116 E8
Hyde SK14 . . . . 113 C8
Crosscliffe St **3** M16 . . . . 97 F4
Crossdale Rd
Bolton BL2 . . . . 42 F8
Hindley WN2 . . . . 57 A5
Manchester M9 . . . . 64 F4
Crossdale Way WA11 . . . . 71 B1
Crossefield Rd SK8. . . . . . 123 A3
Crossen St BL3 . . . . 148 C1
Crossfell Ave M9 . . . . 64 B5
Crossfield Ave WA3 . . . . . . 91 F2
Crossfield Cl
Denton M34 . . . . 101 A2
Stalybridge SK15 . . . . 86 A1
Wardle OL12 . . . . 15 C6
Cross Field Cl OL2 . . . . 32 C1
Crossfield Dr
Hindley WN2 . . . . 57 C3
Radcliffe M26 . . . . 43 E3
Swinton M27 . . . . 61 E1
Worsley M28 . . . . 78 F7
Crossfield Gr
Marple SK6 . . . . 114 B1
Stockport SK2 . . . . 124 B4
Crossfield Pl OL11 . . . . 31 A5
Crossfield Rd
Altrincham WA15 . . . . 120 B2
Handforth SK9 . . . . 131 D4
Irlam M44 . . . . 94 C4
Wardle OL12 . . . . 15 C6
Crossfields BL7 . . . . 25 C8
Crossfield St BL9 . . . . 44 F4
Crossford Dr BL3 . . . . 40 F1
Crossford St M32 . . . . 96 D1
Crossgate Ave M22 . . . . . 121 D6
Crossgate La SK13 . . . . . . 103 F7
Crossgate Mews **8** M46 110 E2
Crossgates Prim Sch
OL16 . . . . 32 A7
Crossgates Rd OL16 . . . . . 32 A6
Crossgill M29 . . . . 77 B5
Cross Glebe St **3** OL6 . . 166 C3
Cross Gr WA15 . . . . 119 F8
Crosshill St **4** M16 . . . . . . 97 F4
Crosshill Wlk BL3 . . . . 40 E5
Crossings The WA12 . . . . . 89 C3
Cross Keys St M4 . . . . 159 B2
Cross Knowle View M41 . . 95 A4
Cross La
Droylsden M43 . . . . 84 D4
Manchester M18 . . . . 99 D5
Marple SK6 . . . . 125 E5
Newton-le-W WA12 . . . . . . 89 B4
Orrell WN5 . . . . 53 D3
Radcliffe M26 . . . . 44 C4
Ramsbottom BL0 . . . . 138 A2
Salford M5, M6 . . . . 81 B2
Wilmslow SK9 . . . . 137 F8
Crossland Rd
Droylsden M43 . . . . 84 B2
Manchester M21 . . . . 109 A8
Crosslands M25 . . . . 63 A3
Crosslands Cl SK13 . . . . . 116 D8
Crosslands Rd M28 . . . . . . 77 F6
Crosslee Prim Sch M9 . . . 64 F4
Cross Lees OL12 . . . . 15 A4
Crossley Cres OL6 . . . . 85 E6
Crossley Ct M4 . . . . 160 A1
Crossley Pk SK4 . . . . 111 F3
Crossley St
Little Lever BL3 . . . . 43 A3
Manchester M18 . . . . 165 B2
Milnrow OL16 . . . . 31 E6
Royton OL2 . . . . 48 E2
Shaw OL2 . . . . 149 C3
Stalybridge SK15 . . . . 85 F2
Crossmead Dr **3** M9 . . . . 64 E5
Crossmeadow **1** OL11 . . 30 A8
Crossmoor Cres SK6 . . . . 113 C1
Crossmoor Dr BL2 . . . . . . 148 B4
Crossmoor Gr SK6 . . . . . . 113 C2
Cross Ormrod St BL3 . . . . 145 A2
Cross Rd
Gatley SK8 . . . . 131 B7
Manchester M21 . . . . 109 B8
Cross Rise SK13 . . . . 116 E8
Cross St
4 Altrincham WA14 . . . . 119 D4
Ashton-u-L OL6 . . . . 166 A2
Aspull WN2 . . . . 38 B6
Atherton M46 . . . . 58 A4
Bolton BL1 . . . . 145 C4
Bolton, Eagley BL7 . . . . . . 25 A7

Cross St continued
3 Broadbottom SK14 . . . 115 A8
Bury BL9 . . . . 140 C2
Denton M34 . . . . 100 E5
Farnworth BL4 . . . . 60 D8
Glossop SK13 . . . . 104 C1
Golborne WA3 . . . . 90 A7
Hadfield SK13 . . . . 104 A5
Heywood OL10 . . . . 29 B2
Hindley WN2 . . . . 56 D5
Hollingworth SK14 . . . . . . 171 A4
Hyde SK14 . . . . 167 A2
Ince-in-M WN3 . . . . 55 E4
Kearsley BL4 . . . . 61 B6
Leigh WN7 . . . . 76 A4
Little Lever BL3 . . . . 43 B3
Manchester M2 . . . . 158 C1
Manchester, Old Trafford
M16 . . . . 162 A1
8 Middleton M24 . . . . 46 F1
Middleton M24 . . . . 64 F8
Milnrow OL16 . . . . 31 D7
4 Mossley OL5 . . . . 68 C2
Oldham, County End OL4 . . 68 A6
Oldham, Mumps OL4 . . . . . 67 B7
3 Oldham, Salem OL4 . . . 67 E6
Radcliffe M26 . . . . 44 B3
Ramsbottom BL0 . . . . 138 C2
Rochdale OL11 . . . . 30 C2
Sale M33 . . . . 108 B2
Salford M3 . . . . 158 B2
Stalybridge SK15 . . . . 86 D4
Standish WN6 . . . . 19 E1
Stretford M32 . . . . 96 D2
Swinton, Clifton Junction
M27 . . . . 62 D2
Swinton, Hazelhurst M28 . 79 C7
Tyldesley M29 . . . . 76 F8
Urmston M41 . . . . 95 C2
Whitefield M45 . . . . 44 E1
8 Wigan, Lamberhead Green
WN5 . . . . 54 B6
Wigan WN3 . . . . 150 A5
Cross The **1** SK13 . . . . . 104 A5
Crosswaite Rd SK2. . . . . . 124 E6
Crossway
Bramhall SK7. . . . . 132 C5
Droylsden M43 . . . . 100 A7
Manchester M20 . . . . 110 B3
Stockport SK2 . . . . 124 A4
Crossway Cl WN4 . . . . . . 73 E5
Crossway Ho **8** M20 . . . 110 B3
Crossway Rd M23 . . . . . . 107 F1
Crossways
Bramhall SK7. . . . . 123 C1
Oldham OL8 . . . . 67 A1
Cross Yd **7** WN1 . . . . 37 C1
Croston Av PR6 . . . . 21 A8
Croston Cl SK9 . . . . 137 C1
Croston Close Rd BL9,
OL12 . . . . 12 C4
Crostons Rd BL8 . . . . 140 A3
Croston St
Bolton BL3 . . . . 146 C4
Hindley WN2 . . . . 56 C6
Manchester M16 . . . . 162 A1
Croston Wlk M11 . . . . 160 B1
Croton St SK4 . . . . 110 E2
Croughton Cl **8** M11 . . . . 99 D7
Crowbank Wlk M40 . . . . . . 83 A5
Crowborough Cl BL6 . . . . . 22 F1
Crowborough Wlk **9**
M15 . . . . 162 C1
Crowbrook Gr **7** SK9 . . . 131 D1
Crowcroft Park Prim Sch
M12 . . . . 99 A3
Crowcroft Rd M12, M13 . . . 99 A3
Crowden Dr SK13 . . . . 104 B5
Crowden Rd M40 . . . . 65 B2
CROWHILL 84 F4
Crowhill Cotts OL7 . . . . . . 166 A4
Crow Hill N M40 . . . . 64 F7
Crowhill Rd OL7 . . . . 84 F4
Crow Hill S M40 . . . . 64 F6
Crow Hill View OL4 . . . . . . 67 F5
Crowhurst Dr WN1 . . . . . . 37 B3
Crowhurst Wlk **2** M23 . . 120 E7
Crow La BL0 . . . . 138 C2
Crowland Gdns SK8 . . . . . 132 B6
Crowland Rd
Bolton BL2 . . . . 25 C2
Wythenshawe M23 . . . . . . 120 F3
Crowley La OL4 . . . . 49 D1
Crowley Rd
Altrincham WA15 . . . . 120 B6
Manchester M9 . . . . 157 C4
Crown Bsns Ctr M35 . . . . . 83 F8
Crown Ct SK7. . . . . 124 D3
Crown Dr BL7 . . . . 9 D7
Cronweast SK OL11 . . . . . . 30 C7
Crown Fields CE WA12 . . . 89 B5
Crown Gdns
Edgworth BL7 . . . . 9 D6
Newton-le-W WA12 . . . . . . 89 B4
13 Rochdale OL16 . . . . . . 31 A5
Crown Gn WA13 . . . . 117 B4
Crown Gr WN7 . . . . 76 D6
Crowngreen Rd M30 . . . . . 79 E1
Crown Hill OL5 . . . . 86 D8
Crownhill Dr M43 . . . . 84 A2
Crown Ind Est
Altrincham WA14 . . . . 119 E7
Manchester M4 . . . . 159 C2
Crown La
Horwich BL6 . . . . 22 A4
Manchester M4 . . . . 159 A3
Crown Mews SK2 . . . . 124 C4

Crown Park Dr WA12 . . . . . 89 B5
Crown Passages WA15 . . 119 E2
Crown Point BL7 . . . . 9 D6
Crown Point Ave M40 . . . . 83 C5
Crown Point North Sh Pk
M34 . . . . 100 E4
Crown Rd OL10 . . . . 29 B2
Crown Royal Ind Pk SK1 170 C4
Crown Sq M3 . . . . 158 B1
Crown St
Ashton-u-L OL6 . . . . 166 B2
Atherton M46 . . . . 58 B3
Bolton BL1 . . . . 145 C3
Denton M34 . . . . 100 E4
Failsworth M35 . . . . 83 F8
20 Failsworth, Newton Heath
M40 . . . . 83 C5
Hindley WN2 . . . . 56 C6
Manchester M15 . . . . 162 E2
8 Middleton M24 . . . . 64 E8
Newton-le-W WA12 . . . . . . 89 A3
Rochdale OL16 . . . . 31 B5
Romiley SK6 . . . . 112 F4
Salford M3 . . . . 158 B2
Shaw OL2 . . . . 149 B3
Wigan WN3 . . . . 150 B2
Crow Orchard Rd WN6 . . . 19 A1
Crowsdale Pl SK2 . . . . 124 E4
Crowshaw Dr OL12 . . . . . . 14 E3
Crow's Nest BL2 . . . . 42 F5
Crow's Nest Cotts BL3 . . . 42 F5
Crowswood Dr SK15 . . . . . 86 D5
Crowther Ave M5 . . . . 161 A4
Crowther Ct
5 Rochdale OL15 . . . . . . 15 E4
Stalybridge SK15 . . . . 168 A3
Crowther Dr WN3 . . . . 54 E1
Crowther St
Littleborough OL15 . . . . . . 15 E4
Manchester M18 . . . . 99 E5
Rochdale OL16 . . . . 31 B4
Stockport SK1 . . . . 169 C1
Crowthorn Dr M23 . . . . . . 121 A2
Crowthorn Rd
Ashton-u-L OL7 . . . . 84 F1
Edgworth BL7 . . . . 10 B8
Reddish SK4 . . . . 111 D7
Crowton Ave M33 . . . . 107 D2
Crow Tree Ave **4** OL13 . . . 3 B8
Crow Trees La BL7 . . . . 9 C7
Crow Wood Rd
Bramhall SK7. . . . . 1 D6
Golborne WA3 . . . . 74 D1
Croxdale Cl OL7 . . . . 84 E5
Croxdale Wlk M9 . . . . 64 D5
Croxton Ave OL16 . . . . 31 B8
Croxton Cl
Marple SK6 . . . . 125 E5
Sale M33 . . . . 107 D2
Croxton Wlk
8 Horwich BL6 . . . . 22 B4
Manchester M13 . . . . 163 C2
Croyde Cl
Bolton BL3 . . . . 25 F3
Hindley WN2 . . . . 57 D3
Wythenshawe M22 . . . . . . 130 F7
Croydon Ave
Leigh WN7 . . . . 75 F8
Royton OL2 . . . . 48 C6
Trub OL11 . . . . 47 D8
Croydon Cl M5 . . . . 161 B4
Croydon Dr M40 . . . . 83 C4
Croydon Sq OL11 . . . . 47 D8
Crummock Cl BL3 . . . . 42 F3
Crummock Dr
Middleton M24 . . . . 46 E3
Sale M33 . . . . 107 D3
Crummock Rd
Farnworth BL4 . . . . 59 E7
Gatley SK8 . . . . 122 B3
CRUMPSALL 64 B1
Crumpsall La M8 . . . . 64 A1
Crumpsall Lane Prim Sch
M8 . . . . 64 A1
Crumpsall Metro Sta M8 . 64 A1
Crumpsall St BL1 . . . . 143 B3
Crumpsall Vale M9 . . . . . . 64 C2
Crumpsall Way M8 . . . . . . 64 B1
Crundale Rd **7** BL1 . . . . . 24 F6
Cruttenden Rd SK2 . . . . . . 124 B4
Cryer St M43 . . . . 84 C4
Crystal Cl WN2 . . . . 56 A3
Crystal Ho **8** M16 . . . . 97 D3
Cuba Ind Est BL0 . . . . 138 C4
Cube The M1 . . . . 83 A2
Cubley Rd M7 . . . . 155 B4
Cuckoo Gr M25 . . . . 63 B6
Cuckoo La
Bury, Fern Grove BL9 . . . . 141 C3
Prestwich M25 . . . . 63 B6
Cuddington Ave M20 . . . . 110 A7
Cuddington Cres SK3 . . . 170 A2
Cuddington Way **7** SK9 131 D5
Cudworth Rd M9 . . . . 64 A5
Cuerden Wlk M22 . . . . 121 E8
Culand St M12 . . . . 164 B2
Culbert Ave M20 . . . . 110 C3
Culcheth Ave SK6 . . . . 125 F6
CULCHETH 91 E3
Culcheth Ave M40 . . . . . . 157 D5
Culcheth Hall Dr WA3 . . . . 91 F4
Culcheth Hall Farm Barns
WA3 . . . . 91 F4
Culcheth High Sch WA3 . . 92 A3
Culcheth La M40 . . . . 83 C4
Culcheth Prim Sch WA3 . . 92 A3
Culcheth Rd WA14 . . . . . . 119 D3

Culcombe Wlk M13 . . . . . 163 C5
Culcross Ave WN3 . . . . 54 C4
Culford Cl M12 . . . . 164 B1
Culgaith Wlk M9 . . . . 157 A3
Culham Cl BL1 . . . . 143 A2
Cullen Cl WN2 . . . . 56 A8
Cullen Gr M9 . . . . 64 F3
Cullercoats Wlk **3** M12 . . 99 B3
Culmere Rd M22 . . . . 121 D1
Culmington Cl M15 . . . . . 162 B1
Culross Ave
Bolton BL3 . . . . 40 E6
Failsworth M40 . . . . 65 E1
Culvercliffe Wlk M3 . . . . . 162 B4
Culverden Wlk M6 . . . . 80 F6
Culver Rd SK3 . . . . 170 A1
Culvert St
Oldham OL4 . . . . 67 E8
Rochdale OL16 . . . . 31 B2
Wigan WN6 . . . . 37 A3
Culverwell Dr M5 . . . . 161 C4
Culzean Cl WN7 . . . . 76 C4
Cumberbatch Pl WN3 . . . . 55 F4
Cumber Cl SK9 . . . . 136 D4
Cumber Dr SK9 . . . . 136 D4
Cumber La SK9 . . . . 136 D4
Cumberland Ave
Brinnington SK5. . . . . 112 C4
Dukinfield SK16 . . . . 101 E8
Heywood OL10 . . . . 29 A2
Irlam M44 . . . . 105 C5
Swinton M27 . . . . 61 F2
Tyldesley M29 . . . . 58 F2
Cumberland Cl BL9 . . . . . . 44 E6
Cumberland Dr
Altrincham WA14 . . . . 128 B8
Royton OL, OL2 . . . . 48 D2
Cumberland Gr OL7 . . . . . 166 B4
Cumberland Rd
Atherton M46 . . . . 58 F4
Manchester M9 . . . . 64 D1
Partington M31 . . . . 105 E2
Rochdale OL11 . . . . 30 F2
Sale M33 . . . . 108 C2
Urmston M41 . . . . 95 C1
Cumberland St
Salford M7 . . . . 158 A4
2 Stalybridge SK15 . . . . . 85 F2
2 Wigan WN1 . . . . 37 E1
Cumbermere La M29 . . . . . 59 B2
Cumbrae Gdns M5 . . . . . . 154 B1
Cumbrae Rd M19 . . . . 99 C1
Cumbria Ct M25 . . . . 62 F1
Cumbrian Cl
4 Manchester M13 . . . . . 163 C2
Platt Bridge WN2 . . . . 56 B2
Shaw OL2 . . . . 48 F8
Cumbria Wlk M6 . . . . 81 B4
Cummings St OL8 . . . . 66 C2
Cunard Cl M13 . . . . 163 C2
Cundall Wlk M23 . . . . 108 F1
Cundey St BL1 . . . . 142 C1
Cundiff Ct M19 . . . . 99 C1
Cundiff Rd M21 . . . . 109 B6
Cundy St SK14 . . . . 167 B4
Cunliffe Ave
Newton-le-W WA12 . . . . . . 89 B5
Ramsbottom BL0 . . . . 11 A4
Cunliffe Brow BL1 . . . . . . 142 B1
Cunliffe Ct WN7 . . . . 75 A4
Cunliffe Dr
Sale M33 . . . . 108 C3
Shaw OL2 . . . . 49 D7
Cunliffe St
Dukinfield SK14 . . . . 101 C4
Leigh WN7 . . . . 75 C5
Radcliffe M26 . . . . 44 D2
Ramsbottom BL0 . . . . 138 C3
Stockport SK3 . . . . 123 C8
Cunningham Brook
Nature Reserve* BL5 . . . 57 C7
Cunningham Dr
Gatley SK8 . . . . 131 A8
Whitefield BL9 . . . . 45 B2
Cunningham Rd BL5 . . . . . 57 D7
Cunningham Way OL1 . . . 153 C4
Curate Ct SK1 . . . . 112 A1
Curate St SK1 . . . . 112 A1
Curlew Cl OL11 . . . . 29 F7
Curlew Dr M44 . . . . 94 A4
Curlew Rd OL4 . . . . 67 E4
Curlew Way SK13 . . . . 115 F8
Curlew Wlk M12 . . . . 164 E5
Currier La OL6 . . . . 85 D2
Curteis St BL6 . . . . 22 B4
Curteis Ct M28 . . . . 79 C7
Curtis Gr SK13 . . . . 104 A5
Curtis Rd
Reddish M19 . . . . 99 C1
Stockport SK4 . . . . 168 A2
Curtis St
Bolton BL3 . . . . 146 C2
Wigan WN5 . . . . 54 D6
Curven Edge BB4 . . . . 1 A7
Curzon Ave M14 . . . . 98 E4
Curzon Dr WA15 . . . . 120 B6
Curzon Gn SK2 . . . . 124 D7
Curzon Mews SK9 . . . . . . 137 A5
Curzon Rd
Ashton-u-L OL6 . . . . 85 D4
Bolton BL1 . . . . 144 C3
Gatley SK8 . . . . 131 B7
Poynton SK12 . . . . 133 E2
Rochdale OL11 . . . . 30 F2
3 Sale M33 . . . . 108 B5

Curzon Rd continued
Salford M7.................155 A3
Stockport SK2............124 D7
Stretford M32..............96 A4
Curzon St
Mossley OL5................68 C1
Oldham OL1................153 C3
Cutacre Cl M29...........59 B1
Cutacre La BL5...........59 D6
CUTGATE....................30 A8
Cutgate Cl M23..........108 E1
Cutgate Rd OL12.........14 B1
Cuthbert Ave M19........99 B2
Cuthbert Ho M16.........97 E2
Cuthbert Rd SK8........122 E6
Cuthbert St
Bolton BL3................146 B2
9 Bury BL8................27 C2
Chadderton OL9.........152 A4
Oldham OL9...............153 A3
4 Rochdale OL12........139 B4
Stockport SK1, SK2.....170 C3
Daisy Way SK6...........134 F7
Dakerwood Cl 3 M40...83 C5
Dakins Rd WN7............56 A5
Dakley St M11............165 C3
Dakota Ave M50..........96 F8
Dakota S M50..............96 F8
Dalbeatie Rise WN1.......37 F1
Dalbeattie St M9..........64 E1
Dalberg St M12............164 A3
Dalbury Dr M40..........156 C1
Dalby Ave M27.............79 E7
Dalby Gr SK1.............112 A1
Dalby Rd WN2..............57 B5
Dale Ave
Bramhall SK7..............132 F8
Eccles M30..................79 C3
Mossley OL5................68 E3
Dalebank M46...............58 C5
Dalebank Mews M27......61 D5
Dalebeck Cl M45...........63 C8
Dalebeck Wlk M45.........63 C8
Dale Brook Ave SK16...101 D6
Dalebrook Ct SK4........168 C1
Dalebrook Rd M33.......108 C1
Dalecrest WN5.............53 D1
Dale Fields OL3............50 F4
Daleford Sq M13.........163 C3
Dalegarth Ave BL1........40 C7
Dale Gr
Altrincham WA15.........119 F7
Ashton-u-L OL7............85 A5
Irlam M44..................105 E6
Leigh WN7...................75 C4
Dale Grove Prim Ctr
SK14......................167 C1
Dale Grove Special Sch
OL7.........................85 A5
Dalehead Cl M18...........99 F6
Dalehead Dr OL2...........49 D7
Dalehead Gr WN7...........75 C4
Dalehead Pl WA11.........71 B1
Dale Ho OL2..................49 C8
Dale House Fold SK12...134 A4
Dale La OL3..................50 F5
Dale Lee BL5.................58 A8
Dale Mills & Chyd Sch Ctr 1
OL16.........................31 F6
Dale Rd
Golborne WA3...............90 A7
Marple SK6................125 E7
Middleton M24.............47 B2
Dale St W
Ashton-u-L OL6...........166 A2
Horwich BL6................22 D2
Dales Ave
Manchester M8.............63 F2
Whitefield M45.............44 D1
Dalesbrook Cl 1 BL3....43 A4
DALES BROW...............79 E5
Dales Brow
Bolton BL1..................24 F6
Swinton M27................79 E6
Dales Brow Ave OL7......85 A5
Dalesfield Cres OL5.......68 E1
Dalesford Cl WN7...........91 C8
Dales Gr M28...............79 A7
Daleside Ave WN4.........73 A8
Dales La M45...............44 E1
Dalesman Cl M9...........157 C4
Dalesman Dr OL1..........49 D4
Dales Park Dr M27..........79 D6
Dale Sq OL2...................48 F4
Dale St
Ashton-u-L OL6...........86 A6
8 Bacup OL13..............3 C8
Bury BL8.....................27 C4
Farnworth BL4.............42 E1
Ince-in-M WN3..............55 F3
Leigh WN7....................75 C5
Manchester M1...........159 B1
Middleton M24..............65 B7
Milnrow OL16................31 F6
Ramsbottom BL0............1 C1
Rochdale OL16.............31 C7
Shaw OL2...................149 B2
Stalybridge SK15..........85 F1
Stockport SK3.............170 A3
Swinton M27.................79 E6
Westhoughton BL5.........38 D1
Whitefield M45..............44 E1
Dale Street Ind Est M24...44 A2
Daleswood Ave M45........44 D1
Dale View
Denton M34................113 A7
Hyde SK14..................113 D8

Daisyfield 9 BL6..........22 D1
Daisyfield Ct M22........121 C1
Daisyfield Ct BL3.........27 C1
Daisyfield Wlk 4 M28....60 D3
Daisy Hall Dr BL5..........57 E5
DAISY HILL..................57 F6
Daisyhill Cl M33..........108 E4
Daisyhill Cl BL5............57 E5
Daisy Hill Rd OL5...........68 D1
Daisy Hill Dr PR6..........21 A8
Daisy Hill Sta BL5..........57 F6
Daisy Mews SK3..........123 D4
Daisy Nook Ctry Pk ★ OL8..84 E6
Daisy Rd WN5................54 E6
Daisy St
Bolton BL3.................146 C4
9 Bury BL8..................27 C2
Chadderton OL9..........152 A4
Oldham OL9...............153 A3
4 Rochdale OL12........139 B4
Stockport SK1, SK2.....170 C3
Daisy Way SK6............134 F7

Dale View continued
Littleborough OL15.........15 F2
Mottram in L SK14.......103 A3
Newton-le-W WA12........89 E4
Dalham Ave M9.............65 A2
Dalkeith Ave SK5.........111 F7
Dalkeith Gr BL3.............40 F5
Dalkeith Rd
Hindley WN2................57 A5
Reddish SK5...............111 F7
Dalkeith Sq OL10..........29 A1
Dallas Ct M50...............96 E8
Dalley Ave M7.............158 A4
Dallimore Rd M23........120 E6
Dalmahoy Cl M40..........83 C8
Dalmain Cl M8.............155 C2
Dalmeny Terr OL11.........30 F4
Dalmorton Rd M21.......109 D8
Dalny St M19................99 B1
Dalry Wlk 1 M23........121 A5
Dalston Ave M35............84 B8
Dalston Dr
Billinge WA11................71 B1
Bramhall SK7..............132 C5
Manchester M20..........110 C2
Dalston Gr WN3.............54 D3
Dalton Ave
Manchester M14............98 A2
Milnrow OL16................31 D7
Stretford M32................96 A4
Whitefield M45..............63 A7
Dalton Cl
Milnrow OL16................31 D7
Ramsbottom BL0............11 A4
Wigan WN5..................54 B7
Dalton Dr
Pendlebury M27............80 D7
Wigan WN3..................57 E8
Dalton Fold BL5............57 F8
Dalton Gdns M41...........95 B3
Dalton Gr
Ashton-in-M WN4..........73 A4
Stockport SK4.............168 C4
Milnrow OL16...............31 D7
Dalton Rd
Manchester M9...............64 D5
Middleton M24..............64 A7
Dalton St
Bury BL8.....................27 B2
Chadderton OL9..........152 B3
Eccles M30...................79 D3
Failsworth M35.............83 E8
Manchester M4, M40.....159 B4
Oldham OL1.................67 A7
Sale M33....................108 C6
Daltry St OL1................67 A8
Dalveen Ave M41..........95 C4
Dalveen Dr WA15.........119 F7
Dalwood Cl M12.............56 F4
Dalymount Cl BL2..........25 B2
Damask Ave M3...........158 A2
Dame Hollow SK8.........131 D7
Damery Ct SK7.............132 E8
Damery Rd SK7............132 E8
Dame St OL9...............153 A4
Dam Head Dr M9...........64 E3
Dam Head La WA3........105 A5
Damian Dr WA12............89 A5
Damien St M12...............99 B2
Dam La
Ashton-in-M WN4...........73 A4
Hollinfare WA3............105 A4
Dams Head Fold BL5......39 F1
Damson Gn M24............65 D8
Damson Wlk M31..........105 D3
Dan Bank SK6.............125 C6
Danbury Wlk M23........120 D8
Danby Cl SK14.............167 C4
Danby Ct 6 OL1..........153 B4
Danby Pl SK14............167 C4
Danby Rd
Bolton BL3.................147 B3
Hyde SK14.................167 C4
Danby Wlk M9..............64 E1
Dane Ave
Cheadle SK3...............123 A8
Partington M31...........105 F4
DANEBANK.................135 E5
DANE BANK...............100 B2
Dane Bank M24............65 B7
Dane Bank Dr SK12.....135 D6
Danebank Mews M34...100 B2
Dane Bank Prim Sch
SK5.........................100 A2
Danebridge Cl BL4........60 E8
Danebury Cl 10 WN2....56 D4
Dane Cl SK7...............123 D3
Danecroft BL3..............43 C3
Dane Dr SK9................37 D6
Danefield Cl SK8..........131 D8
Danefield Rd M33........108 C6
Dane Hill Cl SK12........135 D5
Dane Ho 4 M33..........108 C4
Daneholme Rd M19......110 E5
Dane Mews M33..........108 B4
Dane Rd
Reddish M34...............100 A2
Sale M33...................108 D5
Dane Road Metro Sta
M33........................108 C6
Danes Ave WN2.............56 E6
Danes Brook Cl WN2......56 E6
Danesbury Cl WN5..........71 E4
Danesbury Rd BL2..........25 B4
Danesbury Rise SK8.....122 D5
Danes Gn WN2..............56 E7
Daneshill M25...............63 B6

Danesmoor Dr BL9........141 B4
Danesmoor Rd M20......110 B5
Danes Rd M14...............98 D2
Dane St
Bolton BL3.................146 C4
Manchester M11...........99 E7
Mossley OL5.................68 D3
6 Oldham OL4..............67 C7
Rochdale OL11/OL12....139 B3
Daneswood
Adlington PR7................20 F8
Manchester M25............63 D2
Pendlebury M27............80 C6
Wigan WN1....................37 B3
Danesway Ct BL1..........143 A2
Danesway Ave
Manchester M9...............64 F4
Whitworth OL12.............14 C8
Daneswood Cl OL12......14 C8
Daneswood Fold OL12...14 C8
Danett Cl M12..............165 B2
Dane Wlk SK5..............169 C4
Dan Fold 5 OL1...........153 B3
Danforth Gr M19..........111 B8
DANGEROUS CORNER
Hindley........................57 D2
Standish......................18 C2
Daniel Adamson Ave
M31........................105 D3
Daniel Adamson Rd
Salford M50................154 A1
Stretford M50................96 D8
Daniel Ct M31.............105 F4
Daniel Fold OL12...........14 B2
Daniel's La SK1............169 C2
Daniel St
Hazel Grove SK7..........124 E2
Heywood OL10..............29 B2
Oldham OL11................67 C8
Royton OL2....................49 A3
Whitworth OL12...............4 D2
Daniel Street Ind Est OL12..4 D2
Danisher La OL8............84 F8
Dannywood Cl SK14.....113 C8
Danson St M40............160 B3
Dantall Ave M9.............65 A3
Dante Cl M6, M30..........80 A4
Danty St SK16.............166 B1
Dantzic St M4..............159 A3
Danube The 9 M15.....162 C3
Danvers Cl M34............101 B1
Darbishire St BL1..........25 A1
Darby La WN2................56 D6
Darby Rd M44..............106 A6
Darbyshire Cl BL1........144 C4
Darbyshire Ho WA15...120 C7
Darbyshire St M26.........44 A3
Darbyshire Wlk 1 M26...44 B2
DARCY LEVER................42 D5
Darcy St BL2................148 C1
Darcy Wlk M14..............98 A4
Darden Cl SK4..............110 E3
Darell Wlk M8..............156 B2
Daresbury Ave
Altrincham WA15..........119 C5
Urmston M41................94 F4
Daresbury Cl
Sale M33....................108 F3
Stockport SK3.............170 A1
4 Wilmslow SK9...........137 C8
Daresbury Rd M21..........96 F1
Daresbury St M8..........156 A3
Dargai St M11................83 D1
Dargle Rd M33.............108 B6
Darian Ave M22...........130 D8
Daric Cl WN7.................75 C1
Dark La
Blackrod BL6.................21 B3
Delph OL3....................50 E6
Manchester M12...........164 A4
Mossley OL5.................68 D2
Romiley SK6................112 D3
Uppermill OL3...............69 A8
Darlbeck Wlk M23........109 C5
Darley Ave
Eccles M30...................95 C8
Farnworth BL4...............42 E1
Gatley SK8.................122 B5
Manchester M21..........109 C5
Darley Ho 6 M5...........154 B1
Darley Rd
Hazel Grove SK7..........133 F7
Manchester M16.............97 C3
Rochdale OL11..............30 F4
Wigan WN3....................55 B3
Darley St
Bolton BL1.................143 A1
Farnworth BL4...............60 E8
Horwich BL6..................22 B5
Manchester M11...........160 C1
Sale M33...................108 B4
Stretford M32................96 E4
Darley Terr 4 BL1.......143 A1
Darlington Cl BL8..........27 B5
Darlington Rd
Manchester M20...........110 A6
Rochdale OL11..............30 F7
Darlington St
Ince-in-M WN3..............56 A7
Tyldesley M29................59 A1
Wigan WN1.................151 A3
Darliston Ave M9...........64 A5
Darlton Wlk 8 M9........157 B4
Darnall Ave M20..........110 A8
Darnbrook Dr 2 M22...121 B1
Darncombe Cl M16.........97 F4

Darnhall St WN3............55 F4
DARN HILL....................28 E2
Darnley Ave M28...........60 C1
Darnley St M16..............97 D4
Darnton Gdns OL6..........85 E3
Darnton Rd OL6, SK15....85 E3
Darran Ave WN3.............54 F3
Darras Rd M18................99 C3
Dart Cl OL9....................65 F8
Dartford Ave
Brinnington SK5...........112 B6
Eccles M30....................79 B2
Dartford Cl M12............164 A2
Dartford Rd M41.............95 C1
Dartington Cl
Altrincham M23............120 D6
Stockport SK7..............123 F2
Dartington Rd WN2.........55 F3
Dartmouth Cl OL8..........66 F4
Dartmouth Cres SK5......112 C5
Dartmouth Rd
Manchester M21...........109 C8
Whitefield M45...............63 A7
Dartnall Cl SK12............135 A6
Darton Ave M40............160 B3
Darul-Uloom Islamic Coll
BL8.............................10 F4
Darvel Ave WN4.............72 C4
Darwell Ave M30............95 C8
Darwen Dr 3 WN2..........56 A2
Darwen Rd BL7..............25 A7
Darwen St M16.............161 C1
Darwin Gr SK7..............132 E6
Darwin St
Ashton-u-L OL7............166 A2
Bolton BL1..................143 A2
Dukinfield SK14............102 A5
Oldham OL4...................67 C5
Dashwood Rd M25..........62 F5
Dashwood Wlk M12......165 A2
Datchett Terr OL11..........30 F4
DAUBHILL....................146 C3
Dauntesy Ave M27.........80 D7
Davehall Ave SK9...........137 A2
Davenfield Gr M20.........110 B3
Davenfield Ho 7 M20....110 B3
Davenfield Rd 2 M20....110 B3
Davenham Rd
Handforth SK9.............131 D4
Reddish SK5..................99 F2
Sale M33....................107 F6
Davenhill Rd M19.........111 A8
DAVENPORT................123 E4
Davenport Ave
Manchester M20...........110 B7
Radcliffe M26................43 F6
Wilmslow SK9..............136 E4
Davenport Dr SK6.........113 B6
Davenport Fold BL2.......26 A3
Davenport Fold Rd BL2...26 A4
Davenport Gdns 8 BL1..145 B2
DAVENPORT GREEN
Hale.........................120 F2
Wilmslow...................119 C7
Davenport La WA14......119 C7
Davenport Lo SK3.........170 C1
DAVENPORT PARK.......124 A5
Davenport Park Rd SK2..124 A5
Davenport Rd SK7........124 D2
Davenport St
2 Ashton-u-L M34.......100 E8
Bolton BL1.................145 E4
Droylsden M43..............83 E2
Davenport Sta M27......170 C1
Daventry Rd
Manchester M21...........109 D8
Rochdale OL11..............30 F3
Daveyhulme St OL12......15 B1
Davey La SK9................137 B2
Daveylands
Urmston M41................94 F5
Wilmslow SK9.............137 D7
David Brow BL3............146 A2
David Cl M34.................100 A4
David Cuthbert Bsns Ctr
M11........................165 C3
David Lewis Cl OL16......31 C6
David Mews M14...........110 C7
David Pegg Wlk M40.......83 B5
David's Farm Cl M24......65 C7
Davids La OL4................67 F7
Davidson Dr M24............65 B6
Davidson Wlk WN5..........54 A7
David's Rd M43..............83 E2
David St
Bacup OL13.....................3 D8
Bury BL8.......................27 C4
Denton M34.................101 A2
2 Oldham OL1.............153 B2
Reddish SK5................111 E8
14 Rochdale OL12........14 F1
Davies Ave
Gatley SK8..................131 B6
Newton-le-W WA12........89 C4
Davies Cl SK6...............113 B2
Davies Rd
Partington M31............106 A3
Romiley SK6................112 D3
Davies Sq M14...............98 A4
Davies St
Ashton-u-L OL7..............84 F1
Kearsley BL4.................61 A7
Oldham OL1................153 A4
Platt Bridge WN2...........56 B3
Davis St M30..................79 F1
Davy Ave M27................62 D2
DAVYHULME..................95 B4

Curzon Rd continued
Salford M7.................155 A3
Stockport SK2............124 D7
Stretford M32..............96 A4

D

Daccamill Dr M27..........79 F6
Dacre Ave M16..............97 B2
Dacre Cl M24.................46 B1
Dacre Rd OL11..............30 E4
DACRES.......................68 F4
Dacres Ave OL3.............68 F4
Dacres Dr OL3...............68 F4
Dacres Rd OL3..............68 F4
Daffodil Cl
Haslingden BB4................1 A8
Rochdale OL12..............14 E3
Daffodil Rd BL4.............42 A1
Daffodil St BL1..............24 F5
Dagenham Rd M14.........98 C4
Dagenham Road Ind Est 19
M14.........................98 C3
Dagmar St M28.............60 C4
Dagnall Ave M21..........109 B6
Dahlia Cl
Manchester M19...........110 F6
Rochdale OL12..............14 D3
Dailton Rd WN8.............53 A7
Daimler St M8..............156 B2
Dain Cl SK16...............101 D8
Daine Ave M23.............109 B1
Dainton St M12............164 A3
Daintry Cl M15.............162 C2
Daintry Rd OL9.............152 C3
Dairybrook Gr 2 SK9....131 C1
Dairydale Cl 3 M44........94 B3
Dairyground Rd SK7.....132 F7
Dairyhouse La WA14.....119 B7
Dairy House La SK7......132 B4
Dairy House Rd SK7......132 B5
Dairy House Small Holdings
SK7..........................132 B4
Dairy St OL9................152 B3
Daisy Ave
Farnworth BL4...............42 A1
Manchester M13.............98 E4
Newton-le-W WA12.........89 C2
Daisy Bank
Failsworth M40...............83 D5
Hyde SK14..................113 C8
Daisy Bank Ave M27......80 C6
Daisybank Cl WN2..........56 D5
Daisy Bank Hall M40......83 D5
Daisy Bank La SK8........122 A1
Daisy Bank Mill Cl WA3...91 E3
Daisy Bank Rd M14.........98 D4
Daisybank Villas M14....98 D4

Davyhulme Circ M41 .... 95 C4
Davyhulme Prim Sch M41 95 D3
Davyhulme Rd
  Stretford M32 .... 96 C3
  Urmston, Calder Bank M41 . 94 F4
  Urmston, Davyhulme M41. . 95 B4
Davy Rd WN2 .... 74 C7
Davy St M40 .... 159 B4
Daw Bank SK3 .... 169 B1
Dawber Delph WN6 ...... 35 D8
Dawber St WN4 .... 73 D4
Dawley Cl
  Ashton-in-M WN4 ...... 73 A3
  Bolton BL3 .... 144 C2
Dawlish Ave
  Brinnington SK5........ 112 C5
  Chadderton OL9........ 47 F1
  Cheadle SK8 .... 131 F7
  Droylsden M43......... 83 E1
Dawlish Cl
  Bramhall SK7.......... 132 E7
  Hattersley SK14........ 102 E3
  Hollinfare WA3 .... 105 B3
Dawlish Rd
  Manchester M21........ 109 C8
  Sale M33 .... 107 E5
Dawlish Way WA3........ 105 B1
Dawn St OL2............. 149 B2
Dawnwood Sq WN5...... 36 C2
Dawson Ave M6 .... 37 A3
Dawson La BL1 .... 145 B3
Dawson Rd
  Altrincham WA14....... 119 D8
  Gatley SK8............. 131 D8
Dawson St
  Atherton M46........... 58 C3
  Bury BL9 .... 141 A4
  Heywood OL10.......... 29 C2
  Hyde SK14 .... 167 B1
  Mancheste M3.......... 158 C2
  Manchesterr, St George's M1,
    M15................. 162 F8
  Oldham, Clarksfield OL4. 67 D6
  Oldham, Salem OL4..... 67 E5
  Pendlebury M27........ 80 A8
  Rochdale OL12......... 139 C4
  Stockport SK1 .... 112 B3
Day Dr M35............... 83 F6
Dayfield WN8.............. 53 B7
Day Gr SK14 .... 103 A3
Daylesford Cl SK8...... 122 D4
Daylesford Cres SK8 .... 122 D4
Daylesford Rd SK8 ..... 122 D4
Deacon Ave M27......... 61 E1
Deacon Cl WA14 .... 119 B1
Deacons Cl SK1......... 112 A1
Deacons Cres BL8 .... 27 A5
Deacons Dr M6.......... 80 D6
Deacon St OL16......... 15 B1
Deacon Trad Est WA12 . 89 A2
Deakins Bsns Pk BL7... 8 D1
Deakins Mill Way BL7 .. 8 D1
Deakin St WN3 .... 151 B1
Deal Ave SK5 .... 112 B6
Deal Cl M40 .... 83 D5
Dealey Rd BL3........... 146 A4
Deal Sq SK14 .... 167 B2
Deal St
  Bolton BL3............. 147 C3
  Bury BL9 .... 141 B2
  Hyde SK14............. 167 B2
  Salford M3............. 158 B2
Deal Wlk OL9 .... 152 A2
Dean Ave
  Failsworth M40......... 83 B6
  Manchester M16........ 97 B3
Deanbank Ave 2 M19.. 110 F8
Dean Bank Dr OL16..... 31 B6
Dean Bradley Ct M40.. 157 B2
Dean Brook Cl M40 ..... 83 B7
Dean Cl
  Billinge WN5 .... 71 D3
  Edenfield BL0........... 1 D3
  Farnworth BL4 .... 59 F8
  Handforth SK9.......... 131 C1
  Partington M31........ 105 F4
  Up Holland WN8 .... 53 C7
  Whitefield M45......... 62 D7
Dean Cres WN5.......... 54 B8
Dean Ct
  Bolton BL1............. 148 A4
  1 Dukinfield SK16..... 166 B1
  Golborne WA3 .... 90 A7
  Manchester M15....... 162 A2
  Rochdale OL11......... 30 F4
Dean Dr
  Altrincham WA14....... 119 B1
  Handforth SK9......... 131 D2
DEANE 40 F4
Deane Ave
  Altrincham WA15....... 120 A5
  Bolton BL3............. 144 B1
  Cheadle SK8 .... 123 B6
Deane Church La BL3 . 146 B4
Deane Rd BL3 .... 145 A2
Deanery CE High Sch & Sixth
  Form Coll The WN1 ... 150 B8
Deanery Ct
  Manchester M8 .... 156 A3
  Wigan WN1 .... 150 B4
Deanery Gdns M7...... 155 A4
Deanery Way SK1...... 169 C2
Deane Wlk BL3.......... 145 B2
Dean Hall M14 .... 98 D4
Dean Head La OL3 ..... 51 D7
Dean La
  Failsworth M40 .... 83 B6

Dean La continued
  Hazel Grove SK7....... 133 E8
Dean Mdw WA12......... 89 C4
Dean Moor Rd SK7..... 124 A1
Dean Oaks Prim Sch
  SK9................... 131 E1
Dean Rd
  Golborne WA3 .... 90 A7
  Handforth SK9......... 131 E3
  Haslingden BB4........ 1 B8
  Irlam M44 .... 105 E6
  Reddish M18........... 99 E4
  Salford M3............. 158 B3
Dean Row Ct 9 SK9 . 131 D1
Dean Row Rd SK9...... 137 F8
Deanroyd Rd OL14 ...... 6 B7
DEANS................... 79 E8
Deanscourt Ave M27.... 79 E8
Deans CP Sch The M27.. 79 E8
Deansgate
  Bolton BL1............. 145 B3
  Hindley WN2 .... 56 E6
  Manchester M2, M3 ... 158 C1
  Manchester M3 .... 162 B3
  Radcliffe M26 .... 44 B3
Deansgate La WA14.... 119 E7
Deansgate Mews M3... 162 B4
Deansgate Sta M3 ..... 162 B4
Deansgate The 6 M4 . 110 C8
Deansgreave Rd OL13 ... 4 B7
Deanshut Rd OL8 .... 67 A2
Deans Rd M27 .... 79 E7
Deans Road Ind Est M27 . 79 F7
Dean St
  Ashton-u-L OL6 .... 166 A3
  Failsworth M35 .... 83 E7
  Hazel Grove SK7....... 125 A3
  Manchester M19........ 99 B1
  Mossley SK15 .... 68 B1
  Radcliffe M26 .... 43 F3
  Rochdale OL16......... 15 B1
  Stalybridge SK15....... 86 A1
Deansway M27.......... 79 E8
Deanswood Dr M9 ...... 64 A5
Dean Terr M14 .... 67 C2
Dean Villas OL14........ 6 B7
Deanwater Cl M13 ..... 163 B3
Deanwater Ct
  Gatley SK8............. 131 D7
  Stretford M32.......... 108 C8
Deanway
  Handforth SK9......... 131 C1
  Manchester M40........ 83 A8
  Urmston M41........... 94 D2
Deanway Trad Est SK9. 131 D3
Dearden Ave M38....... 60 A5
Dearden Clough BL0 .... 1 E2
Dearden Fold BL0....... 1 E2
Deardens Fold BL8...... 27 C1
Dearden St
  Littleborough OL15 ..... 16 B6
  Little Lever BL3 .... 43 A4
  Manchester M15....... 162 B2
  12 Stalybridge SK15... 86 A2
Dearden Way WN8...... 53 A7
Dearmans Pl M3........ 158 B2
Dearnaley Way
  Chadderton OL9....... 152 B1
  Oldham OL9............ 66 B4
Dearncamme Cl BL2 ... 25 B5
Dearne Dr M32 .... 96 E2
DEARNLEY 15 E4
Dearnley Cl OL15 ...... 15 E4
DEBDALE 99 F4
Debdale Ave M18 ...... 99 F4
Debdale La
  Reddish M18........... 99 F4
  Tyldesley M29 .... 76 F4
Debdale Outdoor Ctr M18 99 E5
Deben Cl WN6........... 19 D1
Debenham Ave M40.... 83 C4
Debenham Rd M32..... 96 A2
De Brook Cl M41....... 94 E1
Dee Ave WA15......... 120 D5
Dee Dr BL4.............. 61 B5
Deepcar St M19........ 99 A2
Deepdale
  Leigh WN7.............. 76 C3
  Oldham OL4............ 67 D6
Deepdale Ave
  Billinge WN5 .... 71 C1
  Manchester M20........ 110 A8
  Rochdale OL16......... 31 C2
  Royton OL2 .... 48 C8
Deepdale Cl 1 SK5.... 100 A1
Deepdale Ct M9 .... 65 B3
Deepdale Dr M27....... 80 D7
Deepdale Rd BL2....... 25 F1
Deepdene St M12...... 164 C2
Deeping Ave M16....... 97 D2
Deep La
  Littleborough OL15 ..... 16 C1
  Shaw OL16, OL16 ...... 32 B8
Deeplish Com Prim Sch 20
  OL11................. 31 A5
Deeplish Rd OL11...... 139 C1
Deeplish St OL11....... 139 C1
Deeply Vale La WN3, OL11 . 12 C2
Deeracre Ave SK2...... 124 C6
Deerfold Dr M18....... 99 D5
Deerhurst Dr M8........ 155 C2
Deeroak Cl M18........ 165 B2

Deerpark Rd M16 .... 97 E3
Deerwood Gdns WN1... 37 B7
Deerwood Vale SK14... 102 E1
Defence St 7 BL3...... 145 A2
Defiance St M46......... 58 C3
Deganwy Gr SK5....... 111 F5
Degas Cl M7............ 81 B8
Deighton Ave M20 ..... 110 A8
Deighton Cl WN6....... 53 E6
Delacourt Rd M14...... 110 B8
Delafield Ave M12...... 99 A2
Delaford Ave M28....... 78 E7
Delaford Cl SK3........ 123 E4
Delaford Wlk M40...... 83 D4
Delahayes La WA15.... 120 B5
Delahays Dr WA15..... 120 B2
Delahays Range M38... 99 F4
Delahays Rd WA15..... 120 B2
Delaine Rd M20........ 110 C6
Delamere Ave
  Golborne WA3 .... 90 E6
  Sale M33 .... 108 E3
  Salford M6............. 80 C6
  Shaw OL2.............. 49 D8
  Stretford M32.......... 96 D2
  Whitefield M45......... 62 E8
Delamere Cl
  Hazel Grove SK7....... 125 A3
  Mossley SK15 .... 86 E6
  Romiley SK6........... 113 C5
Delamere Gdns BL1.... 143 A3
Delamere Ho 8 M14... 110 C8
Delamere La SK7....... 124 D2
Delamere Rd
  Gatley SK8............. 122 B5
  Handforth SK9......... 131 E4
  Hazel Grove SK7....... 125 A3
  Manchester M19........ 99 B1
  Reddish M34........... 100 B2
  Rochdale OL16......... 31 C4
  Stockport SK2 .... 124 B4
  Urmston M41........... 94 D2
Delamere Sch M41..... 94 D2
Delamere St
  Ashton-u-L OL6 .... 166 B2
  Bury BL9 .... 28 A5
  Droylsden M11......... 99 F7
  6 Oldham OL8......... 67 B5
Delamere Way WN8..... 53 A7
Delamere Rd M14...... 119 C3
Delaunays Rd
  Manchester M8 .... 64 B2
  Sale M33 .... 107 F4
Delaware Wlk M9...... 157 A3
Delbooth Ave M41...... 94 E4
Delegarte St WN3...... 151 B2
Delfhaven Ct WN6..... 37 A7
Delft Wlk M6............ 81 A5
Delfur Rd SK7.......... 132 F7
Delhi Rd M44 .... 105 F8
Dellar St OL12.......... 14 C1
Dell Ave
  Pendlebury M27........ 80 D7
  Wigan WN6 .... 36 E3
Dell Cl OL4.............. 67 F5
Dellcot Cl
  Manchester M25....... 63 D2
  Salford M6............. 80 B5
Dellcot La M28 .... 78 F5
Dell Gdns OL12......... 14 B2
Dellhide Cl OL4......... 68 A6
Dell Mdw OL12.......... 14 B2
Dell Rd OL12............ 14 B2
Dell Side SK6........... 112 E3
Dellside Cl WN4........ 72 D5
Dellside Gr M28........ 60 E3
Dell Side Way OL12 ... 14 C2
Dell St BL2.............. 25 C5
Dell The
  Appley Bridge WN6 ... 35 D7
  Bolton BL2............. 25 C5
Delph Ave BL7.......... 8 D3
Delph Brook Way BL7 .. 8 D2
Delph Gr WN7.......... 57 D1
Delph Hill BL1.......... 23 E2
Delph Hill Cl BL1....... 23 E2
Delph La
  Ainsworth BL2.......... 26 C1
  Delph OL3.............. 50 F5
Delph Lodge OL3....... 50 F3
Delph Mdw Gdns WN5.. 71 D4
Delph New Rd OL3..... 50 F3
Delph Prim Sch OL3 .. 50 F4
Delph Rd OL3........... 50 C8
Delphside Cl WN5...... 53 D5
Delphside Rd WN5..... 53 D5
Delph St
  Bolton BL3............. 145 A1
  Milnrow OL16.......... 31 F6
  Wigan WN6 .... 37 B1
Delside Ave M40....... 83 A8
Delta Cl OL2............ 48 D2
Delta Ho SK6........... 113 A2
Delta Wlk M40.......... 83 A7
Delvino Wlk M14....... 98 A3
Delwood Gdns M22.... 121 D3
De-Massey Cl SK6..... 113 A4
Demesne Cl SK15...... 86 C1
Demesne Cres SK15... 86 C1
Demesne Dr SK15 ..... 86 C1
Demesne Rd M16 ...... 97 E2
Demmings Rd SK8..... 122 F5

Demmings Road Ind Est
  SK8 .... 122 F5
Dempsey Dr BL9........ 45 B2
Denbigh Cl SK7 .... 133 C8
Denbigh Dr OL2......... 48 F6
Denbigh Gr M46........ 58 C5
Denbigh Pl M5 .... 81 A2
Denbigh Rd
  Bolton BL2............. 148 B1
  Denton M34........... 100 F1
  Swinton M27.......... 62 B2
Denbigh St
  Mossley OL5 .... 86 D8
  Oldham OL8............ 66 F3
  Stockport SK4 .... 169 A3
Denbigh Wlk M15...... 162 A3
Denbury Dr WA14...... 119 B5
Denbury Gn SK7........ 124 A1
Denbury Wlk M9....... 156 C2
Denbydale Way OL2.... 48 C4
Denby La SK4.......... 169 A4
Denby Rd SK16......... 101 C7
Dencombe St M12, M13.. 98 F4
Dene Bank BL2......... 25 C5
Dene Brow M34........ 113 B8
Dene Ct SK4............ 168 C2
Dene Dr M24........... 64 F7
Denefield Cl SK6....... 114 B1
Denefield Pl M30....... 79 F3
Deneford Rd M20...... 110 A2
Dene Hollow SK5....... 100 A1
Denehurst Rd OL11.... 30 C8
Denehurst St M12..... 164 C2
Dene Manor M20....... 110 A2
Dene Pk M20........... 110 A3
Dene Rd M20........... 110 A2
Deneside Cres SK7..... 124 F3
Deneside 6 M9......... 157 B4
Deneside Wlk 7 M9... 75 B4
Denes The 2 SK5..... 100 A1
Denesway M33......... 107 E3
Deneway
  Bramhall SK7........... 132 C7
  High Lane SK6......... 134 F8
  Stockport SK4 .... 168 C2
Deneway Cl SK4........ 168 C2
Deneway Mews SK4... 168 C2
Denewell Ave M13..... 164 A2
Denewell Cl M13....... 164 A2
Denewood Ct 3 SK9.. 137 A6
Denford Cl WN3........ 54 F3
Denham Cl BL1......... 25 A5
Denham Dr
  Bramhall SK7........... 132 D7
  Irlam M44 .... 94 A1
  Wigan WN3 .... 55 A3
Denham St
  Manchester M13....... 98 D4
  Radcliffe M26 .... 43 F6
Den Hill Dr OL4........ 67 F6
Denhill Rd M15......... 97 F4
Denholme 1 WN8...... 53 A7
Denholme Rd OL11.... 30 F4
Denholm Rd M20....... 122 C8
Denhurst Rd OL15..... 16 B6
Denis Ave M16......... 97 E2
Denison Ct M14........ 98 C3
Denison Rd SK4........ 111 B5
Denison Rd
  Manchester M14, M15.. 98 A4
  Sale M33 .... 108 B6
Denmark Rd
  Altrincham WA14....... 119 D4
  Chadderton OL9....... 152 C4
  Rochdale OL16......... 31 A8
Denmark Way OL9 ..... 152 C4
Denmore Rd M40...... 65 D3
Denning Pl M27........ 61 F2
Dennington Dr M41.... 95 C4
Dennis St OL5.......... 68 C2
Dennison Ave M20..... 110 B7
Dennison Rd SK8...... 132 B8
Denshaw Ave M34..... 100 D5
Denshaw Cl M19....... 110 E3
Denshaw Fold OL3..... 33 D5
Denshaw Rd OL3....... 50 D5
Densmore St 6 M35.. 83 F7
Denson Rd WA15...... 120 B8
Denstone Ave
  Eccles M30............. 79 E3
  Sale M33 .... 107 E3
  Urmston M41........... 95 C3
Denstone Cres BL2.... 25 D2
Denstone Rd
  Reddish SK5........... 99 F1
  Salford M6............. 80 D5
  Urmston M41........... 95 C3
Denstone Wlk 15 M9.. 64 E3
Dental Hospl M15..... 163 A2
Dent Cl SK5............ 112 C6
Dentdale Cl BL1........ 143 D1
Dentdale Wlk M22..... 130 C8
DENTON 100 D3
Denton Bsns Pk M34.. 100 D3
Denton Ct M34......... 100 E5
Denton Gr WN5......... 54 B8

Denton OL9.............. 152 A1
Denton Pools M34..... 100 E3
Denton Rd
  Denton M34........... 100 E6
  Little Lever BL2 .... 43 B6
Denton St
  Bury BL9 .... 140 C4
  Heywood OL10.......... 29 C1
  7 Rochdale OL12..... 14 F1
Denton Sta M34........ 100 D3
Denton West End Prim Sch
  M34.................. 100 A3
Denver Ave M40........ 160 A3
Denver Dr 4 WA15.... 120 A6
Denver Rd OL11........ 30 F4
Denville Cres M22..... 121 E3
Denyer Terr 22 SK16.. 166 B1
Denzell Gdns M14..... 119 A3
Depleach Rd SK8...... 122 D5
Deptford Ave M23..... 121 A3
De Quincey Cl WA14 . 107 D1
De Quincey Rd WA14 . 107 D1
Deramore Cl OL6...... 85 E3
Deramore St M14...... 98 B3
Derby Ave M5.......... 154 B2
Derby Cl
  Irlam M44 .... 105 C5
  Newton-le-W WA12.... 89 B3
Derby Ct
  Bury BL9 .... 27 F5
  Oldham OL9............ 152 C1
  Sale M33 .... 108 C3
Derby Gr 2 M19....... 99 B1
Derby High Sch The BL9.. 44 D8
Derby Ho
  Manchester M13....... 163 B3
  Wigan WN1 .... 151 A4
Derby Pk M6............ 21 A8
Derby Range SK4 ..... 168 B4
Derby Rd
  Ashton-u-L OL6....... 85 D3
  Golborne WA3 .... 90 C8
  Hyde SK14 .... 167 B4
  Kearsley BL4........... 61 A8
  Manchester M14....... 110 D7
  New Mills SK22 .... 127 D1
  Prestwich M25, M45 .. 63 A6
  Sale M33 .... 107 E6
  Salford M5............. 154 D4
  Stockport, Heaton Moor
    SK4................. 168 C4
  Urmston M41........... 95 D3
Derbyshire Ave M32... 96 B3
Derbyshire Cres M32.. 96 B3
Derbyshire Gn 3 M32. 96 D2
Derbyshire Gr M32.... 96 C2
Derbyshire La M32.... 96 C2
Derbyshire Level SK13 . 116 F6
Derbyshire Rd
  Failsworth M40........ 83 D4
  Partington M31........ 105 C2
  Poynton SK12.......... 134 D5
  Sale M33 .... 108 D2
  Wigan WN3 .... 54 D1
Derbyshire Row BL1... 143 B3
Derbyshire St M11.... 165 C3
Derby St
  Altrincham WA14....... 119 E5
  Ashton-u-L OL7........ 58 C4
  Atherton M46.......... 58 C4
  Bolton BL3............. 145 B1
  Denton M34........... 100 F5
  1 Failsworth M35..... 66 A1
  Glossop SK13......... 116 C8
  Heywood OL10.......... 29 B2
  Horwich BL6........... 22 D1
  Ince-in-M WN3 .... 55 F4
  Leigh WN7.............. 76 A4
  Manchester M8 .... 158 C4
  Marple SK6............. 125 F6
  Mossley OL5 .... 86 D8
  Newton-le-W WA12.... 89 B3
  Oldham, Factory Fold OL6.. 66 C4
  Oldham OL1............ 153 C2
  Oldham, Werneth OL9. 152 C1
  Prestwich M25......... 63 A4
  Ramsbottom BL0....... 11 D6
  Rochdale OL11......... 31 A5
  Stockport SK3 .... 170 A4
  15 Tyldesley M29...... 59 L4
  Westhoughton BL5 .... 39 F1
Derby Terr M34........ 100 E8
Derby Way
  Bury BL9 .... 140 C3
  7 Marple SK6......... 125 F6
Dereham Cl BL8........ 27 D5
Dereham Way WN3 ... 54 D3
Derg St M6............. 154 C1
Derker St OL1........... 67 B8
Dermot Murphy Cl M20 . 109 F6
Dernford Ave M19..... 110 E3
Derngate Dr WN2...... 37 A7
Derrick Walker Ct OL11 . 139 A1
Derry Ave M22......... 121 D3
Derville Wlk 4 M9.... 157 A4
Derwen Bd SK3........ 170 B3
Derwent Ave
  Altrincham WA15....... 120 D5
  Ashton-u-L OL7........ 166 A4
  Droylsden M43......... 83 E1
  Golborne WA3 .... 74 C1
  Heywood OL10.......... 46 D8
  Ince-in-M WN3 .... 55 F4
  Manchester M21....... 109 D5
  Milnrow OL16.......... 32 B6

Derwent Ave continued
Whitefield M45 . . . . 63 C8
Derwent Cl
Culcheth WA3 . . . . 92 A2
Glossop SK13. . . . . 116 F8
Horwich BL6 . . . . 22 C2
Leigh WN7 . . . . 75 E3
Little Lever BL3 . . . . 42 F4
Manchester M21 . . . . 109 D5
Partington M31 . . . . 105 F4
Reddish M34 . . . . 100 B2
Walkden M28. . . . . 60 B2
Whitefield M45 . . . . 63 B8
Derwent Dr
Bramhall SK7 . . . . 132 C5
Bury BL9 . . . . 44 D7
Chadderton OL9. . . . . . . 152 A3
Handforth SK9 . . . . 131 C5
Kearsley BL4 . . . . 61 B5
Littleborough OL15 . . . . . 15 F2
Sale M33 . . . . 108 A2
Shaw OL2. . . . . 149 A4
Derwent Pl WN5 . . . . . . 54 C7
Derwent Rd
Ashton-in-M WN4 . . . . . . 73 E5
Farnworth BL4 . . . . 59 F7
High Lane SK6 . . . . 134 E8
Hindley WN2 . . . . 56 E5
Middleton M24. . . . . 46 E3
Orrell WN5. . . . . 53 F8
Stretford M32 . . . . 96 D3
Urmston M41. . . . . 94 E2
Derwent St Trad Est M5 .162 A4
Derwent St
Droylsden M43. . . . . 83 D1
Leigh WN7 . . . . 75 E3
Manchester M8 . . . . 156 C2
11 Rochdale OL12 . . . . . 14 F1
Salford M5. . . . . 161 C4
Tyldesley M29 . . . . 77 A7
Derwent Terr SK15. . . . . 86 A4
Derwent Way WN7 . . . . . 75 B1
Derwent Wlk
Oldham OL4. . . . . 67 D7
Whitefield M45 . . . . 63 B8
Desford Ave M16, M21 . . 97 C1
Design St BL3 . . . . 146 B4
Desmond Rd M22. . . . . 121 E4
Desmond St M46. . . . . . 58 A2
De Trafford Dr WN2 . . . . 56 B8
De Trafford Ho **13** M30 . . 79 D1
De Trafford Mews **9**
SK9 . . . . 131 D2
De Traffords The M44 . . . 94 B3
Deva Cl
Hazel Grove SK7 . . . . . . 124 D1
Poynton SK12. . . . . 133 B4
Deva Ctr M16. . . . . 161 C1
Deva Ctr M3. . . . . 158 B2
Devaney Wlk M34. . . . . 100 E1
Deva Sq OL9. . . . . 152 C1
Deva St M13, M15. . . . . 163 B1
Deverill Ave M18. . . . . . . 99 F4
Devine Cl
Royton OL2 . . . . 48 D6
Salford M3. . . . . 158 A2
Devisdale Ct WA14 . . . . 119 C3
Devisdale Grange WA14 .119 B3
Devisdale Rd WA14 . . . . 119 B4
Devoke Ave
Billinge WA11. . . . . 71 A1
Walkden M28. . . . . 60 F2
Devoke Gr BL4. . . . . 59 E8
Devoke Rd M22. . . . . . . 121 B2
Devon Ave
Manchester M19 . . . . . . 110 F8
Up Holland WN8 . . . . 53 B6
Whitefield M45 . . . . 44 E1
Devon Cl
Aspull WN2 . . . . 38 D5
Brinnington SK5. . . . . . . 112 C4
Little Lever BL3 . . . . 43 B4
Salford M6. . . . . 80 A3
Shaw OL2. . . . . 48 F7
Wigan WN6 . . . . 54 C6
Devon Cres BB4 . . . . .1 B8
Devon Dr
Ainsworth BL2. . . . . 26 D1
Diggle OL3. . . . . 51 C4
Standish WN1 . . . . 20 B1
Devon Mews **2** M45 . . . 44 E1
Devonport Cres OL2. . . . 48 F7
Devon Rd
Droylsden M43. . . . . 84 A3
Failsworth M35 . . . . 83 E6
Irlam M44 . . . . 105 D5
Partington M31 . . . . 105 E2
Tyldesley M29 . . . . 59 A2
Urmston M41. . . . . 94 F1
Devonshire Cl
Heywood OL10. . . . . 29 A1
8 Urmston M41. . . . . 95 E2
Wigan WN3 . . . . 151 B1
Devonshire Ct
Bolton BL1. . . . . 144 B3
Salford M7. . . . . 155 A4
Stockport SK2 . . . . 124 A5
Devonshire Dr
Alderley Edge SK9 . . . . . 137 B2
Boothstown M28 . . . . 78 B2
Devonshire Gdns WA12. . 89 C2
Devonshire Park Rd SK2 124 A5
Devonshire Pl
Atherton M46. . . . . 58 C4
Prestwich M25. . . . . 63 A5

Devonshire Rd
Altrincham WA14. . . . . . . 119 D6
Atherton M46. . . . . 58 C5
Bolton BL1. . . . . 144 B4
Eccles M30 . . . . 79 E2
Hazel Grove SK7 . . . . . . 133 F8
Manchester, Chorlton-cum-Hardy
M21. . . . . 109 C8
Rochdale OL11. . . . . 30 F2
Salford M6. . . . . 80 A3
Stockport, Heaton Norris
SK4. . . . . 168 B3
Walkden M28. . . . . 60 E5
Devonshire Road Prim Sch
BL1 . . . . 144 B4
Devonshire St
Manchester M12 . . . . . . 164 A2
Salford M7. . . . . 155 B2
Devon St
Bolton BL2. . . . . 148 A3
Bury BL9 . . . . 44 F8
Farnworth BL4. . . . . 42 D2
Hindley WN2 . . . . 56 E5
Leigh WN7 . . . . 76 E4
Oldham OL9. . . . . 66 C4
Rochdale OL11. . . . . 139 C2
Swinton M27 . . . . 61 F2
Devon Way OL8 . . . . 66 C2
Dewan Ind Est BB4. . . . . .1 B8
Dewar Cl M11 . . . . 83 A1
Dewberry Cl
Swinton M27 . . . . 61 E2
Tyldesley M29 . . . . 59 E1
Dewberry Fields WN8 . . . 53 C7
Dewes Ave M27. . . . . 62 B2
Dewey St M11 . . . . 99 D7
Dewham Cl BL5. . . . . 39 F1
Dewhirst Rd OL12. . . . . . 14 F4
Dewhirst Way OL12 . . . . . 14 F4
Dewhurst Clough Rd BL7. . 8 D2
Dewhurst Ct BL7. . . . . 8 D3
Dewhurst Rd BL2 . . . . . . 25 E3
Dewhurst St
Heywood OL10. . . . . 29 E2
Manchester M8 . . . . 158 C4
Dewint Ave SK6. . . . . . . 126 B8
Dew Meadow Cl OL12 . . . 14 E2
Dewsnap Cl SK16. . . . . . 101 C6
Dewsnap La
Dukinfield SK16 . . . . 101 D6
Mottram in L. SK14. . . . . 103 A6
Dewsnap Way SK14 . . . . 102 E2
Dew Way OL9. . . . . 153 A3
Dexter Rd M9. . . . . 64 A5
Dexter Way WN8. . . . . . . 53 B6
Deyne Ave
Manchester M14 . . . . 98 C4
Prestwich M25. . . . . 63 B4
Deyne St M6. . . . . 154 B2
Dial Ct BL4 . . . . 60 D8
Dial Park Prim Sch SK2 . 124 E6
Dial Park Rd SK2. . . . . . 124 D4
Dial Rd
Altrincham WA15. . . . . . . 129 C8
Stockport SK2 . . . . 124 C5
Dialstone Ctr The SK2. . . 124 D6
Dialstone La SK2. . . . . . 124 C6
Diamond Cl **9** OL6. . . . . 85 D4
Diamond St
8 Ashton-u-l OL6. . . . . . 85 D4
Leigh WN7 . . . . 75 E4
Stockport SK2 . . . . 124 A6
Wigan WN6 . . . . 37 A3
Diamond Terr SK6 . . . . . 125 F3
Diane Rd WN4 . . . . 73 E5
Dibden Wlk **4** M23 . . . . 121 A5
Dicconson Cres **9** WN1. . 37 C1
Dicconson La BL5, WN2. . 39 A4
Dicconson St WN1 . . . . . . 37 C1
Dicconson Terr WN1 . . . . 37 C1
Dicken Gn OL11. . . . . 30 F4
Dicken Green La OL11. . . 30 F4
Dickens Cl SK8 . . . . 132 B5
Dickens Dr WN2 . . . . 74 C8
Dickens La SK12 . . . . . . 133 E2
Dickenson Rd M13, M14. . 98 B3
Dickenson St M12 . . . . . . 56 E4
Dickens Pl WN3. . . . . 54 F4
Dickens Rd
Coppull PR7 . . . . 19 E8
Eccles M30 . . . . 79 D1
Dickens St
Heywood OL10. . . . . 29 B2
Oldham OL1 . . . . 49 E4
Dickinson Cl **13** BL1 . . . . 143 B1
Dickinson Ct **1** BL6. . . . . 22 B4
Dickinson St
Bolton BL1. . . . . 143 B1
Manchester M1 . . . . 163 A4
Oldham OL4. . . . . 67 B7
Salford M3. . . . . 158 B3
Dickinson Terr **12** BL1 . . . 143 B1
Didcot Rd M22. . . . . 121 C1
Didley Sq M12 . . . . 165 A3
DIDSBURY 110 C2
Didsbury CE Prim Sch **11**
M20. . . . . 110 B3
Didsbury Gr WN2 . . . . 56 D5
Didsbury Lodge Hall
M20. . . . . 110 C1
Didsbury Pk M20. . . . . . . 110 C1
Didsbury Prim Sch SK4 . 110 F2
Digby Rd OL11 . . . . 30 F4
Digby Wlk **20** M11. . . . . . 160 C1
Dig Gate La OL16 . . . . . . 31 E3
DIGGLE 51 C4

Diggle Mill Cotts OL3 . . . 51 F5
Diggles La OL11 . . . . 29 E6
Diggle St
Shaw OL2. . . . . 149 B2
Wigan WN6 . . . . 37 A1
Diggle Wlk SK15 . . . . 86 E6
Diglands Ave SK22 . . . . . 127 D1
Diglands Cl SK22. . . . . . 127 D1
Diglea OL3 . . . . 51 D5
Dilham Ct BL1 . . . . 146 C4
Dilham Ct BL1 . . . . 144 C4
Dillicar Wlk M9. . . . . 157 A3
Dillmoss Wlk **22** M15. . . 162 A2
Dillon Dr M12 . . . . 164 B1
Dilworth Cl OL10. . . . . . . 29 A2
Dilworth Ct SK2. . . . . . . 124 E5
Dilworth Ho M13. . . . . . . 163 B1
Dilworth St M13, M15. . . 163 B1
Dimple Pk BL7. . . . . 8 D3
Dimple Rd BL7. . . . . 8 C4
Dingle Ave
Appley Bridge WN6 . . . . . 35 E8
Denton M34. . . . . 101 B2
Row-of-Trees SK9 . . . . . 136 D3
Shaw OL2. . . . . 32 C1
Up Holland WN8 . . . . 53 C8
Dingle Bank Rd SK7. . . . 123 D1
Dinglebrook Gr **5** SK9. . . 131 D1
Dingle Cl
Glossop SK13. . . . . 116 A8
Radcliffe M26 . . . . 44 B1
Romiley SK6. . . . . 113 D2
Dingle Dr M43. . . . . 84 B3
Dingle Gr SK8 . . . . 121 F6
Dingle Rd
Middleton M24. . . . . 64 F6
Up Holland WN8 . . . . 53 B7
Dingle Terr OL6 . . . . 67 B2
Dingle The
Bramhall SK7. . . . . 123 C1
Hyde SK14. . . . . 113 E7
Dingle Wlk
9 Bolton BL1. . . . . 145 C4
Wigan WN6 . . . . 36 D4
Dinglewood Cl SK7. . . . . 123 C1
Dinmore Cl SK2. . . . . . . 124 D5
Dinmor Rd M22. . . . . . . 121 D1
Dinnington Dr M8 . . . . . 155 F2
Dinorwic Cl M8. . . . . 64 A2
Dinsdale Cl M40 . . . . . . 160 A2
Dinsdale Dr BL3 . . . . . . 145 A1
Dinslow Wlk **8** M8 . . . . 155 C3
Dinting Ave M20 . . . . . . 110 B6
Dinting CE Prim Sch
SK13. . . . . 104 A1
Dinting La SK13. . . . . . . 104 A1
Dinting Lane Ind Est
SK13. . . . . 104 A1
Dinting Lodge Ind Est
SK13. . . . . 171 C2
Dinting Rd SK13. . . . . . . 104 B2
Dinting Sta SK13. . . . . . 104 A2
Dinting Vale SK13. . . . . . 104 A1
Dinting Vale Bsns Pk
SK13. . . . . 171 C2
Dinton Ho **8** M5. . . . . . . 154 C1
Dinton St M15. . . . . 161 C3
Dipper Dr WA14 . . . . 107 C1
Dipton Wlk M8 . . . . 156 C2
Dirty La
Delph OL3 . . . . 51 B8
Oldham OL4. . . . . 50 B1
Dirty Leech OL12. . . . . . . 14 F6
DISLEY. 135 C5
Disley Ave M20 . . . . 109 F6
Disley Ho SK3 . . . . 170 B3
Disley Prim Sch SK12 . . . 135 D6
Disley St OL11 . . . . 30 C4
Disley Sta SK12 . . . . 135 C6
Disley Wlk M34 . . . . 101 A1
Distaff Rd SK12 . . . . 133 B4
District CE Prim Sch The
SK12. . . . . 89 A3
Ditton Brook BL5 . . . . . . 39 F1
Ditton Mead Cl OL12 . . . 15 B2
Ditton Wlk **5** M23 . . . . . 120 F6
Divine Mercy RC Prim Sch
The M44 . . . . 98 A2
Division St
Bolton BL3. . . . . 147 C4
4 Rochdale OL12. . . . . . 15 B2
Dixey St OL10 . . . . 28 A3
Dixon Ave
Newton-le-W WA12. . . . . . 89 C5
Salford M7. . . . . 155 B2
Shevington WN6 . . . . 36 A5
Dixon Cl
Haydock WA11. . . . . 89 A8
Sale M33 . . . . 108 D2
Dixon Closes OL11 . . . . . 29 E7
Dixon Ct
Cheadle SK8 . . . . 122 D5
Westhoughton BL5 . . . . . 39 E3
Dixon Dr
Shevington WN6 . . . . 36 A5
Swinton M27 . . . . 61 E4
DIXON GREEN. 60 C8
Dixon Green Dr **11** BL4 . . 60 C8
Dixon Pl **8** WN2 . . . . 56 B1
Dixon Rd M34 . . . . 101 B1
Dixon St
13 Ashton-u-l OL6. . . . . . 85 D4
Failsworth M40 . . . . 83 B6
Horwich BL6 . . . . 22 B3
Irlam M44 . . . . 105 F8
Manchester M6. . . . . 80 F6
Middleton M24. . . . . 47 A2
Oldham, Cold Hurst OL1 . 153 B4

Dixon St continued
Oldham, Greenacres Fold
OL4 . . . . 67 E8
Rochdale OL11. . . . . 30 D4
Westhoughton BL5 . . . . . 39 E3
DOBB BROW. 57 C7
Dobb Brow Rd BL5. . . . . . 57 D7
Dobb Hedge Cl WA15 . . . 129 C6
Dobbin Dr OL11. . . . . 30 F3
Dobbinetts La M23,
WA15. . . . . 120 A2
Dob Brook Cl M35, M40. . 83 C6
DOBCROSS. 51 A1
Dobcross Cl M13. . . . . . . 99 A2
Dobcross New Rd OL3. . . 51 A1
Dobhill St BL4 . . . . 60 D8
Dobroyd Ho OL4 . . . . 67 E8
Dobroyd St M8 . . . . 156 A4
Dobson Cl M40 . . . . 83 B4
Dobson Park Ind Est
WN2 . . . . 151 C2
Dobson Park Way M27. . . 56 A6
Dobson Rd BL1 . . . . 144 C3
Dobson St BL1 . . . . 143 A2
Doctor Fold La OL10 . . . . 46 C5
Doctor La OL4 . . . . 50 C1
Doctors La BL9 . . . . 140 A2
Doctors Nook WN7. . . . . . 75 F5
Dodd Croft OL16 . . . . 31 B3
Doddington La M5. . . . . . 161 A4
Doddington Wlk M34. . . . 100 E1
Dodd La BL5 . . . . 39 D4
Dodd's Farm La WN2. . . . 38 E3
Dodd St M5 . . . . 154 A2
Dodge Fold SK2 . . . . 124 E6
Dodge Hill SK4 . . . . 169 B2
Dodgson St OL16 . . . . . . 31 A6
Dodhurst Rd M24. . . . . . . 56 F6
Dodworth Cl WN4. . . . . . . 73 C3
Doe Brow M27. . . . . 64 E1
Doefield Ave M28 . . . . 78 C8
Doeford Cl WA3 . . . . 91 E5
Doe Hey Gr BL4. . . . . 42 B2
Doe Hey Rd BL3. . . . . 42 B2
DOFFCOCKER. 23 E1
Doffcocker Brow BL1 . . . 142 A1
Doffcocker La BL1 . . . . . . 23 F2
Doffcocker Lodge Nature
Reserve[*] BL1 . . . . 23 E1
Dogford Rd OL2 . . . . 48 D5
DOG HILL. 49 E7
Dog Hill Lne OL2. . . . . . . 49 E6
Dolbey St M5 . . . . 154 B1
Dollond St M9 . . . . 64 E1
Dolman Wlk **8** M8. . . . . 155 C3
Dolphin Pl M12 . . . . 163 C3
Dolphin St M12 . . . . 163 C3
Dolwen Wlk M40. . . . . 83 B6
Doman St BL3 . . . . 145 C1
Dombey Rd SK12. . . . . . 133 D2
Domestic App M90. . . . . 130 C6
Dome The **6** WA14 . . . . . 119 D4
Domett St M9 . . . . 64 D2
Dominic Cl M23. . . . . . . 108 E1
Donald Ave WN4 . . . . . . 167 C1
Donald St M1. . . . . 163 A3
Dona St SK1. . . . . 124 A8
Don Ave M6 . . . . 80 C2
Doncaster Ave M20 . . . . 110 A7
Doncaster Cl
Little Lever BL3 . . . . 42 F3
Oldham OL1. . . . . 49 D3
Doncaster Wlk **4** OL1. . . 153 C3
Donhead Wlk M13 . . . . . 163 C2
Donington Gdns M28. . . . 60 D3
Donkey La SK9. . . . . 137 A5
Donleigh St M35. . . . . . . 83 D6
Donnington **6** OL11 . . . . 139 B2
Donnington Ave SK8 . . . 122 F6
Donnington Cl WN7. . . . . . 75 E1
Donnington Rd
Droylsden M18. . . . . 99 E5
Little Lever M26. . . . . 43 C5
Donnison St M12 . . . . . . 164 C2
Donovan Ave M40. . . . . . 159 C4
Don St
Bolton BL3. . . . . 147 A3
Middleton M24. . . . . 47 C1
Doodfield. 125 E2
Doodson Ave M44. . . . . . 94 A2
Doodson Sq BL4 . . . . 60 D8
Dooley La SK2, SK6 . . . . 125 B7
Dooley's La SK9 . . . . 130 C2
Dootson St
4 Abram WN2 . . . . 56 B1
Hindley WN2 . . . . 57 A6
Dorac Ave SK8. . . . . 131 C7
Dora St BL0 . . . . 11 A4
Dorchester Ave
Bolton BL2. . . . . 25 E1
Denton M34. . . . . 100 F1
Manchester M25. . . . . . . 63 C2
Urmston M41. . . . . 95 F3
Dorchester Cl
Altrincham WA15. . . . . . . 120 C3
Wilmslow SK9 . . . . 137 D8
Dorchester Ct
Bramhall SK8. . . . . 123 B1
Sale M33 . . . . 108 B2
Dorchester Dr
Failsworth M40 . . . . 83 C4
Royton OL2 . . . . 48 E2
Sale M23 . . . . 108 E1
Dorchester Gr OL10 . . . . 46 D8
Dorchester Par SK7 . . . . 124 B1

Dorchester Rd
Hazel Grove SK7 . . . . . . 124 B1
Swinton M27 . . . . 79 F6
Up Holland WN8 . . . . 53 A7
Dorclyn Ave M41. . . . . . . 95 D2
Dorfield Cl SK6 . . . . 112 E3
Doric Ave SK6 . . . . 112 D2
Doric Cl M11. . . . . 160 C1
Doric Gn WN5 . . . . 53 D3
Doris Ave BL2 . . . . 42 D7
Doris Rd SK3 . . . . 123 C8
Doris St M24 . . . . 47 A2
Dorket Gr BL5 . . . . 57 D6
Dorking Ave M40 . . . . 83 B4
Dorking Cl
Bolton BL1. . . . . 143 C2
Stockport SK1 . . . . 124 B7
Dorlan Ave M18. . . . . 99 F4
Dorland Gr SK2 . . . . 124 B7
Dorman St **8** M11 . . . . . . 99 D7
Dormer St BL1 . . . . 143 C3
Dorney St M18. . . . . 99 D5
Dorning Rd M27 . . . . 80 A7
Dorning St
Bury BL8 . . . . 27 B4
6 Eccles M30. . . . . 79 D1
Kearsley BL4 . . . . 60 F8
1 Leigh WN7 . . . . 75 E5
Scot Lane End BL6. . . . . . 38 F7
Tyldesley M29 . . . . 58 F1
Wigan WN1 . . . . 150 B4
Dornton Wlk M8 . . . . 155 C2
Dorothy Gr WN7 . . . . 75 E4
Dorothy Rd SK7. . . . . . . 124 F3
Dorothy St
Ramsbottom BL0 . . . . . . 138 B1
Salford M7. . . . . 155 C3
Dorothy Wlk WN2. . . . . . . 73 F8
Dorrian Mews BL1 . . . . . . 40 F7
Dorrington Rd
Cheadle SK3 . . . . 123 A7
Sale M33 . . . . 107 E4
Dorris St
Bolton BL3. . . . . 146 C3
Manchester M19 . . . . . . 111 B8
Dorrit Cl SK12 . . . . 133 E2
Dorset Ave
Bramhall SK7. . . . . 123 D1
Brinnington SK5. . . . . . . 112 C5
Cheadle SK8 . . . . 123 C5
Diggle OL3. . . . . 51 C4
Droylsden M34. . . . . 100 C8
Farnworth BL4. . . . . 60 C8
Manchester M14 . . . . 98 A2
Shaw OL2. . . . . 48 F7
Tyldesley M29 . . . . 59 A3
Dorset Cl
Farnworth BL4. . . . . 60 C8
Heywood OL10. . . . . 29 A1
Wigan WN5 . . . . 54 C6
Dorset Dr
Bury BL9 . . . . 45 A8
Haslingden BB4 . . . . .1 A8
Dorset Rd
Altrincham WA14. . . . . . . 119 B5
Atherton M46. . . . . 58 C5
Droylsden M43. . . . . 83 F3
Failsworth M35 . . . . 83 F6
Irlam M44 . . . . 105 D5
Reddish M19 . . . . 99 C1
Standish WN1 . . . . 20 B1
Dorset St
Ashton-u-l OL6. . . . . 85 D2
Bolton BL2. . . . . 148 A3
Hindley WN2 . . . . 56 E6
Leigh WN7 . . . . 76 D4
Oldham OL9. . . . . 152 C1
Rochdale OL11. . . . . 139 C2
Stretford M32 . . . . 96 D1
Swinton M27 . . . . 61 F2
Dorsey St M4. . . . . 159 B2
Dorstone Cl
Failsworth M40 . . . . 83 C4
Hindley WN2 . . . . 57 B5
Dorwood Ave M9 . . . . 64 C5
Dottered Cl WN7 . . . . 76 A6
Dougall Wlk M12 . . . . . . 165 A2
Doughty Ave M30 . . . . . . 79 F3
Dougill St BL1 . . . . 142 B1
Douglas Ave
Billinge WN5 . . . . 71 D3
Bury BL8 . . . . 22 C5
Horwich BL6 . . . . 22 C5
Stretford M32 . . . . 96 D3
Up Holland WN8 . . . . 53 B7
Douglas Bank Dr WN6. . . 36 F2
Douglas Cl
Horwich BL6 . . . . 22 C5
Whitefield M45 . . . . 45 C2
Douglas Dr
Orrell WN5. . . . . 53 F7
Shevington WN6 . . . . 35 F5
Douglas Gn M6. . . . . 81 A5
Douglas Ho WN5. . . . . . . 53 A1
Douglas Pk M46. . . . . 58 E3
Douglas Rd
Atherton M46. . . . . 58 E2
Hazel Grove SK7 . . . . . . 124 F2
Leigh WN7 . . . . 75 C7
Shevington Moor WN6. . . 19 B2
Stockport SK3 . . . . 123 E4
Swinton M28 . . . . 79 C4
Wigan WN1 . . . . 37 F0
Douglas Sq OL10. . . . . . . 28 F1
Douglas St
Ashton-u-l OL6. . . . . 85 D3
Atherton M46. . . . . 58 E3
Bolton BL1. . . . . 24 E5

Douglas St *continued*
Failsworth M35 . . . . 84 A7
Hindley WN2 . . . . 56 C4
Hyde SK14 . . . . 167 B2
Manchester M40 . . . . 83 A7
Oldham OL1 . . . . 67 A8
Pendlebury M27 . . . . 80 A7
Ramsbottom BL0 . . . . 138 B2
Salford M7 . . . . 155 A2
Wigan WN5 . . . . 150 A3
Douglas View
Adlington PR7 . . . . 21 A6
Standish M 37 B6
Douglas Way M45 . . . . 45 C1
Douglas Wlk
2 Sale M33 . . . . 107 C5
Whitefield M45 . . . . 45 C2
Doulton St M40 . . . . 83 C8
Dounby Ave M30 . . . . 79 B3
Douro St M40 . . . . 157 C1
Douthwaite Dr SK6 . . . . . . 113 E1
Dove Bank Rd BL3 . . . . . . 43 A4
Dove Bk SK6 . . . . 126 F6
Dovebrook Cl SK15 . . . . . . 86 E7
Dovecote M43 . . . . 84 D3
Dovecote Bsns & Tech Pk
M33 . . . . 108 F4
Dovecote Cl OL7 . . . . 25 B8
Dovecote La
Oldham OL4 . . . . 67 F8
Walkden M38 . . . . 59 E3
Dovecote Mews 5 M21 . 109 A8
Dovedale Ave
Droylsden M43 . . . . 83 E2
Eccles M30 . . . . 79 E3
Manchester, Sedgley Park
M25 . . . . 63 E3
Manchester, Withington
M20 . . . . 110 A7
Urmston M41 . . . . 95 D3
Dovedale Cl SK6 . . . . 134 E7
Dovedale Cres WN4 . . . . . 73 A8
Dovedale Ct
1 Glossop SK13 . . . . 104 F1
7 Middleton M24 . . . . . . 46 E2
Dovedale Dr
Standish WN6 . . . . 19 E2
Wardle OL12 . . . . 15 D6
Dovedale Rd
Ashton-in-M WN4 . . . . 73 A8
Bolton BL2 . . . . 25 F1
Stockport SK2 . . . . 124 D7
Stretford M35 . . . . 83 E7
Dove Dr
Bury BL9 . . . . 141 B4
Irlam M44 . . . . 94 A3
Dovehouse Cl M45 . . . . . . 62 D7
Doveleys Rd M6 . . . . 154 A4
Dover Cl BL8 . . . . 11 A1
Dovercourt Ave SK4 . . . . 110 B3
Dover Gr BL3 . . . . 145 A1
Doveridge Gdns M6 . . . . . 154 C3
Dover Pk M41 . . . . 95 D4
Dover Rd M27 . . . . 62 A2
Dover St
Eccles M30 . . . . 79 B2
Farnworth BL4 . . . . 42 D2
Manchester M13 . . . . 163 B2
Oldham OL9 . . . . 152 C1
1 Reddish SK5 . . . . 111 F7
Rochdale OL16 . . . . 15 B2
Dove St
Bolton BL1 . . . . 143 B4
Golborne WA3 . . . . 74 A2
Oldham OL4 . . . . 67 C6
Rochdale OL11 . . . . 139 A3
Dovestone Cres SK16 . . . 101 F7
Dovestone Wlk M40 . . . . . 65 E1
Doveston Rd M33 . . . . . . 108 B6
Dove Wlk
Farnworth BL4 . . . . 59 F8
Manchester M8 . . . . 156 B1
Dovey Cl M29 . . . . 77 C7
Dower St WN2 . . . . 56 A3
Dow Fold BL8 . . . . 26 F3
Dow La BL8 . . . . 26 F3
Dowland Cl 3 M23 . . . . . 108 F2
Dowling Ct WN6 . . . . 36 D3
Dowling St OL11 . . . . . . 139 C2
DOWNALL GREEN 72 C5
Downall Green Rd WN4 . . 72 E6
Downbrook Way WN4 . . . . 73 F6
Downesway SK9 . . . . . . 136 F1
Downfield Cl BL0 . . . . . . 138 B2
Downfields SK5 . . . . . . 100 A1
Downgate Wlk 8 M8 . . . 156 A2
Downgreen Rd BL2 . . . . . 25 E3
Downhall Gn BL1 . . . . . . 145 C4
Downham Ave
Bolton BL2 . . . . 148 C4
Culcheth WA3 . . . . 91 F2
Downham Chase WA15 . . 120 B6
Downham Cl OL10 . . . . . . 48 D2
Downham Cres M25 . . . . . 63 E3
Downham Gdns M25 . . . . . 63 E3
Downham Gr M25 . . . . . . 63 E3
Downham Rd
Heywood OL10 . . . . 29 A2
Reddish SK5 . . . . 111 D5
Downham Wlk
Longshaw WN5 . . . . 53 D1
Wythenshawe M23 . . . . . 120 E8
Downhill Cl OL1 . . . . 48 E1
Downing Cl
Ashton-u-L OL7 . . . . 84 F6
Platt Bridge WN2 . . . . 56 A2

Downing St
Ashton-u-L OL7 . . . . 84 F5
5 Leigh WN7 . . . . 75 F5
Manchester M1, M12, M13 163 B3
Downing Street Ind Est
M12 . . . . 163 B3
Downley Cl OL12 . . . . 14 B2
Downlow Dr M4 . . . . 159 C2
Downs Dr WA14 . . . . 119 E8
Downshaw Rd OL7 . . . . . 85 A6
Downs The
Altrincham WA14 . . . . 119 C3
Cheadle SK8 . . . . 122 D3
Middleton M24 . . . . 65 B5
Prestwich M25 . . . . 63 A2
Wigan WN3 . . . . 54 C4
Downton Ave 13 WN2 . . . 56 D4
Dowry Rd OL4 . . . . 67 F7
Dowry St OL4 . . . . 67 F7
Dowson Prim Sch SK14 . 113 E8
Dowson Rd SK14 . . . . . . 113 E8
Dowson St BL2 . . . . 148 A3
Dow St SK14 . . . . 101 D5
Doyle Ave SK6 . . . . 112 D3
Doyle Cl OL1 . . . . 49 E4
Doyle Rd BL3 . . . . 40 E2
Drake Ave
Farnworth BL4 . . . . 60 D7
Irlam M44 . . . . 105 E6
Wythenshawe M22 . . . . . 121 B2
Drake Cl OL1 . . . . 153 C4
Drake Ct SK5 . . . . 169 B4
Drake Hall BL5 . . . . 57 E5
Drake Rd
Altrincham WA14 . . . . 119 B8
Calderbrook OL15 . . . . 6 C1
Drake St
Atherton M46 . . . . 58 C2
Rochdale OL11, OL16 . . . . 139 C2
Drapers Ct 3 WA3 . . . . . 90 F7
Draybank Rd 4 WA14 . . . 119 B8
Draycote Ho M13 . . . . . . 98 E3
Draycott Cl WN2 . . . . . . 56 F7
Draycott St BL1 . . . . 143 B2
Drayfields M43 . . . . 84 D2
Drayford Cl 2 M23 . . . . 108 F2
Drayton Cl
Bolton BL1 . . . . 143 A2
12 Handforth SK9 . . . . . 131 D1
Sale M33 . . . . 107 D2
Drayton Dr SK8 . . . . 131 B7
Drayton Gr WA15 . . . . . . 120 A5
Drayton Manor M20 . . . . 122 B8
Drayton St M15 . . . . 162 B1
Drayton Wlk M16 . . . . . . 162 A1
Dresden St M40 . . . . 83 C8
Drewett St M40 . . . . 160 B4
Dreyfus Ave M11 . . . . . . 83 C2
Driffield St
Eccles M30 . . . . 95 C8
Manchester M14 . . . . 98 A3
Drinkwater Rd M25 . . . . . 62 F1
Driscoll St 1 M13 . . . . . 98 F3
Drive The
Altrincham WA15 . . . . . . 129 D8
Brinnington SK5 . . . . 112 C4
Broomedge WA3 . . . . . . 117 D1
Bury BL9 . . . . 27 F8
Cheadle SK8 . . . . 123 C4
Edenfield BL0 . . . . 1 D3
Leigh WN7 . . . . 75 F3
Manchester, Broughton Park
M7 . . . . 63 C1
Manchester, Didsbury
M20 . . . . 110 C4
Marple SK6 . . . . 125 E6
Prestwich M25 . . . . 63 B4
Romiley SK6 . . . . 112 D3
Sale M33 . . . . 107 E1
Droitwich Rd M40 . . . . . . 160 A4
Dronfield St
Salford M6 . . . . 154 A4
Wythenshawe M22 . . . . . 121 D8
Droughts La M25 . . . . . . 63 E8
Drovers Wlk 3 SK13 . . . 104 D1
Droxford Ct SK9 . . . . . . 137 B6
Droxford Gr M46 . . . . . . 58 E5
DROYLSDEN 84 B3
Droylsden Acad
Droylsden M43 . . . . 83 F2
Droylsden M43 . . . . 84 C4
Droylsden Metro Sta M43 84 A1
Droylsden Rd
Droylsden M43 . . . . 100 C8
Failsworth M40 . . . . 83 A8
Droylsden Wharf Rd 6
M43 . . . . 100 A8
Drs Green & Slater Rest Hos
SK4 . . . . 168 A3
Druids Cl BL7 . . . . 8 D3
Druid St WN4 . . . . 73 C2
Drummer's La WN4 . . . . . 72 E7
Drummond Sq WN5 . . . . . 54 E7
Drummond St BL1 . . . . . 143 B4
Drummond Way WN7 . . . . 76 B5
Drury La OL9 . . . . 66 B3
Drury St 13 M19 . . . . . . 99 A1
Dryad Cl M27 . . . . 61 F2
Drybrook Cl M13 . . . . . . 164 B1
Dryburgh Ave BL1 . . . . . 143 A4
Dryclough Wlk OL2 . . . . . 48 E3
Dryden Ave
Ashton-in-M WN4 . . . . . . 72 F6
Cheadle SK8 . . . . 122 F6
Swinton M27 . . . . 79 D7
Dryden Cl
Dukinfield SK16 . . . . 102 B7
Marple SK6 . . . . 125 F4

Dryden Cl *continued*
Wigan WN3 . . . . 150 A1
Dryden Rd 4 M16 . . . . . 97 C3
Dryden St M13 . . . . 163 C2
Dryden Way 10 M34 . . . 113 A8
Dryfield La BL6 . . . . 22 A5
Drygate Wlk 6 M9 . . . . 157 B3
Dryhurst Dr SK12 . . . . . 135 D6
Dryhurst La SK12 . . . . . 135 D6
Dryhurst Wlk M15 . . . . . 163 A2
Drymoss OL8 . . . . 67 A1
Drysdale View BL1 . . . . 143 B4
Dryton Wlk WN2 . . . . . . 38 A2
Drywood Ave M28 . . . . . 79 A5
Ducal St M4 . . . . 159 B4
Duchess Park Cl OL2 . . . 149 B4
Duchess Rd M8 . . . . . . 156 B4
Duchess St OL2 . . . . . . 149 B4
Duchess Wlk BL3 . . . . . 146 B4
Duchy Ave
Over Hulton BL5 . . . . 59 A8
Walkden M28 . . . . 78 D8
Duchy Bank M6 . . . . 80 D6
Duchy Rd M6 . . . . 80 D6
Duchy St
Salford M6 . . . . 154 C3
Stockport SK3 . . . . 170 A3
Ducie Ho M1 . . . . 159 B1
Ducie St
Manchester M1 . . . . 159 B1
Oldham OL8 . . . . 66 F2
Radcliffe M26 . . . . 44 B2
Whitefield M45 . . . . 62 F8
Duckshaw La BL4 . . . . . 60 D8
Duckworth La BB4 . . . . . 1 E8
Duckworth Rd M25 . . . . . 62 F3
Duckworth St
3 Bury BL9 . . . . 141 A4
Shaw OL2 . . . . 149 C3
Duddon Ave BL2 . . . . . . 25 F1
Duddon Cl
Standish WN6 . . . . 36 F7
Whitefield M45 . . . . 63 C8
Duddon Wlk 2 M24 . . . . 46 E2
Dudley Ave
Bolton BL2 . . . . 25 C1
Whitefield M45 . . . . 62 F8
Dudley Cl M15 . . . . 162 B1
Dudley Ct 11 M16 . . . . . 97 D3
Dudley Rd
Irlam M44 . . . . 105 D4
Manchester M16 . . . . 97 D3
Sale M33 . . . . 108 B2
Sale, Timperley WA15 . . . 120 B7
Swinton M27 . . . . 79 C3
Dudley St
Ashton-in-M WN4 . . . . . . 73 A5
Eccles M30 . . . . 79 C1
6 Oldham OL4 . . . . . . 67 D6
Salford M7 . . . . 155 C2
Dudlow Wlk 2 M15 . . . . 162 A2
Dudwell Cl BL1 . . . . . . 147 D5
Duerden St BL3 . . . . . . 146 A2
Duffield Ct M15 . . . . . . 163 A1
Duffield Gdns M9 . . . . . 64 F5
Duffield Rd
Middleton M9 . . . . 64 F5
Salford M6 . . . . 80 D5
Duffins Cl OL12 . . . . . . 14 D3
Dufton Wlk
1 Middleton M24 . . . . . 46 E2
Wythenshawe M22 . . . . . 130 E8
Dugdale Ave M9 . . . . . . 64 E4
Dugie St BL0 . . . . 138 B3
Duke Ave
Cheadle SK8 . . . . 131 F6
Glazebury WA3 . . . . 92 C7
Duke Cl M16 . . . . 162 A1
Dukefield St M22 . . . . . 121 E8
Duke of Norfolk CE Prim Sch
SK13 . . . . 104 D1
Duke of Norfolk CE Prim Sch
(Annexe) SK13 . . . . 104 E2
Duke Pl M3 . . . . 162 D8
Duke Rd
Ainsworth BL2 . . . . 26 C1
Dukinfield SK14 . . . . 101 F5
Dukes Ave BL3 . . . . 43 A4
Dukes Ct M30 . . . . 79 F2
Dukes Fold SK13 . . . . . 116 B7
Dukesgate Prim Sch M38 . 60 A5
Dukes Platting OL6 . . . . 85 F5
Duke's Row M3 . . . . . . 38 B4
Dukes St SK13 . . . . . . 116 C8
Duke St
Alderley Edge SK9 . . . . . 137 B2
Ashton-in-M WN4 . . . . . . 73 C3
Ashton-u-L OL6 . . . . 166 B2
Bolton BL1 . . . . 145 B4
Denton M34 . . . . 100 E3
Eccles M30 . . . . 79 C4
Failsworth M35 . . . . 84 A8
Golborne WA3 . . . . 74 A1
Heywood OL10 . . . . 29 B2
Leigh WN7 . . . . 76 A4
Littleborough OL15 . . . . . 16 A5
Manchester M3 . . . . 158 C2
Manchester M3 . . . . 162 B4
Mossley OL5 . . . . 68 E1
Newton-le-W WA12 . . . . . 89 B3
Platt Bridge WN2 . . . . . . 56 A3
Radcliffe M26 . . . . 44 B2
Ramsbottom BL0 . . . . . . 11 A4
Rawtenstall BB4 . . . . 2 E8
Rochdale OL12 . . . . 14 F1
Salford, Lower Broughton
M7 . . . . 155 A1

Duke St *continued*
Salford, Lower Broughton
M7 . . . . 158 A4
Shaw OL2 . . . . 149 C2
Stalybridge SK15 . . . . . . 85 F1
Stockport SK1 . . . . 169 C1
Tyldesley M29 . . . . 77 C6
Walkden, Linnyshaw M28 . 61 A2
Walkden M38 . . . . 60 A5
Wigan, Goose Green WN3 . 54 F4
Wigan, Swinley WN1 . . . . 37 C2
Duke's Terr 17 SK16 . . . 166 B1
Dukes Wharf M28 . . . . . 78 F5
Dukes Wlk WA15 . . . . . 119 F3
DUKINFIELD 101 D7
Dukinfield Pool SK16 . . . . 101 D7
Dukinfield Rd M18 . . . . . 166 B4
Dukinfield St 5 WN7 . . . 76 A5
Dulford Wlk 4 M13 . . . . 163 C1
Dulgar St M11 . . . . 165 B4
Dulverton Gdns BL3 . . . . 43 B2
Dulverton St M40 . . . . . 83 B6
Dulwich Cl 9 M33 . . . . 107 D3
Dulwich St M4 . . . . 159 B3
Dumbarton Cl SK5 . . . . 111 F6
Dumbarton Dr OL10 . . . . 46 A8
Dumbarton Gn WN6 . . . . 36 E2
Dumbarton Rd
Heywood OL10 . . . . 29 A1
Reddish SK5 . . . . 111 F6
Dumbell St M27 . . . . . . 61 F2
Dumber La M33 . . . . . . 107 F6
Dumers Cl M26 . . . . 44 A2
Dumers La BL9, M26 . . . . 44 E5
Dumfries Ave OL3 . . . . . 33 C2
Dumfries Dr OL3 . . . . . . 33 C2
Dumfries Hollow OL10 . . . 29 F3
Dumfries Wlk OL10 . . . . 29 A1
DUMPLINGTON 95 D7
Dunbar Ave M23 . . . . . 121 A3
Dunbar Dr BL3 . . . . 147 B3
Dunbar Gr OL10 . . . . . . 45 D7
Dunbar St OL1 . . . . 153 B4
Dunblane Ave
Bolton BL3 . . . . 40 E5
Stockport SK4 . . . . 169 A2
Dunblane Gr WN4 . . . . . 72 C4
Dunblane Gr OL10 . . . . . 46 A8
Duncan Ave WA12 . . . . . 89 C5
Duncan Pl WN5 . . . . . . 54 E7
Duncan Rd M13 . . . . . . 98 F3
Duncan St
Dukinfield SK16 . . . . . . 101 C6
1 Horwich BL6 . . . . . . 22 C3
Salford, Higher Broughton
M7 . . . . 81 C6
Salford, New Windsor M5 162 D6
Dunchurch Cl BL6 . . . . . 40 D6
Dunchurch Rd M33 . . . . 107 E4
Dun Cl M3 . . . . 158 A2
Duncombe Cl SK7 . . . . . 124 A3
Duncombe Dr M40 . . . . . 83 B7
Duncombe Rd BL3 . . . . 147 B2
Duncombe St M7 . . . . . 155 B2
Duncote Gr OL2 . . . . . . 149 A1
Dundee Cl 3 M30 . . . . . 79 F2
Dundee Cl OL10 . . . . . . 28 F1
Dundee La BL0 . . . . . . 138 B2
Dundonald Rd
Cheadle SK8 . . . . 132 A7
Manchester M20 . . . . . . 110 C3
Dundonald St SK2 . . . . 170 C2
Dundraw Cl M24 . . . . . . 46 B1
Dundrennan Cl SK12 . . . 133 D5
Dunecroft M34 . . . . . . 101 A4
Dunedin Dr M6 . . . . 80 F6
Dunedin Rd BL8 . . . . . . 10 F2
Dunelm Dr M33 . . . . . . 108 D1
Dunham Ave WA3 . . . . . 73 F1
Dunham Cl BL5 . . . . 57 D5
Dunham Gr WN7 . . . . . . 76 C2
Dunham Lawn WA14 . . . 119 B4
Dunham Massey Hall
WA14 . . . . 118 D3
Dunham Pk WA14 . . . . . 118 D3
Dunham Rd
Altrincham, Bowgreen
WA14 . . . . 118 F1
Altrincham WA14 . . . . . . 119 B4
Dukinfield SK16 . . . . . . 101 D6
Handforth SK9 . . . . 131 D5
Mossbrow WA13 . . . . . . 117 E7
Dunham Rise WA14 . . . . 119 C4
Dunham St
Manchester M15 . . . . . . 162 B2
Oldham OL4 . . . . 67 E8
Dunkeld Gdns 2 M23 . . 120 F6
Dunkeld Rd M23 . . . . . . 120 F6
Dunkerley Ave M35 . . . . 83 F7
Dunkerley Cl M8 . . . . . 155 C4
Dunkerley St
Ashton-u-L OL7 . . . . 85 A5
Oldham OL4 . . . . 67 C7
Royton OL2 . . . . 48 D4
Dunkery Rd M22 . . . . . 121 B4
Dunkirk La SK14 . . . . . . 102 A6
Dunkirk Rd M45 . . . . . . 44 F1
Dunkirk Rise OL12 . . . . 139 B3
Dunkirk St M43 . . . . . . 84 B1
Dunley Cl M12 . . . . 165 A1
Dunlin Ave WA12 . . . . . 89 C4
Dunlin Cl
Bolton BL2 . . . . 148 A1
Hazel Grove SK2 . . . . . . 125 A5
Poynton SK12 . . . . 133 A4
Rochdale OL11 . . . . 29 F7
Dunlin Dr M44 . . . . 94 A3
Dunlin Gr WN7 . . . . 76 B5

Dunlin Wlk 1 WA14 . . . 119 B8
Dunlop Ave OL11 . . . . . 30 E4
Dunmail Ave WA11 . . . . 71 C1
Dunmail Dr M29 . . . . . . 77 C6
Dunmail Dr M24 . . . . . . 46 C1
Dunmaston Ave 6 M23 . 120 D7
Dunmere Wlk M9 . . . . . 156 C2
Dunmore Rd SK8 . . . . . 122 B6
Dunmow Ct SK2 . . . . . . 124 E5
Dunmow Wlk M23 . . . . . 109 A2
Dunne La SK13 . . . . . . 104 E2
Dunnerdale Wlk M13 . . . 163 B1
Dunnisher Rd M23 . . . . 121 B5
Dunnock Cl SK2 . . . . . . 124 F5
Dunollie Rd M33 . . . . . 108 C3
Dunoon Cl OL10 . . . . . . 29 A1
Dunoon Dr BL1 . . . . . . 24 C5
Dunoon Rd
Aspull WN2 . . . . 38 D5
Reddish SK5 . . . . 111 F7
Dunoon Wlk M9 . . . . . . 157 E7
Dunrobin Cl OL10 . . . . . 46 A8
DUNSCAR 24 E8
Dunscar Cl M45 . . . . . . 62 D7
Dunscar Grange BL7 . . . 24 F8
Dunscar Ind Est BL7 . . . 24 E7
Dunscore Rd WN3 . . . . 54 E3
Dunsfold Dr M23 . . . . . 120 D8
Dunsford Ct OL4 . . . . . . 67 F5
Dunsley Ave M40 . . . . . 65 D2
Dunsmore Cl M16 . . . . . 97 E4
Dunsop Dr BL1 . . . . 23 F3
Dunstable M12 . . . . . . 139 C4
Dunstable St M19 . . . . . 99 B1
Dunstall Rd M22 . . . . . 121 E5
Dunstan Ct M40 . . . . . . 83 A8
Dunstan St BL2 . . . . . . 148 C3
Dunstar Ave M34 . . . . . 100 E7
Dunster Ave
Brinnington SK5 . . . . . . 112 C5
Manchester M9 . . . . 64 E4
Rochdale OL11 . . . . 139 B1
Swinton M27 . . . . 62 B2
Dunster Cl
Hazel Grove SK7 . . . . . . 124 C1
Platt Bridge WN2 . . . . . . 56 A1
Dunster Dr M41 . . . . . . 94 C1
Dunster Pl M28 . . . . . . 77 F7
Dunster Rd M28 . . . . . . 77 F7
Dunsters Ave BL8 . . . . . 27 C5
Dunsterville Terr OL11 . . 139 B1
Dunston Pl 7 OL9 . . . . . 48 A1
Dunston St M11 . . . . . . 165 C4
Dunton Gn SK5 . . . . . . 112 B6
Dunton Twrs SK5 . . . . . 112 B6
Dunvegan Rd SK7 . . . . . 124 F1
Dunwood Ave OL2 . . . . 149 C4
Dunwoods Park Courts
OL2 . . . . 32 C1
Dunworth St M14 . . . . . 98 B3
Durant St M4 . . . . 159 B3
Durban Cl OL2 . . . . . . 149 A2
Durban Rd 1 BL1 . . . . . 24 E5
Durban St
Ashton-u-L OL7 . . . . 84 E1
Atherton M46 . . . . 58 A2
Golborne WN2 & WN7 . . . 74 E4
Oldham OL8 . . . . 66 C3
Rochdale OL11 . . . . 30 C2
Durden Mews OL2 . . . . 149 B2
Durham Ave M41 . . . . . 95 E3
Durham Cl
Dukinfield SK16 . . . . . . 101 D6
Little Lever BL3 . . . . 43 B6
Romiley SK6 . . . . 113 A1
Swinton M27 . . . . 61 F2
Tyldesley M29 . . . . 59 A3
Durham Cres M35 . . . . . 84 A6
Durham Dr
Ashton-u-L OL6 . . . . 85 D8
Bury BL9 . . . . 45 A8
Ramsbottom BL0 . . . . . . 11 B3
Durham Gr M44 . . . . . . 105 C6
Durham Ho 6 SK3 . . . . 170 B4
Durham Rd
3 Hindley WN2 . . . . . . 56 E5
Salford M6 . . . . 80 C4
Durham St
Bolton BL1 . . . . 143 C2
Droylsden M43 . . . . 100 A8
12 Manchester M9 . . . . 157 E8
Oldham OL9 . . . . 66 B3
Radcliffe M26 . . . . 44 C5
Reddish SK5 . . . . 99 E2
Rochdale OL11 . . . . 31 A5
Wigan WN1 . . . . 37 E1
Durham Wlk
5 Denton M34 . . . . . . 100 F1
Heywood OL10 . . . . 29 A2
Durley Ave
Manchester M8 . . . . 156 B3
Sale WA15 . . . . 120 B7
Durling St M12 . . . . . . 163 C3
DURN 16 C5
Durnford Ave M41 . . . . . 96 A2
Durnford Cl OL12 . . . . . 13 D2
Durnford St M24 . . . . . . 46 F1
Durnford Wlk M22 . . . . 121 B3
Durn St OL15 . . . . 16 C5
Durrell Way WA3 . . . . . 90 E8
Durrington Wlk 4 M40 . . 65 D3
Dursley Dr WN4 . . . . . . 73 D4

Dutton Gr WN7 76 C2
Dutton St M3 158 C3
Duty St BL1 143 B3
Duxbury Ave
Bolton BL2 25 E5
Little Lever BL3 43 A5
Duxbury Dr BL9 141 C2
Duxbury St BL1 143 A2
Duxford Lo M8 63 F2
Duxford Wlk 1 M40 65 C3
DW Stadium (Wigan Athletic FC & Wigan Warriors RLFC) WN5 54 F8
Dyche St M4 159 B3
Dyehouse La OL16 15 C3
Dye House La SK22 127 C1
Dye La SK6 113 B2
Dyers Cl WA13 117 A4
Dyers Ct OL15 16 A6
Dyers La WA13 117 A4
Dyer St
Golborne WA3 73 F1
Salford M5 161 C3
Dymchurch Ave M26 61 C7
Dymchurch St M40 83 C4
Dysarts Cl OL5 68 E3
Dysart St
4 Ashton-u-L OL6 85 D2
Stockport SK2 124 B5
Dyserth Gr SK5 169 C4
Dyson Cl BL4 60 D8
Dyson Gr OL4 67 F8
Dyson Ho 6 BL4 60 D8
Dyson St
Farnworth BL4 60 D7
Mossley OL5 68 B2
Dystelegh Rd SK12 135 D6

E

Eades St M6 81 A3
Edington St M8 64 A1
Eafield Ave OL16 31 F7
Eafield Cl OL16 31 F7
Eafield Rd
Littleborough OL15 15 E3
Rochdale OL16 15 C1
Eagar St M40 83 C6
Eagle Ct
Delph OL3 50 F5
Salford M15 162 B1
Eagle Dr M6 81 A5
Eagle Lo WA15 119 F2
Eagles Nest M25 63 A3
Eagle St
Bolton BL2 148 A3
3 Manchester M4 159 A2
Oldham OL9 153 B2
Rochdale OL16 31 A6
Eagle Tech Pk OL11 31 A4
EAGLEY 24 F7
EAGLEY BANK 24 F6
Eagley Bank OL12 4 E6
Eagley Brook Way BL1 25 A3
Eagley Brow BL1 24 F7
Eagley Dr BL8 27 A1
Eagley Inf Sch BL7 25 A8
Eagley Jun Sch BL7 25 B8
Eagley View BL8 27 A1
Eagley Way BL1 & BL7 24 F7
Ealand Chase BL6 21 F3
EALEES 16 C5
Ealees OL15 16 C5
Ealees Rd OL15 16 C5
Ealing Ave M14 98 C2
Ealinger Way M27 61 F2
Ealing Pl M19 111 A6
Ealing Rd SK3 170 A4
Eames Ave M26 61 A8
Earby Gr M9 64 F3
Earle Rd SK7 123 E3
Earlesdon Cres M38 60 A5
Earlesfield Cl M33 107 D2
Earle St
Ashton-u-L OL7 84 F2
Newton-le-W WA12 89 A3
EARLESTOWN 89 B2
Earlestown Sta WA12 89 B3
Earl Rd
Handforth SK8, SK9 131 E5
Ramsbottom BL0 138 B2
Stockport SK4 168 C4
Earlscliffe Ct WA14 119 B4
Earl's Lo M35 83 D6
Earl St
Atherton M46 58 B2
6 Heywood OL10 29 C2
Ince-in-M WN2 56 A7
Leigh WN7 76 A4
Mossley OL5 68 B1
Prestwich M25 63 C4
Ramsbottom BL0 11 D6
Reddish M34 100 A4
Salford M7 158 A4
Stockport SK3 170 A4
Trub OL11 47 D8
Wigan WN1 37 C1
Earlston Ave M34 100 A3
Earls Way
Failsworth M35 83 D6
5 Glossop SK13 116 B8
Earlswood Rd OL8 66 E3
Earlswood Wlk
Bolton BL1 147 C4
Earlswood Wlk *continued*
Manchester M18 165 C2
Earl Terr 16 SK16 166 B1
Earl Wlk M12 164 C1
Early Bank SK15 102 C7
Early Bank Rd SK14, SK15, SK16 102 B6
Earnshaw Ave
Rochdale OL12 14 E3
Stockport SK1 112 B1
Earnshaw Cl OL7 84 F5
Earnshaw Clough 2 OL5 86 E8
Earnshaw St
Bolton BL3 146 B3
Hollingworth SK14 171 A4
Easby Cl
Cheadle SK8 132 B6
Poynton SK12 133 D4
Easby Rd M24 46 F3
Easedale Cl M41 94 F3
Easedale Rd
Bolton BL1 144 A4
Failsworth M40 83 C8
Easington Wlk 10 M40 83 A6
Easingwold 2 WA14 119 C4
East Ave
Gatley SK8 131 D8
Golborne WA3 74 C1
Leigh WN7 76 C3
Manchester M19 110 F7
Stalybridge SK15 86 A3
Whitefield M45 44 E2
Eastbank St BL1 143 C2
East Bond St WN7 76 A5
Eastbourne Gr BL1 144 A4
Eastbourne St
Oldham OL8 67 B4
Rochdale OL11 139 C1
East Bridgewater St 4 WN7 76 A4
Eastbrook Ave 2 M26 44 C4
Eastburn Ave M40 159 C3
East Central Dr M27 80 B7
Eastchurch Cl BL4 60 D7
Eastcombe Ave M7 81 B7
Eastcote Ave M11 99 E8
Eastcote Rd SK5 111 F5
Eastcote Wlk 5 BL4 42 E1
East Court Wlk M13 163 C2
East Cres M24 64 F7
East Crompton St George's CE Prim Sch OL2 49 D7
Eastdale WA15 128 F8
Eastdale Pl WA14 119 D7
EAST DIDSBURY 110 C1
East Didsbury Sta M20 110 C1
East Downs Rd
Altrincham WA14 119 C2
Cheadle SK8 122 F2
East Dr
Marple SK6 125 F3
Pendlebury M27 80 B7
Salford M6 80 E5
Whitefield BL9 45 B4
Easterdale OL4 67 C6
Eastern Ave M27 62 D3
Eastern By-Pass M11 83 C2
Eastern By Pass M11 99 D8
Eastern Circ M19 111 A6
Eastfield M6 154 B4
Eastfield Ave
Manchester M40 160 B3
Middleton M24 65 A7
Eastfields M26 43 E5
Eastford Sq M40 159 C4
Eastgarth WN2 56 B2
Eastgarth Wlk 21 M9 64 E3
Eastgate OL12 14 C7
Eastgate St
Ashton-u-L OL7 166 A1
Rochdale OL16 139 C4
East Gr M13 164 A1
East Grange M11 83 C3
Eastgrove Ave BL1 24 E6
Eastham Ave
Bury BL9 27 F6
Manchester M14 98 B1
Eastham Way
11 Handforth SK9 131 D5
Walkden M38 60 B5
Easthaven Ave 4 M11 83 C2
East Hill St 7 OL1 67 A6
Eastholme Dr M19 111 B7
Easthope Cl M20 110 B7
East Lancashire Railway* BB4, BL0 1 C5
East Lancashire Rd
Haydock WA11, WA12, WA3 89 C7
Leigh WA3, WN7, M29 76 D2
Pendlebury M27 80 B6
Swinton M27, M28 79 D7
Tyldesley M28, M29 77 C5
Worsley M28 78 D7
East Lea M34 101 A2
Eastleigh Ave M7 155 B4
Eastleigh Cres WN7 76 B3
Eastleigh Dr M40 160 A3
Eastleigh Gr 2 BL1 145 B4
Eastleigh Rd
Gatley SK8 122 B1
Manchester M25 63 E3
East Lynn Dr M28 61 A3
East Market St M3 158 A2
East Meade
Bolton BL3 147 B2
Manchester, Chorlton-cum-Hardy M21 109 B7
East Meade *continued*
Manchester, Sedgley Park M25 63 D2
Swinton M27 79 E6
East Moor M28 78 A7
Eastmoor Dr M40 83 D4
Eastmoor Gr BL3 146 B2
East Mount WN5 53 F6
East Newton St 8 M4 159 C3
Eastnor Cl M15 162 A2
Easton Cl
Middleton M24 65 C7
Wigan WN3 55 A2
Easton Dr SK8 123 A5
Easton Rd M43 83 E1
East Ordsall La M3, M5 158 A1
East Over SK6 125 A8
Eastpark Cl M13 163 C2
East Park Cl M13 163 C2
East Philip St M3 158 B3
East Rd
Manchester M12 99 A3
Mossley SK15 86 E6
Eastry Ave SK5 112 B6
East St
Ashton-in-M WN4 73 D4
3 Ashton-u-L OL6 85 D4
Bury BL9 140 C1
Denton M34 100 F7
Edenfield BL0 1 D4
Haslingden BB4 1 A7
Hindley WN2 57 B3
Littleborough OL15 16 C5
Milnrow OL16 31 D7
Radcliffe M26 44 B3
Rochdale OL16 31 A8
Tyldesley M46 58 F1
Wardle OL12 15 C6
East Union St M16 161 C2
East Vale SK6 126 A5
Eastview M33 108 B3
East View
4 Middleton M24 64 F8
Ramsbottom, Brooksbottoms BL9 11 C3
Ramsbottom, Chatterton BL0 1 C1
Whitworth OL12 4 D2
Eastville Gdns M19 110 E5
Eastward Ave SK9 136 F6
East Ward Prim Sch BL9 141 B2
Eastway
Middleton M24 46 F1
Sale M33 107 F1
Shaw OL2 149 B2
Urmston M41 94 E3
East Way
Bolton BL1 25 B3
Oldham OL1 48 E1
Eastwell Rd
Ashton-in-M WN4 73 A3
Wigan WN6 36 F3
East Wlk BL7 8 D2
Eastwood M14 98 C1
Eastwood Ave
Droylsden M43 83 E1
Failsworth M40 65 F1
Newton-le-W WA12 89 F3
Urmston M41 95 D2
Walkden M28 60 A2
Eastwood Cl
Bolton BL3 146 A3
Bury BL9 141 B2
Eastwood Ct BL9 141 B2
Eastwood Gr WN7 75 D5
Eastwood Rd M40 65 E1
Eastwood St
Denton M34 100 D7
11 Littleborough OL15 16 B5
Eastwood Terr BL1 40 E8
Eatock Lodge Nature Reserve* BL5 57 D6
Eatock Prim Sch BL5 57 E6
Eatock St WN2 56 B3
Eatock Way BL5 57 D6
Eaton Cl
Cheadle SK8 122 F3
Dukinfield SK16 101 C6
Poynton SK12 134 A3
Swinton M27 61 F2
Eaton Ct
Altrincham WA14 119 C1
Wilmslow SK9 137 A6
Eaton Dr
Alderley Edge SK9 136 F2
Ashton-u-L OL7 84 F4
Sale WA15 120 A8
Eaton Rd
Altrincham WA14 119 C1
Manchester M8 63 F1
Sale M33 108 A4
Eaton St WN2 56 E6
Eaves Knoll Rd SK22 127 A1
Eaves La OL9 152 A1
Ebbdale Cl SK1 124 A8
Ebberstone St M14 98 A2
Ebden St M1 163 B4
Ebenezer St SK13 116 D7
Ebnall Wlk M14 110 D7
Ebor Cl OL2 149 A4
Ebor Ho M21 96 F1
Ebor Rd M22 121 E4
Ebor St OL15 16 B5
Ebsworth St M40 157 C4
Ebury St M26 43 F3
ECCLES 79 F1
Ecclesbridge Rd SK6 125 F4
Eccles Cl M11 165 C4
Eccles Fold 9 M30 79 E2
Eccleshall St M11 83 C1
Eccles Metro Sta M30 79 F1
Eccles New Rd M5, M50 80 C2
Eccles Old Rd M6, M30 80 C3
Eccles Rd
Swinton M27 79 F6
Wigan WN5 36 B1
Eccles St BL0 138 B2
Eccles Sta M30 79 F2
Eccleston Ave
29 Bolton BL2 25 B1
Manchester M14 98 B1
4 Swinton M27 79 D7
Eccleston Cl BL8 27 A1
Eccleston Pl M7 155 A4
Eccleston Rd SK3 123 E4
Eccleston St
Failsworth M35 84 A8
Wigan WN1 37 C1
Eccleston Way 3 SK9 131 D4
Eccups La SK9 136 C8
Echo St M1 163 B4
Eckersley Cl 1 M23 120 F6
Eckersley Fold La M46 58 A1
Eckersley Mill Ind Est WN3 150 B3
Eckersley Rd BL1 143 B3
Eckersley St
Bolton BL3 146 C4
Wigan WN1 37 E1
Eckford St M8 156 B2
Eclipse Cl OL16 31 C7
Edale Ave
Denton, Audenshaw M34 100 D7
Denton, Haughton Green M34 112 F8
Manchester M40 83 A8
Reddish SK5 100 A1
Urmston M41 95 B1
Edale Bank 31 SK13 171 B2
Edale Cl
Altrincham WA14 119 C1
Atherton M46 58 C3
20 Gamesley SK13 171 B2
Gatley SK8 131 D7
Hazel Grove SK7 124 E1
Irlam M44 94 A1
Edale Cres SK13 171 B1
Edale Dr WN6 19 E2
Edale Fold 21 SK13 171 B2
Edale Gr
Ashton-u-L OL6 86 A6
Sale M33 107 E2
Edale Rd
Bolton BL3 146 A4
Farnworth BL4 60 C7
Leigh WN7 76 C4
Stretford M32 96 B3
Edale St M6 81 B5
Edbrook Wlk M13 164 A1
Edburton Ct 5 WA3 90 A8
Eddie Colman Cl M40 83 B5
Eddisbury Ave
Manchester M20 109 F8
Urmston M41 94 D4
Eddisford Dr WA3 91 D4
Edditch Gr BL2 148 C3
Eddleston St WN4 72 F6
Eddystone Cl 6 M5 81 A1
Eden Ave
Edenfield BL0 1 D3
Fowley Common WA3 92 C4
High Lane SK6 134 E7
Eden Bank WN7 76 B6
Edenbridge Dr M26 61 B7
Edenbridge Rd
Cheadle SK8 123 B4
Failsworth M40 83 B4
Eden Cl
Heywood OL10 29 A3
Manchester M15 163 A2
Stockport SK1 124 A8
Wilmslow SK9 136 E5
Eden Ct
Edenfield BL0 1 D2
Manchester, Fallowfield M14 98 B1
Manchester, Levenshulme M19 111 A8
Edendale Dr M22 121 D1
EDENFIELD 1 D3
Edenfield Ave M21 109 D4
Edenfield CE Prim Sch BL0 1 D4
Edenfield La M28 78 F4
Edenfield Rd
Manchester M25 63 E2
Rochdale OL11, OL12 13 C2
Edenfield St OL11 & OL12 14 C1
Eden Gr
Bolton BL1 143 B3
Leigh WN7 75 C5
Edenhall Ave M19 110 F8
Edenhall Gr WN2 56 F3
Edenham Wlk 1 M40 65 D2
Edenhurst BB4 1 D8
Edenhurst Dr 3 WA15 120 B5
Edenhurst Rd SK2 124 B6
Eden Lo BL1 143 B3
Eden Park Rd SK8 131 E8
Eden Pl SK8 122 D6
Edensor Cl WN6 37 A4
Edensor Dr WA15 120 C3
Eden St
Bolton BL1 143 B3
Bury BL9 140 C2
Edenfield BL0 1 D2
Oldham OL1 153 B3
Eden St *continued*
Rochdale OL12 139 A4
Edenvale M28 78 A7
Eden Way OL2 149 A4
Edgar St
Bolton BL3 145 B2
Ramsbottom BL0 138 B1
Rochdale OL16 15 C2
Edgbaston Dr M16 97 A3
Edgecote Cl M22 121 F6
Edgedale Ave M19 110 E5
Edge End OL3 51 A3
Edgefield Ave M9 64 E4
Edge Fold Cres M28 78 D8
Edge Fold Ind Est BL4 146 B1
Edge Fold Rd M28 60 D1
Edge Gn M28 78 C8
EDGE GREEN 73 F3
Edge Green La WA3 73 F2
Edge Green Rd WN4 73 F4
Edge Green St WN4 73 D4
Edge Hall Rd WN5 53 E5
Edge Hill Ave OL2 48 E3
Edgehill Chase SK9 137 E7
Edgehill Cl M5 154 C2
Edgehill Ct M32 96 E1
Edgehill Rd M6 80 C3
Edge Hill Rd
Bolton BL3 146 B3
Royton OL2 48 E3
Edgehill St 8 M4 159 A2
Edge La
Bolton BL1, BL6 23 C5
Britannia OL13 4 C8
Droylsden M11, M43 83 D2
Entwistle BL7 9 A8
Mottram in L SK14 102 F4
Stretford M21, M32 96 E1
Edge Lane Rd OL1 67 A8
Edge Lane St OL2 48 E4
EDGELEY 170 A3
Edgeley Fold SK3 123 C7
Edgeley Rd
Stockport SK3 123 B7
Urmston M41 107 A8
Edgemoor WA14 119 A2
Edgemoor Cl
Oldham OL4 49 D1
Radcliffe M26 43 E5
Whitworth OL12 4 E5
Edgemoor Dr OL11 29 F5
Edgerley Pl WN4 73 A3
Edgerton Rd WA3 90 F8
Edgerton Wlk 3 M28 60 D3
Edge St M4 159 A2
EDGE THE 66 C2
Edge The M3 158 C2
Edge View OL1 47 E1
Edge View La SK9 136 B2
Edgeview Wlk 6 M13 163 B3
Edgeware Ave M25 63 F4
Edgeware Gr WN3 54 D3
Edgeware Rd
Eccles M30 79 A4
Failsworth OL9 65 E3
Edgewater M5 154 A2
Edgeway SK9 137 B5
Edgeway Rd WN3 55 A1
Edgewood WN6 36 A5
Edgeworth Ave BL2 26 D1
Edgeworth Dr
Bury BL8 27 A1
Manchester M14 110 E7
Edgeworth Rd
Golborne WA3 73 F1
Hindley WN2 57 A3
Edgeworth Row SK14 167 B4
Edgeworth Vale BL7 9 E6
Edgmont Ave BL3 147 A4
Edgware Rd M40 83 B4
EDGWORTH 9 D6
Edgworth Cl OL10 29 A2
Edgworth Views BL7 9 D8
Edgy Wlk 19 SK15 86 A1
Edilom Rd M8 63 E2
Edinburgh 5 M30 79 E2
Edinburgh Cl
Cheadle SK8 122 F6
Ince-in-M WN2 56 A8
8 Sale M33 107 D3
Edinburgh Dr
Hindley WN2 57 B3
Romiley SK6 113 C4
Wigan WN5 54 D5
Edinburgh Ho M3 158 A1
Edinburgh Rd BL3 43 A2
Edinburgh Sq M40 160 B4
Edinburgh Way OL11 30 D4
Edinburgh Wlk WN2 38 D5
Edington 7 OL12 139 C4
Edison Rd M30 95 C8
Edison St 1 M11 99 E7
Edith Ave M14 98 A3
Edith Cavell Cl M11 83 C1
Edith Cliff Wlk M40 65 F1
Edith St
Bolton BL1 144 C2
Farnworth BL4 60 D7
Oldham OL8 66 F3
Ramsbottom BL0 11 E8
Wigan WN3 150 B3
Edlestone Gr 2 SK9 131 E1
Edlin Cl M12 164 B1
Edlingham 5 OL11 139 B2
Edlington Wlk 12 M40 83 C6
Edmonds St M24 47 B1
Edmonton Ct SK2 124 A4

Edmonton Rd
Failsworth M40 83 A4
Stockport SK2 124 A4
Edmund Cl SK4 169 B4
Edmund Dr WN7 75 C5
Edmunds Ct BL3 145 A2
Edmunds Fold OL15 15 F6
Edmund St
Droylsden M43 84 A1
Failsworth M35 83 F8
Milnrow OL16 31 F6
8 Radcliffe M26 44 C4
Rochdale OL12 139 A4
Salford M6 154 B3
Shaw OL2 149 C3
Walsden OL14 6 A8
Edna Rd WN7 75 C7
Edna St SK14 167 A2
Edridge Way WN2 56 C4
Edson Rd M9 63 F3
Edstone Cl BL3 40 F4
Edward Ave
Littleborough OL15 15 F3
Manchester M21 109 A8
Romiley SK6 112 E3
Salford M6 80 C3
Edward Charlton Rd M16, M21 97 A2
Edward Ct WA14 119 B7
Edward Dr WN4 73 B4
Edward Mews OL9 152 C1
Edward Onyon Ct M6 154 B2
Edward Rd
Manchester M9 64 D5
Shaw OL2 149 A2
Edwards Cl SK6 125 E5
Edwards Ct 3 M22 121 D3
Edwards Dr M45 63 B8
Edward St
Ashton-u-L OL6 85 E2
Bolton BL3 145 A1
Bury BL9 140 C1
Chadderton OL9 152 A4
Denton, Audenshaw M34 100 D7
Denton M34 100 F4
Droylsden M43 100 A8
Dukinfield SK16 101 C6
Farnworth BL4 42 B2
Glossop SK13 104 C1
Horwich BL6 22 A3
Hyde SK14 101 C3
Kearsley M26 61 B8
Leigh WN7 76 A4
Manchester M9 157 B4
Marple SK6 114 B1
Middleton M24 47 A1
Oldham OL9 152 C1
Prestwich M25 63 A5
Radcliffe M26 44 B2
Rochdale, Newbold Brow OL16 31 A8
Rochdale, Wuerdle OL12 15 D4
Sale M33 108 E4
Salford M7 158 B4
Stockport SK1 170 C4
Westhoughton BL5 57 E8
Whitworth OL12 4 D2
Wigan, Rose Bridge WN1 151 C4
Wigan, Swinley WN1 37 C2
Edward Sutcliffe Cl M14 98 A2
Edwards Way SK6 125 E5
Edwin Rd M11 160 B1
Edwin St
Bury BL9 140 B2
Stockport SK1 124 B8
Wigan WN1 151 B3
Edwin Waugh Gdns OL12 14 D3
Edzell Wlk 18 M11 83 C1
Eeasbrook M41 95 D1
EES 107 F7
Egbert St 19 M40 83 A7
EGERTON 8 E2
Egerton Ave WA13 117 C8
Egerton Cl OL10 29 D1
Egerton Cres
Heywood OL10 29 C1
Manchester M20 110 B7
Egerton Ct
Denton M34 101 A4
6 Hindley WN2 56 E5
Manchester M14 98 C4
Stockport SK3 124 A4
Stretford M21 108 F8
Worsley M28 79 A8
Egerton Dr
Altrincham WA15 120 A3
Sale M33 108 B5
Egerton Gr M28 60 D3
Egerton High Sch M41 95 E4
Egerton Ho 3 M15 162 A3
Egerton Lo
Bolton BL7 8 E1
Denton M34 101 A4
Egerton Mews
Droylsden M43 100 A8
Manchester M14 110 D8
Egerton Moss WA15 128 E5
EGERTON PARK 79 B7
Egerton Park Arts Coll M34 100 E4
Egerton Pk M28 79 B7
Egerton Pl OL2 149 A2
Egerton Prim Sch BL7 8 D3
Egerton Rd
Altrincham WA15 120 A2
Eccles M30 79 D4
Handforth SK9 131 B1
Manchester M14 110 D8
Egerton Rd *continued*
Stockport SK3 124 A4
Walkden M28 60 D3
Whitefield M45 62 F7
Egerton St
Abram Brow WN2 74 B7
Ashton-u-L OL6 166 C3
Denton M34 100 E5
Droylsden M43 84 B1
Eccles M30 79 B2
Farnworth BL4 42 C1
Heywood OL10 29 C1
Littleborough OL15 16 C5
Manchester M15 162 A3
Middleton M24 64 C7
Mossley OL5 68 C2
Oldham OL1 67 A8
Prestwich M25 63 C4
Salford M3 158 A1
Egerton Terr M14 110 D7
Egerton Vale BL7 8 D2
Eggar Cl M29 77 B7
Eggington St M40 156 C1
Egham Ct 18 BL2 25 B1
Egham Ho BL3 146 B2
Egmont St
Manchester M8 156 A4
6 Mossley OL5 86 D8
Pendlebury M6 80 E6
Egremont Ave M20 110 A7
Egremont Cl M45 45 A1
Egremont Ct M7 81 C8
Egremont Gr 2 SK3 123 B8
Egremont Rd OL16 31 F4
Egret Dr M44 94 A3
Egyptian St BL1 143 C1
Egypt La M25 45 E1
Ehlinger Ave SK13 104 A5
Eida Way M17 96 C8
Eight Acre M45 62 C7
Eighth Ave OL8 66 D1
Eighth St M17 96 D6
Eileen Gr M14 98 C2
Eileen Gr W M14 98 B2
Elaine Ave M9 65 B2
Elaine Cl WN4 73 D5
Elbain Wlk M40 83 C5
Elberton Wlk 13 M8 155 C3
Elbe St M12 163 C4
Elbow St M19 99 A1
Elbut La BL9 28 F5
Elcho Rd WA14 119 B3
Elcombe Ave WA3 90 E7
Elcot Cl M40 156 C1
Elderberry Cl
Diggle OL3 51 C5
Wigan WN1 37 B4
Elderberry Way SK9 137 E8
Elderberry Wlk M31 105 E3
Elder Cl
Bury BL8 26 F5
Stockport SK2 124 D8
Eldercot Gr BL3 146 A4
Eldercot Rd BL3 146 A4
Eldercroft Rd WA15 120 D5
Elder Dr BL3 42 E5
Elderfield Dr SK6 112 F4
Elder Gr M40 65 F2
Eldermount Rd M9 64 D2
Elder Rd OL4 67 E6
Elder St OL16 31 B5
Elderwood OL9 65 E7
Eldon Cl M34 100 E7
Eldon Gdns WN4 73 A6
Eldon Pl M30 79 C1
Eldon Precinct OL8 153 B1
Eldon Rd
Irlam M44 94 A2
Stockport SK3 123 C7
Eldon St
Bolton BL2 25 B2
Bury BL9 140 C4
Leigh WN7 75 D6
Oldham OL8 153 C1
Eldridge Dr M40 83 A5
Eldroth Ave M22 121 D3
Eleanor Rd
Manchester M21 109 A8
Royton OL2 48 E3
Eleanor St
Bolton BL1 25 A5
Oldham OL1 153 A4
Wigan WN3 150 A3
Electo St M11 99 E7
Elevator Rd M17 96 E6
Eleventh St M17 96 D6
Elf Mill Cl SK3 170 B2
Elf Mill Terr SK3 170 B2
Elford Gr M18 100 A4
Elgar St M12 99 A4
Elgin Ave
Garswood WN4 72 D4
Manchester M20 110 D3
Elgin Cl WN2 56 A8
Elgin Dr M33 108 E3
Elgin Rd
Dukinfield SK16 101 C6
Oldham OL4 67 C5
Elgin St
Ashton-u-L OL7 166 A4
Bolton BL1 142 C2
Stalybridge SK15 86 B1
Elgol Cl SK3 170 C1
Elgol Dr BL3 40 E6
Elham Cl M26 61 C7
Elim St OL15 16 C7
Elim Terr OL15 16 C7
Eliot Dr WN3 150 A1
Eliot Gdns WN3 150 A1
Eliot Rd M30 79 D1
Eliot Wlk M24 47 C3
Elishaw Row M5 154 C1
Eli St OL9 66 A3
Eliza Ann St
5 Eccles M30 79 C1
Manchester M40 159 C4
Elizabethan Ct 10 M29 58 F1
Elizabethan Dr WN3 55 E4
Elizabethan Way OL16 31 F5
Elizabethan Wlk 1 WN2 56 A2
Elizabeth Ave
Chadderton OL9 66 A3
Denton M34 100 E5
Disley SK12 135 D5
Leigh WN2 56 E1
Royton OL2 48 D3
1 Stalybridge SK15 86 A2
Stockport SK1 170 C4
Elizabeth Cl M32 96 D2
Elizabeth Ct
Manchester M14 110 D7
Reddish M18 99 F3
Stockport SK4 168 C2
8 Tyldesley M29 58 F1
Elizabeth Dr BB4 1 A8
Elizabeth Gr OL2 149 B3
Elizabeth Ho
13 Bury BL8 27 C3
Stockport SK4 168 B2
Elizabeth Rd M31 105 F4
Elizabeth Slinger Rd M20 109 F5
Elizabeth St
Ashton-u-L OL6 166 B4
Atherton M46 58 D3
Denton M34 100 D3
Edenfield BL0 1 D3
2 Heywood OL10 29 C2
Hyde SK14 167 A3
Ince-in-M WN2 56 B8
Leigh WN7 76 B3
Manchester M8 156 A1
Prestwich M25 63 C4
3 Radcliffe M26 44 A3
Rochdale OL11 30 C3
1 Swinton M27 61 F1
Whitefield M45 62 F7
Elizabeth Yarwood Ct M13 163 B2
Eliza St
Manchester M15 162 B2
Ramsbottom BL0 11 D6
Elkanagh Gdns M6 154 C3
Elk Mill Ctr Ret Pk OL1 48 B2
Elkstone Ave M38 60 A6
Elkstone Cl WN3 54 C2
Elkwood Cl WN1 37 B4
Elladene Pk M21 109 C8
Ellanby Cl M14 98 B3
Elland Cl
Westhoughton BL5 39 D3
Whitefield BL9 45 B2
Elland House Sch OL2 48 D3
Ellan Wlk 10 M11 83 C1
Ellaston Dr M41 95 D2
Ellastone Rd M6 80 C4
Ella View Lodge M46 58 A4
Ellbourne Rd M9 64 A3
ELLENBROOK 78 B8
Ellenbrook Cl M12 165 B2
Ellenbrook Com Prim Sch M28 78 C8
Ellenbrook Rd M28 78 B7
Ellen Brook Rd M22 130 D8
Ellendale Grange M28 78 B8
Ellen Gr BL4 61 C5
Ellenhall Cl M9 157 A4
Ellenor Dr M29 77 C7
Ellenroad App OL16 32 A4
Ellenroad Engine Ho* OL16 32 A4
Ellenroad St OL16 32 A4
Ellenrod Dr OL12 14 A2
Ellenrod La OL12 14 A2
Ellenshaw Cl OL12 14 A2
Ellen St
2 Bolton BL1 142 C3
Droylsden M43 100 B8
Oldham OL9 153 A4
Stockport SK4 169 A3
Wigan WN1 151 A3
Ellen Wilkinson Cres M12 165 A1
Elleray Cl BL3 43 C3
Elleray Rd
Middleton M9 64 F5
Salford M6 80 D5
Ellerbeck Cl
Bolton BL2 25 C5
Standish WN6 36 F7
Ellerbeck Cres M28 78 C8
Ellerby Ave M27 62 A3
Ellergreen Rd WN2 57 C3
Ellerslie Ct M14 98 C4
Ellesmere Ave
Ashton-u-L OL6 85 C7
Eccles M30 79 E2
Marple SK6 125 F6
Walkden M28 60 C3
Ellesmere Circ M41 95 D7
Ellesmere Cl SK16 101 E8
Ellesmere Dr SK8 123 A5
Ellesmere Gdns BL3 147 A3
Ellesmere Gn M30 79 E3
Ellesmere Ho 3 M30 79 F3
ELLESMERE PARK 79 E4
Ellesmere Rd
Altrincham WA14 119 E6
Ashton-in-M WN4 72 F4
Bolton BL3 146 C3
Cheadle SK3 123 A7
Culcheth WA3 91 E3
Eccles M30 79 E3
Manchester M21 97 C1
Wigan WN5 54 D6
Ellesmere Ret Pk M28 60 D4
Ellesmere Sh Ctr 1 M28 60 D3
Ellesmere St
Bolton BL3 145 A2
14 Eccles M30 79 D1
Failsworth M35 83 F8
Farnworth BL4 60 D8
Leigh WN7 75 F4
Manchester M15 162 A3
Rochdale OL11 139 C1
Swinton, Clifton Green M27 62 A1
Swinton, Deans M27 79 D7
Tyldesley, Higher Green M29 77 C5
Tyldesley M29 59 A1
Walkden M38 60 C4
Ellesmere Terr M14 110 D7
Ellesmere Wlk 3 BL4 60 D8
Ellingham Cl M11 160 C1
Elliot Sq 11 OL1 67 A8
Elliot St
Bolton BL1 142 C3
Oldham OL4 67 E6
Elliott Ave
Dukinfield SK14 101 D5
Golborne WA3 74 B1
Elliott Dr
Hindley WN2 56 E7
Sale M33 107 E4
Elliott St
Farnworth BL4 60 C7
Rochdale OL12 31 A8
Tyldesley M29 76 F8
Ellisbank Wlk 9 M13 163 B3
Ellis Cres M28 60 B3
Ellis Dr M8 64 B1
Ellis Fold OL12 13 E2
Ellis La M24 64 B8
Ellisland Wlk 1 M40 83 A6
Ellison Cl SK14 103 D5
Ellison Ho 1 OL7 166 A1
Ellison St SK13 104 D1
Ellis Rd WN5 71 D4
Ellis St
Hyde SK14 167 C2
Manchester M15 162 B2
Salford M8 158 B4
Wigan WN1 37 E1
Elliston Sq M12 165 A2
Ellonby Rise BL6 40 C5
Ellor St
Salford M5 81 B2
Salford, Seedley M6 154 C3
Ellwood Rd SK1 112 B1
Elm Ave
Downall Green WN4 72 D5
Golborne WA3 74 A1
Newton-le-W WA12 89 C2
Radcliffe M26 61 F8
Standish WN6 36 F8
Wigan WN5 54 E6
Elmbank Ave M20 109 E4
Elmbank Rd M24 65 C8
Elm Beds Rd SK12 134 C2
Elmbridge Wlk
Bolton BL3 145 A1
2 Manchester M40 83 A6
Elm Cl
Mottram in L SK14 103 A4
2 Partington M31 105 F3
Poynton SK12 133 F3
Elm Cres
Alderley Edge SK9 137 B3
Worsley M28 79 A7
Elm Croft WN1 37 B4
Elm Ct SK1 124 B8
Elmdale Ave SK8 122 B2
Elmdale Wlk 2 M15 163 A2
Elm Dr
Billinge WN5 71 D5
Denton M34 100 D4
Stretford M32 108 C8
Elmfield WN6 36 B6
Elmfield Ave
Atherton M46 58 C4
Wythenshawe M22 121 E8
Elmfield Cl SK9 137 B2
Elmfield Ct SK3 170 C1
Elmfield Dr SK6 125 E6
Elmfield Ho SK3 170 C1
Elmfield Rd
Alderley Edge SK9 137 B2
Droylsden M34 100 C8
Stockport SK3 170 C1
Wigan WN1 37 B5
Elmfield St
Bolton, Back O' Th' Bank BL1 143 C2
Bolton BL1 143 C3
Manchester M8 156 A2
Elmgate Gr M19 99 A1
Elm Gr
Alderley Edge SK9 137 B2
Ashton-u-L OL6 85 C5
Bolton BL7 25 A8
Denton M34 100 D5
Droylsden M43 83 D2
Farnworth BL4 60 B8
Glossop SK13 104 C2
Elm Gr *continued*
Handforth SK9 131 C3
6 Horwich BL6 22 E1
Hyde SK14 167 C2
Manchester M20 110 B3
Newhey OL16 32 A3
Oldham OL4 68 B6
Prestwich M25 63 A6
Rochdale OL11 139 B1
Sale M33 108 B6
Swinton M27 61 B2
Urmston M41 95 E2
Wardle OL12 15 C6
Elmham Wlk M40 159 C4
Elm Ho M16 97 D3
Elmhow Gr WN3 55 A2
Elmhurst Dr M19 110 F5
Elmira Way M5 161 A3
Elmlea WA15 119 F4
Elmley Cl SK2 125 A5
Elmore Wood OL15 15 E6
Elm Park Ct M20 110 B4
Elmpark Gate OL12 14 B3
Elmpark Gr OL12 14 B3
Elmpark Vale OL12 14 B3
Elmpark View OL12 14 B3
Elmpark Way OL12 14 B3
Elm Rd
Abram Brow WN2 74 C7
Altrincham WA15 119 E3
Gatley SK8 122 A5
High Lane SK6 134 F7
Hollinfare WA3 105 A2
Kearsley BL4 60 F5
Little Lever BL3 43 B2
Manchester M20 110 A4
Oldham OL8 66 D2
Westhoughton BL5 57 F7
Elmridge WN7 76 B6
Elmridge Ct WA3 90 F8
Elmridge Dr WA15 129 C8
Elmridge Prim Sch WA15 129 C8
Elms SK9 136 F6
Elms Bank Specialist Arts Coll 7 M45 44 F2
Elmsbury St 1 WN4 72 F5
Elms Cl M45 44 F2
Elmsdale Ave M9 64 D5
Elms Farm 3 M45 44 F2
Elmsfield Ave OL11 13 E1
Elmsleigh Ct M30 79 F3
Elmsleigh Rd SK8 122 A2
Elmsmere Rd M20 110 D4
Elms Rd
Manchester SK4 111 B5
Stalybridge SK15 86 D3
Whitefield M45 44 F1
Elms Sq M45 44 E1
Elms St M45 44 F1
Elm St
Bury BL9 141 B2
Eccles M30 79 D1
Edenfield BL0 1 E3
Failsworth M35 83 F8
Farnworth BL4 42 E1
Heywood OL10 29 D2
Leigh WN7 75 F3
Middleton M24 65 C8
Platt Bridge WN2 56 A2
Ramsbottom BL0 11 D6
Rochdale OL12 14 F1
Romiley SK6 112 F4
Swinton M27 61 E1
4 Tyldesley M29 59 A1
Whitworth OL12 4 D2
Elmstead Ave M20 110 A6
Elmsted Cl SK8 123 B3
Elms The
Golborne WA3 90 F7
Mossley OL5 68 B1
Rochdale OL15 15 E4
4 Whitefield M45 44 F2
Elmstone Cl 7 M9 64 C2
Elmstone Dr OL2 48 E5
Elmstone Gr BL1 143 C1
Elmsway
Altrincham WA15 129 B8
Bramhall SK7 132 C7
High Lane SK6 134 E6
Elmswood Ave M14 97 F2
Elmswood Dr SK14 102 A3
Elmsworth Ave M19 99 B1
Elmton Rd M9 64 E3
Elm Tree Cl
Failsworth M35 84 B7
Stalybridge SK15 102 A8
Elmtree Dr SK4 168 C2
Elm Tree Dr
Dukinfield SK16 101 F7
Wythenshawe M22 121 D3
Elm Tree Rd
Golborne WA3 90 F8
Romiley SK6 112 C3
Elmwood M33 107 C4
Elmwood Ave WN4 73 A2
Elmwood Cl BL5 59 A6
Elmwood Ct M32 108 C8
Elmwood Dr OL2 48 C5
Elmwood Gr
Bolton BL1 144 C4
Farnworth BL4 60 C6
Manchester M9 157 C3
Elmwood Lodge M20 110 A4
Elmwood Pk SK15 86 D3

Elm Wood Prim Sch M24. 65 C8
Elnup Ave WN6 .... 36 B6
Elrick Wlk M11 .... 83 B1
Elsa Rd M19 .... 99 C1
Elsdon Dr
  Atherton M46 .... 58 E4
  Manchester M18 .... 99 D6
Elsdon Gdns 6 BL2 .... 25 B1
Elsdon Rd BL3 .... 98 F2
Elsfield Cl BL1 .... 143 A2
Elsham Cl BL1 .... 24 C5
Elsham Dr M28 .... 60 B3
Elsham Gdns M18 ...... 99 B2
Elsie St BL4 .... 60 C7
Elsinore Ave M44 .... 94 A1
Elsinore Cl M35 .... 84 B7
Elsinore Rd M16 .... 97 A4
Elsinore St 8 BL2 ..... 25 B3
Elsma Rd M40 .... 83 E4
Elsmore Rd M14 ...... 110 A8
Elson Dr SK4 .... 113 D7
Elson St BL8 .... 27 B4
Elstead Gr WN4 .... 72 D4
Elstead Wlk M9 .... 64 A3
Elsted Rd OL3 .... 68 E5
Elston Ave WA12 .... 89 C5
Elstree Ave M40 .... 83 B4
Elstree Ct M41 .... 95 D2
Elswick Ave
  Bolton BL3 .... 144 B1
  Bramhall SK7 .... 132 E7
  Manchester M21 ..... 109 D4
Elsworth Cl M26 .... 44 B1
Elsworth Dr BL1 ...... 143 C4
Elsworth St M3 .... 159 A4
Elterwater Cl
  Bury BL8 .... 27 B4
  Manchester M24 ..... 46 D3
Elterwater Rd BL4 ..... 59 E7
Eltham Ave SK2 .... 124 C5
Eltham Cl WN4 .... 73 D3
Eltham Dr M41 .... 95 C5
Eltham St 6 M19 ...... 99 A2
ELTON 27 C2
Elton Ave
  Farnworth BL4 .... 59 F8
  Manchester M19 .... 111 A8
Elton Bank 6 SK13 ... 171 A1
Elton Brook Cl BL8 .... 27 C3
Elton Cl
  8 Gamesley SK13 ... 171 A1
  Golborne WA3 .... 90 E7
  Handforth SK9 ...... 131 E1
  Whitefield M45 .... 63 A8
Elton Dr SK7 .... 133 E8
Elton High Sch Specialist
  Arts Coll The BL8 .... 27 A4
Elton House WN5 ...... 54 C7
Elton Lea 7 SK13 .... 171 A1
Elton Loft 8 BL8 ...... 27 C2
Elton Prim Sch BL8 ... 27 C4
Elton Rd M33 .... 107 E2
Elton St
  Bolton BL2 .... 148 A3
  Rochdale OL11 .... 30 C1
  Salford M7 .... 158 B3
  Stretford M32 .... 96 F5
Elton's Yd M7 .... 158 A3
Elton Vale Rd BL8 ..... 27 B2
Elvate Cres M8 .... 155 C1
Elverdon Cl M15 ..... 162 B1
Elverston St M22 .... 109 E1
Elverston Way OL9 .. 152 C4
Elvey St M40 .... 157 C1
Elvington Cl WN5 ..... 36 B3
Elvington Cres 7 M28 . 78 C8
Elvira Cl M35 .... 84 B7
Elway Rd WN4 .... 73 C4
Elwick Cl 4 M16 ...... 97 F3
Elworth Way 8 SK9 . 131 D4
Elworthy Gr WN1 ..... 37 E2
Elwyn Ave M22 ...... 121 D7
Ely Ave M32 .... 95 F3
Ely Cl M28 .... 78 B8
Ely Cres M35 .... 83 F5
Ely Dr
  Bury BL8 .... 140 A4
  Tyldesley M29 .... 77 C7
Ely Gdns M41 .... 95 E2
Ely Gr BL1 .... 143 B1
Elysian Fields M6 .... 80 C3
Elysian St M11 ...... 165 C4
Ely St OL9 .... 152 A8
Embankment Bsns Pk The
  SK4 .... 110 F1
Embankment Rd BL7 ... 9 C5
Embassy Wlk M18 .... 99 D4
Ember St M11 .... 83 D2
Embla Wlk 7 BL3 ..... 42 A4
Embleton Cl BL3 .... 145 A1
Embleton Cl BL2 ...... 25 E1
Embleton Wlk M18 .. 165 C2
Embsay Cl BL1 .... 24 D5
Emerald Ave WN7 .... 75 E4
Emerald Cotts BL8 ... 10 F3
Emerald Dr OL1 .... 49 E3
Emerald Rd M22 .... 130 F7
Emerald St
  1 Bolton BL1 .... 143 C3
  Denton M34 .... 100 E3
  Wigan WN6 .... 37 A3
Emerson Ave M30 .... 80 A3
Emerson Dr M24 ..... 46 F1
Emerson St M5 ...... 154 A2

Emery Ave M21 ...... 109 C6
Emery Cl
  Altrincham WA14 .... 119 D7
  Stockport SK4 ...... 168 A4
Emery Ct SK4 .... 110 F1
Emily Beavan Cl M11 . 83 B1
Emlea Gdns WN2 ..... 56 B7
Emily Pl M43 .... 83 F1
Emlyn Gr SK8 .... 123 A6
Emlyn St
  Farnworth BL4 .... 42 C1
  2 Hindley WN2 ...... 56 D5
  Swinton M27 .... 79 D8
  Walkden M28 .... 60 D3
Emmanuel Cl BL3 ... 145 A1
Emmanuel Cl OL6 ... 166 B4
Emmanuel Holcombe CE
  Prim Sch BL8 .... 138 A2
Emmanuel Pl BL3 ... 145 A1
Emma St
  Oldham OL8 .... 66 F3
  Rochdale OL12 ...... 139 B4
Emmaus Wlk M6 .... 154 C3
Emmeline Grange M6 . 154 B2
Emmerson St M27 .... 61 F1
Emmett St OL2 .... 22 B3
Emmott Cl OL10 ...... 29 C2
Emmott Way OL1 ... 153 C2
Empire Rd
  Bolton BL2 .... 42 E7
  Dukinfield SK16 .... 101 C6
Empire St M3, M8 ... 158 C4
Empress Ave 2 SK6 . 125 F5
Empress Bsns Ctr M16 161 C2
Empress Ct M15 .... 161 C2
Empress Dr
  Leigh WN7 .... 76 E6
  Reddish SK4 .... 169 A4
Empress Ind EstWN2 . 151 C3
Empress St
  Bolton BL1 .... 142 B1
  Manchester, City Park
    M16 .... 161 C2
  Salford M8 .... 155 C2
Emsworth Cl 6 BL2 ... 25 B1
Emsworth Dr M33 ... 108 C1
Ena Cres WN7 .... 75 C7
Ena St
  Bolton BL3 .... 42 A3
  Oldham OL1 .... 49 C1
Enbridge St M5 ..... 161 A4
Encombe Pl M3 ..... 158 A2
Endcott Cl M18 ..... 165 B2
Enderby Rd M40 ..... 65 C1
Ending Rake OL12 ... 14 C4
Endon Dr M21 ...... 109 F8
Endon St BL1 .... 142 B1
Endsleigh Gdns 1 M14 . 75 F5
Endsleigh Rd M20 .. 110 C6
Endsley Ave M28 .... 60 C1
Enfield Ave
  Manchester M19 ... 111 A6
  Oldham OL8 .... 66 E3
Enfield Cl
  Bolton BL1 .... 143 B1
  Bury BL9 .... 44 F5
  Eccles M30 .... 95 D8
  Rochdale OL11 ...... 29 E8
Enfield Dr 7 M11 .... 83 C2
Enfield Gr WN7 ...... 76 B6
Enfield Rd 1 M30 ... 95 D8
Enfield Rd
  Eccles M30 .... 79 D4
  Swinton M27 .... 79 E6
Enfield St
  Hyde SK14 .... 113 E7
  Walkden M28 .... 60 D5
  Wigan WN5 .... 54 C5
Enford Ave M22 .... 121 A2
Engel Cl BL0 .... 138 A1
Engell Cl M18 .... 99 C5
Engels Ho
  3 Eccles M30 ...... 95 D8
  Manchester M14 ... 110 D8
Engineer St WN2 .... 56 A7
Engine Fold M28 .... 60 B2
Engine Fold Rd M28. 60 A2
Engine La M29 ...... 59 B4
Engine St OL9 ...... 66 B4
Engledene BL1 ..... 24 D6
Englefield Gr 3 WN3 . 55 A4
English Martyrs' RC Prim Sch
  M41 .... 95 C2
English St WN7 ..... 76 A4
Enid Cl M7 .... 155 A1
Enid Pl WN2 .... 73 F8
Ennerdale Ave
  Ashton-in-M WN4 ... 73 B5
  Billinge WA11 .... 71 B1
  4 Bolton BL2 ...... 25 F1
  Manchester M21 ... 109 D4
  Royton OL2 .... 48 C7
  Swinton M27 .... 79 F6
Ennerdale Cl BL3 ... 42 F3
Ennerdale Dr
  Gatley SK8 .... 122 B3
  Sale, Ashton upon Mersey
    M33 .... 107 E5
  Sale, Timperley WA15 120 A8
  Whitefield BL9 ...... 45 A2
Ennerdale Gdns BL2 . 25 E1
Ennerdale Gr
  Ashton-u-L OL7 ..... 84 F5
  Farnworth BL4 ...... 59 E8
Ennerdale Pl WN2 ... 56 B8

Ennerdale Rd
  Hindley WN2 .... 56 E5
  Leigh WN7 .... 76 C4
  Middleton M24 ...... 46 D5
  Partington M31 .... 105 E3
  Rochdale OL11 ...... 30 B4
  Romiley SK6 .... 113 B4
  Stockport SK1 ..... 124 B7
  Stretford M32 .... 96 C3
  Tyldesley M29 ...... 77 D8
Ennerdale Terr SK15 . 86 A3
Ennis Cl M23 .... 120 E5
Ennismore Ave M5, M30 . 80 A2
Enstone Dr M40 ..... 65 D1
Enstone Way M29 ... 59 C1
Enterprise Pk BL6 ... 39 C8
Enterprise Trad Est
  Manchester M18 .... 99 E6
  Stretford M32 .... 96 A8
Enterprise Way WA3 . 91 A7
Enticott Rd M44 ... 105 C5
Entwisle Ave M41 ... 95 B4
Entwisle Rd OL16 ... 31 A8
Entwisle Row BL4 ... 60 D8
Entwisle St
  1 Farnworth BL4 ... 42 E1
  Milnrow OL16 .... 31 E6
  Swinton M27 .... 61 D1
ENTWISTLE 9 B7
Entwisle Gr WN7 .... 76 C3
Entwistle Hall La BL7 .. 9 B8
Entwistle St BL2 .... 148 B4
Entwistle Sta BL7 .... 9 B8
Enver Rd M8 .... 156 B4
Enville Rd
  Altrincham WA14 ... 119 C3
  Manchester M40 .... 65 B1
  Pendlebury M6 ..... 80 C6
Enville St
  Ashton-u-L OL6 .... 166 C3
  Denton M34 .... 100 F7
  Manchester M7 ..... 64 D3
  Manchester M20 ... 110 B4
  Stockport SK3 .... 123 B8
Envoy Cl WN5 ...... 36 E1
Enys Wlk M6 .... 81 A5
Ephraim's Fold WN2 . 38 D6
Epping Cl
  Ashton-u-L OL6 .... 85 C7
  Chadderton OL9 .... 65 E8
Epping Dr M33 ..... 107 C5
Epping Rd M34 .... 100 B2
Epping St M15 ..... 163 A2
Epplesworth Rise M27 . 62 A2
Epsom Ave
  Handforth SK8, SK9 . 131 E4
  Manchester M19 ... 110 F6
  Sale M33 .... 107 C2
Epsom Cl
  Hazel Grove SK7 ... 124 F2
  Rochdale OL11 ...... 29 F8
Epsom Croft P&6 ... 21 B7
Epsom Dr WN2 ..... 73 F7
Epsom Mews 2 M7 . 155 A2
Epsom Wlk OL9 .... 152 C3
Epworth Ct SK4 .... 168 B3
Epworth Gr 3 BL3 . 146 C3
Epworth St M44 ... 159 C1
Equitable St
  Milnrow OL16 .... 31 F5
  Oldham OL4 .... 67 D8
  3 Rochdale OL11 .. 31 A6
Era St
  Bolton BL2 .... 42 E7
  Sale M33 .... 108 B4
Ercall Ave M12 ..... 164 B2
Erica Ave OL4 ...... 49 F4
Erica Cl 3 SK5 ..... 100 A1
Erica Dr M19 .... 110 E4
Erica Wlk WN7 ..... 75 B5
Eric Brook Cl 6 M14 . 98 B1
Eric Bullows Cl M22 . 121 C1
Eric St
  Littleborough OL15 . 16 A4
  Oldham OL4 .... 67 C6
Erin Cl OL9 .... 152 C5
Erindale Wlk M40 .. 156 C2
Erin St M11 .... 99 E7
Erith Cl SK5 .... 112 B6
Erith Rd OL4 .... 67 C6
Erlesmere Ave M34 . 101 A4
Erlesmere Cl OL4 .. 49 F4
Erlington Ave M16 . 97 B2
Ermen Rd M30 ..... 95 C8
Ermington Ct OL10 . 29 C1
Ermington Dr M8 .. 155 C2
Erneley Cl M12 .... 99 B3
Ernest St
  Bolton BL1 .... 145 A3
  Britannia OL13 ..... 4 C8
  Cheadle SK8 ...... 122 C6
  Prestwich M25 ..... 62 F4
  Stockport SK2 .... 124 A6
Ernest Terr OL12 ... 15 B1
Ernlouen Ave BL1 .. 144 A4
Ernocroft Gr 3 M18 . 99 E6
Ernocroft La SK6 ... 114 E2
Ernocroft Rd SK6 .. 114 B1
Erradale Cres WN3 . 54 D2
Erringdon Cl SK2 .. 124 E6
Errington Cl BL3 ... 40 F5
Errington Dr M7 ... 158 A4
Errol Ave M9 ...... 64 A5
Errwood Cres M19 . 111 A8
Errwood Rd M19 .. 111 A7
Erskine Cl 3 BL5 .. 39 E1
Erskine Pl WN2 .... 56 B1
Erskine Rd
  Manchester M9 .... 64 C5
  Partington M31 ... 105 F3

Erskine St
  Compstall SK6 ...... 114 B3
  Manchester M15 ... 162 A2
Erwin St M40 .... 83 B6
Eryngo St SK1 ...... 112 A1
Escott St 1 M16 .... 97 F3
Esk Ave BL0 .... 1 D5
Esk Cl M41 .... 95 A4
Esk Bank SK8 ...... 122 C4
Eskdale Ave
  Bolton BL2 .... 25 F2
  Bramhall SK7 ...... 132 C5
  Manchester M20 .. 110 A7
  Oldham OL8 .... 66 D4
  Rochdale OL11 ..... 30 B4
  Romiley SK6 .... 113 B5
  Royton OL2 .... 48 D7
  Scot Lane End BL6 .. 38 E7
  Uppermill OL3 ...... 69 B5
  Wigan WN1 .... 37 B3
Eskdale Cl BL9 ..... 45 A3
Eskdale Dr
  Altrincham WA15 .. 120 C7
  Middleton M24 ..... 46 F3
Eskdale Gr BL4 ..... 59 F8
Eskdale Ho 3 M13 .. 98 E4
Eskdale Mews OL3 .. 69 B5
Eskdale Rd
  Ashton-in-M WN4 .. 73 B4
  Hindley WN2 .... 56 E5
Eskdale Terr SK15 .. 86 A4
Eskrick St BL1 ..... 143 A2
Eskrigge Cl M7 .... 155 C4
Esmond Rd M8 .... 156 A3
Esmont Dr M24 .... 46 E3
Esplanade The OL16 . 139 B3
Essa Acad BL3 .... 147 A2
Essex Ave
  Droylsden M43 ..... 84 A3
  Heywood BL9 .... 28 E1
  Manchester M20 .. 110 B4
  Stockport SK3 .... 123 B8
Essex Cl
  Failsworth M35 ..... 83 F5
  Shaw OL2 .... 48 F7
Essex Dr BL9 ...... 45 A8
Essex Gdns M44 .. 105 C4
Essex Pl
  Swinton M27 .... 61 F2
  Tyldesley M29 ..... 58 F3
Essex Rd
  Brimington SK5 ... 112 C5
  Reddish M18 ...... 99 F4
  Standish WN1 ..... 37 B8
Essex St
  Horwich BL6 .... 22 D1
  Manchester M2 ... 158 C1
  Rochdale OL11 .... 139 C2
  Wigan WN1 .... 37 E1
Essex Way M15, M16 . 162 A1
Essingdon St BL3 .. 147 A4
Essington Dr M40 . 157 A2
Essoldo Cl M18 .... 165 C1
Estate St OL8 ...... 66 F4
Est Bank Rd BL0 ... 11 A3
Estcourt Prep Sch for Girls
  OL8 .... 66 F4
Esther Fold BL5 .... 57 E8
Esther St OL4 ...... 67 D7
Esthwaite Dr M29 . 77 A7
Estonfield Dr M41 . 95 F2
Eston St M13 ...... 98 D4
Eswick St M11 ..... 83 C1
Etchells Prim Sch SK8 122 C1
Etchells Rd SK8 ... 122 C1
Etchells St SK1 .... 169 C1
Etchell St M40 .... 156 C1
Etharow Ct SK14 .. 167 B2
Ethel Ave
  Manchester M9 .... 64 D5
  Pendlebury M6 .... 80 B8
Ethel Ct OL16 ...... 31 B6
Ethel St
  Bolton BL3 .... 145 A2
  Oldham OL8 .... 66 F3
  Rochdale OL16 .... 31 B6
  Whitworth OL12 .... 4 D2
Ethel Terr M19 ..... 99 A1
Etherley Cl 5 M44 . 94 A2
Etherow Ave
  Failsworth M40 .... 65 F2
  Romiley SK6 ...... 113 E2
Etherow Brow 8 SK14 . 115 A8
Etherow Country Pk★ SK6 114 C3
Etherow Country Pk Nature
  Reserve★ SK6 ..... 114 C2
Etherow Ind Est SK13 103 E5
Etherow Way SK13 . 103 E5
Etherstone St
  Leigh WN7 .... 75 E4
  Manchester M8 .... 156 C4
Eton Ave OL8 ...... 66 B3
Eton Cl
  Manchester M16 .. 162 A1
  Rochdale OL11 ..... 30 B6
Eton Ct M16 .... 162 A1
Eton Dr SK8 .... 122 D2
Eton Hill Ind Est M26 . 44 D5
Eton Hill Rd M26 .. 44 C5
Eton Pl M26 .... 43 F3
Eton St OL7 .... 75 F3
Eton Terr WN3 ..... 151 B1
Eton Way N M26 .. 53 F8
Eton Way S M26 .. 44 D5
Etruria Cl M13 .... 164 B1

Ettington Cl BL8 ..... 27 A3
Ettrick Cl M11 .... 99 D7
ETZ Chaim Sch 1 M8 . 63 F2
Euan Pl 2 M33 ...... 108 C4
Euclid Cl M11 ...... 160 B1
Euro Ctr The M8 ... 158 B4
Europa Bsns Pk
  Bury BL9 .... 140 C3
  Cheadle SK3 .... 123 B6
Europa Circ M17 .... 96 D5
Europa Gate M17 ... 96 D5
Europa Trad Est M26 . 61 B7
Europa Way
  Cheadle SK3 .... 123 B6
  Kearsley M26 .... 61 B3
  Stretford M17 ...... 96 D5
Eustace St
  Bolton BL3 .... 42 A3
  Chadderton OL9 ... 152 C4
Euston Ave M9 ..... 65 A3
Euxton Cl BL8 ...... 27 A1
Evan Cl WN6 .... 36 D4
Evans Bsns Ctr OL11 . 139 A2
Evans Cl M20 ...... 110 A2
Evans Rd M30 ...... 79 A1
Evans St
  Ashton-u-L OL6 .... 85 D4
  Horwich BL6 .... 22 D4
  Leigh WN7 .... 75 F5
  Middleton M24 ..... 65 B8
  Oldham OL1 .... 153 C4
Evan St M40 .... 157 B1
Evanstone Cl BL6 .. 39 A8
Evanton Wlk 13 M9 . 157 B3
Eva Rd SK3 .... 123 A7
Eva St
  Leigh WN7 .... 75 C7
  Manchester M14 .. 98 C3
  Rochdale OL12 .... 15 A2
Evelyn St
  Manchester M14 .. 110 D8
  Oldham OL1 .... 49 B1
Evenholm WA14 ... 119 B2
Evening St M35 .... 83 F8
Evening Cl 8 M18 .. 99 E6
Everard Cl M28 .... 78 C8
Everard St M5 ..... 161 C3
Everbrom Rd BL3 . 146 A3
Everdingen Wlk OL1 . 49 D3
Everest Ave OL7 ... 85 B5
Everest Cl
  Dukinfield SK14 ... 102 A4
  Dukinfield SK16 ... 166 B1
Everest Pl 6 WN1 . 37 C2
Everest Rd
  Atherton M46 .... 58 C5
  Dukinfield SK14 ... 102 A4
Everest St OL11 .... 31 A2
Everett Ct 4 M20 .. 110 B6
Everett Rd M20 ... 110 B6
Everglade OL8 ..... 67 A1
Evergreen Ave BL6 . 22 B3
Evergreen Mews 2 M7 155 A3
Evergreens The 10 BL6 . 22 E1
Evergreen Wlk 3 M33 107 E6
Everleigh Cl BL2 ... 25 E5
Everleigh Dr M7 ... 155 C2
Eversden Ct M7 ... 158 B4
Eversley Ct M33 .. 108 B2
Eversley Rd M20 .. 110 A3
Everton Rd
  Oldham OL8 .... 66 D3
  Reddish SK5 .... 99 F2
Everton St
  Downall Green WN4 . 72 D5
  Swinton M27 .... 79 E8
Every St
  Bury BL9 .... 140 C4
  Manchester M4 ... 160 A1
  Ramsbottom BL0 ... 11 D6
Evesham Ave
  Glossop SK13 ...... 104 A5
  Stockport SK4 .... 168 B3
  Wythenshawe M23 . 120 D7
Evesham Cl
  1 Bolton BL3 ...... 145 A2
  Leigh WN7 .... 75 E1
  Middleton M24 ..... 65 B5
Evesham Dr
  Farnworth BL3, BL4 . 42 B2
  Handforth SK9 .... 131 C2
Evesham Gdns M24 . 65 A5
Evesham Gr
  Ashton-u-L OL6 .... 85 C7
  Sale M33 .... 108 E4
Evesham Rd
  Cheadle SK8 ...... 123 A4
  Manchester M9 .... 65 A2
  Middleton M24 ..... 65 B5
Evesham Wlk
  10 Bolton BL3 .... 145 A2
  Middleton M24 ..... 65 B5
  Oldham OL8 .... 153 B1
Eveside Cl SK8 .... 123 B4
Eve St OL8 .... 66 F2
Evington Ave M11 . 100 A7
Ewan St M18 ...... 99 D6
Ewart Ave M5 ..... 81 A1
Ewart St BL1 ...... 143 B2
Ewhurst Ave M27 . 79 D6
Ewing Cl M8 .... 64 A1
Ewing St M20 ..... 110 A5
Ewood
  12 Eccles M30 .... 79 F2
  Oldham OL8 .... 85 A8
EWOOD BRIDGE 1 C6
Ewood Dr BL8 ..... 44 A8

Ewood La BB4 . . . . 1 C7
Exbourne Rd M22 . . . . . . 121 C1
Exbridge Wlk M40 . . . . . . 83 D4
Exbury 24 OL12 . . . . 139 B4
Exbury St M14 . . . . 110 D7
Excalibur Way M44 . . . . . 105 F7
Excelsior Ave M44 . . . . . . 46 F8
Excelsior Terr OL15 . . . . . 15 F3
Exchange Quay M5 . . . . . 161 A2
Exchange Quay Metro Sta
M5 . . . . 161 A2
Exchange Sq M4 . . . . . . 158 C2
Exchange St
9 Bolton M1 . . . . 145 C3
Edenfield BL0 . . . . 1 D3
Manchester M2 . . . . . . 158 C1
6 Oldham OL4 . . . . 67 B7
Stockport SK3 . . . . 169 B1
Exeter Ave
Bolton BL2 . . . . 25 B2
Denton M34 . . . . 100 F1
Farnworth BL4 . . . . 59 F8
Radcliffe M26 . . . . 43 C5
Salford M7 . . . . 80 A4
Exeter Cl
Cheadle SK8 . . . . 131 F8
Dukinfield SK16 . . . . . . 101 D6
Exeter Ct
Manchester M20 . . . . . 110 C7
3 Middleton M24 . . . . . 46 F1
Exeter Dr
Ashton-u-L OL6 . . . . . . 85 D7
Aspull WN2 . . . . 38 D5
Irlam M44 . . . . 94 B2
Exeter Gr OL11 . . . . 139 C1
Exeter Rd
Brinnington SK5 . . . . . . 112 C5
Hindley WN2 . . . . 56 E5
Urmston M41 . . . . 95 D4
Exeter St
Rochdale OL11 . . . . . . 139 C1
Salford M6 . . . . 154 B2
Exeter Wlk SK7 . . . . 132 F7
Exford Ave WN3 . . . . 55 B4
Exford Cl
Manchester M40 . . . . . 160 A3
Reddish SK5 . . . . 111 F6
Exford Dr BL2 . . . . 43 A6
Exhall Cl M38 . . . . 60 A6
Exit Road W M90 . . . . . . 130 B7
Exmoor Cl OL6 . . . . 85 C7
Exmouth Ave SK5 . . . . . 112 C5
Exmouth Pl OL16 . . . . . . 31 A3
Exmouth Rd M33 . . . . . 107 D5
Exmouth Sq OL16 . . . . . . 31 A3
Exmouth St OL16 . . . . . . 31 A3
Express Trad Est BL4 . . . . 60 E6
Eyam Cl 15 SK13 . . . . . . 171 A2
Eyam Fold 29 SK13 . . . . 171 A2
Eyam Gdns 28 SK13 . . . . 171 A2
Eyam Gn 16 SK13 . . . . . . 171 A2
Eyam Gr
14 Gamesley SK13 . . . . 171 A2
Stockport SK2 . . . . 124 D5
Eyam La SK13 . . . . 171 B2
Eyam Lea SK13 . . . . 171 B2
Eyam Mews SK13 . . . . . 171 A2
Eyam Rd SK7 . . . . 124 E1
Eycott Dr M24 . . . . 46 D1
Eyebrook Rd M14 . . . . . 119 A2
Eyet St WN7 . . . . 75 E5
Eynford Ave SK5 . . . . . . 112 B6
Eyre St M15 . . . . 163 A1

F

Faber St M4 . . . . 159 A3
FACIT 4 D2
Factory Brow M24 . . . . . . 64 C7
FACTORY FOLD 66 A2
Factory Hill BL6 . . . . 22 D4
Factory La
Adlington PR6 . . . . 21 B8
Manchester M9 . . . . . . 64 D1
Salford M3 . . . . 158 A1
Factory St
Middleton M24 . . . . 64 F8
Radcliffe M26 . . . . 44 B3
Ramsbottom BL0 . . . . 138 C3
Tyldesley M29 . . . . 58 F1
Factory Street W M46 . . . 58 C3
Faggy La WN3 . . . . 150 C3
FAILSWORTH 83 C6
Failsworth Ind Est 2
M40 . . . . 83 C6
Failsworth Rd M40 . . . . . 84 A7
Failsworth Sch M35 . . . . 84 A7
Failsworth Sh Ctr 1 M35. 83 F7
Failsworth Sports Ctr
M35 . . . . 84 A7
Fairacres WN6 . . . . 19 B1
Fair Acres BL2 . . . . 25 E3
Fairacres Rd SK6 . . . . . . 134 E8
Fairbairn St BL6 . . . . 22 B3
Fairbank M43 . . . . 99 A1
Fairbank Ave M14 . . . . . . 98 B4
Fairbank Dr M24 . . . . 46 D2
Fairbottom St OL1 . . . . . 153 C3
Fairbottom Wlk 4 M43 . . 100 A8
Fairbourne Ave
Alderley Edge SK9 . . . . 137 B3
Wigan WN1 . . . . 55 A4
Wilmslow SK9 . . . . 136 F4
Fairbourne Cl SK9 . . . . . 136 F4
Fairbourne Dr
Sale WA15 . . . . 108 B1
Wilmslow SK9 . . . . 136 F4

Fairbourne Rd
Denton M34 . . . . 100 E2
Reddish M19 . . . . 99 C1
Fairbourne Wlk 12 OL1 . . 99 C1
Fairbrook Dr M6 . . . . . . 154 B2
Fairbrother St M5 . . . . . 161 C3
Fairburn St M41 . . . . 95 A4
Fairclough St
Bolton BL3 . . . . 42 A4
Droylsden M11 . . . . 83 A2
Hindley WN2 . . . . 56 D6
Newton-le-W WA12 . . . 89 B3
Wigan WN1 . . . . 151 A3
Fairfax Ave
Altrincham WA15 . . . . . 120 A6
Manchester M20 . . . . . 110 B4
Fairfax Cl SK6 . . . . 125 D7
Fairfax Dr
Littleborough OL15 . . . . 15 F3
Wilmslow SK9 . . . . 136 F4
Fairfax Rd M25 . . . . 63 A5
FAIRFIELD
Bury 28 E3
Droylsden 100 A8
Fairfield Ave
Cheadle SK8 . . . . 122 F2
Droylsden M43 . . . . . . 100 A7
Platt Bridge WN2 . . . . . 56 A3
Romiley SK6 . . . . 113 A4
Wigan WN5 . . . . 54 D5
Fairfield Com Prim Sch
BL9 . . . . 28 D3
Fairfield Ct
5 Droylsden M43 . . . . 100 A8
Manchester M14 . . . . . . 98 D4
Fairfield Dr BL9 . . . . 28 D3
Fairfield General Hospl
BL9 . . . . 28 E4
Fairfield High Sch for Girls
8 M43 . . . . 100 A8
Fairfield Ho 7 M43 . . . . . 84 A1
Fairfield Rd
Altrincham WA15 . . . . . 120 C5
Droylsden M43 . . . . 99 F8
Farnworth BL4 . . . . 60 C7
Irlam M44 . . . . 105 C5
Middleton M24 . . . . 46 E1
Fairfield Road Prim Sch
M43 . . . . 99 F8
Fairfields
Bolton BL1 . . . . 24 F8
Oldham OL8 . . . . 66 E2
Fairfield Sq M43 . . . . . . 100 A8
Fairfield St
Manchester M1, M12 . . 163 C4
Salford M6 . . . . 80 E5
Wigan WN5 . . . . 54 D5
Fairfield Sta M34 . . . . . . 100 A7
Fairfield View M34 . . . . . 100 A7
Fairford Cl SK5 . . . . 111 F5
Fairford Dr BL3 . . . . 145 B1
Fairford Way
Reddish SK5 . . . . 111 F5
Wilmslow SK9 . . . . 137 D7
Fairham Wlk M12 . . . . . 160 A1
Fairhaven Ave
Manchester M21 . . . . . 109 B8
Westhoughton BL5 . . . . . 58 B8
Whitefield M45 . . . . 62 D7
Fairhaven Cl SK7 . . . . . . 132 F8
Fairhaven Rd BL1 . . . . . . 143 C3
Fairhaven St M12 . . . . . 164 C2
Fair Hill BB4 . . . . 1 A7
Fairhills Ind Est 105 F8
Fairhills Rd M44 . . . . . . 106 A8
Fairholme Ave
Altrincham WN4 . . . . . . 73 B4
Urmston M41 . . . . 95 C1
Fairholme Rd
Manchester, Withington
M20 . . . . 110 C6
Stockport, Heaton Norris
SK4 . . . . 168 C3
Fairhope Ave M6 . . . . 80 C3
Fairhurst Ave WN6 . . . . . 19 D3
Fairhurst Dr M28 . . . . . . 59 F2
Fairhurst St
Leigh WN7 . . . . 75 E5
Wigan WN3 . . . . 150 B4
Fairisle Cl M11 . . . . 160 C1
Fairlands Pl OL11 . . . . . . 31 B2
Fairlands Rd
Bury BL9 . . . . 27 F6
Sale M33 . . . . 107 F2
Fairlands St OL11 . . . . . . 31 B2
Fairlands View OL11 . . . . 31 B2
Fairlawn M9 . . . . 169 A3
Fairlawn Cl M14 . . . . 98 A4
Fairlea M20 . . . . 101 A2
Fairlea Ave M20 . . . . . . 110 B4
Fairlee Ave M34 . . . . 84 C1
Fairleigh Ave M6 . . . . 80 C3
Fairless Rd M30 . . . . 79 D1
Fairlie Ave BL3 . . . . 40 F5
Fairlie Dr WA15 . . . . 120 B8
Fairlyn Cl BL5 . . . . 59 A7
Fairlyn Dr BL5 . . . . 59 A7
Fairman Dr WN2 . . . . 56 A3
Fairman St M16 . . . . 97 F3
Fairmead Rd M23 . . . . . 109 C1
Fairmile Dr M20 . . . . . . 122 C8
Fairmount Ave BL2 . . . . . 42 E8
Fairmount Rd M27 . . . . . 79 C6
Fairoak Ct BL3 . . . . 145 A1
Fair Oak Rd M19 . . . . . . 110 F5
Fair St
Bolton BL3 . . . . 146 C2
Manchester M1 . . . . . . 159 C1

Fair St continued
Swinton M27 . . . . 62 A1
Fairstead Cl BL5 . . . . 57 D8
Fairstead St M4 . . . . 99 F7
Fairthorne Grange 7 OL7 84 F1
Fair View
Billinge WN5 . . . . 71 C1
Britannia OL13 . . . . 4 C8
Littleborough OL15 . . . . 16 C7
Fairview Ave
Manchester M19 . . . . . . 98 F2
Reddish M34 . . . . 100 A1
Fair View Ave WN5 . . . . . 71 D5
Fairview Cl
Ashton-in-M WN4 . . . . . 73 B4
Chadderton OL9 . . . . . . 65 F8
Marple SK6 . . . . 125 F7
Rochdale OL12 . . . . 13 C2
Fairview Dr
Adlington PR6, PR7 . . . . 20 F8
Marple SK6 . . . . 125 F7
Fairview Rd
Altrincham WA15 . . . . . 120 C5
Reddish M34 . . . . 100 A1
Fairview Residential Cvn Pk
M46 . . . . 58 B4
Fairway
Bramhall SK7 . . . . 132 D6
Droylsden M43 . . . . . . 100 A8
Gatley SK8 . . . . 122 B3
Manchester M25 . . . . . . 63 D2
Milnrow OL16 . . . . 32 A6
Pendlebury M27 . . . . . . 80 C7
Rochdale OL11 . . . . 30 B1
Whitworth OL12 . . . . . . 14 C7
Fairway Ave
Bolton BL2 . . . . 26 A4
Wythenshawe M23 . . . 120 F8
Fairway Cres OL2 . . . . . . 48 D6
Fairway Ct M34 . . . . 100 B4
Fairway Dr M33 . . . . 107 E2
Fairway Prim Sch SK2 . . 124 E7
Fairway Rd
Oldham OL4 . . . . 67 E4
Whitefield BL9 . . . . 45 A3
Fairways BL6 . . . . 22 C3
Fairways SK13 . . . . 104 F1
Fairways The
Garswood WN4 . . . . 72 D2
6 Oldham OL2 . . . . 48 D5
Westhoughton BL5 . . . . . 57 E8
Whitefield M45 . . . . 62 F6
Fairway The
Failsworth M40 . . . . 83 C8
Stockport SK2 . . . . 124 D7
Fairwood Rd M23 . . . . . 120 E7
Fairy La
Salford M8 . . . . 155 B1
Wythenshawe M23 . . . 109 A3
Fairy St BL8 . . . . 27 C2
Fairywell Cl SK9 . . . . . . 131 D1
Fairywell Dr M33 . . . . . . 108 A1
Fairywell Rd WA15 . . . . . 120 C7
Faith St
Bolton BL1 . . . . 142 A1
Leigh WN7 . . . . 75 C5
Falcon Bsns Ctr OL9 . . . 152 C2
Falcon Cl
Bury BL8 . . . . 141 B4
Leigh WN7 . . . . 76 B5
Rochdale OL12 . . . . 13 E2
Salford M50 . . . . 80 C1
Falcon Cres M27 . . . . 62 C2
Falcon Ct
Manchester M15 . . . . . 162 B1
Salford M7 . . . . 155 A4
Falcon Dr
Chadderton OL9 . . . . . 152 C4
Irlam M44 . . . . 94 B4
Middleton M24 . . . . 46 E3
Walkden M38 . . . . 60 A5
Falconers Gn WN3 . . . . 150 B1
Falcon Ho BL9 . . . . 141 A4
Falcon St OL8 . . . . 153 C1
Falconwood Chase M28 . . 78 C6
Falconwood Cl 12 WN6 . . 37 A1
Falconwood Way M11 . . 164 C4
Falfield Dr M8 . . . . 156 B1
FALINGE FOLD 14 D1
Falinge Fold OL12 . . . . . . 14 D1
Falinge Mews OL12 . . . . 139 B4
Falinge Park High Sch
OL12 . . . . 14 D1
Falinge Rd OL12 . . . . 14 E1
Falkirk Dr
Bolton BL2 . . . . 42 F6
Ince-in-M WN2 . . . . 56 A8
Falkirk Gr WN5 . . . . 54 C8
Falkirk St 5 OL4 . . . . . . 67 C7
Falkirk Wlk 18 M23 . . . 121 A2
Falkland Ave
Manchester M40 . . . . . 160 A4
Rochdale OL11 . . . . 30 C8
Falkland Cl OL4 . . . . 49 E4
Falkland Dr WN4 . . . . 72 C2
Falkland Rd BL2 . . . . 43 A7
Fall Bank SK4 . . . . 111 D6
Fall Birch Rd BL6 . . . . . . 39 F8
Fall Green Ave M40 . . . . . 83 B6
Fallons Rd M28 . . . . 61 C1
Fallow Cl BL5 . . . . 39 E2
FALLOWFIELD 110 B8
Fallowfield Dr OL12 . . . . . 14 D2
Fallow Fields Dr SK5 . . . 100 A1
Fallowfield Sh Ctr M14 . . 98 F1
Fallowfield Way M46 . . . . 58 E1
Fallows The OL9 . . . . . . 152 A1

Falls Gr SK8 . . . . 122 A3
Falmer Cl
Bury BL8 . . . . 27 C6
Droylsden M18 . . . . 99 F6
Falmer Dr M22 . . . . 121 D1
Falmouth Ave
Sale M33 . . . . 107 D5
Urmston M41 . . . . 94 E3
Falmouth Cres SK5 . . . . 112 C5
Falmouth Rd M44 . . . . . . 94 B2
Falmouth St
Manchester M40 . . . . . 160 C4
Oldham OL8 . . . . 66 F4
19 Rochdale OL11 . . . . 31 A5
Falsgrave Cl M40 . . . . . . 83 A5
Falshaw Dr BL9 . . . . 18 B1
Falshaw Way M6 . . . . . . 99 D3
Falshaw Way 11 M40 . . . 83 C5
Falstaff Mews SK6 . . . . . 113 A3
Falston Ave M40 . . . . 65 D2
Falstone Ave BL0 . . . . . . 11 C4
Falstone Cl WN3 . . . . 54 E2
Falterley Rd M23 . . . . . . 120 F8
Falterley Road Prim Sch
M22 . . . . 121 C5
Fane Wlk M9 . . . . 64 B3
Faraday Ave
Manchester M8 . . . . . . 156 A2
Swinton M27 . . . . 62 D2
Faraday Cl WN6 . . . . . . 150 A4
Faraday Dr BL1 . . . . 143 B1
Faraday Ho BL1 . . . . 143 B1
Faraday Rise OL12 . . . . . 14 B1
Faraday St M1 . . . . 159 B1
Farcroft Ave M26 . . . . . . 44 C6
Farcroft Cl
Lymm WA13 . . . . 117 C5
Stockport SK2 . . . . 124 E7
Far Cromwell Rd SK6 . . . 112 D7
Fardale OL2 . . . . 149 B2
Farden Dr M23 . . . . 120 D8
Farditch Fold WN3 . . . . . . 54 F3
Farefield Ave WA3 . . . . . . 73 F2
Farewell Cl 1 OL11 . . . . . 30 C2
Far Hey Cl M26 . . . . 43 E3
Farholme OL2 . . . . 48 C2
Farholme La OL13 . . . . . . 3 D8
Faringdon 4 OL12 . . . . . 139 B2
Faringdon Wlk BL3 . . . . . 145 B1
Far La M18 . . . . 99 D4
Farland Pl BL3 . . . . 40 F5
Farlands Dr M20 . . . . . . 122 B7
Farlands Rise OL16 . . . . . 31 C3
Farleigh Cl BL5 . . . . 40 A2
Farley Ave M18 . . . . 100 A4
Farley Ct SK8 . . . . 122 F3
Farley La WN8 . . . . 35 A3
Farley Rd M33 . . . . 108 C2
Farley Way SK5 . . . . 111 F5
Farman St BL3 . . . . 147 A3
Farm Ave
Adlington PR6 . . . . 21 A8
Stretford M32 . . . . 96 A4
Farm Cl
Bury BL8 . . . . 26 F6
Reddish SK4 . . . . 111 C6
Farmers Cl M33 . . . . . . 109 A3
Farmer St SK4 . . . . 169 B3
Farmfield M33 . . . . 107 E6
Farmfold SK9 . . . . 130 F3
Farm Hill M25 . . . . 62 F5
Farm La
Eccles M28 . . . . 78 F5
High Lane SK12 . . . . . . 135 A6
Hyde SK14 . . . . 113 D8
Middleton M25 . . . . 63 D8
Wigan WN2 . . . . 38 A2
Farmlands Wlk OL1 . . . . . 49 C4
Farm Meadow Rd WN5 . . 53 D5
FAR MOOR 53 D4
Farm Rd OL8 . . . . 84 C8
Farmside Ave M44 . . . . . 94 A3
Farm Side Pl 10 M19 . . . 99 A1
Farm St
Chadderton OL9 . . . . . . 48 B1
Failsworth M35 . . . . 83 E6
Heywood OL10 . . . . 46 E8
Farmstead Ct M35 . . . . . 84 C6
Farmway M22 . . . . 65 A7
Farm Way M12 . . . . 89 E1
Farm Wlk
Altrincham WA14 . . . . . 118 E1
Littleborough OL15 . . . . 15 F5
Rochdale OL15 . . . . 15 C1
Farm Yd M19 . . . . 99 A1
Far Ridings SK6 . . . . 113 D3
Farnborough Rd
Bolton BL1 . . . . 24 E6
Manchester M40 . . . . . 160 D4
Farncombe Cl 2 M23 . . . 120 D7
Farndale Gr WN4 . . . . . . 73 C2
Farndale Sq M38 . . . . . . 60 C3
Farndale Wlk 17 M9 . . . 157 B4
Farndon Ave SK7 . . . . . . 124 F4
Farndon Cl M33 . . . . . . 108 E3
Farndon Dr WA15 . . . . . 120 A6
Farndon Rd SK5 . . . . 99 E2
Farnham Ave M9 . . . . 64 D5
Farnham Cl
21 Bolton BL1 . . . . . . 143 B1
Cheadle SK8 . . . . 132 A7
Leigh WN7 . . . . 94 B1
Farnham Dr M44 . . . . 94 B1
Farnhill Wlk M23 . . . . . . 108 E1
Farnley Cl OL12 . . . . 13 F2
Farnsfield WN1 . . . . 37 F1
Farnsworth Ave OL7 . . . . 85 B5

Farnsworth Cl OL7 . . . . . 85 B5
FARNWORTH 60 A7
Farnworth Dr M14 . . . . . . 98 C2
Farnworth L Ctr BL4 . . . . 60 D8
Farnworth Park Ind Est 5
BL4 . . . . 60 D8
Farnworth St
Bolton BL3 . . . . 146 C4
7 Heywood OL10 . . . . . 29 C2
4 Leigh WN7 . . . . 76 B4
Farnworth Sta BL4 . . . . . 42 E1
Farrand Rd OL8 . . . . 66 B2
Farrant Rd M12 . . . . 99 A4
Farrar Rd M43 . . . . 99 F8
Farr Cl WN3 . . . . 54 F5
Farrell St
Salford M7 . . . . 158 B3
Wigan WN5 . . . . 54 C5
Farrer Rd M13 . . . . 98 F3
Far Ridings SK6 . . . . 113 D3
Farrier Cl 8 M33 . . . . . . 108 F3
Farrier's Croft WN6 . . . . . 36 E3
Farriers La OL11 . . . . 30 B4
Farrier Way WN6 . . . . 35 C7
Farringdon Dr M26 . . . . . 43 E4
Farringdon St M6 . . . . . . 154 B3
Farrington Ave M20 . . . . 110 A7
Farrington Rd OL13 . . . . . 4 A8
Farrowdale Ave OL2 . . . . 149 B2
Farrowdale House Sch
OL2 . . . . 149 B2
Farrow St OL2 . . . . 149 B2
Farrow Street E OL2 . . . . 149 B2
Far St SK3 . . . . 170 A4
Farsley Pk BL5 . . . . 39 D4
Farwood Cl M16 . . . . . . 161 C1
Far Woodseats La SK13 . 114 F5
Fastnet St M11 . . . . 165 A4
Fatherford Cl OL3 . . . . . . 51 D5
Faulkenhurst Mews OL1 . 48 C1
Faulkenhurst St OL1, OL9 . 48 C1
Faulkner Ct 1 M1 . . . . . 163 A4
Faulkner Dr WA15 . . . . . 120 B5
Faulkner Rd M32 . . . . . . 96 E2
Faulkner St
Bolton BL3 . . . . 145 B1
Manchester M1 . . . . . . 163 A4
Rochdale OL16 . . . . . . 139 C3
Fauvel Pl SK13 . . . . 104 C1
Fauvel Rd SK13 . . . . 104 C2
Faversham Brow 9 OL1 . 153 B4
Faversham St M40 . . . . . . 83 B7
Fawborough Rd M23 . . . 108 F1
Fawcetts Fold BL5 . . . . . . 39 E4
Fawcett St 1 BL2 . . . . . 148 B3
Fawley Ave SK14 . . . . . . 167 A1
Fawley Gr M22 . . . . 121 D4
Fawns Keep
Stalybridge SK15 . . . . . 102 E6
Wilmslow SK9 . . . . 137 D7
Faye Ave M9 . . . . 65 B2
Fay Gdns SK13 . . . . 171 B4
Faywood Dr SK6 . . . . . . 126 A6
Fearn Dene 2 OL12 . . . . 14 B2
Fearney Side BL3 . . . . . . 42 F3
Fearnham Cl WN7 . . . . . . 75 E1
Fearnhead Ave BL6 . . . . . 22 B5
Fearnhead Cl BL4 . . . . . . 60 E8
Fearnley Way WA12 . . . . 89 C1
Fearns Moss OL13 . . . . . . 3 A8
Fearn St OL10 . . . . 29 C2
Featherstall Brook View 3
OL15 . . . . 16 A5
Featherstall Ho OL9 . . . . 152 C1
Featherstall Road N OL1,
OL9 . . . . 153 A4
Featherstall Road S OL9 . 153 A2
Featherstall Sq 1 OL15 . . 16 A5
Fecit La BL0 . . . . 12 C8
Federation St
Manchester M4 . . . . . . 159 A2
Prestwich M25 . . . . 62 F5
Feldom Rd M23 . . . . . . 108 F2
Fellbridge Cl BL5 . . . . . . 40 B1
Fellbrigg Cl M18 . . . . 99 C3
Fellfoot Cl M28 . . . . 77 F5
Fell Foot Mdw BL5 . . . . . 40 A2
Felling Wlk 6 M14 . . . . . 98 B3
Fellpark Rd M23 . . . . . . 109 A2
Fells Gr M28 . . . . 60 F1
Fellside
Bolton BL2 . . . . 26 A3
Oldham OL1 . . . . 153 B3
Wigan WN1 . . . . 37 D2
Fellside Cl BL8 . . . . 10 F1
Fellside Gdns OL15 . . . . . 15 F7
Fellside Gn SK15 . . . . . . 86 A3
Fell St
Bury BL9 . . . . 27 C2
Leigh WN7 . . . . 75 B4
Felltop Ct OL4 . . . . 68 C5
Felltop Dr SK5 . . . . 112 A8
Felsham Cl BL4 . . . . 42 C1
Felskirk Rd M22 . . . . . . 130 C8
Felsted BL1 . . . . 144 B8
Felt Ct M34 . . . . 100 C2
Felthorpe Dr M8 . . . . . . 155 C2
Felton Ave M22 . . . . 121 D3
Felton Cl BL9 . . . . 45 A5
Felton Wlk BL1 . . . . 143 B2
Fencegate Ave SK4 . . . . 111 D5

Fence St SK2 . . . . 124 D4
Fenchurch Ave M40 . . . . . . 83 C4
Fencot Dr M12 . . . . 99 A4
Fenella St M13 . . . . 98 E4
Fenham Cl M40 . . . . 156 C1
Fenmore Ave M18 . . . . 99 B3
Fenn St M40 . . . . 158 C2
Fenners Cl BL3 . . . . 147 A3
Fenney St M7 . . . . 155 A1
Fenney Street E M7 . . . . . 155 B2
Fenn St M15 . . . . 162 B2
FENNY HILL 67 B4
Fenside Rd M22 . . . . 121 E5
Fenstock Wlk M40 . . . . 83 D4
Fentewan Wlk SK14 . . . . . 102 E3
Fenton Ave SK7 . . . . 124 D4
Fenton Mews OL11 . . . . . . 139 C1
Fenton St
　Bury BL8 . . . . 27 C3
　Manchester M12 . . . . 165 A1
　5 Oldham OL4 . . . . 67 B6
　Rochdale OL12 . . . . 139 B1
　Shaw OL2 . . . . 149 B1
Fenton Way WN2 . . . . 56 F4
Fenwick Cl BL5 . . . . 57 F6
Fenwick Dr
　Manchester SK4 . . . . 110 E3
　Middleton M24 . . . . 46 D1
Fenwick St
　Manchester M15 . . . . 163 A2
　Rochdale OL12 . . . . 139 B3
Ferdinand St M40 . . . . 160 A4
Fereday St M28 . . . . 60 D4
Ferguson Ct M19 . . . . 110 F8
Ferguson Gdns OL12 . . . . . 14 F3
Ferguson Rise WN5 . . . . . . 54 E8
Ferguson Way OL4 . . . . . . 49 D1
Fernacre M33 . . . . 108 C5
Fernally St SK14 . . . . 167 B2
Fern Ave M41 . . . . 95 A2
FERN BANK 86 C1
Fernbank M26 . . . . 62 A8
Fern Bank
　Failsworth M40 . . . . 83 C7
　Stalybridge SK15 . . . . . . 86 C1
Fern Bank Cl SK15 . . . . . . 102 C8
Fern Bank Dr M23 . . . . . . 120 E8
Fern Bank St M18 . . . . . . 113 E8
Fernbeck Cl BL4 . . . . 60 E7
Fernbray Ave M19 . . . . . . 110 D4
Fernbray Rd WN2 . . . . 57 A5
Fernbrook Cl M13 . . . . . . 164 A1
Fernbrook Wlk **12** M8 . . . 155 C3
Fern Cl
　Atherton M46 . . . . 58 D2
　Marple SK6 . . . . 125 F6
　Middleton M24 . . . . 65 D8
　Oldham OL4 . . . . 67 F6
　Shevington WN6 . . . . 36 A6
Fern Clough BL1 . . . . 40 F7
Fernclough Rd M9 . . . . . . 157 A3
Fern Common OL2 . . . . . . 149 B3
Fern Cres SK15 . . . . 86 C1
Ferndale SK14 . . . . 102 A6
Ferndale Ave
　Royton OL16 . . . . 48 C8
　Stockport SK2 . . . . 124 B4
　Whitefield M45 . . . . 62 C7
Ferndale Cl OL4 . . . . 67 D4
Ferndale Dr WN6 . . . . 35 E7
Ferndale Gdns M19 . . . . . 110 E6
Ferndale Mews OL9 . . . . . 140 C3
Ferndale Rd M33 . . . . 108 B2
Ferndale Wlk WN7 . . . . 75 B5
Ferndene Gdns M20 . . . . . 110 B5
Ferndene Rd
　Manchester M20 . . . . . . 110 B5
　Prestwich M25, M45 . . . . 63 C7
Ferndown Ave
　Chadderton OL9 . . . . 65 E7
　Hazel Grove SK7 . . . . . . 124 C1
Ferndown Dr M44 . . . . 94 A3
Ferndown Rd
　Bolton BL2 . . . . 25 E3
　Wythenshawe M23 . . . . . 120 D8
Ferneyfield Rd OL9 . . . . . . 65 F7
Ferngate Dr M20 . . . . 110 B6
FERN GROVE 141 C4
Ferngrove BL9 . . . . 28 B5
FERNHILL 140 B4
Fernhill SK6 . . . . 126 B6
Fernhill Ave
　Bacup OL13 . . . . 3 E8
　Bolton BL3 . . . . 146 A4
Fernhill Cl
　Bacup OL13 . . . . 3 E8
　Glossop SK13 . . . . 104 D3
Fernhill Cres **1** OL13 . . . . 3 E8
Fernhill Dr
　Bacup OL13 . . . . 3 E8
　Manchester M18 . . . . 99 B4
FERNHILL GATE 146 A4
Fernhill Gr **2** OL13 . . . . . . 3 E8
Fern Hill La OL12 . . . . 14 A3
Fernhill Pk OL13 . . . . 3 E8
Fernhills BL7 . . . . 8 E4
Fernhills Bsns Ctr BL9 . . . 140 C4
Fernhill St BL9 . . . . 140 C3
Fernhill Way **4** OL13 . . . . . 3 E8
Fern Ho M40 . . . . 121 A4
Fernholme Ct OL8 . . . . 66 C4
Fernhurst Cl WN3 . . . . . . 151 C3
Fernhurst Gr **8** BL1 . . . . . 143 B1
Fernhurst Rd M20 . . . . . . 110 C5
Fernhurst St OL1, OL9 . . . . 48 C1

Fernie St M4 . . . . 159 A3
Fernilee Cl SK22 . . . . 127 C1
Fern Isle Cl OL12 . . . . 14 B6
Fernlea
　Altrincham WA15 . . . . . . 119 F1
　Gatley SK8 . . . . 122 B1
　Manchester SK4 . . . . 111 C5
Fern Lea
　Ashton-u-L OL6 . . . . 85 C8
　Hollingworth SK14 . . . . . 103 D6
Fernlea Ave OL1 . . . . 48 C1
Fernlea Cl
　Glossop SK13 . . . . 171 B4
　1 Rochdale OL12 . . . . . 14 B2
Fernlea Cres M27 . . . . 79 E7
Fernleaf St M14 . . . . 98 A4
Fernlea Gr WN4 . . . . 72 D5
Fern Lea Gr M38 . . . . 59 F4
Fernlea Lo BL4 . . . . 60 E7
Fern Lea St BB4 . . . . 2 D8
Fernleigh
　Bolton BL1 . . . . 143 B4
　10 Horwich BL6 . . . . . . 22 D1
Fernleigh Ave M19 . . . . . . 99 C1
Fernleigh Dr M16 . . . . 162 A1
Fernley Ave M34 . . . . 101 A2
Fernley Rd SK2 . . . . 124 B6
Fern Lodge Dr OL6 . . . . . . 85 D5
　Fers Gr BL1 . . . . 144 B3
Fernside M26 . . . . 61 C6
Fernside Ave M20 . . . . . . 110 D5
Fernside Ct M26 . . . . 61 C6
Fernside Gr
　Walkden M28 . . . . 60 E4
　Wigan WN3 . . . . 54 D1
Fernside Way OL12 . . . . . . 14 A1
Fern St
　Bolton BL3 . . . . 144 C2
　Bury BL9 . . . . 140 C3
　Chadderton OL9 . . . . . . 152 A4
　Farnworth BL4 . . . . 42 E1
　Manchester M4, M8 . . . . 159 A4
　Manchester, Openshaw
　　M11 . . . . 165 B3
　Oldham OL8 . . . . 153 A1
　Ramsbottom BL0 . . . . . . 11 D7
　Rochdale OL11 . . . . 139 A2
　Wardle OL12 . . . . 15 C6
Fernstead BL3 . . . . 144 C2
Ferns The
　Britannia OL13 . . . . 4 A8
　Dukinfield SK14 . . . . . . 102 A5
Fernstone Cl BL6 . . . . 22 A3
Fernthorpe Ave OL3 . . . . . . 51 C1
Fern View WA15 . . . . 120 E5
Fernview Dr BL0 . . . . 11 A1
Fernville Terr **6** OL13 . . . . 3 D8
Fernwood M26 . . . . 126 C7
Fernwood Ave M18 . . . . . . 99 D3
Fernwood Gr SK9 . . . . . . 137 C8
Ferrand Lodge OL15 . . . . . 16 C7
Ferrand Rd OL15 . . . . 16 B6
Ferrer St WN4 . . . . 72 F6
Ferring Wlk OL9 . . . . 152 B2
Ferris St M11 . . . . 99 D8
Ferrous Way M44 . . . . . . 105 F6
Ferryhill Rd M44 . . . . 94 A2
Ferrymasters Way M44 . . . 94 A1
Ferry Rd M44 . . . . 94 B2
Ferry St M11 . . . . 164 B4
Festival Theatre* SK14 . . . 167 A2
Fettler Cl M27 . . . . 79 F7
Feversham Cl M30 . . . . 79 F4
Fewston Cl BL1 . . . . 24 E5
Fiddlers La M44 . . . . 94 B4
Fiddlers Lane Prim Sch
　M44 . . . . 94 B3
Field Bank Gr M19 . . . . 99 C1
Fieldbrook Wlk BL5 . . . . . . 40 A1
Field Cl
　Bramhall SK7 . . . . 132 D4
　Marple SK6 . . . . 125 D5
Fieldcroft OL11 . . . . 30 B7
Fielden Ave M21 . . . . 97 A1
Fielden Ct M21 . . . . 109 D5
Fielden Rd M20 . . . . 109 F4
Fielden St OL15 . . . . 15 E2
Fielders Way M27 . . . . 61 E4
Fieldfare Ave M40 . . . . 83 B4
Fieldfare Way OL7 . . . . 85 B7
Fieldhead Ave
　Bury BL8 . . . . 27 A2
　Rochdale OL11 . . . . 30 B7
　Tyldesley M29 . . . . 77 B5
Fieldhead Mews SK9 . . . . 137 E8
Fieldhead Rd SK9 . . . . . . 137 E8
Fieldhouse Ind Est OL12 . . 14 F2
Field House La SK6 . . . . . 126 A6
Fieldhouse Rd OL12 . . . . . 14 F2
Fieldhouse Way SK12 . . . 133 E2
Fielding Pl PR6 . . . . 21 B8
Fieldings Cl WN5 . . . . 54 D5
Fielding St
　Eccles M30 . . . . 79 C1
　Middleton M24 . . . . 47 A2
Fieldings Wharf M43 . . . . 100 A8
Field La OL6 . . . . 85 D5
Field Mews M34 . . . . 100 E2
Field Pl **8** M20 . . . . 110 B3
Field Rd
　Milnrow OL16 . . . . 31 D7
　Sale M33 . . . . 107 E6
Fields Cres SK14 . . . . 103 D6
Fieldsend Cl SK15 . . . . . . 102 D8
Fieldsend Dr WN7 . . . . 91 C8
Field End Fold M30 . . . . . . 94 C4
Fields Farm Cl SK14 . . . . 102 D1
Fields Farm Rd SK14 . . . . 102 D1

Fields Farm Wlk **5**
　SK14 . . . . 102 D2
Fields Gr SK14 . . . . 103 D5
Fieldside Cl SK7 . . . . 132 D4
Fields New Rd OL9 . . . . . . 152 B1
Field St
　Droylsden M43 . . . . 99 F8
　Dukinfield SK14 . . . . . . 101 D5
　Failsworth M35 . . . . 83 E7
　Hindley WN2 . . . . 56 E4
　Ince-in-M WN3 . . . . 55 F4
　Manchester M18 . . . . 99 E6
　11 Rochdale OL11 . . . . 31 A4
　Romiley SK6 . . . . 113 A3
　Salford M6 . . . . 154 C2
　Wigan WN6 . . . . 150 B4
Fields The
　Aspull WN2 . . . . 38 C4
　Standish WN6 . . . . 36 F8
Fields Way OL8 . . . . 66 E2
Field Vale Dr SK5 . . . . . . 100 A1
Fieldvale Rd M33 . . . . 107 E1
Fieldview **2** WN8 . . . . 53 A7
Field View Wlk M16 . . . . . . 97 F2
Fieldway
　Platt Bridge WN2 . . . . . . 56 B2
　Rochdale OL16 . . . . 31 B3
Field Wlk
　Altrincham WA15 . . . . . . 120 B3
　7 Partington M31 . . . . . 105 E3
Fife Ave OL9 . . . . 66 A4
Fifield Cl OL8 . . . . 67 A3
Fifth Ave
　Bolton BL1 . . . . 144 B3
　Bury BL9 . . . . 28 D4
　Droylsden M11 . . . . 83 C2
　Dukinfield SK16 . . . . . . 101 B8
　Little Lever BL3 . . . . 42 F4
　Oldham OL8 . . . . 66 C2
　Stretford M17 . . . . 96 C6
Fifth St
　Bolton BL1 . . . . 23 F4
　Stretford M17 . . . . 96 D5
Filbert St **8** OL11 . . . . 49 C1
Filby Wlk M40 . . . . 160 B4
Fildes St M24 . . . . 65 D7
Filey Ave
　Manchester M16 . . . . 97 C3
　Urmston M41 . . . . 95 A4
Filey Dr M6 . . . . 80 D6
Filey Rd
　Manchester M14 . . . . . . 110 D8
　Stockport SK2 . . . . 124 C7
Filey St OL16 . . . . 15 C3
Filton Ave **3** BL3 . . . . 145 A1
Filton Wlk M9 . . . . 156 C2
Finance St OL15 . . . . 15 F4
Finborough Cl M16 . . . . . . 97 E4
Finchale Dr WA15 . . . . . . 120 C1
Finchcroft OL11 . . . . 153 B3
Finchdale Gdns WA3 . . . . . 91 B8
Finch La WN6 . . . . 18 B1
Finchley Ave M40 . . . . 83 C4
Finchley Cl **8** BL8 . . . . . . 27 B1
Finchley Cres WN2 . . . . . . 38 A2
Finchley Gr M40 . . . . 65 A1
Finchley Rd
　Altrincham WA15 . . . . . . 119 E3
　Manchester M14 . . . . 98 B3
Finch Mill Ave WN6 . . . . . . 35 D7
Finchwood Rd M22 . . . . . 121 E5
Findlay Cl WA12 . . . . 89 C2
Findlay St WN7 . . . . 75 E5
Findon Rd M23 . . . . 121 A6
Finghall Rd M41 . . . . 95 B2
Finland Rd SK3 . . . . 170 A3
Finlan Rd M24 . . . . 47 E5
Finlay Ct WN5 . . . . 54 E8
Finlay St BL4 . . . . 60 D8
Finney Cl SK9 . . . . 131 C2
Finney Dr
　Handforth SK9 . . . . 131 C2
　Manchester M21 . . . . . . 109 A7
FINNEY GREEN 131 E2
Finney La SK8 . . . . 122 C1
Finney St BL3 . . . . 147 C4
Finningley Rd M9 . . . . 64 B5
Finny Bank Rd M33 . . . . . 108 A6
Finsbury Ave M40 . . . . 83 C4
Finsbury Cl OL8 . . . . 67 B4
Finsbury Rd SK5 . . . . 111 E8
Finsbury St OL11 . . . . . . 139 A1
Finsbury Way SK9 . . . . . . 131 E2
Finstock CI M30 . . . . 79 D1
Fintry Gr M30 . . . . 79 D1
Fir Ave SK7 . . . . 132 E8
Firbank CI OL7 . . . . 84 F7
Fir Bank Prim Sch OL2 . . . 48 D7
Firbank Rd
　Wigan WN3 . . . . 55 B3
　Wythenshawe M23 . . . . 121 B4
Fir Bank Rd OL2 . . . . 48 D6
Firbarn Cl OL16 . . . . 31 D7
Firbeck Dr M4 . . . . 160 A2
Fir Cl
　Hazel Grove SK7 . . . . . . 124 C3
　Poynton SK12 . . . . 133 F3
Fircroft Wlk OL16 . . . . 19 A2
Fircroft CI **8** SK3 . . . . . . 123 F4
Fircroft Rd OL8 . . . . 67 A2
Firdale Ave M40 . . . . 65 E1
Firdale Wlk OL9 . . . . 152 C3
Firdon Wlk **17** M9 . . . . . . 157 B3
Firecrest CI M28 . . . . 78 B8
Firefly CI M3 . . . . 158 A1
Fire Station Sq M5 . . . . . . 81 C2
Fire Sta Yd OL11 . . . . 139 C2

Firethorn Ave M19 . . . . . . 110 F6
Firethorn Cl BL5 . . . . 39 F2
Firethorn Dr SK14 . . . . . . 102 A2
Firethorn Wlk **5** M23 . . . 107 C5
Firfield Gr M28 . . . . 60 F3
Fir Gr
　Chadderton OL9 . . . . . . 152 B4
　Manchester M19 . . . . 99 A1
　Wigan WN6 . . . . 37 A3
FIRGROVE 31 D6
Firgrove Ave OL16 . . . . . . 31 D8
Firgrove Bsns Pk OL16 . . 31 D8
Firgrove Gdns OL16 . . . . . 31 D8
Fir La OL2 . . . . 48 D6
Fir Rd
　Bramhall SK7 . . . . 132 E8
　Denton M34 . . . . 101 A3
　Farnworth BL4 . . . . 60 B8
　Marple SK6 . . . . 125 E5
　Swinton M27 . . . . 79 E6
Firs Ave
　Ashton-u-L OL6 . . . . 85 B5
　Failsworth M35 . . . . 83 E7
　Manchester M16 . . . . 97 B2
Firsby Ave SK6 . . . . 112 F4
Firsby St **5** M19 . . . . 99 A1
Firs Cl SK8 . . . . 122 A3
Firsdale Ind Est WN7 . . . . 75 C6
Fir Gr SK8 . . . . 122 A4
Firs La WN7 . . . . 75 C5
FIRS LANE 75 D6
Firs Park Cres WN7 . . . . . 75 C5
Firs Prim Sch The M33 . . 107 D4
Firs Rd
　Gatley SK8 . . . . 122 A4
　Over Hulton BL5 . . . . 59 A6
　Sale M33 . . . . 107 D5
Fir St
　Bolton BL1 . . . . 143 C2
　Bury BL9 . . . . 141 A2
　Eccles M30 . . . . 79 D1
　Failsworth M35 . . . . 83 E7
　Heywood OL10 . . . . 29 E1
　Irlam M44 . . . . 105 D6
　Manchester, Miles Platting
　　M40 . . . . 160 A4
　2 Manchester, Old Trafford
　　M16 . . . . 97 C4
　Radcliffe M26 . . . . 44 B2
　Ramsbottom BL0 . . . . . . 11 D7
　Royton OL2 . . . . 48 D5
　Salford M6 . . . . 154 C2
　Stockport SK4 . . . . 169 B2
　Walsden OL14 . . . . 6 A8
First Ave
　Atherton M46 . . . . 58 D4
　Bury BL8 . . . . 26 F6
　Droylsden M11 . . . . 83 D2
　11 Hindley WN2 . . . . . . 56 D5
　Little Lever BL3 . . . . 43 A4
　Manchester SK5 . . . . 86 E5
　Oldham OL8 . . . . 66 D2
　Poynton SK12 . . . . 133 D1
　Stretford M17 . . . . 96 D6
　Swinton M27 . . . . 79 D5
　Tyldesley M29 . . . . 77 C4
　Wigan WN6 . . . . 37 A2
Firs The M34 . . . . 58 D4
Firs The
　Altrincham WA14 . . . . . . 119 B3
　Wilmslow SK9 . . . . 137 A5
First St BL1 . . . . 23 F4
Firsway WN7 . . . . 75 B5
Firs Way M33 . . . . 107 C3
FIRSWOOD 97 A3
Firswood Dr
　Hyde SK14 . . . . 102 A3
　Royton OL2 . . . . 48 C6
　Swinton M27 . . . . 79 E6
Firswood Mount SK8 . . . . 122 A4
Firswood Sta M16 . . . . 97 B2
Firth Cl M7 . . . . 155 A2
Firth St OL1 . . . . 153 C2
Firtree Ave M33 . . . . 107 C4
Fir Tree Ave
　Golborne WA3 . . . . 90 F8
　Oldham OL8 . . . . 67 A2
　Worsley M28 . . . . 78 B5
Fir Tree Cl SK16 . . . . 101 F8
Fir Tree Cres
　Ince-in-M WN3 . . . . 55 F3
　Stalybridge SK16 . . . . . 101 F8
Fir Tree Dr
　Dukinfield SK14 . . . . . . 101 E5
　Ince-in-M WN3 . . . . 55 F3
Fir Tree La SK16 . . . . 101 F8
Fir Tree Prim Sch SK5 . . . . 99 E2
Fir Tree St WN3 . . . . 55 F4
Fir Tree Way **3** BL6 . . . . . 22 E1
Fir Tree Wlk WA3 . . . . 90 F8
Firvale Ave SK8 . . . . 122 B1
Firvale Cl WN7 . . . . 75 C5
Firwood Ave
　Farnworth BL4 . . . . 60 C7
　Stretford M41 . . . . 96 A1
Firwood Cl SK2 . . . . 124 C8
Firwood Cres M26 . . . . 44 B1
Firwood Gr
　Ashton-in-M WN4 . . . . . . 73 A2
　Bolton BL2 . . . . 25 E2
Firwood La BL2 . . . . 25 C3
Firwood Manor Prep Sch **2**
　OL9 . . . . 48 B1
Firwood Pk OL9 . . . . 48 B1
Firwood Specl Sch BL2 . . . 25 C2
Firwood Stables BL2 . . . . . 25 C3
Fishbourne Sq **8** M14 . . . 98 C3

Fishbrook Ind Est BL4 . . . . 61 A7
Fisher Ave WN2 . . . . 74 C7
Fisher Cl WN3 . . . . 54 F5
Fisher Dr WN5 . . . . 53 E7
Fisherfield OL12 . . . . 13 F1
Fishermore Rd M41 . . . . . . 94 E2
Fisher St OL1 . . . . 153 F6
FISHPOOL 44 D8
Fish Rake La BL0, BB4 . . . . 1 E6
Fishwick St OL16 . . . . 31 A6
Fistral Ave SK8 . . . . 131 C8
Fistral Cres SK15 . . . . 86 D4
Fit City Cadishead M44 . . 105 D5
Fit City Clarendon M5 . . . . 81 A2
Fit City Eccles M30 . . . . . . 79 F1
Fit City Ordsall M50 . . . . 161 A3
Fitton Ave M21 . . . . 109 B6
Fitton Cres M27 . . . . 61 F3
FITTON HILL 67 A3
Fitton Hill Rd OL8 . . . . 67 A4
Fitton Hill Sh Prec OL8 . . . 67 A2
Fitton St
　Rochdale OL16 . . . . 31 A8
　Royton OL2 . . . . 48 F4
　Shaw OL2 . . . . 48 F7
Fitzadam St WN1 . . . . . . 150 B4
Fitzalan St SK13 . . . . 104 C1
Fitzgeorge St M40 . . . . . . 156 C1
Fitzgerald Cl M25 . . . . 62 F2
Fitzgerald Ct **11** M34 . . . 113 A8
Fitzgerald Way M46 . . . . . 154 C3
Fitzhugh St BL1 . . . . 25 A5
Fitzroy St
　Ashton-u-L OL7 . . . . 100 F8
　Droylsden M43 . . . . 100 B8
　Stalybridge SK15 . . . . . . 86 D4
Fitzwarren Ct M6 . . . . 154 C3
Fitzwarren St M6 . . . . 154 C3
Fitzwilliam Ct **8** M14 . . . . 98 D4
Fitzwilliam St M7 . . . . 158 A4
Five Fold Ind Pk OL9 . . . . 153 A2
Five Quarters M26 . . . . . . 43 E5
Fiveways M43 . . . . 84 A2
Fiveways Par SK7 . . . . . . 133 E8
Flagcroft Dr M23 . . . . 121 B5
Flagg Wood Ave SK6 . . . . 125 D7
Flagship Ave M5 . . . . 161 B4
Flag St OL13 . . . . 3 E8
Flake La OL2 . . . . 48 D5
Flamborough Wlk **7** M14 . 98 B3
Flamingo Cl M12 . . . . 165 A2
Flamingo Villas M44 . . . . 120 E6
Flamstead Ave M23 . . . . . 120 E6
Flannel St **4** OL12 . . . . . . 31 A8
Flapper Fold La M46 . . . . . 58 C3
Flash Cotts OL4 . . . . 68 C3
Flashfields M25 . . . . 62 F1
Flash St M40 . . . . 83 C6
Flatley Cl M15 . . . . 163 A1
Flavian Wlk M11 . . . . 165 B4
Flax Cl BB4 . . . . 1 A8
Flaxcroft Rd M22 . . . . 121 B3
Flaxfield Ave SK15 . . . . . . 86 D2
Flaxman Rise OL1 . . . . 49 C4
FLAX MOSS 1 A8
Flax Moss Cl BB4 . . . . 1 A8
Flaxpool Cl M16 . . . . 97 E4
Flax St M3 . . . . 158 A3
Flaxwood Wlk M22 . . . . . 121 B3
Fleece St
　2 Oldham OL4 . . . . 67 B7
　Rochdale OL16 . . . . 139 C3
Fleeson St M14 . . . . 98 C3
Fleet Ho BL1 . . . . 143 B1
Fleet St
　Ashton-u-L OL6 . . . . 166 B2
　Droylsden M18 . . . . 99 F6
　Horwich BL6 . . . . 22 D3
　Hyde SK14 . . . . 167 B3
　Oldham OL4 . . . . 67 A6
　Wigan WN5 . . . . 54 B6
Fleetwood Dr WA12 . . . . . 89 A4
Fleetwood Rd M28 . . . . . . 60 A3
Fleming Cl OL12 . . . . 15 D5
Fleming Dr WN4 . . . . 73 D4
Fleming Rd M22 . . . . 121 D2
Flemish Rd M34 . . . . 101 B2
Flemming Pl OL9 . . . . 153 A2
Fletcher Ave
　Atherton M46 . . . . 58 D5
　Swinton M27 . . . . 62 A3
FLETCHER BANK 11 D6
Fletcher Cl
　Heywood OL10 . . . . 29 D2
　Oldham OL9 . . . . 153 A2
Fletcher Ct M26 . . . . 61 B8
Fletcher Dr
　Altrincham WA14 . . . . . . 119 C1
　High Lane SK12 . . . . 134 F1
Fletcher Fold Rd BL9 . . . . . 44 F6
Fletcher Moss Botanical &
　Parsonage Gdns* M20 . 110 B1
Fletcher's Sq **11** SK1 . . . 169 F1
Fletcher's Rd OL15 . . . . . . 15 E3
Fletcher St
　1 Ashton-u-L OL6 . . . . . 166 C3
　Atherton M46 . . . . 58 C3
　Bolton BL3 . . . . 145 B1
　Bury BL9 . . . . 141 A2
　Farnworth BL4 . . . . 60 D8
　Little Lever BL3 . . . . 43 B3
　Manchester M40 . . . . . . 157 C1
　Radcliffe M26 . . . . 44 C4
　Rochdale OL11 . . . . 31 A5
　Stockport SK1 . . . . 169 C1
Fletsand Rd SK9 . . . . 137 D6
Fletton Cl OL12 . . . . 14 E2
Fletton Mews OL12 . . . . . . 14 E2

Flexbury Wlk M40 . . . . 83 D4
Flint Cl
 Droylsden M11 . . . . 83 B2
 Hazel Grove SK7 . . . . . . 124 C1
Flint Gr M44 . . . . 105 C6
Flint St
 Droylsden M43 . . . . 84 B2
 Oldham OL1 . . . . 67 C8
 Stockport SK3 . . . . 170 B3
Flitcroft St BL3 . . . . 147 C4
Flitcroft St OL8 . . . . 67 C4
FLIXTON 94 F2
Flixton Girls' High Sch
  . . . . 95 A2
Flixton Inf Sch M41 . . . . . 94 F3
Flixton Jun Sch M41 . . . . . 94 F3
Flixton Rd
 Carrington M31 . . . . 106 E7
 Flixton M41 . . . . 94 F1
 Manchester M13 . . . . 164 A1
 Urmston M41 . . . . 95 B2
Flixton Sta M41 . . . . 94 F1
Flixton Wlk M13 . . . . 164 A1
Floatshall Rd M23 . . . . . . 121 A6
Floats Rd M23 . . . . 120 E4
Flockton Ave M46 . . . . 36 D4
Flockton Ct **7** BL6 . . . . . 22 B4
Flora Dr M7 . . . . 158 A4
Floral Ct M7 . . . . 155 A2
Flora St
 Ashton-in-M WN4 . . . . 73 B2
 Bolton BL3 . . . . 147 B4
 Manchester M9 . . . . 64 C3
 Oldham OL1 . . . . 153 B3
Florence Ave BL1 . . . . 24 F5
Florence Ct SK3 . . . . 123 B6
Florence Park Ct M20 . . . 110 C4
Florence St
 Bolton BL3 . . . . 147 A4
 Droylsden M43 . . . . 100 B8
 Eccles M30 . . . . 79 B1
 Failsworth M35 . . . . 83 F8
 Rochdale OL16 . . . . 31 B6
 Sale M33 . . . . 108 B6
 Stockport SK4 . . . . 169 B2
 Wigan WN1 . . . . 151 B4
Florence Way SK14 . . . . . 103 D5
Florian Ho OL1 . . . . 153 C3
Florida St OL8 . . . . 153 B1
Florist St SK3 . . . . 170 B3
Florin Gdns M6 . . . . 154 C3
Flowery Bank OL8 . . . . 67 B4
FLOWERY FIELD 167 A4
Flowery Field SK2 . . . . . . 124 A3
Flowery Field Gn SK4 . . . 101 C4
Flowery Field Ind Pk
 SK14 . . . . 101 D5
Flowery Field Prim Sch
 SK14 . . . . 167 A4
Flowery Field Sta SK14 . . 101 D5
Floyd Ave M21 . . . . 109 C5
Floyer Rd M9 . . . . 64 E5
Foden La
 Alderley Edge SK9 . . . . . . 136 C1
 Bramhall SK7 . . . . 132 D3
Foden Wlk **7** M9 . . . . . . 131 D2
FOGGBROOK 124 F6
Fog La M19, M20 . . . . 110 C4
Fold Ave M43 . . . . 84 B2
Fold Cotts OL3 . . . . 51 A2
Fold Cres SK14 . . . . 86 F6
Fold Gdns OL12 . . . . 14 B3
Fold Gn OL9 . . . . 152 A2
Fold La OL12 . . . . 14 C4
Fold Mews
 5 Bury BL9 . . . . 27 F6
 Hazel Grove SK7 . . . . . . 124 E3
Fold Rd M26 . . . . 61 C7
Folds BL6 . . . . 21 C3
Folds Rd BL1, BL2 . . . . . . 148 A4
Fold St
 Bolton BL1 . . . . 145 C3
 Bury BL9 . . . . 140 A2
 Golborne WA3 . . . . 74 A1
 Heywood OL10 . . . . 29 E3
 Manchester M40 . . . . 83 A8
Fold The
 Manchester M9 . . . . 64 D4
 Royton OL2 . . . . 49 A4
 Urmston M41 . . . . 95 A3
Fold View
 Bolton BL7 . . . . 8 E1
 Oldham OL8 . . . . 67 A2
Fold Way OL7 . . . . 84 F3
Foleshill Ave M9 . . . . 157 A3
Foley Gdns OL10 . . . . 46 E7
Foley St **8** WN6 . . . . 56 D5
Foley Wlk M22 . . . . 130 E8
Foliage Cres SK5 . . . . 112 C5
Foliage Gdns SK5 . . . . . . 112 C5
Foliage Rd SK5 . . . . 112 B4
Folkestone Rd M11 . . . . . . 83 D2
Folkestone Road E M11 . . 83 D2
Folkestone Road W M11 . . 83 C2
Follows St M18 . . . . 99 D6
Folly La M27 . . . . 79 D6
Folly Wlk **20** OL12 . . . . . 14 F1
Fonthill Gr M33 . . . . 107 F1
Fontwell Cl
 3 Manchester M16 . . . . . 97 C3
 Standish WN6 . . . . 19 F1
Fontwell La OL9 . . . . 47 A1
Fontwell Rd BL3 . . . . 43 A2
Fontwell Wlk **6** M40 . . . . 65 D2
Footman Ct M7 . . . . 77 B7
Foot Mill Cres OL12 . . . . . 14 D2
Foot Wood Cres OL12 . . . . 14 D2
Forber Cres M18 . . . . 99 D3

Forbes Cl
 Hindley WN2 . . . . 56 E7
 Sale M33 . . . . 108 C2
 Stockport SK1 . . . . 124 B8
Forbes Pk SK7 . . . . 132 D7
Forbes Rd SK1 . . . . 112 B1
Forbes St SK6 . . . . 112 F4
Fordbank Rd M20 . . . . . . 110 A2
Ford Gdns OL11 . . . . 30 B6
Ford Gr SK14 . . . . 103 A4
Fordham Gr BL1 . . . . 144 C4
Ford La
 Manchester M20 . . . . 110 A2
 Salford M6 . . . . 81 A4
 Wythenshawe M20, M22 . 109 F1
Fordland Cl WA3 . . . . 74 E1
Ford Lodge M20 . . . . 110 B2
Fordoe La OL12 . . . . 13 C4
Ford's La SK7 . . . . 132 D6
Ford St
 Dukinfield SK16 . . . . 101 C6
 Kearsley M26 . . . . 61 A8
 Manchester M12 . . . . 164 A3
 Salford M3 . . . . 158 A2
 Stockport SK3 . . . . 169 A1
Ford Way SK14 . . . . 103 A4
Fordyce Way WN2 . . . . 56 A8
Foreland Cl M40 . . . . 157 A1
Forest Ave WN3 . . . . 36 F3
Forest Cl SK16 . . . . 101 C6
Forest Ct M41 . . . . 94 D3
Forest Dr
 Altrincham WA15 . . . . . . 119 F6
 Sale M33 . . . . 107 E2
 Shevington Moor WN6 . . . 19 A2
 Westhoughton BL5 . . . . . . 58 A8
Forester Dr SK15 . . . . 86 A1
Forester Hill Ave
 Bolton BL3 . . . . 147 C3
 Bolton, Great Lever BL3 . . 42 A3
Forester Hill Cl BL3 . . . . 147 C3
Forest Fold WN6 . . . . 35 E6
Forest Gate Com Prim Sch
 M31 . . . . 105 D3
Forest Gdns M31 . . . . 105 D3
Forest Park Sch M33 . . . . 108 A4
Forest Range M19 . . . . 99 A1
Forest Rd BL1 . . . . 142 B3
Forest St
 Ashton-u-L OL6 . . . . 166 C4
 Eccles M30 . . . . 79 A4
 Oldham OL8 . . . . 66 F2
Forest View OL12 . . . . 14 C2
Forest Way BL7 . . . . 25 C6
Forfar St BL1 . . . . 24 E5
Forge Ind Est OL4 . . . . 67 B7
Forge St
 Oldham OL4 . . . . 67 B7
 Wigan WN1 . . . . 151 B3
Formby Ave
 Atherton M46 . . . . 58 C4
 Manchester M21 . . . . 109 D7
Formby Dr SK8 . . . . 131 B8
Formby Rd M6 . . . . 80 E5
Forres Gr WN4 . . . . 72 D4
Forrester Dr OL2 . . . . 49 D8
Forresters Cl WN2 . . . . 74 E8
Forresters Gn M17 . . . . . . 96 E6
Forrester St M28 . . . . 79 A8
Forrest Rd M34 . . . . 101 B1
Forshaw Ave M18 . . . . 99 F6
Forshaw St M34 . . . . 100 D4
Forster St WA3 . . . . 74 A1
Forston Wlk M8 . . . . 156 B2
Forsythia Wlk **2** M31 . . . 105 E2
Forsyth St OL12 . . . . 13 E2
Fortescue Rd SK2 . . . . . . 124 D7
Forth Pl M26 . . . . 43 F5
Forth Rd M26 . . . . 43 F5
Forth St WN7 . . . . 76 C4
Forton Ave BL2 . . . . 42 E7
Forton Rd WN3 . . . . 54 F2
Fortran Cl M5 . . . . 81 A1
Fort Rd M25 . . . . 63 D2
Fortrose Ct M9 . . . . 64 B3
Fortuna Gr M19 . . . . 110 F8
Fortune St BL3 . . . . 148 B1
Fortuneswell Ct M20 . . . . 110 B3
Fortyacre Dr SK6 . . . . 112 E3
Forum Gr M7 . . . . 155 B1
Forum Leisure M22 . . . . . 121 C3
Forum The SK6 . . . . 113 C2
Forward Ctr BL5 . . . . 39 B4
Fosbrook Ave M20 . . . . . . 110 C4
Foscarn Dr M23 . . . . 121 B5
Fossgill Ave BL2 . . . . 25 C5
Foster Ave WN3 . . . . 151 B2
Foster Ct BL9 . . . . 28 D4
Foster La BL2 . . . . 25 F1
Fosters Bldgs WN6 . . . . . 150 B4
Foster St
 Denton M34 . . . . 100 F3
 Oldham OL4 . . . . 67 C7
 Radcliffe M26 . . . . 43 F3
 Salford M5 . . . . 154 A1
 6 Wigan WN6 . . . . 37 A1
Foster Terr **9** BL1 . . . . . 143 B1
Fotherby Dr M9 . . . . 64 D3
Fotherby Pl WN3 . . . . 55 A3
Foul Clough Rd OL14 . . . . . 5 D8
Foulds Ave BL8 . . . . 27 B2
Foulkes Ho **3** M14 . . . . 110 D8
Foundry La
 Manchester M4 . . . . 159 B2
 Wigan WN3 . . . . 54 D4
Foundry St
 Bolton BL3 . . . . 145 C1

Foundry St *continued*
 Bury BL9 . . . . 140 C2
 Dukinfield SK16 . . . . 101 D8
 Heywood OL10 . . . . 29 C2
 Hindley WN2 . . . . 56 D5
 Leigh WN7 . . . . 76 B4
 Little Lever BL3 . . . . 43 A3
 Newton-le-W WA12 . . . . . 89 B3
 Oldham OL8 . . . . 153 B2
 4 Radcliffe M26 . . . . . . 44 A3
 Swinton M27 . . . . 62 A1
Fountain Ave WA15 . . . . . 120 B2
Fountain Cl SK12 . . . . 133 D4
Fountain Gdns OL1 . . . . . . 48 D1
Fountain Pl BL5 . . . . 57 C5
Fountain Pl
 Poynton SK12 . . . . 133 D4
 Whitefield M45 . . . . 62 F7
Fountains Ave M22 . . . . . . 25 C1
Fountains Cl M29 . . . . 77 C7
Fountains Sq SK12 . . . . . 135 D6
Fountains Rd
 Cheadle SK8 . . . . 132 C6
 Urmston M32 . . . . 95 F3
Fountain St
 Ashton-u-L OL6 . . . . 85 F4
 Bury, Elton BL8 . . . . 27 C2
 Bury, Pimhole BL9 . . . . . 141 A2
 6 Eccles M30 . . . . 95 D8
 Hyde SK14 . . . . 167 C3
 Manchester M2 . . . . 159 A1
 Middleton M24 . . . . 65 A8
 4 Oldham OL1 . . . . 153 B3
Fountain Street N BL9 . . . 141 A3
Fountains Wlk
 Chadderton OL9 . . . . 152 A1
 Dukinfield SK16 . . . . 101 C6
 Golborne WA3 . . . . 91 B8
Fouracres Rd M23 . . . . . . 121 A5
FOUR GATES 39 C4
FOUR LANE ENDS 26 C5
Four Lane Ends BL2 . . . . . 25 E4
Four Lanes SK14 . . . . 103 A4
Four Lanes End Rd OL13 . . 3 B8
Four Lanes Way OL11 . . . . 13 C2
Fourmarts Rd WN5 . . . . . . 36 C2
Four Stalls End BL15 . . . . 16 A5
Fourteen Meadows Rd
 WN3 . . . . 150 B2
Fourth Ave
 Bolton BL1 . . . . 144 B3
 Bury BL9 . . . . 28 D4
 Chadderton OL9 . . . . 152 A1
 Droylsden M11 . . . . 83 C3
 Little Lever BL3 . . . . 42 F4
 Mossley SK15 . . . . 86 E6
 Oldham OL8 . . . . 66 C1
 Stretford M17 . . . . 96 A6
 Swinton M27 . . . . 79 D5
Fourth St BL1 . . . . 23 F4
Fourways M17 . . . . 96 A7
Four Yards M2 . . . . 158 C1
Fowey Wlk
 Hattersley SK14 . . . . 102 E3
 5 Wythenshawe M23 . . 121 A5
Fowler Ave M18 . . . . 99 F7
Fowler Cl WN1 . . . . 151 B4
Fowler Ind Est BL6 . . . . . . 22 C2
Fowler St OL8 . . . . 66 B3
FOWLEY COMMON 92 B5
Fowley Common La WA3 . . 92 C5
Fownhope Ave M33 . . . . . 107 F3
Fownhope Rd M33 . . . . . . 107 F3
Foxall Cl M24 . . . . 64 C7
Foxall St M24 . . . . 64 C7
Fox Bank Ct SK3 . . . . 170 A4
Foxbank St M13 . . . . 98 E4
Fox Bench Cl SK7 . . . . . . 132 C6
Foxbench Wlk M21 . . . . . 109 D6
Fox Cl WA15 . . . . 119 F6
Foxcroft St OL15 . . . . 15 F5
Foxdale Cl BL7 . . . . 9 E7
Foxdale St **3** M11 . . . . . . 83 C1
Foxdene Gr WN3 . . . . 54 E2
Foxendon Dr M32 . . . . 99 F1
6 Foxendon Hall & Park*
 M24 . . . . 65 E6
Foxendon La M24 OL9 . . . 65 F6
Foxendon Wlk M34 . . . . . 100 E1
Foxendale Wlk BL3 . . . . . 145 C1
Foxfield Cl BL8 . . . . 27 B5
Foxfield Dr OL8 . . . . 66 C1
Foxfield Gr WN6 . . . . 36 B6
Foxfield Rd M23 . . . . 121 A3
Foxfold Cl M28 . . . . 77 F7
Foxford Wlk M22 . . . . 121 B1
Foxglove Cl
 Altrincham WA14 . . . . . . 119 C8
 Bury BL9 . . . . 28 D3
Foxglove La SK15 . . . . 86 A3
Foxglove Wlk M31 . . . . . . 105 F2
Foxhall Rd
 Altrincham WA15 . . . . . . 119 F6
 Denton M34 . . . . 100 D4
Foxham Dr M7 . . . . 155 B2
Foxhill
 Altrincham WA14 . . . . . . 119 A5
 Shaw OL2 . . . . 48 E8
Foxhill Chase SK2 . . . . . . 125 A5
Fox Hill Ct SK4 . . . . 168 A2
Foxhill Dr SK15 . . . . 102 C7
Fox Hill Rd M30 . . . . 78 F1
Foxhill Rd OL11 . . . . 47 D8
Foxholes Cl OL12 . . . . 15 A1

Foxholes Rd
 Horwich BL6 . . . . 22 D4
 Hyde SK14 . . . . 113 C8
 Rochdale OL12 . . . . 15 A2
Foxland Rd SK8 . . . . 122 B3
Foxlair Ct M22 . . . . 121 B3
Foxlair Rd M22 . . . . 121 B3
Foxland Rd SK8 . . . . 122 B4
Foxlea SK13 . . . . 115 F8
Foxley Cl
 Droylsden M43 . . . . 99 E8
 Lymm WA13 . . . . 117 A2
Foxley Gr BL3 . . . . 145 A2
Foxley Hall Mews WA13 . 117 A1
Foxley Wlk M12 . . . . 165 A1
Fox Park Rd OL8 . . . . 66 C2
Fox Platt Rd OL5 . . . . 68 B1
Fox Platt Terr OL5 . . . . . . 86 C8
Fox St
 Bury BL9 . . . . 140 C3
 Eccles M30 . . . . 79 F2
 Heywood OL10 . . . . 29 C2
 Horwich BL6 . . . . 22 C2
 Milnrow OL16 . . . . 31 E6
 Oldham OL8 . . . . 66 C2
 Rochdale OL16 . . . . 15 B1
 Stockport SK3 . . . . 170 A4
Foxton St M24 . . . . 64 C7
Foxton Wlk **6** M23 . . . . . 121 A2
Foxwell St **6** WN5 . . . . . . 53 E5
Foxwood Dr
 Hyde SK14 . . . . 167 B4
 Mossley OL5 . . . . 68 D2
Foxwood Gdns M19 . . . . . 110 E5
Foynes Cl M40 . . . . 157 A1
Foy St **2** WN4 . . . . 73 B3
Frame The M11 . . . . 83 A2
Framingham Rd M33 . . . . 108 B2
Framley Rd M20, M21 . . . 109 F7
Frampton Cl M24 . . . . 65 B7
Fram St
 Manchester M9 . . . . 157 C4
 Salford M6 . . . . 154 B2
Frances Ave SK8 . . . . 122 A6
Francesca Wlk M18 . . . . . 165 C2
Frances Pl M46 . . . . 58 A2
Frances St
 Bolton BL1 . . . . 143 A2
 Cheadle SK8 . . . . 122 E6
 Dukinfield SK14 . . . . 101 C3
 Irlam M44 . . . . 105 E5
 Manchester M13 . . . . 163 B2
 Oldham OL1 . . . . 49 A1
 7 Stockport SK1, SK3 . 170 B4
Frances Street W SK14 . . 101 C3
France St
 Hindley WN2 . . . . 56 D6
 Westhoughton BL5 . . . . . . 57 E6
 Wigan WN5 . . . . 54 F7
Francis Ave
 Eccles M30 . . . . 79 E2
 Walkden M28 . . . . 60 F2
Francis Rd
 Irlam M44 . . . . 93 F1
 Manchester M20 . . . . 110 C5
Francis St
 Denton M34 . . . . 113 B8
 Eccles M30 . . . . 79 D3
 Failsworth M35 . . . . 83 F7
 Farnworth BL4 . . . . 42 D1
 Hindley WN2 . . . . 56 E5
 Leigh WN7 . . . . 75 E7
 Manchester M3 . . . . 158 C3
 Tyldesley M29 . . . . 77 D8
Francis Terr **3** SK14 . . . 166 C1
Frandley Wlk **4** M13 . . . 163 B3
Frank Cowan CE M7 . . . . 158 A4
Frank Fold OL10 . . . . 29 A2
Frankford Ave BL1 . . . . . . 142 C2
Frankford Sq BL1 . . . . . . 142 C2
Frankland Cl M11 . . . . 83 B2
Franklin Cl OL1 . . . . 153 B4
Franklin St
 Eccles M30 . . . . 79 D2
 Oldham OL1 . . . . 153 B4
 Rochdale OL16 . . . . 31 B5
Franklyn Ave M41 . . . . 94 E2
Franklyn Rd
 Droylsden M43 . . . . 84 A1
 Manchester M18 . . . . 99 F6
Frank Perkins Way M44 . 105 F7
Frank St
 Bolton BL3 . . . . 143 A2
 Bury BL9 . . . . 140 C1
 Failsworth M35 . . . . 83 E7
 Hyde SK14 . . . . 167 B2
Frank Swift Wlk **5** M14 . . 98 A3
Frankton Rd M45 . . . . 62 F7
Franton Rd M11 . . . . 83 B2
Fraser Ave M33 . . . . 108 B3
Fraser Ho BL1 . . . . 143 A1
Fraser Pl M17 . . . . 96 D5
Fraser Rd
 Manchester M8 . . . . 63 F1
 Wigan WN5 . . . . 54 F7
Fraser St
 Ashton-u-L OL6 . . . . 166 C3
 Rochdale OL16 . . . . 31 B4
 Shaw OL2 . . . . 149 A3
 Swinton M27 . . . . 62 A1
Fraternitas Terr M43 . . . . . 83 E8
Frawley Ave WA12 . . . . . . 89 C5
Frecheville Ct BL9 . . . . . . 140 B1
Freckleton Ave M21 . . . . . 109 C4
Freckleton Dr BL8 . . . . 43 F8
Freckleton St WN1 . . . . . . 37 C2

Freda Wlk M11 . . . . 160 C1
Frederica Gdns WN2 . . . . . 56 A3
Frederick Ave OL2 . . . . . . 149 B1
Frederick Ct BL4 . . . . 60 E8
Frederick Rd M6, M7 . . . . . 81 B4
Frederick St
 Ashton-in-M WN4 . . . . 73 A5
 Ashton-u-L OL6 . . . . 85 E2
 Chadderton OL9 . . . . 152 B4
 Denton M34 . . . . 100 F5
 Farnworth BL4 . . . . 60 D8
 Hindley WN2 . . . . 56 E5
 Ince-in-M WN3 . . . . 151 A2
 Oldham OL8 . . . . 66 D4
 Ramsbottom BL0 . . . . . . 138 B1
 Salford M3 . . . . 158 B2
 Wigan WN1 . . . . 151 B4
Fred Longworth High Sch
 M29 . . . . 58 E1
Fred St M44 . . . . 65 D6
Fred Tilson Cl M14 . . . . . . 98 A3
Freehold Com Prim Sch
 OL9 . . . . 152 C1
Freeholds Rd OL12 . . . . . . 4 E6
Freehold St OL11 . . . . . . 139 B1
Freehold Sta OL12 . . . . . 152 B2
Freeholds Terr OL12 . . . . . 4 E6
Free La BB4 . . . . 1 A6
Freelands M29 . . . . 59 C1
Freeland Wlk M11 . . . . . . 165 C4
Freeman Ave **2** OL6 . . . . 85 D3
Freeman Rd SK16 . . . . . . 101 C7
Freeman Sq M15 . . . . 163 A2
Freemantle St SK3 . . . . . 170 A4
Freesia Ave **9** M28 . . . . . 59 F3
Freestone Cl BL8 . . . . 140 A3
FREE TOWN 141 A4
Freetown SK13 . . . . 116 C8
Freetown Bsns Pk BL9 . . 141 A4
Freetown Cl M14 . . . . 98 A4
Freetrade St OL11 . . . . . . 139 B2
Freiston **3** OL12 . . . . . . 139 C4
Fremantle Ave M18 . . . . . . 99 D3
French Ave
 5 Oldham OL1 . . . . 49 C1
 Stalybridge SK15 . . . . 86 C1
French Barn La M9 . . . . . . 64 C3
Frenches Ct OL3 . . . . 69 A6
French Gr BL3 . . . . 42 D5
French St
 Ashton-u-L OL6 . . . . 85 D4
 Stalybridge SK15 . . . . 86 C1
Frenchwood Ct WN2 . . . . . 38 C4
Frensham Wlk M23 . . . . . 120 F4
Fresca Rd OL2 . . . . 49 D4
Fresh Ct SK13 . . . . 115 F7
Freshfield SK8 . . . . 131 B8
Freshfield Ave
 Atherton M46 . . . . 58 C4
 Bolton BL3 . . . . 147 A2
 Prestwich M25 . . . . 63 C6
Freshfield Cl
 Failsworth M35 . . . . 84 A6
 Marple SK6 . . . . 114 B1
Freshfield Gr BL3 . . . . . . 147 C2
Freshfield Rd
 Hindley WN2 . . . . 56 F5
 Stockport SK4 . . . . 110 F3
 Wigan WN3 . . . . 54 E3
Freshfields M26 . . . . 43 D5
Freshfield Wlk **11** M11 . . 83 C2
Freshford Wlk **2** M22 . . . 121 B1
Freshpool Way M22 . . . . . 121 E6
Freshwater Dr
 Ashton-u-L OL6 . . . . 85 E5
 Denton M34 . . . . 113 B8
Freshwater St **3** M18 . . . . 99 E6
Freshwinds Ct OL4 . . . . . . 67 D4
Fresnel Cl SK14 . . . . 102 B6
Frew Ho M5 . . . . 81 D1
Freeland Ave SK3 . . . . . . 123 F4
Freya Gr M5 . . . . 161 C4
Friarmere Rd OL3 . . . . 50 E5
Friars Cl
 Altrincham WA14 . . . . . . 119 B1
 Tyldesley M29 . . . . 59 D1
Friar's Cl SK9 . . . . 136 E8
Friars Cres OL11 . . . . 30 F2
Friars Ct M5 . . . . 80 B2
Friars Prim Sch The M3 . 158 A3
Friar's Rd M33 . . . . 108 B4
Friendship Ave M18 . . . . . . 99 E4
Frieston Rd WA14 . . . . . . 119 E8
Friezland Cl SK15 . . . . 86 E6
Friezland La OL3 . . . . 69 A4
Friezland Prim Sch OL3 . . 68 E5
Frimley Gdns M22 . . . . . . 121 D3
Frinton Ave M40 . . . . 65 D3
Frinton Cl M33 . . . . 107 F1
Frinton Rd BL3 . . . . 146 B3
Frith Rd M20 . . . . 110 C5
Frith St WN5 . . . . 54 A5
Frobisher Cl M13 . . . . 164 A1
Frobisher Pl SK5 . . . . 169 B4
Frobisher Rd OL16 . . . . 6 C1
Frodsham Ave SK4 . . . . . 168 C3
Frodsham Rd WN6 . . . . 36 D3
Frodsham St M33 . . . . . . 108 C2
Frodsham Way SK9 . . . . . 131 E4
Frodsham St **9** M14 . . . . . 98 B3
Frodsley Wlk M12 . . . . . . 164 C2
Froggbrook Cl SK2 . . . . . 124 F6
Frog La WN1 & WN6 . . . . 150 B4

G

Frogley St **2** BL2 ..... 25 B3
Frogmore Ave SK14 ..... 113 E7
Frome Ave
Stockport SK2 ..... 124 C5
Urmston M41 ..... 95 B1
Frome Cl M29 ..... 77 C6
Frome Dr M8 ..... 156 B3
Frome St OL4 ..... 67 C6
Frostlands St **10** M16 ..... 97 E3
Frost St
Manchester M4 ..... 160 A1
Oldham OL8 ..... 66 E4
Froxmer St M18 ..... 165 C2
Froxmer Street Ind Est
M18 ..... 165 C2
Fryent Cl BL6 ..... 21 D2
Fulbeck Ave WN3 ..... 55 A2
Fulbrook Dr SK8 ..... 132 A6
Fulbrook Way M29 ..... 59 C1
Fulford St **4** M14 ..... 97 C4
Fulham Ave M40 ..... 83 B5
Fulham St OL4 ..... 67 C6
Fullerton Rd SK4 ..... 168 B2
FULLWOOD 149 C2
Fulmar Cl
Poynton SK12 ..... 133 A4
Westhoughton BL5 ..... 57 D6
Fulmar Dr
Hazel Grove SK2 ..... 124 F5
Sale M33 ..... 107 C2
Fulmards Cl SK9 ..... 137 C7
Fulmar Gdns OL11 ..... 29 F7
Fulmead Wlk **10** M8 ..... 155 C2
Fulmer Dr M4 ..... 159 C2
Fulmere Ct M27 ..... 79 D6
Fulneck Sq **2** M43 ..... 100 A8
Fulshaw Ave SK9 ..... 137 A6
Fulshaw Cross SK9 ..... 137 A5
Fulshaw Ct SK9 ..... 137 A5
FULSHAW PARK 137 B5
Fulshaw Park S SK9 ..... 137 A4
Fulshaw Pk SK9 ..... 137 A5
Fulshaw Wlk **12** M13 ..... 163 B3
Fulstone Mews SK2 ..... 124 B6
Fulton Ct M15 ..... 163 A1
Fulwell Ave M46 ..... 76 E8
Fulwood Ave M9 ..... 64 F4
Fulwood Cl BL8 ..... 26 F1
Fulwood Rd WA3 ..... 90 E7
Furbarn Rd OL11 ..... 29 D8
Furberry Ct OL4 ..... 68 B5
Furlong Cl WN2 ..... 73 F7
Furlong Rd M22 ..... 121 B3
Furnace St
Dukinfield SK16 ..... 166 B2
Hyde SK14 ..... 101 C4
Furness Ave
Ashton-u-L OL7 ..... 84 F5
Bolton BL2 ..... 25 B2
Heywood OL10 ..... 29 C3
Littleborough OL15 ..... 16 A6
Oldham OL8 ..... 67 C3
Whitefield M45 ..... 63 A8
Furness Cl
2 Glossop SK13 ..... 116 F8
Milnrow OL16 ..... 31 E6
Poynton SK12 ..... 133 D4
Furness Cres WN7 ..... 57 D1
Furness Gr SK4 ..... 168 A1
Furness Quay M50 ..... 161 A3
Furness Rd
Bolton BL1 ..... 144 B3
Cheadle SK8 ..... 132 C6
Manchester M14 ..... 98 C1
Urmston M41 ..... 95 D3
Furness Sq BL2 ..... 25 B2
Furnival Rd M18 ..... 165 C1
Furnival St
Leigh WN7 ..... 75 F7
Reddish SK5 ..... 99 F2
Furrow Dr M30 ..... 79 B4
Furrows The M32 ..... 96 B4
Further Field OL11 ..... 13 D1
Further Heights Rd **11**
OL12 ..... 14 F1
Further Hey Cl OL4 ..... 67 E7
Further La SK14 ..... 102 E3
Further Pits OL11 ..... 30 C7
Furtherwood Rd OL1 ..... 48 C1
Furze Ave BL5 ..... 57 F7
Furzegate OL4 ..... 31 C3
Furze La OL4 ..... 49 D1
Furze The OL2 ..... 48 D6
Furze Wlk M31 ..... 106 A3
Fushia Gr M7 ..... 155 A2
Fusilier Mus The* BL9 ..... 140 B2
Futura Pk BL6 ..... 22 C1
Futures Pk OL13 ..... 3 E8
Fyfield Wlk **9** M8 ..... 156 B2
Fylde Ave
Bolton BL2 ..... 42 E7
Gatley SK8 ..... 131 C8
Fylde Ct M32 ..... 108 C8
Fylde La M18 ..... 99 D3
Fylde Rd SK4 ..... 168 A2
Fylde St BL4 ..... 42 D2
Fylde Street E BL4 ..... 42 D2

Gabbot St PR7 ..... 21 A7
Gable Ave SK9 ..... 137 A7
Gable Ct M34 ..... 100 F2
Gable Dr M24 ..... 46 E1
Gable St
Manchester M11 ..... 164 C4
Newton-le-W WA12 ..... 89 B3
Gables The M33 ..... 108 B3
Gabriel's Terr **1** M24 ..... 65 C7
Gabriels The OL2 ..... 48 F7
Gadbrook Gr M46 ..... 58 B2
Gadbury Ave M46 ..... 58 B3
Gadbury Fold M46 ..... 58 A2
Gaddum Rd
Altrincham WA14 ..... 119 B1
Manchester M20 ..... 110 C3
Gadfield Ct M46 ..... 58 B3
Gadfield Wlk BL3 ..... 147 B4
Gadwall Cl M28 ..... 78 D8
Gail Ave SK1 ..... 169 A2
Gail Cl
Alderley Edge SK9 ..... 137 B2
Failsworth M35 ..... 83 E5
Gainford Ave SK8 ..... 122 B4
Gainford Gdns M40 ..... 65 B1
Gainford Rd SK5 ..... 99 F1
Gainford Wlk BL3 ..... 147 B4
Gainsborough Ave
Bolton BL3 ..... 146 C3
Manchester M20 ..... 110 C5
Marple SK6 ..... 126 B8
Oldham OL8 ..... 66 E4
Stretford M32 ..... 96 F3
Gainsborough Cl
Wigan WN3 ..... 54 D3
2 Wilmslow SK9 ..... 137 D8
Gainsborough Dr
Cheadle SK8 ..... 122 F6
Rochdale OL11 ..... 30 E3
Gainsborough Ho M33 ..... 107 F3
Gainsborough Rd
Chadderton OL9 ..... 47 E1
Droylsden M34 ..... 84 D1
Ramsbottom BL0 ..... 11 B1
Gainsborough St M7 ..... 155 B3
Gainsborough Wlk
Denton M34 ..... 100 A1
1 Dukinfield SK14 ..... 101 F5
Gairloch Ave M32 ..... 96 B2
Gair Rd SK5 ..... 169 C4
Gair St SK14 ..... 167 A4
Gaitskell Cl M12 ..... 160 B1
Galbraith Rd M20 ..... 110 C3
Galbraith Way OL11 ..... 29 E8
GALE 16 C7
Gale Cl OL15 ..... 16 C7
Gale Dr M24 ..... 46 D2
Gale Rd M25 ..... 62 F3
Gale St
Heywood OL10 ..... 29 B2
Rochdale OL12 ..... 14 F3
Galgate Cl
Bury BL8 ..... 26 F1
Manchester M15 ..... 162 B3
Galindo St BL2 ..... 25 C4
Galland St OL4 ..... 67 D7
Galleria The **10** BL1 ..... 145 C3
Galleries Sh Ctr The
WN1 ..... 150 C4
Galleries The **19** WN1 ..... 150 C4
Gallery of Costume*
M14 ..... 98 C2
Gallery Oldham* OL1 ..... 153 C2
Gallery The M3 ..... 158 C2
Galloway Cl
Bolton BL3 ..... 40 E5
Heywood OL10 ..... 45 F8
Galloway Dr
Swinton M27 ..... 61 F4
Up Holland WN8 ..... 53 B6
Galloway Rd M27 ..... 79 D6
Gallowsclough Rd SK15 ..... 102 E6
Galsworthy Ave M8 ..... 156 A2
Galvin Rd M9 ..... 64 B3
Galway St OL1 ..... 153 C2
Galway Wlk M23 ..... 120 F2
Galwey Gr WN1 ..... 37 C4
Gambleside Cl M28 ..... 78 B8
Gamble St WN7 ..... 76 A5
Gambrel Bank Rd OL6 ..... 85 B6
Gambrel Gr OL6 ..... 85 B6
GAMESLEY 171 A1
Gamesley Com Prim Sch
SK13 ..... 171 B2
Game St OL4 ..... 67 C5
Games Wlk **8** M22 ..... 121 B1
Gamma Wlk M11 ..... 83 B2
Gandy La OL12 ..... 14 D4
Gan Eden **8** M7 ..... 63 E1
Gantley Ave WN5 ..... 53 D3
Gantley Cres WN5 ..... 53 D3
Gantley Rd WN5 ..... 53 D4
Gantock Wlk **10** M14 ..... 98 C3
Ganton Ave M45 ..... 62 D7
Garbrook Ave M9 ..... 64 C5
Garden Ave
Droylsden M43 ..... 84 B2
Stretford M32 ..... 96 D3
1 Swinton M27 ..... 79 D7
Garden City BL0 ..... 11 A2
Garden Cl OL15 ..... 15 F2
Garden Ct OL16 ..... 31 C8
Gardenfold Way M43 ..... 84 B2
Garden Fold Way M43 ..... 84 B2

Garden La
Altrincham WA14 ..... 119 D5
17 Rochdale OL16 ..... 31 A8
Salford M3 ..... 158 B2
Worsley M28 ..... 78 A6
Garden Row
Heywood OL10 ..... 29 B4
Rochdale OL12 ..... 14 D2
Garden St
11 Bacup OL13 ..... 3 C8
Bury BL8 ..... 26 F7
Denton M34 ..... 100 F6
Eccles M30 ..... 79 E1
Farnworth BL4 ..... 60 E8
Heywood OL10 ..... 29 C2
Hyde SK14 ..... 167 B4
Manchester M4 ..... 159 A2
Newhey OL16 ..... 32 B4
Oldham, County End OL4 ..... 67 F5
Oldham, Mumps OL1 ..... 67 A7
Ramsbottom BL0 ..... 138 C2
Ramsbottom, Brooksbottoms
BL9 ..... 11 C3
Stockport SK2 ..... 124 C5
Tyldesley M29 ..... 77 A8
Gardens The
Bolton BL1 ..... 24 F6
Edgworth BL7 ..... 9 D4
Salford M30 ..... 80 A3
Garden Terr OL2 ..... 48 C7
Garden Vale M7 ..... 75 C8
Garden Way OL15 ..... 15 F2
Garden Wlk
Ashton-u-L OL6 ..... 166 C4
3 Denton M34 ..... 101 A2
8 Partington M31 ..... 105 E3
Gardner Cl WN1 ..... 20 B1
Gardner Grange SK5 ..... 112 C4
Gardner Ho **8** M30 ..... 79 C2
Gardner Rd **6** M30 ..... 79 E2
Gardner St
Manchester M12 ..... 165 B2
Salford M6 ..... 81 A3
Garfield Ave M19 ..... 99 B1
Garfield Cl OL11 ..... 13 E1
Garfield Cl SK1 ..... 112 A2
Garfield Gr BL3 ..... 145 A1
Garfield St BL3 ..... 146 C3
Garforth Ave M4 ..... 159 C2
Garforth Cres M43 ..... 84 C3
Garforth Rise **1** BL1 ..... 144 A3
Garforth St OL9 ..... 152 C4
Gargrave Ave BL1 ..... 23 F2
Gargrave St
Manchester M7 ..... 80 F8
2 Oldham OL4 ..... 67 B6
Garland Rd M22 ..... 121 E3
Garlick St
Hyde SK14 ..... 167 C3
Manchester M18 ..... 99 D5
Oldham OL9 ..... 153 B2
Garnant Cl M9 ..... 157 C4
Garner Ave WA15 ..... 108 A1
Garner Cl WA14 ..... 119 D2
Garner Dr
Eccles M30 ..... 79 C3
Salford M5 ..... 154 A3
Tyldesley M29 ..... 77 B5
Garner's La SK3 ..... 170 B1
Garnett Cl SK14 ..... 102 F3
Garnett Rd SK14 ..... 102 F3
Garnett St
Oldham OL1 ..... 67 B8
Ramsbottom BL0 ..... 138 B1
Stockport SK1 ..... 169 C1
Garnett Way **11** SK14 ..... 102 F3
Garnett Wlk M40 ..... 65 A1
Garratt Cl OL2 ..... 149 C3
Garrett Hall Prim Sch
M29 ..... 77 D7
Garrett Hall Rd M28 ..... 77 C7
Garratt La M28, M29 ..... 77 D7
Garrett Wlk SK3 ..... 123 C8
Garrick Theatre* SK1 ..... 169 B1
Garron Wlk **1** M22 ..... 121 A2
Garrowmore Wlk **2** M9 ..... 64 E3
Garsdale Cl BL9 ..... 45 B2
Garside Ave WA3 ..... 90 D7
Garside Gr
Bolton BL1 ..... 142 C2
Garside Hey Rd BL8 ..... 27 B6
Garside St
Bolton BL1 ..... 145 B3
Denton M34 ..... 100 F2
Hyde SK14 ..... 167 B1
Garstang Ave BL2 ..... 42 F7
Garstang Dr BL8 ..... 26 F1
Garstang Ho M13 ..... 163 B1
Garston Ave M46 ..... 58 B5
Garston Cl
Leigh WN7 ..... 57 E1
Stockport SK4 ..... 168 C3
Garston St BL9 ..... 141 A4
GARSWOOD 72 C3
Garswood Cres WN5 ..... 71 E4
Garswood Dr BL8 ..... 27 B6
Garswood Old Rd WA11,
WN4 ..... 71 E1
Garswood Prim Sch WN4 ..... 72 C4
Garswood Rd
Billinge WN5 ..... 71 F4
Bolton BL3 ..... 147 D4
Garswood WA11, WN4 ..... 72 C3
Manchester M14 ..... 98 A2
Garswood St WN4 ..... 73 B3

Garswood Sta WN4 ..... 72 D3
Garth Ave WA15 ..... 119 E6
Garth Hts SK9 ..... 137 C7
Garthland Rd SK7 ..... 124 F3
Garthmere Rd M46 ..... 58 F5
Garthorne Cl M16 ..... 97 D4
Garthorp Rd M23 ..... 108 E1
Garth Rd
Marple SK6 ..... 126 A6
Stockport SK2 ..... 124 C7
Wythenshawe M22 ..... 121 D4
Garth The M5 ..... 154 A2
Garthwaite Ave OL8 ..... 66 E4
Gartside Wlk M8 ..... 156 C4
Garton Dr WA3 ..... 74 E1
Gartside St
Ashton-u-L OL7 ..... 84 E1
Delph OL3 ..... 50 E4
Manchester M3 ..... 158 B1
Oldham OL4 ..... 67 B5
Garwick Rd BL1 ..... 142 B3
Garwood St M15 ..... 162 D3
Gascoyne St M14 ..... 98 B3
Gaskell Cl OL15 ..... 16 A6
Gaskell Com Prim Sch
BL1 ..... 145 B4
Gaskell Rd
Altrincham WA14 ..... 119 D6
Eccles M30 ..... 79 E1
Gaskell St
Bolton BL1 ..... 145 A4
Dukinfield SK16 ..... 166 B1
Failsworth M40 ..... 83 D6
Hindley WN2 ..... 56 E7
Swinton M27 ..... 61 F2
Wigan WN1 ..... 151 A4
Gaskill St OL10 ..... 29 A2
Gas St
Adlington PR7 ..... 21 A6
Ashton-u-L OL6 ..... 166 B3
Bolton BL1 ..... 145 B3
Farnworth BL4 ..... 60 D8
6 Heywood OL10 ..... 29 D2
Hollingworth SK14 ..... 103 D5
Littleborough OL15 ..... 75 F5
Platt Bridge WN2 ..... 56 B2
Rochdale OL11 ..... 139 B3
Stockport SK4 ..... 169 B1
Gaston Wlk M9 ..... 64 E3
Gatcombe Mews **1** SK9 ..... 137 A6
Gatcombe Sq M14 ..... 98 C3
Gateacre Wlk M23 ..... 120 E8
Gate Ctr The SK6 ..... 112 E6
Gatefield Cl M26 ..... 43 E3
Gategill Gr WN5 ..... 53 D3
Gatehead Bsns Pk OL3 ..... 50 F3
Gatehead Croft OL3 ..... 50 F3
Gatehead Ho OL3 ..... 50 F3
Gatehead Mews OL3 ..... 50 F3
Gatehead Rd OL3 ..... 50 F3
Gate House Ct **13** M19 ..... 141 C2
Gatehouse Rd M28 ..... 60 A4
Gate Keeper Fold OL7 ..... 85 A7
Gatemere Cl M28 ..... 78 B8
Gatesgarth Rd M24 ..... 46 C2
Gateshead Cl M14 ..... 98 B4
Gateside Wlk **6** M9 ..... 64 E5
Gates Prim Sch The BL5 ..... 39 F2
Gates Sh Ctr The BL1 ..... 145 C3
Gate St
Dukinfield SK16 ..... 101 A6
Manchester M11 ..... 165 C4
Rochdale OL11 ..... 139 C1
Gates The BL2 ..... 26 A3
Gateway Cres OL9 ..... 65 E4
Gateway Ho M1 ..... 159 B1
Gateway Ind Est M1 ..... 159 B1
Gateway Rd M18 ..... 165 C2
Gateways The M27 ..... 61 F1
Gateway The M40 ..... 157 C2
Gathill Cl SK8 ..... 122 F1
Gathurst La WN5, WN6, ... 36 A4
Gathurst Rd WN5 ..... 53 E8
Gathurst St M18 ..... 99 E6
Gathurst Sta WN6 ..... 36 A3
GATLEY 122 A4
Gatley Ave M14 ..... 98 A1
Gatley Brow OL1 ..... 153 B4
Gatley Carrs Nature
Reserve* SK8 ..... 122 A4
Gatley Cl M29 ..... 59 B1
Gatley Gn SK8 ..... 122 A5
Gatley Prim Sch SK8 ..... 122 A5
Gatley Rd
Cheadle SK8 ..... 122 C5
Sale M33 ..... 108 E3
Gatley Sta SK8 ..... 122 B5
Gatling Ave M12 ..... 99 B2
Gatwick Ave M23 ..... 121 B6
Gavel Wlk M24 ..... 46 E1
Gavin Ave M5 ..... 81 A1
Gawsworth Ave M20 ..... 110 C1
Gawsworth Cl
Altrincham WA15 ..... 120 D6
Bramhall SK7 ..... 132 E6
Glossop SK13 ..... 104 A5
Poynton SK12 ..... 133 F2
Shaw OL2 ..... 48 F7
Stockport SK3 ..... 170 D7
Gawsworth Mews SK8 ..... 122 B5
Gawsworth Pl M22 ..... 121 F1
Gawsworth Rd
Golborne WA3 ..... 73 F1
Sale M33 ..... 108 C1
Gawsworth Way
15 Denton M34 ..... 101 A1

Gawsworth Way continued
Handforth SK9 ..... 131 E4
Gawthorne Cl SK7 ..... 124 C2
Gawthorpe Cl BL9 ..... 45 A5
Gaydon Rd M33 ..... 107 D4
Gaythorne St **5** BL1 ..... 143 C3
Gaythorn St M5 ..... 81 C1
Gayton Cl WN3 ..... 54 D3
Gayton Wlk **7** M40 ..... 65 D2
Gaywood Wlk M40 ..... 156 C4
Geddington Rd WA14 ..... 119 C8
GEE CROSS 113 E7
Gee Cross Fold SK14 ..... 113 E7
Gee Cross Holy Trinity CE
Prim Sch SK14 ..... 113 F8
Gee La
Eccles M30 ..... 79 B3
7 Oldham OL8 ..... 66 B2
Gee St SK3 ..... 170 A3
Gelder Clough Residential
Cvn Pk OL10 ..... 29 C5
Gellert Pl BL5 ..... 57 E6
Gellert Rd BL5 ..... 57 E6
Gellfield La OL3 ..... 51 D1
Gemini Rd M6 ..... 81 C4
Geneva Rd SK7 ..... 123 E3
Geneva Terr OL11 ..... 30 C8
Geneva Wlk
Chadderton OL9 ..... 152 C2
11 Manchester M8 ..... 156 B2
Genista Gr M7 ..... 155 A2
Geoff Bent Wlk M40 ..... 83 B5
Geoffrey St
Bury BL9 ..... 141 A4
Over Hulton BL5 ..... 58 F8
Ramsbottom BL0 ..... 11 A4
Geo. Hampson's Bldgs
M43 ..... 92 C8
George Barton St **23** BL2 ..... 25 B1
George Ct **10** SK16 ..... 166 B1
George H Carnall L Ctr
M41 ..... 95 E4
George La SK6 ..... 113 A4
George Leigh St M4 ..... 159 B2
George Mann Cl M22 ..... 121 C1
George Rd BL0 ..... 138 B1
George Richards Way
WA14 ..... 119 C7
George's Cl SK12 ..... 133 E3
Georges La WN1 ..... 151 C4
George's La BL6 ..... 22 E5
George Sq OL1 ..... 153 B2
George's Rd
Sale M33 ..... 108 B3
Stockport SK4 ..... 169 A2
George's Road E SK12 ..... 133 E3
George's Road W SK12 ..... 133 E3
George's Row **2** BB4 ..... 2 F1
George St
Alderley Edge SK9 ..... 137 A1
Altrincham WA14 ..... 119 D4
Ashton-in-M WN4 ..... 73 C4
Ashton-u-L OL6 ..... 166 C4
3 Atherton M46 ..... 58 D3
4 Bacup OL13 ..... 3 C8
Bury BL9 ..... 140 C2
Chadderton OL9 ..... 152 A3
Compstall SK6 ..... 114 B2
Denton M34 ..... 101 A3
Eccles M30 ..... 79 C1
Failsworth M35 ..... 83 F8
Farnworth BL4 ..... 60 B7
Glossop SK13 ..... 116 C8
Heywood OL10 ..... 29 B3
Hindley WN2 ..... 56 E5
Horwich BL6 ..... 22 C3
Ince-in-M WN2 ..... 151 C3
Irlam M44 ..... 94 A3
1 Littleborough OL15 ..... 16 B5
Manchester, City Centre
M1 ..... 163 A4
Manchester, Hilton Park
M25 ..... 63 B1
Milnrow OL16 ..... 31 E7
Mossley OL5 ..... 68 C1
Newton-le-W WA12 ..... 89 A4
Oldham OL1 ..... 153 B2
Radcliffe M26 ..... 43 F3
Rochdale, Greengate OL16 ..... 15 D3
Rochdale, Newbold Brow
OL16 ..... 31 A8
Shaw OL2 ..... 149 C4
Stalybridge SK15 ..... 86 A2
Stockport SK1 ..... 112 A2
Urmston M41 ..... 95 C2
Westhoughton BL5 ..... 57 F8
Whitefield M45 ..... 44 E1
Whitworth OL12 ..... 14 C8
George Street E SK1 ..... 124 B8
George Street N M7 ..... 155 C4
George Street W SK1 ..... 124 B8
George Thomas Ct WN9 ..... 157 A4
George Tomlinson Sch
BL4 ..... 60 E6
Georgette Dr M3 ..... 158 B3
Georgia Ave M20 ..... 109 F5
Georgiana St **3** BL4 ..... 42 D1
Georgian Ct
3 Leigh WN7 ..... 76 B4
12 Tyldesley M29 ..... 58 F1
Georgian Sq **2** WN2 ..... 56 A2
Georgina Ct BL3 ..... 146 B3
Georgina St BL3 ..... 146 B3
Gerald Ave M8 ..... 156 A4

Gerald Rd M6 .... 81 B5
Gerard Ctr The WN4 .... 73 B3
Gerard St WN4 .... 73 B3
Germain Ct M9 .... 64 C5
Gerrard Ave WA15 .... 120 A8
Gerrard Cl WN2 .... 38 D2
Gerrard Rd WN5 .... 71 E5
Gerrards Cl M44 .... 94 A2
Gerrards Gdns SK14 ... 113 E7
Gerrards Hollow SK14 .. 113 D7
Gerrard St
　Farnworth BL4 .... 60 E8
　Leigh WN7 .... 75 F5
　Rochdale OL11 .... 31 A2
　[2] Salford M6 .... 81 A3
　Stalybridge SK15 ...... 86 B1
　[5] Westhoughton BL5 .. 39 E1
Gerrards The SK14 .... 113 D7
Gerrards Wood SK14 .. 113 D7
Gertrude Cl M5 .... 161 A4
Gertrude St OL12 .... 4 E6
Gervis Cl M40 .... 157 A1
Ghyll Gr
　Billinge WA11 .... 71 B1
　Walkden M28 .... 60 E2
Giants Hall Rd M6 ..... 36 E3
Giants Seat Gr M27 .... 80 D8
Gibb La M23 .... 121 D2
Gibbon Ave M22 ...... 121 D2
Gibbon's Rd WN4 ...... 72 D3
Gibbon St
　Bolton BL3 .... 145 A1
　Droylsden M11 .... 83 A2
Gibb Rd M28 .... 79 B7
Gibbs Cl OL3 .... 68 E5
Gibbs St M5 .... 158 A1
Gib Field M46 .... 58 B4
Gibfield Dr M46 .... 58 A2
Gibfield Park Ave M46 . 58 B4
Gibfield Park Way M46 . 58 A4
Gib La M23 .... 121 B7
Gibraltar La M34 ..... 113 B8
Gibraltar St
　Bolton BL3 .... 145 A2
　Oldham OL4 .... 67 D5
Gibsmere Cl M23, WA15. 120 D6
Gibson Ave M18 .... 99 F6
Gibson Gr M28 .... 60 A3
Gibson La M28 .... 60 A3
Gibson Pl M4 .... 159 A3
Gibsons Rd SK4 ...... 168 B4
Gibson St
　Bolton BL2 .... 25 C1
　Leigh WN2 .... 56 D1
　Oldham OL4 .... 67 C6
　Rochdale OL16 .... 31 C8
Gidlow Ave
　Adlington PR6 .... 21 A7
　Wigan WN6 .... 37 A2
Gidlow La
　Wigan, Springfield WN6 . 37 A2
　Wigan WN6 .... 37 A4
Gidlow St
　[1] Hindley WN2 ...... 56 D6
　Manchester M18 .... 99 E6
Giffard Wlk SK7 ...... 124 A2
Gifford Ave M9 .... 64 F4
Gifford Pl WN2 .... 56 B4
GIGG 45 A7
Gigg La BL9 .... 45 A7
Gigg La (Bury FC) BL9 . 44 F7
Gilbert Bank SK6 ..... 113 B4
Gilbert Rd WA15 ..... 119 E1
Gilbert St
　Eccles M30 .... 95 B8
　Hindley WN2 .... 56 D5
　Manchester M15 ...... 162 B3
　Ramsbottom BL0 .... 1 C1
　Salford M6 .... 154 C1
　Walkden M28 .... 60 D1
Gilbrook Way OL16 ... 31 B2
Gilchrist Rd M44 ..... 105 A4
Gilda Brook Rd M30 .. 80 A2
Gilda Cres Rd M30 .... 80 A2
Gilda Rd M28 .... 77 F7
Gilded Hollins Prim Sch
　WN7 .... 75 C1
Gildenhall M35 .... 84 A7
Gilderdale Cl OL2 .... 149 B4
Gildersdale Dr M9 .... 64 C6
Gildridge Rd M16 ..... 97 E1
Gilesgate [3] M14 .... 98 C3
Giles St M12 .... 99 A4
Gillan Rd WN6 .... 37 B3
Gill Ave WN6 .... 36 B6
GILLBENT 131 F6
Gillbent Rd SK8 ..... 132 A7
Gillbrook Rd M20 .... 110 B2
Gillbrow Cres WN1 ... 37 F1
Gillemere Gr OL2 .... 149 C3
Gillers Gn M28 .... 60 C3
Gilford Ave M9 .... 65 D1
Gilliburns Fold M28 ... 77 F7
Gilliburns Wlk BL5 ... 57 F5
Gillingham Rd M30 ... 79 B2
Gillingham Sq M11 ... 164 C1
Gill St
　Manchester M9 .... 64 F1
　Stockport SK1 .... 112 B3
Gillwood Dr SK6 ..... 112 F1
Gilman Cl M9 .... 64 C2
Gilman St M9 .... 64 C2

Gilmerton Dr [22] M40 . 83 C5
Gilmore Dr M25 .... 63 B5
Gilmore St SK3 ...... 170 B3
Gilmour St M24 .... 65 A8
Gilmour Terr M9 ...... 64 F1
GILNOW 145 A2
Gilnow Gdns BL1 .... 144 C2
Gilnow Gr BL1 .... 145 A2
Gilnow La BL3 .... 145 A2
Gilnow La BL3 .... 145 A3
GILNOW PARK 145 A2
Gilnow Rd BL1 .... 144 C2
Gilpin Pl WN2 .... 55 F2
Gilpin Rd M41 .... 95 F2
Gilpin Wlk M24 .... 46 E1
Gilroy St WN1 .... 151 A4
Giltbrook Ave M40 ... 160 A4
Gilwell Dr M23 .... 120 F4
Gilwood Gr M24 ...... 46 F4
Gin Croft La BL0 .... 1 E4
Gingham Brow BL6 .... 22 C2
Gingham Ct [3] M26 .. 44 C4
Gingham Pk M26 ..... 43 E5
GIN PIT 76 F6
Gipsy La SK2 .... 124 C6
Gird La SK6 .... 114 E1
Girton Ave WN4 ...... 73 C2
Girton St M7 .... 158 B4
Girton Wlk M40 ...... 65 D1
Girvan Ave M40 ...... 65 D2
Girvan Cl BL3 .... 146 C3
Girvan Cres WN4 ..... 72 D4
Girvan Wlk OL10 ..... 28 F1
Gisborne Dr M6 ...... 81 A5
Gisburn Ave
　Bolton BL1 .... 23 E2
　Golborne WA3 .... 73 F2
Gisburn Dr BL8 .... 26 E3
Gisburne Ave M40 .... 65 D2
Gisburn Rd OL11 ..... 31 A3
Gissing Wlk M9 ...... 157 A2
Givendale Dr M8 ...... 64 A2
Givvons Fold [10] OL4 . 67 E4
Glabyn Ave BL6 ...... 39 F8
Gladden Hey Dr WN3 . 54 D1
Glade Brow OL4 ...... 68 A6
Gladeside Cl M22 .... 121 C4
Gladeside Rd M22 .... 121 C4
Glade St BL1 .... 144 C3
Glade The
　Bolton BL1 .... 143 A1
　Shevington WN6 ...... 36 B6
　Stockport SK4 .... 168 A1
Gladewood Cl [1] SK9 . 137 C8
Gladewood Dr M35 ... 84 B8
Gladstone Bsns Pk OL4 . 67 B6
Gladstone Cl
　[6] Bolton BL1 ...... 143 B2
　Glossop SK13 .... 116 D8
Gladstone Cres OL11 . 31 A3
Gladstone Ct
　[3] Ashton-u-L OL7 .. 166 A2
　Farnworth BL4 .... 42 C1
　Manchester, Old Trafford
　　M15 .... 97 E4
　Stockport, Heaton Moor
　　SK4 .... 168 B3
Gladstone Gr SK4 .... 168 A3
Gladstone Mews SK4 . 169 B3
Gladstone Mill SK15 .. 86 B1
Gladstone Pl BL4 ..... 42 C1
Gladstone Rd
　Altrincham WA14 ..... 119 D6
　Eccles M30 .... 79 E2
　Farnworth BL4 .... 42 D1
　Urmston M41 .... 95 E2
Gladstone St
　Bolton BL1 .... 143 B2
　Bury BL9 .... 141 B3
　Glossop SK13 .... 116 D8
　Hadfield SK13 .... 104 A4
　Oldham OL4 .... 67 B6
　Pendlebury M27 .... 80 B8
　Stockport SK2 .... 124 C4
　Westhoughton BL5 ..... 39 E1
Gladstone Terrace Rd
　OL3 .... 69 A4
Gladville Dr SK8 ..... 123 A6
Gladwyn Ave M20 .... 109 E4
Gladys St
　[3] Farnworth BL3 ... 42 D2
　Manchester M16 ...... 97 C4
Glaisdale OL4 .... 67 D6
Glaisdale Cl
　Ashton-in-M WN4 ..... 73 C3
　Bolton BL2 .... 25 B2
Glaisdale St BL2 ..... 25 B2
Glaister La BL2 ...... 25 D1
Glamis Ave
　Droylsden M11 .... 83 B3
　Heywood OL10 .... 46 F8
　Stretford M32 .... 96 A2
Glamis Cl WN7 .... 76 D6
Glamorgan Pl OL9 ... 152 C1
Glandon Dr SK8 ...... 132 C8
Glanford Ave M9 ..... 64 A3
Glanton Wlk M40 ..... 65 D1
Glanvor Rd SK3 ..... 123 C8
Glassbrook St WN6 ... 37 A1
Glasshouse St [6] M4 . 159 C3
Glasson Wlk OL9 .... 152 A2
Glass St BL4 .... 60 E7
Glastonbury [28] OL12 . 139 B4
Glastonbury Ave
　Altrincham WA15 ..... 120 B2
　Cheadle SK8 .... 132 C6
　Golborne WA3 .... 91 C8

Glastonbury Dr SK12 . 133 D5
Glastonbury Gdns [5] M26. 43 E5
Glastonbury Rd
　Tyldesley M29 .... 77 B7
　Urmston M32 .... 95 F3
Glaswen Gr SK5 ..... 169 C4
GLAZEBROOK 105 B6
Glazebrook Cl OL10 .. 29 C1
Glazebrook La WA3 .. 105 B5
Glazebrook Sta WA3 . 105 A5
GLAZEBURY 92 B7
Glazebury CE Prim Sch
　WA3 .... 92 C7
Glazebury Dr
　Westhoughton BL5 .... 39 F2
　Wythenshawe M23 .... 121 B5
Glazedale Ave OL2 ... 48 C5
Glaze La WA3 .... 91 D2
Glaziers La WA3 ..... 91 D2
Gleaves Ave BL2 ..... 26 A4
Gleaves Rd M30 ...... 79 E1
Gleave St
　[10] Bolton BL1 ..... 145 C4
　Sale M33 .... 108 B6
Glebe Ave WN4 .... 73 C2
Glebe Cl WN6 .... 150 B4
Glebe End St WN6 ... 150 B4
Glebe House M24 ..... 47 A2
Glebe House Sch OL16 . 139 B2
Glebe La M23 .... 19 E4
Glebeland WA3 .... 91 E2
Glebeland Rd BL1, BL6 . 144 B1
Glebelands Rd
　Prestwich M25 .... 63 B5
　Sale M33 .... 108 A6
　Wythenshawe M23 .... 120 F6
Glebe Rd
　Standish WN6 .... 19 F1
　Urmston M41 .... 95 D2
Glebe St
　Ashton-u-L OL6 ...... 166 C3
　Bolton BL2 .... 148 A2
　Chadderton OL9 .... 66 A3
　Hindley WN2 .... 57 C2
　Leigh WN7 .... 75 F6
　Radcliffe M26 .... 44 B3
　Shaw OL2 .... 149 B3
　Stockport SK1 .... 112 A1
　Westhoughton BL5 .... 39 E1
Gleden St M40 .... 160 B2
Gledhall St SK15 ..... 86 A2
Gledhill Ave M5 ..... 161 B3
Gledhill Cl OL2 ...... 32 A1
Gledhill St M20 ..... 110 B7
Gledhill Way BL7 ..... 9 A1
Glegg St M11 .... 151 C4
Glemsford Cl
　Failsworth M35 .... 83 B6
　Wigan WN5 .... 53 B3
Glencarse Gdns M18 .. 99 E3
Glenarm Wlk M22 ... 121 E2
Glenart M30 .... 79 E3
Glen Ave
　Bolton BL3 .... 144 B1
　Kearsley BL4 .... 61 B6
　Manchester M9 .... 64 F1
　Sale M33 .... 108 A6
　Swinton M27 .... 79 D8
　Worsley M28 .... 79 A8
Glenavon Dr
　Rochdale OL12 .... 14 D3
　Shaw OL2 .... 48 F8
Glenbarry Cl M13 .... 163 B2
Glenbarry St M12 .... 164 A4
Glenbeck Cl BL6 ..... 22 D1
Glenbeck Rd M45 .... 44 E1
Glenboro Ave BL8 ... 27 C2
Glenboro Ct BL8 ..... 27 C1
Glenborough Ave OL13 . 3 C8
Glenbourne Pk SK7 .. 132 D5
Glenbranter Ave M29 . 56 A8
Glenbrook Gdns BL4 . 42 D2
Glenbrook Hill SK13 . 104 C2
Glenbrook Rd M9 .... 64 A5
Glenburn St BL3 ..... 147 A3
Glenby Ave M22 ..... 121 F3
Glencar OL12 .... 14 C1
Glencar Dr [8] M40 .. 65 D2
Glencastle Rd M18 ... 99 C4
Glen Cl WA3 .... 105 B2
Glencoe BL3 .... 148 B3
Glencoe Cl OL10 ..... 28 E1
Glencoe Dr
　Bolton BL2 .... 42 F6
　Sale M33 .... 107 C2
Glencoe Pl OL11 .... 139 A3
Glencoe St OL8 ...... 66 C2
Glencoyne Dr BL1 ... 24 D6
Glencross Ave M21 .. 97 A2
Glendale M27 .... 62 B2
Glendale Ave
　Ashton-in-M WN4 ..... 73 C4
　Manchester M19 ...... 110 F6
　Whitefield M45 .... 44 F9
Glendale Cl
　Boothstown M28 ...... 77 F7
　[8] Heywood OL10 ... 29 D2
Glendale Ct OL8 ..... 66 F4
Glendale Dr BL3 ..... 40 F6
Glendale Rd
　Boothstown M28 ...... 77 F7
　Manchester M28 ...... 99 C4
　Salford M30 .... 80 A3
Glendene Ave
　Ashton-in-M WN4 ..... 73 C4
　Droylsden M43 .... 84 C3

Glenden Foot OL12 ... 14 D2
Glenden Ct
　Bolton BL3 .... 40 F5
　Ince-in-M WN2 .... 56 A8
Glendevon Pl M45 ... 63 B7
Glendinning St M6 ... 154 B2
Glendon Cres OL6 .... 85 B7
Glendon Ct OL11 .... 49 E4
Glendore M5 .... 80 C2
Glendower Dr M40 .. 156 C1
Glen Dr WN6 .... 18 B2
Gleneagles BL3 ...... 40 F3
Gleneagles Ave
　[10] Droylsden M11 .. 83 C2
　Heywood OL10 .... 46 D8
Gleneagles Cl
　Bramhall SK7 .... 133 A7
　Golborne WA3 .... 90 F7
　Wilmslow SK9 .... 137 D8
Gleneagles Rd
　Gatley SK8 .... 122 C1
　Urmston M41 .... 94 F3
Gleneagles Way BL0 . 138 B1
Glenfield WA14 ..... 119 B4
Glenfield Cl OL4 .... 67 D6
Glenfield Dr
　Poynton SK12 .... 133 D3
　Wigan WN6 .... 37 A5
Glenfield Rd SK4 ... 169 A4
Glenfield Sq [2] BL4 . 42 B2
Glenfyne Rd M6 ..... 80 D5
Glengarth OL3 ...... 69 B7
Glengarth Dr BL1, BL6 . 40 C6
Glen Gdns OL12 ..... 14 F2
Glen Gr
　Middleton M24 .... 65 C7
　Royton OL2 .... 48 D5
Glenham Ct [1] M15 . 97 E4
Glenhaven Ave M41 .. 95 C2
Glenhaven Ho M20 .. 110 A5
Glenholme Rd SK7 .. 132 D7
Glenhurst Rd M19 .. 110 E5
Glenilla Ave M28 ... 78 E7
Glenis Dr M20 ...... 122 B8
Glenluce Wlk BL3 ... 40 E5
Glenmay Ct M32 .... 96 C2
Glen Maye M33 ..... 108 C4
Glenmaye Gr WN2 ... 57 A5
Glenmere Cl M25 ... 62 F6
Glenmere Rd M20 .. 122 C8
Glenmoor Rd [2] SK1 . 112 A1
Glenmore Ave
　Farnworth BL2 & BL4 . 42 A2
　Manchester M20 ..... 109 F4
Glenmore Bglws SK16 . 101 C7
Glenmore Cl
　Bolton BL3 .... 40 E5
　Rochdale OL11 .... 29 E5
Glenmore Dr
　Failsworth M35 .... 84 B8
　Manchester M8 ...... 156 B3
Glenmore Gr SK16 .. 101 C8
Glenmore Rd BL0 .... 10 F2
Glenmore St BL9 ... 140 B1
Glenmuir Cl M44 .... 94 A2
Glenolden St M11 ... 83 D2
Glenpark WN7 .... 76 B6
Glenpark Wlk [5] M9 . 157 B3
Glen Rd
　Oldham OL4 .... 67 C6
　Rawtenstall BB4 .... 2 F8
Glenridding Cl OL1 .. 49 A1
Glenridge Cl BL1 ... 143 C2
Glen Rise WA15 .... 120 A5
Glen Royd [1] OL12 .. 14 C1
Glensdale Dr M40 ... 65 E1
Glenshee Dr BL3 .... 40 E5
Glenside WN6 .... 18 B2
Glenside Ave M18 ... 99 D3
Glenside Dr
　Bolton BL3 .... 147 C2
　Romiley SK6 .... 113 B5
　Wilmslow SK9 .... 137 C6
Glenside Gdns M35 .. 84 B7
Glenside Gr M28 .... 60 E3
Glen St
　Bacup OL13 .... 3 E8
　Ramsbottom BL0 ..... 138 B3
　Salford M50 .... 161 A3
Glen Terr BB4 .... 2 F8
Glentham WA14 .... 119 E1
Glenvale Cl M26 .... 44 B3
Glenview
　Littleborough OL15 .. 16 C7
　Royton OL2 .... 48 D5
Glenview Rd M29 ... 58 F2
Glenville Ct SK18 .. 131 F7
Glenville Rd M8 .... 155 C1
Glenville Way M34 .. 100 F6
Glenville Way M34 .. 101 A2
Glenville Wlk [13] SK15. 86 A1
Glenwood Ave [3] SK14. 101 D5
Glenwood Cl M26 ... 44 B2
Glenwood Dr
　Manchester M9 ...... 157 B3
　Middleton M24 .... 47 C1
Glenwood Gr SK2 ... 124 B4
Glenwyn Ave M9 .... 64 E4
Globe Cl M16 .... 162 A1

Globe La Est [10] M26 . 44 B3
Globe La
　Bolton BL7 .... 8 D3
　Dukinfield SK16 ..... 101 B7
Globe Lane Ind Est SK16. 101 B6
Globe Pk OL16 ...... 31 B6
Globe Sq SK16 ..... 101 A7
Globe St [1] OL1 .... 67 B7
GLODWICK 67 B5
Glodwick OL4 .... 67 B5
GLODWICK BROOK . 67 A4
Glodwick Inf Sch [8] OL4. 67 B5
Glodwick Lows Nature
　Reserve* OL4 .... 67 B5
Glodwick Rd OL4 .... 67 B6
Glossopbrook Bsns Pk
　SK13 .... 104 C1
Glossop Brook Rd SK13. 104 B1
Glossop Central Sta
　SK13 .... 104 C2
Glossopdale Com Coll
　SK13 .... 104 C1
Glossopdale Com Coll
　(Annexe) SK13 ..... 104 A4
Glossop Rd
　Broadbottom SK13 ... 115 D7
　Gamesley SK13 ...... 171 B1
　Marple SK6 .... 114 D3
Glossop Way SK14 .. 56 E4
Gloster St [3] BL2 .. 148 A3
Gloucester Ave
　[2] Golborne WA3 ... 90 B8
　Heywood OL10 .... 46 C8
　Horwich BL6 .... 22 D2
　Manchester M19 ..... 111 B8
　Marple SK6 .... 125 F6
　Rochdale OL12 .... 15 A3
　Whitefield M45 ...... 63 A8
Gloucester Cl OL6 .. 85 D8
Gloucester Cres WN2 . 56 E6
Gloucester Ct BL6 .. 22 D2
Gloucester Dr
　Diggle OL3 .... 51 C4
　Sale M33 .... 107 D4
Gloucester Pl
　Atherton M46 .... 58 D4
　[1] Salford M6 ...... 81 A3
Gloucester Rd
　Droylsden M43 .... 84 A3
　Gatley SK8 .... 131 C7
　Hyde SK14 .... 113 E8
　Middleton M24 .... 65 B6
　Poynton SK12 .... 133 D4
　Reddish M34 .... 100 A2
　Salford M6 .... 80 C4
　Urmston M41 .... 95 D1
　Wigan WN5 .... 54 C6
Gloucester Rise SK16 . 102 A7
Gloucester St
　Atherton M46 .... 58 D3
　[1] Manchester M1 .. 162 C3
　Salford, Ordsall M5 . 161 C4
　Salford, Pendleton M6 . 81 A4
　Stockport SK3 ...... 170 A3
Gloucester Street N OL9. 152 C1
Gloucester Street S OL9. 152 C1
Gloucester Way [4] SK13. 116 B8
Glover Ave M8 ...... 156 B2
Glover Ctr [2] OL5 .. 86 D8
Glover Dr SK14 ..... 167 B2
Glover Field M7 .... 155 A2
Glover Rd PR7 ...... 19 D7
Glover's Pl WN5 .... 54 B8
Glover St
　Horwich BL6 .... 22 B4
　Leigh WN7 .... 75 C8
　Newton-le-W WA12 ... 89 C3
Glyn Ave WA15 .... 120 A2
Glyneath Cl M11 ... 164 C4
Glyniss Cl SK3 .... 170 C2
Glynne St BL4 ...... 60 C8
Glynn Gdns M20 ... 109 D4
Glynrene Dr M27 ... 61 C1
Glynwood Pk BL4 .. 42 C1
GMex Metro Sta M1 . 162 C5
Goadsby St M4 .... 159 A2
GOATS 32 C1
Goats Gate Terr M45 . 44 D2
Godbert Ave M21 .. 109 C5
Goddard La
　Glossop SK13 .... 104 A6
　New Mills SK22 ..... 127 E7
Goddard Rd SK13 .. 104 A4
Goddard St OL8 .... 66 F4
Godfrey Ave M43 ... 83 D3
Godfrey Ermen Meml CE
　Prim Sch M30 ...... 95 C8
Godfrey Mill SK14 .. 167 B3
Godfrey Range M18 . 99 F2
Godfrey Rd M6 ..... 80 C5
Godlee Dr M27 ..... 79 E7
GODLEY 167 C3
Godley Cl M11 ..... 165 C4
Godley Ct SK14 .... 167 C3
GODLEY GREEN ... 102 B1
Godley Hill SK14 .. 102 B2
Godley Hill Rd SK14 . 102 B2
Godley Prim Sch SK14. 167 C3
Godley St SK14 .... 167 C4
Godmond Hall Dr M28. 77 F5
Godolphin Cl M30 .. 79 E4
Godson St OL1 ..... 48 E1

Godward Rd SK22......127 B1
Godwin St M18.......99 E6
Goit PI OL16.........139 C3
GOLBORNE...........90 B7
Golborne Ave M20....109 F7
Golborne Cty Prim Sch
WA3...............90 A8
Golborne Dale Rd WA3,
WA12.............90 A5
Golborne Enterprise Pk
WA3...............74 A1
Golborne Gallery★ 9
WN1..............150 C4
Golborne High Sch WA3..74 C1
Golborne PI WN1......151 B4
Golborne Rd
Ashton-in-M WN4....73 E4
Golborne WA3.......90 C8
Golborne St WA12....89 E4
Goldborne Ho OL2....149 B4
Goldbourne Dr OL2...149 B4
Goldbrook CI 2 OL10..29 E1
Goldcraft CI 4 OL10..29 E1
Goldcrest CI
Walkden M28.......78 B7
Wythenshawe M22...121 F5
Goldenhill Ave M11...83 C3
Golden St
Eccles M30.........79 D1
Shaw OL2..........49 E8
Goldenways WN1.....37 C2
Goldfinch Dr BL9.....141 C4
Goldfinch Way M43...84 C3
Goldie Ave M22......121 F2
Goldrill Ave BL2......42 F8
Goldrill Gdns BL2.....42 F8
Goldsmith Ave
Oldham OL1.........49 E4
Salford M5..........154 A2
Goldsmith PI WN3....55 A4
Goldsmith Rd SK5....99 E1
Goldsmith St BL3.....147 A4
Goldsmith Way 8 M34..113 A7
Gold St M1..........159 A1
Goldstein Rd BL6.....40 B4
Goldsworth Rd OL1...49 E3
Goldsworthy Rd M41...94 E2
Goldwick Wlk M23....108 E1
Golf Rd
Altrincham WA15.....119 F3
Sale M33...........108 F4
Golfview Dr M30......79 D4
Gooch Dr WA12.......89 D2
Gooch St BL6........22 C2
Goodacre SK14......102 B6
Gooden St OL10......29 E1
Goode House Fold
SK14..............122 C4
Goodiers Dr M5......161 B4
Goodier St
Manchester M40.....160 C4
Sale M33...........108 A4
Goodier View SK14...101 F5
Goodison CI BL9.....45 B3
Goodlad St BL8......27 B4
Goodman St M9......64 E1
Goodrich 3 OL11....139 B2
Goodridge Ave M22...121 C1
Goodrington Rd SK9..131 E3
Goodshaw Rd M28....78 C8
Good Shepherd CI OL16..31 B8
Goodwill CI M27......79 F7
Goodwin CI OL19.....66 C3
Goodwin Sq WN3.....157 A3
Goodwin St BL1......148 A4
Goodwood Ave
Sale M33...........107 C4
Wythenshawe M23...120 D7
Goodwood CI BL3....42 F3
Goodwood Cres WA15..120 C6
Goodwood Dr
Oldham OL1.........49 B1
Pendlebury M27.....80 B7
Stockport SK3......170 B1
Goodwood Lodge 15 M16..97 D3
Goodwood Rd SK6...125 E5
Goodworth Wlk M40..43 B7
Goole St M11........165 A4
Goose Cote Hill BL7...8 E1
Goose Gn WA14......119 D4
GOOSE GREEN.......54 E4
Goose La OL12.......139 C4
Goosetrey CI SK9....131 E1
Goostrey Ave 5 M20..110 A8
Gordon Ave
Bolton BL3..........144 C1
Chadderton OL9.....66 A3
Garswood WN4.......72 E4
Hazel Grove SK7....124 D3
Manchester M19.....111 B8
Oldham OL4.........67 C6
Sale M33...........108 B6
Gordon CI WN5.......54 E8
Gordon PI M20.......110 B5
Gordon Rd
Eccles M30.........79 D3
Swinton M27........79 F6
Gordon St
16 Ashton-u-L OL6...85 D4
Bury BL9...........140 B3
Droylsden M18......99 E6
Hyde SK14..........167 B2
Leigh WN7..........75 F6
Manchester M16.....162 A1
Newhey OL16........32 B3

Gordon St continued
Oldham, County End OL4..68 A6
Oldham, White Gate OL9..65 F4
9 Rochdale OL11....31 A5
Salford M7.........158 A4
Shaw OL2..........149 C3
4 Stalybridge SK15...86 B1
Stockport SK4......169 B3
Wigan WN1.........151 B3
Gordonstoun Cres WN5..53 F7
Gordon Terr 2 SK15..86 A2
Gordon Way OL10....28 F1
Gore Ave
Failsworth M35.....84 B7
Salford M5.........154 A2
Gorebrook Ct M12...99 A4
Gore CI BL9.........141 C1
Gore Cres M5.......154 A3
Goredale Ave M18...99 E4
Gore Dr M5.........154 A3
Gore La SK9........136 C3
Gorelan Rd M18.....99 D5
Gore's La WA11.....71 A5
Gore St
Manchester M1......159 B1
Manchester M3......158 B1
Salford, Pendleton M6..81 A3
Wigan WN5.........54 B6
Goring Ave M18.....99 D6
Gorman St 8 WN6...37 A1
Gorman Way OL3....54 F5
Gorrells Way OL11...30 D3
Gorrels CI OL11.....30 D3
Gorrel St 4 OL11....31 A5
Gorse Ave
Droylsden M43......84 C2
Marple SK6.........125 E6
Mossley OL5........68 E1
Oldham OL8.........67 C3
Stretford M32.......96 F3
Gorse Bank BL9.....141 C3
Gorse Bank Rd WA15..129 C7
Gorse Cres M32.....96 F3
Gorse Dr
Stretford M32.......96 F3
Walkden M38.......59 F6
Gorsefield CI M26...44 A4
Gorsefield Dr 1 M27..79 F7
Gorsefield Hey SK9...137 E8
Gorsefield Prim Sch M26..44 A4
Gorse Gr BB4........1 A8
Gorse Hall CI SK16...101 F7
Gorse Hall Dr SK15...85 F5
Gorse Hall Prim Sch SK15 86 A1
Gorse Hall Rd SK16...101 F7
GORSE HILL.........96 E3
Gorse Hill Prim Sch M32..96 E4
Gorse La M32.......96 F3
Gorselands SK8.....132 B5
Gorse Rd
Milnrow OL16.......32 A6
Swinton M27........79 E6
Walkden M28.......60 E2
Gorses Dr WN2.....38 C6
Gorses Mount BL2...148 C1
Gorse Sq M31.......105 D3
Gorse St BL2, BL3...42 D5
Gorse St
Oldham OL9.........65 F4
Stretford M32.......96 E3
Gorse The WA14....128 B8
Gorseway SK5......112 B4
Gorse Way SK13.....116 F7
Gorse Wlk M27......75 B5
Gorsey Ave M22.....121 C4
Gorsey Bank Prim Sch
SK9...............136 F7
Gorsey Bank Rd SK3..123 B8
Gorsey Brow
Billinge WN5........71 E5
Mottram in L SK14...103 A1
Romiley SK6........113 A2
Shevington Moor WN6..19 B2
Stockport SK1......112 A1
Gorsey Brow CI WN5..71 D5
Gorsey Clough Wlk BL8..26 F5
Gorsey Dr M22......121 C4
Gorseyfields M43...100 A8
Gorsey Gr BL5......57 D7
Gorsey Hey BL5....57 E7
Gorsey Hill St OL10..29 D1
Gorsey Intakes SK14..115 A8
Gorsey La
Altrincham WA14....119 B5
Ashton-u-L OL6.....85 F6
Partington WA13....118 B7
Gorsey Mount St SK1..112 A1
Gorsey Rd
Wilmslow SK9......136 F8
Wythenshawe M22...121 C4
Gorsey Way OL6....85 E6
Gorsley Bank OL15...16 C7
Gorston Wlk M22....130 C8
Gort CI BL9.........45 A1
GORTON............99 D4
Gorton Cres M34...100 C2
Gorton Fold BL6....22 C3
Gorton Gr M28......60 C5
Gorton Ind Est M18..165 C2
Gorton La M12, M18..165 C2
Gorton Mount Prim Sch
M18..............99 C3
Gorton Parks M18...165 C2
Gorton Rd
Manchester M11, M12..164 C3
Reddish SK5........99 F2
Gorton Ret Mkt M18..99 D5

Gorton St
11 Ashton-u-L OL7...84 F1
Bolton BL2.........148 A2
Chadderton OL9....152 B2
Eccles M30.........79 B1
Farnworth BL4......60 B7
Heywood OL10......29 E2
Manchester M3.....158 C2
Gorton Sta M18.....99 D6
Gortonvilla Wlk M12..164 C2
Gosforth CI
Bury BL8...........27 C5
Oldham OL1.........49 A1
Gosforth Wlk M23...108 F1
Goshen La BL9......44 F6
Goshen Sports Ctr BL9..45 A6
Gosport Sq M7......155 A1
Gosport Wlk M8.....156 C2
Goss Hall St OL4.....67 C6
Gotha Wlk M13, M13..166 C3
Gotherage CI SK6...113 C2
Gotherage La SK6...113 C2
Gothic CI SK6.......113 C2
Gough St
Heywood OL10......29 E2
Stockport SK3......169 A1
Goulden Rd M20....110 A5
Goulden St
Manchester M4......159 B2
Salford M6.........154 B2
Goulder Rd M18.....99 E3
Gould St
Denton M34.........100 E3
Manchester M4......159 B3
Oldham OL1.........67 B8
Gourham Dr SK8....122 F2
Govan St M22.......109 E1
Govind Ruia Ct M16..97 E2
Gowan Dr M24.......46 D1
Gowanlock's St BL1..143 B2
Gowan Rd M16......97 E1
Gower Ave SK7.....124 C3
Gower Ct SK4.......113 E8
Gowerdale Rd SK5...111 D5
Gower Hey Gdns SK14..167 B1
Gower Rd
Hyde SK14..........167 A1
Reddish SK5........169 A4
Gowers St OL16......31 B8
Gower St
Ashton-u-L OL6.....166 C3
Bolton BL1.........145 A4
Farnworth BL4......42 C1
Leigh WN7..........75 E4
Oldham OL1.........67 A7
Swinton M27........62 A1
Wigan WN5.........150 A3
Gowran Pk 3 OL4...67 D6
Gowy CI SK9........131 E1
Goya Rise OL1......49 D4
Goyt Ave SK6.......125 F4
Goyt Cres
Romiley SK6........112 F3
Stockport SK1......112 B3
Goyt Hey Ave WN5..71 E5
Goyt Rd
Disley SK12........135 D5
Marple SK6........125 F4
Goyt Valley Bsd Sk6..112 F3
Goyt Valley Wlk SK6..112 F3
Goyt Wlk M45.......45 B2
Grace St
Horwich BL6........22 B3
Leigh WN7..........75 C5
6 Rochdale OL12...15 A2
Grace Wlk M4.......160 A1
Gracie Ave 2 OL11...67 B8
Gradwell St SK3.....170 A4
Grafton Ave M30....80 A4
Grafton Ct
Manchester M15....162 B1
14 Rochdale OL16...31 B6
Grafton House Prep Sch
OL6..............166 B2
Grafton St
Adlington PR7......20 F6
Altrincham WA14....119 D4
Ashton-u-L OL6.....85 D2
Atherton M46.......58 A1
5 Bolton BL3.......145 A4
Bury BL9...........44 F8
Failsworth M35.....84 A8
Hyde SK14..........167 A3
Manchester M13.....163 B1
Newton-le-W WA12...89 B3
Oldham OL1.........49 E4
Rochdale OL16......31 B6
Stalybridge SK15...86 D3
Stockport SK4......169 B3
Graham Ave WN6....18 C2
Graham Cres M44...105 C3
Graham Dr SK12.....135 C6
Graham Rd
Salford M6.........80 C4
Stockport SK1......124 B8
Graham St
Ashton-u-L OL7.....84 F1
Manchester M11.....165 A4
Platt Bridge WN2...56 A3
Grainger Ave M12...99 A3
GRAINS BAR........50 A6
Grains Rd
Delph OL3, OL4.....50 C4
Shaw OL1, OL2......49 D7
Grain View M5......161 A4
Gralam CI M33.......108 E1

Grammar School Rd
Lymm WA13.........117 A2
Oldham OL8.........66 B2
Grampian CI OL9.....152 A1
Grampian Way
Golborne WA3.......74 C1
8 Platt Bridge WN2...56 B2
Shaw OL2..........149 A4
Granada Mews M16...97 E1
Granada Rd M34.....100 A3
Granada TV M3......162 B4
Granary La M28......78 F5
Granary Mews SK14..133 E3
Granary Way M30...107 F2
Granby Ho M1.......163 A4
Granby Rd
Cheadle SK8........132 B8
Sale WA15..........108 A1
Stockport SK2......124 B5
Stretford M32.......96 E1
Stretford M32.......79 C7
Granby Row M1.....163 A4
Granby St
Bury BL8...........26 F4
Chadderton OL9.....66 A3
Grandale St 8 M14...98 C3
Grand Arc Sh Ctr WN3..150 C4
Grandidge St OL11...139 B1
Grand Island Way M30..95 D8
Grand Union Way M30..95 D8
Granford CI WA14....119 D7
Grange PR7.........19 D8
Grange Arts Ctr The★
OL9..............153 A3
Grange Ave
Altrincham WA15....120 A2
Cheadle SK8........122 F3
Denton M34.........101 B2
Eccles M30.........79 D4
Little Lever BL3.....43 C3
Manchester M19.....110 F8
Milnrow OL16.......31 F4
Oldham OL8.........66 C4
Reddish SK4........111 D5
Sale WA15..........120 B7
Stretford M32.......96 D2
Swinton M27........79 C6
Urmston M41.......94 E2
Wigan, Poolstock WN3..150 B1
Wigan, The Bell WN5..54 B7
Grange Cl
Golborne WA3.......90 C6
Hyde SK14..........167 C1
Grange Cres M41....95 C1
Grange Ct
Altrincham WA14....119 C1
Oldham OL8.........66 C4
Grange Dr
Coppull PR7........19 D8
Eccles M30.........79 D4
Manchester M9......64 F3
Grangeforth Rd M8..155 C4
Grange Gr M45.......62 F8
Grange La
Delph OL3..........50 F6
Manchester M20.....110 B2
Grange Manor BL7...25 C8
Grange Mill Wlk M40..83 B7
Grange Park Ave
Ashton-u-L OL6.....85 F6
Cheadle SK8........122 D5
Wilmslow SK9......137 A8
Grange Park Rd
Bolton BL7..........25 C7
Cheadle SK8........122 D5
Manchester M9.....65 A3
Grange PI M44......105 E5
Grange Rd
Altrincham WA14....119 C1
Ashton-in-M WN4...72 F6
Bolton, Bromley Cross BL7..25 C8
Bolton, Deane BL3...144 B1
Boothstown M28....77 E7
Bury BL8...........27 B2
Eccles M30.........79 A4
Farnworth BL4......42 A1
Manchester M21....97 A2
Sale M33...........108 A4
Sale, Timperley WA15..120 B7
Slattocks OL11.....47 D6
Stockport SK7......123 F3
Urmston M41.......95 C1
Wilmslow SK9......4 D3
Grange Road N SK14..167 C2
Grange Road S
Compstall SK14....114 A8
Hyde SK14..........102 A1
Grange St
Failsworth M35.....83 D6
Hindley WN2........56 D4
Leigh WN7..........75 E3
Oldham OL9.........153 B3
Salford M6.........154 B2
Grange The
Hyde SK14..........167 C1
Manchester M14.....98 C2
6 Oldham OL1......49 B3
Westhoughton BL5...57 D8
Grangethorpe Dr M19..110 F7
Grangethorpe Rd
Manchester M14.....98 C2
Urmston M41.......95 D1
Grangeway SK9.....131 D4
Grange Wlk M24.....46 E2

Grangewood BL7.....25 C7
Grangewood Dr M9...157 A3
Granite St 4 OL1.....67 B8
Gransden Dr M8.....156 C2
Gransmoor Ave M11..99 F7
Gransmoor Rd M11, M43..99 F7
Grantchester PI BL4..147 C1
Grantchester Way BL2..25 C1
Grant CI M9.........64 D2
Grantham CI BL1....143 B1
Grantham Ct M34...100 F1
Grantham Dr BL8....140 A4
Grantham Gr WN2...37 F2
Grantham Rd SK4...168 C2
Grantham St
Manchester M14.....98 B3
Oldham OL1.........67 A5
Grantley St WN4.....73 A5
Grant Mews BL0.....138 B3
Grant PI WN3........55 A3
Grants La BL0.......138 C2
Grant St
Farnworth BL4......42 B2
Rochdale OL11......30 D2
Grantwood WN4.....73 A5
Granville Ave
Manchester M16....97 C2
Salford M7.........155 B4
Granville CI OL9.....152 C3
Granville Ct
Manchester M16....97 C3
Newhey OL16.......32 B3
Granville Gdns M20..110 A2
Granville Rd
Altrincham WA15....120 C6
Bolton BL3.........146 C3
Cheadle SK3, SK8...123 C5
Droylsden M34......84 B1
Manchester M14.....110 D8
Urmston M41.......95 E3
Wilmslow SK9......136 F5
Granville St
Adlington PR6......21 A7
Ashton-u-L OL6.....85 D2
Chadderton OL9....152 C4
Eccles M30.........79 D3
Farnworth BL4......42 D2
Haslingden BB4.....1 A7
1 Hindley WN2.....56 E5
Leigh WN7..........75 F7
Oldham OL1.........48 E1
Swinton M27........79 F8
Walkden M28.......60 D4
Granville Wlk OL9...152 C4
Graphite Way SK13..104 D1
Grasdene Ave 2 M9..64 E3
Grasmere Ave
Farnworth BL4......59 F7
Heywood OL10......46 D8
Hindley WN2........56 E4
Ince-in-M WN2......56 B4
Little Lever BL3.....43 A4
Orrell WN5.........53 B7
Reddish SK4........111 E6
Swinton M27........61 C2
Up Holland WN8....53 B7
Whitefield M45.....62 C7
Grasmere CI SK15...86 A4
Grasmere Cres
Bramhall SK7.......132 E8
Eccles M30.........79 B4
High Lane SK6......125 E1
Grasmere Dr
Ashton-in-M WN4...73 B5
Bury BL9...........45 A7
Grasmere Gr OL7....84 F4
Grasmere Ho 8 M28..60 E2
Grasmere Rd
Alderley Edge SK9..137 A1
Altrincham WA15....120 C6
Gatley SK8.........122 B3
Haslingden BB4.....1 C8
Oldham OL4.........68 A4
Partington M31.....105 E3
Royton OL2.........48 D6
Sale M33...........108 C2
Stretford M32.......96 D3
Swinton M27........79 F6
Wigan WN5.........54 C7
Grasmere St
Bolton BL1.........143 C2
Leigh WN7..........75 E5
10 Rochdale OL12...14 C1
Grasmere Terr WN2..74 B8
Grasmere Wlk M24...46 F2
Grason Ave SK9.....131 C1
GRASSCROFT.......68 C6
Grasscroft SK5......112 C6
Grasscroft St M14...68 C5
Grasscroft Ind Sch OL4..68 C5
Grasscroft Rd
Hindley WN2........57 A4
Stalybridge SK15...86 A1
Grassfield Ave M7....81 C6
Grassholme Dr SK2..125 A5
Grassingham Gdns M6..154 C3
Grassington Ave M40..65 A1
Grassington Ct BL8..26 F4
Grassington Dr BL9..28 D3
Grassington Dr BL2..25 A1
Grassland Rise M38..59 E4
Grass Mead M34....113 B8
Grassmoor Cres SK13..171 A2
Grathie CI BL3.......142 B1
Grathome Wlk BL3..147 B3
Gratrix Ave M5......161 B3

Gratrix La M33 108 F3
Gratrix St M18 99 E4
Gratten Ct M28 60 C4
Gravel Bank Rd SK6 113 B6
GRAVEL HOLE 48 D7
Gravel La
Manchester M3 158 C2
Wilmslow SK9 136 E5
Gravel Wlks 4 OL4 67 B7
Gravenmoor Dr M7 155 B2
Grave Oak La WN7 76 B1
Graver La M40 83 D5
Graves St M26 43 F6
Gray Cl
Mottram in L SK14 102 F3
Wigan WN2 38 A2
Graymar Rd M38 60 A4
Graymarsh Dr SK12 133 E2
Grayrigg Wlk M9 157 A3
Graysands Rd WA15 119 F3
Grayson Ave M45 63 B8
Grayson Rd M38 60 B4
Grayson's Cl WN1 37 C1
Grayson Way OL3 69 B6
Gray St BL1 145 B4
Grayston Ct SK6 126 B7
Graystones Cl WA15 120 D6
Gray Street N BL1 145 B4
Graythorpe Wlk 5 M5 81 A1
Graythorp Wlk 8 M14 98 B3
Graythwaite Rd BL1 23 F2
Grazing Dr M44 94 B3
Greame St M14, M16 98 A3
Great Acre WN1 37 D1
Great Ancoats St M1, M4 159 C1
Great Arbor Way 11 M24 46 F1
Great Bank Rd BL5 39 D3
Great Bent Cl OL12 15 D4
Great Boys Cl M29 59 E1
Great Bridgewater St M1, M3 162 C4
Great Cheetham Street E M7 155 B3
Great Cheetham Street W M7 81 C5
Great Clowes St M7 155 A1
Great Ducie St M3 158 C3
Great Eaves Rd BL0 138 C3
Great Egerton St SK1, SK4 169 B2
Greater Manchester Police (GMP) Mus* M1 159 B1
Greatfield Rd M22 121 B4
Great Flatt OL12 14 B1
Great Fold WN7 76 E4
Great Gable Cl OL1 67 A8
Great Gates Cl OL11 31 A4
Great Gates Rd OL11 31 A3
Great George St
Rochdale OL16 139 C3
Salford M3 158 A2
Wigan WN3 150 B3
Great Hall Cl M26 44 A4
Great Heaton Cl M24 64 C7
Great Holme BL3 147 C4
GREAT HOWARTH 15 B4
Great Howarth OL12 15 B4
Great Jackson St M15 162 B3
Great John St M3 162 B4
Great Jones St M12 165 A2
Great Lee OL12 14 D3
Great Lee Wlk OL12 14 D2
GREAT LEVER 42 A3
Great Marlborough St 3 M1 163 A3
Great Marld Cl BL1 23 F2
Great Mdw OL2 31 F1
Great Moor Inf Sch SK2 124 B4
Great Moor Jun Sch SK2 124 B4
Great Moor St
Bolton BL1 145 C2
Stockport SK2 124 B5
Great Moss Rd M29 77 C2
Great Newton St M40 83 C5
Great Norbury St SK14 167 A2
Great Northern Leisure Sh M3 162 C4
Great Northern Sq M2 162 C4
Great Oak Dr WA15 119 E4
Great Portwood St SK1 169 C2
Great Southern St M14 98 B3
Greatstone Apartments 2 M32 96 E3
Great Stone Cl M26 43 D3
Great Stone Rd
Manchester M16, M21, M32 97 A3
Stretford M16, M32 96 F3
Great Stones Cl BL7 8 E2
Great Underbank SK1 169 C1
Great Western St M14, M16 97 F4
Great Wood Nature Reserve* SK14 114 E8
GREAVE
Rochdale 30 B8
Romiley 113 D4
Greave SK6 113 D4
Greave Ave OL11 30 B7
Greave Fold SK6 113 D4
Greave Ho OL11 30 B8
Greave Pk OL3 69 B7
Greave Prim Sch SK6 113 D4
Greave Rd SK1, SK2 124 C8
Greaves Ave M35 83 E6
Greaves Cl WN6 35 F8
Greaves Rd SK9 136 E7
Greaves St
Mossley OL5 68 C2
2 Oldham, County End OL4 67 F6
Oldham OL1 153 C2
Shaw OL2 149 C3
Grebe Cl
Poynton SK12 133 B4
Wigan WN3 54 B4
Grebe Wlk SK2 125 A4
Grecian Cres BL3 147 C4
Grecian St M7 81 C5
Grecian Street N M7 81 C5
Grecian Terr M7 81 C5
Gredle Cl M41 95 F2
Greeba Rd M23 120 E6
Greek St
Manchester M1 163 B3
Stockport SK1, SK3 170 B4
Greenacre
Gatley SK8 131 C7
Wigan WN1 37 D1
Green Acre BL5 57 F7
Greenacre Cl BL0 11 E7
Greenacre La M28 78 F4
Greenacre Pk BL1 143 C1
GREENACRES 67 D7
Greenacres BL7 9 E6
Greenacres Cl WA3 91 B8
Greenacres Ct 5 OL12 15 D4
Greenacres Dr M19 110 E4
GREENACRES FOLD 67 E7
GREENACRES MOOR 67 C7
Greenacres Prim Sch OL4 67 C7
Greenacres Rd OL4 67 D7
Greenacres The WA13 117 A4
Greenal St WN4 73 B5
Green Ash OL3 50 C7
Green Ave
Bolton BL3 42 B3
Swinton M27 79 F7
Tyldesley M29 77 A4
Walkden M38 59 E5
Greenbank
Abram Brow WN2 74 B7
Hindley WN2 57 B3
Hollingworth SK13 103 F5
3 Horwich BL6 22 D1
Whitworth OL12 14 C5
Green Bank
Bacup OL13 3 D8
Bolton BL2 25 E3
Farnworth BL4 42 C1
Glossop SK13 115 F7
Reddish SK4 111 D7
Greenbank Ave
Gatley SK8 122 A5
Manchester SK4 110 E2
Orrell WN5 53 D3
Swinton M27 79 D6
Uppermill OL3 51 C1
Greenbank Cres SK6 125 F5
Greenbank Dr OL15 15 F3
Greenbank Ind Est WN2 57 B3
Greenbank Prep Sch 1 SK8 123 A1
Greenbank Prim Sch 26 OL12 14 F1
Greenbank Rd
Bolton BL3 144 B1
Bolton BL3 146 B4
Gatley SK8 122 A6
Marple SK6 114 B1
Radcliffe M26 44 A5
Rochdale OL12 14 F2
Sale M33 107 E5
Salford M6 154 B3
Greenbank Terr
Middleton M24 47 C1
Stockport SK4 169 B2
Greenbarn Way BL6 21 D1
Greenbeech Cl SK6 125 E7
Greenbooth Cl SK16 101 F7
Greenbooth Rd OL11, OL12 13 D2
Green Bridge Cl OL11 30 F4
Greenbridge La OL3 69 B5
Green Bridge N BB4 2 E7
Green Bridge S BB4 2 E7
Greenbrook Cl BL9 141 A4
Greenbrook St 6 BL9 141 A4
Greenbrow Rd M23 121 A4
Green Building Apartments The 3 M1 162 C3
Greenburn Ave WA11 71 C1
Greenburn Dr BL2 25 E2
Green Cl
Gatley SK8 122 A6
Tyldesley M46 58 E1
Green Clough OL15 16 C8
Green Common La BL5 58 B7
Greencourt Dr M38 59 F3
Green Courts WA14 119 B3
Greencourts Bsns Pk M22 131 A8
Green Croft SK6 113 E3
Greencroft Mdw OL2 48 F5
Greencroft Rd M30 79 B4
Greencroft Way
Rochdale OL12 15 D3
1 Salford M7 155 A3
Green Ct WN7 75 B1
Greendale M46 58 E4
Greendale Cres WN7 76 C4
Greendale Dr
Manchester M9 64 E3
Radcliffe M26 44 B1
Greendale Gr M34 113 B8
Green Dr
Altrincham WA15 120 A7
Bolton BL6 40 C7
Handforth SK9 131 D2
Manchester M19 98 F1
GREEN END 110 F5
Green End M34 113 B8
Green End Prim Sch 1 M19 110 F5
Green End Rd M19 110 E5
Greene Way M7 81 A8
Greenfeld Prim Sch OL3 69 B6
GREENFIELD 69 B4
Greenfield Ave
Ashton-u-L OL6 85 C6
Eccles M30 95 A8
Ince-in-M WN2 151 C3
Urmston M41 95 D2
Greenfield Cl
Altrincham WA15 120 C6
Bury BL8 27 A1
Newton-le-W WA12 89 C4
Stockport SK3 170 B2
Westhoughton BL5 40 A1
Greenfield Ct OL10 29 D1
Greenfield Ho SK13 104 A6
Greenfield La
Rochdale, Greengate OL16 15 D3
Rochdale, Lower Place OL11 31 A4
Shaw OL2 149 B2
Greenfield Prim Sch SK14 167 B2
Greenfield Rd
Adlington PR6 21 A8
Atherton M46 58 E5
Walkden M38 60 A4
Greenfields WN6 37 A4
Greenfields Cl WN2 56 F6
Greenfields Cres WN4 73 B4
Greenfield St
Denton M34 100 D7
Glossop SK13 104 A6
Hyde SK14 167 A2
Rochdale OL11 31 A4
Greenfield Sta OL3 69 A6
Greenfield View WN5 71 D4
Green Fold M18 99 F6
Greenfold Ave BL4 60 B7
Green Fold La BL5 57 E7
Green Fold Specl Sch BL4 59 F8
Greenfold Way WN7 76 A3
Greenford Cl
Cheadle SK8 123 B4
Orrell WN5 53 D6
Greenford Rd M8 156 A3
Green Gables Cl SK8 122 B1
Greengage M13 163 C2
GREENGATE 15 D3
GREEN GATE 31 C3
Greengate
Altrincham WA15 129 D7
Manchester M3 158 C2
Middleton OL9, M24, M40 65 C5
Green Gate SK14 113 D8
Greengate Cl
Bury BL9 141 C2
Rochdale OL12 15 D3
Greengate E M40 65 D3
Greengate Ind Pk M24 65 C5
Greengate La
Bolton BL2 42 F8
Prestwich M25 63 A4
Greengate Rd M34 101 A4
Greengate St OL4 67 B6
Greengate W M3 158 B3
Green Grove Bank OL16 15 D3
Greenhalgh La PR6 21 B8
Greenhalgh Moss La BL8 27 B5
Greenhalgh St
Failsworth M35 83 C6
Stockport SK4 169 B2
Green Hall Cl M46 58 F5
Green Hall Mews SK9 137 B6
Green Hall Prim Sch M46 58 F4
Greenham Rd M23 108 F2
Greenhaven WN8 53 B7
Greenhaven Cl M28 60 F3
Green Hayes Ave WN1 37 C3
Greenhead Fold SK6 113 A1
Greenhead Wlk BL3 147 B3
Greenhey WN5 54 B7
GREENHEYS 59 E6
Greenheys
Bolton BL2 25 E3
Droylsden M43 84 A2
Greenheys Cres BL8 10 F1
Greenheys Ctr M15 163 A1
Greenheys La M15 163 A1
Greenheys Lane W M15 162 C1
Greenheys Rd M38 59 E6
GREEN HILL 65 D7
Greenhill M25 63 A4
Green Hill OL15 16 A7
Greenhill Ave
Bolton BL3 144 B1
Farnworth BL4 60 C6
Rochdale OL12 139 B4
Sale M33 108 A6
Shaw OL2 31 E1
Greenhill Cotts OL5 68 D2
Greenhill Cres WN5 71 F5
Greenhill La BL3 40 F4
Greenhill Pass 2 OL1 67 A6
Greenhill Prim Sch
Bury BL8 26 F1
11 Oldham OL4 67 A6
Greenhill Rd
Altrincham WA15 120 C6
Billinge WN5 71 F5
Bury BL8 27 A1
Manchester M8 156 A4
Middleton M24 65 D7
Green Hill Rd SK14 102 A3
Green Hill St SK3 170 A3
Greenhill Terr
Middleton M24 65 C7
5 Oldham OL1 67 A6
Green Hill Terr SK3 170 A3
Greenhill Wlk SK12 135 D6
Green Hollow Fold SK15 86 D5
Greenholm Cl M40 65 D1
Greenhow St M43 99 F8
Greenhurst Cres OL8 67 A2
Greenhurst La OL6 85 E6
Greenhurst Rd OL6 85 D7
Greenhythe Rd SK8 131 C6
Greening Rd M19 99 B2
Green La
Alderley Edge SK9 136 F1
Altrincham WA15 120 B4
Ashton-u-L OL6 85 B5
Bolton BL3 42 B2
Compstall SK14 114 B8
Coppull PR7 20 A8
Delph OL3 50 E4
Disley SK12 135 D4
Eccles M30 79 C2
Failsworth M35 83 F4
Glossop, Brookfield SK13 171 C4
Glossop SK13 115 F8
Golborne WA3 75 A2
Hazel Grove SK7 124 D3
Heywood OL10 29 F1
Hindley WN2 57 B4
Hollingworth SK14 103 D6
Horwich BL6 22 B5
Hyde, Godley SK14 102 A1
Irlam M44 105 E5
Kearsley BL4 61 A7
Leigh WN7 76 C6
Manchester, Gorton M18 99 D6
Middleton, Green Hill M24 65 D7
Middleton, Higher Boarshaw M24 47 C2
Oldham, Moss Grove OL8 66 E2
Oldham, Top o' th' Meadows OL4 50 A2
Orrell WN5 53 D3
Poynton SK12 134 C4
1 Rochdale OL12 139 B4
Romiley SK6 113 B2
Sale M33 107 E6
Standish WN6 36 E8
Stockport, Heaton Norris SK4 168 B3
Stockport SK4 168 C2
Whitefield M45 44 F1
Wilmslow SK9 137 B7
Greenland Ave WN6 19 E1
Greenland Cl M29 77 B6
Greenland La PR6 21 D5
Greenland Rd
Bolton BL3 147 C2
Farnworth BL3, BL4 42 A2
Tyldesley M29 77 B6
Greenlands Cl 3 SK8 131 E8
Greenland St
Salford, Cheetham Hill M8 155 C3
3 Salford, Seedley M6 154 B2
Green Lane Ind Est SK4 168 C1
Green Lane N WA15 120 B5
Greenlaw Ct M16 161 C1
Greenlea Ave M18 99 D3
Greenleach La M28 79 A7
Greenlea Cl WN5 53 D5
Greenleaf Cl M28 77 F6
Greenleas BL6 40 C6
Greenlees St OL12 139 C4
Greenleigh Cl BL1 24 D5
Greenmans La OL3 69 A3
Green Mdw OL12 15 D4
Green Mdw Ind Prim Sch 7 WA3 90 F8
Green Mdws
Golborne WA3 90 E5
Marple SK6 125 F7
Westhoughton BL5 57 D8
Green Meadows Dr SK6 125 F8
Green Meadows Wlk M22 121 E1
GREENMOUNT 10 E1
Greenmount Cl BL8 10 F2
Greenmount Ct BL1 144 A4
Greenmount Dr
Heywood OL10 46 F7
Ramsbottom BL8 10 F2
Greenmount La BL1 144 A4
Greenmount Pk BL4 61 A7
Greenmount Prim Sch BL8 10 F2
Greenoak M26 61 C6
Greenoak Dr
Sale M33 108 C1
Walkden M28 60 C5
Greenock Cl BL3 40 E5
Greenock Dr OL10 28 F1
Greenough St
Atherton M46 58 A1
Wigan WN1 151 A4
Greenpark Cl BL8 10 F1
Greenpark Rd M22 109 D1
Green Park View OL1 49 D2
Green Pastures SK4 110 E1
Green Rd M31 105 E3
Greenrigg Cl WN6 36 F7
Greenroyd Ave BL2 25 E2
Greenroyde OL11 139 B1
Greens Arms Rd BB3, BL7 8 E7
Greensbridge Gdns BL5 39 F1
Greenshall La SK12 135 F5
Greenshank Cl
Leigh WN7 76 B5
Newton-le-W WA12 89 C4
Rochdale OL11 29 F7
GREENSIDE 83 F2
Greenside
Ainsworth BL2 26 C1
Farnworth BL4 42 C1
Stockport SK4 168 A1
Worsley M28 79 A5
Greenside Ave
Kearsley BL4 60 F6
Oldham OL4 49 E2
Greenside Cl
Dukinfield SK16 102 A8
Hawkshaw BL8 10 B3
Greenside Cres M43 83 F2
Greenside Ct M30 79 D3
Greenside Dr
Altrincham WA14 119 E1
Bury BL8 26 F8
Irlam M44 93 F1
Greenside La M43 83 F3
Greenside Pl M34 113 B8
Greenside Prim Sch M43 83 F2
Greenside Sh Ctr M43 84 A1
Greenside St M11 165 C4
Greenside Trad Ctr M43 84 A1
Greenside View SK14 102 A5
Greenside Way M24 65 C5
Greens La
Bacup OL13 3 D7
Haslingden BB4 1 C7
Greenslate Ave WN6 35 E8
Greenslate Ct WN5 53 E3
Greenslate Rd WN5 53 E3
Greenslate Water Mdws Nature Reserve* WN5 53 E4
Greensmith Way BL5 39 E3
Greenson Dr M24 64 E7
Green St
Adlington PR6 21 B8
5 Alderley Edge SK9 137 A1
Bury, Walshaw BL8 26 F4
Eccles M30 95 B8
Edenfield BL0 1 E3
Farnworth BL4 42 C1
Hyde SK14 167 B1
Manchester M14 110 E7
Middleton M24 47 B1
Oldham OL8 153 A2
2 Platt Bridge WN2 56 B2
Radcliffe M26 44 A3
Stockport SK3 170 C2
Stretford M32 108 C8
Tyldesley, Hindsford M46 58 E1
8 Tyldesley M29 59 A1
Wigan WN3 150 C2
Greenstead Ave M8 156 A4
Greens The
Altrincham WA15 129 D7
Whitworth OL12 4 C1
Greenstone Ave BL6 22 B3
Greenstone Dr M6 80 F5
Greensward Cl WN6 19 B1
Greensway Ctr OL2 149 B3
Green The
Cheadle SK8 131 F8
Glossop SK13 116 A7
Handforth SK9 131 E3
Hyde SK14 102 A6
Marple SK6 126 A3
Oldham OL8 67 A3
Partington M31 105 F4
Ramsbottom BL8 10 F1
Rochdale OL11 30 C3
Sale WA15 120 C7
Stalybridge SK15 86 E4
Stockport SK4 168 C2
Swinton M27 62 B2
Wigan WN5 54 B6
Worsley M28 78 F5
Greenthorne Ave SK4 111 D7
Greenthorne Cl BL7 9 E7
Greenthorn Wlk 6 M15 162 C1
Green Tree Gdns SK6 113 B2
Greenvale
Rochdale OL11 29 D8
Shevington WN6 35 F4
Greenvale Dr SK8 122 C6
Green View WA13 117 B5
Greenview Chase OL4 68 B5
Greenview Dr
Manchester M20 122 C8
Rochdale OL11 30 A8
Green Villa Pk SK9 136 E4
Greenwatch Cl 7 M30 79 C1
Green Water Mdw SK14 103 D5
Greenway
Altrincham WA14 119 A5
Ashton-in-M WN4 73 A4
Bramhall SK7 132 D6
Horwich BL6 22 F3
Hyde SK14 167 A1
Middleton M9 64 F5
Rochdale OL11 30 B1
Romiley SK6 113 E1
Shaw OL2 31 F1

Greenway continued
Wilmslow SK9 . . . . **137** B6
Wythenshawe M22 . . . . **121** E8
Green Way
Bolton BL1 . . . . **25** B4
❻ Mottram in L SK14 . . **102** F2
Rochdale OL11 . . . . **30** B1
Greenway Ave ❾ M19 . . **99** B1
Greenway Cl
Bury BL8 . . . . **27** B3
Sale M33 . . . . **107** E3
Green Way Cl BL1 . . . . . . **25** B4
Greenway Dr OL5 . . . . . . **68** C2
Greenway Mews BL0 . . . **11** C4
Greenway Rd
Altrincham WA15 . . . . . **119** F8
Gatley SK8 . . . . **131** C6
Greenways
❼ Ashton-u-L OL7 . . . . . **85** A6
Failsworth M40 . . . . **65** D1
Leigh WN7 . . . . **76** B6
Orrell WN5 . . . . **53** D3
Standish WN6 . . . . **37** A6
Greenwich Cl
Failsworth M40 . . . . **83** D4
Rochdale OL11 . . . . **29** F6
Green Wlk
Altrincham, Bowdon
WA14 . . . . **119** B3
Altrincham, Timperley
WA15 . . . . **120** A7
Gatley SK8 . . . . **122** A6
Manchester M16 . . . . **97** C2
❼ Mottram in L SK14 . . **102** F2
Partington M31 . . . . **105** E3
Stretford M32 . . . . **96** B2
Green Wlks M25 . . . . **63** C3
Greenwood Ave
Ashton-u-L OL6 . . . . **85** C6
Horwich BL6 . . . . **22** D1
Stockport SK2 . . . . **124** C6
Swinton M27 . . . . **62** A8
Walkden M28 . . . . **60** C3
Wigan WN5 . . . . **54** E7
Greenwood Bsns Ctr ❿
M5 . . . . **81** A1
Greenwood Cl
Altrincham WA15 . . . . . **120** D5
Boothstown M28 . . . . **77** E7
Culcheth WA3 . . . . **91** F1
Greenwood Dr SK9 . . . **137** D8
Greenwood Gdns SK6 . . **112** E6
Greenwood La ❶❷ BL6 . . **22** E1
Greenwood Pl M30 . . . . . **79** E4
Greenwood Rd
Standish WN6 . . . . **19** E2
Wythenshawe M22 . . . **121** C5
Greenwoods La BL2 . . . . **25** F4
Greenwood St
❷ Altrincham WA14 . . **119** D4
❷ Littleborough OL15 . . **16** B5
Oldham, County End OL4 . . **67** F5
Oldham, Fitton Hill OL8 . . **66** F1
Oldham, Greenacres OL4 . . **67** C8
Rochdale OL16 . . . . **139** C3
Salford M6 . . . . **81** A4
Greenwood Vale BL1 . . . **143** B3
Greenwood Vale S ❷
BL1 . . . . **143** C3
Greer St M11 . . . . **165** C4
Greetland Dr M9 . . . . **64** F4
Gregge St
❺ Heywood, Hopwood
OL10 . . . . **29** E1
Heywood, Lane End OL10 . . **46** E8
Greg Mews SK9 . . . . **131** B2
Gregory Ave
Atherton M46 . . . . **58** C5
Bolton BL2 . . . . **42** E8
Romiley SK6 . . . . **113** C1
Gregory St
Dukinfield SK14 . . . . . . **101** E5
Hindley WN2 . . . . **56** C6
Leigh WN7 . . . . **75** E4
Manchester M12 . . . . . . **164** C2
Oldham OL8 . . . . **66** C3
Westhoughton BL5 . . . . . **57** A7
Gregory Way SK5 . . . . . **111** F6
Gregson Field BL3 . . . . **147** B4
Gregson Rd SK5 . . . . . . **111** E6
Gregson St ❹ OL1 . . . . **153** C2
Greg St SK5 . . . . **111** E6
Grelley Wlk ❷ M14 . . . . . **98** C3
Grenaby Ave WN2 . . . . . . **56** B5
Grendale Ave
Hazel Grove SK7 . . . . . **124** E1
Stockport SK1 . . . . **112** B1
Grendale Dr M16 . . . . . . **161** C1
Grendon Ave OL8 . . . . . . **66** E4
Grendon St BL3 . . . . . . **146** C3
Grendon Wlk M12 . . . . . **165** A2
Grenfell Cl WN3 . . . . **150** A1
Grenfell Rd M20 . . . . . . **110** B3
Grenham Ave M15 . . . . . **162** A2
Grenville St SK7 . . . . . . **124** D3
Grenville St
Dukinfield SK16 . . . . . . **101** C8
Stalybridge SK15 . . . . . . **86** D4
Stockport SK3 . . . . **170** A4
Grenville Terr ❾ OL6 . . . **85** D2
Grenville Wlk OL15 . . . . . **6** C1
Gresford Cl M21 . . . . . . **109** A8
Gresham Ct M45 . . . . **62** D7

Gresham Dr OL9 . . . . . . **152** C3
Gresham St
Bolton BL1 . . . . **143** C3
Denton M34 . . . . **100** F4
Gresham Way M33 . . . . **108** A1
Gresham Wlk SK4 . . . . . **169** B3
Gresley Ave BL6 . . . . **22** B3
Gresley Cl WN1 . . . . **151** B4
Gresty Ave M22 . . . . . . **121** F1
Greswell Prim Sch M34 . . **100** E2
Greswell St M34 . . . . . . **100** F4
Greta Ave SK8 . . . . **131** C6
Gretna Rd M46 . . . . **58** A1
Greton Cl M13 . . . . **98** E4
Gretton Cl OL2 . . . . **48** F4
Greville St M13 . . . . **98** E4
Grey Cl SK6 . . . . **113** A4
Greyfriars WN4 . . . . **72** F4
Greyfriars Ct M33 . . . . . **158** B3
Greyfriars Rd M22 . . . . **121** B2
Greyhound Dr M6 . . . . . . **81** C5
Grey Knotts M28 . . . . **78** A6
Greylag Cres M28 . . . . . . **78** D8
Greylands Cl M33 . . . . . **107** F4
Greylands Rd M20 . . . . **122** C8
Grey Mare La M11 . . . . . . **83** A1
Greymont Rd ❸ BL9 . . . . **27** F6
Grey Rd
Altrincham WA14 . . . . . **119** C5
Ashton-in-M WN4 . . . . . . **73** A4
Greysham Ct M16 . . . . . . **97** E2
Grey St
Ashton-u-L OL6 . . . . . . **166** C2
Denton M34 . . . . **100** D3
Manchester M12 . . . . . . **164** B2
Middleton M24 . . . . **46** F1
Prestwich M25 . . . . **63** C4
Radcliffe M26 . . . . **44** B3
Stalybridge SK15 . . . . . . **86** A1
Greystoke Ave
Altrincham WA15 . . . . . **120** D5
Reddish M19 . . . . **99** C1
Sale M33 . . . . **108** B3
Greystoke Cres M45 . . . . **44** E2
Greystoke Dr
Alderley Edge SK9 . . . . . **137** A2
Bolton BL1 . . . . **24** E6
Middleton M24 . . . . **46** D2
Greystoke La M35 . . . . . . **83** D6
Greystoke St SK1 . . . . . **112** A1
Greystone Ave
Aspull WN2 . . . . **38** C5
Manchester M21 . . . . . . **109** F8
Greystone Cl BL5 . . . . . . **40** A2
Greystone Wlk SK4 . . . . **111** D7
Greywood Ave ❷ M8 . . . **155** C2
Greytown Cl M6 . . . . **80** F5
Greywood Ave BL9 . . . . **141** B2
Grierson St
Bolton BL1 . . . . **143** B3
❿ Manchester M16 . . . . **97** E4
Griffe La ❸ BL9 . . . . **45** D4
Griffin Bsns Ctr M7 . . . . . **81** C5
Griffin Cl BL9 . . . . **141** B4
Griffin Ho BL9 . . . . **141** A4
Griffin La SK8 . . . . **131** D7
Griffin Rd M35 . . . . **83** D6
Griffin St M7 . . . . **81** C6
Griffiths Cl M7 . . . . **158** A4
Griffiths St ❿ M40 . . . . . . **83** C5
Grimeford La BL6 . . . . . . **21** C5
GRIMEFORD VILLAGE . . **21** D6
Grimes Cotts ❹ OL12 . . . **13** F1
Grimes St OL12 . . . . **13** F1
Grime St BL0 . . . . **11** A4
Grimscott Cl ❼ M9 . . . . . **64** F1
Grimshaw Ave M35 . . . . . **84** A8
Grimshaw Cl SK6 . . . . . **113** A4
Grimshaw Ct WA3 . . . . . . **74** A1
Grimshaw La
Manchester M40 . . . . . . **160** C4
Middleton M24 . . . . **65** C7
Grimshaw St
Failsworth M35 . . . . **83** E8
Golborne WA3 . . . . **74** A1
Stockport SK1 . . . . **112** A1
Grimstead Cl M23 . . . . . **120** E6
Grindall Ave M40 . . . . . . **65** B2
Grindleford Gdns ❿
SK13 . . . . **171** B2
Grindleford Gr ❶❸ SK13 . . **171** B2
Grindleford Lea ❿ SK13 . . **171** B2
Grindleford Wlk
❿ Gamesley SK13 . . . . **171** B2
Manchester M21 . . . . . . **109** D5
Grindle Gn M30 . . . . **95** C8
Grindlow Ave M22 . . . . . **121** D3
Grindley Ave M21 . . . . . **109** D5
Grindlow St M13 . . . . . . **164** B1
Grindlow Wlk WN3 . . . . . **54** C2
Grindon Ave M7 . . . . **63** D6
Grindrod St ❶ M26 . . . . . **44** A4
Grindsbrook Rd M26 . . . . **43** F7
Grinton Ave M13 . . . . **98** F2
Grisdale Dr M24 . . . . **46** E2
Grisdale Rd BL3 . . . . . . **144** C1
Grisebeck Way ❸ OL1 . . **153** B3
Grisedale Ave OL2 . . . . . **48** C8
Grisedale Cl
❹ Manchester M18 . . . . **99** D4
Middleton M24 . . . . **46** D3
Grisedale Rd OL11 . . . . . **30** B4
Gristlehurst La BL9, OL10 . . **29** A1
Gritley Wlk ❼ M22 . . . . **121** C1
Grizebeck Cl M18 . . . . . **165** C2

Grizedale Cl
Bolton BL1 . . . . **23** F2
Mossley SK15 . . . . **86** F7
Grizedale Dr WN2 . . . . . . **56** A7
Grizedale Rd SK6 . . . . . **113** B4
Groby Pl WA14 . . . . **119** C4
Groby Pl WA14 . . . . **119** D5
Groby Rd
Altrincham WA14 . . . . . **119** C4
Denton M34 . . . . **100** E7
Manchester M21 . . . . . . **109** B8
Groby Road N M34 . . . . **100** D8
Groby St
Oldham OL8 . . . . **67** A3
Stalybridge SK15 . . . . . . **86** C1
Groom St M1 . . . . **163** B3
Grosvenor Ave
❸ Golborne WA3 . . . . . . **90** D8
❺ Whitefield M45 . . . . . . **44** E1
Grosvenor Cl
Walkden M28 . . . . **60** C5
Wilmslow SK9 . . . . **137** A4
Grosvenor Cres SK14 . . **101** C1
Grosvenor Ct
❾ Ashton-u-L OL7 . . . . **166** A1
Cheadle SK8 . . . . **122** D6
❼ Manchester M16 . . . . . **97** E3
❹ Sale M33 . . . . **107** F5
Salford M7 . . . . **155** A4
Grosvenor Dr
Poynton SK12 . . . . **133** D3
Walkden M28 . . . . **60** C5
Grosvenor Gdns
Newton-le-W WA12 . . . . . **89** C2
Salford M7 . . . . **158** A4
❸ Stalybridge SK15 . . . . **86** A1
Wythenshawe M22 . . . **121** E6
Grosvenor Ho
Ashton-u-L OL7 . . . . . . **166** A1
Manchester M16 . . . . **97** E3
Grosvenor House Mews
M8 . . . . **63** F2
Grosvenor House Sq ❽
SK15 . . . . **86** A1
Grosvenor Ind Est OL7 . . **166** A1
Grosvenor Pl ❻ OL7 . . . **166** A1
Grosvenor Rd
Altrincham WA14 . . . . . **119** C5
Cheadle SK8 . . . . **123** C4
Eccles M30 . . . . **79** A3
Hyde SK14 . . . . **167** A1
Leigh WN7 . . . . **75** D6
Manchester, Whalley Range
M16 . . . . **97** D2
Marple SK6 . . . . **125** F7
Pendlebury M27 . . . . **80** B7
Sale M33 . . . . **107** F6
Stockport, Heaton Moor
SK4 . . . . **168** B3
Urmston M41 . . . . **95** C2
Walkden M28 . . . . **60** C5
❹ Whitefield M45 . . . . . . **44** E1
Grosvenor Road Prim Sch
M27 . . . . **80** B7
Grosvenor Sq
Sale M33 . . . . **108** A4
Uppermill OL3 . . . . **69** B8
Grosvenor St
Ashton-u-L OL7 . . . . . . **166** A1
Bolton BL2 . . . . **148** A2
Bury BL9 . . . . **44** F8
Denton M34 . . . . **100** D4
Hazel Grove SK7 . . . . . **124** D3
Heywood OL10 . . . . **29** D1
Hindley WN2 . . . . **56** D5
Kearsley BL4 . . . . **60** F7
Little Lever BL3 . . . . **43** B4
Manchester M1 . . . . **163** B3
Prestwich M25 . . . . **63** C4
Radcliffe M26 . . . . **43** F4
Rochdale OL11 . . . . **30** C1
Salford M6 . . . . **80** B4
Urmston M41 . . . . **95** E4
Grosvenor Way
Horwich BL6 . . . . **22** C3
Royton OL, OL2 . . . . **48** D2
GROTTON **68** A5
Grotton Hollow OL4 . . . . . **68** A6
Grotton Mdws OL4 . . . . . . **68** A6
Grouse St OL12 . . . . **14** F1
Grove OL15 . . . . **16** C8
Grove Arc SK9 . . . . **137** A2
Grove Ave
Adlington PR6 . . . . **21** A7
Failsworth M35 . . . . **83** E5
Wilmslow SK9 . . . . **137** B7
Grove Bank OL4 . . . . **68** E5
Grove Cl M14 . . . . **98** C2
Grove Cotts OL3 . . . . **51** D6
Grove Cres PR6 . . . . **21** A7
Grove Ct M33 . . . . **108** D4
Grove Hill M28 . . . . **77** F6
Grove Ho SK8 . . . . **132** B6
Grovehurst M27 . . . . **79** C6
Grove La
Altrincham, Timperley
WA15 . . . . **120** A6
Altrincham, Well Green
WA15 . . . . **120** B3
Cheadle SK8 . . . . **132** A6
Manchester M20 . . . . . . **110** B3
Standish WN6 . . . . **36** F8
Grove Pk ❻ M33 . . . . . . **107** F4
Grove Pl WN6 . . . . **36** F8
Grove Rd
Altrincham WA15 . . . . . **119** E3

Grove Rd continued
Middleton M24 . . . . **47** B2
Stalybridge SK15 . . . . . . **86** D4
Up Holland WN8 . . . . **53** C8
Uppermill OL3 . . . . **69** B7
Grove St
Ashton-in-M WN4 . . . . . . **73** A4
Ashton-u-L OL7 . . . . **84** E5
Bolton BL1 . . . . **143** A2
Droylsden M43 . . . . **99** F8
Farnworth BL4 . . . . **60** E8
Hazel Grove SK7 . . . . . **124** E3
Heywood OL10 . . . . **29** E2
Leigh WN7 . . . . **76** B4
Oldham OL1 . . . . **153** F7
Rochdale OL11 . . . . **139** B1
Salford M7 . . . . **155** B1
Uppermill OL3 . . . . **69** B5
Wilmslow SK9 . . . . **137** B7
Grove Terr OL4 . . . . **67** E8
Grove The
Appley Bridge WN6 . . . . . **18** C2
Bolton BL2 . . . . **148** B1
Cheadle SK8 . . . . **132** A6
Glossop SK13 . . . . **171** C4
Golborne WA3 . . . . **74** D1
Ince-in-M WN2 . . . . **151** C3
Little Lever BL3 . . . . **43** B3
Manchester M20 . . . . . . **110** B1
Sale M33 . . . . **108** B3
Shaw OL2 . . . . **149** A2
Stockport SK2 . . . . **170** B3
Uppermill OL3 . . . . **50** F1
Urmston M41 . . . . **94** F1
Grove Way SK9 . . . . **137** B7
Grovewood Cl OL7 . . . . . . **84** E5
Grovewood Dr WN6 . . . . . **35** E8
Grundey St SK7 . . . . **124** E2
Grundy Ave M25 . . . . **62** F2
Grundy Cl BL9 . . . . **141** A1
Grundy La BL9 . . . . **141** A1
Grundy Rd BL4 . . . . **60** E7
Grundys Bldgs M29 . . . . . **77** A8
Grundy's M29 . . . . **77** C5
Grundy St
Bolton BL3 . . . . **147** A4
Golborne WA3 . . . . **90** A7
Heywood OL10 . . . . **46** E8
Manchester SK4 . . . . . . **110** E2
Walkden M28 . . . . **60** F2
Westhoughton BL5 . . . . . **39** E1
Guardian Angels RC Prim
Sch BL8 . . . . **27** B2
Guardian Cl OL12 . . . . . . **15** D5
Guardian St M33 . . . . . . **108** A5
Guernsey Cl M19 . . . . . . **111** A6
Guest Rd M25 . . . . **63** A6
Guest St WN7 . . . . **76** B5
GUIDE BRIDGE **100** F8
Guide Bridge Ind Est
OL7 . . . . **100** E8
Guide Bridge Sta M34 . . **100** F8
Guide Cl M13 . . . . **1** D4
Guide La M34 . . . . **100** F7
Guide Post Rd M13 . . . . **164** A2
Guide St M50 . . . . **80** C1
Guido St
Bolton BL1 . . . . **143** B2
Failsworth M35 . . . . **83** E7
Guild Ave M28 . . . . **60** D2
Guildford Ave SK8 . . . . . **132** A6
Guildford Cl SK1 . . . . . . **124** B7
Guildford Cres WN6 . . . . . **36** F3
Guildford Dr OL6 . . . . **85** C7
Guildford Gr M24 . . . . **47** C3
Guildford Rd
Bolton BL1 . . . . **142** B2
Dukinfield SK16 . . . . . . **102** A7
Manchester M19 . . . . **99** B2
Salford M6 . . . . **80** B4
Urmston M41 . . . . **95** E4
Guildford St
❷ Mossley OL5 . . . . **86** D8
Rochdale OL16 . . . . **31** A7
Guildhall Cl M15 . . . . . . **163** A1
Guild St BL7 . . . . **25** B7
Guilford Rd M30 . . . . **79** B1
Guinness Circ M17 . . . . . . **96** A8
Guinness Ho ❷ OL16 . . . . **31** B6
Guinness Rd M17 . . . . **96** A8
Guinness Road Trad Est
M17 . . . . **95** F8
Guiseley Cl BL9 . . . . **27** E8
Gullane Cl M40 . . . . **65** D2
Gull Cl SK12 . . . . **133** B3
Gulvain Pl OL9 . . . . **65** F8
Gun Rd SK6 . . . . **115** C2
Gunson Ct ❿ M40 . . . . . **159** C3
Gunson St M40 . . . . **159** C3
Gun St M4 . . . . **159** B2
Gunters Ave BL5 . . . . **57** F6
Gurner Ave M5 . . . . **161** B3
Gurney St M4 . . . . **160** A1
Gutter End BL4 . . . . **140** C2
Guy Fawkes St M5 . . . . . **161** B3
Guywood Cotts SK6 . . . . **113** C3
Guywood La SK6 . . . . . . **113** C3
Gwelo St M11 . . . . **83** A2
Gwenbury Ave SK1 . . . . **112** B1
Gwendor Ave M8 . . . . **63** F2
Gwladys St SK15 . . . . **86** E6
Gwynant Pl M20 . . . . **110** C2
Gylden Cl SK14 . . . . **102** B5
Gypsy La OL11 . . . . **30** C3
Gypsy Moth Cl WA15 . . . **120** D5
Gypsy Wlk SK2 . . . . **124** C6

H
Habergham Cl M28 . . . . . . **78** C7
Hacienda The M1 . . . . . . **162** C4
Hackberry Cl WA14 . . . . **119** B8
Hacken Bridge Rd BL3 . . . **42** D4
Hacken La BL3 . . . . **42** C4
Hackford Cl
Bolton BL1 . . . . **144** C4
Bury BL8 . . . . **27** D5
Hacking St
Bury BL9 . . . . **141** A2
Prestwich M25 . . . . **63** A4
Salford M7 . . . . **155** B2
Hackle St M11 . . . . **83** C2
Hackleton Cl M4 . . . . **160** A1
Hackness Rd M21 . . . . . **108** F8
Hackney Ave M40 . . . . . . **83** B5
Hackney Cl M26 . . . . **44** A5
Hackwood Wlk ❽ M8 . . . **155** C3
Hackworth Cl WN1 . . . . . **151** B4
Hadbutt La M29 . . . . **76** F4
Haddington Dr M9 . . . . . . **64** E3
Haddon Ave M40 . . . . **65** F1
Haddon Cl
Alderley Edge SK9 . . . . . **136** F2
High Lane SK6 . . . . **134** E6
Whitefield BL9 . . . . **45** A5
Haddon Gr
Altrincham WA15 . . . . . **119** F7
Reddish SK5 . . . . **111** E7
Sale M33 . . . . **108** A4
Haddon Hall Rd M43 . . . . **83** E2
Haddon Ho M5 . . . . **154** A3
Haddon Lea M29 . . . . . . **171** A2
Haddon Mews ❿ SK13 . . **171** A2
Haddon Rd
Eccles M30 . . . . **95** C8
Gatley SK8 . . . . **131** C7
Golborne WA3 . . . . **74** D2
Hazel Grove SK7 . . . . . **124** E1
Manchester M21 . . . . . . **109** D5
Swinton M28 . . . . **79** C6
Swinton M27 . . . . **79** C6
Haddon St
❽ Ashton-in-M WN4 . . . . **72** C5
Rochdale OL11 . . . . **30** E4
Salford M6 . . . . **81** B5
Stretford M32 . . . . **96** D4
Haddon Way
❶❼ Denton M34 . . . . . . **101** A1
Shaw OL2 . . . . **149** C4
HADFIELD **104** B5
Hadfield Ave ❹ OL9 . . . . . **66** B4
Hadfield Cl M14 . . . . **98** D3
Hadfield Cres OL6 . . . . . . **85** E5
Hadfield Ind Est SK13 . . **103** F6
Hadfield Inf Sch SK13 . . **103** F5
Hadfield Pl SK13 . . . . . . **116** C8
Hadfield Rd
Glossop SK13 . . . . **171** B4
Hadfield SK13 . . . . **104** A3
Hadfields Ave SK14 . . . . **103** D5
Hadfields La SK13 . . . . . **116** C8
Hadfield St
Dukinfield SK16 . . . . . . **101** A7
Glossop SK13 . . . . **116** C8
Manchester M16 . . . . . . **161** C2
Oldham OL8 . . . . **66** F3
Salford M7 . . . . **155** B2
Hadfield Sta SK13 . . . . . **104** A5
Hadleigh Cl BL1 . . . . **25** A6
Hadleigh Gn BL6 . . . . **40** B4
Hadley Ave M13 . . . . **98** E2
Hadley Cl SK8 . . . . **122** F1
Hadley St M6 . . . . **81** B5
Hadlow Gn SK5 . . . . **112** B6
Hadlow Wlk M40 . . . . . . **160** B3
Hadrian Ho OL1 . . . . **153** C3
Hadwin St BL1 . . . . **143** C1
Hafton Rd M7 . . . . **81** B6
Hag Bank La SK12 . . . . . **135** D7
HAG FOLD **58** C5
Hag Fold Sta M46 . . . . . . **58** C5
HAGGATE **48** C3
Haggate OL2 . . . . **48** C3
Haggate Cres OL2 . . . . . . **48** C3
Hagley Rd M5 . . . . **161** A2
Hags The BL9 . . . . **45** A5
HAGUE BAR **135** E8
Hague Bar Prim Sch
SK22 . . . . **135** E8
Hague Bush Cl WA3 . . . . . **74** E1
Hague Ct ❺ M20 . . . . . . **110** A5
Hague Fold Rd SK22 . . . **135** F8
Hague Ho OL8 . . . . **153** C1
Hague Pl ❸ SK15 . . . . . . **86** A2
Hague Rd
Broadbottom SK14 . . . . **115** A8
Manchester M20 . . . . . . **110** A5
Hague St
Ashton-u-L OL6 . . . . **85** D4
Glossop SK13 . . . . **116** D7
Oldham OL4 . . . . **67** E8
Haig Ave M44 . . . . **105** C4
Haig Ct BL8 . . . . **27** B1
HAIGH **38** B7
Haigh Ave SK4 . . . . **111** E5
Haigh Country Pk WN2 . . . **37** F5
Haigh Hill* WN7 . . . . **37** F5
Haigh Hall Cl BL0 . . . . . . **11** B4
Haigh La M24, OL9 . . . . . . **47** E1
Haigh Lawn WA14 . . . . . **119** B3
Haigh Pk SK4 . . . . **111** E5
Haigh Rd WN2 . . . . **38** C6
Haigh St OL11 . . . . **31** A6

Haigh View
Ince-in-M WN3 151 B2
Wigan WN1 37 D2
Haig Rd
Aspull WN2 38 B7
Bury BL8 27 B1
Stretford M32 96 D3
Haig St
Bolton BL1 145 C4
Wigan WN3 150 B3
Haile Dr M28 77 F6
Hailsham Cl BL8 27 C7
Hailwood St OL11 30 E4
Halbury Gdns OL9 152 A3
Halcyon Cl 6 OL12 14 B2
Haldene Wlk M8 155 C2
Haldon Rd M20 110 D5
HALE 120 A1
Hale Ave SK12 133 D2
Hale Bank BL5 39 F1
Halebank Ave M20 109 F7
HALE BARNS 129 D8
Hale Carr WA15 120 B2
Hale Cl WN7 76 B2
Hale Ct WA14 119 D2
Hale Gr WN4 72 F5
Hale Green Ct WA15 120 A3
Hale La M35, M40 83 E8
Hale Low Rd WA15 119 F3
Hale Prep Sch 2 WA15 119 E3
Hale Rd
Altrincham WA15 120 B1
Stockport SK4 168 C3
Hales Cl M43 83 F3
Halesden Rd SK4 111 D5
Halesfield WN2 57 B2
Hale Sta WA14 119 D2
Halesworth Wlk M40 159 C4
Haletop M22 121 D2
Hale View WA14 119 D2
Hale Wlk 1 SK8 123 A5
Halewood Ave WA3 73 F1
Haley Cl 5 SK5 111 F8
Haley St M8 156 B3
Half Acre M26 43 F6
Half Acre Dr OL11 30 C6
Half Acre La
Blackrod BL6 21 C2
Rochdale OL11 30 B6
Half Acre Mews OL11 30 B6
Halfacre Rd M22 121 C4
Half Acre Rd OL11 30 B6
Half Edge La M30 79 F3
Half Moon La SK2 124 E6
Half Moon St 16 M2 158 C1
Halford Dr M40 83 C8
Halfpenny Bridge Ind Est 1 OL11 31 A6
Half St M3 158 B3
Halifax Rd
Littleborough OL15 16 D7
Rochdale OL12 15 C3
Halifax St OL6 166 B4
Haliwell St OL15 16 C5
Hallam Rd M40 83 B5
Hallam St
Radcliffe M26 44 D4
Stockport SK2 124 A6
Hallas Gr M23 109 B1
Hall Ave
Altrincham WA15 119 F7
Manchester M14 98 D3
Sale M33 107 E6
Stalybridge SK15 86 C5
Hall Bank M30 79 C2
Hallbottom St SK14 101 F5
Hallbridge Gdns
Bolton BL1 25 A3
Up Holland WN8 53 B8
Hall Cl
Mottram in L SK14 103 A5
Shevington WN6 36 B6
Hall Coppice The BL7 8 E1
Hallcroft M31 105 F4
Hallcroft Gdns OL16 31 E6
Hall Dr
Middleton M24 64 F7
Mottram in L SK14 103 A5
Hall Farm Ave M41 95 B3
Hall Farm Cl SK7 125 A3
Hall Fold OL12 14 C8
Hallgate
Westhoughton BL5 57 E5
Wigan WN1 150 C4
Hallgate Dr SK8 122 A2
Hallgate Rd SK1 124 B8
Hall Gdns OL12 14 C2
Hall Gn WN8 53 B7
Hall Gr
Cheadle SK8 122 C6
Manchester M14 98 D3
HALL GREEN 53 A7
Hall Green Cl
Dukinfield SK16 166 C1
Up Holland WN8 53 B7
Hall Green Rd SK16 166 C1
Hall House La WN7 76 C4
Halliday Ct 4 OL15 15 E4
Halliday Rd M40 83 B4
Halliford Rd M40 83 A6
Hallington Cl BL3 145 C1
HALL I' TH' WOOD 25 B4
Hall i' th' Wood La
Bolton, Castle Hill BL1, BL2 25 B3
Bolton, Hall i' th' Wood BL1 25 A4
Hall i 'th' Wood (Mus)* BL1 25 A4
Hall i' th' Wood Sta BL1 25 B3
HALLIWELL 143 A2
Halliwell Ave OL8 66 E3
Halliwell Ind Est BL1 143 A3
Halliwell La M8 155 C3
Halliwell Rd
Bolton BL1 143 A2
Prestwich M25 62 F1
Halliwell St
2 Bolton BL1 143 A2
Milnrow OL16 31 E7
Oldham OL9 66 A2
5 Rochdale OL12 139 B4
Halliwell Street W 17 M8 155 C3
Halliwell Wlk M25 62 F1
Hallkirk Wlk 4 M40 65 D2
Hall La
Appley Bridge WN6 18 D2
Bolton BL3, BL4 42 E3
Farnworth BL4 42 D2
Horwich BL6 39 E7
Orrell WN5 53 F4
Partington M31 105 F4
Pennington Green WN2 38 D2
Romiley SK6 113 B6
Wigan, Lamberhead Green WN3, WN5 54 A4
Wigan, Marylebone WN1 37 D4
Wythenshawe M23 121 B6
Hall Lane Gr WN2 56 D8
Hall Lee Bank Pk Nature Reserve* BL5 58 A7
Hall Lee Dr BL5 40 A1
Hall Mdw SK8 122 E1
Hall Meadow Rd SK13 104 D2
Hall Moss La SK7 132 C4
Hall Moss Rd M9 65 A3
Hallows Ave M21 109 C5
Hallows Farm Ave OL12 14 D2
Hall Pool Dr SK2 124 E7
Hall Rd
Altrincham WA14 119 C1
Ashton-u-L OL6 85 C5
Bramhall SK7 123 D1
Handforth SK9 131 E3
Manchester M14 98 D3
Wilmslow SK9 137 A7
Hallroyd Brow OL1 153 B4
Halls Cotts OL3 69 B7
Hall's Ct SK13 104 C1
Hall St
Ashton-in-M WN2 73 E7
Ashton-u-L OL6 85 E2
Bury, Walshaw BL8 26 E4
Bury, Woodhill BL8 27 C4
Cheadle SK8 122 D6
Denton SK14 101 B3
Failsworth M35 83 D6
1 Farnworth BL4 42 D2
Heywood OL10 29 E1
Ince-in-M WN2 151 C4
Manchester M2 162 C4
3 Oldham OL4 67 B7
Radcliffe M26 43 F6
Ramsbottom BL9 11 C2
Royton OL2 48 D4
Stockport SK1 112 A1
Swinton M27 61 F2
Whitworth OL12 14 B8
Wigan WN1 151 A3
Hallstead Ave M38 59 E4
Hallstead Gr M38 59 E4
Hallsville Rd M19 99 C1
Halls Way OL3 69 B6
Hallsworth Rd M30 79 A1
Hall The SK13 116 A7
Hallview Way M28 59 F3
Hallwood Ave M6 80 C5
Hall Wood Ave WA11 72 F1
Hallwood Rd
Handforth SK9 131 D2
Wythenshawe M23 121 A6
Hallworth Ave M34 84 C1
Hallworth Rd M8 156 B4
Hallworthy Cl WN7 75 B1
Halmore Rd M40 160 A2
Halsall Cl BL9 27 F6
Halsall Dr BL3 147 B2
Halsbury Cl M12 164 B2
Halsey Cl OL9 65 E2
Halsey Wlk 19 M8 155 C3
Halshaw La BL4 60 F7
Halsmere Dr M9 64 E3
Halstead Ave
Manchester M21 109 A7
Salford M6 80 E5
Halstead Dr M44 94 B1
Halstead Gr
Leigh WN7 76 B5
Wythenshawe SK8 121 F5
Halstead St
Bolton BL2 148 A3
Bury BL9 141 A4
Halstead Wlk BL9 28 A5
Halstock Wlk M40 157 A1
Halstone Ave SK9 136 E4
Halston St M15 162 B2
Halter Cl M26 44 A5
Halton 12 OL10 29 C2
Halton Bank M6 154 C4
Halton Dr WA15 108 B1
Halton Ho 4 M5 154 C1
Halton Rd M11 83 C2
Halton St
Bolton BL2 148 B3
Hyde SK14 167 C3
Halvard Ave BL9 27 F6
Halvard Ct BL9 27 F6
Halvis Gr M16 97 B3
Hamble Ct M26 61 B8
Hambleden Cl BL3 40 F5
Hambledon Cl M46 58 E5
Hambleton Cl BL8 26 F1
Hambleton Dr 2 M33 107 D5
Hambleton Rd SK8 131 C8
Hamblett St WN7 75 B5
Hambridge Cl M8 156 A3
Hamel St
Bolton BL3 147 B3
Dukinfield SK14 101 F5
Hamer Cty Prim Sch 7 OL16 15 B2
Hamer Dr M16 162 A1
Hamer Hall Cres OL12 15 B1
Hamer Hill M9 64 C3
Hamer La OL16 15 B1
Hamer St
Bolton BL2 25 B1
Heywood OL10 29 B2
Radcliffe M26 44 C4
Ramsbottom BL0 11 B2
Hamerton Rd M40 159 C4
Hamer Vale OL12 15 B2
Hamilcar Ave M30 79 E2
Hamilton Ave
Eccles M30 79 E1
Irlam M44 105 D4
Royton OL2 48 B3
Hamilton Cl
Bury BL8 27 B3
Prestwich M25 63 A3
Stockport SK4 111 D7
Hamilton Cres SK4 168 B1
Hamilton Ct
3 Little Lever BL3 43 B3
Sale M33 108 B4
Wigan WN5 54 E8
Hamilton Gr M16 162 A1
Hamilton Lodge 6 M14 98 C3
Hamilton Mews
Eccles M30 79 B3
Prestwich M25 63 A3
Hamilton Rd
Garswood WN4 72 D4
Hindley WN2 56 F4
Manchester M13 98 F3
Prestwich M25 63 A3
Tyldesley M29 77 D6
Whitefield M45 62 E8
Hamilton Sq
Stockport SK4 169 B3
Wigan WN5 54 E8
Hamilton St
Ashton-u-L OL7 84 F1
Atherton M46 58 C2
Bolton BL1 24 E5
Bury BL9 140 C4
Chadderton OL9 152 A3
Eccles M30 79 B3
Leigh WN7 75 D6
Manchester M16 162 A1
Oldham OL4 67 B7
Salford M7 155 A3
Stalybridge SK15 85 F2
Swinton M27 61 D1
Hamilton Way OL10 28 E1
Hamlet Dr M33 107 E6
Hamlet The BL6 40 B8
Hammerstone Rd M18 165 C2
Hammer Terr BL9 11 C3
Hammett Rd 4 M21 109 A8
Hammond 13 OL10 29 C2
Hammond Ave
Bacup OL13 3 D8
Reddish SK4 111 E5
Hamnet Cl BL1 25 A5
Hamnett St
Droylsden M11, M43 83 D1
Hyde SK14 167 A3
Hamon Rd WA15 119 E4
Hampden Cres M18 165 C1
Hampden Gr M30 79 D2
Hampden Pl WN5 36 D1
Hampden Rd
Prestwich M25 63 C4
Sale M33 108 A3
Shaw OL2 49 D6
Hampden St
Heywood OL10 29 D1
Rochdale OL11 139 C2
Hampshire Cl
Brinnington SK5 112 C5
Bury BL9 45 A8
Glossop SK13 116 F8
Hampshire Ho SK5 112 C5
Hampshire Rd
Brinnington SK5 112 C5
Chadderton OL9 152 B1
Droylsden M43 84 A3
Partington M31 105 D2
Hampshire Wlk 6 M8 156 B2
Hampson Ave WA3 91 F3
Hampson Cl
Ashton-in-M WN4 73 B2
5 Eccles M30 79 B1
Hampson Cres SK9 131 C4
Hampson Fold M26 43 F4
Hampson Gn WN2 37 E8
Hampson Mill La BL9 44 F5
Hampson Pl OL6 85 E6
Hampson Rd
Ashton-u-L OL6 85 E6
Stretford M32 96 C2
Hampson Sq 5 M26 44 A4
Hampson St
Atherton M46 58 C3
Droylsden M43 84 A2
Eccles M30 79 B1
Horwich BL6 22 B4
Manchester M5 162 A4
Manchester, Miles Platting M40 160 A4
Radcliffe M26 44 A3
Sale M33 108 D4
Salford M3, M5 158 A1
Stockport SK1 124 B8
Swinton M27 62 A1
Hampstead Ave M41 94 E1
Hampstead Dr
Stockport SK2 124 C5
Whitefield M45 44 E1
Hampstead La SK2 124 C5
Hampstead Rd WN6 19 D1
Hampsted Ho SK2 124 C5
Hampton Ct SK9 131 D5
Hampton Gr
Bury BL9 27 F6
Cheadle SK8 122 E2
Leigh WN7 76 E7
Sale WA14 107 F1
Hampton Ho 5 M33 108 C4
Hampton Mews 1 SK3 123 F4
Hampton Rd
Bolton BL3 42 A3
Failsworth M35 84 B8
Irlam M44 105 D4
Stretford M21 96 F1
Urmston M41 95 D2
Hampton St OL8 66 D4
Hamsell Rd M13 163 C3
Hanborough Ct M29 76 F8
Hancock Cl M14 98 B3
Hancock St M32 108 D8
Handel Ave M41 95 A2
Handel Mews M33 108 C4
Handel St
Bolton BL1 143 A3
Whitworth OL12 14 B8
Handford Ho 5 M41 95 E2
HANDFORTH 131 C4
Handforth Gr M13 98 E2
Handforth Rd
Handforth SK9 131 E1
Reddish SK5 111 F5
Handforth Sta SK9 131 D3
Hand La WN7 75 E2
Handley Ave M14 98 B1
Handley Cl SK3 123 C5
Handley Gdns BL1 144 A3
Handley Rd SK7 123 E3
Handley St
Bury BL9 44 F8
Rochdale OL12 139 A4
Hands La OL11 30 A7
Handsworth St M12 164 A3
Hanging Birch M24 64 B7
HANGING CHADDER 48 C7
Hanging Chadder Farm OL2 48 C7
Hanging Chadder La OL2 48 C7
Hanging Lees Cl OL16 32 C4
Hani Ct M8 63 F1
Hanifah Inf Small Sch M13 98 E3
Hani Wells Bsns Pk M19 111 B7
Hankinson Cl M31 105 E2
Hankinson Way M6 81 A3
Hanley Cl
Disley SK12 135 D5
Middleton M24 65 A5
Hanlith Mews M19 110 F8
Hanlon St M8 63 F1
Hanmer St WN2 56 D5
Hannah Baldwin Cl M11 164 C4
Hannah Brown Ho WA15 119 E3
Hannah Lodge M20 110 A4
Hannah St M12 99 A2
Hannerton Rd OL2 49 D7
Hannet Rd M22 121 D2
Hanover Bsns Pk WA14 119 B7
Hanover Cres M14 98 D4
Hanover Ct
4 Ashton-u-L OL7 166 A1
Bolton BL3 144 B1
Swinton M28 79 B6
Hanover Gdns M7 155 B4
Hanover Ho
Bolton BL3 146 B2
13 Manchester M14 110 D8
Oldham OL8 153 A2
Hanover Rd
Altrincham WA14 119 B7
Hindley WN2 56 C6
Hanover St
Bolton BL1 145 B3
Leigh WN7 76 A6
Littleborough OL15 16 A5
Manchester M4 159 A2
Mossley OL5 68 C1
Rochdale OL11 30 C2
Stalybridge SK15 85 F2
Hanover Street N M34 100 E8
Hanover Street S 4 M34 100 E8
Hanover Twrs SK5 169 C3
Hansby Cl OL1 48 E1
Hansdon Cl M8 156 A2
Hansen Wlk 3 M22 121 C2
Hanslope Wlk 14 M9 157 B4
Hansom Dr M46 58 A1
Hanson Cl M24 47 A1
Hanson Dr M46 76 A8
Hanson Mews SK1 112 B2
Hanson Pk M24 47 A1
Hanson Rd M40 83 B7
Hanson St
Adlington PR7 20 F5
Bury BL9 140 C4
Middleton M24 47 A1
Oldham OL4 67 C7
Hanstock Cl WN5 53 E5
Hanwell Cl WN7 75 E1
Hanworth Cl M13 163 B3
Happy Valley Nature Reserve* SK7 133 A8
Hapsford Wlk M40 83 A5
Hapton Ave M32 96 D1
Hapton Pl SK4 169 B3
Hapton St M19 99 A1
Harbern Cl M30 79 D4
Harbern Dr WN7 57 D2
Harbord St M24 65 A8
Harborne Wlk 2 BL8 10 F1
Harboro Ct M33 107 F3
Harboro Gr M33 107 F4
Harboro Rd M33 107 E4
Harboro Way M33 107 F4
Harbour City Metro Sta M50 96 F8
Harbour Farm Rd SK14 101 E5
Harbour La
Edgworth BL7 9 D5
Milnrow OL16 31 F5
Harbour Lane N OL16 31 F6
Harbourne Ave M28 78 C8
Harbourne Cl M28 78 C8
Harbrook Gr WN2, WN7 75 C8
Harburn Wlk M22 130 E8
Harbury Cl
Bolton BL3 146 A3
Wigan WN6 36 F2
Harbury Cres M22 121 C5
Harbury Wlk WN6 36 F2
Harcles Dr BL0 11 B2
Harcombe Rd M20 110 C6
Harcourt Ave M41 95 F1
Harcourt Cl M41 95 F1
Harcourt Ind Ctr M28 60 D5
Harcourt Mews 10 BL6 22 B4
Harcourt Rd
Altrincham WA14 119 D6
Sale M33 108 A6
Harcourt St
Oldham OL1 67 B8
Reddish SK5 111 F8
Stretford M32 96 E3
Walkden M28 60 D5
Hardacre St WN3 151 A2
Hardberry Pl SK2 124 E6
Hardcastle Ave M21 109 C6
Hardcastle Cl BL2 25 C6
Hardcastle Gdns BL2 25 C6
Hardcastle Rd SK3 170 A3
Hardcastle St
Bolton BL1 143 C2
7 Oldham, Mumps OL1 67 A7
Harden Dr BL2 25 D2
Harden Hills OL2 49 D8
HARDEN PARK 137 A3
Harden Pk SK9 137 A3
Hardfield Rd M24 65 B5
Hardfield St OL10 29 D2
Hardicker St M19 111 B7
Hardie Ave BL4 60 B7
Harding St
Adlington PR6 21 B8
Dukinfield SK14 101 D5
Manchester, Bradford M4 160 A1
Manchester M3 158 C2
Salford, Pendleton M6 81 A4
Stockport SK1 112 B1
Hardman Ave
Manchester M25 63 D2
Rawtenstall BB4 2 A8
Romiley SK6 113 A3
Hardman Cl
Radcliffe M26 43 F6
Rawtenstall BB4 2 F7
Hardman Dr BB4 2 F7
Hardman Fold BL3 42 B2
Hardman La M35 83 E8
Hardman Rd SK5 111 F8
Hardmans BL7 24 F7
Hardman's La BL7 24 F8
Hardman's Mews M45 62 F6
Hardman's Rd M45 62 F6
Hardman St
Bury BL9 140 C4
Failsworth M35 83 D7
Farnworth BL4 60 E7
Heywood OL10 29 D2
Manchester M3 158 B1
Milnrow OL16 32 A5
Oldham OL9 66 B3
Radcliffe M26 43 F6
Stockport SK3 169 A1
Stockport SK3 170 A4
Wigan WN3 150 B2
Hardman Terr OL13 3 D8
Hardon Gr M13 98 F2
Hardrow Cl WN3 55 B2
Hardrush Fold M35 84 A6
Hardshaw Cl M13 163 B2
Hardsough La BL0 1 D5
Hardwick Cl
High Lane SK6 134 F6
Little Lever M26 43 B5

Hardwicke Rd SK12 . . . . 133 F4
Hardwicke St OL11 . . . . . 30 E4
Hardwick Rd
Ashton-in-M WN4 . . . . . . 73 A5
Partington M31 . . . . 106 A3
Hardwick St OL7 . . . . 84 F2
Hardwood Cl M8 . . . . . . 156 A3
Hardybutts WN1 . . . . . . 151 A4
Hardy Cl
Dukinfield SK16 . . . . . . 101 C8
Rochdale OL11 . . . . 30 F3
Westhoughton BL5 . . . . . 39 E3
Hardy Dr
Altrincham WA15 . . . . . . 119 F7
Bramhall SK7 . . . . 132 D7
Hardy Farm M21 . . . . . . 109 B6
Hardy Gr
Swinton M27 . . . . 79 D5
Worsley M28 . . . . 78 F8
Hardy La M21 . . . . 109 B6
Hardy Mill Prim Sch BL2 . 25 F4
Hardy Mill Rd BL2 . . . . . . 25 F4
Hardy St
Ashton-u-L OL6 . . . . 85 E6
Eccles M30 . . . . 79 B1
Oldham OL4 . . . . 67 A6
Wigan WN6 . . . . 37 A1
Hardywood Rd 4 M34 . . 113 A7
Harebell Ave 10 M28 . . . 59 F3
Harebell Cl OL12 . . . . . . 14 D3
Harecastle Ave M30 . . . . 95 E8
Haredale Dr M8 . . . . . . 156 B2
Hare Dr BL9 . . . . 45 B4
Harefield Ave OL11 . . . . 139 C1
Harefield Dr
Heywood OL10 . . . . 29 F2
Manchester M20 . . . . . . 110 A2
Wilmslow SK9 . . . . 137 B5
Harefield Rd SK9 . . . . . . 131 E4
Hareford Wlk M9 . . . . . 156 C2
Harehill Cl 5 M13 . . . . 163 B3
Hare Hill Rd
Hattersley SK14 . . . . . . 102 C2
Littleborough OL15 . . . . . 16 B6
Hare Hill Wlk SK14 . . . . 102 C3
Hareshill Rd OL10 . . . . . 46 C7
Hare St
4 Manchester M4 . . . . 159 A2
Rochdale OL11 . . . . 139 C1
Harewood SK14 . . . . . . 115 A8
Harewood Ave
Rochdale OL11 . . . . 13 D2
Sale M33 . . . . 107 D3
Harewood Cl OL11 . . . . . 13 D2
Harewood Ct M33 . . . . . 108 C3
Harewood Dr
Rochdale OL11 . . . . 13 C2
Royton OL2 . . . . 48 C5
Harewood Gr SK5 . . . . . 111 E8
Harewood Lodge SK14 . . 115 A8
Harewood Rd
Hindley WN2 . . . . 56 C5
Irlam M44 . . . . 94 B2
Rochdale OL11 . . . . 13 D2
Shaw OL2 . . . . 49 D8
Harewood Way
Rochdale OL11 . . . . 13 C2
Swinton M27 . . . . 61 F2
Harewood Wlk 12 M34 . . 101 A1
Harford Cl SK7 . . . . 124 A1
Hargate Ave 14 . . . . . . 14 A2
Hargate Cl BL9 . . . . 11 C2
Hargate Dr
Altrincham WA15 . . . . . . 120 A1
Irlam M44 . . . . 94 A3
Hargate Hill La SK13 . . . 115 E7
Hargrave CI M9 . . . . 64 C6
Hargreaves Ho BL3 . . . . 145 B2
Hargreaves Rd WA15 . . . 120 C6
Hargreaves St
Bolton BL1 . . . . 143 B2
Oldham, Alder Root OL9 . 152 C2
Oldham OL1 . . . . 153 C3
Rochdale OL11 . . . . 30 C4
Hargreave's St M4 . . . . 159 A3
Harkerside Cl M21 . . . . 109 C8
Harkness St M12 . . . . . 164 A3
Harland Dr
Ashton-in-M WN4 . . . . . . 73 C3
Manchester M8 . . . . . . 156 B3
Harland Way OL12 . . . . . 14 B2
Harlea Ave WN2 . . . . . . 57 A3
Harlech Ave
Hindley WN2 . . . . 57 B4
Prestwich M25, M45 . . . . 63 B7
Harlech Dr SK7 . . . . 124 D1
Harlech St WN4 . . . . . . 72 F5
Harleen Gr SK2 . . . . . . 124 D7
Harlesden Cres 5 BL3 . . 144 C1
Harley Ave
Ainsworth BL2 . . . . 26 D1
Bolton BL2 . . . . 25 E3
Manchester M14 . . . . . . 98 E3
Harley Ct M24 . . . . 46 F1
Harley Rd
Middleton M24 . . . . 46 F1
Sale M33 . . . . 108 C5
Harley St
Ashton-u-L OL6 . . . . . . 166 B3
Manchester M11 . . . . . . 99 D8
Harling Rd M22 . . . . . . 121 E7
Harlington Cl 3 M23 . . . 120 D7
Harlock Ct M6 . . . . 81 B3
Harlow Dr M18 . . . . 99 D3

Harlyn Ave SK7 . . . . . . 132 F7
Harmer Cl M40 . . . . 83 B5
Harmol Gr OL7 . . . . 84 F6
Harmony Sq M13 . . . . . 164 A1
Harmony St
Milnrow OL16 . . . . 31 F6
Oldham OL4 . . . . 67 A6
Harmsworth Dr SK4 . . . 111 B5
Harmsworth St M6 . . . . 154 B2
Harmuir Cl WN6 . . . . . . 36 E4
Harold Ave
Ashton-in-M WN4 . . . . . . 73 A5
Dukinfield SK16 . . . . . . 101 D8
Reddish M18 . . . . 99 F4
Haroldene St BL2 . . . . . . 25 B2
Harold Lees Rd OL10 . . . 29 F3
Harold Priestnall Cl M40 . 83 B6
Harold St
Aspull WN2 . . . . 38 D5
Bolton BL1 . . . . 143 A2
Failsworth M35 . . . . 83 E7
Manchester M16 . . . . . . 161 C2
Middleton M24 . . . . 46 E1
Oldham OL9 . . . . 153 A3
Prestwich M25 . . . . 62 F4
Rochdale OL16 . . . . 15 C2
Stockport SK1 . . . . 124 B8
Harper Ct SK3 . . . . 170 B3
Harper Fold Cl M26 . . . . 43 E3
Harper Fold Rd M26 . . . . 43 E3
HARPER GREEN 42 B1
Harper Green Com L Ctr
BL4 . . . . 42 B1
Harper Green Rd BL3, BL4 42 B1
Harper Green Sch BL4 . . 42 B1
Harper Ho M19 . . . . 98 F1
Harper Mill OL6 . . . . . . 166 C3
Harper Pl OL6 . . . . 166 C3
Harper Rd M22 . . . . 121 E7
Harper's La BL1 . . . . . . 142 B2
Harper's Sq OL2 . . . . . 149 C3
Harper St
Farnworth BL4 . . . . 42 B2
Hindley WN2 . . . . 56 D5
Oldham OL8 . . . . 66 E4
Rochdale OL11 . . . . 139 B1
Stockport SK3 . . . . 170 B3
Wigan WN1 . . . . 151 B3
Harpford Cl BL2 . . . . . . 43 A5
Harpford Dr BL2 . . . . . . 43 A5
Harp Ind Est OL11 . . . . . 30 D2
Harp Rd M17 . . . . 96 A8
Harp Trad Est M17 . . . . . 96 A8
Harptree Gr WN7 . . . . . 75 D7
HARPURHEY 157 B3
Harpurhey Rd M8, M9 . . 157 A3
Harpur Mount Prim Sch
M9 . . . . 157 A4
Harridge Ave
Rochdale OL11 . . . . 14 C3
Stalybridge SK15 . . . . . . 86 D2
Harridge St OL12 . . . . . . 14 C3
Harridge The OL12 . . . . . 14 C3
Harrier Cl
Leigh WN7 . . . . 76 B5
Walkden M28 . . . . 78 D8
Wythenshawe M22 . . . . 121 E5
Harriet St
Irlam M44 . . . . 105 E5
Walkden M28 . . . . 60 D3
Harriett St
Manchester M4 . . . . . . 159 C2
Rochdale OL16 . . . . 31 A7
Harringay Rd M40 . . . . . 83 B5
Harrington Cl BL9 . . . . . 45 A7
Harrington Rd WA14 . . . 119 B5
Harrington St M18 . . . . . 99 E5
Harris Ave
Reddish M34 . . . . 100 B3
Urmston M41 . . . . 95 D5
Harris Cl
Heywood OL10 . . . . 28 E1
Reddish M34 . . . . 100 B3
Harris Dr
Dukinfield SK14 . . . . . . 102 A4
Whitefield BL9 . . . . 45 B2
Harrison Ave M19 . . . . . 99 B2
Harrison Cl 1 OL12 . . . . 13 F1
Harrison Cres BL6 . . . . . 21 C3
Harrison Rd PR7 . . . . . . 21 A6
Harrison's Dr SK6 . . . . . 113 C5
Harrison St
Britannia OL13 . . . . 4 B8
Eccles M30 . . . . 95 B8
Hindley WN2 . . . . 57 B3
Horwich BL6 . . . . 22 B4
Hyde SK14 . . . . 113 F8
Manchester M4 . . . . . . 160 A1
1 Oldham OL1 . . . . . . 153 C2
Ramsbottom BL0 . . . . . . 138 C3
Salford M7 . . . . 158 A4
Stalybridge SK15 . . . . . . 86 A2
Stockport SK1, SK2 . . . . 170 C3
Walkden M38 . . . . 60 A4
4 Wigan WN5 . . . . . . 54 F6
Harrison Way WA12 . . . 89 C4
Harris Rd WN6 . . . . 19 B3
Harris St
Bolton BL3 . . . . 145 B2
Manchester M8 . . . . . . 158 B4
Harrock La WN6 . . . . . . 18 A5
Harrogate Ave M25 . . . . 63 D2
Harrogate Cl M11 . . . . . 99 E7
Harrogate Dr SK5 . . . . . 111 E8
Harrogate Rd SK5 . . . . . 99 E1
Harrogate Sq BL8 . . . . . 26 F1
Harrogate St WN1 . . . . . 151 A3
Harrop Court Rd OL3 . . . 51 D5

HARROP EDGE 102 E5
Harrop Edge La OL3 . . . . 51 B5
Harrop Edge Rd SK14,
SK15 . . . . 102 E4
Harrop Fold OL8 . . . . . . 67 A1
Harrop Fold Sch M28 . . . 60 B3
Harrop Gn OL3 . . . . 51 D5
Harrop Green La OL3 . . . 51 C5
Harrop Rd WA15 . . . . . 119 F2
Harrop St
Bolton BL3 . . . . 146 A4
Droylsden M18 . . . . 99 F6
10 Stalybridge SK15 . . . 86 A2
Stockport SK1 . . . . 124 A7
Walkden M28 . . . . 60 B3
Harrow Ave
Manchester M19 . . . . . . 111 A6
Oldham OL8 . . . . 66 E3
Rochdale OL11 . . . . 30 A6
Harrowby CI WN5 . . . . . 54 E6
Harrowby Ct BL4 . . . . . . 60 B8
Harrowby Dr M40 . . . . . 157 A1
Harrowby Fold BL4 . . . . 60 C8
Harrowby La BL4 . . . . . . 60 C8
Harrowby Rd
Bolton, Fernhill Gate BL3 . 146 A3
Doffcocker BL1 . . . . 23 F7
Swinton M27 . . . . 79 E7
Harrowby St
Farnworth BL4 . . . . 60 C8
Wigan WN5 . . . . 54 E6
Harrow Cl
Bury BL9 . . . . 44 F5
Orrell WN5 . . . . 53 F8
Wilmslow SK9 . . . . 136 F5
Harrow Cres WN7 . . . . . 75 F3
Harrowdene Wlk 8 M9 . 157 A4
Harrow Dr M33 . . . . . . 108 A2
Harrow Mews OL2 . . . . 149 B3
Harrow Pl WN3 . . . . 55 F4
Harrow Rd
Bolton BL1 . . . . 144 B4
Sale M33 . . . . 108 A2
Wigan WN6 . . . . 36 D1
Harrow St
Manchester M8 . . . . 64 B1
Rochdale OL11 . . . . 31 B2
Harrycroft Rd SK6 . . . . . 113 B5
Harry Hall Gdns M7 . . . . 81 C2
Harry Rd SK5 . . . . 111 F8
Harry Rowley Cl 1 M22 . 121 C2
Harry's Ct 3 WN7 . . . . . 75 D5
Harry St
Oldham OL9 . . . . 152 C2
Rochdale OL11 . . . . 30 B3
Royton OL2 . . . . 48 E2
Harry Thorneycroft Wlk
M11 . . . . 164 B4
Harrytown SK6 . . . . . . 113 A2
Harrytown RC High Sch
SK6 . . . . 113 A2
Harswell Cl WN5 . . . . . . 53 E5
Hart Ave
Droylsden M43 . . . . 84 B1
Sale M33 . . . . 108 F3
HART COMMON 57 C6
Hart Ct OL5 . . . . 68 B2
Hart Dr BL9 . . . . 45 B4
Harter St M1 . . . . 163 A4
Hartfield Cl M13 . . . . . . 163 C2
Hartfield Wlk BL2 . . . . . 148 C4
Hartford Ave
Heywood OL10 . . . . 29 B3
Reddish SK4 . . . . 111 D6
Wilmslow SK9 . . . . 136 F5
Hartford Cl OL10 . . . . . . 29 B3
Hartford Dr BL8 . . . . . . 27 A6
Hartford Gdns WA15 . . . 120 D5
Hartford Gn BL5 . . . . . . 57 F6
Hartford Ind Est OL9 . . . 152 C2
Hartford Rd
Sale M33 . . . . 107 D2
Urmston M41 . . . . 95 E4
Westhoughton BL5 . . . . . 57 F6
Hartford Sq OL9 . . . . . . 152 C2
Hartford St M34 . . . . . . 100 E5
Hart Hill Dr M5 . . . . . . 154 A3
Harthill St M8 . . . . 155 C1
Hartington Cl 4 M41 . . . 95 E2
Hartington Ct OL2 . . . . . 48 E4
Hartington Dr
Droylsden M43 . . . . 83 F2
Hazel Grove SK7 . . . . . . 133 E8
Standish WN6 . . . . 36 F7
Hartington Rd
Altrincham WA14 . . . . . . 119 D8
Bolton BL1 . . . . 144 C4
Bramhall SK7 . . . . 132 E6
Eccles M30 . . . . 79 A3
Gatley SK8 . . . . 131 D8
High Lane SK12, SK6 . . . 134 F7
Manchester M21 . . . . . . 109 B8
Stockport SK2 . . . . 124 D5
Hartington St M14 . . . . . 97 F3
Hartis Ave M7 . . . . 155 B2
Hartland Ave M41 . . . . . 96 A2
Hartland Cl
Poynton SK12 . . . . 133 D5
Stockport SK2 . . . . 124 C8
Tyldesley M29 . . . . 77 B8
Hartland St 3 OL10 . . . . 29 D2
Hartlebury OL11 . . . . . . 139 B2
Hartlepool Cl M14 . . . . . 98 B3
Hartley Ave
Manchester M25 . . . . . . 63 D3
Wigan WN1 . . . . 151 B3
Hartley Gn Gdns WN5 . . 53 D2

Hartley Gr
Irlam M44 . . . . 94 B4
Wigan WN5 . . . . 54 B7
Hartley Hall Gdns M16 . . 97 E1
Hartley La OL11 . . . . 30 E3
Hartley Rd
Altrincham WA14 . . . . . . 119 C5
Manchester M21 . . . . . . 97 A1
Hartley St
Heywood OL10 . . . . 29 D2
Horwich BL6 . . . . 22 B3
Littleborough OL15 . . . . . 16 A5
Manchester M40 . . . . . 157 C4
Milnrow OL16 . . . . 31 D7
Rochdale OL12 . . . . 14 B1
Stalybridge SK15 . . . . . . 86 D3
Stockport SK3 . . . . 170 A4
Wardle OL12 . . . . 15 C6
12 Wigan WN5 . . . . . . 54 B6
Hartley Terr
Rochdale OL11 . . . . 30 E3
Wigan WN3 . . . . 150 C3
Hartley Way WN5 . . . . . 53 D2
Hart Mill Cl OL5 . . . . . . 68 B2
Harton Ave M18 . . . . . . 99 C3
Harton Cl OL2 . . . . 149 A2
Hartridge Cl BL5 . . . . . . 57 F6
Harts Farm Mews WN7 . 75 F7
Hartshead Ave
Ashton-u-L OL6 . . . . 85 C6
Stalybridge SK15 . . . . . . 86 A3
Hartshead Cl
Ashton-u-L OL6 . . . . 85 C4
Droylsden M11 . . . . 100 A7
Hartshead Cres M35 . . . 84 F8
HARTSHEAD GREEN . . 85 F8
Hartshead Rd OL6 . . . . . 85 C6
Hartshead St OL4 . . . . . 67 F5
Hartshead View SK14 . . 167 C1
Hart's Houses BL6 . . . . 22 D5
Hartsop Dr M24 . . . . 46 C2
Hartspring Ave 3 M27 . . 80 A7
Hart St
Altrincham WA14 . . . . . . 119 E5
Droylsden M43 . . . . 84 B1
Manchester M1 . . . . . . 159 A1
Tyldesley M29 . . . . 77 C8
Westhoughton BL5 . . . . . 57 B7
Hartswell Cl WA3 . . . . . 74 A2
Hartswood Cl M34 . . . . 101 A4
Hartswood Rd M20 . . . . 110 D6
Hartwell Cl
Bolton BL2 . . . . 25 C3
Manchester M11 . . . . . . 164 C4
Hartwell Gr 2 SK3 . . . . 123 F4
Harty Ho M30 . . . . 79 E2
Harvard Ct SK6 . . . . . . 113 C5
Harvard Gr M6 . . . . 80 C3
Harvard Rd M18 . . . . . . 165 B1
Harvard St 10 OL11 . . . . 31 A4
Harvest Cl
Salford M6 . . . . 80 E5
Wythenshawe M33 . . . . 109 A3
Harvest Pk BL1 . . . . . . 144 C4
Harvest Way WN2 . . . . . 57 C3
Harvey Cl M11 . . . . 165 A4
Harvey Ct WA3 . . . . 74 A1
Harvey Rd
Golborne WN7 . . . . 75 B1
Stockport SK1 . . . . 169 C1
Harvey La WA3 . . . . 73 F1
Harvey St
Bolton BL1 . . . . 143 A3
Bury BL8 . . . . 27 C3
Ince-in-M WN3 . . . . 151 B2
Rochdale OL12 . . . . 15 B2
Stockport SK1 . . . . 169 C1
Harvin Gr M34 . . . . 101 A2
Harwell Rd WA14 . . . . . 107 C1
Harwich Cl
Brinnington SK5 . . . . . . 112 C6
7 Manchester M19 . . . 99 B1
Harwin Cl OL12 . . . . . . 14 D3
Harwood Cl
Manchester M26 . . . . . . 25 F4
Harwood Ct
Manchester SK4 . . . . . . 110 E2
Salford M6 . . . . 81 B4
Harwood Dr BL8 . . . . . . 27 A1
Harwood Gdns OL10 . . . 29 D1
Harwood Gr 2B BL2 . . . . 25 B1
HARWOOD LEE 25 F5
Harwood Mdw BL2 . . . . 25 E5
Harwood Meadows Prim Sch
BL2 . . . . 25 F3
Harwood Park Prim Sch
OL10 . . . . 29 D1
Harwood Rd
Bury BL2, BL8 . . . . 26 C6
Manchester, Burnage M19 . 110 E6
Manchester, Heaton Mersey
SK4 . . . . 110 E2
Harwood St
Littleborough OL15 . . . . . 15 F5
Stockport SK4 . . . . 169 B3
Harwood Vale BL2 . . . . . 25 E3
Harwood Vale Ct BL2 . . . 25 E3
Harwood Wlk BL8 . . . . . 26 E7
Haseldine St WN4 . . . . . 72 F6
Haseley Cl
Little Lever M26 . . . . . . 43 B5
Poynton SK12 . . . . 133 E5
Tyldesley M29 . . . . 77 A8
Haselhurst Wlk 7 M23 . . 108 F2
Hasguard Cl BL1 . . . . . . 40 F8
Haskoll St BL6 . . . . 22 D1
Haslam Brow BL9 . . . . . 44 E8

Haslam Ct
Bolton BL3 . . . . 144 B1
Manchester M7 . . . . 63 D1
Haslam Hall Mews BL1 . . 40 E7
Haslam La BL2 . . . . 25 B5
Haslam Park Prim Sch
BL3 . . . . 144 B1
Haslam Rd SK3 . . . . . . 170 B2
Haslam St
Bolton BL3 . . . . 145 A1
Bury BL9 . . . . 141 A4
Middleton M24 . . . . 65 C7
Rochdale OL12 . . . . 139 A4
Haslemere Ave WA15 . . 129 C6
Haslemere Dr SK8 . . . . 123 A1
Haslemere Ind Est WN4 . 73 A8
Haslemere Rd
Manchester M20 . . . . . . 110 D6
Urmston M41 . . . . 95 B1
HASLINGDEN 1 B6
Haslingden High Sch BB4 . 1 B8
Haslington Rd M22 . . . . 121 E2
Hasper Ave M20 . . . . . . 110 A7
Hassall Ave M20 . . . . . 109 F7
Hassall St
Radcliffe M26 . . . . 44 E5
5 Stalybridge SK15 . . . 86 B1
Hassall Way 7 SK9 . . . . 131 E5
Hassop Ave M7 . . . . 81 A1
Hassop Cl M11 . . . . . . 160 B1
Hassop Rd SK5 . . . . . . 100 A1
Hastings Ave
Manchester M21 . . . . . . 109 A8
Prestwich M45 . . . . 63 B7
Hastings Cl
Bramhall SK8 . . . . 123 C2
Prestwich M45 . . . . 63 B7
Stockport SK1 . . . . 124 B7
Hastings Dr M41 . . . . . . 94 E3
Hastings Rd
Bolton BL1 . . . . 144 B4
Eccles M30 . . . . 79 A4
Prestwich M25 . . . . 63 C5
Haston Cl SK5 . . . . 169 C4
Hasty La
Altrincham WA15 . . . . . . 129 C5
Hale WA15 . . . . 129 E8
Wythenshawe WA15 . . . 129 F8
Hatchett Rd M22 . . . . . 121 E1
Hatchley St M13 . . . . . 164 A1
Hatchmere Cl
Altrincham WA15 . . . . . . 120 D6
Cheadle SK8 . . . . 122 F4
Hatfield Ave M19 . . . . . 110 F6
Hatfield Cl M13 . . . . 55 F4
Hatfield Rd BL1 . . . . . . 142 C1
Hatford Cl M29 . . . . 59 C1
Hathaway Cl SK8 . . . . . 131 B7
Hathaway Ct WN7 . . . . . 76 B6
Hathaway Dr BL1 . . . . . . 25 A5
Hathaway Gdns SK6 . . . 112 F3
Hathaway Rd BL9 . . . . . 45 A3
Hathaway Wlk WN3 . . . . 54 F3
Hatherleigh Wlk BL2 . . . 42 F6
Hatherley Rd M20 . . . . . 110 D6
HATHERLOW 113 A2
Hatherlow La SK7 . . . . . 124 D2
Hatherop Cl M30 . . . . . . 79 B1
Hathersage Ave M5, M6 . 154 A3
Hathersage Cres SK13 . . 171 B2
Hathersage Dr SK13 . . . 116 F8
Hathersage Rd M13 . . . . 98 D4
Hathersage St OL9 . . . . 152 C2
Hathersage Way 6 M34 . 112 B1
HATHERSHAW 66 E3
Hathershaw La OL8 . . . . 66 F3
Hatherton Ct M28 . . . . . 60 D5
Hatro Ct M41 . . . . 96 A1
Hatters Ct SK1 . . . . 170 C4
HATTERSLEY 102 E2
Hattersley Ctr The 2
SK14 . . . . 102 E2
Hattersley Ind Est SK14 . 102 E1
Hattersley Road E SK14 . 102 E2
Hattersley Road W SK14 . 102 C2
Hattersley Sta SK14 . . . 102 C1
Hattersley Wlk SK14 . . . 102 C3
Hatter St M4 . . . . 159 B2
Hatton Ave
Atherton M46 . . . . 58 D5
Salford M7 . . . . 158 A3
Hattonfold M33 . . . . . . 108 C1
Hatton Fold M46 . . . . . . 58 B3
Hatton Gr BL1 . . . . 25 A5
Hattons Ct M32 . . . . 96 C3
Hattons Rd M17 . . . . . . 96 B6
Hatton St
Adlington PR7 . . . . 20 F6
Manchester M12 . . . . . . 99 A3
Stockport SK1 . . . . 169 D1
Hatton Terr 24 SK16 . . . 166 B1
Hat Works Mus* SK4 . . 169 B1
HAUGH 32 C4
Haugh Farm OL16 . . . . . 32 C4
Haugh Fold OL16 . . . . . . 32 C4
Haugh Hill Rd OL4 . . . . . 49 E3
Haugh La OL16 . . . . 32 C4
Haugh Sq OL16 . . . . 32 C4
Haughton Cl SK6 . . . . . 113 A6
HAUGHTON DALE 113 B7
Haughton Dr M22 . . . . . 109 D1
HAUGHTON GREEN . . . 113 A4

Haughton Green Rd M34 113 B8
Haughton Hall Rd M34 .. 101 A3
Haughton St
 Denton M34.............. 100 F5
 Hyde SK14................ 167 B1
Havana Cl M11............ 160 C1
Have Ct M6................ 154 C4
Haveley Hey Prim Sch
 M22........................ 121 C4
Haveley Rd M22.......... 121 C5
Havelock Dr M7.......... 158 A4
Havelock St OL8 .... 153 C1
Havenbrook Gr BL0 ...... 11 A3
Haven Cl
 Hazel Grove SK7........ 124 C1
 Radcliffe M26............ 43 D5
 Uppermill OL4............ 68 D6
Haven Dr M43 .... 83 E2
Haven La OL4............. 49 E3
Havenscroft Ave M30 .... 95 D8
Havenside Cl OL4 .... 49 E3
Haven St M6.............. 154 B1
Haven The
 Altrincham WA15........ 119 F3
 1 Little Lever BL3 ..... 43 B3
Havenwood Rd WN1 ..... 37 B4
Haverbrook Cl WN3 ..... 54 E3
Havercroft Pk BL1 ...... 40 D8
Haverfield Rd M9 .... 64 E3
Haverford St M12....... 164 C2
Havergate Wlks SK2 .... 124 F5
Haversham Dr BL2 ...... 25 B2
Haversham Rd M8 .... 63 E2
Havers Rd M18 .... 99 B5
Haverty Prec WA12 ...... 99 B1
Havisham Cl BL6......... 40 B4
Hawarde Cl WA12........ 89 A4
Hawarden Ave M16 ...... 97 C2
Hawarden Rd WA14 ..... 119 D6
Hawarden St BL1 .... 24 E5
Haw Clough La OL3 ...... 69 C6
Hawdraw Gn SK2........ 124 E6
Hawes Ave
 Farnworth BL4............ 59 E8
 Manchester M14........ 110 E7
 Swinton M27............. 79 F6
Hawes Cl
 Bury BL8................. 27 B5
 Stockport SK2........... 124 A6
Hawes Cres WN4 .... 73 B5
Haweswater Ave
 Ince-in-M WN2.......... 56 B7
 Tyldesley M29........... 77 B7
Haweswater Cl M34 ..... 100 A2
Haweswater Cres BL9 ... 45 B5
Haweswater Dr M24 ...... 46 E2
Haweswater Mews 5
 M24 .... 46 E2
Hawick Dr M28 .... 78 D8
Hawick Gr OL10.......... 28 E1
Hawk Cl BL9.............. 141 B4
Hawker Ave BL3 .... 147 A3
Hawkeshead Rd M8 ..... 156 B2
Hawke St SK15........... 86 C1
HAWK GREEN............ 126 A3
Hawkhurst Ct WN7 ...... 76 B5
Hawkhurst Pk WN7 ...... 76 B5
Hawkhurst Rd M13...... 98 F3
Hawkhurst St WN7...... 76 B4
Hawkins Cl M9 .... 64 C1
Hawkins St SK5.......... 169 B4
Hawkins Way OL15....... 6 C1
HAWKLEY............... 55 A3
Hawkley Ave WN3....... 54 F2
Hawkley Brook Trad Est
 WN3 .... 54 E2
Hawkley Hall High Sch
 WN3 .... 55 C3
Hawk Rd M44............ 94 A3
Hawkridge Cl BL5....... 57 F6
Hawkridge Dr M23..... 108 F2
Hawkrigg Cl WN6....... 36 F7
HAWKSHAW.............. 10 C2
Hawkshaw Cl
 Hawkshaw BL8 .... 10 B3
 Wigan WN2.............. 38 A3
Hawkshaw Ct 9 M5..... 81 A1
Hawkshaw La BL8 ...... 10 B5
Hawkshaw St SK16...... 23 B5
Hawkshead Cl SK15..... 85 F4
Hawkshead Dr
 Bolton BL3............ 146 A3
 Middleton M24.......... 46 E1
 Royton OL2............. 48 C3
Hawkshead Fold SK13.. 104 E3
Hawkshead Rd
 Glossop SK13........... 104 E3
 Shaw OL2............... 149 A4
Hawksheath Cl BL7...... 8 E1
Hawksley Ind Est OL8 ... 66 C3
Hawksley St
 Horwich BL6............ 22 D2
 Oldham OL8............. 66 C3
Hawksmoor Dr OL2 ... 149 B4
Hawkstone Ave
 Droylsden M43.......... 84 C1
 Whitefield M45......... 62 D7
Hawkstone Cl BL2 .... 25 E3
Hawkswick Dr M23 ..... 109 A2
Hawkworth M29......... 77 B5
Hawk Yard OL3 .... 69 D5
Hawk Yard La OL3 ...... 69 D5
Hawley Dr WA15........ 129 B8
Hawley Gn OL12 .... 14 D2
Hawley La WA15........ 129 B8
Hawley St M19 .... 111 B8
Haworth Ave BL0........ 11 A2

Haworth Cl BL9........... 44 F6
Haworth Ct 8 M26...... 44 B3
Haworth Dr
 Bacup OL13............. 3 C8
 Stretford M32........... 96 A3
Haworth Rd M18........ 99 D4
Haworth St
 Bury BL8................. 26 F4
 Edgworth BL7............ 9 D5
 Hindley WN2............ 56 D6
 Oldham OL1............. 48 E1
 Radcliffe M26........... 44 B3
Haworth Wlk 3 M26.... 44 B3
Hawsworth Cl M15..... 163 B1
Hawthorn Ave
 Altrincham WA15...... 119 F8
 Bury BL8................ 27 C4
 Downall Green WN4 .... 72 D5
 Eccles M30............. 79 D3
 Edenfield BL0........... 1 D2
 Hindley WN2............ 57 A4
 Marple SK6............. 125 D6
 Newton-le-W WA12 .... 89 D3
 Orrell WN5.............. 53 F6
 Radcliffe M26........... 44 B1
 Ramsbottom BL0 .... 11 B3
 Standish WN1........... 37 B6
 Urmston M41............ 95 F1
 Walkden M28........... 60 E1
 Wigan WN5.............. 54 D6
 Wilmslow SK9.......... 137 A2
Hawthorn Bank
 Bolton BL2.............. 25 E4
 Glossop SK13.......... 171 C4
Hawthorn Cl
 Altrincham WA15...... 119 F7
 Billinge WN5............ 71 D5
 Tyldesley M29........... 59 D1
Hawthorn Cres
 Bury BL8................ 26 F7
 Oldham OL8............. 66 F2
 Ramsbottom BL0 .... 11 B3
Hawthornden 1 M20 .. 110 A3
Hawthorn Dr
 Irlam M44.............. 105 D5
 Manchester M19........ 110 F7
 Pendlebury M27......... 80 C7
 Salford M6.............. 80 B4
 Stalybridge SK15...... 101 F8
Hawthorne Ave
 Farnworth BL4.......... 60 B8
 Fowley Common WA3 ... 92 C4
 Horwich BL6............ 22 E1
**Hawthorne Ct PR6......... 20 F8
Hawthorne Gr
 1 Ashton-u-L OL7...... 84 F1
 Chadderton OL9....... 152 B4
 Leigh WN7.............. 75 E7
 Poynton SK12.......... 134 C4
 Romiley SK6........... 112 E4
Hawthorne La OL16 ..... 32 A3
Hawthorne Rd BL3 ..... 146 B4
Hawthorne St BL3 ..... 144 C1
Hawthorn Gn SK9...... 137 A7
Hawthorn Gr
 Bramhall SK7......... 132 C6
 Hollingworth SK14..... 103 D6
 Hyde SK14............. 167 A1
 Stockport SK4......... 168 B3
 Wilmslow SK9......... 137 B7
Hawthorn La
 Sale M33............... 107 D6
 Stretford M32........ 108 F8
 Wilmslow SK9......... 137 A7
Hawthorn Lo 3 SK3 ... 123 F4
Hawthorn Pk SK9....... 137 A7
Hawthorn Rd
 Altrincham WA15...... 119 E3
 Droylsden M43......... 84 C2
 Failsworth M40......... 65 F1
 Gatley SK8............ 122 A5
 Kearsley BL4........... 61 B5
 Manchester M14....... 110 F2
 Oldham OL8............. 66 B1
 Reddish M34........... 100 B4
 Rochdale OL11......... 29 E6
 Stretford M21, M32... 108 E8
 Westhoughton BL5 ..... 57 F7
Hawthorn Road S M43 .. 84 C2
Hawthorns Com Sch
 Denton M34............ 100 E5
 Manchester M34........ 84 C1
Hawthorn St
 Denton M34............ 100 E6
 Manchester M34........ 99 E5
 Wilmslow SK9......... 137 A6
Hawthorns The
 6 Atherton M46........ 58 D3
 Denton M34............ 100 D6
Hawthorn Terr
 10 Mossley SK15....... 68 C2
 Stockport SK4......... 168 B3
 Wilmslow SK9......... 137 A6
Hawthorn View
 Lindow End WA16 ..... 136 B2
 Wilmslow SK9.......... 137 A7
Hawthorn Wlk
 Littleborough OL15 ...... 15 F5
 3 Partington M31.... 105 E3
 Wilmslow SK9......... 137 A7
Hawthorpe Gr OL3 ...... 69 B8
Haxby Rd M18 .... 99 D3
Haxey Wlk BL6.......... 21 C7
Haybarn Rd SK2....... 121 B7
Hayburn Rd SK2........ 124 C8
Haycock Cl SK15........ 102 E7

Haycroft SK8............ 131 E8
Hayden St
 1 Glossop SK13....... 104 C1
 Manchester M40...... 157 A1
Haydn Ave M14.......... 98 B4
Haydn Fold SK13....... 115 D7
HAYDOCK................ 89 A8
Haydock Ave M3....... 107 B2
Haydock Cl M32......... 96 F4
Haydock Dr
 Altrincham WA15...... 120 B5
 Hazel Grove SK7....... 124 F2
 Worsley M28........... 78 B6
Haydock La
 Ashton-in-M WA11..... 72 E1
 Bolton BL7.............. 25 A8
Haydock Lane Ind Est
 WA11..................... 72 E1
Haydock Mews 3 M7.. 155 A2
Haydock Park Gdns SK7 73 B1
Haydock Park Racecourse
 WA12.................... 73 D1
Haydock St
 Ashton-in-M WN4 ...... 73 B2
 Bolton BL1............. 145 C4
 Newton-le-W WA12.... 89 A3
Haydock Wlk OL9...... 152 C3
Haye's Rd M44.......... 105 E5
Hayes Row WA3.......... 74 A1
Hayes St
 Leigh, Plank Lane WN7.. 75 A4
 Leigh, Westleigh WN7.. 75 E7
Hayeswater Circ 7 M41.. 95 C3
Hayeswater Rd M41..... 95 C3
Hayfell Rd WN3.......... 55 A1
Hayfield Ave
 Romiley SK6........... 113 A4
 Tyldesley M29........... 77 C6
Hayfield Cl
 Manchester M12...... 164 B3
 Middleton M24.......... 47 C3
 Oldham OL4............. 49 F4
 Ramsbottom BL8 .... 10 F1
Hayfield Rd
 New Mills SK22........ 127 E2
 Romiley SK6........... 113 A4
 Salford M6.............. 80 B4
Hayfield St M33........ 108 B5
Hayfield Wlk
 Altrincham WA15...... 120 C6
 1 Denton M34........ 113 A8
Haygrove Wlk 10 M9 .. 157 A4
Hay Ho OL4.............. 67 E8
Hayle Rd OL1............ 49 D4
Hayley St M12, M13..... 98 E4
Hayling Cl BL8........... 27 C6
Hayling Rd M33......... 107 E5
Haymaker Rise OL12 ... 15 D6
Hayman Ave WN7 .... 75 B2
Haymans Wlk M13 .... 163 B3
Haymarket St
 Bury BL9............... 140 B2
 Manchester M13...... 163 C1
Haymill Ave M38......... 60 A6
Haymond Cl M6.......... 81 A5
Haynes St
 Bolton BL3............. 146 C3
 Rochdale OL12.......... 14 C3
Haysbrook Ave M28...... 60 A4
Haysbrook Cl OL7........ 85 A7
Hayside Way BL9....... 140 C1
Haythorp Ave M22..... 121 E3
Hayward Ave BL3........ 43 C3
Hayward Gr WN6 .... 19 F2
Haywards Cl SK13..... 104 C3
Hayward St BL8......... 27 C3
Hayward Way 2 SK14.. 102 F3
Haywood Cl WA3....... 74 E1
Hazel Ave
 Ashton-u-L OL6........ 85 E6
 Bury BL9............... 141 B2
 Bury, Tottington BL8.... 27 A5
 Cheadle SK8........... 122 E5
 Kearsley M26........... 61 A8
 Manchester M16........ 97 D2
 Newhey OL16.......... 32 A3
 Pendlebury M27......... 80 A7
 Ramsbottom BL0 .... 11 B1
 Romiley SK6........... 113 D2
 Sale M33............... 108 B3
 Walkden M38........... 59 E5
 Westhoughton BL5 ..... 57 F7
 Wigan WN6.............. 37 A4
Hazel Cl
 Droylsden M43.......... 84 C2
 Marple SK6............. 125 D6
Hazel Ct 13 M16........ 97 D3
Hazeldean Cl 17 SK9.. 131 E1
Hazeldene BL5........... 57 D5
Hazel-Dene Cl BL9....... 44 F4
Hazeldene Rd M40....... 65 E1
Hazel Dr
 Gatley M22............ 131 A8
 Poynton SK12.......... 133 F3
 Stockport SK2......... 124 D6
Hazelfields M28......... 79 C7
Hazel Gr
 Chadderton OL9....... 152 B4
 Farnworth BL4.......... 60 B8
 Golborne WA3.......... 90 B8
 Leigh WN7.............. 75 E7
 Radcliffe M26........... 61 A8
 Salford M7............. 80 C2
 Urmston M41............ 95 C3

HAZEL GROVE......... 124 D2
Hazel Grove High Sch
 SK7...................... 133 C8
Hazel Grove Prim Sch
 SK7...................... 124 E3
Hazel Grove Sta SK7... 124 D2
Hazelhall Cl M28........ 79 B7
Hazel Hall La BL0 .... 11 B1
HAZELHURST
 Ashton-under-Lyne 85 F6
 Ramsbottom............ 11 B4
 Swinton.................. 79 B7
Hazelhurst Cl
 Bolton BL1............. 143 B2
 Ramsbottom BL0 .... 11 A4
Hazelhurst Com Prim Sch
 BL1...................... 11 A4
Hazelhurst Dr M24 ...... 46 F4
Hazelhurst Fold M28.... 79 C7
Hazelhurst Mews OL9 ... 65 F3
Hazelhurst Rd
 Ashton-u-L OL6........ 85 F6
 Stalybridge SK15...... 86 A4
 Swinton M28........... 79 C7
Hazel La OL8............. 66 D2
Hazelmere Ave M30.... 79 C4
Hazelmere Gdns M29.. 56 E4
Hazel Mount BL7......... 8 E2
Hazel Pear Cl BL6....... 21 F3
Hazel Rd
 Altrincham WA15...... 119 D6
 Atherton M46.......... 58 C4
 Cheadle SK8........... 123 B1
 Middleton M24.......... 47 B2
 Stalybridge SK15...... 86 C3
 Whitefield M45......... 63 B8
Hazel St
 Denton M34............ 100 E6
 Hazel Grove SK7....... 124 E3
 Ramsbottom BL0 .... 11 A4
**Hazel Terr M9........... 64 D4
Hazelton Cl WN7......... 75 E1
Hazel View SK6......... 125 F3
Hazel Wlk M31.......... 105 E3
Hazelwood OL9......... 65 E8
Hazelwood Ave 2...... 25 E3
Hazelwood Cl
 Glossop SK13.......... 104 A6
 Hyde SK14............. 102 A2
Hazelwood Ct M41...... 95 D3
Hazelwood Dr
 Bury BL9............... 27 F7
 Denton M34............ 100 F6
Hazelwood Rd
 Altrincham WA15...... 119 C2
 Bolton BL1............. 142 B2
 Hazel Grove SK7....... 124 F3
 Stockport SK2......... 124 A4
 Wigan WN1.............. 37 B4
 Wilmslow SK9.......... 137 D8
 Wythenshawe M22 ... 130 D8
Hazelwood St WA4 ...... 73 C4
Headen Ave WN5......... 54 B5
Headingley Dr M16...... 97 A3
Headingley Rd M14 .... 110 D7
Headingley Way BL1.... 147 A3
Headland Cl WA3........ 90 E6
Headlands Dr M25....... 63 A1
Headlands Rd SK7..... 123 F5
Headlands St OL12 ..... 14 E1
Heady Hill Ct OL10...... 29 A1
**HEADY HILL............ 29 A1
Heady Hill Ct OL10...... 29 A2
Heady Hill Rd OL10...... 29 A2
Heald Cl
 Altrincham WA14...... 119 C2
 Rochdale OL12.......... 14 C3
Heald Gr
 Altrincham WA14...... 119 C2
 Rochdale OL12.......... 14 C3
Heald Gr
 Gatley SK8............ 122 A1
 Manchester M14....... 98 B4
HEALD GREEN......... 131 B8
Heald Green Sta SK8.. 131 A8
Heald La OL15........... 16 A3
Heald Pl M14............ 98 B3
Heald Place Prim Sch
 M14...................... 98 B3
Heald Rd WA14......... 119 C2
Healds Gn OL1.......... 47 F3
**HEALDS GREEN......... 47 F3
Healdwood Rd SK6.... 113 C4
Healey Ave
 Heywood OL10.......... 29 E3
 Rochdale OL12.......... 14 D4
Healey Cl
 Salford M7.............. 81 C8
 Wythenshawe M23 ... 108 F2
Healey Dell Cotts OL12.. 14 B3
Healey Dell Nature Reserve *
 OL12.................... 14 B6
Healey Gr OL12 .... 14 C4
Healey Hall Farm OL12.. 14 C4
Healey Hall Mews OL12.. 14 E4
Healey La OL12 .... 14 E3
Healey Prim Sch OL12 .. 14 E3
Healey St OL16......... 139 D2
Healey Stones OL12..... 14 E4
Healing St BL1.......... 31 A5
Heanor Ave M34....... 113 A8
HEAP BRIDGE.......... 141 C1
Heap Bridge Prim Sch
 BL9 .... 28 D1

Heap Brow BL9 .... 28 D1
Heape St OL11........... 30 C1
Heapfold 8 OL12 .... 14 B2
Heaplands BL6.......... 10 F1
Heap Rd OL12 .... 13 D2
Heapriding Bsns Pk SK4 169 A1
Heaps Farm Ct SK15 .. 102 D7
Heap St
 Bolton BL3............. 147 B4
 Heywood BL9........... 28 D1
 Oldham M24............ 67 C7
 Radcliffe M26........... 44 B3
 Whitefield M45......... 62 F7
Heapworth Ave BL0 .. 138 B2
Heapy Cl BL8............ 26 F1
Heardman Ave 1 WN6.. 37 A1
Heath Ave
 Ramsbottom BL0 .... 11 B1
 Salford M7............. 81 C4
 Urmston M41............ 95 E3
Heathbank Rd
 Cheadle SK8........... 131 F8
 Manchester M9......... 64 C5
 Stockport SK3......... 123 B7
Heathbourne Rd OL13.. 3 C8
Heath Cl BL3............ 146 B2
Heathcote Ave SK4..... 168 C1
Heathcote Gdns SK6.. 113 E1
Heathcote Rd M18...... 99 C4
Heath Cres SK2........ 170 C1
Heather Ave
 Droylsden M43.......... 84 C2
 Irlam M44.............. 105 D6
 Shaw OL2............... 49 D8
Heather Bank
 Bury BL8................ 26 E7
 Littleborough OL15 ..... 16 D6
 Rawtenstall BB4 .... 1 F8
Heather Bank Cl SK13.. 116 A3
Heather Brae WA12.... 89 A4
Heather Brow SK15 ... 102 E7
Heather Cl
 Haslingden BB4 .... 1 A8
 Heywood OL10.......... 46 D8
 Horwich BL6............ 22 B4
 Oldham OL4............. 49 E1
Heather Ct SK14........ 114 D5
**Heatherdale Dr M8 .... 156 A4
Heatherfield
 Bolton BL1.............. 24 D5
 Edgworth BL7............ 9 E6
Heatherfield Ct SK9 .. 137 B8
Heather Gr
 Ashton-in-M WN4 ...... 73 E4
 Droylsden M43........ 100 B8
 Hollingworth SK14..... 103 D6
 Leigh WN7.............. 75 D7
 Wigan WN5.............. 54 E6
Heatherlands OL12...... 4 D4
Heather Lea M34...... 101 A2
Heatherlea Cl WN8...... 53 C7
Heather Rd WA14, WA15.. 119 E1
Heatherside
 Reddish SK5........... 100 A1
 Stalybridge SK5........ 86 D2
Heatherside Ave OL5... 68 E1
Heatherside Rd BL0... 138 C3
Heather St M11......... 83 B2
Heathers The SK2..... 124 B4
Heatherway
 Manchester M14....... 98 B4
 Sale M33............... 107 D5
Heather Way
 Diggle OL3.............. 51 C6
 Marple SK6............. 125 E4
Heather Wlk M31...... 105 E3
Heath Farm La M31 ... 106 B3
Heathfield
 Bolton BL2.............. 25 F3
 Eccles M28............. 78 F5
 Farnworth BL4.......... 41 C1
 Wilmslow SK9......... 137 A5
Heathfield Ave
 Bacup OL13............. 3 C8
 Denton M34............ 100 D1
 Gatley SK8............ 122 B5
 Manchester SK4....... 111 C5
Heathfield Cl M33.... 108 F4
Heathfield Dr
 Bolton BL3............. 146 B2
 Pendlebury M27......... 80 A7
 Tyldesley M29........... 59 D1
Heathfield Prim Sch
 BL3 .... 146 A2
Heathfield Rd
 Bacup OL13............. 3 C8
 Stockport SK2......... 170 C2
 Whitefield BL9, M45 .... 44 F3
Heathfields
 Altrincham WA15...... 119 C3
 Uppermill OL3.......... 69 C8
Heathfields Sq OL3..... 69 C8
Heathfield St M40...... 83 C5
Heath Gdns WN2........ 57 C3
Heath Hill Dr OL13 ...... 3 C8
Heath La
 Culcheth WA3........... 91 A1
 Golborne WA3.......... 90 F2
 Leigh WN7.............. 75 B5
Heathland WN8......... 53 B7
Heathlands Rd M7, M25.. 81 B8
Heathland Terr SK3.... 170 B3
Heathlea WN7........... 57 C2
Heathlea Cl BL1......... 24 E6

Heathlea Gdns WN2 . . . . 57 C2
Heathmoor Ave WA3 . . . . 90 D6
Heath Rd
Altrincham, Rosehill
WA14 . . . . 119 D2
Altrincham, Timperley
WA15 . . . . 119 F8
Ashton-in-M WN4 . . . . 73 C2
Glossop SK13 . . . . 104 D2
Stockport SK2, SK3 . . . . 170 C2
Wardle OL12 . . . . 15 C6
Heathside Gr M28 . . . . 60 E3
Heathside Park Rd SK3 . . . 122 F7
Heathside Rd
Cheadle SK3 . . . . 123 A7
Manchester M20 . . . . 110 D6
Heath St
Ashton-in-M WN4 . . . . 73 C2
Golborne WA3 . . . . 90 A8
Rochdale OL11 . . . . 139 A2
Salford M8 . . . . 155 C3
Heath The
Ashton-u-L OL7 . . . . 85 A7
Glossop SK13 . . . . 104 C3
Middleton M24 . . . . 65 B6
Heath View M7 . . . . 81 A8
Heathway Ave M11 . . . . 83 D2
Heathwood OL3 . . . . 69 C8
Heathwood Rd M19 . . . . 110 E4
HEATLEY 117 C5
Heatley Cl WA13 . . . . 117 A4
Heatley Gdns BL5 . . . . 39 F1
Heatley Rd OL16 . . . . 31 D6
Heatley Way 🟩 SK9 . . . . 131 D4
HEATON 144 A4
Heaton Ave
Bolton, Harwood Lee BL2 . . . 25 E5
Doffcocker BL1 . . . . 23 F1
Farnworth BL4 . . . . 60 C8
Little Lever BL3 . . . . 43 A4
Stockport SK7 . . . . 123 E3
HEATON CHAPEL 111 C6
Heaton Chapel Sta SK4 . 111 C5
Heaton Cl
Stockport SK4 . . . . 168 A3
Up Holland WN8 . . . . 53 A7
Whitefield BL9 . . . . 45 A5
Heaton Court Gdns BL1 . . 40 E7
Heaton Ct
Bury BL9 . . . . 44 E7
Prestwich M25 . . . . 63 C3
Sale M33 . . . . 108 C4
Stockport SK4 . . . . 168 B4
Heaton Dr BL9 . . . . 45 A5
Heaton Fold BL9 . . . . 44 E8
Heaton Grange Dr M9 . . . 144 A3
Heaton Hall ★ M25 . . . . 63 E5
Heaton La SK4 . . . . 169 B1
HEATON MERSEY 110 C5
Heaton Mersey Comm
Nature Reserve ★ SK4 . . 110 E3
HEATON MOOR 168 B4
Heaton Moor Rd SK4 . . . . . 168 B4
HEATON NORRIS 168 C2
HEATON PARK 63 D4
Heaton Park ★ M25 . . . . 63 E5
Heaton Park Metro Sta
M25 . . . . 63 C4
Heaton Park Prim Sch
M45 . . . . 63 B6
Heaton Park Rd M9 . . . . 64 A5
Heaton Park Road W M9 . 64 A5
Heaton Rd
Bolton BL6 . . . . 40 D6
Little Lever BL2 . . . . 43 B5
Manchester, Withington
M20 . . . . 110 C6
Stockport, Heaton Norris
SK4 . . . . 168 A3
Stockport SK4 . . . . 169 A3
Heatons Gr BL5 . . . . 40 A2
Heaton Sch Sch SK4 . . . 111 B5
Heaton St
Aspull WN2 . . . . 38 D5
Denton M34 . . . . 100 D3
Ince-in-M WN3 . . . . 151 B2
Middleton M24 . . . . 64 B7
Milnrow OL16 . . . . 32 A5
Prestwich M25 . . . . 63 C4
Salford M7 . . . . 155 B3
Standish WN1 . . . . 19 E1
Wigan WN1 . . . . 37 C2
Heaton Twrs SK4 . . . . 169 B2
HEAVILEY 124 A7
Heaviley Gr
Horwich BL6 . . . . 22 A5
Stockport SK2 . . . . 124 A6
Hebble Butt Cl OL16 . . . . 31 E6
Hebble Cl BL2 . . . . 25 B5
Hebburn Dr BL8 . . . . 27 C5
Hebden Ave
Fowley Common WA3 . . . . 92 B5
Romiley SK6 . . . . 113 A4
Salford M5, M6 . . . . 80 C3
Hebden Ct BL1 . . . . 145 B4
Hebden Dr SK13 . . . . 116 F8
Hebden Wlk 🟦 M15 . . . . . . 162 C1
Hebdon Cl WN4 . . . . 73 A5
Heber Pl 🔟 OL15 . . . . 16 B5
Heber St
Ince-in-M WN2 . . . . 151 C3
Radcliffe M26 . . . . 44 A3
Hebron St OL16 . . . . 49 A3
Hector Ave OL16 . . . . 31 B8

Hector Rd
Manchester M13 . . . . 98 F3
Wigan WN5 . . . . 36 D1
Heddles Ct WN7 . . . . 75 E4
Heddon Cl SK14 . . . . 110 E3
Heddon Wlk M8 . . . . 156 C2
Hedgelands Wlk 🟦 M33 . 107 C5
Hedgemead 🟧 WN6 . . . . 37 A1
Hedgerow Gdns WN6 . . . . 19 D1
Hedge Rows OL12 . . . . 4 C1
Hedgerows The SK14 . . . . . 102 A3
Hedges St M35 . . . . 84 A8
Hedley St BL1 . . . . 142 C2
Hedley Wlk 🟦 M8 . . . . 155 C3
Heeley St WN1 . . . . 37 B2
Heginbottom Cres OL 85 C5
Height Barn La OL13 . . . . 4 A8
Heights Ave OL12 . . . . 14 E2
Heights Ct OL12 . . . . 14 E2
Heights Ct OL12 . . . . 14 E1
Heights La
Chadderton OL1 . . . . 47 F2
Delph OL3 . . . . 50 E7
Rochdale OL12 . . . . 14 E1
Heights The
Horwich BL6 . . . . 22 D1
Tyldesley M29 . . . . 77 B8
Helena St M6 . . . . 80 C5
Helensville Ave M6 . . . . 80 F5
Helenswhite Wlk M13 . . . 163 B3
Helga St M40 . . . . 160 A4
Helias Cl M28 . . . . 59 F3
Hellidon Cl M12 . . . . 164 A2
Hell Nook WA3 . . . . 73 F1
Helmclough Way M28 . . . . . 78 B8
Helmet St M1, M12 . . . . 163 C4
Helmsdale M28 . . . . 60 C2
Helmsdale Ave BL3 . . . . 40 F6
Helmsdale Cl BL9 . . . . 44 E8
HELMSHORE 1 B7
Helmshore Ave OL4 . . . . 49 E3
Helmshore Ho OL2 . . . . 149 B4
Helmshore Prim Sch 🟦
BB4 . . . . 1 A7
Helmshore Rd
Haslingden BB4 . . . . 1 A7
Ramsbottom BL0, BL8, BB4 . . 1 A3
Helmshore Wlk M13 . . . . . 163 B3
Helmsman Way WN3 . . . . . . 150 B1
Helsby Cl OL4 . . . . 68 A6
Helsby Gdns BL1 . . . . 143 C4
Helsby Rd M33 . . . . 108 E2
Helsby Way
🟦 Handforth SK9 . . . . 131 D4
Wigan WN3 . . . . 54 C2
Helsby Wlk M12 . . . . 164 B4
Helston Cl
Bramhall SK7 . . . . 132 F7
Hattersley SK14 . . . . 102 D1
Irlam M44 . . . . 94 B2
Helston Dr OL2 . . . . 48 F4
Helston Gr SK8 . . . . 131 C8
Helston Way M29 . . . . 77 C8
Helston Wlk SK14 . . . . 102 D1
Helton Wlk M24 . . . . 46 C1
Helvellyn Dr M24 . . . . 46 D2
Helvellyn Rd WN5 . . . . 54 B7
Helvellyn Wlk 🟦 OL1 . . . . . 49 A1
Hembury Ave M19 . . . . 110 F6
Hembury Cl M24 . . . . 47 B2
Hemfield Cl WN2 . . . . 56 B8
Hemfield Ct WN2 . . . . 56 C8
Hemfield Rd WN2 . . . . 56 C8
Hemley Cl BL5 . . . . 57 E6
Hemlock Ave OL8 . . . . 66 E3
Hemming Dr M30 . . . . 79 E1
Hemmington Dr M9 . . . . . . 157 A3
Hemmons Rd M12 . . . . 99 B3
Hempcroft Rd WA15 . . . . . 120 D5
Hempshaw La SK1, SK2 . . 124 B7
Hemsby Cl BL3 . . . . 146 A4
Hemsley St S M9 . . . . 64 E1
Hemsley St M9 . . . . 64 E1
Hemswell Cl M6 . . . . 154 B4
Hemsworth Rd
Bolton BL1 . . . . 145 A4
Manchester M18 . . . . 99 D3
Henbury Dr SK6 . . . . 113 B6
Henbury La SK8 . . . . 131 F6
Henbury Rd SK9 . . . . 131 D4
Henbury St
Manchester M14 . . . . 98 A3
Stockport SK2 . . . . 124 B6
Henderson Ave 🟦 M27 . . 61 F1
Henderson St
Littleborough OL15 . . . . 16 A5
Manchester M19 . . . . 111 B8
Henderville St OL15 . . . . 16 A6
Hendham Cl SK7 . . . . 124 A2
Hendham Dr WA14 . . . . 119 B5
Hendham Vale M9 . . . . 156 C2
Hendham Vale Ind Pk
M8 . . . . 156 C3
Hendon Cl 🟦 SK9 . . . . 137 D8
Hendon Dr
Bury BL9 . . . . 44 F5
Cheadle SK3 . . . . 123 A7
Hendon Gr
Heywood OL10 . . . . 46 E7
Leigh WN7 . . . . 75 F8

Hendon Rd
Manchester M9 . . . . 64 D4
Wigan WN5 . . . . 54 E8
Hendon St WN7 . . . . 75 F8
Hendriff Pl 🟦 OL12 . . . . 14 F1
Henfield Wlk M22 . . . . 121 C3
Henfold Rd M29 . . . . 77 C7
Hengist St
Bolton BL2 . . . . 148 C3
Manchester M18 . . . . 99 D4
Henley Ave
Cheadle SK8 . . . . 122 F2
Irlam M44 . . . . 105 E6
Manchester M16 . . . . 97 B3
Henley Cl BL8 . . . . 44 B8
Henley Dr
Altrincham WA15 . . . . 119 F7
Ashton-u-L OL7 . . . . 84 F4
Henley Gr BL3 . . . . 147 A3
Henley Pl M19 . . . . 111 A6
Henley St
Aspull WN2 . . . . 38 B6
Chadderton OL9 . . . . 66 A4
Oldham OL1 . . . . 153 A4
🟦 Rochdale OL12 . . . . 14 F1
Henley Terr OL11 . . . . 139 B1
Henlow Wlk 🟦 M40 . . . . . . 65 D2
Henniker Rd BL3 . . . . 146 A2
Henniker St M27 . . . . 79 E6
Hennon St BL1 . . . . 143 A1
Henrietta St
Ashton-u-L OL6 . . . . 166 B4
Bolton BL3 . . . . 146 B4
Leigh WN7 . . . . 75 F5
Manchester M16 . . . . 161 C1
Henry Herman St BL3 . . . 146 A3
Henry Lee St BL3 . . . . 146 C3
Henry Park St WN1 . . . . 151 B3
Henry Sq OL6 . . . . 166 A2
Henry St
Bolton BL2 . . . . 148 A2
Denton M34 . . . . 113 B8
🟦 Droylsden M43 . . . . 84 A1
Eccles M30 . . . . 79 C1
Failsworth M35 . . . . 83 F7
Glossop SK13 . . . . 104 C1
Hyde SK14 . . . . 167 A2
Ince-in-M WN3 . . . . 55 E4
Leigh WN7 . . . . 76 A3
Littleborough OL15 . . . . 15 F3
Manchester M4 . . . . 159 A2
Manchester, Old Trafford
M16 . . . . 161 C1
Middleton M24 . . . . 64 F8
Prestwich M25 . . . . 63 C5
Ramsbottom BL0 . . . . 11 D7
Rochdale OL11 . . . . 139 C2
Stockport SK1 . . . . 124 B8
🟦 Tyldesley M29 . . . . 59 A1
Wardle OL12 . . . . 15 E4
🟥 Westhoughton BL5 . . . . . 39 E1
Henshall La WA14 . . . . 118 C6
Henshaw Ct M16 . . . . 97 B4
Henshaw La OL9 . . . . 65 F2
Henshaw St
Oldham OL1 . . . . 153 B3
Stretford M32 . . . . 96 D2
Henshaw Wlk
Bolton, Halliwell BL1 . . . . . . 143 B2
🟦 Manchester M13 . . . . . . 163 B3
Henson Gr WA15 . . . . 120 A4
Henthorn St OL2 . . . . 149 B2
Henton Wlk M40 . . . . 159 C4
Henty Cl M30 . . . . 79 B1
Henwick Hall Ave BL0 . . . 11 B4
Henwood Rd M20 . . . . 110 C5
Hepley Rd SK12 . . . . 134 A3
Hepple Cl SK4 . . . . 110 F3
Heppleton Rd M40 . . . . 65 D2
Hepple Wlk OL7 . . . . 84 E5
Hepton St OL1 . . . . 153 B4
Heptonstall Wlk M18 . . . 165 C1
Hepworth Cl WN3 . . . . 73 F2
Hepworth St SK14 . . . . 113 E7
HERALD GREEN 122 B2
Heraldic Ct M6 . . . . 81 A5
Herbert St
Bacup OL13 . . . . 3 D8
Chadderton OL9 . . . . 152 B3
Denton M34 . . . . 101 A4
Droylsden M43 . . . . 83 F1
Horwich BL6 . . . . 22 B4
Little Lever BL3 . . . . 43 B3
Oldham OL4 . . . . 49 D1
Prestwich M25 . . . . 62 F4
Radcliffe M26 . . . . 43 F5
Salford M8 . . . . 155 C1
Stockport SK3 . . . . 170 A3
Stretford M32 . . . . 96 D2
Westhoughton BL5 . . . . 39 E2
Wigan WN3 . . . . 150 B8
Hereford Cl
Ashton-in-M WN4 . . . . 73 C2
Ashton-u-L OL6 . . . . 85 D7
Shaw OL2 . . . . 149 B3
Hereford Cres BL3 . . . . 43 A4
Hereford Dr
Bury BL9 . . . . 44 F8
Handforth SK9 . . . . 131 E3
Manchester M25 . . . . 63 C2
Swinton M27 . . . . 79 F6
Hereford Gr
Up Holland WN8 . . . . 53 B6
Urmston M41 . . . . 95 C2
Hereford Rd
Bolton BL1 . . . . 144 B4
Brinnington SK5 . . . . 112 C5

Hereford Rd continued
Cheadle SK8 . . . . 123 A4
Hindley WN2 . . . . 56 F6
Salford M30 . . . . 80 A5
Hereford St
Bolton BL1 . . . . 143 C2
Oldham OL9 . . . . 152 C1
🔟 Rochdale OL11 . . . . 31 A5
Sale M33 . . . . 108 B4
Hereford Way
Middleton M24 . . . . 47 C2
Stalybridge SK15 . . . . 102 D7
Hereford Wlk
🟦 Denton M34 . . . . 100 F1
Romiley SK6 . . . . 113 A1
Herevale Grange M28 . . . . 78 B7
Herevale Hall Dr BL0 . . . . . 11 B4
Heristone Ave M34 . . . . . . 100 F3
Heritage Gdns M20 . . . . . . 110 B2
Heritage Ho M3 . . . . 162 B4
Heritage Wharf OL7 . . . . . . 166 A1
Herle Dr M22 . . . . 121 C1
Hermitage Ave SK6 . . . . . . 113 F2
Hermitage Cl WN6 . . . . 35 F3
Hermitage Ct WA15 . . . . . . 120 A3
Hermitage Gdns SK6 . . . . 113 F2
Hermitage Green La WA2,
WA12 . . . . 89 F1
Hermitage Rd
Altrincham WA15 . . . . 120 A3
Manchester M8 . . . . 64 A1
Hermon Ave OL8 . . . . 66 E4
Herne St M11 . . . . 165 A4
Heron Ave
Dukinfield SK16 . . . . 101 E7
Farnworth BL4 . . . . 59 F7
Heron Cl SK13 . . . . 116 F8
Heron Ct
Salford M6 . . . . 80 B3
Stockport SK3 . . . . 170 B3
Herondale Cl M40 . . . . 83 B5
Heron Dr
Droylsden M34 . . . . 84 C1
Irlam M44 . . . . 94 A3
Poynton SK12 . . . . 133 A3
Wigan WN3 . . . . 54 E2
Heron La OL5 . . . . 68 D3
Heron Pl WN5 . . . . 54 C8
Heron St
Manchester M15 . . . . 162 B1
Oldham OL8 . . . . 66 D3
Stockport SK4 . . . . 170 A3
Swinton M27 . . . . 62 A1
Heron's Way BL2 . . . . 148 A2
Herons Wharf WN6 . . . . 35 D7
Heron View SK13 . . . . 115 F8
Herries St OL6 . . . . 85 D6
Herristone Rd M8 . . . . 64 A2
Herrod Ave SK4 . . . . 111 E5
Herschel St M40 . . . . 83 A8
Hersey St M6 . . . . 154 B2
Hersham Wlk 🟦 M9 . . . . . 157 B4
Hertford Dr M29 . . . . 59 A3
Hertford Gr M44 . . . . 105 C6
Hertford Rd M9 . . . . 157 C3
Hertfordshire Park Cl
OL2 . . . . 149 B4
Hertford St OL7 . . . . 166 A1
Hesford Ave M9 . . . . 157 C3
Hesketh Ave
Bolton BL1 . . . . 24 F5
Manchester M20 . . . . 110 A3
Shaw OL2 . . . . 149 B1
Hesketh Cl
Atherton M46 . . . . 58 C4
🟦 Manchester M20 . . . . . 110 A3
Hesketh Dr WN6 . . . . 19 A2
Hesketh Fletcher CE High
Sch M46 . . . . 58 C4
Hesketh Manor M46 . . . . . . 58 C3
Hesketh Meadow La WA3 . 90 F8
Hesketh Rd
Rochdale OL16 . . . . 31 C7
Sale M33 . . . . 107 F3
Hesketh St
Atherton M46 . . . . 58 C4
Leigh WN7 . . . . 75 D5
Stockport SK4 . . . . 169 B3
Wigan WN5 . . . . 54 F7
Hesketh Wlk
🟦 Farnworth BL4 . . . . 60 D8
Middleton M24 . . . . 46 E2
Hesnall Cl WA3 . . . . 92 C8
Hessel St M50 . . . . 154 A1
Hester Wlk 🟦 M15 . . . . . . 162 F1
Heston Ave M13 . . . . 98 F2
Heston Dr M41 . . . . 95 C3
Heswall Ave
Culcheth WA3 . . . . 91 E4
Manchester M20 . . . . 110 B2
Heswall Dr BL8 . . . . 26 F5
Heswall Rd SK5 . . . . 99 F1
Hethering ton Wlk M12 . . 99 A4
Hethorn St M40 . . . . 83 C5
Hetton Ave M13 . . . . 98 E2
Heversham Ave OL2 . . . . . . 49 D7
Heversham Wlk M18 . . . . 165 C2
Hewart Cl M40 . . . . 159 C4
Hewart Dr BL9 . . . . 141 C3
Hewitt Ave M34 . . . . 99 F3
Hewitt Bsns Pk WN5 . . . . . . 53 F4
Hewitt St M15 . . . . 162 C3
Hewlett Rd M21 . . . . 97 A1
Hewlett St
Bolton BL2 . . . . 148 A3
Westhoughton BL5 . . . . 57 B7
Wigan WN1 . . . . 150 C4

Hexham Ave
Bolton BL1 . . . . 23 F1
Wigan WN3 . . . . 54 F4
Hexham Cl
Atherton M46 . . . . 58 E4
Chadderton OL9 . . . . 152 D3
Shaw OL2 . . . . 149 B3
Stockport SK2 . . . . 124 E5
Hexham Rd M18 . . . . 99 C3
Hexon Cl M6 . . . . 154 B3
Hexworth Wlk SK7 . . . . 124 A2
Hey Bottom La OL12 . . . . . . 15 A6
Heybrook Rd M45 . . . . 63 C8
Heybrook Prim Sch OL12 . 15 A1
Heybrook Rd M23 . . . . 121 B5
Heybrook St OL16 . . . . 31 B6
Heybrook Wlk M45 . . . . 63 C8
Heybury Cl M11 . . . . 164 C4
Hey Cres OL4 . . . . 68 B6
Hey Croft M45 . . . . 62 C7
Heycrofts View BL0 . . . . 1 E3
Heyden Bank 🟨 SK13 . . 171 A2
Heyden Fold 🟧 SK13 . . . . 171 A2
Heyden Terr 🟨 SK13 . . . . 171 A2
Heyes Ave WA15 . . . . 120 B7
Heyes Dr WA15 . . . . 120 B7
Heyes La
Alderley Edge SK9 . . . . 137 B3
Sale WA15 . . . . 120 B8
Heyes Lane Jun & Inf Schs
WA15 . . . . 120 B8
Heyes Leigh WA15 . . . . 120 B7
Heyes Rd WN5 . . . . 53 E6
Heyes St WN6 . . . . 35 C7
Heyes Terr WA15 . . . . 120 B8
Hey Flake La OL3 . . . . 50 E7
Heyford Ave M40 . . . . 65 D2
Heyford Rd WN5 . . . . 54 D8
Hey Head Ave BB4 . . . . 3 A8
Hey Head La OL15 . . . . 6 B1
HEYHEADS 86 E7
Heyheads New Rd SK15 . 86 E7
Hey Hill Cl OL2 . . . . 149 A1
Hey House Mews BL8 . . . . 10 F4
Heyland Rd M23 . . . . 121 A6
Heylee OL7 . . . . 100 F8
Heyridge Dr M22 . . . . 109 D1
HEYROD 86 C4
Heyrod St
Manchester M1 . . . . 163 C4
Mossley SK15 . . . . 86 D5
Heyrose Wlk 🔞 M15 . . . . 162 A2
Heys Ave
Romiley SK6 . . . . 113 E3
Swinton M27 . . . . 61 D2
Wythenshawe M23 . . . . 109 A1
Heysbank Rd SK12 . . . . . . 135 D5
Heys Cl OL16 . . . . 32 B5
Heys Close N M27 . . . . 61 C2
Heyscroft Rd
Manchester, Withington
M20 . . . . 110 C6
Stockport, Heaton Mersey
SK4 . . . . 168 A2
Heys Farm Cotts SK6 . . . 113 E3
Heysham Ave M20 . . . . 109 F2
Heysham Rd WN5 . . . . 54 B7
Heyshaw Wlk M23 . . . . 108 F1
Hey Shoot La WA3 . . . . 92 C5
HEYSIDE 49 A4
Heyside OL2 . . . . 49 A3
Heyside Ave OL2 . . . . 49 A3
Heyside Cl SK15 . . . . 86 E6
Heys La
Heywood OL10 . . . . 29 A1
Romiley SK6 . . . . 113 E3
Heys Prim Sch The 🟦
OL6 . . . . 85 D3
Heys Rd
Ashton-u-L OL6 . . . . 85 D3
Prestwich M25 . . . . 63 B5
Heys St St BL8 . . . . 140 A2
Hey St
Ince-in-M WN3 . . . . 55 F3
Rochdale OL16 . . . . 31 B8
Heys The
Ashton-u-L OL6 . . . . 85 D3
Prestwich M25 . . . . 63 B5
Reddish SK5 . . . . 100 A1
Heys View M25 . . . . 63 B4
Heythrop Cl M45 . . . . 44 E1
Hey Top OL3 . . . . 69 D3
Heyward Ho M46 . . . . 58 C3
Hey-with-Zion Prim Sch
OL4 . . . . 67 E7
HEYWOOD 29 F2
Heywood Ave
Golborne WA3 . . . . 74 B1
Oldham OL4 . . . . 68 A8
Swinton M27 . . . . 62 B2
Heywood Cl SK9 . . . . 137 B2
Heywood Com High Sch
OL10 . . . . 28 E1
Heywood Ct M25 . . . . 63 B7
Heywood Distribution Pk BL9,
OL10 . . . . 45 F8
Heywood Fold Rd OL4 . . . . 67 F7
Heywood Gdns
Bolton BL3 . . . . 147 B4
Golborne WA3 . . . . 74 B1
Prestwich M25 . . . . 63 B4
Heywood Hall Rd OL10 . . 29 D3
Heywood Ho
Oldham OL3 . . . . 153 C1
🟦 Salford M6 . . . . 80 C3
Heywood La OL4 . . . . 68 A7

Hey–Hil 219

Heywood Old Rd M24,
OL10 . . . . 46 B3
Heywood Park View BL3 147 B4
Heywood Rd
Alderley Edge SK9 . . . . 137 B2
Prestwich M25 . . . . 63 C7
Rochdale OL11 . . . . 30 C1
Sale M33 . . . . 108 B3
Heywood's Hollow BL1 . . 143 C3
Heywood Sports Complex
OL10 . . . . 29 C3
Heywood St
Bolton BL1 . . . . 145 C4
Bury BL9 . . . . 141 A2
Failsworth M35 . . . . 83 D7
Little Lever BL3 . . . . 43 B3
Manchester M8 . . . . 156 A2
Oldham OL4 . . . . 67 E8
Swinton M27 . . . . 79 E8
Heywood Sta★ OL10 . . . . 29 E1
Heywood Way M6 . . . . 154 C3
Heyworth Ave SK6 . . . . 113 D3
Heyworth St 4 M5 . . . . 154 B1
Hibbert Ave
Denton M34 . . . . 100 E5
Hyde SK14 . . . . 167 B1
Hibbert Cres M35 . . . . 84 A6
Hibbert La SK6 . . . . 125 F5
Hibbert St
Bolton BL1 . . . . 143 C2
Manchester M14 . . . . 98 C3
Oldham OL4 . . . . 67 E7
Reddish SK4, SK5 . . . . 111 E5
Hibernia St BL3 . . . . 144 C1
Hibernia Way M32 . . . . 96 A5
Hibson Ave OL12 . . . . 13 E2
Hibson Cl OL12 . . . . 15 C6
Hic Bibi, Copull Nature
Reserve★ WN1 . . . . 19 F5
Hic Bibi La PR7 . . . . 19 E6
Hickenfield Rd SK14 . . . . 101 F5
Hicken Pl SK14 . . . . 101 F5
Hickton Dr WA14 . . . . 119 B6
Hieland Rd WN1 . . . . 37 E2
Higgingshaw La OL2 . . . . 49 A2
HIGGINSHAW 49 A2
Higginshaw Rd OL1 . . . . 67 A8
Higginson Rd SK5 . . . . 111 E8
Higginson St WN7 . . . . 76 A5
Higgs Cl OL4 . . . . 67 D7
Higham Cl OL2 . . . . 149 A1
Higham La SK14 . . . . 114 A7
Higham St SK8 . . . . 123 A1
Higham View M6 . . . . 81 A3
High Ash Gr M34 . . . . 100 D7
High Ave BL2 . . . . 42 E7
Highbank SK13 . . . . 103 F7
High Bank
Altrincham WA14 . . . . 119 D5
Bolton BL7 . . . . 24 F7
Manchester M18 . . . . 99 E5
Over Hulton M46 . . . . 59 A6
High Bank Ave SK15 . . . . 102 D7
High Bank Cl M44 . . . . 105 D6
Highbank Cres OL4 . . . . 68 E5
High Bank Cres M25 . . . . 63 C3
Highbank Dr M20 . . . . 122 B8
High Bank Gr M25 . . . . 63 C3
High Bank Grange BL6 . . . 40 B8
High Bank La BL6 . . . . 40 B8
Highbank Private Hospl
BL8 . . . . 26 F4
Highbank Rd
Glossop SK13 . . . . 116 F7
Newhey OL16 . . . . 32 C4
High Bank Rd
Droylsden M43 . . . . 99 F8
Hyde SK14 . . . . 167 C3
Pendlebury M27 . . . . 80 B7
Whitefield BL9 . . . . 44 F3
High Bank Side SK1 . . . . 169 C1
High Bank St BL2 . . . . 148 C3
High Barn Cl OL11 . . . . 139 B1
High Barn La OL12 . . . . 4 C3
High Barn Rd
Middleton M24 . . . . 65 A7
Royton OL2 . . . . 48 F4
High Barn St OL2 . . . . 48 E4
High Beeches BL2 . . . . 43 B5
High Beeches Cres WN4 . . 73 A6
High Bent Ave SK8 . . . . 132 A6
Highbridge Cl BL2 . . . . 43 A6
Highbrook Gr 14 BL1 . . . . 143 B1
High Brow M38 . . . . 59 E3
Highbury SK4 . . . . 110 F2
Highbury Ave
Irlam M44 . . . . 94 A1
Urmston M41 . . . . 94 E2
Highbury Cl BL5 . . . . 57 D6
Highbury Rd
Manchester M16 . . . . 97 E1
Reddish SK4 . . . . 111 C6
Highbury Way OL2 . . . . 48 D6
Highclere Ave M7, M8 . . . 155 C2
Highclere Rd M8 . . . . 63 F2
Highcliffe Ct WN6 . . . . 36 F7
Highcliffe Rd M9 . . . . 64 A3
Highclove La M28 . . . . 77 F5
High Crest Ave SK8 . . . . 121 F5
Highcrest Gr M29 . . . . 59 D1
Highcroft
Bolton BL1 . . . . 25 A3
Hyde SK14 . . . . 113 F6
Highcroft Ave M20 . . . . 109 E4
High Croft Cl SK16 . . . . 102 A8
Highcroft Rd SK6 . . . . 113 C3
Highcroft Way OL12 . . . . 14 F4
HIGH CROMPTON 48 F8
Highdales Rd M23 . . . . 121 B5
Highdown Wlk 26 M9 . . . 157 B4
High Elm Dr WA15 . . . . 129 C8
High Elm Rd WA15 . . . . 129 D7
High Elms SK8 . . . . 132 B5
Higher Ainsworth Rd M26 43 E7
Higher Ardwick M12 . . . . 163 C3
Higher Arthurs OL3 . . . . 69 B6
Higher Bank Rd OL15 . . . . 16 A3
Higher Barlow Row SK1 . 170 C4
Higher Barn BL6 . . . . 22 F3
Higher Barn Rd SK13 . . . . 171 C4
HIGHER BARROWSHAW . . . 49 D2
Higher Bents La SK6 . . . . 113 A3
HIGHER BLACKLEY 64 B5
Higher Blue Bell Cotts
BL5 . . . . 39 C4
HIGHER BOARSGREAVE . . . 3 A6
HIGHER BOARSHAW 47 C2
Higher Bridge St BL1 . . . . 145 C4
Higherbrook Cl BL6 . . . . 22 D1
HIGHER BROUGHTON 155 A3
Higher Bury St SK4 . . . . 169 A2
Higher Calderbrook OL15 . 6 C1
Higher Calderbrook Rd
OL15 . . . . 6 C2
Higher Cambridge St
M15 . . . . 163 A2
Higher Carr La OL3 . . . . 69 B7
Higher Chatham St M15 . 163 A2
Higher Cleggswood Ave
OL15 . . . . 16 A3
Higherclough Cl BL3 . . . . 146 A4
Higher Count Hill OL4 . . . 49 E2
Higher Croft
Eccles M30 . . . . 95 C8
Whitefield M45 . . . . 62 C6
Higher Crossbank OL4 . . . 67 F8
Higher Cross La OL3 . . . . 69 C8
Higher Damshead BL5 . . . 57 F8
Higher Darcy St BL2 . . . . 148 C1
Higher Dean St M26 . . . . 43 E3
HIGHER DINTING 104 A2
Higher Dinting SK13 . . . . 104 A2
HIGHER DISLEY 135 E4
Higher Downs WA14 . . . . 119 C3
Higher Drake Mdw BL5 . . . 57 E5
Higher Dunscar BL7 . . . . 8 E1
HIGHER END 53 D3
Higher Failsworth Prim Sch
M35 . . . . 84 A8
Higher Fold M24 . . . . 47 B3
Higher Fold La BL0 . . . . 11 E7
HIGHER FOLDS 76 E6
Higher Folds Enterprise Ctr
WN7 . . . . 76 E6
Higher Folds Prim Sch
WN7 . . . . 76 D7
Higher Fullwood OL1 . . . . 49 D4
Higher Gn
10 Ashton-u-L OL6 . . . . 85 D4
Ashton-u-L OL6 . . . . 166 C4
HIGHER GREEN 77 C5
Higher Green La M29 . . . . 77 C6
HIGHER HARTSHEAD 67 F2
Higher Henry St SK14 . . . . 167 B1
Higher Hillgate SK1, SK2 . 170 C4
Higher House Cl OL9 . . . . 66 A4
HIGHER HURST 85 E5
HIGHER INCE 151 C4
Higher Kinders OL3 . . . . 69 C6
Higher Knowles BL6 . . . . 22 E2
Higher La
Aspull WN2 . . . . 38 A4
Disley SK12 . . . . 135 E1
Lymm WA13 . . . . 117 B1
Up Holland WN8 . . . . 53 C7
Whitefield M45 . . . . 62 E8
Higher Lane Prim Sch
M45 . . . . 62 F7
Higher Lime Rd OL8 . . . . 84 C8
Higher Lo OL11 . . . . 13 D2
Higher Lomax La OL10 . . . 29 A3
Higher Lydgate Pk OL4 . . . 68 C6
Higher Market St BL4 . . . . 60 E8
Higher Mdws M19 . . . . 111 C8
Higher Moulding BL9 . . . . 28 E5
Higher Newtons OL5 . . . . 68 D2
Higher Noon Sun SK22 . . . 127 F2
Higher Openshaw Com Sch
M11 . . . . 99 D8
Higher Ormond St M13,
M15 . . . . 163 A2
Higher Oswald St 2 M4 . 159 A2
Higher Park OL2 . . . . 32 C2
Higher Pit La M26 . . . . 43 E8
HIGHER POYNTON 134 B2
Higher Rd M41 . . . . 95 E2
Higher Ridings BL7 . . . . 24 F7
Higher Rise OL2 . . . . 32 A1
Higher Row BL9 . . . . 141 B3
Higher Shady La BL7 . . . . 25 C7
Higher Shore Rd OL15 . . . . 15 F7
Higher Southfield BL5 . . . . 57 E7
Higher Sq SK13 . . . . 104 A7
HIGHER SUMMERSEAT . . . 11 B1
Higher Summerseat BL0 . 11 B2
Higher Swan La BL3 . . . . 147 A3
Higher Tame St SK15 . . . . 86 B2
Higher Turf La OL4 . . . . 50 B1
Higher Turf Pk OL2 . . . . 48 E3
Higher View WN8 . . . . 53 C6
Higher Wharf St OL6,
OL7 . . . . 166 B2
Higher Wheat La OL16 . . . 31 C8
HIGHER WOODHILL 27 E6
Higher Wood St M24 . . . . 46 F1
Higher York St M13 . . . . 163 B2
HIGHFIELD
Farnworth 59 F8
Wigan 54 D4
Highfield
Gatley SK8 . . . . 122 C3
Sale M33 . . . . 108 C3
Wigan WN3 . . . . 54 D4
High Field WA14 . . . . 118 B2
Highfield Ave
Atherton M46 . . . . 58 E5
Bolton BL2 . . . . 26 A3
Boothstown M28 . . . . 77 F7
Golborne WA3 . . . . 89 F8
Heywood OL10 . . . . 29 A2
Leigh WN7 . . . . 76 C3
Radcliffe M26 . . . . 44 C1
Romiley SK6 . . . . 112 F2
Sale M33 . . . . 108 C3
Shevington WN6 . . . . 36 A6
Wigan WN1 . . . . 37 E1
Highfield Cl
Adlington PR6 . . . . 21 A7
Dukinfield SK14 . . . . 101 F6
Stockport SK3 . . . . 123 F4
Stretford M32 . . . . 108 C8
Highfield Cres SK9 . . . . 131 C1
Highfield Ct
Farnworth BL4 . . . . 60 B7
Mottram in L SK14 . . . . 103 A4
Highfield Ctry Pk Nature
Reserve★ M19 . . . . 111 C8
Highfield Dr
Eccles M30 . . . . 79 D3
Farnworth BL4 . . . . 60 A7
Middleton M24 . . . . 64 F7
Mossley OL5 . . . . 86 C8
Pendlebury M27 . . . . 80 C7
Royton OL2 . . . . 48 E2
Standish WN6 . . . . 36 F7
4 Urmston M41 . . . . 95 C3
Highfield Est SK9 . . . . 131 C1
Highfield Gdns
Hollingworth SK14 . . . . 103 D5
Hyde SK14 . . . . 167 C3
Highfield Glen OL6 . . . . 85 F5
Highfield Gr WN2 . . . . 38 C5
Highfield Grange Ave
WN3 . . . . 54 E2
Highfield Ho
5 Farnworth BL4 . . . . 59 F8
Stockport SK3 . . . . 170 C1
Highfield Hospl (Private) The
OL11 . . . . 139 B1
Highfield Ind Est OL9 . . . 153 A3
Highfield La
Town of Lowton WA3 . . . . 90 C5
Whitefield M45 . . . . 44 F3
Highfield Mdw OL5 . . . . 86 C8
Highfield Park Rd SK6 . . . 112 F3
Highfield Parkway SK7 . . 132 D4
Highfield Pk SK4 . . . . 110 F2
Highfield Pl
Prestwich M25 . . . . 63 A5
Reddish M18 . . . . 99 F4
Highfield Prim Sch
Farnworth BL4 . . . . 60 A8
Urmston M41 . . . . 95 F2
Highfield Range M18 . . . . 99 F4
Highfield Rd
Adlington PR6 . . . . 21 A7
Altrincham WA15 . . . . 120 B5
Altrincham, Well Green
WA15 . . . . 120 A3
Blackrod BL6 . . . . 21 E1
Bolton BL1 . . . . 142 B2
Cheadle SK8 . . . . 122 F1
Eccles M30 . . . . 79 D4
Edenfield BL0 . . . . 1 D3
Farnworth BL4 . . . . 60 A8
Glossop SK13 . . . . 116 D8
Hazel Grove SK7 . . . . 125 A2
Hindley WN2 . . . . 56 D7
10 Marple SK6 . . . . 125 F6
Mellor SK6 . . . . 126 B6
Milnrow OL16 . . . . 32 A6
Poynton SK12 . . . . 133 A4
Prestwich M25 . . . . 63 A5
Reddish M19 . . . . 99 C1
Rochdale OL11 . . . . 13 E1
Salford M6 . . . . 154 C2
Stockport SK7 . . . . 123 F3
Stretford M32 . . . . 108 C8
Walkden M38 . . . . 59 F5
Highfield Road N PR6 . . . 21 A8
Highfield St Matthews CE
Prim Sch WN3 . . . . 54 C4
Highfield St
Denton M34 . . . . 100 E5
Dukinfield SK16 . . . . 166 B1
Kearsley BL4 . . . . 61 A6
Middleton M24 . . . . 65 B8
Oldham OL9 . . . . 153 A3
Salford M7, M8 . . . . 155 C3
2 Stockport SK3 . . . . 123 C8
Highfield Street W SK16 . 166 B1
Highfield Terr
Ashton-u-L OL7 . . . . 85 A7
Manchester M9 . . . . 157 A4
Highgate
Altrincham WA14 . . . . 119 B3
Bolton BL3 . . . . 40 C2
Highgate Ave M41 . . . . 95 A4
Highgate Cres
Appley Bridge WN6 . . . . 35 E7
Manchester M18 . . . . 99 D3
Highgate Ctr 4 SK6 . . . . 112 F3
Highgate Dr
Royton OL2 . . . . 48 C7
Highgate Dr continued
Walkden M38 . . . . 59 E5
Highgate Ho 7 OL8 . . . . 66 D2
Highgate La
Walkden M38 . . . . 59 E5
Whitworth OL12 . . . . 14 C5
Highgate Rd
Altrincham WA14 . . . . 119 B4
Up Holland WN8 . . . . 53 B7
High Gates M33 . . . . 108 E5
Highgrove WA15 . . . . 108 A1
Highgrove Cl BL1 . . . . 143 C3
Highgrove Mews 2 SK9 . 137 A6
High Grove Rd
Cheadle SK8 . . . . 122 C5
Uppermill OL4 . . . . 68 E5
Highgrove The BL1 . . . . 23 D1
High Hill Rd SK22 . . . . 127 D1
High Hurst Cl M24 . . . . 64 C7
High Knowls OL4 . . . . 68 A4
High La
Broadbottom SK13 . . . . 115 E7
Manchester M21 . . . . 109 B8
Romiley SK6 . . . . 113 B4
Highland Ave SK6 . . . . 113 A2
Highland Lo WN6 . . . . 19 D1
Highland Rd
Bolton BL7 . . . . 25 C8
Horwich BL6 . . . . 22 E1
Highlands
Littleborough OL15 . . . . 16 A3
Royton OL2 . . . . 48 C3
Highlands Dr SK2 . . . . 124 F6
Highlands Rd
Hazel Grove SK2 . . . . 124 F6
Rochdale OL11 . . . . 29 E5
Royton OL2 . . . . 48 C3
Shaw OL2 . . . . 149 A4
Highlands The 3 OL5 . . . . 68 C1
Highland View 1 OL5 . . . 68 C2
Highland Wlk M35 . . . . 83 D6
HIGH LANE 134 E8
High Lane Prim Sch SK6 134 F8
High Lawn Prim Sch BL1 . 24 E6
High Lea
Adlington PR6 . . . . 21 A8
Cheadle SK8 . . . . 122 C5
High Lee Ho M33 . . . . 108 D4
High Lee La OL4 . . . . 50 B4
High Legh Rd M11 . . . . 99 D8
High Level Rd OL11 . . . . 31 A6
Highmarsh Cres WA12 . . . 89 B4
High Marsh Cres M20 . . . 109 F5
High Mdw 2 SK8 . . . . 131 E8
High Mdws
Bolton BL7 . . . . 25 B8
Glossop SK13 . . . . 116 B7
Romiley SK6 . . . . 113 C3
Highmeadow
Radcliffe M26 . . . . 43 F1
Up Holland WN8 . . . . 53 A6
Highmead St M18 . . . . 99 D5
Highmead Wlk M16 . . . . 162 A1
High Moor Cres OL4 . . . . 49 E1
High Moor La WN6 . . . . 18 B4
High Moor View OL4 . . . . 49 E1
Highmore Dr M9 . . . . 64 E3
High Mount BL2 . . . . 25 E3
Highnam Wlk M22 . . . . 121 A1
Highover Ho M20 . . . . 109 F4
High Peak OL15 . . . . 16 F5
High Peak Rd
Ashton-u-L OL6 . . . . 86 A6
Whitworth OL12 . . . . 14 C6
High Peak St M40 . . . . 83 B6
High Pk WN6 . . . . 36 C6
High Rid La BL6 . . . . 23 B1
Highshore Dr M8 . . . . 155 C3
High St
Altrincham WA14 . . . . 119 D4
Atherton M46 . . . . 58 D3
Bolton BL3 . . . . 145 A1
Bolton BL3 . . . . 147 B4
Bury BL8 . . . . 26 F4
Chapeltown BL7 . . . . 9 C4
Cheadle SK8 . . . . 122 D6
Delph OL3 . . . . 50 F5
Droylsden M43 . . . . 84 B1
Golborne WA3 . . . . 90 A8
Hazel Grove SK7 . . . . 124 F2
Heywood OL10 . . . . 29 B2
Horwich BL6 . . . . 22 B4
Hyde SK14 . . . . 167 C3
Ince-in-M WN3 . . . . 151 B2
Leigh WN7 . . . . 76 A5
5 Littleborough OL15 . . . . 15 F5
Little Lever BL3 . . . . 43 B3
Manchester M1, M4 . . . . 159 A1
Middleton M24 . . . . 47 A1
Middleton M24 . . . . 47 A2
Mossley OL5 . . . . 68 D2
Newton-le-W WA12 . . . . 89 D4
Oldham, Lees OL4 . . . . 67 E6
Oldham OL1 . . . . 153 C3
Rochdale OL12 . . . . 139 C4
Royton OL2 . . . . 48 D4
Shaw OL2 . . . . 149 B2
Stalybridge SK15 . . . . 85 F1
Stalybridge SK15 . . . . 86 A1
Standish WN6 . . . . 19 E1
Stockport SK1 . . . . 169 C1
Tyldesley, Lark Hill M29 . . . 77 B5
Tyldesley M29 . . . . 58 F1
Uppermill OL3 . . . . 69 B8
Walkden M28 . . . . 60 D3
Wigan, New Springs WN2 . . 38 B3
Wigan, Swinley WN1 . . . . 37 D2
High Stile La OL3 . . . . 51 D2
High Stile St BL4 . . . . 60 E7
Highstone Dr M8 . . . . 156 C2
Highstones Gdns SK13 . . 104 F2
High Street E SK13 . . . . 104 D1
High Street W SK13 . . . . 104 B1
Highthorne Gn OL2 . . . . 48 C8
High Trees Dr M20 . . . . 109 F5
Highview SK13 . . . . 116 A7
High View St
Bolton, Sharples BL1 . . . . 24 E6
1 Bolton, Willows BL3 . . . 146 C4
Highview Wlk M9 . . . . 64 E3
Highwood OL11 . . . . 13 E1
Highwood Cl
3 Bolton BL2 . . . . 25 F1
Glossop SK13 . . . . 116 B8
High Wood Fold SK6 . . . . 126 C8
Highwoods Cl WN4 . . . . 73 B5
Highworth Cl BL3 . . . . 145 B1
Highworth Dr M40 . . . . 65 D2
Higson Ave
Eccles M30 . . . . 95 C8
Manchester M21 . . . . 109 B7
Romiley SK6 . . . . 112 F2
Hilary Ave
Atherton M46 . . . . 58 C5
Gatley SK8 . . . . 131 D8
Golborne WA3 . . . . 74 D1
Oldham OL8 . . . . 84 F8
Hilary Cl SK4 . . . . 169 A2
Hilary Gr BL4 . . . . 60 D7
Hilary Rd M22 . . . . 121 C1
Hilary St OL11 . . . . 30 D1
Hilberry Ho OL5 . . . . 68 E3
Hilbre Ave OL1 . . . . 48 D2
Hilbre Rd M19 . . . . 110 F8
Hilbury Ave M9 . . . . 64 D1
Hilda Ave
Bury BL8 . . . . 26 F6
Cheadle SK8 . . . . 122 E5
Hilda Gr SK5 . . . . 169 C4
Hilda Rd SK14 . . . . 113 D7
Hilda St
Heywood OL10 . . . . 29 D3
Leigh WN7 . . . . 75 D6
Oldham OL9 . . . . 153 A3
Reddish SK5 . . . . 169 C4
Hilden Ct M16 . . . . 97 D4
Hilden St
Bolton BL2 . . . . 148 A2
4 Leigh WN7 . . . . 75 F5
Hilditch Cl M23 . . . . 121 B6
Hildyard St WN5 . . . . 54 F6
Hiley Rd M30 . . . . 79 A1
Hilgay Cl WN3 . . . . 54 D3
Hillam Cl M41 . . . . 95 F1
Hillary Ave
Ashton-u-L OL7 . . . . 85 B5
Wigan WN5 . . . . 54 D5
Hillary Rd SK14 . . . . 102 A5
Hillbank WN6 . . . . 37 A7
Hillbank Cl BL1 . . . . 142 C3
Hill Bank Cl SK15 . . . . 86 D5
Hillbank St OL11 . . . . 47 D6
Hillbeck Cres WN4 . . . . 72 D4
Hillbrae Ave WA11 . . . . 71 A1
Hillbre Way 1 SK9 . . . . 131 D4
Hillbrook Ave M40 . . . . 65 B2
Hillbrook Rd
Bramhall SK7 . . . . 132 D6
Stockport SK1 . . . . 124 C8
Hillbrow Wlk 9 M8 . . . . 155 C3
Hillbury Rd SK7 . . . . 123 F1
Hill Cl WN6 . . . . 35 E8
Hillcote Wlk M18 . . . . 165 B2
Hill Cot Rd BL1 . . . . 24 F5
Hill Court Mews SK6 . . . . 113 B2
Hillcourt Rd
High Lane SK6 . . . . 134 F7
Romiley SK6 . . . . 113 C4
Hillcourt St M1 . . . . 163 A3
Hill Cres
Leigh WN7 . . . . 75 C8
Manchester M9 . . . . 64 A3
Hillcrest
Hyde SK14 . . . . 113 F7
Middleton M24 . . . . 46 F3
Platt Bridge WN2 . . . . 56 B2
Salford M6 . . . . 80 A3
Hill Crest M46 . . . . 58 F5
Hillcrest Ave
Heywood OL10 . . . . 29 A3
Stockport SK4 . . . . 168 A2
Hill Crest Ave WN7 . . . . 75 C8
Hillcrest Cres OL10 . . . . 29 A3
Hillcrest Dr
Denton M34 . . . . 101 B1
Reddish M19 . . . . 111 C7
Hillcrest Gram Sch SK3 . 170 C2
Hillcrest Rd
Prestwich M25 . . . . 62 F2
Rochdale OL11 . . . . 30 D2
Stockport, Bramhall Green
SK7 . . . . 123 F1
Stockport, Stockport Great Moor
SK2 . . . . 124 C7
Tyldesley M29 . . . . 77 D8
Hillcroft
Oldham OL8 . . . . 67 A1
Stockport SK2 . . . . 124 E6
Hillcroft Cl M8 . . . . 156 A4
Hillcroft Rd WA14 . . . . 119 A5
Hilldale Ave M9 . . . . 64 E4
Hilldean WN8 . . . . 53 C8
Hill Dr SK9 . . . . 131 E3

Hillel Ho M15 . . . . **163** A1
Hillend SK14 . . . . **103** A1
Hillend La SK14 . . . . **103** A1
Hillend Pl M23 . . . . **109** A2
Hillend Rd M23 . . . . **109** A2
Hill End Rd OL3 . . . . **50** F4
Hill Farm Cl OL8 . . . . **67** B3
Hillfield M5 . . . . **154** A2
Hillfield Cl M13 . . . . **164** A1
Hillfield Dr
  Bolton BL2 . . . . **25** B1
  Worsley M28 . . . . **78** A7
Hillfield Wlk **10** BL2 . . . . . **25** B1
Hillfoot Wlk **28** M15 . . . . **162** A2
Hillgate Ave M5 . . . . **161** B3
Hillgate Bsns Ctr SK1 . . . **170** C4
Hillgate St OL6 . . . . **166** C4
Hillhead Wlk M8 . . . . **156** A1
Hillhouse Ct OL12 . . . . **30** B3
Hill House Fold La WN6 . . **18** C5
Hill House La WN6 . . . . . . **18** C5
Hillier St M9 . . . . **157** B4
Hillier Street N M9 . . . . . . **157** B4
Hillingdon Cl OL8 . . . . **84** B8
Hillingdon Dr M9 . . . . **65** B2
Hillington Rd
  Sale M33 . . . . **107** F5
  Stockport SK3 . . . . **123** C8
Hillkirk Dr OL12 . . . . **14** C3
Hillkirk St M11 . . . . **160** B1
Hill La
  Blackrod BL6 . . . . **21** C2
  Bolton BL2 . . . . **148** A4
  Manchester M9 . . . . **64** D4
Hillman Cl M40 . . . . **157** A1
Hill Mount SK16 . . . . **102** A8
Hillock The
  Bolton BL2 . . . . **25** D5
  Tyldesley M29 . . . . **77** B5
Hill Pond Ave SK22 . . . . . **127** D1
Hillreed WN6 . . . . **36** F1
Hill Rise
  Altrincham WA14 . . . . . . **119** A5
  Ramsbottom BL0 . . . . **11** A4
  Romiley SK6 . . . . **113** B5
Hillsborough Dr BL9 . . . . . **45** B2
Hill's Ct **3** BL8 . . . . **27** B4
Hillsdale Gr BL2 . . . . **25** E3
Hillside WA13 . . . . **117** E1
Hill Side BL1 . . . . **40** F7
Hillside Ave
  Ashton-in-M WN4 . . . . . . **72** F8
  Atherton M46 . . . . **58** E4
  Blackrod BL6 . . . . **21** E1
  Bolton BL7 . . . . **25** C8
  Diggle OL3 . . . . **51** C3
  Farnworth BL4 . . . . **60** C7
  Horwich BL6 . . . . **22** C4
  Hyde SK14 . . . . **113** F6
  Mossley SK15 . . . . **86** F6
  Oldham, Clarksfield OL4 . . **67** C7
  Oldham, Grotton OL4 . . . . **68** B5
  Royton OL2 . . . . **48** E5
  Salford M7 . . . . **81** A8
  Shaw OL2 . . . . **49** D8
  Walkden M28 . . . . **60** C4
  Whitefield M45 . . . . **44** E2
Hillside Cl
  Billinge WN5 . . . . **71** D5
  Bolton, Harwood Lee BL2 . **25** E5
  Bolton, Hunger Hill BL3 . . **40** D2
  Bramhall SK7 . . . . **133** A7
  Disley SK12 . . . . **135** E6
  Glossop SK13 . . . . **171** B3
  Manchester M40 . . . . **65** A1
  Wigan WN3 . . . . **54** D3
Hillside Cres
  Ashton-u-l OL6 . . . . **85** F5
  Bury BL9 . . . . **27** F6
  Horwich BL6 . . . . **22** C4
Hillside Ct BL1 . . . . **40** F7
Hillside Dr
  Middleton M24 . . . . **47** B1
  Pendlebury M27 . . . . **80** D6
Hillside Gr SK6 . . . . **114** B1
Hillside Ho BL1 . . . . **40** F7
Hillside Rd
  Altrincham WA15 . . . . . . **120** A3
  Hyde SK14, Sk6 . . . . **113** D5
  Ramsbottom BL0 . . . . . . **138** A1
  Stockport SK2 . . . . **124** D7
Hillside St **5** BL3 . . . . . . **145** A1
Hillside View
  Denton M34 . . . . **113** A4
  Milnrow OL16 . . . . **32** A6
Hillside Way OL12 . . . . **4** C1
Hillside Wlk OL12 . . . . **14** D4
Hills La BL9 . . . . **45** C2
Hillspring Rd OL4 . . . . **68** A6
Hill St
  Altrincham WA14 . . . . . . **119** C8
  Ashton-u-l OL6, OL7 . . . . **166** B2
  Bolton BL7 . . . . **9** D4
  Bury BL8 . . . . **26** F4
  Dukinfield SK16 . . . . **166** B1
  Heywood OL10 . . . . **29** C2
  Hindley WN2 . . . . **56** D6
  Hyde SK14 . . . . **113** F8
  Leigh WN7 . . . . **75** E5
  Manchester M20 . . . . . . **110** B7
  Middleton M24 . . . . **47** A3
  Oldham OL4 . . . . **67** B7

Hill St continued
  Radcliffe M26 . . . . **43** F4
  Ramsbottom BL9 . . . . **11** C3
  Rochdale OL16 . . . . **31** A7
  Romiley Sk6 . . . . **113** B2
  Salford M7 . . . . **155** A2
  Shaw OL2 . . . . **149** C2
  Wigan WN6 . . . . **37** B1
Hillstone Ave OL12 . . . . **14** D4
Hillstone Cl BL8 . . . . **10** F2
HILLTOP **137** B8
HILL TOP **60** D4
Hilltop OL12 . . . . **14** C5
Hill Top
  Altrincham WA15 . . . . . . **120** A1
  Bolton BL1 . . . . **143** A3
  Chadderton OL1 . . . . **47** F2
  Little Lever BL3 . . . . **43** A4
  Over Hulton M46 . . . . **58** F5
  Romiley Sk6 . . . . **113** B3
Hilltop Ave
  Manchester M9 . . . . **64** D3
  Whitefield M45 . . . . **63** B8
Hill Top Ave
  Cheadle SK8 . . . . **132** B8
  Prestwich M25 . . . . **63** B4
  Wilmslow SK9 . . . . **137** B8
Hilltop Ct
  Manchester, Crumpsall
    M8 . . . . **63** F2
  Manchester M14 . . . . **98** D1
  Walkden M28 . . . . **60** D4
Hill Top Ct SK8 . . . . **123** B1
Hilltop Dr
  Bury BL8 . . . . **26** E6
  Haslingden BB4 . . . . **1** C7
  Marple SK6 . . . . **125** C7
  Royton OL2 . . . . **48** E2
Hill Top Dr
  Altrincham WA15 . . . . . . **120** A1
  Rochdale OL11 . . . . **30** F2
Hill Top Fold **1** WN2 . . . . **56** E6
Hilltop Gr M45 . . . . **63** B8
Hill Top La OL3 . . . . **50** C4
Hilltop Rd SK13 . . . . **104** B3
Hill Top Rd
  Heywood OL10 . . . . **46** B8
  Walkden M28 . . . . **60** D4
Hillview OL15 . . . . **6** D1
Hill View
  Delph OL3 . . . . **50** F4
  Stalybridge SK15 . . . . . . **102** E6
Hill View Cl OL1 . . . . **49** C2
Hillview Ct BL1 . . . . **143** B4
Hill View Dr PR7 . . . . **19** D8
Hillview Rd BL1 . . . . **143** B4
Hill View Rd M34 . . . . **100** A1
Hillwood Ave M8 . . . . **63** F3
Hillwood Dr SK13 . . . . **116** F8
Hillyard St **7** BL8 . . . . . . **27** C3
Hilly Croft BL7 . . . . **24** F8
Hilmarton Cl BL2 . . . . **25** E5
Hilrose Ave M41 . . . . **95** F2
Hilson Ct **1** M43 . . . . **84** A1
Hilton Arc OL1 . . . . **153** C3
Hilton Ave
  Horwich BL6 . . . . **22** A3
  Urmston M41 . . . . **95** D2
Hilton Bank M28 . . . . **60** B3
Hilton Cl WN7 . . . . **76** A5
Hilton Cres
  Ashton-u-l OL6 . . . . **85** C5
  Manchester M25 . . . . **63** B2
  Worsley M28 . . . . **78** B6
Hilton Ct SK3 . . . . **170** B4
Hilton Dr
  Ashton-u-l OL7 . . . . **84** F5
  Irlam M44 . . . . **105** C5
  Manchester M25 . . . . **63** B2
Hilton Fold La M24 . . . . **47** B1
Hilton Gr
  Poynton SK12 . . . . **133** D4
  Walkden M28 . . . . **60** B3
HILTON HOUSE **39** A6
Hilton La
  Prestwich M25 . . . . **63** A2
  Walkden M28 . . . . **60** B2
Hilton Lane Prim Sch
    M28 . . . . **60** B3
Hilton Lo M25 . . . . **63** B2
HILTON PARK **63** B2
Hilton Pl WN2 . . . . **38** C6
Hilton Rd
  Bury BL9 . . . . **140** C2
  Disley SK12 . . . . **135** B7
  Poynton SK12 . . . . **134** C5
  Stockport SK7 . . . . **123** F1
  Wythenshawe M22 . . . . . **121** E5
Hiltons Cl OL8 . . . . **153** B1
Hiltons Farm Cl M34 . . . . . **100** E6
Hilton Sq M27 . . . . **62** A1
Hilton St
  Ashton-in-M WN4 . . . . **73** C3
  Bolton BL2 . . . . **148** C3
  Bury BL9 . . . . **140** C4
  Dukinfield SK16 . . . . **101** F5
  Ince-in-M WN3 . . . . **151** B2
  Manchester M1, M4 . . . . . **159** B2
  Salford M7 . . . . **155** A1
  Stockport SK3 . . . . **170** A4
  Walkden M38 . . . . **60** A4
  Wigan WN1 . . . . **37** D1
Hilton Street N M7 . . . . . . **155** A2
Hilton Wlk M24 . . . . **64** C8
Himley Rd M11 . . . . **83** C3
Hincaster Wlk M18 . . . . . . **165** C1
Hinchcombe Cl M38 . . . . . . **60** A6
Hinchley Rd M9 . . . . **65** B3

Hinchley Way M27 . . . . **61** F2
Hinckley St M11 . . . . **164** C4
Hindburn Cl M45 . . . . **45** B1
Hindburn Dr M28 . . . . **78** A8
Hindburn Wlk M45 . . . . **45** B1
Hinde St M40 . . . . **83** A8
Hindhead Wlk M40 . . . . **83** D4
Hind Hill St OL10 . . . . **29** D1
Hindle Dr OL2 . . . . **48** C3
Hindles Cl M46 . . . . **58** A1
Hindle St
  Bacup OL13 . . . . **3** D8
  Radcliffe M26 . . . . **44** A3
Hindle Terr OL3 . . . . **50** F4
HINDLEY **56** D6
Hindley All Saints CE Prim
    Sch WN2 . . . . **56** E5
Hindley Ave M22 . . . . **121** B2
Hindley Bsns Ctr **10** WN2 . **56** D5
Hindley Cl **2** OL7 . . . . **84** F1
HINDLEY GREEN **57** B2
Hindley Green Bsns Pk
    WN2 . . . . **57** B2
Hindley Green Prim Sch
    WN2 . . . . **57** B3
Hindley High Sch WN2 . . . . **56** F5
Hindley Ho WN3 . . . . **150** A1
Hindley L Ctr WN2 . . . . **56** F7
Hindley Mill La WN2 . . . . . . **56** F7
Hindley Pool WN2 . . . . **56** E6
Hindley Prim Sch **7** WN2 . **56** E5
Hindley Rd BL5, WN2 . . . . . **57** D5
Hindley St
  Ashton-u-l OL7 . . . . **84** F1
  Stockport SK1 . . . . **170** C4
Hindley Sta WN2 . . . . **56** D7
Hindley Wlk **1** WN1 . . . . **150** C4
Hind Rd WN5 . . . . **54** D8
HINDSFORD **58** C1
Hindsford CE Prim Sch
    M46 . . . . **58** C1
Hindsford Cl M23 . . . . **108** C1
Hindsford St M46 . . . . **58** F1
Hind's Head Ave WN6 . . . . . **18** F6
Hinds La
  Bury BL8 . . . . **27** C1
  Radcliffe BL8, BL9 . . . . . . **44** C7
Hind St BL2 . . . . **148** C3
Hinkler Ave BL3 . . . . **147** B3
Hinstock Cres M18 . . . . **99** D5
Hinton **19** OL12 . . . . **139** B4
Hinton Cl OL11 . . . . **29** E6
Hinton Gr SK14 . . . . **114** A8
Hinton Mews SK1 . . . . **112** B1
Hinton St
  Manchester M4 . . . . **159** B3
  Oldham OL8 . . . . **153** C1
Hipley Cl SK6 . . . . **113** A5
Hirons La OL4 . . . . **68** A5
Hirst Ave M28 . . . . **60** C5
Hitchen Cl SK16 . . . . **101** F7
Hitchen Dr SK16 . . . . **101** F7
Hitchin Wlk M13 . . . . **163** C1
Hive St OL8 . . . . **66** B2
Hives The M17 . . . . **96** C7
Hoade St WN2 . . . . **56** E7
Hobart Cl SK7 . . . . **132** F4
Hobart St
  Bolton BL1 . . . . **143** A2
  Manchester M18 . . . . **99** E5
Hobby Gr WN7 . . . . **76** B5
Hob Hey La WA3 . . . . **91** D3
Hob Hill **1** SK15 . . . . **85** F1
Hob Hill Mdws SK13 . . . . . **116** D7
Hob La OL4 . . . . **9** C7
Hob Mill Rise OL5 . . . . **68** E4
Hobson Cres M34 . . . . **100** E6
Hobson Moor Rd SK14 . . . **103** A7
Hobson St
  Droylsden M11 . . . . **100** A7
  Failsworth M35 . . . . **83** D6
  Oldham OL1 . . . . **153** C2
  Reddish SK5 . . . . **99** F2
Hockenhull Cl M22 . . . . . . **121** E2
Hockerley Cl M33 . . . . **107** D5
Hockery View WN2 . . . . **56** C4
HOCKLEY **134** A3
Hockley Cl SK12 . . . . **134** A3
Hockley Paddock SK12 . . . **133** F3
Hockley Rd
  Poynton SK12 . . . . **134** A3
  6 Wythenshawe M23 . . **120** F6
Hodder Ave
  Littleborough OL15 . . . . . . **15** F6
  Platt Bridge WN2 . . . . **55** F2
Hodder Bank SK12 . . . . . . **124** E5
Hodder Cl WN5 . . . . **54** D7
Hodder Way M45 . . . . **63** C8
Hoddesdon St M8 . . . . **156** B3
Hodge Clough Inf Sch
    OL1 . . . . **49** D3
Hodge Clough Jun Sch
    OL1 . . . . **49** D3
Hodge Clough Rd OL1 . . . . . **49** D3
HODGEFOLD **114** F8
Hodge Fold SK14 . . . . **114** F8
Hodge La
  Broadbottom SK14 . . . . . **114** F8
  Salford M5, M6 . . . . **154** C1
Hodge Rd
  Oldham OL1 . . . . **49** D3
  Walkden M28 . . . . **60** D2
Hodges St WN6 . . . . **37** A2
Hodge St M9 . . . . **64** F1
Hodgson Dr WA15 . . . . . . **120** A8
Hodgson St
  Ashton-u-l OL6 . . . . **166** A2

Hodgson St continued
  Salford M8 . . . . **155** C1
Hodnet Dr WN4 . . . . **73** C3
Hodnett Ave M41 . . . . **94** E1
Hodnet Wlk M34 . . . . **100** E1
Hodson Fold OL8 . . . . **67** A1
Hodson Rd M27 . . . . **61** E2
Hodson St
  Salford M3 . . . . **158** B2
  Wigan WN3 . . . . **150** C3
Hogarth Rd
  Marple SK6 . . . . **126** B8
  Rochdale OL11 . . . . **30** F3
Hogarth Rise OL1 . . . . **49** D4
Hogarth Wlk M8 . . . . **156** C2
Hoggs Bridge Cl M27 . . . . . **80** D8
Hoghton Ave OL13 . . . . **4** A8
Holbeach Cl
  Bury BL8 . . . . **27** D5
  Hindley WN2 . . . . **56** E4
Holbeck M29 . . . . **77** B5
Holbeck Ave OL12 . . . . **14** D4
Holbeck Cl BL6 . . . . **39** D8
Holbeck Gr M14 . . . . **163** A1
Holberton Cl M8 . . . . **155** B1
Holberton Cl SK7 . . . . **124** A3
Holborn Ave
  Failsworth M35 . . . . **84** B7
  Leigh WN7 . . . . **75** F8
  Radcliffe M26 . . . . **43** D4
  Wigan WN3 . . . . **150** B1
Holborn Dr M8 . . . . **156** B1
Holborn Gdns OL11 . . . . . . **139** A1
Holborn Sq OL11 . . . . **139** A1
Holborn St OL11 . . . . **139** A1
Holbrook Ave M38 . . . . **60** A6
Holbrook St M1 . . . . **163** A4
HOLCOMBE **138** A2
Holcombe Ave
  Bury BL8 . . . . **27** B2
  Golborne WA3 . . . . **90** C8
HOLCOMBE BROOK **11** B2
Holcombe Brook Prim Sch
    BL0 . . . . **11** A2
Holcombe Cl
  Altrincham WA14 . . . . . . **119** B6
  Kearsley BL4 . . . . **61** A6
  Oldham OL4 . . . . **68** A7
  Salford M6 . . . . **81** A2
Holcombe Cres BL4 . . . . **61** A6
Holcombe Ct BL0 . . . . **10** F2
Holcombe Gdns M19 . . . . . **110** E5
Holcombe Lee BL0 . . . . **11** A4
Holcombe Mews BL0 . . . . . **10** F3
Holcombe Old Rd BL8 . . . . **138** A1
Holcombe Prec BL0 . . . . . . **10** F3
Holcombe Rd
  Haslingden BB4 . . . . **1** A6
  Little Lever BL3 . . . . **42** F3
  Manchester M14 . . . . **110** E7
  Ramsbottom BL8 . . . . **10** F2
Holcombe View Cl OL4 . . . . **49** D2
Holcombe Village BL8 . . . . **138** A2
Holcombe Wlk SK4 . . . . . . **111** D7
Holcroft Dr WN2 . . . . **74** C7
Holcroft La WA3 . . . . **92** D2
Holcroft Rd
  Manchester M18 . . . . **99** E4
  Golborne WA3 . . . . **91** A1
  see Holcroft Rd
Holcroft St
  Bolton BL1 . . . . **24** E6
  Bury BL9 . . . . **28** E4
  Manchester M16 . . . . **97** E1
  Ramsbottom BL0 . . . . **11** A3
Holden Brook Cl WN7 . . . . . **76** B5
Holden Clough Com Prim
    Sch OL6 . . . . **85** D7
Holden Clough Dr OL7 . . . . **85** B7
HOLDEN FOLD **48** C2
Holden Fold La OL1, OL2 . . **48** D3
Holden Lea BL5 . . . . **39** E3
Holden Rd
  Leigh WN7 . . . . **76** B5
  Manchester M7 . . . . **63** D1
Holden St
  Adlington PR7 . . . . **20** F7
  Ashton-u-l OL6 . . . . **166** C4
  Oldham OL8 . . . . **66** F3
  5 Rochdale OL12 . . . . . **15** A2
Holden Wlk WN5 . . . . **54** E5
Holder Ave BL3 . . . . **43** B5
Holderness Dr OL2 . . . . **48** C2
Holdgate Cl M15 . . . . **162** B1
Holding St WN2 . . . . **56** D6
Holdsworth St M27 . . . . **79** D7
Holebottom OL6 . . . . **85** C6
Hole House Fold SK6 . . . . . **113** B2
Holford Ave M14 . . . . **98** B2
Holford Ct M34 . . . . **100** F3
Holford Cres SK9 . . . . **136** C7
Holford Dr SK9 . . . . **136** C7
Holford Way M41 . . . . **89** F3
Holford Wlk OL16 . . . . **31** D7
Holgate Dr WN5 . . . . **53** E6
Holgate St OL4 . . . . **49** E1
Holhouse La BL8 . . . . **10** F2
Holiday La SK2 . . . . **124** F6
Holkar Mdws BL7 . . . . **25** B8
Holker Cl
  Manchester M13 . . . . **164** A1
  Poynton SK12 . . . . **133** F4
Holker Way **21** M34 . . . . **101** A1
Holkham Cl **6** M4 . . . . . . **159** C2
Holland Ave SK15 . . . . **86** A2
Holland Cl OL3 . . . . **50** E4
Holland Ct
  Manchester M8 . . . . **63** F2
  Poynton SK12 . . . . **133** E3
  Radcliffe M26 . . . . **44** C4
  Stockport SK1 . . . . **124** A7
Holland Gr OL6 . . . . **85** B6

Holland Rd
  Bramhall SK7 . . . . **132** E7
  Dukinfield SK14 . . . . **101** F5
  Manchester M8 . . . . **63** F2
Holland Rise **7** OL12 . . . **139** B4
Holland St
  Bolton BL1 . . . . **143** C4
  Denton M34 . . . . **100** D4
  Heywood OL10 . . . . **29** D2
  Manchester M40 . . . . **160** A3
  Radcliffe M26 . . . . **44** C4
  Rochdale OL12 . . . . **139** B4
  Rochdale, Wuerdle OL16 . . **15** D4
  Salford M6 . . . . **80** D3
Holland Street E M34 . . . . **100** E4
Holland Street W M34 . . . **100** D4
Holland Wlk M6 . . . . **81** A5
Hollies Ct SK3 . . . . **108** B4
Hollies Dr SK6 . . . . **126** A5
Hollies La SK9 . . . . **137** F7
Hollies The
  10 Atherton M46 . . . . . . **58** D3
  Bolton BL2 . . . . **42** F8
  Gatley SK8 . . . . **122** B5
  Manchester, West Didsbury
    M20 . . . . **109** F3
  Pendlebury M27 . . . . **80** B7
  Salford M6 . . . . **80** B3
  Stockport, Heaton Moor
    SK4 . . . . **168** B3
  Wigan WN1 . . . . **37** D3
Hollin Acre BL5 . . . . **57** F7
Hollin Bank SK4 . . . . **111** D7
Hollinbrook WN6 . . . . **36** F2
Hollin Cres OL3 . . . . **68** E5
Hollin Cross La SK13 . . . . . **116** C8
Hollin Dr M24 . . . . **46** F4
Holliney Ave M22 . . . . **121** F1
Holliney Rd M22 . . . . **121** F1
HOLLINFARE **105** A3
Hollington Way WN3 . . . . . . **54** C2
Hollingwood Cl WN4 . . . . . . **73** A3
HOLLINGWORTH
  Glossop **103** C6
  Littleborough **16** A3
Hollingworth Ave M40 . . . . . **65** F2
Hollingworth Business and
  Enterprise Coll OL16 . . . . **32** A6
Hollingworth Cl **8** SK1 . . **170** C4
Hollingworth Dr SK6 . . . . . **125** F3
Hollingworth La OL14 . . . . . . **6** B8
Hollingworth Lake Ctry Pk*
  OL15 . . . . **16** B2
Hollingworth Lake Water
  Activity Ctr* OL15 . . . . . . **16** B2
Hollingworth Prim Sch
  SK14 . . . . **103** C5
Hollingworth Rd
  Littleborough OL15 . . . . . . **16** B4
  Romiley SK6 . . . . **112** E4
Hollingworth St OL9 . . . . . . **66** B3
Hollinhall St OL4 . . . . **67** C7
Hollin Hey Cl WN5 . . . . **71** D3
Hollin Hey Rd BL1 . . . . **23** E3
Hollinhey Terr SK14 . . . . . **103** C5
Hollin House M24 . . . . **47** A3
Hollinhurst Dr BL6 . . . . **40** C7
Hollinhurst Rd M26 . . . . **44** C1
Hollin La
  Middleton M24, OL10 . . . . **46** F4
  Rochdale OL11 . . . . **29** E6
  Styal SK9 . . . . **130** F5
Hollin Prim Sch M24 . . . . . . **47** A3
HOLLINS
  Middleton **47** A3
  Oldham **66** D2
  Radcliffe **45** A5
Hollins Ave
  Hyde SK14 . . . . **113** E7
  Leigh WN7 . . . . **75** F8
Hollins Bank **41** SK13 . . . **171** A2
Hollins Brook Cl BL9 . . . . . . **45** B5
Hollins Brook Way BL9 . . . . **45** B6
Hollins Brow BL9 . . . . **44** F4
Hollins Cl
  40 Gamesley SK13 . . . . **171** A2
  Garswood WN4 . . . . **72** D4
  Tyldesley M29 . . . . **77** B8
  Whitefield BL9 . . . . **45** B4
Hollinsclough Cl M22 . . . . **121** E5
Hollinscroft Ave WA15 . . . . **120** D5
Hollins Fold **43** SK13 . . . **171** A2
Hollins Gdns **46** SK13 . . . **171** A2
Hollins Gn M24 . . . . **47** A3
Hollins Gr
  42 Gamesley SK13 . . . . **171** A2
  Manchester M12 . . . . **99** A3
  Sale M33 . . . . **108** A4
HOLLINS GREEN
  Irlam **105** B2
  Oldham **66** D2
Hollins Green Rd SK6 . . . . **125** F6
Hollins Grundy Prim Sch
  BL9 . . . . **45** A5
Hollinshead M7 . . . . **155** B2
Hollins Ind Pk SK13 . . . . . **104** B5
Hollins La
  Edenfield BL0 . . . . **1** E2
  Marple, Marple Bridge
    SK6 . . . . **126** C8
  Marple SK6 . . . . **125** F6
  Mossley OL5 . . . . **68** D1
  Uppermill OL3 . . . . **69** D5
  Whitefield BL9 . . . . **45** B4
Hollins Mews
  44 Gamesley SK13 . . . . **171** A2
  Whitefield BL9 . . . . **45** C4

Hollinsmoor Rd SK6,
SK22 . . . . **127** D7
Hollins Mount SK6 . . . . . **126** B8
Hollins Rd
  Hindley WN7 . . . . **57** A5
  Oldham, Greenacres Fold
  OL4 . . . . **67** F8
  Oldham, Hollins OL8 . . . . **66** D2
Hollins Sq BL9 . . . . **45** B3
Hollins St
  Bolton BL2 . . . . **148** B2
  ❸ Oldham OL4 . . . . **67** F6
  Stalybridge SK15 . . . . . . **101** F8
  Walsden OL14 . . . . **6** B8
Hollins Terr ❷ SK6 . . . . . **125** F6
HOLLINS THE **57** A5
Hollins The ❹ SK6 . . . . . **125** F6
HOLLINS VALE **45** B5
Hollins Vale Nature
  Reserve* BL9 . . . . **45** B5
Hollins Way ❸ SK13 . . . . . **171** A2
Hollins Wlk M22 . . . . **121** D2
Hollinswood Rd
  Bolton BL2 . . . . **148** B2
  Worsley M28 . . . . **78** B6
Hollinwell Cl M24 . . . . **46** F4
HOLLINWOOD **66** B1
Hollinwood Ave M40, OL9 . **65** E2
Hollinwood Branch Canal
  Nature Reserve* M43. . **84** C4
Hollinwood Bsns Ctr M35 **66** B1
Hollinwood La SK6. . . . . . **126** B2
Hollinwood Rd SK12 . . . . **135** D6
Holllins Ave ❹❼ SK13 . . . **171** A2
Holloway Dr M27, M28 . . . . **61** C1
Hollowbrook Way ❹
  OL12 . . . . **14** D2
Hollowell La BL6 . . . . **22** D1
Hollow End SK5. . . . . **112** D7
Hollowfield OL11 . . . . **13** D1
Hollowgate M28 . . . . **79** B6
Hollow Mdws M26 . . . . **61** C6
Hollows Ct SK14 . . . . **167** B2
Hollowspell OL12 . . . . **15** C3
Hollows The Sk8 . . . . **122** C1
Hollow The SK8. . . . . **122** C1
Hollow Vale Dr SK5 . . . . . **112** A8
Holly Ave
  Cheadle SK8 . . . . **122** D5
  Newton-le-W WA12 . . . . . . **89** D3
  Urmston M41 . . . . **95** B2
  Walkden M28. . . . . **60** E2
Hollybank M43 . . . . **84** C3
Holly Bank
  Ashton-u-L OL6 . . . . **85** D2
  Entwistle BL7 . . . . **9** B7
  Failsworth M40 . . . . **83** C7
  Glossop SK13. . . . . **116** E8
  Hollingworth SK14 . . . . . **103** D5
  ❷ Royton OL2 . . . . **48** D6
  Sale M33 . . . . **108** C3
Holly Bank Cl M15 . . . . . . **161** C2
Holly Bank Ct Sk8 . . . . . . **123** A1
Holly Bank Rd SK9 . . . . . . **131** B1
Hollybank Rise SK16 . . . . **101** F8
Hollybank St M26 . . . . **43** F3
Hollybrook OLL **48** B3
Hollybrook Dene SK6 . . . **113** E2
Hollybush Sq WA3 . . . . **74** E1
Hollybush St M18 . . . . **99** E6
Holly Cl WA15 . . . . **120** A6
Hollycroft Ave
  Bolton BL2 . . . . **42** E5
  Wythenshawe M22 . . . . . **121** D6
Holly Ct
  Bury BL9 . . . . **141** A2
  Hyde SK14 . . . . **102** A2
  ❶ Irlam M44 . . . . **94** B3
  ❽ Manchester M20 . . . . . **110** B6
  Stockport SK3 . . . . **170** B1
Hollydene WN2 . . . . **38** B5
Holly Dene Dr BL6 . . . . **40** B7
Holly Dr M33 . . . . **108** A4
Holly Dr M25. . . . . **63** A2
Holly Fold M45 . . . . **44** F1
Holly Gr
  Bolton BL1 . . . . **142** C1
  Bolton BL6 . . . . **40** B7
  Chadderton OL9. . . . . **152** B4
  Denton M34 . . . . **101** A3
  Dukinfield SK15. . . . . **101** E8
  Farnworth BL4. . . . . **60** A8
  Leigh WN7 . . . . **75** E7
  Oldham OL4 . . . . **67** E7
  Sale M33 . . . . **108** D4
Holly Grange
  Altrincham WA14 . . . . . . **119** D2
  Stockport SK7 . . . . **123** F3
Holly Heath Dr WN1. . . . . . **37** B4
Hollyhedge Ave M22 . . . . **121** D5
Hollyhedge Court Rd
  M22 . . . . **121** D5
Hollyhedge Ct M22 . . . . . **121** C4
Hollyhedge Rd M22, M23 . **121** C5
Hollyhey Dr M23 . . . . **109** C2
Holly Heys ❹ M33 . . . . . . **108** D4
Hollyhouse Dr SK6 . . . . . **113** A5
Holly House Dr M41. . . . . . **94** F2
Hollyhurst M28 . . . . **79** B6
Holly La
  Oldham OL8 . . . . **66** C2
  Wythenshawe M23 . . . . . **130** E5
Holly Mill Cres BL1. . . . . . **143** C4
Hollymount
  Failsworth M40 . . . . **65** D3
  Manchester M16 . . . . **97** B4

Holly Mount
  ❷ Glossop SK13 . . . . **104** D1
  Haslingden BB4 . . . . **1** A7
Hollymount Ave SK2 . . . . **124** C5
Hollymount Dr
  Oldham OL4 . . . . **49** E3
  Stockport SK2 . . . . **124** C5
Hollymount Gdns SK2 . . . **124** D5
Hollymount La BL8 . . . . **10** E1
Holly Mount RC Prim Sch
  BL8. **1** A7
Hollymount Rd SK2 . . . . . **124** D5
Holly Oak Gdns OL10 . . . . **29** C1
Holly Rd
  Aspull WN2 . . . . **38** B5
  Bramhall SK7 . . . . **132** E5
  Golborne WA3 . . . . **90** C8
  High Lane SK6 . . . . **134** F7
  Lymm WA13 . . . . **117** B2
  Poynton SK12 . . . . **133** E3
  Reddish SK4 . . . . **111** C5
  Swinton M27 . . . . **79** D6
  Wigan WN5 . . . . **54** E6
Holly Road N SK9 . . . . . . **137** B6
Holly Road S SK9 . . . . **137** B5
Holly Royde Ct M20 . . . . . **110** B6
Holly St
  Bolton BL1. . . . . **143** C4
  Bury BL9 . . . . **141** A2
  Bury, Tottington BL8. . . . . **26** F6
  Droylsden M43. . . . . **83** D2
  Manchester M11 . . . . **164** B4
  Ramsbottom BL9 . . . . **11** C3
  Stockport SK1 . . . . **112** B1
  Wardle OL12 . . . . **15** C6
Hollythorn Ave SK8 . . . . . **132** C7
Hollyville OL3. . . . . **69** C5
Hollyway M22 . . . . **121** E8
Holly Wlk M31 . . . . **105** D3
Hollywood
  Altrincham WA14. . . . . . . **119** D2
  Bolton BL1. . . . . **142** B2
Hollywood Rd
  Bolton BL1. . . . . **142** B2
  Marple SK6 . . . . **126** A1
Hollywood Towers SK3. . **170** A4
Hollywood Way SK3, SK4. **169** A1
Holmbrook M29 . . . . **59** C1
Holmcroft Rd M18 . . . . **99** D3
Holm Ct M6 . . . . **81** A3
Holmdale Ave M19 . . . . . . **110** E5
Holme Ave
  Bury BL8 . . . . **27** C5
  Wigan WN1 . . . . **37** C2
Holmebrook Dr BL6 . . . . . . **22** D1
Holme Cres OL2 . . . . **48** C2
Holmecroft Chase BL5 . . **40** A3
Holme Ct ❼ WN1. . . . . **37** C2
Holmedale Ct ❸ M33 . . . **108** C4
Holmefield M33. . . . . **108** B4
Holme House St OL15 . . . . **6** D1
Holme La
  Haslingden BB4 . . . . **1** D8
  Rawtenstall BB4 . . . . **1** E8
Holme Park Gdns M28 . . . **78** A5
Holme Park Way M35 . . . . **84** B7
Holme Rd M20. . . . . **110** E3
Holmes Cotts BL1 . . . . . . **142** C3
Holmes Ct SK1. . . . . **169** C1
Holmes House Ave WN3. . **54** D3
Holmes Rd OL12 . . . . **139** A3
Holmes St
  Bolton BL3 . . . . **42** A4
  Cheadle SK8 . . . . **122** E6
  Rochdale, Greengate OL12 . **15** C3
  Rochdale, Spotland Bridge
  OL12 . . . . **139** A3
  Stockport SK2 . . . . **170** B3
Holme St
  Bacup OL13 . . . . **3** D8
  Hyde SK14 . . . . **167** A2
Holmes Way M34 . . . . **112** F7
Holmeswood Cl SK9 . . . . **137** C8
Holmeswood Pk BB4 . . . . . **1** E8
Holmeswood Rd BL3 . . . . **147** A2
Holme Terr
  Calderbrook OL15 . . . . **6** D1
  Haslingden BB4 . . . . **1** D8
  Wigan WN1 . . . . **37** B3
Holme Vale BL4 . . . . **1** A6
Holmfield Ave
  Manchester, Harpurhey
  M9. . . . . **157** C3
  Manchester, Sedgley Park
  M25. . . . . **63** A5
Holmfield Avenue W M9 **157** C3
Holmfield Cl SK4. . . . . **169** A3
Holmfield Dr SK8 . . . . **132** B8
Holmfield Gn BL3 . . . . **40** F4
Holmfirth Rd
  Diggle OL3 . . . . **52** D1
  Oldham OL3 . . . . **70** A8
Holmfirth St M13 . . . . **98** F4
Holmfoot Wlk ❻ M9 . . . . . **157** A3
Holmlea Rd M43 . . . . **83** E2
Holmleigh Ave M9 . . . . **64** E1
Holmpark Rd M11. . . . . **99** F7
Holmrook WA14 . . . . **119** B5
Holmsfield Cl WN2. . . . . . . **38** A2
Holmside Gdns M19. . . . . **110** E4
Holmwood WA14 . . . . **119** A3
Holmwood Cl WN4. . . . . . . **73** A5
Holmwood Ct M20 . . . . . . **110** B4
Holmwood Rd M20. . . . . . **110** B5
Holroyd St
  Manchester M11 . . . . **165** A4
  Rochdale OL16. . . . . **31** A7
Holset Dr WA14 . . . . **119** B5

Holset Wlk SK7 . . . . **124** A2
Holset Ave M8 . . . . **156** A2
Holstein Ave OL12 . . . . **14** D4
Holstein St M13. . . . . **164** A1
Holt Ave WN5. . . . . **71** D4
Holtby St M9 . . . . **64** E1
Holt Cres WN5. . . . . **71** D4
Holt Ho M20 . . . . **110** B2
Holthouse Rd BL8. . . . . **26** F5
Holt La M35 . . . . **84** B7
HOLT LANE END. **84** A7
Holt Lane Mews M35. . . . . **84** B7
Holt Mill Rd BB4 . . . . **2** D8
Holton Way WN3. . . . . **54** E1
HOLTS **67** E4
Holts La OL4. . . . . **67** E4
Holt's La SK9 . . . . **130** F3
Holt St
  Altrincham WA14. . . . . . . **119** C8
  Ashton-u-L M34 . . . . **100** E8
  Bolton BL3 . . . . **145** A1
  Calderbrook OL15 . . . . **6** D2
  Eccles M30 . . . . **95** C8
  Hindley WN2 . . . . **56** C5
  Leigh WN7 . . . . **75** E7
  Manchester M40 . . . . **157** C1
  Milnrow OL16 . . . . **32** A5
  Oldham OL4 . . . . **67** C8
  Orrell WN5. . . . . **53** D5
  Ramsbottom BL0 . . . . **11** D6
  ❾ Rawtenstall BB4. . . . . . . **2** E8
  Stockport SK1 . . . . **170** C4
  Swinton M27 . . . . **61** F2
  Tyldesley M29 . . . . **59** A1
  Whitworth OL12 . . . . **4** C1
  Wigan, Scholes WN1 . . . . **151** C4
  Wigan, Springfield WN6 . . **36** F2
  Wigan, Worsley Mesnes
  WN3 . . . . **55** A4
Holt's Terr OL12 . . . . **14** E2
Holt Street W BL0. . . . . . . **138** B1
Holtswell OL3 . . . . **74** E1
Holt Town M4, M40. . . . . . **160** B2
Holt Town Sta M4 . . . . . . **160** B2
Holtwood Wlk SK5. . . . . . **112** C7
Holway WN7 . . . . **156** C3
Holwick Rd M23 . . . . **109** E8
Holwood Dr M16. . . . . **109** E8
Holybourne Wlk M23. . . . **120** D8
Holy Cross & All Saints RC
  Prim Sch ❷ M30 . . . . . . **95** D8
Holy Cross CE VA Prim Sch
  OL1. . . . . **153** C4
Holy Cross Coll BL9 . . . . . **44** E8
Holy Cross Jun Sch OL1 **153** C4
Holy Family RC & CE Coll
  OL10. . . . . **29** C1
Holy Family RC Prim Sch
  Boothstown M28 . . . . **77** E7
  Oldham OL8 . . . . **84** D8
  Platt Bridge WN2. . . . . **56** A3
  ❶ Sale M33 . . . . **108** E4
  Wigan WN2 . . . . **38** A2
Holy Family VA RC Prim Sch
  OL11 . . . . **30** F2
Holy Harbour St BL1 . . . . **142** C2
Holyhurst Wlk ❷❽ BL1 . . . **143** B2
Holy Inf RC Prim Sch
  BL1 . . . . **143** B4
Holy Name RC Prim Sch
  M15. . . . . **163** A1
Holyoake Rd M28 . . . . **60** E2
Holyoake St M43. . . . . **84** C2
Holyoak St M40. . . . . **83** C6
Holyrood Cl
  Leigh WN7 . . . . **76** E7
  Prestwich M25. . . . . **63** C6
Holyrood Ct M25. . . . . **63** C6
Holyrood Dr
  Prestwich M25. . . . . **63** C6
  Swinton M27 . . . . **79** D7
Holyrood Gr M25 . . . . **63** C6
Holyrood Rd M25 . . . . **63** C6
Holyrood St
  Failsworth M40 . . . . **83** E4
  Oldham OL1 . . . . **49** A1
Holy Rosary RC Prim Sch
  OL8 . . . . **66** F2
Holy St OL16. . . . . **31** B2
Holy Trinity CE Dobcross Sch
  OL3 . . . . **50** F2
Holy Trinity CE Prim Sch
  Ashton-u-L OL6 . . . . **166** A3
  Bury BL9 . . . . **140** C1
  Littleborough OL15 . . . . . . **16** B5
  Manchester M9 . . . . **157** B4
Holy Trinity Stacksteads CE
  Prim Sch ❿ OL13 . . . . **3** C8
Holywood St ❻ M14 . . . . . **98** B3
Homebeck Ho Sk8 . . . . . . **122** A5
Homebury Dr M11. . . . . **83** B2
Home Dr M24. . . . . **47** A1
Home Farm Ave SK14 . . . **102** F1
Homelands Cl M33. . . . . . **107** F2
Homelands Rd M33 . . . . . **107** F2
Homelands Wlk M33 . . . . **157** A3
Homelaurel Ho M33. . . . . **108** B2
Homer Dr SK6. . . . . **126** B8
Homer St ❺ M26. . . . . **43** E3
Homerton Rd M40 . . . . **83** B4
Homestead Cl M31. . . . . . **106** A4
Homestead Cres M19 . . . **110** D3
Homestead Gdns OL12 . . . **15** D4
Homestead Rd SK12. . . . **135** C6
Homestead The ❽ M33 . . **108** D4
Homewood Rd M22 . . . . . **121** C1
Homewood Rd M22 . . . . . **109** D1
Honduras St ❶ OL4. . . . . . **67** B7

Hondwith Cl BL2. . . . . **25** C5
Honeybourne Cl M29. . . . . **59** C1
Honeycombe Cotts SK8 . **122** E5
Honey Hill OL4. . . . . **67** F5
Honey St M8. . . . . **159** B4
Honeysuckle Ave WN6 . . . **36** F3
Honeysuckle Cl
  Romiley SK6. . . . . **113** A5
  Sale M23 . . . . **108** C1
Honeysuckle Dr SK15 . . . . **86** C2
Honeysuckle Way OL12 . . **14** D3
Honeysuckle Wlk M33. . . **107** D6
Honeywell La OL8. . . . . **66** F3
Honeywood Cl BL0. . . . . . . **11** A3
Honford Rd M22 . . . . **121** C3
Hong Kong Ave M90 . . . . **130** A8
Honister Dr M24. . . . . **46** F2
Honister Rd
  Manchester M9 . . . . **157** C3
  Wigan WN5 . . . . **54** B6
Honister Way OL11. . . . . . . **30** B4
Honiton Ave SK14 . . . . . . **102** D2
Honiton Cl
  Chadderton OL9. . . . . **47** E1
  Heywood OL10. . . . . **46** B7
  Hindley WN7 . . . . **57** D2
Honiton Dr BL2. . . . . **43** A6
Honiton Gr M26. . . . . **43** D4
Honiton Way WA14 . . . . . **119** B6
Honiton Wlk ❸ SK14 . . . . **102** D2
Honor St M13 . . . . **98** F3
Honsham Wlk M23 . . . . . **108** E1
Hood Cl M29 . . . . **59** D1
Hood Dr WN7. . . . . **76** B3
Hood Sq OL4 . . . . **68** A5
Hood St M4 . . . . **159** B2
Hood Wlk ❸ M34. . . . . **113** A7
Hook St WN2 . . . . **151** C3
Hoole Cl SK8. . . . . **123** A5
HOOLEY BRIDGE **29** C4
Hooley Bridge Ind Est
  OL10. . . . . **29** C4
HOOLEY BROW. **29** D3
HOOLEY HILL **100** F6
Hooley Range SK4 . . . . . . **168** B3
Hooper St
  Manchester M12 . . . . **164** A4
  Stockport SK1, SK4 . . . . . **169** B1
HOOTEN GARDENS **76** C3
Hooton La WN7 . . . . **76** C3
Hooton St
  Bolton BL3 . . . . **146** C3
  Manchester M40 . . . . **160** C3
Hooton Way ❶❹ SK9 . . . . **131** D5
Hopcroft Cl M6 . . . . **80** A4
Hope Ave
  Bolton, Harwood Lee BL2 . **25** E5
  Bolton, Springfield BL2. . . **148** B2
  Handforth SK9 . . . . **131** C3
  Stretford M32 . . . . **96** B3
  Walkden M38. . . . . **60** C4
Hope Carr La WN7 . . . . **76** B2
Hope Carr Rd WN7 . . . . **76** A3
Hope Carr Way WN7 . . . . . **76** A3
Hope Carr Wildlife Reserve*
  WN7 . . . . **76** B2
Hopecourt Cl M6 . . . . **80** B4
Hope Cres WN6 . . . . **36** B6
Hope Ct ❶ OL12 . . . . **139** C4
Hopedale Cl M11 . . . . **160** C1
Hopedale Rd SK5 . . . . **111** F6
Hope Ent Ctr WN5 . . . . **36** E1
Hopefield Rd WA13 . . . . . **117** B4
Hopefield St BL3 . . . . **147** A4
Hope Fold Ave M46 . . . . . . **58** B2
Hopefold Dr M28 . . . . **60** D3
Hope Green Way SK10. . **133** D2
Hope Hey La M38 . . . . **59** F5
Hope La
  Leigh WA3, WN7 . . . . **76** C2
  Midway SK10. . . . . **133** D1
  Wardsend SK10. . . . . **133** E1
Hopelea St M20. . . . . **110** B7
Hope Park Cl M25. . . . . **63** B3
Hope Park Rd M25 . . . . **63** B3
Hope Pl OL11. . . . . **30** C1
Hope Rd
  Manchester M14 . . . . **98** D4
  Prestwich M25. . . . . **63** A2
  Sale M33 . . . . **108** B4
Hopes Carr SK1. . . . . **169** C1
Hope Sch WN3. . . . . **54** F2
Hope St
  Adlington PR6 . . . . **21** B8
  Ashton-in-M WN4 . . . . **73** D5
  Ashton-u-L OL6 . . . . **85** D4
  Aspull WN2 . . . . **38** A4
  Denton M34 . . . . **100** F5
  Dukinfield SK16 . . . . **101** B8
  Eccles M30 . . . . **79** F2
  Glossop SK13. . . . . **104** E2
  Hazel Grove SK7. . . . . . . **124** D3
  Heywood OL10. . . . . **46** F8
  Hindley WN2 . . . . **56** F6
  Horwich BL6 . . . . **22** C4
  Ince-in-M WN3 . . . . **55** E4
  Leigh WN7 . . . . **75** F6
  Manchester M1 . . . . **159** A1
  Newton-le-W WA12 . . . . . . **89** B3
  Oldham OL1 . . . . **67** A7
  Pendlebury M27. . . . . **80** A8
  Ramsbottom BL0 . . . . **138** B1
  Rochdale OL12. . . . . **139** C4
  Salford, Higher Broughton
  M7. . . . . **155** A3
  Salford, New Windsor M5 . **81** C1
  Scot Lane End BL6. . . . . . **38** E3

Hope St continued
  Shaw OL2 . . . . **149** B3
  Stockport SK4 . . . . **169** A1
  ❸ Swinton M27 . . . . **79** D7
  Tyldesley M29 . . . . **77** B5
  Walkden M38. . . . . **60** A4
  Wigan WN1 . . . . **150** C4
Hope Street N BL6 . . . . . . **22** B5
Hope Terr
  Dukinfield SK16 . . . . **101** B8
  Stockport SK3 . . . . **170** B4
Hopgarth Wlk M40 . . . . **83** D5
Hopkin Ave OL1. . . . . **67** B8
Hopkin Mill OL4 . . . . **67** D6
Hopkins Bldgs OL5. . . . . . **68** E3
Hopkins Field WA14 . . . . . **119** B1
Hopkinson Ave M34 . . . . . **100** C5
Hopkinson Cl OL3. . . . . **69** B8
Hopkinson Rd M9. . . . . **64** D5
Hopkins St
  Hyde SK14 . . . . **167** B4
  Manchester M12 . . . . **99** A3
Hopkin St OL1 . . . . **153** C3
Hoppet La M43 . . . . **84** C2
Hopton Ave M22 . . . . **121** F3
Hopton Ct M15 . . . . **163** A2
HOPWOOD **29** E1
Hopwood Ave
  Eccles M30 . . . . **79** D3
  Heywood OL10. . . . . **46** D8
  Horwich BL6 . . . . **22** C4
Hopwood Cl
  ❺ Golborne WA3 . . . . **90** F8
  Whitefield BL9 . . . . **44** F3
Hopwood Ct M24 . . . . **47** A4
Hopwood Ct Mews ❺
  OL10 . . . . **46** E8
Hopwood Hall Coll
  (Middleton Campus)
  M24. . . . . **47** A5
Hopwood Hall Coll (Rochdale
  Campus) OL12 . . . . **139** B3
Hopwood Prim Sch OL10. **46** E8
Hopwood Rd M24. . . . . **47** A4
Hopwood St
  Failsworth M40 . . . . **83** B6
  Pendlebury M27. . . . . **80** A8
Hopwood Woodlands Nature
  Reserve* M24. . . . . **47** A5
Horace Barnes Cl M14 . . . **98** A3
Horace Gr SK4. . . . . **169** B4
Horace St BL1 . . . . **143** A2
Horatio St ❹ M18. . . . . **99** F6
Horbury Ave M18 . . . . **99** D3
Horbury Dr BL8. . . . . **27** C2
Horden Wlk ❽ OL2 . . . . . . **48** E4
Hordern Cl SK13 . . . . **104** A4
Horeb St BL3 . . . . **145** A1
Horest La OL3 . . . . **50** B7
Horley Cl BL8. . . . . **27** C7
Hornbeam Cl
  Altrincham WA15 . . . . . . **120** E5
  Sale M33 . . . . **107** C5
Hornbeam Cres WN4. . . . . **73** B3
Hornbeam Rd M19 . . . . **99** B2
Hornbeam Way M4 . . . . . **159** A3
Hornby Ave M9 . . . . **64** E5
Hornby Dr BL3 . . . . **40** D3
Hornby Gr WN7 . . . . **76** D7
Hornby Lodge M25. . . . . . . **63** B3
Hornby Rd M16, M32. . . . . **96** F4
Hornby St
  Bury BL9 . . . . **140** C4
  Heywood OL10. . . . . **29** D2
  Manchester M8 . . . . **158** C4
  Middleton M24. . . . . **65** A8
  Oldham OL8 . . . . **153** A1
  Wigan WN1 . . . . **37** C2
Horncastle Cl
  Bury BL8 . . . . **27** D5
  ❹ Golborne WA3 . . . . **90** F8
Horncastle Rd M40. . . . . . . **65** B1
Hornchurch Ct
  Heywood OL10. . . . . **46** E7
  ❷ Manchester M15 . . . . . **162** D2
Hornchurch St M15 . . . . . **162** B2
Horncliffe Cl BB4 . . . . **1** E8
Horncliffe Rd BL1 . . . . **1** B8
Horncliffe View BB4 . . . . . . **1** B8
Horne Gr WN3 . . . . **54** F5
Horne St BL9. . . . . **44** E8
Hornet Cl OL11. . . . . **31** A3
Horniman Ho M13 . . . . . . **163** B1
Hornsea Cl
  Bury BL8 . . . . **26** F2
  Chadderton OL9. . . . . **47** F1
Hornsea Rd SK2 . . . . **125** A5
Hornsea Wlk M11. . . . . **83** A1
Hornsey Gr WN3 . . . . **54** D3
Horridge Ave WA12 . . . . . **89** C5
Horridge Fold BL7 . . . . **8** E3
Horridge Fold Ave BL3 . . . **39** F4
Horridge Fold BL7 . . . . **27** B4
Horrobin Fold BL7 . . . . **9** C2
Horrobin La BL7 . . . . **9** C2
Horrocks Fold BL1 . . . . . . **24** C7
Horrocks Fold Ave BL1 . . **24** D6
Horrocks Rd BL7. . . . . **9** C6
Horrocks St
  Leigh WN7 . . . . **75** A4
  Radcliffe M26 . . . . **44** C4
  Tyldesley M46 . . . . **58** E1
Horsa St BL2 ❿ **25** B1
Horsedge St OL1. . . . . . . **153** C3
Horsefield Ave OL12 . . . . . **14** C6

Horsefield Cl M21........ 109 E7
Horseshoe La
 Alderley Edge SK9........ 137 A2
 Bolton BL7........ 25 A8
 Oldham OL9........ 65 F6
Horsfield St BL3........ 144 A1
Horsfield Way SK6........ 112 F6
Horsforth La OL3........ 69 A4
Horsham Ave SK7........ 124 C1
Horsham Cl
 Bury BL8........ 27 C7
 Westhoughton BL5........ 57 F6
Horsham Gr WN2........ 37 F2
Horsham St M6........ 154 B2
Horstead Wlk M19........ 99 A2
Horton Ave BL1........ 24 E6
Horton Mill Prim Sch OL4 67 B6
Horton Rd OL2........ 98 A2
Horton Sq OL2........ 149 B2
Horton St
 Stockport SK1........ 124 A7
 Wigan WN6........ 36 E3
Hortree Rd M32........ 96 E2
HORWICH........ 22 D4
Horwich Bsns Pk BL6........ 22 C4
*Horwich Heritage Ctr**........
 BL6........ 22 C4
Horwich L Ctr BL6........ 22 C3
Horwich Parish CE Prim Sch
 BL6........ 22 C4
Horwich Parkway Sta BL6 39 C7
Horwood Cres M20........ 110 D5
Hoscar Dr M19........ 110 F7
HOSKER'S NOOK........ 57 D6
Hoskers Nook BL5........ 57 D7
Hoskers The BL5........ 57 D6
Hoskins Cl M12........ 165 A1
Hospital Ave M30........ 79 E2
Hospital Cotts M25........ 62 E5
Hospital Rd
 Bolton BL7........ 25 A8
 Pendlebury M27........ 80 B7
Hotel Rd M90........ 130 C7
Hotel St
 Bolton BL1........ 145 C3
 Newton-le-W WA12........ 89 C3
Hothersall Rd SK5........ 111 F8
Hotspur Cl M14........ 110 A8
HOUGH........ 21 D2
Hough Cl OL8........ 67 A2
Hough End Ave M21........ 109 C6
Houghend Cres M21........ 109 E6
Hough Fold Way BL2........ 25 E4
Hough Gn WA15........ 128 E5
Hough Hall Rd M40........ 157 C4
Hough Hill Rd SK15........ 102 B8
Hough La
 Alderley Edge SK9........ 137 D3
 Bolton BL7........ 24 F7
 Dukinfield SK14........ 101 F6
 Stake Hill M24........ 47 F4
 Tyldesley M29........ 77 C8
Hough Rd M20........ 110 A7
Hough St
 Bolton BL3........ 146 A4
 Tyldesley M29........ 77 D8
Houghton BL3........ 145 B1
Houghton Ave
 Oldham OL8........ 66 D2
 Wigan WN5........ 36 E2
Houghton Cl
 Newton-le-W WA12........ 89 B3
 Rochdale OL16........ 31 C6
*Houghton Dale Nature
 Reserve** M34........ 101 C1
Houghton La
 Shevington WN6........ 35 F6
 Swinton M27........ 79 D5
Houghton Rd M8........ 64 A1
Houghton St
 Bury BL9........ 140 B1
 Leigh WN7........ 75 F6
 Newton-le-W WA12........ 89 B3
 Pendlebury M27........ 80 D6
 Royton OL2........ 48 E2
Hough Wlk M7........ 158 A3
Houghwood Grange WN4 72 F3
Houldsworth Ave WA14 119 E7
*Houldsworth Mill Bsns & Art
 Ctr* SK4,SK5........ 111 E7
Houldsworth Sq SK5 111 E7
Houldsworth St
 Manchester M1........ 159 B2
 2 Radcliffe M26........ 43 F5
 Reddish SK5........ 111 E7
Houseley Ave OL9........ 66 A3
Houseman Cres M20 109 F5
Houseman Gr WN6........ 37 A2
Housley Cl WN3........ 150 A1
Houson St OL3........ 153 C1
Houston Pk M50........ 154 C1
Hove Cl BL8........ 10 F1
Hoveden St M8........ 158 C4
Hove Dr M14........ 110 B7
Hove St BL3........ 144 C1
Hovey Cl M8........ 155 C3
Hovingham St OL16........ 31 B8
Hovington Gdns M19...... 110 E6
Hovis St M11........ 165 C4
Howard Ave
 Bolton BL3........ 146 A4
 Cheadle SK8........ 123 A1
 Eccles M30........ 79 D3
 Kearsley BL4........ 60 F7
 Lymm WA13........ 117 B4

Howard Ave continued
 Reddish SK4........ 111 C6
Howard Cl
 Glossop SK13........ 104 B2
 Romiley SK6........ 113 A2
Howard Cl OL6........ 166 C3
Howard Dr WA15........ 120 A1
Howard Hill BL9........ 45 A5
Howardian Cl OL8........ 66 E2
Howard La M34........ 100 F4
Howard Pl
 8 Hyde SK14........ 167 A2
 Rochdale OL16........ 139 C4
Howard Rd
 Culcheth WA3........ 92 A2
 Wythenshawe M22........ 109 D1
Howards La WN5........ 53 F7
Howard's La OL5........ 68 F1
Howards Mdw SK13........ 116 B7
Howard Spring Wlk M8 155 C4
Howard St
 Ashton-u-L OL7........ 166 A4
 Bolton BL1........ 143 C1
 Denton M34........ 100 E5
 Glossop SK13........ 104 C1
 Manchester M8........ 158 C4
 Oldham OL4........ 49 E1
 Radcliffe M26........ 44 B3
 Rochdale OL12........ 139 C4
 Salford M5........ 161 A4
 Shaw OL2........ 149 A3
 Stalybridge SK15........ 86 D4
 Stockport SK1........ 169 C2
 Stretford M32........ 96 D2
 Wigan WN5........ 54 C5
Howard Way OL15........ 6 C3
Howarth Ave M28........ 79 C7
Howarth Cl M11........ 83 A1
HOWARTH CROSS........ 15 C2
Howarth Cross St 5 OL16 15 B2
Howarth Ct SK2........ 124 B5
Howarth Dr M44........ 93 F1
Howarth Farm Way OL12 15 C3
Howarth Gn OL12........ 15 C3
Howarth Sq OL16........ 31 A8
Howarth St
 Farnworth BL4........ 60 D7
 Leigh WN7........ 76 B4
 Littleborough OL15........ 16 B6
 Manchester M16........ 97 C4
 Westhoughton BL5........ 57 F8
Howbridge Cl M28........ 78 C8
Howbro Dr OL7........ 84 E5
Howbrook Wlk 7 M15 162 C2
How Clough Cl M28........ 60 F2
How Clough Dr M28........ 60 F2
Howcroft Cl BL1........ 145 B4
Howcroft St BL3........ 145 A1
Howden Cl SK5........ 99 E2
Howden Dr WN3........ 55 B4
Howden Rd
 Manchester M9........ 64 C5
 New Mills SK22........ 127 C1
HOWE BRIDGE........ 58 B1
Howe Bridge Cl M46........ 58 B1
Howe Bridge Sports Ctr
 M46........ 58 B1
Howe Dr BL0........ 11 B2
Howell Croft N 7 BL1........ 145 C3
Howell Croft S BL1........ 145 C3
Howells Ave M33........ 108 B5
Howell's Yd 5 BL1........ 145 C3
Howe St
 Ashton-u-L OL7........ 100 F8
 Salford M7........ 155 A3
Howgill Cres OL8........ 66 E3
Howgill St M11........ 83 D1
How Lea Dr BL9........ 27 F6
Howley Cl M44........ 94 B1
Howsin Ave BL2........ 25 B4
Howton Cl M12........ 99 A4
Howty Cl SK9........ 131 D1
Hoxton Cl SK6........ 113 A4
Hoy Dr M41........ 95 D5
Hoylake Cl
 Failsworth M40........ 83 D8
 Leigh WN7........ 75 D2
Hoylake Rd
 Bacup OL13........ 3 E8
 2 Bolton BL1........ 143 B4
 Manchester M12........ 163 C4
 Middleton M24........ 65 C6
 Radcliffe M26........ 44 C1
 Whitworth OL12........ 4 D3
Hoyle's Terr OL16........ 31 E6
Hoyle Street Ind Est
 M12........ 163 C3
Hoyle Wlk M13........ 163 C2
Hubert Worthington Ho 8
 SK9........ 137 A1
Hucclecote Ave M22...... 121 C2
Hucklow Ave M23........ 121 A3
Hucklow Bank 30 SK13 171 A2
Hucklow Cl 30 SK13...... 171 A2
Hucklow Fold 34 SK13... 171 A2
Hucklow Lanes 33 SK13 171 A2
Huddart Cl M5........ 161 B4
Huddersfield Rd
 Denshaw OL3........ 33 E2
 Diggle OL3........ 51 D5
 Newhey OL16, OL3........ 32 D5

Huddersfield Rd continued
 Oldham OL1, OL4........ 67 D8
 Stalybridge OL5, SK15...... 86 E4
Hudson Gr 3 WA3........ 90 E8
Hudson Rd SK14........ 113 E7
Hudsons Pas OL15........ 16 C7
Hudson Sq OL1........ 48 D1
Hudson St OL9........ 66 A2
Hudsons Wlk OL11........ 30 C7
Hudswell Cl M45........ 62 E8
Hugh Bsns Pk BB4........ 2 F8
Hughendon Cl BL8........ 26 F7
Hughes Ave BL6........ 22 A4
Hughes Cl
 Bury BL9........ 141 A3
 Failsworth M35........ 83 E8
Hughes St
 Bolton BL1........ 143 A2
 Manchester M11........ 164 B4
Hughes Way M30........ 79 A1
Hugh Fold OL4........ 67 E5
Hughley Cl OL2........ 49 A4
Hugh Lupus St BL1........ 25 A5
HUGH MILL........ 2 F8
Hugh Oldham Dr M7........ 81 C6
Hugh St
 Glossop SK13........ 104 B1
 Rochdale OL16........ 31 A8
Hughtrede St OL16........ 31 B3
Hugo St
 Farnworth BL4........ 42 B2
 Manchester M40........ 83 A7
 Rochdale OL11........ 30 D2
Hulbert St
 Bolton BL1........ 27 C1
 Middleton M24........ 47 B1
Hullet Cl WN6........ 35 E8
Hull Mill La OL3........ 50 F5
Hull Sq M3........ 158 A2
Hully St SK15........ 85 F2
HULME........ 162 C2
Hulme Court Prep Sch 1
 OL8........ 66 D4
Hulme Ct M15........ 162 B3
Hulme Dr WA15........ 120 C7
Hulme Gr WN7........ 75 C6
Hulme Gram Schs 2 OL8 66 D4
Hulme Hall Ave SK8...... 132 B8
Hulme Hall Cl SK8........ 123 A1
Hulme Hall Cres SK8.... 132 A8
Hulme Hall Grammar Sch 2
 SK8........ 123 A1
Hulme Hall La M40........ 160 B4
Hulme Hall Rd
 Cheadle SK8........ 123 A1
 Manchester M15........ 162 A3
Hulme Pl M5........ 81 C2
Hulme Rd
 Bolton BL2........ 25 E5
 Kearsley M26........ 61 C7
 Leigh WN7........ 75 C6
 Reddish, Dane Bank M34 . 100 B3
 Reddish, Heaton Chapel
  SK4........ 111 C6
 Sale M33........ 108 B3
Hulmes Rd M35, M40...... 83 E5
Hulme St
 Ashton-u-L OL6........ 85 D4
 Bury BL8........ 140 A3
 Manchester M1, M15...... 162 C3
 Oldham OL8........ 66 E4
 Salford M5........ 81 C1
 Stockport SK1........ 124 B7
Hulme's Terr BL2........ 43 C8
Hulton Ave M28........ 60 B3
Hulton Cl SK3........ 123 B6
Hulton District Ctr M28 .. 60 A4
Hulton Dr BL3........ 146 A3
Hulton La BL3........ 146 A3
HULTON LANE ENDS...... 59 A8
Hulton St
 Denton M34........ 100 E4
 Failsworth M35........ 83 E7
 Manchester M16........ 97 E4
 Salford M5........ 161 A3
Humber Dr BL9........ 27 F7
Humber Pl WN5........ 54 C7
Humber Rd
 Milnrow OL16........ 32 A6
 Tyldesley M29........ 77 C7
Humber St
 Manchester M8........ 156 B3
 Salford M50........ 154 A1
Humberstone Ave M15 .. 162 C2
Hume St
 Manchester M19........ 111 B8
 Rochdale OL16........ 31 A5
Humphrey Booth Gdns
 M6........ 154 B3
Humphrey Cres M41...... 96 A2
Humphrey La M41........ 96 A2
Humphrey Park Sta M32 96 A3
Humphrey Pk M41........ 96 A2
Humphrey St M16........ 161 B1
Humphrey St
 Ince-in-M WN2........ 56 A7
 Salford M8........ 155 C4
Humphries Cl M40........ 159 C4
Huncoat Ave SK4........ 111 D5
Huncote Dr M9........ 64 E1
Hungerford Wlk 6 M23 120 D7
HUNGER HILL
 Bolton........ 40 D3
 Standish........ 18 F4
Hunger Hill Ave BL3...... 40 E2
Hunger Hill La OL12...... 13 F3
Hunmanby Ave M15...... 162 C3
Hunstanton Dr BL8........ 27 D5

Hunston Rd M33........ 107 F2
Hunt Ave OL7........ 85 B5
Hunter Dr M26........ 44 A5
Hunter Rd WN5........ 36 E1
Hunters Chase WN5...... 53 E1
Hunters Cl
 Handforth SK9........ 131 F1
 6 Romiley SK6........ 112 F3
Hunters Ct
 Dukinfield SK16........ 101 F7
 Stalybridge SK15........ 102 D8
Hunters Ct BL0........ 11 C7
Hunters Hill BL9........ 45 B4
Hunters Hill La OL3........ 51 C6
Hunters La SK13........ 115 F8
Hunter's La
 Oldham OL11........ 153 C3
 Rochdale OL12, OL16...... 139 C4
Hunters Lodge SK9........ 131 F1
Hunters Mews
 Sale M33........ 108 A5
 Wilmslow SK9........ 137 C7
Hunterston Ave M30...... 80 A2
Hunter's View SK9........ 131 C3
Hunt Fold Dr BL8........ 10 F1
Huntingdon Ave OL9...... 152 B1
Huntingdon Cres SK5.... 112 C5
Huntingdon Rd SK8...... 131 C7
Huntingdon St M9........ 157 B8
Huntingdon Wlk 20 BL1 143 B2
Huntingdon Ave M20...... 110 A7
Huntley Mount Rd BL9 .. 141 B3
Huntley Rd
 Manchester M8........ 63 E2
 Stockport SK3........ 123 B7
Huntley St BL1........ 143 B3
Huntly Chase SK9........ 137 C7
Huntly Rd OL10........ 28 E1
Hunt Rd SK14........ 102 A5
Huntroyde Ave 28 BL2... 25 B1
Hunt's Bank
 Manchester M3........ 158 C2
 Westhoughton BL5........ 57 F6
Huntsbottom La M44...... 93 E2
Huntsman Dr M44........ 105 F7
Huntsman Rd M9........ 157 C4
Hunts Rd 2 M6........ 80 D5
Hunt St
 Atherton M46........ 58 D3
 Manchester M9........ 64 D1
 Wigan WN1........ 151 B3
Hurdlow Ave M7........ 81 C6
Hurdlow Gn 10 SK13...... 171 A1
Hurdlow Lea 11 SK13.... 171 A1
Hurdlow Mews SK13...... 171 A1
Hurdlow Way 12 SK13 ... 171 A1
Hurdlow Wlk M9........ 157 A3
Hurdsfield Rd SK2........ 124 D4
Hurford Ave M18........ 99 D6
Hurlbote Cl SK9........ 131 D5
Hurley Dr SK8........ 122 E2
Hurlston Rd BL3........ 147 A2
HURST........ 85 D5
Hurst Ave
 Cheadle SK8........ 132 C6
 Sale M33........ 107 C3
Hurstbank Ave M19...... 110 D4
Hurst Bank Rd OL6........ 85 E6
Hurstbourne Ave M11 ... 83 B2
HURST BROOK........ 166 C4
Hurstbrook Cl OL4........ 104 F1
Hurst Brook Cl OL6...... 166 C4
Hurstbrook Dr M32........ 95 F2
Hurst Cl
 Glossop SK13........ 104 E1
 Hulton BL5........ 58 F7
*Hurst Clough Nature
 Reserve** SK14........ 102 F2
Hurst Cres SK13........ 116 E8
Hurst Cross OL6........ 85 D5
Hurst Ct
 Ashton-u-L OL6........ 85 E5
 Wythenshawe M23........ 120 F4
HURSTEAD........ 15 C4
Hurstead 2 OL12........ 15 C4
Hurstead Cl M8........ 156 A2
Hurstead Gn 8 OL12...... 15 D4
Hurstead Rd OL16........ 31 F6
Hurstfield Ind Est SK4,
 SK5........ 111 E6
Hurstfield Rd M28........ 78 B8
Hurstfold Ave M19........ 110 D3
Hurst Gr OL6........ 85 E5
Hurst Green Cl BL8........ 43 F8
Hurst Hall Dr OL6........ 85 E5
Hursthead Inf Sch SK8 .. 132 C6
Hursthead Jun Sch SK8 132 C7
Hursthead Rd SK8........ 132 B7
Hursthead Wlk M13...... 163 B3
Hurst Hill Cres OL6........ 85 D4
HURST KNOLL........ 85 D4
Hurst Knoll CE Prim Sch
 OL6........ 166 C4
Hurst La WA3........ 92 C7
Hurst Mdw
 Ashton-u-L OL6........ 85 D5
 Rochdale OL16........ 31 C3
Hurst Mill La WA3........ 92 C8
Hurst Mills Ind Est 8
 SK13........ 104 F1
Hurst Rd SK13........ 104 F1
Hurst St
 Bolton BL3........ 146 C3
 Bury BL9........ 141 A2
 Hindley WN2........ 56 C6
 Leigh WN7........ 76 B3

Hurst St continued
 Oldham OL9........ 153 A3
 Reddish SK5........ 111 E7
 Rochdale OL11........ 31 A5
 Walkden M28........ 60 D6
Hurstvale Ave SK8........ 122 B1
Hurstville Rd M21........ 109 B6
Hurstway Dr 33 M9........ 64 E3
Hurst Wlk 4 M22........ 121 A2
Hurstwood
 Ashton-u-L OL6........ 85 F6
 Bolton BL3........ 24 E5
Hurstwood Cl OL8........ 67 C4
Hurstwood Ct
 Bolton BL3........ 42 C4
 Leigh WN7........ 76 B2
Hurstwood Rd SK2........ 124 B4
Huskisson Way WA12 .... 89 B4
Hus St 1 M43........ 100 A8
Hustads La OL3........ 50 E1
Husteads La OL3........ 50 F1
Hutchins La OL4........ 49 D1
Hutchinson Rd OL11...... 13 D2
Hutchinson St
 4 Radcliffe M26........ 44 C4
 Rochdale OL11........ 30 C6
Hutchinson Way M26..... 44 A3
Hutchinson Wlk 4 M34... 100 A8
Hutton Ave
 Ashton-u-L OL6........ 85 E3
 Boothstown M28........ 77 F6
Hutton Cl WA3........ 91 E5
Hutton Lodge M20........ 110 C7
Hutton St WN1........ 20 A3
Hutton Wlk 7 M13........ 163 C2
Huxley Ave M8........ 156 A2
Huxley Cl SK7........ 132 E7
Huxley Dr SK7........ 132 E7
Huxley Pl WN3........ 150 A1
Huxley St
 Altrincham WA14........ 119 D7
 Bolton BL1........ 142 C2
 6 Oldham OL4........ 67 C6
Huxley Terr 4 WA14...... 119 C1
Huxton Gn SK7........ 124 A2
Huyton Rd BL6, PR7........ 21 A6
Huyton Terr PR6........ 21 B6
Hyacinth Cl SK3........ 170 A1
Hyatt Cres WN6........ 19 C3
HYDE........ 167 C2
Hyde Bsns Ctr SK14........ 167 A2
Hyde Central Sta SK14 .. 101 C2
Hyde Cl WN3........ 150 A1
Hyde Clarendon Sports Hall
 SK14........ 167 B3
Hyde Dr M28........ 60 C2
Hyde Fold Cl M19........ 110 F6
Hyde Gr
 Manchester M13........ 163 B4
 Sale M33........ 108 B4
 Walkden M28........ 60 C2
Hyde Ho SK4........ 111 C5
Hyde Leisure Pool SK14 167 C2
Hyde North Sta SK16...... 101 C1
Hyde Pl M13........ 163 C1
Hyde Rd
 Denton M34........ 101 A3
 Manchester, Gorton M12,
  M18........ 99 D4
 Manchester, West Gorton
  M12........ 164 B2
 Mottram in L SK14........ 103 A4
 Oldham M24........ 65 E6
 Romiley SK14, SK6........ 113 B5
 Walkden M28........ 60 C2
HYDES........ 85 F1
Hyde's Cross M4........ 159 A2
Hyde Sq M24........ 46 E1
Hyde St
 Bolton BL3........ 146 C3
 Droylsden M43........ 84 C4
 Dukinfield SK16........ 101 D8
Hydes Terr 1 SK15........ 86 B2
Hydon Brook Wlk OL11... 30 C4
Hydra Cl M7........ 81 C3
Hydrangea Cl
 Bolton BL3........ 57 F6
 8 Sale M33........ 107 C6
Hyldavale Ave SK8........ 122 B6
Hylton Dr SK8........ 132 C8
Hyman Goldstone Wlk 4
 M8........ 155 C3
Hyndman Ct M5........ 154 A2
Hypatia St BL2........ 148 B3
Hythe Cl M14........ 98 C3
Hythe Rd SK3........ 123 B8
Hythe St BL3........ 146 A4
Hythe Wlk OL9........ 152 B2**

I

Ibberton Wlk 8 M9........ 64 F1
Ibsley PR7........ 20 B3
Ice House Cl 5 M28........ 59 F3
Iceland St M6........ 154 C2
Idonia St BL1........ 143 A3
Ifco Ct M14........ 98 C3
Ilex Gr M7........ 155 A2
Ilford St M11........ 83 B2
Ilfracombe Rd SK2........ 124 D6
Ilfracombe St M40........ 83 D6
Ilkeston Dr WN2........ 38 F3
Ilkeston Wlk
 5 Denton M34........ 113 A8
 4 Manchester M40........ 83 A6

Ilkley Cl
Bolton BL2 . . . . **148** C3
Chadderton OL9 . . . . **152** B2
Ilkley Cres SK5 . . . . **111** E8
Ilkley Dr M41 . . . . **95** A4
Ilkley St M40 . . . . **83** A8
Ilk St M11 . . . . **95** B3
Illingworth Ave SK15 . . . . **86** C2
Illona Dr M7 . . . . **81** A8
Ilminster OL11 . . . . **139** B2
Ilminster Wlk ⁊ M9 . . . . . . **64** E5
Ilthorpe Wlk ⁊ M40 . . . . . . **83** A6
Imex Bsns Pk M13 . . . . **98** F3
Imogen Cl M5 . . . . **161** C4
Imperial Dr WN7 . . . . **76** D6
Imperial Point M50 . . . . . . **96** F7
Imperial Terr M33 . . . . . . **108** A4
Imperial War Mus North*
M17 . . . . **96** E7
Ina Ave BL1 . . . . **23** F1
Ince CE Prim Sch WN2 . . . **56** A7
Ince Cl
Manchester M20 . . . . **110** B7
Stockport SK4 . . . . **169** B3
Ince Green La WN2, WN3 . **151** C2
Ince Hall Ave WN2 . . . . . . **151** C4
INCE-IN-MAKERFIELD . . . **151** B3
Ince St SK3 . . . . **169** B3
Ince Sta WN3 . . . . **151** C2
Ince Wlk WN1 . . . . **150** C4
Inchcape Dr M9 . . . . **64** B4
Inchfield Cl OL11 . . . . **29** E8
Inchfield Rd
Manchester M40 . . . . **65** B1
Walsden OL14 . . . . **6** A8
Inchley Rd M13 . . . . **163** B3
Inchwood Mews OL4 . . . . . **49** E4
Incline Rd OL8 . . . . **66** C2
Independent St BL3 . . . . . . **43** A3
Ind Est The ⁊ BL1 . . . . . . **143** A2
India Ho M1 . . . . **163** A4
India St BL9 . . . . **11** C3
Indigo St M6 . . . . **80** F5
Indigo Wlk M6 . . . . **80** F5
Indus Pl M7 . . . . **81** C4
Industrial Cotts M4 BB4 . . . **2** F8
Industrial St
Ramsbottom BL0 . . . . **1** C1
Westhoughton BL5 . . . . . . **57** F7
Industry Rd
Chadderton OL9 . . . . **66** A4
⁊ Littleborough OL15 . . . **16** B5
⁊ Rochdale OL11 . . . . . . **13** E1
Whitworth OL12 . . . . **4** D2
Infant St M25 . . . . **63** C4
Infirmary St M11 . . . . **145** C3
Ingersol Rd M11 BL6 . . . . . **22** E1
Ingham Ave WA12 . . . . **89** C1
Ingham Rd WA14 . . . . **107** D1
Inghams La OL15 . . . . **16** B5
Ingham St
Bury BL9 . . . . **141** A1
Failsworth M40 . . . . **83** E4
Leigh WN7 . . . . **75** E8
⁊ Oldham OL1 . . . . **67** A7
Inghamwood Cl M7 . . . . . . **155** C3
Ingleby Ave M9 . . . . **64** F4
Ingleby Cl
Shaw OL2 . . . . **149** A4
Standish WN6 . . . . **19** D2
Westhoughton BL5 . . . . **40** A2
Ingleby Ct M32 . . . . **96** E1
Ingleby Way OL2 . . . . **149** A4
Ingledene Ave M7 . . . . **63** E1
Ingledene Cl BL1 . . . . **63** E1
Ingledene Gr BL1 . . . . **142** A2
Ingle Dr SK2 . . . . **124** C7
Inglefield OL11 . . . . **13** F1
Inglehead Cl M34 . . . . **101** A2
Inglenook Cl M31 . . . . **106** F6
Ingle Nook Cl M31 . . . . . . **106** F6
Inglenook Court Leigh
M46 . . . . **76** A8
Ingle Rd SK8 . . . . **123** A6
Ingles Fold OL2 . . . . **78** B7
Inglesham Cl
Leigh WN7 . . . . **75** E1
Wythenshawe M23 . . . . . **121** B6
Ingleton Ave M8 . . . . **64** A2
Ingleton Cl
Bolton BL2 . . . . **25** D4
Cheadle SK8 . . . . **122** C6
Newton-le-W WA12 . . . . . . **89** B4
Royton OL2 . . . . **48** D5
Ingleton Dr WA11 . . . . **71** B1
Ingleton Mews BL8 . . . . . . **27** B4
Ingleton Rd SK3 . . . . **123** C7
Inglewhite Ave WN1 . . . . . **37** C2
Inglewhite Cl ⁊ WN1 . . . . . **37** C2
Inglewhite Pl ⁊ WN1 . . . . . **37** C2
Inglewood WA14 . . . . **119** B3
Inglewood Ave WN1 . . . . . **151** B3
Inglewood Cl
Ashton-u-L OL7 . . . . **84** F5
Bury BL9 . . . . **141** C4
Partington M31 . . . . **105** F4
Inglewood Ct ⁊ WN5 . . . . . **54** D5
Inglewood Hollow SK15 . . **102** C8
Inglewood Rd M41 . . . . **95** C3
Inglewood Wlk M13 . . . . . **163** C2
Inglis St OL15 . . . . **16** B6
Ingoe Cl OL10 . . . . **29** F3
Ingoldsby Ave M13 . . . . **98** D4
Ingram Dr SK4 . . . . **110** E3
Ingram St
Platt Bridge WN2 . . . . **56** A3

Ingram St continued
Wigan WN6 . . . . **36** F2
Ings Ave OL12 . . . . **14** B2
Ings La OL12 . . . . **14** C2
Inkerman St
Hyde SK14 . . . . **167** A4
Manchester M40 . . . . **157** A2
⁊ Rochdale OL12 . . . . . . **14** F1
Ink St OL16 . . . . **139** C3
Inman St
Bury BL9 . . . . **44** E8
Denton M34 . . . . **100** F3
Innes St M12 . . . . **99** B3
Innis Ave M40 . . . . **83** C5
Inscape House Salford
M28 . . . . **60** E1
Inscape House Sch SK8 . . **122** D3
Institute St BL1 . . . . **148** A3
Instow Cl
Chadderton OL9 . . . . **47** F1
Manchester M13 . . . . **164** A2
Intake La OL3 . . . . **69** B3
International App M90 . . . **130** C7
Invar Rd M27 . . . . **61** D1
Inverbeg Dr BL2 . . . . **43** A7
Invergarry Wlk ⁊ M11 . . . . **83** C1
Innerlael Ave BL1 . . . . **144** B4
Inverness Ave M9 . . . . **65** A4
Inverness Cl WN7 . . . . **38** D5
Inverness Rd SK16 . . . . . . **101** C7
Inver Wlk M40 . . . . **65** D2
Inward Dr WN6 . . . . **36** A5
Inwood Wlk M8 . . . . **156** C2
Inworth Cl BL5 . . . . **57** F6
Inworth Wlk M8 . . . . **155** C3
Iona Pl BL2 . . . . **25** C2
Iona Way M41 . . . . **95** E5
Ionian Gdns ⁊ M7 . . . . **81** C5
Ipswich St OL11 . . . . **139** C1
Ipswich Wlk
⁊⁰ Denton M34 . . . . **101** A1
Manchester M12 . . . . **164** B1
Iqbal Cl M12 . . . . **165** A1
Irby Wlk SK8 . . . . **123** A4
Ireby Cl M24 . . . . **46** C2
Iredale Cres WN6 . . . . **36** F7
Iredine St ⁊ M11 . . . . **83** C1
Irene Ave SK14 . . . . **101** E5
Iris Ave
Farnworth BL4 . . . . **42** A1
Kearsley BL4 . . . . **60** F5
Manchester M11 . . . . **99** D8
Iris St
Oldham OL4 . . . . **66** F3
Ramsbottom BL0 . . . . **138** B2
Iris Wlk ⁊ M31 . . . . **105** E2
Irkdale St M8 . . . . **156** C2
Irk St M4 . . . . **159** A3
Irk Vale Dr OL1, OL9 . . . . . . **47** F1
Irk Valley Com Sch M8 . . . **156** C4
Irk Way M45 . . . . **45** B2
IRLAM **105** F7
Irlam Ave M30 . . . . **79** D2
Irlam & Cadishead Com High
Sch M44 . . . . **94** A2
Irlam Endowed Prim Sch ⁊
M44 . . . . **94** A2
Irlam Ind Est M44 . . . . **105** E7
Irlam Prim Sch ⁊ M44 . . . . **94** A1
Irlam Rd
Sale M33 . . . . **108** C4
Urmston M41 . . . . **94** D2
IRLAMS O' TH' HEIGHT . . . **80** E5
Irlam Sq M6 . . . . **80** D5
Irlam St
Bolton BL1 . . . . **143** B3
Manchester M40 . . . . **157** B1
Irlam Sta M44 . . . . **105** E7
Irlam Wharf Rd M44 . . . . . **106** A6
Irmass Ind Est M17 . . . . **96** D6
Irma St BL1 . . . . **143** C3
Iron St
Horwich BL6 . . . . **22** C2
Manchester M40 . . . . **160** B3
Iron Works The OL2 . . . . **48** D3
Irvin Dr M22, SK8 . . . . **131** A8
Irvine Ave ⁊ M28 . . . . **78** A6
Irvine St WN7 . . . . **75** F6
Irving Cl SK2 . . . . **124** A3
Irving Ho ⁊ BL1 . . . . **143** B2
Irving St
Bolton BL1 . . . . **143** B2
Oldham OL8 . . . . **66** B2
Irwin St M40 . . . . **83** C6
Irwell Ave
Eccles M30 . . . . **79** F1
Walkden M38 . . . . **60** B4
Irwell Cl ⁊ M26 . . . . **44** B2
Irwell Gr M30 . . . . **79** F1
Irwell Ho ⁊ M15 . . . . **162** A3
Irwell Pl
Eccles M30 . . . . **79** F1
Kearsley M26 . . . . **61** B8
Salford M5 . . . . **81** C2
Wigan WN5 . . . . **54** C6
Irwell Rd WN5 . . . . **53** F7
Irwell St
Bury BL9 . . . . **140** B2
Kearsley M26 . . . . **61** A8
Manchester M3 . . . . **158** B1
Manchester, Strangeways M7,
M8 . . . . **158** B4
Radcliffe M26 . . . . **44** B2
Ramsbottom BL0 . . . . **138** C2
IRWELL VALE **1** C5
Irwell Vale Rd BB4, BL0 . . . . **1** C6
Irwell Vale Sta BL0 . . . . **1** C5
Irwell Wlk OL8 . . . . **66** C3

Irwin Ct SK8 . . . . **122** F3
Irwin Dr SK8 . . . . **131** C5
Irwin Rd WA14 . . . . **119** D8
Irwin St M34 . . . . **100** E3
Isaac Cl M5 . . . . **161** A4
Isaac St BL1 . . . . **144** C4
Isabella Cl M16 . . . . **97** C4
Isabella Sq WN1 . . . . **151** B4
Isabella St OL12 . . . . **15** A2
Isabel Wlk BL3 . . . . **145** A1
Isaiah St OL8 . . . . **66** F4
Isa St BL0 . . . . **11** A4
Isca St M11 . . . . **160** C1
Isel Wlk M24 . . . . **46** D2
Isherwood Dr SK6 . . . . **125** D6
Isherwood Fold BL7 . . . . **9** D7
Isherwood Rd M31 . . . . . . **106** F6
Isherwood St
Heywood OL10 . . . . **29** C1
Leigh WN7 . . . . **75** E8
Rochdale OL11 . . . . **31** A6
Isis Cl M7 . . . . **81** A8
Island Cotts BL9 . . . . **11** C2
Island Row WN2 . . . . **56** C4
Island The BL9 . . . . **11** C2
Islington Rd SK2 . . . . **124** C4
Islington St M3 . . . . **158** A1
Islington Way M3 . . . . **158** A1
Isobel Cl
Eccles M30 . . . . **79** B1
⁊ Manchester M16 . . . . . . **97** F4
Ivanhoe Ave WA3 . . . . **74** D1
Ivanhoe Ct BL3, BL4 . . . . . . **42** C2
Ivanhoe St
Farnworth BL3, BL4 . . . . . . **42** C2
Oldham OL1 . . . . **49** C1
Iveagh Ct ⁊ OL16 . . . . **31** B6
Iver Ho ⁊ M5 . . . . **154** C5
Ivor St OL11 . . . . **30** B3
Ivy Ave WA12 . . . . **89** B4
Ivy Bank Cl BL1 . . . . **24** E5
Ivy Bank Rd BL1 . . . . **24** E5
Ivybridge Cl M13 . . . . **164** A1
Ivybridge Ho BL3 . . . . **144** C1
Ivy Cl
Droylsden M43 . . . . **83** F3
⁊ Rawtenstall BB4 . . . . **2** F8
Shaw OL2 . . . . **149** B3
Ivy Cotts
Denton M34 . . . . **113** A7
⁊ Rawtenstall BB4 . . . . **2** F8
Ivycroft SK13 . . . . **171** B4
Ivydale Dr WN7 . . . . **76** C5
Ivy Dr M24 . . . . **64** E8
Ivy Farm Gdns WA3 . . . . . . **91** D4
Ivy Gr
Farnworth BL4 . . . . **60** B8
Kearsley BL4 . . . . **60** F7
Walkden M38 . . . . **59** F4
Ivy Graham Cl M40 . . . . **83** B6
Ivygreen Dr OL4 . . . . **67** F6
Ivygreen Rd M21 . . . . **109** A8
Ivy Ho M27 . . . . **79** D1
Ivy House Rd WA3 . . . . **74** D1
Ivyleaf Sq M7 . . . . **155** B2
Ivylea Rd M19 . . . . **110** E4
Ivylodge Cl SK15 . . . . **86** E4
Ivy Rd
Bolton BL1 . . . . **142** B1
Bury BL8 . . . . **27** B2
Golborne WA3 . . . . **90** B8
Poynton SK12 . . . . **133** E3
Westhoughton BL5 . . . . **57** F7
Ivy St
Ashton-in-M WN4 . . . . **73** B3
Bolton BL3 . . . . **146** C4
Eccles M30 . . . . **79** D1
Manchester M40 . . . . **83** A8
Ramsbottom BL0 . . . . **10** F3
⁊ Rawtenstall BB4 . . . . **2** F8
Wigan WN1 . . . . **150** B4
Ivy Terr OL15 . . . . **6** D2
Ivy Wlk M31 . . . . **105** D3

J

J2 Bsns Pk BL9 . . . . **141** C2
Jack Brady Cl M23 . . . . . . **120** E4
Jackdaw Rd BL8 . . . . **10** F2
Jackie Brown Wlk M40 . . . **157** A1
Jack La
Droylsden M43 . . . . **84** C2
Urmston M41 . . . . **95** E2
Jack McCann Ct ⁊⁰ OL16 . **31** A8
Jackman Ave OL10 . . . . **46** D7
Jack's La BL5 . . . . **57** F1
Jackson Ave
Culcheth WA3 . . . . **91** E3
⁊ Dukinfield SK16 . . . . . . **101** D8
Jackson Cl
Manchester M21 . . . . **96** F1
Urmston M41 . . . . **95** A3
Jackson Gdns M34 . . . . . . **100** D2
Jackson Mews OL4 . . . . **49** D1
Jackson Pit ⁊ OL1 . . . . . . **153** B2
Jackson Pl OL16 . . . . **31** B8
Jackson's Brickworks Nature
Reserve* SK12 . . . . **134** D6
Jacksons Edge Rd SK12 . . **135** B6
Jackson's La SK7 . . . . **133** C8
Jackson's Row M2 . . . . **158** C1

Jackson St
Ashton-u-L OL6 . . . . **166** B4
Cheadle SK8 . . . . **122** E6
Failsworth M35 . . . . **83** D6
Farnworth BL4 . . . . **60** D8
Glossop, Padfield SK13 . . **104** C5
Glossop SK13 . . . . **116** C7
Hyde SK14 . . . . **167** A2
Ince-in-M WN2 . . . . **56** A2
Kearsley BL4 . . . . **60** F7
Middleton M24 . . . . **65** B8
Mottram in L SK14 . . . . . . **103** A3
Oldham, County End OL4 . . **67** F6
Oldham, Greenacres Moor
OL4 . . . . **67** B7
Radcliffe M26 . . . . **44** B2
Sale M33 . . . . **108** D5
Stretford M32 . . . . **96** C1
Walkden M28 . . . . **60** C4
Wardle OL12 . . . . **15** C6
Whitefield M45 . . . . **62** F7
Jackson Warehouse M1 . . **159** B1
Jack St BL2 . . . . **25** C1
Jack Taylor Ct OL12 . . . . . . **15** B1
Jacob Brigth Mews ⁊
OL12 . . . . **14** F2
Jacobite Cl M7 . . . . **63** C1
Jacobsen Ave SK14 . . . . . . **167** C4
Jacob St WN2 . . . . **56** D6
Jaffrey St ⁊ WN7 . . . . **75** E5
James Andrew St M24 . . . . **65** B8
James Bentley Wlk ⁊
M40 . . . . **83** C5
James Brindley Basin
M1 . . . . **159** C1
James Brindley Prim Sch
M28 . . . . **60** C1
James Butterworth Ct ⁊
OL16 . . . . **31** B6
James Butterworth St ⁊
OL16 . . . . **31** B6
James Cl SK16 . . . . **101** E8
James Corbett Rd M50 . . . **154** A1
James Ct ⁊⁰ M18 . . . . **99** D5
James Dr SK14 . . . . **167** B2
James Henry Ave M5 . . . . **161** B4
James Hill St OL15 . . . . **16** B5
James Leech St SK1, SK3 . **170** B4
James Leigh St M1 . . . . . . **163** A4
James Nasmyth Way M30 . **79** C2
Jameson St OL11 . . . . **30** B2
James Pl
Coppull PR7 . . . . **19** E8
Standish WN6 . . . . **19** D2
James Rd OL2 . . . . **149** B3
James Sq WN6 . . . . **19** D2
James St
Ashton-in-M WN2 . . . . **73** E7
⁊ Ashton-u-L M34 . . . . . **100** E8
Bacup OL13 . . . . **3** B7
Bolton BL7 . . . . **8** D3
Bury BL9 . . . . **141** A1
Denton M34 . . . . **101** A4
Droylsden M43 . . . . **84** B2
Dukinfield SK15, SK16 . . . **101** E8
Failsworth M35 . . . . **84** A2
⁊ Glossop SK13 . . . . **116** C8
Heywood OL10 . . . . **29** D3
Horwich BL6 . . . . **21** F3
Ince-in-M WN3 . . . . **151** A2
Kearsley BL4 . . . . **60** F8
Little Lever BL3 . . . . **43** B3
Manchester M40 . . . . **160** A3
Oldham OL4 . . . . **49** D3
Prestwich M25 . . . . **63** A5
Radcliffe M26 . . . . **44** B2
Rochdale, Dearnley OL15 . . **15** C4
Rochdale, Hursted OL12 . . **15** C4
⁊ Rochdale, Newbold Brow
OL12 . . . . **31** A8
Romiley SK6 . . . . **113** A5
Royton OL2 . . . . **149** A1
Sale M33 . . . . **108** D4
Salford M3 . . . . **158** A1
Stockport SK3 . . . . **170** B3
Tyldesley M29 . . . . **76** F8
Westhoughton BL5 . . . . **39** E2
Whitworth OL12 . . . . **4** D2
James Street N M26 . . . . . . **44** B2
James Street S OL9 . . . . . . **152** A3
Jameston Rise ⁊⁰ OL10 . . . **28** B4
Jamieson Cl M8 . . . . **155** B1
Jane Barter Ho ⁊ BL4 . . . . **60** C2
Jane St
Chadderton OL9 . . . . **152** B2
Rochdale OL12 . . . . **139** B4
Whitworth OL12 . . . . **4** E1
Janus Dr OL1 . . . . **48** D1
Japan St M7 . . . . **155** C3
Jardine Way OL9 . . . . **65** F4
Jarvis St M34 . . . . **100** E2
Jarvis St
⁊⁰ Oldham OL4 . . . . **67** A6
Rochdale OL12 . . . . **14** F1
Jasmine Ave M43 . . . . **84** C2
Jasmine Cl M23 . . . . **108** E1
Jasmine Ct BL3 . . . . **147** B3
Jasmine Rd WN5 . . . . **54** D7
Jasmine Wlk M31 . . . . **105** F2
Jauncey St BL3 . . . . **144** C1
Jaxons Ct WN1 . . . . **150** C4
Jayton Ave M20 . . . . **122** B8
Jean Ave WN7 . . . . **75** E1
Jean Cl M19 . . . . **99** A2
Jedburgh Ave BL1 . . . . **144** B4
Jefferson Way OL12 . . . . . . **14** F3
Jeffreys Dr SK16 . . . . **101** D8

Jeffrey St WN2 . . . . **56** A8
Jeffrey Wlk OL10 . . . . **29** A2
Jehlum Cl M8 . . . . **156** B3
Jellicoe Ave M44 . . . . **105** E6
Jenkinson St WN2 . . . . **56** D6
Jenkyn Wlk ⁊ M11 . . . . . . **160** C1
Jennaby Wlk BL3 . . . . **143** B2
Jennet Hey WN4 . . . . **72** F6
Jennet's La WA3 . . . . **76** C1
Jennings Ave M5 . . . . **161** A4
Jennings Cl SK14 . . . . **102** B5
Jennings Park Ave WN2 . . . **74** C7
Jennings St SK3 . . . . **170** A3
Jenison Cl M18 . . . . **165** B2
Jenny Beck Gr BL3 . . . . **147** B4
Jenny La SK7 . . . . **132** E4
Jenny Lind Cl ⁊ BL4 . . . . . . **42** C2
Jenny St OL8 . . . . **66** C2
Jepheys Pl ⁊ OL12 . . . . **14** F1
Jepheys St OL12 . . . . **14** F1
Jepson St SK2 . . . . **124** A6
JERICHO **28** E4
Jericho Rd BL9 . . . . **28** E4
Jermyn St OL12 . . . . **31** A8
Jerrold St ⁊ OL15 . . . . **16** B5
Jersey Cl M19 . . . . **110** F7
Jersey Rd SK5 . . . . **169** C4
Jersey St
Ashton-u-L OL6 . . . . **166** B4
Manchester M4 . . . . **159** C2
Jerusalem Pl M2 . . . . **162** C4
Jesmond Ave M25 . . . . **63** B2
Jesmond Dr BL8 . . . . **27** C5
Jesmond Gr SK8 . . . . **132** B8
Jesmond Rd BL1 . . . . **142** B4
Jesmond Wlk M9 . . . . **64** D5
Jespersen St OL1 . . . . **153** C3
Jessamine Ave M7 . . . . **158** A4
Jessel Cl M13 . . . . **163** C2
Jessica Way WN7 . . . . **75** B4
Jessie St
Bolton BL3 . . . . **144** C1
Failsworth M40 . . . . **83** A6
Jessop Dr SK6 . . . . **125** F8
Jessop Forge BL3 . . . . **43** A3
Jessop St M18 . . . . **99** D5
Jethro St
Bolton, Bradshaw BL2 . . . . **25** C4
Bolton, Tonge Fold BL2 . . **148** C4
Jetson St M18 . . . . **99** F6
Jevington Wlk ⁊ M13 . . . . **163** C2
Jewell Cl M41 . . . . **95** B2
Jewish Senior Boys Sch
M7 . . . . **155** A4
Jimmy McMullen Wlk ⁊
M14 . . . . **98** A3
Jinnah Cl
Manchester M11 . . . . **165** C4
Oldham OL4 . . . . **67** C5
Joan St M40 . . . . **83** A7
Jobling St M11 . . . . **164** C4
Jocelyn St M40 . . . . **157** B1
Joddrell St M3 . . . . **158** B1
Joe Connolly Way ⁊ BL4 . . . **2** E8
Joel La SK14 . . . . **113** F7
Johannesburg Gdns
M23 . . . . **120** F4
John Ashworth St OL12 . . . **15** B1
John Atkinson Ct M5 . . . . . **154** A2
John Ave SK8 . . . . **122** E6
John Beeley Ave M11 . . . . . **99** D8
John Booth St OL4 . . . . **67** F5
John Boste Ct BL3 . . . . **42** C3
John Brown St ⁊ BL1 . . . . **145** B4
John Clynes Ave M40 . . . . **159** C3
John Cross St BL3 . . . . **147** B4
John Dalton St
Glossop SK13 . . . . **103** E5
Manchester M2 . . . . **158** C1
John Foran Cl M40 . . . . **83** B6
John Gilbert Way M17 . . . . . **96** E5
John Henry St OL12 . . . . **4** D4
John Heywood St M11 . . . . **83** B2
John Kemble Ct OL11 . . . . . **30** D4
John Kennedy Gdn SK14 . . **103** A3
John Kennedy Rd SK14 . . . **102** F3
John Knott St OL4 . . . . **67** F6
John Lee Fold M24 . . . . **47** A1
John Lloyd Ct M44 . . . . **105** F8
John Milne Ave OL16 . . . . . **31** D3
Johnny King Cl M40 . . . . . . **157** A1
John Roberts Cl OL11 . . . . **139** B1
John Robinson Wlk ⁊
M40 . . . . **83** A7
Johns Cl M21 . . . . **109** B8
John Shepley St SK14 . . . . **167** B2
John Smeaton Ct M1 . . . . . **159** C1
Johnson Ave
Leigh WN7 . . . . **56** E1
Newton-le-W WA12 . . . . . . **89** B5
Oldham OL1 . . . . **49** E5
Johnsonbrook Rd SK14,
SK16 . . . . **101** D6
Johnson Cl WN7 . . . . **75** B4
JOHNSON FOLD **23** F3
Johnson Fold Ave BL1 . . . . **23** F3
Johnson Fold Com Prim Sch
BL1 . . . . **23** F3
Johnson Gr M24 . . . . **64** E8
Johnson's Sq M40 . . . . **160** A4
Johnson St
Atherton M46 . . . . **58** A1
Bolton BL1 . . . . **145** C4
Manchester M15 . . . . **162** A4
Pendlebury M27 . . . . **80** D6

Johnson St *continued*
Radcliffe M26 . . . . 44 B1
Rochdale OL11 . . . . 30 C4
Salford M3 . . . . 158 B2
Tyldesley M29 . . . . 59 A1
[16] Wigan WN5 . . . . 54 B6
Johnson Terr [22] SK16 . . 166 B1
John's Pl SK6 . . . . 113 C2
John St
Altrincham WA14 . . . . . 119 D4
Ashton-in-M WN4 . . . . . 73 D5
Ashton-u-L OL7 . . . . . . 166 A1
Bolton BL7 . . . . 25 A7
Bredbury SK6 . . . . 113 A4
Bury BL9 . . . . 140 C3
Compstall SK6 . . . . 114 B3
Denton M34 . . . . 100 F4
Droylsden M43 . . . . 83 F1
Eccles M30 . . . . 79 B1
Failsworth M35 . . . . 65 F1
Farnworth BL4 . . . . 60 E8
Glossop SK13 . . . . 116 C8
Golborne WA3 . . . . 90 A8
Hazel Grove SK7 . . . . . 124 D3
Heywood OL10 . . . . 29 D2
Hindley WN2 . . . . 57 B3
Irlam M44 . . . . 105 E5
Leigh WN7 . . . . 75 F5
[2] Littleborough OL15 . . 16 A5
[11] Little Lever BL3 . . . . 43 B3
Manchester M4 . . . . . . 159 A2
Marple SK6 . . . . 126 A5
Middleton M25 . . . . 63 E8
Oldham, Bank Top OL8 . 153 B2
Oldham, County End OL4 . 68 A6
Pendlebury M27 . . . . . . 80 A8
Rochdale OL16 . . . . 15 C3
Romiley SK6 . . . . 113 C2
Royton OL2 . . . . 48 D4
Sale M33 . . . . 108 B5
Salford, Lower Broughton
 M7 . . . . 158 A4
Salford M3 . . . . 158 B2
Shaw OL2 . . . . 149 A1
Stalybridge SK15 . . . . . 86 C5
Stockport SK1 . . . . 169 C1
Stockport SK1 . . . . 170 C4
[7] Tyldesley M29 . . . . . 59 A1
Walkden M28 . . . . 60 D4
Whitworth OL12 . . . . 4 D2
[4] Wigan, Pemberton WN5 . 54 D5
Wigan, Scholes WN1 . . . 151 A4
Johnston [21] OL12 . . . . 139 B4
Johnston Ave OL15 . . . . 15 F3
Johnstone Ct M32 . . . . . 96 A3
John Street E OL7 . . . . . 84 F1
John Street W OL7 . . . . 100 F8
John William St
 Droylsden M11 . . . . . . 83 C1
 Eccles M30 . . . . 79 F2
Joiner St
 Manchester M4 . . . . . . 159 A1
 Salford M5 . . . . 81 C1
Join Rd M33 . . . . 108 D4
Jolly Brows BL2 . . . . . . 25 D3
Jolly Tar La PR7 . . . . . . 20 B7
Jonas St M9 . . . . 157 B4
Jonathan Cl BB4 . . . . 1 A8
Jones Sq SK1 . . . . 124 A7
Jones St
 Bolton BL1 . . . . 145 C4
 Glossop SK13 . . . . . . 104 A5
 Horwich BL6 . . . . 22 B4
 Oldham OL1 . . . . 67 A8
 Radcliffe M26 . . . . 44 B4
 Rochdale OL16 . . . . . . 31 A6
 Royton OL2 . . . . 48 E2
 Salford M6 . . . . 154 C2
Jonquil Dr M28 . . . . 59 F3
Jopson St M24 . . . . 47 B1
Jordan Ave OL2 . . . . 49 D8
Jordan St
 Glossop SK13 . . . . . . 104 E1
 Manchester M15 . . . . . 162 B3
Joseph Adamson Ind Est
 SK14 . . . . 101 C2
Joseph Dean Ct [13] M40 . 83 F4
Josephine Dr [2] M27 . . . 80 A7
Joseph Jennings Ct OL7 . 85 A6
Joseph Johnson Mews
 M22 . . . . 109 C1
Joseph St
 Eccles M30 . . . . 79 B1
 Failsworth M35 . . . . . . 83 F8
 [1] Farnworth BL4 . . . . . 42 D1
 Littleborough OL15 . . . . 16 B6
 Marple SK6 . . . . 126 A6
 Middleton M24 . . . . 46 F1
 Radcliffe M26 . . . . 44 B2
 [3] Rochdale OL12 . . . . 14 D2
Joshua La M24 . . . . 65 D7
Josslyn Rd M5 . . . . 154 A3
Jo St M5 . . . . 81 A1
Joule Cl M5 . . . . 161 A4
Joules Ct [2] SK1 . . . . . 170 C4
Joule St M9 . . . . 64 E1
Jowett St
 Oldham OL1 . . . . 49 C1
 Reddish SK5 . . . . 169 C4
Jowett's Wlk OL7 . . . . . 166 A2
Jowkin La OL11 . . . . 29 B1
Joyce St M40 . . . . 83 B7
Joynson Ave M7 . . . . . . 158 A4
Joynson St M33 . . . . . . 108 B5

Joy Pl [3] OL12 . . . . . . 14 F2
Joy St
 Ramsbottom BL0 . . . . 138 B2
 Rochdale OL12 . . . . . . 14 F2
JUBILEE 32 C2
Jubilee OL2 . . . . 32 C2
Jubilee Ave
 Orrell WN5 . . . . 53 D4
 Radcliffe M26 . . . . 44 C1
 Stalybridge SK16 . . . . . 85 E1
Jubilee Cl M30 . . . . 79 D3
Jubilee Cotts M28 . . . . . 60 C3
Jubilee Ct
 Golborne WA3 . . . . 74 A1
 [2] Handforth SK9 . . . . 131 E5
 Manchester M16 . . . . . . 97 B4
 Reddish SK5 . . . . 99 F2
Jubilee Ho BL1 . . . . . . 145 B2
Jubilee Pool BL1 . . . . . 143 A1
Jubilee Rd M24 . . . . 47 B1
Jubilee St
 [3] Ashton-u-L OL7 . . . . 84 F1
 Bolton BL1 . . . . 146 C3
 Salford M6 . . . . 154 C2
 Shaw OL2 . . . . 149 C2
Jubilee Terr M24 . . . . . . 47 B2
Jubilee Way BL9 . . . . . 140 A2
Judith St OL12 . . . . 14 C3
Judson Ave M21 . . . . . 109 C6
Julia Mews [4] BL6 . . . . 22 B4
Julian Ho OL1 . . . . 153 C3
Julia St
 Horwich BL6 . . . . 22 B4
 Manchester M3 . . . . . . 158 C3
 Rochdale OL12 . . . . . . 139 B4
Julius St M19 . . . . 111 B8
July St M13 . . . . 164 A1
Jumbles Beck BL2 . . . . . 9 D4
Jumbles Ctry Pk* BL7 . . . 9 D4
JUMBO 9 D6
Junction 19 Ind Pk OL10 . 29 F1
Junction 22 Bsns Pk OL9 . 65 F1
Junction Ho M1 . . . . . . 159 B1
Junction La WA12 . . . . . 89 B3
Junction Rd
 Bolton BL3 . . . . 144 A1
 Stockport SK1, SK2, SK3 . 170 C3
Junction Road W BL6 . . . 40 D5
Junction St
 Dukinfield SK14 . . . . . 101 C5
 Oldham OL8 . . . . 66 E4
Junction Terr WN3 . . . . 151 B2
Junction Works M1 . . . . 159 B1
June Ave
 Leigh WN7 . . . . 75 C6
 Stockport SK4 . . . . . . 168 B2
June St OL7 . . . . 166 A2
Juniper Bank SK5 . . . . . 112 A8
Juniper Cl
 Bolton BL1 . . . . 143 B1
 Oldham OL4 . . . . 49 F4
 Sale M33 . . . . 108 A6
Juniper Cres M43 . . . . . 99 E8
Juniper Dr
 Hindley WN2 . . . . 57 A3
 Milnrow OL16 . . . . 31 D7
Jupiter Gr WN3 . . . . 54 E2
Jupiter Wlk M40 . . . . . . 83 A5
Jura Cl SK16 . . . . 101 D8
Jura Dr M41 . . . . 95 E5
Jura Gr OL10 . . . . 29 B1
Jurby Ave M9 . . . . 64 D4
Jury St
 Leigh WN7 . . . . 75 E7
 Manchester M8 . . . . . 158 C4
Justene Cl WA3 . . . . 74 A2
Justin Cl M13 . . . . 163 B3
Jutland Ave OL11 . . . . . . 30 C8
Jutland Gr BL5 . . . . 39 F1
Jutland Ho M1 . . . . 159 B1
Jutland St M1 . . . . 159 B1

K

Kale St M13 . . . . 163 B3
Kalima Gr M7 . . . . 155 A2
Kandel Pl OL12 . . . . 4 D1
Kane Ct WA3 . . . . 75 A1
Kansas Ave M50 . . . . . . 96 E8
Kara St M6 . . . . 154 B2
Karen Rd WN1 . . . . 151 C4
Karmo Ind Est OL11 . . . 139 A2
Kaskenmoor Sch OL8 . . . 66 B2
Kassim Darwish Gram Sch
 for Boys M16 . . . . 97 E1
Kate St BL0 . . . . 138 B2
Kathan Cl OL16 . . . . 31 B7
Katherine Ct M46 . . . . . 161 C1
Katherine Rd SK2 . . . . . 124 C5
Katherine St OL6 . . . . . 166 A2
Kathkin Ave M8 . . . . 64 B2
Kathleen Gr M14 . . . . . . 98 D2
Kathleen St OL16 . . . . . 139 A3
Kay Ave SK6 . . . . 112 D3
Kay Brow
 Heywood OL10 . . . . 29 B2
 Ramsbottom BL0 . . . . 138 C2
Kay Cl WN1 . . . . 151 A4
Kaye Ave WA3 . . . . 91 F3
Kayfields BL2 . . . . 25 E4
Kayley Ind Est OL7 . . . . 84 F3
Kay Lodge M14 . . . . . . 110 C8
Kaymar Ct BL1 . . . . . . 142 A1
Kay's Ave SK1 . . . . . . 112 B1
Kays Gdns M3 . . . . . . 158 A2
Kay St
 Atherton M46 . . . . 58 D2

Kay St *continued*
 Bolton BL1 . . . . 145 C4
 Bury BL9 . . . . 141 A3
 Chapeltown BL7 . . . . . . 9 C4
 Heywood OL10 . . . . 29 C2
 Little Lever BL3 . . . . . . 43 A3
 Manchester, Charlestown
 M6 . . . . 80 F6
 Manchester, West Gorton
 M11 . . . . 164 C3
 Ramsbottom BL9 . . . . . 11 C3
 Rochdale OL11 . . . . . . 139 B1
 [10] Stalybridge SK15 . . 86 A1
 Stalybridge SK15 . . . . 102 A8
Kays Wood Rd SK6 . . . 125 D6
Keadby Cl M30 . . . . 95 D8
Keal Dr M44 . . . . 94 B4
Keane Cl M8 . . . . 156 A3
Keane St OL7 . . . . 166 A3
Kean Pl M30 . . . . 79 D1
Kearnes Cl WN2 . . . . . . 74 C6
KEARSLEY 61 A6
Kearsley Com L Ctr BL4 . 60 F6
Kearsley Dr BL3 . . . . . . 42 B3
Kearsley Hall Rd M26 . . . 61 C7
Kearsley Mount Sh Prec
 BL4 . . . . 61 B6
Kearsley Rd
 Kearsley M26 . . . . 61 D8
 Manchester M8 . . . . . . 64 A2
Kearsley St
 Eccles M30 . . . . 79 B2
 Leigh WN7 . . . . 75 D5
 Wigan WN6 . . . . 37 B1
Kearsley Vale M26 . . . . . 61 A7
Kearsley Vale M26 . . . . . 61 B8
Kearsley West Prim Sch
 M26 . . . . 60 E7
Kearton Dr M30 . . . . 80 A1
Keary Cl M18 . . . . 99 D6
Keasdon Ave M22 . . . . 121 D4
Keaton Cl M6 . . . . 154 B4
Keats Ave
 Denton M34 . . . . 113 A8
 Droylsden M43 . . . . . . 84 A2
 Longshaw WN5 . . . . . . 53 D5
 Rochdale OL12 . . . . . . 14 A1
 Wigan, Poolstock WN3 . 150 B1
 Wigan, Standish Lower Ground
 WN6 . . . . 36 E3
Keats Cl M46 . . . . 58 E5
Keats Cres M26 . . . . . . 43 E4
Keats Fold SK16 . . . . . 102 B7
Keats Mews M23 . . . . . 120 C8
Keats Rd
 Eccles M30 . . . . 79 D1
 Oldham OL1 . . . . 49 B1
 Ramsbottom BL8 . . . . . 11 A6
Keats St WN7 . . . . 75 D7
Keats Way M34 . . . . 56 B1
Keats Wlk [2] BL1 . . . . 143 B2
Keb La OL8 . . . . 85 A8
Keble Ave OL8 . . . . 66 E3
Keble Gr WN7 . . . . 75 C8
Keble St WN2 . . . . 151 C3
Kedington Cl [8] M40 . . 156 C1
Kedleston Ave M14 . . . . 98 E4
Kedleston Gn SK2 . . . . 124 D7
Kedleston Wlk M34 . . . . 100 F1
Keele Cl SK2 . . . . 124 B6
Keele Wlk M40 . . . . . . 159 C3
Keeley Cl M40 . . . . 83 C4
Keepers Dr OL12 . . . . . . 13 E2
Keep The BL1 . . . . 40 F7
Keighley Ave M43 . . . . . 84 A3
Keighley Cl BL8 . . . . . . 26 F2
Keighley St BL1 . . . . . . 142 C2
Keith Ave M33 . . . . . . 108 A1
Keith Dr SK3 . . . . 123 B7
Keith Wlk M40 . . . . . . 160 A3
Kelboro Ave M34 . . . . . 100 D7
Kelbrook Ct SK2 . . . . . 124 E5
Kelbrook Rd M11 . . . . . 165 B4
Kelby Ave M23 . . . . . . 121 B7
Kelday Wlk M8 . . . . . . 156 C2
Keld Cl BL8 . . . . 27 B5
Keld Wlk M18 . . . . 165 C1
Kelfield Ave M23 . . . . . 109 A2
Kelham Wlk [3] M40 . . . . 65 C1
Kellaton Cl WN3 . . . . . 151 B2
Kellbank Rd WN3 . . . . . 54 E3
Kellbrook Cres
 Manchester M7 . . . . . . 63 B1
 Salford M7 . . . . 81 A8
Kellett St WN5 . . . . 36 D1
Kellett St
 [4] Bolton BL1 . . . . 24 F6
 Rochdale OL16 . . . . . . 31 B8
Kellet Wlk M11 . . . . 83 B2
Kelling Wlk M15 . . . . . . 162 A3
Kells Gr WN6 . . . . 37 A2
Kelmarsh Cl [7] M11 . . . . 99 D7
Kelmscott Lodge M41 . . . 95 B3
Kelsall Cres SK3 . . . . . 170 A2
Kelsall Dr
 Altrincham WA15 . . . . 120 C6
 Droylsden M43 . . . . . . 83 F3
Kelsall Rd SK8 . . . . . . 123 A5
Kelsall St
 Manchester M12 . . . . . 164 C2
 Oldham OL9 . . . . 153 A2
 Rochdale OL16 . . . . . . 139 C4
 Sale M33 . . . . 108 B4
Kelsall Way [6] SK9 . . . 131 D5
Kelsey [14] OL10 . . . . . . 29 C2
Kelsey Wlk M9 . . . . 64 B5
Kelso Cl OL8 . . . . 66 F1
Kelso Gr WN2 . . . . 56 D4

Kelson Ave OL7 . . . . . . 166 A4
Kelstern Ave M13 . . . . . 98 E3
Kelstern Cl BL2 . . . . . . 148 C4
Kelstern Sq M13 . . . . . . 98 E3
Kelton Cl SK5 . . . . 111 F5
Kelverlow St OL4 . . . . . 67 C6
Kelvin Ave
 Middleton M24 . . . . 64 B6
 Sale M33 . . . . 108 B4
Kelvin Cl WN4 . . . . 72 D4
Kelvindale Dr WA15 . . . 120 C7
Kelvin Gr
 Manchester M8 . . . . . . 156 A2
 Wigan WN3 . . . . 54 F2
Kelvington Dr M9 . . . . . 157 A2
Kelvin St
 Ashton-u-L OL7 . . . . . 100 F8
 Manchester M4 . . . . . 159 A2
Kelway Terr WN1 . . . . . 37 D1
Kelwood Ave BL9 . . . . . 28 D5
Kemball St M30 . . . . . . 79 F2
Kemble Ave M23 . . . . . 109 C1
Kemble Cl BL6 . . . . 22 B5
Kemmel Ave M22 . . . . . 121 E5
Kemnay Wlk [11] M11 . . 83 C1
Kemp Ave OL11 . . . . . . 139 A1
Kempley Cl M12 . . . . . . 164 C2
Kempnough Hall Rd M28 . 78 F7
Kemp Rd SK6 . . . . 126 C7
Kempsey St OL9 . . . . . 152 B3
Kempsey Wlk M40 . . . . 65 D1
Kempsford Cl M23 . . . . 121 B6
Kemp St
 Hyde SK14 . . . . 167 B4
 Middleton M24 . . . . 64 F8
Kempster St M7 . . . . . . 158 A4
Kempston Gdns [24] BL1 . 143 B2
Kempton Ave
 Little Lever BL3 . . . . . . 43 A2
 Sale M33 . . . . 107 D3
Kempton Cl
 Droylsden M43 . . . . . . 84 C2
 Hazel Grove SK7 . . . . 125 A1
 Newton-le-W WA12 . . . . 89 D5
Kempton Rd M19 . . . . . 111 A8
Kempton Way OL9 . . . . 152 C3
Kemsing Wlk M5 . . . . . 81 A1
Kenchester Ave M11 . . . 99 D8
Kendal Ave
 Ashton-u-L OL7 . . . . . . 84 F4
 Denton M34 . . . . 101 A1
 Dukinfield SK14 . . . . . 101 C5
 Sale M33 . . . . 108 C3
 Urmston M41 . . . . 94 E4
Kendal Cl
 Altrincham WA15 . . . . 120 D5
 Heywood OL10 . . . . . . 46 E8
Kendal Ct
 Stalybridge SK15 . . . . . 86 A3
 Wythenshawe M22 . . . 121 E6
Kendal Dr
 Bramhall SK7 . . . . . . 132 C5
 Bury BL9 . . . . 44 D7
 Gatley SK8 . . . . 122 C4
 Shaw OL2 . . . . 49 D7
Kendal Gdns SK6 . . . . . 113 B4
Kendal Gr
 Ashton-in-M WN4 . . . . . 73 B4
 Leigh WN7 . . . . 75 D5
 Walkden M28 . . . . 60 F8
 Whitefield M45 . . . . . . 62 F8
Kendal Ho SK15 . . . . . . 86 A3
Kendall Rd M9 . . . . 63 F3
Kendal Rd
 Bolton BL1 . . . . 144 C4
 Boothstown M28 . . . . . 77 E7
 Hindley WN2 . . . . 56 E5
 Ince-in-M WN2 . . . . . . 56 B2
 Ramsbottom BL0 . . . . . 11 A2
 Salford M6 . . . . 80 C5
 Stretford M32 . . . . 96 D3
Kendal Road W BL0 . . . . 10 F2
Kendal St WN6 . . . . . . 150 B4
Kendal Terr [4] SK16 . . . 166 C1
Kendon Wlk M24 . . . . . 46 E1
Kendon Gr M34 . . . . . . 100 E3
Kendrew Rd BL3 . . . . . 146 A4
Kendrew Wlk M9 . . . . . . 64 E1
Kendrick Pl WN1 . . . . . 151 B4
Kenford Dr WN3 . . . . . . 54 E2
Kenford Wlk M8 . . . . . . 155 C2
Kenhall Rd WN7 . . . . . . 76 C4
Kenilworth [1] OL11 . . . 139 B2
Kenilworth Ave
 Chadderton OL9 . . . . . 47 E1
 Cheadle SK8 . . . . 123 A3
 Handforth SK9 . . . . . . 131 D3
 Manchester M20 . . . . . 109 F5
 Swinton M27 . . . . 62 B3
 Whitefield M45 . . . . . . 63 A7
Kenilworth Cl
 Marple SK6 . . . . 125 F8
 Oldham OL4 . . . . 67 C5
 Radcliffe M26 . . . . 43 F6
Kenilworth Dr
 Hazel Grove SK7 . . . . 133 D8
 Hindley WN2 . . . . 56 F4
 Leigh WN7 . . . . 76 E7
Kenilworth Gdns [4] M29 . 89 C1
Kenilworth Gr M34 . . . . 100 C8
Kenilworth Rd
 Cheadle SK3 . . . . 122 F7
 Golborne WA3 . . . . 90 E7
 Royton OL16 . . . . 48 C8
 Sale M33 . . . . 107 E4
 Urmston M41 . . . . 94 C2
Kenilworth Sq [5] BL1 . . 142 B1

Kenion Rd OL11 . . . . . . 30 B6
Kenion St OL16 . . . . . . 139 C3
Kenley Dr OL10 . . . . . . 46 F7
Kenley Wlk M8 . . . . . . 156 C2
Kenmay Ave BL3 . . . . . 40 F6
Kenmere Gr M40 . . . . . 65 B8
Kenmor Ave BL8 . . . . . 27 A1
Kenmore Cl M45 . . . . . 63 B8
Kenmore Dr WA15 . . . . 120 B3
Kenmore Gr
 Garswood WN4 . . . . . . 72 D4
 Irlam M44 . . . . 105 D6
Kenmore Rd
 Sale M33 . . . . 107 C1
 Whitefield M45 . . . . . . 63 B8
 Wythenshawe M22 . . . 121 D7
Kenmore Way M45 . . . . 63 B8
Kennard Cl M9 . . . . 64 F1
Kennard Pl WA14 . . . . 119 E6
Kennedy Cl WN6 . . . . . 36 F8
Kennedy Dr
 Little Lever BL3 . . . . . . 43 C3
 Whitefield BL9 . . . . 45 B2
Kennedy Rd
 Salford M5 . . . . 80 C2
 Tyldesley M29 . . . . 59 C1
Kennedy Sq [3] SK14 . . 102 F3
Kennedy St
 Bolton BL2 . . . . 148 C3
 Manchester M2 . . . . . 158 C1
 Oldham OL8 . . . . 153 B1
Kennedy Way
 Denton M34 . . . . 100 D2
 Stockport SK4 . . . . . . 168 C2
Kennerley Ct
 Stockport SK2 . . . . . . 124 A5
 Wilmslow SK9 . . . . . . 137 A7
Kennerley Lo SK3 . . . . 170 C1
Kennerley Rd SK2 . . . . 124 A5
Kennerley's La SK9 . . . 137 A7
Kennet [15] OL10 . . . . . 29 C2
Kennet Cl
 Handforth SK9 . . . . . . 131 D2
 Westhoughton BL5 . . . . 39 E1
Kenneth Ave WN7 . . . . . 75 D6
Kenneth Collis Ct M22 . . 121 C3
Kenneth Gr WN7 . . . . . 75 D6
Kenneth Sq M7 . . . . . . 155 B2
Kennett Dr SK6 . . . . . . 112 F4
Kennett Rd M23 . . . . . . 121 A3
Kennet Way WN7 . . . . . 75 F7
Kenninghall Rd M22 . . . 121 D3
Kennington Ave M40 . . . 83 B4
Kennington Fold BL3 . . . 147 A3
Kenny Cl OL4 . . . . 67 C5
Kenside St [8] M16 . . . . 97 F3
Kensington Ave
 Ashton-u-L OL6 . . . . . . 85 E4
 Chadderton OL9 . . . . . 65 E8
 [2] Hyde SK14 . . . . . . 167 B1
 Manchester M14 . . . . . 98 D4
 Radcliffe M26 . . . . 43 D4
 Royton OL2 . . . . 48 C6
Kensington Cl
 Milnrow OL16 . . . . 32 A6
 Ramsbottom BL8 . . . . . 11 A1
Kensington Ct
 Bolton BL1 . . . . 145 B3
 [1] Hyde SK14 . . . . . . 167 B1
 Reddish M34 . . . . 100 B4
 Salford M7 . . . . 81 C8
 Wilmslow SK9 . . . . . . 137 A6
Kensington Dr
 Bury BL8 . . . . 44 A8
 Horwich BL6 . . . . 22 D3
 Leigh WN7 . . . . 76 E7
 Salford M7 . . . . 154 A3
Kensington Gdns
 Altrincham WA15 . . . . 119 F1
 Hyde SK14 . . . . 167 C1
Kensington Gr
 Altrincham WA15 . . . . 119 E8
 Reddish M34 . . . . 100 B4
 [14] Stalybridge SK15 . . 86 A1
Kensington Rd
 Failsworth M35 . . . . . . 84 B8
 Manchester M21 . . . . . 97 B2
 Oldham OL8 . . . . 66 D4
 Stockport SK3 . . . . . . 123 B7
 [3] Wigan WN5 . . . . . . 54 D5
Kensington St
 Bolton BL1 . . . . 145 B3
 Hyde SK14 . . . . 167 B1
 Manchester M14 . . . . . 98 A3
 Rochdale OL16 . . . . . . 139 B1
Kensington The M20 . . . 110 B5
Kenslow Ave M8 . . . . . 63 F2
Kensworth Cl
 [6] Altrincham M23 . . . 120 D6
 Bolton BL1 . . . . 143 A1
Kensworth Dr BL1 . . . . 143 A1
Kent Ave
 Chadderton OL9 . . . . . 152 B2
 Cheadle SK8 . . . . 123 C5
 Droylsden M43 . . . . . . 83 E1
 Platt Bridge WN2 . . . . . 56 A2
Kent Cl
 Diggle OL3 . . . . 51 C4
 Walkden M28 . . . . 60 B2
Kent Ct
 Bolton BL1 . . . . 145 B4
 Manchester M14 . . . . . 98 C3
Kent Dr
 Bury BL9 . . . . 45 A8
 Kearsley BL4 . . . . 61 B6
Kentford Dr M40 . . . . . 159 C4
Kentford Gr [8] BL4 . . . . 60 C8
Kentford Rd BL1 . . . . . 143 C1

Kent Gr M35 . . . . 83 E6
Kentmere Ave
  Billinge WA11 . . . . 71 C1
  Rochdale OL16 . . . . 15 B3
Kentmere Cl SK8 . . . . . . 122 B3
Kentmere Ct M9 . . . . 65 B4
Kentmere Dr
  Middleton M24 . . . . 46 E3
  Tyldesley M29 . . . . 77 B7
Kentmere Gr BL4 . . . . . . 59 F7
Kentmere Prim Sch ☑
  OL12 . . . . 15 B3
Kentmere Rd
  Altrincham M23, WA15 . . 120 D6
  Bolton BL2 . . . . 25 F1
Kentmere Cl
  Manchester, Heaton Mersey
   SK4 . . . . 110 E2
  Manchester, West Gorton
   M12 . . . . 165 A3
Kenton Ave M18 . . . . 99 C3
Kenton Cl
  Bolton BL2 . . . . 143 A1
  Denton M34 . . . . 100 D7
Kenton Rd OL2 . . . . 149 A3
Kenton St OL8 . . . . 67 C5
Kent Rd
  Atherton M46 . . . . 58 C4
  Glossop SK13 . . . . 104 D1
  Irlam M44 . . . . 105 C5
  Partington M31 . . . . 105 C2
  Reddish M34 . . . . 100 A2
  Stockport SK3 . . . . 123 B8
  Tyldesley M29 . . . . 59 A2
Kent Road E M14 . . . . . . 98 D3
Kent Road W M14 . . . . . . 98 D3
Kentsford Dr M26 . . . . . . 43 B5
Kent St
  Bolton BL1 . . . . 145 B4
  Leigh WN7 . . . . 76 E4
  ☑ Manchester M2 . . . . . 158 C1
  Oldham OL6 . . . . 66 F4
  Rochdale OL11 . . . . 139 C2
  Salford M7 . . . . 158 A4
  Swinton M27 . . . . 61 F2
  Wigan WN1 . . . . 151 A3
Kentstone Ave SK4 . . . . 110 E3
Kentucky St OL4 . . . . . . 67 C6
Kent Way M12 . . . . 89 C1
Kentwell Cl SK16 . . . . . 101 B7
Kent Wlk
  Haslingden BB4 . . . . 1 A8
  Heywood OL10 . . . . 29 A1
Kenwick Dr M40 . . . . . . 65 E2
Kenwood Ave
  Altrincham WA15 . . . . . 119 F7
  Bramhall SK7 . . . . 132 D5
  Gatley SK8 . . . . 122 F4
  Leigh WN7 . . . . 76 C5
  Manchester M19 . . . . . . 110 F6
Kenwood Cl
  Leigh WN7 . . . . 76 C4
  Stretford M32 . . . . 96 E2
Kenwood Ct M32 . . . . . . 96 E1
Kenwood La M28 . . . . . . 78 F5
Kenwood Rd
  Bolton BL1 . . . . 142 B3
  Oldham OL1 . . . . 48 C1
  Reddish SK5 . . . . 99 E2
  Stretford M32 . . . . 96 E1
Kenworthy Ave OL6 . . . . 85 E5
Kenworthy Cl SK14 . . . . 102 E2
Kenworthy Gdns OL3 . . . 51 B1
Kenworthy La M22 . . . . 109 D1
Kenworthy St
  Rochdale OL16 . . . . 31 C7
  ☑ Stalybridge SK15 . . . . 86 A1
Kenworthy Terr ☑ OL16 . 31 C7
Kenwright St M4 . . . . . . 159 A2
Kenwyn St M40 . . . . . . 160 B3
KENYON 90 F3
Kenyon Ave
  Dukinfield SK16 . . . . . . 101 F5
  Oldham OL8 . . . . 66 F3
  Sale M33 . . . . 108 E2
Kenyon Bsns Pk BL3 . . . 145 B1
Kenyon Cl SK14 . . . . . . 101 F5
Kenyon Cres ☑ BL9 . . . . 27 F6
Kenyon Fold OL11 . . . . . 29 E5
Kenyon Gr M38 . . . . 59 E4
Kenyon La
  Culcheth WA3 . . . . 91 A4
  Kenyon WA3 . . . . 90 F3
  Manchester M40 . . . . . . 83 A8
  Middleton M24 . . . . 65 C8
  Prestwich M25 . . . . 63 C4
Kenyon Rd
  Little Lever BL2 . . . . . . 43 B5
  Standish WN6 . . . . 19 D2
  Wigan WN1 . . . . 37 C2
Kenyon St
  Ashton-u-L OL6 . . . . . . 166 B3
  Britannia OL13 . . . . 4 B8
  Bury BL9 . . . . 141 A3
  Droylsden M18 . . . . 99 F6
  Dukinfield SK16 . . . . . . 101 B8
  Heywood OL10 . . . . 29 C2
  Leigh WN7 . . . . 75 D8
  Radcliffe M26 . . . . 44 B3
  Ramsbottom BL0 . . . . . 138 C2
Kenyon Terr M38 . . . . . . 59 E3
Kenyon Way
  Bury BL8 . . . . 26 F5
  Walkden M38 . . . . 59 E4
Keppel Rd M21 . . . . 97 B1
Keppel St OL6 . . . . 166 C3
Kepplecove Mdw M28 . . . 77 F5

Kepwick Dr M22 . . . . . . 121 E1
Kerans Dr BL5 . . . . 57 F1
Kerenhappuch St BL0 . . 138 B1
Kerfield Wlk ☑ M13 . . . . 163 B3
Kerfoot Cl M22 . . . . 121 E8
Kerfoot St WN7 . . . . 76 C4
Kermishaw Nook M29 . . . 77 B6
Kermoor Ave BL1 . . . . . . 24 E6
Kerne Gr M23 . . . . 109 A1
Kerrera Dr M5 . . . . 154 A1
Kerridge Dr SK6 . . . . . . 112 F4
Kerrier Cl M30 . . . . 80 A2
Kerris Cl M22 . . . . 121 E1
Kerr St M9 . . . . 64 D3
Kerry Gr BL2 . . . . 148 B4
Kerry Wlk M23 . . . . 120 F3
KERSAL 81 B8
Kersal Ave
  Pendlebury M27 . . . . . . 80 C8
  Walkden M38 . . . . 60 B4
Kersal Bank M7 . . . . 81 C8
Kersal Bar M7 . . . . 63 C1
Kersal Cell M7 . . . . 80 F8
Kersal Cl
  Manchester M25 . . . . . . 63 A1
  ☑ Prestwich M7 . . . . . . 63 C1
Kersal Crag M7 . . . . 63 C1
KERSAL DALE 155 A3
Kersal Dr WA15 . . . . . . 120 C5
Kersal Hall Ave ☑ M7 . . . 81 A8
Kersal Moor Nature
  Reserve* M8 . . . . 63 B1
Kersal Rd M25, M7 . . . . . 63 A1
Kersal Vale Ct M7 . . . . . 81 A8
Kersal Vale Rd M7, M25 . . 80 F8
Kersal Way M7 . . . . 81 B7
Kerscott Rd M23 . . . . . 108 F2
Kersh Ave M19 . . . . 111 B8
Kershaw Ave
  Little Lever BL3 . . . . . . 43 A4
  Prestwich M25 . . . . 62 F2
  Sale M33 . . . . 108 E2
Kershaw Bsns Ctr BL3 . . 145 A1
Kershaw Dr OL9 . . . . 65 E8
Kershaw Gr M34 . . . . . . 100 C8
Kershaw La M34 . . . . . . 100 C8
Kershaw Rd M35 . . . . . . 83 F7
Kershaw St
  Ashton-u-L OL7 . . . . . . 100 F8
  Bolton BL3 . . . . 145 A1
  Bolton, Bradshaw BL2 . . . 25 C5
  Bury BL9 . . . . 141 A2
  Droylsden M43 . . . . 83 F1
  Glossop SK13 . . . . 116 C8
  Heywood OL10 . . . . 29 B2
  ☑ Rochdale OL12 . . . . 139 C4
  Royton OL2 . . . . 48 D5
  Shaw OL2 . . . . 149 B3
  Tyldesley M29 . . . . 59 A1
  Wigan WN5 . . . . 54 B6
Kershaw Street E OL2 . . 149 B3
Kershaw Way WA12 . . . . 89 C5
Kershaw Wlk M12 . . . . . 164 A2
Kershope Gr M5 . . . . . . 161 A4
Kersley St OL4 . . . . 67 B6
Kerswell Wlk M40 . . . . . 83 A6
Kerwin Wlk M11 . . . . . . 165 A4
Kerwood Dr OL2 . . . . . . 48 E3
Kesteven Rd M9 . . . . . . 157 A3
Keston Ave
  Droylsden M43 . . . . 83 C1
  Manchester M9 . . . . 65 A3
Keston Cres SK5 . . . . . 112 B6
Keston Rd ☑ OL1 . . . . . 49 C1
Kestor St BL2 . . . . 148 B3
Kestrel Ave
  Droylsden M34 . . . . 84 C1
  Farnworth BL4 . . . . 59 F7
  Oldham OL4 . . . . 67 F8
  Swinton M27 . . . . 62 B2
  Walkden M38 . . . . 60 A5
Kestrel Cl
  Hyde SK14 . . . . 167 B4
  Marple SK6 . . . . 126 A3
  Prestwich M25 . . . . 63 B6
Kestrel Dr
  Ashton-in-M WN4 . . . . . 73 C6
  Bury BL9 . . . . 141 B4
  Irlam M44 . . . . 94 F4
Kestrel Rd M17 . . . . 95 F8
Kestrel St ☑ BL1 . . . . . 148 A4
Kestrel View SK13 . . . . 115 F8
Kestrel Wlk M12 . . . . . . 165 A2
Keswick Ave
  Ashton-u-L OL7 . . . . . . 84 F5
  Chadderton OL9 . . . . . . 152 A3
  Denton M34 . . . . 100 D4
  Dukinfield SK14 . . . . . . 101 C4
  Gatley SK8 . . . . 122 B4
  Oldham OL8 . . . . 67 C3
  Urmston M41 . . . . 94 E1
Keswick Cl
  Irlam M44 . . . . 105 D4
  Manchester M13 . . . . . . 164 A1
  Middleton M24 . . . . 46 D2
  Stalybridge SK15 . . . . . 86 A4
Keswick Ct
  ☑ Middleton M24 . . . . . 46 D2
  Wythenshawe M22 . . . . 121 E6
Keswick Dr
  Bramhall SK7 . . . . 132 C5
  Bury BL9 . . . . 44 D7
Keswick Gr M6 . . . . 154 C2
Keswick Pl WN2 . . . . . . 56 A7
Keswick Rd
  Altrincham WA15 . . . . . 120 D6
  High Lane SK6 . . . . 134 E8
  Reddish SK4 . . . . 111 D7

Keswick Rd *continued*
  Stretford M32 . . . . 96 C3
  Walkden M28 . . . . 60 F2
Keswick St
  Bolton BL1 . . . . 143 C2
  Rochdale OL11 . . . . 30 B2
Ketley Wlk ☑ M22 . . . . 121 F3
Kettering Rd M19 . . . . . . 99 B2
Kettleshulme Way SK12 . 134 A3
Kettleshulme Wlk ☑
  SK9 . . . . 131 E1
Kettlewell Wlk M18 . . . 165 C1
Ketton Cl M11 . . . . 99 E7
Kevin Ave OL2 . . . . 48 E2
Kevin Cl SK2 . . . . 124 B4
Kevin St M19 . . . . 111 B8
Kew Ave SK14 . . . . 167 B1
Kew Dr
  Cheadle SK8 . . . . 122 E2
  Urmston M41 . . . . 95 A4
Kew Gdns M40 . . . . 65 A1
Kew Rd
  Failsworth M35 . . . . 84 A8
  Oldham OL4 . . . . 67 C5
  Rochdale OL11 . . . . 31 A3
Key Cl M44 . . . . 113 A8
Keyhaven Wlk M40 . . . . 157 A1
Keymer St M11 . . . . . . 160 B2
Keynsham Rd M11 . . . . . 83 B3
Keystone Cl M6 . . . . . . 154 B4
Key West Cl M11 . . . . . 160 C1
Keyworth Wlk M40 . . . . 160 B4
Kibbles Brow BL7 . . . . . 25 B8
Kibboth Crew BL0 . . . . . 138 B3
Kibworth Cl M45 . . . . . . 62 D8
Kibworth Wlk ☑ M9 . . . . 64 E5
Kidacre Wlk ☑ M40 . . . . 83 A7
Kidderminster Way OL9 . 47 F1
Kidd Rd SK13 . . . . 116 E6
Kid Glove Rd WA3 . . . . . 74 B1
Kidwall Wlk ☑ M9 . . . . . 64 F1
Kiel Cl M30 . . . . 95 E8
Kielder Cl WN4 . . . . 72 F7
Kielder Hill M24 . . . . . . 46 F4
Kielder Sq M5 . . . . 154 C1
Kiers Ct BL6 . . . . 22 E4
Kilbride Ave BL2 . . . . . . 42 F6
Kilbuck La WA11 . . . . . . 89 A8
Kilburn Ave
  Ashton-in-M WN4 . . . . . 73 D4
  Manchester M9 . . . . 64 D5
Kilburn Cl
  Gatley SK8 . . . . 131 B7
  Leigh WN7 . . . . 57 D1
Kilburn Ct ☑ M14 . . . . . 98 D4
Kilburn Dr WN6 . . . . 36 A7
Kilburn Gr WN3 . . . . 54 D3
Kilburn Rd
  Orrell WN5 . . . . 53 C5
  Radcliffe M26 . . . . 43 E4
  Stockport SK3 . . . . 123 C7
  ☑ Wigan WN6 . . . . 37 A1
Kilcoby Ave M27 . . . . . . 80 D8
Kildale Cl BL3 . . . . 40 E4
Kildare Cres OL11 . . . . . 30 F2
Kildare Grange WN2 . . . . 56 C5
Kildare Rd
  Manchester M21 . . . . . 109 D8
  Swinton M27 . . . . 79 E6
Kildare St
  Farnworth BL4 . . . . 60 C7
  Hindley WN2 . . . . 56 C5
  Wigan WN3, WN5 . . . . . 54 F6
Kildonan Dr BL3 . . . . . . 40 F6
Killer St BL0 . . . . 138 C2
Killington Cl WN3 . . . . . . 55 B2
Killingworth Mews ☑
  BL6 . . . . 22 D1
Killon St BL9 . . . . 141 A1
Kilmaine Dr BL3 . . . . . . 40 E5
Kilmarsh Wlk ☑ M8 . . . 155 C3
Kilmington Dr M8 . . . . . 155 C2
Kilmory Dr BL2 . . . . 42 F6
Kilmory Fold SK13 . . . . 104 E3
Kiln Bank OL12 . . . . 4 C2
Kiln Brow BL7 . . . . 25 C8
Kiln Croft SK6 . . . . 112 F1
Kiln Croft La SK9 . . . . . 131 E4
Kilner Cl BL9 . . . . 45 B4
Kilnerdeyne Terr OL16 . . 139 B2
Kilner Wlk M40 . . . . . . 159 C8
Kiln Field BL7 . . . . 24 F8
Kiln Hill Cl OL1 . . . . 47 F2
Kiln Hill La OL1 . . . . 47 F2
Kilnhurst Wlk ☑ BL1 . . . 145 A4
Kiln La
  Glossop SK13 . . . . 104 A5
  Milnrow OL16 . . . . 31 F6
Kilnside Dr M9 . . . . 157 A3
Kilnsey Wlk M40 . . . . . 160 A4
Kilnsley St WN5 . . . . . . 54 C5
Kilton Wlk M40 . . . . . . 159 C4
Kilvert Dr M33 . . . . 107 F5

Kilworth Ave M33 . . . . . 107 F3
Kilworth Dr BL6 . . . . 40 D6
Kilworth St OL11 . . . . . 139 A1
Kimberley Ave SK6 . . . . 113 C2
Kimberley Pl WN4 . . . . . 73 C3
Kimberley Rd BL1 . . . . . 24 E5
Kimberley St
  Bacup OL13 . . . . 3 A7
  Oldham OL8 . . . . 66 C3
  Salford M7 . . . . 155 B3
  Stockport SK3 . . . . 170 B3
Kimberley Wlk M15 . . . . 162 A3
Kimberly St WN6 . . . . . . 37 A1
Kimble Cl BL8 . . . . 10 F2
Kimbolton Cl M12 . . . . . 165 A2
Kimnel Ave M7 . . . . 80 D2
Kinburn Rd M19 . . . . . . 110 D2
Kinbury Wlk M40 . . . . . 159 C4
Kincardine Ct M13 . . . . 163 B2
Kincardine Rd M13 . . . . 163 B2
Kincraig Cl
  Bolton BL3 . . . . 40 E4
  Droylsden M11 . . . . 83 C1
Kinder Ave
  Ashton-u-L OL6 . . . . 86 A6
  Oldham OL4 . . . . 67 D5
Kinder Cl SK13 . . . . 116 A8
Kinder Ct SK3 . . . . 170 B3
Kinder Dr SK6 . . . . 126 A6
Kinder Fold SK15 . . . . . 102 D6
Kinder Gr
  Ashton-in-M WN4 . . . . . 72 F6
  Newhey OL16 . . . . 113 E2
Kinder Ho M5 . . . . 154 A3
Kinderlee Way SK13 . . . 115 B5
Kinder Mews OL3 . . . . . 69 B5
Kinders Cl M31 . . . . . . 106 D6
Kinders Cres OL3 . . . . . 69 B5
Kinders Fold OL15 . . . . . 15 F7
Kinders La OL3 . . . . 69 B6
Kinder St
  Stalybridge SK15 . . . . . 86 A2
  Stockport SK3 . . . . 170 B3
Kinderton Ave M20 . . . . 110 B7
Kinder Way
  Middleton M24 . . . . 46 F2
  Mottram in L SK14 . . . . 102 F3
King Charles Ct SK13 . . 116 D7
Kingcombe Wlk ☑ M9 . . 157 B4
King Cup Cl SK13 . . . . . 116 A8
King David High Sch M8 . 63 F1
King David Jun & Inf Schs
  M8 . . . . 63 F1
King Edward Ave SK13 . . 104 D1
King Edward St SK14 . . . 113 E8
King Edward Rd SK14 . . 113 E8
King Edward's Bldgs M7 . 155 C4
King Edward St
  Eccles M30 . . . . 79 C2
  ☑ Manchester M19 . . . . 99 B1
  Salford M5 . . . . 161 B4
Kingfisher Ave M34 . . . . 84 C1
Kingfisher Cl M12 . . . . . 164 B1
Kingfisher Com Specl Sch
  The OL9 . . . . 65 F5
Kingfisher Ct
  Ashton-in-M WN4 . . . . . 73 B6
  Rochdale OL12 . . . . 15 C4
  ☑ Wigan WN6 . . . . 37 A1
Kingfisher Ctr OL13 . . . . 3 E8
Kingfisher Dr
  Bury BL9 . . . . 141 B4
  Farnworth BL4 . . . . 59 F7
Kingfisher Mews SK6 . . 126 A6
Kingfisher Rd SK2 . . . . 124 B2
Kingfisher Way SK13 . . . 115 F8
King George Cl WN4 . . . 73 B3
King George Rd
  Haydock WA11 . . . . 89 A7
  Hyde SK14 . . . . 113 E8
Kingham Dr M4 . . . . . . 159 C2
Kingholm Gdns BL1 . . . 143 A1
King La OL1 . . . . 49 E4
Kingmoor Ave SK6 . . . . . 44 B4
King of Kings Sch The
  M4 . . . . 159 A3
King of Prussia Yd WN1 . 150 C4
King's Acre WA14 . . . . . 119 A1
Kings Ave
  Gatley SK8 . . . . 122 A4
  Manchester M8 . . . . . . 156 B4
  Whitefield M45 . . . . 44 E2
King's Ave WA3 . . . . 90 F7
Kingsbridge Ave
  Ainsworth BL2 . . . . 26 D1
  Hattersley SK14 . . . . . 102 C2
Kingsbridge Cl SK6 . . . . 125 E7
Kingsbridge Ct M9 . . . . 157 A3
Kingsbridge Dr SK16 . . . 101 B7
Kingsbridge Ho BL3 . . . 144 C1
Kingsbridge Rd
  Manchester M9 . . . . . . 157 A3
  ☑ Oldham OL4 . . . . 67 B5
Kingsbrook Ct M21 . . . . 109 E8
Kingsbrook Rd M16, M21, 109 E8
Kingsbury Ave BL1 . . . . 142 A1
Kingsbury Ct BL8 . . . . . . 27 A6
Kingsbury Court Lo BL1 . 142 A1
Kingsbury Ct BL1 . . . . . 142 A1
Kingsbury Dr SK9 . . . . . 131 D1
Kingsbury Rd ☑ M11 . . . 83 C2
Kingscliff
  Prestwich M25 . . . . 63 C5
  Wilmslow SK9 . . . . 137 A6
King's Cl
  Droylsden M18 . . . . 99 F6
  Stockport SK7 . . . . 123 F2

Kingscliffe St M9 . . . . . 157 B4
Kingscourt Ave BL1 . . . . 142 C2
Kings Cres M16 . . . . 97 B3
King's Cres M46 . . . . 76 E8
Kingscroft Ct WN1 . . . . 151 A3
Kings Ct
  ☑ Glossop SK13 . . . . . 116 C8
  Stockport SK5 . . . . 169 C3
  ☑ Tyldesley M29 . . . . . 58 F1
Kingsdale Cl BL9 . . . . . . 45 A7
Kingsdale Rd M18 . . . . . 100 A4
Kingsdown Cres WN1 . . . 37 C4
Kingsdown Dr BL1 . . . . 143 C1
Kingsdown Gdns ☑ BL1 . 143 C1
Kingsdown Rd
  Abram Brow WN2 . . . . . 74 B7
  Wythenshawe M22 . . . . 121 C1
Kingsdown Wlk SK5 . . . 112 B5
Kings Dr SK8 . . . . 123 A3
King's Dr
  Marple SK6 . . . . 125 E7
  Middleton M24 . . . . 64 D8
  Stockport SK8 . . . . 168 A3
Kingsfield Dr M20 . . . . . 110 C2
Kingsfield Way M29 . . . . 77 B8
Kings Fold M46 . . . . 58 E3
Kingsfold Ave M40 . . . . 159 C4
Kingsfold Cl BL2 . . . . . . 42 E6
Kingsford St M5 . . . . . . 154 A2
Kingsgate Bsns Ctr SK4 . 169 B2
Kingsgate Rd M22 . . . . 121 C1
King's Gdns WN7 . . . . . . 76 C5
Kings Gr
  Rochdale SK16 . . . . 15 C4
  Stretford M32 . . . . 96 F3
Kingshill Ct WN6 . . . . . . 36 F7
Kingshill Rd M21 . . . . . 109 A8
Kingsholme Rd M22 . . . 121 C2
Kings La M32 . . . . 96 F3
Kingsland Cl M40 . . . . . 160 A3
Kingsland Rd
  Cheadle SK3 . . . . 123 A7
  Farnworth BL4 . . . . 42 A1
  Rochdale OL11 . . . . 30 B3
Kingslea PR7 . . . . 20 F8
Kingslea Rd M20 . . . . . 110 C5
Kingsleigh Rd SK4 . . . . 110 F4
Kingsley Ave
  Handforth SK9 . . . . . . 131 C2
  Manchester M9 . . . . . . 157 C3
  Salford M7 . . . . 81 A7
  Stockport SK4 . . . . 169 B4
  Stretford M32 . . . . 96 F3
  Urmston M41 . . . . 95 B2
  Whitefield M45 . . . . 63 B8
  Wigan WN3 . . . . 54 F3
Kingsley Cl
  Ashton-u-L OL6 . . . . 86 A5
  Denton M34 . . . . 100 D1
Kingsley Dr
  Cheadle SK8 . . . . 123 A3
  Oldham OL4 . . . . 67 E7
Kingsley Gr M34 . . . . . . 100 C8
Kingsley Ho M1 . . . . . . 159 B1
Kingsley Rd
  Altrincham WA15 . . . . . 120 B7
  Hindley WN2 . . . . 56 F5
  Middleton M24 . . . . 47 B2
  Oldham OL4 . . . . 67 C6
  Swinton M27 . . . . 61 D1
  Walkden M28 . . . . 60 C1
  Wythenshawe M22 . . . . 121 D8
Kingsley St
  Bolton BL1 . . . . 143 A2
  Bury BL8 . . . . 27 B2
  Leigh WN7 . . . . 75 C7
King's Lynn Cl SK20 . . . 110 B3
Kingsmead Mews M9 . . . 64 C5
Kingsmede WN1 . . . . . . 37 D3
Kingsmere Ave M19 . . . . 98 F1
Kingsmill Ave M19 . . . . 111 B8
Kingsmoor Fields SK13 . 104 D3
Kingsmoor Rd SK13 . . . 104 D3
Kingsnorth Cl ☑ BL1 . . . 143 C1
Kingsnorth Rd M41 . . . . 94 E4
Kings Oak Cl WN1 . . . . 151 A4
Kings Pk
  Leigh WN7 . . . . 76 A8
  Stretford M17 . . . . 96 B4
King Sq M12 . . . . 153 B2
Kings Rd
  Cheadle SK8 . . . . 123 A3
  Failsworth OL9 . . . . 65 E3
  Golborne WA3 . . . . 90 A7
  Hazel Grove SK7 . . . . . 124 E3
  Irlam M44 . . . . 105 E6
  Manchester, Chorlton-cum-Hardy
   M21 . . . . 109 B6
  Manchester, Firswood M16 . 97 B3
  Sale M33 . . . . 107 F4
  Shaw OL2 . . . . 149 A2
  Stretford M32 . . . . 96 E2
King's Rd
  Ashton-in-M WN4 . . . . . 73 A5
  Ashton-u-L OL6 . . . . 85 E5
  Manchester M25 . . . . . . 63 C1
  Oldham OL8 . . . . 153 C1
  Oldham OL8 . . . . 100 B6
  Rochdale OL16 . . . . 31 B5
  Romiley SK6 . . . . 113 A3
  Wilmslow SK9 . . . . 136 E8
Kings Reach Bsns Pk
  SK4 . . . . 168 C1
Kings Road Prim Sch
  M16 . . . . 97 A3

Kings Street Rdbt OL1 . . . 153 B2
King St
 Bolton BL1 . . . . 145 B3
 Bolton, Bradshaw Chapel
 BL2 . . . . 25 C5
 5 Bolton, Cox Green BL7. . 24 F8
 Broadbottom SK14. . . . . . 115 A8
 Delph OL3 . . . . 50 F4
 Denton M34. . . . . 100 F3
 Droylsden M43. . . . . 100 A8
 Dukinfield SK16 . . . . 101 C7
 Eccles M30 . . . . 79 F1
 Failsworth M35 . . . . 83 D6
 Farnworth BL4. . . . . 60 D8
 Glossop SK13. . . . . 116 C8
 Heywood OL10. . . . . 29 D1
 Hindley WN2 . . . . 56 D6
 Hollingworth SK14. . . . . . 103 D5
 Horwich BL6 . . . . 22 A4
 Hyde SK14. . . . . 167 A3
 Ince-in-M WN2 . . . . 56 A7
 Leigh WN7 . . . . 75 F4
 Manchester M2. . . . . 158 C1
 Middleton M24. . . . . 47 A1
 Mossley OL5 . . . . 68 D1
 Newton-le-W WA12. . . . . . 89 B3
 Oldham OL8 . . . . 153 B2
 Radcliffe M26 . . . . 44 B2
 Ramsbottom BL0 . . . . 138 C2
 Rawtenstall BB4 . . . . 2 E8
 Rochdale OL16. . . . . 139 C3
 10 Royton OL2. . . . . 48 D4
 Salford, Higher Broughton
 M7. . . . . 155 B3
 Salford, Irlams o' th' Height
 M6. 80 D5
 Salford M3. . . . . 158 B2
 5 Stalybridge SK15. . . . . 86 A2
 Stretford M32 . . . . 96 D1
 Westhoughton BL5 . . . . . . 39 F1
 Whitworth OL12. . . . . 4 D3
 Wigan WN1 . . . . 150 C3
Kings Terr M32 . . . . 96 F3
King's Terr **14** SK16 . . . . 166 B1
KINGSTON 101 B3
Kingston Arc **8** SK14 . . 102 E2
Kingston Ave
 Bolton BL2 . . . . 25 C1
 Chadderton OL9. . . . . 66 A4
 Manchester M20 . . . . 110 B1
 5 Oldham OL1 . . . . 49 B1
Kingston Cl
 Bury BL8 . . . . 44 B8
 Hattersley SK14. . . . . 102 E2
 Sale M33 . . . . 107 D2
 Salford M7. . . . . 155 A4
 Shaw OL2. . . . . 149 B4
 Wigan WN3 . . . . 55 B3
Kingston Cres BB4 . . . . 1 A7
Kingston Ct
 14 Handforth SK9 . . . . . 131 E1
 Manchester M20 . . . . 110 B1
Kingston Dr
 Royton OL2 . . . . 48 C6
 Sale M33 . . . . 108 D5
 Urmston M41. . . . . 107 B8
Kingston Gdns SK14. . . . 101 B3
Kingston Gr M9. . . . . 64 F4
Kingston Hill SK8 . . . . . . 122 D4
Kingston Pl SK8 . . . . 122 E2
Kingston Rd
 Failsworth M35 . . . . 84 B7
 Handforth SK9 . . . . 131 D5
 Manchester M20 . . . . 110 B1
 Radcliffe M26 . . . . 44 C6
Kingston St SK3 . . . . 169 A1
Kingstreet SK7 . . . . 132 B1
King Street E
 Rochdale OL11. . . . . 139 C2
 Stockport SK1 . . . . 169 C2
King Street S OL11 . . . . . 139 B1
King Street W
 Manchester M3 . . . . 158 C1
 Stockport SK3 . . . . 169 B1
 Wigan WN1 . . . . 150 C4
Kingsway
 Altrincham WA14. . . . . . . 119 D5
 Cheadle M20, SK8 . . . . . . 122 C5
 Dukinfield SK16 . . . . 101 E7
 Ince-in-M WN2 . . . . 151 C3
 Kearsley BL4 . . . . 60 F6
 Manchester M14, M19,
 M20. . . . . 110 D4
 Middleton M24. . . . . 65 B6
 Newton-le-W WA12. . . . . . 89 C2
 Pendlebury M27. . . . . 80 C6
 Rochdale OL16. . . . . 31 C5
 Romiley SK6. . . . . 112 E3
 Stockport SK7 . . . . 123 F2
 Stretford M32 . . . . 96 C1
 Walkden M28. . . . . 78 D8
 Wigan WN1 . . . . 37 C2
Kingsway Ave M19 . . . . . . 98 F1
Kingsway Bldgs M19 . . . 110 E5
Kingsway Cl OL8 . . . . 153 B1
Kingsway Cres M19 . . . . 110 E5
Kingsway Pk M41. . . . . 95 D4
Kingsway Prim Sch M41. 95 E4
Kingsway Sch **20** WN1. . 37 C1
Kingsway Sch The SK8 . . 122 C4
Kingsway West Ind Pk
 OL16 . . . . 31 B5
Kingswear Dr BL1 . . . . . . 142 C1

Kings Wlk M43. . . . . 100 A8
Kings' Wlk OL6 . . . . 85 D5
Kingswood Gr SK5 . . . . 99 F1
Kingswood Rd
 Eccles M30 . . . . 79 B4
 Manchester M14 . . . . 110 E8
 Middleton M24. . . . . 46 F3
 Prestwich M25. . . . . 62 F5
Kingthorpe Gdns BL3 . . 147 C4
King William Ent Pk
 M50. . . . . 161 A4
King William St
 Eccles M30 . . . . 79 A3
 Salford M50. . . . . 161 A4
 Tyldesley M29 . . . . 76 F8
Kingwood Ave BL1. . . . . . 40 F8
Kingwood Cres WN5 . . . . 54 D6
Kinlay Rd BL4. . . . . 147 C1
Kinlet Rd WN3 . . . . 54 C4
Kinlett Wlk **11** M40. . . . . 65 D2
Kinley Cl M12. . . . . 164 C2
Kinloch Dr BL1 . . . . 144 B3
Kinloch Gdns OL8. . . . . . . 67 A4
Kinloch St
 Kinmel Ave SK5. . . . . 112 C4
 Kinmel Wlk **4** M23 . . . 120 F6
Kinmount Wlk M9 . . . . . . 157 A2
Kinnaird Cres SK1 . . . . . 124 B8
Kinnaird Rd M20. . . . . . . 110 C5
Kinnerly Gr M28 . . . . 60 A1
Kinniside Cl WN3 . . . . 55 A2
Kinross Ave
 Garswood WN4 . . . . 72 C4
 Oldham, Mumps OL1 . . . . 67 B8
 Stockport SK2 . . . . 124 A3
Kinross Cl BL0 . . . . 11 A2
Kinross Dr BL3. . . . . 40 F5
Kinross Rd M14. . . . . 98 E3
Kinsale Wlk M23. . . . . . . 120 F3
Kinsey Ave M23. . . . . 120 F7
Kinsley Dr M28 . . . . 60 C2
Kintbury St WN2 . . . . 73 F7
Kintore Ave SK7 . . . . 124 F3
Kintore Wlk **5** M40 . . . . 156 C1
Kintyre Ave M5 . . . . 154 B1
Kintyre Cl **3** M11 . . . . 83 C1
Kintyre Dr BL3 . . . . 40 E5
Kinver Cl BL3 . . . . 146 C3
Kinver Rd M40. . . . . 65 C2
Kipling Ave
 Denton M34. . . . . 113 A7
 Droylsden M43. . . . . 84 A3
 Wigan WN3 . . . . 55 A4
Kipling Cl SK2 . . . . 124 E7
Kipling Gr WN7 . . . . 75 D7
Kipling Rd OL1. . . . . 49 B2
Kipling St M7. . . . . 155 A2
Kippax St M14 . . . . 98 B3
Kirby Ave
 Atherton M46. . . . . 58 C5
 Failsworth OL9 . . . . 65 D3
 Swinton M27 . . . . 79 D5
Kirby Rd WN7. . . . . 75 F5
Kirby Wlk
 3 Manchester M4 . . . . . 159 C2
 Shaw OL2. . . . . 149 B4
Kiribati Way WN7 . . . . 75 E6
Kirkbank St OL9 . . . . 153 A3
Kirkbeck WN7 . . . . 76 C3
Kirkburn View BL6 . . . . . . 27 C5
Kirkby Ave
 Manchester M40 . . . . 83 B7
 Sale M33 . . . . 108 B7
Kirkby Cl BL9 . . . . 44 E7
Kirkby Dr M33. . . . . 108 D2
Kirkby Rd
 Bolton BL1. . . . . 144 B4
 Culcheth WA3 . . . . 91 F3
Kirkdale Ave M40 . . . . 65 D2
Kirkdale Dr OL2. . . . . 48 C5
Kirkdale Gdns WN8 . . . . . 53 A7
Kirkebrok Rd BL3 . . . . . . 146 A4
Kirkfell Dr
 High Lane SK6. . . . . 134 E8
 Tyldesley M29 . . . . 77 B7
Kirkfell Wlk OL1 . . . . 48 F1
Kirkgate Cl **5** M40. . . . . 159 C3
Kirkhall La
 Bolton BL1. . . . . 144 C4
 Leigh WN7. . . . . 75 E7
Kirkhall Wkshps The
 BL1. . . . . 144 C4
Kirkham Ave
 Golborne WA3 . . . . 90 E6
 Manchester M18 . . . . 99 D6
Kirkham Cl M34. . . . . 100 F3
Kirkham Rd
 Gatley SK8. . . . . 131 C8
 Leigh WN7. . . . . 75 D2
KIRKHAMS 63 B6
Kirkham St
 Abram WN2 . . . . 74 B8
 Bolton BL2. . . . . 25 C1
 Oldham OL9 . . . . 153 B3
 Salford M5. . . . . 154 B1
 Walkden M28. . . . . 60 A5
Kirkhaven Sq M40. . . . . . 160 B4
Kirkhill Grange BL5 . . . . . 40 A2
Kirkhill Wlk **12** M40. . . . . 65 D2
KIRKHOLT 30 F3
Kirkholt Wlk **11** M9 . . . . . 64 E3
Kirkhope Dr BL1. . . . . 143 A1
Kirkhope Wlk BL1. . . . . . 143 A1
Kirklands
 Bolton BL2. . . . . 25 D2
 Sale M33 . . . . 108 A2
Kirklee Ave OL9. . . . . 48 A1
Kirklee Rd OL11. . . . . 30 D2

Kirklees Cl BL8 . . . . 26 F7
Kirklees St
 Bury BL8 . . . . 26 F7
 Wigan WN1 . . . . 151 B4
Kirklees Wlk M45 . . . . 63 B8
Kirkless Ind Est WN2 . . . . 38 B1
Kirkless La WN2 . . . . 38 B1
Kirkless St WN2 . . . . 38 A3
Kirkless Villas WN2 . . . . . 38 A2
Kirkley St SK14 . . . . 167 B1
Kirklinton Dr M9. . . . . . . 157 A2
Kirkman Ave M30. . . . . 79 B4
Kirkman Cl M18. . . . . 99 D4
Kirkmanshulme La M12,
 M18. . . . . 165 B1
Kirkman St BL9. . . . . 44 F3
Kirkpatrick St WN2 . . . . . 57 B3
Kirk Rd M19 . . . . 111 B7
Kirk St M18. . . . . 99 D5
Kirkstall **22** OL12. . . . . . . 139 B4
Kirkstall Ave
 Heywood OL10. . . . . 29 C3
 Littleborough OL15 . . . . . . 16 A7
Kirkstall Cl SK12 . . . . . . 133 D4
Kirkstall Gdns **7** M26. . . 43 E5
Kirkstall Rd
 Middleton M24. . . . . 46 F3
 Urmston M41. . . . . 95 E3
Kirkstall Sq M13 . . . . 163 C2
Kirkstead Cl M11 . . . . 165 A4
Kirkstead Rd SK8 . . . . . . 132 C6
Kirkstead Way WA3 . . . . . 90 A8
Kirkstile Cres WN3. . . . . . 54 E2
Kirkstile Pl M27. . . . . 61 E4
Kirkstone Ave M28. . . . . . 60 F1
Kirkstone Cl OL1. . . . . 48 F1
Kirkstone Dr
 Middleton M24. . . . . 46 E2
 Royton OL2 . . . . 48 D6
Kirkstone Rd
 Dukinfield SK14 . . . . 101 C5
 Failsworth M40. . . . . 65 C2
Kirktown Wlk M11 . . . . . . 165 C4
Kirkwall Dr BL2 . . . . 148 B1
Kirkway
 Manchester M9 . . . . 65 A4
 Middleton M24. . . . . 65 A7
 Rochdale OL11. . . . . 30 F2
Kirkwood Cl WN2 . . . . 37 F2
Kirkwood Dr M40 . . . . . . 159 C4
Kirtley Ave M30. . . . . 79 D3
Kirtlington Cl OL2. . . . . . 149 A1
Kirton Lo M25 . . . . 63 C4
Kirton Wlk M9 . . . . 64 C5
Kitchener Ave M44. . . . . . 105 C4
Kitchener St
 Bolton BL3. . . . . 42 B3
 Bury BL8 . . . . 27 B1
Kitchener Way BL4. . . . . . 147 C1
Kitchen St **14** OL16. . . . . . 31 A8
Kite Gr WN7 . . . . 76 B5
Kitepool St M30 . . . . 79 A3
Kitter St OL12. . . . . 15 C3
KITT GREEN 54 C8
Kitt Green Rd WN5. . . . . . 54 C8
Kittiwake Cl SK2 . . . . 77 A7
Kittiwake Cl SK2 . . . . 124 F5
KITT'S MOSS 132 D6
Kitt's Moss La SK7 . . . . . 132 D6
Kitty Wheeldon Gdns
 M33. . . . . 108 A5
Kiveton Cl M28. . . . . 60 C2
Kiveton Dr WN4. . . . . 73 C2
Kiwi Pk M17. . . . . 96 C5
Knacks La OL12. . . . . 14 A5
Knaresborough Cl SK5 . . 99 E1
Knaresborough Rd WN2. . 56 E4
Knarr Barn La OL3 . . . . . . 50 D3
Knarr La OL3 . . . . 50 E2
Kneller Wlk OL1 . . . . 49 D4
Knight Cres M24. . . . . 46 D3
Knightley Wlk M40. . . . . . 157 A1
Knightsbridge M45. . . . . 169 C2
Knightsbridge Cl
 13 Handforth SK9 . . . . . 131 D1
 Salford M7. . . . . 155 A4
Knightsbridge Mews
 M20. . . . . 110 B4
Knight's Cl SK9. . . . . 137 B5
Knightscliffe Cres WN6 . . 35 D6
Knights Ct M5. . . . . 80 A2
Knights Gr M27 . . . . 79 D6
Knightshill Cres WN6 . . . . 37 A1
Knight St
 Ashton-u-L OL7 . . . . 84 F2
 Bolton BL1. . . . . 145 C4
 Bury BL8 . . . . 27 C2
 Hyde SK14. . . . . 167 B1
 Manchester M20 . . . . 110 B4
Knightswood BL3 . . . . 40 F3
Knightswood Rd M8 . . . . 156 A3
Kniveton Rd M12 . . . . 164 C2
Kniveton St SK14. . . . . . . 167 C3
Knob Hall Gdns M23 . . . 120 F3
Knole Ave SK12. . . . . 133 F4
Knoll St
 Rochdale OL11. . . . . 30 C2
 Salford M7. . . . . 155 A3
Knoll Street Ind Pk M7. . 155 A3
Knoll The
 Mossley OL5 . . . . 68 B1
 Shaw OL2. . . . . 149 C2
Knot Hill Resr Nature
 Reserve * OL6 . . . . 85 F7
Knott Fold SK14 . . . . 167 A1
Knott Hill La OL3. . . . . 50 E3
Knott Hill St OL12. . . . . 4 E6

Knott La
 Bolton BL1. . . . . 23 F2
 Hyde SK14. . . . . 113 E8
Knott Lanes OL8 . . . . 84 F8
Knotts Brow BL7 . . . . 7 F4
Knott's Hos WN7. . . . . 91 B8
Knowe Ave **6** M22. . . . . . 121 D1
Knowl Cl BL10 . . . . 11 C4
Knowldale Way M12 . . . . 164 B1
Knowle Ave OL7 . . . . 166 A4
Knowle Dr M25 . . . . 63 A2
Knowle Gn SK9 . . . . 131 C3
Knowle Pk SK9 . . . . 131 C3
Knowle Rd SK6 . . . . 126 D6
Knowles Ave WN3 . . . . 54 F4
Knowles Ct M6. . . . . 80 B3
Knowles Edge St BL1. . . 142 C2
Knowles Pl
 1 Manchester M15 . . . . 162 C2
 Wigan WN1 . . . . 151 B4
Knowles St
 Ince-in-M WN3 . . . . 151 A2
 Radcliffe M26 . . . . 44 A4
Knowle Way SK14 . . . . . . 102 F2
Knowl Hill Dr OL12. . . . . . 13 E2
Knowl Hill View OL10 . . . . 29 A2
Knowl La OL12 . . . . 13 B5
Knowl Mdw BB4 . . . . 1 A6
Knowl Rd
 Milnrow OL16 . . . . 31 D6
 Oldham OL2 . . . . 149 C1
Knowls La OL4 . . . . 67 F5
Knowl St
 Oldham OL8 . . . . 66 C2
 Stalybridge SK15. . . . . 86 B2
Knowls The OL8 . . . . 66 C1
Knowl Syke St OL12. . . . . 15 C7
Knowl Top La OL3. . . . . . . 69 D7
Knowl View
 Bury BL8 . . . . 27 A6
 Littleborough OL15 . . . . . . 15 F2
Knowsley OL4 . . . . 68 A7
Knowsley Ave
 Atherton M46. . . . . 58 C4
 Golborne WA3 . . . . 74 B1
 Oldham OL4. . . . . 68 A7
 Salford M5. . . . . 161 B4
 Urmston M41. . . . . 95 C4
Knowsley Cres
 Stockport SK1 . . . . 124 B8
 Whitworth OL12. . . . . 4 E6
Knowsley Dr
 Leigh WN7 . . . . 75 E2
 Oldham OL4. . . . . 68 A7
 Swinton M27 . . . . 79 D5
Knowsley Gn
 Oldham OL4. . . . . 68 A7
 Salford M5. . . . . 161 B4
Knowsley Gr **8** BL6. . . . . 22 D1
Knowsley Grange BL1. . . 40 D7
Knowsley Jun Sch OL4 . . 68 A7
Knowsley Park Way BL4. . 1 B8
Knowsley Rd
 Ainsworth BL2. . . . . 26 C1
 Bolton BL1. . . . . 142 B2
 Haslingden BB4 . . . . 1 B8
 Hazel Grove SK7 . . . . 133 F8
 Stockport SK1 . . . . 124 B8
 Whitefield M45 . . . . 62 F8
 Wigan WN6 . . . . 37 A3
Knowsley Road Ind Est
 BB4. 1 B8
Knowsley St
 Bolton BL1. . . . . 145 C3
 Bury BL9 . . . . 140 B1
 Leigh WN7 . . . . 75 D5
 Manchester M8. . . . . 159 A4
 Rochdale OL12. . . . . 139 B4
Knowsley Terr
 Oldham OL4. . . . . 68 A7
 Stockport SK1 . . . . 124 B8
Knutsford Ave
 Manchester M16 . . . . 97 D3
 Reddish SK4. . . . . 111 D7
 Sale M33 . . . . 108 C4
Knutsford Rd
 Manchester M18 . . . . 99 C4
 Row-of-Trees SK9, WA16. 136 D3
Knutsford St M6 . . . . 154 B2
Knutsford View WA15 . . 129 C8
KNUTSHAW BRIDGE 40 F3
Knuttshaw Cres BL3 . . . . 40 E2
Knypersley Ave SK2 . . . . 124 C7
Krester Ct M20 . . . . 110 A5
Krokus Sq OL9. . . . . 152 A3
Kyle Cl SK7 . . . . 124 F1
Kylemore Ave BL3 . . . . . 144 B1
Kylemore Pl BL4 . . . . 60 C7
Kylemore Way M11 . . . . . 164 C4
Kyle Rd SK7 . . . . 124 F1
Kynder St M34. . . . . 100 F3

L

Labrador Quay M50 . . . . . . 96 F7
Labtec St M27 . . . . 62 B1
Laburnum Ave
 Ashton-u-L OL6 . . . . 85 C6
 Atherton M46. . . . . 58 E3
 Bury BL8 . . . . 26 F7
 Chadderton OL9. . . . . 48 C1
 Droylsden M34. . . . . 84 C1
 Eccles M30 . . . . 95 A8
 Failsworth M35 . . . . 83 F6
 Hyde SK14. . . . . 113 D8
 Ince-in-M WN3 . . . . 151 C2
 Leigh WN7 . . . . 75 E8
Laburnum Ave continued
 Shaw OL2. . . . . 149 B2
 Stalybridge SK15, SK16. . 101 F8
 Swinton M27 . . . . 79 E6
 Whitefield M45 . . . . 62 F7
Laburnum Cl **4** WA15. . . 120 B5
Laburnum Ct
 Bury BL8 . . . . 26 F7
 Lymm WA13. . . . . 117 B4
Laburnum Dr
 Whitefield BL9. . . . . 45 A1
 Wigan WN6 . . . . 37 A4
Laburnum Gr
 Horwich BL6 . . . . 22 E1
 Prestwich M25. . . . . 63 A5
 Tyldesley M29 . . . . 59 D1
Laburnum La
 Altrincham WA15. . . . . . . 128 E8
 Newhey OL16. . . . . 32 A3
Laburnum Pk BL2. . . . . . . 25 B5
Laburnum Rd
 Farnworth BL4. . . . . 60 B8
 Golborne WA3 . . . . 90 F7
 Haslingden BB4 . . . . 1 A7
 Irlam M44 . . . . 105 D5
 Manchester M18 . . . . 99 D4
 Middleton M24. . . . . 65 C8
 Oldham OL8. . . . . 84 C8
 Reddish M34 . . . . 99 F3
 Urmston M41. . . . . 95 B4
 Walkden M28. . . . . 60 L1
Laburnum St
 Ashton-in-M WN4 . . . . 73 B2
 Atherton M46. . . . . 58 E3
 7 Bolton BL1 . . . . 145 A4
 Salford M6. . . . . 154 C2
Laburnum Terr OL11 . . . . 30 B4
Laburnum Way
 Littleborough OL15 . . . . . . 15 F5
 Stockport SK3 . . . . 123 B6
Laburnum Wlk **1** M33 . . 107 C5
Lacerta Mews M7 . . . . 81 C3
Lacey Ave SK9. . . . . 131 B1
Lacey Ct SK9 . . . . 131 B1
Lacey Gn SK9 . . . . 131 B1
Lacey Gr SK9 . . . . 131 B1
LACEY GREEN 131 B1
Lacey Green Prim Sch
 SK9. . . . . 131 B1
Lackford Dr M40. . . . . 159 C4
Lacrosse Ave OL8 . . . . 66 C4
Lacy Gr M32 . . . . 96 D1
Lacy St
 Stockport SK1 . . . . 170 C4
 Stretford M32 . . . . 96 D1
Lacy Wlk M12. . . . . 164 B4
Ladbrooke Cl OL6 . . . . . . 166 C4
Ladbrooke Rd OL6 . . . . . . 85 C5
Ladcastle Rd OL3 . . . . 69 A7
Ladhill La OL3 . . . . 69 B5
Ladies La WN2 . . . . 56 D6
Ladybarn Ave WA3 . . . . . . 89 F7
Ladybarn Cres
 Bramhall SK7. . . . . 132 F6
 Manchester M14 . . . . 110 D6
Ladybarn Ho **1** M14 . . . . 110 D6
Ladybarn La M14 . . . . 110 D6
Ladybarn Manor SK7. . . . 132 E8
Ladybarn Mews **2** M14. 110 D6
Ladybarn Prim Sch M20 . 110 D6
Ladybarn Rd M14. . . . . . . 110 D6
Ladybower SK8 . . . . 123 C4
Ladybower Ct SK13 . . . . 104 C1
Ladybridge Ave M28 . . . . 78 C8
Lady Bridge Brow BL1. . . 40 F7
Ladybridge High Sch BL3. 40 F4
Lady Bridge La BL1, BL3. . 40 F7
Ladybridge Prim Sch
 Bolton BL3. . . . . 40 F5
 Cheadle SK8 . . . . 123 B4
Ladybridge Rd SK8. . . . . 123 B3
Ladybridge Rise SK8 . . . 123 C3
Ladybrook Ave WA15. . . 120 B8
Ladybrook Gr **9** SK9 . . . 131 D2
Ladybrook Prim Sch SK7. 132 F7
Ladybrook Rd SK7 . . . . . 123 C1
Ladyburn Ct M14. . . . . . . 110 D7
Ladyfield St SK9 . . . . 137 B7
Ladyfield Terr SK9 . . . . . 137 C7
Lady Harriet Wlk M28 . . . 60 C3
Ladyhill View M28 . . . . 78 C8
LADY HOUSE 31 E4
Ladyhouse Cl OL16. . . . . . 32 A5
Ladyhouse La OL16 . . . . . 32 A5
Lady Kelvin Rd WA14. . . 119 C2
Lady La
 Culcheth WA3 . . . . 91 C1
 Wigan WN3 . . . . 54 E3
Ladylands Ave **12** M11 . . 83 C2
Ladymeadow Cl BL3 . . . . 25 B3
Ladymere Dr M28 . . . . 78 B8
Lady Rd OL4 . . . . 67 E6
Ladys Cl SK12. . . . . 133 E4
Ladyshore Cl M6. . . . . . . 154 C1
Ladyshore Rd BL3. . . . . . . 43 C2
Ladysmith Ave
 Ashton-in-M WN4 . . . . 73 C3
 Bury BL9 . . . . 28 A5
Ladysmith Dr OL6. . . . . . . 85 F5
Ladysmith Rd
 Ashton-u-L OL6 . . . . 85 F5
 Manchester M20 . . . . 110 C3
 Stalybridge SK15. . . . . 86 A4
Ladysmith Sh Ctr OL6 . . 166 B3

Ladysmith St
Oldham OL8 . . . . 66 C3
Stockport SK3 . . . . 170 B3
Ladysmith The OL6 . . . . . . 85 F5
Ladythorn Ave SK6 . . . . . 126 A5
Ladythorn Cres SK7 . . . . 132 F6
Ladythorn Ct M25 . . . . . . 63 A2
Ladythorne Ave M25 . . . 63 A2
Ladythorne Dr M25 . . . . 63 A2
Ladythorn Gr SK7 . . . . . . 132 F6
Ladythorn Rd SK7 . . . . . 132 E6
Ladywell Ave M38 . . . . . . 60 A5
Ladywell Cl SK7 . . . . 124 A2
Ladywell Gr M38 . . . . 60 A5
Ladywell Metro Sta M5 . 80 A2
Ladywood Sch BL3 . . . . . 43 B4
Lafford La WN8 . . . . 35 C2
Lagan Wlk M22 . . . . 121 E2
Lagos Cl M14 . . . . 98 A4
Laindon Rd M13, M14 . . . 98 E4
Lainton Ct 6 BL3 . . . . . . 123 C8
LAITHWAITE 54 D8
Laithwaite Rd WN5 . . . . . 54 E7
Lake Bank OL15 . . . . 16 A3
Lake Dr M24 . . . . 64 F7
Lakeland Ave M14 . . . . . . 73 C4
Lakeland Cres BL9 . . . . . 44 E6
Lakeland Cl 1 M24 . . . . . 46 D2
Lakeland Dr OL2 . . . . 48 C8
Lakelands Dr BL3 . . . . . . 40 F5
Lakenheath Cl 2 BL1 . . . 24 F6
Lakenheath Dr BL1 . . . . . 25 A6
Lake Rd
Denton M34 . . . . 100 F4
Stalybridge SK15 . . . . 85 F4
Stretford M17 . . . . 96 C7
Lakes Dr WN5 . . . . 53 E6
Lakeside
Gatley SK8 . . . . 122 C3
Prestwich M7 . . . . 63 D1
Wilmslow/Alderley Edge
SK9 . . . . 136 C7
Lake Side
Bury BL9 . . . . 44 F5
Glossop SK13 . . . . 104 A6
Leigh WN7 . . . . 75 D6
Littleborough OL15 . . . . . . 16 A2
Lakeside Ave
Ashton-u-L OL7 . . . . 84 F4
Bolton BL3 . . . . 42 A2
Orrell WN5 . . . . 53 E3
Walkden M28 . . . . 60 D5
Lakeside Cl M18 . . . . 99 F6
Lake Side Cotts WN1 . . 20 C1
Lakeside Dr SK12 . . . . . 133 E5
Lakeside Gn SK2 . . . . . . 124 C6
Lakeside Rise M9 . . . . . 64 A3
Lakeside Way BL9 . . . . 140 C1
Lakes Rd
Dukinfield SK16 . . . . 101 C8
Marple SK6 . . . . 126 B6
Lake St
Bolton BL3 . . . . 145 C1
Leigh WN7 . . . . 76 A6
Stockport SK2 . . . . 124 B5
Lakes Terr WN2 . . . . 56 A7
Lake View
Manchester M9 . . . . 65 A2
Stalybridge SK15 . . . . 85 F4
Lake Wlk WN5 . . . . 54 B7
Lakin St M40 . . . . 83 A7
Laleham Gn SK7 . . . . . . 123 D3
Lamb Cl M12 . . . . 164 C1
Lamb Ct M3 . . . . 158 E2
LAMBERHEAD GREEN . . 54 B5
Lamberhead Green Com
Prim Sch WN5 . . . . 54 B6
Lamberhead Ho WN5 . . 54 B6
Lamberhead Ind Est WN5. 54 C5
Lamberhead Rd WN5 . . 54 C6
Lambert Dr M33 . . . . . . 107 E6
Lamberton Dr M23 . . . . 120 E6
Lambert St OL7 . . . . 100 F8
Lambeth Ave M35 . . . . . . 84 B8
Lambeth Cl BL6 . . . . 22 D3
Lambeth Gr SK6 . . . . . . 113 A5
Lambeth Rd
Failsworth M40 . . . . 83 C4
Reddish SK5 . . . . 111 F7
Lambeth St M46 . . . . 58 B3
Lambeth Terr OL11 . . . . 139 A1
Lambgates SK13 . . . . . . 104 A5
Lambgates La SK13 . . . 104 A5
Lamb La
Ashley WA14 . . . . 128 D4
Salford M3 . . . . 158 E2
Lambley Cl WN7 . . . . 75 D8
Lambourn Cl
Bolton BL3 . . . . 145 B1
Poynton SK12 . . . . 133 D4
Lambourne Cl M22 . . . . 130 D8
Lambourne Gr 4 OL16 . . 31 F5
Lambourn Rd M41 . . . . . 94 D4
Lambrook Wlk M40 . . . . 83 D4
Lambs Fold SK4 . . . . . . 111 D5
Lamb St WN1 . . . . 37 E1
Lambton Rd
Manchester M21 . . . . . . 109 D8
Swinton M28 . . . . 79 C7
Lambton St
Bolton BL3 . . . . 146 C2
Eccles M30 . . . . 79 B3
Wigan WN5 . . . . 54 E4
Lamburn Ave M40 . . . . . . 65 D2
Lamb Wlk 1 M34 . . . . . 113 A7
Lamerton Way SK9 . . . . 131 E2
Lamorna Cl M7 . . . . 81 B7
Lamphey Cl BL1 . . . . 40 D8

Lamplight Way M27 . . . . 80 E7
Lamport Cl M1 . . . . 163 B3
Lamport Ct M1 . . . . 163 B3
Lampson St M8 . . . . 158 B4
Lampton Cl WA14 . . . . . 119 D7
Lamsholme Cl 7 M19 . . 99 A2
Lanark Ave M22 . . . . . . 121 E8
Lanark Cl
Hazel Grove SK7 . . . . . . 125 A2
Heywood OL10 . . . . 28 F1
Lanbury Dr M8 . . . . 155 C3
Lancashire Ct OL9 . . . . 152 C1
Lancashire Health & Racquet
Club M24 . . . . 46 B2
LANCASHIRE HILL 169 B3
Lancashire Hill SK1, SK4,
SK5 . . . . 169 B3
Lancashire Rd M31 . . . . 105 E2
Lancaster Ave
Atherton M46 . . . . 58 E2
Failsworth M35 . . . . 83 E7
Golborne WA3 . . . . 90 C8
Haslingden BB4 . . . . 1 B8
Horwich BL6 . . . . 22 D2
Middleton M24 . . . . 65 C7
Ramsbottom BL0 . . . . 11 A4
Stalybridge SK15 . . . . 86 A3
Tyldesley M29 . . . . 59 A3
Urmston M41 . . . . 95 E3
Whitefield M45 . . . . 63 A7
Lancaster Cl
Adlington PR6 . . . . 21 B7
Bolton BL2 . . . . 148 A3
Hazel Grove SK7 . . . . . . 133 D8
Romiley SK6 . . . . 113 A1
Lancaster Cres
Failsworth M40 . . . . 83 C4
2 Leigh WN7 . . . . 76 B4
3 Manchester M19 . . . . 110 F8
Lancaster Dr
Bury BL9 . . . . 27 F8
Little Lever BL3 . . . . 43 B4
Manchester M25 . . . . 63 C2
Lancaster Ho
3 Royton OL2 . . . . 48 D5
5 Stockport SK3 . . . . . . 170 B4
Lancasterian Sch M20 . 109 E4
Lancaster Pl PR6 . . . . . . 21 A8
Lancaster Rd
Denton M34 . . . . 100 F1
Droylsden M43 . . . . 83 F3
Handforth SK9 . . . . 131 E1
Hindley WN2 . . . . 56 F5
Irlam M44 . . . . 105 D5
Manchester M20 . . . . . . 110 A3
Salford M6 . . . . 80 B4
Wigan WN5 . . . . 36 D1
Lancaster Sq 2 OL2 . . . 48 D5
Lancaster St
Chadderton OL9 . . . . 66 A3
Ince-in-M WN3 . . . . 151 A2
Mossley OL5 . . . . 68 B1
2 Radcliffe M26 . . . . 43 E3
Stockport SK1 . . . . 112 A2
Lancaster Terr
2 Bolton BL1 . . . . 143 B2
Rochdale OL11 . . . . 13 D2
Lancaster Way BL5 . . . . 39 D2
Lancelot Rd M22 . . . . . . 121 F2
Lancelyn Dr SK9 . . . . . . 137 D8
Lance Wood Pl WN5 . . . 54 D6
Lanchester Dr BL3 . . . . 145 A1
Lanchester St M40 . . . . 160 B3
Lancing Ave M20 . . . . . 110 D3
Lancing Wlk OL9 . . . . . . 152 A2
Landau Dr M28 . . . . 59 F3
Landcross Rd M14 . . . . . 98 C1
Landedmans BL5 . . . . . . 57 D5
Landells Wlk M40 . . . . . 83 A5
Lander Gr M9 . . . . 64 F3
LAND GATE 73 A8
Land Gate OL12 . . . . 4 F5
Landgate Ind Est WN4. . 73 A8
Land Gate La WN4 . . . . . 73 B8
Landgate Sch The WN4. . 73 A7
Landkey Cl 1 M23 . . . . 120 F1
Land La SK9 . . . . 137 C6
Landmark Ct BL1 . . . . . . 23 F1
Landor Cl WA3 . . . . 90 E8
Landor St M34 . . . . 99 F3
Landore Cl M26 . . . . 44 B4
Landos Ct 12 M40 . . . . 159 C3
Landos Rd M40 . . . . . . 159 C3
Landrace Dr M28 . . . . . . 78 B6
Landsberg Rd M35 . . . . . 84 B8
Landsberg Terr M35 . . . . 84 B8
Landseer Dr SK6 . . . . . . 126 B7
Landseer St OL4 . . . . 67 A5
Lands End Rd M24 . . . . . 64 B7
LANDSIDE 75 F1
Landside WN7 . . . . 75 F2
Land St WN6 . . . . 19 D2
Lane Brow OL4 . . . . 68 B5
Lane Ct 1 M41 . . . . 98 D4
LANE END 46 F8
Lane End
Eccles M30 . . . . 79 F1
Heywood OL10. . . . . 46 F8
Shaw OL2 . . . . 48 A6
Lane End Prim Sch SK8 . 123 C2
Lane End Rd
Britannia OL13 . . . . 4 A8
Manchester M19, SK4 . . 110 E4
LANE ENDS 114 D1

Lane Ends
Romiley SK6 . . . . 113 D3
5 Wigan WN5 . . . . 54 D5
Lanegate SK14 . . . . 113 D8
LANE HEAD 90 E6
Lane Head Ave WA3 . . . . 90 F8
Lane Head Rd
Mossley OL4, OL5 . . . . . . 68 A3
Oldham OL4 . . . . 67 F4
Lane Mdw OL2 . . . . 149 A2
Lanesfield Wlk M8 . . . . 156 C4
Laneside Ave OL2 . . . . . 49 D7
Laneside Cl OL15 . . . . . . 16 A6
Laneside Dr SK7 . . . . . . 124 A1
Laneside Rd
Manchester M20 . . . . . . 122 C8
New Mills, Rowarth SK22 . 127 E6
Laneside Wlk OL16 . . . . . 31 F7
Lane The BL1 . . . . 40 D7
Lanfield Dr M8 . . . . 155 C3
Langcliffe Cl WA3 . . . . . . 91 E3
Langcliffe Pl M26 . . . . . . 61 C8
Langcliffe Wlk M18 . . . . 165 C1
Langcroft Dr 4 M40 . . . . 83 C5
Langdale Ave
Golborne WA3 . . . . 74 C1
Ince-in-M WN2 . . . . 151 A8
Manchester M19 . . . . . . 111 B8
Oldham OL8 . . . . 66 D4
Royton OL16 . . . . 48 C8
Wigan WN1 . . . . 37 B3
Langdale Cl
Altrincham WA15 . . . . . . 119 E5
Denton M34 . . . . 100 E1
Gatley SK8 . . . . 122 C3
High Lane SK6 . . . . 134 E8
Langdale Cres
Abram WN2 . . . . 74 B8
Wigan WN5 . . . . 54 B8
Langdale Ct M8 . . . . 156 B2
Langdale Dr
Middleton M24 . . . . 46 F3
Walkden M28 . . . . 60 D5
Whitefield BL9 . . . . 45 A3
Langdale Gr M29 . . . . . . 56 B2
Langdale Mews 9 BL9 . . 27 F5
Langdale Rd
Bramhall SK7 . . . . 132 C5
Hindley WN2 . . . . 56 E5
Manchester M14 . . . . 98 D4
Partington M31 . . . . 105 E3
Reddish SK4 . . . . 111 C6
Romiley SK6 . . . . 113 B4
Sale M33 . . . . 107 E1
Stretford M32 . . . . 96 C3
Wigan WN5 . . . . 54 B7
Langdale St
Bolton BL3 . . . . 147 B3
Farnworth BL4 . . . . 60 C7
Leigh WN7 . . . . 75 E5
Langdale Terr SK15 . . . . 86 A4
Langden Cl
Culcheth WA3 . . . . 91 D4
Shaw OL2 . . . . 149 A4
Langdon Cl BL1 . . . . 143 A1
Langdon Coll 1 M7 . . . . 63 F1
Langfield WA3 . . . . 90 E7
Langfield Ave M16 . . . . . 97 D3
Langfield Cres M43 . . . . 84 C2
Langfield Wlk M5 . . . . . 154 C2
Langford Dr
Irlam M44 . . . . 94 A1
Leigh WN7 . . . . 75 E2
Langford Gdns BL3. . . . 147 B4
Langford Rd
Manchester, Withington
M20. . . . . 110 A6
Stockport, Heaton Moor
SK4 . . . . 168 C4
Langford St M34 . . . . . . 100 F3
2 **Langham Cl** BL1 . . . . . 25 A5
Langham Ct
Manchester M20 . . . . . . 109 F4
Stretford M32 . . . . 96 A4
Langham Gr WA15 . . . . 120 B8
Langham Ho SK4 . . . . . 168 B2
Langham Rd
Altrincham WA14 . . . . . . 119 C2
Oldham OL8 . . . . 66 E4
Salford M6 . . . . 154 C2
Standish WN6 . . . . 19 D1
Stockport SK4 . . . . 168 B1
Langham St OL7 . . . . 85 A5
Langholm Cl WN3 . . . . . . 54 D3
Langholm Dr BL2 . . . . . . 42 F6
Langholme Cl M15 . . . . 162 A3
Langholme Pl M30 . . . . . 79 B2
Langholme Way OL10 . . 28 F1
Langholm Rd WN4 . . . . . 72 C4
Langland Cl
Manchester, Charlestown
M9. . . . . 64 E4
Manchester, North Reddish
M19 . . . . 99 D2
Langland Dr M30 . . . . . . 95 C7
LANGLEY 46 D2
Langley Ave
Hazel Grove SK7 . . . . . . 124 B1
Middleton M24 . . . . 46 C1
Newton-le-W WA12 . . . . . 89 C1
Oldham OL4 . . . . 68 B5
Prestwich M25 . . . . 63 B6
Langley Cl
Golborne WA3 . . . . 74 C1
Standish WN6 . . . . 19 E2
Urmston M41 . . . . 95 E2
Langley Cres M25 . . . . . . 63 B6

Langley Ct
Glossop SK13 . . . . 104 A5
9 Manchester M7 . . . . . 63 E1
Langley Dr
3 Bolton BL3 . . . . 144 C1
Boothstown M28 . . . . 77 F6
Glossop SK13 . . . . 116 F8
Handforth SK9 . . . . 131 E3
Langley Gdns M25 . . . . . 63 B6
Langley Gr M25 . . . . 63 B6
Langley Grange M25 . . . 63 B6
Langley Hall Rd M25 . . . 63 B6
Langley Ho M24 . . . . 47 A3
Langley La M24 , OL10 . . 46 D4
Langley Platt La M29, M46 76 D8
Langley Rd
Manchester, Charlestown M6,
M27. . . . . 80 F7
Manchester M14 . . . . 98 D1
Prestwich M25 . . . . 63 A5
Sale M33 . . . . 107 E4
Langley Road S M6, M27 . 81 A5
Langley St WN5 . . . . 54 D6
Langness St 2 M11 . . . . 83 C1
Lango St 1 M16 . . . . 97 C4
Langport Ave M12 . . . . . 164 B2
Langroyd Wlk M8 . . . . . 155 C3
Langset Ave 2 WN2 . . . . 56 D6
Langsett Ave
Salford M6 . . . . 154 C1
Langsett Gn 15 SK13 . . 171 A1
Langsett Gr 18 SK13 . . 171 A1
Langsett La SK13 . . . . . 171 A2
Langsett Lea 25 SK13 . . 171 A1
Langsett Terr 24 SK13 . . 171 A1
Langshaw Rd BL3 . . . . . 144 C1
Langshaw St
Manchester M16 . . . . 97 C4
Salford M6, M6 . . . . 154 C1
Langshaw Wlk BL3 . . . . 144 C1
Langside Ave M9 . . . . . . 64 E4
Langside Dr BL3 . . . . . . 40 E4
Langstone Cl BL6 . . . . . . 22 B3
Langston Gn SK7 . . . . . 124 A1
Langston St M3 . . . . 158 C3
Langthorne St M19 . . . . 111 B8
Langthorne Wlk BL3 . . . 145 A1
Langton Ave WN6 . . . . . . 19 E1
Langton Cl
Newton-le-W WA12 . . . . . 89 A4
Oldham M35 . . . . 84 C8
Langton Pl WN6 . . . . 19 E1
Langton St
Heywood OL10 . . . . 29 D3
Middleton M24 . . . . 65 A8
Salford M6. . . . . 154 B2
Langton Terr OL11 . . . . . 30 E4
Langtree Cl M28 . . . . 78 B8
Langtree La WN6 . . . . . . 19 D3
Langworthy Ave M38 . . . 60 A4
Langworthy Metro Sta
M50. . . . . 154 B1
Langworthy Rd
Manchester M40 . . . . 83 A7
Salford M6. . . . . 154 C1
Langworthy Road Prim Sch
M6 . . . . 154 C3
Lanhill Dr M8 . . . . 156 C2
Lankro Way M30, M17 . . 79 F1
Lanreath Wlk 10 M8 . . . 156 B2
Lansbury Ho BL6 . . . . . . 97 D3
Lansbury St WN5 . . . . . . 54 A6
Lansdale Gdns M19 . . . 110 E5
Lansdale St
Eccles M30 . . . . 95 A8
Walkden M28 . . . . 60 D5
Lansdown Cl SK8 . . . . . 132 C7
Lansdowne WA3 . . . . 91 E2
Lansdowne Ave
Droylsden M34 . . . . 84 C1
Romiley SK6 . . . . 113 D2
Lansdowne Cl
11 Bolton BL2 . . . . 25 B1
Ramsbottom BL0 . . . . . . 138 B1
Lansdowne Cl OL9 . . . . 152 B2
Lansdowne Dr M28 . . . . 60 C1
Lansdowne Ho M20 . . . 110 B2
Lansdowne Rd
Altrincham WA14 . . . . . . 119 D6
Bolton BL2 . . . . 25 B2
Chadderton OL9 . . . . 152 C2
Eccles M30 . . . . 79 D3
Flixton M41 . . . . 106 E8
Manchester M8 . . . . 64 A1
Over Hulton M46 . . . . 58 F5
Sale M33 . . . . 108 A6
Lansdowne Road N M41. . 94 E1
Lansdowne St OL11 . . . . 30 C7
Lanstead Dr M40 . . . . . . 160 B2
Lantern View SK22 . . . . 127 B1
Lapwing Cl
Newton-le-W WA12 . . . . . 89 C3
Rochdale OL11 . . . . 29 E7
Stalybridge SK15 . . . . 86 A4
Lapwing Ct 4 M20 . . . . . 110 A5
Lapwing Ctr The SK5 . . 112 C6
Lapwing La
Brinnington SK5 . . . . 112 C6
Manchester M20 . . . . . . 110 A5

Larch Cl
Billinge WN5 . . . . 71 D5
Failsworth M35 . . . . 83 F6
Golborne WA3 . . . . 90 F6
Marple SK6 . . . . 125 E5
Poynton SK12 . . . . 133 F3
Rawtenstall BB4 . . . . 1 F8
Sale M23 . . . . 120 C8
Larches The OL5 . . . . 68 E1
Larch Gdns M8 . . . . 156 A1
Larch Gr
Atherton M46 . . . . 58 C4
Chadderton OL9. . . . . . . 152 B4
Oldham OL4 . . . . 67 E8
Swinton M27 . . . . 61 B2
Larchlea WA15 . . . . 119 F4
Larch Rd
Denton M34 . . . . 101 A3
Eccles M30 . . . . 79 A4
Leigh WN7 . . . . 75 E8
Partington M31 . . . . 105 E3
Larch St
Bury BL9 . . . . 141 B2
Oldham OL8 . . . . 153 A2
Larchview Rd M24 . . . . . 65 C8
Larchway
Bramhall SK7 . . . . 132 C7
High Lane SK6 . . . . 134 F7
Milnrow OL16 . . . . 31 D7
Larch Way SK13 . . . . . . 116 F8
Larchwood
Chadderton OL9 . . . . 65 E8
Cheadle SK8 . . . . 122 D6
Larchwood Ave M9 . . . 157 C3
Larchwood Cl M33 . . . . 107 C4
Larchwood Dr
Wigan WN1 . . . . 37 B3
Wilmslow SK9 . . . . 137 E8
Larchwood St BL1 . . . . 143 C2
Larden Wlk 1 M8 . . . . . 155 C2
Larel Trad Est OL2 . . . . . 49 A2
Largs Wlk 7 M23 . . . . . 120 F6
Lark Rise M20 . . . . 109 F3
Larkfield Ave
Walkden M38. . . . . 59 F5
Wigan WN1 . . . . 37 B4
Larkfield Cl
Ashton-u-L OL7 . . . . 85 B7
Ramsbottom BL8 . . . . 10 F1
Larkfield Gr
Bolton BL2 . . . . 148 B4
Walkden M38. . . . . 59 F5
Larkfield Mews M38 . . . 59 F5
Larkhall Rise M22 . . . . . 121 E5
LARK HILL 77 A5
Lark Hill
Farnworth BL4 . . . . 60 E7
Stalybridge SK15 . . . . 86 A4
Larkhill Ave WN6 . . . . . . 36 F8
Larkhill Cl WA15 . . . . . . 120 B6
Lark Hill Cl 1 M24 . . . . . 65 A8
Lark Hill La OL4 . . . . 51 A4
Lark Hill Pl OL12 . . . . . . 14 E1
Lark Hill Prim Sch
Salford M6. . . . . 154 C2
Stockport SK3 . . . . 123 C8
Lark Hill Rd SK8 . . . . . . 123 C5
Lark Hill Rd
Stockport SK3 . . . . 123 C8
Uppermill OL3 . . . . 51 A3
Larkside Ave M28 . . . . . 60 E3
Larkspur Cl
Bolton BL1 . . . . 25 B3
Leigh WN7 . . . . 75 F3
Larks Rise M43 . . . . 84 D3
Lark St
Bolton BL1 . . . . 145 C4
Farnworth BL4 . . . . 60 D7
Oldham OL4 . . . . 49 D3
Larkswood Dr SK2 . . . . 124 F5
Larkwood Cl SK15 . . . . . 86 E7
Larmuth Ave M21 . . . . . 109 C6
Larne Ave
Stockport SK3 . . . . 123 B7
Stretford M32 . . . . 96 C2
Larne St M11 . . . . 165 A4
Larwood Ave SK4 . . . . . 168 B1
Lascar Ave M5 . . . . 161 A4
Lashbrook Cl M40 . . . . . 160 A4
Lassell Fold SK14 . . . . . 102 B6
Lassell St M11 . . . . 99 F7
Last Drop Village The ★
BL7 . . . . 9 A1
Lastingham St M40 . . . . 83 C6
Latchford St OL7 . . . . . . 166 A4
Latchmere Rd M14 . . . . 110 C8
Latham Ave WA12 . . . . . 89 C4
Latham Cl SK6 . . . . 112 F5
Latham Ho WA12 . . . . . . 89 B4
Latham La WN5 . . . . 54 A8
Latham Rd BL6 . . . . 21 C3
Latham Row BL7 . . . . . . 22 F3
Latham St
Bolton BL1 . . . . 143 C2
Droylsden M11. . . . . 99 F7
Lathbury Rd M40, M9 . . 157 A2
Lathom Gr M33 . . . . 108 E3
Lathom Hall Ave OL4 . . . 68 A7
Lathom Rd
Irlam M44 . . . . 105 B8
Manchester M20 . . . . . . 110 D7
Lathom St 8 BL9 . . . . . 141 A4
Latimer Cl 2 WN5 . . . . . 53 F7
Latimer St OL4 . . . . 67 A6

Latin St OL16 . . . . 139 B2
Latrigg Cres M24 . . . . 46 C2
Latrobe St M43 . . . . 100 A8
Lauderdale Cres M13 . . 163 C2
Launceston Cl
  Bramhall SK7 . . . . 132 F7
  Oldham OL8 . . . . 67 C4
Launceston Rd
  Hindley WN2 . . . . 57 C3
  Radcliffe M26 . . . . 43 D5
Laundry St M6 . . . . 154 C4
Laura St BL9 . . . . 11 C2
Laureate's Pl OL4 . . . . 68 B7
Laureate Way M34 . . . . 113 A7
Laurel Ave
  Bolton, Darcy Lever BL3 . . 42 E5
  Chadderton OL9 . . . . 65 E8
  Cheadle SK8 . . . . 122 D5
  Manchester M14 . . . . 98 A2
  Newton-le-W WA12 . . . . . . 89 D3
Laurel Bank
  Hyde SK14 . . . . 113 C8
  Stalybridge SK15 . . . . 102 B8
Laurel Bank Gdns M9 . . . 64 E3
Laurel Cres WN2 . . . . 57 A3
Laurel Ct
  [10] Rochdale OL16 . . . . 31 B6
  Stockport SK4 . . . . 168 B4
Laurel Dr
  Altrincham WA15 . . . . 120 B4
  Walkden M38 . . . . 60 A4
Laurel End La SK4 . . . . . 168 A3
Laurel Gn M34 . . . . 101 A2
Laurel Gr
  Ashton-in-M WN4 . . . . 73 B4
  Golborne WA3 . . . . 90 D8
  Leigh WN7 . . . . 75 E8
  Salford M5 . . . . 80 C2
Laurel Ho SK4 . . . . 168 B4
Laurel Rd SK4 . . . . 168 B4
Laurels Dr OL15 . . . . 15 F2
Laurel St
  Bolton BL1 . . . . 144 C3
  Bury BL9 . . . . 141 B2
  Bury, Tottington BL8 . . . . . 26 F6
  Middleton M24 . . . . 65 D6
  [6] Oldham OL4 . . . . 67 B6
  Stockport SK4 . . . . 169 B2
  Wigan WN5 . . . . 54 F7
Laurels The
  [2] Bolton BL1 . . . . 145 C4
  High Lane SK6 . . . . 134 E8
  Mossley OL5 . . . . 68 D1
Laurel Way SK8 . . . . 132 C8
Laurel Wlk M31 . . . . 105 E2
Laurence Cl M12 . . . . 165 B2
Laurence Lowry Ct [2]
  M27 . . . . 61 F1
Lauren Cl [15] OL4 . . . . 67 F6
Lauria Terr BL2 . . . . 26 D1
Laurie Pl [2] OL12 . . . . . . 14 F1
Laurieston Ct SK8 . . . . . 122 C5
Lausanne Rd
  Manchester M20 . . . . 110 B7
  Stockport SK7 . . . . 123 E3
Lavender Cl
  Altrincham M23 . . . . 108 C1
  Sale M33 . . . . 107 C5
Lavender Hill BL4 . . . . 1 F8
Lavender Rd
  Farnworth BL4 . . . . 42 A1
  Oldham OL4 . . . . 67 E4
  Wigan WN6 . . . . 36 F3
Lavenders Brow SK1 . . . 169 C1
Lavender St M26 . . . . 43 D3
Lavender Wlk
  Downall Green WN4 . . . . . 72 D5
  [3] Partington M31 . . . . . . 105 E2
Lavenham Ave M11 . . . . . 83 D1
Lavenham Bsns Ctr OL9 152 C2
Lavenham Cl
  Hazel Grove SK7 . . . . 133 E8
  Whitefield BL9 . . . . 44 F3
Laverton Cl BL9 . . . . 28 E1
Lavington Ave SK8 . . . . . 123 A6
Lavington Gr M18 . . . . 99 D4
Lavinia St M30 . . . . 79 B2
Lavister Ave M19 . . . . . . 110 E3
Lawefield Cres M27 . . . . . 61 D4
Lawers Ave OL9 . . . . 152 A4
Lawflat OL12 . . . . 15 C5
Lawler Ave M5 . . . . 161 B2
Lawnbank Cl M24 . . . . 46 E1
Lawn Cl OL8 . . . . 67 C3
Lawn Closes OL8 . . . . 67 C3
Lawndale Cl M26 . . . . 44 B2
Lawndale Dr M28 . . . . 78 B8
Lawn Dr
  Altrincham WA15 . . . . 119 C6
  Swinton M27 . . . . 79 E7
Lawnfield Cl SK7 . . . . . . 123 D2
Lawnfold SK11 . . . . 171 B4
Lawngreen Ave M21 . . . . 109 A7
Lawnhurst Ave M23 . . . . 120 F8
Lawnhurst Trad Est SK3 123 B5
Lawns Ave WN5 . . . . 53 C5
Lawnside Mews M20 . . . 110 A5
Lawn St BL1 . . . . 143 A1
Lawns The
  Altrincham WA15 . . . . 119 C3
  Hindley WN2 . . . . 56 C5
  Wilmslow SK9 . . . . 136 E4
Lawnswood OL11 . . . . 30 C3
Lawnswood Dr
  Pendlebury M27 . . . . 80 B6

Lawnswood Dr continued
  Tyldesley M29 . . . . 59 D1
Lawnswood Park Rd M27. 80 B6
Lawrence Cl [2] OL12 . . . . 14 A1
Lawrence Ct [6] WN2 . . . . 56 B1
Lawrence Pl SK12 . . . . . 133 D2
Lawrence Rd
  Altrincham WA14 . . . . 119 C6
  Hazel Grove SK7 . . . . 124 E3
  Urmston M41 . . . . 94 E3
Lawrence St
  Bury BL9 . . . . 44 F4
  Stockport SK1 . . . . 169 B1
Lawrie Ave BL0 . . . . 138 B1
Lawson Ave
  Gatley SK8 . . . . 122 B5
  Horwich BL6 . . . . 22 C4
  Leigh WN7 . . . . 57 E1
Lawson Cl
  Middleton M24 . . . . 47 A4
  Swinton M28 . . . . 79 C7
Lawson Dr WA15 . . . . 120 A6
Lawson Gr M33 . . . . 108 A6
Lawson Rd BL1 . . . . 142 C2
Lawson St
  [1] Bolton BL1 . . . . 143 B4
  Manchester M9 . . . . 64 C2
Lawson Wlk M34 . . . . 112 F8
Law St
  Rochdale OL11 . . . . 30 C4
  Walsden OL14 . . . . 6 B7
Lawton Ave SK7 . . . . 132 E8
Lawton Cl
  Culcheth WA3 . . . . 91 E3
  Romiley SK6 . . . . 112 F1
Lawton Fold OL4 . . . . 68 B7
Lawton Moor Rd M23 . . . 109 A1
Lawton Rd SK4 . . . . 168 C4
Lawton Sq OL3 . . . . 50 F4
Lawton St
  Delph OL3 . . . . 50 F4
  Droylsden M43 . . . . 84 B2
  Hyde SK14 . . . . 167 B3
  Manchester M11 . . . . 99 D7
  Rochdale OL12 . . . . 15 A1
Laxey Ave M46 . . . . 58 E2
Laxey Cres WN7 . . . . 75 C7
Laxey St M40 . . . . 83 B7
Laxfield Dr M41 . . . . 94 D3
Laxford Gr BL3 . . . . 40 E6
Laxley Cl OL9 . . . . 152 B1
Layard St OL6 . . . . 166 A3
Laycock Ave
  Bolton BL2 . . . . 25 B3
  Stalybridge SK15 . . . . 86 E4
Laycock Cres [4] M35. . . . 83 F7
Laycock Dr SK16 . . . . . . 102 A7
Laycock Gr M35. . . . . 83 F7
Laycock St OL16 . . . . 15 D3
Laycock Way M34 . . . . . . 112 F8
Layfield Cl BL8 . . . . 26 D7
Layland Ave WA3 . . . . 91 E4
Laystall St M1 . . . . 159 B1
Laythe Barn Cl OL16 . . . . 31 E6
Layton Ave SK14 . . . . . . 101 C2
Layton Cl
  Stockport SK1 . . . . 124 A8
  [2] Wigan WN5 . . . . 54 D5
Layton Dr
  Kearsley BL4 . . . . 60 F6
  Romiley SK6 . . . . 113 C3
Layton St M40 . . . . 160 A2
Lazarette Way BL2 . . . . . . 25 A2
Lazenby Cres WN4 . . . . . . 72 F3
Lazonby Ave WN2 . . . . 38 F3
Lazonby Wlk [7] M13 . . . . 98 F4
Leabank St [5] M19 . . . . . . 99 A2
Leabrook Dr M40 . . . . 83 E8
Leaburn Dr M19 . . . . 110 E4
Leach Cl OL16 . . . . 15 C2
Leaches Rd BL0 . . . . 11 D8
Leach Mews M25 . . . . 62 F4
Leach St
  Bolton BL3 . . . . 145 B1
  [4] Farnworth BL4 . . . . 42 E1
  Manchester M18 . . . . 165 B2
  Milnrow OL16 . . . . 31 F5
  Prestwich M25. . . . . 62 F4
  Rochdale OL16 . . . . 31 B6
  Shaw, Moss Hey OL2 . . . . 149 C2
  Shaw, Shaw Side OL2 . . . 149 A1
Leach Wlk OL4 . . . . 67 E8
Leaconfield Dr M28 . . . . . 78 F7
Leacroft WN4 . . . . 72 F6
Leacroft Rd BL2. . . . . 42 D5
Leacroft Rd M21 . . . . 109 D5
Lea Ct
  Failsworth M35 . . . . 83 E7
  Stockport SK4 . . . . 168 B4
Leadale Cl WN6. . . . . 19 D1
Leadale Rise OL4 . . . . 68 A6
Leader St
  Wigan, Norley WN5 . . . . . . 54 C6
  Wigan, Scholes WN1 . . . . 151 B4
Leader Williams Rd M44 . 93 F1
Lea Dr M9 . . . . 64 F3
Leafield Ave M20 . . . . 110 D4
Leafield Cl M26 . . . . 43 E3
Leafield Dr
  Cheadle SK8 . . . . 131 F6
  Worsley M28 . . . . 78 A6
Leafield Rd SK12 . . . . . . 135 C6
Leaford Ave M34. . . . . 100 D4
Leaford Cl M34 . . . . 100 D4
Leaf St
  Bolton BL3 . . . . 148 C1

Leaf St continued
  Manchester M15 . . . . 162 C2
  Reddish SK5. . . . . 111 F7
Leagate M41. . . . . 95 E1
Lea Gate BL2 . . . . 25 D5
Lea Gate Cl
  Bolton BL2. . . . . 25 D5
  Wigan WN3 . . . . 54 E3
Leaholme Cl M40 . . . . 83 D5
Leah St [3] OL15. . . . . 16 B5
Leak St M16 . . . . 161 C2
Leal Holme Ave WN2. . . . . 38 A3
Leamington Ave
  Bury BL9 . . . . 27 E8
  Manchester M20 . . . . 109 F4
  Newton-le-W WA12 . . . . . . 89 C1
Leamington Ct [3] SK5. . . 111 E7
Leamington Ho M13 . . . . . 163 B1
Leamington Rd
  Eccles M30 . . . . 79 B3
  Reddish SK5. . . . . 111 E7
  Urmston M41. . . . . 95 C3
Leamington St
  Manchester M11 . . . . 99 D7
  Oldham OL4 . . . . 67 D8
  Rochdale OL12. . . . . 14 C2
Leamore Wlk [1] M9. . . . . . 64 E3
Lea Mount Dr BL9. . . . . . . 28 D4
Leam St OL6 . . . . 85 D4
Leander Cl
  Manchester M9 . . . . 64 E2
  Manchester M26. . . . . 43 E5
  Oldham OL11 . . . . 30 D1
Lean Town SK13 . . . . 116 D6
Lea Rd
  Gatley SK8. . . . . 122 B1
  Stockport SK4 . . . . 168 C4
Leaside Ave OL4 . . . . 48 B2
Leaside Cl OL12. . . . . 14 D2
Leaside Dr M20 . . . . 110 D5
Leaside Gr M28 . . . . 60 E3
Leaside Way SK9. . . . . . . 137 C6
Lea St WN3 . . . . 150 A3
Leas The WA15 . . . . 120 C3
Leaton Ave M23 . . . . 121 A6
Leavale Cl M38. . . . . 59 F4
Leavengreave Ct OL12. . . . 4 D4
Lea View
  Royton OL2 . . . . 48 C3
  Wigan WN1 . . . . 37 F1
Leaway
  Ince-in-M WN2 . . . . 151 C3
  Wardle OL12 . . . . 15 C6
Le Bas Ho M20. . . . . 109 F6
Lecester Rd M8. . . . . 156 B2
Leckenby Cl [2] M28. . . . . 78 A6
Leconfield Dr M9 . . . . 64 E4
Leconfield Rd M30. . . . . . . 78 F4
Lecturers Cl BL3 . . . . 145 C1
Ledbrooke Cl M5 . . . . 161 B4
Ledburn Cl M15. . . . . 162 A2
Ledburn Cl M15. . . . . 162 A2
Ledbury Ave M41 . . . . 95 C3
Ledbury Cl M24 . . . . 65 A6
Ledbury Rd M35 . . . . 83 E4
Ledbury St WN7 . . . . 75 F6
Ledbury Wlk M9. . . . . 64 C3
Ledgard Ave WN7 . . . . 75 D4
Ledge Ley SK8 . . . . 131 E8
Ledmore Gr M46 . . . . 72 D3
Ledsham Ave M9 . . . . 64 A5
Ledson Rd M23 . . . . 120 F5
Ledward La WA14 . . . . . . 119 B2
Lee Ave
  Altrincham WA14 . . . . 119 C7
  Bolton BL3 . . . . 147 A3
Leebangs Rd SK14 . . . . . 115 A8
Lee Bank BL5 . . . . 58 B8
Leech Ave OL6 . . . . 85 E5
Leech Brook Ave M34. . . 100 E5
Leech Brook Cl M34. . . . . 100 E6
Leech St
  Hyde SK14 . . . . 167 C2
  Stalybridge SK15. . . . . 86 A1
Lee Cl M44 . . . . 93 F2
Lee Cres M32 . . . . 96 E2
Lee Ct M22. . . . . 121 E8
Lee Dale Cl M34. . . . . 101 A2
Leedale St M12 . . . . 99 A2
Leeds Cl BL9 . . . . 45 B3
Leeds St WN3. . . . . 150 B3
Leeds Street Ind Est
  WN3 . . . . 150 B3
Leefields Cl OL3. . . . . 69 B8
Lee Fold M29. . . . . 77 C7
Leegate Cl SK4 . . . . 110 F4
Leegate Dr M9 . . . . 64 F4
Leegate Gdns SK4 . . . . . 168 A4
Leegate Rd SK4 . . . . 168 A4
Lee Gr BL4 . . . . 59 F8
Leegrange Rd M9. . . . . 64 E1
Lee Head SK13 . . . . 115 C5
Lee Ho M22 . . . . 121 E8
Leek St M26 . . . . 43 E3
Lee La
  Abram WN2 . . . . 74 B8
  Horwich BL6 . . . . 22 B4
Leemans Hill St BL8. . . . . 27 A5
Lee Mount SK13 . . . . 116 C7
Lee Rd OL13 . . . . 3 E8
LEES 67 E6
Lees Ave M34 . . . . 100 E3
Lees Brook Pk OL4. . . . . . 67 D6
Lees Cotts BL7. . . . . 9 C2
Lees Gr OL4 . . . . 67 D5
Leeshall Cres M14. . . . . . 110 D1
Lees Hall Ct [9] M14. . . . . 110 D8

Leeside SK4 . . . . 168 A1
Lee Side OL3 . . . . 51 D4
Lee La Wardle 35 B6
Lees New Rd OL4, OL6 . . . 67 D2
Lees Park Ave M43. . . . . . . 84 C2
Lees Park Way M43 . . . . . 84 C2
Lees Rd
  Adlington PR6 . . . . 21 B8
  Ashton-u-L OL6 . . . . 85 D7
  Bramhall SK7 . . . . 132 D5
  Oldham OL4 . . . . 67 C6
  Lees Row SK13 . . . . 104 C5
Lees Sq OL6 . . . . 166 C3
Lees St
  Ashton-u-L OL6 . . . . 166 B4
  Droylsden M43 . . . . 84 B2
  Manchester M11, M18. . . . . 99 E6
  Middleton M24 . . . . 65 D7
  [2] Mossley OL5 . . . . 68 C2
  Oldham OL4 . . . . 85 A8
  Shaw OL2 . . . . 149 B3
  [5] Stalybridge SK15 . . . . 86 A2
  Swinton M27 . . . . 61 F1
Lees St E OL13 . . . . 4 C8
Lees Street E OL12 . . . . 149 C3
Lee St
  Atherton M46 . . . . 58 D2
  Bury BL9 . . . . 27 F8
  Littleborough OL15 . . . . . . 16 B6
  Middleton M24 . . . . 46 F3
  Oldham OL8 . . . . 153 B1
  Stockport SK1 . . . . 169 C1
  Uppermill OL3 . . . . 69 B8
Leestone Rd M22 . . . . . . 121 E6
Leesway Dr M34 . . . . 101 A2
Leeswood M21 . . . . 109 C6
Lee Vale Dr SK13 . . . . . . 115 D7
Leewood M27. . . . . 61 D4
Leewood Ct SK4 . . . . 168 B3
Left Bank M3 . . . . 158 B1
Le Gendre St BL2. . . . . 25 B2
Legh Cl SK12 . . . . 133 E4
Legh Ct M33. . . . . 108 E3
Legh Dr
  Droylsden M34 . . . . 84 B1
  Romiley SK6. . . . . 113 B6
Leghorn Wlk [14] M11 . . . 160 C1
Legh Rd
  High Lane SK12 . . . . 135 A6
  Salford M7 . . . . 155 A4
Legh St
  Ashton-in-M WN4 . . . . 73 B2
  Eccles M30 . . . . 79 C1
  Golborne WA3 . . . . 90 A8
  Manchester M13 . . . . 163 C1
  Newton-le-W WA12. . . . . . . 89 A3
  Salford M7 . . . . 155 A3
Legion Gr M7. . . . . 155 B2
Legwood Ct M41 . . . . 95 C2
Leicester Ave
  Denton M34 . . . . 100 F1
  Droylsden M43 . . . . 83 F3
  Hindley WN2 . . . . 56 F6
  Horwich BL6 . . . . 22 A3
  Sale M15 . . . . 120 A8
  Salford M7 . . . . 155 C4
Leicester Cl M7. . . . . 63 F1
Leicester Dr SK13 . . . . . . 116 F8
Leicester Rd
  Altrincham WA15 . . . . 119 F2
  Failsworth M35 . . . . 84 A6
  Sale M33 . . . . 108 B5
  Salford M7. . . . . 155 B3
  Tyldesley M29 . . . . 59 A2
  Whitefield M45 . . . . 44 D1
Leicester St
  Ashton-u-L OL7 . . . . 166 B4
  Oldham OL4 . . . . 67 B6
  Reddish SK5. . . . . 99 F2
  Rochdale OL11 . . . . 31 A5
Leicester Wlk M7. . . . . . . 155 B2
LEIGH 75 E6
Leigh Arc [4] WN1. . . . . . . 150 C4
Leigh Ave
  Marple SK6 . . . . 125 E6
  Swinton M27 . . . . 79 D5
Leighbrook Rd M14 . . . . . 110 B8
Leigh Bsns Pks WN7 . . . . 76 B3
Leigh CE Inf Sch [4] WN7. 75 E5
Leigh CE Jun Sch WN7 . . 75 E5
Leigh Central Prim Sch
  WN7 . . . . 75 F5
Leigh Cl BL8. . . . . 27 B3
Leigh Commerce Pk WN7 76 B2
Leigh Common BL5 . . . . . . 39 E1
Leigh Fold SK14 . . . . 101 E5
Leigh High Appartments
  SK14 . . . . 167 B2
Leigh Infmy WN7 . . . . 76 A6
Leigh La BL8. . . . . 27 B3
Leigh Prim Sch SK14. . . . 167 C2
Leigh Rd
  Altrincham WA15 . . . . 119 E2
  Atherton M46. . . . . 58 B2
  [2] Bolton BL5 . . . . 57 F7
  Hindley WN2 . . . . 57 B2
  Leigh WN7 . . . . 75 F6
  Westhoughton BL5 . . . . . . 57 F6
  Wilmslow SK9 . . . . 136 D5
  Worsley M28 . . . . 78 C6
Leighs Cotts WA15 . . . . . 120 C4
Leigh Sports Village WN7 75 D3
Leigh St
  Aspull WN2 . . . . 38 F3
  Bury BL8 . . . . 26 F4
  Farnworth BL4 . . . . 60 D8

Leigh St continued
  [1] Heywood OL10 . . . . 29 C2
  Hyde SK14 . . . . 167 B2
  Leigh WN2 . . . . 57 B1
  Wigan WN7 . . . . 75 C5
  Milnrow OL16. . . . . 31 D7
  Westhoughton BL5 . . . . . . 39 E1
  Wigan WN1 . . . . 151 A3
Leighton Ave
  Atherton M46. . . . . 58 B3
  Bolton BL1 . . . . 144 B4
  Littleborough OL15 . . . . . . 15 F2
Leighton Dr
  Golborne WN7. . . . . 75 B1
  Marple SK6 . . . . 126 C8
Leighton Rd M16. . . . . 97 C4
Leighton St
  Atherton M46. . . . . 58 B3
  Manchester M40 . . . . 83 A8
Leigh Westleigh Meth Prim
  Sch WN7 . . . . 75 D8
Leinster Rd M27. . . . . 79 E7
Leinster St BL4. . . . . 60 C7
Leith Ave M33 . . . . 108 E4
Leith Pl OL8 . . . . 66 E3
Leith Rd M33 . . . . 108 E4
Le Mans Cres BL1. . . . . . 145 C3
Lemnos St OL1 . . . . 67 A7
Lemonpark Ind Est OL10. . 46 E8
Lemon St M29 . . . . 76 F8
Lena St
  Bolton BL1 . . . . 143 C2
  Manchester M1 . . . . 159 B1
Lench Rd BB4 . . . . 2 D8
Lench St [5] BB4 . . . . 2 F8
Len Cox Wlk [3] M4. . . . . 159 B2
Lenfield La OL1 . . . . 48 E1
Leng Rd M40 . . . . 83 D5
Lenham Ave M30 . . . . 79 B2
Lenham Cl SK5 . . . . 112 B6
Lenham Gdns BL2. . . . . . . 42 E6
Lenham Mews SK5. . . . . . 112 B6
Lenham Wlk M22 . . . . 130 D8
Lennox Gdns BL3 . . . . 40 F5
Lennox St OL6 . . . . 166 C3
Lennox Wlk OL10 . . . . 28 F1
Lenora St BL3 . . . . 146 B4
Lenten Gr OL10 . . . . 46 E7
Lenthall Wlk [20] M8. . . . 155 C1
Lentmead Dr M40 . . . . 65 A1
Lenton Gdns M22. . . . . . . 121 E5
Lentworth Dr M28 . . . . . . 60 C5
Leominster Dr M22 . . . . . 121 F2
Leominster Rd M24 . . . . . . 65 B6
Leonard Ct WN7 . . . . 75 B4
Leonardin Cl OL2 . . . . 48 F8
Leonard St
  Bolton BL3 . . . . 147 B3
  Rochdale OL11 . . . . 30 C1
Leonard Way OL2 . . . . 48 F3
Leopold Ave M20 . . . . 110 A5
Leopold St
  Rochdale OL11 . . . . 139 A3
  Wigan WN5 . . . . 54 C5
Lepp Cres BL8 . . . . 27 C5
Leroy Dr M9 . . . . 64 E2
Lerryn St SK7 . . . . 123 D1
Lesley Rd M32. . . . . 96 A1
Leslie Ave
  Oldham OL9 . . . . 66 B3
  Whitefield BL9 . . . . 44 F3
Leslie Gr WA15 . . . . 120 A6
Leslie Hough Way M6 . . . . 81 B4
Leslie St
  Bolton BL2 . . . . 25 B1
  Manchester M14 . . . . 98 B3
Lessingham Ave WN1 . . . . 37 B3
Lester Rd M38 . . . . 59 E5
Lester St M32 . . . . 96 C2
Letchworth Ave [2] OL11. . 31 A5
Letchworth St M14 . . . . . . 98 B3
Letcombe Cl WN7 . . . . 75 F7
Letham St OL8 . . . . 66 F2
Letitia St BL6. . . . . 22 A3
Levedale Rd M9 . . . . 64 B4
Leven Ave BL4 . . . . 61 B5
Levengreave Cl WN2 . . . . . 57 C3
Levenhurst Rd M8 . . . . . . 155 C3
Levens Dr BL2. . . . . 25 E1
Levens St
  Salford M6. . . . . 154 E3
  Manchester M40 . . . . 83 A7
LEVENSHULME 99 B1
Levenshulme High Sch
  M19. . . . . 111 A7
Levenshulme Rd M18 . . . . 99 D4
Levenshulme Sta M19. . . . 99 A1
Levenshulme Swimming Pool
  M19. . . . . 99 A1
Levenshulme Terr [8] M19 99 A1
Levenshulme Trad Est
  M19. . . . . 99 C3
Levens Pl
  Ince-in-M WN2 . . . . 56 A8
  Wigan WN5 . . . . 54 C7
Levens Rd SK7 . . . . 124 C2
Levens St Wlk
  Chadderton OL9 . . . . 152 A1
  Wigan WN5 . . . . 54 C7
Leven Wlk
  Whitefield M45 . . . . 63 D1
  [2] Wilmshawe M23 . . . . . 121 A5
Lever Ave M27 . . . . 62 B2
Lever Bridge Pl BL3. . . . . . 42 D5
Lever Cl [7] M29. . . . . 58 F1
Lever Ct M7. . . . . 81 B8
Lever Dr BL3 . . . . 147 C4

LEVER EDGE 147 A2
Lever Edge La BL3 ..... 147 B3
Lever Edge Prim Sch
BL3 .... 147 B2
Leverett Cl WA14 ...... 119 A5
Lever Gr BL2 .... 148 A1
Lever Hall Rd BL2 ...... 42 D7
Leverhulme Ave BL3 ... 42 A3
Leverhulme Com Prim Sch
BL2 .... 42 E7
Lever Park Ave BL6 .... 22 B5
Lever Park Sch BL6 .... 22 C3
Lever Sh Par BL3 .... 147 B4
Lever St
Bolton BL3 .... 147 C4
Hazel Grove SK7 .... 124 D3
Heywood OL10 .... 29 D3
Little Lever BL3 .... 43 A4
Manchester M1 .... 159 B1
Middleton M24 .... 47 A1
Radcliffe M26 .... 43 F5
Ramsbottom BL0 ...... 138 C2
Tyldesley M29 .... 58 F1
Westhoughton BL5 ..... 39 E3
Lever Wlk M24 .... 64 F7
Levington Dr OL8 ...... 85 A8
Levi St BL1 .... 23 F1
Lewes Ave M40 .... 100 F1
Lewes Wlk OL9 .... 152 B2
Lewis Ave
Manchester M9 .... 64 E1
Urmston M41 .... 95 D5
Lewis Cl
Adlington PR7 .... 20 E6
Wigan WN3 .... 150 A1
Lewis Dr OL10 .... 28 F1
Lewisham Ave M40 .... 83 B4
Lewisham Cl OL2 ...... 48 C6
Lewis Rd
Droylsden M43 .... 83 E2
Reddish SK5 .... 99 F1
Lewis St
Eccles M30 .... 79 D1
Heywood OL10 .... 29 E3
Manchester M40 .... 160 A3
Shaw OL2 .... 149 B1
Lewis Street Prim Sch
M30 .... 79 D1
Lewtas St M30 .... 79 E1
Lexton Ave M8 .... 64 B2
Leybourne Ave M19 ... 99 B2
Leybourne St BL1 ...... 143 B2
Leybrook Rd M22 ..... 121 C3
Leyburn Ave
Royton OL2 .... 48 D4
Stretford M32 .... 96 C3
Urmston M41 .... 95 A1
Leyburn Cl
Whitefield M45 .... 62 E8
Wigan WN1 .... 151 C4
Leyburn Rd SK2 .... 124 D6
Leyburn Gr
Farnworth BL4 .... 42 D1
Romiley SK6 .... 113 C2
Leyburn Ho BL2 .... 98 E4
Leyburn Rd M40 .... 65 C2
Leycett Dr M23 .... 109 A1
Ley Cres M29 .... 77 B6
Leycroft St M1 .... 163 B4
Leyden Wlk M23 ...... 121 A4
Ley Dr OL10 .... 46 E7
Leyfield Ave SK6 ...... 113 C2
Leyfield Rd OL16 ...... 31 E6
Leygate View SK22 .... 127 B1
Ley Hey Ave SK6 ...... 125 F7
Ley Hey Ct SK6 .... 125 F7
LEY HEY PARK 125 F7
Ley Hey Rd SK6 .... 125 F7
Ley La SK6 .... 126 D8
Leyland Ave
Gatley SK8 .... 122 B6
Hindley WN2 .... 56 E3
Irlam M44 .... 94 B4
Manchester M20 .... 110 D3
Leyland Green Rd WN4 . 72 C5
Leyland Mill Farm WN1 . 37 D4
Leyland Mill La WN1 .. 37 C3
Leylands La SK14 ...... 114 F7
Leyland St
Abram WN2 .... 56 B1
Bury BL9 .... 44 F4
Hindley WN2 .... 56 C4
Stockport SK1 .... 169 B1
Ley Rd M29 .... 77 A7
Leys Rd WA14 .... 119 E8
Leyton Ave M40 .... 83 B7
Leyton Cl BL4 .... 147 C1
Leyton Dr BL9 .... 44 F5
Leyton St 2 OL12 ..... 15 A2
Leywell Dr OL1 .... 49 D3
Leywell Rd M9 .... 157 C4
Library La OL9 .... 153 A4
Library St
Westhoughton BL5 ..... 57 F8
Wigan WN1 .... 150 C4
Libra St BL1 .... 143 A2
Lichens Cres OL8 ..... 67 A3
Lichfield Ave
Altrincham WA15 ...... 120 C3
Ashton-u-L OL6 .... 85 D8
Bolton BL2 .... 25 B2
Golborne WA3 .... 90 D8
Reddish SK5 .... 111 E8
Tyldesley M29 .... 77 C7
Lichfield Cl
Farnworth BL4 .... 60 A8
Radcliffe M26 .... 43 D5

Lichfield Dr
Bury BL8 .... 140 A4
Chadderton OL9 .... 48 A1
Manchester, Cheetham Hill
M8 .... 156 B3
Manchester, Sedgley Park
M25 .... 63 C2
Swinton M27 .... 79 F6
Lichfield Gr WN4 ...... 73 C2
Lichfield Rd
Eccles M30 .... 79 F4
Radcliffe M26 .... 43 D5
Urmston M41 .... 95 D3
Lichfield St
Salford M6 .... 81 B5
Wigan WN5 .... 54 C5
Lichfield Terr OL16 ... 31 C4
Lidbrook Wlk M12 .... 164 E1
Liddington Hall Dr BL0 . 11 B4
Lidgate Cl WN3 .... 54 D3
Lidgate Gr
7 Farnworth BL4 ...... 60 C8
4 Manchester M20 .... 110 A3
Lidgett Cl M38 .... 60 C5
Lidiard St M8 .... 64 A1
Lido Ho OL4 .... 68 A6
Lieutenant Wlk M5 ... 161 B4
Liffey Ave M22 .... 121 E3
Lifton Ave M40 .... 160 B4
Light Alders La SK12 .. 135 A6
Lightborne Rd M33 ... 107 E4
Lightbounds Rd BL1 .. 23 F3
Lightbourne Ave 5 M27 . 79 F7
LIGHT BOURNE GREEN . 79 F6
Lightbowne Rd M40 .. 65 C2
Lightburn Ave OL15 .. 15 E4
Lightburne Ave
Bolton BL1 .... 144 B3
Leigh WN7 .... 75 E3
Lightfoot Wlk 6 M11 .. 160 C1
Lighthorne Ave SK3 .. 122 F7
Lighthorne Gr SK3 .... 122 F7
Lighthorne Rd SK3 ... 122 F7
Lighthouse OL15 ...... 6 C1
Lighthouse Christian Sch
M9 .... 157 C3
Light Oaks Inf & Jun Schs
M6 .... 80 B4
Light Oaks Rd
Fowley Common WA3 .. 92 C6
Salford M6 .... 80 C4
Lightowlers La OL15 .. 16 D7
Lightshaw La WA3 .... 74 B8
Lightwood M28 .... 78 B8
Lightwood Cl 7 BL4 ... 42 E1
Lignum Ave OL9 ...... 152 B4
Lilac Ave
Bury BL9 .... 44 D7
Downall Green WN4 ... 72 D5
Hyde SK14 .... 113 D8
Leigh WN7 .... 75 E7
Newhey OL16 .... 32 A3
Pendlebury M27 .... 80 A8
Wigan WN6 .... 37 A3
Lilac Ct 5 M6 .... 81 A2
Lilac Gdns WN3 .... 55 F4
Lilac Gr
Billinge WN5 .... 71 D4
Chadderton OL9 .... 152 B4
Manchester M40 .... 65 A1
Prestwich M25 .... 63 A6
Lilac La OL8 .... 66 D2
Lilac Rd
Altrincham WA15 ...... 120 A3
Golborne WA3 .... 74 A1
Rochdale OL11 .... 30 F2
Lilac St SK2 .... 124 C2
Lilac Terr 2 OL13 ...... 3 D8
Lilac View Cl OL2 ..... 49 D6
Lilac View Rd OL2 .... 149 C2
Lila St M9 .... 157 C3
Lilburn Cl BL0 .... 11 C4
Lily St OL16 .... 31 A7
Lilford Cl M12 .... 165 A2
Liliford St
Atherton M46 .... 58 B2
Leigh WN7 .... 75 E4
Lilian Dr WN6 .... 37 A3
Lilian Gr SK5 .... 111 F8
Lillian St M16 .... 97 C4
Lilly St
Bolton BL1 .... 145 A4
Hyde SK14 .... 113 F8
Lilmore Ave
Failsworth M40 .... 83 C6
Manchester M8 .... 156 C2
Lilstock Wlk 10 M9 ... 64 E3
Lily Ave
Farnworth BL4 .... 42 B1
Newton-le-W WA12 ... 89 D2
Lily Cl SK3 .... 170 A1
LILY HILL 44 E2
Lily Hill St M45 .... 44 E2
Lily La
Ashton-in-M WN4 ..... 73 E5
Eccles M30 .... 79 B1
Middleton M24 .... 65 C8

Lily St continued
Milnrow OL16 .... 31 F6
Oldham OL1 .... 48 E1
Royton OL2 .... 48 F4
Lily Thomas Ct 3 M11 . 99 D7
Lima St M19 .... 141 B3
Limbert Circ M8 ...... 64 C1
Lime Ave
Leigh WN7 .... 75 E8
New Mills SK22 .... 127 D1
Swinton M27 .... 79 C6
Urmston M41 .... 95 B2
Whitefield M45 .... 62 F7
Lime Bank St M12 .... 164 A4
Limebrook Cl M11 .... 99 E7
Lime Cl
Abram Brow WN2 ..... 74 C7
Dukinfield SK16 .... 101 D6
Hollinfare WA3 .... 105 A2
Salford M6 .... 81 A3
Lime Cres M16 .... 97 B4
Limeditch Rd M35 .... 84 A8
Lime Gdns
Dukinfield SK16 .... 101 B8
Middleton M24 .... 64 E8
Lime Gn OL8 .... 66 D1
Lime Gr
Altrincham WA15 ...... 120 B7
Ashton-u-L OL6 .... 85 C5
Bury BL9 .... 27 F7
Cheadle SK8 .... 122 D6
Denton M34 .... 100 F4
Dukinfield SK15 .... 101 E8
Heywood OL10 .... 29 C3
Hindley WN2 .... 56 F3
Littleborough OL15 ... 15 F6
Manchester M16 ...... 97 B4
Prestwich M25 .... 63 A6
Ramsbottom BL0 ...... 11 D7
Royton OL2 .... 48 D6
Walkden M28 .... 60 D1
Lime Green Rd OL8 ... 84 D8
LIMEHURST 85 A6
Limehurst Ave
8 Ashton-u-L OL7 ..... 85 A6
Manchester M20 ...... 109 F8
Limehurst Ct OL8 ..... 66 D1
Limehurst Prim Sch OL8 . 84 D8
Limehurst Rd OL7 .... 85 A6
Limekiln La M12 ...... 164 A4
Lime Kiln La SK6 ...... 126 A5
Lime La M35 .... 84 C7
Lime Pl SK16 .... 101 B8
Lime Rd M32 .... 96 D1
Limers Gate OL12 .... 14 F5
Limerston Dr M40 .... 83 A5
Limes Ave WN6 .... 37 B6
Limesdale Cl BL2 ..... 43 B5
LIME SIDE 66 D1
Limeside Prim Sch OL8 . 66 D1
Limeside Rd OL8 ...... 66 C1
Limes Sch The OL7 ... 166 A4
Lime St
Atherton M46 .... 57 F3
Bury BL9 .... 27 F6
Chadderton OL1 .... 48 C1
Dukinfield SK16 .... 101 B8
Eccles M30 .... 79 D1
Farnworth BL4 .... 60 C7
Rochdale OL11 .... 30 C4
Romiley SK6 .... 112 E4
Tyldesley M29 .... 58 F1
Wigan WN1 .... 151 A4
Limestead Ave M8 ... 156 A4
Limes The
Culcheth WA3 .... 91 D4
Golborne WA3 .... 90 D6
Mossley, Micklehurst OL5 . 68 B1
Mossley, Mossley Cross OL5 . 68 B1
Standish WN6 .... 37 A6
Stockport SK3 .... 170 A3
Lime Tree Cl M41 ..... 95 E1
Lime Tree Gr M35 .... 84 B7
Lime Tree Prim Sch
M33 .... 108 E3
Limetrees Rd M24 .... 64 F8
Lime Vale WN3 .... 55 F4
Lime Vale Rd WN5 .... 71 C3
Lime Wlk
6 Handforth SK9 ...... 131 D1
Partington M31 .... 105 D3
Limewood Cl
Bridge End BB4 .... 1 A7
Haslingden BB4 .... 1 A7
Limewood Mdw M29 .. 77 C6
Limley Gr M21 .... 109 C7
Linacre Ave BL3 ...... 147 B2

Linacre Way SK13 .... 116 F7
Linbeck Gr WA3 ...... 74 E1
Linby St M15 .... 162 B3
Lincoln Ave
Denton M34 .... 100 F1
Droylsden M43 .... 84 A3
Gatley SK8 .... 131 B7
Golborne WA3 .... 74 D1
Irlam M44 .... 105 C4
Little Lever BL3 .... 43 A2
Manchester M19 ...... 99 B1
Manchester M32 ...... 95 F3
Lincoln Cl
Ashton-u-L OL6 .... 85 D8
Golborne WN7 .... 91 C8
Rochdale OL11 .... 31 A6
Tyldesley M29 .... 59 A2
Lincoln Ct
Failsworth M40 .... 83 B4
14 Manchester M7 .... 63 E1
Lincoln Dr
Altrincham WA15 ..... 120 B5
Ashton-in-M WN4 .... 73 D2
Aspull WN2 .... 38 D5
6 Bury BL9 .... 44 F8
Littleborough OL15 .. 16 A3
Manchester M25 ...... 63 C2
Lincoln Gn SK5 .... 112 C6
Lincoln Gr
Atherton M46 .... 58 B3
Bolton BL2 .... 25 F4
Manchester M13 ..... 163 C1
Manchester M33 ..... 108 F4
Lincoln Leach Ct OL11 . 139 C1
Lincoln Mill (Bolton Ent Ctr)
BL3 .... 144 C2
Lincoln Minshull 12
M23 .... 108 F2
Lincoln Pl WN5 .... 36 C1
Lincoln Rd
Bolton BL1 .... 144 B4
Failsworth M35 .... 84 A6
Handforth SK9 .... 131 E1
Hindley WN2 .... 56 E5
7 Manchester M24 ... 65 C5
7 Swinton M27 .... 79 E7
Lincoln Rise SK6 ..... 113 A1
Lincoln Sq M2 .... 158 C1
Lincoln St
Eccles M30 .... 79 C1
Manchester M13 ..... 98 F4
Oldham OL9 .... 152 C1
Rochdale OL11 .... 31 A6
Lincoln Way 5 SK13 .. 116 F8
Lincoln Wlk OL10 .... 29 A2
Lincombe Rd M22 .... 130 D8
Lincroft Rd M22 ...... 57 A3
Linda Dr SK7 .... 124 D2
Lindale Ave
Bolton BL1 .... 40 F8
Chadderton OL9 ...... 152 A2
Failsworth M40 .... 65 D2
Urmston M41 .... 94 F3
Whitefield BL9 .... 45 A3
Lindale Cl M28 .... 78 F7
Lindale Dr M24 .... 46 E3
Lindale Rise OL2 ..... 49 D7
Lindbury Ave SK2 .... 124 C7
Linden Ave
Altrincham WA15 ..... 119 C5
Ashton-in-M WN4 .... 72 F5
Atherton M46 .... 58 B2
Denton M34 .... 100 D7
Little Lever BL3 .... 43 A5
Oldham OL4 .... 67 D8
Orrell WN5 .... 53 E6
Pendlebury M6 .... 80 E6
Ramsbottom BL0 ..... 11 D6
Sale M33 .... 107 F4
2 Swinton M27 .... 79 D7
Linden Cl
Denton M34 .... 101 A3
Edenfield BL0 .... 1 D2
Lymm WA13 .... 117 A4
Linden Cres WN5 ..... 53 E6
Linden Dr M5 .... 161 A4
Linden Gr
Billinge WN5 .... 71 C3
Bramhall SK7 .... 132 D4
Leigh WN7 .... 75 E7
Manchester M14 ..... 110 D8
Orrell WN5 .... 53 E6
Stockport SK2 .... 124 B4
Linden Lea
Rawtenstall BB4 ...... 1 F8
Sale M33 .... 108 B2
Linden Mews M28 .... 77 F6
Linden Pk M19 .... 111 A8
Linden Rd
Boothstown M28 ..... 77 F6
Cheadle SK8 .... 123 A3
Denton M34 .... 101 A3
Hindley WN2 .... 57 A2
Manchester M20 ..... 110 A4
Stalybridge SK15 .... 102 D7
Linden Road Prim Sch
M34 .... 101 A3
Linden St WN5 .... 54 C5
Linden Way
Droylsden M43 .... 99 E8
High Lane SK6 .... 135 A7

Linden Wlk
Bolton BL2 .... 25 B5
Orrell WN5 .... 53 E6
Lindenwood OL9 ...... 65 E8
Lindeth Ave M18 ..... 99 D4
Lindfield Dr BL1 ...... 143 B3
Lindfield Estate N SK9 . 137 A6
Lindfield Estate S SK9 . 136 F6
Lindfield Rd SK5 ..... 99 F1
Lindinis Ave M6 ...... 81 B2
Lindisfarne 17 OL12 . 139 B4
Lindisfarne Ave WN3 . 91 C8
Lindisfarne Cl M33 ... 108 B2
Lindisfarne Dr OL7 ... 84 E5
Lindisfarne Pl BL2 ... 25 C2
Lindisfarne Rd OL7 .. 84 E5
Lindley Ave WN5 ..... 53 C5
Lindley Gr SK3 .... 170 A1
Lindley St
Kearsley BL4 .... 61 B6
Little Lever BL3 .... 43 B3
Lindleywood Rd M14 . 110 E8
Lindow Comm Nature
Reserve★ SK8 .... 136 E7
Lindon Park Rd BB4 .. 1 C7
Lindop Rd WA15 ..... 119 F1
Lindow Cl BL8 .... 27 B6
Lindow Court Pk WA16 . 136 B5
Lindow Ct
Romiley SK6 .... 112 D3
4 Sale M33 .... 108 F3
Wilmslow SK9 .... 136 F6
LINDOW END 136 B2
Lindow Fold Dr SK9 .. 136 D5
Lindow La SK9 .... 136 E6
Lindow Par SK9 ...... 136 F6
Lindow Prim Sch SK9 . 136 D3
Lindow Rd M16 ...... 97 C2
Lindow St
Leigh WN7 .... 75 D6
Sale M33 .... 108 F3
Lindrick Ave M45 .... 62 D6
Lindrick Cl M40 ...... 83 C7
Lindrick Terr BL3 .... 145 A1
Lindsay Ave
Bramhall SK8 .... 123 B1
Manchester M19 ..... 98 F1
Swinton M27 .... 79 E7
Lindsay Cl OL4 .... 49 D2
Lindsay Rd M19 ...... 110 F8
Lindsay St
Horwich BL6 .... 22 D1
Stalybridge SK15 .... 86 B1
Lindsay Terr WN2 ... 38 B5
Lindsell Rd WA14 .... 119 C8
Lindsgate Dr WA15 .. 120 B6
Lindside Wlk 8 M9 .. 64 E3
Lind St M40 .... 160 B2
Lindum Ave M16 ..... 97 C4
Lindum Ct OL10 ...... 29 E2
Lindum St M14 .... 98 B3
Lindwall Cl M23 ...... 109 B2
Linear View WA12 ... 89 C1
Linehan Cl SK4 ...... 110 C1
Lineholme OL2 ...... 48 C2
Linen Cl M33 .... 158 A3
Lines Rd
Droylsden M43 .... 84 B1
Irlam M44 .... 105 F8
Linfield Cl BL2 .... 25 D4
Linfield St M11 .... 83 B1
Linford Ave M40 ..... 65 C2
Lingard Cl M34 ...... 100 C8
Lingard La SK6 ...... 112 D5
Lingard Rd M22 ..... 109 D1
Lingards La M29 ..... 77 A4
Lingard St
Leigh WN7 .... 76 B4
Reddish SK5 .... 111 F8
Lingard Terr M34 ... 100 C8
Lingcrest Rd M19 ... 111 C7
Lingdale Rd SK8 .... 122 F2
Lingdale Wlk M40 .. 83 A7
Ling Dr M46 .... 58 D2
Lingfield 2 M16 ..... 97 D3
Lingfield Ave
Hazel Grove SK7 ..... 124 F2
Sale M33 .... 107 B2
Lingfield Cl
Bury BL8 .... 27 C7
Farnworth BL4 .... 60 C7
Lingfield Cres WN6 .. 36 E3
Lingfield Rd M11 .... 83 C2
Lingfield Wlk OL9 .. 152 C3
Lingholme Dr M24 .. 46 C2
Lingmell Ave WA11 .. 71 C1
Lingmell Cl
Bolton BL1 .... 40 F8
Middleton M24 .... 46 D2
Urmston M41 .... 95 A4
Lingmoor Cl
Middleton M24 .... 46 D2
Wigan WN3 .... 55 A1
Lingmoor Dr M29 ... 77 B7
Lingmoor Rd BL1 ... 23 F1
Lingmoor Wlk 1 M15 . 162 C1
Lings Wlk M22 .... 130 D8
Linguard Bsns Pk 6 OL16 . 31 A6
Linhope Cl SK4 ...... 110 E3
Link 25 Bsns Pk WN4 . 72 F8
Link Ave M41 .... 96 A1
Linkfield Dr M28 .... 77 F6
Link La OL8 .... 66 E2

Link Rd
Oldham OL4 . . . . 67 F7
Sale M33 . . . . 107 D2
Links Ave M35 . . . . 83 F5
Links Cres M25 . . . . 63 E2
Links Ct M27 . . . . 61 F2
Links Dr BL6 . . . . 40 B7
Linksfield M34 . . . . 100 F5
Linkside Ave OL2 . . . . 48 D5
Links Pl OL6 . . . . 85 E6
Links Rd
Bolton, Harwood BL2 . . . . . . 26 A3
Bolton, Lostock Junction
BL6 . . . . 40 B7
Heywood OL10 . . . . 46 D8
Marple SK6 . . . . 125 F4
Romiley SK6 . . . . 113 D2
Wilmslow SK9 . . . . 136 E4
Links Rise M41 . . . . 95 A4
Links The
Failsworth M40 . . . . 83 C7
Hyde SK14 . . . . 102 A6
Links View
Manchester M25 . . . . 63 A1
Rochdale OL11 . . . . 30 B6
Linksview Ct M45 . . . . 62 D7
Linksway
Gatley SK8 . . . . 122 A4
Manchester M25 . . . . 63 D2
Pendlebury M27 . . . . 80 A6
Links Way OL9 . . . . 152 C4
Linksway C5 M44 . . . . 111 A5
Linksway Dr BL9 . . . . 45 B3
Linnell Dr OL11 . . . . 29 E8
Linnet Cl
Droylsden M34 . . . . 84 C1
Hazel Grove SK2 . . . . 124 F5
Manchester M12 . . . . 98 F4
Newton-le-W WA12 . . . . 89 C3
Linnet Dr
Bury BL9 . . . . 141 B4
Irlam M44 . . . . 94 A3
Leigh WN7 . . . . 76 B5
Linnet Hill OL11 . . . . 30 C6
Linnet's Wood Mews M28 60 E3
Linney La OL2 . . . . 149 C3
Linney Rd SK7 . . . . 123 D2
Linney Sq WN1 . . . . 151 B4
Linn St M8 . . . . 64 A1
LINNYSHAW 60 F3
Linnyshaw Cl BL3 . . . . 146 A3
Linnyshaw Ind Est M28 . . . 60 E4
Linslade Gdns BL3 . . . . . . 145 B1
Linslade Ho 10 M5 . . . . . . 154 C1
Linslade Wlk 7 M9 . . . . . . 157 A3
Linstead Dr M8 . . . . 155 C2
Linstock Way M46 . . . . 58 B3
Linthorpe Wlk BL3 . . . . . . 146 B4
Linton Ave
Bury BL9 . . . . 27 F5
Golborne WA3 . . . . 73 F2
Reddish M34 . . . . 100 A3
Linton Cl M4 . . . . 164 A4
Linton Rd M33 . . . . 108 C6
Linton Vale M26 . . . . 61 B8
Linton Wlk M7 . . . . 80 F8
Linwood Cl 2 WN2 . . . . 56 C4
Linwood Gr M12 . . . . 99 A2
Linwood St M35, M40 . . . . . 83 C6
Lion Brow M9 . . . . 64 D3
Lion Fold La M9 . . . . 64 D3
Lion La BL6 . . . . 21 C2
Lions Dr M27 . . . . 80 A7
Lion St M9 . . . . 64 D2
Liptrot St WN5 . . . . 54 F7
Lisbon St 7 OL12 . . . . 14 C1
Lisburn Ave
Manchester M16, M21 . . . . . . 97 C1
Sale M33 . . . . 108 A3
Lisburne Ave SK2 . . . . 124 D7
Lisburne Cl SK2 . . . . 124 D6
Lisburne La SK2 . . . . 124 D6
Lisburn Rd M40 . . . . 83 A8
Liscard Ave M14 . . . . 98 B1
Liscard St M46 . . . . 58 B3
Lisetto Ave 1 OL4 . . . . 67 B5
Liskeard Ave OL2 . . . . 48 F4
Liskeard Cl OL16 . . . . 15 C1
Liskeard Dr SK7 . . . . 132 F7
Lisle St 3 OL12 . . . . 31 A8
Lismore Ave
Bolton BL3 . . . . 40 F5
6 Stockport SK3 . . . . 123 B8
Lismore Rd SK16 . . . . 101 D7
Lismore Way WA15 . . . . . . 119 E2
Lismore Wlk M22 . . . . 130 E8
Lissadel St M6 . . . . 81 B4
Lisson Gr WA15 . . . . 119 E2

Lister Rd M24 . . . . 64 B6
Lister St BL3 . . . . 146 B3
Liston St SK16 . . . . 101 F8
Litcham Cl M1 . . . . 163 B3
Litchfield Cl OL3 . . . . 33 C2
Litchfield Ct M24 . . . . 64 C7
Litchfield Gr M28 . . . . 79 A7
Litherland Ave M22 . . . . . 121 E2
Litherland Rd
Bolton BL3 . . . . 147 B2
Sale M33 . . . . 108 A3
Little 66 BL9 . . . . 45 B7
Little Ancoats St M4, M4 . 159 B2
Little Bank St 4 OL4 . . . . . 67 B6
LITTLE BOLLINGTON 118 B2
Little Bollington CE Prim Sch
WA14 . . . . 118 B2
Little Bolton Terr M5 . . . . . 80 C2
LITTLE BOLTON 80 B1
LITTLEBOROUGH 16 B5
Littleborough Coach House
& Heritage Ctr* 18
OL15 . . . . 16 B5
Littleborough Com Prim Sch
OL15 . . . . 16 B7
Littleborough Sp Ctr
OL15 . . . . 16 B7
Littleborough Sta OL15 . . . 16 B5
Littlebourne Wlk BL1 . . . . . 25 A6
Littlebrook Cl
10 Bolton BL2 . . . . 25 B1
Cheadle SK8 . . . . 123 C4
Glossop SK13 . . . . 104 A4
Littlebrooke Cl BL2 . . . . . . 148 B4
Little Brook Rd M33 . . . . . . 107 C1
Little Brow BL7 . . . . 25 A7
Little Church St 3 WN5 . . . 54 B6
LITTLE CLEGG 15 D5
Little Clegg Rd OL15 . . . . . 15 F2
Littledale St OL12 . . . . 139 B4
Little David St M1 . . . . 163 A4
Little Ees La M33 . . . . 107 F7
Little Egerton St SK1 . . . . 169 B2
Little Factory St M29 . . . . . 58 F1
Littlefields SK14 . . . . 103 A4
Little Flatt OL12 . . . . 14 B1
Littlegate BL5 . . . . 57 E5
Littlegreen Gdns M6 . . . . . 154 C3
Littleham Wlk M18 . . . . . . 165 C1
Little Harwood Lee 25 E3
Littlehaven Cl M12 . . . . . . 164 B1
Little Heath La WA14 . . . . . 118 D5
Little Heaton VC CE Prim Sch
M24 . . . . 64 C7
Little Hey St OL2 . . . . 49 B8
Littlehills Cl M24 . . . . 46 E1
Little Holme St M4 . . . . . . 160 A1
Little Holme Wlk BL3 . . . . 147 C4
Little Howarth Way 1
OL12 . . . . 15 C4
LITTLE HULTON 60 A4
Little John St M3 . . . . 162 E8
Little La WN3, WN5 . . . . 54 E4
LITTLE LEVER 43 C4
Little Lever L Ctr BL3 . . . . 42 F3
Little Lever Sch (Specialist
Lang Coll) BL3 . . . . 42 F3
Little Lever St 8 M1, M4. 159 B2
Little London 8 WN1 . . . . . 37 C1
Little Mdws BL7 . . . . 8 E2
Little Meadow Rd WA14 . . 119 B1
Little Moor Clough BL7 . . . . 8 E2
Littlemoor Cotts SK1 . . . . 124 B8
Littlemoor Ct 3 SK13 . . . . 116 C8
Littlemoor Ho 1 OL4 . . . . . 67 C8
Littlemoor La OL3 . . . . 51 B4
Little Moor OL4 . . . . 67 C8
Littlemoor Prim Sch 7
OL4 . . . . 67 C8
Littlemoor Rd SK14 . . . . . . 103 A2
LITTLEMOSS 84 C3
Littlemoss Bsns Pk M43 . . 84 C3
Little Moss La M27 . . . . 61 F2
Littlemoss Rd M43 . . . . 84 C3
Little Nelson St 1 M4 . . . . 159 A3
Little Oak Cl OL4 . . . . 67 F8
Little Overwood WA14 . . . . 107 B1
Little Pasture WN7 . . . . 75 D7
Little Peter St M15 . . . . . . 162 B3
Little Pitt St M1 . . . . 159 B1
Little Quay St M3 . . . . 158 B1
Littler Ave M21 . . . . 109 C5
Littlers Point M17 . . . . 96 D5
LITTLE SCOTLAND 21 B2
Little Scotland BL6 . . . . 21 B2
Little St SK1 . . . . 124 B8
Little Stones Rd BL7 . . . . . . 8 E2
Littleton Gr WN6 . . . . 19 E2
Littleton Rd M6, M7, M25 . 81 A6
LITTLE TOWN 91 C1
Little Town OL8 . . . . 66 C4
Little Underbank SK1 . . . . 169 F2
Littlewood OL2 . . . . 49 A4
Littlewood Ave 1 BL2 . . . . 27 F5
Littlewood Rd M22 . . . . . . 121 D4
Littlewood St M6 . . . . 154 B2
Litton Bank SK13 . . . . 171 B1
Littondale Cl OL2 . . . . 48 E5
Litton Fold 10 SK13 . . . . . . 171 B1
Litton Gdns 9 SK13 . . . . . 171 B1
Litton Mews SK13 . . . . 171 B1
Liverpool Cl SK5 . . . . 111 E7
Liverpool Rd
Ashton-in-M WN4 . . . . 73 A3
Eccles M30 . . . . 79 C1
Garswood WA11, WN4 . . . . . 72 D2
Irlam, Cadishead M44 . . . . . 105 D4
Irlam M30, M44 . . . . 94 D4

Liverpool Rd continued
Manchester M3 . . . . 162 B4
Platt Bridge WN2 . . . . 56 C3
Liverpool St
7 Reddish SK5 . . . . 111 E7
Salford M5 . . . . 81 B1
Liverstudd Ave SK5 . . . . . 111 F8
Liverton Ct M9 . . . . 64 B5
Livesey St
Manchester, Levenshulme
M19 . . . . 111 B8
Manchester M4 . . . . 159 C3
Oldham OL1 . . . . 67 C8
Livingston Ave M22 . . . . . 121 B2
Livingstone Ave 2 OL5 . . . 68 C1
Livingstone Pl M16 . . . . . . 161 B1
Livingstone Prim Sch OL5 86 C8
Livingstone St
2 Ashton-in-M WN4 . . . . . . 73 A5
Oldham, County End OL4 . . . 68 A6
Oldham, Lees OL4 . . . . 67 E5
Stalybridge SK15 . . . . 101 D6
Livsey La OL10 . . . . 29 A2
Livsey St
Rochdale OL16 . . . . 31 A7
Whitefield M45 . . . . 62 F8
Lizard St M1 . . . . 159 B1
Liza St WN7 . . . . 75 E8
Lizmar Terr M40, M9 . . . . . 157 C4
Llanberis Rd SK8 . . . . 122 C1
Llanfair Rd 3 SK3 . . . . 123 C8
Lloyd Ave SK8 . . . . 122 A6
Lloyd Ct M12 . . . . 164 C2
Lloyd Gdns WA14 . . . . 119 D3
Lloyd Rd M19 . . . . 111 B7
Lloyd's Ct WA14 . . . . 119 D3
Lloyd Sq 7 WA14 . . . . 119 D4
Lloyd St
Altrincham WA14, WA15 . . . 119 D4
Heywood OL10 . . . . 29 D1
Manchester M2 . . . . 158 C1
Rochdale OL11 . . . . 30 D4
Stockport SK4 . . . . 169 A3
Whitworth OL12 . . . . 4 C1
Lloyd Street N M14, M15 . 163 A1
Lloyd Street S M14 . . . . . . 98 A2
Lloyd Wright Ave M11 . . . 164 B4
Lobden Cres OL12 . . . . 14 D8
Lobelia Ave BL4 . . . . 42 A1
Lobelia Wlk 6 M31 . . . . . . 105 E2
Lobley Cl OL12 . . . . 15 B2
Local Board St WN2 . . . . . 151 C3
Lochawe Cl OL10 . . . . 29 A1
Lochinver Gr OL10 . . . . 29 A1
Lochmaddy Cl SK7 . . . . . . 124 F1
Loch St WN5 . . . . 54 B6
Lock Cl OL10 . . . . 46 E8
Locke Ind Est BL6 . . . . 22 B3
Lockerbie Pl WN3 . . . . 54 E2
Locker La WN4 . . . . 73 F4
Lockett Bsns Pk WN4 . . . . 73 C5
Lockett Gdns M3 . . . . 158 A2
Lockett Rd WN4 . . . . 73 C6
Lockett St
Manchester M8 . . . . 158 B4
Salford M6 . . . . 81 A5
Lock Flight Bldgs WN3 . . . 54 F2
Lockhart Cl M12 . . . . 165 A1
Lockhart St OL16 . . . . 31 B5
Lockingate St OL6 . . . . 85 B6
Locking Gate Rise OL4 . . . 49 E1
Lock Keepers Mews M27 80 D8
Lock La
Bolton BL3, BL6 . . . . 40 D3
Partington M31 . . . . 105 E3
Locklands La M44 . . . . 94 A2
Lock Rd WA14 . . . . 119 C6
Lockside SK6 . . . . 126 A6
Lockside Mews WN1 . . . . . 151 A3
Lockside View OL5 . . . . 68 E3
Locksley Cl SK4 . . . . 168 C2
Locks The M44 . . . . 94 B1
Locks View M41 . . . . 151 C4
Lockton Cl
Manchester M1 . . . . 163 B3
Reddish SK5 . . . . 111 E6
Lockton Ct M1 . . . . 163 B3
Lock View M26 . . . . 61 B8
Lockwood St 7 M12 . . . . . . 99 B3
Locomotion Ind Est BL6 . . 22 B2
Lodden Wlk 21 M9 . . . . . . 157 E4
Lodge Ave M41 . . . . 95 E2
Lodge Bank
Glossop SK13 . . . . 104 A6
Horwich BL6 . . . . 21 F2
Lodge Bank Est BL6 . . . . . . 21 F3
Lodge Bank Rd OL15 . . . . . 15 F3
Lodge Brow M26 . . . . 44 B2
Lodge Cl
Dukinfield SK16 . . . . 101 E7
Lymm WA13 . . . . 117 B4
Lodge Ct
Manchester SK4 . . . . 110 F2
Mottram in S SK14 . . . . 103 A4
Lodge Dr
Culcheth WA3 . . . . 91 F3
Tyldesley M29 . . . . 77 B6
Lodge Farm SK7 . . . . 123 E2
Lodge Fold M43 . . . . 84 B2
Lodge Gn SK16 . . . . 101 E7
Lodge Gr M46 . . . . 58 E1
Lodge Hill La BL0 . . . . 12 A8
Lodge La
Delph OL3 . . . . 50 E5
Dukinfield SK16 . . . . 101 E8
Haydock WA11, WA12, WN4 89 B8
Hyde SK14 . . . . 167 A4

Lodge La continued
Leigh WN7 . . . . 76 E4
Tyldesley M46 . . . . 58 D1
Lodge Mews BL0 . . . . 138 C2
Lodge Mill La BL0 . . . . 2 A1
Lodgepole Cl M30 . . . . 94 F8
Lodge Rd
Orrell WN5 . . . . 53 E4
Radcliffe M26 . . . . 44 B2
Tyldesley M46 . . . . 58 E1
Lodgeside Cl M43 . . . . 84 B2
Lodge St
Ashton-u-L OL7 . . . . 84 F1
Dukinfield SK14 . . . . 101 E5
Littleborough OL15 . . . . 16 B5
Manchester M40 . . . . 157 B1
Middleton M24 . . . . 47 A1
Ramsbottom BL0 . . . . 138 C2
Lodge The SK13 . . . . 104 A6
Lodge Vale
Droylsden M43 . . . . 84 B2
Ramsbottom BL0 . . . . 12 A8
Loeminster Pl WN2 . . . . . . 151 C3
Loen Cres BL1 . . . . 142 C3
Loganberry Ave M6 . . . . . . 81 A3
Logan St BL1 . . . . 24 E5
Logwood Ave
Bramhall SK7 . . . . 140 A3
Wigan WN5 . . . . 54 E7
Logwood Ho WN5 . . . . 54 E8
Logwood Pl WN5 . . . . 54 E8
Loire Dr WN5 . . . . 54 F8
Loisine Cl OL11 . . . . 30 B3
Lok Fu Gdns M8 . . . . 155 B1
Lomas Cl M19 . . . . 110 E3
Lomas La BB4 . . . . 1 F8
Lomas St
Failsworth M35 . . . . 66 A1
Middleton M24 . . . . 47 B1
Stockport SK3 . . . . 170 A3
Lomax's Bldgs BL2 . . . . . 145 C2
Lomax St
Bolton BL1 . . . . 143 B2
Bury BL9 . . . . 141 A3
6 Farnworth BL4 . . . . 42 C2
Manchester M1, M4 . . . . . . 159 C1
4 Platt Bridge WN2 . . . . . . 56 B2
Radcliffe M26 . . . . 44 A2
Ramsbottom BL8 . . . . 10 F1
Whitefield M45 . . . . 44 E2
Lombard Cl SK6 . . . . 112 F4
Lombard Gr M14 . . . . 110 C8
Lombard St
Atherton M46 . . . . 58 B3
Oldham OL1 . . . . 153 B3
Rochdale OL12 . . . . 139 A4
Lombardy Ct 9 M6 . . . . . . 81 A3
Lomond Ave
Altrincham WA15 . . . . 120 A3
Stretford M32 . . . . 96 D3
Lomond Cl SK2 . . . . 124 A3
Lomond Dr BL8 . . . . 27 B4
Lomond Pl BL3 . . . . 40 E6
Lomond Rd M22, SK8 . . . . 121 F2
Lomond Terr OL16 . . . . 31 C4
London Cl WN5 . . . . 54 E8
London Fields WN5 . . . . . . 71 E5
London Pl SK1 . . . . 169 C1
London Rd
Alderley Edge SK9 . . . . 137 A1
Hazel Grove SK2, SK7 . . . . 124 D3
Manchester M1 . . . . 163 B4
Midway SK10, SK12 . . . . . . 133 C1
Oldham OL1 . . . . 49 B1
London Road N SK12 . . . . 133 E5
London Road S SK12 . . . . 133 D3
London Sq SK1 . . . . 169 C1
London St
Bolton BL3 . . . . 147 B4
Salford M6 . . . . 81 B4
Whitefield M45 . . . . 62 F7
Longacre WN2 . . . . 75 B8
Long Acres Dr OL12 . . . . . . 4 D2
Longacres La OL12 . . . . 4 D2
Longacres Rd WA15 . . . . . 129 D7
Longacre St M1, M4 . . . . . 159 C1
Longbow Ct M7 . . . . 155 A1
Longbridge Rd M17 . . . . . . 96 A6
Longbrook WN6 . . . . 36 B7
Longbutt La WA13 . . . . 117 A2
Longcliffe Wlk 5 BL1 . . . . 143 C2
Long Clough OL2 . . . . 49 C7
Longclough Dr SK13 . . . . . 116 A8
Longcrag Wlk 4 M15 . . . . 163 A1
Longcroft M29 . . . . 76 E4
Longcroft Cotts BL9 . . . . . . 11 F1
Longcroft Dr WA14 . . . . . . 119 B4
Longcroft Gr
Droylsden M34 . . . . 100 B8
Wythenshawe M23 . . . . 120 F7
Long Croft La SK8 . . . . 122 F1
Long Cswy
Farnworth BL4 . . . . 60 D7
Leigh M46 . . . . 76 B8
Longdale Cl OL2 . . . . 48 C4
Longdale Dr SK14 . . . . 103 A3
Longdale Gdns SK14 . . . . . 103 A3
Longdell Wlk 11 M9 . . . . . . 157 E8
Longden Ave OL4 . . . . 49 E3
Longden Ct SK7 . . . . 132 E5
**Longdendale Com Language
Coll** SK14 . . . . 103 C5
Longden Rd
Ashton-in-M WN4 . . . . 73 A3

Longden Rd continued
Manchester M19 . . . . 99 B2
Longden St 8 BL1 . . . . 144 C4
Longendale Rd WN6 . . . . . . 36 E8
Longfellow Ave BL3 . . . . . 146 B3
Longfellow Cl WN3 . . . . . . 150 A1
Longfellow Cres OL1 . . . . . 49 D4
Longfellow Wlk 5 M34 . 113 A7
Longfield Ave
Altrincham WA15 . . . . 120 C6
Gatley SK8 . . . . 131 C7
Urmston M41 . . . . 95 C1
Longfield Cl SK14 . . . . 101 E6
Longfield Cres OL4 . . . . 67 D8
Longfield Dr M41 . . . . 95 B2
Longfield Pk OL2 . . . . 149 A2
Longfield Rd
Bolton BL3 . . . . 146 B3
Rochdale OL11 . . . . 30 C8
Shaw OL2 . . . . 149 A2
Wythenshawe M23 . . . . 120 F8
Longfield Sh Ctr M25 . . . . . 63 A5
Longfield St 2 WN2 . . . . . . 37 F2
Longford Ave
Bolton BL1 . . . . 142 C2
Stretford M32 . . . . 96 E2
Longford Cl M32 . . . . 96 E3
Longford Cotts M32 . . . . . . 96 F2
Longford Ho 4 M21 . . . . . . 96 F1
Longford Park Speci Sch
M32 . . . . 96 F2
Longford Pl M14 . . . . 98 E4
Longford Rd
Manchester M21 . . . . 97 A1
Reddish SK5 . . . . 99 F1
Stretford M32 . . . . 99 E3
Longford Road W SK5 . . . . 99 E1
Longford St
Heywood OL10 . . . . 29 D2
Manchester M18 . . . . 99 D6
Longford Trad Est M32 . . . 96 D3
Longford Wharf 2 M32 . . . . 96 E2
Long Grain Pl SK2 . . . . 124 D5
Longham Cl
Bramhall SK7 . . . . 123 D1
Manchester M11 . . . . 160 B1
Long Hey WA15 . . . . 120 A3
Longhey Rd M22 . . . . 121 D5
Long Heys La WN8 . . . . 35 A6
Long Heys or Back La
WN8 . . . . 35 B6
Longhill OL11 . . . . 30 D4
Longhill Wlk 8 M40 . . . . . . 83 A6
Longhirst Cl BL1 . . . . 142 B3
Longhope Rd M22 . . . . 121 C2
Longhurst La
Marple SK6 . . . . 126 C6
Stockport SK6 . . . . 126 D3
Longhurst Rd
Hindley WN2 . . . . 57 A4
Manchester M9 . . . . 64 B5
Long La
Bolton BL2, BL3 . . . . 42 E6
Broadbottom SK13 . . . . 115 C7
Bury BL3 . . . . 27 E7
Hindley WN2 . . . . 57 A4
Oldham OL9 . . . . 65 F3
Uppermill OL3 . . . . 51 A3
Westhoughton BL5 . . . . 39 D2
Longlands Dr SK14 . . . . . . 102 B3
Longlevens Rd M22 . . . . . 121 C3
Longley Dr M28 . . . . 79 B6
Longley La M22 . . . . 121 E7
Longley Rd M28 . . . . 60 D2
Longley St
Oldham OL1 . . . . 153 C2
Shaw OL2 . . . . 149 B1
Long Marl Dr SK9 . . . . 131 F4
Long Mdw
Bolton BL7 . . . . 25 C7
Dukinfield SK14 . . . . 101 F6
Longmead Ave
Ashton-in-M WN4 . . . . 73 C4
Hazel Grove SK7 . . . . 124 D1
Longmeade Gdns SK9 . . . 137 C6
Longmeadow SK8 . . . . 132 C7
Longmeadow Gr M34 . . . . 100 E2
Long Meadow Pas SK14 . . 167 A3
Longmead Rd M6 . . . . 154 F3
Longmead Way M24 . . . . . . 47 B1
Longmere Ave M22 . . . . . 121 D3
Long Millgate
Manchester M3 . . . . 158 C2
Manchester M3, M4 . . . . . . 159 A2
Longmoor Rd SK13 . . . . . . 116 A7
Longmoor St OL8 . . . . 153 A2
Longnor Mews 1 SK13 . . . 171 A2
Longnor Rd
Gatley SK8 . . . . 131 D8
Hazel Grove SK7 . . . . 133 E7
Longnor Way 17 SK13 . . . . 171 A2
Longport Ave M20 . . . . 110 A7
Longridge BL7 . . . . 25 C8
Longridge Ave
Stalybridge SK15 . . . . 86 A4
Standish WN6 . . . . 36 F8
Longridge Cres BL1 . . . . . . 23 F2
Longridge Dr
Bury BL8 . . . . 44 A8
Heywood OL10 . . . . 28 F2
Longridge Way WN6 . . . . . 36 F8
Low Row SK15 . . . . 86 F7
Long Rushes OL2 . . . . 48 F8
LONGSHAW 53 E1
Longshaw Ave
Longshaw WN5 . . . . 53 E1
Swinton M27 . . . . 61 F1
Longshaw Cl WN5 . . . . 53 E1

Longshaw Comm
Billinge WN5 . . . . 71 E8
Longshaw WN5 . . . . 53 E1
Longshaw Dr M28. . . . . . . 60 A4
Longshaw Ford Rd BL1. . . 23 F5
Longshaw Old Rd WN5 . . 53 F1
LONGSHOOT 37 E1
Longshoot Cl WN1 . . . . . . 37 D1
Longshut La SK1, SK2. . . 170 C3
Longshut Lane W SK2 . . . 170 C3
Longsides Rd WA15. . . . . 129 C7
LONGSIGHT. 164 C1
LONG SIGHT 48 E2
Longsight BL2 . . . . 25 E5
Longsight Ind Est M12 . . 98 F4
Longsight La
Bolton BL2 . . . . 25 D4
Cheadle SK8 . . . . 131 F6
Longsight Rd
Manchester M18 . . . . . . 99 B3
Ramsbottom BL0, BL8. . . 11 A2
Longsight Sh Ctr M12 . . . 98 F4
Longson St BL1 . . . . 25 A1
Longsons The SK5 . . . . . 169 E2
Long St
Manchester M18 . . . . . . 99 E6
Middleton M24. . . . . 47 A1
Swinton M27 . . . . 79 F7
Longthwaite Cl ⊡ M24 . . 46 D2
Longton Ave
Golborne WA3 . . . . 90 C7
Manchester M20 . . . . . 110 A5
Longton Rd
Manchester M9 . . . . 64 C4
Salford M6. . . . . 80 C5
Longton St
Bury BL9 . . . . 44 F4
Hindley WN2 . . . . 56 C4
Longtown Gdns ⊿ BL1 . . 143 B2
Longview Dr M27 . . . . 61 C1
Longwall Ave M28 . . . . . . 78 C8
Long Wlk M31 . . . . 105 D3
Longwood Ave SK2 . . . . 124 B6
Longwood Cl SK6 . . . . . . 113 E3
Longwood Rd M22 . . . . . 121 E3
Long Wood Rd M17 . . . . . 96 B6
Longworth Ave BL6 . . . . . 21 C3
Longworth Cl M41. . . . . . 94 E1
Longworth Clough BL7. . . 8 D2
Longworth La BL7 . . . . 8 C2
Longworth Rd
Bolton BL7. . . . . 8 B3
Horwich BL6 . . . . 22 C4
Longworth St
Bolton BL2 . . . . 148 C3
Manchester M3 . . . . . . 162 B4
SK12. . . . . 133 B3
Lonsdale Ave
Leigh WN7 . . . . 75 D2
Reddish SK5 . . . . 99 F3
Rochdale OL16. . . . . 31 B5
Swinton M27 . . . . 79 D5
Urmston M41 . . . . 95 B4
Lonsdale Gr ⊡ BL4 . . . . . 60 C8
Lonsdale Rd
Bolton BL1. . . . . 144 B4
Manchester M19 . . . . . . 99 B2
Oldham OL8 . . . . 66 B2
Lonsdale St
Bury BL8 . . . . 27 C2
Failsworth M40 . . . . 83 C6
Lonsdale Wlk WN5 . . . . . 54 B8
Loom St M4 . . . . 159 B2
Loonies Ct ⊡ SK1. . . . . . 170 C4
Lord Ave
Bacup OL13 . . . . 3 C8
⊡ Hindley M46. . . . . . . 58 E1
Lord Bank Rd SJ M50. . . 154 C1
Lord Derby Rd SK14. . . . 113 E7
Lord Gr ⊡ M4. . . . . 54 F2
Lord Kitchener Ct M33 . . 108 B5
Lord La M35. . . . . 83 F6
Lord Napier Dr M5. . . . . 161 B3
Lord North St M40 . . . . . 160 C4
Lord's Ave M5 . . . . 154 A2
Lords Coll BL2 . . . . 148 A2
Lordsfields Ave OL7. . . . 166 B4
Lord Sheldon Way OL7 . . 84 F2
Lordship Cl M9 . . . . 64 F1
Lordsmead St M15. . . . . 162 A2
Lord's St M44. . . . . 105 C5
Lord's Stile La BL7. . . . . 25 B7
Lord St
Ashton-in-M WN4 . . . . . 73 D4
Ashton-u-L OL6 . . . . . . 166 B4
Bury BL9 . . . . 140 C2
Bury, Heap Bridge BL9. . . 141 C1
Farnworth BL4 . . . . 60 E8
Glossop SK13. . . . . 104 D1
Hindley WN2 . . . . 56 D4
Hollingworth SK14. . . . . 171 A4
Horwich BL6 . . . . 22 B4
Ince-in-M WN2 . . . . 56 A7
Leigh WN7 . . . . 75 F5
Little Lever BL3 . . . . 43 B3
Manchester M3, M4 . . . 159 A3
Middleton M24. . . . . 47 A2
Newton-le-W WA12 . . . . 89 A3
Oldham OL1. . . . . 67 C7
Radcliffe M26 . . . . 44 A3
Reddish M34 . . . . 100 A4
Salford M7. . . . . 81 C4
Stalybridge SK15, SK16. . 101 F8
Stockport SK1 . . . . 169 C1
Tyldesley, Gin Pit M29 . . 76 F6
Tyldesley, Hindsford M46. . 58 E1
Westhoughton BL5 . . . . . 39 E1
Wigan WN1 . . . . 37 C1

Lord Street Prim Sch BL6 22 B4
Lord Street S WN7 . . . . . 76 A5
Lordy Cl WN6 . . . . 37 B7
Loreto Chorlton RC High Sch
(Upper Sch) M21 . . . . . 109 D7
Loreto Gram Sch ⊡
WA14. . . . . 119 C4
Loreto Prep Sch WA14 . . 119 C5
Loreto Sixth Form Coll
M15. . . . . 162 B1
Loretto Rd M41. . . . . 95 F1
Lorgill Cl SK3. . . . . 123 E8
Loring St M40 . . . . 83 C5
Lorland Rd SK3. . . . . . . 123 B7
Lorna Gr SK8 . . . . 121 F6
Lorna Rd SK8 . . . . 123 B2
Lorna Way M44 . . . . 106 A8
Lorne Ave OL2. . . . . 48 B3
Lorne Gr
Stockport SK3 . . . . 170 B2
Urmston M41. . . . . 95 C2
Lorne Rd M14 . . . . 110 C8
Lorne St
Bolton BL1. . . . . 145 C3
Eccles M30 . . . . 95 B8
Farnworth BL3, BL4. . . . 42 C2
Heywood OL10. . . . . 29 D1
Mossley OL5 . . . . 68 F4
Oldham OL8 . . . . 66 F4
Rochdale OL12. . . . . 15 B3
Wigan WN1 . . . . 151 B4
Lorne Way OL10 . . . . 28 F1
Lorraine Cl ⊡ OL10 . . . . . 46 E8
Lorraine Rd WA15. . . . . 120 B5
Lorton Cl
Boothstown M28 . . . . . . 77 F6
Middleton M24. . . . . 46 C2
Lorton Gr BL2 . . . . 42 F8
LOSTOCK
Bolton 40 B6
Horwich 39 F8
Lostock Ave
Hazel Grove SK7 . . . . . 124 B1
⊡ Manchester M19 . . . . 99 B1
Poynton SK12. . . . . 133 B4
Sale M33 . . . . 108 C4
Urmston M41. . . . . 95 B3
Lostock Cl
Billinge WN5 . . . . 71 E5
Heywood OL10. . . . . 29 B3
Lostock Coll M32 . . . . . . 96 A3
Lostock Dr M32 . . . . 95 F4
Lostock Dr BL9 . . . . 27 E8
Lostock Gr M32. . . . . 96 B3
Lostock Hall Prim Sch
SK12. . . . . 133 B3
Lostock Hall Rd SK12. . . 133 B3
Lostock Ind Est BL6. . . . . 39 E7
Lostock Junction La BL6 . 40 C7
LOSTOCK JUNCTION 40 D5
Lostock La
Horwich BL5, BL6 . . . . . 39 E6
Horwich BL6 . . . . 39 E8
Lostock Park Dr BL6 . . . . 40 A7
Lostock Prim Sch BL4, BL6. 40 C6
Lostock Rd
Four Gates BL5 . . . . 39 C4
Poynton SK12. . . . . 133 D2
Salford M5. . . . . 154 B2
Urmston M41. . . . . 95 D4
Lostock St M40 . . . . 160 A3
Lostock Sta BL6 . . . . 40 C6
Lostock Way SK9 . . . . . . 131 D4
Lostock Wlk
Leigh WN7 . . . . 75 D6
⊡ Whitefield M45. . . . . . 45 C1
Lothian Ave M30. . . . . . . 79 B3
Lottery Row BL1. . . . . . . 145 C3
Lottery St SK3 . . . . 169 A1
Lottie St M27 . . . . 80 A8
Loughborough Cl ⊡
M33. . . . . 107 D3
Loughfield M41. . . . . 95 A2
Loughrigg Ave
Billinge WA11 . . . . 71 B1
Royton OL2 . . . . 48 C8
Loughrigg Cl M29. . . . . . . 77 B7
Louisa St
Bolton BL1. . . . . 143 B2
Manchester M11 . . . . . . 99 D8
Walkden M28. . . . . 60 D4
Louis Ave BL9 . . . . 140 C4
Louise Cl OL12. . . . . 15 C3
Louise Gdns
Rochdale OL12. . . . . 15 C3
Westhoughton BL5 . . . . . 57 F6
Louise St OL12. . . . . 15 C3
Louvaine Ave BL1. . . . . . 23 F4
Louvaine Cl M18. . . . . . . 99 E5
Louvain St M35. . . . . 83 F7
Lovalle St BL1 . . . . 142 C1
Lovat Rd BL2 . . . . 43 A7
Lovatt Ct WA13. . . . . 117 B4
Love La
Edenfield BL0. . . . . 1 E1
Stockport SK4 . . . . 169 B2
Lovell Ct M8. . . . . 63 F2
Lovell Dr SK14. . . . . 167 C4
Lovers La
Atherton M46. . . . . 58 A1
Uppermill OL4 . . . . 68 D6
Lovett Wlk M22 . . . . 121 E8
Low Bank OL12 . . . . 15 C3
Low Bank Rd WN4 . . . . . 72 F4
Lowbrook Ave M9 . . . . . . 65 B3
Low Comm WN7 . . . . 76 B2

Lowcroft Cres OL9 . . . . . 65 F8
LOW CROMPTON 48 F6
Low Crompton Rd OL2 . . 48 E6
Lowcross Rd M40 . . . . . . 83 A6
Lowe Ave M46. . . . . 58 C5
Lowe Gn OL2 . . . . 48 E5
Lowe Mill La WN2. . . . . . 56 D5
Lower Albion St M1. . . . 163 B4
Lower Alma St SK16. . . . 166 B1
LOWER ARTHURS 69 B6
Lower Bamford Cl ⊡
M24 . . . . 47 A2
Lowerbank M34 . . . . 100 F5
Lower Bank SK13 . . . . . . 116 D8
Lower Bank Cl SK13. . . . 171 C3
Lower Bank St BL9. . . . . 140 B2
Lower Barn Rd SK13 . . . 171 B4
Lower Beechwood OL11. . 139 A4
Lower Bennett St SK14. . 101 C5
Lower Bents La SK6. . . . 112 F4
Lower Birches OL4 . . . . . 67 F4
Lower Blue Bell Cotts
BL5. . . . . 39 C4
LOWER BOARSGREAVE . . . 3 A6
LOWER BREDBURY 112 E2
Lower Bridgeman St
BL2. . . . . 148 A2
Lower Broadacre SK15. . 102 E6
Lowerbrook Cl BL6. . . . . 22 D1
Lower Brook Farm BL5. . 58 F7
Lower Brook La M28 . . . . 79 A5
Lower Brooklands Par ⊡
M8 . . . . 63 E2
LOWER BROUGHTON . . . 158 A4
Lower Broughton Rd
Salford, Higher Broughton
M7. . . . . 81 C6
Salford, Lower Broughton
M7. . . . . 158 A4
Lower Bury St SK4 . . . . . 169 A2
Lower Byrom St M3. . . . 162 B4
Lower Calderbrook OL15. . 6 C1
Lower Carr La OL3 . . . . . 69 B6
Lower Carrs
Ashton-u-L OL6 . . . . 85 D5
Stockport SK1 . . . . 169 C1
Lower Chatham St M1. . . 163 A3
Lower Clowes BB4 . . . . . . 1 E8
Lower Clowes Rd BB4. . . . 1 E8
Lower Count Hill OL4 . . . 49 E2
Lower Crimble OL11 . . . . 29 F4
Lower Croft M45. . . . . . . 62 C6
Lowercroft Bsns Pk BL8. . 26 F3
Lowercroft Prim Sch BL8. 26 F2
Lowercroft Rd BL8. . . . . . 26 F2
Lower Crossbank OL4 . . . 67 F8
Lower Darcy St BL2 . . . . 148 C1
Lower Dingle OL1. . . . . . . 49 C4
LOWER DINTING 104 B1
Lower Drake Fold BL5. . . 57 E5
Lower Edge Ave OL1 . . . 153 B4
Lower Falinge OL12 . . . . 139 B5
Lowerfield Dr SK2 . . . . . 124 F5
Lowerfield Gdns WA3 . . . 74 C1
Lowerfields OL8 . . . . 66 E4
Lower Fields SL5 . . . . . . 51 A1
Lower Fields Rise OL2. . . 149 B4
LOWER FOLD 14 C3
Lower Fold
Bolton BL2. . . . . 25 F4
Denton M34. . . . . 101 A2
Marple SK6 . . . . 126 B8
Lower Fold Ave OL2. . . . . 49 A4
Lower Fold Cl OL12 . . . . . 14 C4
Lower Fold Cott SK6 . . . 134 D7
Lower Fold La OL12 . . . . . 14 C4
Lower Fold Dr OL12 . . . . . 14 C4
Lowerfold Way OL12 . . . . 14 C4
Lower Frenches Dr OL3 . . 69 A5
Lower Gates OL16. . . . . . 139 C3
Lower Goodwin Cl BL2. . . 25 E2
LOWER GREEN 77 C3
Lower Green
Ashton-u-L OL6 . . . . . . 166 C4
Middleton M9. . . . . 64 F5
⊡ Rochdale OL12. . . . . . 14 C1
Lower Green La M29 . . . . 77 C3
Lower Greenshall La
SK12. . . . . 135 F6
Lower Hague SK22 . . . . . 135 E8
LOWER HEALEY 14 D4
Lower Hey La OL5. . . . . . 68 E3
Lower Highgum Visitor ~*
SK14. . . . . 114 A8
Lower Hillgate SK1 . . . . 169 C1
LOWER HINDS 44 D8
Lower House Dr BL6 . . . . 40 C7
Lower House La OL12 . . . 15 B7
Lower House St ⊡ OL1. . . 67 B8
Lower House Wlk BL7 . . . 25 A8
Lower Hyde Green Farm
SK15 . . . . 86 E4
LOWER INCE 151 A4
Lower Jowkin La OL11 . . . 29 D7
LOWER KERSAL 81 A7
Lower Kersal Prim Sch
M7 . . . . 81 B6
Lower Knoll Rd OL3. . . . . 51 C5
Lower La OL15. . . . . 15 C4
Lower Landedmans BL5. . 57 F7
Lowerlea SK12. . . . . 135 C6
Lower Leigh Rd BL5. . . . . 57 F5
Lower Lime Rd OL8 . . . . . 84 C7
Lower Longshoot WN1. . . 151 A4
Lower Lyndon Ave WN6 . . 36 A6
Lower Makinson Fold ⊡
BL6. . . . . 22 D1

Lower Market St SK14. . . 115 B8
Lower Marlands BL7. . . . 24 F8
Lower Mead BL7. . . . . 8 F1
Lower Meadow BL7 . . . . . . 9 D6
Lower Meadow Rd SK9. . 131 E4
Lower Moat Cl SK4. . . . . 169 B3
Lower Monton Rd M30 . . 79 F2
LOWER MOOR 47 A8
Lower Mosley St M1, M2. 162 C4
Lower Moss La
Manchester M15. . . . . . 162 A3
Whitefield M45 . . . . 62 D3
Lower New Row M28. . . . 60 A1
Lower Ormond St M15 . . 163 A3
Lower Park Cres SK12. . . 133 C6
Lower Park Prim Sch
SK12. . . . . 133 C4
Lower Park Rd
Manchester M14 . . . . . . 98 C3
Poynton SK12. . . . . 133 B5
LOWER PLACE 31 B4
Lowerplace Prim Sch
OL16. . . . . 31 B4
LOWER POOLS 142 A2
Lower Rawson St BL4 . . . 42 E1
Lower Rd BL0 . . . . 11 E8
LOWER RUSHCROFT 149 A4
Lower St Stephen St ⊡
WN6 . . . . 37 A1
Lower Seedley Rd M6. . . 154 B3
Lower Sherriff St OL12 . . 139 B4
Lower Southfield BL5. . . . 57 E7
Lower Square SK13 . . . . 104 A7
Lower St
Farnworth BL4. . . . . 60 C7
⊡ Rochdale OL16. . . . . . 31 A4
Lower Stones OL3 . . . . . . 50 E3
Lower Strines Rd SK6. . . 126 A5
LOWER SUMMERSEAT . . . 11 C1
Lower Sutherland St M27 79 E8
Lower Tenterfield OL11 . . 13 D2
Lower Tong BL7 . . . . 24 F7
Lower Turf La OL4 . . . . . . 68 B8
Lower Tweedale St
OL11 . . . . 139 A6
Lower Vickers St M40. . . 160 A3
Lower Victoria St OL9. . . 152 B3
Lower Wharf St OL6. . . . 166 C2
Lower Wheat End OL16. . 31 B8
Lower Woodhill Rd BL8 . . 140 A3
Lowerwood La ⊿ BL2. . . . 25 E1
Lower Wrigley Gn OL3 . . . 51 C3
Lower Rd BL9 . . . . 28 A6
Lowe St
Denton M34. . . . . 101 B3
⊡ Golborne WA3 . . . . . . 90 A8
Radcliffe M26 . . . . 43 F4
Stockport SK1 . . . . 169 C1
Lowestead Rd ⊡ M11. . . . 83 C2
Lowes The WA14. . . . . . . 119 B1
Lowestoft St M14 . . . . . . 98 B2
Loweswater Ave M29. . . . 77 A7
Loweswater Rd
Farnworth BL4. . . . . 59 E7
Gatley SK8. . . . . 122 B5
Loweswater Terr SK15. . . 86 A4
Lowfell Wlk M18. . . . . . . 99 D3
Lowfield Ave
Ashton-u-L OL6 . . . . 85 F5
Droylsden M43. . . . . 83 F3
Lowfield Gdns WA3 . . . . 92 C7
Lowfield Gr SK2, SK3 . . . 170 C3
Lowfield Rd SK2, SK3 . . . 170 B3
Lowfield Wlk ⊡ M9 . . . . . 64 E3
Low Gate OL3 . . . . 34 A1
Lowgill Wlk M18 . . . . 99 D5
Low Gn M46 . . . . 58 F5
Low Grove La OL3 . . . . . . 68 E5
Low Lea Rd SK6. . . . . . . 126 B6
Low Mdws OL2 . . . . 48 D6
Lowndes Cl SK2. . . . . . . 124 B7
Lowndes La SK1, SK2 . . . 124 B7
Lowndes St BL1. . . . . . . 142 A1
Lowndes Wlk ⊡ M13. . . . 163 C2
Lownorth Rd M22 . . . . . . 130 E8
Lowood Ave M41 . . . . 94 F4
Lowood Cl OL16 . . . . 31 F6
Lowood St WN7. . . . . 75 D5
Lowry Wlk ⊡ M9 . . . . . . 157 B3
Lowry Rd M30 . . . . 79 E2
Lowry Ct SK14. . . . . 103 A4
Lowry Dr
Marple SK6 . . . . 126 B8
Swinton M27 . . . . 61 F1
Lowry Ho ⊿ M14 . . . . . . 110 D8
Lowry Outlet Mall M50. . . 96 F7
Lowry The ⊡ M14 . . . . . 110 C8
Lowry The ~ M50. . . . . . 96 F7
Lowry Wlk BL1. . . . . 143 A1
Lowry Cl SK14 . . . . 8 E1
Lowstern Cl BL7. . . . . 8 E1

Lows The OL4 . . . . 67 B5
Lowther Ave
Altrincham WA15. . . . . . 120 A6
Culcheth WA3 . . . . 91 F4
Manchester M18 . . . . . . 99 B3
Royton OL2 . . . . 48 C8
Lowther Cl M25. . . . . 63 A3
Lowther Cres M24 . . . . . . 46 D1
Lowther Ct M25. . . . . 62 F3
Lowther Dr WN7 . . . . 76 E7
Lowther Gdns M41. . . . . 94 D3
Lowther Rd
Manchester M8 . . . . 64 A1
Prestwich M25. . . . . 62 F3
Rochdale OL11. . . . . 30 E4
Lowther St BL3 . . . . 42 A3
Lowther Terr WN6 . . . . . . 35 C8
Lowthorpe St M14 . . . . . 98 B2
LOWTON 90 E8
Lowton Ave M9 . . . . 157 C3
Lowton Bsns Pk WA3. . . . 91 A7
LOWTON COMMON 91 A8
Lowton Gdns WA3 . . . . . 90 B5
LOWTON HEATH 90 C6
Lowton High Sch WA3. . . 91 B8
Lowton Jun & Inf Sch
WA3 . . . . 91 A7
Lowton Rd
Golborne WA3 . . . . 74 C1
Sale M33 . . . . 107 D2
LOWTON ST MARY'S 90 F8
Lowton St Mary's CE Prim
Sch WA3 . . . . 91 A8
Lowton St M26 . . . . 44 A4
Lowton West Prim Sch
WA3 . . . . 90 D8
Low Wood Cl SK7 . . . . . . 123 C1
Low Wood Rd M34 . . . . . 100 A4
Loxford Ct M15 . . . . 162 C2
Loxford St M15 . . . . 162 C2
Loxham St BL4. . . . . 42 D2
Loxley Wlk M40. . . . . . . 160 B4
Loxton Cres WN3 . . . . . . 55 B3
Loynd St BL0 . . . . 11 D6
Lubeck St M9 . . . . 157 B4
Lucas St
Bury BL9 . . . . 141 A3
Oldham OL4 . . . . 67 B7
Lucas Wlk M11 . . . . 164 C4
Lucerne Cl OL9 . . . . 152 C2
Lucerne Rd SK7. . . . . . . 123 E3
Lucien Cl M12. . . . . 164 B1
Lucknow St OL11 . . . . . . 139 C1
Lucy St
Bolton BL1. . . . . 145 D7
Manchester M15. . . . . . 162 A2
Stockport SK3 . . . . 170 B4
Ludford Gr M33. . . . . . . 107 F1
Ludgate Hill M4 . . . . 159 B3
Ludgate Rd
Failsworth M40 . . . . 83 C4
Rochdale OL11. . . . . 31 A2
Ludgate St M4. . . . . 159 A3
Ludlow Ave
Hindley WN2 . . . . 57 A4
Prestwich M25, M45. . . . 63 B6
Swinton M27 . . . . 62 A2
Ludlow Dr WN7 . . . . 76 E7
Ludlow Pk ⊡ OL4 . . . . . . 67 D8
Ludlow Rd SK2 . . . . 124 C8
Ludlow St WN6 . . . . 19 D3
Ludovic Cres WN1. . . . . . 37 C4
Ludwell Wlk ⊡ M8. . . . . 156 A7
Ludworth Prim Sch SK6. 126 B8
Lugano Rd SK7 . . . . 123 E3
Luke Kirby Ct M27 . . . . . 61 F1
Luke Rd M43 . . . . 84 B1
Luke St
Ashton-in-M WN4 . . . . . 73 D5
⊡ Bacup OL13 . . . . 3 C8
Luke Wlk M8 . . . . 156 B2
Lullington Cl M22. . . . . . 121 C1
Lullington Rd M6 . . . . . . 154 A4
Lulworth Ave M41 . . . . . . 94 F2
Lulworth Cl BL8. . . . . 27 C6
Lulworth Cres M35. . . . . 84 B8
Lulworth Dr WN7 . . . . . . 57 A4
Lulworth Gdns M23 . . . . 120 F8
Lulworth Rd
Bolton BL3. . . . . 146 A3
Eccles M30 . . . . 79 C3
Middleton M24. . . . . 47 A2
LUMB 1 B4
Lumb Carr Ave BL0 . . . . . 11 A4
Lumb Carr Rd BL0, BL8. . . 11 A4
Lumb Cl SK7 . . . . 132 E6
Lumb Cotts BL0. . . . . 1 B4
Lumber La M28 . . . . 78 E8
Lumb Flats BL0. . . . . 1 B4
Lumb Holes La BB4 . . . . . 2 E7
Lumb La
Bramhall SK7. . . . . 132 E6
Droylsden, Littlemoss M34, M43,
OL7. . . . . 84 D4
Droylsden M34. . . . . 84 D3
Droylsden M43. . . . . 84 C3
Lumn Head Prim Sch SK6 122 B3
Lumiere Bldgs ⊡ M15. . . 162 C3
Lumley Cl M14 . . . . 98 B4
Lumn Hollow SK14 . . . . . 167 B2
Lumn Rd SK14 . . . . 167 B2
Lumn's La M27 . . . . 62 C1
Lumn St BL9. . . . . 27 F8

Lumsdale Rd M32 .... 96 A5
Lumsden St BL3 .... 145 B1
Lum St BL1 .... 148 A4
Lumwood BL1 .... 142 B3
Luna St M4 .... 159 B2
Lundale Wlk 15 M40 .... 83 A6
Lund Ave M26 .... 62 B8
Lund St M16 .... 161 C2
Lundy Ave M21 .... 109 C5
Lune Cl M45 .... 45 A1
Lunedale 7 WN2 .... 56 B2
Lunedale Gn SK2 .... 124 E6
Lune Dr M45. .... 63 A8
Lune Gr
 Heywood OL10. .... 29 B3
 Leigh WN7 .... 75 C5
Lunehurst 12 WA3 .... 90 E8
Lune Rd WN2. .... 56 A2
Lune St
 Oldham OL8. .... 66 E4
 Tyldesley M29 .... 76 F8
Lune Way SK5 .... 111 F5
Lune Wlk
 Droylsden M43. .... 100 B8
 Whitefield M45 .... 63 A8
Lunn Ave M18 .... 99 D4
Luntswood Gr WA12 .... 89 A4
Lupin Ave BL4 .... 42 A1
Lupin Cl OL1. .... 49 E3
Lupton St M3 .... 100 F4
Lurden Wlk 2 OL9. .... 66 B4
Lurdin La WN1, WN6. .... 37 B7
Lurgan Ave M33 .... 108 C3
Lutener Av WA14 .... 119 C8
Luton Dr M23. .... 121 A4
Luton Gr M46. .... 58 B3
Luton Rd SK5. .... 111 F8
Luton St
 Bolton BL3 .... 42 A4
 3 Bury BL8. .... 27 B1
Luxhall Wlk M40 .... 83 B4
Luxor Gr M34. .... 99 F5
LUZLEY 86 B7
LUZLEY BROOK 48 F5
Luzley Brook Rd OL2 .. 149 A1
Luzley Rd OL5, OL6. .... 86 B7
Lyceum Pas 1 OL16 .. 139 C3
Lyceum Pl M15 .... 163 A3
Lychgate Cl OL4 .... 67 E4
Lychgate Mews
 8 Manchester, Chorlton-cum-
 Hardy M21 .... 109 A8
 Manchester, Heaton Mersey
 SK4 .... 110 E2
Lychwood 11 SK6 .... 125 F6
Lydbrook Cl BL1. .... 145 B2
Lydden Ave M11 .... 83 D3
Lydford OL11. .... 139 B2
Lydford Gdns BL2. .... 42 F6
Lydford Gn WN6 .... 36 F8
Lydford Rd M6 .... 81 B4
Lydford Wlk M13. .... 163 C2
LYDGATE 68 D5
Lydgate Ave BL2 .... 42 E8
Lydgate Cl
 Denton M34 .... 101 B1
 Mossley SK15 .... 86 E6
 Whitefield M45 .... 45 A1
Lydgate Dr OL4 .... 67 D5
Lydgate Fold OL4 .... 68 C5
Lydgate Rd
 Droylsden M43. .... 83 E2
 Sale M33 .... 108 C2
Lydgate The OL15. .... 16 E6
Lydgate Wlk M45 .... 45 A1
Lydiate Cl BL3 .... 147 C2
Lydiat La SK9 .... 137 A1
Lydney Ave SK8. .... 131 C7
Lydney Rd M41 .... 94 D3
Lyefield Ave WN1 .... 37 F1
Lyefield Wlk 16 OL16 .. 31 B6
Lymbridge Dr BL6. .... 21 D1
Lyme Ave SK9 .... 131 B1
Lyme Clough Way M24 .. 46 F4
Lyme Ct
 Hazel Grove SK7 .... 124 D3
 Hyde SK14 .... 167 B3
Lymefield Dr M28 .... 78 A7
Lymefield Gr SK2 .... 124 B6
Lymefield Terr SK13 ... 115 C7
Lymefield Visitor Ctr*
 SK14 .... 115 B8
Lyme Gr
 Altrincham WA14 .... 119 C4
 Droylsden M43. .... 99 F8
 Marple SK6 .... 125 F5
 Romiley SK6. .... 113 D2
 Stockport SK2 .... 170 C3
Lyme Lea Cl SK8 .... 132 B8
Lyme Park* SK12. .... 135 B1
Lyme Park Ctry Pk*
 SK12 .... 135 B2
Lyme Rd
 Hazel Grove SK7 .... 124 D3
 High Lane SK12 .... 135 A4
 Poynton SK12. .... 134 C3
Lyme St
 Hazel Grove SK7 .... 124 D3
 Manchester SK4 .... 110 F2
Lyme Terr 1 SK16 .... 166 B1
Lymewood Dr
 Disley SK12 .... 135 C6
 Wilmslow SK9 .... 137 E8
Lymington Cl M24 .... 65 B5

Lymington Dr M23 .... 108 D1
LYMM 117 A3
Lymm Cl
 Stockport SK3 .... 170 A2
 Walkden M28. .... 60 A3
Lymm High Sch WA13 .. 117 B3
Lymm Rd WA14 .... 118 B1
Lymm Wlk 5 SK8 .... 123 A5
Lymn St WN2 .... 56 B3
Lynbridge Cl WN5. .... 53 E5
Lyncombe Cl M24 .... 132 B6
Lyndale Ave
 Reddish SK5. .... 99 F3
 Swinton M27 .... 79 D6
Lyndale Dr OL15 .... 16 A6
Lyndene Ave M28 .... 79 A8
Lyndene Ct OL10. .... 29 C3
Lyndene Gdns SK8 .... 122 B6
Lyndene Rd M22 .... 121 D5
Lyndhurst Ave
 Ashton-u-L OL6 .... 85 B5
 Denton M34. .... 100 E3
 Hazel Grove SK7 .... 124 C1
 Irlam M44 .... 94 B3
 Manchester M25 .... 63 E3
 Oldham OL9 .... 65 F5
 Romiley SK6. .... 112 F4
 Sale M33 .... 107 F3
 Trub OL11 .... 47 D8
 Urmston M41. .... 95 C4
Lyndhurst Cl SK9 .... 136 D5
Lyndhurst Com Prim Sch
 SK16 .... 166 C1
Lyndhurst Dr WA15 .... 120 A2
Lyndhurst Prim Sch OL8 .. 66 D3
Lyndhurst Rd
 Manchester M20 .... 110 B5
 Oldham OL8. .... 66 D3
 Reddish SK5. .... 99 E2
 Stretford M32 .... 96 B3
Lyndhurst St M6 .... 154 B2
Lyndhurst View SK16 ... 166 C1
Lyndon Ave M46 .... 36 A7
Lyndon Cl
 Bury BL8 .... 26 F6
 Oldham OL4 .... 68 B8
Lyndon Croft OL8 .... 66 C4
Lyndon Rd M44 .... 93 F2
Lyne Ave SK13 .... 116 A8
Lyne Edge Cres SK6 ... 101 F7
Lyne Edge Rd SK16. ... 102 A7
Lyneham Wlk M7 .... 155 C2
Lyne View SK14 .... 101 F8
Lyngard Cl SK9 .... 131 E1
Lyngate Cl SK1 .... 124 A8
Lyn Gr OL10 .... 29 A3
Lynham Dr OL10 .... 46 D8
Lynmouth Ave
 Manchester M20 .... 110 A6
 Oldham OL8. .... 66 F3
 10 Reddish SK5. .... 111 E7
 Royton OL2 .... 48 C3
 Urmston M41. .... 107 B8
Lynmouth Cl
 Chadderton OL9. .... 47 E1
 Radcliffe M26 .... 44 C4
 Wigan WN6 .... 37 A2
Lynmouth Ct M25. .... 62 F3
Lynmouth Gr M25. .... 62 F3
Lynn Ave M33 .... 108 D6
Lynn Dr M43. .... 83 E2
Lynne Cl SK13 .... 116 F8
Lynn St OL9 .... 66 C4
Lynnwood Dr OL11. .... 30 B8
Lynnwood Rd M19 .... 110 D2
Lynroyle Way OL11 .... 30 D3
Lynside Wlk M22. .... 130 E8
Lynsted Ave BL3 .... 42 A3
Lynstock Way BL6. .... 39 E6
Lynthorpe Ave M44 ... 105 D6
Lynthorpe Rd M40 .... 65 D2
Lynton Ave
 Hattersley SK14. .... 102 C2
 Irlam M44 .... 94 A3
 Oldham OL8. .... 66 C2
 Rochdale OL11. .... 30 B3
 Royton OL2 .... 48 C3
 Swinton M27 .... 61 F1
 Urmston M41. .... 94 C2
 Wigan WN6 .... 37 A3
Lynton Cl OL9 .... 47 F1
Lynton Cres M28. .... 78 D8
Lynton Dr
 High Lane SK6 .... 134 E8
 Manchester M19 .... 110 F7
 Prestwich M25. .... 63 C6
Lynton Gr WA15 .... 119 F5
Lynton La SK9 .... 137 A2
Lynton Lea M26. .... 44 C4
Lynton Mews 3 SK9 ... 137 A2
Lynton Park Rd SK8 ... 131 F8
Lynton Rd
 Bolton BL3 .... 146 C2
 Cheadle SK8 .... 122 C5
 Hindley WN2 .... 56 F6
 Manchester, Chorlton-cum-Hardy
 M21. .... 97 A1
 Manchester, Heaton Chapel
 SK4 .... 111 C5
 Swinton M27 .... 61 F1
 Tyldesley M29 .... 77 D8
Lynton St
 Leigh WN7 .... 75 D5
 Manchester M14 .... 98 B2
Lyntonvale Ave SK8 ... 122 B6
Lynton Wlk SK14 .... 102 C2
Lyntown Trad Est M30 .. 79 E2
Lynway Dr M20 .... 110 B5

Lynway Gr M24 .... 47 B2
Lynwell Rd M30. .... 79 D2
Lynwood
 Altrincham WA15 .... 129 A8
 Wilmslow SK9 .... 137 A6
Lynwood Ave
 Bolton BL3. .... 42 B2
 Eccles M30 .... 79 D2
 Golborne WA3 .... 90 E6
 Manchester M16 .... 97 C2
Lynwood Cl OL7 .... 85 A7
Lynwood Ct M8. .... 63 F2
Lynwood Dr OL4 .... 67 E8
Lynwood Gr
 Atherton M46. .... 58 B3
 Bolton BL2. .... 25 D4
 Droylsden M34. .... 84 C1
 Reddish SK4. .... 111 C6
 Sale M33 .... 108 C5
Lyon Gr M28 .... 79 A8
Lyon Ind Est WA14 ... 119 B7
Lyon Rd
 Altrincham WA14 .... 119 C7
 Kearsley BL4 .... 60 E6
 Wigan WN6 .... 37 A2
Lyon Road Ind Est M28 .. 60 F6
Lyons Dr BL8 .... 27 A1
Lyons Fold M33. .... 108 B6
Lyon St M17 .... 96 A7
Lyon St
 Ashton-in-M WN4 .... 72 F7
 Shaw OL2. .... 149 B3
 Swinton M27 .... 79 E7
 Wigan WN3 .... 150 B3
Lyra Pl M7 .... 81 C3
Lysander Cl M14 .... 110 B8
Lytham Ave M21 .... 109 C7
Lytham Cl OL6 .... 85 E6
Lytham Ct OL6 .... 85 E6
Lytham Dr
 Bramhall SK7 .... 133 A7
 Heywood OL10. .... 29 C1
Lytham Rd
 Ashton-in-M WN4 .... 72 F5
 Gatley SK8 .... 122 B6
 Manchester M14, M19. .... 98 F1
 Urmston M41. .... 94 C2
Lytham St
 Rochdale OL12. .... 14 E3
 Stockport SK3 .... 170 C2
Lytherton Ave M44 .... 105 D4
Lyth St M14. .... 110 D7
Lytton Ave M8 .... 156 A2
Lytton Rd M43 .... 84 A2
Lytton St BL1 .... 143 A2

M

Mabel Ave
 Bolton BL3. .... 42 A3
 Worsley M28 .... 79 A7
Mabel Rd M35. .... 66 A1
Mabel's Brow BL4. .... 60 E7
Mabel St
 7 Bolton BL3. .... 144 C4
 Failsworth M40 .... 83 D5
 2 Rochdale OL12. .... 14 D2
 Westhoughton BL5 .... 57 F6
 Wilmslow SK9 .... 54 E6
Maberry Cl WN6 .... 35 D7
Mabfield Rd M14 .... 98 C1
Mableden Cl SK8 .... 131 D8
Mab's Cross Ho 5 WN1 .. 37 C1
Mab's Cross Prim Sch
 WN1 .... 37 D1
Mabs Ct OL6. .... 85 D2
MacAulay St
 Rochdale OL11. .... 30 D2
 Royton OL2 .... 48 E4
MacAuley Cl SK16. .... 102 A7
MacAuley Pl WN3. .... 54 F4
MacAuley Rd
 Manchester M16 .... 97 B2
 Reddish SK5. .... 99 E1
MacAuley Way 7 M34 .. 113 A8
McCall Wlk M11 .... 83 B2
Macclesfield Cl WN2. ... 56 C5
Macclesfield Rd
 Alderley Edge SK9 ... 137 B1
 Hazel Grove SK7 .... 133 F8
 Wilmslow SK9 .... 137 D6
McConnell Rd M40. .... 83 A7
McCormack Dr M1 ... 151 A4
MCCready Dr M5 .... 161 B4
MacDonald Ave
 Farnworth BL4. .... 60 B7
 Wigan WN3 .... 55 A3
MacDonald Rd M44 .... 105 E8
MacDonald St
 Oldham OL8. .... 66 F4
 Wigan WN5 .... 54 B6
McDonna St BL1 .... 142 C3
Mcdonough Ct OL8. .... 67 A3
Macefin Ave M21 .... 109 D4
Mcellen Rd WN2 .... 74 C7
Macfarren St M12. .... 99 A3
McGinty Pl M1. .... 163 A4
McKean St BL3 .... 42 A4
Mackenzie Ave WN3 .... 55 A3
Mackenzie Ind Pk SK3 .. 123 B6
Mackenzie Rd M7. .... 81 B6
Mackenzie St
 Bolton BL1. .... 143 A4
 Manchester M12. .... 99 A3
Mackenzie Wlk OL1. .... 49 E5
Mackeson Dr OL6. .... 85 E4

Mackeson Rd OL6. .... 85 E4
Mckie Cl OL8 .... 67 A3
Mackintosh Way OL1 .. 153 C3
Mackworth St M15. .... 162 B1
McLaren Ct M21 .... 97 A1
McLaren Dr M8. .... 63 E1
McLean Dr M44. .... 94 B4
Maclure Rd OL11. .... 139 C2
Macnair Ct SK6. .... 126 A5
Macnair Mews SK6. .... 126 A5
McNaught St 8 OL16 ... 31 B6
Madams Wood Rd M28 .. 60 A3
Maddison Rd M43. .... 99 F8
Madeira Pl M30. .... 79 C2
Madeley Cl
 Altrincham WA14 .... 128 E8
 Wigan WN3 .... 54 E3
Madeley Dr OL9. .... 152 B2
Madeley Gdns
 Bolton BL1. .... 143 B2
 Rochdale OL12. .... 14 C1
Maden's Sq 9 OL15. ... 16 B5
Maden St OL9 .... 76 F6
Maden Wlk OL9 .... 152 B4
Madison Apartments
 M16 .... 161 B1
Madison Ave
 Cheadle SK8 .... 123 A2
 Droylsden M34. .... 100 C8
Madison Gdns BL5 .... 40 A2
Madison Pk BL5 .... 40 A2
Madison Pl M40 .... 83 A6
Madison St M18 .... 99 F6
Madrasatul Iman Muhammed
 2 BL1. .... 143 C2
Madras Rd SK3 .... 123 C7
Maesbrook Dr M29. .... 77 A8
Zakariya 3 BL1. .... 143 C2
Mafeking Ave BL9. .... 28 A5
Mafeking Pl WN4 .... 73 C3
Mafeking Rd BL2 .... 42 E7
Mafeking St OL8. .... 66 C3
Magdala St
 Heywood OL10. .... 46 E8
 Oldham OL1. .... 153 B4
Magdalen Dr WN4 .... 72 F4
Magda Rd SK2. .... 124 D5
Magenta Ave M44. .... 94 B4
Magna Carta Ct M6, M27. .. 80 B6
Magnolia Cl
 6 Partington M31 .... 105 E2
 Sale M33 .... 107 C6
Magnolia Ct
 8 Sale M33 .... 107 C6
 8 Salford M6 .... 81 A2
Magpie La M43 .... 84 C3
Magpie Cl M11 .... 67 E4
Magpie Wlk 8 M11 .... 160 C1
Maguire Ave SK13 .... 104 A6
Maher Gdns M15. .... 97 E4
Mahogany Wlk 11 M33 .. 107 C5
Mahood St SK3 .... 170 A3
Maida St M12 .... 99 B2
Maiden Cl
 5 Ashton-u-L OL7. .... 85 A6
 Rawtenstall BB4 .... 2 F8
Maiden Mews 4 M27 ... 79 F7
Maidford Cl
 Manchester M4 .... 160 A1
 Stretford M32 .... 96 E2
Maidstone Ave M21. .... 97 A1
Maidstone Mews 2 M21 .. 97 A1
Maidstone Rd SK4. .... 110 D3
Maidstone Wlk 5 M34 .. 101 A1
Maidstone Rd SK4 .... 110 D3
Main Ave M19 .... 110 C1
Main Dr OL1. .... 48 D1
Maine Rd M14 .... 98 A3
Mainhill Wlk M40 .... 83 C5
Main La WN3 .... 90 F3
Mainprice Cl M6 .... 154 C4
Main Rd OL9. .... 152 C3
Mains Ave WN2 .... 73 F7
Main St
 Billinge WN5 .... 71 E5
 Failsworth M35 .... 83 F8
 Hyde SK14 .... 167 A4
Mainwaring Dr SK9 ... 137 D8
Mainwaring Terr M23 .. 109 A2
Mainway M24. .... 64 F6
Mainway E M24 .... 65 C6
Mainwood Rd WA15... 120 C5
Mainwood Rd M22 ... 121 B1
Maitland Ave M21. .... 109 D5
Maitland Cl
 Rochdale OL12. .... 15 C3
 Walsden OL14 .... 6 A8
Maitland St
 Stockport SK1 .... 124 B7
 Walsden OL14 .... 6 A8
Maitland Wlk OL9. .... 152 B4
Maizefield Cl M33. .... 108 F4
Majestic Mews WN5 ... 53 D5
Major St
 Manchester M1. .... 163 A4
 Milnrow OL16. .... 31 F6
 Ramsbottom BL0 .... 138 B2
 Wigan WN5 .... 54 C6
Major Wlk M5 .... 161 B4
Makants Cl
 Over Hulton M46. .... 58 F5
 Tyldesley M29 .... 77 E8
Makepeace Wlk M8. .... 63 E2
Makerfield Dr WA12 ... 89 A5
Makerfield Way WN2. ... 56 B7
Makin Ct OL10 .... 29 D1
Makinson Arc 15 WN1 .. 150 C4
Makinson Ave
 Hindley WN2 .... 56 E7

Makinson Ave continued
 Horwich BL6 .... 22 E1
Makinson La BL6. .... 22 F4
Makin St M1. .... 163 A3
Makkah Cl M40 .... 83 A5
Malaga Ave M90 .... 130 B7
Malakoff St SK15 .... 85 E1
Malbern Ind Est M43 ... 100 C4
Malbrook Wlk 3 M13 .. 163 C2
Malby St OL1 .... 153 C4
Malcolm Ave M27 .... 62 A3
Malcolm Dr M27 .... 62 A2
Malcolm St OL11. .... 30 D3
Malden Gr M23 .... 121 A7
Maldon Cl
 Hazel Grove SK2 .... 125 A6
 Little Lever BL3 .... 43 A3
 Wigan WN2 .... 37 F2
Maldon Cres M27 .... 79 F6
Maldon Dr M30 .... 79 E4
Maldon Rd WN6 .... 36 F8
Maldon St OL11. .... 139 C1
Maldwyn Ave
 Bolton BL3. .... 146 C2
 Manchester M8 .... 64 A2
Malgam Dr M20. .... 122 B8
Malham Ave WN3 .... 55 A2
Malham Cl
 Leigh WN7 .... 75 C5
 Royton OL2 .... 48 D4
Malham Ct SK2. .... 124 D6
Malham Dr M45. .... 63 A8
Malham Gdns 4 BL3. .. 146 C3
Malika Pl WN4 .... 72 E6
Malmison Bourne M7 .. 155 A2
Mallaig Wlk M11. .... 165 C4
Mallard Cl
 Dukinfield SK16 .... 101 E7
 Hazel Grove SK8 .... 122 A5
 8 Oldham OL8 .... 66 D2
Mallard Cres SK12 .... 133 A4
Mallard Ct SK8 .... 131 B8
Mallard Dr BL6 .... 22 A3
Mallard Gn WA14 .... 119 B8
Mallards Reach SK6. ... 112 A3
Mallard St M1. .... 163 A3
Mallet Cres BL1. .... 23 F2
Malley Gdns 1 OL5. ... 86 D8
Malley Wlk 18 M9. .... 64 E3
Malling Rd M23. .... 121 A4
Mallison St BL1. .... 143 C3
Mallory Ave OL7. .... 85 B5
Mallory Ct WA14 .... 119 C3
Mallory Dr WN7. .... 76 C5
Mallory Rd SK14 .... 102 A4
Mallory Wlk M23. .... 120 D8
Mallow Croft OL16. .... 31 C4
Mallowdale M28 .... 78 B8
Mallowdale Ave 1 M14 .. 110 B8
Mallowdale Cl BL1. .... 40 D7
Mallowdale Rd SK2 ... 124 E5
Mallow Wlk M31 .... 105 F2
Mall The
 Bury BL9 .... 140 C2
 5 Eccles M30 .... 79 F2
 6 Hyde SK14 .... 167 A2
 Sale M33 .... 108 B5
 4 Sale M33 .... 108 B5
 Stalybridge SK15. .... 102 E6
Malmesbury Cl SK12 ... 133 D4
Malmesbury Rd SK8. .. 132 B6
Malpas Ave WN1. .... 37 E1
Malpas Cl
 Cheadle SK8 .... 123 A4
 Handforth SK9 .... 131 E1
Malpas Dr WA14 .... 107 E1
Malpas St
 Manchester M12 .... 165 A2
 Oldham OL1. .... 153 C3
Malpas Wlk M16 .... 162 A1
Malrae WA15 .... 119 E1
Malsham Rd M23 .... 108 F2
Malta Cl M24 .... 65 D8
Malta St
 Manchester M4 .... 160 A1
 Oldham OL4. .... 67 D6
Maltby Ct OL4 .... 67 F5
Maltby Dr BL3 .... 146 C3
Maltby Rd M23 .... 120 F6
Maltings La 7 OL11. ... 30 C2
Malton Ave
 Bolton BL3. .... 146 A4
 Golborne WA3 .... 90 E7
 Manchester M21 .... 109 B8
 Whitefield M45 .... 44 F8
Malton Cl
 Chadderton OL9. .... 47 F1
 Leigh WN7 .... 75 C5
 1 Whitefield M45 .... 44 F8
Malton Dr
 Altrincham WA14 .... 119 A4
 Hazel Grove SK7 .... 133 D7
Malton Rd
 Boothstown M28 .... 77 F7
 Stockport SK4 .... 168 A4
 Wigan WN5 .... 153 A1
Malt St M15 .... 162 D3
Malus Ct M6. .... 81 A3
Malverley Dr WN7 .... 76 C5
Malvern Ave
 Ashton-u-L OL6 .... 85 C7
 Atherton M46. .... 58 F5
 Bolton BL1. .... 142 A1
 Bury BL9 .... 84 C2
 Droylsden M43. .... 57 A4
 Urmston M41. .... 95 B2
 Wythenshawe SK8. ... 121 F5

Malvern Cl
Ashton-in-M WN4 ..... 73 B4
[2] Farnworth BL4 ..... 59 F8
Horwich BL6 ..... 22 C5
Milnrow OL16 ..... 32 A7
Pendlebury M27 ..... 80 D6
Prestwich M25 ..... 63 C5
Royton OL2 ..... 48 C3
[5] Shaw OL2 ..... 48 F8
Stockport SK4 ..... 169 A3
Wigan WN3 ..... 54 C3
Malvern Cres WN3 ..... 55 F4
Malvern Dr
Altrincham WA14 ..... 119 B5
Pendlebury M27 ..... 80 D6
Malvern Gr
Manchester M20 ..... 110 A6
Manchester M6 ..... 80 C3
Walkden M28 ..... 60 D3
Malvern Rd M24 ..... 65 A5
Malvern Rise SK13 ..... 104 A5
Malvern Row [1] M15 ..... 162 A2
Malvern St
Manchester M15 ..... 162 A2
Oldham OL8 ..... 153 A1
Malvern Street E OL11 ..... 30 C7
Malvern Street W OL11 ..... 30 C7
Malvern Terr WN7 ..... 75 F3
Malvern Way BB4 ..... 1 A7
Manby Rd M18 ..... 99 B4
Manby Sq M18 ..... 99 B4
Mancentral Trad Est M3 158 A1
MANCHESTER. 159 B3
Manchester Acad M15 .. 98 B4
Manchester Airport M90 130 A7
Manchester Airport Sta
M90 ..... 130 B7
Manchester Aquatics Ctr
M13 ..... 163 B2
Manchester Arndale Sh Ctr
M4 ..... 159 A2
Manchester Art Gall★ [1]
M1 ..... 159 A1
Manchester Bsns Pk
M22 ..... 130 D8
Manchester Bsns Sch
M15 ..... 163 A2
Manchester Central
Convention Complex M2,
M3 ..... 162 C4
Manchester Central School
of English M2 ..... 159 A1
Manchester Chambers
OL1 ..... 153 B3
Manchester Coll The
(Abraham Moss Campus)
M8 ..... 156 B4
Manchester Coll The
(Fielden Campus) M20. 109 F4
Manchester Coll The
(Malcolm Ho & Fernside)
M40 ..... 83 E4
Manchester Coll The
(Moston Campus) M9 .. 157 C4
Manchester Coll The
(Nicholls Campus)
M12 ..... 164 A3
Manchester Coll The
(Northenden Campus)
M23 ..... 109 C1
Manchester Coll The (North
Manchester Sixth Form)
M9 ..... 157 B4
Manchester Coll The (One
Central Park) M40 ..... 157 C2
Manchester Coll The
(Openshaw Campus)
M11 ..... 165 B3
Manchester Coll The
(Preston St) M18 ..... 165 C2
Manchester Coll The (Shena
Simon Campus) M1 ... 163 A4
Manchester Coll The (St
John's Ctr) M3 ..... 158 B1
Manchester Coll The (St
Matthew's Ctr) M40 ... 65 C1
Manchester Coll The (The
Ctr for Music) M1 ..... 159 B2
Manchester Coll The (The
Manchester Sch of
Building) M1 ..... 165 C2
Manchester Coll The
(Wythenshawe Campus) [1]
M22 ..... 121 D4
Manchester Creative &
Media Acad for Boys
M9 ..... 65 B3
Manchester Creative &
Media Acad for Girls
M40 ..... 65 A1
Manchester Enterprise Acad
M22 ..... 121 C3
Manchester Evening News
Arena★ M3 ..... 158 C3
Manchester Fort Sh Pk
M8 ..... 156 B1
Manchester Gram Sch The
M13 ..... 98 E2
Manchester Health Acad
M23 ..... 120 E7
Manchester High Sch for
Girls M14 ..... 98 C3
Manchester Ind Ctr M3 162 A4
Manchester Ind Pk M40 157 C1
Manchester Islamic High Sch
for Girls [11] M21 ..... 109 A8

Manchester Jewish Mus★
M8 ..... 159 A4
Manchester Jun Girls Sch
M7 ..... 63 E1
Manchester Mesivta Sch
M25 ..... 63 B3
Manchester Met Univ (All
Saints Campus) M1, M13,
M15 ..... 163 A3
Manchester Met Univ
(Aytoun Campus) M1 .. 163 B4
Manchester Met Univ
(Didsbury Campus)
M20 ..... 110 B2
Manchester Met Univ
(Elizabeth Gaskell Campus)
M13 ..... 98 C4
Manchester Met Univ
(Hollings Campus) M14. 98 D2
Manchester Museum The★
M13 ..... 163 B2
Manchester Muslim Prep Sch
M20 ..... 110 B6
Manchester National Squash
Ctr M11 ..... 160 C2
Manchester New Rd
Middleton M24, M9 ..... 64 F6
Partington M31 ..... 105 F3
Manchester Old Rd
Bury BL9 ..... 140 B1
Middleton M24 ..... 64 E4
Manchester Oxford Road Sta
M1 ..... 163 A3
Manchester Rd
Altrincham WA14 ..... 119 D7
Ashton-u-L M34, M43, OL7 . 84 F1
Bolton BL3 ..... 42 B4
Bury BL9 ..... 140 B1
Bury, Blackford Bridge BL9,
M45 ..... 44 F5
Carrington M31 ..... 106 B6
Cheadle M20, SK8 ..... 122 D7
Denton M34 ..... 100 E3
Droylsden M34 ..... 100 B8
Dukinfield SK14 ..... 101 C3
Glossop SK13, SK14 ..... 103 E7
Handforth SK9 ..... 131 C2
Haslingden BB4 ..... 1 D7
Heywood OL10 ..... 46 D7
Hollinfare, Hollins Green
WA3 ..... 105 B3
Hollinfare WA3 ..... 105 A2
Ince-in-M WN2, WN1, .. 56 A7
Kearsley BL4, M27 ..... 61 D4
Leigh WN7, WN7 ..... 76 D4
Manchester M16, M21, .. 97 B1
Manchester M21 ..... 109 A8
Mossley OL3, OL5, SK15 .. 68 D3
Oldham OL8 ..... 66 F5
Pendlebury M27 ..... 80 B7
Ramsbottom BL0, BL9 ... 11 E4
Reddish M34 ..... 100 B4
Rochdale OL11 ..... 30 C4
Scot Lane End BL6 ..... 38 E8
Shaw OL2 ..... 149 A1
Stockport SK4 ..... 169 B4
Swinton M27, M28 ..... 61 C2
Tyldesley M29 ..... 77 C8
Walkden M28 ..... 60 E2
Westhoughton BL5 ..... 40 B1
Manchester Regional
Athletics Arena M11 ... 160 C2
Manchester Regional
Gymnastics Ctr M18 .. 165 C1
Manchester Regional Hockey
Ctr M12 ..... 165 B1
Manchester Regional Tennis
Ctr M11 ..... 160 C2
Manchester Road E M38. 60 B4
Manchester Road Prim Sch
M43 ..... 83 E1
Manchester Road S M34 100 E3
Manchester Road W M38. 59 E5
Manchester Royal Infmy
M13 ..... 163 C1
Manchester Science Pk
M15 ..... 163 A1
Manchester St
Heywood OL10 ..... 29 E1
Manchester M16 ..... 161 C1
Oldham OL8, OL9 ..... 153 A2
Manchester Technology Ctr
M1 ..... 163 A2
Manchester United Mus★
M32 ..... 96 F5
Manchester Velodrome★
M11 ..... 83 A2
Manchester Victoria Sta
M3 ..... 159 A3
Mancroft Ave BL3 ..... 147 A4
Mancroft Terr BL3 ..... 147 A4
Mancroft Wlk [1] M11 .. 163 B3
Mancunian Rd M34 ..... 113 A8
Mancunian Way
Manchester M1, M12,
M15 ..... 163 B3
Manchester, St George's
M15 ..... 162 A3
Mandalay Gdns SK6 ..... 125 D7
Mandarin Gn [3] M41 .. 95 B4
Mandarin Wlk [3] M6 ... 81 A3
Mandeville Cl WN5 ..... 54 D2
Mandeville St M19 ..... 111 B8
Mandeville Terr BL8 ..... 10 B2
Mandley Ave M40 ..... 65 D2

Mandley Cl BL3 ..... 43 A5
Mandley Park Ave M7 . 155 B3
Mandon Cl M26 ..... 43 E5
Manesty Cl M24 ..... 46 C2
Manet Cl M7 ..... 81 B8
Mangle St M1 ..... 159 B1
Mango Pl M6 ..... 81 A2
Manifold Dr SK6 ..... 134 F6
Manifold St M6 ..... 81 B5
Manilla Wlk [1] M11 ... 160 C1
Manipur St M11 ..... 164 C4
Manley Ave
Golborne WA3 ..... 73 F2
Swinton M27 ..... 61 E4
Manley Cl
Leigh WN7 ..... 75 D8
Ramsbottom BL9 ..... 11 C2
Manley Cres BL5 ..... 40 B1
Manley Gr
Bramhall SK7 ..... 132 E6
Mottram in L SK14 ..... 102 F3
Manley Park Prim Sch
M16 ..... 97 C2
Manley Rd
Manchester M16, M21, .. 97 D1
Oldham OL8 ..... 66 E4
Rochdale OL11 ..... 30 C3
Sale M33 ..... 107 F1
Manley St
Ince-in-M WN3 ..... 151 B2
Salford M7 ..... 155 A2
Manley Terr BL1 ..... 143 B4
Manley Way SK14 ..... 103 A3
Manning Ave WN6 ..... 37 A2
Manningford Ct WN3 .. 151 B1
Manningham Rd BL3 .. 144 B1
Mannington Dr M9 ..... 156 C3
Mannion Ho WN1 ..... 151 A4
Mannock St OL8 ..... 153 A2
Manns Cl OL3 ..... 68 F5
Manns The OL3 ..... 68 F5
Manor Ave
Golborne WA3 ..... 90 C8
Little Lever BL3 ..... 43 C3
Manchester M16 ..... 97 D2
Sale M33 ..... 107 D4
Urmston M41 ..... 95 D1
Manor Cl
Bramhall SK8 ..... 123 C1
Chadderton OL9 ..... 152 C4
Denton M34 ..... 101 B2
Garswood WN4 ..... 72 C3
Uppermill OL4 ..... 68 E5
Wilmslow SK9 ..... 136 F8
Manor Ct
Bury BL9 ..... 27 E7
Golborne WA3 ..... 90 C8
Sale M33 ..... 107 D4
[5] Stockport SK1 ..... 112 A1
Stretford M32 ..... 96 B1
Manordale Wlk M40 ... 156 C2
Manor Dr
Manchester M21 ..... 109 D4
Royton OL2 ..... 48 E3
Manor Farm Cl OL7 ... 84 F5
Manor Farm Rise OL4 .. 67 D7
Manorfield Cl M41 ..... 95 B4
Manor Gate Rd BL2 ... 43 A8
Manor Gdns SK9 ..... 137 D7
Manor Gr
Aspull WN2 ..... 38 B5
Leigh WN7 ..... 76 C3
Wigan WN5 ..... 54 B8
Manor Green Prim Sch [17]
M34 ..... 113 A8
Manor High Sch M33 .. 107 D5
Manor Hill Rd SK6 ..... 125 F7
Manor Ho SK9 ..... 136 D3
Manor House CW WA11 .. 71 B1
Manorial Dr M38 ..... 59 E5
Manor La OL3 ..... 51 E8
Manor Lo
Bramhall SK8 ..... 123 C1
Pendlebury M27 ..... 80 D8
Manor Mill Cl OL12 ..... 15 D3
Manor Park Rd SK13 .. 104 E1
Manor Park View SK13 . 104 E2
Manor Pk M45 ..... 95 D1
Manor Pl WN3 ..... 151 C2
Manor Rd
Altrincham WA15 ..... 119 E4
Bramhall SK7, SK8 ..... 123 C1
Brinnington SK5 ..... 112 C4
Denton M34 ..... 101 B1
Droylsden, Fairfield M34 . 100 B7
Droylsden, Greenside M43 . 83 F1
Dukinfield SK14 ..... 101 F5
Hindley WN2 ..... 56 F5
Horwich BL6 ..... 22 D4
Manchester M19 ..... 99 B2
Marple SK6 ..... 125 F7
Middleton M24 ..... 65 A6
Oldham OL4 ..... 67 C4
Romiley SK6 ..... 113 B5
Sale M33 ..... 108 B5
Salford M6 ..... 154 A4
Shaw OL2 ..... 149 B7
Shevington WN6 ..... 36 A6
Stretford M32 ..... 96 B2
Swinton M27 ..... 79 F6
Tyldesley M29 ..... 77 C6
Wilmslow SK9 ..... 136 E8
Manor St
Bolton BL1 ..... 145 C3
Bury BL9 ..... 141 A2
Denton M34 ..... 100 F7
Farnworth BL4 ..... 60 C7
Glossop SK13 ..... 104 D1

Manor St continued
Golborne WA3 ..... 74 B1
Kearsley BL4 ..... 61 B5
Manchester M12 ..... 163 C3
Middleton M24 ..... 47 A2
Mossley OL5 ..... 68 C2
Oldham OL2 ..... 49 A2
Ramsbottom BL0 ..... 138 B3
Wigan WN1 ..... 150 C4
Wigan, Worsley Hall WN5 . 54 F6
Manor View SK6 ..... 125 F5
Manor Way PR7 ..... 19 D8
Manor Wlk M14 ..... 100 F7
Mansart Cl WN4 ..... 73 D3
Manse Ave WN6 ..... 18 F5
Manse Gdns WA12 ..... 89 D4
Mansell Way BL6 ..... 39 D8
Manse The OL5 ..... 86 C8
Mansfield Ave
Denton M34 ..... 100 D5
Manchester M9 ..... 64 D4
Ramsbottom BL0 ..... 11 B2
Mansfield Cl
Ashton-u-L OL7 ..... 84 F1
Denton M34 ..... 100 D5
Mansfield Cres M34 ... 100 D4
Mansfield Dr M9 ..... 64 E4
Mansfield Gr BL1 ..... 142 B1
Mansfield Grange OL11 . 30 C6
Mansfield Rd
Hyde SK14 ..... 167 C1
Manchester M9 ..... 64 E4
Mossley OL5 ..... 68 E1
[7] Oldham OL8 ..... 67 B5
Rochdale OL11 ..... 29 E7
Urmston M41 ..... 95 B1
Mansfield St
Ashton-u-L OL7 ..... 84 F1
Golborne WA3 ..... 73 F1
Mansfield View OL5 ..... 68 E1
Mansford Dr M40 ..... 157 C1
Manshaw Cres M34 ... 100 A7
Manshaw Rd M11, M34 . 100 A7
Mansion Ave M45 ..... 44 E3
Mansion The WA3 ..... 91 D3
Manson Ave M15 ..... 162 A3
Manstead Wlk M40 ... 160 B2
Manston Dr SK8 ..... 123 A2
Manswood Dr M8 ..... 156 A3
Mantell Wlk M40 ..... 83 A5
Manthorpe Ave M20 .. 79 A7
Mantley La OL3 ..... 50 A7
Manton Ave
Manchester M9 ..... 65 B2
Reddish M34 ..... 100 A3
Manton Cl M7 ..... 155 C2
Manvers St SK5 ..... 169 B3
Manwaring St M35 ..... 83 E8
Manway Bsns Pk WA14 . 119 E8
Maple Ave
Altrincham WA15 ..... 120 E5
Atherton M46 ..... 58 B4
Bolton BL1 ..... 142 B1
Bury BL9 ..... 141 B2
Cheadle SK8 ..... 122 F2
Droylsden M34 ..... 84 B1
Eccles M30 ..... 95 D8
Golborne WA3 ..... 90 F7
Hindley WN2 ..... 56 F3
Ince-in-M WN2 ..... 151 C2
Manchester M21 ..... 109 B8
Marple SK6 ..... 125 F4
Newton-le-W WA12 ..... 89 D2
Poynton SK12 ..... 133 F3
Stalybridge SK15 ..... 101 F8
Stretford M32 ..... 96 D1
Whitefield M45 ..... 62 F6
Maple Cl
Billinge WN5 ..... 71 D5
Chadderton OL9 ..... 48 B1
Kearsley BL4 ..... 60 F8
Middleton M24 ..... 65 D8
Sale M33 ..... 107 C4
Salford M6 ..... 154 C3
Shaw OL2 ..... 48 F8
Stockport SK2 ..... 124 B6
Maple Cres WN7 ..... 75 F7
Maplecroft SK1 ..... 124 B8
Maple Ct SK4 ..... 168 C4
Mapledon Rd M9 ..... 157 C4
Maple Dr WN2 ..... 74 B7
Maplefield Dr M28 ..... 78 B7
Maple Gr
Bury BL8 ..... 27 A5
Failsworth, Holt Lane End
M35 ..... 83 E5
Failsworth, New Moston
M40 ..... 65 F2
Prestwich M25 ..... 63 A6
Ramsbottom BL0 ..... 11 D6
Walkden M28 ..... 78 D8
Wigan WN6 ..... 37 A3
Maple Lo M23 ..... 120 C8
Maple Rd
Alderley Edge SK9 ..... 137 B3
Bramhall SK7, SK8 ..... 132 E6
Chadderton OL9 ..... 48 B1
Farnworth BL4 ..... 60 A8
Partington M31 ..... 105 E3
Sale M23 ..... 108 C1
Swinton M27 ..... 79 E6
Maple St
Ashton-in-M WN4 ..... 73 A6
Bolton BL3 ..... 145 A1

Maple St continued
Bolton, Bradshaw BL2 ... 25 C5
Oldham OL8 ..... 66 C3
Rochdale OL11 ..... 139 A2
Walsden OL14 ..... 6 A7
Maple Wlk BL3 ..... 42 E5
Maplewood Cl
[3] Manchester M9 ..... 64 C2
Royton OL2 ..... 48 C2
Maplewood Ct M7 ..... 155 A3
Maplewood Gdns BL1 . 143 C2
Maplewood Gr SK15 ... 86 C3
Maplewood Ho BL1 ... 143 B1
Maplewood Rd SK9 ... 137 E8
Maplin Cl M13 ..... 163 C3
Maplin Dr SK2 ..... 125 A5
Maranatha Ct [8] M30 .. 95 D8
Marble St
Manchester M2 ..... 159 A1
Oldham OL1 ..... 67 B8
Marbury Ave M14 ..... 98 B1
Marbury Cl
Cheadle SK3 ..... 123 A7
Urmston M41 ..... 94 D3
Marbury Dr WA14 ..... 107 E1
Marbury Gr WN6 ..... 36 E8
Marbury Rd
Handforth SK9 ..... 131 B1
Reddish SK4 ..... 111 D7
Marcer Rd M40 ..... 160 A2
March Ave SK4 ..... 168 B2
Marchbank WN3 ..... 38 A2
Marchbank Dr SK8 .... 122 C6
March Dr BL8 ..... 27 D5
Marchers Mews [7] M30 79 B1
Marches Cl OL2 ..... 49 B4
Marchmont Cl [8] M18 . 99 F6
Marchwood Ave M21 .. 97 D1
Marcliffe Dr
Reddish M19 ..... 99 C1
Rochdale OL11 ..... 30 B6
Marcliffe Ind Est SK7 .. 124 E1
Marcliff Gr SK4 ..... 168 B2
Marcroft Pl [6] OL11 .... 31 A4
Marcus Garvey Ct M16 . 97 E2
Marcus Gr M14 ..... 98 C3
Marcus St BL1 ..... 142 B1
Mardale Ave
Manchester M20 ..... 110 C5
Royton OL2 ..... 48 C8
Swinton M27 ..... 61 C2
Urmston M41 ..... 94 F3
Mardale Cl
Atherton M46 ..... 58 C5
Bolton BL2 ..... 25 F1
[8] Oldham OL4 ..... 67 D8
Prestwich M25 ..... 63 C7
Stalybridge SK15 ..... 86 A3
Mardale Dr
[1] Bolton BL2 ..... 25 F1
Gatley SK8 ..... 122 B6
Mardale Rd M27 ..... 79 D6
Marden Rd M23 ..... 121 A5
Mardyke OL12 ..... 139 B4
Maretgate Sh Ctr WN3 . 150 A4
Marfield Ave OL9 ..... 152 A1
Marford Cl M22 ..... 121 D6
Marford Cres M33 ..... 107 F2
Margaret Ashton Cl M9 . 157 C3
Margaret Ave
Rochdale OL16 ..... 31 C7
Wigan WN6 ..... 36 C4
Margaret Ho [5] OL6 ... 166 A2
Margaret Rd
Denton M34 ..... 101 A4
Droylsden M43 ..... 83 E2
Margaret Sands St [9]
M15 ..... 162 A2
Margaret St
Ashton-u-L OL7 ..... 166 A1
[1] Bury BL9 ..... 140 C1
Heywood OL10 ..... 29 B2
Hindley WN2 ..... 56 D6
Oldham OL8 ..... 66 B2
Reddish SK5 ..... 111 E7
Shaw OL2 ..... 149 B2
Wigan WN6 ..... 37 A1
Margaret Terr OL6 ..... 166 A2
Margate Ave M40 ..... 83 B5
Margate Rd SK5 ..... 111 F7
Margrove Chase BL6 ... 40 C5
Margrove Cl M35 ..... 84 C7
Margrove Rd M6 ..... 80 A4
Margrove Cl OL12 ..... 15 A2
Margueritta Rd M40 ... 83 D4
Marham Cl M21 ..... 109 E6
Maria St BL1 ..... 143 B2
Marie Cl M34 ..... 100 F2
Marie St M7 ..... 155 B3
Marigold St
Rochdale OL11 ..... 139 C1
Wigan WN5 ..... 54 D7
Marigold Terr M24 ..... 65 D7
Mariman Dr M8 ..... 64 A2
Marina Ave M34 ..... 101 A1
Marina Cl SK9 ..... 131 D5
Marina Cres M11 ..... 83 B3
Marina Dr
Marple SK6 ..... 125 C7
Wigan WN5 ..... 54 D5
Marina Rd
Droylsden M43 ..... 84 B2

Marina Rd *continued*
Romiley SK6 112 E4
Marine Ave M31 105 D3
Mariners Way M44 105 F8
Marion Pl WN2 73 F8
Marion St
Farnworth BL3 42 C2
Oldham OL8 66 F3
Maritime Cl WA12 89 C5
Maritime Ct 5 M33 107 F4
Marjorie Cl M18 165 B2
Mark Ave M6 81 B4
Markenfield Dr OL2 48 F7
Market App 3 WN4 73 B3
Market Arc 2 SK13 104 C1
Market Ave OL6 166 B3
Market Chambers BL0 138 C3
Market Par BL9 140 C2
Market Pl
Adlington PR7 21 A7
Ashton-u-L OL6 166 B3
13 Atherton M46 58 D3
Bury BL9 140 B2
Compstall SK6 114 A2
Edenfield BL0 1 D3
Farnworth BL4 60 D8
Heywood OL10 29 D2
Hyde SK14 167 A2
Leigh WN7 75 F5
Middleton M24 47 A1
Mottram in L SK14 103 A3
Oldham OL1 153 B3
Ramsbottom BL0 138 C3
11 Royton OL2 48 E4
Standish WN6 19 E1
Stockport SK1 169 C2
Wigan WN1 150 C4
Market Pl Sh Ctr BL1 145 C4
Market Prec BL4 60 D8
Market Sq OL2 48 D4
Market St
Adlington PR7 21 A6
Altrincham WA14 119 D4
Ashton-u-L OL6 166 B3
Atherton M46 58 C3
Bolton BL1 145 C3
Broadbottom SK14 115 A8
Bury BL9 140 C1
Bury, Gigg BL9 44 F8
Bury, Tottington BL8 26 F6
Denton M34 100 F3
Disley SK12 135 D6
Droylsden M43 84 B1
Edenfield BL0 1 D4
Farnworth BL4 42 D1
Glossop SK13 104 C1
Heywood OL10 29 C2
Hindley WN2 56 D5
Hollingworth SK14 103 D5
Hyde SK14 167 A2
Kearsley M26 61 B8
Leigh WN7 75 F5
Little Lever BL3 43 B3
Manchester M1 159 A1
Manchester M4 158 C2
Marple SK6 125 F6
5 Middleton M24 46 F1
Mossley OL5 68 C1
Mottram in L SK14 103 A4
Newton-le-W WA12 89 A3
11 Rawtenstall BB4 2 E8
Rochdale OL12 4 E7
Shaw OL2 149 B2
Stalybridge SK15 86 A2
Standish WN6 19 E1
Swinton M27 62 A1
Tyldesley M29 58 F1
Westhoughton BL5 57 E8
Whitworth OL12, OL13 4 D4
Wigan WN1 150 C4
Market Street Metro Sta
M1 159 A1
Market Way
Rochdale OL16 139 C4
Salford M6 154 C3
Market Wlk 3 M33 108 B4
Markfield Ave M13 164 A1
Markham Cl
Dukinfield SK14 101 D6
Manchester M12 164 B4
Markham St SK14 101 D5
Markington St M14 98 A3
Mark Jones Wlk M40 83 B5
Mark La OL2 49 D6
Markland Ct WN6 150 A4
MARKLAND HILL 40 E8
Markland Hill BL1 40 E8
Markland Hill Cl BL1 23 F1
Markland Hill La BL1 23 F1
Markland Hill Prim Sch
BL1 23 A8
Marklands Rd
Horwich BL6 22 E5
Tyldesley M29 77 A4
Markland St
6 Bolton BL3 145 C2
Hyde SK14 167 B1
Ramsbottom BL0 138 C2
Wigan WN1 151 B4
Markland Tops BL1 23 F1
Marks St M26 44 A3
Mark St
Bacup OL13 3 C8
Boothstown M28 77 F7
Oldham OL9 153 A3
Mark St *continued*
Rochdale OL12 15 B1
Mark Wood Rd OL3 50 F4
MARLAND 30 A4
Marland Ave
Cheadle SK8 122 F2
Oldham OL8 67 A1
Rochdale OL11 30 B4
Marland Cl OL11 30 B5
Marland Cres SK5 111 F8
Marland Fold OL11 30 B5
Marland Fold La OL8 66 F1
Marland Gn OL11 30 B4
Marland Hill Prim Sch
OL11 30 C5
Marland Hill Rd OL11 30 C4
Marland Old Rd OL11 30 B4
Marlands Sq 15 M29 58 F1
Marland St OL9 66 A3
Marland Way M32 96 D3
Marlborough Ave
Alderley Edge SK9 137 B2
Cheadle SK8 123 B2
Ince-in-M WN3 55 F4
Manchester M16 97 C2
Marlborough Cl
Ashton-u-L OL7 100 E8
Denton M34 100 F3
Marple SK6 125 D7
Ramsbottom BL0 11 C3
Whitworth OL12 14 C7
Marlborough Ct BL1 23 E2
Marlborough Dr
Failsworth M35 83 E6
Reddish SK4 169 A4
Marlborough Gdns 3 BL4 59 F8
Marlborough Gr M43 84 C2
Marlborough Rd
Altrincham WA14 119 D2
Atherton M46 58 F4
Hyde SK14 113 E8
Irlam M44 94 B3
Royton OL2 48 E2
Sale M33 108 B4
Salford, Ellesmere Park
M30 80 A4
Salford, Higher Broughton
M7 155 C3
Salford M7, M8 155 C2
Stretford M32 96 C3
Urmston M41 94 F2
Marlborough Road Prim Sch
M7 155 C2
Marlborough St
5 Ashton-u-L OL7 84 F1
Bolton BL1 145 A4
Heywood OL10 46 E8
Oldham OL4 67 A6
14 Rochdale OL12 14 C1
Marlbrook Dr BL5 57 E5
Marlbrook Wlk BL3 147 C4
Marlcroft Ave SK4 168 B2
Marlcroft Cl M23 121 A7
Marld Cres BL1 23 F2
Marle Ave OL5 68 E1
Marle Croft M45 62 C6
Marled Hey BL7 9 D5
Marle Rise OL5 68 E1
Marler Rd SK14 167 B4
Marley Cl WA15 119 F7
Marley Dr M33 108 A6
Marleyer Cl M40 83 C7
Marleyer Rise SK6 125 A8
Marley Rd
Manchester M19 111 B8
Poynton SK12 133 E2
Marlfield Ave WA13 117 A2
Marlfield Ct M41 94 E1
Marlfield Rd
Altrincham WA15 129 D7
Shaw OL2 48 E8
Marlfield St M9 64 E1
Marl Gr WN5 53 D4
Marlhill Cl SK2 124 E5
Marlhill Ct SK2 124 E5
Marlinford Dr M40 83 C5
Marloes WA14 119 B2
Marlor Ct OL10 29 B2
Marlor St M34 100 E4
Marlow Brow SK13 104 A4
Marlow Cl
2 Bolton BL2 25 F1
Cheadle SK8 122 F2
Marlow Ct PR7 20 F6
Marlow Dr
Altrincham WA14 118 F2
Handforth SK9 131 C5
Irlam M44 94 A3
Swinton M27 79 E6
Marlowe Cl WN3 150 A1
Marlowe Dr M20 110 B4
Marlowe Wlk 15 M34 113 A7
Marlowe Wlks SK6 112 F2
Marlow Ho 9 M5 154 C1
Marlow Rd M9 64 F1
Marlow St 5 SK13 104 A5
Marlton Wlk M9 64 E4
Marlwood Rd BL1 23 F2
Marlwood Way OL2 48 C2
Marmion Cl WA3 74 E1
Marmion Dr M21 109 A8
Marne Ave
Ashton-u-L OL6 85 F5
Wythenshawe M22 121 E5
Marne Cres OL11 30 C7
Marnland Gr BL3 40 E4
Marnock Cl WN2 74 F8
Maroon Rd M22 130 F7
MARPLE 125 D5
Marple Ave BL1 25 A4
MARPLE BRIDGE 126 B8
Marple Cl
Oldham OL8 66 D2
Shevington Moor WN6 19 B2
Marple Ct SK1 124 A7
Marple Gr M32 96 C3
Marple Hall Dr SK6 125 D7
Marple Hall Sch SK6 125 C7
Marple Old Rd SK2 125 A6
Marple Rd
Broadbottom SK13 115 B5
Stockport SK2 124 E6
MARPLERIDGE 126 A2
Marple St M15 162 A1
Marple Sta SK6 126 A7
Marquis Ave BL9 140 B4
Marquis Dr SK8 131 D7
Marquis St M19 99 D1
Marrick Ave SK8 122 C5
Marrick Cl WN3 55 A2
Marriott St
Manchester M20 110 B6
Stockport SK1 170 C4
Marron Pl M2 162 C4
Marryat Ct M12 164 C2
Mars Ave BL3 146 C3
Marsden Cl
Ashton-u-L OL7 84 E5
Mossley OL5 68 B1
Royton OL16 48 C8
Marsden Dr WA15 120 C6
Marsden Rd
Bolton BL1 145 B3
Romiley SK6 113 C3
Marsden St
Boothstown M28 77 F6
Bury BL9 140 C3
Eccles M30 79 C3
Glossop SK13 104 A4
Ince-in-M WN3 55 F4
10 Manchester M2 158 C1
2 Middleton M24 65 C7
Walkden M28 61 B2
Westhoughton BL5 57 E8
Wigan WN1 150 C4
Wigan, Worsley Hall WN5 54 F6
Marsett Cl OL12 14 A1
Marsett Wlk 9 M23 108 F2
Marshall Ct
6 Ashton-u-L OL6 85 D2
1 Oldham OL1 153 B4
Marshall Rd M19 99 A1
Marshall St
Leigh WN7 75 E4
Manchester, Brunswick
M12 163 C2
Manchester M4 159 B2
Rochdale OL16 31 C7
Marshall Stevens Way
M17 96 B5
Marsham Cl
7 Manchester M13 98 E4
Oldham OL4 68 B5
Marsham Dr SK6 126 A5
Marsham Rd
Hazel Grove SK7 124 C1
Westhoughton BL5 57 F6
Marshbank 16 BL5 39 E1
Marshbrook Cl WN2 57 A6
Marsh Brook Cl WA3 105 A2
Marshbrook Dr M9 64 C2
Marsh Brook Fold BL5 57 A7
Marshbrook Rd 1 M41 95 C3
Marsh Cl SK3 170 A2
Marshdale WN7 75 D6
Marshdale Rd BL1 40 F8
Marshfield Rd WA15 120 C6
Marshfield St 10 M13 163 C2
Marsh Fold La BL1 144 C4
Marsh Gn WN5 36 D1
MARSH GREEN 36 D1
Marsh Green Cty Prim Sch
WN5 36 D1
Marsh Hey Cl M38 59 F6
Marsh La
Ashley WA16 128 A4
Farnworth BL4 60 A8
Little Lever BL3 43 B4
Wigan WN1 150 C4
Marsh Rd
Little Lever BL3 43 B4
Walkden M38 60 B4
Marsh Row WN2 57 A4
Marsh St
11 Bolton BL1 143 B2
Bolton BL5 39 E1
Horwich BL6 22 A4
Walkden M28 60 F2
Westhoughton BL5 39 E1
Marshway Dr WA12 89 B5
Marsland Ave WA15 120 B8
Marsland Cl M34 100 B3
Marsland Green La M29 76 E3
Marsland Rd
Altrincham WA15 120 B6
Marple SK6 125 D7
Sale M33 108 B3
Marslands OL3 51 B3
Marsland St
Hazel Grove SK7 124 D2
Stockport SK1 169 C3
Marsland Street Ind Ctr
SK7 124 E2
Marsland Street N M7 155 C3
Marsland Street S M7 155 C3
Marsland Terr SK1 124 B8
Mars St
Edgworth BL7 9 E6
Oldham OL9 152 C3
Marston Cl
Failsworth M35 84 C6
Horwich BL6 39 F8
Whitefield M45 63 C8
Marston Dr M44 94 B1
Marston Ho 8 M5 154 C1
Marston Rd
Salford M7 155 B4
Stretford M32 96 F2
Marston St M40 157 A1
Martens Rd M44 105 E5
Marthall Dr M33 108 E1
Marthall Way 8 SK9 131 E5
Martham Dr SK2 125 A6
Martha St
6 Bolton BL3 147 A4
Oldham OL1 153 A4
Martha's Terr OL16 15 C3
Martin Ave
Little Lever BL3 43 C3
Newton-le-W WA12 89 C5
8 Oldham OL4 67 C6
Martin Cl
Denton M34 100 F5
Hazel Grove SK2 124 F5
Martindale Cl OL2 48 E5
Martindale Cres
Manchester M12 164 B1
Middleton M24 46 D3
Wigan WN5 54 F6
Martindale Gdns BL1 143 B2
Martindale Rd WA11 71 C2
Martin Dr M44 94 A4
Martingale Cl M26 44 A5
Martingale Ct M8 156 A3
Martingale Way M43 84 D2
Martin Gr BL4 60 F7
Martin Ho M14 98 D3
Martin La OL12 14 B1
Martin Rd M27 62 B2
Martinsclough BL6 40 C6
Martinscroft Rd M23 121 B5
Martins Ct WN2 57 A6
Martins Field OL12 13 F1
Martin St
8 Atherton M46 58 D3
Bury BL9 28 D3
Denton M34 100 F7
Edgworth BL7 9 D4
Hyde SK14 167 B2
Salford M5 154 B2
Martland Ave
Golborne WA3 90 E7
Shevington WN6 35 F5
Martland Cres WN6 36 E3
Martland Mill Bsns Pk
WN5 36 C2
Martland Mill Ind Est
WN5 36 C1
Martland Mill La WN5 36 D2
Martland Pk WN5 36 B2
Martlesham Wlk 4 M4 159 A2
Martlet Ave
Disley SK12 135 C6
Rochdale OL11 29 F7
Martlet Cl M14 98 B1
Martlew Dr M46 58 F4
Martock Ave M22 121 E3
Marton Ave
Bolton BL2 148 C4
Manchester M20 110 C2
Marton Cl WA3 91 E4
Marton Dr M46 58 E4
Marton Gn SK3 170 A1
Marton Gr SK4 111 E6
Marton Grange M25 63 E3
Marton Pl M33 108 A4
Marton St WN1 37 C1
Marton Way 5 SK9 131 E5
Marus Ave WN3 54 F3
MARUS BRIDGE 54 F2
Marus Bridge Prim Sch
WN3 54 E2
Marvic Ct M13 98 E3
Marwick Cl WN6 19 D2
Marwood Cl
Altrincham WA14 119 B6
Kearsley M26 61 A8
Marwood Dr M23 120 F3
Maryfield Cl WA3 90 A7
Mary France St M15 162 B2
Mary Hulton Ct BL5 58 A8
Maryland Ave BL2 42 D7
MARYLEBONE 37 D3
Marylebone Ct WN1 37 D3
Marylebone Pl WN1 37 D3
Marylon Dr M22 121 E8
Maryport Dr WA15 120 D7
Mary St
Cheadle SK8 122 D6
Denton M34 101 A4
Droylsden M43 84 B1
Dukinfield SK16 166 B1
Farnworth BL4 60 D7
Heywood OL10 29 C2
Hyde SK14 167 A3
Manchester M3 158 C3
Ramsbottom BL0 138 B1
Rochdale OL16 15 D4
Stockport SK1 112 A2
Tyldesley M29 77 A8
Mary Street E BL6 22 B4
Mary Street W BL6 22 A4
Masboro St M8 155 C3
Masbury Cl BL1 24 E7
Masefield Ave
Leigh WN7 75 D7
Prestwich M25 62 F3
Radcliffe M26 43 E4
Wigan WN5 54 A6
Masefield Cl SK16 102 B7
Masefield Cres 4 M43 84 A1
Masefield Dr
Farnworth BL4 60 B7
Stockport SK4 168 A2
Wigan WN3 54 F5
Masefield Gr SK5 99 E1
Masefield Prim Sch BL3 43 B4
Masefield Rd
Droylsden M43 84 A1
Little Lever BL3 43 B4
Oldham OL1 49 B2
Mason Cl WN4 73 D4
Mason Gdns BL3 145 B2
Mason La M46 58 E2
Mason Row
Bolton BL7 8 E2
Oldham OL4 50 C1
Masons Gr SK13 104 A6
Mason St
Abram WN2 74 B8
10 Ashton-u-L OL7 84 F1
Bolton BL7 8 E1
Bury BL9 141 A2
Heywood OL10 29 B2
Horwich BL6 22 B3
Manchester M4 159 B2
Rochdale OL16 139 C3
Wigan WN3 150 B3
Mason Street Ind Est
WN3 150 B3
Massey Ave
Ashton-u-L OL6 85 C6
Failsworth M35 84 B8
Massey Croft OL12 14 C8
Massey Rd
Altrincham WA15 119 E4
Sale M33 108 E4
Massey St
6 Alderley Edge SK9 137 A1
Bury BL9 141 B3
Salford M5 81 C1
Stockport SK1 169 C1
Massey Wlk M22 121 F1
Massie St SK8 122 D6
Matchmoor La BL6 23 A4
Matham Wlk M15 163 A3
Mather Ave
Eccles M30 79 E2
Golborne WA3 90 E6
Manchester M25 63 C1
Whitefield M45 44 F1
Mather Fold Rd M28 60 B1
Mather La WN7 76 A4
Mather Rd
Bury BL9 27 F7
Eccles M30 79 E2
Mather St
2 Atherton M46 58 D3
Bolton BL3 145 B2
Failsworth M35 83 E7
Farnworth BL4 60 E8
Radcliffe M26 44 A3
Mather Street Prim Sch
M35 83 D7
Mather Way 4 M6 81 A3
Matheson Dr WN5 54 E8
Matisse Way M7 81 B8
MATLEY 102 D5
Matley Cl SK14 102 B5
Matley Gn SK5 112 C6
Matley La SK14, SK15 102 D6
Matley Park La SK15 102 D6
Matlock Ave
Ashton-u-L OL6 85 F6
Denton M34 113 A8
Manchester M20 109 F6
Salford M7 81 A7
Urmston M41 107 B8
Matlock Bank 8 SK13 171 B1
Matlock Cl
Atherton M46 58 D2
Farnworth BL4 42 E1
Sale M33 108 C4
Matlock Ct BL6 22 E4
Matlock Dr SK7 133 E8
Matlock Gdns 5 SK13 171 B1
Matlock La 7 SK13 171 B1
Matlock Mews WA14 119 E5
Matlock Pl 6 SK13 171 B1
Matlock Rd
Gatley SK8 131 C7
Reddish SK5 100 A1
Stretford M32 96 A3
Matlock St M30 95 C8
Matson Wlk 3 M22 121 A2
Matt Busby Cl M27 80 B7
Matterdale Terr SK15 86 A4
Matthew Cl
Glossop SK13 103 F7
Oldham OL8 67 C4
Matthew Moss High Sch
OL11 30 B4
Matthew Moss La OL11 30 B4
Matthews Ave BL4 60 F7
Matthews La M12, M19 99 B2
Matthew's St M12 164 C3
Matthias Ct M3 158 A3
Mattison St M11 99 E7
Maudsley Cl M7 155 C2
Maudsley St BL9 140 B1
Maud St
Bolton BL2 25 C5

Maud St continued
Rochdale OL12. . . . . 15 A2
Mauldeth Cl SK4. . . . . . . 168 A3
Mauldeth Rd
Manchester, Burnage
M19. . . . . 110 F6
Manchester M14, M19,
M20. . . . . 110 D7
Stockport, Heaton Moor SK4,
M19. . . . . 168 A4
Stockport M19 & SK4 . . 110 F4
Mauldeth Road Prim Sch
M14. . . . . 110 E7
Mauldeth Road Sta M14. 110 E7
Mauldeth Road W M20,
M21. . . . . 109 D8
Maunby Gdns M38 . . . . . 60 C3
Maureen Ave M8 . . . . . . 156 A4
Maureen St OL12 . . . . . . 15 A2
Maurice Cl SK16 . . . . . . 101 E8
Maurice Dr M9 . . . . 154 C4
Maurice Pariser Wlk M8 155 C3
Maurice St M6. . . . . 154 C4
Maveen Cl SK2 . . . . 124 A4
Maveen Gr SK2. . . . . . . 124 A4
Mavis Gr OL16 . . . . 32 A6
Mavis St OL11 . . . . 30 C1
Mawdsley Dr M8. . . . . . 156 C4
Mawdsley St BL1. . . . . . 145 C3
Maxton Ho BL4 . . . . 60 E8
Maxwell Ave SK2 . . . . . . 124 C5
Maxwell St
Bolton BL1. . . . . 143 B4
Bury BL9 . . . . 141 B3
Max Woosnam Wlk 3
M14. . . . . 98 A3
Mayall St OL5. . . . . 68 C1
Mayall Street E 8 OL4 . 67 C7
Mayan Ave M3 . . . . 158 A2
May Ave
Abram Brow WN2 . . . . . . 74 C7
Cheadle SK8 . . . . 132 B6
Leigh WN7 . . . . 75 D6
Stockport SK4 . . . . 168 C2
Maybank St BL3 . . . . . . 145 A1
Maybreck Ave M8 . . . . . . 64 A2
Maybreck Cl BL3. . . . . . 144 C1
Maybrook Wlk 1 M9. . 157 A4
Mayburn Cl M24 . . . . 65 C5
Maybury St M18 . . . . 99 E6
Maycroft SK5. . . . . 112 B6
Maycroft Ave M20 . . . . 110 C5
May Ct 14 M16. . . . . 97 D3
May Dr M19 . . . . 110 F6
Mayer St SK2 . . . . 124 C7
Mayes Ct M14 . . . . 110 D7
Mayes Gdns M4. . . . . . 160 A1
Mayes St M4 . . . . 159 A2
Mayfair
Horwich BL6 . . . . 22 D3
1 Manchester M7 . . . . . 63 C1
Mayfair Ave
Radcliffe M26 . . . . 43 D4
Salford M6. . . . . 80 B3
Urmston M41. . . . . 95 B2
Whitefield M45 . . . . 62 F7
Mayfair Cl
Dukinfield SK16 . . . . . . 102 A8
Haslingden BB4 . . . . 1 A7
Poynton SK12. . . . . 133 E4
Stalybridge SK15. . . . . 101 F8
Mayfair Cotts WN1 . . . . 20 C1
Mayfair Cres M35 . . . . . 84 B8
Mayfair Ct
Altrincham WA15. . . . . 120 B7
3 Manchester, Fallowfield
M14. . . . . 110 C8
Manchester, West Didsbury
M20. . . . . 109 F3
Mayfair Dr
Atherton M46. . . . . 58 F4
Irlam M44 . . . . 94 A2
Pennington Green WN2. . 38 D2
Royton OL2 . . . . 48 D2
Sale M33 . . . . 107 E2
Wigan WN3 . . . . 54 F2
Mayfair Gdns
Rochdale OL11. . . . . . . 139 A1
Whitefield M45 . . . . 62 F7
Mayfair Gr M45 . . . . 62 F7
Mayfair Rd M22. . . . . . 121 E4
Mayfair The M20. . . . . . 110 B5
Mayfield
Bolton BL2. . . . . 25 D5
Radcliffe M26 . . . . 43 E2
Mayfield Ave
Adlington PR6 . . . . 21 A7
Bolton BL3 . . . . 42 B3
7 Denton M34. . . . . . . 113 A7
Farnworth BL4. . . . . 60 C7
Oldham OL4. . . . . 68 A7
Reddish SK5. . . . . 111 F5
Sale M33 . . . . 108 E4
Stretford M32 . . . . 96 B1
Swinton M27 . . . . 79 C6
Walkden M28. . . . . 60 D3
Mayfield Cl
Altrincham WA15. . . . . 120 B6
Ramsbottom BL0 . . . . . . 11 A2
Mayfield Ct WN5 . . . . . . 54 B8
Mayfield Dr WN7 . . . . . . 91 C8
Mayfield Gr
Manchester M18 . . . . . . 99 F3
Reddish SK5. . . . . 111 F5
Wilmslow SK9 . . . . 136 E5
Mayfield Ind Est M44 . . . 94 C3
Mayfield Mans M16 . . . . 97 E3

Mayfield Prim Sch 7 OL1 49 B1
Mayfield Rd
Altrincham WA15. . . . . 120 B6
Bramhall SK7. . . . . 132 E4
Manchester, Broughton Park
M7. . . . . 63 C1
Manchester, Whalley Range
M16. . . . . 97 E3
Marple SK6 . . . . 114 B1
Oldham OL1. . . . . 49 B1
Ramsbottom BL0 . . . . . . 11 A2
Up Holland WN8 . . . . . . 53 B7
Mayfield St
Ashton-in-M WN4 . . . . . 73 A3
Atherton M46. . . . . 58 C2
Denton M34. . . . . 100 E5
Rochdale OL16. . . . . 15 B1
Mayfield Terr OL16. . . . . 15 B1
Mayflower Ave M5 . . . . 161 B4
Mayflower Cl SK13. . . . 116 B8
Mayflower Cotts WN1 . . 37 C8
Mayford Rd M19 . . . . 99 B2
Maygate OL9 . . . . 153 A4
May Gr M19 . . . . 111 B8
Mayhill Dr
Salford M6. . . . . 80 A4
Worsley M28. . . . . 79 A8
Mayhurst Ave M21. . . . 109 D3
Maynard Rd M31 . . . . . 119 C8
Mayorlowe Ave SK5. . . 112 C4
Mayor's Rd WA15 . . . . . 119 E4
Mayor St
Bolton BL1. . . . . 145 A2
Bury BL8 . . . . 27 C3
Chadderton OL9. . . . . . 152 C3
Bolton St M12 . . . . 164 A1
May Pl 9 OL11 . . . . 31 A4
Maypole M31 . . . . 106 D6
Maypole Cres WN2. . . . . 74 C7
Maypool Dr SK5. . . . . . 111 F6
May Rd
Cheadle SK8 . . . . 132 B6
Manchester M16 . . . . . . 97 D3
Pendlebury M27. . . . . . . 80 B6
Maysmith Mews 1 M7. 155 A2
May St
Bolton BL3. . . . . 148 A3
Eccles M30 . . . . 79 C4
Edgworth BL7 . . . . 9 E6
Failsworth M40 . . . . 83 C5
Golborne WA3 . . . . 74 B2
Heywood OL10. . . . . 46 B8
Leigh WN7 . . . . 75 C5
Oldham OL8. . . . . 66 C4
Radcliffe M26 . . . . 44 A3
Mayton St M11 . . . . 165 A4
Maytree Ct M4 . . . . 20 F8
May Tree Dr WN1 . . . . . . 37 B4
Mayville Dr M20 . . . . . . 110 B5
May Wlk 2 M31 . . . . . . 105 E3
Maywood Ave M20 . . . . 122 B8
Maze St BL3 . . . . 42 D5
Meachin Ave M21 . . . . . 109 C5
Meade Cl M41 . . . . 95 C2
Meade Gr M13 . . . . 98 F3
Meade Hill Rd M25, M8 . . 63 E3
Meade Hill Sch M8 . . . . . 64 C6
Meade Manor M21 . . . . 109 B7
Meade The
Bolton BL3. . . . . 147 B2
Manchester M21 . . . . . 109 B7
Wilmslow SK9 . . . . 137 C8
Meadfoot Ave M25 . . . . . 63 C3
Meadfoot Rd M18 . . . . . . 99 D5
Meadland Gr BL1 . . . . . 143 C4
Meadow Ave
Altrincham WA15. . . . . 120 B3
Swinton M27 . . . . 62 B1
Meadow Bank OL7. . . . . 85 B6
Meadow Bank
Altrincham WA15. . . . . 120 A7
Glossop SK13. . . . . 115 F7
Hollingworth SK14. . . . 103 D6
Manchester M21 . . . . . 109 A7
Romiley SK6. . . . . 112 F5
Stockport SK4 . . . . 168 B2
Meadowbank Ave M46 . . 58 D4
Cheadle SK8 . . . . 122 F5
Meadowbank Rd BL3. . . 146 B2
Meadowbrook BL3. . . . . . 40 B3
Bury BL9 . . . . 141 C4
Meadow Brook Way SK8 123 B4
Meadow Brow SK9 . . . . . 137 C8
Meadownurn Nook M30. . 79 B4
Meadow Cl
Altrincham WA15. . . . . 120 B3
Denton M34. . . . . 113 A4
Heywood OL10. . . . . 29 C2
High Lane SK6. . . . . 134 F8
Little Lever BL3 . . . . 43 B2
Mossley OL5 . . . . 68 E3
Newton-le-W WA12. . . . . 89 A3
Romiley SK6. . . . . 113 A5
Stretford M32 . . . . 96 E1
Wilmslow SK9 . . . . 136 E4
Meadow Cotts OL12. . . . . 4 D3
Meadowcroft
Ashton-in-M WN4 . . . . . 72 F6
Mottram in L SK14. . . . 103 A4

Meadowcroft continued
Radcliffe M26 . . . . 43 F5
Westhoughton BL5 . . . . . 57 F7
Meadow Croft
Hazel Grove SK7. . . . . . 124 E4
Whitefield M45 . . . . 62 C6
Meadowcroft Ho OL11 . . 29 F6
Meadowcroft La
1 Oldham OL11 . . . . . . 49 B1
Rochdale OL11. . . . . 29 F6
Meadowcroft Way WN7 . 76 B2
Meadow Ct
2 Altrincham WA15. . . 120 D6
Altrincham, Well Green
WA15 . . . . 120 C3
Salford M6. . . . . 80 B3
Stretford M21 . . . . 108 F8
7 Wigan WN6. . . . . 37 A1
Meadowfield
Bolton BL5. . . . . 40 C7
Rochdale OL16. . . . . 31 B3
18 Up Holland WN8. . . . 53 A7
Meadow Field WN2 . . . . . 75 B8
Meadowfield Cl SK13. . . 171 C3
Meadowfield Ct SK14 . . 167 A4
Meadowfield Dr M28 . . . 78 B6
Meadow Fold OL3. . . . . . 69 C8
Meadowgate
Urmston M41. . . . . 95 D1
Worsley M28. . . . . 36 E2
Worsley M28. . . . . 78 B8
Meadowgate Rd M6. . . . . 80 C3
Meadow Head Ave OL12. 14 D6
Meadow Ind Est
Manchester M35 . . . . . . 83 D6
Stockport SK1 . . . . 169 C3
Meadow La
Bolton BL2. . . . . 43 A7
Denton M34. . . . . 113 A4
Disley SK12. . . . . 135 D6
Dukinfield SK16. . . . . . 101 D8
Eccles M28 . . . . 78 F5
Oldham OL8. . . . . 66 E2
Meadow Pit La WN2 . . . . 37 F8
Meadow Pk BL0 . . . . 1 C4
Meadow Rd
Manchester M24 . . . . . . 64 E6
Salford M7. . . . . 81 C3
Urmston M41. . . . . 95 D1
Meadow Rise
Glossop SK13. . . . . 115 F7
Shaw OL2. . . . . 32 A1
Meadows Cl
Hazel Grove SK7. . . . . . 124 E3
4 Hindley WN2 . . . . 56 D5
Meadowside
Bramhall SK7. . . . . 123 C2
Newhey OL16. . . . . 32 C3
Meadowside Ave
Ashton-in-M WN4 . . . . . 73 A8
Bolton BL2. . . . . 148 C3
Bolton, Breightmet BL2 . 42 D8
Irlam M44 . . . . 94 A2
Walkden M28. . . . . 60 E4
Wythenshawe M22 . . . . 121 E4
Meadowside Cl M26 . . . . 44 A5
Meadowside Gr M28 . . . . 60 E3
Meadowside Rd SK7 . . . . 133 B1
Sale La BL2. . . . . 25 F5
Meadows Rd
Cheadle SK8 . . . . 131 F8
Gatley SK8 . . . . 122 B1
Reddish SK4. . . . . 111 C6
Sale M33 . . . . 108 C6
Meadows Sch The M9 . . . 64 F4
Meadows St WN6 . . . . . . 37 A1
Meadow The
Hyde SK14. . . . . 167 B1
Stockport SK1 . . . . 124 C5
Meadows The
Irlam M44 . . . . 105 E6
Middleton M24. . . . . 65 B6
Oldham OL4. . . . . 68 A6
Prestwich M25. . . . . 63 C3
Radcliffe M26 . . . . 44 A2
Rochdale OL12. . . . . 13 A4
Romiley SK6. . . . . 113 B4
Uppermill OL3 . . . . 69 B7
Whitefield M45 . . . . 62 C7
Whitworth OL12. . . . . 4 C1
Meadow The
Bolton BL6. . . . . 40 C7
Delph OL3. . . . . 50 F5
Meadow Wlk SK5 . . . . . . 54 C6
Meadow View
Adlington PR6 . . . . 20 F8
Rochdale OL11. . . . . 14 A1
Wigan WN5 . . . . 53 E8
Meadow Way
Altrincham WA15. . . . . 120 B3
Blackrod BL6 . . . . 21 E1
Bury BL8 . . . . 26 E6
Coppull PR7. . . . . 19 D8
Edgworth BL7 . . . . 9 E6
Manchester M40 . . . . 9 E1
Ramsbottom, Summerseat
BL9 . . . . 11 C2
Wilmslow SK9 . . . . 136 E4
Meadow Wlk
Farnworth BL4. . . . . 60 A8
Littleborough OL15 . . . . 15 F5
Partington M31 . . . . . . 105 E3
Romiley SK6. . . . . 112 F3
Tyldesley M29 . . . . 77 B4
Meadscroft Dr SK9. . . . 136 F1
Meads Gr
Farnworth BL4. . . . . 59 E8
Tyldesley M29 . . . . 77 C6

Meads The OL9 . . . . . . 152 A2
Mead The M5. . . . . 154 A4
Meadway
Bramhall SK7. . . . . 132 E5
Bury BL9 . . . . 44 F6
Dukinfield SK16. . . . . . 101 E7
Failsworth OL9 . . . . 65 E2
Golborne WA3 . . . . 90 D8
High Lane SK6. . . . . 134 F8
Ince-in-M WN2 . . . . 151 C3
Poynton SK12. . . . . 133 B4
Ramsbottom BL0 . . . . . . 1 C4
Rochdale OL11. . . . . 30 C4
Stalybridge SK15. . . . . 102 E6
Tyldesley M29 . . . . 59 D1
Mead Way M34 . . . . 112 F8
Meadway Cl
Horwich BL6 . . . . 22 D3
Sale M33 . . . . 107 C2
Meadway Rd SK8 . . . . . 123 B3
Meadhouse Brow SK1 . . 169 C11
Mealhouse Ct M46. . . . . 58 C3
Mealhouse La
Atherton M46. . . . . 58 C3
Bolton BL1. . . . . 145 C3
Meal St SK4 . . . . 169 B3
Meanley Rd M29 . . . . 59 A1
Meanley St 16 M29. . . . . 59 A1
Meanwood Brow 19 OL12. 14 C1
Meanwood Fold OL12 . . 139 A4
Meanwood Prim Sch
OL12. . . . . 14 C1
Measham Mews M1. . . . 163 A3
Meburn Wlk M14 . . . . . . 98 B4
Mechinoh Sch 10 M7. . . . 63 E1
Media City UK Metro Sta
M50. . . . . 96 E7
Medina Cl SK8 . . . . 123 B4
Medlar Way WN4 . . . . . . 72 F5
Medley St OL12 . . . . 14 F1
Medlock Cl BL4. . . . . 60 B8
Medlock Ct M11 . . . . . . 165 B3
Medlock Dr M24. . . . . . . 65 B7
Medlock Ho 8 M15. . . . 162 A3
Medlock L Ctr WA3. . . . . 84 B2
Medlock Prim Sch M13 163 C3
Medlock Rd M35. . . . . . . 84 B5
Medlock St
Droylsden M43. . . . . 84 B2
Manchester M15 . . . . . 162 C3
MEDLOCK VALE 84 A4
Medlock Valley Com Sch
OL8 . . . . 67 A2
Medlock Way
Oldham OL4 . . . . 67 E6
Platt Bridge WN2. . . . . . 56 A2
Whitefield M45 . . . . 63 C8
Medowell Wlk M8 . . . . . . 64 B2
Medway Cl
Ashton-in-M WN4 . . . . . 72 F6
Golborne WN7 . . . . 91 C8
Handforth SK9 . . . . 131 D2
Oldham OL8. . . . . 66 C3
Salford M5. . . . . 154 A3
Medway Cres WA14 . . . 119 C6
Medway Dr
Horwich BL6 . . . . 22 D3
Kearsley BL4 . . . . 61 B5
Medway Pl WN5 . . . . 54 D7
Medway Rd
Culcheth WA3 . . . . 92 A2
Oldham OL8. . . . . 66 C3
Shaw OL2. . . . . 149 B4
Walkden M28. . . . . 78 B8
Medway The OL10 . . . . . 29 B3
Medway Wlk
Manchester M40 . . . . . 160 A3
Wigan WN5 . . . . 54 D7
Meech St M11 . . . . 165 C4
Meek St OL2. . . . . 49 A2
Meerbrook Rd SK3. . . . . 123 A8
Mee's Sq M30 . . . . 95 D8
Megfield BL5. . . . . 57 E6
Megna Cl OL9 . . . . 153 A3
Melandra Castle Rd
SK13 . . . . 171 A2
Melandra Cres SK14 . . . 102 E2
Melandra Rd SK13 . . . . . 171 B3
Melanie Cl SK13 . . . . . . 116 A8
Melanie St SK5. . . . . . . 111 F8
Melba St M11. . . . . 83 A2
Melbecks Wlk 5 M23 . . 108 F2
Melbourne Ave
Chadderton OL9 . . . . . . 152 B3
2 Stretford M32. . . . . . 96 D2
Wythenshawe M90 . . . . 130 A8
Melbourne Cl
Horwich BL6 . . . . 22 C3
Rochdale OL11. . . . . 31 B2
Melbourne Mews
Chadderton OL9 . . . . . . 152 B3
Salford M7. . . . . 155 B1
Melbourne Rd
Bolton BL1. . . . . 144 B1
Bramhall SK7. . . . . 132 F5
Rochdale OL11. . . . . 31 A2
Melbourne St
Chadderton OL9 . . . . . . 152 B3
Denton M34. . . . . 100 E2
Manchester, Harpurhey
M9. . . . . 157 B4
Pendlebury M27. . . . . . . 80 B8
Reddish SK5. . . . . 111 F8
Salford M7. . . . . 155 B1
Stalybridge SK15. . . . . . 86 A1

Melbourne Street N OL6. 166 C4
Melbourne Street S OL6. 166 C4
Melbury Ave M20 . . . . . 110 D4
Melbury Dr BL6. . . . . 39 F8
Melbury Rd SK8. . . . . . . 132 B6
Meldon Rd M13. . . . . 98 E2
Meldreth Dr M12 . . . . . . 99 F4
Meldrum St OL8 . . . . 66 F4
Melford Ave
Ashton-in-M WN4 . . . . . 73 A4
Orrell WN5. . . . . 53 D3
Melford Dr
Ashton-in-M WN4 . . . . . 73 A4
Manchester M40 . . . . . . 65 E1
Melford Dr
Ashton-in-M WN4 . . . . . 73 A4
Manchester M40 . . . . . . 65 E1
Melford Rd
8 Denton M34. . . . . . . 113 A7
Manchester M40 . . . . . . 65 E1
Melford Rd SK7 . . . . . . 124 F1
Melfort Ave M32 . . . . 96 E1
Melia Ho M4. . . . . 159 A3
Meliden Cres
Bolton BL1. . . . . 142 B1
Wythenshawe M22 . . . . 121 E3
Melksham Cl 4 M5 . . . . 81 B2
Mellalieu St
Middleton M24. . . . . 46 F1
Royton OL2 . . . . 48 E2
Melland Ave M21 . . . . . 109 C5
Melland High Sch M18 . . 99 C3
Melland Rd M18 . . . . 99 C3
Meller Rd M13. . . . . 98 F3
Melling Ave
Chadderton OL9. . . . . . . 47 E1
Reddish SK4. . . . . 111 E6
Melling Cl
Adlington PR6 . . . . 21 B7
Leigh WN7. . . . . 75 F1
Melling Rd OL4 . . . . 67 C6
Melling St
Manchester M12 . . . . . . 99 A4
Wigan WN5 . . . . 54 E5
Mellington Ave M20. . . . 122 C8
Melling Way WN3. . . . . . 54 D1
Mellodew Dr OL1 . . . . . . 49 F7
Mellor Cl
Ashton-u-L OL6 . . . . 85 E2
Standish WN6 . . . . 19 E2
Mellor Ct SK2. . . . . 124 E6
Mellor Dr
Bury BL9 . . . . 44 D7
Walkden M28. . . . . 60 C1
Mellor Gr BL1 . . . . 142 B1
Mellor Prim Sch SK6. . . 126 C8
Mellor Rd
Ashton-u-L, Higher Hurst
OL6. . . . . 85 F4
Ashton-u-L, Stamford Park
OL6. . . . . 85 E3
Cheadle SK8 . . . . 123 B1
New Mills SK6, SK22 . . 127 C3
Mellors Cl M16 . . . . 162 A1
Mellors Rd M17 . . . . 96 B7
Mellor St
Droylsden M43. . . . . 83 F1
Eccles M30 . . . . 79 D1
Failsworth M35 . . . . 83 D6
Manchester, Ardwick M12 163 C4
Manchester, Miles Platting
M40. . . . . 160 A3
Oldham, Lees OL4 . . . . . 67 E6
6 Oldham, The Edge OL8 . 66 C2
Prestwich M25. . . . . 62 F4
2 Radcliffe M26. . . . . . 44 B2
Rochdale OL11, OL12. . 139 A3
Royton OL2 . . . . 48 D5
Stretford M32 . . . . 96 E4
Mellor Way 1 OL9. . . . . 66 B4
Mellowstone Dr M21. . . 109 F8
Melloy Pl M8 . . . . 159 A4
Melmerby Cl WN4. . . . . . 72 F3
Melmerby Ct M5. . . . . . 154 C1
Melon Pl 4 M6. . . . . 81 B2
Melrose 12 OL12 . . . . . 139 B4
Melrose Apartments M13. 98 C4
Melrose Ave
Bolton BL1. . . . . 142 A1
Bury BL8 . . . . 27 C3
Cheadle SK3 . . . . 122 F7
Eccles M30 . . . . 79 B4
Heywood OL16. . . . . 32 A5
Leigh WN7. . . . . 57 D1
Littleborough OL15 . . . . 16 A7
Manchester M20 . . . . . 110 C3
Sale M33 . . . . 108 B4
Melrose Cl 6 M45. . . . . . 44 F2
Melrose Cres
Altrincham WA15. . . . . 120 B1
Garswood WN4 . . . . 72 C3
Poynton SK12. . . . . 134 D5
Stockport SK3 . . . . 123 D4
Melrose Ct
Chadderton OL9. . . . . . . 66 A4
15 Handforth SK9 . . . . 131 E1
Melrose Dr WN3. . . . . . . 54 D3
Melrose Gdns M26 . . . . . 43 E5
Melrose Rd
Little Lever BL3 . . . . 42 F3
6 Radcliffe M26. . . . . . 43 E5
Melrose St
Failsworth M40 . . . . 83 C5
3 Oldham M41 . . . . 49 B1
Ramsbottom BL9 . . . . . . 11 B2
Rochdale OL11. . . . . . . 139 A3
Melsomby Rd M23 . . . . . 109 A2
Meltham Ave M20. . . . . . 110 A6

Meltham Cl SK4 . . . . 110 E1
Meltham Pl **5** BL3 . . . . 147 A4
Meltham Rd SK4 . . . . 110 E1
Melton Ave
  Reddish M34 . . . . 100 A3
  Urmston M41 . . . . 94 D3
Melton Cl
  Heywood OL10 . . . . 29 B1
  Tyldesley M29 . . . . 77 B8
  Walkden M28 . . . . 60 C2
Melton Dr BL9 . . . . 45 A5
Melton Rd M8 . . . . 63 E1
Melton Row M26 . . . . 43 F4
Melton St
  Heywood OL10 . . . . 29 B1
  Manchester M9 . . . . 64 F1
  Radcliffe M26 . . . . 43 F4
  Reddish SK5 . . . . 169 C4
Melton Way M26 . . . . 43 F4
Melton Wlk M26 . . . . 43 F4
Melverley Rd M9 . . . . 64 A5
Melverley St WN3 . . . . 150 A3
Melville Cl M11 . . . . 99 E7
Melville Ct **3** M20 . . . . . . 110 A2
Melville Rd
  Irlam M44 . . . . 105 C5
  Kearsley BL4 . . . . 60 F6
  Stretford M32 . . . . 96 B3
Melville St
  Ashton-u-L OL6 . . . . 166 B3
  Bolton BL3 . . . . 42 A4
  Oldham OL4 . . . . 67 E5
  Rochdale OL11 . . . . 30 D1
  Salford M3 . . . . 158 A2
Melvin Ave M22 . . . . 121 E4
Melyncourt Dr SK14 . . . . . 102 E3
Memorial Rd M28 . . . . 60 D2
Menai Gr SK8 . . . . 123 A6
Menai Rd SK3 . . . . 170 B2
Mendip Ave
  Wigan WN3 . . . . 54 C3
  Wythenshawe M22 . . . . . 121 F4
Mendip Cl
  Bolton BL2 . . . . 43 A7
  Chadderton OL9 . . . . 152 A1
  Gatley SK8 . . . . 131 B7
  Horwich BL6 . . . . 22 C5
  Royton OL2 . . . . 48 C3
  Stockport SK4 . . . . 169 B3
Mendip Cres BL8 . . . . 27 B3
Mendip Ct SK4 . . . . 169 B3
Mendip Dr
  Bolton BL2 . . . . 43 A6
  Milnrow OL16 . . . . 32 A7
Mendip Rd OL8 . . . . 66 D3
Mendips Cl **3** OL2 . . . . . . 48 F8
Menston Ave M40 . . . . 65 E1
Mentmore Rd OL16 . . . . . . 31 D8
Mentone Cres M22 . . . . . . 121 E4
Mentone Rd SK4 . . . . 168 C3
Mentor St M13 . . . . 98 F3
Menzies Ct M21 . . . . 97 B1
Mercer Cres BB4 . . . . 1 A8
Mercer La OL11 . . . . 29 E8
Mercer Rd
  Heywood OL10 . . . . 46 D7
  Manchester M18 . . . . 99 D5
Mercer St
  Droylsden M43 . . . . 84 B2
  Manchester M19 . . . . 99 B1
  Newton-le-W WA12 . . . . . 89 D4
Merchants Cres WA3 . . . . . 74 E1
Merchants Quay M50 . . . . 161 A2
Mercian Mall OL6 . . . . 166 B3
Mercian Way M29 . . . . 59 D3
Mercia St BL3 . . . . 144 C5
Mercury Bldgs M1 . . . . 159 B1
Mercury Pk M41 . . . . 95 F5
Mercury Way M41 . . . . 95 F6
Mere Ave
  Droylsden M43 . . . . 99 E8
  Leigh WN7 . . . . 75 D5
  Middleton M24 . . . . 65 A6
Merebank Cl OL11 . . . . 29 E8
Mere Bank Cl M28 . . . . 60 C3
Merebrook Cl M26 . . . . 44 B1
Mere Cl
  Reddish M34 . . . . 100 B2
  Sale M33 . . . . 108 F3
  Whitefield BL9 . . . . 45 A2
Mereclough Ave M28 . . . . . 60 F1
Meredew Ave M27 . . . . 79 E6
Meredith Ct **6** M15 . . . . . 163 A2
Meredith St
  Bolton BL3 . . . . 147 C3
  Manchester M14 . . . . 110 D7
Mere Dr
  Swinton M27 . . . . 110 B4
  Swinton M27 . . . . 62 A2
Merefield Ave OL11 . . . . . . 139 B1
Merefield Cl WN2 . . . . 56 E4
Merefield Rd WA15 . . . . . . 120 C5
Merefield St OL11 . . . . 139 B1
Merefield Terr OL11 . . . . . . 139 B1
Merefold BL6 . . . . 21 F3
Mere Fold M28 . . . . 60 B3
Mere Gdns BL1 . . . . 145 B4
Mere Gr WA11 . . . . 71 B1
Merehall Cl BL1 . . . . 145 B4
Merehall Dr BL1 . . . . 145 B4
Merehall St BL1 . . . . 143 B1
Mere Ho SK4 . . . . 110 E1
Mere La OL11 . . . . 139 C1
Mereland Ave M20 . . . . . . 110 C4

Mereland Cl WN5 . . . . 53 E6
Meremanor M28 . . . . 60 F1
Merepool Cl SK6 . . . . 125 C7
Mere Rd
  Ashton-in-M WN4 . . . . 73 C4
  Newton-le-W WA12 . . . . . 89 F4
Mereside SK15 . . . . 85 F4
Mereside Cl SK8 . . . . 122 F4
Mereside Gr M28 . . . . 60 E3
Mereside Sch SK4 . . . . . . 168 B2
Mereside Wlk **15** M15 . . . 162 A2
Mere St
  7 Leigh WN7 . . . . 75 D5
  Rochdale OL11 . . . . 139 C2
  Wigan WN5 . . . . 54 F6
Mere The
  Ashton-u-L OL6 . . . . 85 E6
  Cheadle SK8 . . . . 123 A4
Mere Wlk BL1 . . . . 145 B4
Merewood Ave M22 . . . . . 121 D6
Meriden Cl M26 . . . . 43 F6
Meriden Gr BL6 . . . . 40 D6
Meridian Pl M20 . . . . 110 A4
Merinall Cl OL16 . . . . 31 C7
Meriton Rd SK9 . . . . 131 D4
Meriton Wlk M18 . . . . 99 B4
Merlewood Ave
  6 Droylsden M34 . . . . . . 84 B1
  Methuen St M12 . . . . 111 C7
  Uppermill OL3 . . . . 69 B8
Merlewood Dr
  Swinton M27 . . . . 79 C6
  Tyldesley M29 . . . . 77 B8
Merlin Cl
  Hazel Grove SK2 . . . . 125 A6
  Littleborough OL15 . . . . . . 16 A2
  Oldham OL8 . . . . 85 A8
Merlin Ct WA14 . . . . 119 A6
Merlin Gr M27 . . . . 62 B2
Merlin Gr BL1 . . . . 142 B1
Merlin Ho **3** M19 . . . . . . 110 D4
Merlin Rd
  Irlam M44 . . . . 94 A4
  Milnrow OL16 . . . . 31 F6
Merlyn Ave
  Denton M34 . . . . 100 E2
  Manchester M20 . . . . 110 C4
  Sale M33 . . . . 108 C6
Merlyn Ct M20 . . . . 110 C4
Merrick Ave M22 . . . . 121 E4
Merrick St OL10 . . . . 29 E1
Merridale Rd M40 . . . . 65 C1
Merridale The WA15 . . . . . 129 A8
Merridge Wlk **8** M8 . . . . 155 C2
Merrill St M4 . . . . 160 A1
Merriman St BL4 . . . . 97 E4
Merrion St BL4 . . . . 42 C2
Merrow Wlk M1 . . . . 163 B3
Merrybent Cl SK2 . . . . 124 D4
Merrybower Rd M7 . . . . . . 155 B4
Merrydale Ave M30 . . . . . . 79 F4
Merryman Hall OL16 . . . . . 15 B2
Merseybank Ave M21 . . . . 109 D4
Mersey Bank Rd SK13 . . . 171 C4
Mersey Cl
  Hindley WN2 . . . . 57 C3
  Whitefield M45 . . . . 45 B1
Mersey Cres M20 . . . . 109 D3
Mersey Dr
  Partington M31 . . . . 106 A4
  Whitefield M45 . . . . 45 B1
Mersey Drive Prim Sch
  M45. . . . . 45 C2
Mersey Ind Est
  Manchester SK4 . . . . 110 E1
  Oldham M35 . . . . 66 B1
Mersey Mdws M20 . . . . . 109 F3
Mersey Rd
  Manchester, Heaton Mersey
    SK4. . . . . 110 F2
  Manchester, West Didsbury
    M20. . . . . 109 F3
  Orrell WN5 . . . . 53 F7
  Platt Bridge WN2 . . . . 56 B2
  Sale M33 . . . . 108 B6
Mersey Road N M35 . . . . . . 66 B1
Mersey Sq
  Stockport SK1 . . . . 169 B1
  Whitefield M45 . . . . 45 B1
Mersey St
  Droylsden M11 . . . . 99 E7
  Leigh WN7 . . . . 75 C5
  Stockport SK1 . . . . 112 A2
Mersey Vale Nature Pk
  (Reserve)* SK4 . . . . 168 A1
Mersey Vale Prim Sch
  SK4. . . . . 168 A1
Mersey Valley Visitor Ctr*
  M33. . . . . 108 F6
Merseyway SK1 . . . . 169 B2
Merseyway Sh Ctr SK4 . . . 169 B1
Merston Dr M20 . . . . 122 C8
Merton Ave
  Hazel Grove SK7 . . . . 133 F8
  Oldham OL8 . . . . 66 D3
  Romiley SK6 . . . . 113 A4
Merton Cl BL3 . . . . 144 C1
Merton Dr M43 . . . . 83 E1
Merton Gr
  Altrincham WA15 . . . . 120 B6
  Failsworth OL9 . . . . 65 D3
  Tyldesley M29 . . . . 77 C6
Merton Rd
  Poynton SK12 . . . . 133 B4
  Prestwich M25 . . . . 63 C5
  Sale M33 . . . . 108 A6
  5 Stockport SK3 . . . . . . 123 B8

Merton Rd continued
  Wigan WN3 . . . . 54 C4
Merton St BL8 . . . . 140 A3
Merton Wlk **10** M9 . . . . . 157 B3
Merville Ave M40 . . . . 64 F1
Mervyn Pl WN3 . . . . 55 B4
Mervyn Rd M7 . . . . 81 B6
Merwell Rd M41 . . . . 94 E1
Merwood Ave SK8 . . . . . . 131 D8
Merwood Gr M14 . . . . 98 E4
Meshaw Cl M23 . . . . 108 E2
Mesnefield Rd **1** M7 . . . . 81 A8
Mesne Lea Gr M28 . . . . 78 E8
Mesne Lea Prim Sch M28 . 60 E1
Mesne Lea Rd M28 . . . . . . 60 E1
Mesnes Ave WN3 . . . . 150 A1
Mesnes Rd WN1 . . . . 37 C3
Mesnes St WN1 . . . . 150 C4
Mesnes Terr **12** WN1 . . . . 37 C1
Metal Box Way BL5 . . . . . . 40 A2
Metcalfe Cl
  Romiley SK6. . . . . 113 B2
  Walkden M38. . . . . 59 F4
Metcalfe Dr SK6 . . . . 113 B2
Metcalf Mews OL3 . . . . 69 B8
Metcalf Terr BL2 . . . . 26 D1
Metfield Pl **6** BL1 . . . . . . 144 C4
Metfield Wlk **19** M40 . . . . 65 D2
Methodist Cotts BL5 . . . . . 39 D3
Methuen St M12 . . . . 111 C7
Methwold St BL3 . . . . 146 C4
Mevagissey Wlk **3** OL4 . . 67 C8
Mews The
  Bolton BL1 . . . . 144 B4
  Gatley SK8 . . . . 122 B5
  12 Hindley WN2 . . . . 56 D5
  Leigh WN7 . . . . 76 A7
  Manchester M40 . . . . 160 D3
  Prestwich M25 . . . . 63 B3
  Sale M33 . . . . 108 C3
  Whitefield M45 . . . . 62 D8
  Wilmslow SK9 . . . . 130 D4
  Worsley M28 . . . . 78 E6
Mexborough St **7** OL4 . . . 67 B8
Meyer St SK2, SK3 . . . . . . 170 C2
Meynell Dr WN7 . . . . 75 F2
Meyrick Cl
  Newton-le-W WA12 . . . . . 89 A3
  Wigan WN3 . . . . 54 C2
Meyrick Rd M6 . . . . 81 A3
Meyrick St WN5 . . . . 54 F6
Miall St OL11 . . . . 139 C2
Micawber Rd SK12 . . . . . . 133 E2
Michael Cl M19 . . . . 110 D2
Michaels Hey Par M23 . . . 108 E2
Michael St M24 . . . . 64 F8
Michael Wife La BL0 . . . . . . 1 A7
Michigan Ave M50 . . . . 96 F8
Mickleby Wlk M40 . . . . . . 160 A3
MICKLEHURST 86 F4
Micklehurst All Saints' CE
  Prim Sch OL5. . . . . 68 E1
Micklehurst Ave M20 . . . . 109 E4
Micklehurst Gn SK2 . . . . . 124 E5
Micklehurst Rd OL5 . . . . . . 68 E1
Mickleton M46. . . . . 58 E4
Midbrook Wlk **6** M22 . . . 121 B1
Middlebourne St M6 . . . . . 154 B2
Middlebrook Dr BL6 . . . . . . 40 D6
Middlebrook Sh Ctr BL6. . . 39 D8
Middlecot Cl **2** WN5 . . . . . 53 E5
Middlefield OL8. . . . . 65 A8
Middle Field OL8 . . . . 13 E1
Middlefields SK8 . . . . 123 B4
Middlegate M40 . . . . 65 D3
Middle Gate OL8 . . . . 66 E2
Middle Gn OL6 . . . . 166 C4
Middleham St M14 . . . . 98 A2
MIDDLE HEALEY 14 D4
Middle Hill OL12 . . . . 14 F4
Middle Hillgate SK1 . . . . . 170 C4
Middle Newgate OL15 . . . . . 16 A5
Middlesex Dr **7** BL9 . . . . 44 F8
Middlesex Rd
  Brinnington SK5. . . . . 112 C6
  Manchester M8 . . . . 64 D2
Middlesex Wlk OL9 . . . . . . 153 A2
Middle St OL12 . . . . 14 F4
Middlestone Dr M9 . . . . . . 157 A3
MIDDLETON 65 B8
Middleton Ave M35 . . . . . . 83 F7
Middleton Cl M26 . . . . 43 F7
Middleton Gdns **8** M24. . . 64 F3
Middleton Gdns **8** M24 . . . 64 F8
MIDDLETON JUNCTION . . . 65 D6
Middleton Old Rd M9 . . . . . 64 D2
Middleton Parish Church Sch
  M24. . . . . 46 F2
Middleton Rd
  Chadderton, Chadderton Park
    OL9. . . . . 65 D8
  Chadderton, Westwood
    OL9. . . . . 152 B3
  Heywood OL10. . . . . 46 E7
  Manchester M8, M9 . . . . . . 63 F3
  Middleton M24. . . . . 64 A6
  Reddish SK5. . . . . 99 F2
  Royton OL2. . . . . 48 C3
Middleton Sch Ctr M24. . . . 64 E8
Middleton Tech Sch M24 . . 65 C8
Middleton View M24 . . . . . . 65 B8
Middleton Way M24. . . . . . . 64 F8
Middle Turn BL7. . . . . 9 D7
Middleway OL4 . . . . 67 C8
Middlewich Wlk M18. . . . . . 165 C1
MIDDLEWOOD 134 C5
Middlewood WA3 . . . . 90 E8

Middlewood Ct OL9 . . . . . 152 A4
Middlewood Dr SK4. . . . . . 168 A1
Middlewood Gn OL9 . . . . . 152 A4
Middle Wood La OL15 . . . . . 15 E6
Middlewood Rd
  Hazel Grove SK7, SK12 . . 134 C7
  High Lane SK6 . . . . 134 D7
  Poynton SK12. . . . . 134 B4
Middlewood St M5. . . . . . . 158 A1
Middlewood Sta SK6 . . . . . 134 D6
Middlewood View M34. . . . 134 D7
Middlewood Wlk M9 . . . . . 157 A3
Midford Ave M30 . . . . 79 B2
Midford Dr BL1 . . . . 24 E7
Midford Wlk **12** M8 . . . . . 156 A2
Midge Hall Dr OL11 . . . . . . 30 A6
Midge Hill OL5. . . . . 68 D4
Midgley Ave M18 . . . . 99 E6
Midgley Cres OL6 . . . . 85 E4
Midgley Dr OL16 . . . . 31 C2
Midgley St M27 . . . . 79 D6
Midgrove OL3 . . . . 50 F3
Midgrove La OL3. . . . . 50 F4
Midhurst Ave M40 . . . . 83 B4
Midhurst Cl
  1 Bolton BL1 . . . . 143 B1
  Cheadle SK8 . . . . 131 F8
Midhurst St OL11 . . . . 139 C1
Midhurst Way OL9 . . . . . . 152 B2
Midland Cl OL7 . . . . 75 C6
Midland Rd
  Reddish SK5. . . . . 99 F2
  Stockport SK7. . . . . 123 E3
Midland St M12 . . . . 164 A3
Midland Wlk SK7 . . . . 123 E3
Midlothian St M11 . . . . 83 B2
Midmoor Wlk **5** M9 . . . . . 64 E3
Midway SK8 . . . . 132 B5
Midway Dr SK12 . . . . 133 D2
Midway St M19 . . . . 99 A2
Milan St M7 . . . . 155 B3
Milburne Rd BL9. . . . . 27 F6
Milburn Ave M23 . . . . 109 B2
Milburn Dr BL2 . . . . 42 F8
Milbury Dr OL15 . . . . 16 A2
Milden Cl M20. . . . . 110 C4
Mildred Ave
  Manchester M25 . . . . 63 C1
  Oldham OL4. . . . . 68 B5
  Royton OL2. . . . . 48 E2
Mildred St M7 . . . . 81 C5
MILE END 124 B5
Mile End La SK2 . . . . 124 B6
Mile La BL8. . . . . 26 F1
Miles Ave OL13 . . . . 3 D8
Miles La
  Appley Bridge WN6 . . . . . . 35 E6
  Shevington WN6 . . . . 36 A6
MILES PLATTING 160 A3
Miles St
  Farnworth BL4. . . . . 60 C8
  Hyde SK14. . . . . 167 C2
  Manchester M12 . . . . 165 A3
  Oldham OL1 . . . . 67 B8
Milford Ave **2** OL8 . . . . . . 66 C2
Milford Cres OL15. . . . . 16 B6
Milford Dr M19 . . . . 111 C7
Milford Gr SK2 . . . . 124 C7
Milford Rd
  Bolton, Harwood BL2. . . . . 25 F4
  Bolton, Lever Edge BL3 . . 147 B3
  4 Wigan WN2 . . . . 37 F2
Milford St
  Ince-in-M WN3 . . . . 151 B2
  Manchester M9 . . . . 64 B4
  6 Rochdale OL12 . . . . . . 14 F1
  Salford M6. . . . . 154 B2
Milking Green Ind Est
  OL4. . . . . 67 F5
Milk St
  Hyde SK14. . . . . 167 A2
  Manchester M2 . . . . 159 A1
  2 Oldham OL4 . . . . 67 C7
  Ramsbottom BL0. . . . . . . 138 B1
  Rochdale OL11. . . . . 139 C2
  Tyldesley M29 . . . . 59 A1
  Wigan WN3 . . . . 150 C3
Milkstone Pl OL11. . . . . . . 139 C2
Milkstone Rd OL11. . . . . . . 139 C2
Milkwood Gr **2** M18. . . . . . 99 D4
Millais St M40 . . . . 83 A8
Millar Barn La
  6 Rawtenstall BB4. . . . . . 2 E8
  Rawtenstall BB4 . . . . 2 F8
Millard St OL9 . . . . 152 A3
Mill Bank
  Appley Bridge WN6. . . . . . 35 D7
  Radcliffe M26 . . . . 44 B2
Millbank Ct OL10. . . . . 29 B2
Millbank St
  Heywood OL10. . . . . 29 B2
  Manchester M1, M4 . . . . . 159 C1
Millbeck Ct **4** M24 . . . . . . 46 D2
Millbeck Gr WA11. . . . . 71 B2
Millbeck Rd M24. . . . . 46 D2
Millbeck St **15** M15. . . . . 163 A6
Millbrae Gdns OL2 . . . . 48 F7
MILLBROOK 86 D4
Millbrook Ave
  Atherton M46. . . . . 58 E5
  Denton M34 . . . . 100 D1
Millbrook Bank OL11. . . . . . 13 D1

Millbrook Bsns Ctr M23 . 120 E6
Millbrook Cl
  Fowley Common WA3 . . . . 92 C5
  Shaw OL2. . . . . 49 D6
Millbrook Fold SK7 . . . . . . 133 F8
Millbrook Gr **1** SK9. . . . . 131 D1
Millbrook Ho
  2 Farnworth BL4. . . . . . . 60 E8
  Hollingworth SK14. . . . . . 103 E6
Millbrook Ind Est M23. . . . 120 E6
Millbrook Prim Sch
  Mossley SK15 . . . . 86 E5
  Shevington WN6 . . . . 36 B6
Millbrook Rd M23. . . . . . . 121 A4
Millbrook St SK1. . . . . 170 C4
MILL BROW 126 E8
Mill Brow
  4 Broadbottom SK14. . . 115 A8
  Chadderton OL1. . . . . 48 A2
  Manchester M9 . . . . 64 C2
  Marple SK6 . . . . 126 D8
  Oldham OL6. . . . . 67 C2
  Worsley M28 . . . . 78 F6
Mill Brow Rd SK6 . . . . 126 E8
Mill Court Dr M26 . . . . 61 B8
Millcrest Cl M28 . . . . 77 F5
Mill Croft
  Bolton BL1 . . . . 145 A4
  Shaw OL2. . . . . 149 C2
Millcroft Ave WN5 . . . . 53 D5
Mill Croft Cl OL12 . . . . 13 C2
Mill Croft La OL3. . . . . 51 A7
Millcroft Tea Gdns* OL11 . 13 B1
Mill Ct
  Glossop SK13. . . . . 104 C1
  Urmston M41. . . . . 95 C1
Milldale Cl
  Atherton M46. . . . . 58 C3
  Bolton BL6. . . . . 40 B7
Milldale Rd WN7 . . . . 75 B1
Millennium Wood Nature
  Reserve* SK12 . . . . 135 E3
Miller Meadow Cl OL2. . . . 149 C4
Miller Rd OL8. . . . . 66 C3
Millers Brook Cl OL10 . . . . 29 D3
Millers Cl M23 . . . . 109 A3
Millers Ct
  Salford M5. . . . . 80 A2
  5 Stalybridge SK15 . . . 101 F8
Millersdale Ct **3** SK13 . . 104 F1
Millers La WA13 . . . . 117 B5
Miller's La
  Atherton M46. . . . . 58 E1
  Platt Bridge WN2. . . . . 56 A2
Millers Nook WN8 . . . . 53 E7
Millers Row SK4 . . . . 169 B4
Millers St M30. . . . . 79 C2
Miller St
  Ashton-u-L OL6 . . . . 166 C4
  Bolton BL1 . . . . 143 B4
  Heywood OL10. . . . . 29 D2
  Manchester M4 . . . . 159 A2
  Radcliffe M26 . . . . 43 F6
  Ramsbottom BL9. . . . . 11 C2
  Scot Lane End BL6. . . . . . 38 E7
Millers Wharf SK15 . . . . . . 86 B2
Millet Terr BL9 . . . . 28 E7
Millett St
  Bury BL9 . . . . 140 A2
  Ramsbottom BL0. . . . . 11 D7
Millfield Ct WA15 . . . . 119 E2
Millfield Dr M28 . . . . 78 B6
Millfield Gr OL16 . . . . 31 B6
Millfield La WN4, WA11 . . . 72 E1
Millfield Rd BL2 . . . . 43 A7
Millfield Wlk **2** M40 . . . . . 65 C2
Millfold OL12 . . . . 4 D2
Mill Fold Gdns OL15. . . . . . 16 A4
Mill Fold Rd M24. . . . . 64 F8
Millford Ave M41. . . . . 94 E2
Millford Gdns M41 . . . . 94 E2
MILLGATE 4 D4
Millgate
  Bolton BL7. . . . . 8 D2
  Delph OL3. . . . . 50 F4
  Rochdale OL16. . . . . 15 C2
  Stockport SK1 . . . . 169 C2
  Wigan WN1 . . . . 150 C4
Mill Gate OL8 . . . . 66 D2
Millgate Ind Est M4 . . . . . 159 A3
Millgate La M20 . . . . 110 B1
Mill Gate Sh Ctr BL9 . . . . 140 B2
Millgate Terr OL12. . . . . 4 E5
Millgreen Cl WN8 . . . . 53 A7
Mill Green Specl Sch
  WA12 . . . . 89 E3
Mill Green St **2** M12. . . . . 164 A4
Millhall Cl M15 . . . . 162 B1
Millhead Ave M40. . . . . . . 160 B2
MILL HILL 148 A4
Mill Hill M38. . . . . 59 E6
Mill Hill Ave SK12 . . . . 133 D7
Mill Hill Gr SK14 . . . . 102 F2
Mill Hill Hollow SK12 . . . . 133 D7
Mill Hill St BL2. . . . . 148 A4
Mill Hill Way **3** SK14. . . . 102 F2
Mill Ho OL9. . . . . 27 F8
Millhouse Ave M23 . . . . . . 121 A4
Mill House Cl OL12 . . . . 15 D4
Millhouse St BL0 . . . . 11 E8
Mill House View WN8 . . . . . 53 C7
Milliner Ct SK2. . . . . 124 C7
Millingford Ave WA3 . . . . . 73 F2
Millingford Gr WN4 . . . . . . 73 B3
Millingford Ind Est WA3. . . 90 A8
Milling St M1 . . . . 162 C4
Millington Gdns WA13. . . . 117 C5
Millington Wlk **12** M15 . . 162 A2

Mill La
Altrincham WA15 129 E4
Appley Bridge WN6 35 D7
Ashton-u-L OL6 166 B2
Aspull WN2 38 F3
Bolton BL6 39 F7
4 Bury BL8 27 B4
Cheadle Hulme SK8 123 B3
Cheadle SK8 122 D6
Denton M34, SK14 101 B2
Failsworth M35 83 C7
Hazel Grove SK7 133 F8
Horwich BL6 22 D4
Leigh WN7 76 B4
Lymm WA13 117 C4
Marple SK6 125 B7
Mossley OL5 68 C2
Newton-le-W WA12 89 E3
Oldham OL9 66 C4
Reddish, North Reddish SK5 99 F1
Reddish, Reddish Vale SK5 112 B8
Romiley SK6 113 A5
Royton OL2 48 C4
Up Holland WN8 53 A8
Uppermill OL4 50 D1
Westhoughton BL5 57 E5
Wythenshawe M22 109 E1
Mill Mdw WA12 89 E3
Mill Nook OL12 14 F3
Millom Ave M23 109 B1
Millom Cl OL16 15 C1
Millom Dr BL9 45 A2
Millom Pl SK8 122 B3
Millow St M4 159 A3
Mill Point M1 163 B4
Mill Pond Ave
3 Bolton BL3 42 A3
New Mills SK22 127 D1
Mill Pond Cl
Shaw OL2 149 B2
Stockport SK6 113 B5
Millpool Wlk 1 M9 157 A4
Mill Rd
Bury BL9 27 F8
Orrell WN5 53 D5
Wilmslow SK9 137 B7
Millrise OL1 153 B4
Mills Farm Cl OL8 67 A1
Mills Hill Prim Sch OL9 65 E8
Mills Hill Rd M24 65 D8
Mills Hill Sta M24 47 D1
Mills St
Heywood OL10 29 B2
Whitworth OL12 4 D1
Mill St
Adlington PR6 21 B8
Altrincham WA14 119 E5
Ashton-in-M WN4 73 C2
9 Bolton, Cox Green BL7 24 F8
Bolton, Mill Hill BL1 148 A4
Bury BL8 26 F8
Dukinfield SK14 101 E5
Failsworth M35 83 D7
Farnworth BL4 60 C8
Glossop SK13 104 D1
Golborne WA3 90 A8
Hazel Grove SK7 124 D3
Hindley WN2 56 D5
Leigh WN7 76 A4
Manchester M11 165 A4
Mossley OL5 86 C8
Radcliffe M26 44 B2
Ramsbottom BL0 11 A4
Royton OL2 48 D4
Salford M6 81 A4
Stalybridge SK15 86 C1
Tyldesley M46 58 E1
Uppermill OL3 69 B8
Westhoughton BL5 57 F8
Wigan WN3 150 B3
Wilmslow SK9 137 B7
Worsley M28 78 A6
Millstone Cl
Poynton SK12 133 F5
Romiley SK6 113 A3
Millstone Rd BL1 23 F1
Millstream La M40 83 E4
Mill Street Ind Est BL1 148 A3
Milltown SK13 104 D1
Milltown Cl 3 M26 44 B2
Milltown St M26 44 B3
Mill View Ct OL8 66 D3
Mill View La BL6 22 E4
Millwall Cl M18 99 D5
Millway WA15 129 C7
Millway Wlk 19 M40 83 C5
Millwell La 5 BL1 145 C3
Millwood Cl
Ashton-in-M WN4 73 A5
4 Cheadle SK8 131 E8
Millwood Ct BL9 44 F6
Millwood Prim Specl Sch
BL9 44 F6
Millwood Terr 3 SK14 167 A2
Millwood View 6 SK15 86 B2
Millwright St M40 83 C5
Mill Yd BL9 141 A3
Milne Cl
Dukinfield SK16 101 C8
Manchester M12 165 A2
Milner Ave
Altrincham WA14 119 B7
Bury BL9 27 F5
Milner St
Manchester M16 97 D4
Pendlebury M27 80 A8
Radcliffe M26 43 E3
Whitworth OL12 4 C1
Milnes Ave WN7 75 F2
Milne St
Chadderton OL9 152 B3
Haslingden BL0 1 C5
Oldham, Higginshaw OL1 49 A2
Oldham OL9 152 C1
Rochdale OL11 30 C2
Shaw OL2 149 B2
Milngate Cl OL16 31 C3
Milnholme BL1 142 B3
MILNROW 31 E4
Milnrow CE Prim Sch
OL16 31 F6
Milnrow Cl M13 163 B3
Milnrow Rd
Littleborough OL15 16 A2
Rochdale OL16 31 B7
Shaw, Jubilee OL16, OL2 32 C2
Shaw OL2 149 B3
Shaw, Small Brook OL2 149 C4
Milnthorpe Rd BL2 42 F8
Milnthorpe St M6 81 B5
Milnthorpe Way M12 164 B2
Milo St M9 64 D3
Milsom Ave BL3 146 C3
Milstead Wlk M40 83 A5
Milston Wlk M8 156 A2
Milton Ave
3 Droylsden M43 84 A1
Irlam M44 105 E6
Little Lever BL3 43 B4
Newton-le-W WA12 89 B3
Salford M5 154 A2
Stalybridge SK15 86 E4
Milton Cl
Atherton M46 58 D5
Dukinfield SK16 102 B7
Haslingden BB4 1 A7
Marple SK6 125 F4
Stretford M32 96 E3
Milton Cres
Cheadle SK8 122 C5
Farnworth BL4 60 B6
Milton Ct
Bramhall SK7 132 F6
3 Eccles M30 79 D2
5 Manchester, Broughton Park
M7 63 E1
Manchester, Green End
M19 110 E4
Milton Dr
Chadderton OL9 152 A2
Poynton SK12 133 D4
Sale, Brooklands WA15 108 A1
Sale M33 108 B6
Milton Gr
Longshaw WN5 53 D1
Manchester M16 97 C2
Orrell WN5 53 F6
Sale M33 108 A6
Wigan, Marylebone WN1 37 C3
Wigan, Redwood WN5 54 A6
Milton Ind Ct SK6 112 F5
Milton Lo M16 97 C2
Milton Mount 1 M18 99 D4
Milton Pl M6 81 B3
Milton Rd
Bramhall SK7 132 E7
Coppull PR7 19 E8
Droylsden M34 84 D1
Golborne WA3 90 D7
Prestwich M25 63 C5
Radcliffe M26 43 E4
Stretford M32 96 E3
Swinton M27 61 D1
Milton St John's CE Prim Sch
12 OL5 68 C2
Milton St
Eccles M30 79 D2
Hyde SK14 167 A4
Leigh WN7 75 E5
Middleton M24 46 F1
Mossley OL5 68 C2
Ramsbottom BL0 138 B2
Rochdale OL16 139 C3
Royton OL2 48 E4
Salford M7 158 B4
Milton View OL5 68 D2
Milverton Ave SK14 102 C2
Milverton Cl BL6 40 D5
Milverton Dr SK7 132 B5
Milverton Rd M14 98 D3
Milverton Wlk SK14 102 C2
Milwain Dr SK4 111 C6
Milwain Rd
Manchester M19 111 A8
Stretford M32 96 C1
Mimosa Dr M27 61 F2
Mimosa Rd 2 OL9 65 F8
Mincing St 2 M4 159 A3
Minden Cl
Bury BL8 27 B2
Manchester M20 110 D4
Minden Par BL9 140 C2
Minehead Ave
Hindley WN7 57 D2
Manchester M20 109 F6
Urmston M41 107 B8
Miners Mews The M28 78 B7
Minerva Rd
Ashton-u-L OL6, SK16 166 C2
Farnworth BL4 42 A2
Mine St OL10 29 D4
Minford Cl M40 83 B6
Minnie St
Bolton BL3 146 B3
Whitworth OL12 4 D2
Minoan Gdns M7 81 C5
Minorca Ave M11 83 D2
Minorca Cl OL11 29 E8
Minorca St BL3 147 B4
Minor St
Failsworth M35 66 A1
Oldham OL8 153 B1
Rochdale OL11 30 C1
Minshull St M1 159 A1
Minshull Street S M1 163 B4
Minsmere Cl 1 M8 156 A2
Minsmere Wlks SK2 124 F4
Minstead Cl SK14 102 A1
Minstead Wlk 2 M22 121 B2
Minster Cl
Bolton BL2 25 C2
Dukinfield SK16 101 D6
Minster Dr
Altrincham WA14 128 A8
Cheadle SK8 123 A5
Urmston M41 95 A3
Minster Gr M29 77 B7
Minsterley Par M22 121 C1
Minster Rd
Bolton BL2 25 C2
Manchester M9 157 C4
Minster Way OL9 48 A1
Minstrel Cl
Abram Brow WN2 74 B7
Swinton M27 79 D7
Minton Ct BL3 146 A4
Minton St
Failsworth M40 83 C8
Oldham OL4 67 A5
Minto St OL7 166 A4
Mintridge Cl 9 M11 99 E7
Mint St BL0 1 C2
Mirabel St M3 158 C3
Miranda Ct M5 161 C4
Mirfield Ave
Manchester M9 64 D4
Oldham OL8 66 E4
Stockport SK4 168 B2
Mirfield Cl WA3 90 D7
Mirfield Dr
Eccles M30 79 D4
Middleton M24 46 F1
Urmston M41 95 C4
Mirfield Rd M9 64 D4
Miriam Gr WN7 76 A4
Miriam St M35 83 D5
Mirrlees Dr SK7 124 C2
Miry La
Westhoughton BL5 57 E6
Wigan WN3, WN6 150 A4
Miry Lane Ind Est WN6 150 A4
Missenden Ho 12 M5 154 C1
Mission St OL10 29 C2
Missouri Ave M50 154 B1
Mistletoe Gr M3 158 A3
Mistral Ct M30 79 E3
Mitcham Ave M9 65 A3
Mitchell Cl SK8 121 F6
Mitchell Fold SK6 134 D1
Mitchell Gdns M22 121 E4
MITCHELL HEY 139 B3
Mitchell Hey OL12 139 B3
Mitchell Rd WN5 71 E5
Mitchells Quay M35 83 E7
Mitchell St
Ashton-in-M WN4 73 C2
Bury BL8 27 C4
Eccles M30 79 C3
Failsworth M40 83 B5
Golborne WA3 90 A8
Ince-in-M WN2 56 A7
Leigh WN7 75 B5
Manchester M11 164 C4
13 Middleton M24 46 F1
Oldham OL1 153 B4
Rochdale, Greengate OL16 15 C3
Rochdale, Spotland Bridge
OL12 139 A4
Wigan WN5 54 E6
Mitcheson Gdns M6 154 C3
Mitford Ct M14 110 C7
Mitford Rd M14 110 C7
Mitford St M32 96 C1
Mitre Rd M12, M13 98 F4
Mitre St
Bolton BL1 143 B4
Failsworth M35 83 F8
Mitton Cl
Bury BL8 26 F2
Culcheth WA3 91 E5
Heywood OL10 28 F2
Mizpah Gr BL8 27 B2
Mizzy Rd OL12 14 F1
Moadlock SK6 113 C4
Moat Ave M22 121 C5
Moat Gdns M22 121 C4
Moat Hall Ave M30 95 A8
Moat Hall Sp Ctr M30 79 A1
Moat House Sch SK4 169 B3
Moat House St WN2 56 A7
Moat Rd M22 121 C4
Moat Wlk SK5 112 C7
Mobberley Cl M19 110 E4
Mobberley Rd
Ashley WA14, WA15,
WA16 128 E3
Bolton BL2 42 E8
Wilmslow SK9 130 D1
Mocha Par M7 158 A3
Modbury Cl SK7 124 A1
Modbury Wlk 13 M8 156 A2
Mode Hill La M45 45 C1
Mode Hill Wlk M45 63 C8
Mode Wheel Circ M17 96 C7
Mode Wheel Rd M5, M50 154 A1
Mode Wheel Road S
M50 154 A1
Mode Wheel Wkshp M50 96 D8
Modwen Rd M5 161 B2
Moelfre Dr SK8 132 C7
Moffat Cl BL2 42 F6
Moffat Ct 27 SK16 166 B1
Moggie La SK10 133 F1
Moisant St BL3 147 A3
Moison Ho SK2 124 A6
Mold St
Bolton BL1 143 B3
Oldham OL1 153 B4
Molesworth St OL16 31 A7
Mollets Wood M34 101 A5
Mollington Rd M22 130 E8
Mollis Gr OL1 49 E3
Molyneux Rd
Reddish M19 99 C1
Westhoughton BL5 40 B1
Molyneux St
Rochdale OL12 139 A4
Wigan WN1 151 A4
Mona Ave
Cheadle SK8 122 D1
Stretford M32 96 C3
Monaco Dr M22 109 D2
Monarch Cl
Irlam M44 105 E6
Royton OL2 48 E2
Mona Rd OL9 152 B1
Monart Rd M9 64 E1
Mona St
Hyde SK14 167 B2
Salford M6 81 A4
Wigan WN1 150 B4
Monastry The★ M12 165 B2
Mona Way M44 106 B8
Moncrieffe St
Bolton BL3 145 C2
Bolton, Rose Hill BL4 148 A1
Monde Trad Est M17 96 A6
Mond Rd M44 94 B4
Money Ash Rd WA15 119 E3
Monfa Ave SK2 124 A4
Monica Ave M8 63 F2
Monica Gr M19 110 F8
Monica Terr WN4 73 B2
Monks Cl
Manchester M8 64 B2
Milnrow OL16 31 E6
Monks Ct M5 80 B2
Monksdale Ave M41 95 B2
Monks Hall Gr M30 79 F2
Monks La BL2 25 D2
Monk's Rd SK13 116 A4
Monkswood OL1 153 B3
Monkton Ave M18 99 C3
Monkwood Dr 3 M9 157 B4
Monmouth Ave
Bury BL9 27 F5
Sale M33 107 F5
Monmouth Cres WN4 73 D2
Monmouth Rd SK8 123 B1
Monmouth St
2 Manchester M18 99 E6
Middleton M24 65 C8
Oldham OL9 152 C1
Rochdale OL11 139 C2
Monroe Cl
Salford M6 154 B4
Wigan WN3 55 A3
Monsal Ave
Salford M7 81 A7
Stockport SK2 124 D7
Monsall Cl BL9 45 A2
Monsall Rd M40, M9 157 B2
Monsall St
Manchester M40 157 A1
Oldham OL8 66 E3
Monsall Sta M40 157 B2
Mons Ave OL11 30 C8
Montague Ho SK3 170 A4
Montague Rd
Ashton-u-L OL6 85 D3
Manchester M16 161 A1
Sale M33 108 B4
Montague St BL3 146 B3
Montague Way SK15 86 A2
Montagu Rd SK2 124 D8
Montagu St SK6 114 B2
Montana Ho 4 M1 163 A3
Montana Sq M11 99 E7
Montcliffe Cres M16 97 F2
Monteagle St M9 64 B4
Montford Rise WN2 38 A2
Montford St M50 96 F8
Montfort Cl BL5 57 D6
Montgomery OL11 139 B2
Montgomery Dr BL9 45 B2
Montgomery Ho OL8 66 B1
Montgomery Rd M13 98 F2
Montgomery St
Oldham OL8 66 B1
Rochdale OL11 30 C4
Montgomery Way M26 43 C5
Montmano Dr M20 109 F6
MONTON 79 D4
Monton Ave M30 79 E3
Monton Bridge Ct M30 79 C4
Montondale M30 79 C3
Montonfields Rd M30 79 C3
Monton Gn M30 79 D4
Monton Green Prim Sch
M30 79 E4
Monton Ho SK5 112 B4
Monton La M30 79 E2
Monton Lodge M30 79 C4
Monton Mews 4 WN1 37 B3
Monton Mill Gdns M30 79 C3
Monton Rd
Brinnington SK5 112 C4
Eccles M30 79 D3
Monton St
Bolton BL3 147 B3
Manchester M14 98 A4
Radcliffe M26 43 F3
Montpellier Mews 10 M7 63 E1
Montpellior Rd M22 121 D2
Montreal St
Abram Brow WN7 74 E4
3 Manchester M19 99 B1
Oldham OL8 66 F4
Montrey Cres WN4 72 C3
Montrose 2 M30 79 E2
Montrose Ave
Bolton BL2 25 C1
Dukinfield SK16 101 C7
Laithwaite WN5 54 D8
2 Manchester M20 110 A5
Ramsbottom BL0 11 A2
Stockport SK2 124 A3
Stretford M32 96 B2
Wigan WN5 54 D7
Montrose Cres 3 M19 99 A1
Montrose Dr BL7 25 B7
Montrose Gdns OL2 48 F4
Montrose Sch WN5 54 D7
Montrose St OL11 30 C1
Montserrat Brow BL1 23 D2
Montserrat Rd BL1 23 E2
Monument Mansions 6
WN1 37 C2
Monument Rd WN1 37 D2
Monyash Ct 32 SK13 171 A1
Monyash Gr 31 SK13 171 A1
Monyash Lea 33 SK13 171 A1
Monyash Mews 30 SK13 171 A1
Monyash Pl 29 SK13 171 A1
Monyash View WN2 56 F3
Monyash Way 1 SK13 171 B1
Moody St WN6 19 E1
Moon Gr M14 98 D3
Moon St OL9 152 C3
Moor Allerton Sch M20 109 F4
Moor Ave WN6 35 E8
Moorbottom Rd BL8 10 E5
Moorby Ave M19 110 E4
Moorby St 7 OL1 67 A8
Moorby Wlk BL3 145 C1
Moor Cl M26 43 E5
MOORCLOSE 65 C8
Moorcock Ave M27 80 B8
Moorcot Ct M23 120 F7
Moor Cres OL3 51 B3
Moorcroft
Edenfield BL0 1 D2
Rochdale OL11 30 F3
Moorcroft Dr M19 110 F4
Moorcroft Rd M23 108 F1
Moorcroft Sq SK14 101 E6
Moorcroft St
1 Droylsden M43 84 B1
Oldham OL8 66 C2
Moorcroft Wlk M19 110 F4
Moordale Ave OL4 49 E1
Moordale St M20 110 A5
Moordown Cl M8 156 B2
Moor Edge Rd OL5, SK15 86 F8
Mooredge Terr OL2 48 E2
Moore Gr WA13 117 B5
Moore Ho 4 M30 95 D8
MOOREND 127 A6
Moor End M22 121 D8
Moor End Ave M7 81 C8
Moor End Ct M7 81 C8
Moor End Rd SK6 127 A5
Moore's Ct 3 BL1 144 C4
Moores La WN6 19 D2
Moore St
Rochdale OL16 139 C3
Wigan WN1 37 E1
Moore Street E WN1 37 E1
Moore Wlk 10 M34 113 A7
Moorfield
Boothstown M28 77 F6
Edgworth BL7 9 D6
Manchester M7 63 C1
Radcliffe M26 43 E4
Worsley M28 78 F8
Moorfield Ave
Denton M34 101 A2
Littleborough OL15 16 A7
Manchester M20 110 C7
Stalybridge SK15 102 D7
Moorfield Chase BL4 60 D7
Moorfield Cl
3 Eccles M30 79 D1
Irlam M44 94 B3
Swinton M27 79 D6
Moorfield Com Prim Sch
M44 94 A3
Moorfield Cres WA3 91 A7
Moorfield Dr
Dukinfield SK14 101 E5
Wilmslow SK9 136 E5
Moorfield Gr
Bolton BL2 25 B1
Sale M33 108 D3
Stockport SK4 168 B4
Moorfield Hamlet OL2 48 F7

Moorfield Hts
Hollingworth SK15 87 A6
Mossley SK15 86 E7
Moorfield Mews OL2 149 B3
Moorfield Par M44 94 B3
Moorfield Pl 3 OL12 14 F1
Moorfield Prec SK14 103 D5
Moorfield Prim Sch SK7 124 C1
Moorfield Rd
Irlam M44 94 B3
Manchester M20 109 F4
1 Oldham OL8 66 B2
Salford M6 80 D5
Swinton M27 79 C6
Moorfield St
Hollingworth SK14 103 D5
1 Manchester M20 110 B7
Platt Bridge WN2 56 B3
Moorfield Terr
Hollingworth SK14 103 D5
Mossley SK15 86 E7
Moorfield Wlk M41 95 D2
Moorgate BL9 141 A3
Moor Gate BL2 25 D5
Moorgate Ave
Manchester M20 109 F6
Rochdale OL11 30 A7
Moorgate Ct 26 BL2 25 B1
Moorgate Dr
Mossley SK15 86 E6
Tyldesley M29 77 C5
Moor Gate La OL15 15 E7
Moorgate Mews SK15 86 E7
Moorgate Prim Sch BL2 148 B4
Moorgate Rd
Mossley SK15 86 E7
Radcliffe M26 43 E8
Moorgate Ret Pk BL9 140 C3
Moorgate St OL3 69 B8
Moorhead St M4 159 B3
MOORHEY 67 B6
Moorhey Rd M38 59 F6
Moorhey St OL4 67 B6
Moor Hill OL11 29 F8
Moorhill Ct 7 M7 63 C1
Moorhouse Farm OL16 31 E6
Moorhouse Fold OL16 31 E6
Moorhouse Prim Sch OL16 31 E6
Moorings Cl WN1 151 C4
Moorings Rd M17 96 B8
Moorings The
Disley SK12 135 E6
Mossley OL5 68 E3
Worsley M28 79 A5
Moor La
Bolton BL1, BL3 145 B2
Bramhall SK7 132 E3
Leigh WN7 75 E8
Manchester M7 63 C1
Rochdale OL12 13 F3
Salford M7, M25 81 B8
Uppermill OL3 51 C2
Urmston M41 95 A3
Wilmslow SK9 136 E5
Wythenshawe M23 109 A2
Moorland Ave
Droylsden M43 83 E1
Manchester M8 63 F2
Milnrow OL16 32 A6
Rochdale OL11 29 F8
Sale M33 108 C3
Uppermill OL3 50 F2
Whitworth OL12 14 C7
Moorland Cres OL12 14 C7
Moorland Dr
Cheadle SK8 131 F8
Horwich BL6 22 F3
Walkden M38 60 A6
Moorland Fold SK15 102 E7
Moorland Gr BL1 142 A2
Moorland Rd
Ashton-in-M WN4 73 E5
Hindley WN2 56 C5
Manchester M20 110 B3
Mossley SK15 86 E5
Stockport SK2 124 B4
Moorlands Ave
Leigh WN7 75 F3
Urmston M41 95 B3
Moorlands Cres OL5 68 D1
Moorlands Dr OL5 68 E3
Moorlands Home BL1 142 B3
Moorlands Jun Sch M33 108 E5
Moorland St
Littleborough OL15 16 C7
Rochdale OL12 14 E1
Shaw OL2 149 C3
Moorlands View
Bolton BL3 146 A2
Edenfield BL0 1 D5
Moorland Terr OL12 14 A1
Moorlea M35 83 F8
Moor Lodge SK4 168 B4
Moor Nook M33 108 D3
Moor Park Ave OL11 30 B2
Moor Park Rd M20 122 C8
Moor Platt M33 108 D3
Moor Platt Cl BL6 22 F3
Moor Rd
Calderbrook OL15 6 C1
Haslingden BB4 1 A5
Orrell WN5 53 E6
Ramsbottom BL8 138 A2
Wythenshawe M23 120 E8
Moorsbrook Gr 9 SK9 131 E1
Moorsholme Ave 8 M40 83 A7
MOORSIDE
Eccles 79 D7
Shaw 49 E3
Moorside
Littleborough OL15 16 D6
Rochdale OL11 30 F3
Moorside Ave
Ainsworth BL2 26 D1
Bolton BL1 142 A1
Droylsden M43 84 C2
Farnworth BL4 60 B7
Horwich BL6 22 C4
Moorside Cl SK13 116 B7
Moorside Cres M43 84 C2
Moorside Ct
Denton M34 101 A4
Sale M33 108 B4
Moorside High Sch M27 79 D7
Moorside Ho WA15 120 C7
Moorside La M34 101 A4
Moor Side La BL0 12 A7
Moorside Lo M27 79 D8
Moorside Prim Sch
Droylsden M43 84 B1
Swinton M27 79 D7
Moorside Rd
Bury BL8 26 E5
Manchester M8 64 A1
Mossley OL5 68 E1
Salford M7 81 C8
Stockport SK4 168 A2
Swinton M27 79 D8
Urmston M41 94 E3
Moorside St M43 84 C2
Moorside Sta M27 61 D1
Moorside View
Bury BL8 26 F6
Shaw OL2 149 C4
Moorside Wlk WN5 54 B8
Moorsley Dr M9 64 F4
Moor St
Aspull WN2 38 C5
Bury BL9 140 C3
Eccles M30 79 B1
Heywood OL10 29 B2
Oldham OL1 67 B7
Shaw OL2 149 A2
Swinton M27 79 F7
Moors View BL0 138 B2
Moorton Ave M19 110 F7
Moorton Pk M19 110 F7
Moortop Cl M9 64 C6
Moor Top Pl SK4 168 B3
Moor View
Bacup OL13 3 B7
Rawtenstall BB4 2 F6
Moor View Cl OL12 13 F2
Moorville Rd M6 80 C5
Moor Way BL8 10 C3
Moorway Dr M9 65 A4
Moorwood Dr
Oldham OL8 67 C4
Sale M33 107 E3
Mopmakers Gn 2 SK9 137 B7
Mora Ave OL9 48 B1
Moran Cl SK9 131 E2
Morano Dr WN2 56 A3
Moran Wlk 4 M15 162 C2
Morar Dr BL2 43 A7
Morar Rd SK16 101 D7
Mora St M9 157 C4
Moravian Cl SK16 166 C1
Moravian Field 3 M43 100 A8
Moray Cl BL0 11 A4
Moray Rd OL9 66 A4
Morbourne Cl M12 164 B2
Morden Ave
Ashton-in-M WN4 73 B3
17 Droylsden M11 83 C2
Morecambe Cl M40 83 B6
Morelands The BL1 144 A3
Morely St OL4 49 E1
Moresby Cl WN7 75 D5
Moresby Dr M20 122 B8
Moreton Ave
Bramhall SK7 132 E5
Sale M33 107 F3
Stretford M32 96 D2
Whitefield M45 44 F1
Moreton Cl
Dukinfield SK16 101 D6
Golborne WA3 73 F1
Moreton Dr
Bury BL8 27 B3
Handforth SK9 131 E3
Leigh WN7 75 E1
Poynton SK12 133 F4
Moreton Ho WA14 119 B4
Moreton La SK2 124 C7
Moreton St OL9 65 F8
Moreton Way SK14 102 F3
Moreton Wlk SK2 124 D7
Morgan Pl SK5 169 C4
Morgan St OL15 16 B5
Morgans Way WA3 91 A8
Morillon Rd M44 94 A4
Morland Rd M16 97 C4
MORLEY 130 C2
Morley Ave
Manchester M14 98 A1
Swinton M27 79 E6
MORLEY GREEN 130 C1
Morley Green Rd SK9 130 C1
Morley Ho M22 121 F7
Morley Rd M26 43 D4
Morley's La M29 76 F3
Morley St
Atherton M46 58 C2
Bolton BL3 145 A2
Bury BL9 44 F8
Glossop SK13 116 D8
Rochdale OL16 15 B1
Whitefield M45 62 F8
Morley Way OL3 69 B5
Morna Wlk M12 164 A4
Morningside WA14 119 B5
Morningside Cl
Droylsden M43 100 A7
23 Rochdale OL16 31 B6
Morningside Dr M20 122 C8
Mornington Ave SK8 122 D4
Mornington Cres M14 110 B8
Mornington Ct 5 OL1 153 B4
Mornington Rd
Adlington PR6 21 B8
Bolton BL1 144 B4
Cheadle SK8 122 D4
Hindley WN2 56 F5
Over Hulton M46 58 F6
Rochdale OL11 31 A3
Sale M33 108 D5
Morpeth Cl
Ashton-u-L OL7 84 E4
Manchester M12 164 B1
Morpeth St M27 79 E6
Morrell Rd M22 121 E8
Morris Ct 4 M14 110 C8
Morris Fold Dr BL6 40 C6
Morris Gn BL3 146 C2
Morris Gr M41 106 E8
Morris Green Bsns Pk BL3 146 C4
Morris Green La BL3 146 C3
Morris Green St BL3 146 C2
Morris Hall 8 M14 98 D4
Morris Ho WN1 151 A4
Morrison St BL3 147 B3
Morrison Wlk M40 83 A5
Morris Rd WN8 53 A7
Morris St
Bolton BL1 148 A3
1 Hindley WN2 56 D5
Ince-in-M WN3 55 E4
Manchester M20 110 B7
Oldham OL4 67 A5
Radcliffe M26 44 E5
Tyldesley M29 58 F1
Wigan WN1 151 A4
Morrowfield Ave M8 155 C3
Morse Rd M40 83 B5
Morston Cl M28 78 B8
Mortar St
Oldham OL4 67 C7
Oldham OL4 67 C8
Mortfield Gdns BL1 145 A4
Mortfield La BL1 145 A4
Mort Fold M38 60 A5
Mortimer Ave M9 64 E4
Mortimer Ho SK4 168 C2
Mortimer St OL1 67 A8
Mort La M28, M29, M38 59 E2
Mortlake Cl M28 59 F3
Mortlake Dr M40 83 B5
Morton Ave WN3 150 B1
Morton Cl WN3 54 C2
Morton St
Failsworth M35 83 C6
Middleton M24 47 A1
Radcliffe M26 44 B2
Stockport SK4 169 B4
Mortons The BL5 39 E2
Morton Terr
18 Denton M34 101 A1
Romiley SK6 113 B5
Mort St
Farnworth BL4 60 B8
Hindley WN2 57 A5
Horwich BL6 22 B4
Leigh WN7 75 B5
Wigan WN6 37 A1
Morven Ave SK7 124 F3
Morven Dr M23 121 A5
Morven Gr BL2 42 F7
Morville Dr WN3 55 B4
Morville Rd M21 97 D1
Moschatel Wlk M31 106 A3
Moscow Rd SK3 170 A3
Moscow Road E SK3 170 A3
Mosedale Ave WA11 71 B1
Mosedale Cl
Tyldesley M29 77 C6
Wythenshawe M23 120 E6
Mosedale Rd M24 46 E2
Moseldene Rd SK2 124 D5
Moseley Ct
Cheadle SK8 122 F3
Manchester M19 98 F1
Moseley Grange SK8 122 F3
Moseley Rd
Cheadle SK8 122 F3
Manchester M14 110 E8
Moseley St SK3 170 B4
MOSES GATE 42 C2
Moses Gate Ctry Pk★ BL3 42 E3
Moses Gate Nature Reserve★ BL3 42 E1
Moses Gate Sta BL4 42 C2
Moses Gate Wkshps 2 BL3 42 D2
Mosley Ave
Bury BL9 27 F5
Ramsbottom BL0 11 B2
Mosley Cl WA15 119 F7
MOSLEY COMMON 77 F8
Mosley Common Rd M28, M29 77 F7
Mosley Rd
Altrincham WA15 120 B6
Stretford M17 96 C6
Mosley St
Manchester M1, M2 159 A1
Radcliffe M26 43 F4
Mosley Street Metro Sta M1 159 A1
MOSLEY VILLAGE 96 C5
Mossack Ave 4 M22 121 D1
Moss Ave
Leigh WN7 76 B5
Orrell WN5 53 D3
Rochdale OL16 31 C6
Moss Bank
Bramhall SK7 132 C5
Manchester M8 156 A4
Moss Bank Ave M43 84 C2
Mossbank Cl SK13 171 B4
Moss Bank Cl BL1 143 B4
Moss Bank Ct M43 84 C2
Mossbank Gr OL10 29 C3
Moss Bank Gr M27 61 D2
Moss Bank Ho BL1 142 A3
Moss Bank Rd
Billinge WA11 71 B2
Swinton M27 61 D2
Moss Bank Way
Bolton, Smithills BL1 142 B3
Doffcocker BL1 23 E1
Mossbray Ave M19 110 D4
Moss Bridge Rd OL16 31 B6
Mossbrook Ct M40 159 C4
Mossbrook Dr M38 59 E6
Moss Brook Rd M9 157 B3
MOSSBROW 117 E7
Moss Cl
Haslingden BB4 1 A8
Radcliffe M26 43 D5
Mossclough Ct M9 157 B3
Moss Colliery Rd M27 61 E4
Mosscot Wlk M13 163 B3
Moss Croft Cl M41 94 E3
Mossdale Ave BL1 40 D7
Mossdale Rd
Ashton-in-M WN4 73 A8
Sale M33 107 F1
Wythenshawe M23 108 F1
Mossdown Rd OL2 49 A3
Moss Dr BL6 22 F3
Moss Farm Cl M24 65 B6
MOSSFIELD 96 B4
Mossfield Cl
Bury BL9 141 B4
Stockport SK4 168 B2
Tyldesley M29 77 A8
Mossfield Ct BL1 145 B4
Mossfield Cty Prim Sch M27 61 F1
Mossfield Dr M9 65 A4
Mossfield Gn M30 94 C4
Mossfield Rd
Altrincham WA15 120 D6
Farnworth BL4 60 B8
Kearsley BL4 60 F5
Swinton M27 61 F2
Mossfields WN6 18 F6
Moss Fold M29 77 C8
Mossgate Rd OL2 32 A1
Moss Gn M31 106 F6
Moss Gr
Lymm WA13 117 B4
Shaw OL2 31 E1
Standish WN6 36 E8
Moss Grange Ave M16 97 D4
MOSS GROVE 66 E1
Moss Grove Ct 2 M15 97 E4
Mossgrove Rd WA15 119 F6
Mossgrove St 8 OL8 66 D2
Mosshall Cl M15 162 A2
Moss Hall Farm BL5 59 D7
Moss Hall Rd BL9, OL10 45 E7
MOSS HEY 149 C2
Moss Hey Dr M23 109 B1
Moss Hey Prim Sch SK7 132 C5
Moss Hey St OL2 149 C2
Moss House La M28 78 A5
Moss House Terr M9 64 C1
Moss Ind Est
Golborne WN7 75 B1
Rochdale OL16 31 B5
Moss La
Alderley Edge SK9 137 B1
Altrincham WA15 119 F7
Altrincham WA15 120 A5
Appley Bridge WN6 18 E3
Ashton-u-L OL7 84 E2
Bolton BL1 142 B3
Bramhall SK7 132 D5
Broadbottom SK14 114 F8
Fowley Common WA3 92 D5
Hale WA14, WA15 119 E4
Horwich BL6 21 F2
Irlam M44 105 D5
Kearsley BL4 61 B5
Middleton M9 64 F5
Paddockhill WA16 136 A4
Partington M31 105 F3
Partington M31, WA13 106 A2
Platt Bridge WN2 56 A3
Rochdale OL12 14 B7
Rochdale OL16 31 A6
Royton OL2 49 A3
Sale M33 107 B2
Swinton M27 61 D2
Town of Lowton WA3 90 B5
Moss La *continued*
Tyldesley M29 77 A1
Urmston M41 95 D5
Walkden M28 60 E4
Whitefield M45 62 F8
Wythenshawe SK9 130 E6
Moss La (Altrincham FC) WA15 119 F3
Mossland Cl OL10 46 D8
Mossland Gr BL3 40 D2
Moss Lane E M14, M16 98 A4
Moss Lane Ind Est
Manchester M45 45 A1
Oldham OL2 49 A3
Moss Lane W M15, M16 97 E4
Moss Lea BL1 143 A4
Mosslee Ave M8 63 F3
MOSSLEY 68 C1
MOSSLEY BROW 68 C1
MOSSLEY CROSS 68 B1
Mossley Hollins High Sch OL5 68 E1
Mossley Rd
Ashton-u-L, Higher Hurst OL6 85 E4
Ashton-u-L OL6 166 C3
Uppermill OL4 68 D5
Mossley Sta OL5 68 C1
Moss Lodge La OL7 84 D2
Moss Manor M33 107 E3
Moss Mdw BL5 39 E2
Moss Meadow Rd M6 80 C4
Mossmere Rd SK8 123 A4
Moss Mill St OL16 31 B5
MOSS NOOK 130 F7
Moss Park Inf Sch M32 96 B2
Moss Park Jun Sch M32 96 B2
Moss Park Rd M32 96 B2
Moss Pit Row WN2 38 B4
Moss Pl 5 BL9 44 E8
Moss Rd
Alderley Edge SK9 137 C2
Irlam M44 105 C7
Kearsley BL4 60 E5
Orrell WN5 53 D3
Stretford M32 96 C3
Moss Rose SK9 137 B2
Moss Row
Bury BL9 140 C1
Rochdale OL11 13 D1
Moss Shaw Way M26 43 E5
MOSS SIDE 97 F4
Moss Side La WA3 105 A2
Moss Side L Ctr M15 162 C1
Moss Side Rd M44 105 E6
Moss Side St OL12 4 E5
Moss St
Bury BL9 140 B2
Droylsden M34 84 B1
2 Farnworth BL4 42 E1
5 Heywood OL10 29 C2
Hollingworth SK14 103 D5
Ince-in-M WN3 55 F3
Oldham OL4 67 E8
Platt Bridge WN2 56 A3
Ramsbottom BL9 11 D2
Rochdale OL16 31 B6
Salford M7 155 A1
9 Wigan, Redwood WN5 54 B6
Wigan, Springfield WN6 37 A1
Moss Street E OL6 166 B3
Moss Street W OL7 84 F2
Moss Terr
Ashton-u-L OL6 166 A2
Rochdale OL16 31 B6
3 Wigan WN5 54 B5
Wilmslow SK9 137 F8
Moss The M24 65 B6
Moss Vale Cres M32 95 F3
Moss Vale Rd M41 95 E2
Moss View Com Sch M31 106 A3
Moss View Rd
Bolton BL2 42 E8
Partington M31 106 A3
Mossway M24, M9 64 F5
Moss Way M33 107 E4
Mossways Gn SK9 136 C7
Mossways Pk SK9 136 C7
Mosswood Pk M20 122 B8
Mosswood Rd SK9 131 E1
MOSSY LEA 18 F6
Mossylea Cl M24 65 B5
Mossy Lea Fold WN6 19 A3
Mossy Lea Rd WN6 18 F5
MOSTON 65 B1
Moston Bank Ave M9 157 C3
Moston Fields Prim Sch M40 65 A1
Moston La
Manchester M9, M40 157 C4
Manchester, Moston M40 65 B2
Moston Lane E OL9, M40 65 E1
Moston Lane Prim Sch M9 157 C4
Moston Rd M24 65 D5
Moston St
Reddish SK5 111 F8
Salford M7 155 C3
Moston Sta M40 65 D2
Mostyn Ave
Bury BL9 27 F5
Cheadle SK8 122 E1
Manchester M14 110 E8
Mostyn Rd SK7 124 C1
Mostyn St SK15, SK16 101 F8
Motcombe Farm Rd SK8 122 B1
Motcombe Gr SK8 122 A3

Motcombe Rd SK8 ...... **122** A2
Motherwell Ave 2 M19 .. **99** A1
Mottershead Ave BL3 .... **43** A4
Mottershead Rd M22 .... **121** C4
Mottram Ave M21 .... **109** C5
Mottram CE Prim Sch
SK14 .... **103** A3
Mottram Cl SK8 .... **123** A5
Mottram Dr
Altrincham WA15 .... **120** A5
Wigan WN3 .... **150** B1
Mottram Fold
Mottram in L SK14 ...... **103** A3
Stockport SK1 .... **170** C4
MOTTRAM IN LONGDENDALE **103** B4
Mottram Mews 6 BL6 ... **22** B4
Mottram Moor SK14 ..... **103** B4
Mottram Old Rd
Compstall SK14 .... **114** B8
Stalybridge SK15 .... **102** D7
Mottram Rd
Alderley Edge SK9 .... **137** D1
Broadbottom SK14 .... **115** A8
Hattersley SK14 .... **102** C3
Sale M33 .... **108** F3
Stalybridge SK15 .... **102** D7
MOTTRAM RISE **102** E7
Mottram St
Horwich BL6 .... **22** B4
5 Stockport SK1 .... **170** C4
Mough La OL9 .... **65** E3
Mouldsworth Ave
Manchester M20 .... **110** A7
Reddish SK4 .... **111** D6
Moulton St Prec M8 .... **158** B4
Moulton St M8 .... **158** B4
Mouncey St M1 .... **163** A3
Mountain Ash OL12 ...... **14** B3
Mountain Ash Cl
Rochdale OL12 .... **14** B3
9 Sale M33 .... **107** C5
Mountain Ash Cotts OL3 .. **33** D1
Mountain Gr M28 .... **60** C4
Mountain Rd PR7 .... **19** E8
Mountain St
Failsworth M40 .... **83** D4
Mossley OL5 .... **68** C1
Stockport SK1 .... **112** A2
Walkden M28 .... **60** C4
Mount Ave
Littleborough OL15 .... **16** A7
Rawtenstall BB4 .... **2** F8
Rochdale OL12 .... **15** E4
Mountbatten Ave SK16 .. **101** F6
Mountbatten Cl BL9 ...... **45** C2
Mountbatten St M18 ..... **165** C1
Mount Carmel Cres M5 .. **161** C3
Mount Carmel Ct M5 .... **161** C3
Mount Carmel RC Prim Sch
M9 .... **64** D2
Mount Cres
Orrell WN5 .... **53** F6
Stockport SK4 .... **169** A2
Mount Dr
Marple SK6 .... **125** F5
Urmston M41 .... **95** F2
Mountfield M25 .... **63** B4
Mountfield Ct WN5 ...... **53** F7
Mountfield Rd
Bramhall SK7 .... **132** E5
Stockport SK3 .... **123** C7
Mountfield Wlk
5 Bolton BL1 .... **143** B1
11 Manchester M11 ..... **160** C1
Mountfold M24 .... **65** B7
Mountford Ave M8 .... **63** F2
Mount Gr SK8 .... **121** F6
Mountheath Ind Pk M25 .. **63** B1
Mount La OL3 .... **50** E1
Mountmorres Cl BL5 ..... **59** A7
Mount Pleasant
Adlington PR6 .... **21** A8
16 Bacup OL13 .... **3** C8
Bolton BL3 .... **148** C1
Edgworth BL7 .... **9** D5
Hazel Grove SK7 .... **124** D3
Middleton, Rhodes M24 .... **64** C8
Middleton, Simister M25 ... **63** F8
Ramsbottom BL9 .... **11** F3
Wilmslow SK9 .... **137** B8
Mount Pleasant Bsns Ctr
OL4 .... **67** B7
Mount Pleasant Rd
Denton M34 .... **100** F2
Farnworth BL4 .... **59** F8
Mount Pleasant St
Ashton-u-L OL6 .... **166** C3
Denton M34 .... **100** F7
2 Horwich BL6 .... **22** D1
Oldham OL4 .... **67** B7
Mount Pleasant Trad Est
OL6 .... **166** C4
Mount Pleasant Wlk M26 . **44** A4
Mount Rd
Compstall SK14 .... **114** A6
Manchester M18, M19 ..... **99** C3
Middleton M24 .... **65** A7
Prestwich M25 .... **63** C6
Stockport SK4 .... **168** C2
Mountroyal Cl SK14 ..... **102** A5
Mount St Joseph Business & Enterprise Coll 1 BL4 .. **42** A2
Mount St Joseph's Rd
BL3 .... **144** B1
Mountside Cl OL12 .... **14** F2
Mountside Cres M25 ..... **62** F4
Mount Sion Rd M26 ...... **43** E2
Mount Skip La M38 ...... **60** A4
Mount St
Bolton BL1 .... **143** B1
Denton M34 .... **101** B1
Eccles M30 .... **95** C8
Glossop SK13 .... **116** C8
Heywood OL10 .... **29** D1
Horwich BL6 .... **22** D2
Hyde SK14 .... **167** B2
Leigh WN7 .... **75** C4
Manchester M2 .... **162** C4
Ramsbottom BL0 .... **138** B2
Rochdale, Castleton OL11 .. **30** C1
Rochdale OL12 .... **139** B4
Royton OL2 .... **48** E3
Salford M3 .... **158** A3
Swinton M27 .... **79** F7
Mount Terr M43 .... **83** E3
Mount The
Altrincham WA14 .... **119** D5
Ashton-u-L OL6 .... **85** D3
Brinnington SK5 .... **112** B4
Hale WA15 .... **129** C8
Mount View
Ince-in-M WN3 .... **151** A1
Uppermill OL3 .... **69** B8
Mount View Rd OL2 ...... **49** D6
Mount Zion Rd BL9 ...... **44** F5
Mousell St M8 .... **159** A4
Mouselow Cl SK13 ...... **171** C3
Mowat Ct M14 .... **110** D8
Mowbray Ave
Manchester M25 .... **63** C1
Sale M33 .... **108** C3
Mowbray St
Ashton-u-L OL7 .... **166** A2
Bolton BL1 .... **142** B1
5 Oldham OL1 .... **153** C2
Rochdale OL11 .... **30** B3
Stockport SK1 .... **170** C4
Mowbray Wlk 4 M24 ..... **46** E2
Mow Halls La OL3 .... **51** A1
Moxley Rd M8 .... **63** F1
Moxon Way WN4 .... **73** D4
Moyse Ave BL8 .... **26** F5
Mozart Cl M4 .... **159** C2
MUDD **103** A2
Mudhurst La SK12 .... **135** E3
Muirfield Ave SK6 .... **113** A4
Muirfield Cl
Bolton BL3 .... **40** F3
Failsworth M40 .... **83** C7
Heywood OL10 .... **29** D1
Prestwich M25 .... **63** B5
Wilmslow SK9 .... **137** D8
Muirfield Dr M29 .... **77** C7
Muirhead Ct M6 .... **81** A5
Mulberry Ave WA3 .... **90** F7
Mulberry Cl
Gatley SK8 .... **131** C7
Radcliffe M26 .... **44** A2
Rochdale OL11 .... **139** B1
Wigan WN5 .... **54** D6
Mulberry Ct
Altrincham WA14 .... **119** D6
8 Horwich BL6 .... **22** D1
7 Salford M6 .... **81** A3
6 Urmston M41 .... **95** E2
Mulberry Mews SK4 ..... **169** B2
Mulberry Mount St SK3 . **170** B4
Mulberry Rd M6 .... **81** A3
Mulberry St
2 Ashton-u-L OL6 .... **166** C3
Manchester M2 .... **158** C1
Mulberry Wlk
Droylsden M43 .... **99** E8
Sale M33 .... **107** D6
Mule St BL2 .... **148** A3
Mulgrave Rd M28 .... **79** A8
Mulgrave St
Bolton BL3 .... **146** C2
Swinton M27 .... **61** D1
Mulgrove Wlk 29 M9 ..... **64** E3
Mullacre Rd M22 .... **121** D6
Mull Ave M12 .... **164** C1
Mulliner St 1 BL1 ...... **143** C1
Mullineux St M28 .... **60** D2
Mullins Ave WA12 .... **89** C5
Mullion Cl M19 .... **99** D2
Mullion Dr WA15 .... **119** E6
Mullion Wlk M8 .... **156** B2
Mulmount Cl OL8 .... **66** C3
MUMPS **67** A7
Mumps OL1 .... **67** A7
Munday St M4 .... **160** A1
Municipal Cl 2 OL10 ..... **29** D2
Munn Rd M9 .... **64** C5
Munro Ave
Orrell WN5 .... **53** E6
Wythenshawe M22 .... **121** F2
Munslow Wlk M9 .... **64** F3
Munster St M4 .... **159** A3
Muriel St
Heywood OL10 .... **29** E2
Rochdale OL16 .... **31** B5
Salford M7 .... **155** A1
Murieston Rd WA15 ..... **119** E2
Murphy Cl WN3 .... **150** A1
Murrayfield OL11 .... **29** E6
Murray Rd BL9 .... **140** C2
Murray St
Atherton M46 .... **58** B2
Manchester M4 .... **159** C2
Salford M7 .... **155** A2
Murrow Wlk 3 M9 .... **157** A4
Murton Terr BL1 .... **143** C4
Musbury Ave SK8 .... **123** B2
Musden Ave BB4 .... **1** A7
Musden Wlk SK4 .... **111** D7
Museum St M2 .... **162** C4
Musgrave Gdns BL1 ..... **144** C4
Musgrave Rd
Bolton BL1 .... **144** C4
Wythenshawe M22 .... **121** D3
Muslin St M5 .... **81** C1
Mus of Science & Ind (MOSI)★ M3 .... **162** B4
Mus of the Manchester Regiment★ OL6 .... **166** B3
Mus of Transport★ M8 .. **156** B2
Mus of Wigan Life★
WN1 .... **150** C3
Mustard La WA3 .... **91** B1
Muter Ave M22 .... **121** F2
Mutual St OL10 .... **29** E3
Mycroft Cl WN7 .... **75** E8
Myerscroft Cl M40 .... **65** E1
Myrrh St BL1 .... **143** B2
Myrrh Wlk 4 BL1 .... **143** B3
Myrtle Ave
Ashton-in-M WN4 .... **72** F6
Leigh WN7 .... **75** E7
Newton-le-W WA12 .... **89** C2
Myrtle Bank M25 .... **63** A1
Myrtle Cl OL8 .... **153** B1
Myrtle Gdns BL9 .... **141** B2
Myrtle Gr
Billinge WN5 .... **71** D4
Droylsden M43 .... **84** C2
Manchester M25 .... **63** B2
Reddish M34 .... **99** F3
Whitefield M45 .... **44** D2
Myrtleleaf Gr M5 .... **154** A2
Myrtle Pl M7 .... **81** C4
Myrtle Rd
Middleton M24 .... **47** C2
Partington M31 .... **105** D3
Myrtle St
Bolton BL1 .... **145** A4
Manchester, Beswick M11 **164** C4
3 Manchester, Old Trafford
M16 .... **97** C4
Stockport SK3 .... **123** B8
Wigan WN1 .... **150** B4
Myrtle Street N BL9 ..... **141** B2
Myrtle Street S BL9 ..... **141** B2
My St M5 .... **154** B1
Mytham Gdns BL3 .... **43** B2
Mytham Prim Sch BL3 ... **43** B3
Mytham Rd BL3 .... **43** B2
Mytholme Ave M44 ...... **105** C3
Mythorn Wlk M40 .... **83** B5
Mytton Rd BL1 .... **142** B4
Mytton St M15 .... **162** C1

N

Nabbs Fold BL8 .... **10** F3
Nabbs Way BL8 .... **11** A1
Nab La SK6 .... **125** E7
Naburn Cl SK5 .... **112** C6
Naburn Dr WN5 .... **53** E5
Naburn St M13 .... **98** D4
Nada Lo M8 .... **63** F1
Nada Rd M8 .... **63** F1
Naden View 5 OL11 ...... **13** D1
Naden Wlk M45 .... **63** A8
Nadine St M6 .... **154** B3
Nadin St 1 OL8 .... **66** E3
Nailers Gn 1 BL8 .... **10** F1
Nailgate OL16 .... **31** C2
Nairn Cl
Manchester M40 .... **160** B3
Standish WN6 .... **19** D1
Nall St
Manchester M19 .... **111** B7
Milnrow OL16 .... **31** E6
Nameplate Cl M30 .... **79** B2
Nancy St M15 .... **162** A2
Nandywell BL3 .... **43** B3
Nangreave Rd SK2 ...... **124** B6
NANGREAVES **11** F2
Nangreaves St WN7 ...... **75** C5
Nangreave St M5 .... **158** A1
Nan Nook Rd M23 .... **108** F1
Nansen Ave M30 .... **79** C3
Nansen Cl M32 .... **96** E4
Nansen Rd SK8 .... **122** A4
Nansen St
Salford M6 .... **154** B2
Stretford M32 .... **96** E4
Nansmoss La SK9 .... **130** D1
Nantes Ct BL1 .... **143** A2
Nantwich Ave OL12 ...... **14** F3
Nantwich Cl 3 SK8 ..... **123** A5
Nantwich Rd M14 .... **98** A1
Nantwich Way 6 SK9 .... **131** E5
Nantwich Wlk BL3 ...... **147** B4
Napier Ct
Hyde SK14 .... **167** B1
Manchester, City Park
M15 .... **161** C2
Stockport, Heaton Moor
SK4 .... **168** B3
Napier Dr BL6 .... **22** D1
Napier Gn M5 .... **161** B3
Napier Ho OL14 .... **6** A8
Napier Rd
Eccles M30 .... **79** C3
Manchester, Chorlton-cum-Hardy
M21 .... **109** B8
Stockport, Heaton Moor
SK4 .... **168** B3
Napier St
Hazel Grove SK7 .... **124** D3
Napier St *continued*
Hyde SK14 .... **167** B1
Shaw OL2 .... **149** B4
Swinton M27 .... **79** D7
Napier Street E OL8 .... **153** A1
Napier Street W OL8 .... **153** A1
Naples Rd SK3 .... **123** B7
Naples St M4 .... **159** A3
Narbonne Ave M30 .... **80** A4
Narborough Cl WN2 ...... **56** E4
Narbuth Dr M8 .... **155** C3
Narcissus Ave BB4 .... **1** A8
Narcissus Wlk 6 M28 .... **59** F3
Narrowgate Brow OL2 .... **48** D7
Narrow La SK10 .... **134** A1
Narrows The WA14 ...... **119** C4
Naseby Ave M9 .... **64** F4
Naseby Ct M25 .... **63** C5
Naseby Pl M25 .... **63** C5
Naseby Rd SK5 .... **99** F1
Naseby Wlk M45 .... **63** C8
Nash Rd M17 .... **95** F8
Nash St M15 .... **162** B2
Nasmyth Ave M34 .... **101** A4
Nasmyth Bsns Ctr M30 ... **79** C2
Nasmyth Rd M30 .... **95** C8
Nasmyth St
Horwich BL6 .... **22** C3
Manchester M8 .... **156** C1
Nately Rd M16 .... **97** A2
Nathan Dr M3 .... **158** B2
Nathaniel Ct WN2 .... **56** B3
Nathans Rd M22 .... **121** C4
National Dr M5 .... **161** A4
National Trad Est SK7 ... **124** C3
Naunton Ave WN7 .... **75** C5
Naunton Rd M24 .... **65** B7
Naunton Wlk 24 M9 ..... **157** B4
Naval St M4 .... **159** C2
Navenby Ave M16 .... **97** C4
Navenby Rd WN3 .... **55** A2
Navigation Bank WN6 .... **36** D3
Navigation Cl WN7 .... **75** E4
Navigation Ho
Leigh WN7 .... **76** A4
Manchester M1 .... **159** B1
Navigation Prim Sch 2
WA14 .... **119** D6
Navigation Rd WA14 .... **119** D6
Navigation Sta & Metro
WA14 .... **119** E6
Naylor Ave WA3 .... **90** B8
Naylor Ct 15 M40 .... **159** C3
Naylorfarm Ave WN6 ..... **35** F5
Naylor St
Atherton M46 .... **58** C2
Manchester M40 .... **160** A3
Oldham OL1 .... **153** B3
Nazarene Ct BL5 .... **39** E2
Nazarene Theological Coll 8
M20 .... **110** A3
Nazeby Wlk OL9 .... **152** C1
Naze Ct 3 OL1 .... **153** B4
Naze Wlk SK5 .... **112** C6
Neal Ave
Ashton-u-L OL6 .... **85** D3
Gatley SK8 .... **122** A1
Neale Ave OL3 .... **69** B5
Neale Rd M21 .... **109** B7
NEAR BARROWSHAW **49** E1
Near Birches Par OL4 .... **67** E4
Nearbrook Rd M22 ...... **121** C4
Nearcroft Rd M23 ...... **121** B7
Near Hey Cl M26 .... **43** E3
Nearmaker Ave M22 ..... **121** C4
Nearmaker Rd M22 ...... **121** C4
Neary Way M41 .... **95** C5
Neasden Gr 5 BL3 ...... **144** C1
Neath Ave M22 .... **121** D7
Neath Cl
Poynton SK12 .... **133** D5
Prestwich M45 .... **63** C7
Neath Fold BL3 .... **147** A3
Neath St OL9 .... **153** A3
Nebo St BL3 .... **147** A4
Nebraska St BL1 .... **143** B1
Neden Cl M11 .... **165** B4
Needham Ave M21 ...... **109** B8
Needwood Cl M40 ...... **157** A1
Needwood Rd SK6 ...... **113** C5
Neenton Sq M12 .... **165** A3
Neild Gdns WN7 .... **75** E4
Neild St
Manchester M1 .... **163** B4
Oldham OL8 .... **66** F4
Neill St M8 .... **158** B4
Neilson Cl M24 .... **65** C7
Neilson Ct M23 .... **121** A6
Neilston Ave M40 .... **83** B7
Neilston Rise BL1 .... **40** D7
Nellie St OL10 .... **29** B2
Nell La M20, M21 .... **109** D6
Nell St BL1 .... **143** C4
Nel Pan La WN7 .... **75** D8
Nelson Ave
Eccles M30 .... **79** D3
Poynton SK12 .... **134** A3
Nelson Bsns Ctr M34 .... **100** F4
Nelson Cl SK12 .... **134** A3
Nelson Ct
Manchester, Miles Platting
M40 .... **160** A4
Manchester, Old Trafford
M15 .... **97** E4
Nelson Dr
Droylsden M43 .... **83** E2
Ince-in-M WN2 .... **56** A8
Irlam M44 .... **105** E6
Nelson Fold M27 .... **62** A1
Nelson Mandela Ct 9
M16 .... **97** E3
Nelson Rd M9 .... **64** D5
Nelson Sq BL1 .... **145** C3
Nelson St
Atherton M46 .... **58** B3
Bolton BL3 .... **148** A1
Britannia OL13 .... **4** C8
5 Bury BL9 .... **44** F8
Denton, Hooley Hill M34 .. **100** F6
Denton M34 .... **100** F4
Eccles M30 .... **79** D2
Farnworth BL4 .... **60** E8
Hazel Grove SK7 .... **124** F4
Heywood OL10 .... **29** D1
8 Hindley WN2 .... **56** D6
Horwich BL6 .... **22** D3
Hyde SK14 .... **167** B2
7 Littleborough OL15 ..... **16** B5
5 Little Lever BL3 .... **43** B3
Manchester, Brunswick
M13 .... **163** B1
Manchester, Miles Platting
M40 .... **160** B4
Middleton M24 .... **65** C7
Newton-le-W WA12 .... **89** A3
Oldham OL4 .... **67** E5
Rochdale OL16 .... **139** C3
Salford M7 .... **155** A1
Salford, Weaste M5 ..... **154** B1
Stretford M32 .... **96** D1
Tyldesley M29 .... **77** B8
Walsden OL14 .... **6** A8
Nelson Way OL9 .... **66** B4
Nelstrop Cres SK4 ...... **111** D6
Nelstrop Rd SK4 .... **111** D6
Nelstrop Wlk SK4 ...... **111** C6
Nene Gr WN2 .... **56** E4
Nepaul Rd M9 .... **64** E1
Neptune Gdns 11 M7 ..... **81** C5
Nesbit St 4 BL2 .... **25** B3
Nesfield Rd M23 .... **108** F2
Neston Ave
Bolton BL1 .... **24** F5
Manchester M20 .... **110** A6
Sale M33 .... **108** E2
Neston Cl OL2 .... **49** D7
Neston Gr SK3 .... **170** A1
Neston Rd
Bury BL8 .... **26** F5
Rochdale OL16 .... **31** C4
Neston St M11 .... **99** F7
Neston Way SK9 .... **131** D3
Neswick Wlk 4 M23 .... **108** F2
Netherbury Cl M18 ...... **99** C3
Netherby Rd WN6 .... **37** A3
Nethercote Ave M23 .... **121** B6
Nethercott Ct M29 .... **58** E1
Nethercroft OL11 .... **13** E1
Nethercroft Ct WA14 .... **119** C5
Nethercroft Rd WA15 .... **120** C5
Netherfield Cl OL8 .... **66** C4
Netherfield Rd BL3 ..... **147** B2
Netherfields WN7 .... **75** D7
Netherhey La OL2 .... **48** C2
Nether Hey St OL8 .... **67** B4
Netherhouse Rd OL2 .... **149** A3
Netherland St M5 ...... **161** A4
NETHER LEES **67** D4
Netherlees OL4 .... **67** D5
Netherley Rd PR7 .... **19** E8
Netherlow Ct SK14 ...... **167** B2
Nether St
Hyde SK14 .... **113** F8
Manchester M12 .... **163** C4
Netherton Gr BL4 .... **42** B2
Netherton Rd M14 .... **98** A1
Nethervale Dr M9 .... **157** B3
Netherwood M35 .... **84** B8
Netherwood Ct WN6 ...... **36** A6
Netherwood Gr WN3 ...... **54** E1
Netherwood Rd M22 .... **121** C7
Netherwood Way BL5 ..... **40** A2
Netley Ave OL12 .... **14** F3
Netley Gdns 2 M26 ...... **43** E5
Netley Rd M23 .... **121** A4
Nettlebarn Rd M22 ..... **121** C5
Nettleford Rd M16 ...... **109** E8
Nettleton Gr M9 .... **64** F1
Network Ctr M27 .... **80** E7
Nevada St
18 Bolton BL1 .... **143** B1
Manchester M13 .... **164** A1
Nevendon Dr M23 ...... **120** F4
Nevern Cl BL1 .... **40** F8
Nevile Ct M7 .... **81** B8
Nevile Rd M7 .... **81** B8
Neville Cardus Wlk 12
M14 .... **98** C3
Neville Cl BL1 .... **145** B4
Neville Dr M44 .... **94** A4
Neville St
Chadderton OL9 .... **152** C3
Hazel Grove SK7 .... **124** D3
Newton-le-W WA12 .... **89** A3
Platt Bridge WN2 .... **56** A3
Nevill Rd SK7 .... **123** E2
Nevill Road Inf Sch SK7 . **123** E2
Nevill Road Jun Sch SK7 **123** E2
Nevin Ave SK8 .... **122** E1
Nevin Cl SK7 .... **133** A7
Nevin Rd M40 .... **65** D1
Nevis Gr BL1 .... **24** D5
Nevis St OL11 .... **31** A2

Nevy Fold Ave BL6 . . . . **22** F3
New Acre Ct SK6 . . . . **113** B2
New Allen St M4, M40 . . **159** C3
Newall Gr WN7 . . . . **75** F6
NEWALL GREEN **121** A3
Newall Green High Sch
M23 . . . . **120** F3
Newall Green Prim Sch
M23 . . . . **121** B4
Newall Rd M23 . . . . **120** F3
Newall St
Littleborough OL15 . . . . . **16** B6
Oldham OL9 . . . . **66** B2
Walsden OL14 . . . . **6** A8
Newark Ave
Little Lever M26 . . . . . . **43** C5
3 Manchester M14 . . . . . **98** B3
Newark Park Way OL2 . . **48** C6
Newark Rd
Hindley WN2 . . . . **56** C4
Reddish SK5 . . . . **111** F5
Rochdale OL12 . . . . **14** F3
Swinton M27 . . . . **62** B2
Newark Sq OL12 . . . . **14** F3
Newark St WN6 . . . . **36** F1
Newarth Dr WA13 . . . . . **117** A2
New Bailey Sch OL8 . . . . **158** B1
Newbank Chase OL9 . . . **152** A4
Newbank Cl M24 . . . . **65** C7
New Bank Cl OL3 . . . . **50** F1
New Bank St
Hadfield SK13 . . . . **104** A5
Manchester M12 . . . . . . **164** C1
Tyldesley M29 . . . . **77** A8
Newbank Towers M3 . . . **158** B3
New Barn
Haslingden BB4 . . . . **1** B6
Shaw OL3 . . . . **50** C6
Uppermill OL3 . . . . **69** E3
New Barn Ave WN4 . . . . . **73** C3
Newbarn Cl OL2 . . . . **149** A3
New Barn La
Leigh WN7 . . . . **75** E2
Rawtenstall BB4 . . . . **2** A8
Rochdale OL11 . . . . **30** E4
New Barns Rd OL8 . . . . . **67** A2
New Barns Ave M21 . . . **109** D6
New Barn St
Bolton BL1 . . . . **142** B1
11 Rochdale OL16 . . . . . . **31** A5
Shaw OL2 . . . . **149** A3
New Barton St M6 . . . . . **80** C5
Newbeck Cl BL6 . . . . **22** D1
Newbeck St **1** M4 . . . . . **159** A2
New Beech Rd SK4 . . . . . **110** E2
New Beech St SK14 . . . . **167** A3
New Belvedere Cl **4** M32 **96** D2
Newberry Gr SK3 . . . . . . **170** A1
NEWBOLD **31** C7
NEWBOLD BROW **31** B8
Newbold Cl SK16 . . . . . . **101** C8
Newbold Hall Dr **3** OL16 **31** C7
Newbold Hall Gdns **2**
OL16 . . . . **31** C7
Newbold Moss OL16 . . . **31** B8
Newbold St
Bury BL8 . . . . **27** C2
Rochdale OL16 . . . . **31** C7
Newbold Sta OL16 . . . . . **31** C6
Newbolt St SK5 . . . . **122** E6
Newbourne Cl SK7 . . . . . **124** D3
Newbreak Cl **2** OL4 . . . . **67** D8
Newbreak St **3** OL4 . . . . **67** D8
NEWBRIDGE **96** B8
Newbridge Cl
Garswood WN4 . . . . **72** D3
Manchester M15 . . . . . . **162** E6
Newbridge Gdns BL2 . . . **25** E4
New Bridge Gdns M26 . . **44** E5
New Bridge La SK1 . . . . **112** A2
Newbridge Learning Com
WN2 . . . . **56** A3
New Bridge St M3 . . . . . **158** C3
Newbridge View OL16 . . **86** D8
New Briggs Fold BL7 . . . . **8** E2
New Broad La OL16 . . . . . **31** C3
Newbrook Ave M21 . . . . **109** D4
Newbrook Rd BL5, M46 . **58** F6
New Brunswick St BL6 . . **22** B3
New Buildings Pl **4**
OL16 . . . . **139** C4
Newburn Ave M9 . . . . . . **64** F4
Newburn Cl WN3 . . . . **54** E4
NEW BURY **60** B7
Newbury Ave M33 . . . . . **107** C4
Newbury Cl SK8 . . . . **132** A6
Newbury Cl SK9 . . . . **137** A6
Newbury Dr
Eccles M30 . . . . **79** B3
Urmston M41 . . . . **95** C5
Newbury Gr OL10 . . . . . . **46** C8
Newbury Pl M7 . . . . **155** A3
Newbury Rd
Gatley SK8 . . . . **131** C7
Little Lever BL3 . . . . **42** F3
Newbury Wlk
Bolton BL1 . . . . **143** B1
Chadderton OL9 . . . . **152** C3
Manchester M9 . . . . **157** A2
Newby Cl BL9 . . . . **45** A7
Newby Dr
Altrincham WA14 . . . . . . **119** D6

Newby Dr continued
Gatley SK8 . . . . **122** A6
Middleton M24 . . . . **46** F3
Sale M33 . . . . **108** E3
Newby Rd
Bolton BL2 . . . . **25** F2
Hazel Grove SK7 . . . . . . **124** D2
Stockport SK4 . . . . **168** B2
Newby Road Ind Est SK7 **124** D2
Newby Sq WN5 . . . . **54** B5
Newcastle St **5** M15 . . . **162** C3
Newcastle Wlk **2** M34 . . **101** A1
New Cathedral St M1 . . **158** C2
New Century Apartments
BL0 . . . . **138** C3
New Chapel La BL6 . . . . . **22** F2
New Charter Acad
(Greenhurst Campus)
OL6 . . . . **85** E7
New Charter Acad (Silver
Springs Campus) OL6 . . **85** E4
Newchurch OL8 . . . . **85** A8
Newchurch Com Prim Sch
WA3 . . . . **91** E2
Newchurch Ct **6** M26 . . . . **44** B3
New Church St M45 . . . . . **62** F7
Newchurch La WA3 . . . . . **91** F2
Newchurch Pl OL11 . . . . . **30** C1
Newchurch Rd
Bacup OL13 . . . . **3** C8
Rawtenstall BB4, OL13 . . . **2** F8
New Church Rd BL11 . . . . **23** F2
Newchurch St
Manchester M11 . . . . . . **164** C4
Rochdale OL11 . . . . **30** D1
New Church St M26 . . . . . **44** B3
Newchurch Wlk **5** M26 . . **44** B3
New City Rd M38 . . . . **59** F8
Newcliffe Rd M9 . . . . **64** F4
New Coin St OL2 . . . . **48** D3
New Collier's Row BL1 . . . **23** E6
Newcombe Cl M11 . . . . . **160** C1
Newcombe Ct **3** M33 . . . **107** F4
Newcombe Dr M38 . . . . . . **59** F6
Newcombe Rd BL0 . . . . . **138** C2
Newcombe St M3 . . . . . **158** C3
New Copper Moss WA15 **119** F4
New Court Dr BL7 . . . . **8** E3
Newcroft M35 . . . . **84** B6
Newcroft Cres M41 . . . . . **95** F1
Newcroft Dr
Manchester M9 . . . . **64** C1
Stockport SK3 . . . . **170** A2
Stretford M41 . . . . **96** A1
Newcroft Rd M41 . . . . **95** F1
New Cross St M1 . . . . **159** B2
New Cross St
Pendlebury M27 . . . . **80** A7
Salford M5 . . . . **80** C2
Newdale Rd M12 . . . . **99** B2
New Devonshire Sq M7 . **155** B2
New Drake Gn BL5 . . . . . . **57** E5
Newearth Rd M28 . . . . . . **78** B8
New Earth St
Mossley OL5 . . . . **68** D2
Oldham OL4 . . . . **67** C5
New Ellesmere App M28 . **60** A4
New Elm Rd M3 . . . . **162** A4
Newenden Rd WN1 . . . . . . **37** B4
New Farm Cotts WA3 . . . **105** A7
New Field Ct
Radcliffe M26 . . . . **43** E3
Rochdale OL16 . . . . **31** B8
Newfield Ct WA13 . . . . . **117** A5
Newfield Head La OL16 . . **32** B5
Newfield View OL16 . . . . . **32** A6
New Fold WN5 . . . . **53** C4
New Forest Rd M23 . . . . . **120** C8
NEWGATE **53** A6
Newgate OL16 . . . . **139** C3
New Gate BL5 . . . . **146** A1
Newgate Ave WN6 . . . . . . **35** E8
Newgate Dr M38 . . . . **60** A6
Newgate Rd
Sale M33 . . . . **107** C1
Wilmslow SK9 . . . . **136** D7
New George St
8 Bury BL8 . . . . **27** C3
Manchester M4 . . . . **159** A2
New Green BL2 . . . . **25** E6
Newhall Ave
Eccles M30 . . . . **95** A7
Little Lever BL3 . . . . **43** B6
New Hall Ave
Gatley SK8 . . . . **131** B7
Salford M7 . . . . **155** A4
Newhall Dr M23 . . . . **109** B2
New Hall La
Bolton BL1 . . . . **144** A4
Culcheth WA3 . . . . **92** A2
Culcheth, Wigshaw WA3 . . **91** E1
New Hall Mews BL1 . . . . . **23** D1
New Hall Pl BL1 . . . . **144** A4
Newhall Rd SK5 . . . . **100** A2
New Hall Rd
Bury BL9 . . . . **28** E4
Sale M33 . . . . **108** F4
Salford M7 . . . . **155** A4
Newham Ave M11 . . . . . . **83** B2
Newham Dr **7** BL8 . . . . . . **27** B1
Newhart Gr M28 . . . . **60** C2
Newhaven Ave
Droylsden M11 . . . . **99** F7
Leigh WN7 . . . . **75** F8
Newhaven Bsns Pk M30 . . **79** E1
Newhaven Cl
Bramhall SK8 . . . . **123** C2

Newhaven Cl continued
Bury BL8 . . . . **27** C7
Newhaven Wlk **4** BL2 . . . . **25** B1
New Herbert St M6 . . . . . **80** C5
NEWHEY **32** B4
Newhey Ave M22 . . . . . . **121** D5
Newhey Com Prim Sch **1**
OL16 . . . . **32** A3
Newhey Rd
Milnrow OL16 . . . . **32** A5
Wythenshawe M22 . . . . . **121** D5
New Hey Rd SK8 . . . . **122** E6
New Heys Way SK14 . . . . **32** B4
New Heys Way BL2 . . . . . **25** D6
New Ho OL4 . . . . **48** A5
New Holder St BL1 . . . . . **145** B3
Newholme Ct
Manchester M20 . . . . . . **110** C6
Stretford M32 . . . . **96** E2
Newholme Gdns M28 . . . . **60** C3
Newholme Rd M20 . . . . . **109** F5
Newhouse Cl OL12 . . . . . . **15** C6
Newhouse Cres OL11 . . . . **29** E8
Newhouse Dr WN3 . . . . . . **54** D1
Newhouse Rd OL10 . . . . . **46** D8
NEW HOUSES **54** C1
Newhouse St OL12 . . . . . . **15** C6
Newick Wlk **8** M9 . . . . . . **64** E3
Newington Ave M8 . . . . . **63** F3
Newington Dr
Bolton BL1 . . . . **143** C1
Bury BL8 . . . . **27** A1
Newington Wlk **7** BL1 . . **143** C1
New Islington M4 . . . . . **159** C2
New Islington Sta M4 . . . **160** A1
New Kings Head Yd M3 . **158** C2
New La
Bolton BL2 . . . . **25** E2
Eccles M30 . . . . **79** B1
Middleton M24 . . . . **47** A1
Royton OL2 . . . . **48** D4
Newland Ave WN5 . . . . . . **54** D5
Newland Dr BL5 . . . . **58** F8
Newland Mews WA3 . . . . . **91** E5
Newlands
Failsworth M35 . . . . **83** E4
Wilmslow/Alderley Edge
SK9 . . . . **136** C7
Newlands Ave
Bolton BL2 . . . . **25** F1
Bramhall SK7 . . . . **132** F8
Cheadle SK8 . . . . **132** A7
Eccles M30 . . . . **94** F7
Irlam M44 . . . . **94** A2
Rochdale OL12 . . . . **14** F3
Tyldesley M29 . . . . **77** A6
Whitefield M45 . . . . **44** E1
Newlands Cl
Cheadle SK8 . . . . **132** A4
Rochdale OL12 . . . . **14** F3
Newlands Dr
Glossop SK13 . . . . **171** C4
Golborne WA3 . . . . **90** D8
Manchester M20 . . . . . . **122** C8
Pendlebury M27 . . . . **80** C6
Prestwich M25 . . . . **63** A5
Scot Lane End BL6 . . . . . . **38** E7
Wilmslow SK9 . . . . **136** E5
Newlands Rd
Cheadle SK8 . . . . **122** D6
Leigh WN7 . . . . **75** F3
Wythenshawe M23 . . . . . **120** F8
Newland St M8 . . . . **64** A1
Newland Wlk M46 . . . . . . **46** B3
New Lane Ct BL2 . . . . **25** E2
New Lane End WA3 . . . . . **91** A2
New Lawns SK5 . . . . **100** A1
Newlea Cl BL1 . . . . **142** C2
New Lees St OL6 . . . . **85** D5
New Lester Cl M29 . . . . . . **59** B1
New Lester Way M38 . . . . **59** E4
New Line OL13 . . . . **4** B8
New Line Ind Est OL13 . . . **4** A8
New Lodge WN1 . . . . **37** D2
New Lyme Ave SK15 . . . . . **86** D3
Newlyn Cl SK7 . . . . **124** D1
Newlyn Dr
Ashton-in-M WN4 . . . . **73** B1
Romiley SK6 . . . . **113** A3
Sale M33 . . . . **108** C1
Newlyn St M14 . . . . **98** B2
Newman Ave WN6 . . . . . . **37** A2
NEW MANCHESTER **60** A1
Newman Cl WN2 . . . . **56** C6
Newman St
Ashton-u-L OL6 . . . . **166** A3
Hyde SK14 . . . . **167** B3
Rochdale OL16 . . . . **15** C3
Wigan WN1 . . . . **37** E2
New Market M2 . . . . **158** C1
Newmarket Cl M33 . . . . . **107** B2
Newmarket Gr OL7 . . . . . . **84** F1
Newmarket Mews M7 . . . **155** A2
Newmarket Rd
Ashton-u-L OL7 . . . . **84** F5
Little Lever BL3 . . . . **43** A2
New Market St WN1 . . . . **150** C4
New Meadow BL6 . . . . **40** C7
New Miles La WN6 . . . . . . **35** F5
New Mill St OL15 . . . . **16** A5
Newmill Wlk **2** M8 . . . . **156** A4
New Moor La SK7 . . . . . . **124** D3
New Moss Rd M44 . . . . . **105** D6
NEW MOSTON **65** E1

New Moston Prim Sch
M40 . . . . **65** E2
New Mount St **4** M4 . . . . **159** A3
Newnham St BL1 . . . . . . **143** C4
New Oak Cl M35 . . . . **84** B6
New Oak Com High Sch
M6 . . . . **81** A5
New Park High Sch M30 . **79** C2
New Park Rd M5 . . . . **161** B3
Newpark Wlk **5** M8 . . . . **156** A2
Newport Ave SK5 . . . . . . **111** F7
Newport Mews BL4 . . . . . **60** D7
Newport Rd
Bolton BL3 . . . . **42** A3
Denton M34 . . . . **113** B8
Manchester M21 . . . . **97** A1
Newport St
Bolton BL1, BL3 . . . . **145** C2
Bury BL8 . . . . **27** A5
Farnworth BL4 . . . . **60** D7
Manchester M14 . . . . **98** B3
Middleton M24 . . . . **47** C1
Oldham OL8 . . . . **153** A1
Salford M6 . . . . **154** B2
Newquay Ave
Ainsworth BL2 . . . . **26** D1
Reddish SK5 . . . . **111** E7
Newquay Dr SK7 . . . . . . **132** F7
Newquay Ho **3** OL9 . . . . . **48** A1
Newquay Wlk M23 . . . . . **158** B1
New Radcliffe St OL1 . . . **153** B3
New Rd
Adlington PR6 . . . . **21** D8
Aspull WN2 . . . . **38** A5
Glossop SK13 . . . . **103** F7
Littleborough OL15 . . . . . . **15** F5
Oldham OL8 . . . . **66** E4
Radcliffe M26 . . . . **44** B2
Whitworth OL12 . . . . **4** B1
New Ridd Rise SK14 . . . . **113** D8
New Riven Ct BL3 . . . . **43** A3
New Rock BL5 . . . . **57** F5
New Royd Ave OL4 . . . . . . **67** F8
Newry Rd M30 . . . . **95** E8
Newry St BL1 . . . . **143** A3
Newry Wlk M9 . . . . **64** B3
Newsham Cl BL3 . . . . **145** A1
Newsham Rd SK3 . . . . . . **170** B2
Newsham Wlk
2 Manchester M12 . . . . . **99** B3
Wigan WN6 . . . . **36** F1
Newshaw La SK13 . . . . . **171** C4
Newsholme Cl WA3 . . . . . **91** F3
Newsmith St **3** M6 . . . . **155** C3
New Smithfield Mkt
M18 . . . . **165** C3
NEW SPRINGS **38** A3
New Springs BL1 . . . . . . **142** B3
New St
Altrincham WA14 . . . . . . **119** D4
Ashton-in-M WN4 . . . . **73** D4
Blackrod BL6 . . . . **21** D2
Bolton BL1 . . . . **145** B2
5 Broadbottom SK14 . . . **115** A8
Eccles M30 . . . . **79** C1
Littleborough OL15 . . . . . . **15** F4
Manchester M40 . . . . . . **160** B4
Manchester/Salford M3 . . **158** B2
Milnrow OL16 . . . . **32** A5
Oldham OL4 . . . . **67** E6
Platt Bridge WN2 . . . . **56** A2
Radcliffe M26 . . . . **44** B2
Rochdale OL12 . . . . **14** E2
Stalybridge SK15 . . . . . . **102** A8
Swinton M27 . . . . **62** A2
Uppermill OL3 . . . . **69** B8
Wigan WN5 . . . . **54** B5
Wilmslow SK9 . . . . **136** E5
Newstead **4** OL12 . . . . . . **139** B4
Newstead Ave
Ashton-u-L OL6 . . . . **85** C7
Manchester M20 . . . . . . **110** D5
Newstead Cl SK12 . . . . . **133** D5
Newstead Dr BL3 . . . . . . **146** A2
Newstead Gr SK6 . . . . . . **112** F3
Newstead Rd
Urmston M41 . . . . **95** E3
Wigan WN3 . . . . **54** F3
Newstead Terr WA15 . . . **119** F7
New Tame OL3 . . . . **50** C7
New Tempest Rd BL6 . . . . **40** C4
New Thomas St M6 . . . . . **81** A4
NEWTON **101** F5
Newton Ave
Manchester, Longsight
M12 . . . . **98** F4
Manchester, Withington
M20 . . . . **110** A6
Newton Bank Prep Sch
WA12 . . . . **89** E4
Newton Bsns Pk SK14 . . **102** A5
Newton Cl WN1 . . . . **37** D2
Newton Com Hosp WA12 **89** B2
Newton Cres M24 . . . . . . **46** D3
Newtondale Ave OL2 . . . . **48** C4
Newton Dr BL8 . . . . **11** A1
Newton for Hyde Sta
SK14 . . . . **167** C4
New Tong Field BL7 . . . . . **24** F7
Newton Gn SK14 . . . . . . **101** F5
Newton Hall Ct SK14 . . . **101** C5
Newton Hall Rd SK14 . . . **101** C5
NEWTON HEATH **83** B5
Newton Heath & Moston
Metro Sta M40 . . . . **83** B6

Newton Ho M14 . . . . **110** D8
Newtonhurst SK14 . . . . . **102** A5
Newton La WA12 . . . . **89** E6
NEWTON-LE-WILLOWS . . **89** B2
Newton-le-Willows High Sch
WA12 . . . . **89** D5
Newton-le-Willows Prim Sch
WA12 . . . . **89** C3
Newton-le-Willows Sta
WA12 . . . . **89** E3
Newton Moor Ind Est
SK14 . . . . **101** F5
Newtonmore Wlk M11 . . . **83** B1
Newton Park Dr WA12 . . . **89** F3
Newton Rd
Altrincham WA14 . . . . . . **119** E7
Billinge WN5 . . . . **71** F6
Failsworth M35 . . . . **83** F5
Golborne, Lowton Common WA3,
WN7 . . . . **91** A8
Hadfield SK9 . . . . **131** A1
Manchester M24 . . . . **64** B6
Newton-le-W WA12 . . . . . **89** F1
Town of Lowton WA3,
WA12 . . . . **90** D5
Urmston M41 . . . . **95** C2
Newton St
Ashton-u-L OL6 . . . . **166** C3
Bolton BL1 . . . . **143** B2
Bury BL9 . . . . **27** F6
Droylsden M43 . . . . **84** C3
Failsworth M40 . . . . **83** C6
Hyde SK14 . . . . **167** A4
Leigh WN7 . . . . **75** F5
Manchester M1 . . . . **159** B1
Rochdale OL16 . . . . **31** A5
8 Stalybridge SK15 . . . . . **85** F2
Stockport SK3 . . . . **170** B4
Stretford M32 . . . . **96** E2
Newton Terr
22 Bolton BL1 . . . . **143** B2
20 Dukinfield SK16 . . . . . **166** B1
Newton Wlk BL1 . . . . . . **143** B2
Newton Westpark Prim Sch
WN7 . . . . **75** C8
NEWTON WOOD **101** B6
Newton Wood Rd SK16 . . **101** B6
NEWTOWN
Poynton **134** A3
Swinton **61** F1
Wigan **54** E6
Newtown Ave M34 . . . . . **100** F2
Newtown Cl
Manchester M11 . . . . . . **165** B4
Swinton M27 . . . . **61** F1
Newtown Ct
Manchester M40 . . . . . . **159** C4
Prestwich M25 . . . . **63** C4
Newtown St
Prestwich M25 . . . . **63** C4
Shaw OL2 . . . . **149** B2
New Union St M4 . . . . . . **159** C2
New Vernon St **12** BL9 . . **140** C4
New Viaduct St M11,
M40 . . . . **160** B2
New Vine St M15 . . . . . . **162** C2
New Wakefield St
2 Manchester M1 . . . . . **162** C3
Manchester M1 . . . . **163** A3
New Way OL12 . . . . **4** C1
New Welcome St M15 . . **162** C2
New William Cl M31 . . . . **105** F4
NEW WINDSOR **81** B1
New York BL3 . . . . **40** F5
New York St
Heywood OL10 . . . . **29** B2
Manchester M1 . . . . **159** A1
New Zealand Rd SK1 . . . **112** B2
Neyland Cl BL1 . . . . **40** F7
Ney St OL7 . . . . **84** F6
Niagara Ho SK2 . . . . **124** A4
Niagara St SK2 . . . . **124** A4
Nicholas Croft M4 . . . . . **159** A2
Nicholas Cl M20 . . . . **110** C4
Nicholas Owen Cl M11 . . **165** C4
Nicholas Rd **1** OL8 . . . . . **66** E4
Nicholas St
Bolton BL2 . . . . **148** A3
Manchester M1, M2 . . . . **159** A1
Nicholls St M12 . . . . **164** A3
Nicholson Rd SK14 . . . . . **101** C5
Nicholson Sq SK16 . . . . . **101** B8
Nicholson St
Oldham OL4 . . . . **67** E6
Rochdale OL11 . . . . **139** C1
Stockport SK4 . . . . **169** E2
Nichols St M6 . . . . **81** B3
Nickleby Rd SK12 . . . . . **133** E3
Nicolas Rd M21 . . . . **97** A1
Nicol Mere Dr WN4 . . . . . **73** A5
Nicol Mere Sch WN4 . . . . **73** A5
Nicol Rd WN4 . . . . **73** B5
Nield Rd M34 . . . . **100** F3
Nield's Brow WA14 . . . . . **119** C2
Nield St OL5 . . . . **68** B2
Nields Way SK6 . . . . **126** D4
Nigel Rd M9 . . . . **157** C3
Nigher Moss Ave SK6 . . . **31** C6
Nightingale Cl SK9 . . . . . **131** B1
Nightingale Cl **1** WN6 . . . **37** A1
Nightingale Dr M34 . . . . **101** A2
Nightingale Gdns M23 . . **109** A1
Nightingale Rd BL6 . . . . . **21** C3
Nightingale St M3 . . . . . **159** A3
Nightingales Wlk **2** BL3 **147** C3
Nile St
Ashton-u-L OL7 . . . . **100** F8

Nile St continued
Bolton BL3 . . . . 145 C1
Oldham OL3 . . . . 153 B4
Rochdale OL16 . . . . 31 A8
Nile Terr M7 . . . . 155 A1
Nile The ⑪ M15 . . . . 162 C3
NIMBLE NOOK 152 A1
Nimble Nook OL9 . . . . 152 A1
Nina Dr M40 . . . . 65 C3
Nine Acre Ct M5 . . . . 161 B3
Nine Acre Dr M5 . . . . 161 B3
Ninehouse La BL3 . . . . 147 C4
Ninfield Rd M23 . . . . 121 B4
Ninian Ct ② M24 . . . . 46 F1
Ninian Gdns M24 . . . . 60 D3
Ninth Ave OL8 . . . . 66 D1
Nipper La M45 . . . . 44 E2
Nisbet Ave M22 . . . . 121 E3
Nixon Rd BL3 . . . . 163 C3
Nixon St M13 . . . . 146 C3
Nixon Road S BL3 . . . . 146 C3
Nixon St
  Failsworth M35 . . . . 83 E7
  Rochdale OL11 . . . . 30 B3
  Stockport SK3 . . . . 170 B4
No 2 Pas SK3 . . . . 169 A1
No 11 Pas M20 . . . . 109 F5
Noahs Ark La M40 . . . . 136 A1
NOB END 43 A2
Nob End Nature Reserve*
  BL3 . . . . 42 F1
Noble Mdw OL12 . . . . 15 D4
Noble St
  Bolton BL3 . . . . 145 B1
  ⑦ Leigh WN7 . . . . 76 A5
  Oldham OL8 . . . . 66 F4
Noel Dr M33 . . . . 108 D4
Noel St BL1 . . . . 145 B3
Nolan St M9 . . . . 157 B4
Nona St M6 . . . . 154 B3
NOOK 49 D7
Nook Farm Ave OL12 . . . . . 14 F3
Nook Fields BL2 . . . . 25 E3
Nook La
  Ashton-u-L OL6 . . . . 85 E6
  Golborne WA3 . . . . 90 B8
  Tyldesley M29 . . . . 77 D2
Nook Terr ⑩ OL12 . . . . . . 14 F3
Nook The
  Appley Bridge WN6 . . . . 35 E7
  Bramhall SK7 . . . . 132 D5
  Eccles M30 . . . . 79 A4
  Uppermill OL3 . . . . 69 C4
  Urmston M41 . . . . 95 D1
  Worsley M28 . . . . 78 F8
Noon Ct WA12 . . . . 89 B1
Noon Sun Cl OL3 . . . . 69 A4
Noon Sun St OL3 . . . . 14 F1
Norbet Wlk ⑧ M9 . . . . . . 157 B3
Norbreck Ave
  Cheadle SK8 . . . . 123 A6
  Manchester M21 . . . . 109 B7
Norbreck Cres M6 . . . . 37 A2
Norbreck Gdns BL2 . . . . . 148 C4
Norbreck St BL2 . . . . 148 C4
Norburn Rd M13 . . . . 98 F2
Norbury Ave
  Billinge WN5 . . . . 71 D6
  Hyde SK14 . . . . 167 A2
  Marple SK6 . . . . 125 E6
  Sale M33 . . . . 107 F4
  ⑦ Salford M7 . . . . 80 D5
  Uppermill OL4 . . . . 68 C6
Norbury Cl M40 . . . . 160 B4
Norbury Cres SK7 . . . . 124 D2
Norbury Dr SK6 . . . . 125 F6
Norbury Gr
  Bolton BL1 . . . . 25 A4
  Hazel Grove SK7 . . . . 124 E2
  Swinton M27 . . . . 61 F1
Norbury Hall Prim Sch
  SK7 . . . . 124 E1
Norbury Ho ⑭ OL4 . . . . . . 67 B5
Norbury Hollow Rd SK7 . . 134 B8
Norbury La OL8 . . . . 67 D3
Norbury Mews SK6 . . . . . . 125 E6
NORBURY MOOR 124 E1
Norbury St
  Leigh WN7 . . . . 75 D5
  Rochdale OL16 . . . . 31 B4
  Salford M7 . . . . 155 B2
Norbury Way ⑧ SK9 . . . . . 131 D5
Norcliffe Wlk M18 . . . . 99 B4
Norcot Wlk ⑱ M15 . . . . . 162 A2
Norcross Cl M7 . . . . 124 D5
Nordale Pk OL12 . . . . 13 D2
Nordek Cl OL2 . . . . 48 D5
Nordek Dr OL2 . . . . 48 D5
NORDEN 13 E2
Norden Ave M20 . . . . 110 A6
Norden Cl OL11 . . . . 13 C2
Norden Com Prim Sch
  OL12 . . . . 13 F2
Norden Ct BL3 . . . . 147 B4
Norden Lodge OL11 . . . . . 29 E8
Norden Rd OL11 . . . . 29 E6
Norden St M11 . . . . 99 D1
Nordens Rd ⑧ OL9 . . . . . . 65 F8
Nordens St OL9 . . . . 152 A4
Norden Way OL11 . . . . 13 C2
Noreen Ave M25 . . . . 63 C5
Norfield Cl SK16 . . . . 101 C8
Norfolk Ave
  Droylsden M43 . . . . 83 F3
  Heywood OL10 . . . . 29 A2
  Manchester M18 . . . . 99 C4
  Reddish, Debdale M34 . . . 99 F3

Norfolk Ave continued
  Reddish, Heaton Chapel
  SK4 . . . . 111 C6
  Whitefield M45 . . . . 63 A8
Norfolk Cl
  Calderbrook OL15 . . . . . . 6 C1
  Hindley WN2 . . . . 57 A6
  Irlam M44 . . . . 105 C5
  Little Lever BL3 . . . . 43 B4
  Shaw OL2 . . . . 48 F7
Norfolk Cres M35 . . . . 83 E6
Norfolk Dr BL4 . . . . 42 D1
Norfolk Gdns M41 . . . . 94 D3
Norfolk Ho
  ③ Manchester M7 . . . . . . 63 E1
  ① Sale M33 . . . . 108 D4
Norfolk Rd
  Atherton M46 . . . . 58 C5
  Longshaw WN5 . . . . 53 E1
  Manchester M18 . . . . 99 C4
Norfolk Sq ⑧ SK13 . . . . . . 104 C1
Norfolk St
  Glossop SK13 . . . . 104 D1
  Hyde SK14 . . . . 167 A2
  Manchester M2 . . . . 159 A1
  Oldham OL9 . . . . 66 C4
  Rochdale OL11 . . . . 139 E2
  Salford M6 . . . . 81 A5
  Walkden M28 . . . . 60 D6
  Wigan, Springfield WN6 . . 37 A2
  ⑨ Wigan, Worsley Hall
  WN5 . . . . 54 F6
Norfolk Way OL2 . . . . 48 D2
Norford Way OL11 . . . . 29 E7
Norgate St M20 . . . . 110 B3
Norlan Ave M34 . . . . 100 E7
Norland Wlk M40 . . . . 83 A5
Norleigh Rd M22 . . . . 121 D8
NORLEY 54 C6
Norley Ave M32 . . . . 96 F3
Norley Cl OL1 . . . . 48 B2
Norley Dr
  Manchester M19 . . . . 99 C2
  Sale M33 . . . . 108 E4
Norley Hall Ave WN5 . . . . . 54 C6
Norley Rd
  Leigh WN7 . . . . 75 B4
  Wigan WN5 . . . . 54 C7
Norman Ave
  Haydock WA11 . . . . 89 A7
  Hazel Grove SK7 . . . . 124 C3
  Newton-le-W WA12 . . . . . 89 E3
Normanby Chase WA14 . . 119 B4
Normanby Gr M27 . . . . 61 E1
Normanby Rd M28 . . . . 60 C1
Normanby St
  Bolton BL3 . . . . 146 C2
  Manchester M14 . . . . 98 A4
  Swinton M27 . . . . 61 E1
  Wigan WN5 . . . . 54 B6
Norman Cl M24 . . . . 47 C1
Normandale Ave BL1 . . . . 142 A1
Normandy Cres M26 . . . . . 43 F3
Norman Gr
  Manchester M12 . . . . 99 A4
  Reddish SK5 . . . . 111 E7
Norman Rd
  Altrincham WA14 . . . . . . 119 C6
  Ashton-u-L OL6 . . . . 85 C6
  Manchester M14 . . . . 98 D2
  Rochdale OL11 . . . . 139 A2
  Sale M33 . . . . 108 B3
  Salford M7 . . . . 155 B3
  Stalybridge SK15 . . . . . . 87 B3
  Stockport, Heaton Norris
  SK4 . . . . 168 B3
Norman Road W M9 . . . . . 157 C3
Norman's Pl WA14 . . . . . . 119 D4
Norman St
  Bury BL9 . . . . 141 B4
  Failsworth M35 . . . . 66 A1
  Hyde SK14 . . . . 167 B2
  Manchester M12 . . . . 165 B1
  Middleton M24 . . . . 47 B2
  Oldham OL1 . . . . 153 A4
  Radcliffe M26 . . . . 44 D4
Normanton Ave M6 . . . . . . 80 C3
Normanton Cl WN6 . . . . . . 36 E4
Normanton Dr M9 . . . . 64 E4
Normanton Rd SK3, SK8 . . 123 A6
Normington St ⑪ OL4 . . . 67 C7
Norreys Ave M41 . . . . 94 E3
Norreys St OL16 . . . . 31 A8
Norris Ave M34 . . . . 168 C1
Norris Bank Prim Sch
  SK4 . . . . 168 C1
Norris Bank Terr SK4 . . . . 168 C1
Norris Hill Dr SK4 . . . . 168 C2
Norris Rd M33 . . . . 108 D2
Norris St
  Bolton BL3 . . . . 145 B1
  Little Lever BL3 . . . . 43 A3
  Tyldesley M29 . . . . 77 A8
Norris Twrs SK4 . . . . 169 B2
Nortex Mill Bsns Ctr BL1 . 145 A4
Northallerton Rd M7 . . . . . 81 B6
Northam Cl WN6 . . . . 17 D1
Northampton Rd M40 . . . . 157 C2
Northampton Way ⑪
  M34 . . . . 101 A1
NORTH ASHTON 72 E6
North Ave
  Farnworth BL4 . . . . 60 B8
  Golborne WN7 . . . . 74 F4
  Leigh WN7 . . . . 76 C3
  Manchester M19 . . . . 110 F7
  Ramsbottom BL8 . . . . . . 10 F1

North Ave continued
  Stalybridge SK15 . . . . . . 86 A3
  Uppermill OL3 . . . . 69 B5
  Whitefield BL9 . . . . 45 B4
Northaven Cl M30 . . . . 80 A1
North Back Rock BL9 . . . . 140 C2
Northbank Gdns M19 . . . . 110 E6
Northbank Ind Pk M44 . . . 105 F6
Northbank Wlk M20 . . . . . 109 D3
North Blackfield La M7 . . . 81 C8
Northbourne St M6 . . . . . . 154 B2
Northbrook Ave M8 . . . . . . 63 F4
North Brook Rd SK13 . . . . 171 B4
North Broughton St M3 . . 158 B2
North Butts St WN7 . . . . . . 76 B3
North Cestrian Gram Sch
  WA14 . . . . 119 C5
North Chadderton Sch
  OL9 . . . . 48 A2
North Chadderton Sch
  (Lower) OL9 . . . . 152 A4
North Cheshire Jewish Prim
  Sch SK8 . . . . 122 C2
North Circ M45 . . . . 63 A6
North City Sh Ctr M9 . . . . 157 B4
North Cl SK13 . . . . 103 F7
North Cliffen La M7 . . . . . 155 B2
Northcliffe Rd SK2 . . . . . . 124 C8
Northcombe Rd SK3 . . . . . 170 B1
Northcote Ave M22 . . . . . 121 D4
Northcote Rd SK7 . . . . 132 F7
North Cres
  Droylsden M11 . . . . 83 D3
  Failsworth M40 . . . . 65 D3
  Manchester M11 . . . . 37 F1
North Croft
  Atherton M46 . . . . 58 B5
  Oldham OL8 . . . . 67 A3
Northdale Rd M9 . . . . 64 B5
North Dean St M27 . . . . . . 62 A1
Northdene Dr OL11 . . . . . . 29 F6
Northdown Ave
  Manchester M15 . . . . 162 A2
  Romiley SK6 . . . . 113 C5
Northdowns Rd OL2 . . . . . 48 F8
North Downs Rd SK8 . . . . 122 F3
North Dr
  Appley Bridge WN6 . . . . 18 C2
  Droylsden M34 . . . . 84 C1
  Pendlebury M27 . . . . 80 B7
  ⑩ North Edge WN7 . . . . 76 B6
NORTHENDEN 121 D8
Northenden Prim Sch
  M22 . . . . 109 D1
Northenden Rd
  Gatley SK8 . . . . 122 A6
  Sale M33 . . . . 108 A4
Northenden View M20 . . . 110 B2
North End Rd SK15 . . . . . . 86 B2
Northen Gr M20 . . . . 109 F4
Northern Ave M27 . . . . 62 C3
Northern Gr BL1 . . . . 142 C1
NORTHERN MOOR 109 A1
Northfield Ave M40 . . . . . . 65 F2
Northfield Ct WN3 . . . . 74 C1
Northfield Dr SK9 . . . . 137 D8
Northfield Rd
  Bury BL9 . . . . 27 F6
  Failsworth M40 . . . . 65 F2
Northfield St BL3 . . . . 144 C1
Northfleet Rd M30 . . . . 94 F8
Northgate OL12 . . . . 14 C7
North Gate OL8 . . . . 66 E2
Northgate Ct BL6 . . . . 22 C1
Northgate La OL1 . . . . 49 E3
Northgate Rd SK3 . . . . 123 C8
North George St M3 . . . . . 158 A2
North Gr
  Manchester M13 . . . . 164 A1
  Urmston M41 . . . . 95 C2
  Walkden M28 . . . . 60 C3
North Grecian Street Prim
  Sch M7 . . . . 81 C5
North Hill St M3 . . . . 158 A3
North La
  Rochdale OL12 . . . . 139 C4
  Tyldesley M29 . . . . 77 A6
Northland Rd
  Bolton BL1 . . . . 24 F6
  Manchester M9 . . . . 65 A3
Northlands M26 . . . . 43 E5
Northleach Cl BL8 . . . . 27 B3
Northleigh Dr M25 . . . . . . 63 D3
Northleigh Ho ⑪ M16 . . . 97 B2
Northleigh Rd M16 . . . . . . 97 B3
North Lonsdale St M32 . . . 96 F4
North Manchester General
  Hospl M8 . . . . 64 B1
North Meade M21 . . . . 109 B7
NORTH MOOR 153 A3
Northmoor Rd M12 . . . . . . 99 A3
North Nook OL4 . . . . 67 F8
Northolme Gdns M19 . . . . 110 E5
Northolt Ave WN7 . . . . 75 F8
Northolt Cl M11 . . . . 83 D2
Northolt Dr BL3 . . . . 147 C4
Northolt Fold OL10 . . . . . . 46 E7
North Par M23 . . . . 108 F1
North Par
  ⑰ Manchester M2 . . . . . 158 C1
  Newhey OL16 . . . . 32 A5
  Sale M33 . . . . 108 D2
North Park Rd SK7 . . . . . . 123 E3
North Pl SK1 . . . . 169 C1
North Quarry Bsns Pk
  WN6 . . . . 18 D1
North Rd
  Altrincham WA14 . . . . . . 129 A8

North Rd continued
  Atherton M46 . . . . 58 B5
  Droylsden, Clayton M11 . . 83 C2
  Droylsden M34 . . . . 84 D1
  Glossop SK13 . . . . 104 C3
  Prestwich M25 . . . . 62 F5
  Stretford M17 . . . . 96 C5
NORTH REDDISH 99 F1
North Reddish Jun & Inf
  Schs ⑤ SK5 . . . . 99 F1
North Ridge High Sch
  M12 . . . . 64 C6
Northridge Rd M9 . . . . 64 D6
North Rise OL3 . . . . 69 B5
Northside Ave M41 . . . . . . 94 F1
North St
  Ashton-in-M WN4 . . . . . . 73 D5
  Ashton-u-L OL6 . . . . 166 A2
  Heywood OL10 . . . . 29 B2
  Manchester M8 . . . . 159 A4
  Middleton M24 . . . . 47 A2
  Radcliffe M26 . . . . 44 C4
  Ramsbottom BL0 . . . . . . 1 C2
  Rochdale OL16 . . . . 31 A8
  ⑪ Royton OL2 . . . . 48 D4
  Whitworth OL12 . . . . 4 C1
North Stage M50 . . . . 96 F8
North Star Dr M3 . . . . 158 A1
Northstead Ave M34 . . . . 101 B2
Northumberland Ave
  OL7 . . . . 166 A4
Northumberland Cl
  M16 . . . . 161 C1
Northumberland Cres
  M16 . . . . 161 C1
Northumberland Rd
  Brimington SK5 . . . . 112 B6
  Manchester M16 . . . . 161 C1
  Partington M31 . . . . 105 E2
Northumberland St
  Salford M7 . . . . 155 B3
  Wigan WN1 . . . . 37 E1
Northumberland Way
  M22 . . . . 121 E6
Northumbria St ⑧ BL3 . . 144 C1
Northurst Dr M8 . . . . 63 F3
North Vale Rd WA15 . . . . . 119 F6
North Veiw M45 . . . . 44 E2
North View
  Mossley OL5 . . . . 68 E1
  Ramsbottom, Higher
  Summerseat BL9 . . . . 11 B2
  Ramsbottom, Strongstry BL0 . 1 C2
North View Cl OL4 . . . . 68 C5
North Walkden Prim Sch
  M28 . . . . 60 C5
Northward Rd SK9 . . . . . . 136 F6
Northway
  Altrincham WA14 . . . . . . 119 E6
  Droylsden M43 . . . . 100 A8
  Eccles M30 . . . . 79 F2
  Wigan WN1 . . . . 37 C1
North Way
  Bolton BL1 . . . . 25 B4
  Brinnington SK5 . . . . 112 C6
  Hyde SK14 . . . . 167 B2
Northways WN6 . . . . 19 D2
Northwell St ⑧ WN7 . . . . 75 E8
North Western St
  Manchester, Ardwick
  M12 . . . . 164 A3
  Manchester, Levenshulme
  M19 . . . . 111 A8
  Manchester M1, M12 . . . 163 C4
Northwold Cl WN3 . . . . . . 54 D3
Northwold Dr
  Bolton BL1 . . . . 40 E8
  Manchester M9 . . . . 65 B3
Northwood BL2 . . . . 25 D4
Northwood Ave WA12 . . . . 89 F3
Northwood Cres BL3 . . . . 144 C1
Northwood Gr M33 . . . . . . 108 B4
North Woodley ⑥ M26 . . 44 C1
Norton Ave
  Manchester M12 . . . . 99 B3
  Reddish M34 . . . . 100 A3
  Sale M33 . . . . 107 D6
  Urmston M41 . . . . 95 A4
Norton Gr SK4 . . . . 168 B1
Norton Grange M25 . . . . . . 63 D3
Norton Rd
  Boothstown M28 . . . . 77 E7
  Rochdale OL12 . . . . 14 F3
Norton St
  Bolton BL1 . . . . 143 C1
  Manchester M1 . . . . 159 C1
  Manchester M3 . . . . 158 C2
  Manchester, Miles Platting
  M40 . . . . 160 B4
  Manchester, Old Trafford
  M16 . . . . 97 C4
  Salford, Higher Broughton
  M7 . . . . 155 B3
Norview Dr M20 . . . . 122 B8
Norville Ave M40, M9 . . . . 65 D3
Norway Gr SK5 . . . . 169 C4
Norway St
  Bolton BL1 . . . . 143 A2
  Manchester M6 . . . . 154 B2
  Stretford M32 . . . . 96 E3
Norweb Way WN7 . . . . 76 B3
Norwell Rd M22 . . . . 121 E5
Norwich Ave
  Ashton-in-M WN4 . . . . . . 73 D3
  Chadderton OL9 . . . . 48 A1
  Denton M34 . . . . 100 F1
  Golborne WA3 . . . . 90 D8
  Rochdale OL11 . . . . 30 B7

Norwich Cl
  Ashton-u-L OL6 . . . . 85 D8
  Dukinfield SK16 . . . . 102 A7
Norwich Dr BL8 . . . . 140 A3
Norwich Rd M32 . . . . 95 F3
Norwich St OL11 . . . . 31 A5
Norwich St ⑤ BL3 . . . . . . 40 E4
Norwood M25 . . . . 63 B2
Norwood Ave
  Ashton-in-M WN4 . . . . . . 72 F6
  Bramhall SK7 . . . . 132 D5
  Cheadle SK8 . . . . 123 A3
  Golborne WA3 . . . . 90 F7
  High Lane SK6 . . . . 134 D7
  Manchester M20 . . . . 110 D4
  Salford M7 . . . . 81 B8
  Tyldesley M29 . . . . 77 B6
  Wigan WN6 . . . . 37 A3
Norwood Cl
  Adlington PR6 . . . . 21 A8
  Shaw OL2 . . . . 149 A4
  Walkden M28 . . . . 78 E8
Norwood Cres OL2 . . . . . . 48 E2
Norwood Ct M32 . . . . 96 E1
Norwood Dr
  Altrincham WA15 . . . . . . 120 D5
  Swinton M27 . . . . 79 D7
Norwood Gr
  Bolton BL1 . . . . 144 C4
  Royton OL2 . . . . 48 E2
Norwood Lo M7 . . . . 81 B8
Norwood Pk WA14 . . . . . . 119 C5
Norwood Rd
  Gatley SK8 . . . . 122 B6
  Stockport SK2 . . . . 124 B4
  Stretford M32 . . . . 96 E2
Noseby Ct M25 . . . . 63 C5
Nostell Rd WN4 . . . . 73 A5
Nottingham Ave SK5 . . . . 112 C6
Nottingham Cl SK5 . . . . . . 112 C5
Nottingham Dr
  Ashton-u-L OL6 . . . . 85 B7
  Bolton BL1 . . . . 143 B1
  Failsworth M35 . . . . 83 A6
Nottingham Pl WN1 . . . . . 37 E1
Nottingham Way ⑧ M34 101 A1
Nowell Ct M24 . . . . 47 A3
Nowell House M24 . . . . . . 47 A3
Nowell Rd M24 . . . . 47 A3
Nudger Cl OL3 . . . . 50 F2
Nudger Gn OL3 . . . . 51 A2
Nuffield Cl BL1 . . . . 142 B1
Nuffield Rd M22 . . . . 121 E4
Nugent House Sch WN5 . . 71 C4
Nugent Rd BL3 . . . . 147 B3
Nugget St OL4 . . . . 67 B6
Nuneaton Dr M40 . . . . 160 A3
Nuneham Ave M20 . . . . . . 110 C7
Nunfield Cl M40 . . . . 65 B2
NUN HILLS 3 C7
Nunnery Rd BL3 . . . . 146 B4
Nunthorpe Dr M8 . . . . 156 C4
Nursery Ave WA15 . . . . . . 128 E8
Nursery Cl
  ④ Glossop SK13 . . . . . . 116 C8
  Sale M33 . . . . 108 D4
  Stockport SK2 . . . . 124 D7
Nursery Dr SK12 . . . . 133 D4
Nursery Gdns OL16 . . . . . 31 C8
Nursery Gr M31 . . . . 105 E4
Nursery La
  Cheadle SK3 . . . . 123 A7
  Wilmslow SK9 . . . . 136 F5
Nursery Rd
  Cheadle SK8 . . . . 123 A1
  Dukinfield SK14 . . . . 101 C3
  Failsworth M35 . . . . 84 A7
  Prestwich M25 . . . . 63 A6
  Stockport SK4 . . . . 168 C2
Nursery St
  Manchester M16 . . . . 97 F3
  Salford M6 . . . . 154 C3
Nut Bank La M24 . . . . 64 E5
Nuthatch Ave M28 . . . . . . 78 D8
Nuthurst Rd M40 . . . . 65 D1
Nutsford Vale M12, M18 . . 99 B4
NUTTALL 11 C4
Nuttall Ave
  Horwich BL6 . . . . 22 A3
  Little Lever BL3 . . . . 43 C3
  Whitefield M45 . . . . 62 F8
Nuttall Cl OL3 . . . . 138 C1
Nuttall Hall Cott's BL0 . . . 11 D5
Nuttall Hall Rd BL0 . . . . . . 11 D5
Nuttall La BL0 . . . . 138 B1
NUTTALL LANE 138 B1
Nuttall Mews M45 . . . . 62 F8
Nuttall Rd BL0 . . . . 11 D4
Nuttall Sq BL9 . . . . 44 F5
Nuttall St
  Atherton M46 . . . . 58 B3
  Bury BL9 . . . . 141 A1
  Irlam M44 . . . . 105 B6
  Manchester, City Park
  M16 . . . . 161 C1
  Manchester M11 . . . . 165 A3
  Oldham OL8 . . . . 67 B4
  Rochdale OL11 . . . . 31 A7
Nutt La M25 . . . . 63 E8
Nutt St WN1 . . . . 37 E2
Nutwood Ct SK5 . . . . 111 E7

O

Oadby Cl M12. . . . . 99 A4
Oadby Pl **2** SK5 . . . . 99 F2
Oak Ave
 Abram Brow WN2 . . . . 74 C7
 Cheadle SK8 . . . . 123 A2
 Golborne WA3 . . . . 90 B8
 Hindley WN2 . . . . 57 A3
 9 Horwich BL6 . . . . 22 E1
 Irlam M44 . . . . 105 D5
 Little Lever BL3 . . . . 43 B3
 Manchester M21 . . . . 109 B8
 Middleton M24 . . . . 65 A7
 Newton-le-W WA12 . . . . . . 89 C3
 Ramsbottom BL0 . . . . 11 A2
 Romiley SK6 . . . . 113 C2
 Royton OL2 . . . . 48 D6
 Standish WN6 . . . . 36 F8
 Stockport, Heaton Norris
  SK4 . . . . 168 B2
 Whitefield M45 . . . . 62 F7
 Wilmslow SK9 . . . . 136 F5
OAK BANK 63 A8
Oakbank WN2 . . . . 56 B3
Oak Bank
 Alderley Edge SK9 . . . . . . 137 A2
 Manchester M9 . . . . 157 A4
 Mossley, Carrbrook SK15 . . 86 F7
 Prestwich M25 . . . . 62 F1
Oakbank Ave OL9 . . . . 65 F8
Oak Bank Ave M9 . . . . 64 F1
Oak Bank Cl M45 . . . . 63 B8
Oakbank Dr BL1 . . . . 24 D6
Oakbarton BL6 . . . . 40 C4
Oak Brow Cotts SK9 . . . . . . 130 E4
Oak Cl
 Mottram in L SK14 . . . . . . 103 A4
 Whitworth OL12 . . . . 4 D4
 Wilmslow SK9 . . . . 136 F6
Oakcliffe Rd
 Rochdale OL12 . . . . 15 D4
 Wythenshawe M23 . . . . . . 121 A7
Oak Coppice BL1 . . . . 144 A3
Oak Cotts SK9 . . . . 130 E4
Oakcroft SK15 . . . . 102 E8
Oakcroft Way M22 . . . . 121 E6
Oak Ct SK6 . . . . 113 A5
Oakdale BL2 . . . . 25 E4
Oakdale Cl M45 . . . . 62 D8
Oakdale Ct
 Altrincham WA14 . . . . 119 C5
 Delph OL3 . . . . 50 E3
 Stalybridge SK15 . . . . 86 B2
Oakdale Dr
 Gatley SK8 . . . . 122 B2
 Manchester M20 . . . . 110 C1
 Tyldesley M29 . . . . 77 C6
Oakdale Specl Sch SK16 . . 101 E6
Oakden Dr M34 . . . . 100 C2
Oakdene M27 . . . . 79 B6
Oak Dene OL3 . . . . 69 A4
Oakdene Ave
 Gatley SK8 . . . . 131 C7
 Reddish SK4 . . . . 111 D5
Oakdene Cres SK6 . . . . 125 F7
Oakdene Ct SK9 . . . . 131 B1
Oakdene Gdns SK6 . . . . 125 F7
Oakdene Rd
 Marple SK6 . . . . 125 F7
 Middleton M24 . . . . 65 C8
 Sale WA15 . . . . 120 B8
Oakdene St M9 . . . . 157 C4
Oak Dr
 Cheadle SK7 . . . . 132 C7
 Marple SK6 . . . . 125 D6
 Reddish M34 . . . . 100 A4
Oaken Bank Rd M24 . . . . 47 A3
Oakenbottom Rd BL2 . . . . . . 42 D7
Oakenclough OL1 . . . . 153 B3
Oaken Clough **3** OL7 . . . . . 85 A5
Oakenclough Cl SK9 . . . . . . 131 D2
Oakenclough Dr BL1 . . . . . . 23 F2
Oaken Clough Dr **1** OL7 . 85 A6
Oaken Clough Terr OL7 . . . 84 F6
Oakenden Cl WN4 . . . . 73 A6
Oakengates WN6 . . . . 19 F1
Oakenrod Hill OL11 . . . . 30 C6
Oakenshaw Ave OL12 . . . . . 14 C6
Oakenshaw View OL12 . . . . 14 C6
Oaken St OL7 . . . . 85 A6
Oaker Ave M20 . . . . 109 E4
Oaker Pl M20 . . . . 109 E4
Oakes St BL4 . . . . 60 F7
Oakes The SK13 . . . . 116 A7
Oakfield
 Dukinfield SK16 . . . . 101 E6
 Gatley SK8 . . . . 122 C2
 Manchester M25 . . . . 63 D3
 Sale M33 . . . . 108 A5
Oakfield Ave
 Atherton M46 . . . . 58 C4
 Cheadle SK8 . . . . 122 E6
 Droylsden M43 . . . . 83 F1
 Golborne WA3 . . . . 73 F1
 Manchester, Firswood M16 . 97 A3
 Manchester, Whalley Range
  M16. . . . . 97 D3
 Mossley SK15 . . . . 86 E6
Oakfield Cl
 Alderley Edge SK9 . . . . . . 137 B3
 Bramhall SK7 . . . . 132 E4
 Horwich BL6 . . . . 22 F2

Oakfield Cres WN2 . . . . 38 C5
Oakfield Ct WA15 . . . . 119 F6
Oakfield Dr M38 . . . . 59 E5
Oakfield Gr
 Farnworth BL4 . . . . 60 C6
 Manchester M18 . . . . 99 D4
Oakfield High Sch WN2 . . 57 A5
Oakfield Mews
 1 Sale M33 . . . . 108 A4
 Stockport SK3 . . . . 170 C1
Oakfield Prim Sch SK14 . 101 E5
Oakfield Rd
 Alderley Edge SK9 . . . . . . 137 B2
 Altrincham WA15 . . . . 119 E4
 Cheadle SK8 . . . . 122 C2
 Dukinfield SK14 . . . . 101 E5
 Glossop SK13 . . . . 171 B3
 Manchester M20 . . . . 110 A3
 Poynton SK12 . . . . 133 F4
 Stockport SK3 . . . . 170 C1
Oakfield St
 Altrincham WA15 . . . . 119 E5
 Manchester M8 . . . . 156 A2
Oakfield Terr OL11 . . . . 30 C8
Oakfield Trad Est WA15 . . 119 E5
Oakfold Ave OL6 . . . . 85 D6
Oakford Ave M40 . . . . 159 C3
Oakford Wlk BL3 . . . . 146 C4
Oak Gates BL7 . . . . .8 E1
Oak Gr
 Ashton-u-L OL6 . . . . 85 D6
 Cheadle SK8 . . . . 122 E5
 Eccles M30 . . . . 79 B1
 Poynton SK12 . . . . 133 D4
 Urmston M41 . . . . 95 E2
Oakgrove Sch SK8 . . . . 131 C7
Oakham Ave M20 . . . . 110 A8
Oakham Cl BL8 . . . . 27 D5
Oakham Mews M7 . . . . 63 D1
Oakham Rd M34 . . . . 101 A1
Oakhaven WN7 . . . . 76 C3
Oak Hill OL15 . . . . 15 F5
Oakhill Cl BL2 . . . . 43 A7
Oak Hill Cl WN1 . . . . 37 B4
Oakhill Ct M7 . . . . 155 B3
Oakhill Trad Est M28 . . . . . 60 C6
Oakhill Way M8 . . . . 155 C3
Oak Ho M14 . . . . 98 D1
Oakhouse Dr M21 . . . . 109 B7
Oakhurst Chase SK9 . . . . . 137 A2
Oakhurst Dr SK3 . . . . 123 B5
Oakhurst Gdns M25 . . . . . . 63 A4
Oakhurst Gr BL5 . . . . 57 C7
Oakington Ave **10** M14 . . 98 B3
Oak La
 Whitefield M45 . . . . 63 B8
 Wilmslow SK9 . . . . 136 F6
Oakland Ave
 Manchester M19 . . . . 110 E4
 Salford M6 . . . . 80 B4
 Stockport SK2 . . . . 124 D6
Oakland Gr BL1 . . . . 142 A2
Oaklands BL1 . . . . 40 F7
Oaklands Ave SK8 . . . . 123 A2
Oaklands Cl SK9 . . . . 131 E1
Oaklands Ct OL4 . . . . 68 F5
Oaklands Dene SK14 . . . . . 102 A2
Oaklands Dr
 Hazel Grove SK7 . . . . 124 E1
 Hyde SK14 . . . . 102 A2
 Prestwich M25 . . . . 63 B4
 Sale M33 . . . . 108 A5
Oaklands Ho M14 . . . . 98 C1
Oaklands Pk OL4 . . . . 68 F5
Oaklands Private Hospl
 M6 . . . . 80 B4
Oaklands Rd
 Edenfield BL0 . . . . 1 D2
 Golborne WA3 . . . . 90 F2
 Royton OL2 . . . . 48 E2
 Salford M7 . . . . 81 A8
 Swinton M27 . . . . 79 D6
 Uppermill OL4 . . . . 68 F5
Oaklea
 1 Manchester M16 . . . . 97 C3
 Shevington Moor WN6 . . . . 19 A2
Oak Lea Ave SK9 . . . . 137 A5
Oaklea Rd M33 . . . . 107 E5
Oakleigh
 4 Stockport, Davenport
  SK3. . . . . 123 F4
 Stockport, Heaton Moor
  SK4 . . . . 168 B3
Oakleigh Ave
 Altrincham WA15 . . . . 120 A7
 Bolton BL3 . . . . 42 A2
 1 Manchester M19 . . . . 110 F7
Oakleigh Cl OL10 . . . . 46 E7
Oakleigh Rd SK8 . . . . 131 E8
Oakley Ave WN5 . . . . 71 E6
Oakley Cl
 Failsworth M40 . . . . 83 C5
 Radcliffe M26 . . . . 62 A8
Oakley Dr
 Oldham OL1 . . . . 49 D4
 Wigan WN5 . . . . 54 E6
Oakley Gr BL5 . . . . 40 F7
Oakley St OL15 . . . . 15 E4
Oakley Villas SK4 . . . . 168 B3
Oaklings The WN2 . . . . 57 A3
Oak Lo SK7 . . . . 132 F7
Oakmere Ave M30 . . . . 79 C4
Oakmere Cl M21 . . . . 121 D4
Oakmere Rd
 Cheadle SK8 . . . . 122 E5
 Handforth SK9 . . . . 131 D5

Oak Mews SK9 . . . . 131 C1
Oakmoor Dr M7 . . . . 81 B8
Oakmoor Rd M23 . . . . 121 A6
Oak Rd
 Altrincham WA15 . . . . 119 E3
 Cheadle SK8 . . . . 122 E5
 Failsworth M35 . . . . 83 F6
 Manchester M20 . . . . 110 B5
 Oldham OL8 . . . . 66 D2
 Paddockhill WA16 . . . . . . 136 B5
 Partington M31 . . . . 105 D2
 Sale M33 . . . . 108 A5
 Salford M7 . . . . 81 C5
Oakridge Wlk **3** M9 . . . . 157 A3
Oaks Ave BL2 . . . . 25 E4
Oaks Bsns Pk The M23 . . . 120 E8
Oak Shaw Cl M9 . . . . 64 D2
Oakshaw Dr OL12 . . . . 14 A1
Oakside Cl SK8 . . . . 122 E6
Oaks La BL2 . . . . 25 B4
Oaks Prim Sch The BL1 . . 24 F6
Oak St
 Atherton M46 . . . . 58 A1
 Denton M34 . . . . 100 F6
 Eccles M30 . . . . 79 D1
 Glossop SK13 . . . . 104 C1
 Hazel Grove SK7 . . . . 124 D3
 Heywood OL10 . . . . 29 B3
 Hyde SK14 . . . . 167 E3
 Leigh WN7 . . . . 75 F3
 Littleborough OL15 . . . . . . 16 C5
 Manchester M4 . . . . 159 A2
 2 Manchester M4 . . . . 159 B2
 Middleton M24 . . . . 65 D7
 Newhey OL16. . . . . 32 B4
 Radcliffe M26 . . . . 44 C1
 Ramsbottom BL0 . . . . 138 B1
 Rochdale OL16 . . . . 139 C3
 Shaw OL2 . . . . 149 C3
 Stockport SK3 . . . . 123 B8
 Swinton M27 . . . . 62 A1
 Tyldesley M29 . . . . 59 A1
 Whitworth OL12. . . . . 4 D5
 Wigan WN1 . . . . 151 B3
Oaks The
 Gatley SK8 . . . . 122 A2
 Hyde SK14 . . . . 102 A3
Oak Terr
 Littleborough OL15 . . . . 6 D2
 Rawtenstall BB4 . . . . 1 E8
Oak Tree Cl
 Atherton M46 . . . . 58 A1
 Hyde SK14 . . . . 102 A2
 Stockport SK2 . . . . 124 D8
Oaktree Cotts SK8 . . . . 122 F3
Oak Tree Cres SK15 . . . . . . 102 B8
Oak Tree Ct SK8 . . . . 122 E5
Oak Tree Dr SK16 . . . . 101 F7
Oak View
 Oldham OL11 . . . . 48 D1
 Whitworth OL12. . . . . 4 D4
Oak View Rd OL3 . . . . 69 B5
Oakville Dr M6 . . . . 80 A4
Oakville Terr **11** M40 . . . . 64 F1
Oakwater Ave SK8 . . . . 122 C2
Oakway
 Manchester M24 . . . . 122 C8
 Middleton M24 . . . . 46 F4
Oakwell Dr
 Manchester M7 . . . . 63 E1
 Whitefield BL9 . . . . 45 B3
Oakwell Mans M7 . . . . 63 E1
Oak Wlk M34 . . . . 100 E6
OAKWOOD 86 E4
Oakwood
 Chadderton OL9 . . . . 65 F7
 Glossop SK13. . . . . 115 F8
 Sale M33 . . . . 107 C4
Oakwood Ave
 Ashton-in-M WN4 . . . . 73 A2
 Denton M34 . . . . 100 F7
 Failsworth M40 . . . . 65 D1
 Gatley SK8 . . . . 122 B5
 Shevington WN6 . . . . 35 F5
 Swinton M27 . . . . 61 A4
 Walkden M28 . . . . 60 F2
 Wilmslow SK9 . . . . 136 E6
Oakwood Cl BL8 . . . . 27 B3
Oakwood Ct WA14 . . . . 128 B8
Oakwood Dr
 Bolton BL1 . . . . 40 F8
 Leigh WN7 . . . . 75 E1
 Manchester M8 . . . . 63 F2
 Walkden M28 . . . . 60 F2
Oakwood Est M5 . . . . 154 A1
Oakwood High Sch M30 . . 79 F4
Oakwood La WA14 . . . . 119 B1
Oakwood Mews M24 . . . . . . 65 C8
Oakwood Rd
 Disley SK12 . . . . 135 D6
 Romiley SK6 . . . . 113 C2
Oakwood Sq SK8 . . . . 122 C2
Oak Wood View OL5 . . . . . . 86 C6
Oakworth Croft OL4 . . . . . . 49 F4
Oakworth Dr BL1 . . . . 24 D5
Oakworth St M9 . . . . 64 C3
Oasis Acad Media City . . .
Oatlands Rd M22 . . . . 121 C2
Oat St SK11 . . . . 124 A7
Oban Ave
 Failsworth M40 . . . . 83 A4
 Oldham M41 . . . . 49 B1
Oban Cres SK11 . . . . 123 D4
Oban Dr
 Garswood WN4 . . . . 72 C4
 Sale M33 . . . . 108 C3

Oban Gr BL1 . . . . 24 E5
Oban Way WN2 . . . . 38 D5
Oberlin St
 Oldham OL4 . . . . 67 D7
 Rochdale OL11 . . . . 139 A1
Oberon Cl **1** M30 . . . . 79 D2
Occlestone Cl M33 . . . . . . 108 E1
Occupation Rd **1** WA14 119 D6
Ocean Ho M15 . . . . 163 A1
Ocean St WA14 . . . . 119 B6
Ocean Street Trad Est
 WA14 . . . . 119 B6
Ocean Wlk **3** M15 . . . . . . 162 C1
Ockendon Dr M9 . . . . 157 B3
Octavia Dr M40 . . . . 83 C4
Odell St M11 . . . . 165 B3
Odessa Ave M6 . . . . 80 B4
Odette St M18 . . . . 99 C4
OFFERTON 124 E6
Offerton Dr SK2 . . . . 124 D6
Offerton Fold SK2 . . . . 124 C7
Offerton Gn SK2 . . . . 124 F6
OFFERTON GREEN 125 A6
Offerton Ind Est SK1,
 SK2 . . . . 124 C7
Offerton La SK1, SK2 . . . . 124 C8
Offerton Rd SK2, SK7 . . . . 125 A4
Offerton St SK2 . . . . 124 E8
Offerton Sch
 Offerton SK2 . . . . 125 A6
 Horwich BL6 . . . . 22 A3
 Stockport SK1 . . . . 112 B2
Off Grove Rd SK15 . . . . 86 D4
Off Ridge Hill La **3** SK15 . 85 F2
Off Stamford St SK15 . . . . . 86 D4
Off Vaudrey La **4** M34 . . 101 A2
Ogbourne Wlk **9** M13. . . 163 C2
OGDEN 32 F5
Ogden Cl
 Haslingden BB4 . . . . 1 A7
 Heywood OL10. . . . . 29 A2
 Whitefield M45 . . . . 45 A1
Ogden Ct SK14 . . . . 167 B2
Ogden Dr BB4 . . . . 1 A7
Ogden Gdns SK16 . . . . 101 E8
Ogden Gr SK8 . . . . 121 F4
Ogden La
 Manchester M11 . . . . 99 D7
 Newhey OL16. . . . . 32 D5
Ogden Rd
 Bramhall SK7 . . . . 132 D5
 Failsworth M35 . . . . 83 F6
Ogden Sq SK16 . . . . 101 B8
Ogden St
 Broadbottom SK14 . . . . . . 115 B8
 Chadderton OL9 . . . . 152 C4
 4 Manchester M20 . . . 110 B3
 2 Middleton M24 . . . . . 65 A8
 9 Oldham OL4 . . . . 67 D6
 Prestwich M25 . . . . 63 C4
 Rochdale OL11 . . . . 30 C2
 Swinton M27 . . . . 79 F7
Ogden Wlk M45 . . . . 63 A8
Ogmore Wlk M40 . . . . 65 C2
Ogwen Dr M25 . . . . 63 B5
Ohio Ave M50 . . . . 96 F8
O'Kane Ho **10** M30 . . . . . 79 D1
Okehampton Cl M26 . . . . . . 43 C5
Okehampton Cres M33 . . . 107 D5
Okeover Rd M7 . . . . 75 D6
Oldacres Dr M17 . . . . 155 A4
Olaf St **3** BL2 . . . . 25 B1
Olanyian Dr M8 . . . . 155 B1
Old Bakery The **3** BL5 . . 57 F8
Old Bank Cl SK6 . . . . 113 A3
Old Bank St M2 . . . . 158 C1
Old Bank The M15 . . . . . . 163 A2
Old Bank View OL1 . . . . 49 C4
Old Barn Pl BL7 . . . . 25 A8
Old Barton Rd M17, M30 . . 95 C7
Old Bedians Sports Ctr
 M20. . . . . 122 A8
Old Beechfield Gdns
 WN6. . . . . 19 D1
Old Birley St M15 . . . . 162 C1
OLD BIRTLE. 28 C2
OLD BOSTON 89 A8
Old Boston WA11 . . . . 89 A7
Old Boston Trad Est
 WA11 . . . . 89 B8
Oldbridge Dr WN2 . . . . 56 D6
Old Broadway M20 . . . . . . 110 B5
Old Brook Cl OL12 . . . . 49 D8
Oldbrook Fold WA15 . . . . 120 B4
Old Brow OL5 . . . . 68 C1
Old Brow La OL16 . . . . 15 C3
Old Brown Ct OL5 . . . . 86 C8
Oldbury Cl
 Heywood OL10. . . . . 46 D7
 Manchester M40 . . . . 160 A3
Oldcastle Ave M20 . . . . . . 110 A8
Old Chapel St SK3 . . . . . . 170 A3
Old Church Mews **2**
 SK16 . . . . 101 E8
Old Church St
 Failsworth M40 . . . . 83 C6
 Oldham OL1 . . . . 153 C3
Old Clay Dr OL12 . . . . 15 D4
Old Clough La M28 . . . . 60 F1
Old Colliery Yd WN4 . . . . . . 72 C3
Old Croft St OL4 . . . . 67 F5
Old Croft OL4 . . . . 68 A6
Old Croft Mews SK1 . . . . . 124 B7
Old Crofts Bank M41 . . . . . 95 C3
Old Cross St OL6 . . . . 104 E2
Old Cross St OL6 . . . . 166 C3
Old Ctyd The M22 . . . . 121 F5

Old Dairy Mews SK14 . . . . 101 C5
Old Delph Rd OL11 . . . . 13 F1
Old Doctors St BL8. . . . . . . 26 F7
Old Eagley Mews BL1 . . . . 24 F6
Old Edge La OL12 . . . . 48 C2
Old Elm St M12, M13. . . . . 163 C4
Old Engine Ho The BL0. . . 138 C2
Old Engine La BL0 . . . . 11 D6
Oldersaw Dr M9 . . . . 157 A2
Old Farm Cres M43 . . . . . . 99 F8
Old Farm Dr SK2. . . . . 124 F6
Old Farm La M46 . . . . 132 C7
OLDFIELD BROW 119 A5
Oldfield Brow Prim Sch
 WA14 . . . . 119 A5
Oldfield Cl **1** BL5. . . . . . . 57 F8
Oldfield Dr WA15 . . . . 119 F6
Oldfield Gr M33. . . . . 108 C5
Oldfield La WA14 . . . . 118 F4
Oldfield Mews WA14 . . . . . 119 C5
Oldfield Rd
 Altrincham WA14 . . . . 119 B5
 Prestwich M25 . . . . 63 C7
 Sale M33 . . . . 108 C5
 Salford M5 . . . . 161 C4
Oldfield St M11 . . . . 83 C1
Old Fold M30 . . . . 79 C4
Old Fold Rd
 Aspull WN2 . . . . 38 D5
 Westhoughton BL5 . . . . . . 57 C7
Old Gardens St BL3 . . . . . 170 C4
Old Garden The WA15 . . . . 120 B7
Oldgate Wlk M15 . . . . 162 A2
OLD GLOSSOP 104 E2
Old Green
 Bolton BL2 . . . . 25 F2
 Ramsbottom BL8 . . . . 10 F1
Old Greenwood La BL6 . . . 22 D1
Old Ground St BL0 . . . . . . 138 C2
Old Hall Cl
 Bury BL8 . . . . 27 B7
 Glossop SK13. . . . . 104 D2
Old Hall Clough BL6. . . . . . 40 C7
Oldhall Cres SK9 . . . . 131 E3
Old Hall Ct
 Sale M33 . . . . 108 A4
 Whitefield M45 . . . . 62 C7
Old Hall Dr
 Ashton-in-M WN4 . . . . 73 A2
 Manchester M18 . . . . 99 D4
 Stockport SK2 . . . . 124 E6
Old Hall Drive Prim Sch
 M18. . . . . 99 D4
Old Hall Farm BL3 . . . . 42 E4
Old Hall La
 Bolton BL6 . . . . 23 C1
 Manchester M25 . . . . 64 A6
 Manchester, Rusholme M13, M14,
  M19. . . . . 98 E2
 Marple SK6 . . . . 126 C5
 Mottram in L SK14 . . . . . . 103 A5
 Westhoughton BL5 . . . . . . 57 E6
 Whitefield M45 . . . . 62 C6
 Woodford SK7 . . . . 132 D1
 Worsley M28 . . . . 78 E7
Old Hall Mill La M46 . . . . . . 76 A8
Old Hall Prim Sch BL8 . . . . 27 B7
Old Hall Rd
 Failsworth M40 . . . . 83 B7
 Gatley SK8 . . . . 122 A6
 Manchester M7 . . . . 63 D1
 Stretford M32 . . . . 96 A4
 Whitefield M45 . . . . 62 C7
Old Hall Sq **3** SK13 . . . . 104 A5
Old Hall St
 Dukinfield SK16 . . . . 101 A7
 Farnworth BL4 . . . . 60 E7
 Ince-in-M WN3 . . . . 151 B2
 3 Manchester M11 . . . . 99 E7
 Middleton M24 . . . . 47 C1
Old Hall Street N BL1 . . . . 145 C3
OLDHAM 153 B3
Oldham Ave SK1 . . . . 112 B1
Oldham Bsns Ctr OL4 . . . 153 C2
Oldham Central Trad Pk Pk
 OL1. . . . . 67 A8
Oldham Coll The OL9. . . . 153 B3
Oldham Ct **11** M40 . . . . . 159 C3
Oldham Dr SK6 . . . . 113 A4
OLDHAM EDGE 48 F1
Oldham Rd
 Ashton-u-L OL7 . . . . 85 A5
 Delph OL3, OL4 . . . . 50 D2
 Failsworth M35, M40. . . . . 83 D6
 Middleton M24 . . . . 65 A8
 Rochdale OL11, OL16 . . . . 31 A3
 Royton OL11, OL2 . . . . . . 48 E3
 Shaw OL1, OL4. . . . . 50 B7
 Shaw, Shaw Side OL2 . . . 149 B1
 Uppermill OL4, OL3 . . . . . 68 F7
 OL3 . . . . 153 B2
Oldhams La
 Bolton BL1 . . . . 143 A4
 Bolton, Sharples BL1 . . . . 24 D5
Oldham Sports Ctr OL1 . . 153 C3
Oldham St
 Denton M34 . . . . 100 C3
 Glossop SK13. . . . . 84 B2
 Hyde SK14 . . . . 167 A2
 Manchester M1, M4 . . . . . 159 A1
 8 Manchester M5 . . . . 111 E7
 Salford M5 . . . . 158 A1
Oldhams Terr BL1 . . . . 143 A4
Oldham Way OL1, OL4, OL8,
 OL9 . . . . 153 B2

Oldham West Bsns Ctr
OL9 . . . . 152 B3
Old Heyes Rd WA15 . . . 120 B8
Old Hey Wlk WA12 . . . . 89 C1
Old House Terr OL6 . . . . 85 E5
Old Kiln OL13 . . . . 3 D8
Old Kiln La
 Bolton BL1 . . . . 23 D1
 Oldham OL4 . . . . 68 B4
Oldknow Rd SK6 . . . . . 126 A6
Old La
 Bury BL9 . . . . 27 F8
 Horwich BL6 . . . . 22 F2
 Manchester M11 . . . . . . 99 D7
 Oldham, Werneth OL9 . . 68 A8
 Oldham, Wood Brook OL4 . 68 A8
 Shevington WN6 . . . . . . 36 B6
 Uppermill, Lydgate OL4 . . 68 E6
 Uppermill OL3 . . . . 51 B2
 Walkden M38 . . . . 59 F6
 Westhoughton BL5 . . . . 57 D8
 Whitworth OL12, OL13 . . 4 E6
 Wigan WN1 . . . . 37 B4
Old Lansdowne Rd M20 . 110 A4
Old Lees St OL6 . . . . . . 85 D5
Old Links Cl BL1 . . . . . . 23 E2
Old Lord's Cres BL6 . . . 22 B5
Old Manor Pk M46 . . . . 58 A2
Old Market Pl 4 WA14 . 118 D5
Old Market St M9 . . . . 64 D2
Old Meadow Dr M34 . . 100 F5
Old Meadow La WA15 . . 120 B3
Old Medlock St M3 . . . 162 B4
Old Mill Cl
 Lymm WA13 . . . . 117 C6
 Pendlebury M27 . . . . . . 80 B8
Old Mill Ho OL4 . . . . . . 68 A5
Old Mill La
 Hazel Grove SK7 . . . . . 134 A8
 Oldham OL4 . . . . 68 A5
Old Mills Hill M24 . . . . . 47 D1
Oldmill St OL12 . . . . . 139 C4
Old Mill St M4 . . . . . . 159 C1
Olivia Ct M20 . . . . 110 B7
Old Moat Phram Sch M20 110 A7
Old Moor Rd SK6 . . . . . 112 E5
Old Moss La WA13 . . . . 92 E6
Old Mount St M4 . . . . . 159 B3
Old Nans La BL2 . . . . . . 25 E4
Old Nursery Fold BL2 . . . 25 E4
Old Oak Cl BL2 . . . . 43 B5
Old Oak Dr M34 . . . . . . 101 A3
Old Oake Cl M28 . . . . . . 60 E2
Old Oak St M20 . . . . . . 110 B3
Old Orchard SK9 . . . . . 137 A7
Old Orch The WA15 . . . 120 B8
Old Packhorse Rd OL15 . . 16 F6
Old Pack Horse Rd OL3 . . 51 B6
Old Park La M17 . . . . . . 155 E6
Old Parrin La M30 . . . . . 79 B3
Old Pasture Cl SK2 . . . . 124 E7
Old Pepper La WN6 . . . . 19 B2
Old Quarry La BL7 . . . . . . 8 F1
Old Rake BL6 . . . . 22 E5
Old Rd
 Ashton-in-M WN4 . . . . . 73 A4
 Ashton-u-L OL6 . . . . . . 86 A6
 Bolton BL1 . . . . 143 B3
 Cheadle SK8 . . . . 122 F6
 Dukinfield SK16 . . . . . . 166 C1
 Failsworth M35 . . . . . . 83 E8
 Glossop SK13 . . . . 104 A7
 Handforth SK9 . . . . 131 D3
 Hyde SK14 . . . . 167 A4
 Manchester M9 . . . . . . 64 D2
 Mottram in L SK14 . . . . 102 F5
 Rochdale OL16 . . . . 15 E4
 Stalybridge SK15 . . . . . 102 C8
 Stockport SK4 . . . . 169 B3
 Wilmslow SK9 . . . . 137 B8
Old Rectory Gdns SK8 . . 122 D5
Old River Cl M44 . . . . . . 94 A2
Old School Ct
 Eccles M30 . . . . 79 D4
 Manchester M9 . . . . . . 64 C2
Old School Dr M9 . . . . . 64 C2
Old School House The
 OL15 . . . . 15 F6
Old School La
 Adlington PR7 . . . . 20 E5
 Cheadle SK8 . . . . 132 A8
Old School Mews
 2 Bacup OL13 . . . . 3 C8
 4 Dukinfield SK15, SK16 . 101 E8
Old School Pl WN9 . . . . . 73 A3
Old School Rooms The 2
 BL1 . . . . 145 C2
Old Shaw St M5 . . . . . . 161 B4
Old Sirs BL5 . . . . 57 F5
Old St 6 OL6 . . . . 166 C3
Old St
 Ashton-u-L OL6 . . . . . . 166 B3
 Broadbottom SK14 . . . . 115 A8
 Oldham OL4 . . . . 67 D5
 Stalybridge SK15 . . . . . 86 A2
Old Stables The M34 . . . 100 F6
Old Station St 8 M30 . . 79 C1
Oldstead Gr BL1 . . . . . . 40 F3
Oldstead Wlk M9 . . . . . 157 A2
Old Swan Cl BL7 . . . . 8 E2
Old Swan Cotts BL7 . . . . . 8 E2
OLD TAME 50 B8
Old Tannery The SK14 . . 113 E8
Old Thorn La OL3 . . . . . 69 D6
Old Towns Cl BL8 . . . . . . 26 F7
OLD TRAFFORD 161 B1
Old Trafford Com Sch
 M16 . . . . 161 C2

Old Trafford (Lancashire Cty
 Cricket Club) M32 . . . . . 96 F4
Old Trafford (Man Utd FC)
 M17 . . . . 96 F5
Old Trafford Metro Sta
 M16 . . . . 97 A4
Old Vicarage BL5 . . . . . . 57 E5
Old Vicarage Gdns M28 . . 60 D3
Old Vicarage Mews BL5 . . 57 E5
Old Vicarage Rd BL6 . . . . 22 F3
Old Wargrave Rd WA12 . . 89 C3
Oldway Wlk M40 . . . . . . 83 B5
Old Wellington Rd M31 . . 79 E2
Old Wells Cl M38 . . . . . . 60 A6
Old Well Wlk M33 . . . . . 107 C2
Oldwood Rd M23 . . . . . 121 A3
Old Wool La SK8 . . . . . . 122 F4
Old York St M15 . . . . . . 162 B2
Oleo Terr M44 . . . . 94 C3
Olga St BL1 . . . . 143 A2
Olivant St BL9 . . . . 44 E8
Olive Bank BL8 . . . . 27 B4
Olive Gr WN6 . . . . 36 F3
Olive Rd WA15 . . . . 120 A8
Oliver Cl OL15 . . . . 15 F5
Oliver Fold Cl M28 . . . . . 77 E6
Oliver St
 Atherton M46 . . . . 58 D3
 Manchester, Beswick M11 . 164 C4
 Stockport SK1, SK3 . . . . 170 C4
Old Shapley Ave M20 . . . 110 B3
Olive St
 Bacup OL13 . . . . 3 E8
 Bolton BL3 . . . . 147 A4
 Bury BL8 . . . . 140 A2
 Failsworth M35 . . . . . . 83 E8
 Heywood OL10 . . . . 29 E2
 Radcliffe M26 . . . . 44 C3
 Rochdale OL11 . . . . 30 C1
Olive Terr 2 SK14 . . . . 115 A8
Olive Wlk 5 M33 . . . . . 107 C6
Olivia Ct M5 . . . . 161 A8
Olivia Gr M14 . . . . 98 D3
Ollerbarrow Rd WA15 . . 119 E2
Ollerbrook Ct 4 BL1 . . . 143 C2
Ollersett Ave SK22 . . . . 127 D1
Ollersett La SK22 . . . . . 127 E1
Ollerton 10 OL12 . . . . . 139 B4
Ollerton Ave
 Manchester M16 . . . . . . 97 C3
 Sale M33 . . . . 107 D5
Ollerton Cl
 Wigan WN2 . . . . 38 A2
 Wythenshawe M22 . . . . 109 E1
Ollerton Dr M35 . . . . . . 83 F6
Ollerton Rd SK9 . . . . . . 131 E5
Ollerton St
 1 Adlington PR6 . . . . . 21 A8
 Bolton BL1 . . . . 24 F6
Ollerton Terr BL1 . . . . . . 24 F6
Olney Ave M12 . . . . 99 B2
Olney OL11 . . . . 139 B2
Olney Ave M22 . . . . 121 D6
Olney St M13 . . . . 98 D4
Olsberg Cl M26 . . . . 44 C4
Olwen Ave M12 . . . . . . 164 B1
Olwen Cres SK5 . . . . . . 111 F8
Olympia Ct 2 M44 . . . . 94 A2
Olympia Trad Est M15 . . 162 B3
Olympic Ct M50 . . . . 96 F8
Olympic St M11 . . . . . . 164 B4
Omer Ave M13 . . . . 98 F2
Omer Dr M19 . . . . 110 E7
Onchan Ave OL4 . . . . . . 67 B6
One Ash Cl OL12 . . . . . . 14 F2
One Oak Ct SK7 . . . . . . 123 C2
One Oak La SK9 . . . . . . 137 F7
Ongar Wlk M9 . . . . 64 B3
Onslow Ave M40 . . . . . . 65 E1
Onslow Cl OL1 . . . . 153 B4
Onslow Rd SK3 . . . . 123 C8
Onslow St OL11 . . . . . . 30 C4
Onward St SK14 . . . . . . 167 A2
OOZEWOOD 48 B6
Oozewood Rd M2, OL2 . . 48 B5
Opal Ct 5 M14 . . . . . . 110 D8
Opal Gr WN7 . . . . 75 E4
Opal St M19 . . . . 111 B8
OPENSHAW 165 C4
Openshaw Fold Rd BL9 . . 44 D8
Openshaw La M44 . . . . . 105 E6
Openshaw Pl BL4 . . . . . . 60 B8
Openshaw Wlk 15 M11 . . 83 C1
Opera House* M3 . . . . . 158 B1
Oracle Ct M28 . . . . 60 D2
Orama Ave M6 . . . . 80 A4
Oram St BL9 . . . . 44 B2
Orange Hill Rd M25 . . . . . 63 C5
Orbital 24 Bsns Pk M43 . 100 D3
Orbital Way M11 . . . . . 100 D3
Orchard Ave
 Bolton BL1 . . . . 143 C3
 Partington M31 . . . . . . 105 F4
 Reddish M18 . . . . 99 E4
 Worsley M28 . . . . 78 B7
Orchard Brow WA3 . . . . 105 A2
Orchard Cl
 Cheadle SK8 . . . . 132 C7
 Leigh WN7 . . . . 75 F7
 Poynton SK12 . . . . 133 E3
 Shevington WN6 . . . . . . 36 A7
 Wilmslow SK9 . . . . 136 F5
Orchard Ct
 Bury BL9 . . . . 44 E7
 Orrell WN5 . . . . 53 D3

Orchard Ct *continued*
 Stockport SK2 . . . . 124 D6
Orchard Dr
 Altrincham WA15 . . . . . 120 A3
 Gamesley SK13 . . . . . . 171 B1
 Handforth SK9 . . . . 131 E2
Orchard Gdns
 Bolton BL2 . . . . 25 F3
 Mossy Lea WN6 . . . . . . 18 F6
Orchard Gn SK9 . . . . . . 137 B1
Orchard Gr
 Manchester M20 . . . . . 109 F5
 Shaw OL2 . . . . 149 A3
Orchard House Day Hospl
 OL2 . . . . 48 E4
Orchard Ind Est M6 . . . . 81 A5
Orchard La WN7 . . . . . . 76 A7
Orchard Pl
 Poynton SK12 . . . . 133 D4
 1 Sale M33 . . . . 108 B5
 Sale WA15 . . . . 120 B7
Orchard Rd
 Altrincham WA15 . . . . . 119 E5
 Compstall SK6 . . . . 114 B2
 Failsworth M35 . . . . . . 83 F7
 Lymm WA13 . . . . 117 B5
Orchard Rise SK14 . . . . 113 F7
Orchard Road E M22 . . . 109 E2
Orchard Road W M22 . . . 109 D2
Orchard St
 Ashton-in-M WN4 . . . . . 73 C3
 Heywood OL10 . . . . 29 E3
 Hyde SK14 . . . . 167 B2
 Manchester M20 . . . . . 109 F5
 Salford M6 . . . . 81 A4
 Stockport SK1 . . . . 169 F2
 Wigan WN1 . . . . 151 A4
Orchards The
 Heywood OL10 . . . . 29 E2
 3 Orrell WN5 . . . . 53 E5
Orchard The
 Disley SK12 . . . . 135 D6
 Oldham OL4 . . . . 67 C3
 4 Westhoughton BL5 . . 39 E1
Orchard Trad Est M6 . . . 80 F5
Orchard Vale SK3 . . . . . 123 C6
Orchard Wlk BL8 . . . . . . 10 F1
Orchid Ave BL4 . . . . 42 B1
Orchid Cl
 Irlam M44 . . . . 105 E8
 Oldham OL1 . . . . 48 D1
 Up Holland WN8 . . . . . . 53 B6
Orchid Dr BL9 . . . . 45 A7
Orchid Gdns SK8 . . . . . 121 F6
Orchid St M9 . . . . 157 A3
Orchid Way OL12 . . . . . . 14 D7
Ordell Wlk 1 M9 . . . . . 64 E3
ORDSALL 161 B3
Ordsall Ave M38 . . . . . . 60 B8
Ordsall District Ctr M5 . . 161 B4
Ordsall Hall (Mus)* M5 . 161 B3
Ordsall La M5 . . . . 161 C4
Oregon Ave OL1 . . . . . . 48 E1
Oregon Cl M13 . . . . 163 C2
Orford Ave SK12 . . . . . . 135 D6
Orford Cl
 Bury BL8 . . . . 140 A4
 High Lane SK6 . . . . 134 E7
Orford Ct WN7 . . . . 76 B2
Orford Rd
 Failsworth M40 . . . . . . 83 C5
 Prestwich M25 . . . . 63 B5
Organ St
 Hindley WN2 . . . . 57 B3
 Leigh WN7 . . . . 75 E5
Organ Way SK14 . . . . . 103 D5
Oriel Ave OL8 . . . . 66 E3
Oriel Cl
 Chadderton OL9 . . . . . . 152 A1
 Stockport SK2 . . . . 124 B6
Oriel Ct 7 M33 . . . . . . 108 B5
Oriel Rd
 Ashton-in-M WN4 . . . . . 72 F4
 Manchester M20 . . . . . 110 A4
Oriel St
 Bolton BL3 . . . . 144 C1
 Rochdale OL11 . . . . . . 139 C1
Orient Ho M1 . . . . 163 A4
Orient Rd M6 . . . . 80 B4
Orient St M7 . . . . 155 C3
Oriole Cl M28 . . . . 78 B8
Oriole Ho 6 M19 . . . . . 110 D4
Orion Bsns Pk SK3 . . . . 123 B5
Orion Pl M7 . . . . 81 C4
Orkney Cl
 Radcliffe M26 . . . . 44 B4
 Wythenshawe M23 . . . . 121 A4
Orkney Dr M41 . . . . 95 D5
Orlanda Ave M6 . . . . . . 80 B4
Orlanda Dr M7 . . . . 155 C2
Orlando St BL3 . . . . 148 A1
Orleans Way OL1 . . . . . 153 B3
Orme Ave
 Middleton M24 . . . . 65 A7
 Salford M6 . . . . 80 B4
Orme Cl
 Manchester M11 . . . . . 160 B1
 Urmston M41 . . . . 95 F2
Ormerod Ave OL2 . . . . . 48 E3
Ormerod Cl SK6 . . . . . . 113 A1
Ormerod St OL10 . . . . . 29 E1
Orme St
 Alderley Edge SK9 . . . . 137 A1
 Oldham OL4 . . . . 67 A5
Ormonde Ave M6 . . . . . 80 B4
Ormonde Ct OL6 . . . . . 166 C4
Ormonde St OL6 . . . . . 166 C4

Ormond St
 Bolton BL3 . . . . 42 D5
 Bury BL9 . . . . 141 A3
Ormrod Ct BL9 . . . . 141 A2
Ormrod St
 Bolton BL3 . . . . 145 B2
 Bolton, Hall i' th' Wood BL2 . 25 C4
 Bury BL9 . . . . 141 A2
 10 Farnworth BL4 . . . . 60 C8
Ormrods The BL9 . . . . . . 28 F5
Ormsby Ave M18 . . . . . . 99 B4
Ormsby Cl
 Standish WN6 . . . . 19 E2
 Stockport SK3 . . . . 123 E4
Orms Gill Pl SK2 . . . . . . 124 E6
Ormsgill St M15 . . . . . . 162 C2
Ormside Cl WN2 . . . . . . 57 C4
Ormskirk Ave M20 . . . . 109 F6
Ormskirk Cl BL8 . . . . . . 44 A8
Ormskirk Rd
 1 Reddish SK5 . . . . . 111 F6
 Up Holland WN8 . . . . . . 53 A7
 Wigan WN5 . . . . 54 D6
Ornston Ave BL6 . . . . . . 22 C5
Ornston Gr WN7 . . . . . . 75 F7
Ornatus St BL1 . . . . 24 A1
Oronsay Gr M5 . . . . 154 B1
Orphanage St SK4 . . . . 169 B3
Orpington St M40 . . . . . 83 E8
Orpington Rd 2 M9 . . . 157 B3
Orpington Wlk WN5 . . . . 54 C6
ORRELL 53 E5
Orrell Arc 3 WN1 . . . . 150 C4
Orrell Gdns WN5 . . . . . . 53 F6
Orrell Hall Cl WN5 . . . . . 54 B8
Orrell Holgate Prim Sch 4
 WN5 . . . . 53 E5
Orrell Newfold Com Prim
 Sch WN5 . . . . 53 D4
ORRELL POST 53 E7
Orrell St
 Bury BL8 . . . . 140 A3
 Manchester M11 . . . . . . 99 D8
Orrell Sta WN5 . . . . 53 E4
Orrell Water Pk* WN5 . . 53 E4
Orrel St M6 . . . . 154 B2
Orrishmere Prim Sch
 SK8 . . . . 123 A3
Orrismere Rd SK8 . . . . . 122 F3
Orron St OL15 . . . . 16 A5
Orsett Cl M40 . . . . 159 C3
Orthes Gr SK4 . . . . 111 D5
Orton Ave M23 . . . . 109 A1
Orton Rd M23 . . . . 109 A1
Orton Way WN4 . . . . 72 F3
Orvietto Ave M6 . . . . . . 80 B4
Orville Dr M19 . . . . 110 F7
Orwell Ave
 Reddish M34 . . . . 100 A3
 Wythenshawe M22 . . . . 121 D6
Orwell Cl
 Bury BL8 . . . . 140 A4
 Handforth SK9 . . . . 131 D2
 Wigan WN6 . . . . 36 E3
Orwell Rd BL1 . . . . 142 B2
Osborne Cl BL4 . . . . 44 B8
Osborne Cl M46 . . . . 58 C3
Osborne Dr M27 . . . . . . 80 C7
Osborne Gr
 Bolton BL1 . . . . 142 C1
 Gatley SK8 . . . . 122 A3
 Leigh WN7 . . . . 76 D6
Osborne Ho
 Eccles M30 . . . . 79 C2
 7 Radcliffe M26 . . . . . 43 E3
Osborne Ind Est OL9 . . . 152 C4
Osborne Pl SK13 . . . . . . 104 A5
Osborne Rd
 Altrincham WA15 . . . . . 119 E5
 Ashton-in-M WN4 . . . . . 73 A4
 Golborne WA3 . . . . 90 E7
 Hyde SK14 . . . . 167 B1
 3 Manchester, Harpurhey
 M9 . . . . 157 B3
 Manchester, Levenshulme
 M19 . . . . 110 A3
 Manchester, Didsbury
 M20 . . . . 110 A3
 Oldham OL9 . . . . 153 A1
 Salford M6 . . . . 80 A2
 Stockport SK2 . . . . 170 C3
Osborne St
 Heywood OL10 . . . . 29 D1
 Manchester, Didsbury
 M20 . . . . 110 A3
 Manchester M40 . . . . . 159 C4
 Oldham OL9 . . . . 152 C4
 Rochdale OL16 . . . . . . 139 C1
 Romiley SK6 . . . . 112 D3
 Salford M6 . . . . 154 C2
 Shaw OL2 . . . . 149 B2
Osborne Terr
 10 Ashton-u-L OL6 . . . 166 C3
 Bacup OL13 . . . . 3 D8
 Bolton BL3 . . . . 108 B4
Osbourne Cl
 Farnworth BL4 . . . . 42 D1
 Wilmslow SK9 . . . . 137 D6
Osbourne Pl 9 WA14 . . 119 D4
Osbourne Wlk 6 M26 . . 43 E3
Oscar St
 Bolton BL1 . . . . 142 C2
 Manchester M40 . . . . . 160 D1
Oscott Cl M8 . . . . 155 C2

Oscroft Wlk M14 . . . . . 110 D7
Osmond St OL4 . . . . 67 C7
Osmund Ave OL4 . . . . . . 42 D7
Osprey Ave BL5 . . . . 57 D6
Osprey Cl
 Dukinfield SK16 . . . . . . 101 E7
 Manchester M15 . . . . . 162 B1
Osprey Ct M15 . . . . 162 B1
Osprey Dr
 Droylsden M43 . . . . 84 C3
 Irlam M44 . . . . 94 A3
 Wilmslow SK9 . . . . 137 C8
Ospreys The WN3 . . . . . 54 C4
Ossington Ct M23 . . . . . 109 A3
Ossington Wlk M23 . . . . 109 A3
Osterley Rd M9 . . . . 65 A3
Ostlers Gate M43 . . . . . . 84 D2
Ostrich La M25 . . . . 63 C3
Oswald Cl M6 . . . . 81 A5
Oswald La M21 . . . . 97 B1
Oswald Rd M21 . . . . 97 A1
Oswald Road Prim Sch
 M21 . . . . 97 A1
Oswald St
 Bolton BL3 . . . . 146 C4
 Manchester, Bradford M4 . 160 A1
 Manchester M4 . . . . . . 159 A3
 Oldham OL9 . . . . 153 A4
 Reddish SK5 . . . . 99 F3
 Rochdale OL16 . . . . 31 B8
 Shaw OL2 . . . . 149 C4
Oswestry Cl BL8 . . . . . . 26 F8
Otago St 2 OL4 . . . . . . 49 C1
Othello Dr 2 M30 . . . . . 79 D2
Otley Ave M6 . . . . 80 C3
Otley Cl OL9 . . . . 152 B2
Otley Gr SK3 . . . . 123 D4
Otmoor Way OL2 . . . . . . 49 A4
Otranto Ave M6 . . . . 80 B4
Otterburn Pl SK2 . . . . . . 124 E6
Otterbury Cl BL8 . . . . . . 26 F2
Otter Dr
 Salford M8 . . . . 155 B1
 Whitefield BL9 . . . . 45 B4
Otterham Wlk M40 . . . . 83 D5
Otterspool Rd SK6 . . . . 125 B8
Otterwood Sq WN5 . . . . 36 C2
Ottery Wlk 8 M40 . . . . 65 D2
Ottowa Cl M23 . . . . 120 F4
OUGHTRINGTON 117 C4
Oughtrington Cres
 WA13 . . . . 117 B4
Oughtrington La WA13 . . 117 A2
Oughtrington Prim Sch
 WA13 . . . . 117 B4
Oughtrington View
 WA13 . . . . 117 B4
Oulder Hill OL11 . . . . . . 30 B7
Oulder Hill Com Sch &
 Language Coll OL11 . . . 30 B7
Oulder Hill Dr OL11 . . . . 30 B7
Ouldfield Cl 22 OL16 . . 30 E5
Oultan Ave M33 . . . . . . 108 E5
Oulton Cl 1 WN7 . . . . . 76 A4
Oulton St BL1 . . . . 25 A5
Oulton Wlk M40 . . . . . . 160 A1
Oundle Cl M14 . . . . 98 C3
Our Lady Immaculate RC
 Prim Sch M14 . . . . 72 E6
Our Lady of Grace RC Prim
 Sch M25 . . . . 63 A6
Our Lady of Lourdes RC Prim
 Sch
 Bury BL8 . . . . 27 C6
 Farnworth BL4 . . . . 60 A8
 Partington M31 . . . . . . 105 E3
Our Lady of Mount Carmel
 RC Prim Sch 7 OL6 . . 85 D4
Our Lady of the Rosary RC
 Prim Sch M41 . . . . . . 95 C4
Our Lady & St Anselm's RC
 Prim Sch OL12 . . . . . . 4 D2
Our Lady & St Paul's RC Prim
 Sch OL12 . . . . 28 F1
Our Lady's RC High Sch
 Manchester M9 . . . . . . 64 D5
 Royton OL2 . . . . 48 D3
Our Lady's RC Prim Sch
 Aspull WN2 . . . . 38 C5
 Manchester M16 . . . . . . 97 D3
 Oldham OL4 . . . . 49 E3
 8 Stockport SK3 . . . . . 170 E4
Ouse St M50 . . . . 80 C1
Outram Cl SK6 . . . . 125 F4
Outram Ho M26 . . . . . . 159 C1
Outram Mews OL3 . . . . . 51 B1
Outram Rd SK14, SK16 . . 101 B6
Outram Sq M43 . . . . . . 100 A4
Outrington Dr M11 . . . . 165 A4
Outterside St PR7 . . . . . 21 A6
OUTWOOD 61 F8
Outwood Ave M27 . . . . . 61 F8
Outwood Dr SK8 . . . . . . 131 A8
OUTWOOD GATE 62 B8
Outwood Gr BL1 . . . . . . 24 E5
Outwood La M90 . . . . . 130 C7
Outwood Lane W M90 . . 130 B8
Outwood Prim Sch SK8 . 131 D7
Outwood Rd
 Gatley SK8 . . . . 131 B7
 Radcliffe M26 . . . . 44 A1
Oval Dr SK16 . . . . 101 B7
Oval The
 Gatley SK8 . . . . 131 B8

Oval The continued
Shevington WN6 . . . . 35 F5
Oval View SK6 . . . . 113 B5
Over Ashberry 1 WA14 . 107 B1
Overbeck Cl WN6 . . . . . . 37 A4
Overbridge Rd M7, M8 . 158 B4
Overbrook Ave M40 . . . . 157 A1
Overbrook Dr M25 . . . . . 63 B3
Overcombe Wlk 1 M40 . 156 C1
Overdale
 1 Marple SK6 . . . . 125 F6
 Pendlebury M27 . . . . 80 A6
Overdale Cl OL1 . . . . 48 E1
Overdale Cres M41 . . . . . 94 F2
Overdale Dr
 Bolton BL1 . . . . 144 A3
 Glossop SK13 . . . . 116 B8
Overdale Rd
 New Mills SK12 . . . . 135 F6
 Romiley SK6 . . . . 125 A8
 Wythenshawe M22 . . . . 121 D5
Overdell Dr OL12 . . . . . . 14 C4
Overdene Cl BL6 . . . . 40 C6
Overens St OL4 . . . . 67 B7
Overfield Way OL12 . . . . 14 E2
Overgreen BL2 . . . . 25 F3
Overhill Dr SK9 . . . . 137 E7
Overhill La SK9 . . . . 137 E7
Overhill Rd
 Chadderton OL9 . . . . 65 F8
 Wilmslow SK9 . . . . 137 D7
Overhill Way WN3 . . . . . 54 D3
Over Hos BL7 . . . . 9 F4
OVER HULTON 58 F7
Overlea Dr M19 . . . . 110 E5
Overlinks Dr M6 . . . . 80 B5
Overshores Rd BL7 . . . . . 9 B8
Overstone Dr M8 . . . . . 155 C3
Overton Ave M22 . . . . . 121 D5
Overton Cl M26 . . . . 44 B1
Overton Cres
 Hazel Grove SK7 . . . . . . 124 E4
 Sale M33 . . . . 107 D1
Overton Rd M22 . . . . . . 121 D5
Overton St WN7 . . . . 75 E4
Overton Way 2 SK9 . . . 131 D5
Over Town La
 Rochdale OL12 . . . . 13 A3
 Rochdale, Wolstenholme
  OL12 . . . . 13 C3
Overt St OL11 . . . . 139 C1
Overwood Rd M22 . . . . 121 D8
Ovington Wlk 6 M40 . 156 C1
Owen Fold OL4 . . . . 67 F7
Owenington Gr M38 . . . . 60 A5
Owens Cl OL9 . . . . 65 E8
Owens Farm Dr SK2 . . . 124 E7
Owen's Row 3 BL6 . . . . 22 C3
Owen St
 Eccles M30 . . . . 79 B1
 2 Leigh WN7 . . . . 75 D5
 Oldham OL1 . . . . 49 E3
 Salford M6 . . . . 81 A5
 Stockport SK3 . . . . 169 A1
OWLER BARROW 27 A3
Owlerbarrow Rd BL8 . . . 27 A3
Owler La OL9 . . . . 65 E3
Owlsfield WA12 . . . . 89 E3
Owls Gate OL4 . . . . 67 E6
Owlwood Cl M38 . . . . . . 59 E3
Owlwood Dr M38 . . . . . . 59 E3
Owsten Ct BL3 . . . . 21 F3
Oxbow Way M45 . . . . . . 63 A8
Oxbridge Cl 8 M33 . . . . 107 D3
Oxburgh Rd WN3 . . . . . . 55 F4
Oxendale Dr M24 . . . . . . 46 D1
Oxendon Ave M11 . . . . . . 83 B3
Oxenholme Wlk 12 M18 . 99 D3
Oxenhurst Gn SK2 . . . . . 124 E5
Oxford Ave
 Droylsden M43 . . . . 83 F3
 Rochdale OL11 . . . . 30 A6
 Sale M33 . . . . 107 D4
 Whitefield M45 . . . . 63 A8
Oxford Cl BL4 . . . . 59 F8
Oxford Ct
 Manchester, City Centre
  M2 . . . . 162 C4
 3 Manchester, Hulme
  M15 . . . . 162 C2
 Manchester, Hulme M15 . 163 A2
 Manchester, Old Trafford
  M16 . . . . 162 A1
 Wigan WN1 . . . . 37 D1
Oxford Dr
 Middleton M24 . . . . 47 C2
 Romiley SK6 . . . . 113 C4
Oxford Gr
 Bolton BL1 . . . . 142 C1
 Irlam M44 . . . . 105 C6
Oxford Grove Prim Sch
  BL1 . . . . 142 C1
Oxford Ho OL9 . . . . 152 C2
Oxford Park Com Sports Ctr
  OL7 . . . . 100 F1
Oxford Pl
 Manchester M14 . . . . 98 C4
 14 Rochdale OL16 . . . . 31 A5
Oxford Rd
 Altrincham WA14 . . . . . 119 D3
 Atherton M46 . . . . 58 B5
 Dukinfield SK16 . . . . . . 101 D8
 Horwich BL6 . . . . 39 F8
 Hyde SK14 . . . . 113 E8
 Little Lever BL3 . . . . 42 F3

Oxford Rd continued
 Manchester M1, M13 . . 163 B2
 Orrell WN5 . . . . 53 F8
 Salford M6 . . . . 80 B4
Oxford St
 Adlington PR7 . . . . 21 A6
 Bolton BL1 . . . . 145 C3
 Bury BL9 . . . . 141 A1
 Eccles M30 . . . . 79 E1
 Hindley WN2 . . . . 56 F7
 Leigh WN7 . . . . 75 F6
 Manchester, City Centre M1, M60,
  M2 . . . . 163 A4
 Manchester, Old Trafford
  M16 . . . . 162 A1
 Newton-le-W WA12 . . . . 89 B3
 Oldham OL9 . . . . 152 C1
 Shaw OL2 . . . . 149 B3
 Stalybridge, Copley SK15 . 86 C1
 Stalybridge, Millbrook SK15 86 D4
Oxford Street E OL7 . . . 166 A1
Oxford Street W OL7 . . . 100 F8
Oxford Way
 Rochdale OL12 . . . . 14 E2
 Stockport SK4 . . . . 169 A3
Oxford Wlk 4 M34 . . . . 101 A1
Ox Gate BL1 . . . . 25 D5
Ox Hey Cl
 Horwich BL6 . . . . 39 E8
 Ramsbottom BL0 . . . . . . 138 C3
Ox Hey La
 Denshaw OL3 . . . . 33 E1
 Horwich BL6 . . . . 39 F7
Oxhill Wlk 17 M40 . . . . . 65 D2
Oxhouse Rd WN5 . . . . . . 53 D4
Oxlea Gr BL5 . . . . 57 E2
Oxney Rd M14 . . . . 98 C4
Ox St BL0 . . . . 138 B1
Oxted Wlk 8 M8 . . . . . . 156 A2
Oxton Ave M22 . . . . 121 C4
Oxton St M11 . . . . 99 F7
OYY Lubavitch Girls Sch
  M7 . . . . 63 D1
Ozanam Ct M7 . . . . 155 A3

P

Pacific Rd WA14 . . . . . . 119 A6
Pacific Way M50 . . . . . . 96 C8
Packer St
 1 Bolton BL1 . . . . 142 C2
 Rochdale OL16 . . . . 139 C3
Pack Horse Yd 5 OL16 . 139 C3
Packwood Chase 9 . . . . 65 F8
Padbury Cl M41 . . . . 94 D3
Padbury Ho 7 M6 . . . . . 154 C1
Padbury Way BL2 . . . . . . 25 E1
Padbury Wlk M40 . . . . . 157 C1
Padden Brook SK6 . . . . . 113 B2
Padden Brook Mews
  SK6 . . . . 113 B2
Paddington Ave M40 . . . 83 B5
Paddington Cl M6 . . . . . . 81 A2
Paddison St 2 M27 . . . . . 79 E7
Paddock Chase SK7 . . . 133 F6
Paddock Cl M46 . . . . 58 E5
Paddock La
 Failsworth M35 . . . . 83 F5
 Lymm WA13 . . . . 117 C7
 Partington WA13, WA14 . 118 B5
Paddock Rd SK14 . . . . . 113 D8
Paddock Rise WN6 . . . . . 36 E3
Paddock St M12 . . . . . . 163 C3
Paddocks The SK3 . . . . 124 A4
Paddock The
 Altrincham WA15 . . . . . 120 B4
 Ashton-in-M WN4 . . . . . 72 F6
 Bramhall SK7 . . . . 123 D1
 Cheadle SK8 . . . . 122 E5
 Handforth SK9 . . . . 131 D4
 Hollingworth SK14 . . . . 103 E5
 Ramsbottom BL0 . . . . . . 138 B3
 Uppermill OL3 . . . . 68 F4
 Worsley M28 . . . . 78 E7
Paderborn Ct BL1 . . . . . 145 B2
PADFIELD 104 C5
Padfield Gate SK13 . . . . 116 D7
Padfield Main Rd SK13 . 104 C5
Padfield Prim Sch SK13 . 104 B5
Padiham Cl
 Bury BL9 . . . . 44 D7
 Leigh WN7 . . . . 76 A5
Padstow Cl SK14 . . . . . . 102 D3
Padstow Dr SK7 . . . . . . 132 F7
Padstow Pl 2 OL9 . . . . . 48 A1
Padstow St M40 . . . . . . 160 B3
Padstow Wlk SK14 . . . . 102 D3
Padworth Wlk M23 . . . . 120 D8
Pagan St OL16 . . . . 139 C4
Pagefield Cl 15 WN6 . . . 37 A1
Pagefield Ind Est WN6 . 150 A4
Pagefield St WN6 . . . . . . 37 A1
Paget St M40 . . . . 157 A1
Pagnall Ct OL9 . . . . 152 B8
Paignton Ave
 Hattersley SK14 . . . . . . 102 D2
 Manchester M19 . . . . . . 110 F8
Paignton Cl WN5 . . . . . . 71 E8
Paignton Dr M33 . . . . . . 107 D5
Paignton Gr SK5 . . . . . . 111 F7
Paignton Wlk SK14 . . . . 102 C2
Pailin Dr M43 . . . . 84 C2
Pailton Cl BL6 . . . . 40 D6
Painswick Rd M22 . . . . . 121 B1

Paisley Pk BL4 . . . . 42 D1
Paiton St BL1 . . . . 144 C3
Palace Arc 1 WN4 . . . . . 73 B3
Palace Ct 8 BL1 . . . . . 145 C4
Palace Gdns OL1 . . . . . . 48 D2
Palace Gr WN7 . . . . 76 D6
Palace Rd
 Ashton-u-L OL6 . . . . 85 E5
 Sale M33 . . . . 108 A5
Palace St
 Bolton BL1 . . . . 145 C4
 Bury BL9 . . . . 141 A2
 Oldham OL9 . . . . 152 C3
Palace Theatre★ M1 . . . 163 A4
Palatine Ave
 Manchester M20 . . . . . . 110 B6
 Rochdale OL11 . . . . 30 A8
Palatine Cl
 Irlam M44 . . . . 93 F1
 Wigan WN1 . . . . 54 E4
Palatine Cres M20 . . . . . 110 B5
Palatine Dr BL9 . . . . 27 F8
Palatine Ho 4 SK3 . . . . 170 B4
Palatine Mews M34 . . . 100 E5
Palatine Rd
 Manchester M20 . . . . . . 110 B6
 Rochdale OL11 . . . . 30 A8
 Wythenshawe M20, M22 . 109 E2
Palatine Sq WN7 . . . . . . 75 D5
Palatine St
 4 Bolton BL1 . . . . 145 C3
 Denton M34 . . . . 100 E4
 Ramsbottom BL0 . . . . . . 138 C2
 Rochdale OL16 . . . . 31 C7
Palatine Terr OL11 . . . . . 30 A8
Palewood Cl WN5 . . . . . . 37 E1
Palfrey Pl M12 . . . . 163 C3
Palgrave Ave M40 . . . . . 157 A1
Palin St WN2 . . . . 57 B3
Palin Wood Rd SK15 . . . . 50 F5
Pall Mall 158 C1
Pallotine Wlk OL11 . . . . 139 A1
Palma Ave M40 . . . . 130 B8
Palm Ave WN4 . . . . 72 D5
Palm Bsns Ctr OL9 . . . . 152 B3
Palm Cl M33 . . . . 107 D5
Palmer Ave SK8 . . . . 122 F6
Palmer Cl
 Manchester M8 . . . . 64 B2
 Oldham OL8 . . . . 66 F4
Palmer Gr WN7 . . . . 57 E1
Palmer St
 Dukinfield SK16 . . . . . . 166 B1
 6 Sale M33 . . . . 108 A4
 Salford M7 . . . . 81 C5
Palmerston Ave M16 . . . 97 D2
Palmerston Cl
 Hindley WN2 . . . . 56 C4
 Ramsbottom BL0 . . . . . . 11 C4
 Reddish M34 . . . . 100 B3
Palmerstones Ct BL1 . . 144 A3
Palmerston Rd
 Reddish M34 . . . . 100 B3
 Stockport SK2 . . . . 124 B3
Palmerston St M12 . . . . 160 B1
Palm Gr
 Chadderton OL9 . . . . . . 152 B4
 Wigan WN5 . . . . 54 D6
Palm St
 Bolton BL1 . . . . 143 C3
 Droylsden M43 . . . . 83 E2
 Manchester M13 . . . . . . 98 F3
 Oldham OL4 . . . . 67 C8
Paltine Ct 1 M34 . . . . . 100 E5
Pandora St M20 . . . . . . 110 A6
Panfield Rd M22 . . . . . . 121 D4
Pangbourne Ave M41 . . 95 E3
Pangbourne Cl SK3 . . . . 123 F2
Pankhurst Wlk 11 M14 . 98 B3
Panmure St OL8 . . . . 66 F4
Pansy Rd BL4 . . . . 60 A8
Panton St BL6 . . . . 22 C3
Paperhouse Cl 8 OL11 . 13 D1
Paper Mill Rd BL7 . . . . . 25 A7
Paprika Cl M11 . . . . 160 A1
Parade Rd M90 . . . . 130 C7
Parade The
 1 Alderley Edge SK9 . . 137 A1
 Culcheth WA3 . . . . 91 E3
 Romiley SK6 . . . . 113 A1
 Swinton M27 . . . . 79 F8
 8 Whitefield M45 . . . . . 44 F2
Paradise St
 Denton M34 . . . . 100 F7
 Glossop SK13 . . . . 104 A5
 Ramsbottom BL0 . . . . . . 138 B2
Paragon Bsns Pk BL6 . . 39 E8
Paragon Ind Est OL15 . . 15 F3
Paramel Ave M26 . . . . . . 43 B5
Parbold Ave M20 . . . . . . 110 A6
Parchments The WA12 . 89 D4
Pardoners Ct M5 . . . . . . 80 B2
Pargate Chase OL11 . . . 30 A4
Parham Wlk 4 M9 . . . . . 64 E3
Paris Ave
 Salford M5 . . . . 161 B3
 Wigan WN3 . . . . 54 C3
Parish View M5 . . . . 161 B4
Parish Wk BL2 . . . . 26 D1
Paris St BL3 . . . . 146 B4
Park Ave
 Altrincham WA14 . . . . . 119 E8
 Bolton BL1 . . . . 143 B4
 Bramhall SK7 . . . . 132 D5
 Chadderton OL9 . . . . 48 B1
 Cheadle, Cheadle Heath
  SK3 . . . . 122 F7

Park Ave continued
 Cheadle SK8 . . . . 122 F1
 Failsworth M35 . . . . 83 D8
 Gatley WA3 . . . . 119 E5
 Hale WA15 . . . . 119 F1
 Hyde SK14 . . . . 167 A4
 Longshaw WN5 . . . . 53 E1
 Manchester, Levenshulme
  M19 . . . . 99 A1
 Manchester, Old Trafford
  M16 . . . . 161 C1
 Pendlebury M27 . . . . 80 A7
 Poynton SK12 . . . . 133 E4
 Prestwich M25 . . . . 63 B4
 Radcliffe M26 . . . . 44 D4
 Ramsbottom BL0 . . . . . . 11 D6
 Romiley SK6 . . . . 113 C2
 Sale M33 . . . . 108 A6
 Salford M7 . . . . 155 C4
 Shevington WN6 . . . . 36 B7
 Swinton M27 . . . . 79 F8
 Whitefield M45 . . . . 62 D6
 Wilmslow SK9 . . . . 137 C8
Park Avenue N WA12 . . 89 C2
Park Avenue S WA12 . . 89 C2
Park Bank M7 . . . . 58 F6
Park Bglws 4 SK6 . . . . . 125 F5
PARK BRIDGE 67 C1
Park Bridge Her Ctr★
  OL6 . . . . 67 C1
Park Bridge Rd
 Oldham OL7, OL8 . . . . . . 85 A8
 Oldham, Park Bridge OL6 . 67 B1
Parkbridge Wlk M13 . . . 163 B2
Park Brook La WN6 . . . . 36 B7
Parkbrook Rd M23 . . . . 121 B7
Park Brow Cl M21 . . . . . 109 C7
Park Cl
 Altrincham WA14 . . . . . 119 F8
 Chadderton OL9 . . . . 48 B1
 Glossop SK13 . . . . 104 D2
 Stalybridge SK15 . . . . . . 85 F3
 Whitefield M45 . . . . 62 F6
Park Cotts
 Shaw OL2 . . . . 48 E8
 Uppermill OL3 . . . . 68 E5
Park Court Mews SK8 . . 122 E4
Park Cres
 Ashton-u-L OL6 . . . . 85 E2
 Bacup OL13 . . . . 3 F8
 Chadderton OL9 . . . . 47 F1
 Glossop SK13 . . . . 104 D2
 Handforth SK9 . . . . 131 B1
 Manchester M14 . . . . . . 98 C3
 Wigan WN1 . . . . 37 B1
Park Crescent W WN1 . . 37 B1
Park Ct
 Droylsden M11 . . . . 83 D2
 Manchester M25 . . . . . . 63 E2
 Rochdale OL16 . . . . 139 C2
 Sale M33 . . . . 108 A5
 Wythenshawe M22 . . . . 121 D3
Parkdale
 Chadderton OL9 . . . . 48 B1
 Tyldesley M29 . . . . 77 B5
Parkdale Ave
 Denton M34 . . . . 100 D7
 Manchester M18 . . . . . . 82 C1
Parkdale Rd BL2 . . . . . . 25 C1
Parkdene Cl BL2 . . . . 25 D4
Park Dene Dr SK13 . . . . 104 C2
Park Dr
 Altrincham, Timperley
  WA15 . . . . 120 A7
 Altrincham WA15 . . . . . 119 F1
 Eccles M30 . . . . 79 D4
 Hale SK14 . . . . 167 A4
 Manchester M16 . . . . . . 97 C2
 Stockport SK4 . . . . 168 B2
Park Edge BL5 . . . . 58 A7
Parkedge Cl WN7 . . . . . . 75 E3
Parkend Dr WN7 . . . . . . 75 D2
Parkend Rd M23 . . . . . . 121 A5
Parker St
 Bury BL9 . . . . 141 A2
 Manchester M1 . . . . 159 A1
Parkfield
 Chadderton OL9 . . . . 48 B1
 Droylsden M43 . . . . 84 A2
 1 Middleton M24 . . . . . 64 F8
 Salford M5 . . . . 154 A2
 Shevington WN6 . . . . 36 B7
Parkfield Ave
 Farnworth BL4 . . . . 60 C7
 Manchester M14 . . . . . . 98 B3
 Manchester, Sedgley Park
  M25 . . . . 63 D3
 Marple SK6 . . . . 125 F6
 2 Oldham OL8 . . . . 66 B2
 Tyldesley M29 . . . . 77 B6
 Urmston M41 . . . . 95 B1
Parkfield Cl
 Leigh WN7 . . . . 76 A7
 Tyldesley M29 . . . . 77 B6
Parkfield Ct
 Altrincham WA14 . . . . . 119 C4
 Manchester M20 . . . . . . 110 A3
Parkfield Dr
 Middleton M24 . . . . 64 E8
 Tyldesley M29 . . . . 59 D1
Parkfield Ind Est M24 . . 64 F8
Parkfield Lodge M20 . . . 110 A4
Parkfield Prim Sch M24 . 46 E1
Parkfield Rd
 Altrincham WA14 . . . . . 119 C3
 Bolton BL3 . . . . 147 C3
 Cheadle SK8 . . . . 122 F1
 Uppermill OL4 . . . . 68 E6

Parkfield Road N M40 . . 65 F1
Parkfield Road S M20 . . 110 A4
Parkfields
 Abram Brow WN2 . . . . . . 74 B6
 Stalybridge SK15 . . . . . . 86 D3
Parkfield St
 Manchester M14 . . . . . . 98 B4
 Rochdale OL16 . . . . 31 B2
Parkgate
 Altrincham WA14 . . . . . 119 B4
 Bury BL8 . . . . 26 F5
 Droylsden OL16 . . . . 48 B1
Park Gate Ave M20 . . . . 110 B6
Park Gate Cl SK6 . . . . . . 112 C5
Parkgate Dr
 Bolton BL1 . . . . 25 A5
 Pendlebury M27 . . . . 80 A7
 Stockport SK2 . . . . 124 B4
Parkgate Rd M14 . . . . . . 119 C8
Park Gates Ave SK8 . . . 123 C1
Park Gates Dr SK8 . . . . 123 C1
Parkgate Way
 7 Handforth SK9 . . . . 131 D4
 Shaw OL2 . . . . 49 D7
Park Gr
 Manchester M19 . . . . . . 99 A2
 Radcliffe M26 . . . . 43 F4
 Stockport, Heaton Moor
  SK4 . . . . 168 B4
 Walkden M28 . . . . 78 D8
Park Grange WN2 . . . . . 56 E4
Parkham Cl BL5 . . . . 57 F6
Park Hey Dr WN6 . . . . . . 35 E7
Park Hill
 Manchester M25 . . . . . . 63 D2
 2 Rochdale OL12 . . . . . 14 F1
Parkhill Ave M8 . . . . 64 B2
Park Hill Cl SK22 . . . . . . 127 C1
Park Hill Dr M45 . . . . . . 62 E8
Park Hill Rd M45 . . . . . . 120 A1
Parkhills Rd BL9 . . . . . . 44 F3
Park Hill St BL1 . . . . . . 145 A4
Park Ho
 Droylsden M43 . . . . 100 A8
 Manchester, Levenshulme
  M19 . . . . 99 A1
 Manchester M20 . . . . . . 110 A4
 Sale WA15 . . . . 120 C7
Park House Bridge Est
  M6 . . . . 80 F7
Park House Bridge Rd
  M6 . . . . 80 E6
Parkhouse St M11 . . . . . 165 B4
Parkhurst Ave M40 . . . . 65 E1
Parkin Cl SK16 . . . . 101 C8
Park Ind Est WN4 . . . . . . 72 E3
Parkinson St
 Bolton BL3 . . . . 144 C1
 Bury BL9 . . . . 27 F5
Park St M12 . . . . 99 A3
Park La
 Altrincham WA15 . . . . . 120 A1
 Dukinfield SK16 . . . . . . 101 C8
 Golborne WN2 & WN7 . . 74 D6
 Horwich BL6 . . . . 22 D3
 Leigh WN7 . . . . 76 C4
 Little Bollington WA14 . . 118 B2
 Oldham OL8 . . . . 66 F2
 Pendlebury M27 . . . . 80 D7
 Poynton SK12 . . . . 133 F3
 Rochdale OL16 . . . . 139 C4
 Royton OL2 . . . . 48 D4
 Salford, Irlams o' th' Height
  M6 . . . . 80 C5
 Salford M7 . . . . 155 A4
 Stockport SK1 . . . . 124 B8
 Uppermill OL3 . . . . 69 C5
 Whitefield M45 . . . . 62 D7
Parklake Ave M7 . . . . . . 155 B4
Parkland Ave SK22 . . . . 127 C1
Parklands
 Romiley SK6 . . . . 113 C3
 Royton OL2 . . . . 48 C7
 Sale M33 . . . . 108 C5
 Shaw OL2 . . . . 49 D8
 Whitefield M45 . . . . 62 D7
Parklands Dr
 Aspull WN2 . . . . 38 C6
 Sale M33 . . . . 107 D2
Parklands Rd M23 . . . . . 120 F7
Parklands The
 Horwich BL6 . . . . 39 D7
 Kearsley M26 . . . . 61 B7
 Stockport SK4 . . . . 169 B4
Parklands Way SK12 . . . 133 E4
PARK LANE 62 D7
Park Lane Ct
 Salford M7 . . . . 155 A4
 Whitefield M45 . . . . 62 D7
Parklea Ct 6 M7 . . . . . . 63 E1
Parklee Prim Sch M46 . . 58 B2
Parkleigh Dr M40 . . . . . . 65 E2
Park Lodge
 Manchester, Heaton Moor
  SK4 . . . . 111 B5
 1 Manchester, Levenshulme
  M19 . . . . 99 A1
 Manchester, Whalley Range
  M16 . . . . 97 E3
Park Lodge Cl SK8 . . . . 122 E4
Park Lodge Ind Hospl
  SK6 . . . . 113 D3
Park Mdw BL5 . . . . 58 A8
Park Mews M16 . . . . 97 C2
Park Mill Ind Est OL5 . . 68 D3
Park Mount SK8 . . . . . . 122 A5

Parkmount Rd M9 . . . . 64 E1
Park Par
Ashton-u-L OL6 . . . . 166 B2
Shaw OL2. . . . . 32 C1
Park Parade Ind Est OL6 166 A2
Park Pl
Manchester SK4. . . . . 110 F2
Manchester, Strangeways
M4. . . . . 159 A3
Prestwich M25. . . . . 63 C5
Salford M6. . . . . 80 A3
Park Range M14 . . . . 98 D3
Park Rd
Adlington PR7 . . . . 20 F6
Altrincham, Ashley Heath
WA15 . . . . 119 F1
Altrincham, Bowdon WA14 119 A2
Altrincham, Timperley
WA15 . . . . 119 A2
Bolton BL1. . . . . 144 C3
Bramhall SK8. . . . . 123 C1
Bury BL9 . . . . 140 B4
Cheadle SK8. . . . . 122 E6
Denton M34. . . . . 100 E3
Droylsden M34. . . . . 100 D8
Eccles M30 . . . . 79 D4
Edgworth BL7 . . . . 9 E5
Glossop SK13. . . . . 104 A4
Golborne WA3 . . . . 90 A7
High Lane SK12 . . . . 135 A6
Hindley WN2 . . . . 56 E3
Hyde SK14 . . . . 167 A4
Little Lever BL3 . . . . 42 F4
Longshaw WN5 . . . . 53 F1
Manchester, Heaton Moor
SK4 . . . . 111 B5
Manchester M25, M8. . . . 63 E2
Middleton M24. . . . . 65 A8
Oldham, Glodwick OL4, OL8. 67 A5
Oldham OL8 . . . . 153 C1
Partington M31 . . . . 106 A3
Partington, Warburton
WA13 . . . . 117 C8
Ramsbottom BL0 . . . . 10 F3
Rochdale OL12. . . . . 15 A1
Romiley SK6. . . . . 113 C3
Sale, Ashton upon Mersey
M33. . . . . 108 A6
Sale, Timperley WA15 . . 120 B7
Salford M6. . . . . 80 A3
Stalybridge SK15, SK16 . . 85 D1
Standish WN6 . . . . 36 E8
Stretford M17, M32. . . . . 96 C3
Walkden M28. . . . . 60 D1
Westhoughton BL5 . . . . . 58 A8
Wigan, Redwood WN5 . . 54 B6
Wigan, Springfield WN6 . . 37 A1
Wilmslow SK9 . . . . 136 F7
Wythenshawe SK8. . . . . 121 F5
Park Rise
Romiley SK6. . . . . 113 C3
Stalybridge SK15. . . . . . . 85 F3
Park Road S
Newton-le-W WA12. . . . . 89 E4
Urmston M41. . . . . 95 C2
Park Row
3 Bolton BL1 . . . . 24 F6
Manchester SK4 . . . . . . 110 F2
Park Seventeen M45 . . . . 44 F1
Parkside
Hindley WN2 . . . . 56 E6
Manchester M14 . . . . 98 C1
Middleton M24. . . . . 65 A7
Whitworth OL12. . . . . 4 D2
Parkside Ave
Ashton-in-M WN4 . . . . . . 72 A5
Eccles M30 . . . . 79 C1
Failsworth M35 . . . . 83 F5
Walkden M28. . . . . 60 D1
Park Side Ave OL2 . . . . . 149 C4
Parkside Bsns Pk WA3 . . 90 A8
Parkside Cl
High Lane SK12 . . . . 134 D8
Radcliffe M26 . . . . 44 D4
Parkside Cres WN5 . . . . . 53 F6
Parkside Ind Est OL2. . . . 48 E4
Parkside La SK6 . . . . 126 C6
Parkside Mews M45. . . . . 44 F1
Parkside Rd
Golborne WA12, WA2 . . . 90 B2
Manchester M14 . . . . 98 A2
Sale M33 . . . . 108 D3
Parkside St BL2. . . . . 25 C1
Parkside Wlk
Bury BL9 . . . . 140 C1
Stockport SK7 . . . . 123 E3
Park Sq
Ashton-u-L OL6 . . . . 85 E4
Manchester M16 . . . . 97 A2
Park St
Ashton-u-L OL7 . . . . 166 A2
Ashton-u-L OL7 . . . . 166 B2
Atherton M46. . . . . 58 E4
Bolton BL1. . . . . 145 A4
Denton M34. . . . . 100 D3
Droylsden M43. . . . . 84 C2
Farnworth BL4. . . . . 42 D1
Heywood OL10. . . . . 46 E8
Manchester M3 . . . . 158 C3
Mossley OL5 . . . . 86 C8
Oldham OL8 . . . . 153 B2

Park St continued
Pendlebury M27. . . . . 80 A7
Prestwich M25. . . . . 63 C4
Radcliffe M26 . . . . 44 C4
Rochdale OL16. . . . . 139 C2
Romiley SK6. . . . . 112 F3
Royton OL2 . . . . 48 E4
Salford, Kersal Dale M7 . 155 A4
Salford M3. . . . . 158 A1
Shaw OL2. . . . . 149 C3
Stalybridge SK15. . . . . . . 86 B1
Stockport SK1 . . . . 169 E2
1 Tyldesley M29. . . . . . . 59 A1
Wigan WN3 . . . . 150 B2
Parkstead Dr M9. . . . . . . 157 A2
Parks The WA12 . . . . 73 B1
Parkstone Ave
Droylsden M18. . . . . 99 F6
Whitefield M45 . . . . 62 D6
Parkstone Cl BL8. . . . . . . 26 F2
Parkstone Dr M27 . . . . . . 80 B6
Parkstone La M28. . . . . . . 78 F4
Parkstone Rd M44 . . . . . . 94 A3
Parksway
Manchester, Higher Blackley
M9. . . . . 64 B6
Manchester, Sedgley Park
M25. . . . . 63 C2
Pendlebury M27. . . . . 80 C6
Parks Yd BL9 . . . . 140 B2
Park Terr
Heywood OL10. . . . . 29 D3
Mossley OL5 . . . . 86 C8
Westhoughton BL5 . . . . . 39 F1
Whitefield M45 . . . . 62 D7
Park The
Stretford M32. . . . . 96 E4
Uppermill, Lydgate OL4. . 68 D6
Uppermill OL3 . . . . 69 C5
Park View
Abram WN2 . . . . 56 B1
Ashton-in-M WN4 . . . . . . 73 B2
Chadderton OL9. . . . . 48 B1
Cheadle SK3 . . . . 122 F7
Droylsden M34. . . . . 100 D8
Farnworth BL4. . . . . 42 D1
Gatley SK8 . . . . 122 A6
Hazel Grove SK7 . . . . . . 134 B8
Ince-in-M WN2 . . . . 56 B7
Kearsley BL4 . . . . 60 F7
Little Bollington WA14. . . 118 B2
Littleborough OL15 . . . . . 16 B6
Manchester, Burnage M14. 110 C7
Manchester, Collyhurst
M9. . . . . 156 C2
7 Manchester M21 . . . . . . 96 F1
Manchester, Moss Side M14 98 A4
Newton-le-W WA12. . . . . 89 E3
Romiley SK6. . . . . 112 C3
Stalybridge SK6. . . . . 85 F4
Stockport SK1 . . . . 124 B7
Park View Com Sch M40 160 B4
Parkview Ct M32. . . . . . . 96 E1
Park View Ct
Poynton SK12 . . . . 133 E4
Prestwich M25. . . . . 63 B3
Romiley SK6. . . . . 113 C2
Parkview Pk WA13 . . . . . 117 D1
Park View Prim Sch M25 . 63 B3
Park View Rd
Bolton BL3. . . . . 146 C4
Prestwich M25. . . . . 63 B3
Park View Rise SK22 . . . 127 C1
Parkville Rd
Manchester M20 . . . . . . 110 C5
Prestwich M25. . . . . 63 C6
Parkway
Chadderton OL9. . . . . 48 A1
Cheadle SK3 . . . . 122 F7
Denton M34. . . . . 100 C3
New Mills SK22 . . . . 127 C1
Rochdale OL11. . . . . 30 B8
Shevington Moor WN6. . . 19 A2
Stockport SK3 . . . . 123 E2
Walkden M38. . . . . 59 F4
Westhoughton BL5 . . . . . 57 D6
Wilmslow SK9 . . . . 137 B6
Park Way
Eccles M17, M41. . . . . . . 96 A6
Urmston M32, M41. . . . . . 95 F5
Parkway Bsns Ctr M14 . . 97 F2
Parkway Circ M17 . . . . . . 96 A6
Parkway Four Ind Est
M17. . . . . 96 A6
Parkway Gr M38. . . . . 59 E4
Parkway Ind Est M17. . . . 96 A6
Parkway Trad Est M32. . . 96 A5
Parkwood BL7 . . . . 8 D2
Parkwood Dr M38 . . . . . 151 B2
Parkwood Dr BL5. . . . . . . 58 F7
Parkwood Rd M23 . . . . . 121 C7
Parliament Pl BL9 . . . . . . 140 B1
Parliament St
Bury BL9 . . . . 140 B1
Ince-in-M WN3 . . . . 151 A2
Up Holland WN8 . . . . 53 C7
Parndon Dr SK2. . . . . . . 124 C7
Parnell Ave M22 . . . . . . 121 D8
Parnell Cl M29. . . . . 77 B5
Parnham Cl M26 . . . . 43 B5
Parochial CE Prim Sch **5**
OL6. . . . . 85 D3
Parrbrook Cl M45. . . . . . . 45 A1
Parrbrook Wlk M45. . . . . . 45 B1
PARR BROW 77 E8
Parr Cl BL4. . . . . 60 B8
Parrenthorn High Sch
M25. . . . . 63 D7

Parrenthorn Rd M25 . . . . 63 C7
Parrenthorn Sports Ctr
M25. . . . . 63 D7
Parfield Rd M28 . . . . 79 A7
Parr Fold BL9. . . . . 45 B2
Parr Fold Ave M28 . . . . . . 60 C1
Parr Ho OL8 . . . . 153 C1
Parrin La M30 . . . . 79 C3
Parrot St
Bolton BL3. . . . . 145 B1
Droylsden M11. . . . . 83 C1
Parrs Ct M44 . . . . 93 F2
Parrs Mount Mews SK4 . 110 F2
Parr St
Droylsden M11. . . . . 99 E7
Eccles M30 . . . . 79 D1
Tyldesley M29 . . . . 76 F8
Parrs Wood Ave M20. . . 110 C2
Parrs Wood Entertainment
Ctr M20. . . . . 110 D1
Parrs Wood La M19, M20 110 D2
Parrs Wood Rd
Manchester, Burnage
M20. . . . . 110 C2
Manchester, East Didsbury
M20. . . . . 122 B8
Parrs Wood Tech Coll
M20. . . . . 110 D1
Parry Mead SK6. . . . . . . 113 A4
Parry Rd M12 . . . . 99 A4
Parry Wlk **12** OL6 . . . . 85 D4
Parslow Ave M8 . . . . 156 A4
Parsonage M3. . . . . 158 C1
Parsonage Brow WN8. . . 53 A8
Parsonage Cl
Bury BL9 . . . . 141 A3
Salford M5. . . . . 161 C4
Up Holland WN8 . . . . 53 A7
Parsonage Ct
5 Manchester, Withington
M20. . . . . 110 B6
Stockport, Heaton Moor
SK4 . . . . 168 B4
Parsonage Dr M28 . . . . . . 60 C2
Parsonage Gdns SK6. . . 126 A4
Parsonage Gn SK9 . . . . . 137 B7
Parsonage La M3 . . . . . . 158 C2
Parsonage Rd
Kearsley M26. . . . . 61 C7
Manchester, Withington
M20. . . . . 110 C7
Stockport, Heaton Moor
SK4 . . . . 168 C4
Urmston M41. . . . . 94 E1
Walkden M28. . . . . 57 B7
Parsonage Ret Pk WN7. . 75 E5
Parsonage St
Bury BL9 . . . . 141 A3
Hyde SK14 . . . . 167 A1
Manchester, Crumpsall M8 . 63 F1
Manchester, Hulme M15 . 162 B1
Radcliffe M26 . . . . 44 A3
Stockport SK4 . . . . 169 B2
Parsonage Way
Cheadle SK8 . . . . 123 B5
Leigh WN7 . . . . 75 E6
Parsonage Wlk OL16 . . . . 31 F7
Parsons Dr M24. . . . . 46 F2
Parson's Field M6. . . . . . . 81 A5
Parson's La BL9. . . . . . . 140 C3
PARSON'S MEADOW . . . 150 A2
Parsons St OL9 . . . . 152 C2
Parsons Way WN1 . . . . . . 37 B1
Parth St BL0. . . . . 28 D1
PARTINGTON 105 F4
Partington Ct
Farnworth BL4. . . . . 42 C1
2 Glossop SK13. . . . . . . 104 F1
Partington La M27 . . . . . . 79 E7
Partington Pk
M31. . . . . 105 F3
Partington Pl **3** M33. . . . . 108 B5
Partington Prim Sch
M31. . . . . 105 F3
Partington Sh Ctr M44 . . 105 F3
Partington Sports Village
M31. . . . . 105 F2
Partington St
Bolton BL3. . . . . 146 C2
Eccles M30 . . . . 79 D3
Failsworth M35 . . . . 83 F7
Heywood OL10. . . . . 29 A2
Manchester M40 . . . . . . 157 C1
4 Oldham OL1 . . . . 67 A7
Rochdale OL11. . . . . 30 B2
Swinton M28 . . . . 79 C8
Wigan WN5 . . . . 54 E8
Partridge Ave M23 . . . . . 121 C6
Partridge Cl
Irlam M44 . . . . 94 A4
Rochdale OL11. . . . . 29 F7
Partridge Ct SK2. . . . . . . 124 B5
Partridge Rd M35 . . . . . . 84 D3
Partridge Rise M43 . . . . . 84 D3
Partridge St **8** M16 . . . . . 96 F5
Partridge Way OL9 . . . . . 65 E8
Part St BL5 . . . . 39 E2
Parvet Ave M43 . . . . 83 F3
Pascal St M19 . . . . 111 A8
PASSMONDS 14 B1
Passmonds Cres OL11 &
OL12 . . . . 14 B1
Passmonds Way OL11 . . 30 B8

Pass St OL9. . . . . 153 A2
Pass The OL16. . . . . 31 A8
Paston Rd M22 . . . . 121 D7
Pasture Cl
Ashton-in-M WN4 . . . . . . 72 E6
Heywood OL10. . . . . 29 B1
Pasturefield Cl **1** M33. . . 108 F3
Pasture Field Rd M22 . . . 121 F1
Pasturegreen Way M44 . . 94 B3
Pastures La OL4 . . . . 68 B8
Patch Croft Rd M22 . . . . 121 F1
Patchett St
Manchester M12 . . . . . . 164 C2
9 Tyldesley M29. . . . . . . 59 A1
Patey St M12 . . . . 99 A3
Pathfield Wlk **2** M9 . . . . 157 A4
Patience St **11** OL12 . . . . 14 C1
Patmos St BL10. . . . . 11 D6
Paton Ave BL3 . . . . 42 A3
Paton Ct **2** BL3 . . . . 42 A3
Paton St
Manchester M1 . . . . 159 B1
Rochdale OL12. . . . . 14 D3
Patricia Dr M28 . . . . 60 E2
Patrick Roddy Ct M18 . . 165 C1
Patricroft Rd WN2 . . . . . 151 C2
Patricroft Sta M30 . . . . . . 79 C2
Patten St M20 . . . . 110 B6
Patterdale Ave
Oldham OL1. . . . . 49 A1
Rochdale OL11. . . . . 30 B3
Stalybridge SK15. . . . . . . 86 A3
Patterdale Cl
Bury BL9 . . . . 44 E7
Middleton M24. . . . . 46 E2
Patterdale Pl WN2 . . . . . . 56 A7
Patterdale Rd
Ashton-in-M WN4 . . . . . . 73 A8
Ashton-u-L OL7 . . . . 84 F5
Bolton BL2. . . . . 25 F4
Leigh WN7 . . . . 76 C4
Partington M31 . . . . 105 E3
Romiley SK6. . . . . 113 B4
Stockport SK1 . . . . 124 B7
Wythenshawe M22 . . . . 121 E8
Patterdale Wlk WA15 . . . 120 D5
Patterson Ave M21 . . . . . 97 A1
Patterson St
Bolton BL3. . . . . 146 A4
Denton M34. . . . . 100 F4
Newton-le-W WA12 . . . . . 89 B3
Westhoughton BL5 . . . . . 57 B7
Patting Cl M44. . . . . 94 C3
Pattishall Cl M4 . . . . 160 A1
Pattison Cl OL12 . . . . 14 D3
Pattison Cl BL9 . . . . 45 C2
Patton Cl BL9 . . . . 28 C1
Paul Ct **6** SK1 . . . . 112 A1
Paulden Ave
Manchester M23 . . . . . . 121 B6
Paulden Dr M35 . . . . 84 A7
Paulette St BL1 . . . . 145 A8
Paulhan Rd M20. . . . . . . 110 D4
Paulhan St BL3 . . . . 147 B3
Pauline St WN2 . . . . 57 B1
Paul Row OL15. . . . . 6 D1
Pavilion Cl **2** OL12. . . . . . 14 F2
Pavilion Dr OL6 . . . . 85 D5
Pavilion Ho M20 . . . . 110 A4
Pavilion Rd SK9 . . . . 137 E8
Pavilions The SK8 . . . . . 122 D4
Pavilion Wlk M26 . . . . 43 F3
Paxford Pl SK9 . . . . 137 A5
Paythorne Cl WA3 . . . . . . 91 F3
Paythorne Gn SK2 . . . . . 124 E5
Peabody St BL3. . . . . . . 147 B4
Peacefield SK6 . . . . 125 E5
Peacehaven Ave **12** M11. . 83 C2
Peace St
Atherton M46. . . . . 58 E3
Bolton BL3. . . . . 145 A1
3 Failsworth M35 . . . . . . 66 A1
Tyldesley M29 . . . . 76 F7
Peach Bank M24. . . . . 65 A8
Peach Bank Ho M24. . . . . 65 A8
Peach Rd OL4 . . . . 49 D1
Peach St M25 . . . . 63 C5
Peach Tree Cl M7 . . . . . . 155 C2
Peach Tree Ct **1** M6 . . . . 81 A2
Peacock Ave **8** M6. . . . . . 80 D5
Peacock Cl
Glossop SK13. . . . . 171 B4
Manchester M18 . . . . . . 165 C2
Peacock Dr SK8 . . . . 131 B6
Peacock Fold WN7. . . . . . 75 D6
Peacock Gr M18 . . . . 99 D4
Peacock La OL16. . . . . 6 B6
Peak Ave **5** SK9 . . . . 131 D5
Peak Bank SK6 . . . . 113 B3
Peak Cl OL4 . . . . 49 F4
Peakdale Ave
Gatley SK8. . . . . 122 B1
Manchester M8 . . . . 156 B4
Peakdale Rd
Droylsden M43. . . . . 83 E3
Glossop SK13. . . . . 171 B3
Marple SK6 . . . . 126 A4
Peak Ho SK13. . . . . 104 A5

Par–Pee **245**

Peaknaze Cl
Glossop SK13. . . . . 116 B8
Pendlebury M27. . . . . 80 B8
Peak St
Bolton BL1. . . . . 143 A2
Manchester M1 . . . . 159 B1
Oldham OL9. . . . . 152 C2
Stockport SK1 . . . . 112 A2
Peak View SK13. . . . . . . 171 C4
Pear Ave BL9 . . . . 141 C3
Pear Cl M24 . . . . 65 B6
Peardale Cl M30 . . . . 95 C8
Pearl Ave M7 . . . . 63 E1
Pearl Brook Ind Est BL6. . 22 B3
Pearl Mill Cl OL8. . . . . 67 B4
Pearl St
Denton M34. . . . . 100 E3
Hazel Grove SK7 . . . . . . 124 E4
Rochdale OL11. . . . . 30 C8
Wigan WN6 . . . . 37 B3
Pearl Way M14 . . . . 103 A2
Pearly Bank OL1 . . . . 49 D4
Pear Mill Ind Est SK6 . . . 112 C2
Pearn Ave M19 . . . . 110 F5
Pearn Rd M19 . . . . 110 F5
Pearson Cl
Milnrow OL16 . . . . 31 F7
Partington M31 . . . . 106 A3
Pearson Gr **7** OL4 . . . . . . 67 E6
Pearson Ho **5** M30 . . . . . . 95 D8
Pearson Mews SK16. . . . 101 C6
Pearson St
Bury BL9 . . . . 141 B3
Dukinfield SK16 . . . . 101 C6
Reddish SK5. . . . . 169 C3
Rochdale OL16. . . . . 31 C8
Peart Ave SK6 . . . . 113 C6
Pear Tree Cl
Glossop SK13. . . . . 171 B4
Marple SK6 . . . . 126 B8
Salford M6. . . . . 81 A2
Peartree Cres WA12. . . . . 89 C2
Pear Tree Ct
Aspull WN2 . . . . 38 C6
3 Salford M6 . . . . 81 A2
Pear Tree Dr
Farnworth BL4. . . . . 60 A7
Stalybridge SK15. . . . . . . 86 B2
Pear Tree Gr M29 . . . . 59 E1
Pear Tree Pl BL4. . . . . 60 A7
Peartree Wlk M22 . . . . . . 121 B4
Pear Tree Wlk **10** M33 . . 107 C5
Peart St M34 . . . . 100 E3
Peary St M4 . . . . 159 B3
Peaslake Cl SK6 . . . . 113 D2
Peatfield Ave M27 . . . . . . 61 E2
Peatfield Wlk **8** M15 . . . . 162 D7
Pebble Cl SK15 . . . . 86 A4
Pebworth Cl M24, M9. . . . 64 F5
Peckford St M40 . . . . 83 A5
Peckforton Cl SK8 . . . . . 122 A5
Peckforton Wlk **11** SK9 . 131 E1
Peckmill Cl M23. . . . . . . 121 A5
Pedder St BL1 . . . . 142 C1
Pedler Brow La OL12. . . . 13 E6
Pedley Wlk M13 . . . . 163 B3
Peebles Cl WN4. . . . . 72 C4
Peebles Dr M40. . . . . 83 D4
PEEL. 59 F4
Peel Ave
Altrincham WA14. . . . . . 119 D2
Ramsbottom BL0 . . . . . . 138 A1
PEEL BROW 11 C4
Peel Brow BL0. . . . . 11 D6
Peel Brow Prim Sch BL0 . 11 D6
Peel Cl M46 . . . . 58 E3
Peel Green Rd M30. . . . . . 95 B8
Peel Green Trad Est M30 . 95 B8
Peel Hall Ave M29 . . . . . . 59 B1
Peel Hall Prim Sch M22 . 121 F3
Peel Hall Rd
Ramsbottom BL0, BL9 . . . 11 B2
Wythenshawe M22 . . . . 121 F2
Peel House Ct M38 . . . . . 59 F3
Peel La
Heywood OL10. . . . . 29 B3
Manchester M8 . . . . 159 B4
Tyldesley M29 . . . . 77 C4
Walkden M28, M38 . . . . . 59 F3
Peel Mills Ind Est BL9. . . 140 B3
Peel Moat Ct SK4. . . . . . 111 B5
Peel Moat Rd SK4. . . . . . 111 B5
Peel Moat Sports Ctr
SK4 . . . . 111 B5
Peel Mount
Ramsbottom BL0 . . . . 11 A4
Salford M6. . . . . 81 B3
Peel Park Cres M38 . . . . . 59 F4

Peel Rd WA15 . . . . 119 E3
Peels Ave OL4 . . . . 68 A7
Peel Sq M18 . . . . 99 D5
Peel St
Adlington PR6 . . . . 21 B8
Ashton-u-L OL6 . . . . 166 B3
Chadderton OL9 . . . . 152 B3
Denton, Audenshaw M34 . 100 E6
Denton M34 . . . . 100 E4
Droylsden M43 . . . . 99 F8
Dukinfield SK16 . . . . 166 C1
Eccles M30 . . . . 79 F2
Failsworth M35 . . . . 83 D6
Farnworth BL4 . . . . 60 E8
Glossop SK13 . . . . 104 C5
Heywood OL10 . . . . 29 B2
Hyde SK14 . . . . 167 C1
Leigh WN7 . . . . 75 E5
Littleborough OL15 . . . . . 16 B5
Newton-le-W WA12 . . . . . 89 B3
Platt Bridge WN2 . . . . 56 A2
1 Radcliffe M26 . . . . 44 B2
Rochdale OL12 . . . . 139 B4
Shaw OL2 . . . . 149 A3
Stalybridge SK15 . . . . 85 F1
Stockport SK2 . . . . 170 C2
Westhoughton BL5 . . . . . . 39 E1
Peel Terr
10 Dukinfield SK16 . . . . 166 B1
Westhoughton BL5 . . . . . . 39 E2
Peel Twr ★ BL8 . . . . 10 F5
Peel View BL8 . . . . 27 A6
Peel Way BL9 . . . . 140 B2
Peelwood Ave BL4 . . . . 60 A4
Peelwood Gr M46 . . . . 58 E2
Peerglow Pk Est WA14 . . 119 E8
Peers CI M41 . . . . 94 D4
Peers St BL8 . . . . 27 C2
Pegamoid St BL2 . . . . 25 B1

Pegasus Ct
Rochdale OL11 . . . . 30 C6
Sale M33 . . . . 108 D5
Pegasus Sq M7 . . . . 81 C3
Pegwell Dr M7 . . . . 155 B1
Pekin St OL6 . . . . 166 C4
Pelham Gr WN2 . . . . 56 D4
Pelham PI M8 . . . . 64 B2
Pelham St
Ashton-u-L OL7 . . . . 84 E1
Bolton BL3 . . . . 146 C3
Oldham OL8 . . . . 66 F2
Pellowe Rd 3 OL8 . . . . . . 66 E4
Pelton Ave M27 . . . . 61 D2
Pelton Wlk M40 . . . . 157 A1
PEMBEC WN5 . . . . 54 C7
Pemberlei Rd WN2 . . . . 38 D2
PEMBERTON 54 C5
Pemberton Ho OL2 . . . . . . 149 B4
Pemberton St WN3, WN5 . . 54 B2
Pemberton St
Bolton BL1 . . . . 143 B4
Manchester M16 . . . . 97 C4
3 Rochdale OL11 . . . . . 30 C2
Walkden M38 . . . . 60 A4
Pemberton Sta WN5 . . . . 54 D4
Pemberton Way OL2 . . . . 149 B4
Pembridge Fold M24 . . . . . 65 C8
Pembridge Rd M9 . . . . 64 F4
Pembroke Ave
Eccles M30 . . . . 79 D2
Sale M33 . . . . 107 F5
Pembroke CI
Cheadle SK8 . . . . 122 E2
Horwich BL6 . . . . 22 A4
Manchester M13 . . . . 164 A2
Pembroke Ct
Hazel Grove SK7 . . . . . . 124 E2
Pendlebury M27 . . . . 80 B8
14 Rochdale OL12 . . . . . 14 F1
Romiley SK6 . . . . 112 F2
Pembroke Dr
Bury BL9 . . . . 44 E7
Oldham OL4 . . . . 49 E4
Pembroke Gr M44 . . . . . . 105 C6
Pembroke Ho 3 SK3 . . . . 170 B4
Pembroke Rd
Hindley WN2 . . . . 57 C3
Wigan WN5 . . . . 36 D1
Pembroke St
Bolton BL1 . . . . 145 A4
Littleborough OL15 . . . . . 16 B6
Oldham OL8 . . . . 153 A2
Salford, Higher Broughton
M7 . . . . 155 B2
3 Salford, Seedley M6 . 154 B1
Pembroke Way 6 M34 . . 101 A1
Pembry CI SK5 . . . . 112 B5
Pembury CI M22 . . . . 121 C3
Penarth Rd
Bolton BL3 . . . . 146 B4
Wythenshawe M22 . . . . . 121 D8
Penbury Rd WN1 . . . . 37 B5
Pencarrow CI M20 . . . . . . 109 F3
Pencombe CI M12 . . . . . . 165 A1
Pencroft Way M15 . . . . . . 163 A1
Pendeen CI
Tyldesley M29 . . . . 77 A7
Wythenshawe M22 . . . . 121 E1
Pendennis 2 OL11 . . . . . 139 B2
Pendennis Ave BL6 . . . . . . 40 D5
Pendennis CI M26 . . . . 43 C5
Pendennis Cres WN2 . . . . 57 A3
Pendennis Rd SK4 . . . . . . 168 C3
Pendle Ave BL1 . . . . 24 E6
PENDLEBURY 80 C8

Pendlebury CI M25 . . . . 62 F2
Pendlebury Ct SK3 . . . . . . 124 A4
Pendlebury Fold BL3 . . . . . 40 D2
Pendlebury La WN1, WN2 . 37 D6
Pendlebury Rd
Gatley SK8 . . . . 122 B6
Swinton M27 . . . . 79 F8
Pendlebury St BL1 . . . . . . 143 C3
Pendlebury Twrs SK5 . . . . 169 C3
Pendle CI
Bury BL8 . . . . 27 B3
Oldham OL4 . . . . 67 D5
Wigan WN5 . . . . 54 D5
Pendlecroft Ave M27 . . . . . 80 C7
Pendle Ct
Bolton BL1 . . . . 143 A3
Leigh WN7 . . . . 76 B4
Pendle Dr BL6 . . . . 22 C5
Pendle Gdns WA3 . . . . 91 E2
Pendle Gr OL2 . . . . 48 C3
Pendle Rd
Denton M34 . . . . 100 F2
Golborne WA3 . . . . 74 C1
PENDLETON 81 A3
Pendleton Gn 3 M6 . . . . . 154 C3
Pendleton Way 10 M6 . . . . 81 A3
Pendleway M27 . . . . 62 A1
Pendle Wlk SK5 . . . . 112 A4
Pendragon PI M35 . . . . 84 A7
Pendrell Wlk 2 M9 . . . . . . 64 E3
Penelope Rd 4 M6 . . . . . . 80 D5
Penerly Dr M9 . . . . 157 A2
Penfair CI M11 . . . . 83 A1
Penfield CI M1 . . . . 163 B3
Penfold Wlk M12 . . . . 164 C2
Pengarth Rd BL6 . . . . 22 C4
Pengham Wlk M23 . . . . . . 109 A1
Pengwern Ave 1 BL3 . . . . 146 B4
Penhale Mews SK7 . . . . . . 132 F7
Penhall Wlk M40 . . . . 83 A5
Peninsula M7 . . . . 81 B7
Penistone Ave
Manchester M9 . . . . 65 A3
Rochdale OL16 . . . . 31 C6
Salford M6 . . . . 80 C3
Penketh Ave
Manchester M18 . . . . 99 B4
Tyldesley M29 . . . . 77 B6
Penketh St M6 . . . . 37 B2
Penleach Ave WN7 . . . . . . 76 B5
Penmere Gr M33 . . . . 107 E1
Penmoor Chase SK7 . . . . 124 B1
Penmore CI OL2 . . . . 49 D7
Pennant Dr M25 . . . . 63 A5
Pennant Ind Est 9 OL1 . . 67 B8
Pennant St OL1 . . . . 67 B8
Pennell Dr WN3 . . . . 54 F5
Pennell St M11 . . . . 83 D1
Penn Gn SK8 . . . . 123 B1
Penn House CI SK7 . . . . . . 132 E8
Pennine Ave
Chadderton OL9 . . . . . . 152 A1
Wigan WN3 . . . . 54 C2
Pennine CI
Bury BL8 . . . . 27 B3
Horwich BL6 . . . . 22 C5
Manchester M9 . . . . 64 F4
Pennine Ct
Stalybridge SK15 . . . . 86 D3
Swinton M27 . . . . 62 A1
Pennine Dr
Altrincham WA14 . . . . . . 119 B5
Ashton-u-L OL6 . . . . 85 E4
Milnrow OL16 . . . . 32 A6
Wardle OL12 . . . . 15 C6
Pennine Gr
Ashton-u-L OL6 . . . . 85 E6
Leigh WN7 . . . . 75 C8
Pennine La WA3 . . . . 74 C1
Pennine Prec 3 OL16 . . . . 31 F5
Pennine Rd
Glossop SK13 . . . . 116 A8
Horwich BL6 . . . . 22 C5
Romiley SK6 . . . . 113 C6
Stockport SK7 . . . . 124 B1
Pennine Sq OL11 . . . . 30 C5
Pennine Terr 2 SK16 . . . . 166 C1
Pennine Vale OL2 . . . . . . 149 C4
Pennine View
Denton M34 . . . . 100 E5
Littleborough OL15 . . . . . . 6 D2
Mossley OL5 . . . . 68 D1
Royton OL2 . . . . 48 E4
Stalybridge SK15 . . . . 86 C4
Pennine Wlk WN2 . . . . 56 B2
PENNINGTON 75 E3
Pennington Ave WN7 . . . . . 75 E3
Pennington CI
Pennington Green WN2 . . 38 E2
Walkden M38 . . . . 59 E4
Pennington Dr WN7 . . . . . . 75 B1
Pennington Dr WA12 . . . . . 89 E3
Pennington Flash Ctry Pk★
WN7 . . . . 75 B3
Pennington Gdns WN7 . . . . 75 E1
PENNINGTON GREEN 38 E1
Pennington Green La
WN2 . . . . 38 E2
Pennington La
Ince-in-M WN2 . . . . 56 A8
Standish WN2 . . . . 37 E8
Pennington Mews WN7 . . . 75 E2
Pennington Rd
Bolton BL3 . . . . 147 C3
Leigh WN7 . . . . 75 F3
Pennington St
Bury BL8 . . . . 26 F4

Pennington St *continued*
7 Hindley WN2 . . . . 56 D6
Manchester M12 . . . . 99 A2
Oldham OL9 . . . . 66 B3
11 Walkden M28 . . . . 60 E3
Pennistone CI 5 M44 . . . . . 94 B3
Pennon CI M7 . . . . 155 B2
Penn St
Farnworth BL4 . . . . 60 C8
Heywood OL10 . . . . 29 D1
Horwich BL6 . . . . 22 C3
Manchester M40 . . . . . . 157 C4
Oldham OL8 . . . . 153 A1
Rochdale OL16 . . . . 139 C4
Penny Black Chambers
M28 . . . . 78 F5
Penny Bridge La M41 . . . . . 95 A2
Penny Brook Fold SK7 . . . 124 F3
Pennybutts CI WA3 . . . . . . 73 F2
Penny Gate WN7 . . . . 56 D6
Pennyhurst St WN3 . . . . . 150 B3
Penny La
Haydock WA11 . . . . 89 B7
Stockport SK5 . . . . 169 C3
Penny Mdw OL6 . . . . 166 C3
Pennymoor Dr WA14 . . . . 119 B6
Penrhos Ave SK8 . . . . 121 F4
Penrhyn Ave
Cheadle SK8 . . . . 122 E1
Middleton M24 . . . . 65 A7
Penrhyn Cres SK7 . . . . . . 133 C8
Penrhyn Dr
Hazel Grove SK7 . . . . . . 124 D1
Prestwich M25 . . . . 63 B4
Penrhyn Gr M46 . . . . 58 C5
Penrhyn Rd SK3 . . . . 123 C8
Penrice CI M26 . . . . 43 D5
Penrice Fold M28 . . . . 78 B7
Penrith Ave
Ashton-u-L OL7 . . . . 84 F5
Bolton BL1 . . . . 142 A1
Droylsden M11 . . . . 83 B3
Oldham OL8 . . . . 66 C4
Prestwich M45 . . . . 63 B7
Reddish SK5 . . . . 99 F1
Sale M33 . . . . 108 C2
Walkden M28 . . . . 60 F2
Penrith CI M31 . . . . 105 E4
Penrith Cres WN4 . . . . 73 B4
Penrith St OL11 . . . . 139 C1
Penrod PI M6 . . . . 81 B4
Penrose CI M8 . . . . 156 A4
Penrose Gdns M24 . . . . . . 47 B1
Penrose St BL2 . . . . 148 C3
Penrose Wlk M24 . . . . 47 A4
Penroy Ave M20 . . . . 109 D3
Penroyson CI M12 . . . . . . 164 C2
Penruddock Wlk 4 M13 . . 98 F4
Penry Ave M44 . . . . 105 C4
Penryn Ave
Royton OL2 . . . . 48 F3
Sale M33 . . . . 108 C1
Penryn Ct M7 . . . . 63 D1
Pensarn Ave M14 . . . . 110 E8
Pensarn Gr SK5 . . . . 169 C4
Pensby CI M27 . . . . 80 C7
Pensby Wlk M40 . . . . 157 A1
Pensford Ct BL2 . . . . 25 E6
Pensford Rd M23 . . . . 120 F3
Penshaw Ave WN3 . . . . . . 55 B3
Penshurst Rd SK5 . . . . . . 112 B6
Penshurst Wlk 20 M34 . . 101 A1
Penson St WN1 . . . . 37 D2
Penswick Rd WN7 . . . . 57 C3
Penthorpe Dr OL2 . . . . 48 F3
Pentland Ave M40 . . . . 65 C2
Pentland CI SK7 . . . . 124 B1
Pentlands Ave M7 . . . . . . 155 A1
Pentlands The 1 OL2 . . . . 48 F8
Pentland Terr BL1 . . . . . . 143 B1
Pentland Way SK14 . . . . . 102 B6
Pentwyn Gr M23 . . . . 121 B2
Penwell Fold OL1 . . . . 48 E1
Penydarren View 8 BL4 . . 42 C2
Penzance PI 3 OL9 . . . . . . 48 A1
Penzance St M40 . . . . 160 B3
Peoples History Mus★
M3 . . . . 158 B1
People's History Mus
(Archive & Study Ctr)★
M1 . . . . 163 A4
Peover Ave M33 . . . . 108 E4
Peover Rd SK9 . . . . 131 E5
Peover Wlk 4 SK8 . . . . . . 123 A5
Pepler Ave M23 . . . . 109 B2
Peploe Wlk M23 . . . . 108 D1
Pepper CI M22 . . . . 121 D6
Pepper Ct SK9 . . . . 137 A6
Pepperhill Rd M16 . . . . 97 F4
Pepper La WN6 . . . . 19 B3
Pepper Mill La WN1 . . . . . 151 A3
Peppermint CI OL16 . . . . . 32 C4
Pepper St M4 . . . . 159 A2
Pepper St WA16 . . . . 128 F1
Pepperwood Dr WN3 . . . . . 54 E2
Pepys PI WN3 . . . . 54 D4
Perceval Way WN2 . . . . . . 56 D4
Perch St 4 WN1 . . . . 37 E1
Percival CI M8 . . . . 155 C2
Percival Rd M43 . . . . 84 B1
Percival Wlk OL2 . . . . 48 E3
Percy Dr M5 . . . . 161 B3
Percy Rd M34 . . . . 100 C2
Percy St
Bolton BL1 . . . . 143 C2
Bury BL9 . . . . 141 B3
Farnworth BL4 . . . . 60 E7
Oldham OL4 . . . . 67 C7

Percy St *continued*
Ramsbottom BL0 . . . . . . 138 B1
Rochdale OL16 . . . . 31 B5
Stalybridge SK15 . . . . 86 B2
Stockport SK1 . . . . 169 C2
Whitworth OL12 . . . . 4 E6
Peregrine Dr WN7 . . . . 76 B5
Peregrine Cres M43 . . . . . . 84 C3
Peregrine Dr M44 . . . . 94 A3
Peregrine Rd SK2 . . . . 125 A4
Peregrine St M15, M16. . . 162 C1
Perendale Rise BL1 . . . . . . 143 B4
Periton Wlk 8 M9 . . . . 64 E3
Perivale Dr OL8 . . . . 67 B4
Perkins Ave M7 . . . . 155 B1
Pernham St OL4 . . . . 67 C7
Perrin St SK14 . . . . 167 A2
Perry Ave SK14 . . . . 102 A4
Perrybrook Wlk WN4 . . . . . 73 D4
Perry Ct OL11 . . . . 139 A1
Perrygate Ave M20 . . . . . . 110 A6
Perrymead M25 . . . . 63 C6
Perryn PI WN6 . . . . 19 F1
Perry Rd WA15 . . . . 120 B6
Pershore 8 OL12 . . . . 139 B4
Pershore Rd M24 . . . . 47 A3
Pershore 4 M30 . . . . 79 E2
Perth Ave
Chadderton OL9 . . . . 66 A4
Ince-in-M WN2 . . . . 56 A8
Perth CI SK7 . . . . 132 F5
Perth Rd OL11 . . . . 31 B2
Perth St
Bolton BL3 . . . . 146 C3
Royton OL2 . . . . 49 A4
Swinton M27 . . . . 79 D7
Peru St M3 . . . . 158 A2
Peterborough CI OL6 . . . . . 85 B6
Peterborough Dr BL1 . . . . 143 B1
Peterborough St 1 M18 . . 99 F6
Peterborough Wlk 10
BL1 . . . . 143 C1
Peterchurch Wlk M11 . . . 165 C4
Peterhead CI BL1 . . . . 143 A1
Peterhead Wlk 4 M5 . . . . 81 A1
Peterhouse Gdns SK6 . . . 113 C4
Peterhouse Wlk WM4 . . . . 72 F4
Peterloo Ct 5 M6 . . . . . . 154 B2
Peterloo Terr 8 M24 . . . . . 47 A2
Peter Martin St 2 BL6 . . . . 22 B4
Peter Moss Way M19 . . . . . 99 C1
Petersburg Rd SK3 . . . . . . 170 A2
Peters Ct WA15 . . . . 120 D5
Petersfield Dr M23 . . . . . . 120 D7
Petersfield Wlk M5 . . . . . . 81 A1
Petersfield Wlk 1 BL1 . . . 145 B4
Peter St
Altrincham WA14 . . . . . . 119 D3
Ashton-in-M WN4 . . . . . . 73 C3
Bury BL9 . . . . 140 C3
Denton M34 . . . . 101 A3
Eccles M30 . . . . 79 D1
Glossop SK13 . . . . 104 A6
Golborne WA3 . . . . 90 A8
Hazel Grove SK7 . . . . . . 124 D3
Hindley WN2 . . . . 56 D5
Leigh WN7 . . . . 76 B4
Manchester M2, M3 . . . . 162 C4
Oldham OL1 . . . . 153 C2
Stockport SK1 . . . . 112 A2
Tyldesley M29 . . . . 58 F1
Westhoughton BL5 . . . . . . 57 A7
Wigan WN5 . . . . 54 B8
Peterswood Ct M22 . . . . . 121 B3
Peterwood Gdns M32 . . . . 96 A1
Petheridge Dr 2 M22 . . . . 121 B1
Petrel Ave SK12 . . . . 133 B4
Petrel CI
Droylsden M43 . . . . 84 C3
Rochdale OL11 . . . . 29 F7
Stockport SK3 . . . . 170 A2
Tyldesley M29 . . . . 77 A8
Petrie Ct M6 . . . . 81 B4
Petrie St OL12 . . . . 139 C4
Petrock Wlk 5 M40 . . . . . . 83 C5
Petticoat La WN2 . . . . 56 B7
Petts Cres OL15 . . . . 16 B6
Petunia Wlk 8 M28 . . . . . . 59 F3
Petworth Ave WN3 . . . . . . 54 D2
Petworth CI M22 . . . . 121 E5
Petworth Rd OL9 . . . . 152 B2
Pevensey Ct M9 . . . . 65 A2
Pevensey Rd M6 . . . . 80 E5
Pevensey Wlk OL9 . . . . . . 152 B2
Peveril Ave SK22 . . . . 127 C1
Peveril CI M45 . . . . 63 A2
Peveril Ct M41 . . . . 97 A2
Peveril CI 1 SK13 . . . . 116 F8
Peveril Dr SK7 . . . . 133 F8
Peveril Rd
Altrincham WA14 . . . . . . 119 C7
Oldham OL1 . . . . 49 C1
Salford M5 . . . . 154 B1
Peveril St BL3 . . . . 146 C2
Peveril Terr SK14 . . . . . . 113 F8
Pewfist Gn BL5 . . . . 57 E6
Pewfist Spinney The BL5 . 57 D7
Pewfist The BL5 . . . . 57 E7
Pewsey Rd M22 . . . . 121 F3
Pexhill CI SK14 . . . . 168 A2
Pexwood OL1 . . . . 47 E5
Pheasant Dr M21 . . . . 109 D7
Pheasant Rise WA14 . . . . 119 D1
Phelan CI M40 . . . . 156 C1
Phethean St
Bolton BL2 . . . . 148 A3

Phethean St *continued*
Farnworth BL4 . . . . 42 C2
Philip Ave M34 . . . . 100 E5
Philip CI 6 WN5 . . . . 54 D5
Philip Dr M33 . . . . 108 B2
Philip Godlee Lodge
M20 . . . . 110 B1
Philip Howard Ct 2 BL4 . . 60 C8
Philip Howard Rd SK13 . . 116 C8
Philips Ave BL4 . . . . 60 D7
Philips Ct 5 M14 . . . . 98 D4
Philips Dr M45 . . . . 62 D6
Philips High Sch M45 . . . . 62 E8
Philips Park 83 A3
*Philips Park Nature
Reserve*★ M45 . . . . 62 D5
Philips Park Rd
Manchester M11 . . . . . . 160 B2
Whitefield M45 . . . . 62 F6
Whitefield, Park Lane M45 . 62 D6
Philip St
Bolton BL3 . . . . 145 A1
Eccles M30 . . . . 79 D1
Oldham OL4 . . . . 67 C8
Rochdale OL11 . . . . 139 C1
Phillimore St OL4 . . . . 67 E5
Phillips PI M45 . . . . 62 F7
Phillips St WN7 . . . . 75 E1
Phillip Way 1 SK14 . . . . . 102 E1
Phipps St M28 . . . . 60 C4
Phoebe St
8 Bolton BL3 . . . . 146 C4
Salford M5 . . . . 161 B4
Phoenix CI OL10 . . . . 29 F1
Phoenix Ct SK4 . . . . 111 E5
Phoenix Ind Est M35 . . . . 84 A8
Phoenix Park Ind Est
OL10 . . . . 29 F1
Phoenix PI OL4 . . . . 67 F7
Phoenix St
Bolton BL1 . . . . 148 A4
Bury BL9 . . . . 140 B2
Farnworth BL4 . . . . 60 D7
Littleborough OL15 . . . . . 16 B6
Manchester M2 . . . . 159 A1
Oldham, County End OL4 . . 67 F7
Oldham OL1 . . . . 153 C2
Rochdale OL11 . . . . 83 A1
Phoenix Way
Ince-in-M WN3 . . . . 151 B1
Radcliffe M26 . . . . 44 A2
Urmston M41 . . . . 95 E6
Phyllis St
Middleton M24 . . . . 65 C7
Rochdale OL12 . . . . 14 B1
Piccadilly
Manchester M1 . . . . 159 B1
Stockport SK1 . . . . 169 C1
Piccadilly Gardens Metro Sta
M1 . . . . 159 A1
Piccadilly Gdns M1 . . . . . 159 A1
Piccadilly Lofts M1 . . . . . 159 A1
Piccadilly Metro Sta
M60 . . . . 163 B4
Piccadilly Plaza M1 . . . . . 159 A1
Piccadilly Sta M1 . . . . . . 163 B4
Piccadilly Trad Est M1. . . 159 B1
Pickering CI
Altrincham WA15 . . . . . . 120 A7
Bury BL8 . . . . 27 B5
Kearsley M26 . . . . 61 A8
Urmston M41 . . . . 95 B2
Pickering St M15 . . . . 162 B1
Pickford Ave BL3 . . . . 43 C3
Pickford Ct
Dukinfield SK16 . . . . 101 C8
Manchester M15 . . . . . . 162 B1
Pickford La SK16 . . . . 101 C8
Pickford Mews 3 SK16 . . 101 C8
Pickford's Brow SK1 . . . . 169 C1
Pickford St M4 . . . . 159 B2
Pickford Wlk OL2 . . . . 48 E3
Pickhill La OL3 . . . . 69 B8
Pickhill Mews OL3 . . . . . . 69 B8
Pickley Gn WN7 . . . . 57 E1
PICKLEY GREEN 57 E1
Pickmere Ave M20 . . . . . . 110 B8
Pickmere CI
4 Droylsden M43 . . . . . . 84 B1
Stockport SK3 . . . . 123 C6
Wythenshawe M33 . . . . . 108 F2
Pickmere Ct 10 SK9 . . . . . 131 D5
Pickmere Gdns SK8 . . . . . 122 F4
Pickmere Mews OL3 . . . . . 69 B8
Pickmere Rd SK9 . . . . 131 D5
Pickmere Terr 8 SK16 . . . 166 B1
Picksley St WN7 . . . . 76 B4
Pickthorn CI WN2 . . . . 56 B3
Pickup St
Ashton-u-L OL7 . . . . 85 A6
Salford M7 . . . . 158 A3
Pickwick Rd SK12 . . . . . . 133 D3
Picton CI M3 . . . . 158 B2
Picton Dr SK9 . . . . 131 E2
Picton Sq 8 OL6 . . . . 47 A6
Picton St
Ashton-u-L OL7 . . . . 85 A6
Salford M7 . . . . 158 A3
Picton Wlk 5 M16 . . . . 97 F3
Pictor Speci Sch WA15 . . 120 A7
Picton CI OL1 . . . . 49 C1
Piercy Ave M7 . . . . 158 A4
Piercy St
Failsworth M35 . . . . 83 E7
Manchester M4 . . . . 160 A2
Piethorne CI OL16 . . . . 32 C4
Pigeon St M1 . . . . 159 B1
Pigginshaw SK9 . . . . 136 E8

Piggott St BL4 . . . . 60 C7
Pigot St 2 WN5 . . . . 54 B6
Pike Ave
Atherton M46 . . . . 58 A2
Failsworth M35 . . . . 84 C6
Pike Fold La M9 . . . . 64 C3
Pike Fold Prim Sch M9 . . 64 C3
Pikehouse Cotts OL15 . . 16 D7
Pike Nook Wkshp BL3 . . 145 A1
Pike Rd BL3 . . . . 147 A4
Pike's La SK13 . . . . 116 B8
Pikes Lane Prim Sch
BL3 . . . . 145 A2
Pike St OL11 . . . . 139 C1
Pike View BL6 . . . . 22 D4
Pike View Cl OL4 . . . . 67 B5
Pilgrim Dr M11 . . . . 160 C1
Pilgrims Way WN6 . . . . . . 37 A7
Pilgrim Way OL1 . . . . 49 D3
Pilkington Dr M45 . . . . . . 45 B2
Pilkington Rd
Kearsley BL4 . . . . 60 F6
Manchester M9 . . . . 65 A3
Radcliffe M26 . . . . 43 F4
Pilkington St
Bolton BL3 . . . . 145 B1
Hindley WN2 . . . . 56 D6
Middleton M24 . . . . 47 C1
Ramsbottom BL0 . . . . 138 B1
Pilkington Way M26 . . . . 44 A2
Pilling Field BL7 . . . . 8 E1
Pilling St
Bury BL8 . . . . 27 C3
Denton M34 . . . . 100 F3
Leigh WN7 . . . . 75 D5
8 Rawtenstall BB4 . . . . . . 2 F8
Rochdale OL12 . . . . 139 A4
Pilling Wlk OL9 . . . . 152 A2
Pilning St BL3 . . . . 42 A4
Pilot Ind Est BL3 . . . . 42 B4
Pilot St BL9 . . . . 140 C1
Pilsley Cl WN5 . . . . 36 A1
Pilsworth Cotts M45 . . . 45 C5
Pilsworth Rd
Bury BL9, OL10 . . . . 45 D7
Heywood OL10 . . . . 46 A8
Whitefield BL9 . . . . 45 A6
Pilsworth Way BL9 . . . . . 45 A6
Pimblett St
Golborne WA3 . . . . 90 A7
Manchester M3 . . . . 158 C3
Pimbo La WN8 . . . . 53 A4
PIMHOLE 141 A1
Pimhole Bsns Pk BL9 . . . 141 A1
Pimhole Rd BL9 . . . . 141 A2
Pimlico Cl M7 . . . . 155 A2
Pimlott Gr
Dukinfield SK14 . . . . 101 D5
Prestwich M25 . . . . 62 F2
Pimlott Rd BL1 . . . . 25 B3
Pimmcroft Way WN3 . . . 109 A3
Pincher Wlk 10 M11 . . . . 83 C1
Pinder Wlk 5 M15 . . . . . 162 C2
Pineacre Cl 3 WA14 . . . 107 B1
Pineapple St SK7 . . . . . . 124 E2
Pine Ave
Newton-le-W WA12 . . . . . 89 D2
Whitefield M45 . . . . 62 F6
Pine Cl
Denton M34 . . . . 100 E6
Marple SK6 . . . . 125 E4
Pine Ct
Manchester M20 . . . . . . 110 A4
Stockport SK7 . . . . 123 D2
Pine Gr
Denton M34 . . . . 101 A3
Eccles M30 . . . . 79 E4
Farnworth BL4 . . . . 60 B8
Golborne WA3 . . . . 90 C8
Manchester M13, M14 . . . 98 E4
Prestwich M45 . . . . 63 A6
Royton OL2 . . . . 48 D6
Sale M33 . . . . 107 D6
Stalybridge SK16 . . . . . . 101 E8
Swinton M27 . . . . 79 D7
Westhoughton BL5 . . . . . 57 E7
Worsley M28 . . . . 78 E8
Pinehurst Rd M40 . . . . . . 157 B1
Pinelea WA15 . . . . 119 F4
Pine Lo SK7 . . . . 132 F7
Pine Mdw M26 . . . . 61 C6
Pine Rd
Bramhall SK7 . . . . 132 F8
Dukinfield SK15 . . . . 101 E8
Manchester M20 . . . . . . 110 B4
Poynton SK12 . . . . 133 F3
Wigan WN5 . . . . 54 E6
Pine St
Ashton-u-L OL6 . . . . 166 B4
Bolton BL1 . . . . 143 C2
Bury BL9 . . . . 141 B2
Chadderton OL9 . . . . 152 A4
Dukinfield SK14 . . . . 101 D5
Heywood OL10 . . . . 29 D2
Littleborough OL15 . . . . 16 B6
Manchester M1 . . . . 159 A1
Middleton M24 . . . . 65 C7
Newhey OL16 . . . . 32 B4
Radcliffe M26 . . . . 44 A3
Rochdale OL16 . . . . 31 B7
Romiley SK6 . . . . 113 B5
5 Tyldesley M29 . . . . . . 59 A1
Pines The
Leigh WN7 . . . . 75 D3
Manchester M23 . . . . . . 109 B1
Sale M33 . . . . 108 B2
Pine Street N BL9 . . . . . . 141 B3
Pine Street S BL9 . . . . . . 141 B2

Pinetop Cl M21 . . . . 109 D7
Pine Tree Rd OL8 . . . . . . 66 D1
Pinetree St M18 . . . . 165 C1
Pinevale WN6 . . . . 37 A2
Pineview WN3 . . . . 54 B1
Pine Way OL4 . . . . 67 F6
Pine Wlk 1 M31 . . . . 105 E3
Pinewood
Altrincham WA14 . . . . . . 119 A2
Ashton-in-M WN4 . . . . . . 73 A2
Chadderton OL9 . . . . 65 E7
Sale M33 . . . . 107 D4
Pinewood Cl
Abram Brow WN2 . . . . . . 74 C7
29 Bolton BL1 . . . . 143 B2
Dukinfield SK16 . . . . 166 C1
Stockport SK4 . . . . 168 A3
Pinewood Cres
Ince-in-M WN2 . . . . 151 C2
Orrell WN5 . . . . 53 E6
Ramsbottom BL0 . . . . 11 B2
Pinewood Ct
Altrincham WA14 . . . . . . 119 E1
Sale M33 . . . . 108 D5
Pinewood Rd
Manchester M21 . . . . . . 109 A7
Wilmslow SK9 . . . . 137 E8
Pinfold SK13 . . . . 171 B4
Pinfold Ave M9 . . . . 65 A2
Pinfold Cl
Altrincham WA15 . . . . . . 129 D7
Westhoughton BL5 . . . . . 57 D5
Pinfold Ct
Cheadle SK8 . . . . 123 A1
Prestwich M25 . . . . 62 F5
Pinfold Dr
Cheadle SK8 . . . . 123 A1
Whitefield M45 . . . . 62 E8
Pinfold La
Romiley SK6 . . . . 113 E4
Whitefield M45 . . . . 62 F8
Wythenshawe M90, WA15 . 129 F6
Pinfold Prim Sch SK14 . 102 C1
Pinfold Rd M28 . . . . 60 C2
Pinfold St WN2 . . . . 56 A7
Pingate Dr SK8 . . . . 132 A6
Pingate La SK8 . . . . 132 A6
Pingate Lane S SK8 . . . . 132 A6
Pingle La OL3 . . . . 50 E5
Pingot Ave M27 . . . . 209 A1
Pingot OL2 . . . . 32 D1
Pingot Ct 6 WN5 . . . . . . 75 D5
Pingot Rd WN5 . . . . 71 E5
Pingot The
Irlam M44 . . . . 94 B3
Leigh WN7 . . . . 75 D5
Pingott La SK13 . . . . 104 A5
Pinhigh Pl M6 . . . . 80 B6
Pink Bank La M12 . . . . . . 99 A4
Pin Mill Brow M12 . . . . . 164 C4
Pinnacle Bsns Ctr SK4 . 169 B3
Pinnacle Dr BL7 . . . . 8 E2
Pinner Fold SK15 . . . . . . 86 D3
Pinner Pl M19 . . . . 111 A6
Pinners Cl BL0 . . . . 138 B3
Pinnington La M32 . . . . . 96 D2
Pinnington Rd M18 . . . . . 99 D6
Pintail Ave SK3 . . . . 170 A2
Pintail Cl 5 OL12 . . . . . . 14 B2
Pinwood Cl 3 SK9 . . . . . 131 E1
Pioneer Cl BL6 . . . . 22 C4
Pioneer Ind Est WN5 . . . 54 E6
Pioneer Rd M27 . . . . 62 D2
Pioneers St 4 OL11 . . . . 31 A6
Pioneer St
Droylsden M11 . . . . 83 B2
Horwich BL6 . . . . 22 C4
4 Littleborough OL15 . . . 16 B5
Walsden OL14 . . . . 6 A7
Pioneers Villa OL16 . . . . 32 E4
Piperhill Ave M22 . . . . . . 109 D2
Piper Hill Sch M23 . . . . . 121 B4
Pipers Cl OL11 . . . . 29 D8
Pipers Ct M44 . . . . 94 C3
Pipers The WA3 . . . . 90 F8
Pipewell Ave M18 . . . . . . 165 C1
Pipit Ave M12 . . . . 89 C3
Pipit Cl M34 . . . . 84 C2
Pirie Wlk 4 M40 . . . . 83 C6
Pitcairn Ho 12 M30 . . . . 79 D1
Pitchcombe Rd M22 . . . 121 B2
Pitcombe Cl BL1 . . . . 24 D7
Pitfield Gdns M23 . . . . . 120 F7
Pitfield La BL2 . . . . 25 F4
Pitfield St BL2 . . . . 148 B3
Pit La OL16, OL2 . . . . 31 D1
Pitman St M11 . . . . 165 A4
Pitmore Wlk 3 M40 . . . . 65 D2
Pitses Cl OL4 . . . . 67 C6
PITSES 67 C6
Pits Farm Ave OL11 . . . . 30 C7
Pitsford Rd M40 . . . . 157 B1
Pitshouse OL12 . . . . 13 E2
Pitshouse La OL12 . . . . . 13 E2
Pit St
Denton M34 . . . . 100 F3
Oldham OL9 . . . . 66 B4
Pittbrook St M12 . . . . . . 164 A3
Pitt St
Denton M34 . . . . 100 F6
Heywood OL10 . . . . 29 C2
Hyde SK14 . . . . 167 A3
Ince-in-M WN3 . . . . 151 A2
Oldham OL4 . . . . 67 A5
Radcliffe M26 . . . . 43 E3
Rochdale OL12 . . . . 139 C4
Stockport SK3 . . . . 170 A4
Wigan WN3 . . . . 150 B3

Pitt Street E OL4 . . . . 67 B5
Pixmore Ave BL1 . . . . 25 B4
Place Rd WA14 . . . . 119 C6
Place The M1 . . . . 159 B1
Plain Pit St SK14 . . . . . . 101 C5
Plainsfield St 8 M16 . . . . 97 E4
Plane Ave WN5 . . . . 54 E7
Plane Ct 4 M6 . . . . 81 A2
Plane Rd M35 . . . . 83 F5
Plane St OL4 . . . . 67 C7
Plane Tree Cl SK6 . . . . . . 125 D5
Plane Tree Gr WA11 . . . . 89 A7
Planetree Rd WA15 . . . . 120 A2
Plane Tree Rd M31 . . . . . 105 D3
Planetree Wlk M23 . . . . 120 E8
Planet Way M34 . . . . 100 E5
Planewood Gdns 1 WA3 . 90 F7
Plank La WN7 . . . . 75 B4
PLANK LANE 75 B4
Plantagenet Wlk M40 . . 83 D4
Plantation Ave M28 . . . . 60 C4
Plantation Gates WN1 . . 37 E2
Plantation Gr BL9 . . . . . . 45 C4
Plantation Ind Est OL6 . . 85 D2
Plantation Rd BL7 . . . . 9 F7
Plantation St
Ashton-u-L OL6 . . . . 85 D2
Bacup OL13 . . . . 3 C8
Manchester M18 . . . . 99 E5
Plantation View BL9 . . . . 11 C3
Plant Cl M33 . . . . 108 A5
Plant Hill Arts Coll M9 . . 64 C4
Plant Hill Rd M9 . . . . 64 D4
Plasden Ct M23 . . . . 121 A5
Plasman Ind Ctr M19 . . . 99 D1
Plate St OL1 . . . . 153 C3
Platinum Rd M41 . . . . . . 95 F6
Plato St OL9 . . . . 153 A3
Platt Ave OL6 . . . . 85 C6
PLATT BRIDGE 56 A2
Platt Bridge Com Sch
WN2 . . . . 56 B2
Plattbrook Cl M14 . . . . . . 98 B1
Platt Cl OL16 . . . . 32 A5
Platt Croft WN7 . . . . 76 C4
Platt Ct M14 . . . . 98 C2
Platt Fold Rd WN7 . . . . . . 76 A6
Platt Fold St WN7 . . . . . . 76 A6
Platt Hill Ave BL3 . . . . . . 146 A4
Platting Gr OL7 . . . . 84 F5
Platting La OL11 . . . . 31 A4
Platting Rd OL4 . . . . 68 C7
Platt La
Hindley WN2 . . . . 56 D5
Manchester M14 . . . . 98 B2
Standish WN1 . . . . 19 E1
Uppermill OL3 . . . . 50 F2
Westhoughton BL5 . . . . . 58 B7
Wigan WN1 . . . . 37 E1
Platt St
Cheadle SK8 . . . . 122 E6
Dukinfield SK16 . . . . 101 A7
Glossop SK13 . . . . 104 B5
Leigh WN7 . . . . 75 F6
8 Oldham OL4 . . . . 67 F6
Platt Wlk M15 . . . . 162 A2
Playfair Cl OL10 . . . . 46 E7
Playfair St
Bolton BL1 . . . . 24 F6
Manchester M14 . . . . 98 B4
Playhouse 2 * SK1 . . . . 169 B1
Plaza The * SK1 . . . . 169 B1
Pleachway SK4 . . . . 110 F2
Pleasance Way M31 . . . . 89 D4
Pleasant Ct 5 OL11 . . . . 30 C2
Pleasant Gdns BL1 . . . . . 145 B4
Pleasant Rd M30 . . . . 79 E1
Pleasant St
Bury BL8 . . . . 26 F4
Heywood OL10 . . . . 29 C4
Manchester M9 . . . . 157 A3
Rochdale OL12 . . . . 30 C2
Standish WN6 . . . . 19 E1
Pleasant Way SK8 . . . . . 132 C6
Pleasington Dr
Bury BL8 . . . . 26 E2
Failsworth M40 . . . . 65 C1
Plevna St BL2 . . . . 148 A3
Plodder La BL4, BL5 . . . . 59 D8
Plodder Lane Prim Sch 1
BL4 . . . . 60 B8
Ploughbank Dr M21 . . . 109 D7
Plough Cl M41 . . . . 94 C1
Ploughfields BL5 . . . . 39 E3
Plough Fields M28 . . . . . 78 A5
Plough St 6 SK16 . . . . . 101 D8
Plover Cl
Glossop SK13 . . . . 116 F8
Newton-le-W WA12 . . . . . 89 C3
Rochdale OL11 . . . . 29 F7
Plover Dr
Altrincham WA14 . . . . . . 119 B8
Bury BL9 . . . . 141 B4
Irlam M44 . . . . 94 A4
Plover Terr M21 . . . . 109 D7
Plover Way WA3 . . . . 90 E8
Plowden Ave BL3 . . . . . . 146 C3
Plowden Rd M22 . . . . . . 121 B2
Plowley Cl M20 . . . . 110 B2

Plucksbridge Rd SK6 . . . 126 B3
Plumbley Dr M16 . . . . 97 C3
Plumbley St 11 M11 . . . . 99 E7
Plumley Cl SK3 . . . . 170 C1
Plumley Rd SK9 . . . . 131 D5
Plummer Ave M21 . . . . . 109 B6
Plumpton Cl OL1, OL2 . . . 48 E1
Plumpton Dr BL9 . . . . 27 E6
Plumpton Rd OL11 . . . . . 48 C8
Plumpton Wlk 6 M13 . . . 98 F4
Plum Tree Ct M6 . . . . . . 80 C8
Plum Tree Cl OL10 . . . . . 153 A1
Plum Tree Ct 2 M5 . . . . 81 A2
Plunge Rd BL0 . . . . 1 E3
Pluto Cl M6 . . . . 81 C4
Plymouth Ave M13 . . . . 164 B1
Plymouth Cl OL6 . . . . 85 C7
Plymouth Dr
Bramhall SK7 . . . . 132 F7
1 Farnworth BL4 . . . . . . 59 F8
Plymouth Gr
Manchester M13 . . . . . . 164 A1
Radcliffe M26 . . . . 43 D5
Standish WN6 . . . . 37 A7
Stockport SK3 . . . . 123 B7
Plymouth Grove Prim Sch
M13 . . . . 164 B1
Plymouth Grove W M13 . 164 B1
Plymouth Ho M13 . . . . . 163 C2
Plymouth Rd M33 . . . . . 107 D5
Plymouth St OL8 . . . . 66 F4
Plymouth View M13 . . . . 163 C2
Plymouth Village M12 . . 164 A1
Plymtree Cl M8 . . . . 63 E2
Pobgreen La OL3 . . . . 51 D1
Pochard Dr
Altrincham WA14 . . . . . . 119 B7
Poynton SK12 . . . . 133 A4
Pochin St M40 . . . . 160 B3
Pocket Nook BL6 . . . . 40 B3
Pocket Nook La WN2 . . . 91 B7
Pocket Nook Rd BL6 . . . . 40 B3
Pocket Wkshps The BL3 . 144 C2
Pockington Dr M23 . . . . 120 F7
Podnor La SK6 . . . . 127 A6
Podsmead Rd M22 . . . . . 121 B2
Poet's Nook WN7 . . . . . . 75 E4
Poet Ret Pk The OL16 . . . 31 A7
Poise Brook Dr SK2 . . . . 124 F5
Poise Brook Rd SK2 . . . . 124 F5
Poise Cl SK7 . . . . 125 A3
Poke St 1 WN5 . . . . 54 B6
Poland St
1 Ashton-u-L M34 . . . . . 100 E8
Manchester M4 . . . . 159 C2
Poland Street Ind Est
M4 . . . . 159 C2
Polden Cl 5 OL8 . . . . 66 E3
Polden St WN3 . . . . 55 E4
Poleacre La SK6 . . . . 113 C6
Polebrook Ave M12 . . . . 164 A2
Polebrook Cl M12 . . . . . . 164 A2
Polefield App M25 . . . . . 63 B6
Polefield Circ M25 . . . . . 63 B6
Polefield Gdns M25 . . . . 63 B6
Polefield Gr M25 . . . . 63 B6
Polefield Grange M25 . . . 63 B6
Polefield Hall Rd M25 . . . 63 B6
Polefield Rd
Manchester M9 . . . . 64 C2
Prestwich M25 . . . . 63 C6
Polegate Dr WN2 . . . . 57 D2
Pole La
Failsworth M35 . . . . 83 F8
Whitefield M45 . . . . 45 D1
Whitefield, Unsworth BL9,
M45 . . . . 45 C3
Pole Lane Ct BL9 . . . . 45 C3
Pole St
Ashton-u-L OL7 . . . . 166 B4
Bolton BL1 . . . . 25 B1
Standish WN6 . . . . 19 E1
Polesworth Cl M12 . . . . . 165 A2
Police St
1 Altrincham WA14 . . . . 119 D5
Eccles M30 . . . . 79 C2
Manchester M2 . . . . 158 C1
Pollard Ct 4 OL1 . . . . . . 153 F8
Pollard Gr OL15 . . . . 16 C8
Pollard Ho BL3 . . . . 146 B2
Pollard La BL9 . . . . 11 C2
Pollard Sq M31 . . . . 106 A3
Pollard St M4 . . . . 160 A1
Pollard Street E M4, M40 160 A2
Pollen Cl M33 . . . . 108 B2
Pollen Rd WA14 . . . . 119 C6
Polletts Ave SK5 . . . . 112 C6
Pollit Croft SK6 . . . . 112 F1
Pollitt Ave OL6 . . . . 85 C5
Pollitt Cl M12 . . . . 164 C2
Pollitt St M30 . . . . 79 B2
Pollitts St M26 . . . . 44 C3
Polonia Ct OL8 . . . . 66 C3
Polperro Cl OL2 . . . . 49 A4
Polperro Wlk SK14 . . . . . 102 D3
Polruan Rd M21 . . . . 97 A2
Polruan Wlk SK14 . . . . . . 102 E3
Polworth Rd M9 . . . . 64 E1
Polygon Ave M12, M13 . . 163 C2
Polygon Rd M8 . . . . 63 F1
Polygon St M13 . . . . 163 C3

Pig–Por 247

Polygon The
Eccles M30 . . . . 80 A2
Salford M7 . . . . 81 C5
Pomfret St
Manchester M12 . . . . . . 165 A2
Salford M6 . . . . 80 C5
Pomona Cres M5 . . . . . . 161 B3
Pomona Metro Sta M5,
M16 . . . . 161 B2
Pomona St OL11 . . . . . . 139 C1
Pomona Strand M16, M5 . 161 B2
Ponds Cl M21 . . . . 97 B1
Pond St WA3 . . . . 91 A8
Pondwater Cl M28 . . . . . 60 A3
Ponsford Ave M9 . . . . . . 65 A3
Ponsonby Rd M32 . . . . . 96 D3
Pontefract Cl M27 . . . . . . 80 B7
Poolbank Cl WN2 . . . . . . 57 C3
Pool Bank St M24 . . . . . . 64 B7
Poolcroft M33 . . . . 108 F3
Poole Cl SK7 . . . . 123 D1
Pooley Cl M24 . . . . 46 B1
Poolfield Cl M26 . . . . 43 E3
Pool Fold
Bolton BL1 . . . . 142 A2
Failsworth M35 . . . . 84 A6
Pool House Rd SK12 . . . 134 D5
Pool Pl BL1 . . . . 142 A2
Pool Rd WA3 . . . . 105 A3
Pool St
Bolton BL1 . . . . 145 B3
Hindley WN2 . . . . 56 D4
Oldham OL8 . . . . 66 F4
Wigan WN3 . . . . 150 B2
POOLSTOCK 150 B2
Poolstock La WN3 . . . . . . 55 A4
Pool Terr BL1 . . . . 142 A2
Poolton Rd M9 . . . . 64 B4
Poorfield St OL8 . . . . 153 B1
Poot Hall OL12 . . . . 14 F3
Pope Way 5 M34 . . . . . . 113 A8
Poplar Ave
Altrincham WA14 . . . . . . 119 E6
Bolton, Astley Bridge BL1 . 24 F5
Bolton, Bradshaw BL2 . . . 25 C6
Bury BL9 . . . . 141 B3
Culcheth WA3 . . . . 91 F3
Dowmall Green WN3 . . . . 72 D5
Horwich BL6 . . . . 22 E1
Manchester M19 . . . . . . 111 B7
New Mills SK22 . . . . 127 D1
Newton-le-W WA12 . . . . . 89 D3
Oldham OL8 . . . . 66 D2
4 Rochdale OL12 . . . . . . 14 C1
Uppermill OL4 . . . . 68 C4
Wilmslow SK9 . . . . 136 F5
Poplar Cl
Gatley SK8 . . . . 122 B5
Manchester M29 . . . . 59 A1
Poplar Ct
Denton M34 . . . . 100 F7
Manchester M8 . . . . 98 D1
Poplar Dr M25 . . . . 63 A2
Poplar Gr
Ashton-u-L OL6 . . . . 85 C5
Hindley WN2 . . . . 57 B3
Irlam M44 . . . . 105 D6
Manchester M18 . . . . 99 D4
Ramsbottom BL0 . . . . 11 D7
Sale M33 . . . . 108 B3
Stockport SK2 . . . . 124 C4
Tyldesley M29 . . . . 77 A8
Westhoughton BL5 . . . . . 57 E8
Poplar Rd
Dukinfield SK16 . . . . 101 F7
Eccles M30 . . . . 79 E4
Manchester M19 . . . . . . 110 D3
Stretford M32 . . . . 108 C8
Swinton M27 . . . . 79 D7
Walkden M28 . . . . 60 E1
Poplars Rd SK15 . . . . 86 E3
Poplar St
Denton M34 . . . . 100 F7
Failsworth M35 . . . . 83 D6
Golborne WA3 . . . . 74 B1
Leigh WN7 . . . . 75 F4
Manchester M24 . . . . . . 110 F2
Middleton M24 . . . . 65 D7
Poplars The
Adlington PR7 . . . . 20 F6
Golborne, Bank Heath WA3 . 74 B1
Golborne WN7 . . . . 91 C8
Mossley OL5 . . . . 68 C3
Poplar Street Prim Sch
M34 . . . . 100 E6
Poplar Way SK6 . . . . 135 C4
Poplar Wlk
Chadderton OL9 . . . . 152 B4
Partington M31 . . . . 105 D3
Poplin Dr M3 . . . . 158 B3
Poppy Cl
Chadderton OL9 . . . . 65 E7
Sale M33 . . . . 108 E1
Poppyfield Ho 4 OL9 . . . 65 F8
Poppyfield View OL11 . . . 29 E8
Poppythorn La M25 . . . . 63 A5
Popular St WN2 . . . . 59 A1
Porchester Dr M26 . . . . . 43 C5
Porchfield Sq M3 . . . . . . 162 B4
Porlock Ave
Droylsden M34 . . . . 100 C8
Hattersley SK14 . . . . 102 C2

Porlock Cl
Platt Bridge WN2.......... **56** A1
Stockport SK1..........**124** C8
Porlock Rd
Urmston M41..........**107** B8
Wythenshawe M23 ....**121** B6
Porlock Wlk SK14 ....**102** C2
Porritt Cl OL11..........**29** E6
Porritt St BL9..........**141** A4
Porritt Way BL0..........**138** C1
Portal Ct M24..........**65** C8
Portal Gr M34..........**101** B1
Portal Wlk 9 M9 ....**157** A4
Porter Ave WA12..........**89** C5
Porter Dr M40 ....**157** A2
Porterfield Dr M29....**77** A8
Porter St
Bury BL9 ....**140** C4
Oldham OL9..........**153** E7
Porters Wood Cl WN5 ....**54** B7
Portfield Cl BL1..........**40** F8
Portfield Wlk 18 M40..**83** A6
Porthleven Cres M29....**77** C8
Porthleven Dr M23....**120** E6
Porthrowan Wlk SK14....**102** E3
Portico Liby & Gall★
M2 ....**159** A1
Portinscale Cl BL8....**27** B3
Portland Basin Mus★
OL7 ....**166** A1
Portland Chmbrs 3 SK15 **86** B2
Portland Cl
Abram WN2..........**74** A8
Hazel Grove SK7..........**124** B1
Platt Bridge WN2..........**56** A1
Portland Cres M13....**164** A1
Portland Ct M20..........**110** B3
Portland Gr SK4..........**168** B4
Portland Ho
3 Ashton-u-L OL6....**166** A1
Marple SK6 ....**125** E5
Salford M6..........**80** A3
Portland Ind Est BL9....**141** A4
Portland Pl
Ashton-u-L OL7..........**166** A2
Horwich BL6 ....**22** C3
Portland Rd
Altrincham WA14..........**119** D3
Manchester M13..........**98** F3
New Mills SK22..........**127** D1
Pendlebury M27..........**80** B7
Salford M30..........**80** A4
Stretford M32..........**96** E4
Walkden M28..........**60** C5
Portland St
Bolton BL1..........**143** B2
Bury BL9..........**141** A4
5 Leigh WN7 ....**75** F5
Manchester M1..........**159** A1
Rochdale OL16..........**139** C4
Wigan WN5 ....**54** E6
Portland Street N OL6..**166** A3
Portland Street S OL6,
OL7 ....**166** A2
Portland Terr OL6..........**166** A2
Portland The 10 M14 ..**110** D8
Portloe Rd SK8..........**131** B7
Portman Rd M19..........**97** E3
Portman St OL5..........**68** C1
Porton Wlk 1 M22..........**121** B1
Portrea Cl SK3..........**170** C1
Portree Cl M30..........**79** B2
Portrush Rd M22..........**121** E2
Portside Cl M29..........**78** B5
Portslade Wlk M23..........**120** F4
Portsmouth Cl M7..........**155** A1
Portsmouth St M13..........**163** B1
Port Soderick Ave M5....**81** A1
Port St
Manchester M1..........**159** A1
Oldham OL8 ....**66** F4
Stockport SK1..........**169** B2
Portstone St 11 M16....**97** E4
Portugal Rd M25..........**63** B2
Portugal St
Ashton-u-L OL7..........**84** F1
Bolton BL2..........**148** B3
9 Manchester M4..........**154** C2
Portugal Street E M1..**163** C4
Portville Rd M19..........**99** A2
Portway M22..........**121** C1
PORTWOOD **112** A2
Portwood Ind Est SK1..**112** B2
Portwood Pl SK1..........**169** C2
Portwood Wlk 9 M9 ..**157** A4
Postal St M1..........**159** B1
Post Office St WA14..**119** D5
Post St SK13..........**104** B5
Potato Wharf M3 ....**162** A4
Pot Gn BL0..........**11** A3
Pot Hill OL6..........**166** C4
Pot Hill Sq OL6..........**166** C4
Potterdale Cl OL11..........**49** A1
Potter Ho OL8..........**153** C1
Potter St M26..........**43** C2
Potters House Sch 7 BL9 **27** F6
Potters La M9..........**157** C3
Potter St
Bury BL9 ....**141** A4
Radcliffe M26 ....**44** D4
Pottery La M11, M12....**165** A3
Pottery Rd WN3..........**150** B3
Pottery Terr WN3 ....**150** B3

Pottinger St OL7..........**84** F1
Pott St
1 Altrincham WA14 ....**119** D4
Swinton M27..........**61** F2
Poulton Ave BL2..........**42** E7
Poulton Dr 7 WN4....**72** F5
Poundswick La M22....**121** D3
Powder Mill Cl M44 ....**94** B1
Powell Ave SK14..........**167** B3
Powell Ct 8 BL9..........**140** C3
Powell Dr WN5 ....**71** D3
Powell Rd 9 BL9 ....**140** C3
Powell St
Abram WN2..........**56** B1
Bury BL8 ....**27** B1
Droylsden M11..........**83** D2
Manchester M16..........**97** C4
13 Wigan WN1..........**37** C1
Powicke Dr SK6..........**112** F1
Powicke Wlk SK6..........**113** A1
Powis Rd M41..........**94** C1
Pownall Ave
Bramhall SK7..........**132** F7
4 Manchester M20 ....**110** A8
Pownall Ct SK9..........**136** E8
POWNALL GREEN **132** F7
Pownall Green Prim Sch
SK7..........**132** E7
Pownall Hall Sch SK9 ..**136** F8
POWNALL PARK **136** F7
Pownall Pl SK7..........**132** E7
Pownall Rd
Altrincham WA14..........**119** D3
Cheadle SK8..........**123** A1
Wilmslow SK9..........**136** F8
Pownall St
Hazel Grove SK7..........**124** D3
1 Leigh WN7 ....**76** A5
Powys St M46..........**58** E1
Poynings Dr M22..........**121** C1
Poynt Chase M28..........**78** B6
Poynter St M40..........**65** C1
Poynter Wlk 1 OL1....**49** D4
POYNTON **133** E4
Poynton Coppice Nature
Reserve★ SK12..........**134** B2
Poynton High Sch &
Performing Arts Coll
SK12..........**133** F2
Poynton Ind Est SK12 ..**133** D1
Poynton L Ctr SK12 ....**133** F2
Poynton St
Bury BL9 ....**141** A1
Manchester M15 ....**162** C2
Poynton Sta SK12..........**133** C4
Praed Rd M17..........**96** C6
Praeson Cl M46..........**58** A1
Pratt Wlk 1 M11..........**160** C1
Precinct The
2 Cheadle SK8..........**123** A2
Rochdale OL11..........**29** E7
Stockport SK2..........**124** D6
Preece Cl SK14..........**102** A4
Preesall Ave SK8..........**131** B8
Preesall Cl BL8..........**26** F1
Prefect Pl WN5..........**54** C8
Premier Rd M8..........**158** C4
Premier St M16..........**97** D4
Prentice Wlk M11..........**83** A1
Prenton St M11..........**99** E8
Prenton Way BL8..........**26** F5
Presall St 2 BL2..........**148** C4
Presbury Ct 1 M20 ..**110** A2
Presbyterian Fold 6
WN2..........**56** D6
Prescot Ave
Atherton M46..........**58** E5
Tyldesley M29 ....**59** D1
Prescot Cl 8 WN9..........**141** A1
Prescot Rd
Altrincham WA15..........**119** F2
Manchester M9..........**157** A3
Prescott Ave WA3..........**73** F2
Prescott La WN5 ....**54** B8
Prescott Rd SK9..........**131** B1
Prescott St
Bolton BL3..........**146** C4
Golborne WA3..........**74** A1
Hindley WN2 ....**56** D5
Leigh WN7..........**75** F6
Rochdale OL16..........**15** C2
Walkden M28..........**60** B3
Wigan WN3, WN1, WN6...**150** B4
Prescott Wlk M34..........**101** B1
Press St M11..........**99** D7
Prestage St
Manchester, Levenshulme
M12..........**99** B2
Manchester, Old Trafford
M16..........**97** D4
Salford M16..........**161** C1
Prestbury Ave
Altrincham WA15..........**119** E6
Manchester M14..........**97** F1
Wigan WN3 ....**54** E2
Prestbury Cl
Bury BL9 ....**141** A1
Stockport SK2..........**124** D4
Prestbury Ct 1 M28....**60** D2
Prestbury Dr
Oldham OL1..........**48** D1
Romiley SK6..........**112** E3
Prestbury Rd
Bolton BL1..........**25** A5
Wilmslow SK9..........**137** E5
Prestfield Rd M45..........**63** A7
Presto Gdns BL3..........**146** B4
PRESTOLEE..........**61** A8

Prestolee Ct M27..........**80** E8
Prestolee Prim Sch M26..**61** B8
Prestolee Rd
Kearsley M26..........**43** B1
Little Lever BL3 ....**43** A1
Preston Ave
Irlam M44..........**105** F7
Salford M30..........**80** A3
Preston Cl M30..........**80** A3
Preston Rd
Manchester M19..........**111** A8
Standish PR7, WN6 ....**19** D5
Preston St
1 Bolton BL3 ....**42** B4
Manchester M18..........**165** C2
Middleton M24..........**65** A8
Oldham OL4..........**67** A6
16 Rochdale OL12 ....**14** C1
Presto St
Bolton BL3..........**146** B4
Farnworth BL4..........**60** E8
PRESTWICH..........**63** A4
Prestwich Arts Coll M25..**63** B5
Prestwich Ave
Culcheth WA3 ....**91** E3
Leigh WN7 ....**76** B5
Prestwich Cl SK2..........**124** E7
Prestwich Forest Pk★
M25..........**62** D4
Prestwich Hills M25....**63** A2
Prestwich Hospl (Secure
Unit) M25..........**62** F5
Prestwich Ind Est M46....**58** B3
Prestwich Metro Sta M25 **63** A4
PRESTWICH PARK..........**63** B3
Prestwich Park Road S
M25..........**63** A3
Prestwich Prep Sch M25 **63** C5
Prestwich St M46..........**58** B3
Prestwick Wlk 1 M40....**65** C2
Prestwood Cl BL1..........**143** A1
Prestwood Dr BL1 ....**143** A1
Prestwood Rd
Farnworth BL4..........**42** A1
Salford M6..........**80** C4
Pretoria Rd
Ashton-in-M WN4 ....**73** B4
Bolton BL2..........**42** B8
Oldham OL8 ....**66** C3
Pretoria St 2 OL12 ....**14** C1
PRETTYWOOD..........**28** E2
Price St
Bury BL9 ....**141** A1
Dukinfield SK16..........**101** C8
Farnworth BL4..........**42** D1
Prichard St M32..........**96** D2
Prickshaw La OL12 ....**14** B6
Prickshaw La OL12..........**14** B6
Pride Cl WA12..........**89** E2
Pridmouth Rd M20..........**110** C6
Priest Ave SK8..........**122** A4
Priestfields WN7..........**76** B5
Priest Hill 6 OL1..........**153** B3
Priestley Rd M27, M28 ..**79** C8
Priestley Way OL2..........**49** D7
Priestnall Ct SK4..........**110** F3
Priestnall Rd SK4..........**110** F3
Priestnall Sch SK4..........**110** F3
Priestners Way WN7....**75** E6
Priest St
Oldham OL9..........**66** B4
Stockport SK1..........**170** C3
Priestwood Ave OL4....**49** F4
Primary Cl M44..........**105** D5
Primley Wlk 8 M9....**157** B4
Primrose Ave
Farnworth BL4..........**42** A1
Hyde SK14..........**113** D8
Marple SK6..........**125** E6
Uppermill OL3 ....**51** C1
Urmston M41..........**95** D2
Walkden M28..........**60** B2
Primrose Bank
2 Altrincham WA14 ....**119** C1
1 Bacup OL13 ....**3** C8
Bury BL8 ....**26** E7
Oldham OL8..........**153** B1
Uppermill OL3 ....**69** B5
Walkden M28..........**60** B2
Primrose Cl
Bolton BL2..........**26** A4
Salford M5..........**154** C2
Primrose Cottage Sch
BL9..........**141** A4
Primrose Cotts 1 WA14..**119** C1
Primrose Cres
1 Glossop SK13..........**116** B8
Hyde SK14..........**113** D8
Primrose Dr
Bury BL9 ....**28** D4
Droylsden M43..........**84** C3
Primrose Gr WN5..........**54** E7
Primrose Hill SK13....**116** B8
Primrose Hill Com Prim Sch
M5 ....**161** B4
Primrose Hill Ct 7 OL2..**48** F8
Primrose La
Glossop SK13..........**116** B8
Marple SK6..........**127** A4
Standish WN6..........**19** D2
Primrose St
9 Bacup OL13 ....**3** C8
Bolton BL1..........**143** C4
Farnworth BL4..........**60** E7
4 Leigh WN7 ....**75** D5
Manchester M4..........**159** B2
Rochdale OL12..........**139** A4
Tyldesley M29 ....**59** A1

Primrose Street N M29...**59** A1
Primrose Street S M29...**77** A8
Primrose Terr
2 Glossop SK13..........**116** B8
Urmston M41..........**95** C6
Primrose View WN4....**73** C2
Primrose Wlk
Marple SK6..........**125** E6
Oldham OL8..........**153** B1
Primula Dr WA3..........**90** D8
Primula St BL1..........**24** F5
Prince Albert Ave 4 M19..**99** A2
Prince Charlie St OL1....**67** C8
Princedom St M9..........**157** B4
Prince Edward Ave
Denton M34..........**100** F2
7 Oldham OL4..........**67** C8
Prince George St 3 OL1..**49** C1
Prince Lee Gdns SK4....**111** A5
Prince Mead Pl M17....**96** B5
Prince of Wales Ind Units 8
OL1..........**67** C8
Prince Rd SK12..........**134** C5
Princes Ave M44..........**94** C3
Prince's Ave
Little Lever BL3 ....**43** B4
Manchester M20..........**110** C4
Romiley SK6..........**113** A3
Tyldesley M29 ....**77** B6
Princes Ct
Manchester M20..........**110** B5
Ramsbottom BL0..........**138** C2
Princes Dr M33..........**108** D3
Prince's Dr SK6..........**125** E7
Princes Gdns WN7....**76** C5
Prince's Pk WN6..........**35** F4
Princes Rd
Altrincham WA14..........**119** D6
Sale M33..........**108** D3
Stockport SK4..........**168** A4
Prince's Rd SK6..........**113** A3
Princess Ave
Ashton-in-M WN4 ....**73** C3
Atherton M46..........**58** D5
Cheadle SK8..........**123** A3
Denton M34..........**100** E3
Haydock WA11..........**89** A7
Kearsley BL4..........**60** F6
Manchester M25..........**63** C2
Rochdale OL12..........**15** C4
Princess Cl
Dukinfield SK16..........**101** D8
Heywood OL10..........**29** D1
Mossley OL5..........**86** E8
Princess Ct M15..........**162** A2
Princess Dr M24..........**64** E8
Princess Gr BL4..........**60** D8
Princess Ho 5 M1..........**163** A3
Princess Par
Bury BL9 ....**140** C2
Manchester M14..........**109** F8
Princess Parkway M20, M22,
M23..........**109** C2
Princess Rd
Adlington PR6 ....**21** B8
Ashton-in-M WN4 ....**73** C3
Bolton BL6..........**40** B8
Failsworth OL9 ....**65** E3
Manchester, Moss Side M14,
M16..........**97** F4
Manchester, West Didsbury M14,
M20, M21, M15..........**109** E6
Milnrow OL16..........**31** D7
Prestwich M25..........**63** C4
Shaw OL2..........**149** A2
Urmston M41..........**95** B2
Wigan WN6..........**36** C4
Wilmslow SK9..........**136** F5
Princess St
Altrincham WA14..........**119** C8
Ashton-u-L OL6..........**85** D4
Bolton BL1..........**145** C3
Eccles M30 ....**79** C2
Failsworth M35..........**83** E7
Glossop SK13..........**116** C8
Hindley WN2 ....**56** C5
Hyde SK14..........**167** B2
Manchester M1, M60, M2 ..**163** A4
Manchester, St George's
M15..........**162** A2
Oldham OL4..........**67** E6
Pendlebury M27..........**80** B7
11 Radcliffe M26..........**43** E3
Rochdale OL12..........**14** F1
Salford M6..........**81** A4
Whitworth OL12..........**14** C8
Wigan WN3 ....**150** C3
Princes St WA12..........**89** B3
Prince's St SK1..........**169** B2
Princess Wlk SK7..........**133** A7
Prince St
Ashton-in-M WN4 ....**73** A5
Bolton BL1..........**145** B4
Britannia OL13..........**4** D7
Heywood OL10..........**29** D2
6 Oldham OL4..........**67** A7
Ramsbottom BL0..........**138** C2
Rochdale OL16..........**31** B5
Princeton Cl BL6..........**22** C2
Princeton St 1 M6....**80** C3
Prince Way OL2..........**48** C6
Prinknash Rd M22....**121** D1
Printers Fold SK14....**103** D5
Printers La BL2, BL7....**25** C6
Printers Pk SK14..........**103** E5

Printer St
Droylsden M11..........**99** D8
Oldham OL1..........**153** C2
Printon Ave M9..........**64** B3
Printshop La M46..........**58** E1
Printworks La M19....**99** C1
Printworks Rd SK15....**86** C3
Printworks The M4....**159** A2
Priorsleigh SK4..........**110** F2
Prior St OL8..........**67** B5
Priory Ave
Leigh WN7 ....**57** D1
Manchester M21..........**109** B8
Salford M7..........**81** C6
Priory Cl
Dukinfield SK16..........**101** D6
Oldham OL8..........**66** D3
Sale M33..........**108** D6
1 Wigan WN5..........**54** B5
Priory Ct
3 Altrincham WA14 ....**119** C1
Eccles M30 ....**79** E2
Reddish SK5..........**111** E8
Priory Gdns M20..........**110** B4
Priory Gr
Chadderton OL9..........**66** A4
Salford M7..........**81** C6
Priory Hospl Altrincham
(private) The WA15....**129** A7
Priory La SK5..........**111** E8
Priory Nook WN8 ....**53** C7
Priory Pl BL2..........**25** C2
Priory Rd
Altrincham WA14..........**128** B8
Ashton-in-M WN4 ....**72** F5
Cheadle SK8..........**123** A5
Sale M33..........**108** D5
Swinton M27..........**79** E8
Up Holland WN8 ....**53** C7
Wilmslow SK9..........**136** E8
Priory St WA14..........**119** C1
Priory The M7..........**81** C6
Pritchard St M1..........**163** A3
Private La BL4..........**1** C8
Privet St OL4..........**49** D1
Proctor Cl WN5..........**36** E1
Proctor St BL8..........**27** C1
Proctor Way M30..........**94** F7
Prodesse Ct WN2..........**56** D6
Proe's Ct WN1..........**150** B4
Progress Ave M34....**100** F6
Progress St
Ashton-u-L OL6..........**166** A3
Bolton BL1..........**143** C1
Hindley WN2 ....**56** D5
Rochdale OL11..........**30** C1
Promenade OL10..........**29** C2
Propps Hall Dr M35....**83** E6
Propps Hall Prim Sch
M35..........**83** E6
Prospect Ave
Bolton BL2..........**26** A3
Farnworth BL4..........**60** C7
Irlam M44..........**105** E6
Prospect Cotts WN2 ....**38** A6
Prospect Cl BL8..........**26** F7
Prospect Dr
Altrincham WA15..........**129** D8
Failsworth M35..........**83** F5
Prospect Hill BL2..........**25** F4
Prospect Ho
Manchester M9..........**157** B3
Standish WN6..........**36** E8
Prospect Ind Ctr 15 WN2..**56** D5
Prospect Pl
Ashton-u-L OL6..........**85** D5
Bury BL9 ....**45** A4
Farnworth BL4..........**60** C7
Heywood OL10..........**29** D3
Prospect Rd
Ashton-u-L OL6..........**85** E5
Dukinfield SK16..........**101** D8
Irlam M44..........**105** E6
Oldham OL9..........**152** C3
Stockport SK4..........**36** E7
Prospect St
Bolton BL1..........**143** C1
Heywood OL10..........**46** E8
Hindley WN2 ....**56** D5
Littleborough OL15 ....**16** B6
Rochdale OL11..........**30** E4
Tyldesley M29 ....**58** F1
Prospect Terr
Bacup OL13 ....**3** E7
Bury BL8 ....**140** A4
Prospect Vale SK8 ....**122** B1
Prospect Vale Prim Sch
SK8..........**122** B1
Prospect View M27....**80** A7
Prospect Villas 3 M9....**64** F1
Prosperity St M29....**77** D8
Prosser Ave M46..........**58** A2
Protector Way M44 ..**105** F8
Prout St M12..........**99** A3
Provender Cl WA14 ..**119** D3
Providence Ho OL4....**67** E8
Providence St
4 Ashton-u-L OL6..........**85** D4
Bolton BL3..........**145** C1
Denton M34..........**100** F7
Manchester M4..........**160** A1
Walsden OL14..........**6** A7
Provident Ave M19....**99** C1
Provident St OL2..........**149** B3
Provident Way WA15..**120** A7
Provis Rd M21..........**109** B7
Prubella Ave M34....**100** E5
Pryce Ave WN2..........**151** C3

Pryce St BL1. . . . . 143 A1
Pryme St M15. . . . . 162 B3
Pudding La SK14. . . . . 102 C3
Puffin Ave SK12. . . . . 133 B4
Puffingate Cl SK15. . . . . . . 86 E7
Pugin Wlk M9 . . . . 157 A2
Pulborough Cl BL8. . . . . . . 27 B7
Pulford Ave M21. . . . . 109 D4
Pulford Rd M33. . . . . 108 D2
Pullman Cl M18. . . . . 111 B8
Pullman Dr M32 . . . . 95 F3
Pullman St OL11. . . . . 139 C1
Pulman Ct BL3. . . . . 148 A1
Pump St
  10 Hindley WN2. . . . . 56 D5
  9 Oldham OL9 . . . . 66 B2
Punch La BL5. . . . . 40 D1
Punch St BL3. . . . . 145 A2
PUNGLE THE 57 D5
Pungle The BL5. . . . . 57 D5
Purbeck Cl M22. . . . . 121 C1
Purbeck Dr
  Bury BL8 . . . . 27 C6
  Horwich BL6 . . . . 22 C5
Purbeck Way M29 . . . . 77 B7
Purcell Cl BL1. . . . . 143 A1
Purcell St M11. . . . . 99 A3
Purdon St 2 BL9 . . . . 27 F6
Purdy Ho OL8. . . . . 153 B1
Puritan Wlk 7 M40. . . . . . 156 C1
Purley Ave M23. . . . . 109 B1
Purley Dr M44. . . . . 105 C5
Purslow Cl M12. . . . . 160 B1
Purton Wlk 8 M9. . . . . . . 157 B3
Putney Cl OL1 . . . . 48 E1
Puzzletree Ct SK2. . . . . . . 124 C7
Pye Cl WA11. . . . . 89 B8
Pyegrove SK13. . . . . 104 F1
Pyegrove Rd SK13 . . . . . . 104 E1
Pyke St WN1. . . . . 37 D1
Pymgate Dr SK8. . . . . 122 A2
Pym St
  Eccles M30 . . . . 79 D2
  Heywood OL10. . . . . 29 D1
  Manchester M40 . . . . 157 C4
Pyramid Ct M7 . . . . 155 A2
Pyrus Cl M30 . . . . 94 F8
Pytha Fold Rd M20. . . . . . 110 D5

Q

Quadrant The
  Droylsden M43. . . . . 83 F1
  Manchester M9 . . . . 65 D1
  Romiley SK6. . . . . 113 A2
  Stockport SK1 . . . . 112 B1
Quail Dr M44 . . . . 94 A3
Quail St OL4. . . . . 67 C6
Quainton Ho 5 M5 . . . . . 154 C1
Quakerfields BL5 . . . . 57 D7
Quakers' Pl WN6. . . . . 19 E3
Quakers Field BL8. . . . . . . 26 F8
Quakers Terr WN6 . . . . 19 D3
Quantock Cl
  Stockport SK4 . . . . 169 B2
  Wigan WN3 . . . . 54 C2
Quantock Dr OL8 . . . . 66 F3
Quantock St 7 M16. . . . . . 97 E4
Quarlton Dr BL8 . . . . 10 B3
Quarmby Rd M18 . . . . 99 F4
Quarry Bank Mill 8 SK9 . . 130 F2
Quarry Bank Rd SK9 . . . . 130 F3
Quarry Cl SK13 . . . . 104 D1
Quarry Clough SK15. . . . . 102 D8
Quarry Hill OL12 . . . . 14 E3
Quarry Hts 4 SK15. . . . . . 101 F8
Quarry La OL3 . . . . 50 D1
Quarrymans View WA15. . 120 B6
Quarry Pl WN1. . . . . 151 B4
Quarry Pond Rd M28 . . . . . 59 F3
Quarry Rise
  Romiley SK6. . . . . 113 B3
  Stalybridge SK15, SK16. . . 101 F8
Quarry St
  Radcliffe M26 . . . . 44 B3
  Ramsbottom BL0 . . . . 11 D6
  Rochdale OL12. . . . . 14 C1
  Romiley SK6. . . . . 113 B3
  Stalybridge SK15. . . . . . . 85 F1
  Whitworth OL12. . . . . 4 E6
Quarry Wlk 17 M11. . . . . . 160 C1
Quay 5 M5. . . . . 161 B3
Quayside WN7 . . . . 75 E4
Quayside M28 . . . . 78 B5
Quays Reach M50 . . . . . . 154 B1
Quay St
  Heywood OL10. . . . . 29 E1
  Salford M3. . . . . 158 B2
Quays The M50 . . . . 96 E7
Quay View M5 . . . . 161 A4
Quebec Cl
  Abram Brow WN2 & WN7 . . 74 E5
  Bolton BL3. . . . . 145 A1
  Denton M34. . . . . 100 E4
  Oldham OL9. . . . . 153 C2
Queen Alexandra Cl M5 . 161 C4
Queen Ann Cl BL9. . . . . 45 C4
Queen Ann Dr M28. . . . . . . 78 B7
Queen Anne Ct SK9 . . . . . 137 C6
Queen Elizabeth Hall *
  OL1 . . . . 153 B3
Queenhill Dr SK14. . . . . . 102 A5

Queenhill Rd M22. . . . . . . 109 E1
Queens Ave
  Manchester M18 . . . . 165 B1
  Rochdale OL12. . . . . 15 C4
Queen's Ave
  Ashton-in-M WN4 . . . . 73 B3
  Atherton M46. . . . . 58 C5
  Bolton BL3. . . . . 25 A7
  Glazebury WA3 . . . . 92 C7
  Little Lever BL3 . . . . 43 A4
  Romiley SK6. . . . . 113 A3
Queensbridge Prim Sch
  BL4 . . . . 60 C8
Queensbrook BL1. . . . . . . 145 B3
Queensbury Cl
  Bolton BL1. . . . . 24 D5
  16 Handforth SK9 . . . . . . 131 D1
  Wilmslow SK9 . . . . 137 D8
Queensbury Ct M40. . . . . 160 B3
Queensbury Par M40. . . . 160 B3
Queens Cl
  Hyde SK14. . . . . 113 E7
  Mosley Common M28 . . . . 77 F7
  Stockport SK4 . . . . 168 A2
  Walkden M28. . . . . 60 D3
Queenscroft 2 M30. . . . . . 79 F3
Queens Ct
  Manchester, Collyhurst
    M40. . . . . 157 A1
  Stockport SK4 . . . . 168 A3
  Urmston M41. . . . . 94 E2
Queen's Ct
  3 Manchester M21 . . . . . . 97 B2
  Manchester, Withington
    M20. . . . . 110 A4
  Marple SK6 . . . . 126 A6
Queens Dr
  Cheadle SK8 . . . . 123 A2
  Golborne WA3 . . . . 90 C8
  Hyde SK14. . . . . 113 F7
  Newton-le-W WA12. . . . . . 89 C5
  Rochdale OL11. . . . . 30 E3
Queen's Dr
  Glossop SK13. . . . . 104 F1
  Manchester, Sedgley Park
    M25. . . . . 63 C2
  Stockport SK4 . . . . 168 A2
Queensferry St M40. . . . . . 83 C6
Queensgate
  Bolton BL1. . . . . 144 C4
  Bramhall SK7. . . . . 132 E5
Queensgate Dr OL2 . . . . . . 48 C6
Queensgate Prim Sch
  SK7. . . . . 132 E4
Queens Gdns WN7 . . . . . . 76 C5
Queen's Gdns SK8 . . . . . . 122 E6
Queen's Gr M12 . . . . 164 E5
Queensland Rd M18. . . . . 165 B1
Queensmere Dr M27 . . . . . 62 A2
Queen's Park Rd OL10. . . . 29 D3
Queens Pl BL9 . . . . 11 C2
Queen Sq OL6 . . . . 85 D3
Queens Rd
  Bolton BL3. . . . . 146 B4
  Chadderton OL9. . . . . . . 152 A3
  Haydock WA11. . . . . 89 A7
  Manchester, Cheetham Hill M8,
    M9. . . . . 156 B2
  Manchester, Collyhurst M40,
    M9. . . . . 157 A1
  Orrell WN5. . . . . 53 C5
  Sale M33 . . . . 107 F5
Queen's Rd
  Altrincham WA15. . . . . . . 119 F3
  Ashton-u-L OL6 . . . . 85 D5
  Cheadle SK8 . . . . 123 A3
  Hazel Grove SK7 . . . . . . 124 E3
  Romiley SK6. . . . . 113 A3
  Urmston M41. . . . . 95 D1
  Wilmslow SK9 . . . . 137 A6
Queens Road Prim Sch
  SK8. . . . . 123 A3
Queen St
  Ashton-u-L OL6 . . . . 166 C3
  3 Bacup OL13 . . . . 3 E8
  5 Bolton BL1. . . . . 145 F8
  Bury, Pimhole BL9. . . . . . 141 A2
  Bury, Tottington BL8 . . . . . 27 A5
  Cheadle SK8 . . . . 122 F6
  Denton, Hooley Hill M34 . . 100 F6
  Dukinfield SK16. . . . . 166 B1
  Failsworth M35 . . . . 83 E7
  Farnworth BL4. . . . . 60 D8
  Glossop SK13. . . . . 116 B8
  6 Golborne WA3 . . . . 90 C8
  Hadfield SK13 . . . . 104 A4
  Heywood OL10. . . . . 29 E1
  9 Hindley WN2. . . . . 56 D6
  Horwich BL6 . . . . 22 B3
  Hyde SK14. . . . . 167 B1
  Leigh WN7 . . . . 76 A5
  Littleborough OL15 . . . . . . 16 B5
  Manchester M2 . . . . 158 C1
  Marple SK6 . . . . 126 A6
  Middleton M24. . . . . 65 C8
  Mossley OL5 . . . . 68 C1
  Newton-le-W WA12. . . . . . 89 B3
  10 Oldham, County End OL4 . 67 F6
  Oldham OL1. . . . . 153 C2
  Platt Bridge WN2. . . . . . . 56 A2
  Radcliffe M26 . . . . 44 A2
  Ramsbottom BL0 . . . . . . 138 B2
  Rochdale OL12. . . . . 139 C4
  Royton OL2 . . . . 48 D4

Queen St continued
  Salford, Irlams o' th' Height
    M6. . . . . 80 D5
  Salford M3. . . . . 158 B2
  Shaw OL2. . . . . 149 B2
  Stalybridge SK15. . . . . . . 86 A2
  Walkden M38. . . . . 60 B3
  Westhoughton BL5 . . . . . . 57 E8
  Wigan, Norley WN5. . . . . . 54 B6
  Wigan, Pemberton WN5 . . . 54 D5
  Wigan WN3 . . . . 150 C3
Queens Terr SK9. . . . . 131 D3
Queen's Terr
  3 Bacup OL13 . . . . 3 E8
  7 Dukinfield SK16. . . . . . 166 B1
Queenston Rd M20. . . . . . 110 A4
Queen Street W M20 . . . . 110 A4
Queens View OL15 . . . . 16 A3
Queensway
  Dukinfield SK16 . . . . 101 F7
  Gatley SK8. . . . . 131 C8
  Ince-in-M WN2 . . . . 56 A8
  Irlam M44 . . . . 93 F2
  Kearsley BL4. . . . . 60 F5
  Leigh WN7 . . . . 76 D6
  Manchester M19 . . . . 110 E8
  Mossley OL5 . . . . 86 D8
  Partington M31. . . . . 105 F4
  Poynton SK12. . . . . 133 D3
  Rochdale OL11. . . . . 30 E3
  Shevington WN6 . . . . 35 F4
  Swinton M27 . . . . 62 A2
  Swinton M27 . . . . 62 B3
  Urmston M41. . . . . 95 C1
  Walkden M28. . . . . 78 C8
  Wigan WN1 . . . . 37 F4
Queens Wlk M43. . . . . 84 A1
Queen Victoria St
  Eccles M30 . . . . 79 C2
  Rochdale OL11. . . . . 31 A4
Quendy St M15 . . . . 162 A3
Quendon Ave M7 . . . . 158 B4
QUICK 68 D4
Quick Edge La OL4 . . . . . . 68 B4
Quickedge Rd OL4, OL5 . . 68 C3
Quickmere Ct 7 OL5. . . . . 68 C2
Quick Rd OL4, OL5. . . . . . . 68 D3
Quick View OL5 . . . . 68 E3
QUICKWOOD. 68 D3
Quickwood OL5. . . . . 68 D3
Quill Ct M44. . . . . 105 E6
Quilter Gr M9. . . . . 64 C2
Quinney Cres M16 . . . . 97 F4
Quinn St M11. . . . . 83 A1
Quinton 10 OL12 . . . . 139 B4
Quinton Wlk M13 . . . . 163 B2
Quintrell Brow BL7. . . . . . . 25 A8

R

Raby St M14, M16 . . . . 97 F4
Racecourse Pk SK9 . . . . . 136 F6
Racecourse Rd SK9 . . . . . 136 F6
Racecourse Wlk M26 . . . . . 43 F4
Racefield Hamlet OL2. . . . . 48 A4
Racefield Rd WA14. . . . . . 119 C4
Race The SK9. . . . . 131 D2
Rachel Ho BL9. . . . . 141 D3
Rachel Rosing Wlk M8 . . . 155 C4
Rachel St M12. . . . . 163 C3
Rack House Prim Sch
  M23. . . . . 109 A1
Rackhouse Rd M23. . . . . . 109 B1
Radbourne Cl M12. . . . . . 165 A2
Radbourne Gr BL3. . . . . . . 40 F4
RADCLIFFE 44 A3
Radcliffe Ave WA3 . . . . 91 E3
Radcliffe Gr WN7 . . . . 75 F7
Radcliffe Hall CE/Meth Prim
  M26. . . . . 44 A4
Radcliffe Metro Sta M26 . . 44 D3
Radcliffe Moor Rd BL2,
  M26. . . . . 43 C5
Radcliffe New Rd M45,
  M26. . . . . 44 D2
Radcliffe Park Cres M6. . . . 80 C5
Radcliffe Park Rd M6 . . . . . 80 C5
Radcliffe Pool & Fitness
  Ctr. 44 A3
Radcliffe Prim Sch M26. . . 43 E4
Radcliffe Rd
  2 Bolton BL3. . . . . 43 A4
  Bolton, Darcy Lever BL2,
    BL3 . . . . 42 D5
  Bolton, Springfield BL2 . . 148 B3
  Bury BL9 . . . . 44 E7
  Oldham OL4. . . . . 49 D2
Radcliffe Riverside Sch
  M26. . . . . 44 B4
Radcliffe St
  Oldham, Cold Hurst OL1 . . 153 C4
  Oldham, Grotton OL4. . . . . 68 A6
  Royton OL2 . . . . 48 E4
Radcliffe Athletics Ctr
  OL9 . . . . 152 A3
Radclyffe Sch The OL9 . . . 65 F7
Radclyffe St
  Chadderton OL9. . . . . 152 C4
  Middleton M24. . . . . 47 A3
  10 Oldham OL1 . . . . 153 C8
Radelan Gr M26 . . . . 43 D4
Radford Cl SK2. . . . . 124 C7
Radford Dr
  Irlam M44 . . . . 94 A3
  2 Manchester M9 . . . . . . 157 B4
Radford Ho SK2. . . . . 124 C7
Radford St M7. . . . . 81 C8
Radium St M4 . . . . 159 C2

Radlett Dr WA15. . . . . 120 A8
Radlett Wlk 3 M13 . . . . . 163 C1
Radley Cl
  Bolton BL1. . . . . 142 A1
  7 Sale M33 . . . . 107 D3
Radley St
  Droylsden M43. . . . . 99 E8
  Manchester M16 . . . . 97 F3
Radnor Ave M34. . . . . 100 B3
Radnor Cl WN2 . . . . 57 A3
Radnor Dr WN7 . . . . 75 C5
Radnormere Dr SK8. . . . . 123 A4
Radnor St
  Manchester, Gorton M18. . . 99 C4
  Manchester, Moss Side M15 . 97 F4
  Oldham OL9. . . . . 152 C1
  Stretford M32 . . . . 96 D1
Radstock Cl
  Bolton BL1. . . . . 24 E7
  Manchester M14 . . . . 98 B1
Radstock Rd M32 . . . . 96 C2
Radway M29. . . . . 59 C1
Raeburn Dr SK6. . . . . 126 B8
Rae St SK3 . . . . 123 C8
Raglan Ave
  Prestwich M25, M45. . . . . . 63 B7
  Swinton M27 . . . . 62 B2
Raglan Cl M11. . . . . 160 C1
Raglan Dr WA14 . . . . 119 E8
Raglan Rd
  Sale M33 . . . . 108 A3
  Stretford M32 . . . . 96 B3
Raglan St
  Bolton BL1. . . . . 143 A2
  Hyde SK14. . . . . 101 C2
  Rochdale OL11. . . . . 30 C1
Raglan Wlk 6 M15. . . . . . 162 C2
Ragley Cl SK12. . . . . 133 F4
Raikes Clough Ind Est
  BL3. . . . . 42 C4
Raikes La BL3. . . . . 42 C4
Raikes Lane Ind Est BL3 . . 42 C4
Raikes Rd BL3 . . . . 42 D5
Raikes Way BL3. . . . . 42 D5
Railgate OL13. . . . . 4 C8
Rail Pl 8 M15 . . . . 163 A2
Railside Terr M40. . . . . 80 A2
Railton Ave M16 . . . . 97 D2
Railton Terr M6 . . . . 80 D4
Railway App 4 OL11 . . . . . 30 C2
Railway Bank SK14. . . . . . 101 C2
Railway Brow OL11. . . . . . . 30 C1
Railway Cotts
  Hollinfare WA3 . . . . 105 B5
  Romiley SK6. . . . . 112 F4
Railway Rd
  Adlington PR6, PR7. . . . . . 21 A7
  Golborne WA3 . . . . 74 B1
  Leigh WN7 . . . . 75 E5
  Oldham, Factory Fold OL9. . 66 A2
  Oldham OL9. . . . . 153 A2
  Stockport SK1, SK3 . . . . . 170 B4
  Stretford M32 . . . . 96 F5
  Urmston M41. . . . . 95 E2
Railway Road Ind Est
  M26. . . . . 44 D3
Railway St
  Altrincham WA14. . . . . . . 119 D4
  Atherton M46. . . . . 58 B4
  Bacup OL13 . . . . 3 B8
  Dukinfield SK16. . . . . 166 B1
  Farnworth BL4. . . . . 42 E1
  Glossop SK13. . . . . 104 C1
  Hadfield SK13 . . . . 104 A5
  Heywood OL10. . . . . 29 E1
  Hindley WN2. . . . . 56 E7
  Hyde SK14. . . . . 167 A2
  Littleborough OL15 . . . . . . 16 B5
  Manchester M18 . . . . 99 D6
  Newhey OL16. . . . . 32 B4
  Newton-le-W WA12. . . . . . 89 B3
  Radcliffe M26 . . . . 44 A3
  Ramsbottom BL0 . . . . . . 138 C2
  Ramsbottom, Summerseat
    BL9 . . . . 11 C2
  Rochdale OL16. . . . . 31 A6
  Stockport SK4 . . . . 169 B2
  Wigan WN6 . . . . 37 A1
Railway Street Ind Est
  M18. . . . . 99 D6
Railway Terr
  Bury BL8 . . . . 27 C1
  Disley SK12 . . . . 135 D6
  Entwistle BL7. . . . . 9 B8
  3 Manchester M21 . . . . . . 97 B2
Railway View
  3 Oldham OL4 . . . . 67 F6
  Shaw OL2. . . . . 149 C4
Raimond St BL1. . . . . 143 A2
Rainbow Cl M21. . . . . 109 B7
Rainbow Dr M46. . . . . 58 D5
Raincliff Ave M13 . . . . 98 F2
Raines Crest OL16 . . . . 32 A6
Rainford Ave
  Altrincham WA15. . . . . . . 120 A6
  Manchester M20 . . . . 110 A8
Rainford Ho BL1 . . . . 145 C5
Rainford Rd WA11, WN5. . . 71 C5
Rainford St BL2. . . . . 25 D6
Rainforth St M13. . . . . 98 F3
Rainham Dr
  Bolton BL1. . . . . 143 B1
  Manchester M8 . . . . 156 A3
Rainham Gr 2 BL1. . . . . . 143 B1
Rainham Way
  Brinnington SK5. . . . . 112 B6
  Chadderton OL9. . . . . . . 152 B2
Rainhill Wlk M40 . . . . 83 D4
Rainow Ave M43 . . . . 83 E1
Rainow Dr SK12. . . . . 134 A2

Radlett Dr WA15. . . . . 120 A8
Rainow Rd SK3 . . . . 123 C6
Rainow Way 10 SK9 . . . . . 131 E1
Rainshaw St
  Bolton BL1. . . . . 143 C4
  3 Oldham OL4 . . . . 67 D8
  Royton OL2 . . . . 48 D4
RAINSOUGH 63 A1
Rainsough Ave M25. . . . . . 63 A1
Rainsough Brow M25 . . . . . 62 F1
Rainsough Cl M25 . . . . 63 A1
Rainton Wlk 2 M40. . . . . . 65 D2
Rainwood OL9 . . . . 65 E8
Raithby Dr WN3. . . . . 55 A3
Raja Cl M8 . . . . 156 B3
Rake
  Ramsbottom BL0 . . . . . . 138 B2
  Rochdale OL15. . . . . 29 D8
Rake Fold BL8 . . . . 138 A2
RAKE HEAD. 3 A7
Rake Head Barn La OL14 . . 6 A8
Rake Head La OL13 . . . . . . 3 B8
Rakehead Wlk 4 M15. . . . 162 C1
Rake La M27. . . . . 62 B2
Rake St BL9 . . . . 140 C4
Rake Terr OL15 . . . . 16 C6
Rakewood Dr OL4. . . . . 49 E4
Rakewood Rd OL15 . . . . . . 16 C2
Raleigh Cl
  Manchester M20 . . . . 110 A5
  Oldham OL1. . . . . 153 C4
Raleigh Gdns OL15. . . . . . . 6 C1
Raleigh St
  Reddish SK5. . . . . 169 B4
  Stretford M32 . . . . 96 E2
Ralli Courts M3 . . . . 158 B1
Ralph Ave SK14 . . . . 113 E7
Ralph Green St OL9 . . . . . . 66 B3
Ralph Sherwin Ct OL12. . . 15 D4
Ralphs La
  Dukinfield SK16 . . . . 101 C7
  Oldham OL3. . . . . 33 D2
Ralph St
  Bolton BL1. . . . . 143 A2
  Droylsden M11. . . . . 83 D1
  Rochdale OL12. . . . . 15 A1
Ralston Cl M7 . . . . 155 C4
Ralstone Ave OL8. . . . . 66 F4
Ramage Wlk M12 . . . . 160 B1
Ramillies Ave SK8. . . . . . . 123 C1
Ramillies Hall Sch SK8 . . 123 C2
Ramp Road E M90 . . . . . . 130 C7
Ramp Road S M90 . . . . . . 130 C7
Ramp Road W M90. . . . . . 130 B7
Ramsay Ave BL4 . . . . 60 B7
Ramsay Pl OL16. . . . . 31 A8
Ramsay St
  Bolton BL1. . . . . 143 B4
  Rochdale OL16. . . . . 31 A8
Ramsay Terr 10 OL16. . . . . 31 A8
RAMSBOTTOM 138 C1
Ramsbottom La BL0. . . . . 138 C3
Ramsbottom Pool & Fitness
  Ctr BL0. . . . . 138 C3
Ramsbottom Sta* BL0. . . 138 C2
Ramsbury Dr M40. . . . . . . 65 D2
Ramsdale Rd SK7. . . . . . . 132 E8
Ramsdale St OL9. . . . . . . 152 A3
Ramsden Cl
  Glossop SK13. . . . . 104 D2
  Oldham OL1. . . . . 153 B3
  Wigan WN3 . . . . 150 A1
Ramsden Cres OL1. . . . . . 153 B4
Ramsden Fold M27 . . . . . . 61 F2
Ramsden La OL14 . . . . 5 F7
Ramsden Rd
  Calderbrook OL12 . . . . 5 C2
  Wardle OL12 . . . . 15 C6
Ramsden St
  Ashton-u-L OL6 . . . . 166 B4
  Bolton BL3. . . . . 42 D5
  Oldham OL1. . . . . 153 B3
  Walsden OL14. . . . . 6 A7
Ramsden Wood Rd OL14 . . 6 A7
Ramsey Ave M19. . . . . 99 D1
Ramsey Cl
  Ashton-in-M WN4 . . . . 73 B3
  Atherton M46. . . . . 58 E2
  Ramsey Gr BL8 . . . . 27 B2
Ramsey St
  Chadderton OL9. . . . . . . 152 B1
  3 Leigh WN7 . . . . 76 A4
  Manchester M40 . . . . 83 B7
  Oldham OL1. . . . . 67 B8
Ramsgate Rd
  Failsworth M40. . . . . 83 C4
  Reddish SK5. . . . . 111 F7
Ramsgate St M7, M8. . . . . 155 B1
Ramsgill Cl M23 . . . . 108 F1
Ramsgreave Cl BL9 . . . . . . 44 D7
Ram St M38 . . . . 59 F5
Ramwell Cl BL3. . . . . 42 B3
Ramwell Gdns BL3 . . . . . . 145 A1
Ramwells Brow BL7 . . . . . . 25 A8
Ramwells Ct BL7. . . . . 25 B8
Ranby Ave M9 . . . . 64 F4
Randale Dr BL9. . . . . 45 A6
Randal St M16 . . . . 36 A5
Randall Cl WA12 . . . . 89 B4
Randall Wlk 22 M11. . . . . 160 C1
Randal St BL3 . . . . 146 C4
Randerson St M12 . . . . . . 163 C3
Randlesham St M25. . . . . . 63 C4

Randle St **1** WN2 . . . . 56 D6
Randolph Pl SK3 . . . . 170 B3
Randolph Rd BL4 . . . . 60 F7
Randolph St
  Bolton BL3 . . . . 145 A2
  Manchester M19 . . . . . . 99 B4
  Oldham OL8 . . . . 66 C2
Rands Clough Dr M28 . . 78 B6
Rand St **6** OL1 . . . . 49 D1
Ranelagh Rd M27 . . . . . . 80 C7
Ranelagh St M11 . . . . 83 B2
Raneley Gr OL11 . . . . 31 A2
Ranford Rd M19 . . . . 111 A8
Range Dr SK6 . . . . 113 C6
Range Hall Ct **7** SK1 . . 112 A1
Range La OL1 . . . . 33 D1
Rangemore Ave M22 . . 121 D8
Range Rd
  Dukinfield SK16 . . . . . . 102 B7
  Manchester M16 . . . . . . 97 E3
  Stalybridge SK15 . . . . . 102 B8
  Stockport SK3 . . . . 170 B3
Range St
  Bolton BL3 . . . . 147 A4
  Manchester M11 . . . . . 165 C4
Ranicar St WN2 . . . . 57 C3
Rankine Terr BL3 . . . . . . 145 A1
Ranmore Ave
  Garswood WN4 . . . . 72 D4
  Manchester M11 . . . . . . 99 D8
Rannoch Rd BL2 . . . . 43 A7
Ransfield Rd M21 . . . . . . 97 B1
Ranulph Ct **1** M6 . . . . . 80 D5
Ranworth Ave SK4 . . . . 110 F2
Ranworth Cl BL1 . . . . 25 A6
Raper St OL4 . . . . 67 C8
Rapes Highway OL3 . . . . 33 F5
Raphael St BL1 . . . . 143 A2
Rappax Rd WA15 . . . . . 129 A8
Rasbottom St BL3 . . . . . 145 B1
Raspberry La M44 . . . . . . 94 A5
Rassbottom Brow **6** SK15 85 F2
Rassbottom Ind Est SK15 . 85 F2
Rassbottom St SK15 . . . . 85 F2
Rassey Cl WN6 . . . . 37 A7
Rastell Wlk **2** M9 . . . . . 64 E3
Ratcliffe Ave M44 . . . . . . 94 A2
Ratcliffe Rd WN2 . . . . . . 38 C6
Ratcliffe St
  Leigh WN7 . . . . 75 F6
  Manchester M19 . . . . . . 99 B1
  6 Stockport SK1 . . . . 170 C4
  Tyldesley M29 . . . . 59 B1
  Wigan WN6 . . . . 37 A1
Ratcliffe Terr OL5 . . . . . 86 C8
Rathan Rd M41 . . . . 95 C4
Rathbone St OL16 . . . . . . 31 C7
Rathbourne Ave M9 . . . . 64 D4
Rathen Ave WN2 . . . . 56 A8
Rathen Rd M20 . . . . 110 C5
Rathmell Cl WA3 . . . . 91 E3
Rathmel Rd M23 . . . . . . 108 F2
Rathmore Ave M40 . . . . 157 B1
Rathvale Dr M22 . . . . . . 130 C8
Rath Wlk **10** M40 . . . . . . 83 C5
Rathybank Cl **3** BL1 . . 142 C2
Rattenbury Ct M6 . . . . . . 80 C5
Raveden Cl BL1 . . . . 142 C3
Raveley Ave M14 . . . . . . 110 D8
Ravelston Dr M9 . . . . . . 157 A3
Raven Ave
  Chadderton OL9 . . . . . . 152 A1
  Haslingden BB4 . . . . 1 A7
Raven Cl
  Droylsden M43 . . . . 84 C3
  Sale WA15 . . . . 108 B1
Raven Ct WA4 . . . . 1 B8
Raven Ct BB4 . . . . 1 B8
Raven Ct M15 . . . . 162 B1
Ravendale Cl OL12 . . . . . 14 A1
Raven Dr M44 . . . . 94 A3
Ravenfield Gr **10** BL1 . . 145 A4
Ravenglass Dr M44 . . . . 46 D3
Ravenhead Cl **16** M14 . 110 D8
Ravenhead Dr WN8 . . . . 53 A7
Ravenhead Sq SK15 . . . . 86 E5
Ravenhurst M6 . . . . 81 A5
Ravenhurst **4** M47 . . . . 63 E1
Ravenhurst Dr BL1 . . . . . 40 D6
Ravenna Ave M20 . . . . . 120 D7
Ravenoak Ave M19 . . . . 111 C8
Ravenoak Dr M35 . . . . . . 84 A8
Ravenoak Park Rd SK8 . . 132 B8
Ravenoak Rd
  Cheadle SK8 . . . . 132 B8
  Stockport SK2 . . . . 124 A4
Raven Pk BB4 . . . . 1 B8
Raven Rd BL3 . . . . 146 A4
Ravensbury Com Prim Sch
  M11 . . . . 83 B2
Ravensbury St M11 . . . . 83 B2
Ravenscar Cres M22 . . 130 D8
Ravenscar Wlk BL4 . . . . 60 D7
Ravens Cl
  Glossop SK13 . . . . 115 F8
  Manchester M25 . . . . . . 63 E2
Ravenscraig Rd M38 . . . 60 B6
Ravensdale Gdns M30 . . 79 E3
Ravensdale Rd BL1 . . . . . 40 D7
Ravensdale St M14 . . . . . 98 C3
Ravensfield Ind Est BL3 . 146 B4
Ravensfields Prim Sch
  SK16 . . . . 101 B8
Ravensfield Way SK16 . . 101 B8
Ravens Holme BL1 . . . . . 40 E7
Ravenside Pk OL9 . . . . . 152 A1

Raven St
  Bury BL9 . . . . 140 C4
  Manchester M12 . . . . . 163 C4
  Rochdale OL11 . . . . 13 E1
Ravenstonedale Dr OL2 . 48 E5
Ravenstone Dr M33 . . . 108 E5
Ravenstones Dr OL3 . . . 51 C3
Ravensway M25 . . . . 63 D2
Ravenswood M20 . . . . . 109 H4
Ravens Wood BL1 . . . . . . 40 E7
Ravenswood Ave
  Stockport SK4 . . . . 168 A1
  Wigan WN3 . . . . 54 D3
Ravenswood Brow WN5 . 71 E6
Ravenswood Ct **5** SK3 . 123 F4
Ravenswood Dr
  Bolton BL1 . . . . 40 E7
  Cheadle SK8 . . . . 132 B8
  Hindley WN2 . . . . 56 E7
  Wigan WN2 . . . . 64 E3
Ravenswood Rd
  Stretford M32 . . . . 96 F4
  Wilmslow SK9 . . . . 136 E4
Raven Terr **1** SK16 . . . . 166 C1
Raven Way
  Salford M6 . . . . 154 C3
  6 Salford, Pendleton M6 . 81 A3
Ravenwood OL9 . . . . 65 D7
Ravenwood Dr
  Altrincham WA15 . . . . . 129 D7
  Denton M34 . . . . 100 E6
Ravine Ave M9 . . . . 157 C3
Rawcliffe Ave BL2 . . . . . . 42 F7
Rawcliffe St M14 . . . . 98 B3
Rawdon Cl **3** M19 . . . . . 99 B1
Rawkin Cl M15 . . . . 162 B1
Rawlinson St **13** BL6 . . . 22 B4
Rawlyn Rd BL1 . . . . 142 A2
Rawpool Gdns M23 . . . . 121 A7
Rawson Ave BL4 . . . . 42 E1
Rawson Rd BL1 . . . . 142 C1
Rawson Rake BL0, BL8 . 138 A2
Rawsthorne Ave
  Edenfield BL0 . . . . 1 D2
  Manchester M18 . . . . . . 99 D2
Rawsthorne St
  Bolton BL1 . . . . 143 B2
  Tyldesley M29 . . . . 77 D8
Rawstron St OL12 . . . . . . 4 C1
Rawthey Pl WN2 . . . . 55 F2
Raycroft Ave M9 . . . . 65 A2
Raydale Cl WA3 . . . . 74 E1
Rayden Cres BL5 . . . . . . 57 E6
Raydon Ave M40 . . . . . . 157 A1
Raylees BL0 . . . . 11 C4
Rayleigh Ave M11 . . . . . . 99 F7
Raymond Ave
  Bury BL9 . . . . 27 F5
  Oldham OL9 . . . . 66 B4
Raymond Rd M23 . . . . . 109 B2
Raymond St M27 . . . . . . 61 F1
Rayner La
  Ashton-u-L OL7 . . . . 84 F3
  Droylsden M34, M43, OL7 . 84 D2
Rayners Cl SK15 . . . . 85 F1
Rayner St SK1 . . . . 124 B8
Raynham Ave M20 . . . . 110 B3
Raynham St OL6 . . . . . . 166 C3
Rayson Hill Dr M9 . . . . . 64 C2
Reabrook Ave M12 . . . . 164 C2
Reach The M28 . . . . 60 E2
Read Cl
  Bury BL9 . . . . 44 D7
  Shaw OL2 . . . . 149 B2
Reade Ave M41 . . . . 94 F1
Reade Ho M41 . . . . 94 F1
Reading Cl M11 . . . . 165 C4
Reading Dr M33 . . . . . . 108 A5
Reading St M6 . . . . 81 B5
Reading Wlk **1** M34 . . . 100 F1
Readitt Wlk M11 . . . . 83 B2
Read St SK14 . . . . 101 C3
Read Street W SK14 . . . 101 C3
Reaney Wlk M12 . . . . . . 165 A2
Reather Wlk M40 . . . . . . 159 C3
Rebecca St M8 . . . . 156 A4
Rechar Way M27 . . . . . . 61 F1
Recreation Ave WN4 . . . 73 D4
Recreation Dr WN5 . . . . 71 E5
Recreation Rd M35 . . . . 66 B1
Recreation St
  Bolton BL3 . . . . 147 B4
  Bolton, Harwood Lee BL2 . 25 E5
  Prestwich M25 . . . . 63 C4
Rectory CE Prim Sch
  WN4 . . . . 72 D5
Rectory Cl
  Denton M34 . . . . 101 A2
  Radcliffe M26 . . . . 44 D4
Rectory Ct **8** SK6 . . . . 125 F5
Rectory Fields SK1 . . . . 112 A1
Rectory Gdns
  Prestwich M25 . . . . 63 B4
  Westhoughton BL5 . . . . 57 E5
Rectory Gn
  Prestwich M25 . . . . 63 B4
  Stockport SK1 . . . . 112 A1
Rectory Gr M25 . . . . 63 B3
Rectory Hill BL9 . . . . 28 D4
Rectory La
  Bury BL9 . . . . 28 D4
  Prestwich M25 . . . . 63 A4

Rectory La continued
  Radcliffe M26 . . . . 44 B3
  Standish WN1, WN6 . . . 20 A1
Rectory Rd
  Downall Green WN4 . . . 72 D5
  Manchester M8 . . . . 63 F1
Rectory St M24 . . . . 46 F1
Redacre SK12 . . . . 133 F6
Redacre Rd M18 . . . . 99 E5
Red Bank
  Bury BL9 . . . . 28 E6
  Manchester M4, M8 . . . 159 A3
Red Bank Ave M42 . . . . . 89 F1
Red Bank Rd M26 . . . . . . 43 F5
Redbarn Cl SK6 . . . . 112 F4
Red Barn Rd WN5 . . . . . . 71 C6
Redbourne Dr M41 . . . . . 94 F4
Redbrick Ct **8** OL7 . . . . 166 A1
Red Bridge BL2 . . . . 26 A1
Redbridge Gr **9** M21 . . 109 A8
Redbrook Ave M40 . . . . 157 B1
Redbrook Cl BL4 . . . . 42 E1
Redbrook Gr **2** SK9 . . . 131 D1
Redbrook Rd
  Altrincham WA15 . . . . . 120 D5
  Ince-in-M WN3 . . . . 151 B2
  Partington M31 . . . . 105 E2
Red Brook St OL11 . . . . 139 A3
Redburn Ave M23 . . . . . 121 B7
Redburn Rd M23 . . . . . . 121 B7
Redby St M11 . . . . 165 B3
Redcar Ave
  Manchester M20 . . . . . 110 B6
  Urmston M41 . . . . 95 A4
Redcar Cl
  Hazel Grove SK7 . . . . . 125 A1
  Oldham OL1 . . . . 49 B1
  Stockport SK7 . . . . 124 B2
Redcar Rd
  Bolton BL1 . . . . 142 B4
  Little Lever BL3 . . . . . . 43 A3
  Pendlebury M27 . . . . . . 80 C7
Redcar St OL12 . . . . 139 B4
Red Cedar Pk BL2 . . . . . 42 D5
Redcliffe Ct M25 . . . . . . 63 B2
Redclyffe Ave M14 . . . . . 98 C3
Redclyffe Rd
  Eccles M41 . . . . 95 D7
  Manchester M20 . . . . . 110 A5
Redcot Ct M45 . . . . 62 C7
Redcote St M40 . . . . 83 A8
Redcourt Ave M20 . . . . 110 B4
Redcroft Gdns **2** M19 . 110 E4
Redcroft Rd M33 . . . . . . 107 E6
Redcross St
  Rochdale OL12 . . . . 14 F1
  Rochdale, Town Head
    OL12 . . . . 139 C4
Redcross Street N OL12 . 14 F1
Reddaway Cl M6 . . . . 81 A5
REDDISH 111 D8
Reddish Cl BL2 . . . . 25 E6
REDDISH GREEN 111 F7
Reddish La
  Lymm WA13 . . . . 117 A5
  Reddish M18, SK5 . . . . . 99 E4
Reddish North Sta SK5 . 99 F2
Reddish Rd SK5 . . . . 111 F5
Reddish South Sta SK5 . 111 E5
Reddish Vale Ctry Pk*
  SK5 . . . . 112 B7
Reddish Vale Nature
  Reserve* SK5 . . . . 112 A5
Reddish Vale Rd SK5 . . . 112 A7
Reddish Vale Tech Coll
  SK5 . . . . 111 F7
Reddy La WA14 . . . . 118 B1
Reddyshore Brow OL15 . 16 C8
Reddyshore Scout Gate
  OL14 . . . . 6 B5
Redesmere Cl
  Altrincham WA15 . . . . . 120 D6
  Droylsden M43 . . . . 84 B1
Redesmere Dr
  Alderley Edge SK9 . . . . 137 A1
  Cheadle SK8 . . . . 132 E7
Redesmere Pk M41 . . . . 107 B8
Redesmere Rd SK9 . . . . 131 D5
Redfearn Wood OL12 . . . 14 B2
Redfern Ave M33 . . . . . . 108 E3
Redfern Cl SK13 . . . . . . 104 A6
Redfern Cotts OL11 . . . . 13 D1
Redfern Ho SK6 . . . . 113 A2
Redfern St M4 . . . . 159 A2
Redfern Way OL11 . . . . . 13 D1
Redfield Cl M11 . . . . 160 C1
Redfield Croft WN7 . . . . . 76 A5
Redford Cl WN7 . . . . 76 A5
Redford Dr SK7 . . . . 124 A2
Redford Rd M8 . . . . 63 D3
Redford St BL8 . . . . 27 C3
Red Gables OL7 . . . . 166 A4
Redgate
  Glossop SK13 . . . . 104 C4
  Hyde SK14 . . . . 113 D8
Redgate La
  Manchester, Longsight
    M12 . . . . 164 C1
  Manchester M12 . . . . . . 99 A4
Redgate Rd M44 . . . . 73 B6
Redgate Way BL4 . . . . . 147 C1
Redgrave Pas OL4 . . . . . 67 D8
Redgrave Rise WN3 . . . . 54 D3
Redgrave St OL4 . . . . . . 67 B8
Redgrave Wlk M19 . . . . . 99 C1
Red Hall St OL4 . . . . 67 C6

Redhill Dr SK6 . . . . 112 E3
Redhill Gr BL1 . . . . 143 B1
Redhill St M4 . . . . 159 C2
Red Hill Way WN2 . . . . . 56 D6
Redhouse La
  Disley SK12 . . . . 135 E7
  Romiley SK6 . . . . 113 A4
Red House La WA14 . . . 118 C8
Redington Cl M28 . . . . . . 78 A5
Redisher Cl BL0 . . . . 10 F3
Redisher Croft BL0 . . . . . 10 F3
Redisher La BL8 . . . . 10 E3
Redisher Wood Nature
  Reserve* 10 F4
Red La
  Bolton BL2 . . . . 25 E1
  Disley SK12 . . . . 135 C5
  Rochdale OL12 . . . . 15 B2
Redland Ave SK5 . . . . . . 111 F5
Redland Cl OL15 . . . . 16 B6
Redland Cres M21 . . . . . 109 B6
Redland Dr M40 . . . . 73 E7
Red Lane Com Sch BL2 . 25 F1
Red Lion St M4 . . . . 159 A2
Red Lodge SK12 . . . . 135 A6
Red Lumb St OL12 . . . . . 13 A3
Redlynch Wlk M8 . . . . . . 156 A3
Redmain Gr WA3 . . . . . . 90 E8
Redmans Cl M30 . . . . . . 79 B1
Redmayne Cl WA12 . . . . 89 B4
Redmere Dr BL9 . . . . 45 A8
Redmere Gr M14 . . . . . . 110 C8
Redmire Mews SK16 . . . 101 F7
Redmires Ct **7** M5 . . . . 81 A1
Redmond Cl M34 . . . . . . 100 E7
Redmoor Sq **3** M13 . . . 163 B3
Rednal Wlk WN3 . . . . . . 150 B2
Red Pike Wlk **2** OL1 . . . 67 A8
Redpol Ave WN7 . . . . . . 76 B5
Redpoll Cl M28 . . . . 78 B7
RED ROCK 37 D8
Red Rock Brow WN1 . . . 37 C8
Red Rock La
  Kearsley M26 . . . . 61 E6
  Standish WN1, WN2 . . . 37 D8
Red Rose Cres M19 . . . . 111 C7
Red Rose Gdns M38 . . . 60 A4
Red Rose Ret Pk M5 . . . 161 B4
Red Rose Wks OL2 . . . . 48 F4
Red Row SK7 . . . . 134 B8
Redruth St M14 . . . . 98 B2
Redruth Wlk **4** OL9 . . . 48 A1
Redscar Wlk M24 . . . . . . 46 E1
Redshank Gr WN7 . . . . . 76 B4
Redshaw Ave BL2 . . . . . . 25 B6
Redshaw Cl M14 . . . . 98 D1
Redstart Cl **7** WA3 . . . . 90 E8
Redstart Gr M28 . . . . 78 D8
Redstock Cl BL5 . . . . 40 B1
Redstone Rd M19 . . . . . 110 D3
Redthorn Ave **2** M19 . . 110 E4
Redthorpe Cl **3** BL2 . . . 25 B1
Redvale Rd M7 . . . . 155 B2
REDVALES 44 E6
Redvales Rd BL9 . . . . 44 E7
Redvers St OL1 . . . . 153 A4
Redwater Cl **9** M28 . . . . 78 A6
Red Waters WN7 . . . . . . 76 A6
Redwing Ctr M17 . . . . . . 96 C6
Redwing Rd BL0 . . . . 10 F2
REDWOOD 54 A5
Redwood
  Chadderton OL9 . . . . . . 65 D7
  Sale M33 . . . . 107 C4
  Shevington WN6 . . . . . . 36 B6
  Westhoughton BL5 . . . . 57 D6
Redwood Ave
  Wigan, Beech Hill WN6 . 36 F3
  Wigan WN5 . . . . 54 A6
Redwood Cl
  Bolton, Darcy Lever BL2 . 42 E5
  Cheadle SK3 . . . . 123 B8
  Rochdale OL12 . . . . 14 B3
Redwood Dr
  Denton M34 . . . . 100 E6
  Manchester M8 . . . . 156 B1
  Rawtenstall BB4 . . . . . . 1 F8
  Romiley SK6 . . . . 112 F3
Redwood Ho M22 . . . . . 109 E1
Redwood La OL4 . . . . . . 67 D7
Redwood Park Gr OL16 . 31 D7
Redwood Rd OL3 . . . . . . 69 C7
Redwood St M6 . . . . 30 B7
Redwood St M6 . . . . 81 A4
Reebok Stad (Bolton
  Wanderers FC) BL6 . . . 39 D7
Reece Ct **4** SK16 . . . . . 101 D8
Reeceton Gdns M23 . . . 144 A3
Reedbank M26 . . . . 62 A8
Reedbank Cl M26 . . . . . . 60 C8
Red Cres WN5 . . . . 55 A4
Reed Ct **8** OL1 . . . . 153 B4
Reedham Cl BL1 . . . . . . 144 C4
Reedham Wlk
  Manchester M40 . . . . . 160 A4
  Oldham OL9 . . . . 66 C4
Reed Hill OL16 . . . . 139 C4
Reedley Dr M28 . . . . 78 C8
Reedmace Cl M28 . . . . . 60 E1
Reedmaker Pl M27 . . . . . 79 E8
Reedshaw Bank SK2 . . . 124 D5
Reedshaw Rd M9 . . . . . . 156 C2
Reedsmere Cl WN5 . . . . 54 F6
Reed St
  Manchester M18 . . . . . . 99 D6

Reed St continued
  9 Oldham OL1 . . . . . . 67 A7
Reedymoor BL5 . . . . 57 E4
Reeman Cl SK4 . . . . 113 A4
Reeman Ct SK9 . . . . 131 B2
Reepham Cl WN3 . . . . . . 54 D3
Reeve Cl SK2 . . . . 124 F5
Reeves Ct M5 . . . . 80 A2
Reeves Rd M21 . . . . 109 B7
Reeves St WN7 . . . . 75 F6
Reeve St WA3 . . . . 91 B8
Reevey Ave SK7 . . . . 124 C2
Reform St OL12 . . . . 139 C4
Reform Wlk M11 . . . . . . 165 B4
Refuge St OL12 . . . . 149 B2
Regaby Gr WN2 . . . . 57 A5
Regal Cl M45 . . . . 63 B8
Regal Fold OL12 . . . . 15 B4
Regal Ind Est M12 . . . . . 165 A3
Regal Wlk M40 . . . . 83 C6
Regan Ave M21 . . . . 109 D7
Regan St
  Bolton BL1 . . . . 143 A3
  8 Radcliffe M26 . . . . . 44 B2
Regatta Cl M9 . . . . 66 A3
Regatta St M6 . . . . 80 C6
Regency Chambers BL9 . 140 B2
Regency Cl
  4 Glossop SK13 . . . . 104 D1
  Manchester M40 . . . . . 157 A1
  Oldham OL8 . . . . 66 D4
Regency Ct
  Altrincham WA15 . . . . . 120 C5
  1 Cheadle SK8 . . . . . 123 A2
  5 Manchester M21 . . 97 A1
  Rochdale OL11 . . . . 29 F7
  Sale M33 . . . . 107 F4
  Stockport SK2 . . . . 124 A6
  Wigan WN1 . . . . 151 A4
Regency Gdns
  Cheadle SK8 . . . . 131 E8
  Hyde SK14 . . . . 167 C4
Regency Ho **4** M1 . . . . 163 A4
Regency Pk SK9 . . . . 63 J3
Regency Pk SK9 . . . . 136 F3
Regency Wharf WN7 . . . 76 C4
Regent Ave
  Ashton-in-M WN4 . . . . . 72 F5
  Manchester M14 . . . . . . 98 A2
  Walkden M38 . . . . 60 C4
Regent Bank SK9 . . . . . . 136 F5
Regent Cl
  Bramhall SK7 . . . . 132 D4
  Cheadle SK8 . . . . 123 C4
  Heywood OL10 . . . . 29 B1
  Wilmslow SK9 . . . . 136 F5
Regent Ct
  Failsworth M35 . . . . 83 E4
  Royton OL2, OL9 . . . . . 48 D2
Regent Ct
  Altrincham WA14 . . . . . 119 D4
  Hale WA15 . . . . 129 C8
  Manchester, Broughton Park
    M7 . . . . 63 D1
  Manchester SK4 . . . . . . 111 C5
Regent Dr
  Bolton BL6 . . . . 40 B7
  Denton M34 . . . . 100 D1
  Leigh WN7 . . . . 76 D7
  Mossley OL5 . . . . 86 D8
Regent Ho M14 . . . . 98 D3
Regent Pl M14 . . . . 98 C4
Regent Ho
  Altrincham WA14 . . . . . 119 D4
  Bolton BL6 . . . . 40 B6
  Platt Bridge WN2 . . . . . 56 A3
  Salford M5 . . . . 81 A1
  Stockport SK2 . . . . 124 A6
Regent Ret Pk M50 . . . . 161 B4
Regents Hill BL6 . . . . 40 C6
Regent Sq M5 . . . . 161 B4
Regent St
  Bury BL9 . . . . 140 C2
  Eccles M30 . . . . 79 F2
  Failsworth M40 . . . . 83 D5
  Glossop, Padfield SK13 . 104 B5
  Glossop SK13 . . . . 104 D1
  Heywood OL10 . . . . 29 B2
  3 Hindley WN2 . . . . . 56 D5
  Littleborough OL15 . . . . 16 B5
  Middleton M24 . . . . 46 F2
  Newton-le-W WA12 . . . 89 A3
  Oldham OL1 . . . . 67 A7
  Ramsbottom BL0 . . . . . 11 A4
  Rochdale OL12, OL16 . . 15 A1
  Shaw OL2 . . . . 149 B3
  Tyldesley M46 . . . . 58 C2
Regents The SK9 . . . . . . 137 C8
Regent Trad Est M5 . . . . 158 A1
Regent Wlk BL4 . . . . 60 D8
Regina Ave SK15 . . . . . . 86 A2
Regina Cres WN7 . . . . . . 76 F5
Regina Ct M6 . . . . 80 A3
Reginald Latham Ct M40 160 A3
Reginald St
  Bolton BL3 . . . . 146 A2
  2 Droylsden M11 . . . . 99 F7
  Eccles M30 . . . . 95 A8
  Swinton M27 . . . . 61 D1
Regional Science Ctr
  OL1 . . . . 153 B2
Reid Cl M34 . . . . 113 A8
Reidys Cl BL8 . . . . 27 B1
Reigate Rd M41 . . . . 106 E8
Reilly St M15 . . . . 162 C2
Reins Lee Ave OL8 . . . . . 67 A2
Reins Lee Rd OL7 . . . . . . 85 A2
Reliance St M40 . . . . 83 C6

Reliance Street Ent Pk [1]
M40.......................83 C6
Reliance Ret Est M40.....83 C6
Rena Ct SK4...............169 A3
Rena Ct SK4...............169 A3
Rendel Cl
Newton-le-W WA12.......89 D2
Stretford M32.............96 D2
Renfrew Cl WN3...........55 A3
Renfrew Dr BL3............40 F3
Renfrew Rd WN2...........38 D5
Rennie Cl M32.............98 E2
Renshaw Ave M40.........79 D1
Renshaw Dr BL9..........141 C3
Renshaw St
Altrincham WA14.........119 E5
Eccles M30................79 D1
Renton Rd
Bolton BL3...............146 B3
Stretford M32............96 E3
Wythenshawe M22........121 D4
Renwick Gr BL3...........146 C3
Renwick Sq WN4...........72 F3
Repton Dr
Droylsden M43............83 D3
Failsworth M40...........65 E1
Hyde SK14................167 B3
Ince-in-M WN3............55 F4
Oldham OL8...............66 D3
Reddish M34..............100 A3
Urmston M41...............94 D2
Repton Cl
Bacup OL13.................4 B8
[6] Sale M33.............107 D3
Reservoir Gdns M28......60 D4
Reservoir Rd SK3.........170 A3
Reservoir St
Aspull WN2................38 F3
Ince-in-M WN2............56 A8
Rochdale OL16............15 C1
Salford M3...............158 B3
Salford, Seedley M6.....154 C2
Residences The M25......63 C3
Restormel Ave WN2.......38 D5
Retford Ave M46..........31 B4
Retford Cl BL8...........27 E5
Retford St OL1...........67 B5
Retiro St OL1...........153 C2
Retreat The
Romiley SK6..............113 C1
Worsley M28..............78 F8
Reuben St SK4...........169 B4
Revers St BL8...........140 A3
Reveton Gn SK7..........124 A2
Rex Bldgs SK9...........137 B6
Rexcine Way SK14........104 B5
Reynard Ct [5] M14......98 E4
Reynard Rd M21..........109 B7
Reynard St SK14.........167 A3
Reynell Rd M13...........98 F2
Reyner St
Ashton-u-L OL6...........85 E2
Manchester M1...........163 A4
Reynolds Cl BL5..........58 F6
Reynolds Dr
Manchester M18...........99 D6
Marple SK6...............126 B8
Over Hulton BL5..........58 F7
Reynolds Mews SK9......137 E8
Reynolds Rd M16.........97 C4
Reynold St SK14.........167 A2
Rhine Cl BL8.............26 F7
Rhine Dr M8.............155 B1
Rhine The [10] M15......162 C3
Rhiwlas Dr BL9...........44 F8
Rhode Hos SK6..........125 F3
RHODES.................64 B7
Rhodes Ave
Haslingden BB4...........1 A7
Oldham OL4...............67 F5
Uppermill OL3............51 C1
Rhodes Bank OL1.........67 A6
Rhodes Bsns Pk M24.....64 C7
Rhodes Cres OL11........30 F3
Rhodes Dr BL9............45 A2
Rhodes Gn M24...........64 B8
Rhodes Hill OL4..........67 F5
Rhodes St
Dukinfield SK14.........101 C3
Glossop SK13............104 B5
Oldham, County End OL4..67 F7
Oldham, Mumps OL1......67 A7
Rochdale OL12............11 B3
Royton OL2...............49 A3
Rhode St BL8.............26 F6
Rhodes Top SK13.........104 B5
Rhodeswood Dr SK13.....104 A6
Rhos Ave
Cheadle SK8.............122 E1
Manchester M14..........110 E8
Middleton M24............65 A7
Rhos Dr SK7.............124 D1
Rhosleigh Ave BL1.......143 B4
Rhyddings The BL9.......28 E7
Rialto Gdns M7..........155 B2
Ribbesford Rd WN3.......54 C4
Ribble Ave
Bolton BL2................42 E7
Chadderton OL9...........47 F1
Littleborough OL15.......15 F6
Ribble Cl WN3...........91 F2
Ribble Cres WN5.........71 C3
Ribble Dr
Boothstown M28...........77 F6
Bury BL9..................27 F8
Kearsley BL4.............61 B5
Whitefield M45...........45 A1
Wigan WN5................54 C7

Ribble Drive Prim Sch
M45......................45 A1
Ribble Gr
Heywood OL10.............29 A3
Leigh WN7................75 C5
Ribblehead Ct M26.......61 C8
Ribble Rd
Oldham OL8...............66 C3
Platt Bridge WN2.........56 A2
Shevington Moor WN6.....19 B2
Ribblesdale Cl OL10......46 D7
Ribblesdale Dr M40......156 C1
Ribblesdale Rd BL3......147 A4
Ribble St
Britannia OL13.............4 A8
Rochdale OL11............30 E4
Ribbleton Cl BL8.........26 F1
Ribble Wlk M43..........100 A8
Ribchester Dr BL1........44 D7
Ribchester Gdns WA3.....92 A3
Ribchester Gr BL2........25 E1
Riber Bank [14] SK13...171 B1
Riber Cl [20] SK13.....171 B1
Riber Fold [18] SK13...171 B1
Riber Gn [19] SK13.....171 B1
Ribston St M15..........162 B2
Rice St M3..............162 B4
Richard Burch St [3] BL9.140 C3
Richard Gwyn Cl BL5.....57 D6
Richard Reynolds Ct
M44.....................105 C6
Richards Cl M34..........100 F6
Richardson Cl M45........44 F1
Richardson Rd M30.......79 E2
Richardson St
[3] Manchester M11......99 E7
Stockport SK1...........124 A7
Richards Rd WN6..........19 B3
Richard St
Ince-in-M WN3...........151 A2
Ramsbottom BL0...........11 E7
Rochdale OL11...........139 C2
Salford M3..............158 A2
Richbell Cl M44.........105 F7
Richborough Cl M7.......155 B1
Richelieu St BL3.........42 A4
Richmond Ave
Chadderton OL9...........66 A4
Handforth SK9...........131 D4
Manchester M25...........63 C1
Royton OL2...............48 D4
Urmston M41..............95 E2
Richmond Cl
Bury BL8.................26 F6
Culcheth WA3.............91 D4
Dukinfield SK16.........101 D6
Glossop SK13...........104 A5
Lymm WA13...............117 B4
Mossley OL5..............86 B8
Rochdale OL16............31 C3
Sale M33................108 F3
Shaw OL2................149 B1
Stalybridge SK15.........86 A1
Standish WN1.............37 B7
Whitefield M45...........62 D7
Richmond Cres OL5.......86 E8
Richmond Ct
Altrincham WA14.........119 B2
Cheadle SK8.............122 C5
Denton M34..............100 E6
Salford M6..............158 A2
Stockport SK2...........124 D5
Richmond Dr
Leigh WN7................76 D7
Lymm WA13..............117 B4
Swinton M28..............79 C8
Richmond Gdns
Bolton BL3................42 B3
Newton-le-W WA12........89 C2
Richmond Gn WA14.......119 B2
Richmond Gr
Bramhall SK7............132 F6
Cheadle SK8.............122 F1
Eccles M30................79 E3
Farnworth BL4............42 A1
Leigh WN7................76 E6
Manchester M13..........98 F1
Richmond Grove E M12...164 B1
Richmond Hill
Hyde SK14...............167 C1
Wigan WN5................54 C6
Richmond Hill Rd SK8...122 C6
Richmond Ho [7] SK15....86 A1
Richmond Pk M14.........98 F1
Richmond Prim Sch OL9..153 A2
Richmond Rd
Altrincham, Rosehill
WA14..................119 C2
Altrincham WA15........119 D5
Ashton-in-M WN4.........72 F5
Boothstown M28..........77 E7
Dukinfield SK16.........101 D6
Eccles M17...............96 A7
Failsworth M35...........84 B8
Hindley WN2...............57 A3
Manchester, Heaton Mersey
SK4.....................110 F2
Manchester M14..........110 D8
Reddish M34.............100 A3
Romiley SK6.............113 C3
Richmond St
Ashton-u-L OL7...........84 F3
Atherton M46.............58 C2
Bury BL9.................44 E8
Denton M34..............100 F6
Droylsden M43............84 C2
Horwich BL6..............22 B3

Richmond St continued
Hyde SK14...............167 B2
Manchester M1...........163 A4
Salford M3..............158 B3
Stalybridge SK15.........86 C2
Wigan WN1...............150 B4
Wigan, Worsley Mesnes
WN3.....................150 A1
Richmond Terr SK6......126 B1
Richmond Wlk
Oldham OL9..............153 A2
Radcliffe M26............43 E6
Ricroft Rd SK6..........114 B3
Riddell Cl M5............80 C2
Ridding Ave M22.........121 E3
Ridding Cl SK2..........124 D6
Riddings Ct WA15.......119 F8
Riddings Rd
Altrincham WA15.........119 F2
Sale WA15...............120 A8
Riders Gate BL9..........28 F4
Ridge Ave
Altrincham WA15.........129 D6
Marple SK6..............126 A4
Standish WN1.............37 B7
Ridge Cl
Glossop SK13............171 B3
Romiley SK6.............113 F2
Ridge Cres
Marple SK6..............126 A3
Whitefield M45...........63 B8
Ridgecroft OL7...........85 B6
Ridgedale Ctr [3] SK6..125 F6
Ridgedales The OL1.......49 E4
Ridge End Fold SK6.....126 A2
Ridgefield M2...........158 C1
Ridgefield St M35........83 E6
Ridge Gr M45.............63 B8
Ridgegreen M28...........78 A5
RIDGE HILL..............86 A4
Ridge Hill La SK15......86 A3
Ridge Hill Prim Sch SK15.85 F3
Ridge La OL3.............51 D5
Ridgemont Ave SK4......168 B2
Ridgemont Wlk [10] M23..108 F2
Ridge Pk SK7............132 D6
Ridge Rd SK6............126 A3
Ridge The SK6...........126 A3
Ridgeway
Golborne WA3.............90 E7
Swinton M27..............62 B2
Wilmslow SK9...........137 F7
Ridgeway Gates [3] BL1..145 C3
Ridgeway Rd WA15.......120 C5
Ridgewell Ave [4] WA3...90 D8
Ridge Wlk M9.............64 B8
Ridgewood Ave
Chadderton OL9...........65 E8
Manchester M40.........157 A1
Ridgewood Cl WN7........57 C3
Ridgmont Cl BL6..........22 F3
Ridgmont Dr
Boothstown M28..........77 F6
Horwich BL6..............22 F3
Ridgmont Rd SK7........132 E5
Ridgway
Disley SK12.............135 C6
Romiley SK6.............113 A1
Riding Cl
Sale M33................108 F4
Tyldesley M29............77 D7
Riding Fold M43..........84 D3
Riding Fold La M28......77 F6
Riding Gate BL2..........25 E6
Riding Gate Mews BL2....25 E6
Riding Head La BL0.......11 F8
Riding La WN4............73 F5
Ridings Cl OL3...........51 A2
Ridings Rd SK13.........103 F5
Ridings St M40..........157 C1
Riding St
Chorley PR6..............21 A7
Manchester M3...........158 B1
Ridings The SK9.........136 D4
Ridings Way OL9.........152 B2
Ridley Dr WA14..........107 E1
Ridley Gr M33...........108 F3
Ridley St OL4............67 A6
Ridley Wlk M15..........163 A1
Ridling La SK14..........167 B3
Ridsdale Ave M20........110 A6
Ridsdale Wlk M6.........81 A5
Ridyard St
Platt Bridge WN2.........56 B3
Walkden M38.............60 C4
Wigan WN5................54 E7
Rifield Cl BL1..........142 B3
Rifle Rd M21,M33........108 F5
Rifle St OL1............153 C4
Riga Rd M14..............98 C1
Riga St M4..............159 A2
Rigby Ave
Blackrod BL6............21 C2
Radcliffe M26............44 C5
Rigby Ct
Bolton BL3..............147 C4
Rochdale OL11............30 E4
Rigby Gr M38.............59 E4
Rigby La BL2.............25 C5
Rigby St
Altrincham WA14.........119 D3
Ashton-in-M WN4..........73 A3
[2] Golborne WA3.........90 A8
Hindley WN2..............56 E6
Salford M7..............155 A2

Rigby's Yd [6] WN5.......54 B6
Rigby Wlk M7............155 B2
Rigel St M3.............159 B2
Rigton Cl M12...........165 A1
Riley Cl M33............107 B1
Riley Ct [3] BL1.........143 C1
Riley La WN7..............38 B7
Riley Sq WN1............151 A4
Riley St M46..............58 A1
Rileywood Cl SK6........112 F1
Rilstone Wlk OL11........57 D8
Rilston Ave WA3..........91 D3
Rimington Ave WA3.......74 C1
Rimington Fold M24......46 D3
Rimmer Cl M11...........160 B1
Rimmington Cl M9.........65 A2
Rimmon Cl OL3...........69 B5
Rimsdale Cl SK8.........122 A3
Rimsdale Dr M40..........83 C8
Rimsdale Wlk BL3.........40 E5
Rimworth Dr M40........159 C4
Rindle Rd M29............93 C8
Ringcroft Gdns M40......65 B1
Ringford Wlk M40........157 B1
RINGLEY................61 D7
Ringley Ave WA3.........73 F1
Ringley Chase M45.......62 E8
Ringley Cl M45...........62 D8
Ringley Cl M27...........80 E8
Ringley Dr M45...........62 D7
RINGLEY FOLD............61 D6
Ringley Gr BL1...........24 E5
Ringley Hey M45.........62 D8
Ringley Mdw M26..........61 C7
Ringley Old Brow M26....61 E8
Ringley Park View M45...62 D8
Ringley Rd
Kearsley, Ringley M26...61 D8
Kearsley, Stoneclough M26.61 D8
Whitefield M45...........62 C7
Ringley Road W M26......61 E8
Ringley St M9...........157 A4
Ringlow Ave M27..........79 C7
Ringlow Park Rd M27.....79 C7
Ring Lows La OL12........15 A4
Ringmer Dr [4] M22.....121 C1
Ringmere Ct [7] OL1....153 B4
Ringmore Rd SK7........124 A2
Rings Cl M35............83 F6
Ringstead Cl SK9.......131 D1
Ringstead Dr
Handforth SK9...........131 D1
Manchester M40.........159 C3
Ringway Ave M7...........75 F8
Ringway Gr M33.........108 E2
Ringway Prim Sch M22...130 D8
Ringway Rd M22,M90......130 D7
Ringway Road W
M90....................130 D8
Ringway Trad Est M22...130 E8
Ringwood Ave
Compstall SK14.........114 A8
Droylsden M34............84 C1
Hazel Grove SK7........124 B1
Hyde SK14...............102 A1
Radcliffe M26............44 B1
Ramsbottom BL0..........11 A4
Ringwood Way OL9........152 C4
Rink St M14.............110 D7
Ripley Ave
Cheadle SK8.............132 B5
Stockport SK2...........124 B4
Ripley Cl
Hazel Grove SK7........133 E8
Manchester M4...........164 A4
Ripley Cres M41..........94 F5
Ripley Dr
Leigh WN7................75 F6
Wigan WN3................54 C4
Ripley St BL2............25 B4
Ripley Way M34..........112 F8
Ripon Ave
Bolton BL2................23 F1
Golborne WA3.............90 D8
[1] Wigan WN6............37 B3
Ripon Cl
Altrincham WA15.........120 C1
Chadderton OL9..........152 B2
Little Lever BL2..........42 F3
Radcliffe M26............44 D5
Stockport SK1...........170 C4
[5] Whitefield M45.......44 F2
Ripon Ct
Ashton-u-L OL6..........166 C3
Manchester M15.........163 A1
Oldham OL1.............153 A4
Ripon Dr
Ashton-in-M WN4..........73 D2
Bolton BL1................23 F1
Ripon Gr M33...........107 F6
Ripon Ho M14.............98 E4
Ripon Rd M32.............95 F3
Ripon St
Ashton-u-L OL6..........166 C3
Manchester M15.........163 A1
Oldham OL1.............153 A4
Rippenden Ave M21.......97 A2
Rippingham Rd M20......110 B7
Rippleton Rd M22........121 E4
Rippon Rd
Denshaw OL3.............33 D3
Oldham OL1,OL4..........49 E3
Ripponden St [10] OL11..49 C1

Rel–Riv 251

Ripton Wlk M9............64 B4
Risbury Wlk [5] M40.....83 C6
Rises The SK13..........103 F5
Rise The
Oldham OL4...............67 F7
Wigan WN6................36 C3
Rishton Ave BL3.........147 C2
Rishton La BL3..........147 C2
Rishworth Cl SK2........124 D5
Rishworth Dr M40........83 E8
Rishworth Rise OL2.......32 A1
Rising La OL8............66 E2
Rising Lane Cl OL8......66 E2
Risings The SK22........127 B1
Risley Ave M9............64 D1
Risley St OL1...........153 B2
Rissington Ave M23.....121 B6
Rita Ave [4] M14........98 B3
Ritson Cl M18...........165 B2
Riva Rd M19.............110 D2
Riverbank OL3.............50 F1
Riverbank Dr BL8........140 A3
Riverbank Gdns BL8......140 A3
Riverbank Lawns M3.....158 B3
Riverbanks BL2..........148 C1
Riverbank The M26.......61 A8
Riverbank Tower M3.....158 B3
Riverbank Way BL3.......116 F7
Riverbrook Rd WA14.....107 C1
Riverdale Cl WN6.........36 D4
Riverdale Rd M9..........64 B3
River La M31............105 F4
Rivermead OL16...........32 B3
Rivermead Ave M34......113 A7
Rivermead Rd M34.......113 B7
Rivermead Way M45......63 A8
Riverpark Rd M40........83 A3
River Pl
Manchester M15.........162 B3
Milnrow OL16............31 F6
Riversdale Ct M25........63 A1
Riversdale Dr OL8........67 A1
Riversdale Rd SK8......122 C5
Riversdale View SK6.....113 A5
Rivers Edge The OL12......4 C1
Rivershill M33..........108 A6
Rivershill Dr OL10.......29 B1
Rivershill Gdns WA15...129 D6
Riverside
Bolton BL1................25 A2
Chadderton OL1...........47 E1
Dukinfield SK16.........166 C1
Salford M7..............158 A3
Riverside Ave
Irlam M44................94 B1
Manchester M21.........109 D3
Wigan WN1................37 D1
Riverside Bsns Pk SK9...137 D7
Riverside Cl SK13.......104 D1
Riverside Ct
Manchester M20.........109 F3
Milnrow OL16..............4 D4
Riverside Dr
Kearsley M26.............61 B8
Ramsbottom BL9..........11 B2
Rochdale OL16............15 C2
Urmston M41..............95 B2
Riverside Gdns M33.....108 A6
Riverside Ho OL3.........69 B8
Riverside Ind Pk SK16..166 C1
Riverside Lodge M20.....109 F3
Riverside Mews M15.....162 B3
Riverside Rd M26.........44 D4
Riverside Wlk BL7.........8 A7
Riverside Works BL2....148 B4
Rivers La M41............95 C5
Riversleigh Cl BL1........23 F3
Riversmeade
Bolton BL7................25 C7
Leigh WN7................76 A6
Rivers St WN5............53 E6
River St
Bolton BL2..............148 A2
Heywood OL10.............29 D3
Manchester, Ardwick M12.163 C4
Manchester M15.........162 C3
Radcliffe M26............44 B2
Ramsbottom BL0..........11 D3
Stockport SK1...........170 B3
Wilmslow SK9...........137 B8
Riverstone Bridge OL15..16 B5
Riverstone Dr M23......120 D7
Riverton Rd M20.........122 B8
Riverview BL4...........110 F1
River View SK5..........112 A7
River View Cl SK14.......62 F2
Riverview Cotts [3] SK13.116 C7
Riverview Ct
Oldham OL5...............68 C1
Salford M7...............81 C8
River View Wlk BL1......145 A2
River Way WN1...........150 C4
Riviera Ct OL12..........13 C2
Rivington Ave
Adlington PR6............21 B7
Golborne WA3.............74 C1
Pendlebury M27...........80 C8
Rivington & Blackrod High
Sch BL6.................22 B6
Rivington Cres M27.......80 C7

Rivington Ct M45 . . . . 62 C7
Rivington Ctry Pk★ BL6 . . 22 A8
Rivington Dr
  Bickershaw WN2 . . . . 74 F8
  Bury BL8 . . . . 27 A1
  Shaw OL2 . . . . 49 D7
  Up Holland WN8 . . . . 53 C7
Rivington Gr
  Droylsden M34 . . . . 100 C8
  Irlam M44 . . . . 105 D6
  Rivington Hall Barn★ BL6 . 22 A8
Rivington Hall Cl BL0 . . . 11 C4
Rivington La
  Adlington PR6 . . . . 21 D6
  Horwich BL6 . . . . 22 A7
Rivington Park Ind Sch
  BL6 . . . . 22 B6
Rivington Pl PR7 . . . . . . 19 D6
Rivington Rd
  Altrincham WA15 . . . . . . 119 F2
  Oldham OL4 . . . . 68 A7
  Salford M6 . . . . 80 C4
Rivington St
  Atherton M46 . . . . 58 B2
  Blackrod BL6 . . . . 21 D2
  Oldham OL1 . . . . 48 F1
  Rochdale OL12 . . . . 14 F1
  Rivington Way WN6 . . . . . 36 F8
  Rivington Wlk M12 . . . . . 164 C11
  Rixson St OL4 . . . . 49 D2
  Rix St BL1 . . . . 143 B2
  Rixton Ct M16 . . . . 97 B3
  Rixton Dr M29 . . . . 77 B8
  Rixtonleys Dr M44 . . . . . . 94 B1
RL Hughes Prim Sch WN4 73 A3
Roach Bank Rd BL9 . . . . . 45 B7
Roach Ct M40 . . . . 159 C3
ROACHES 68 D3
Roaches Ind Est OL5 . . . . 68 B4
Roaches Mews OL5 . . . . . 68 D3
Roaches Way OL5 . . . . . . 68 E3
Roach Gn WN1 . . . . 37 E1
Roachill Cl WA14 . . . . . . 119 B5
Roach Pl OL16 . . . . 31 A8
Roach St
  Bury, Blackford Bridge
    BL9 . . . . 44 F4
  Bury, Heap Bridge BL9 . . . 141 C2
  Roach Vale OL16 . . . . 15 C2
  Roachwood Cl OL9 . . . . . . 65 E7
  Roading Brook Rd BL2 . . . 26 B3
  Road Knowl OL2 . . . . 149 C2
  Road La OL12 . . . . 14 D4
  Roads Ford Ave OL16 . . . . 31 F7
  Roadside Cl WA3 . . . . 90 C8
  Roaring Gate La WA15 . . . 120 E2
Robert Hall St M5 . . . . . 161 B4
Robert Harrison Ave
  M20 . . . . 109 F6
Robert Lawrence Ct M41 . 95 A1
Robert Malcolm Cl M40 . 157 A1
Robert Owen Gdns M22 . 121 D8
Robert Owen St M43 . . . . 84 C2
Robert Salt Ct WA14 . . . . 119 E6
Roberts Ave M14 . . . . 98 B4
Robert Saville Ct OL11 . . 30 C6
Robertscroft Cl M22 . . . . 121 C3
Robertshaw Ave M21 . . . 109 B6
Robertshaw St WN7 . . . . 75 E7
Robertson St M26 . . . . . . 44 A4
Roberts St M30 . . . . 79 D1
Robert St
  Bolton BL2 . . . . 25 E5
  Bury BL8 . . . . 27 C3
  Dukinfield, Kingston SK14 101 C3
  Dukinfield SK16 . . . . 101 B8
  ⑨ Failsworth M35 . . . . . . 66 A1
  ⑨ Heywood OL10 . . . . . . 46 E8
  Manchester M3 . . . . 158 C3
  Oldham OL8 . . . . 66 B3
  Platt Bridge WN2 . . . . 56 A3
  Prestwich M25 . . . . 63 C4
  Radcliffe M26 . . . . 44 A4
  Ramsbottom BL0 . . . . 1 C1
  ⑩ Rochdale OL16 . . . . . . 31 A8
  Sale M33 . . . . 108 E4
  Tyldesley M46 . . . . 58 E1
  Robeson Way M22, SK8 . . 121 F6
  Robe Wlk ⑤ M18 . . . . 99 D6
Robin Cl
  Bramhall SK7 . . . . 132 E7
  Droylsden M43 . . . . 84 C3
  Robins La WA3 . . . . 91 D2
Robin's La
  Billinge WA11 . . . . 71 A8
  Bramhall SK7 . . . . 132 D7
Robinson Pk SK15 . . . . . 85 E1
Robinson's Cl OL6 . . . . . 166 B4

Robinson St
  Chadderton OL9 . . . . 152 B2
  Dukinfield SK15 . . . . 101 E8
  ⑮ Horwich BL6 . . . . 22 B4
  Hyde SK14 . . . . 167 C3
  Leigh WN7 . . . . 76 A4
  Rochdale OL16 . . . . 31 A7
  Stockport SK3 . . . . 170 A3
  ⑱ Tyldesley M29 . . . . 59 A1
Robinsway WA14 . . . . . . 119 C1
Robinswood Rd M22 . . . . 121 D2
Robinwood Lodge ⑱
  SK13 . . . . 171 B1
Rob La WA12 . . . . 89 E5
Robson Ave M41 . . . . 95 E7
Robson Pl WN2 . . . . 74 B8
Robson St OL1 . . . . 153 C2
Robson Way ⑧ WA3 . . . . 90 F8
Roby Ct M1 . . . . 159 B1
ROBY MILL 35 B3
Roby Mill WN8 . . . . 35 B3
Roby Mill CE Prim Sch
  WN8 . . . . 35 B3
Roby Rd M30 . . . . 95 C8
Roby St M1 . . . . 159 B1
Roby Well Way WN5 . . . . 71 D5
Roch Ave OL10 . . . . 29 A2
Roch Bank M9 . . . . 63 F3
Rochbury Cl OL11 . . . . . . 29 F6
Roch Cl M45 . . . . 45 B1
Roch Cres M45 . . . . 45 C1
ROCHDALE 139 A3
  Rochdale Canal★ OL16 . . 31 C6
Rochdale Exchange Sh Ctr
  OL16 . . . . 139 C3
Rochdale Girls Sch ㉗
  OL12 . . . . 14 F1
Rochdale Ho M15 . . . . . . 162 B3
Rochdale Infmy OL12 . . . 14 F1
Rochdale La
  Heywood OL10 . . . . 29 D2
  Royton OL2 . . . . 48 D5
Rochdale Metro Sta
  OL16 . . . . 139 C2
Rochdale Old Rd BL9 . . . 28 D4
  Rochdale Pioneers Mus★
  OL12 . . . . 139 C4
Rochdale Rd
  Britannia OL13 . . . . 4 B8
  Bury BL9 . . . . 141 B2
  Denshaw OL3 . . . . 33 B3
  Edenfield BL0 . . . . 1 F2
  Heywood OL10 . . . . 29 C2
  Littleborough OL15, HX6 . . 7 E1
  Manchester, Collyhurst M40, M8,
    M9 . . . . 157 A2
  Manchester M9 . . . . 64 D3
  Middleton M24, OL11 . . . . 47 C4
  Milnrow OL16 . . . . 31 E7
  Oldham, Cold Hurst OL1 . . 153 B4
  Oldham OL1 . . . . 48 E1
  Ramsbottom BL0 . . . . 12 B7
  Royton OL2 . . . . 48 D6
  Shaw, High Crompton OL2,
    OL16 . . . . 48 F8
  Shaw OL2 . . . . 149 B3
  Walsden OL14 . . . . 6 B6
Rochdale Road E OL10 . . 29 F3
Rochdale Sta OL11 . . . . 139 C2
Roche Gdns SK8 . . . . . . 132 B6
Roche Rd OL3 . . . . 50 E5
  Rocher Vale Nature
    Reserve★ OL6 . . . . . . 67 C2
Rochester Ave
  Bolton BL2 . . . . 25 E1
  Manchester M21 . . . . . . 109 D6
  Manchester, Sedgley Park
    M25 . . . . 63 C2
  Walkden M28 . . . . 60 C1
Rochester Cl
  Ashton-u-L SK16 . . . . 85 C7
  Dukinfield SK16 . . . . 102 A7
  Golborne WA3 . . . . 90 A8
Rochester Dr WA14 . . . . 107 E1
Rochester Gr SK7 . . . . . 124 E3
Rochester Rd M41 . . . . . . 95 D4
Rochester Way OL9 . . . . 152 B2
Rochford Ave M45 . . . . . . 62 D7
Rochford Cl M45 . . . . 62 D7
Rochford Ho M34 . . . . . . 100 E6
Rochford Rd M30 . . . . 94 F8
Roch Mills Cres OL11 . . . 30 C5
Roch Mills Gdns OL11 . . 139 A1
Roch Pl WN2 . . . . 55 F2
Roch St OL16 . . . . 15 B1
Roch Valley Way OL11 . . 30 C5
Roch Way M45 . . . . 45 B1
Roch Wlk M45 . . . . 45 B1
Rockall Wlk M11 . . . . . . 160 C1
Rock Ave BL1 . . . . 142 C2
  Rockbourne Cl ⑥ WN2 . . . 56 D4
Rockdove Ave M15 . . . . . 162 C3
Rocket Way M3 . . . . 158 A1
Rockfield Dr ⑧ M9 . . . . 157 B4
Rock Fold BL7 . . . . 8 F1
Rock Gdns SK14 . . . . . . 113 E7
Rockhampton St M18 . . . 99 E5
Rockhaven Ave BL6 . . . . . 22 C4
Rockhouse Cl M30 . . . . . 95 C8
Rockingham Cl
  Manchester M12 . . . . . . 164 A2
  Shaw OL2 . . . . 48 E8
  Rockingham Dr WN2 . . . . 57 A3
Rockland Wlk ⑥ M40 . . . 65 C2
Rockley Gdns M6 . . . . . . 81 B4
Rocklyn Ave M40 . . . . 65 C2
Rocklynes SK6 . . . . 113 B2
Rockmead Dr M9 . . . . 64 E3

Rock Nook OL15 . . . . 6 D1
Rock Rd
  Urmston M41 . . . . 95 F2
  Worsley M28 . . . . 78 B2
  Rock Sh Ctr The BL9 . . . . 140 C2
Rock St
  Ashton-u-L OL7 . . . . 85 A5
  Droylsden M11 . . . . 99 E8
  Golborne WA3 . . . . 74 A2
  ⑧ Heywood OL10 . . . . . . 29 E1
  Horwich BL6 . . . . 22 B3
  Hyde SK14 . . . . 113 E7
  Oldham OL1 . . . . 153 C3
  Radcliffe M26 . . . . 44 B2
  Ramsbottom BL0 . . . . 11 E7
  Salford M7 . . . . 155 A2
Rock Terr
  Bolton BL7 . . . . 8 F1
  Mossley OL5 . . . . 68 D3
  Rock The BL7 . . . . 140 C2
Rocky Bank Terr WN3 . . 151 B1
Rocky La M27, M30 . . . . . 79 D4
Roda St M9 . . . . 157 C3
Rodborough Rd M23 . . . 121 A3
Rodeheath Cl SK9 . . . . . 137 D7
Rodenhurst Dr ⑲ M40 . . 83 A7
Rodepool Cl SK9 . . . . . . 131 D2
Rodgers Cl BL5 . . . . 57 E6
Rodgers Way BL5 . . . . . . 57 E6
Rodmell Ave M40 . . . . . . 157 A1
Rodmell Cl BL7 . . . . 24 F7
Rodmill Ct M14 . . . . 98 C1
Rodmill Dr SK8 . . . . 122 A4
Rodney Ct ⑦ M4 . . . . . . 159 C3
Rodney Dr SK6 . . . . 113 A5
  Rodney House Sch M19 . 110 F8
Rodney St
  Ashton-u-L OL6 . . . . 85 D4
  Atherton M46 . . . . 58 C2
  Manchester M4 . . . . 159 C2
  Rochdale OL11 . . . . 30 B2
  Salford M3 . . . . 158 A1
  Wigan WN1 . . . . 150 C3
  Roeacre Bsns Pk OL10 . . 29 E2
Roeacre St OL10 . . . . . . 29 E2
Roebuck Gdns ⑬ M33 . . 108 A4
Roebuck La
  Oldham OL4 . . . . 50 A3
  Sale M33 . . . . 108 A4
  Roebuck Low OL4 . . . . . . 50 A3
  Roebuck St WN2 . . . . 57 C3
  Roeburn Wlk M45 . . . . . . 63 C8
  Roecliffe Cl WN3 . . . . . . 150 B2
  Roe Cross Gn SK14 . . . . 102 F5
  Roe Cross Ind Est SK14 . 103 A5
  Roe Cross Rd SK14, SK15 . 102 F5
  Roedean Gdns M41 . . . . . 94 D2
  Roefield Terr OL12 . . . . . . 30 A8
  Roe Gn M28 . . . . 79 A8
  Roe Green Ave M28 . . . . . 79 A8
ROE GREEN 79 A8
  Roe La OL4 . . . . 67 D5
Roe St
  Manchester M4 . . . . 159 C3
  Rochdale OL12 . . . . 14 C1
  Rogate Dr M23 . . . . 121 A5
  Roger Byrne Cl M40 . . . . . 83 B5
  Roger Cl SK6 . . . . 112 F2
  Roger Hay ⑥ SK8 . . . . . . 123 A2
  Rogerson Cl WA15 . . . . . 120 C7
  Roger St M8 . . . . 159 A3
  Rogerstead BL3 . . . . . . 144 C2
  Rogerton Cl WN7 . . . . 76 B4
  Rok Ct M34 . . . . 100 C3
Rokeby Ave
  Golborne WA3 . . . . 74 D1
  Stretford M32 . . . . 96 D1
  Rokeden WA12 . . . . 89 D4
  Roker Ave M13 . . . . 98 F2
  Roker Ind Est OL1 . . . . . . 67 B7
  Roker Park Ave M34 . . . . 100 D7
Roland Rd
  ② Bolton BL3 . . . . 146 C4
  Reddish SK5 . . . . 111 F7
Rolla St M3 . . . . 158 B2
Rollesby Cl BL8 . . . . 27 D5
Rolleston Ave M40 . . . . . 160 A2
Rollins La SK6 . . . . 114 A1
Rolls Cres M15 . . . . 162 B1
Rollswood Dr M40 . . . . . . 83 A6
Romana Sq WA14 . . . . . 119 E8
Roman Cl
  Newton-le-W WA12 . . . . . 89 C2
  Wigan WN3 . . . . 54 F4
  Roman Ct M47 . . . . 155 A1
Roman Rd
  Ashton-in-M WN4 . . . . . . 73 A5
  Manchester M25 . . . . 63 A1
  Oldham M35, OL8 . . . . . . 66 B3
  Royton OL2 . . . . 48 E3
  Stockport SK4 . . . . 169 B2
Roman St
  Ashton-u-L OL7 . . . . 166 A1
  Manchester M4 . . . . 159 A2
  Mossley OL5 . . . . 68 D3
  ④ Radcliffe M26 . . . . 43 E3
  Romer Ave ③ M40 . . . . . . 65 E1
  Rome Rd M40 . . . . 159 C3
  Romer St BL2 . . . . 148 C3
Romford Ave
  Denton M34 . . . . 101 A4
  Leigh WN7 . . . . 75 F6
  Romford Cl OL8 . . . . 153 B1
  Romford Pl WN2 . . . . 56 E5
  Romford Rd M33 . . . . . . 107 E6
  Romford St WN2 . . . . 56 E5
  Romford Wlk M9 . . . . 64 A3
ROMILEY 113 D2

Romiley Cres BL2 . . . . . . 42 D8
Romiley Dr BL2 . . . . 42 D8
Romiley Prec SK6 . . . . . 113 C2
Romiley Prim Sch SK6 . . 113 C2
Romiley Sq WN6 . . . . 36 E8
Romiley St
  Salford M6 . . . . 80 D5
  Stockport SK1 . . . . 112 B3
  Romiley Sta SK6 . . . . . . 113 C2
Romley Rd M41 . . . . 95 D4
Romney Ave OL11 . . . . . . 30 F2
Romney Chase BL1 . . . . 143 B4
Romney Rd BL1 . . . . 23 E2
Romney St
  Ashton-u-L OL6 . . . . 166 C3
  Manchester M40 . . . . 83 A8
  Salford M6 . . . . 81 B5
  Romney Twrs SK5 . . . . . . 112 B6
Romney Way
  Brinnington SK5 . . . . . . 112 B6
  Wigan WN1 . . . . 37 B3
Romney Wlk OL9 . . . . . . 152 B2
Romsey ⑫ OL12 . . . . . . 139 B4
Romsey Ave M24 . . . . . . 46 F3
Romsey Dr SK8 . . . . 132 C6
Romsey Gdns M23 . . . . . 121 A6
Romsey Gr WN3 . . . . 54 D2
Romsey Cl M12 . . . . 165 A2
Romsley Dr BL3 . . . . 146 C3
Rona Cl M12 . . . . 164 C1
Ronaldsay Gdns M5 . . . . 154 B1
Ronald St
  Droylsden M11, M43 . . . . 83 D1
  Oldham OL4 . . . . 67 C7
  Rochdale OL11 . . . . 30 C1
Ronan Ct SK4 . . . . 168 B4
Rondin Cl M12 . . . . 164 B3
Rondin Rd M12 . . . . 164 B3
Ronnis Mount OL7 . . . . . 85 A7
Ronton Wlk M8 . . . . 156 C4
Roocroft Ct BL1 . . . . 143 A1
Roocroft Sq BL6 . . . . 21 C2
Rooden Ct M25 . . . . 63 C4
Roods La OL1 . . . . 13 C1
Rookery Ave
  Appley Bridge WN6 . . . . . 35 E8
  Ashton-in-M WN4 . . . . . . 73 B2
  Droylsden M18 . . . . 99 F6
Rookery Cl SK15 . . . . . . 102 E7
Rookerypool Cl SK9 . . . 131 D2
Rookery The WA12 . . . . . 89 D4
Rooke St M30 . . . . 95 A8
Rookfield M33 . . . . 108 C5
Rookfield Ave M33 . . . . . 108 C5
Rookley Wlk ⑪ M14 . . . . 98 C3
Rook St
  Manchester M15 . . . . . . 162 B1
  Oldham OL4 . . . . 67 C5
  Ramsbottom BL0 . . . . . . 138 C2
Rookswood Dr OL11 . . . . 30 B3
Rookway M24 . . . . 65 A7
Rookwood OL11, OL9 . . . 47 E1
Rookwood Ave M23 . . . . 120 F7
Rookwood Hill SK7 . . . . 123 E1
Rooley Moor Rd
  Bacup OL12, OL13 . . . . . . 3 C4
  Rochdale OL12 . . . . 14 A3
  Rochdale, Spotland Fold
    OL12 . . . . 14 C1
  Rooley St OL11 & OL12 . . 14 C1
  Roosevelt Rd BL4 . . . . . . 60 F7
  Rooth St SK4 . . . . 169 A2
  Ropefield Way OL12 . . . . . 14 E3
  Rope St M12 . . . . 139 C4
  Rope Wlk M3 . . . . 158 B3
  Ropeworks The ⑫ M15 . 162 C3
  Ropley Wlk ④ M9 . . . . . . 64 F1
  Rosa Gr M7 . . . . 155 A2
  Rosalind Ct M5 . . . . 154 C1
  Rosamond Dr M3 . . . . . 158 A2
  Rosamond St BL3 . . . . . 146 C4
  Rosamond Street W M13,
    M15 . . . . 163 A2
  Rosary Cl OL8 . . . . 66 F2
  Rosary Rd OL8 . . . . 67 A1
  Roscoe Ave WA12 . . . . . . 89 E3
  Roscoe Cl BL5 . . . . 57 F7
  Roscoe Lowe Brow PR6 . . 21 D7
  Roscoe Rd M44 . . . . 93 E1
Roscoe St
  Oldham OL1 . . . . 67 A6
  Stockport SK3 . . . . 170 A4
  Wigan WN1 . . . . 151 B3
  Roscow Ave BL2 . . . . 42 E8
  Roscow Rd BL4 . . . . 61 A7
  Rose Acre M28 . . . . 78 B7
  Roseacre Cl BL2 . . . . . . 148 C4
  Roseacre Dr SK8 . . . . . . 122 C1
Rose Ave
  Abram Brow WN2 . . . . . . 74 B7
  Farnworth BL4 . . . . 42 C1
  Irlam M44 . . . . 93 F1
  Littleborough OL15 . . . . . 15 F3
  Rochdale OL11 . . . . 13 D2
  Wigan WN6 . . . . 37 A4
Rosebank
  Bolton BL3 . . . . 40 C7
  Edenfield BL0 . . . . 1 C1
  Rosebank Cl BL2 . . . . 26 C1
Rose Bank Cl
  Hollingworth SK14 . . . . 103 D5
  Wigan WN1 . . . . 37 B4
Rosebank Rd
  Failsworth M40 . . . . 83 B4
  Irlam M44 . . . . 105 C4
  Rosebay Cl OL2 . . . . 48 F4
  Roseberry Ave ④ OL1 . . . 49 B1
  Roseberry Cl BL1 . . . . 11 C3

Roseberry Rd WN4 . . . . . 73 A5
Roseberry St
  Bolton BL3 . . . . 146 C4
  Oldham OL8 . . . . 153 A2
  Stockport SK2 . . . . 124 D4
Rosebery St
  Manchester M14 . . . . 97 F3
  Westhoughton BL5 . . . . . . 57 F8
ROSE BRIDGE 151 C4
  Rosebridge Ct WN1 . . . . 151 C3
  Rose Bridge High Sch
    WN1 . . . . 151 C4
  Rosebridge Way WN1 . . . 151 C3
Rosebury St M5 . . . . 81 B5
Rose Cottage Rd M14,
  M20 . . . . 110 B8
  Rose Cotts ⑫ M14 . . . . 110 D8
  Rose Cres M44 . . . . 93 F1
  Rosecroft Cl SK3 . . . . . . 123 E4
  Rose Ct WN1 . . . . 151 C4
Rosedale Ave
  Atherton M46 . . . . 58 D3
  Bolton BL1 . . . . 24 E5
  Golborne WA3 . . . . 90 C7
  Rosedale Cl OL1 . . . . 49 B1
  Rosedale Ct M34 . . . . . . 100 E3
  Rosedale Dr WN7 . . . . . . 76 C5
Rosedale Rd
  Manchester M14 . . . . 98 A2
  Reddish SK4 . . . . 169 A4
  Rosedale Sh Ctr ⑳ M40 . 83 C5
  Rosedale Way SK16 . . . . 101 C6
  Rosefield Cl SK3 . . . . . . 170 B1
  Rosefield Cres OL16 . . . . 31 C7
  Rosefinch Dr M44 . . . . . . 94 B1
  Rosegarth Ave M20 . . . . 109 D4
Rose Gr
  Bury BL8 . . . . 27 A2
  Kearsley BL4 . . . . 60 F7
  Rosehay Ave M34 . . . . . 100 F2
  Rose Hey La M35 . . . . 83 E4
ROSEHILL 119 C2
ROSE HILL
  Ashton-in-Makerfield 72 F7
  Bolton 148 A1
Rose Hill
  Bolton BL2 . . . . 148 A1
  Delph OL3 . . . . 50 F4
  Denton M34 . . . . 100 E3
  Ramsbottom BL0 . . . . . . 138 B2
  Stalybridge SK15 . . . . . . 102 A8
Rose Hill Ave
  Failsworth M40 . . . . 83 B4
  Wigan WN5 . . . . 54 C6
  Rosehill Cl M6 . . . . 154 C2
Rose Hill Cl
  Ashton-u-L OL6 . . . . 85 F5
  Bolton BL7 . . . . 25 A7
  Rose Hill Cres OL6 . . . . . 85 F5
Rosehill Ct
  Oldham OL4 . . . . 67 E8
  Salford M6 . . . . 154 C2
  Rose Hill Dr BL7 . . . . 25 A7
  Rose Hill Marple Sta
    SK6 . . . . 125 E6
  Rosehill Methodist Com Prim
    Sch OL6 . . . . 85 E6
  Rose Hill Prim Sch SK6 . 125 E6
  Rosehill Rd M27 . . . . 61 F2
  Rose Hill Rd OL6 . . . . 85 F5
  Rose Hill St OL10 . . . . . . 29 B2
  Rose Hill View WN4 . . . . . 72 F7
  Rose La SK6 . . . . 125 E6
  Roseland Ave M20 . . . . . 110 B4
  Roseland Dr M25 . . . . 63 C6
  Roselands Ave M33 . . . . 107 F2
  Rose Lea BL2 . . . . 25 E4
  Roseleigh SK4 . . . . 111 C5
  Rose Leigh M41 . . . . 95 D2
  Roseleigh Ave M19 . . . . 110 F7
  Rosemary Cres WN1 . . . . 37 D2
Rosemary Dr
  Hyde SK14 . . . . 113 D7
  Littleborough OL15 . . . . . 15 F6
  Newton-le-W WA12 . . . . . 89 F3
  Rosemary Gr M7 . . . . 81 C5
Rosemary La
  Over Hulton BL5 . . . . 59 B6
  Stockport SK1 . . . . 112 A1
  Rosemary Rd OL9 . . . . . . 65 E8
  Rosemary Wlk M31 . . . . 105 F2
  Rosemead Ct ⑤ SK5 . . . 111 F6
  Rosemount M24 . . . . . . 101 D5
  Rosemount Ave M44 . . . . 46 F2
  Rosemount Cres SK14 . . 101 D5
  Roseneath SK7 . . . . 123 D1
  Roseneath Ave M19 . . . . . 99 C1
  Roseneath Gr BL3 . . . . . 147 A3
Roseneath Rd
  Bolton BL3 . . . . 147 A3
  Urmston M41 . . . . 95 C2
  Rosen Sq OL9 . . . . 152 B3
Rose St
  Bolton BL2 . . . . 148 A1
  Chadderton OL9 . . . . 66 A3
  Hindley WN2 . . . . 56 D5
  Middleton M24 . . . . 65 C8
  Reddish SK5 . . . . 169 C2
  Wigan WN1 . . . . 151 C4
  Rose Terr SK15 . . . . 86 A1
  Rose Thorns Cl M24 . . . . . 64 F4
  Rosette Wlk ⑧ M27 . . . . . 79 F7
  Rose Vale SK8 . . . . 122 B1
  Rosevale Ave M19 . . . . . 110 E5
  Rosevale Cl ⑫ WN2 . . . . . 56 D4
  Roseville Mews M33 . . . 108 B4
  Roseway SK7 . . . . 123 F2
  Rosewell Cl M40 . . . . . . 160 A4

Rose Wlk
Marple SK6 . . . . 125 E6
5 Partington M31 . . . . . 105 E3
Rosewood
Hyde SK14 . . . . 103 D5
Rochdale OL11. . . . . 13 E1
Westhoughton BL5 . . . . . 57 D6
Rose Wood M34 . . . . 100 D3
Rosewood Ave
Bury BL8 . . . . 27 A6
Droylsden M43. . . . . 84 C3
Stockport SK4 . . . . 168 A1
Rosewood Cl
Abram Brow WN2 . . . . . . 74 B7
Dukinfield SK16. . . . . . . 101 D6
Rosewood Cres OL9. . . . . 48 B1
Rosewood Ct
Salford M6 . . . . 124 C5
Rosewood Gdns
6 Sale M33 . . . . 108 F3
Wythenshawe SK8 . . . . . 121 F6
Rosewood Rd M9 . . . . . . 64 E5
Rosewood Wlk M23 . . . . 120 C8
Rosford Ave M14 . . . . . . 98 B2
Rosgill Cl SK4 . . . . 110 E2
Rosgill Dr M24 . . . . 46 D1
Rosgill Wlk M18 . . . . . . 165 C1
Rosina Cl WN4 . . . . 72 F6
Rosina St M11 . . . . 99 F7
Rosley Rd M9 . . . . 55 B3
Roslin Gdns BL1 . . . . . . 142 C3
Roslin St M11. . . . . 83 D2
Roslyn Ave M41. . . . . . . 94 E1
Roslyn Rd SK3. . . . . 170 B1
Rossall Ave
5 Radcliffe M26. . . . . . . 44 C1
Stretford M32 . . . . 96 C3
Rossall Cl BL2 . . . . 148 C4
Rossall Cres WN7 . . . . . . 76 A3
Rossall Dr SK7. . . . . 132 E6
Rossall Rd
Bolton BL2 . . . . 148 C4
Rochdale OL12. . . . . 15 A2
Rossall St 1 BL2 . . . . . . 148 C4
Rossall Way M6. . . . . . . 81 A3
Ross Ave
Manchester M19 . . . . . . 98 F1
Oldham OL9 . . . . 65 F4
Stockport SK3 . . . . 170 B1
Whitefield M45 . . . . 62 F6
Ross Cl
Billinge WN5 . . . . 71 E6
Wigan WN2 . . . . 37 F2
Rossdale Gr WN6 . . . . . . 37 A2
Ross Dr M27. . . . . 61 E4
Rossenclough Rd SK9 . . 131 D1
Rossendale Ave 3 M9 . . 64 F1
Rossendale Cl OL2 . . . . . 49 D7
Rossendale Rd SK8 . . . . 131 C8
Rossendale Sch BL0 . . . . 12 A7
Rossendale Way OL2 . . . 149 B4
Rossett Ave
Sale WA15. . . . . 120 A8
1 Wythenshawe M22. . . 130 D8
Rossett Cl WN3 . . . . 54 D2
Rossett Dr M41 . . . . 95 A4
Rossetti Wlk 2 M34 . . . . 113 A7
Ross Gr M41. . . . . 95 C2
Rosshill Wlk 20 M15 . . . 162 A2
Rossington St M40. . . . . 83 D5
Rossini St BL1 . . . . 143 A3
Rosslare Rd M22. . . . . . . 121 E2
Ross Lave La M34. . . . . . 100 C1
Rosslave Wlk SK5. . . . . . 112 C7
Rosslyn Gr WA15. . . . . . 120 A6
Rosslyn Rd
Cheadle SK8 . . . . 122 D1
Manchester M16 . . . . . . 97 A2
Manchester, Moston M40 . . 65 A1
Rossmere Ave OL11 . . . . 30 C6
Rossmill La WA15. . . . . . 129 B7
Ross St OL8 . . . . 153 A1
Rostherne Ave
Golborne WA3 . . . . 90 D8
High Lane SK6 . . . . 134 E8
Manchester, Fallowfield
M14. . . . . 98 A1
Manchester, Old Trafford
M16. . . . . 97 C3
Rostherne Ct 8 WA14. . . 119 D3
Rostherne Gdns BL3 . . . 146 B4
Rostherne Rd
Sale M33 . . . . 108 F3
Stockport SK3 . . . . 170 B1
Wilmslow SK9 . . . . 136 F4
Rostherne St
1 Altrincham WA14. . . . 119 D3
1 Salford M6 . . . . 154 B1
Rosthermere Rd SK8. . . . 122 F4
Rosthwaite Cl
Middleton M24. . . . . 46 C1
Wigan WN3 . . . . 55 A2
Rosthwaite Gr WA11 . . . 71 B1
Roston Ct M7. . . . . 155 B4
Roston Rd M7 . . . . 155 B4
Rostrevor Rd SK3 . . . . . 170 B1
Rostron Ave M12 . . . . . . 164 B2
Rostron Rd BL0 . . . . 138 B2
Rostron St 6 M19 . . . . . 99 B1
Rothay Cl
Bolton BL2. . . . . 148 A4
Prestwich M45. . . . . 63 C8
Rothay Dr
Middleton M24. . . . . 46 E3
Reddish SK5. . . . . 111 F8
Rothay St M9 . . . . 76 B4
Rothbury Ave WN7. . . . . 84 E5
Rothbury Cl BL8 . . . . 26 F2

Rothbury Ct BL3 . . . . . . 146 B3
Rotherby Rd M22 . . . . . . 121 E5
Rotherdale Ave WA15 . . 120 D5
Rotherhead Cl BL6. . . . . 21 F2
Rothermere Wlk 5 M23. 120 E7
Rotherwood Ave M32 . . . 96 E3
Rotherwood Rd SK9. . . . 136 D6
Rothesay Ave SK16. . . . . 101 C7
Rothesay Cres M33 . . . . 107 C2
Rothesay Rd
Bolton BL3. . . . . 146 B3
Manchester M8 . . . . 63 E2
Oldham OL1. . . . . 49 C1
Pendlebury M27. . . . . . . 80 C7
Rothesay Terr OL16 . . . . 31 C4
Rothiemay Rd M41 . . . . . 94 E2
Rothley Ave M22. . . . . . . 121 D5
Rothman Cl M40. . . . . . . 83 C6
Rothwell Cres M38 . . . . . 59 E5
Rothwell La M38. . . . . . . 59 E5
Rothwell Rd
Adlington PR6 . . . . 21 B7
Golborne WA3 . . . . 74 C1
Rothwell St
Bolton BL3. . . . . 145 B1
Failsworth M35 . . . . 83 F7
Failsworth, Newton Heath
M40. . . . . 83 C6
Ramsbottom BL0 . . . . . . 138 B2
Rochdale OL12. . . . . 15 B1
Royton OL2 . . . . 48 D3
Walkden M28. . . . . 60 F3
Rottingdene Dr 3 M22. . 121 C1
Roughey Gdns M22 . . . . 121 D4
Rough Hill La BL9 . . . . . . 28 A8
Roughlea Ave WA3. . . . . 91 D4
Roughlee Ave M27. . . . . 79 D7
Roughtown Rd OL5 . . . . . 68 D2
Roundcroft SK6. . . . . . . 113 E3
Round Hey OL5 . . . . 86 C8
Round Hill Cl SK13. . . . . 171 C3
Roundhill Way OL4. . . . . 49 E1
Round House Ave WN1. . 37 C1
Roundmoor Rd WN6 . . . 37 A7
ROUNDTHORN 37 E4
Roundthorn Bsns Pk
M23. . . . . 120 E5
Roundthorn Ct M23 . . . . 120 F7
Roundthorn Ind Est M23 120 E6
Roundthorn La BL5 . . . . . 57 E7
Roundthorn Prim Sch
OL4. . . . . 67 C5
Roundthorn Rd
Middleton M24. . . . . 65 B7
Oldham OL4. . . . . 67 C5
Wythenshawe M23. . . . . 120 F6
Roundthorn Wlk 8 M23. 120 F6
Roundway SK7. . . . . 132 D6
Roundwood Rd M22. . . . 121 D7
Rousdon Cl M40 . . . . . . 157 A1
Rouse Cl M11. . . . . 160 C1
Rouse St OL11 . . . . 30 C4
Routledge Wlk M9 . . . . . 157 D4
Roving Bridge Rise M27. 80 D8
Rowan Ave
Golborne WA3 . . . . 90 F7
2 Horwich BL6. . . . . 22 E1
Manchester M16 . . . . . . 97 D3
Sale M33 . . . . 108 C2
Urmston M41. . . . . 95 D3
Wigan WN6 . . . . 36 F3
Rowan Cl
Failsworth M35 . . . . 83 F6
Rochdale OL12. . . . . 14 B3
Rowan Cres SK16. . . . . . 101 F7
Rowan Ct
Hyde SK14 . . . . 167 B1
Manchester M14 . . . . . . 110 D7
Wilmslow SK9 . . . . 137 B7
Rowan Dr
Bury BL9 . . . . 141 B3
Cheadle SK8 . . . . 132 C8
Rowanhill WN1 . . . . 37 D1
Rowan Lo SK7 . . . . 132 F7
Rowan Pl M25 . . . . 63 B3
Rowan St SK15. . . . . 86 C3
Rowanside Dr SK9 . . . . . 137 E8
Rowans St BL8. . . . . 27 C4
Rowan St SK14. . . . . 167 C1
Rowans The
6 Adlington PR6. . . . . . 21 A8
Bolton BL1. . . . . 40 F7
Mossley OL5 . . . . 68 D1
Rowanswood Dr SK14. . 102 A3
Rowan Tree Dr M33. . . . 108 B1
Rowan Tree Rd
Oldham OL8. . . . . 66 D1
Paddockhill WA16. . . . . 136 B5
Rowan Way M7. . . . . 155 A3
Rowan Wlk
Glossop SK13. . . . . 171 B4
Partington M31 . . . . 105 E2
Rowanwood OL9. . . . . . . 65 E7
Rowany Cl M25. . . . . 63 A2
ROWARTH 127 C7
Rowarth Ave
Denton M34. . . . . 113 A8
3 Gamesley SK13. . . . . 171 A2
Rowarth Bank 9 SK13 . . 171 A2
Rowarth Cl 10 SK13. . . . 171 A2
Rowarth Fold 7 SK13 . . 171 A2
Rowarth Rd M23. . . . . . . 121 A2
Rowarth Way 4 SK13 . . . 171 A2
Rowbotham St 13 SK14. 113 E8
Rowbottom Sq WN1. . . . 150 C4
Rowbottom Wlk OL8 . . . 153 B1

Rowcon Cl M34. . . . . 100 E6
Rowdell Wlk M23 . . . . . . 109 B2
Rowden Rd OL4. . . . . 67 E4
Rowe Gn M34. . . . . 100 F2
Rowena St M34 . . . . 42 C2
Rowendale St M1 . . . . . . 162 C4
Rowe St M29 . . . . 77 B8
Rowfield Dr M23. . . . . . . 120 F3
Rowland Ave M41. . . . . . 95 E3
Rowland Ct 17 OL16. . . . 31 B6
ROWLANDS. 11 D2
Rowlands Rd BL9 . . . . . . 11 D2
Rowland St
Atherton M46. . . . . 58 D2
16 Rochdale OL16 . . . . . 31 B6
Salford M5. . . . . 161 A4
Rowlandsway M22 . . . . . 121 D2
Rowland Way OL4 . . . . . 67 E7
Rowley Rd SK7 . . . . 133 E8
Rowley St OL6. . . . . 85 D6
ROW-OF-TREES. 136 D3
Rowood Ave
Manchester M8 . . . . 156 B2
Reddish SK5. . . . . 99 F2
Rowrah Cres M24 . . . . . . 46 C1
Rowsley Ave
Bolton BL1. . . . . 142 A1
Manchester M20 . . . . . . 109 E4
Rowsley Cl 22 SK13 . . . . 171 B2
Rowsley Gn 24 SK13. . . . 171 B2
Rowsley Gr
25 Gamesley SK13. . . . . 171 B2
Reddish SK5. . . . . 111 E7
Rowsley Mews SK13 . . . 171 B2
Rowsley Rd
Eccles M30 . . . . 95 C8
Stretford M32 . . . . 96 A3
Rowsley St
Manchester M11 . . . . . . 160 C1
Salford M6. . . . . 81 B5
Rowsley Wlk 23 SK13. . . 171 B2
Rowson Dr M44. . . . . 105 D6
Rowton Rise WN1. . . . . . 37 B8
Rowton St 8 BL2 . . . . . . 25 B3
Roxalina St BL3 . . . . . . 147 B4
Roxburgh St 5 M18. . . . . 99 D5
ROXBURY 67 B5
Roxbury Ave OL4. . . . . . . 67 D5
Roxby Cl M28. . . . . 60 B3
Roxby Wlk 18 M40 . . . . . 65 D2
Roxholme Wlk M22 . . . . 130 C8
Roxton Cl BL6 . . . . 22 B5
Roxton Rd SK4. . . . . 111 C6
Roxwell Wlk 8 M9 . . . . . 157 A4
Royal Albert Edward Infmy
WN1. . . . . 37 C2
Royal Arc 9 WN1. . . . . . 150 C4
Royal Ave
Bury BL9 . . . . 27 F5
Droylsden M43. . . . . 84 B2
Heywood OL10. . . . . 29 D1
Manchester M21 . . . . . . 109 A8
Urmston M41. . . . . 95 D2
Royal Bolton Hospl BL4 147 C1
Royal Coll Manchester
SK8. . . . . 131 E6
Royal Court Dr BL1. . . . . 145 A4
Royal Cres SK8 . . . . 122 C2
Royal Dr WN7 . . . . 76 E6
Royal Exchange Arc 20
M2 . . . . 158 C1
Royal Exchange Sh Ctr
M2 . . . . 158 C2
Royal Exchange Theatre* 22
M2 . . . . 158 C2
Royal Eye Hospl M13 . . . 163 B1
Royal Gdns
Altrincham WA14. . . . . . 118 F2
Ramsbottom BL0 . . . . . . 11 A3
Royal George Cotts OL3 . 68 E5
Royal George Mills OL3 . 68 E5
Royal George St SK1,
SK3. . . . . 170 C4
Royal Ho BL1 . . . . 144 B2
Royal Manchester Children's
Hospl M13. . . . . 163 C1
Royal Oak Ind Est SK1. . 170 C3
Royal Oak Rd M23 . . . . . 121 A7
Royal Oak Yd M1. . . . . . 169 C1
Royal Oldham Hospl OL1 48 D1
Royal Par OL1 . . . . 48 D3
Royal Rd SK12 . . . . 135 D5
Royal School Manchester
SK8. . . . . 131 D6
Royal St OL16. . . . . 15 C3
Royal The M3. . . . . 158 A4
Royalthorn Ave M22 . . . 121 D6
Royalthorn Dr M22. . . . . 121 C6
Royalthorn Rd M22 . . . . 121 D6
Royce Ave WA15. . . . . . . 119 E5
Royce Cres Prim Sch
M15. . . . . 162 B1
Royce Ct 25 M15 . . . . . . 162 A2
Royce Rd M15 . . . . 162 A2
Royce Trad Est M17 . . . . 95 F7
Roydale St M40. . . . . 160 B3
Royden Ave
Irlam M44 . . . . 105 F8
Manchester M9 . . . . 64 D5
Wigan WN3 . . . . 55 A2
Royden Cres WN5. . . . . . 71 E5
Royden Rd WN5 . . . . 71 E5
Roydes St M24 . . . . 47 B2
Royds Cl
Bury BL8 . . . . 27 A5
Manchester M13 . . . . . . 164 A1

Royds Pl 15 OL16. . . . . . 31 A5
Royds Rd OL13 . . . . 3 A7
Royds St
Bury, Tottington BL8. . . . 26 F7
Bury, Woodgate Hill BL9 . 28 D4
Littleborough OL15 . . . . 16 C6
Milnrow OL16 . . . . 32 A5
Rochdale OL16. . . . . 31 B5
Royds Street W OL16. . . 31 A5
Royds St 6 OL16. . . . . . . 31 A5
Roy Ho OL2. . . . . 48 D6
Royland Ave BL3. . . . . . . 42 A3
Royland Ct BL3 . . . . 147 C3
Royle Ave SK13 . . . . 104 D1
Royle Barn Rd OL11 . . . . 30 C3
Royle Cl
Oldham OL8 . . . . 66 F3
Stockport SK2 . . . . 124 A5
Royle Gn Rd M22. . . . . . 121 D8
Royle Green Rd M22 . . . 121 D8
Royle Higginson Ct M41. 95 C1
Roylelands Bglws OL11 . 30 C3
Royle Pennine Trad Est
OL11. . . . . 30 D3
Royle Rd OL11 . . . . 30 D3
Royle Sq 2 SK9 . . . . 137 A1
Royle St
Denton M34. . . . . 100 F5
Manchester M14 . . . . . . 110 D7
Salford M6. . . . . 154 C1
Stockport SK1 . . . . 170 C3
Walkden M28. . . . . 60 D2
ROYLEY 48 D3
Royley OL2 . . . . 48 D3
Royley Carr Flats SK6 . . 113 A3
Royley Cres OL2 . . . . 48 C3
Royley House OL2. . . . . . 48 C3
Royley Way OL2 . . . . 48 C3
Roynton Rd BL6. . . . . 22 B7
Royon Dr SK3. . . . . 123 B7
Roy St OL2 . . . . 48 D4
Royston Ave
Bolton BL3. . . . . 148 C4
Manchester M16 . . . . . . 97 D3
Reddish M34 . . . . 100 A3
Royston Cl
2 Golborne WA3 . . . . . . 90 E8
Ramsbottom BL8 . . . . . . 10 F1
Royston Ct 6 M16 . . . . . 97 D3
Royston Rd
Manchester M41. . . . . . . 95 E3
Salford M6. . . . . 154 C1
ROYTON 48 E4
Royton Ave M33 . . . . . . 108 E2
Royton & Crompton Sch
OL2. . . . . 49 A4
Royton Hall Prim Sch OL2 48 E4
Royton Hall Wlk OL2 . . . 48 E4
ROYTON MOSS. 49 B3
Rozel Sq M3. . . . . 162 B4
Ruabon Cres WN2 . . . . . 57 A4
Ruabon Rd M20. . . . . . . 110 C2
Rubens Cl SK6. . . . . 126 C8
Ruby Gr WN7 . . . . 75 E4
Ruby St
Bolton BL1. . . . . 143 C3
Denton M34. . . . . 100 E3
Manchester M15. . . . . . 163 A2
Ramsbottom BL9 . . . . . . 11 C3
Rudcroft Cl M13 . . . . . . 163 B2
Rudding St OL2 . . . . 49 A2
Ruddpark Rd M22. . . . . . 121 D1
Rudd St M40. . . . . 83 A7
Rudgwick Dr BL8 . . . . . . 27 C7
Rudman Ave M20 . . . . . . 110 A7
Rudman Dr M5 . . . . 161 C4
Rudman St OL12 . . . . . . 14 E2
Rudolph St BL3 . . . . 147 C3
Rudston Ave M40. . . . . . 65 B2
Rudyard Ave
Middleton M24. . . . . 47 C3
Standish WN6. . . . . 19 E2
Rudyard Gr
Reddish SK4. . . . . 111 D6
Rochdale OL11. . . . . 30 F2
Sale M33. . . . . 107 E2
Rudyard Rd M6 . . . . 80 C5
Rudyard St M7 . . . . 155 A2
Ruecroft Cl WN6 . . . . . . 35 D7
Rufford Ave
Hyde SK14 . . . . 167 C2
Rochdale OL11. . . . . 30 D4
Rufford Cl
Ashton-u-l OL6 . . . . 85 C7
Shaw OL2. . . . . 48 F7
Whitefield M45 . . . . 45 A2
Rufford Dr
Bolton BL3. . . . . 147 A2
Whitefield M45 . . . . 44 F2
Rufford Gr BL3 . . . . 147 A2
Rufford Pl
Reddish M18 . . . . 99 F4
Tyldesley M29 . . . . 76 F4
Rufford Rd M16 . . . . 97 D3
Rufford St 4 WN4 . . . . . 72 F5
Rufus St M14 . . . . 110 E7
Rugby Cl WN5 . . . . 53 E5
Rugby Dr
Orrell WN5. . . . . 53 F8
Sale M33. . . . . 108 A2
Rugby Rd
Leigh WN7 . . . . 75 F3
Rochdale OL12, OL16. . . 15 A1
Salford M6. . . . . 80 A3
Rugby Road Ind Est OL12. 15 A1
Rugby St M7, M8 . . . . . . 158 B4

Rugeley St M6. . . . . 81 B5
Ruins La BL2 . . . . 25 E4
Ruislip Ave M40 . . . . . . 157 B2
Ruislip Cl OL8 . . . . 67 B4
Rumbles La OL3 . . . . 50 F4
Rumbold St M18. . . . . . . 99 E6
Rumworth Rd BL6. . . . . . 40 C6
Rumworth St BL3 . . . . . . 40 F4
Runcorn St M15 . . . . . . 161 C3
Runfield Cl WN7 . . . . 76 A5
Runger La M90, WA15. . . 129 F8
Runhall Cl M12 . . . . 165 A2
Running Hill Farm OL3 . . 51 D2
Running Hill Gate OL3. . 51 D1
Running Hill La OL3 . . . . 51 D2
Runnymeade M6, M27 . . 80 B5
Runnymede Cl SK3. . . . . 123 C6
Runnymede Ct
Bolton BL3. . . . . 145 A1
Royton OL2 . . . . 48 E4
Stockport SK3 . . . . 123 C6
Runshaw Ave WN6 . . . . . 35 E8
Rupert St
Bolton BL3. . . . . 147 C3
Failsworth M40 . . . . 83 E4
Radcliffe M26 . . . . 44 B1
Reddish SK5. . . . . 111 E7
Rochdale OL11. . . . . 14 C1
Wigan WN1. . . . . 151 B3
Rupert Terr 5 SK5. . . . . 111 E7
Ruscombe Fold M24 . . . . 46 D3
Rush Acre Cl M26. . . . . . 43 E3
Rushall Wlk M23. . . . . . 120 F2
Rush Bank OL2 . . . . 48 F8
Rushbrooke Ave 1 M11. . 83 C2
Rushbury Dr OL2. . . . . . . 49 A4
Rushcroft Ct M9 . . . . 65 A2
Rushcroft Prim Sch OL2. 149 B4
Rushcroft Rd OL2 . . . . . . 48 F8
Rushden Ave M19. . . . . . 99 B2
Rushden Rd M19. . . . . . . 99 B2
Rushen St 8 M11. . . . . . . 83 C1
Rushes Mdw WA13. . . . . 117 B5
Rushes The SK13 . . . . . . 171 C4
Rushey Ave M22 . . . . . . 121 C6
Rushey Cl WA15 . . . . . . 129 D7
Rushey Field BL7 . . . . . . 24 F8
Rushey Fold Ct 6 BL1. . . 143 A2
Rushey Fold La BL1 . . . . 143 A2
Rusheyleas Cl BL1 . . . . . 142 C2
Rushey Rd M22 . . . . 121 C6
Rushfield Dr M13 . . . . . . 98 F3
Rushfield Rd SK8 . . . . . . 132 A6
Rushford Ave M19 . . . . . 99 A2
Rushford Ct 1 M19 . . . . . 99 A2
Rushford Gr BL1. . . . . . . 143 C4
Rushford St M12. . . . . . . 99 A3
RUSHGREEN 117 A4
Rushgreen Rd WA13 . . . 117 A4
Rushgrove OL3 . . . . 69 B7
Rush Hill Rd OL3. . . . . . . 69 B7
Rush Hill Terr OL3 . . . . . 69 B7
Rushlake Dr BL1. . . . . . . 143 B1
Rushlake Gdns OL11 . . . 29 E8
Rushley Ave M7. . . . . 81 B7
Rushmere
Ashton-u-l OL6 . . . . 85 E6
Glossop SK13. . . . . 116 E8
Rushmere Ave M19 . . . . 99 B1
Rushmere Dr BL8 . . . . . . 27 C5
Rushmere Wlk M16 . . . . 162 A1
Rushmoor WN4. . . . . 73 E4
Rushmoor Cl M44. . . . . . 94 A2
Rush Mount OL2 . . . . 48 F8
RUSHOLME 98 E2
Rusholme Gdns 3 M14. . 98 C2
Rusholme Gr M14. . . . . . 98 C3
Rusholme Pl M14 . . . . . . 98 C2
Rushside Rd SK8. . . . . . . 132 A6
Rush St SK16. . . . . 101 F8
Rushton Ave
Leigh WN7 . . . . 75 D8
Newton-le-W WA12. . . . . 89 B4
Rushton Dr
Marple SK6 . . . . 125 F5
Romiley SK6. . . . . 113 C3
Stockport SK7 . . . . 123 D2
Rushton Gdns SK7. . . . . 123 D2
Rushton Gr
Manchester M11 . . . . . . 99 F7
Oldham OL4. . . . . 49 E3
Rushton Rd
Bolton BL1. . . . . 142 B1
Cheadle SK8 . . . . 132 A6
Stockport SK3 . . . . 123 B7
Rushton St
3 Bacup OL13 . . . . 3 E8
Manchester M20 . . . . . . 110 B2
Walkden M28. . . . . 60 D2
Rushway Ave M9. . . . . . . 65 B2
Rushwick Ave M40 . . . . 157 B1
Rushwood Pk WN6. . . . . 19 D2
Rushworth Bldgs OL13 . . 3 C8
Rushycroft SK14 . . . . . . 111 C5
Rushyfield Cres SK6. . . . 113 D3
Rushy Hill View 18 OL12. 14 C1
Rushy View WA12. . . . . . 89 A4
Ruskin Ave
Denton M34. . . . . 100 C1
Droylsden M34. . . . . 100 F7
Kearsley BL4 . . . . 60 F7
Manchester M14 . . . . . . 98 B4

Ruskin Ave continued
Newton-le-W WA12...... 89 C4
Oldham OL9................. 65 F3
Wigan WN3.................. 54 F3
Ruskin Cres
Abram WN2................... 56 B1
Prestwich M25............. 62 F3
Ruskin Dr M33........... 107 D4
Ruskin Gdns SK6..... 113 A3
Ruskin Gr SK6.......... 113 A3
Ruskington Dr M9..... 157 A3
Ruskin Rd
Droylsden M43............. 84 A2
Little Lever BL3............ 43 B4
Manchester M16........... 97 C3
Prestwich M25............. 62 F3
Reddish SK5................. 99 E1
Rochdale OL11............. 30 F2
Ruskin St
Oldham OL1............... 153 A4
Radcliffe M26............. 44 C4
Rusland Ct
Manchester M9............ 65 A3
Sale M33................... 108 A5
Rusland Dr BL2........ 25 E2
Rusland Wlk 8 M22.. 121 C2
Russeldene Rd WN3.. 54 E3
Russell Ave
High Lane SK6............ 134 E7
Manchester M16.......... 97 D2
Sale M33................... 108 D5
Russell Cl BL1........ 144 C4
Russell Ct
Farnworth BL4............. 60 E7
Manchester M16........... 97 D2
Walkden M38............... 60 C3
Russell Ctr The M20.. 110 C7
Russell Dr M44......... 94 A2
Russell Gdns SK4.... 168 B1
Russell Pl 1 M33.... 108 B5
Russell Rd
Manchester M16........... 97 D3
Partington M31........... 106 A3
Salford M6................... 80 B5
Russell Scott Prim Sch
M34...................... 100 E4
Russell St
6 Ashton-u-L OL6..... 85 D4
Atherton M46............. 58 C3
Bolton BL1............... 145 A4
5 Bury BL9............. 140 C4
Chadderton OL9.......... 152 B3
Compstall SK6............ 114 B3
Dukinfield SK16........ 101 C8
Eccles M30................. 79 F2
Farnworth BL4............. 60 E8
Heywood OL10............ 29 E1
Hindley WN2............... 57 C2
Hyde SK14................ 167 A3
Ince-in-M WN2............ 56 A8
Manchester M8........... 158 C4
Manchester, Moss Side M16 97 F3
Prestwich M25............ 63 C4
Rochdale OL11.......... 139 B1
Stockport SK4............ 124 A6
Walkden M38............... 60 C3
Russet Rd M9........... 64 D1
Russet Way SK9....... 136 E3
Russet Wlk BL1....... 143 B4
Rustons Wlk 2 M40.. 65 E1
Ruth Ave M40.......... 65 E1
Ruthen La M16......... 97 B4
Rutherford Ave 2 M14.. 98 B3
Rutherford Cl SK14.. 167 A2
Rutherford Dr BL5.... 58 F7
Rutherford Gall SK14.. 167 B2
Rutherford Way SK14.. 167 A2
Rutherglade Cl M40.. 156 C2
Rutherglen Dr BL3.... 40 F6
Rutherglen Wlk M40.. 157 B1
Ruthin Ave
Cheadle SK8............ 122 E2
Manchester M9............ 64 C5
Middleton M24............. 65 A6
Ruthin Cl OL8........... 66 B2
Ruth St
Bolton BL1............... 145 B4
10 Bury BL9........... 140 C4
Edenfield BL0............. 1 D2
Manchester M18........... 99 D3
Oldham OL1.............. 153 C4
Rochdale OL11.......... 139 B2
Rutland Ave
Denton M34............... 101 B2
Golborne WA3............. 90 D7
Manchester, Firswood M16.. 97 A3
Manchester, Withington
M20...................... 110 A5
Over Hulton M46......... 58 F4
Swinton M27............... 61 F2
Urmston M41............... 95 E3
Rutland Cl
5 Ashton-u-L OL6..... 85 D2
Gatley SK8............... 122 B6
Little Lever BL3............ 43 B4
Rutland Cres SK5.... 112 D6
Rutland Ct
Manchester M20......... 110 B5
Stockport, Heaviley SK2.. 124 B7
Stockport SK2............ 124 A5
Rutland Dr
Ashton-in-M WN4....... 73 C4
Bury BL9.................... 45 A8
Manchester M7............ 63 D1

Rutland Gr
Bolton BL1............... 142 C1
Farnworth BL4............. 60 C7
Rutland La M33........ 108 F4
Rutland Rd
Altrincham WA14........ 119 D6
Droylsden M43............. 83 E2
Eccles M30................. 79 F3
Hazel Grove SK7........ 133 E8
Hindley WN2............... 56 F6
Irlam M44................ 105 D5
Partington M31.......... 105 E2
Tyldesley M29............. 58 F2
Walkden M28............... 60 D1
Rutland St
Ashton-u-L OL6.......... 85 D2
Bolton BL3............... 147 A4
Dukinfield SK14........ 101 D5
Failsworth M35............ 83 F8
Heywood OL10............ 29 D3
Leigh WN7................. 76 E4
4 Manchester M18.... 99 E6
Oldham OL9.............. 152 C1
Swinton M27............... 61 E1
Rutland Way OL2..... 149 C3
Rutland Wlk BB4....... 1 A8
Rutter's La SK7........ 124 C2
Ryall Ave M5........... 161 B4
Ryall Avenue S M5.. 161 B4
Ryan St M11............. 99 E7
Ryburn Sq OL11........ 29 E6
Rydal Ave
Chadderton OL9.......... 47 F1
Droylsden M43............. 83 E1
Dukinfield SK14......... 101 C5
Eccles M30................. 79 B4
Hazel Grove SK7........ 124 C3
High Lane SK6.......... 134 E8
Hindley WN2............... 56 E5
Middleton M24............. 64 F6
Orrell WN5................. 53 F7
Royton OL2................. 48 C8
Sale M33................... 107 F5
Urmston M41............. 107 A8
Rydal Cl
Ashton-in-M WN4....... 73 C4
Blackrod BL6............... 21 C3
Bury BL9.................... 44 E7
Gatley SK8............... 122 B4
Reddish M34............. 100 B2
Tyldesley M29............. 77 A7
Rydal Cres
Swinton M27............... 79 F7
Walkden M28............... 60 E1
Rydal Dr WA15...... 129 D8
Rydal Gr
Ashton-u-L OL7........ 166 A4
Farnworth BL4............. 59 F7
Heywood OL10............ 46 D8
Whitefield M45............ 63 A8
Rydal Ho 4 M28..... 60 E2
Rydal Mount 4 SK5.. 99 F2
Rydal Pl
Abram WN2................. 74 B8
Ince-in-M WN2............ 56 B8
Rydal Rd
Bolton BL1............... 144 A4
Haslingden BB4............ 1 C8
Little Lever BL3............ 43 A3
Stretford M32............... 96 D3
Rydal St
Leigh WN7................. 75 E5
Newton-le-W WA12..... 89 C3
Rydal Wlk
Oldham OL4............... 67 D7
Stalybridge SK15......... 86 A3
Wigan WN7................. 54 C7
Ryde Ave
Denton M34............... 113 B8
Stockport SK4............ 168 B2
Ryder Ave WA14..... 119 E7
Ryder Brow M18....... 99 D4
Ryderbrow Rd M18.... 99 D4
Ryder Brow Sta M18.. 99 D4
Ryder Gr WN7.......... 76 C2
Ryder St
Bolton BL1............... 142 C2
Heywood OL10............ 29 D2
Manchester M40......... 160 A4
Ryde St
Bolton BL1............... 146 A4
Wigan WN5................. 54 E6
Rydings La OL12...... 15 A5
Rydings Rd OL12...... 15 B4
Rydley St BL2......... 148 B2
Ryebank Gr OL6........ 85 D5
Ryebank Mews 3 M21.. 96 F1
Ryebank Rd M21....... 96 F1
Rye Bank Rd M16..... 97 B3
Ryeburn Ave M22.... 121 D3
Ryeburn Dr BL2........ 25 B5
Ryeburne St OL4....... 67 C7
Ryeburn Wlk M41..... 94 F4
Rye Croft M45.......... 62 C7
Ryecroft Ave
Bury BL8................... 26 F6
Golborne WA3............. 74 E1
Heywood OL10............ 29 E2
Rye Croft Ave M6..... 80 C3
Ryecroft Bsns Pk 12 OL7.. 84 F1
Ryecroft Cl OL9......... 65 F3
Ryecroft Dr BL5......... 39 D3
Ryecroft Gr M23...... 121 A7
Ryecroft Ho OL7...... 166 A1
Ryecroft La
Denton M34............... 100 F7
Eccles M28................. 78 F4
Ryecroft Rd M32....... 96 C1

Ryecroft St OL7........ 84 F1
Ryecroft View M34... 100 C8
Ryedale Ave M40..... 157 A1
Ryedale Cl SK4........ 168 B3
Ryefield
6 Ashton-u-L OL7..... 84 F1
Pendlebury M6........... 80 D6
Ryefield Cl WA15.... 120 C5
Ryefield Rd M33...... 107 C2
Ryefields
6 Rochdale, Hurstead
OL12...................... 15 C4
Rochdale OL11.......... 30 A6
Ryefields Dr OL3....... 51 B1
Ryefield St BL1......... 25 A1
Ryeford Cl WN3...... 151 C2
Rye Hill BL5............. 57 F8
Ryeland Cl OL16...... 31 B4
Ryelands BL5............ 57 F8
Ryelands Cl 2 BL5.. 57 F8
Rye St OL10............. 29 E3
Rye Wlk
Chadderton OL9......... 152 A2
Manchester M13........ 163 C1
Rygate Wlk 3 M8.... 155 C2
Rylance Rd WN3....... 54 D1
Rylance St M11....... 164 B4
Ryland Cl SK5........... 99 F1
Ryland Ho 1 M21.... 109 A8
Rylands Ct 8 M15.. 162 A2
Rylands Ho 7 M14.. 110 D8
Rylands St WN6........ 37 A2
Rylane Wlk M40...... 157 A1
Rylatt Cl 1 M33...... 107 F5
Ryley Ave BL3.......... 144 B1
Ryleys Farm SK9..... 136 F1
Ryleys La SK9.......... 136 F1
Ryleys Sch The SK9.. 136 F1
Ryley St 3 BL3....... 144 C2
Rylstone Ave M21.... 109 D3
Ryther Gr M9............ 64 B5
Ryton Ave M18......... 99 C3
Ryton Cl WN3.......... 150 B2

S

Sabden Brook Dr WN2.. 55 F2
Sabden Cl
Bury BL9.................... 27 F7
Heywood OL10............ 29 A2
Manchester M40.......... 160 B3
Sabden Rd BL1........... 23 E2
Sabrina St M8......... 155 B1
Sack St 4 SK14....... 101 D5
Sackville Cl OL2........ 32 A1
Sackville St
Ashton-u-L OL6......... 166 B3
1 Bolton BL2......... 148 C3
Manchester M1.......... 163 A4
6 Rochdale OL11..... 30 C2
Salford M3................ 158 B2
Sacred Heart RC Prim Sch
Hindley WN2............... 57 B3
3 Leigh WN7.......... 75 E5
Manchester M18........... 99 C4
Oldham OL1.............. 49 C2
Rochdale OL16........... 31 C6
Tyldesley M46............. 58 E1
Westhoughton BL5........ 39 F1
Wigan WN6................. 36 F2
Wythenshawe M23..... 120 F6
Saddleback Cl 3 M28.. 78 B6
Saddleback Cres WN5.. 54 B7
Saddleback Rd WN5.... 54 B7
Saddle Cote M28........ 78 A6
Saddlecote OL8........ 156 B4
Saddle Cl 6 WN5..... 54 F6
Saddle Gr M43........... 84 D3
Saddle St BL2............ 25 B2
Saddlewood Ave M19.. 110 D2
Saddleworth Bsns Ctr
OL3...................... 50 F4
Saddleworth Bsns Pk OL3 51 C4
Saddleworth Fold OL3.. 51 C1
Saddleworth Mus & Art
Gall* OL3.................. 69 B8
Saddleworth Prep Sch
OL4...................... 68 C8
Saddleworth Sch OL3.. 51 B1
Sadie Ave M32.......... 96 A4
Sadler Ct M15......... 162 B1
Sadler St
Bolton BL3................. 42 A4
Middleton M24............ 46 F1
Safflower Ave M27..... 79 D8
Saffron Cl WA3.......... 90 E8
Saffron Dr OL4......... 49 D2
Saffron Wlk
Partington M31.......... 105 F2
3 Wythenshawe M22.. 121 D1
Safton Cl BL9............ 27 B6
Sagars Rd
Handforth SK9........... 131 C3
Styal SK9................ 131 B4
Sagar St M8............ 158 C4
St Aelred's RC Tech Coll
WA12.................... 89 D4
St Agnes CE Prim Sch
Manchester M13.......... 98 F3
Oldham OL4............... 68 A4
St Agnes Rd M13...... 98 F2
St Agnes St SK5......... 99 F2
St Aidan & St Oswald's RC
Prim Sch OL2............ 48 E3
St Aidan's CE Prim Sch
WN5...................... 71 E5

St Aidan's Cl
Billinge WN5............. 71 E6
Rochdale OL11.......... 139 A1
St Aidan's Gr M7....... 81 B6
St Aidans RC Prim Sch
M23...................... 109 B1
St Aidan's RC Prim Sch
WN3...................... 54 D2
St Aiden's Cl M26..... 44 A1
St Albans Ave
Ashton-u-L OL6.......... 85 C7
Failsworth M40............ 83 B5
St Alban's Ave SK4.. 111 C5
St Albans Cl
Haydock WA11............ 89 A7
Oldham OL8............... 66 F4
St Albans Cres WA14.. 119 C8
St Alban's Ct OL11.. 139 B2
St Alban's St OL16.. 139 B2
St Alban's Terr
Rochdale OL11.......... 139 B2
Salford M8............... 155 C1
St Aldates SK6........ 112 F2
St Aldwyn's Rd M20.. 110 B5
St Alphonsus RC Prim Sch
M16...................... 162 A1
St Ambrose Barlow RC High
Sch 8 M27............. 79 F7
St Ambrose Barlow RC Prim
Sch M29................. 77 A5
St Ambrose Coll WA15.. 129 B8
St Ambrose Ct 13 OL1.. 49 C1
St Ambrose Gdns M6.. 154 C2
St Ambrose Prep Sch
WA15.................... 129 B8
St Ambrose RC Prim Sch
Manchester M21.......... 109 D4
Stockport SK3.......... 170 B1
St Ambrose Rd
Oldham OL1.............. 49 C1
Tyldesley M29............. 77 A5
St Andrews Ave M30.. 79 E1
St Andrew's Ave
Altrincham WA15....... 119 F7
Droylsden M43............ 83 E1
St Andrews CE Jun Sch
SK13.................... 171 C4
St Andrews CE Prim Sch
BL5...................... 59 A8
St Andrew's CE Prim Sch
Eccles M30................. 79 E1
Manchester M19......... 111 B8
Radcliffe M26............. 43 F6
Ramsbottom BL0......... 138 B1
Wigan WN6................. 36 F2
Worsley M28............... 78 A6
St Andrew's CE Prim Sch
Dearnley OL12............ 15 E4
St Andrews Cl
Rochdale OL15............ 15 E4
Sale M33................ 107 C1
Stockport SK4............ 168 B4
St Andrew's Cl
Ramsbottom BL0......... 138 C1
Romiley SK6.............. 113 B1
St Andrew's Cres WN2.. 56 D5
St Andrews Ct
Altrincham WA15....... 119 F3
Glossop SK13............ 104 A4
Stockport SK1............ 112 A1
St Andrews Dr
Heywood OL10............ 46 D8
Leigh WN7................. 76 C5
St Andrew's Dr
Heywood OL10............ 29 D1
Wigan WN6................. 36 F2
St Andrews Ho M38.. 60 B3
St Andrews Meth Prim Sch
M28...................... 60 B3
St Andrews Rd
Bolton BL6................. 40 B7
Gatley SK8............... 122 C1
Stockport SK4............ 168 B4
St Andrew's Rd
Radcliffe M26............. 43 F6
Stretford M32............... 96 B2
St Andrew's Sq M1..... 163 C4
St Andrew's St
Radcliffe M26............. 43 F6
St Andrews View M26.. 43 F7
St Annes Acad M24..... 46 F4
St Anne's Ave
Royton OL2................. 48 E3
Salford M6................ 154 B3
Tyldesley M46............. 58 E1
St Anne's CE Jun & Inf Sch
OL2...................... 48 E3
St Anne's CE Lydgate Prim
Sch OL4.................. 68 C6
St Anne's CE Prim Sch
Sale M33................ 108 D4
Wigan WN6................. 36 D3
St Anne's Cres OL4.... 68 B5
St Anne's Ct
Denton M34............... 100 E6
Sale M33................ 108 C4
Shevington WN6......... 35 F5
St Anne's Dr
Denton M34............... 101 A4
Shevington WN6......... 36 A5
St Anne's Fulshaw CE Prim
Sch SK9................. 136 F6
St Anne's Gdns OL10.. 29 F2
St Anne's Prim Sch
Denton M34............... 101 A4
Manchester, Bradford M4.. 160 A1

St Annes RC High Sch
SK4...................... 169 A4
St Anne's RC Prim Sch
Droylsden M34.......... 100 A7
Manchester, Cheetham Hill
M8...................... 156 A4
Oldham OL4............... 67 C7
St Annes Rd
Denton M34............... 100 F6
Horwich BL6............... 22 C4
Manchester M21........ 109 B7
St Anne's Rd M34..... 101 A4
St Annes Sq OL3...... 50 F4
St Annes St 6 SK14.. 115 A8
St Anne's St BL9..... 140 C4
St Anns Churchyard
M2...................... 158 C1
St Anns Cl M25........ 63 A3
St Ann's Pas M2..... 158 C1
St Ann's RC Prim Sch 6
M32...................... 96 D2
St Ann's Rd
Hazel Grove SK7....... 124 C1
Prestwich M25........... 63 A3
Rochdale OL11........... 31 D8
St Ann's Road N SK8.. 122 B2
St Ann's Road S SK8.. 131 C8
St Ann's Sq
Gatley SK8............... 131 C8
Manchester M2.......... 158 C1
St Anns St M33........ 108 F3
St Ann's St M27....... 79 E8
St Ann St
Bolton BL1............... 143 B1
Manchester M2.......... 158 C1
St Anthonys Dr OL5.. 68 D2
St Anthony's RC Prim Sch
M22...................... 121 D1
St Antony's RC Coll M41.. 95 F2
St Asaphs Dr OL6...... 85 B6
St Asaph's Dr M7.... 155 C4
St Aubin's Rd BL2.... 148 B2
St Aubyn's Rd WN1.... 37 C4
St Augustine of Canterbury
RC High Sch 1 OL8... 66 D3
St Augustine's CE Prim Sch
Manchester M40.......... 157 B1
Pendlebury M27........... 80 B8
St Augustine's Ct 27 BL2.. 25 B1
St Augustine's Rd SK3.. 123 B8
St Augustine St
Bolton BL1............... 143 A2
Manchester M40......... 157 B1
St Austell Ave M29.... 77 C8
St Austell Dr
Gatley SK8............... 131 B8
Ramsbottom BL0......... 10 F2
St Austell Ho M16..... 97 E1
St Austell Pl 18 OL9.. 48 B1
St Austell Rd M16..... 97 E1
St Austells Dr M25.... 63 B5
St Austell's Dr M27.... 80 C7
St Barnabas' CE Prim Sch
M11...................... 165 B4
St Barnabas's Dr OL15.. 16 A6
St Barnabas Sq M11.. 165 B4
St Bartholomew's CE Prim
Sch OL12................ 14 C8
St Bartholomew St 2
BL3...................... 42 A4
St Bede CE Prim Sch
BL3...................... 146 C2
St Bede's Ave BL3.... 146 B2
St Bede's Coll M16... 97 E3
St Bees Cl
Gatley SK8............... 122 B3
Manchester M14........... 98 A4
St Bees Rd BL2......... 25 C2
St Bees Wlk 8 M24... 46 E2
St Benedict's Ave M12.. 164 C2
St Benedicts RC Prim Sch
WN2...................... 56 C6
St Benedict's RC Prim Sch
SK9...................... 131 E3
St Bernadette's RC Prim Sch
Brinnington SK5........... 112 B4
Shevington WN6........... 36 A6
6 Whitefield M45..... 44 F2
St Bernard's Ave 1 M6.. 81 C5
St Bernard's Cl M6.... 81 B5
St Bernard's RC Prim Sch
Bolton BL3................. 40 E5
Manchester M19........ 110 E5
St Boniface RC Prim Sch
M7...................... 81 C6
St Boniface Rd M7.... 81 C4
St Brannocks Rd SK8.. 132 B7
St Brannock's Rd M21.. 97 C1
St Brelades Dr M7.... 155 C4
St Brendan's RC Prim Sch
BL2...................... 25 E4
St Brendan's Rd M20.. 110 B7
St Brendan's Road N
M20...................... 110 B7
St Brides Gr M20....... 110 A4
St Brides Way M16.. 162 A1
St Brigid's RC Prim Sch
M11...................... 160 D1
St Catherine's Acad BL2.. 25 E2
St Catherine's CE Prim Sch
Horwich BL6............... 22 B3
St Catherine's Rd M20.. 110 A4
St Catherine's CE Prim Sch
Wigan WN1.............. 151 B4
St Catherines Ct BL6.. 22 B3
St Catherines Dr BL4.. 59 F8
St Catherine's RC Prim Sch
Golborne WA3............ 90 E7
2 Manchester M20... 110 C3

St Catherine's Rd M20 . . . . 110 B7
St Chad's Ave SK6 . . . . 113 C2
St Chad's CE Prim Sch
    OL3 . . . . 51 C1
St Chad's Cl OL16 . . . . 139 C3
St Chads Cres OL3 . . . . 69 C8
St Chad's Ct OL16 . . . . 139 C3
St Chad's Gr SK6 . . . . 113 C2
St Chad's RC Prim Sch
    M8 . . . . 156 A1
St Chad's Rd M20 . . . . 110 D7
St Charles St M4, M8 . . . . . 159 A4
St Charles St3 . . . . 103 F5
St Charles RC Prim Sch
    SK3 . . . . 103 E5
St Charles's RC Prim Sch
    M27 . . . . 79 D8
St Christopher's Ave OL6 . 85 E6
St Christophers Cl M20 . . 109 F6
St Christopher's Dr SK6 . 113 A2
St Christopher's RC Prim Sch
 ■ Ashton-u-L OL6 . . . . . . 85 E6
 ■ Romiley SK6 . . . . 113 A2
St Christopher's Rd OL6 . . 85 E6
St Chrysostom's CE Prim Sch
    M13 . . . . 164 A1
St Clair Rd BL8 . . . . 10 F3
St Clare's RC Prim Sch
    M9 . . . . 64 C5
St Clare Terr BL6 . . . . 39 F8
St Clement Ct M41 . . . . 95 D1
St Clement's Ct
    M11 . . . . 99 E7
St Clements Ct OL11 . . . . . . 30 C8
St Clement's Ct
 ■ Irlam M44 . . . . 94 B3
    Oldham OL8 . . . . 153 C1
    Prestwich M25 . . . . 63 C4
    Wigan WN3 . . . . 150 A1
St Clement's Dr M5 . . . . . 161 B3
St Clements Fold M41 . . . . 95 E2
St Clement's Rd
    Manchester M21 . . . . . . 109 A4
    Wigan WN1 . . . . 37 C4
St Clement's St WN3 . . . . . 55 F4
St Columba's RC Prim Sch
    BL2 . . . . 25 B4
St Cuthberts Fold OL8 . . . . 67 A1
St Cuthbert's RC High Sch
    OL16 . . . . 31 B1
St Cuthbert's RC Prim Sch
    Manchester M20 . . . . . . 110 C6
    Wigan WN5 . . . . 54 D6
St Damian's RC Science Coll
    OL6 . . . . 85 E7
St David's Ave SK6 . . . . . . 113 B2
St Davids CE Prim Sch
    WN2 . . . . 38 B7
St David's Cl M33 . . . . 108 A3
St David's Cl OL16 . . . . 85 D7
St David's Cres WN2 . . . . . 38 B5
St Davids Rd SK8 . . . . 123 A6
St David's Rd SK7 . . . . 124 C1
St Davids Wlk M32 . . . . 96 A2
St Domingo St OL9 . . . . . . 153 B2
St Dominics Mews BL3 . . . 146 C3
St Dominics Way M24 . . . . 65 A7
St Dunstan's RC Prim Sch
    M40 . . . . 83 A8
St Dunstan Wlk M40 . . . . . 83 A6
St Edmund Arrowsmith RC
    High Sch WN4 . . . . 73 B2
St Edmund Hall Cl BL0 . . . 11 C4
St Edmunds RC Prim Sch
    M40 . . . . 157 B2
St Edmund St BL1 . . . . 145 B3
St Edwards CE Prim Sch
    OL11 . . . . 30 C2
St Edward's RC Prim Sch
    OL4 . . . . 67 E7
St Elisabeth's CE Prim Sch
    SK5 . . . . 111 E8
St Elisabeth's Way SK5 . . 111 E8
St Elizabeth's RC Prim Sch
    M22 . . . . 121 E2
St Elizabeth's Rd WN2 . . . 38 B5
St Elmo Ave SK2 . . . . 124 D7
St Elmo Pk SK12 . . . . 134 C4
SS Osmund & Andrew RC
    Prim Sch BL2 . . . . 42 F6
SS Simon & Jude's CE Prim
    Sch ■ BL3 . . . . 42 A3
St Ethelbert's Ave BL3 . . 144 B1
St Ethelbert's RC Prim Sch
    BL3 . . . . 144 B1
St Francis RC Prim Sch
    M12 . . . . 165 B2
St Gabriel Cl WN8 . . . . 35 C3
St Gabriel's CE Prim Sch
    M24 . . . . 65 D7
St Gabriel's Cl OL11 . . . . . 30 D1
St Gabriels Mews ■ M24 . 65 C7
St Gabriel's RC High Sch
    BL9 . . . . 140 A1
St Gabriel's Prim Sch
    Leigh WN7 . . . . 76 E7
    Rochdale OL11 . . . . 30 D1
ST GEORGE'S 162 A3
St George's Ave
    Manchester M15 . . . . . . 162 A3
    Sale WA15 . . . . 120 A8
    Westhoughton BL5 . . . . . 57 F7
St George's Central CE Prim
    Sch ■ M29 . . . . 59 A1

St Georges CE Prim Sch
    BL5 . . . . 57 D7
St George's CE Prim Sch
 ■ Atherton M46 . . . . 58 C4
    Hyde SK14 . . . . 167 A1
    Mossley OL5 . . . . 68 B1
    Salford M6 . . . . 81 A5
    Stockport SK2 . . . . 170 C2
St George's Cres
    Sale WA15 . . . . 120 B8
    Salford M6 . . . . 80 A3
    Walkden M28 . . . . 60 D2
St George's Ct
    Hyde SK14 . . . . 167 B2
    Manchester M15 . . . . . . 162 A3
    Tyldesley WN7 . . . . 76 F8
St George's Dr
    Altrincham WA14 . . . . . 119 B7
 ■ Bolton BL1 . . . . 145 B4
    Eccles M30 . . . . 79 F1
 ■ Stretford M32 . . . . 96 C1
    Whitefield BL9 . . . . 45 C3
St Georges Dr SK14 . . . . . 167 A1
St George's Dr M40 . . . . . . 83 B7
St George's Gdns M34 . . . 101 A1
St George's Pl
    Atherton M46 . . . . 58 B4
    Salford M6 . . . . 81 A5
St George's RC High Sch
    M28 . . . . 60 C2
St Georges Rd
    Stretford M32 . . . . 96 C1
    Whitefield BL9 . . . . 45 C4
St George's Rd
    Bolton BL1 . . . . 145 B4
    Carrington M31 . . . . 106 D6
    Droylsden M43 . . . . 83 F3
    Manchester M14 . . . . . . 110 E7
    Rochdale OL11 . . . . 29 F8
St George's Sq OL9 . . . . . 65 E3
St George's St
    Bolton BL1 . . . . 145 C4
    Stalybridge SK15 . . . . . . 86 A3
    Tyldesley M29 . . . . 76 F8
St George's Terr BB4 . . . . . . 3 A6
St George's Way M46 . . . . . 81 A4
St Germain St BL4 . . . . 60 C8
St Gilbert's RC Prim Sch
    SK14 . . . . 79 B2
St Giles Dr SK14 . . . . 167 C2
St Gregorys Cl BL4 . . . . . . 60 C8
St Gregory's RC Prim Sch ■
    BL4 . . . . 60 E8
St Gregorys Rd M13 . . . . . 163 C3
St Helena Rd BL1 . . . . 145 B3
St Helens CE Prim Sch
    WA3 . . . . 105 B2
St Helens Cl WA13 . . . . . . 105 B2
St Helens Coll (Newton
    Campus) WA12 . . . . 89 B4
St Helens Rd
    Bolton BL3, BL5 . . . . . . 146 B3
    Leigh WN7 . . . . 75 C2
St Helier's Dr M7 . . . . 155 C4
St Helier Sq M19 . . . . 110 F5
St Heliers St BL3 . . . . 147 A4
St Herberts Ct OL9 . . . . . . 152 B3
St Herberts RC Prim Sch
    OL9 . . . . 152 A3
St Hilarys Pk ■ SK9 . . . . . 137 A1
St Hilda's CE Prim Sch
 ■ Manchester M16 . . . . . . 97 B2
    Oldham OL1 . . . . 153 A4
    Prestwich M25 . . . . 63 C4
St Hilda's Cl M22 . . . . 109 E1
St Hilda's Dr OL1 . . . . 153 A4
St Hilda's Rd
    Denton M34 . . . . 100 F6
    Manchester M16 . . . . . . 161 C1
    Wythenshawe M22 . . . . 109 D1
St Hilda's View M45 . . . . . 62 F8
St Hugh of Lincoln RC Prim
    Sch ■ M32 . . . . 96 C3
St Hugh's CE Prim Sch
    OL4 . . . . 67 E3
St Hugh's Cl WA14 . . . . . . 119 E8
St Hugh's RC Prim Sch
    WA15 . . . . 119 F8
St Ignatius Wlk M5 . . . . . . 161 B4
St Ives Ave SK8 . . . . 123 A6
St Ives Cres M33 . . . . 108 B6
St Ives Rd M14 . . . . 98 B2
St Ives Way OL2 . . . . 49 A4
St James Ave BL2 . . . . 42 E7
St James' Sq ■ BL8 . . . . . 27 B4
St James CE Prim Sch
    Farnworth BL4 . . . . 60 C7
    Wardle OL12 . . . . 15 C6
St James' CE Prim Sch
    Ashton-u-L OL6 . . . . . . 166 C3
    Manchester M18 . . . . . . 99 D5
    Manchester, Rusholme M14 98 D2
    Shaw OL2 . . . . 149 B3
    Wigan WN3 . . . . 54 F5
St James CE Prim Sch Daisy
    Hill BL5 . . . . 57 F5
St James CE Sch ■
    SK13 . . . . 116 B8
St James Ct
    Glossop SK13 . . . . 116 C7
    Salford M6 . . . . 80 B3
St Jame's Cl OL2 . . . . 48 C8
St James Cres WN2 . . . . . . 74 F8
St James Ct
    Altrincham WA15 . . . . . 119 E4
 ■ Bury BL8 . . . . 27 B4
    Cheadle SK8 . . . . 131 F6
    Manchester M20 . . . . . . 122 B8

St James Ct continued
 ■ Oldham OL4 . . . . 67 C8
    Standish WN6 . . . . 19 D2
St James' Ct
 ■ Hattersley SK14 . . . . . 102 D2
    Salford M6 . . . . 80 B3
St James Dr M33 . . . . 108 A3
St James' Dr SK9 . . . . 137 A6
St James Gr WN3 . . . . 150 B2
St James' Gr ■ OL10 . . . . . 29 C2
St James Lo SK3 . . . . 124 A4
St James' RC High Sch
    SK8 . . . . 131 F6
St James' RC Prim Sch
    Hattersley SK14 . . . . . . 102 D2
    Orrell WN5 . . . . 53 D4
St James Rd
    Manchester M4 . . . . 111 B5
    Salford M7 . . . . 155 B2
St James' Rd WN5 . . . . 53 D4
St James's CE Sec Sch &
    Sports Coll BL4 . . . . 60 D6
St James's Gr WA15 . . . . . 169 B3
St James's Wlk M44 . . . . . 107 F1
St James's RC Prim Sch
    M6 . . . . 154 C3
St James's Sq ■ M46 . . . . 58 C4
St James's St OL1 . . . . 67 B7
St James St
    Ashton-u-L OL6 . . . . 85 D2
    Eccles M30 . . . . 79 E2
    Farnworth BL4 . . . . 60 B7
    Heywood OL10 . . . . 29 C2
    Manchester M1 . . . . 163 A4
    Milnrow OL16 . . . . 31 F6
    Shaw OL2 . . . . 149 B3
    Westhoughton BL5 . . . . . 57 F5
St James' St BB4 . . . . 3 A7
St James' Way SK8 . . . . . . 131 F6
St John Bosco RC Prim Sch
    M9 . . . . 65 A3
St John Fisher RC High Sch
    WN6 . . . . 36 F2
St John Fisher RC Prim Sch
    Denton M34 . . . . 101 B1
    Middleton M24 . . . . 47 B3
St John Fisher & St Thomas
    More RC Prim Sch
    M22 . . . . 121 D4
St John Rigby Coll WN5 . . 35 F7
St John's Ave
    Droylsden M43 . . . . 84 B2
    Westhoughton BL5 . . . . . 39 D3
    Failsworth M35 . . . . 83 F8
    Leigh WN7 . . . . 75 F6
St John's CE Inf Sch
    M35 . . . . 84 A7
St John's CE Jun Sch
    Dukinfield SK16 . . . . . . 101 E8
    Farnworth BL4 . . . . 60 E8
    Hindley WN2 . . . . 57 B3
    Manchester, Heaton Mersey
    SK4 . . . . 110 E2
    Manchester M13 . . . . . . 98 E4
    Radcliffe M26 . . . . 44 B1
    Salford M24 . . . . 80 C6
    Slattocks M24 . . . . 47 E6
    Wigan WN5 . . . . 54 B6
St John's Cl
    Dukinfield SK16 . . . . . . 101 E8
    Romiley SK6 . . . . 113 B2
St Johns Ct
    Oldham OL4 . . . . 67 F7
    Ramsbottom BL0 . . . . . 138 C2
    Westhoughton BL5 . . . . . 39 E3
St John's Ct
 ■ Abram WN2 . . . . 56 B1
    Altrincham WA14 . . . . . 119 D3
    Hyde SK14 . . . . 167 C3
    Radcliffe M26 . . . . 44 C2
 ■ Rochdale OL16 . . . . 31 B6
    Salford M7 . . . . 155 A2
St John's Dr
    Hyde SK14 . . . . 167 C3
 ■ Rochdale OL16 . . . . 31 B6
St John's Gdns OL5 . . . . . . 68 D2
St John's Ind Est OL4 . . . . 67 E6
St John's Mews BL8 . . . . . 26 F7
St Johns Mosley Common
    CE Prim Sch M28 . . . . . . 77 F7
St John's Pass M3 . . . . . . 162 B4
St John's Pl SK4 . . . . 110 E3
St John's RC Prim Sch
    Manchester M21 . . . . . . 97 A1
    Rochdale OL11 . . . . 139 C2
St John's Rd
    Altrincham WA14 . . . . . 119 D3
    Aspull WN2 . . . . 38 B5
    Bolton BL6 . . . . 40 B4
    Boothstown M28 . . . . . . 77 F7
    Denton M34 . . . . 100 F5
    Hazel Grove SK7 . . . . . . 124 B1
    Manchester, Heaton Mersey
    SK4 . . . . 110 E2
    Manchester, Longsight M13 98 F4
    Manchester, Old Trafford
    M16 . . . . 97 C4
    Wilmslow SK9 . . . . 136 E3
St Johns Sq M3 . . . . 158 A2
St John's St
    Abram WN2 . . . . 56 B1
    Farnworth BL4 . . . . 60 E8
    Failsworth M24, M40 . . . 65 D3
    Prestwich M25 . . . . 63 D7

St John St
    Atherton M46 . . . . 58 D3
    Dukinfield SK16 . . . . . . 101 E8
 ■ Eccles M30 . . . . 79 D1
    Horwich BL6 . . . . 22 B3
    Irlam M44 . . . . 94 A2
    Manchester M3 . . . . 162 B4
    Newton-le-W WA12 . . . . 89 A3
 ■ Oldham OL4 . . . . 67 F6
    Pendlebury M27 . . . . 80 B6
    Walkden M28 . . . . 60 D4
St Johns Wlk ■ SK3 . . . . . 123 B8
St John's Wlk OL9 . . . . . . 152 C2
St Johns Wood Rd 40 B4
St John the Evangelist RC
    Prim Sch BL7 . . . . 9 D4
St John Vianney Sch M16 . 97 B2
St John with St Mark CE
    Prim Sch BL9 . . . . 140 C4
St John with St Michael CE
    Prim Sch OL12 . . . . 4 E5
St Joseph & St Bedes RC
    Prim Sch BL9 . . . . 141 B4
St Josephs Ave M45 . . . . . 63 C7
St Josephs Cl OL2 . . . . . . 149 C4
St Joseph's Dr
    Rochdale OL16 . . . . 31 B4
    Salford M5 . . . . 161 B4
St Joseph's RC High Sch &
    Sports Coll ■ BL4 . . . . . 22 E1
St Joseph's RC Inf Sch ■
    SK5 . . . . 111 E8
St Joseph's RC Jun Sch ■
    SK5 . . . . 111 E8
St Joseph's RC Prim Sch
    Adlington PR6 . . . . 21 B8
 ■ Denton OL13 . . . . 3 D8
    Bolton BL1 . . . . 142 C1
    Heywood OL10 . . . . 29 C1
 ■ Leigh WN7 . . . . 76 A4
    Manchester M13 . . . . . . 98 E4
    Mossley OL5 . . . . 68 C1
    Ramsbottom BL0 . . . . . 138 B2
 ■ Sale M33 . . . . 108 B4
    Shevington Moor WN6 . . 19 A3
    Shaw OL2 . . . . 149 B1
    Stockport SK1 . . . . 169 C1
St Joseph's The Worker RC
    Prim Sch M44 . . . . 94 A3
St Jude's RC Prim Sch
    SK4 . . . . 54 F5
St Katherines Dr BL6 . . . . . 21 C3
St Kentigern's RC Prim Sch
    M14 . . . . 98 A1
St Kilda Ave BL4 . . . . 60 F6
St Kilda's Ave M43 . . . . 83 F3
St Kilda's Dr M7 . . . . 155 C4
St Lawrence Quay M50 . . . 96 F7
St Lawrence Rd M34 . . . . . 101 A3
St Lawrence St M7 . . . . . . 162 A2
St Leonard's Ave BL6 . . . . 22 F1
 ■ St Leonards Ct ■ M33 . 107 F4
St Leonard's Rd SK4 . . . . 111 D5
St Leonard's Sq ■ M24 . . 47 A1
St Leonard's St M24 . . . . . 47 A1
St Lesmo Ct SK3 . . . . 123 C7
St Lesmo Rd SK3 . . . . 123 C7
St Lewis RC Prim Sch
    WA3 . . . . 91 B1
St Luke's Ave WA3 . . . . . . 90 D8
St Lukes CE Prim Sch
    OL9 . . . . 152 A3
    Bury BL9 . . . . 44 F8
    Glossop SK13 . . . . 104 C1
    Manchester M12 . . . . . . 164 B1
    Salford M5 . . . . 161 B4
St Luke's Cres SK16 . . . . . 101 C8
St Lukes Ct
    Bolton BL1 . . . . 144 C4
    Chadderton OL9 . . . . . . 152 A3
 ■ Manchester M9 . . . . 53 E4
St Lukes Ho WN4 . . . . 73 C4
St Luke's RC Prim Sch
    M6 . . . . 80 C5
St Luke's Rd M6 . . . . 154 B2
St Luke St OL11 . . . . 139 C1
St Lukes Wlk ■ M40 . . . . . 83 A6
St Malachy's RC Prim Sch
    M40 . . . . 156 C1
St Malo Rd M45 . . . . 37 C4
St Margaret Mary's RC Prim
    Sch M40 . . . . 65 D4
St Margaret's Ave M19 . . 110 F6
St Margaret's CE Prim Sch
 ■ Heywood OL10 . . . . 29 A1
    Manchester M16 . . . . . . 97 D2
 ■ Oldham OL8 . . . . 66 B2
    Prestwich M25 . . . . 63 D7
St Margaret's Cl
    Altrincham WA14 . . . . . 119 C4
 ■ Bolton BL1 . . . . 144 B4
    Prestwich M25 . . . . 63 C6
St Margaret's Gdns OL8 . . 66 C3
St Margaret's RC Prim Sch
    SK13 . . . . 115 D8
St Margaret's Rd
    Altrincham WA14 . . . . . 119 C4
    Bolton BL1 . . . . 144 B4
    Cheadle SK8 . . . . 123 A6
    Failsworth M24, M40 . . . 65 D3
    Prestwich M25 . . . . 63 C7
St Margaret Ward RC Prim
    Sch M33 . . . . 107 C2

St Marie's RC Prim Sch
    Bury BL9 . . . . 140 C1
    Standish WN6 . . . . 19 E2
St Mark's Ave
    Altrincham WA14 . . . . . 119 A5
    Royton OL2 . . . . 49 A4
    Wigan WN5 . . . . 54 F7
St Marks CE Prim Sch
    WN5 . . . . 54 F6
St Mark's CE Prim Sch
    Romiley SK6 . . . . 113 A4
    Worsley M28 . . . . 78 F6
St Mark's Cl OL2 . . . . 49 A4
St Mark's Cres OL8 . . . . . . 60 D1
St Mark's Ct OL9 . . . . 152 B8
St Mark's La M7, M8 . . . . 155 C4
St Mark's RC Prim Sch
    M27 . . . . 62 A2
St Mark's Sq ■ BL9 . . . . . 140 C4
St Mark's St
    Bolton BL3 . . . . 145 C1
    Reddish M19 . . . . 99 C1
    Romiley SK6 . . . . 113 A4
St Mark St SK16 . . . . 166 B1
St Mark's View BL3 . . . . . 145 C1
St Mark's Wlk BL3 . . . . . . 147 B4
St Martin's Ave SK4 . . . . . 168 C2
St Martin's CE Jun & Inf Sch
    OL8 . . . . 67 B2
St Martin's Cl
    Droylsden M43 . . . . 83 F3
    Hyde SK14 . . . . 167 C2
St Martin's Dr M7 . . . . 155 C4
St Martins Rd M33 . . . . . . 107 E6
St Martin's Rd
    Marple SK6 . . . . 126 A6
    Oldham OL8 . . . . 67 B2
St Martin's St OL11 . . . . . . 30 D1
St Mary's Ave
    Billinge WN5 . . . . 71 C4
    Bolton BL3 . . . . 144 B1
    Denton M34 . . . . 113 A8
St Mary's CE Prim Sch
    Bolton BL3 . . . . 146 A4
 ■ Droylsden M43 . . . . 84 B1
    Failsworth M40 . . . . 65 C5
    Hawkshaw BL8 . . . . 10 C2
    Ince-in-M WN3 . . . . 55 F4
    Irlam M44 . . . . 105 C5
    Prestwich M25 . . . . 63 A4
    Reddish SK5 . . . . 112 A6
    Rochdale OL11 . . . . 31 A4
 ■ Sale M33 . . . . 108 A4
    Uppermill OL3 . . . . 69 C4
    Urmston M41 . . . . 95 C4
St Mary's CE Prim Sch High
    Crompton OL2 . . . . 48 F8
St Marys Cl M25 . . . . 63 A4
St Mary's Cl
    Ashton under Lyne SK16 . 166 B1
 ■ Manchester M19 . . . . . . 99 A1
St Mary's Ct
    Failsworth M40 . . . . 83 B8
    Golborne WA3 . . . . 91 B8
    Hollingworth SK14 . . . . 103 C5
    Manchester M8 . . . . 63 F1
    Partington M31 . . . . 105 F4
    Prestwich M25 . . . . 63 A4
St Mary's Dr
    Cheadle SK8 . . . . 122 F6
    Manchester SK5 . . . . . . 111 F6
    Uppermill OL3 . . . . 69 C5
St Mary's Gate
    Manchester M3 . . . . 158 C2
    Rochdale OL12, OL16 . . . 139 E4
    Shaw OL2 . . . . 149 B3
    Uppermill OL3 . . . . 69 B8
St Mary's Hall Rd M8 . . . . 63 F1
St Mary's Ind Pk SK14 . . . 102 A6
St Mary's Parsonage M3 . 158 C1
St Mary's Pk M25 . . . . 63 A4
St Mary's Pl BL9 . . . . 140 B2
St Mary's RC High Sch M16 . 97 B4
St Mary's RC Inf Sch
    WA12 . . . . 89 C4
St Mary's RC Jun Sch
    WA12 . . . . 89 B3
St Mary's RC Prim Sch
    Denton M34 . . . . 100 D3
    Dukinfield SK16 . . . . . . 101 E6
    Eccles M30 . . . . 79 E1
    Failsworth M35 . . . . 83 E6
    Glossop SK13 . . . . 116 D8
    Horwich BL6 . . . . 22 C2
    Littleborough OL15 . . . . 16 A5
    Manchester M19 . . . . . . 111 A8
    Marple SK6 . . . . 126 B7
    Middleton M24 . . . . 46 E2
    Radcliffe M26 . . . . 44 A4
    Stockport SK4 . . . . 169 B2
 ■ Swinton M27 . . . . 79 F8
St Mary's Rd
    Altrincham WA14 . . . . . 119 C3
    Aspull WN2 . . . . 38 C5
    Disley SK12 . . . . 135 D5
    Dukinfield SK14 . . . . . . 101 F5
 ■ Eccles M30 . . . . 79 F2

St Mary's Rd continued
Failsworth M40 . . . . 83 B7
Glossop SK13 . . . . 116 C8
Prestwich M25 . . . . 63 B4
Sale M33 . . . . 107 F5
Walkden M28 . . . . 60 C5
St Mary's & St John's RC
Prim Sch 2 WN1 . . . . . . 37 C1
St Marys St OL1 . . . . 153 C4
St Mary's St
Manchester, Hulme M15 . . 162 B1
Manchester M3 . . . . 158 C1
St Marys View 3 SK14 . . 101 F5
St Mary's Way
2 Leigh WN7 . . . . 75 F5
Oldham OL1 . . . . 153 C3
Stockport SK1 . . . . 112 A2
St Matthew's CE Inf Sch
 . . . . 47 F2
St Matthew's CE Prim Sch
M32 . . . . 108 C8
St Matthew's CE Prim Sch
Bolton BL1 . . . . 143 B1
Little Lever BL3 . . . . 43 A3
Stockport SK3 . . . . 170 B4
St Matthew's CI WN8 . . . 54 C4
St Matthews St M32 . . . . 96 C1
St Matthew's Dr OL1 . . . 48 A2
St Matthews Grange
BL1 . . . . 143 B1
St Matthew's RC High Sch
M40 . . . . 65 C2
St Matthew's Rd SK3 . . 170 A4
St Matthew's Terr
8 Bolton BL1 . . . . 143 B1
Stockport SK3 . . . . 170 A4
St Matthew's Wlk BL1 . . 143 B1
St Mawes Ct M26 . . . . . . 43 C5
St Maxentius CE Prim Sch
BL2 . . . . 25 D5
St Michael's Ave
Atherton M46 . . . . 58 A1
Bolton BL3 . . . . 42 B2
Bramhall SK7 . . . . 132 E8
St Michael's CE Aided Prim
Sch M41 . . . . 94 F1
St Michael's CE Prim Sch
Atherton M46 . . . . 58 B2
Bolton BL3 . . . . 42 C3
Heywood OL10 . . . . 29 D5
Middleton M24 . . . . 65 A5
St Michaels CI BL8 . . . . . 43 F8
St Michaels Ct M33 . . . 107 E6
St Michael's Ct
Eccles M30 . . . . 95 A8
8 Wigan WN1 . . . . 37 C2
St Michaels Gdns M45 . . 45 B1
St Michael's RC Prim Sch 7
M45 . . . . 45 B1
St Michael's Rd SK14 . . 102 A2
St Michael's Sq
6 Ashton-u-L OL6 . . . . 166 C3
3 Manchester M4 . . . . . 159 A3
St Modwen Rd M32 . . . . 96 A5
St Monica's RC High Sch
M25 . . . . 63 C3
St Monica's RC Prim Sch
M41 . . . . 94 E2
St Nicholas Rd
Golborne WA3 . . . . 75 A1
Manchester M15 . . . . 162 B2
St Osmund's Dr BL2 . . . . 42 E7
St Osmund's Gr BL2 . . . . 42 E7
St Oswalds CI PR7 . . . . . 19 E8
St Oswald's RC Prim Sch
Ashton-in-M WN4 . . . . 73 B3
Coppull PR7 . . . . 19 D8
St Oswald's Rd WN4 . . . 73 A2
St Oswalds Rd M19 . . . . 99 B2
St Patrick's RC High Sch &
Arts Coll M30 . . . . 79 B1
St Patrick's RC Prim Sch
Manchester M4 . . . . 159 C3
Oldham OL8 . . . . 153 A2
Wigan WN1 . . . . 151 A4
St Patrick's St WN1 . . . . 151 A4
St Patrick's VA RC Prim Sch
OL12 . . . . 15 A1
St Patricks Way WN1 . . 151 A3
St Paul's Ave WN3 . . . . . 54 F4
St Pauls CE Prim Sch
1 Salford M5 . . . . 81 B1
Walkden M28 . . . . 60 E3
St Paul's CE Prim Sch
Adlington PR6 . . . . 21 A7
Bolton BL1 . . . . 112 B4
Brinnington SK5 . . . . 141 B4
Bury BL9 . . . . 141 A3
Manchester M20 . . . . 110 C6
Royton OL2 . . . . 48 C3
Salford M7 . . . . 81 B8
Stalybridge SK15 . . . . 86 C2
Walkden M28 . . . . 60 F2
Wigan WN1 . . . . 54 F3
St Paul's CI
Adlington PR6 . . . . 21 A8
Stalybridge SK15 . . . . 86 C2
St Pauls Ct
3 Manchester M7 . . . . . 63 C1
Stalybridge SK15 . . . . 86 C2
2 Walkden M28 . . . . . . 60 D2
St Paul's Ct M26 . . . . . . 44 A1
St Pauls Gdns 4 M7 . . . 63 C1
St Paul's Gdns SK14 . . . 167 B3
St Paul's Hill Rd SK14 . . 167 C2

St Pauls Ho 9 OL2 . . . . 48 D4
St Paul's Peel CE Prim Sch
M38 . . . . 59 F5
St Paul's PI 1 BL1 . . . . 142 C3
St Paul's RC High Sch
M23 . . . . 121 B4
St Paul's RC Prim Sch
Hyde SK14 . . . . 167 C4
Poynton SK12 . . . . 133 E2
St Pauls Rd M28 . . . . . . 60 E2
St Paul's Rd
Manchester, Sedgley Park
M7 . . . . 63 C1
Manchester, Withington
M20 . . . . 110 C6
Stockport, Heaton Moor
SK4 . . . . 168 A4
St Paul's Rise 4 M7 . . . . 63 C1
St Paul's St
Bury BL9 . . . . 141 A3
Hyde SK14 . . . . 167 B3
Ramsbottom BL0 . . . . 138 C2
Stockport SK1 . . . . 112 A3
St Pauls Trad Est SK15 . 86 C2
St Paul's Villas BL9 . . . . 141 A3
ST PETERFIELD 146 A2
St Peter & St Paul's RC Prim
Sch BL3 . . . . 145 B1
St Peter's Ave BL1 . . . . 142 A2
St Peter's CE Inf Sch
WN7 . . . . 75 C5
St Peter's CE Jun Sch
WN7 . . . . 75 C5
St Peter's CE Prim Sch
Ashton-in-M WN4 . . . . 72 F6
Ashton-u-L OL7 . . . . 166 A1
Bury BL9 . . . . 44 E6
Farnworth BL4 . . . . 60 D7
Hindley WN2 . . . . 56 C5
Newton-le-W WA12 . . . . . 89 E4
Swinton M27 . . . . 79 F8
St Peters CI OL7 . . . . 84 F2
St Peter's CI WA13 . . . . 117 A4
St Peter's Ct 1 M32 . . . . 96 E3
St Peter's Dr SK14 . . . . . 167 C2
St Petersgate SK1 . . . . . 169 C1
St Peter's Gate OL14 . . . 6 B8
St Peter's Ho BL2 . . . . . . 148 B2
St Peter's RC High Sch
(Upper) M12 . . . . 99 A4
St Peter's RC High Sch Visual
Arts Coll WN5 . . . . 53 F7
St Peter's RC Prim Sch
Hazel Grove SK7 . . . . 124 D1
Middleton M24 . . . . 65 A7
Stalybridge SK15 . . . . 86 A1
Wythenshawe M23 . . . . . 121 A3
St Peter's Rd
Bury BL9 . . . . 44 F6
Swinton M27 . . . . 79 F8
St Peter's Smithills Dean CE
Prim Sch BL1 . . . . 142 B4
St Peter's Sq
Manchester M1 . . . . 162 C4
Stockport SK1 . . . . 169 C1
St Peter's Sq Metro Sta
M2 . . . . 162 C4
St Peter's Sq
6 Ashton-u-L OL6 . . . . 166 A2
Rochdale OL16 . . . . 31 B6
St Peter's Terr BL4 . . . . . 60 D7
St Peter's VC CE Prim Sch
OL16 . . . . 31 B5
St Peter's Way
Bolton, Burnden BL1, BL2, BL3,
BL4 . . . . 42 B4
Bolton, Mill Hill BL1 . . . . 145 C4
St Philip Howard RC Sports
Coll 7 SK13 . . . . 116 B8
St Philip's Ave BL3 . . . . 147 A4
St Philips CE Prim Sch
M45 . . . . 162 C2
St Philip's CE Prim Sch
M46 . . . . 58 E3
St Philip's CE Sch M3 . . 158 A1
St Philip's PI M3 . . . . . . 158 A2
St Philip's RC Prim Sch
Manchester M7 . . . . 63 C1
Stockport SK2 . . . . 124 E6
St Philip's Rd M18 . . . . . 99 D4
St Philips Sq M3 . . . . . . 158 A2
St Philip's Dr OL1, OL2 . . 48 E1
St Raphael's RC Prim Sch
SK15 . . . . 86 E4
St Richard's CI M46 . . . . 58 C4
St Richard's RC Prim Sch
1 Atherton M46 . . . . . . 58 C4
Manchester M12 . . . . 99 B3
St Saviour CE Prim Sch
M26 . . . . 61 C7
St Saviour's Com Prim Sch
OL13 . . . . 4 A8
St Saviour's Rd SK2 . . . 124 C5
Saintsbridge Rd M22 . . . 121 C2
St Sebastian's RC Prim Sch
M6 . . . . 81 A5
St Simons CI SK3 . . . . . 124 C8
St Simon's RC Prim Sch
SK7 . . . . 124 C4
St Simon St M3 . . . . . . 158 A3
St Stephen & All Martyrs' CE
Prim Sch BL2 . . . . 148 C1
St Stephen's Ave
Manchester L M34 . . . . . . 100 E8
Wigan WN1 . . . . 151 A4
St Stephen's CE Prim Sch
5 Ashton-u-L M34 . . . . 100 E8
Bury BL8 . . . . 27 B1

St Stephen's CE Prim Sch
continued
Kearsley M26 . . . . 61 A6
Tyldesley M29 . . . . 77 B6
St Stephens CI M29 . . . . 77 A5
St Stephen's CI
Bolton BL2 . . . . 148 C1
Manchester M13 . . . . 164 A1
St Stephen's Gdns
Kearsley BL4 . . . . 61 A6
10 Middleton M24 . . . . . 47 A2
St Stephen's RC Sch M43 44 A2
St Stephen's Rd WN6 . . . 19 C1
St Stephen St
6 Oldham OL8 . . . . 67 A8
Salford M3 . . . . 158 B2
St Stephens View M43 . . 84 A2
St Teresa's RC Prim Sch
Irlam M44 . . . . 105 E8
Little Lever BL3 . . . . 43 A3
Manchester M16 . . . . 97 A3
Up Holland WN8 . . . . 35 B1
St Teresa's Rd M16 . . . . 97 A3
St Teresa's RC Prim Sch
Ashton-in-M WN4 . . . . 73 C3
Golborne WA3 . . . . 74 B1
7 Leigh WN7 . . . . 76 B4
Oldham OL8 . . . . 153 A1
Westhoughton BL5 . . . . . . 40 B1
St Thomas' CE Prim Sch
Newhey OL16 . . . . 32 B4
Reddish SK4 . . . . 111 C6
Stockport SK1 . . . . 170 C4
St Thomas CI BB4 . . . . . . 1 A7
St Thomas' CI M26 . . . . . 44 A3
St Thomas Ct BL9 . . . . . 141 A2
St Thomas's Leesfield CE Prim
Sch OL4 . . . . 67 E5
St Thomas Moorside CE (VA)
Prim Sch OL1 . . . . 49 E4
St Thomas More RC Coll
M34 . . . . 100 F2
St Thomas More RC Prim
Sch M24 . . . . 65 A5
St Thomas More Sports Ctr
M34 . . . . 100 F2
St Thomas of Canterbury
Prim Sch BL1 . . . . 144 A4
St Thomas of Canterbury RC
Prim Sch M7 . . . . 155 B2
St Thomas Par OL4 . . . . . 67 E6
St Thomas' PI M8 . . . . . 159 A4
St Thomas's CE Prim Sch
Bolton BL1 . . . . 143 A2
Bury BL1 . . . . 141 B1
St Thomas's Circ OL8 . . 153 A1
St Thomas's Ct WN8 . . . . 53 C7
St Thomas's PI SK1 . . . . 170 C4
St Thomas St
Bolton BL1 . . . . 143 A2
Wigan WN3 . . . . 150 C3
St Thomas Street N OL8 153 B1
St Thomas Street S OL8 . 153 B1
St Thomas the Martyr CE
Prim Sch WN6 . . . . 53 B7
St Veronica's RC Prim Sch
BB4 . . . . 1 B7
St Vincent's RC Inf Sch
WA15 . . . . 119 E5
St Vincent's RC Jun Sch
WA15 . . . . 119 E5
St Vincents RC Prim Sch 5
OL12 . . . . 14 A1
St Vincent St M4 . . . . . . 159 C2
St Werburgh's Rd M21,
M16 . . . . 109 C8
St Werburgh's Rd Sta
M21 . . . . 109 C8
St Wilfred's CE Prim Sch
WN6 . . . . 19 F1
St Wilfred's Dr OL12 . . . . 14 D4
St Wilfrids CE Prim Sch 1
M22 . . . . 121 E8
St Wilfrid's CE Prim Sch
M40 . . . . 83 D5
St Wilfrid's Ent Ctr M15 162 B2
St Wilfrid's RC Prim Sch
WN4 . . . . 73 D4
St Wilfrid's RC Prim Sch
M15 . . . . 162 B2
St Wilfrid's Rd WN6 . . . . 19 F1
St Wilfrid's St M15 . . . . 162 B2
St Wilfrid's Way WN6 . . . 19 E1
St William Rd PR6 . . . . . . 21 A8
St Williams Ave BL3 . . . 147 B3
St William's RC Prim Sch
WN2 . . . . 151 C3
St Winifred's PI 2 SK15 . 85 F2
St Winifred's Rd OL12 . . 14 A3
SK4 . . . . 168 A2
Salcombe Ave BL2 . . . . . 26 D1
Salcombe CI
Sale M33 . . . . 107 E5
Wigan WN1 . . . . 37 E2
Salcombe Gr BL2 . . . . . . 42 F6
Salcombe Rd
Droylsden M11, M43 . . . . 99 D8
Stockport SK2 . . . . 124 C8
Salco Sq WA14 . . . . 119 D6
Salcot Wlk 2 M40 . . . . . 159 C3
SALE 108 C4
Sale Gram Sch M33 . . . . 108 C3
Sale Heys Rd M33 . . . . . . 107 F3
Sale High Sch M33 . . . . . 108 D2
Sale La M29 . . . . 77 D8

Sale L Ctr M33 . . . . 108 C5
SALEM 67 D6
Sale Metro Sta M33 . . . . 108 B4
Salem Gr OL4 . . . . 67 D6
Sales's La BL9 . . . . 80 C3
Salesbury Way WN3 . . . . 55 A3
Sale's La BL9 . . . . 12 B3
Sale St OL15 . . . . 16 B6
Sale Water Pk * M33 . . 108 E7
SALFORD 81 A2
Salford App M3 . . . . . . 158 C2
Salford Art Gallery & Mus *
M6 . . . . 81 A3
Salford Cath * M3 . . . . 158 C2
Salford Central Sta M3 . 158 B1
Salford City Acad M30 . . 78 F1
Salford City Coll M30 . . . 79 F4
Salford City Coll (City
Campus Skills Ctr) M6 . . 81 B4
Salford City Coll (De la Salle
Ctr) 8 M6 . . . . 80 C3
Salford City Coll (Eccles
Sixth Form Ctr) M30 . . . 79 F5
Salford City Coll (Pendleton
Sixth Form Ctr) M6 . . . . 154 A4
Salford City Coll (Walkden
Sixth Form Ctr) M28 . . . 60 D1
Salford Crescent Sta M5 . 81 B2
Salford Foyer M6 . . . . . . 154 C3
Salford Quays Metro Sta
M50 . . . . 161 A3
Salford RC Cath * M3 . . 158 A2
Salford Rd BL5 . . . . 59 C7
Salford Royal Hospl M6 . 80 B3
Salford Shopping City
M6 . . . . 154 C3
Salford St
Bury BL9 . . . . 141 A4
Oldham OL4 . . . . 67 C5
Salford Univ Bsns Pk M6/
M7 . . . . 81 C3
Salford Watersports Ctr
M50 . . . . 161 A3
Salik Gdns OL11 . . . . . . 139 C1
Salisbury Ave
Heywood OL10 . . . . 46 C8
Hindley WN2 . . . . 56 E6
Salisbury Cres OL6 . . . . . 85 D7
Salisbury Dr
Dukinfield SK16 . . . . 102 A7
Manchester M25 . . . . 63 C2
Salisbury House M3 . . . 158 B2
Salisbury Rd
Altrincham M41 . . . . 119 D7
1 Ashton-in-M WN4 . . . 73 A5
Horwich BL6 . . . . 22 F1
Manchester M21 . . . . 97 C1
Oldham OL4 . . . . 67 B6
Radcliffe M26 . . . . 43 E5
Salford M30 . . . . 80 A4
Swinton M27 . . . . 79 F7
Urmston M41 . . . . 95 D4
Salisbury St
Bolton BL3 . . . . 145 A2
Glossop SK13 . . . . 104 A5
4 Golborne WA3 . . . . . . 90 A8
Manchester M14 . . . . 98 A4
Middleton M24 . . . . 47 B1
Reddish SK5 . . . . 111 F8
Whitefield M45 . . . . 62 F8
Salisbury Terr BL3 . . . . . 43 C3
Salisbury Way M29 . . . . . 77 B8
Salix Ct M6 . . . . 81 A3
Salkeld Ave WN4 . . . . . . 72 F3
Salkeld St OL11 . . . . 139 C1
Salley St OL15 . . . . 6 C2
Sallowfields WN5 . . . . . . 53 D5
Sally Barn Cotts BB4 . . . . 1 E8
Salmon Fields OL2 . . . . . 48 F3
Salmon Fields Bsns Village
OL2 . . . . 48 F3
Salmon St
Manchester M4 . . . . 159 A2
1 Wigan WN1 . . . . 37 E1
Salmsbury Hall CI BL0 . . 11 B4
Salop St
Bolton BL2 . . . . 148 A2
Salford M6 . . . . 81 A4
Saltash CI M22 . . . . 121 C1
Saltburn Wlk 23 M9 . . . 157 B4
Saltdene Rd M22 . . . . . . 121 C1
Saltergate CI BL3 . . . . . . 40 F4
Saltergate Mews M5 . . . 81 A1
Salter Rake Gate OL14 . . . 6 A8
Saltersbrook Gr 12 SK9 . 131 E1
Salters Ct M46 . . . . 58 D3
Salterton Dr BL3 . . . . 40 F2
Saltford Ave M4 . . . . . . 160 E1
Saltford Ct M4 . . . . 160 E1
Salthill Ave OL10 . . . . . . 46 E7
Salthill Dr M22 . . . . 121 E2
Saltire Gdns M7 . . . . . . 155 B4
Saltney Ave M20 . . . . . . 109 F7
Saltram CI M26 . . . . 43 C5
Saltram Rd WN3 . . . . 55 A3
Saltrush Rd M22 . . . . . . 121 D1
Salts Dr OL15 . . . . 16 A6
Salts St OL2 . . . . 149 B3
Saltwood Gr BL1 . . . . . . 143 C1
Salutation St 10 M15 . . 162 C2
Salvin CI WN4 . . . . 73 D3
Salvin Wlk 27 M9 . . . . . 64 E3
Salwick CI WN3 . . . . 54 E4
Sam Cowan CI M14 . . . . 98 A3
Samian Gdns M7 . . . . . . 81 C5

Samlesbury CI
Manchester M20 . . . . 109 F3
Oldham OL2 . . . . 48 F7
Sammy Cockson CI M14 . 98 A3
Samouth CI M40 . . . . . . 160 A3
Sampson Sq M14 . . . . . . 98 A4
Sam Rd OL3 . . . . 51 C5
Samson St OL16 . . . . 31 C8
Sam Swire St M15 . . . . 162 C1
Samuel Laycock Specl Sch
SK15 . . . . 85 F4
Samuel St
Bury BL9 . . . . 141 A3
Failsworth M35 . . . . 83 F8
Hollingworth M14 . . . . . . 103 C4
Manchester M24 . . . . 111 B8
Middleton M24 . . . . 30 C2
Rochdale OL11 . . . . 30 A7
Stockport SK4 . . . . 169 A3
Tyldesley M46 . . . . 58 F1
Samwoods Ho WN4 . . . . 73 A5
Sanby Ave M18 . . . . 99 C4
Sanby Rd M18 . . . . 99 C4
Sanctuary CI M15 . . . . . 163 B1
Sanctuary The M15 . . . . 162 B2
Sandacre Rd M23 . . . . . 121 B7
Sandal St M40 . . . . 160 B3
Sandbach Rd BL5 . . . . . . 57 D6
Sandalwood Dr WN6 . . . . 36 F3
Sandbach Ave M14 . . . . 109 F8
Sandbach Rd
Reddish SK5 . . . . 99 E2
Sale M33 . . . . 108 F3
Sandbach Wlk SK8 . . . . 123 A4
Sandbank Gdns OL12 . . . 4 C2
Sand Banks BL1 . . . . 24 F6
Sandbed La
Delph OL3 . . . . 51 A5
Mossley OL5 . . . . 68 C2
Sand Beds La BL0, BB4 . . 2 B5
Sandbrook Com Prim Sch
OL11 . . . . 30 F3
Sandbrook Gdns WN5 . . . 53 C5
Sandbrook Rd WN5 . . . . . 53 C5
Sandbrook Way
Denton M34 . . . . 101 A5
Rochdale OL11 . . . . 30 E4
Sandby CI OL13 . . . . 4 A8
Sandby Dr SK6 . . . . 126 B8
Sandering Dr M8 . . . . . . 155 B1
Sandering CI BL5 . . . . . . 57 D6
Sanderling Dr WN7 . . . . . 76 A6
Sanderling Rd
Hazel Grove SK7 . . . . 125 A4
Newton-le-W WA12 . . . . . 89 C4
Sanderson CI M28 . . . . . . 79 A7
Sanderson Ct M40 . . . . . 157 B1
Sanderson La PR7 . . . . . . 18 A8
Sanderson's Croft WN7 . . 76 C4
Sanderson St
Bury BL9 . . . . 141 A3
1 Leigh WN7 . . . . 75 D5
Manchester M40 . . . . 157 B1
Sanderstead Dr M9 . . . . 64 E3
Sandfield CI 3 WA3 . . . . 90 E8
Sandfield Cres WA3 . . . . 90 C7
Sandfield Dr BL6 . . . . 40 C6
Sandfield Rd OL16 . . . . . 31 B5
Sandfold SK5 . . . . 99 E2
Sandford Ave M18 . . . . . 99 D6
Sandford CI BL2 . . . . 25 E4
Sandford La SK5 . . . . 99 D2
Sandford Rd
Orrell WN5 . . . . 53 C5
Sale M33 . . . . 108 F3
Sandford St M26 . . . . . . 44 D4
Sandgate Ave
Droylsden M11 . . . . 83 D2
Kearsley M26 . . . . 61 C7
Sandgate Dr M41 . . . . . . 95 C4
Sandgate Rd
Chadderton OL9 . . . . 152 B2
Prestwich M45 . . . . 63 B7
Sandham St BL3 . . . . . . 147 C4
Sandheys M34 . . . . 100 F5
Sandheys Gr M18 . . . . . . 99 E4
Sandhill CI BL3 . . . . 147 C4
Sandhill La
Broadbottom SK6 . . . . . . 115 A2
Marple SK6 . . . . 114 E1
Sandhill St SK14 . . . . . . 167 C4
Sandhill Wlk M22 . . . . . 121 B2
Sandhole La OL11 . . . . . . 29 E5
Sand Hole La OL11 . . . . . 30 F1
Sand Hole Rd BL4 . . . . . . 61 A6
Sandhurst Ave M20 . . . . 110 A6
Sandhurst CI BL8 . . . . . . 27 D2
Sandhurst Ct BL2 . . . . . . 42 E6
Sandhurst Dr
Bolton BL2 . . . . 42 E6
2 Wilmslow SK9 . . . . . 137 C8
Sandhurst Rd
Manchester M20 . . . . 110 B2
Stockport SK2 . . . . 124 B5
Sandhurst Rd M9 . . . . . . 64 D1
Sandiacre WN6 . . . . 36 E8
Sandilands Prim Sch
M23 . . . . 120 D8
Sandilands Rd M23 . . . . 120 D7
Sandilea Ct M7 . . . . 63 A1
Sandileigh Ave
Altrincham WA15 . . . . . . 119 F3
Brinnington SK5 . . . . 112 B4
Cheadle SK8 . . . . 123 A6
Manchester M20 . . . . 110 B5

Sandileigh Dr
Altrincham WA15 . . . . . 119 F3
Bolton BL1 . . . . 25 B3
Sandimoss Ct 🔳 M33 . 107 F4
Sandiway
Glossop SK13 . . . . 116 F7
Heywood OL10 . . . . 29 E2
Irlam M44 . . . . 94 A2
Romiley SK6 . . . . 112 F3
Stockport SK7 . . . . 123 E2
Sandiway Cl SK6 . . . . 125 F8
Sandiway Dr M20 . . . . 110 A3
Sandiway Pl WA14 . . . 119 D5
Sandiway Rd
Altrincham WA14 . . . . . 119 D6
Handforth SK9 . . . . 131 D5
Sale M33 . . . . 107 F4
Sandling Dr WA3 . . . . 74 A2
Sandmere Wlk 🔳 M9 . 64 E3
Sandmoor Pl WA13 . . 117 A2
Sandon St BL3 . . . . . . 147 A4
Sandown Ave M6 . . . . 154 B2
Sandown Cl
Culcheth WA3 . . . . 91 F4
🔳 Oldham OL1 . . . . 49 A1
Wilmslow SK9 . . . . 137 D8
Sandown Cres
Little Lever BL3 . . . . 43 A2
Manchester M18 . . . . . . 99 D3
Sandown Dr
Altrincham WA14 . . . . . 129 D6
Denton M34 . . . . 113 B8
Sale M33 . . . . 107 E3
Sandown Gdns M41 . . 95 A2
Sandown Rd
Bolton BL2 . . . . 25 E3
Hazel Grove SK7 . . . . . 125 A2
Stockport SK3 . . . . 123 B8
Whitefield BL9 . . . . 45 A2
Wigan WN6 . . . . 36 E3
Sandown St M18 . . . . 99 F6
Sandpiper Cl
Dukinfield SK16 . . . . . . 101 E7
Farnworth BL4 . . . . 59 F7
Newton-le-W WA12 . . . . 89 C4
Rochdale OL11 . . . . 29 F7
Sandpiper Dr SK3 . . . 170 A2
Sandpiper Rd WN3 . . . 54 B4
Sandpits Bsns Pk SK14 102 E3
Sandra Dr WA12 . . . . . 89 E3
Sandray Cl BL3 . . . . . . 40 F5
Sandray Gr M5 . . . . . . 154 B1
Sandridge Cl BL4 . . . . 60 E8
Sandridge Wlk M22 . . 148 B2
Sandringham Ave
Denton M34 . . . . 100 D6
Reddish M34 . . . . 100 A3
Stalybridge SK15 . . . . . 86 A3
Sandringham Cl
Adlington PR7 . . . . 20 E6
Altrincham WA14 . . . . . 118 F1
Wigan WN5 . . . . 54 E5
Sandringham Ct
Golborne WA3 . . . . 90 E7
🔳 Wilmslow SK9 . . . . . 137 A6
Sandringham Dr
Dukinfield SK16 . . . . . . 101 F7
Leigh WN7 . . . . 76 E7
Milnrow OL16 . . . . 32 A6
Poynton SK12 . . . . 133 D3
Ramsbottom BL8 . . . . . 11 A1
Stockport SK4 . . . . 168 A1
Sandringham Grange
M25 . . . . 63 E3
Sandringham Rd
Cheadle SK8 . . . . 123 A3
Hazel Grove SK7 . . . . . 124 F2
Hindley WN2 . . . . 56 E4
Horwich BL6 . . . . 22 E2
Hyde SK14 . . . . 113 E7
Romiley SK6 . . . . 112 D3
Worsley M28 . . . . 78 A6
Sandringham St M18 . 99 C4
Sandringham Way
Royton OL2 . . . . 48 C6
🔳 Wilmslow SK9 . . . . . 137 A6
Sands Ave OL9 . . . . . . 65 E8
Sands Cl SK14 . . . . . . 102 D1
Sandsend Cl M8 . . . . . 155 B1
Sandsend Rd M41 . . . 95 C3
Sandst
Manchester M40 . . . . . 159 C4
Stalybridge SK15 . . . . . 101 F8
Sandstone Rd
Milnrow OL16 . . . . 31 F7
Wigan WN2 . . . . 54 E2
Sandstone Way M21 . 109 D6
Sands Wlk SK14 . . . . . 102 D1
Sandway WN6 . . . . . . 36 F2
Sandwell Dr M33 . . . . 108 B6
Sandwich Rd M30 . . . . 79 F3
Sandwich St M28 . . . . 60 D2
Sandwick Cres BL3 . . 145 A1
Sandwith Cl WN5 . . . . 53 B8
Sandwood Ave BL3 . . 40 E6
Sandy Acre OL5 . . . . . 86 C8
Sandyacre Cl BL5 . . . . 59 A6
Sandy Ave OL8 . . . . . . 66 D3
Sandy Bank OL2 . . . . . 48 F8
Sandy Bank Ave SK14 102 D1
Sandybank Cl SK13 . . 171 B4
Sandy Bank Rd
Edgworth BL7 . . . . 9 D5
Salford M6 . . . . 155 C4
Sandybrook Cl BL8 . . . 26 F6
Sandybrook Dr M9 . . . 64 C2
Sandy Brow M9 . . . . . 64 D2
Sandy Brow La WA3 . . 90 E2

Sandy Cl BL9 . . . . 44 F4
Sandycroft Ave
🔳 Wigan WN1 . . . . 37 C1
Wythenshawe M22 . . . 121 D3
Sandy Ct WN7 . . . . 75 A1
Sandygate Cl M27 . . . 79 E7
Sandy Gr
Dukinfield SK16 . . . . . . 101 D8
Salford M6 . . . . 154 B3
Swinton M27 . . . . 79 F8
Sandy Haven Cl SK14 102 D1
Sandy Haven Wlk SK14 102 D1
Sandyhill Rd M9 . . . . . 64 B3
Sandyhills BL3 . . . . . . 147 B4
Sandy La
Adlington PR7 . . . . 20 F6
Broadbottom SK13 . . . 115 A4
Culcheth WA3 . . . . 91 A1
Droylsden M43 . . . . . . 84 C2
Dukinfield SK16 . . . . . . 101 D8
Golborne, Aspull Common
  WA3 . . . . 75 A1
Irlam M44 . . . . 94 A2
Lymm WA13 . . . . 117 B4
Manchester M21 . . . . . 109 C8
Middleton M24 . . . . . . 65 C8
Orrell WN5 . . . . 53 D4
Prestwich M25 . . . . . . 63 A2
Reddish SK4, SK5 . . . . 169 B3
Rochdale OL11 . . . . . . 30 C7
Romiley SK6 . . . . 113 D3
Royton OL2 . . . . 48 D4
Salford M6 . . . . 154 B3
Stretford M32 . . . . 96 C1
Tyldesley M29 . . . . 77 B1
Tyldesley, Town Lane M29 77 A4
Uppermill OL3 . . . . 51 B2
Wilmslow SK9 . . . . 136 E8
Wythenshawe M23 . . . 120 E7
Sandylands Dr M25 . . 63 A1
Sandy Meade M25 . . . 63 A3
Sandy Pk WN2 . . . . . . 57 A6
Sandyshot Wlk 🔳 M21 121 F3
Sandy Vale SK16 . . . . 85 E1
Sandywarps M44 . . . . 106 A8
Sandyway M25 . . . . . . 63 A3
Sandy Way WN2 . . . . . 56 C2
Sandyway Cl BL5 . . . . 57 D8
Sandywell Cl M11 . . . . 99 D7
Sandywell St M11 . . . . 99 D8
Sandy Wlk 🔳 OL2 . . . 48 D4
Sandy Wood M6 . . . . . 154 B3
Sanfold La M19 . . . . . 99 C2
Sangster Ct M5 . . . . . 161 A4
Sankey Gr M9 . . . . 64 B3
Sankey St
Bury BL9 . . . . 140 A2
🔳 Golborne WA3 . . . . . 90 A8
Newton-le-W WA12 . . . . 89 A3
Sankey Valley Ind Est
WA12 . . . . 89 A2
Santiago St M14 . . . . 98 B3
Santley St M11 . . . . . . 99 A3
Santon Ave M14 . . . . . 110 E8
Santon Dr WA3 . . . . . . 90 E8
Sapling Gr M33 . . . . . 107 D2
Sapling Rd
Bolton BL3 . . . . 146 C2
Swinton M27 . . . . 79 D5
Sarah Butterworth Ct 🔳
OL16 . . . . 31 B6
Sarah Butterworth St 🔳
OL16 . . . . 31 B6
Sarah St
Britannia OL13 . . . . 4 C8
🔳 Eccles M30 . . . . 79 B1
Edenfield BL0 . . . . 1 E3
Hindley WN2 . . . . 57 B2
Manchester M11 . . . . . 164 C4
Middleton M24 . . . . . . 64 C8
🔳 Oldham OL4 . . . . 66 D2
🔳 Rochdale OL11 . . . . . 31 A6
Shaw OL2 . . . . 149 A1
Sargent Dr M16 . . . . . 97 E4
Sargent Rd SK6 . . . . . 112 D2
Sark Rd M21 . . . . 97 A2
Sarn Ave M22 . . . . 121 D4
Sarnesfield Cl M12 . . . 99 A4
Sarnia Ct M7 . . . . 155 A3
Sarsfield Ave 🔳 WA3 . 90 D8
Satinwood Cl WN4 . . . 72 F2
Satinwood Wlk M33 . . 158 B3
Saturn Gr M6 . . . . 81 C4
Saunton Ave BL2 . . . . 25 F3
Saunton Rd M11 . . . . . 99 D8
Sautridge Cl OL11 . . . 47 D7
Savernake Rd SK6 . . . 113 C5
Savick Ave BL2 . . . . . . 42 F7
Saville St
Bolton BL2 . . . . 148 A2
Middleton M24 . . . . . . 65 D7
Saviour CE Prim Sch
M40 . . . . 156 C1
Saviours Terr BL3 . . . 144 C1
Savio Way M24 . . . . . . 65 A7
Savoy Cl M45 . . . . 44 E2
Savoy Dr OL2 . . . . 48 D2
Savoy St
Oldham OL4 . . . . 67 B5
Rochdale OL11 . . . . 30 C8
Sawley Ave
Golborne WA3 . . . . 74 D1
Littleborough OL15 . . . . 16 A7
Oldham OL4 . . . . 67 D4

Sawley Ave continued
Whitefield M45 . . . . 44 F2
Wigan WN6 . . . . 36 F2
Sawley Cl WA3 . . . . . . 92 A2
Sawley Dr SK8 . . . . . . 132 C6
Sawley Rd M40 . . . . . 160 B4
Sawmill The BL9 . . . . 140 C1
Sawmill Way 🔳 OL15 . 16 A5
Sawpit St WA13, WA14 118 A6
Saw St BL1 . . . . 143 B2
Sawston Wlk M40 . . . . 65 C3
Sawyer Brow SK14 . . . 167 C4
Sawyer Dr WN4 . . . . . . 73 D3
Sawyer St
Bury BL8 . . . . 27 B4
🔳 Rochdale OL11 . . . . . 14 F1
Saxby Ave BL7 . . . . . . 24 F8
Saxby St M6 . . . . 80 C5
Saxelby Dr M8 . . . . . . 156 B3
Saxfield Dr M23 . . . . . 121 C6
Saxholme Wlk 🔳 M22 121 C2
Saxon Ave
Dukinfield SK16 . . . . . . 101 C8
Manchester M8 . . . . . . 64 A2
Saxon Cl BL8 . . . . 27 B3
Saxon Dr
Chadderton OL9 . . . . . . 65 E8
Denton M34 . . . . 100 C1
Droylsden M43 . . . . . . 84 B2
Saxon Ho 🔳 M16 . . . . 97 D3
Saxonholme Rd OL11 . 47 C7
Saxon Rd OL5 . . . . 68 D3
Saxon St
Denton M34 . . . . 100 F3
Droylsden M43 . . . . . . 84 B2
Manchester M40 . . . . . 160 B3
Middleton M24 . . . . . . 65 B8
Oldham OL4 . . . . 67 C7
Radcliffe M26 . . . . 43 F3
Saxons The BL3 . . . . . 146 A2
Saxthorpe Cl
🔳 Sale M33 . . . . 107 D5
Wigan WN3 . . . . 54 D3
Saxthorpe Wlk M40 . . 164 B1
Saxwood Ave M9 . . . . 64 D1
Saxwood Cl OL12 . . . . 13 F1
Scafell Ave OL7 . . . . . . 84 F4
Scafell Cl
High Lane SK6 . . . . 134 E8
Oldham OL1 . . . . 48 F1
Scafell Dr WN5 . . . . . . 54 B6
Scafell Gr WN5 . . . . . . 56 B2
Scalby Wlk 🔳 M22 . . . 121 D1
Scale St M5 . . . . 81 A1
Scarborough St M40 . . 83 A8
Scarcroft Rd M12 . . . . 165 A1
Scarfield Dr OL11 . . . . 13 E1
Scargill Cl 🔳 M14 . . . 110 C8
Scargill Rd BL3 . . . . . . 146 A4
Scarisbrick Ave M20 . . 110 D3
Scarisbrick Rd M19 . . . 110 F8
Scarisbrick St 🔳 WN1 . 37 C1
Scarr Ave M26 . . . . 44 C2
Scarr Dr OL12 . . . . 14 C2
Scarr La OL2 . . . . 49 D7
Scarr Terr OL12 . . . . . . 4 D2
Scarsdale Ave M14 . . . 142 A1
Scarsdale Rd M14 . . . . 98 E4
Scarsdale St BL1 . . . . . 81 B3
Scarthwood Cl BL2 . . . 25 E5
Scawfell Ave BL2 . . . . 25 B2
Scawton Wlk M9 . . . . . 64 B3
Sceptre Cl WA12 . . . . . 89 A3
Schofield Cl M24 . . . . . 47 A3
Schofield Gdns WN7 . . 75 E3
Schofield Hall Rd OL15 16 C1
Schofield La M46 . . . . . 57 F3
Schofield Pl OL15 . . . . 6 D2
Schofield Rd
Calderbrook OL15 . . . . . 6 D2
Droylsden M11 . . . . . . 83 C2
Failsworth M35 . . . . . . 83 F8
Haslingden BB4 . . . . 1 A6
Heywood OL10 . . . . 29 D1
Leigh WN7 . . . . 75 E4
Littleborough OL15 . . . . 16 C1
Milnrow OL16 . . . . 32 A5
Oldham OL8 . . . . 66 F3
Radcliffe M26 . . . . 44 B4
Scholar Green Rd M32 96 A5
Scholars Cl M27 . . . . . 61 F3
Scholars Dr
Manchester M20 . . . . . 110 A7
Stockport SK3 . . . . 123 B7
Scholars Rise BL7 . . . . 24 F7
Scholars Way
🔳 Middleton M24 . . . . . 46 F1
Scholes CE Prim Sch
SCHOLES 151 B4
Scholes Bank BL6 . . . . 22 A5
Scholes Cl M7 . . . . 155 C4
Scholes Dr M40 . . . . . . 65 E2
Scholes La M25 . . . . . . 63 C3
Scholes Prec WN1 . . . 151 A4
Scholes St
Bury BL8 . . . . 27 C3
Chadderton OL9 . . . . . . 66 A4
Failsworth M35 . . . . . . 66 A1
🔳 Oldham OL1 . . . . 67 A7

Scholes St continued
Pendlebury M27 . . . . . . 80 A8
Rochdale OL11 . . . . . . 30 C1
Scholes Wlk M25 . . . . 63 B3
Scholey St BL2 . . . . . . 148 A1
Scholfield Ave M41 . . . 95 F1
School Ave
Ashton-u-l OL6 . . . . 85 D6
Stretford M32 . . . . 96 F3
Wigan WN1 . . . . 37 E1
School Brow
Billinge WN5 . . . . 71 E5
Bury BL9 . . . . 140 C2
Romiley SK6 . . . . 113 A2
Worsley M28 . . . . 78 F6
School Cl
Glossop SK13 . . . . 103 E5
Poynton SK12 . . . . 133 F3
School Cres SK15 . . . . 86 A4
School Ct
Bolton BL7 . . . . 8 E2
Edenfield BL0 . . . . 1 D2
Manchester M4 . . . . . . 159 C2
Stockport SK3 . . . . 170 C2
School Dr
Billinge WN5 . . . . 71 E5
Dukinfield SK16 . . . . . . 101 E6
Lymm WA13 . . . . 117 C5
School Gr
Manchester M20 . . . . . 110 D6
Prestwich M25 . . . . . . 63 A2
School Hill BL1 . . . . . . 145 B4
School Ho The 🔳 BL7 . 24 F7
Schoolhouse M17 . . . . 96 D5
School House Flats 🔳
OL8 . . . . 66 C2
School La
Aspull WN2 . . . . 37 E7
Bury BL9 . . . . 27 E8
Carrington M31 . . . . . . 106 E6
Compstall SK6 . . . . 114 B4
Edgworth BL7 . . . . 9 E8
Garswood WN4 . . . . . . 72 C3
Hollinfare WA3 . . . . 105 A2
Hyde SK14 . . . . 113 E7
Irlam, Cadishead M44 . 105 D5
Irlam M44 . . . . 93 F2
Manchester, Didsbury M19,
  M20 . . . . 110 C3
Manchester M9 . . . . . . 64 C2
Mossley SK15 . . . . 86 E7
Partington WA14 . . . . . 118 D5
Poynton SK12 . . . . 133 F4
Reddish SK4 . . . . 111 C5
Rochdale, Bagslate Moor
  OL11 . . . . 29 C8
Rochdale OL16 . . . . . . 139 C3
Simister M25 . . . . 19 D1
Up Holland, Roby Mill WN8 53 B3
Up Holland WN5, Orrell . 53 C7
Wigan WN1 . . . . 151 A4
School Mews
Bramhall SK7 . . . . 132 E7
Newhey OL16 . . . . 32 B4
School Rd
Altrincham WA15 . . . . . 119 F3
Eccles M30 . . . . 95 C8
Failsworth M35 . . . . . . 83 F7
Handforth SK9 . . . . 131 D4
Oldham OL8 . . . . 66 B2
Stretford M32 . . . . 96 C2
Schools Hill SK8 . . . . . 122 D3
Schoolside Cl M8 . . . . 156 A2
Schoolside La M24 . . . 64 C7
Schools Rd M18 . . . . . 99 E5
School St
Ashton-in-M WN4 . . . . . 73 D5
Atherton M46 . . . . 58 B2
Bacup OL13 . . . . 3 B8
Bolton BL7 . . . . 24 F7
Bury BL9 . . . . 141 B1
Eccles M30 . . . . 79 B3
Golborne WA3 . . . . 90 A8
Hazel Grove SK7 . . . . . 124 E2
Heywood OL10 . . . . 29 C2
Horwich BL6 . . . . 22 C3
Ince-in-M WN2 . . . . . . 151 C3
Leigh WN7 . . . . 75 E8
Littleborough OL15 . . . . 15 E5
Little Lever BL3 . . . . . . 43 B3
Manchester M4 . . . . . . 159 B3
Newton-le-W WA12 . . . . 89 B3
Oldham, Grotton OL4 . . 68 A6
Oldham OL8 . . . . 153 A1
Radcliffe M26 . . . . 44 A3
Ramsbottom BL0 . . . . . 138 B1
Rochdale OL12 . . . . . . 139 E4
Tyldesley, Gin Pit M29 . 76 F7
Tyldesley M29 . . . . 76 F8
Uppermill OL3 . . . . 69 B8
Westhoughton BL5 . . . . 57 E8
Wigan WN1 . . . . 151 A4
School Street Ind Est
SK7 . . . . 124 E2
School Terr
Golborne WA3 . . . . 90 A8
Whitworth OL12 . . . . . . 4 C1
School View BL7 . . . . . 9 D8
School Way WN5 . . . . . 54 C6
School Wlk M16 . . . . . 162 A1
Schuster Rd M14 . . . . 98 D3
Schwabe St M24 . . . . . 64 C8
Scobell St 🔳 BL8 . . . . 27 A5
Scoltock Way OL1 . . . . 153 C3
Score St M11 . . . . 83 A1
Scorton Ave BL2 . . . . . 42 F7
Scorton St 🔳 BL1 . . . . 144 C4
Scorton Wlk 🔳 M40 . . 65 D2

Scotforth Cl M15 . . . . 162 B3
Scotia Wlk 🔳 WA3 . . . 90 F8
Scot La
Aspull BL6, WN2 . . . . . 38 C3
Wigan, Marsh Green WN5,
  WN6 . . . . 36 E1
Wigan, Worsley Hall WN5 54 F7
Scotland 🔳 M19 . . . . 159 A3
Scotland Hall Rd M40 . 83 C4
Scotland La BL9 . . . . . 28 D8
Scotland Pl BL0 . . . . . 138 C2
Scotland St
Ashton-u-l OL6 . . . . 166 C2
Failsworth M40 . . . . . . 83 C5
SCOT LANE END 38 F7
Scott Ave
Bury BL9 . . . . 44 F6
Eccles M30 . . . . 79 C3
Hindley WN2 . . . . 56 E6
Manchester M21 . . . . . 97 B2
Scott Cl SK5 . . . . 169 C4
Scott Court Appts M27 80 D8
Scott Dr
Altrincham WA15 . . . . . 119 F4
Marple SK6 . . . . 126 B8
Scottfield OL8 . . . . 153 C1
Scottfield Rd OL8 . . . . 153 C1
Scott Gate M34 . . . . . . 100 F7
Scott Ho
Manchester M19 . . . . . 99 A2
Walsden OL14 . . . . 6 A8
Scott Rd
Denton M34 . . . . 100 E1
Droylsden M43 . . . . . . 84 A1
Golborne WA3 . . . . 74 D2
Prestwich M25 . . . . . . 62 F3
Scotts Ind Est OL16 . . 31 A6
Scott St
Kearsley M26 . . . . 61 D7
Leigh WN7 . . . . 75 D5
Oldham OL8 . . . . 153 C1
Tyldesley M29 . . . . 77 C4
Walsden OL14 . . . . 6 A8
Westhoughton BL5 . . . . 39 E2
Wigan WN6 . . . . 37 B1
Scott Wlk WA12 . . . . . 89 C1
Scotty Brook Cres SK13 103 E8
Scout Dr M23 . . . . 120 F4
Scout Gn M24 . . . . 47 A3
Scout Moor Wind Farm*
BL0 . . . . 2 D1
Scout Rd
Bolton BL1 & BL2 . . . . . 24 B7
Bolton BL2 . . . . 2 A2
Scout View BL8 . . . . . . 27 A6
Scovell St M7 . . . . 155 A2
Scowcroft La OL2 . . . . 149 A2
Scowcroft St 🔳 BL2 . . 25 B1
Scroggins La M31 . . . . 105 F4
Scropton St M40 . . . . . 157 A2
Seabright Wlk M11 . . . 160 C1
Seabrook Cres M41 . . . 95 D4
Seabrook Rd M40 . . . . 83 C4
Seacombe Ave M14 . . . 98 A1
Seacombe Gr SK3 . . . . 123 B8
Seaford Rd
Bolton BL2 . . . . 25 E6
Salford M6 . . . . 81 B4
Seaford Wlk
Chadderton OL9 . . . . . . 152 B2
Manchester M9 . . . . . . 64 C3
Seaforth Ave M46 . . . . 58 C4
Seaforth Rd BL1 . . . . . 24 E5
Seaham Dr BL8 . . . . . . 27 C5
Seaham Wlk 🔳 M14 . . 98 B3
Sealand Cl M33 . . . . . . 108 C2
Sealand Dr M30 . . . . . 95 A8
Sealand Ho M25 . . . . . 63 C5
Sealand Rd M23 . . . . . 120 D7
Sealand Way 🔳 SK9 . . 131 D4
Seale Ave M34 . . . . . . 100 D7
Sealey Wlk M40 . . . . . 160 B4
Seal Rd SK7 . . . . 133 A7
Seaman Way WN2 . . . 56 A6
Seamon's Dr WA14 . . . 119 A6
Seamons Wlk WA14 . . . 119 A6
Seamons Wlk WA14 . . . 119 B5
Searby Rd M18 . . . . . . 99 B4
Searness Rd M24 . . . . 46 D2
Seascale Ave M11 . . . . 83 B3
Seascale Cres WN1 . . . 37 C3
Seascale Wlk 🔳 M24 . . 46 E2
Seathwaite
Middleton M24 . . . . . . 46 D2
Wigan WN7 . . . . 77 A7
Seathwaite Rd M41 . . . 59 F7
Seatoller Cl OL2 . . . . . 48 E4
Seatoller Dr M24 . . . . . 46 C1
Seatoller Pl WN5 . . . . . 54 B7
Seaton Cl SK7 . . . . 124 D1
Seaton Mews OL7 . . . . 84 F4
Seaton Rd BL1 . . . . 143 D2
Seaton Way M14 . . . . . 98 A4
Sebastian Cl SK6 . . . . 126 B7
Second Ave
Atherton M46 . . . . 58 C4
Bolton BL1 . . . . 144 B3
Bury BL9 . . . . 28 D4
Droylsden M11 . . . . . . 83 D2
Little Lever BL3 . . . . . . 42 F4
Mossley SK15 . . . . 86 E5
Oldham OL8 . . . . 66 D1
Poynton SK12 . . . . 133 D1

Second Ave continued
Stretford M17 . . . . 96 D5
Swinton M27 . . . . 79 D5
Tyldesley M29 . . . . 77 B4
Wigan WN6 . . . . 37 A2
Second St BL1 . . . . 23 F4
Section St 7 BL3 . . . . . . 145 C2
Sedan Cl M5 . . . . 81 A1
Sedburgh Cl M33 . . . . . . 107 D3
Sedbury Cl M23 . . . . 108 F1
Seddon Ave
Manchester M18 . . . . 99 D6
Radcliffe M26 . . . . 44 D5
Seddon Cl
Atherton M46 . . . . 58 C3
Radcliffe M26 . . . . 44 A4
Seddon Gdns M26 . . . . . . 61 A8
Seddon House Dr WN6 . . 36 E3
Seddon La M26 . . . . 61 A8
Seddon Rd M14 . . . . 119 D2
Seddons Ave BL8 . . . . . . 44 A8
Seddon St
7 Little Lever BL3 . . . . . 43 B3
Manchester M12 . . . . 99 B2
Radcliffe M26 . . . . 44 A3
Walkden M38 . . . . 59 E3
Westhoughton BL5 . . . . . 59 E3
Sedgeborough Rd M16 . . 97 E3
Sedge Cl SK5 . . . . 112 A8
Sedgefield Cl M5 . . . . . . 81 A2
Sedgefield Dr
Bolton BL1 . . . . 142 B3
Wigan WN6 . . . . 36 E3
Sedgefield Pk 1 OL4 . . . 67 D6
Sedgefield Rd M26 . . . . . 62 A8
Sedgefield Wlk M23 . . . 108 F2
Sedgeford Cl SK9 . . . . . 131 D1
Sedgeford Rd M40 . . . . . 157 A1
Sedgely Ave M7 . . . . 37 A7
Sedgemoor Cl SK8 . . . . 123 B2
Sedgemoor Vale BL2 . . . 25 F2
Sedgemoor Way OL1 . . . 153 B3
Sedgley Ave
Manchester M25 . . . . 63 C2
Prestwich M25 . . . . 62 F5
Rochdale OL16 . . . . 31 B4
Sedgley Bldgs M43 . . . . 100 A8
Sedgley Cl M24 . . . . 65 C7
Sedgley Dr BL5 . . . . 57 E5
SEDGLEY PARK 63 C2
Sedgley Park Com Prim Sch
M25 . . . . 63 D2
Sedgley Park Rd M25 . . . 63 C2
Sedgley Park Trad Est
M25 . . . . 63 B1
Sedgley Rd M8 . . . . 156 A4
Sedgley St M24 . . . . 65 C7
Sedgwick Cl
Atherton M46 . . . . 58 E3
Westhoughton BL5 . . . . . 57 F6
Sedwyn St 7 WN1 . . . . . 37 E1
SEEDFIELD 27 F5
Seedfield Rd BL9 . . . . . . 27 F5
SEEDLEY 154 B3
Seedley Ave M38 . . . . . . 60 B4
Seedley Park Rd M6 . . . 154 B2
Seedley Prim Sch M6 . . 154 B2
Seedley Rd M6 . . . . 154 C3
Seedley St M14 . . . . 98 B3
Seedley View Rd M6 . . . 154 B2
Seed St BL1 . . . . 144 C3
Seel St OL5 . . . . 68 B1
Sefton Ave
Atherton M46 . . . . 58 C5
Orrell WN5 . . . . 53 D5
Sefton Cl
Manchester M13 . . . . . . 163 B2
Middleton M24 . . . . 64 E8
Oldham OL1 . . . . 49 D4
Orrell WN5 . . . . 53 D5
Sefton Cres M33 . . . . . . 108 B6
Sefton Ct
8 Bolton BL1 . . . . 145 B4
4 Bury BL9 . . . . 27 F6
Sefton Dr
Bury BL9 . . . . 28 A6
Handforth SK9 . . . . 131 C2
Swinton M27 . . . . 79 D6
Worsley M28 . . . . 79 A8
Sefton Fold Dr WN5 . . . . 71 D5
Sefton Fold Gdns WN5 . . 71 D5
Sefton La BL6 . . . . 22 E1
Sefton Rd
Ashton-in-M WN4 . . . . . . 72 F6
Bolton BL1 . . . . 142 B2
Manchester M21 . . . . . . 109 B8
Middleton M24 . . . . 64 E8
Orrell WN5 . . . . 53 D5
Sale M33 . . . . 108 B5
Swinton M27 . . . . 61 F1
Wigan WN3 . . . . 54 F4
Sefton St
Bury BL9 . . . . 27 F6
Glossop SK13 . . . . 116 C8
Heywood OL10 . . . . 29 C1
Leigh WN7 . . . . 75 F5
Manchester M8 . . . . 156 A4
Oldham OL9 . . . . 66 B2
Radcliffe M26 . . . . 44 C1
Rochdale OL11 . . . . 139 C1
Whitefield M45 . . . . 62 F7
Sefton View WN5 . . . . . . 53 D5
Segal Cl M7 . . . . 155 A3
Selborne Rd M21 . . . . . . 97 B1

Selbourne Cl
Reddish SK5 . . . . 99 E2
Westhoughton BL5 . . . . . 40 A1
Selbourne St
Leigh WN7 . . . . 75 F7
Oldham OL8 . . . . 67 A1
Selby Ave
Chadderton OL9 . . . . 47 F1
Whitefield M45 . . . . 44 F2
Selby Cl
Milnrow OL16 . . . . 31 E6
Poynton SK12 . . . . 133 D5
Radcliffe M26 . . . . 44 D5
Stretford M32 . . . . 96 A3
Selby Dr
Salford M6 . . . . 80 B3
Urmston M41 . . . . 94 F5
Wigan WN3 . . . . 54 C4
Selby Gdns SK8 . . . . . . 132 C6
Selby Rd
Middleton M24 . . . . 46 F3
Stretford M32 . . . . 96 A3
Selby St
Manchester M11 . . . . . . 165 A4
Reddish SK5 . . . . 169 A4
Rochdale OL16 . . . . 31 B8
Selby Wlk BL8 . . . . 26 F1
Selden St OL8 . . . . 153 A1
Selham Wlk M13 . . . . . . 163 C3
Selhurst Ave M11 . . . . . . 83 C2
Selkirk Ave
Garswood WN4 . . . . 72 C4
Oldham OL8 . . . . 66 D4
Selkirk Dr M9 . . . . 64 F3
Selkirk Gr WN5 . . . . 54 C8
Selkirk Pl OL10 . . . . 29 A1
Selkirk Rd
Bolton BL1 . . . . 24 D5
Chadderton OL9 . . . . 66 A4
Sellars Sq M43 . . . . 100 A8
Sellars St M43 . . . . 99 E8
Sellers Way OL9 . . . . 66 A3
Selsby Ave M30 . . . . 79 B2
Selsey Ave
Cheadle SK3 . . . . 122 F7
Sale M33 . . . . 107 F3
Selsey Dr M20 . . . . 122 C8
Selside WN3 . . . . 55 B2
Selside Ct M26 . . . . 61 B8
Selside Wlk 2 M14 . . . . 110 C8
Selstead Rd M22 . . . . . . 121 C1
Selston Rd M9 . . . . 64 A4
Selwood Wlk 6 M9 . . . . 157 A3
Selworth Ave M33 . . . . . 108 E4
Selworth Cl 4 WA15 . . . 119 E6
Selworthy Rd M16 . . . . . . 97 E4
Selwyn Ave M9 . . . . 64 D1
Selwyn Cl M12 . . . . 89 B5
Selwyn Dr SK8 . . . . 132 C7
Selwyn St
Bolton BL2 . . . . 148 A2
Leigh WN7 . . . . 75 F6
Oldham OL8 . . . . 153 B1
Semple Way OL9 . . . . . . 65 F3
Senecar Cl WN2 . . . . 38 B2
Senior Ave M14 . . . . 110 E7
Senior Rd M30 . . . . 95 A8
Senior St M3 . . . . 158 B3
Sennicar La WN1 . . . . 37 D6
Sepal Cl SK5 . . . . 100 A1
Sephton Ave WA3 . . . . . . 91 E3
Sephton St WN3 . . . . . . 151 C2
Sepia Gr M24 . . . . 46 F1
Sequoia St M9 . . . . 157 B4
Sergeants La M45 . . . . . 62 C7
Serin Cl
Hazel Grove SK7 . . . . . . 124 F5
Newton-le-W WA12 . . . . . 89 C3
Service St SK3 . . . . 123 B8
Sesame Gdns M44 . . . . . 94 C3
Setantii Mus * OL6 . . . . 166 B3
Set St SK15 . . . . 85 F1
Settle Cl BL8 . . . . 26 F2
Settle St
Bolton BL3 . . . . 147 B3
Little Lever BL3 . . . . 43 C3
Settstones La OL3 . . . . . 51 D1
Seven Acres OL3 . . . . . . 50 F5
Seven Acres Ctry Pk *
BL2 . . . . 13 E2
Seven Acres La OL12 . . . 13 E2
Seven Acres Nature
Reserve * BL2 . . . . 42 D8
Seven Oaks WN7 . . . . . . 76 A6
Sevenoaks Ave
Manchester SK4 . . . . . . 111 A5
Urmston M41 . . . . 95 D4
Sevenoaks Dr
Bolton BL3 . . . . 147 B3
Pendlebury M27 . . . . 80 A6
Sevenoaks Gr SK8 . . . . 122 B6
Sevenoaks Wlk 1 M13 . . 163 C1
Seven Stars Bridge WA3 150 A3
Seven Stars Rd WN3 . . . 150 A3
Seven Stiles Dr SK6 . . . 125 E7
Seventh Ave OL8 . . . . . . 66 D1
Severn Cl
Altrincham WA14 . . . . . . 119 C6
Billinge WN5 . . . . 71 D3
Bury BL9 . . . . 27 F7
Severn Dr
Bramhall SK7 . . . . 132 C6
Hindley WN2 . . . . 57 C3
Milnrow OL16 . . . . 32 A6
Wigan WN5 . . . . 54 D7
Severn Rd
Ashton-in-M WN4 . . . . . . 73 E5
Chadderton OL9 . . . . 65 F8

Severn Rd continued
Culcheth WA3 . . . . 91 F2
Heywood OL10 . . . . 29 A3
Oldham OL8 . . . . 66 C1
Severnside Trad Est M17 . 96 B5
Severn St M7 . . . . 76 B4
Severn Way
Kearsley BL4 . . . . 61 B6
Reddish SK5 . . . . 111 F5
Seville's Bldgs OL5 . . . . 68 C2
Seville St
Royton OL2 . . . . 48 E2
Shaw OL2 . . . . 149 A1
Sewell Way M38 . . . . 59 F3
Sewerby St M16 . . . . 97 F4
Sexa St M11 . . . . 99 D8
Sexton St
Glossop SK13 . . . . 103 F7
Heywood OL10 . . . . 29 C2
Seymour Ave M11 . . . . . . 83 D2
Seymour Cl M16 . . . . . . 161 C1
Seymour Ct
Manchester SK4 . . . . . . 110 E2
2 Radcliffe M26 . . . . 44 B3
Salford M7 . . . . 155 C4
Seymour Dr BL2 . . . . 25 C6
Seymour Gr
Altrincham WA15 . . . . . . 120 A5
Farnworth BL4 . . . . 42 A1
Manchester M16 . . . . 97 B4
Marple SK6 . . . . 125 E6
Rochdale OL16 . . . . 31 B3
Sale M33 . . . . 108 A4
Seymour Ho 16 SK9 . . . . 131 C1
Seymour Park Prim Sch
M16 . . . . 97 B4
Seymour Rd
Bolton BL1 . . . . 143 C3
Cheadle SK8 . . . . 132 A8
Manchester M7, M8 . . . . . 63 F1
Stockport SK2 . . . . 124 B5
Seymour Road Prim Sch
M11 . . . . 83 D2
Seymour Road S M11 . . . 83 D2
Seymour St
Denton M34 . . . . 100 D4
Heywood OL10 . . . . 29 C1
Manchester M18 . . . . 99 D6
Radcliffe M26 . . . . 44 B3
Seymour Wlk 4 M26 . . . . 44 B3
Shackleton Ct M40 . . . . . 83 C4
Shackleton St BL1 . . . . . 143 D1
Shackleton St M30 . . . . . 79 C3
Shackliffe Rd M40 . . . . . . 65 B2
Shaddock Ave OL12 . . . . 13 F1
Shade Ave OL4 . . . . 67 F5
Shade Terr SK6 . . . . 134 F7
Shadowbrook Ave M23 . 121 A4
Shadowbrook Cl OL1 . . . 48 C1
Shadowmoss Rd M22 . . 130 E8
Shadows La OL5 . . . . 68 E4
Shadows Mews OL5 . . . . 68 E4
Shadwell Gr WN7 . . . . . . 75 C8
Shadwell Street E OL10 . 29 E3
Shadwell Street W OL10 . 29 D3
Shadworth Cl OL5 . . . . . . 68 E4
Shadworth La OL3, OL5 . . 68 F3
Shady La
Bolton BL7 . . . . 25 B7
Wythenshawe M23 . . . . 120 D7
Shady Oak Rd SK2 . . . . . 124 F6
Shaftesbury Ave
Altrincham WA15 . . . . . . 120 C6
Bramhall SK8 . . . . 123 C1
Eccles M30 . . . . 95 C8
Horwich BL6 . . . . 39 F8
Littleborough OL15 . . . . . 15 F3
Shaftesbury Cl BL6 . . . . . 39 F8
Shaftesbury Dr OL12 . . . 15 D6
Shaftesbury Gdns M41 . . 94 D2
Shaftesbury Rd
Cheadle SK3 . . . . 123 B6
Manchester M8 . . . . 156 A3
Swinton M27 . . . . 79 F7
Shafton Wlk 22 M40 . . . . 65 D2
Shaftsbury Cl 20 BL1 . . 143 B1
Shaftsbury Dr 1 WA15 . . 120 D6
Shaftsbury Dr OL10 . . . . 46 C8
Shaftsbury Rd WN5 . . . . 54 A8
Shakeley La M46, M29 . . 58 F4
Shakerley Rd M29 . . . . . . 58 F1
Shakespeare Ave
Bury BL9 . . . . 44 F6
Denton M34 . . . . 112 F8
Radcliffe M26 . . . . 43 E4
Stalybridge SK15 . . . . . . 86 E4
Shakespeare Cl OL15 . . . 6 C1
Shakespeare Cres
Droylsden M43 . . . . 84 A2
Eccles M30 . . . . 79 D2
Shakespeare Dr SK8 . . . 122 F6
Shakespeare Gr WN3 . . . 55 A4
Shakespeare Rd
Droylsden M43 . . . . 84 A2
Oldham OL1 . . . . 49 C2
Prestwich M25 . . . . 62 F3
Romiley SK6 . . . . 112 F2
Swinton M27 . . . . 79 E8
Shakespeare Wlk M13 . . 163 C2
Shalbourne Rd M28 . . . . 60 C3
Shaldon Dr M40 . . . . 83 E4
Shalebrook Cl M46 . . . . . 58 A2
Shalemoor Ct M46 . . . . . 58 A2
Shalewood Ct M46 . . . . . 58 A2
Shalfleet Cl BL2 . . . . 25 E5

Shandon Ave M22 . . . . . 109 D1
Shanklin Cl
Denton M34 . . . . 113 B8
Manchester M21 . . . . 97 A1
Shanklin Rd 4 M21 . . . . . 97 A1
Shanklin Wlk BL3 . . . . . 148 C1
Shanklyn Ave 2 M41 . . . 95 C2
Shanley Cl OL9 . . . . 152 B4
Shannon Cl OL10 . . . . . . 29 A3
Shannon Rd M22 . . . . . . 121 E4
Shanter Cl OL12 . . . . 4 H6
Shap Ave WA15 . . . . 120 D5
Shap Cres M28 . . . . 60 F1
Shap Dr M28 . . . . 60 F1
Shap Gate WN5 . . . . 54 B7
Shapwick Cl 5 M9 . . . . . 157 A4
Sharcott Cl 7 M16 . . . . . 97 F4
Shardlow Cl M40 . . . . . . 160 A4
Shared St WN1 . . . . 151 A3
Shargate Cl SK9 . . . . . . 131 C1
Sharman St BL3 . . . . . . 148 B1
Sharnbrook Wlk
9 Bolton BL2 . . . . 25 B1
4 Manchester M8 . . . . . . 63 E2
Sharnford Cl BL2 . . . . . . 148 B2
Sharnford Sq M12 . . . . . 165 A2
Sharon Ave OL4 . . . . 68 C5
Sharon Cl OL7 . . . . 84 E1
Sharon Sq WN2 . . . . 73 F8
SHARPLES 143 B4
Sharples Ave BL1 . . . . . . 24 E5
Sharples Com L Ctr BL1 . 24 F5
Sharples Dr BL8 . . . . 26 F3
Sharples Gn BL7 . . . . 9 D6
Sharples Hall 1 BL1 . . . . 24 F6
Sharples Hall Dr BL1 . . . 24 F6
Sharples Hall Fold BL1 . . 24 F5
Sharples Hall Mews BL1 . 24 F5
Sharples Hall St OL4 . . . . 67 D8
Sharples Mdw BL7 . . . . . . 9 D6
Sharples Pk BL1 . . . . . . 143 A4
Sharples Prim Sch BL1 . . 25 A5
Sharples Sch BL1 . . . . . . 24 F5
Sharples St SK4 . . . . . . 169 B3
Sharp St
Bury BL8 . . . . 27 B4
Ince-in-M WN3 . . . . 151 B2
Manchester M4 . . . . 159 B3
Middleton M24 . . . . 65 A8
Prestwich M25 . . . . 62 E8
Walkden M28 . . . . 60 E3
Sharrington Dr M23 . . . . 120 E6
Sharrow Wlk M9 . . . . . . 157 A3
SHARSTON 121 D5
Sharston Ind Area M22 . 121 E7
Sharston Rd M22 . . . . . . 121 E7
Shaving La M28 . . . . 60 D1
SHAW 149 B3
Shaw Ave SK14 . . . . 113 F8
Shawbrook Ave M28 . . . . 78 B8
Shawbrook Rd M19 . . . . 111 A5
Shawbury Cl BL6 . . . . 21 D1
Shawbury Gr M33 . . . . . 107 F2
Shawbury Rd M23 . . . . . 121 B4
Shawbury St M24 . . . . . . 65 C7
Shawclough Cl OL12 . . . . 14 C2
Shawclough Com Prim Sch
OL12 . . . . 14 E3
Shawclough Dr OL12 . . . . 14 D3
Shawclough Rd OL12 . . . 14 C3
Shawclough Trad Est 6
OL12 . . . . 14 D2
Shawclough Way OL12 . . 14 D3
Shawcroft Cl OL2 . . . . . 149 A1
Shawcroft View 2 BL3 . . 25 B3
Shawcross Fold SK1 . . . 169 C2
Shawcross La M22 . . . . . 121 B8
Shawcross St
Hyde SK14 . . . . 113 F8
Salford M6 . . . . 154 C1
Stockport SK1 . . . . 170 C4
Shawdene Rd M22 . . . . . 121 D8
Shawe Hall Ave M41 . . . 107 A8
Shawe Hall Cres M41 . . . 107 A8
Shawe Rd M41 . . . . 95 A2
Shawes Dr PR6 . . . . 21 C7
SHAWFIELD 4 D6
Shawfield Cl M14 . . . . . . 110 A8
Shawfield Ct SK2 . . . . . . 124 D5
Shawfield Gr OL12 . . . . . . 13 F2
Shawfield La
Rochdale, Norden OL12 . . 13 F2
Rochdale OL12 . . . . 14 A2
Shawfield Rd SK13 . . . . . 171 C3
Shawfields SK15 . . . . 86 D3
Shawfold OL2 . . . . 149 B3
Shawford Cres M40 . . . . . 65 C2
Shawford Rd M40 . . . . . . 65 C2
SHAWFORTH 4 D6
Shawgreen Cl M15 . . . . . 162 A2
Shaw Hall 7 M14 . . . . . . 98 D4
Shaw Hall Ave SK14 . . . 102 B5
Shaw Hall Bank Rd OL3 . . 68 F5
Shaw Hall Cl OL3 . . . . . . 68 F5
Shaw Head Dr M35 . . . . . 83 F6
SHAW HEATH 170 B3
Shaw Heath SK3 . . . . . . 170 B3
Shawheath Cl M15 . . . . . 162 A2
Shawhill Wlk M40 . . . . . . 160 B2
Shaw Ho
Atherton M46 . . . . 58 D4
Farnworth BL4 . . . . 60 D7
Shaw La SK13 . . . . 171 C3
Shawlea Ave M19 . . . . . 110 E6
Shaw Moor Ave SK15 . . . 86 C1
Shaw Rd
Horwich BL6 . . . . 22 B5

Shaw Rd continued
Newhey OL16 . . . . 32 B3
Oldham OL1 . . . . 67 A8
Royton, Buersil Head OL16 . 31 B1
Royton OL2 . . . . 48 F4
Stockport SK4 . . . . 168 B4
Shaw Road S SK3 . . . . . 170 B2
Shaws OL3 . . . . 69 C7
Shaws Fold SK9 . . . . . . 130 F3
SHAW SIDE 149 B1
Shaw's La OL3 . . . . 69 C7
Shaw's Rd 12 WA14 . . . 119 D4
Shaw St
Ashton-in-M WN4 . . . . . . 73 B5
Ashton-u-L OL6 . . . . 85 D3
Bolton BL3 . . . . 145 B1
Bury BL9 . . . . 141 B3
Culcheth WA3 . . . . 92 A3
Farnworth BL4 . . . . 42 C2
Glossop SK13 . . . . 116 C8
Manchester M3 . . . . 158 C3
Mottram in L SK14 . . . . . 103 A4
Oldham, Grotton OL4 . . . . 68 A6
Oldham OL1 . . . . 153 C4
2 Rochdale OL12 . . . . . . 15 B2
Royton OL2 . . . . 48 E4
Uppermill OL3 . . . . 69 B6
Wigan WN1 . . . . 37 C1
Shaw Terr 5 SK16 . . . . . 166 C1
Shaw The SK13 . . . . 171 C3
Shay Ave WA15 . . . . 120 E1
Shayfield Ave
Chadderton OL9 . . . . 65 E8
Wythenshawe M22 . . . . 121 D6
Shayfield Dr M22 . . . . . . 121 D6
Shayfield Rd M22 . . . . . . 121 D5
Shay La WA15 . . . . 120 D1
Sheader Dr M5 . . . . 80 C2
Sheaf Field Wlk M26 . . . . 44 A4
Sheard Ave OL6 . . . . 85 D6
Sheard Ct OL2 . . . . 149 B2
Sheardhall Ave SK12 . . . 135 E5
Shearing Ave OL12 . . . . . 13 F1
Shearsby Cl M15 . . . . . . 162 B1
Shearwater Ave M29 . . . . 77 A8
Shearwater Dr
Walkden M28 . . . . 60 C3
Westhoughton BL5 . . . . . 57 D6
Shearwater Gdns M30 . . . 95 A8
Shearwater Ho 19 M19 . 110 D4
Shearwater Rd SK2 . . . . 125 A5
Sheddings The BL3 . . . . . 42 A4
Sheepfoot La
Manchester M25, M8 . . . . 63 B3
Oldham OL1 . . . . 48 D1
Sheepfoot Wlk OL1 . . . . . 48 D1
Sheep Gap OL12 . . . . 14 B1
Sheep Gate Dr BL8 . . . . . 26 E5
Sheerness St M18 . . . . . . 99 D5
Sheffield Rd
Glossop SK13 . . . . 104 F1
Hyde, Godley SK14 . . . . 102 A3
Hyde SK14 . . . . 167 C4
Sheffield St
Manchester M1 . . . . 163 C4
Stockport SK4 . . . . 169 B3
Shefford Cl M11 . . . . 164 C4
Shefford Cres WN3 . . . . . 54 C2
Sheiling Ct WA14 . . . . . . 119 C4
Sheilings The M33 . . . . . . 90 F8
Shelbourne Ave BL1 . . . 142 B1
Shelburne Dr WN2 . . . . . 56 C4
Shelden Cl 4 SK13 . . . . . 171 A1
Shelden Fold 3 SK13 . . . 171 A1
Shelden Mews SK13 . . . . 171 A1
Shelden Pl 5 SK13 . . . . . 171 A1
Shelderton Cl 5 M40 . . . . 83 A7
Sheldon Ave
Standish WN6 . . . . 19 E2
Urmston M41 . . . . 95 B2
Sheldon Cl
Farnworth BL4 . . . . 42 B2
Partington M31 . . . . 105 F3
Sheldon Ct OL7 . . . . 85 B5
Sheldon Rd
Hazel Grove SK7 . . . . . . 133 E8
Poynton SK12 . . . . 134 C2
Sheldon St M11 . . . . 83 B2
Sheldrake Cl SK16 . . . . . 101 E7
Sheldrake Rd WA14 . . . . 119 B8
Sheldwich Cl WN7 . . . . . . 75 F3
Shelfield Cl OL11 . . . . 13 F1
Shelfield Cl OL11 . . . . 13 F1
Shelfield La OL11 . . . . 13 F1
Shelford Ave M18 . . . . . . 99 B4
Shellbrook Gr 3 SK9 . . . 131 D1
Shelley Ave M24 . . . . 47 B3
Shelley Cl PR7 . . . . 19 F5
Shelley Ct SK8 . . . . 123 A1
Shelley Dr
Abram WN2 . . . . 56 B1
Wigan WN5 . . . . 54 A6
Shelley Gr
Droylsden M43 . . . . 84 A1
Dukinfield SK14 . . . . 101 D5
Stalybridge SK15 . . . . . . 86 E4
Shelley Rd
9 Oldham, Broadbent
OL1 . . . . 49 C1
Oldham OL9 . . . . 65 F3
Prestwich M25 . . . . 62 F3
Reddish SK5 . . . . 99 E1
Swinton M27 . . . . 79 E8
Walkden M38 . . . . 60 A5
Shelley Rise SK16 . . . . . 102 B7
Shelley St
Failsworth M40 . . . . 83 C8
Leigh WN7 . . . . 75 D7

Shelley Way M34 .... 112 F8
Shelley Wlk
Atherton M46........... 58 D5
Bolton BL1............. 143 A1
Shellingford Cl WN6 ...... 35 D7
Shelmerdine Cl 1 SK14 . 102 F2
Shelmerdine Gdns M6 ... 80 C4
Shelton Ave M33........ 107 D4
Shenfield Wlk M40....... 160 A3
Shenhurst Cl SK9 .... 136 E4
Shentonfield Rd M22.... 121 E6
Shenton Park Ave M33 .. 107 C2
Shenton St SK14 .... 101 C4
Shepherd Cross St Ind Est 12
BL1..................... 143 A2
Shepherd Cross St BL1 .. 142 C1
Shepherd Ct 1 OL16....... 31 B6
Shepherd's Brow WA14 . 119 A3
Shepherds Cl
Blackrod BL6............ 21 C3
Ramsbottom BL8.......... 10 F1
Shepherd's Dr BL6........ 23 A3
Shepherds Gn OL3 .... 69 D5
Shepherd St
Bury BL9 .... 140 C1
3 Bury BL9.............. 141 A1
Bury, Greenmount BL8..... 26 F8
Heywood OL10............ 29 C2
Manchester M9 .... 64 E1
Rochdale, Norden OL11..... 13 D1
Rochdale, Town Head
OL12.................. 139 C4
Royton OL2 .... 48 E3
Shepherds Way OL16....... 31 F5
Shepherd Wlk M34....... 112 F8
Shepley Ave BL3......... 144 C1
Shepley Cl
2 Dukinfield SK16 .... 101 D8
Hazel Grove SK7 .... 133 D8
Shepley Dr SK7 .... 124 E1
Shepley Ind Est North
M34.................... 101 A7
Shepley Ind Est South
M34.................... 101 A6
Shepley La SK6 .... 125 F3
Shepley Lane Ind Est
SK6.................... 125 F3
Shepley Rd M34, SK16 .... 100 F6
Shepley St
Denton M34............. 100 F7
Failsworth M35 .... 66 A1
Glossop, Brookfield SK13 . 171 B3
Glossop, Old Glossop SK13 104 F2
Hyde SK14.............. 167 B2
4 Oldham OL4 .... 67 E6
11 Stalybridge SK15 ...... 86 A2
Shepton Ave WN2......... 56 A1
Shepton Cl BL1 .... 24 D7
Shepton Dr M23 .... 121 A2
Shepway Ct M30 .... 79 B2
Sheraton Cl WN5 .... 36 B1
Sheraton Rd OL8.......... 66 E4
Sherborne Ave WN2 ...... 57 A5
Sherborne House M24 ... 47 A3
Sherborne Rd
Cheadle SK3 .... 123 A7
Urmston M41............. 95 E3
Wigan WN5 .... 54 A8
Sherborne St M3, M8 .... 158 C4
Sherborne Street W M3 . 158 B3
Sherborne Trad Est M8 .. 156 A1
Sherbourne Cl
Cheadle SK8 .... 132 B6
Oldham OL8.............. 67 C4
Radcliffe M26 .... 43 D5
Sherbourne Ct M25 ...... 63 A4
Sherbourne Dr OL10 ...... 29 A3
Sherbourne Pl WN3...... 151 B1
Sherbourne Rd
Bolton BL1.............. 142 A1
Middleton M24............ 47 A3
Sherbourne St M25 .... 63 A4
Sherbrook Cl M33 .... 107 F3
Sherbrooke Ave OL3 ...... 51 C1
Sherbrooke Rd SK12 .... 135 D6
Sherbrook Rise SK9...... 137 C6
Sherdley Ct M8 .... 64 A1
Sherdley Rd M8........... 64 A1
Sherford Cl SK7 .... 124 A2
Sheridan Ave WA3 .... 90 D7
Sheridan Ct M40......... 157 B1
Sheridan Way
Chadderton OL9.......... 65 E8
Denton M34............. 112 F8
Sheri Dr WA12............ 89 E2
Sheriffs Dr M29........... 59 D1
Sheriff St
Bolton BL2............... 25 B1
Milnrow OL16 .... 32 A5
Rochdale OL12........... 139 B4
Sheringham Dr
Bury BL8 .... 27 D5
Hyde SK14.............. 102 A3
Swinton M27 .... 79 F6
Sheringham Pl BL3 ..... 145 A1
Sheringham Rd M14 .... 110 D7
Sherlock St M14......... 110 D7
Sherratt St M4.......... 159 B2
Sherrington St M12 ...... 99 A3
Sherway Dr WA15........ 120 C6
Sherwell Rd M9........... 64 B3
Sherwin Way OL11 .... 30 D1
Sherwood Ave
Ashton-in-M WN4 .... 73 C4
Cheadle SK8 .... 122 F2
Droylsden M43............ 84 C2
Manchester M14 .... 110 C8
Radcliffe M26 .... 43 F8
Sherwood Ave *continued*
Sale M33 .... 108 D5
Salford M7.............. 81 B7
Stockport SK4 .... 168 A1
Tyldesley M29 .... 77 A6
Sherwood Bsns Pk OL11.. 30 D2
Sherwood Cl
Ashton-u-L OL6 .... 85 C7
Bury BL8 .... 26 F7
Marple SK6 .... 125 F4
Salford M5.............. 154 A3
Sherwood Cres
Platt Bridge WN2......... 56 A2
Wigan WN5 .... 54 D7
Sherwood Dr
Pendlebury M27.......... 80 B7
Wigan WN5 .... 54 D6
Sherwood Fold SK13..... 115 D7
Sherwood Gr
Leigh WN7 .... 76 B2
Wigan WN5 .... 54 D7
Sherwood Ind Pk OL11 ... 30 D2
Sherwood Rd
Reddish M34 .... 100 B3
Romiley SK6............ 113 B5
Sherwood St
3 Bolton BL1 .... 143 C3
Manchester M14 .... 110 C8
Oldham OL1............. 153 A4
Rochdale OL11............ 30 D2
Sherwood Way OL2 .... 48 E8
Shetland Rd M40 .... 160 A3
Shetland Way
Radcliffe M26 .... 44 A5
Urmston M41............. 95 D5
SHEVINGTON 36 B5
Shevington Com Prim Sch
WN6..................... 35 F6
Shevington Gdns M23.... 109 B1
Shevington High Sch
WN6..................... 36 B7
Shevington La WN6 ...... 36 B7
SHEVINGTON MOOR 19 A2
Shevington Moor WN6 ... 19 A2
SHEVINGTON VALE 35 E7
Shevington Vale Prim Sch
WN6..................... 35 E8
Shieldborn Dr M9........ 157 B3
Shield Cl OL8 .... 153 B2
Shield Dr M28 .... 79 C8
Shield St SK3 .... 170 B4
Shiel St M28.............. 60 D3
Shiers Dr SK8........... 122 E4
Shiffnall St BL2......... 148 A2
Shildon Cl WN2........... 37 F2
Shilford Dr M4 .... 159 C3
Shillingford Rd
Farnworth BL4............ 60 C8
Manchester M18.......... 99 D2
Shillingstone Cl BL2 ..... 26 A3
Shillingten Cl 1 M28 .... 59 F3
Shiloh La OL4............. 50 B3
Shiloh Rd SK22, SK6 ..... 127 B6
Shilton Gdns BL3 .... 145 B1
Shilton St BL0 .... 138 B1
Shilton Wlk 21 M40 ...... 65 D2
Ship Canal Ho M15....... 162 B4
Shipham Cl WN7.......... 75 D8
Ship La OL3, OL4 .... 50 B5
Shipla Cl OL9 .... 153 B3
Shipley Ave M6 .... 80 C3
Shipley View M41......... 94 F5
Shipper Bottom La BL0... 11 D5
Shippey St M14.......... 110 D7
Shipston Cl BL8........... 27 B3
Shipton St BL1.......... 142 B1
Shirburn 8 OL11 .... 139 B2
Shirebrook Dr
Glossop SK13............ 116 F8
Glossop, Whitfield SK13 . 116 E8
Radcliffe M26 .... 44 B4
Shireburn Ave BL2 ...... 148 C4
Shiredale Cl SK8........ 123 B4
Shiredale Dr M9 .... 157 A3
Shire Gdns M26........... 43 F4
Shiregreen Ave M40 ..... 156 C1
Shire Hill Hospl SK13 ... 104 E3
Shirehills M25 .... 63 A3
Shireoak Rd M20 .... 110 D7
Shires Cl WN2 .... 56 E4
Shires The
Droylsden M43............ 84 D3
Radcliffe M26 .... 44 A5
Shire Way SK13 .... 104 E3
Shirewell Rd WN5 .... 53 E5
Shirley Ave
Droylsden M34.......... 100 C8
Dukinfield SK14.......... 101 D5
Eccles M30 .... 95 C8
Failsworth OL9 .... 65 E2
Gatley SK8.............. 131 C6
Marple SK6 .... 125 E6
Pendlebury M27.......... 80 C7
Reddish M34 .... 99 F3
Salford M7............... 81 A7
Stretford M32 .... 96 F3
Shirley Cl SK7 .... 124 C2
Shirley Ct M33.......... 108 C4
Shirley Gr SK3.......... 170 B1
Shirley Rd M8 .... 156 A3
Shirley St OL11 .... 30 C2
Shoecroft Ave M34...... 100 E2
Shoemaker Gdns WN2 ... 38 C5
SHOLVER 49 D4
Sholver Hey La OL1 ...... 49 D4
Sholver Hill Cl OL1 ...... 49 E4
Sholver La OL1 .... 49 D4
Shone Ave M22.......... 121 F2
SHORE 15 F6
Shore Ave OL2............ 32 C1
Shoreditch Cl SK4 ...... 111 B5
SHORE EDGE 49 E8
Shorefield Cl OL16........ 31 F7
Shore Fold OL15 .... 15 F6
Shore Gn M23 .... 121 A3
Shoreham Cl 5 M16 ..... 97 E4
Shoreham Wlk OL9 ...... 152 A2
Shore Hill OL15 .... 16 C6
Shore Lea OL15........... 15 F6
Shore Mount OL15 .... 15 F6
Shore Rd OL15........... 15 F7
Shore St
Milnrow OL16 .... 31 F6
Oldham OL1.............. 67 A7
Shoreswood BL1.......... 24 D5
Shorland St M27.......... 79 C7
Shorrocks St BL8 .... 26 F3
Short Ave M43............ 99 F8
Shortcroft St M15...... 162 C3
Shortland Cres M19..... 110 D3
Shortland Pl WN2......... 75 A8
Shortlands Ave BL9 ...... 44 F8
Short St
Bacup OL13 .... 3 B8
Golborne WA3 .... 74 B1
Hazel Grove SK7 .... 124 D3
Heywood OL10............ 29 B1
Manchester M4 .... 159 A1
Salford M7.............. 158 B3
Stockport SK4 .... 169 B3
3 Tyldesley M46.......... 58 F1
11 Wigan WN5............ 54 B6
Short Street E SK4 ...... 169 B3
Shortwood Cl 17 M40 ..... 83 A6
Shottery Wlks SK6 .... 112 F3
Shotton Wlk 4 M14....... 98 C3
Shottwood Fold OL15 .... 16 C8
Shrewsbury Cl WN2....... 56 F6
Shrewsbury Ct M16 ..... 162 A1
Shrewsbury Gdns SK8... 132 C6
Shrewsbury Rd
Bolton BL1.............. 144 B4
Droylsden M43............ 84 A3
Prestwich M25............ 63 A3
Sale M33 .... 108 A2
Shrewsbury St
Glossop SK13............ 104 C1
Manchester M16 .... 162 A1
Oldham OL4 .... 67 C8
Shrewsbury Way 7 M34 101 A3
Shrigley Cl SK9 .... 131 D1
Shrigley Road N SK12 ... 134 C3
Shrigley Road S SK10,
SK12 .... 134 C2
Shrivenham Wlk M23 ... 120 F7
Shropshire Ave SK5..... 112 C6
Shropshire Dr SK13 ..... 116 F8
Shropshire Rd M35 ...... 84 A6
Shropshire Sq M12 ..... 164 C2
Shrowbridge Wlk M12 .. 165 A2
Shrubbery The BL6 .... 40 C7
Shrub St BL3 .... 146 C2
Shudehill M4 .... 159 A2
Shudehill Metro Sta M4 159 A2
Shudehill Rd M28......... 60 A1
Shurdington Rd BL5, M46 . 58 F6
Shurmer St BL3......... 146 C4
Shutt La OL3.............. 50 F2
Shuttle Hillock Rd WN2 .. 74 F7
Shuttle St
6 Eccles M30 .... 79 F2
Hindley WN2 .... 56 E6
Radcliffe M26 .... 44 C1
Tyldesley M29 .... 59 A1
SHUTTLEWORTH 11 E8
Shuttleworth Cl M21 .... 109 E8
Shutts La SK15.......... 102 D8
Siam St M11............ 164 C4
Sibley Ave WN4........... 73 D4
Sibley Rd SK4........... 168 B3
Sibley St M18............ 99 D5
Siblies Wlk 7 M22...... 121 B1
Sibson Ct 3 M21 .... 97 A1
Sibson Rd
Manchester M21........... 97 A1
Sale M33 .... 108 B4
Sickle St
Manchester M1, M2 ..... 159 A1
Oldham OL4 .... 67 A5
Sidbrook St WN2 .... 56 C5
Sidbury Rd M21.......... 109 C8
Sidcup Rd M23 .... 120 F5
Siddall St
Heywood OL10............ 46 E8
Manchester M12 .... 99 A2
Oldham OL1............. 153 C4
2 Radcliffe M26.......... 44 A4
Shaw OL2............... 149 B3
Siddal Moor Sports Coll
OL10..................... 46 D7
Siddeley St WN7......... 75 D5
Siddington Ave
Manchester M20......... 110 A7
Stockport SK3 .... 170 A2
Siddington Rd
Handforth SK9........... 131 D5
Poynton SK12........... 133 F2
Siddow Comm WN7........ 76 A4
SIDDOW COMMON 76 A3
Side Ave WA14.......... 119 C1
Sidebottam St SK6 ...... 112 F4
Sidebottom St
Droylsden M43............ 83 F1
Oldham OL4.............. 67 E8
Stalybridge SK15......... 86 A2
Side St
Droylsden M11............ 83 B2
Oldham OL8.............. 66 C2
Sidford Cl BL3 .... 42 D5
Siding St OL13............ 3 C8
Sidings The
Bolton BL7 .... 9 C4
Britannia OL13............ 4 A8
Bury BL9 .... 140 B1
Worsley M28 .... 79 A5
Sidlaw Cl OL8............ 66 F2
Sidley Ave M9 .... 64 F4
Sidley Pl SK14 .... 167 C3
Sidley St SK14 .... 167 C3
Sidmouth Ave M41....... 94 E3
Sidmouth Dr M9 .... 64 D2
Sidmouth Gr
Cheadle SK8 .... 131 F7
Wigan WN3 .... 54 E3
Sidmouth Rd M33 .... 107 D5
Sidmouth St
Denton M34............. 100 D7
Oldham OL9 .... 152 B1
Sidney Rd M9............. 64 D1
Sidney St
Bolton BL3.............. 145 C1
Leigh WN7 .... 76 A5
Manchester M1 .... 163 A3
3 Manchester M3 .... 158 C1
Oldham OL1.............. 49 A1
Salford M3.............. 158 A2
Sidwell Wlk M4.......... 160 A1
Siemens Rd
Irlam M44 .... 105 E5
Manchester M20......... 109 E5
Siemens St BL6 .... 22 C2
Sienna Cl M44 .... 105 E6
Sighthill Wlk M9........ 157 A4
Signal Cl M30............. 79 B2
Signal Dr M40 .... 157 A2
Signet Wlk M8........... 156 B1
Silas St OL6 .... 85 D5
Silburn Way M24, M9 ..... 64 D7
Silbury Wlk M8 .... 155 C1
Silchester Dr M40....... 157 A2
Silchester Way BL2 ...... 25 E1
Silchester Wlk 3 OL1 ... 153 C3
Silcock St WA3 .... 74 A1
Silfield Cl M11 .... 160 B1
Silkhey Gr M28 .... 60 D1
Silkin Cl M13 .... 163 B3
Silkin Ct M13 .... 163 B3
Silk Mill SK12........... 133 C4
Silk Mill Way 11 M24 ..... 64 F8
Silk St
Eccles M30 .... 79 F1
Failsworth M40 .... 83 C6
Glossop SK13............ 104 E1
Leigh WN7 .... 75 F5
Manchester M4 .... 159 C2
Middleton M24............ 64 F8
Rochdale OL11............ 30 D4
Salford M3.............. 158 A3
Westhoughton BL5 .... 39 E1
Silkstone St M11 .... 165 C3
Sillavan Way M3......... 158 B2
Sillitoe Dr WN6 .... 37 A1
Silsbury Gr WN6 .... 37 A8
Silsden Ave
Golborne WA3 .... 91 B8
Manchester M9 .... 64 B5
Silsden Wlk M7........... 80 F8
Silton St M9............ 157 C4
Silvamere Cl M6 .... 154 B3
Silverbirch Cl M33 ...... 107 D2
Silver Birches M34 ..... 101 B1
Silver Birch Gr
Ashton-in-M WN4 .... 73 A5
Pendlebury M27.......... 80 B6
Silver Birch Mews SK16 . 101 E7
Silverbirch Way 3 M35 .. 83 F7
Silver Blades Ice Rink
WA15................... 119 E4
Silver Cl SK16........... 101 B7
Silvercroft St M15 ...... 162 B3
Silver Ct 3 M45 .... 44 E1
Silverdale
Altrincham WA14........ 119 C4
5 Romiley SK6.......... 112 F3
Swinton M27 .... 62 A2
Wigan WN1 .... 37 C2
Silverdale Ave
Chadderton OL9......... 152 A2
Denton M34............. 101 A2
Ince-in-M WN2 .... 56 A8
Irlam M44 .... 94 B3
Manchester M25 .... 63 E2
Walkden M38............. 60 A5
Silverdale Cl
Bury BL9 .... 45 A8
High Lane SK6 .... 134 E8
Silverdale Ct WN1 ...... 151 A4
Silverdale Dr
Oldham OL4 .... 67 F6
Wilmslow SK9 .... 137 A4
Silverdale Rd
Bolton BL1.............. 144 C3
Farnworth BL4............ 42 A1
Gatley SK8.............. 122 B4
Hindley WN2 .... 56 F5
Manchester M21 .... 97 C1
Newton-le-W WA12........ 89 B4
Stockport SK4 .... 168 C4
Wigan WN5 .... 54 B8
Silverdale St M11 .... 99 F8
Silver Hill OL16 .... 31 F7
Silver Hill Rd SK14 ..... 167 B1
Silver Jubilee Wlk 4
M4..................... 159 B2
Silverlace Ave M11....... 99 E8
Silverlea Dr M9........... 64 C2
Silvermere OL6 .... 85 E6
Silvermere Cl BL0....... 138 B1
Silver Spring SK14 ...... 113 F8
Silver St
Bury BL9 .... 140 B2
Irlam M44 .... 94 B3
Manchester M1 .... 159 A1
Manchester M1 .... 163 A4
Oldham OL1............. 153 B2
5 Platt Bridge WN2...... 56 B2
Ramsbottom BL0 .... 138 C2
Rochdale OL12.......... 139 A4
Walsden OL14 .... 6 A7
Whitefield M45 .... 44 E1
Silverstone Dr M40 ...... 83 D4
Silver Terr WN1.......... 151 A3
Silverthorne Cl 12 SK15 .. 86 A1
Silverton Cl SK14 .... 102 E2
Silverton Gr
Bolton BL1.............. 143 C4
Middleton M24............ 46 D4
Silverton Ho M6 .... 80 A3
Silverwell La BL1, BL2 ... 145 C3
Silverwell St
Bolton BL1.............. 145 C3
Failsworth M40 .... 83 D5
Horwich BL6 .... 22 B4
Silverwood OL9........... 65 E7
Silverwood Ave M21 .... 109 B8
Silvington Way WN2 ..... 38 A2
Simeon St
Manchester M4 .... 159 B3
Milnrow OL16 .... 31 F6
Walsden OL14 .... 6 A8
Simfield Cl WN6 .... 19 D1
SIMISTER 63 E8
Simister Dr BL9........... 45 A2
Simister Gn M25 .... 63 E8
Simister La
Middleton, Bowlee M24,
M25..................... 46 A1
Middleton, Simister M25 .. 63 E8
Simister Rd M35 .... 83 F7
Simister St 10 M9....... 157 B4
SIMMONDLEY 116 A7
Simmondley Gr SK13.... 116 A8
Simmondley La SK13.... 116 A8
Simmondley New Rd
SK13................... 116 A7
Simmondley Prim Sch
SK13................... 116 A8
Simms Cl
Bury BL0 .... 138 A1
Salford M3.............. 158 A2
SIMM'S LANE END........ 72 B5
Simm's Sq WN2........... 38 D4
Simonbury Cl BL8......... 26 F2
Simon Freeman Cl M19 . 111 C6
Simon La M24 .... 46 A2
Simons Cl
Glossop SK13............ 116 A7
Sale M33 .... 108 A3
Simonsway M22, SK8 .... 121 D2
Simons Wlk SK13 .... 116 A8
Simpkin St WN2 .... 56 B1
Simpson Ave M27......... 62 C2
SIMPSON CLOUGH......... 29 C5
Simpson Gr M28 .... 78 A6
Simpson Hill Cl OL10..... 29 F3
Simpson Rd M28.......... 78 A6
Simpson Sq OL9 .... 66 C3
Simpson St
Droylsden M11............ 83 A1
Hyde SK14.............. 167 A2
Manchester M4 .... 159 B3
Oldham OL9.............. 66 B4
Wilmslow SK9 .... 136 F6
Sinclair Ave M8.......... 63 F1
Sinclair Pl WN5.......... 54 E8
Sinclair St OL11.......... 30 D3
SINDERLAND GREEN...... 106 C1
Sinderland La WA14..... 106 D1
Sinderland Rd WA14 .... 119 C8
Sindsley Ct M27 .... 61 D1
Sindsley Gr BL3......... 147 B3
Sindsley Rd M27 .... 61 D2
Singapore Ave M90 ..... 130 A8
Singleton Ave
Bolton BL2............... 42 F7
Horwich BL6 .... 22 C5
Singleton Cl M7 .... 63 C1
Singleton Gr BL5.......... 40 B1
Singleton Lo M7 .... 63 D1
Singleton Rd
Manchester M7........... 63 D1
Stockport, Heaton Moor
SK4.................... 168 B4
Singleton St M26 .... 43 D4
Sion St M26 .... 44 A2
Sirdar St M11............. 99 F8
Sir Isaac Newton Way
OL16 .... 31 E4
Sirius Pl M7 .... 158 A3
Sir Matt Busby Way M17 . 96 F5
Sir Richard Fairey Rd
SK4 .... 111 B7
Sir Williams Ct M23..... 121 B6
Siskin Cl
Leigh WN7 .... 76 B5
Newton-le-W WA12........ 89 C3
Siskin Rd SK2.......... 124 F5

Sisley Cl M7 .... 81 B8
Sisson St M3 .... 83 F7
Sisters' St M43 .... 100 A8
Sitch La SK22 .... 127 F3
Sittingbourne Rd WN1 .. 37 C4
Sixpools Gr **6** M28 .... 78 C8
Sixth Ave
    Bolton BL1 .... 144 B3
    Bury BL9 .... 28 D4
    Little Lever BL3 .... 42 F4
    Oldham OL8 .... 66 C1
Sixth St M17 .... 94 F1
Size House Pl **7** WN7 .. 76 A4
Size St OL12 .... 4 D1
Skagen Ct BL1 .... 143 B1
Skaife Rd M33 .... 108 E4
Skarratt Cl M12 .... 164 C2
Skegness Cl BL8 .... 27 D5
Skellorn Green La SK10 133 F1
Skelton Gr
    Bolton BL2 .... 42 F8
    Manchester M13 .... 98 F2
Skelton Rd
    Altrincham WA14 ..... 119 E7
    Stretford M32 .... 96 D3
Skelton St WN4 .... 72 F6
Skelwith Ave BL3 .... 147 C2
Skelwith Cl M41 .... 95 A4
Skerry Cl M13 .... 163 B3
Skerton Rd M16 .... 97 B4
Skiddaw Cl M24 .... 46 D3
Skiddaw Pl WN5 .... 54 C6
Skilgate Wlk **10** M40 83 C6
Skip Pl M3, M4 .... 159 A3
Skipton Ave
    Chadderton OL9 .... 47 F1
    Failsworth M40 .... 65 D1
    Hindley WN2 .... 57 A4
Skipton Cl
    Bury BL8 .... 26 F2
    Hazel Grove SK7 ...... 133 C8
    Reddish SK5 .... 111 E8
Skipton Dr M41 .... 94 F5
Skipton St
    Bolton BL2 .... 148 C4
    Oldham OL8 .... 67 B4
Skipton Wlk BL2 .... 148 C3
Skull House La WN6 .... 35 D8
Skull House Mews WN6 35 D8
Skye Cl OL10 .... 28 F1
Skye Rd M41 .... 95 D5
Skyes Cres WN3 .... 54 C1
Skyes Ct **8** OL16 ... 31 B6
Skye Wlk M23 .... 121 A4
SLACKCOTE 50 B7
Slackcote OL3 .... 50 C7
Slackey Brow BL4 .... 61 C6
Slackey Fold WN2 .... 57 B1
Slack Fold La BL4 ...... 147 A1
Slack Gate OL12 .... 14 F8
Slack Gate La OL3 ...... 50 D8
Slack Hall OL4 .... 67 F8
Slack La
    Bolton BL2 .... 25 E7
    Delph OL3 .... 50 D6
    Swinton M27 .... 62 A1
    Westhoughton BL5 .... 39 F3
Slack Rd M9 .... 64 D1
Slack St
    Hyde SK14 .... 167 C4
    Rochdale OL16 .... 139 C3
Slade Gr M13 .... 98 F3
Slade Hall Rd M12 ...... 99 A2
Slade La M13, M19 ..... 98 F2
Slade Mount M19 ...... 110 F8
Sladen Fold OL15 .... 16 D8
Sladen St OL12 .... 14 F1
Slade St BL3 .... 43 A3
Slades View Cl OL3 ..... 51 C5
Slag La WA3 .... 74 F2
Slaidburn Ave M22 ..... 42 F6
Slaidburn Cl
    6 Milnrow OL16 .. 31 F5
    Wigan WN3 .... 55 A3
Slaidburn Cres WA3 .... 73 F2
Slaidburn Dr BL8 .... 26 F3
Slaithwaite Dr **5** M11 83 C2
Slant Cl SK13 .... 116 E8
Slateacre Rd SK14 ..... 113 F7
Slate Ave M4 .... 159 C1
Slate La
    Ashton-u-l OL7 .... 84 E1
    Droylsden M34 ...... 100 C8
Slatelands Ave SK13 .. 116 B8
Slatelands Rd SK13 ... 116 B8
Slater Ave BL6 .... 22 C4
Slaterfield BL3 .... 145 B1
Slater La BL1 .... 25 A1
Slater's Nook **10** BL5 39 E1
Slater St
    Bolton BL1 .... 143 C1
    Eccles M30 .... 79 B2
    Failsworth M35 .... 65 F1
    Farnworth BL4 .... 60 D8
    Oldham OL9 .... 153 B2
Slater Street N WN7 ... 75 D5
Slater Way **3** SK14 104 F2
Slate Wharf M15 .... 162 A3
SLATTOCKS 47 D6
Slaunt Bank OL12 ...... 13 D2
Slawson Way OL10 ..... 29 F3
Sleaford Cl
    Bury BL8 .... 27 D5
    Manchester M40 .... 160 A3

Sledbrook St WN5 .... 54 C5
Sleddale Cl SK2 .... 124 D5
Sledmere Cl
    Bolton BL1 .... 143 C2
    Droylsden M11 .... 83 A1
Sledmoor Rd M23 ..... 108 F1
Slimbridge Cl BL2 .... 26 A1
Sloane Ave OL4 .... 67 F8
Sloane St
    5 Ashton-u-l OL6 166 C3
    Bolton BL3 .... 146 B3
Slough Ind Ctr M5 ..... 161 C4
SMALLBRIDGE 15 D2
Smallbridge Cl **8** M28 78 C8
Smallbridge Ind Pk **6**
    .... 15 B2
SMALL BROOK 149 C4
Smallbrook La WN7 ..... 57 E3
Smallbrook Rd OL2 ..... 32 C1
Smalldale Ave M16 ..... 97 F3
Smalley St
    Rochdale OL11 .... 30 C2
    Standish WN6 .... 19 E1
Smallfield Dr M9 ...... 157 A4
Smallridge Cl M40 ... 160 A3
SMALLSHAW 85 C3
Smallshaw Cl **1** OL6 85 B5
Smallshaw Fold **2** OL6 85 B5
Smallshaw La OL6 ..... 85 C5
Smallshaw Rd OL12 .... 14 A4
Smallshaw Sq **1** OL6 85 B5
Smallwood St M40 ...... 83 C6
Smart St M12 .... 99 A3
Smeaton Cl M32 .... 96 E2
Smeaton St
    Horwich BL6 .... 22 C2
    Manchester M8 ...... 156 C2
Smedley Ave
    Bolton BL3 .... 42 A3
    Manchester M8 ...... 156 C2
Smedley La M8, M9 ... 156 C3
Smedley Pl SK13 ...... 104 E2
Smedley Rd M40, M8 156 C2
Smedley St M8 .... 156 B2
Smethurst Hall Pk WN5 53 C2
Smethurst Hall Rd BL9 28 F4
Smethurst La
    Bolton BL3, BL4 ..... 146 B2
    Wigan WN5 .... 54 C5
Smethurst Rd WN5 ..... 53 C2
Smethurst St
    Heywood OL10 .... 29 B2
    Manchester M9 .... 64 D1
    Middleton M24 .... 65 D7
Smith Ave WN5 .... 54 B8
Smith Fold La M28 ...... 60 A3
Smith Hill OL16 .... 32 A6
Smithies Ave M24 ...... 47 A2
Smithies St OL10 .... 29 E2
SMITHILLS 142 B3
Smithills Country Pk *
    BL1 .... 24 B5
Smithills Croft Rd BL1 142 B3
Smithills Dean Rd BL1 142 B4
Smithills Dr BL1 .... 23 F2
Smithills Hall Cl BL0 138 C1
Smithill's Hall (Mus) *
    BL1 .... 142 B4
Smithills Open Farm *
    BL1 .... 24 C5
Smithills Sch BL1 ..... 142 C3
Smithills Sports Ctr BL1 142 C3
Smith La BL7 .... 8 F1
Smith's La WN2 .... 56 B8
Smiths Lawn SK9 ..... 137 A5
Smith's Pl **8** M6 ..... 58 D3
Smith's Rd BL3 .... 42 D3
Smith St
    Adlington PR7 .... 20 F6
    Ashton-u-l OL7 .... 84 F1
    Aspull WN2 .... 38 C5
    Atherton M46 .... 58 C3
    Bury BL9 .... 141 A3
    Cheadle SK8 .... 122 F6
    Denton M34 .... 100 F2
    Dukinfield SK14 ...... 101 D5
    Dukinfield SK16 ...... 101 A8
    7 Heywood OL10 .. 29 D2
    9 Leigh WN7 .... 76 A5
    Littleborough OL15 .... 16 B5
    Manchester M16 .... 161 C2
    Mossley OL5 .... 68 B2
    Oldham OL4 .... 67 E8
    Ramsbottom BL0 .... 138 B1
    Rochdale OL16 ...... 139 C3
    Walkden M28 .... 60 D3
Smithwood Ave WN2 ... 56 F6
SMITHY BRIDGE 15 F4
Smithy Bridge Prim Sch
    OL15 .... 15 F3
Smithy Bridge Rd OL15 15 F3
Smithy Bridge Sta OL15 15 F3
Smithy Brow WN6 ...... 18 C8
Smithy Cl SK13 .... 104 D1
Smithy Croft BL7 .... 24 F8
Smithy Dr WA14 ...... 118 D3
Smithy Fold
    Glossop SK13 .... 104 D1
    Rochdale OL16 .... 14 C1
Smithy Fold Rd **3** SK14 167 B1
Smithy Glen Dr WN5 ... 53 E4
Smithy Gn
    Cheadle SK8 .... 132 A8
    Ince-in-M WN2 .... 151 C3
    Newhey OL16 .... 32 E4
    Romiley SK6 .... 113 B5
Smithy Gr OL6 .... 166 C4

SMITHY GREEN 132 B7
Smithy Hill BL3 .... 146 A4
Smithy La
    Altrincham WA14 .... 118 D3
    Hyde SK14 .... 167 B1
    Marple SK6 .... 114 F1
    Partington M31 ...... 105 F3
    Uppermill OL3 .... 69 B8
Smithy Nook OL15 .... 6 C1
Smithy St
    Hazel Grove SK7 .... 124 D3
    Leigh WN7 .... 75 F4
    Ramsbottom BL0 .... 138 C2
    Westhoughton BL5 .... 39 E3
Smock La WN4 .... 72 C4
Smyrna St
    Heywood OL10 .... 29 C1
    7 Oldham OL4 ..... 67 C6
    Radcliffe M26 .... 43 F4
    Salford M5 .... 154 B1
Smyrna Wlk M26 .... 43 F4
Snapebrook Gr **6** SK9 131 E1
Snape St M40 .... 83 F6
Snell St M4 .... 160 A1
Snipe Ave OL11 .... 29 F7
Snipe Cl SK12 .... 133 A4
Snipe Rd OL8 .... 67 B2
Snipe Ret Pk OL7 ..... 100 D8
Snipe St BL3 .... 147 C4
Snipe Way OL7 .... 100 D8
Snowberry Wlk M31 .. 105 E3
Snowden Ave
    Urmston M41 .... 107 B8
    Wigan WN5 .... 55 A4
Snowden St
    Bolton BL1 .... 145 B4
    Heywood OL10 .... 46 E8
    1 Oldham M4 .... 65 C2
Snowden Wlk **4** M40 65 C2
Snowdon Dr
    Cheadle SK8 .... 122 E2
    Horwich BL6 .... 22 C5
Snowdon Rd M30 .... 80 A3
Snowdon St OL11 .... 31 A2
Snowdrop Cl BB4 .... 1 A8
Snowdrop Wlk M7 .... 155 A2
Snow Hill Rd BL3 .... 42 D5
Snowshill Dr WN3 ...... 54 C4
Snydale Cl BL5 .... 40 B2
Snydale Way BL3, BL5 40 C1
Soane Cl M4 .... 73 D3
Soap St M4 .... 159 A2
Soapstone Way M44 .. 106 A8
Society St OL2 .... 149 B3
Sofa St BL1 .... 142 B1
Soham Cl WN2 .... 56 E4
Soho St
    Bolton BL3 .... 145 C2
    Oldham OL4 .... 67 B7
    Wigan WN5 .... 54 F7
Solent Ave M8 .... 64 A1
Solent Dr BL3 .... 42 D5
Sole St WN1 .... 37 E1
Solness St BL9 .... 27 F6
Soloman Rd WA14 .... 107 C1
Solway Cl
    Ashton-in-M WN4 ..... 73 A4
    Bolton BL3 .... 147 A3
    Swinton M27 .... 61 E4
Solway Rd M22 .... 121 C1
Somerby Dr M22 ...... 121 C1
Somerdale Ave BL1 .. 144 A3
Somerfield Rd M9 ..... 64 D2
Somerford Ave M20 .. 110 A8
Somerford Ho SK12 .. 133 E4
Somerford Rd M40 ..... 99 F2
Somerford Way **3** SK9 131 E5
Somersby Ct SK7 ..... 123 E1
Somersby Dr BL7 ...... 24 F8
Somersby Wlk BL3 ... 145 C1
Somerset Ave
    Shaw OL2 .... 48 F7
    Tyldesley M29 .... 59 F3
Somerset Cl
    Brinnington SK5 ...... 112 C4
    Irlam M44 .... 105 D6
Somerset Gr BL9 .... 44 F8
Somerset Gr OL11 ...... 30 A8
Somerset Pl M33 ...... 108 B6
Somerset Rd
    Altrincham WA14 .... 119 D6
    Atherton M46 .... 58 C5
    Bolton BL1 .... 144 B4
    Droylsden M43 .... 84 A3
    Failsworth M35 .... 83 E6
    Salford M30 .... 80 A4
    Wigan WN5 .... 54 C7
Somerset St OL4 .... 67 C6
Somerset Wlk BB4 ...... 1 B8
Somers Rd SK5 .... 169 F1
Somers Wlk M9 .... 64 B3
Somerton Ave
    Sale M33 .... 108 C3
    Wythenshawe M22 .. 121 C3
Somerton Cl WN6 ...... 19 D1
Somerton Ct M9 .... 65 A3
Somerton Rd BL2 .... 43 A6
Somerton Wlk **8** OL9 48 A1
Somerville Gdns WA15 119 F7
Somerville Rd WN7 .... 37 C3
Somerville Sq BL1 ... 142 C3
Somerville St BL1 .... 142 C3
Sommerville Ct M47 .. 155 A4
Sonning Dr BL3 .... 146 A2
Sonning Wlk **1** M8 156 A6
Sopwith Dr M14 .... 98 B1
Sorby Rd M44 .... 106 A7

Sorrel Bank M6 .... 154 C4
Sorrel Dr OL15 .... 15 F6
Sorrell Bank SK5 ...... 100 A1
Sorrel St M15 .... 162 B2
Sorrel Way OL4 .... 49 E2
Sorting Ho The M1 ... 159 B2
Sorton St M3 .... 163 A3
Soudan Rd SK2 .... 124 A6
Soudan St M24 .... 65 B5
Sougher's La WN4 ...... 72 F7
Sougher's Lane End WN4 72 E6
Sound The OL3 .... 50 F4
SOURACRE 86 C3
Souracre Fold SK15 .... 86 B3
South Acre Dr SK9 ... 131 D3
Southall St M3 .... 158 C4
Southampton Cl M7 .. 155 A1
Southam St M7 .... 155 C3
South Ave
    Golborne WN7 .... 74 F4
    Heywood OL10 .... 29 B2
    Kearsley BL4 .... 60 F6
    Leigh WN7 .... 76 C3
    Manchester M19 .... 110 F7
    Manchester M41 ...... 95 D5
    Uppermill OL3 .... 69 B6
    Whitefield M45 .... 44 E1
South Bank Cl SK9 ... 137 B2
South Bank Rd M19 .. 110 D5
South Bank Rd BL9 ... 140 B1
Southbourne Ave M41 95 F2
Southbourne St M6 .. 154 B2
Southbourne Ave M9 .. 63 F3
Southbrook Cl SK13 .. 171 B4
Southbrook Gr BL3 ... 147 C3
South Chadderton Sch
    OL9 .... 65 F3
South Chadderton Sta
    OL9 .... 66 A3
Southchurch Par M40 159 C4
South Cl
    Glossop SK13 .... 103 F7
    Whitefield BL9 .... 45 A3
    Wilmslow SK9 .... 137 B6
Southcliffe Rd **3** SK5 111 F6
South Cliffe St **11** M11 99 F7
Southcombe Wlk M15 . 97 F4
Southcourt WN7 .... 76 B6
South Cres
    Droylsden M11 .... 83 D2
    Failsworth M40 .... 65 D3
South Croft OL8 .... 67 B3
Southcross Rd M18 .... 99 D3
South Cross St **1** M26 140 C2
South Croston St M16 97 D4
South Cross St OL16 .. 31 A8
Southdene Ave M20 .. 109 E4
Southdown Cl
    Rochdale OL11 .... 30 C5
    Stockport SK4 .... 169 B2
Southdown Cres
    Cheadle SK8 .... 131 F8
    Manchester M9 .... 65 A2
Southdown Dr M28 ..... 77 F6
South Downs Cl **2** WA14 119 D1
South Downs Rd WA14 119 D1
South Dr
    Altrincham WA15 .... 120 A7
    Appley Bridge WN6 ... 18 C2
    Bolton BL2 .... 25 D3
    Gatley SK8 .... 122 A4
    Manchester M21 .... 109 B6
    Wilmslow SK9 .... 137 B6
Southend Ave M15 ... 162 A2
Southend St BL3 ...... 146 C3
Southern App M27 ..... 62 C2
Southernby Cl **9** M13 98 F4
Southern Cl
    Denton M34 .... 112 F8
    Stockport SK7 .... 123 F1
Southern Cres SK7 ... 123 F1
Southern Cross Sch
    M21 .... 109 C5
Southern Ho **3** BL1 . 143 A1
Southern Ind Est M18 . 60 D5
Southern Rd M33 ..... 108 A6
Southern's Fold WN2 .. 38 A3
Southern St
    Manchester M3 ...... 162 B4
    Salford M6 .... 154 B2
    Walkden M28 .... 60 D5
    Wigan WN5 .... 54 D5
Southery Ave WN3 ..... 54 D3
Southey Cl OL15 .... 15 F2
Southey Ct M34 ...... 113 A8
Southey Wlk **6** M34 113 A7
South Failsworth Prim Sch
    M35 .... 83 F5
Southfield WN2 .... 56 B2
Southfield Ave BL9 ..... 27 F6
Southfield Cl
    Dukinfield SK16 ...... 101 D6
    Handforth SK9 .... 131 C3
Southfield Dr BL5 .... 57 E7
Southfield Est M17 ..... 96 C6
Southfield Rd BL0 ...... 11 A2
Southfields Ave **2** M11 83 C2
Southfields Dr M33 .. 120 B7
Southfield St **1** BL3 .. 42 B4
Southgarth Rd M6 ... 154 B3
Southgate
    Bolton BL2 .... 25 E4
    Manchester, Chorlton-cum-Hardy
    M21 .... 109 B7

Southgate *continued*
    Manchester, Heaton Chapel
    SK4 .... 111 C5
Manchester M3 .... 158 C1
Uppermill OL3 .... 51 A2
Urmston M41 .... 107 B8
Whitworth OL12 .... 14 C7
Southgate Ave M40 .... 83 A4
Southgate Cl **3** M33 . 108 C5
Southgate Ind Est OL10 29 E1
Southgate Mews SK4 . 111 C5
Southgate Rd
    Failsworth OL9 .... 65 E3
    Whitefield BL9 .... 44 F3
Southgate St OL1 .... 153 C2
Southgate Way **11** OL2 166 A1
South Gr
    9 Alderley Edge SK9 137 A1
    Manchester M13 .... 164 A1
    Sale M33 .... 108 B3
    Walkden M28 .... 60 C2
Southgrove Ave BL1 ... 24 E6
South Hall St M5 ...... 161 C7
South Hey WN7 .... 75 C5
South Hill St OL4 .... 67 F5
South Hill St OL4 .... 67 A6
South King St
    Eccles M30 .... 79 B2
    Manchester M2 ...... 158 C1
South La M29 .... 77 A5
South Lancashire Ind Est
    .... 73 B6
Southlands Ave
    Eccles M30 .... 95 A8
    Standish WN6 .... 36 E8
South Langworthy Rd
    M50 .... 154 C1
Southlawn SK9 .... 137 A5
Southleigh Dr M19, M20 110 D1
Southleigh Dr BL2 ..... 43 A6
Southlink OL4 .... 67 A6
Southlink Bsns Pk OL4 67 A6
Southlink Wkshps OL4 67 A6
South Lonsdale St M32 96 E3
South Marlow St SK13 104 A4
South Mead SK12 ..... 133 B5
South Meade
    Altrincham WA15 .... 120 A7
    Manchester M21 .... 109 B7
    Manchester, Sedgley Park
    M25 .... 63 D2
    Swinton M27 .... 79 E6
South Meadway SK6 . 134 F7
Southmere Cl **2** M40 65 C3
South Mesnefield Rd M7 81 A8
Southmill St M2 .... 162 C4
Southmoor M23 ...... 120 F7
Southmoor Bsns Pk M23 120 F2
Southmoor Rd M23 .. 120 F5
Southmoor Wlk BL3 .. 145 B1
South Oak La SK9 .... 136 F5
Southolme Gdns M19 110 E4
Southover BL5 .... 57 E6
South Par
    Rochdale OL16 .... 139 C3
    Stockport SK7 .... 123 F2
South Park Dr SK12 .. 133 E5
South Park Rd SK8 ... 122 B6
South Pl **11** OL16 ... 31 A8
Southpoint OL4 .... 67 C6
Southpool Cl SK7 .... 124 A2
South Pump St M1 ... 163 B4
South Radford St M7 .. 81 A7
South Rd
    Altrincham, Ashley Heath
    WA14 .... 128 E8
    Altrincham, Rosehill WA14 119 D1
    Manchester M20 .... 110 B2
    Swinton M27 .... 62 D2
South Reddish St M18 111 E5
Southridge M34 ...... 100 F5
South Row M25 .... 62 F1
South Royd St BL8 ..... 26 F7
Southsea St M11 .... 99 D7
Southside SK6 .... 112 E6
South Side SK14 ..... 113 F8
Southside Ind Pk M46 . 58 B4
South St
    Alderley Edge SK9 .. 137 A1
    Ashton-u-l OL7 .... 100 E8
    Bolton BL3 .... 147 B3
    Heywood OL10 .... 29 B2
    Manchester, Longsight
    M12 .... 164 B1
    Manchester M11 .... 165 C3
    Oldham OL8 .... 66 B2
    Rochdale OL16 .... 31 A8
    Tyldesley M46 .... 58 E1
South Stage M50 .... 96 F8
South Terr
    12 Alderley Edge SK9 137 A1
    Bury BL9 .... 44 D7
    Ramsbottom BL0 .... 1 C2
South Terrace Ct **12** OL16 31 A8
South Vale Cres WA15 119 F5
South View
    Atherton M46 .... 58 C3
    2 Manchester M14 98 C2
    Mossley SK15 .... 99 F3
    Reddish SK5 .... 99 F3
    Rochdale OL11 .... 29 E6
    Romiley SK6 .... 113 C6
South Views SK8 ..... 122 C3
South View Rd
    Glossop SK13 .... 116 F7
    Rochdale OL12 .... 15 E3
South View St BL2 ... 148 C3

South View Terr OL16 .... 15 E4
South Villa Ct WN6 ..... 36 E8
Southward Rd WA11 .... 89 A7
Southwark Dr SK16 .... 101 D6
Southway
  Altrincham WA14 ...... 119 C6
  Ashton-u-L OL7 .... 85 B6
  Droylsden M43 .... 100 A8
  7 Eccles M30 .... 79 F2
  Failsworth OL9 .... 65 F2
  Oldham OL8 .... 66 E2
Southwell Cl
  13 Bolton BL1 .... 145 A4
  Golborne WA3 .... 90 C8
  Romiley SK6 .... 113 A1
Southwell Ct 8 M42 .... 96 C1
Southwell Dr WN7 ..... 157 B3
Southwell Rd M21 ..... 109 A2
South William St M43 .. 158 A1
South Wlk 15 SK15 .... 86 A1
Southwold Cl M19 ..... 99 C1
Southwood Cl BL3 ..... 147 C3
Southwood Dr M9 ..... 64 A5
South Woodley Mans M26 62 C8
Southwood Rd SK2 .... 124 B4
Southworth Ct M43 .... 158 A2
Southworth Rd WA12 .. 89 F4
Southyard St M19 ..... 111 B8
Sovereign Bsns Pk WN1 .. 151 C8
Sovereign Ent Pk M50 .. 161 A3
Sovereign Fold Rd WN7 . 57 E1
Sovereign Rd M41 ..... 151 A3
Sovereign St M6 ...... 81 A4
Sowerby Cl BL8 .... 26 F2
Sowerby Wlk M9 ...... 64 B4
Spa Cl SK5 .... 111 E8
Spa Cres M38 .... 60 A6
Spa Gr M38 .... 60 A6
Spa La
  Oldham OL4 .... 67 E5
  Walkden M38 .... 60 A6
Spalding Dr M23 ...... 121 A2
Spa Rd
  Atherton M46 .... 58 D5
  Bolton BL1 .... 145 A3
Sparkford Ave M23 .... 108 D1
Sparkle St M1 .... 163 B4
Spark Rd M23 .... 120 F7
Spa Road Ind Est BL1 .. 145 B3
Sparrow Cl
  Manchester M13 ..... 164 A1
  Reddish SK5 .... 99 E2
Sparrowfield Cl SK15 .. 86 E7
Sparrow Hill
  Appley Bridge WN6, WN8 .. 18 A2
  Rochdale OL16 .... 139 C3
Sparrow St OL2 .... 48 E2
Sparta Ave M28 ...... 60 D2
Sparta Wlk M11 ...... 165 A4
Sparth Bottoms Rd OL11 139 A1
Sparth Ct SK4 .... 169 A3
Sparthfield Ave OL11 .. 139 B1
Sparthfield Rd SK4 .... 169 A3
Sparth Hall SK4 ...... 169 A3
Sparth La SK4 .... 169 A3
Sparth Rd M40 .... 83 D5
Spa St M13, M15 ..... 163 B1
Spathfield Ct SK4 .... 169 A3
Spath Holme 2 M20 .. 110 A3
Spath La SK8 .... 131 F5
Spath Lane E SK8 .... 132 B5
Spath Rd M20 .... 110 A3
Spath Wlk SK8 ...... 132 B5
Spawell Cl WA3 ...... 90 E8
Spaw St M3 .... 158 B2
Speakman Ave
  Leigh WN7 .... 76 B5
  Newton-le-W WA12 .. 89 C5
Speakmans Dr WN6 .. 35 C6
Spean Wlk 8 M11 .... 83 C1
Spear St M1, M4 ..... 159 B2
Specialist Learning Ctr The
  M35 .... 83 D7
Spectator St M4 ..... 160 A2
Specton Wlk 5 M12 .. 99 B3
Spectrum Bsns Pk SK3 . 123 B6
Spectrum Way SK3 ... 123 C6
Speedwell SK13 ...... 103 F7
Speedwell Cl
  Glossop SK13 .... 103 F7
  10 Golborne WA3 .... 90 E8
Speke Wlk M34 ...... 100 E1
Spelding Dr WN6 .... 36 E4
Spencer Ave
  1 Dukinfield SK14 ... 101 D5
  Little Lever BL3 ..... 43 A3
  Manchester M16 .... 97 C2
  Whitefield M45 ..... 44 E2
Spencer La OL11 ..... 29 E5
Spencer Rd WN1 ..... 37 C3
Spencer Road W WN6 . 37 A3
Spencer's La WN5 ... 53 D7
Spencer St
  Bury BL8 .... 27 C3
  1 Dukinfield SK14 .. 101 C8
  Eccles M30 .... 79 C1
  Littleborough OL15 .. 16 C6
  Mossley OL5 .... 68 B1
  Oldham, Lower Moor OL1 . 67 A8
  Oldham OL9 .... 66 C4
  Radcliffe M26 ...... 44 B3
  Ramsbottom BL0 .... 138 B1
  Reddish SK5 .... 111 F8
Spender Ave M8 .... 156 A2
Spendmore La PR7 .. 19 D8
Spen Fold
  Bury BL8 .... 44 A8

Spen Fold continued
  Littleborough OL15 ... 16 A4
Spenleach La BL8 .... 10 D3
Spenlow WN7 .... 76 C3
Spenlow Cl SK12 .... 133 E1
Spennithorne Rd M41 .. 95 B2
Spenser Ave
  Denton M34 .... 113 A8
  Radcliffe M26 ...... 43 E4
Spenwood Rd OL15 .. 15 F5
Spey Cl
  Altrincham WA14 .... 119 C6
  Standish WN6 .... 19 D1
Spey Ho 7 SK5 ...... 99 F2
Speyside Cl M45 .... 63 A8
Spilsby Sq WN3 ..... 55 A2
Spindle Ave SK15 ... 86 C3
Spindle Croft BL4 ... 60 D8
Spindle Ct OL2 ..... 48 E4
Spindle Hillock WN4 . 72 D5
SPINDLE POINT 86 C3
Spindlepoint Dr 4 M28 . 78 C8
Spindle Point Prim Sch
  BL4 .... 61 B5
Spindles Sh Ctr The OL1 . 153 B2
Spindles The OL5 ... 86 D8
Spindle Wlk BL5 .... 39 F2
Spindlewood Cl SK15 . 86 D2
Spindlewood Rd WN3 .. 151 C2
Spingdale M38 ...... 59 D6
Spinks St OL4 ...... 67 B5
Spinnerbottom SK22 . 127 F2
Spinnerette Cl WN7 . 76 A5
Spinners Gdns OL12 . 15 C4
Spinners Gn OL12 .. 14 F2
Spinners La SK12 ... 133 C4
Spinners Mews BL1 .. 145 A8
Spinners Way OL4 .. 49 E4
Spinney Apts WN8 .. 35 C1
Spinney Cl
  Glossop SK13 ...... 104 C2
  Handforth SK9 ..... 131 C3
Spinney Dr
  Bury BL9 .... 27 E6
  Sale M33 .... 107 D2
Spinney Gr M34 .... 100 F5
Spinney Nook OL2 .. 25 D2
Spinney Rd M23 .... 121 B7
Spinney The
  Bolton BL1 .... 144 B3
  Chapeltown BL7 .... 9 C2
  Cheadle SK8 .... 122 E3
  Oldham OL4 .... 68 A8
  Urmston M41 .... 95 A2
  Whitefield M45 .... 62 C7
  Wigan WN5 .... 54 E5
Spinningfields BL1 .. 145 A4
Spinning Gate Sh Ctr
  WN7 .... 75 F4
Spinning Jenny Way WN7 75 F4
Spinning Jenny Wlk 2
  M4 .... 159 C2
Spinning Mdw BL1 .. 145 A4
Spinnings The BL9 .. 11 C3
Spion Kop WN4 .... 73 A3
Spiredale Brow WN6 . 19 F8
Spire Hollin SK13 ... 104 C2
Spire Hollin Ho SK13 . 104 C2
Spire Manchester Hospl
  (Private) M16 ...... 97 D3
Spires Croft WN7 .. 76 B5
Spire Wlk M12 ...... 164 A4
Spirewood Gdns SK6 . 113 A2
Spodden Cotts OL12 . 14 C8
Spodden Fold OL12 . 14 C8
Spodden St OL12 ... 139 A4
Spodden Wlk M45 .. 45 C1
Spodgemere La WA14 . 118 C1
Spod Rd OL12 ...... 14 D1
Spokeshave Way OL16 . 15 C2
Spooner Rd 6 M30 . 79 C1
Sportcity M11 ...... 160 C2
Sportcity Stadium Metro Sta
  M11 .... 160 C2
Sportcity-velodrome Sta
  M11 .... 83 A1
Sportcity Way M11 . 160 C2
Sportside Ave M28 . 60 E4
Sportside Cl M28 ... 60 E4
Sportside Gr M28 .. 60 E4
Sportsmans Dr OL8 . 67 A3
Sportsman St WN7 . 75 D5
SPOTLAND BRIDGE .. 139 A4
Spotland Bridge Ind Ctr
  OL11 .... 30 C8
SPOTLAND FOLD 14 C1
Spotland Prim Sch OL12 139 A4
Spotland Rd OL12 .. 139 B4
Spotland Stadium (Rochdale
  AFC) OL11 .... 30 C8
Spotland Tops OL12 . 14 B1
Spreadbury St 7 M40 . 83 A7
Spring Ave
  Hyde SK14 .... 113 F8
  Whitefield M45 .... 44 E2
SPRING BANK 54 D6
Springbank
  Chadderton OL9 .... 152 A3
  Glossop SK13 ...... 103 F5
  Uppermill OL3 ..... 69 B8
Spring Bank
  Altrincham WA14 ... 119 D3
  Appley Bridge WN6 .. 35 C8
  Salford M6 .... 154 B3
  Stalybridge SK15 ... 102 B8
  Whitworth, Broadley OL12 . 14 D4

Spring Bank continued
  Whitworth OL12 ..... 4 D1
Spring Bank Ave
  Ashton-u-L OL6 .... 85 B5
  Denton M34 .... 100 D7
Springbank Cl SK6 .. 113 C6
Springbank Ct
  Manchester M8 ..... 63 F1
  Romiley SK6 .... 113 B5
Springbank Gdns WA13 . 117 B5
Spring Bank La
  Rochdale OL1 ...... 29 E8
  Stalybridge SK15 .. 86 C5
Spring Bank Pl SK1 . 170 B4
Springbank Rd SK6 . 113 C6
Spring Bank St OL8 . 66 C4
Spring Bank Terr M41 . 100 C7
Spring Bottom OL14 . 5 F7
Springbourne M6 .. 36 F2
Springbridge Rd M16 . 97 F1
Spring Brook Sch OL8 . 66 D3
Springburn
  Horwich BL6 .... 22 D1
  1 Worsley M28 .... 78 A6
Springburn Way OL3 . 69 B7
Spring Cl
  Ashton-u-L OL7 .... 85 A6
  Bury BL8 .... 26 E6
  Oldham OL4 .... 67 D5
  Ramsbottom BL0 .. 138 B2
Spring Clough M28 . 79 B6
Spring Clough Ave M28 . 60 F2
Spring Clough Dr
  Oldham OL8 .... 67 C4
  Walkden M28 .... 60 F2
Spring Cotts OL5 ... 68 C2
Spring Ct Mews SK14 . 103 C8
Springdale Gdns M20 . 110 A3
SPRINGFIELD
  Bolton 148 B2
  Wigan 37 A2
Springfield
  Broadbottom SK13 .. 115 C6
  Kearsley M26 ...... 61 C6
  1 Urmston M41 .... 95 C2
Springfield Ave
  Golborne WA3 ..... 89 F8
  Hazel Grove SK7 ... 124 D3
  Littleborough OL15 . 16 B8
  Lymm WA13 .... 117 B5
  Marple SK6 .... 156 B4
  Reddish SK5 .... 111 E7
Springfield Cl
  Failsworth M35 .... 83 F8
  Glossop SK13 ...... 171 B4
  5 Heywood OL10 .. 29 E1
Springfield Dr SK9 . 136 D5
Springfield Gdns BL4 . 61 A6
Springfield Ind Est M33 . 83 E8
Springfield La
  Irlam M44 .... 93 F2
  Rochdale OL16 .... 15 B5
  Royton OL2 .... 48 C7
  Salford M3 .... 158 B3
Springfield Prim Sch
  M33 .... 108 B4
Springfield Rd
  Adlington PR6 ..... 21 A8
  Altrincham WA15 .. 119 D5
  Atherton M46 ..... 58 E4
  Bolton BL1 .... 24 E7
  Coppull PR7 .... 19 E8
  Droylsden M43 .... 83 F3
  Farnworth BL4 .... 42 A1
  Gatley SK8 .... 122 B5
  Hindley WN2 ...... 56 C6
  Horwich BL6 ...... 22 E1
  Kearsley BL4 ...... 60 F6
  Middleton M24 .... 46 F2
  Ramsbottom BL0 .. 11 A2
  Sale M33 .... 108 B4
  Wilmslow SK9 ..... 137 A2
Springfield Road N PR7 . 19 E8
Springfield St
  Ashton-u-L OL6 .... 85 E5
  5 Bolton BL3 ...... 42 A4
  Denton M34 .... 100 F6
  Heywood OL10 .... 29 A2
  Wigan WN1 .... 151 A3
Spring Gardens St 4 BB4 . 2 F8
Spring Garden St 11 OL2 . 48 D4
Spring Gdns
  Altrincham WA15 .. 120 C5
  1 Atherton M46 .. 58 D3
  Bolton BL2 .... 25 F4
  Glossop SK13 ...... 104 A5
  Hazel Grove SK7 .. 124 D3
  Hindley WN2 ...... 56 C6
  Manchester M1, M2 . 159 A1
  Middleton M24 .... 47 A1
  Rawtenstall BB4 ... 2 F6
  8 Royton OL2 ..... 48 D4
  Salford M6 .... 154 C3
  Stockport SK1 ..... 112 A1
  Wigan WN1 .... 150 B4
Spring Gr
  Uppermill OL3 ..... 69 B5
  Wigan WN1 .... 151 A3
Spring Grove Mews .. 44 E2
Spring Hall Rise OL4 . 49 F4
Springhead Ave
  Manchester M20 ... 110 A7
  Oldham OL4 .... 68 A5
Springhead Com Inf & Fst
  Sch OL4 .... 68 A6

SPRING HILL 67 D8
Springhill OL2 ...... 48 D4
Springhill Ave OL13 . 3 D8
Spring Hill Ct 5 OL4 . 67 F7
Springhill High Sch OL16 . 31 B5
Springhill Sports Ctr &
  Athletics Arena OL16 . 31 C5
Springhill Villas OL13 . 3 D8
Spring La
  Lymm WA13 .... 117 F3
  Oldham OL4 .... 67 E5
  Radcliffe M26 ..... 44 B3
Springlawn BL1 ..... 40 F8
Springlea SK7 ...... 124 D3
Spring Meadow La OL3 . 69 C8
Spring Mill OL3 .... 69 B8
Spring Mill Cl BL3 .. 147 B4
Spring Mill Wlk OL16 . 15 C2
Springmount WA3 .. 90 E7
Spring Pl OL12 ..... 4 D3
Springpool WN3 .... 54 B2
Spring Rd
  Altrincham WA14 .. 119 D2
  9 Cheadle SK3 .... 123 C8
  Orrell WN5 .... 53 F8
  Poynton SK12 ..... 133 F2
  Wigan WN5 .... 36 A1
Spring Rise
  Glossop SK13 ...... 115 F7
  Shaw OL2 .... 32 A1
  Stalybridge SK15 .. 85 F3
Springside SK4 ..... 111 D7
Spring Side
  Rawtenstall BB4 ... 2 F6
  Whitworth OL12 .... 4 D4
Springside Ave M28 . 60 E3
Springside Cl M28 .. 60 E3
Springside Cotts BL7 . 8 A2
Springside Cty Prim Sch
  BL9 .... 27 E7
Springside Gr M28 . 60 E3
Springside Rd BL9 . 27 E8
Springside Sch OL16 . 15 B2
Springside View BL8 . 27 C7
Springside Wlk M15 . 162 A2
Springs La SK15 ... 86 C3
Springs Rd M24 .... 65 E6
Spring St
  Bolton BL3 .... 145 C1
  Broadbottom SK14 . 115 A8
  Bury BL9 .... 140 C1
  Bury, Tottington BL8 . 26 F7
  Bury, Walshaw BL8 . 26 C2
  Farnworth BL4 .... 42 D1
  Glossop SK13 ..... 104 B1
  Hollingworth SK14 . 103 C5
  Horwich BL6 .... 22 B4
  Ince-in-M WN3 .... 55 E4
  Manchester M12 .. 99 A2
  Oldham, County End OL4 . 68 A6
  Oldham OL4 .... 67 C8
  Ramsbottom, Bank La BL0 . 11 D7
  Ramsbottom, Tanners BL0 . 138 B2
  Stalybridge SK15 .. 86 A2
  Uppermill OL3 .... 69 B8
  Wigan WN1 .... 151 A3
  Wilmslow SK9 .... 137 A7
Springs The
  Altrincham WA14 .. 119 B2
  Rochdale OL16 .... 29 E2
Spring Terr
  4 Bacup OL13 ..... 3 D8
  Bury BL8 .... 26 F7
  Chadderton OL9 ... 152 A3
  Newhey OL16 ...... 32 C4
  Rochdale OL11 .... 14 A1
Spring Thyme Fold OL15 . 16 A5
Springvale M24 .... 9 E6
Spring Vale
  Hazel Grove SK7 .. 124 E2
  Middleton M24 .... 47 B1
  Prestwich M25 .... 63 A2
Springvale Cl OL7 .. 84 F5
Springvale Ct M24 . 65 B8
Spring Vale Dr BL8 . 26 E6
Spring Vale St BL8 . 26 E6
Spring Vale Terr OL15 . 16 B5
Spring Vale Way OL2 . 149 A1
SPRING VIEW 55 F4
Springville Ave M9 . 157 C3
Springwater Ave BL0 . 11 A3
Springwater Cl BL2 . 25 E3
Springwell Cl 1 M6 . 154 F3
Springwell Gdns SK14 . 102 E1
Springwell Way 2 SK14 . 102 E1
Springwood
  Delph OL3 .... 50 E5
  Glossop SK13 ..... 115 F8
Springwood Ave
  Chadderton OL9 ... 47 E1
  Pendlebury M27 .. 80 B6
Springwood Cres SK6 . 112 F7
Springwood Hall OL7 . 85 A7
Springwood Hall Rd OL7 . 85 A7
Springwood La SK6 . 113 F3
Springwood Prim Sch
  M27 .... 80 A7
Spring Wood St OL13 . 3 D8
Springwood Way OL7 . 85 A6
Sprodley Dr WN6 .. 18 B2
Spruce Ave BL9 .... 141 B2
Spruce Cl 3 SK13 .. 90 F7
Spruce Cres 2 BL9 . 27 F7

Spruce Ct 1 M6 ..... 81 B2
Spruce Lo SK8 ..... 122 D6
Spruce Rd WN6 .... 36 F3
Spruce St
  Manchester M15 ... 162 B2
  Rochdale OL16 .... 31 B6
Spruce Wlk
  7 Sale M33 .... 107 C6
  Walsden OL14 ..... 6 A8
Sprucewood OL9 ... 65 D8
Spurn La OL3 ...... 51 B4
Spurstow Mews SK8 . 132 C8
Spur The OL8 ...... 67 A3
Spur Wlk M8 ...... 155 C3
Square Rd OL14 .... 6 A8
Square Sh Ctr The 2
  M33 .... 108 B4
Square St BL0 ...... 138 C2
Square The
  Altrincham WA15 .. 129 C8
  Bury BL9 .... 140 C2
  Hyde SK14 .... 167 A2
  Stockport SK4 .... 168 C3
  Swinton M27 ...... 79 E5
  17 Tyldesley M29 . 59 A1
  Uppermill, Dobcross OL3 . 51 A2
  Uppermill OL3 .... 69 B8
Squires Ct WA3 .... 91 B3
Squire Rd M8 ...... 155 C3
Squires Ct M5 ..... 80 A2
Squires La M46 .... 76 E8
Squires Mews M31 . 105 E3
Squirrel Dr WA14 .. 119 C8
Squirrel La BL6 .... 22 A4
Squirrel's Jump SK9 . 137 C1
Stablefold OL5 ..... 86 C8
Stable Fold
  Eccles M30 .... 79 A5
  Radcliffe M26 ..... 44 A4
Stableford Ave M30 . 79 C4
Stable St OL9 ...... 66 A2
Stables The
  Culcheth WA3 ..... 91 D3
  Droylsden M43 .... 84 D3
  Leigh WN7 .... 76 A7
  Prestwich M25 .... 63 C3
  4 Sale M33 .... 108 A4
  Whitworth OL12 .... 4 C1
Stable Yd The M20 .. 110 C7
Stablings The SK9 . 137 A5
Stack La OL13 ..... 4 B8
STACKSTEADS 3 B8
Stadium Dr M11 ... 164 B4
Stadium Way
  Wigan, Marsh Green WN5 . 36 E1
  Wigan, Wallgate WN5,
  WN6 .... 150 A3
Stafford Cl 6 SK13 . 116 F8
Stafford Ct
  2 Rochdale OL16 .. 15 E4
  3 Sale M33 .... 108 A3
Stafford Rd
  Eccles M30 .... 79 E3
  Failsworth M35 ... 84 A5
  Swinton M27 ...... 79 F8
  Walkden M28 ..... 60 C1
Stafford St
  Bury BL8 .... 140 A4
  Hindley WN2 ...... 56 C5
  Leigh WN7 .... 76 D4
  New Mills SK22 ... 127 C1
  Oldham OL9 .... 66 C4
Stafford Wlk 12 M34 . 101 A1
Stage La WA13 ..... 117 C4
Stag Ind Est WA14 . 119 B6
Stag Pasture Rd OL8 . 66 D1
Stainburn Cl WN6 .. 35 E6
Stainburn Rd M11 . 165 B4
Staindale OL4 ..... 67 D6
Stainer Cl WA12 ... 89 B5
Stainer St M12 .... 99 A3
Stainforth Cl
  Bury BL8 .... 26 F3
  Culcheth WA3 .... 91 D4
Stainforth St M11 .. 164 C4
Stainmoor Ct SK2 . 124 D6
Stainmore Ave OL6 . 85 D7
Stainsbury St BL3 . 146 C4
Stainton Ave M18 .. 99 E4
Stainton Cl M26 ... 43 F5
Stainton Dr M24 ... 46 D3
Stainton Rd M26 .. 43 F5
Stairgate WN1 ..... 150 C4
Staithes Rd M22 .. 130 D8
Stakeford Dr M8 .. 156 C4
STAKE HILL 47 E5
Stakehill Ind Est M24 . 47 D4
Stakehill La M24 ... 47 D5
Staley Ct SK15 .... 86 C2
Staleydene Prep Sch 8
  SK16 .... 101 C8
Staley Farm Cl SK15 . 86 C3
Staley Hall Cres SK15 . 86 C3
Staley Hall Rd SK15 . 86 C3
Staley Rd OL5 ..... 86 C8
Staley St
  Oldham, Moorhey OL4 . 67 B6
  10 Oldham OL4 .... 67 F6
Stalham Cl M40 ... 160 A3
Stalmine Ave SK8 . 131 B8
STALYBRIDGE 86 B3
Stalybridge Ctry Pk*
  SK15 .... 87 A2
Stalybridge Rd SK14 . 103 A4

Stalyhill Dr SK15......... 85 F2
Stalyhill Inf Sch SK15 .. 102 E7
Stalyhill Jun Sch SK15 .. 102 D7
Staly Ind Est ⁊ SK15 ..... 85 F2
Stamford Arc ⁊ OL6 .... 166 C3
Stamford Ave
  Altrincham WA14 .... 119 A5
  Ashton-u-L SK15 .... 85 E2
Stamford Ct SK15 .... 85 E2
Stamford Ct
  3 Ashton-u-L OL6 ...... 85 D2
  Manchester M13 .... 98 F3
Stamford Dr
  Failsworth M35 .... 84 B6
  Stalybridge SK15 .... 85 F2
Stamford Gr SK15 .... 85 E2
Stamford Grange ❶
  WA14 .... 119 C4
Stamford New Rd WA14 119 D4
STAMFORD PARK 119 C5
Stamford Park Jun & Inf
  Schs ❶ WA15 .... 119 E3
Stamford Park Rd WA15. 119 E3
Stamford Pl M33......... 108 C4
Stamford Rd
  Alderley Edge SK9 ..... 137 B1
  Altrincham WA14 ...... 119 C2
  Carrington M31 .... 106 D7
  Denton M34 .... 100 E6
  Handforth SK9 .... 131 A1
  Little Bollington WA14 .. 118 B2
  Manchester M13 .... 98 F3
  Oldham OL4 .... 67 F7
  Salford M7 .... 81 B6
  Urmston M41 .... 95 B2
Stamford Sq
  ❷ Altrincham WA14 ... 119 D5
  Ashton-u-L OL6 .... 85 D2
Stamford St
  Altrincham WA14 ...... 119 D5
  Atherton M46 .... 58 E4
  Heywood OL10 .... 29 E1
  Manchester M16 .... 97 D4
  Manchester, Old Trafford
    M16.................. 161 C1
  Mossley OL5 .... 68 B1
  ❿ Oldham OL4 .... 67 E6
  Rochdale OL16 .... 31 B6
  Sale M33 .... 108 A6
  Stalybridge, Millbrook SK15 86 D4
  Stalybridge OL6, SK15.. 85 F2
  Swinton M27 .... 62 C8
Stamford Street Central
  OL6 .... 166 B2
Stamford Street E OL6.. 85 D2
Stamford Street W OL6 . 166 A2
Stamford Way ❷ WA14.. 119 D5
Stampstone St OL1....... 67 B8
Stanage Ave M40 ...... 64 F4
Stanbank St SK4 .... 169 B4
Stanbourne Dr BL1...... 143 C4
Stanbridge Ct SK4 ..... 169 B2
Stanbrook St M19....... 111 C8
Stanbury Cl BL9 .... 28 D1
Stanbury Dr SK16 ...... 101 D8
Stanbury Wlk M40 ..... 160 A3
Stancliffe Gr WN2...... 38 C6
Stancliffe Rd M22 ...... 121 E5
Stancross Rd M23....... 120 C8
STAND 62 C8
Standall Wlk M9 .... 64 E1
Stand Ave M45 .... 44 E1
Stand Cl M45 .... 62 C8
Standedge Foot Rd OL3 . 51 D8
Standedge Rd OL3 ..... 51 C5
Standedge Wlk SK15 ... 86 E6
Standfield Ctr ❷ M28 . 78 A6
Standfield Dr M28 ..... 78 A7
STANDISH 19 F2
Standish Gallery ⒔
  WN1 .... 150 C4
Standishgate WN1...... 150 C4
Standish Ho SK14 ..... 167 B2
STANDISH LOWER
  GROUND.............. 36 E4
Standish Rd M14....... 110 D8
Standish St M29 .... 77 A8
Standish Wlk M34 ..... 100 E1
Standish Wood La
  Standish WN6 .... 36 E7
  Wigan, Beech Hill WN6 . 36 E5
Stand La
  Radcliffe M26, M45 .... 44 C1
  Whitefield M26, M45.... 62 C8
Standmoor Ct M45 ..... 62 D7
Standmoor Rd M45 .... 62 D7
Standon Wlk ❷ M40 ... 65 D2
Standrick Hill Rise SK15. 86 E5
Standring Ave BL8 ..... 44 A8
Stand Rise M26 .... 62 B8
Stanedge Cl BL0 .... 11 C4
Stanedge Gr WN3...... 55 B2
Stanford Cl M26 .... 61 C7
Stanford Hall Cres BL0.. 11 B4
Stanhope Ave
  Denton M34 .... 100 E5
  Prestwich M25 .... 63 A5
Stanhope Cl
  Denton M34 .... 100 E5
  Wilmslow SK9 .... 137 D8
Stanhope Ct M25 ...... 63 A5

Stanhope Rd
  Altrincham WA14 ...... 119 A2
  Salford M6 .... 80 E5
Stanhope St
  Ashton-u-L OL6 .... 85 D4
  Denton M34 .... 100 E5
  Leigh WN7 .... 75 D6
  Manchester M19 .... 99 B1
  Mossley OL5 .... 86 C8
  Reddish SK5 .... 111 E7
  Rochdale OL11 .... 139 C1
Stanhope Way M35 ..... 83 E8
Stanhorne Ave M8 ..... 64 A2
Stanier Ave M30 ...... 79 D3
Stanier Pl BL6 .... 22 C2
Stanier St M9 .... 157 B4
Stanion Gr SK16 .... 101 D8
Stan Jolly Wlk M11 .... 165 C4
Stanlaw M30 .... 79 E1
Stanley Ave
  Hazel Grove SK7 ...... 124 D3
  Hyde SK14 .... 167 B4
  Manchester M14 ...... 98 D3
  Marple SK6 .... 125 D7
Stanley Avenue N M25 . 63 A6
Stanley Avenue S M25 . 63 A6
Stanley Cl
  Manchester M16 ...... 161 C1
  Westhoughton BL5 .... 57 F7
  Whitefield M45 .... 44 F1
Stanley Cl M16 .... 161 C1
Stanley Dr
  Altrincham WA15 ..... 120 A5
  Gatley SK8, SK9 ...... 131 D6
  Leigh WN7 .... 75 D8
  Whitefield M45 .... 62 F6
Stanley Gn Bsns Pk SK8. 131 E5
Stanley Gr
  Horwich BL6 .... 22 D1
  Manchester, Belle Vue M12,
    M18................... 99 B4
  ❽ Manchester M21 ... 109 A8
  Stockport, Heaton Moor
    SK4.................. 168 B4
  Urmston M41 .... 95 D2
STANLEY GREEN 131 E6
Stanley Green Ind Est
  SK8 .... 131 E5
Stanley Green Ret Pk
  SK8 .... 131 E5
Stanley Grove Com Prim Sch
  M12.................... 99 A4
Stanley Ho M16......... 97 E2
Stanley La WN2 .... 38 E7
Stanley Mews BL2 ...... 42 D7
Stanley Mount M33 .... 108 A3
Stanley Park Wlk BL2 . 148 C4
Stanley Pl
  Rochdale OL12......... 139 B4
  Wigan WN1 .... 151 B4
Stanley Rd
  Aspull WN2 .... 38 C6
  Bolton BL1 .... 142 B1
  Eccles M30 .... 95 C8
  Farnworth BL4 .... 59 E8
  Handforth SK8, SK9.... 131 E6
  Manchester, Old Trafford
    M16.................. 161 C1
  Manchester, Whalley Range
    M16.................. 97 E2
  ❿ Oldham OL4 .... 66 B4
  Pendlebury M27 .... 80 A8
  Platt Bridge WN2 ...... 56 A3
  Radcliffe M26 .... 43 E6
  Reddish M34 .... 100 B3
  Salford M7 .... 155 A4
  Stockport SK4 .... 168 B3
  Up Holland WN8 ...... 53 B7
  Walkden M28 .... 60 D2
  Whitefield M45 .... 44 F1
Stanley Road Prim Sch
  OL9 .... 66 B4
Stanley Sq SK15 .... 85 F1
Stanley St
  Atherton M46 .... 58 C3
  Chadderton OL9....... 152 B4
  Heywood OL10......... 29 D1
  Manchester M43 ...... 158 B1
  Manchester M11 ...... 99 E7
  Manchester M40 ...... 157 C1
  Manchester, Stangeways
    M8................... 159 A4
  Newton-le-W WA12..... 89 A3
  Oldham, Nether Lees OL4 . 67 E5
  Oldham OL4 .... 68 A6
  Prestwich M25 .... 63 C4
  Ramsbottom BL0 ...... 138 B1
  Rochdale OL12......... 139 B4
  ❸ Stalybridge SK15 ... 85 F1
  Stockport SK1 .... 112 A2
  Tyldesley M29 .... 59 A1
  Whitefield M45 .... 44 F1
  Wigan WN5 .... 54 F6
Stanley Street S BL3 .. 145 B2
Stanmer St CL8......... 10 B3
Stanmoor Dr WN2 ..... 38 D6
Stanmore Ave M32..... 96 B2
Stanmore Dr BL3 ...... 144 C1
Stannard Rd M30 ..... 79 F4
Stanneybrook Cl OL11. 31 B8
Stanney Cl OL16 ...... 31 E5
Stanneylands Cl SK9 .. 131 C2
Stanneylands Dr SK9.. 131 B2
Stanneylands Rd SK9.. 131 B2
Stanrose Cl BL7......... 8 E1
Stansbury Pl SK2...... 124 E6

Stansby Gdns M12 ... 164 B2
Stansfield Cl WN7 .... 76 C2
Stansfield Dr OL11 ... 13 F1
Stansfield Hall OL15 ... 51 D5
Stansfield Hall CE/Free
  Church Prim Sch OL15.. 16 D8
Stansfield Rd
  Bolton BL2............ 148 B4
  Failsworth M35 .... 84 A8
  Hyde SK14 .... 167 B4
  Rawtenstall BB4 .... 2 E8
Stansfield St
  ❷ Bacup OL13 .... 3 C8
  Chadderton OL9....... 152 B1
  Droylsden M11........ 99 D8
  Failsworth M40 .... 83 D4
  Oldham OL1 .... 153 B4
Stanstead Cl WN2..... 37 F2
Stansted Wlk M23 .... 108 D1
Stanthorne Ave M20 .. 110 A7
Stanton Ave
  Manchester M20 ...... 109 E4
  Salford M7 .... 81 B7
Stanton Cl WN3........ 55 B3
Stanton Ct M32 .... 96 D4
Stanton Gdns
  Manchester M20 ...... 109 E4
  Stockport SK4 .... 168 B1
Stanton St
  Droylsden M11........ 83 C2
  ❸ Oldham OL9 .... 66 B3
  Stretford M32 .... 96 D4
Stanway Ave ❸ BL3.. 145 A2
Stanway Cl
  ❻ Bolton BL3 .... 145 A2
  Middleton M24........ 65 B6
Stanway Dr WA15..... 119 F3
Stanway Rd M45 ...... 63 B8
Stanway St
  Manchester M9 .... 157 B4
  Stretford M32 .... 96 D4
Stanwell Rd
  Failsworth M40 .... 65 C1
  Swinton M27 .... 79 F7
Stanwick Ave M9 ...... 64 A4
Stanworth Ave BL2.... 42 E6
Stanworth Cl ❻ M16.. 97 E3
Stanyard Ct M5........ 161 B7
STANYCLIFFE 47 C3
Stanycliffe La M24 .... 47 B3
Stanyforth St SK13 ... 104 A4
Stapleford Cl
  Over Hulton BL5 .... 59 A6
  Sale M33 .... 108 E5
  Wythenshawe M23 .... 120 F4
Stapleford Gr BL8..... 27 A2
Stapleford Wlk M34.. 100 F1
Staplehurst Cl WN7 ... 57 C2
Staplehurst Rd M40 ... 83 B4
Staplers Wlk ❾ M14 .. 98 C3
Stapleton Ave BL1 .... 40 E8
Stapleton St
  Platt Bridge WN2 ...... 56 A2
  Salford M6 .... 80 C5
Star Bank OL13 .... 3 D7
Starbeck Cl BL8........ 26 F2
Starcliffe St BL3, BL4.. 42 D2
Starcross Wlk M40 .... 83 B6
Starfield Ave OL15 .... 15 F2
Star Gr M7 .... 155 B2
Starkey St OL10 .... 29 D3
Starkie Rd BL2 .... 25 B1
Starkies BL9........... 44 E7
Starkie St M28 .... 79 A8
Star La BL6 .... 21 F3
STARLING 26 E1
Starling Cl
  Droylsden M43......... 84 D3
  Wythenshawe M22 ... 121 E6
Starling Dr BL4 .... 59 F7
Starling Rd M26 ...... 43 E8
Starmoor Dr M8 ...... 156 A2
Starmount Cl BL2 .... 43 B6
Starring La OL15 ...... 15 E5
Starring Rd OL15...... 15 E5
Starring Way OL15 ... 15 F5
Startham Ave WN5 .... 71 D3
Starting Chair OL4 ... 68 C8
Stash Gr M23 .... 121 B7
Statham St M34....... 101 A3
Statham Fold SK14 ... 102 A4
Statham St M6 .... 81 B2
Statham Wlk ⒉ M13.. 163 B3
Station App
  Delph OL3 .... 50 F3
  Manchester, East Didsbury
    M20.................. 110 C1
  Manchester M1 .... 163 A4
Station Approach Bsns Ctr
  OL11.................. 139 C2
Station Ave
  Leigh WN2 .... 56 D1
  Orrell WN5 .... 53 D5
Station Bridge M4 ..... 95 D2
Station Cl
  ❶ Hyde SK14 .... 167 A2
  Manchester M26 ...... 43 F5
Station Cotts SK8 .... 123 B2
Stationers Entry ❹ OL16 139 C3
Station La
  Oldham OL4 .... 68 B5
  Uppermill OL3 .... 69 A5
Station Lofts OL7 ..... 166 B2
Station Mews
  Garswood WN4 .... 72 D3
  Manchester M35 ...... 83 E8
Station Rd
  Adlington PR7 .... 21 A6

Station Rd continued
  Blackrod BL6 .... 21 E1
  Chapeltown BL7....... 9 C4
  Cheadle SK8 .... 123 B1
  Diggle OL3 .... 51 D5
  Eccles M30 .... 79 D1
  Garswood WN4 .... 72 C3
  Glossop SK13......... 104 A5
  Handforth SK9 .... 131 D3
  Haslingden BB4 .... 1 A7
  Hyde SK14 .... 102 B2
  Irlam M44 .... 105 E7
  Kearsley BL4 .... 61 A7
  ❾ Littleborough OL15. 16 B5
  Manchester, Crumpsall M8.. 64 A1
  Manchester SK4 ...... 110 E1
  Marple SK6 .... 125 F6
  Marple, Strines SK6, SK22 126 D1
  Milnrow OL16 .... 31 F5
  Mossley OL5 .... 68 D1
  Oldham OL4 .... 68 A8
  Partington M44 .... 118 B5
  Ramsbottom BL8 .... 10 F1
  Reddish SK5........... 99 E2
  Rochdale OL11 .... 139 C2
  Romiley SK6........... 113 B5
  Stockport SK1 .... 169 B1
  Stretford M32 .... 96 D3
  Styal SK9 .... 131 A4
  Swinton M27 .... 61 F1
  Uppermill OL3 .... 69 B8
  Urmston M41.......... 95 D2
  Whitworth, Broadley OL12 . 14 C5
  Whitworth OL12........ 4 D3
  Wigan WN1 .... 150 C4
  Wilmslow SK9 .... 137 B7
Station Rd
  Bolton BL3 .... 145 C2
  Dukinfield SK16 ...... 166 B1
  Glossop SK13......... 104 D1
  Hazel Grove SK7 ..... 124 D2
  Oldham OL4 .... 67 F6
Station View M43 ... 100 A7
Staton Ave BL2 ...... 148 C4
Staton St M11 .... 165 C4
Statter St BL9 .... 45 A4
Staveleigh Mall OL6.. 166 B3
Staveley Ave
  Bolton BL1 .... 24 E6
  Stalybridge SK15 ..... 86 A3
Staveley Cl
  Middleton M24........ 46 E2
  Shaw OL2 .... 49 D6
Staveley Wlk ❽ OL2.. 48 E4
Staverton Cl M13 .... 163 C3
Stavesacre WN7 .... 75 F3
Staveton Cl SK7....... 124 A3
Stavordale ⒒ OL12 . 139 B4
Staycott St M16....... 97 F4
Staythorpe St SK15... 86 C2
Stayley Dr OL5......... 86 D8
Stead St BL0 .... 138 C2
Steadway OL3 .... 69 C5
Stean Cl Manchester M1 160 B1
Steeles Ave SK14 ..... 167 B3
Steeple Cl M8 .... 155 C1
Steeple Dr M5 .... 161 A4
Steeple View OL2 .... 48 D4
Stein Ave WA3 .... 90 E8
Stelfox Ave
  Manchester M14 ...... 98 A1
  Sale WA15 .... 120 C7
Stelfox La M34........ 100 E7
Stelfox St M30 .... 95 B8
Stella Maris Sch ❻ SK4.. 110 E2
Stella St M9 .... 64 B4
Stelling St M18 .... 99 C5
Stenbury Cl M14 ..... 98 C3
Stenner La M20....... 110 B1
Stenner Woods & Milgate
  Fields Nature Reserve
  M20.................. 110 A1
Stenson Sq ❶ M11... 99 D7
Stephen Cl ❷ BL8 ... 27 C2
Stephen Lowry Wlk ❶
  M40.................... 83 A7
Stephen Oake Cl M8 . 155 C1
Stephenson Ave M43 . 84 A1
Stephenson Rd
  Newton-le-W WA12..... 89 D2
  Stretford M32 .... 96 E2
Stephenson St
  Abram WN2 .... 74 B8
  Failsworth M35 .... 66 A1
  Horwich BL6 .... 22 B2
  ❹ Oldham OL4 .... 67 D8
Stephens Rd
  Manchester M20 ...... 110 D6
  Stalybridge SK15 ..... 85 F4
Stephens St BL2....... 42 D8
Stephen St
  Bury BL8 .... 27 C2
  Platt Bridge WN2 ..... 56 A2
  Stockport SK1 .... 124 B8
  Urmston M41.......... 95 E2
Stephens Terr ❻ M20. 110 B3
Stephen Street S BL8 . 27 C1
Stephen's Way WN3 .. 54 E5
STEPPING HILL 124 D4
Stepping Hill Hospl SK2 124 C4
Steps Mdw OL12 ...... 15 D4
Steptoe Dr OL1 .... 48 D1
Sterling Pl OL10 ...... 28 F1
Stern Ave M5.......... 161 A4
Sterndale Ave WN6 ... 19 E2
Sterndale Rd
  Boothstown M28 ...... 77 F6

Sterndale Rd continued
  Romiley SK6........... 113 B1
  Stockport SK3 .... 170 B1
Sterratt St BL1........ 145 A2
Stetchworth Dr M28 ... 78 B7
Steuber Dr M44........ 105 F5
Steven Ct M21 .... 109 C8
Stevenson Cl WN3 ... 150 B1
Stevenson Ct BL4 ..... 60 E7
Stevenson Dr OL1..... 49 E4
Stevenson Pl M1...... 159 B1
Stevenson Rd M27 ... 61 E1
Stevenson Sq
  Manchester M1 ...... 159 B1
  Rochdale OL11 .... 15 C3
Stevenson St
  Salford M3............ 158 A1
  Walkden M28 .... 60 B3
Stevens St SK9 .... 137 A1
Stewart Ave BL4 ...... 60 B7
Stewart Ho BL1 ...... 143 B1
Stewart Rd WN3 ...... 55 A3
Stewart St
  Ashton-u-L OL7 .... 84 F2
  Bolton BL1 .... 143 B2
  Bury BL8 .... 27 B3
  Newhey OL16.......... 32 B3
Stewerton Cl WA3 .... 7 B3
Steynton Cl BL1........ 40 F8
Stickens Lock La ❸ M44 . 94 B1
Stile Cl M41 .... 94 C2
Stiles Ave SK6 .... 125 F7
Stiles Cl SK13......... 103 E5
Stillwater Dr M11 .... 83 A2
Stilton Dr M11........ 165 A4
Stirling ❻ M30 .... 79 E2
Stirling Ave
  Hazel Grove SK7 ..... 124 D1
  Ince-in-M WN2 .... 56 A2
  Manchester M20 ..... 109 F8
  ❷ Marple SK6......... 125 F5
Stirling Cl
  Leigh WN7 .... 76 D6
  Stockport SK3 .... 123 C6
Stirling Dr
  Garswood WN4 .... 72 D4
  Stalybridge SK15 ..... 86 A3
Stirling Gr M45 .... 63 A8
Stirling Ind Est BL6 .. 22 C2
Stirling Rd
  Bolton BL1 .... 24 E5
  Hindley WN2 .... 56 D4
  Oldham OL9 .... 65 F4
Stirling St
  Oldham OL9 .... 152 C3
  Wigan WN1 .... 37 C2
Stirrup Brook Gr M28 . 77 F5
Stirrup Field ❻ WA3 .. 90 A8
Stirrup Gate M28 ..... 79 A5
Stitch La M24 .... 169 A3
Stitch-Mi-Lane BL2... 25 F2
Stiups La OL16 .... 31 B4
Stobart Ave M25 ...... 63 C2
STOCK BROOK 152 B3
Stockburn Dr M35 .... 84 C7
Stockbury Gr ❻ BL1 . 143 C1
Stock Cl OL12.......... 14 E2
Stockdale Ave SK3 ... 170 C1
Stockdale Gr BL2 ..... 25 F2
Stockdale Rd M9 ..... 64 E4
Stockfield Mount OL9 . 152 B2
Stockfield Rd OL9..... 152 B3
Stock Gr OL16......... 31 F7
Stockholm Rd SK3 ... 170 B2
Stockholm St M11 ... 83 B2
Stock La OL9 .... 152 B2
Stockland Cl M13 .... 163 B3
Stockley Ave BL2 ..... 25 E2
Stockley Dr WN6..... 35 E8
Stockley Wlk ⒉ M15. 162 A2
Stockmar Grange BL1.. 40 E8
STOCKPORT 123 B1
Stockport Acad SK3.. 123 B7
Stockport Air Raid Shelters
  (Mus)* SK1 .... 169 B1
Stockport Coll (Heaton Moor
  Campus) SK4 .... 111 B5
Stockport Coll (Town Centre
  Campus) SK1 .... 170 C4
Stockport Coll (Woodley
  Sports Ctr) SK6...... 112 E3
Stockport Gram Sch
  SK2.................. 124 A5
STOCKPORT GREAT
  MOOR............... 124 C5
STOCKPORT LITTLE
  MOOR............... 124 D8
Stockport Rd
  Altrincham, Timperley
    WA15................ 120 B6
  Altrincham WA15..... 119 F5
  Ashton-u-L OL7 ...... 100 F8
  Broadbottom SK14.... 114 D8
  Cheadle SK8 .... 122 E6
  Denton M34........... 100 F2
  Hattersley SK14....... 102 E2
  Hyde SK14............ 113 E2
  Manchester M12, M13,
    M19................. 164 A1
  Marple SK6 .... 125 E6
  Mossley OL5 .... 68 C2
  Romiley SK6........... 113 B2
  Uppermill OL4 .... 68 C5
Stockport Road E SK6.. 112 D3
Stockport Road W SK6.. 112 D3
Stockport Sch SK2.... 124 B5
Stockport Sta SK3 ... 170 B4
Stockport Trad Est SK4. 123 B8

Stocks Brow SK13 104 A7
Stocksfield Dr
  ③ Manchester M9 64 E3
  Walkden M38 59 F5
Stocksgate OL12 14 B2
Stocks Gdns SK15 86 C1
Stocks Ho M41 94 F1
Stocks Ind Est M30 79 C2
Stocks La SK15 86 C1
Stocks Park Dr BL6 22 C3
Stocks St
  Manchester M4, M8 159 A4
  Rochdale OL11 30 B2
Stocks Street E M4, M8 159 A4
Stock St BL8 27 E5
Stocks The SK13 104 A7
Stockton Ave ④ SK3 123 B8
Stockton Dr BL8 27 B5
Stockton Pk OL4 67 D6
Stockton Rd
  Manchester M21 109 A8
  Wilmslow SK9 136 F4
Stockton St
  Farnworth BL4 42 C2
  Littleborough OL15 16 A5
  ④ Manchester M9 97 E4
  Swinton M27 79 E7
Stockwell WN3 54 D3
Stockwood Wlk M9 157 A3
Stoke Abbott Cl SK7 132 E7
Stokesay Cl
  Bury BL9 44 F5
  Royton OL2 49 A4
Stokesay Dr SK7 124 C1
Stokesay Rd BL3 147 B3
Stokes Ct The ⑥ WA3 90 D8
Stokesley Wlk BL3 147 B3
Stokes Mill ⑤ SK15 86 B2
Stokes St M11 83 D1
Stokoe Ave WA14 119 A6
Stonall Ave M15 162 A3
Stoneacre BL6 39 F8
Stoneacre Ct M27 79 F7
Stoneacre Rd M22 121 C2
Stonebeck Ct BL5 58 F8
Stonebeck Rd M23 120 F5
Stonebreaks Rd OL4 68 B7
Stonebridge Cl BL2 40 E6
Stonebridge Mews M29 77 A5
Stonechat Cl
  Droylsden M43 84 C3
  ⑩ Golborne WA3 90 E8
  Walkden M28 78 B8
Stonechurch BL3 145 A1
Stone Cl BL0 11 A4
Stonecliffe Ave SK15 86 A2
Stonecliffe Terr SK15 86 A3
STONECLOUGH 61 B7
Stoneclough Mews OL1 48 E1
Stoneclough Rd BL4, M26 61 B8
Stoneclough Rise M26 61 B8
Stonecroft ② OL1 153 B3
Stonecroft Ct M20 110 A4
Stonecrop WN6 13 B8
Stonedelph Cl BL2 26 D1
Stonefield M30 59 C1
Stonefield Dr M8 155 B1
Stonefield St ① OL16 31 F1
Stoneflat Ct OL12 139 A4
Stone Gdns WN7 76 A5
Stonehall La WN8 35 A5
Stonehaven BL3 40 F3
Stone Haven WN3 54 D2
Stonehead St M9 157 C3
Stonehewer St M26 44 B2
Stonehill Cres OL12 14 A3
Stonehill Dr OL12 14 A3
Stone Hill Ind Est BL4 60 D6
Stone Hill La OL12 14 A2
Stonehill Rd OL12 14 A3
Stone Hill Rd BL4 60 D6
Stonehouse BL7 25 B7
Stonehouse Rd WN5 36 D2
Stonehouse Wlk ③ M23 120 E7
Stonelands Way M9 157 C3
Stone Lea Way M46 58 A3
Stoneleigh M14 98 C1
Stoneleigh Ave M33 107 E5
Stoneleigh Dr M26 61 B7
Stoneleigh Mews M9 64 B4
Stoneleigh Prim Sch OL1 49 B2
Stoneleigh Rd OL4 68 A7
Stoneleigh St OL1 67 B8
Stone Lee Cl M15 162 C2
Stonely Dr OL14 6 A7
Stonemead SK6 113 E3
Stone Mead Ave WA15 129 C7
Stonemead Cl BL3 147 C4
Stonemead Dr M9 64 D4
Stonemere Dr M26 44 C1
Stone Mill Cotts BL7 9 D4
Stonemill Terr SK5 169 C3
Stonepail Cl SK8 121 F5
Stonepail Rd SK8 122 A5
Stone Pale M45 62 F7
Stone Pit Cl WA3 74 F1
Stone Pit La WA3 90 F2
Stone Pits BL0 1 E3
Stoneridge SK13 103 F5
Stone Row
  Marple SK6 126 A6
  Wigan WN2 38 A3

Stoner Rd PR7 20 F7
Stones Bank Rd BL7 8 B5
Stonesby Cl M16 97 D4
Stonesdale Cl OL2 48 E5
Stone St
  Bolton BL3 25 B1
  Manchester M3 162 B4
  Milnrow OL16 31 F5
  Rawtenstall BB4 2 F8
Stonesteads Dr BL7 25 A8
Stonesteads Way BL7 25 A8
Stoneswood Dr OL5 68 D2
Stoneswood Rd OL3 50 F4
Stonethwaite Cl WN3 55 A2
Stoney Bank M26 61 C7
Stoney Bridge La WA15 120 A7
Stoney Brow WN8 35 B1
Stoneycroft Ave BL4 24 C4
Stoneycroft Cl BL6 22 D5
STONEYFIELD 139 C1
Stoneyfield SK15 86 A4
Stoneyfield Cl M16 97 F2
Stoneygate La WN6 18 B2
Stoneygate Wlk M11 99 D7
Stoneyholme Ave M8 156 C3
Stoneyhurst Cres WA3 91 D5
Stoney Knoll M7 155 A2
Stoney La
  Adlington PR7 20 E4
  Delph OL3 50 D7
  Wilmslow SK9 136 F5
Stone Royd OL12 4 D1
Stoneyside Ave M28 60 E4
Stoneyside Gr M28 60 E4
Stoneyvale Ct OL11 30 F4
Stonyford Rd M33 108 D4
Stonyhurst Ave
  Bolton BL1 24 F5
  Ince-in-M WN3 151 A2
Stopford Ave BL6 43 C3
Stopford Wlk M34 100 F3
Stopforth St WN6 37 A1
Stopley Wlk M11 165 A4
Stores Rd M90 130 A6
Stores St M25 63 C4
Store St
  Ashton-u-L OL7 85 A6
  Horwich BL6 22 C4
  Manchester, Ancoats M1, M4 159 C1
  Manchester, Openshaw M11 165 B3
  Radcliffe M26 44 D4
  ⑦ Radcliffe OL11 13 E1
  Shaw OL2 149 C4
  Stockport SK2 124 C4
Storeton Cl M22 121 E2
Stortford Dr M23 109 B2
Storth Bank SK13 115 F7
Storth Meadow Rd SK13 115 F7
Storwood Cl WN5 53 E5
Stothard Rd M32 96 C1
Stott Dr M41 94 D1
Stottfield OL2 48 B3
Stott Ho OL8 153 B1
Stott La
  Bolton BL2 25 B1
  Middleton M24, OL10 46 F5
  Salford M6, M5 80 B2
Stott Milne St OL9 152 B1
Stott Rd
  Failsworth OL9 65 E3
  Swinton M27 79 D6
Stott's La M35 83 D6
Stott St
  Failsworth M35 83 D6
  Milnrow OL16 31 F4
  ⑦ Rochdale, Hurstead OL16 15 D4
  Rochdale OL12 14 F1
Stott Wharf WN7 76 B4
Stourbridge Ave M38 60 A6
Stour Cl WA14 119 C6
Stourport Cl SK13 113 A1
Stourport St OL4 67 A8
Stour Rd M29 77 B7
Stout St WN7 75 C5
Stovell Ave M12 99 A2
Stovell Rd M40 83 A8
Stowell St
  Bolton BL3 143 B1
  Salford M5 154 B1
Stowell Tech Ctr
  Salford M5 161 A4
  Stretford M50 96 F8
Stowell Cl M9 64 B4
Stow Gdns M20 110 A6
Stracey St M40 160 B3
Stradbroke Cl
  Golborne WA3 91 A7
  ⑥ Manchester M18 165 C1
Strain Ave M9 64 D4
Straits The M29 77 C6
Strand Ave WN4 73 B4
Strand Ct M32 108 C8
Strand The
  Ashton-in-M WN4 73 B4
  Horwich BL6 22 D3
  Rochdale OL11 30 F2

Strand Way OL1, OL2 48 D2
Strange Rd WN4 72 D3
Strange St WN7 75 B4
STRANGEWAYS 158 C4
Strangford St M26 43 D4
Strang St BL0 11 C6
Stranraer Rd WN5 36 D1
Stranton Dr M28 79 C8
Stratfield Ave M23 108 D1
Stratford Ave
  Bolton BL1 142 A1
  Bury BL9 27 D8
  Eccles M30 95 C8
  Manchester M20 109 F5
  Oldham OL8 66 F3
  Rochdale OL11 139 B1
Stratford Cl BL4 147 C1
Stratford Gdns SK6 112 F3
Stratford Rd M24 65 B5
Stratford Sq SK8 131 C7
Stratford St WN6 37 A1
Strathavon Pl OL10 28 E1
Strathblane Cl M20 110 B7
Strathfield Dr ⑧ M11 83 C2
Strathmere Ave M32 96 D3
Strathmore Ave
  Ashton-in-M WN4 73 A5
  Denton M34 101 B2
  ④ Manchester M16 97 B2
Strathmore Cl BL0 11 C4
Strathmore Rd BL2 25 E1
Stratton Dr WN2 55 F1
Stratton Gr BL6 22 B5
Stratton Rd
  Manchester M16 97 B2
  Stockport SK2 124 C8
  Swinton M27 61 F1
Strawberry Bank M6 81 B3
Strawberry Cl WA14 119 B7
Strawberry Hill M6 81 B3
Strawberry Hill Rd BL2 148 B1
Strawberry La
  Uppermill OL5 68 C4
  Wilmslow SK9 136 E6
Strawberry Rd M6 81 B3
Stray St M11 99 E8
Stray The BL3 25 B4
Streamside Cl WA15 120 B4
Stream Terr SK1 112 B1
Street Bridge Rd OL1, OL2 48 A2
STREET END 84 B8
Streetgate M38 59 F5
Streethouse La OL3 50 F1
Street La M26 43 F8
Street Lodge OL1 30 B1
STRETFORD 96 C2
Stretford Gram Sch M32 96 E1
Stretford High Sch Com
  Language Coll M32 96 F4
Stretford Ho ⑦ M32 96 C1
Stretford L Ctr M32 96 C1
Stretford Mall M32 96 C1
Stretford Meml Hospl
  M16 97 B3
Stretford Metro Sta M32 96 D1
Stretford Motorway Est
  M32 96 A3
Stretford Rd
  Manchester M15, M16 162 B2
  Urmston M41 95 E1
Stretton Ave
  Billinge WN5 71 E5
  Golborne WA3 90 E7
  Manchester M20 110 C3
  Sale M33 107 E4
  Stretford M32 96 A3
Stretton Cl
  Manchester M40 157 A1
  Standish M40 36 E8
Stretton Rd
  Bolton BL3 146 B4
  Ramsbottom BL0 11 B2
Stretton Way ③ SK9 131 D5
Striding Edge Wlk ① OL1 49 A1
STRINES 126 C2
Strines Cl WN2 56 D6
Strines Ct SK14 167 B4
Strines Rd
  Marple SK6 126 B4
  New Mills SK6 135 D8
Strines St OL14 6 A7
Strines Sta SK6 126 D1
Stringer Ave M14 102 F2
Stringer Cl SK14 102 F2
Stringer St
  Leigh WN7 75 F5
  Stockport SK1 112 A2
Stringer Way SK14 102 F2
Stroma Gdns M41 95 C5
Stromness Gr OL10 28 F1
Strong St M7 158 B4
STRONGSTRY 1 C2
Strongstry Rd BL0 1 C2
Strontian Wlk ⑨ M11 83 C1
Stroud Ave M30 79 B3
Stroud Cl
  Middleton M24 65 A5
  Wigan WN2 37 F2
Stuart Ave
  Bacup OL13 3 D8
  Hindley WN2 57 C3
  Irlam M44 93 F2
  Marple SK6 125 C7
Stuart Cl WN5 71 E5
Stuart Ho M43 100 A8
Stuart Rd
  Altrincham WA14 119 B7

Stuart Rd continued
  Brinnington SK6 112 D6
  Stretford M32 96 D3
Stuart St
  Droylsden M11 83 A2
  Manchester M24 65 C8
  Oldham OL8 153 B1
  Rochdale OL16 31 A6
Stuart Street E M11 83 A2
Stuart Wlk M24 64 F7
STUBBINS 1 B1
Stubbins Cl M23 108 E1
Stubbins La BL0 138 C4
Stubbins Prim Sch BL0 1 C1
Stubbins St BL0 1 C1
Stubbins Vale Rd BL0 1 B1
Stubbins Vale Terr BL0 1 B1
Stubbs Cl M7 81 B8
Stubbylee La OL13 3 F8
STUBLEY 15 E5
Stubley Gdns ⑤ OL15 16 A5
Stubley La OL15 15 F4
Stubley Mill Rd
  Littleborough, Dearnley OL15 15 F4
  Littleborough OL15 16 A5
STUBSHAW CROSS 73 D5
Student Village M1 163 A3
Studforth Wlk ⑧ M15 163 A1
Studland Rd M22 121 F3
Studley Cl OL2 49 A4
Studley St M29 58 F1
Sturton Ave WN3 54 E3
STYAL 130 F4
Styal Ave
  Reddish SK5 111 F6
  Stretford M32 96 A3
Styal Cross SK9 130 E4
Styal Ctry Pk* SK9 130 E3
Styal Gn SK9 130 F3
Styal Gr SK8 122 A3
STYAL GREEN 131 A3
Styal Ho M22 121 F7
Styal Prim Sch SK9 130 E4
Styal Rd
  Gatley M22, SK8, SK9 122 A3
  Wilmslow SK9 137 B8
  Wythenshawe M22 130 F7
Styal St BL1 144 B4
Styal View SK9 131 B2
Styhead Dr M44 46 D3
Style St M4 159 A3
Styperson Way SK12 133 E3
Sudbrook Cl WA3 90 E8
Sudbury Cl
  Manchester M16 161 C1
  Wigan WN3 55 B2
Sudbury Dr
  Bolton BL6 40 C6
  Gatley SK8 131 C8
Sudbury Rd SK7 123 E8
SUDDEN 30 D4
Sudden Cl SK14 30 C4
Sudell Bank M40 157 A1
Sudell Street Ind Est M4 159 B3
Sudley Rd OL11 139 A1
Sudlow St OL16 15 B2
Sudren St BL8 26 F3
Sue Patterson Wlk M40 157 A1
Suez St WA12 89 B3
Suffield St M24 65 A8
Suffield Wlk ① M22 121 D1
Suffolk Ave M43 84 A3
Suffolk Cl
  Little Lever BL3 43 B5
  Standish WN1 37 B8
Suffolk Dr
  Brinnington SK5 112 C6
  Handforth SK9 131 C1
Suffolk Gr WN7 75 C5
Suffolk Rd WA14 119 B5
Suffolk St
  Oldham OL9 66 B4
  Rochdale OL11 139 C2
  Salford M6 81 A5
Sugar La OL3 51 A2
Sugar Mill Sq M5 154 A1
Sugden Sports Ctr M1 163 A3
Sugden St ① OL6 85 D3
Sulby Ave M32 96 E2
Sulby St
  Kearsley M26 61 B7
  Manchester M40 83 A8
Sulgrave Ave SK12 133 F4
Sullivan St M12 99 A3
Sullivan Way WN1 37 D1
Sultan St BL9 44 F8
Sulway Cl M27 80 A7
Sumac St M11 83 D2
Summer Ave M14 95 E2
Sumberland Ho M27 62 B2
Summerbottom St SK14 115 A8
Summer Castle OL16 31 A7
Summercroft Ct WA3 90 A7
Summer Ct M33 107 C2
Summerdale Dr BL0 11 B2
Summerfield Ave M43 83 E1
Summerfield Cl ② M21 96 F1
Summerfield Dr
  Middleton M24 47 C1
  Tyldesley M29 77 B8
Summerfield Pl SK9 137 A5
Summerfield Rd
  Bolton BL3 42 B4
  Worsley M28 79 A8
  Wythenshawe M22 121 C2

Summerfields PR7 19 F7
Summerfields Ctr ⑩ SK9 131 D1
Summerfield View OL8 67 C3
Summerhill View OL3 33 D1
Summerlea SK8 132 B8
Summer Pl ① M14 98 C2
Summersales Ind Est
  WN3 54 C4
Summers Ave SK15 86 C2
SUMMERSEAT 11 C2
Summerseat Cl
  Oldham OL4 68 A7
  Salford M5 161 A4
Summerseat La BL0 11 A2
Summerseat Meth Prim Sch
  BL9 11 D2
Summerseat Sta* BL9 11 C1
Summersgill Cl OL10 29 E1
Summershades La OL4 68 D6
Summershades Rise OL4 68 D6
Summer St
  Horwich BL6 22 B4
  Rochdale OL16 31 A7
Summerton Ho ③ M5 81 A1
Summerville Ave M9 157 C3
Summerville Prim Sch M6 80 D5
Summerville Rd M6 80 D5
SUMMIT
  Calderbrook 6 D1
  Heywood 29 A2
  Royton 48 C7
Summit Cl BL9 28 E3
Summit St OL10 28 F3
Sumner Ave BL2 26 C1
Sumner Rd M6 80 D5
Sumners Pl SK13 104 B1
Sumner St
  Aspull WN2 38 D5
  Atherton M46 58 C3
  Bolton BL3 146 B2
  Glossop SK13 116 C8
  Shaw OL2 149 B1
Sumner Way M41 95 D2
Sunadale Cl BL3 144 B1
Sunbank Cl OL12 14 D2
Sunbank La WA15 129 E6
Sunbeam St WA12 89 C3
Sunbeam Wlk ⑩ M11 160 C1
Sunbury Cl
  Handforth SK9 131 E2
  Stalybridge SK16 101 F8
Sunbury Dr M40 83 D4
Sundance Ct M50 96 D8
Sunderland Ave OL6 166 C4
Sunderland Pl WN5 36 D1
Sundew Pl M24 65 D7
Sundial Cl SK14 102 D3
Sundial Rd SK2 124 D7
Sundial Wlk SK14 102 D3
Sundridge Cl BL3 146 A3
Sunfield SK6 113 C3
Sunfield Ave OL4 49 E4
Sunfield Cres OL2 48 E3
Sunfield Dr OL2 48 E3
Sunfield Est OL3 51 C4
Sunfield La OL3 51 C4
Sunfield Rd OL1 153 B4
Sunfield Way OL4 67 E7
Sunflower Gr ③ OL9 65 F8
Sunflower Mdw M44 94 B3
Sun Gate OL15 15 F1
Sunhill Cl OL5 68 E1
Sun Inn Mews OL3 33 D3
Sunk La OL10 29 D2
Sunlaws Ct SK13 116 B8
Sunlaws St SK13 116 B8
Sunleigh Rd WN2 56 E6
Sunlight Rd BL1 144 C3
Sunningdale Ave
  Droylsden M11 83 B2
  Radcliffe M26 43 D4
  Sale M33 108 E3
  Whitefield M45 62 C7
Sunningdale Cl
  Bury BL8 44 A8
  Dukinfield SK14 101 F5
Sunningdale Ct
  Reddish M34 100 B4
  Sale M33 108 E3
Sunningdale Dr
  Bramhall SK7 133 A7
  Glossop SK13 104 E1
  Heywood OL10 46 D8
  Irlam M44 93 F3
  Prestwich M25 63 B5
  Salford M6 80 B5
  Stockport SK3 123 A8
Sunningdale Gr WN7 76 D7
Sunningdale Rd
  Cheadle SK8 132 A7
  Denton M34 101 B1
  Urmston M41 95 B1
Sunningdale Wlk ① BL3 145 A1
Sunninghey Ct SK9 136 E1
Sunning Hill Prim Sch
  BL3 147 A4
Sunning Hill St ⑨ BL3 147 A4
Sunny Ave BL9 27 F5
SUNNY BANK 45 A4
Sunny Bank
  Kearsley M26 61 A8
  Oldham OL4 67 C5

Sunny Bank continued
Wilmslow, Fulshaw Park
SK9 . . . . 137 B6
Sunnybank Ave
Droylsden M43 . . . . 83 F1
Eccles M30 . . . . 79 F3
Manchester SK4 . . . . . . 110 F4
Sunnybank Cl WA12 . . . . 89 C4
Sunny Bank Cl BB4 . . . . . . 1 A6
Sunnybank Dr SK9 . . . . . 136 D4
Sunny Bank Prim Sch
BL9 . . . . 45 A3
Sunnybank Rd
Bolton BL1 . . . . 142 C2
Droylsden M43 . . . . 83 F1
Tyldesley M29 . . . . 77 B6
Sunny Bank Rd
Altrincham WA14 . . . . . 128 C8
Haslingden BB4 . . . . 1 A6
Manchester M13 . . . . . . 98 E3
Whitefield BL9 . . . . 45 A3
Sunny Banks ⬛ SK13 . . 116 B8
Sunny Bower St BL8 . . . 26 F6
Sunny Brow Rd
Manchester M18 . . . . . . 99 C4
Middleton M24 . . . . 64 E8
Sunny Dr
Orrell WN5 . . . . 53 F6
Prestwich M25 . . . . 62 F4
Sunnyfield Rd
Manchester SK4 . . . . . . 110 F3
Prestwich M25 . . . . 63 C7
Sunnyfields WN3 . . . . . . 54 C2
Sunny Garth BL5 . . . . . . 57 E8
Sunnylea Ave M19 . . . . 119 B1
Sunnymead Ave BL1 . . . 143 C4
Sunnymede Vale BL0 . . . 11 A3
Sunnyside OL7 . . . . 84 F5
Sunny Side M32 . . . . 96 F2
Sunnyside Ave M43 . . . . 83 F4
Sunny Side Cotts OL12 . . 13 B2
Sunnyside Cres ⬛ OL6 . . 85 D2
Sunnyside Ct
Droylsden M43 . . . . 83 F3
Manchester M20 . . . . . . 110 C3
Sunnyside Gr OL6 . . . . . . 85 D2
Sunnyside Rd
Ashton-in-M WN4 . . . . . . 72 F7
Bolton BL1 . . . . 142 C2
Droylsden M43 . . . . 84 A3
Sunnywood Dr BL8 . . . . . 27 A6
Sunnywood La BL8 . . . . . 27 A6
Sunset Ave M22 . . . . . . 109 D2
Sunset Bsns Ctr BL4 . . . 61 C5
Sunshine Pl M14 . . . . . . 98 A2
Sun St
Mossley OL5 . . . . 68 C1
Ramsbottom BL0 . . . . . 138 B3
Sun Vale Ave OL14 . . . . . 6 B7
Sun View OL2 . . . . 49 A3
Sunwell Terr SK6 . . . . . 125 F3
Surbiton Rd M40 . . . . . . 83 B4
Surma Cl
Oldham OL9 . . . . 153 A3
Rochdale OL16 . . . . 31 B5
Surrey Ave
Droylsden M43 . . . . 83 F3
Leigh WN7 . . . . 76 E4
Shaw OL2 . . . . 48 F7
Surrey Cl BL3 . . . . 43 B4
Surrey Dr BL9 . . . . 44 F8
Surrey Park Cl OL2 . . . . 149 B4
Surrey Rd M9 . . . . 64 D2
Surrey St
Ashton-u-L OL6 . . . . 85 D5
Glossop SK13 . . . . 104 C1
Manchester M9 . . . . 64 C2
Oldham OL9 . . . . 152 C1
Surrey Way SK5 . . . . . . 112 C4
Surtees Rd M23 . . . . . . 109 A2
Sussex Ave
Heywood OL10 . . . . 28 E1
Manchester M20 . . . . . 110 B4
Sussex Cl
Chadderton OL9 . . . . . . 152 B2
Hindley WN2 . . . . 57 A5
Standish WN1 . . . . 20 B1
Swinton M27 . . . . 62 A2
Sussex Dr
Bury BL9 . . . . 44 F8
Droylsden M43 . . . . 84 A3
Haslingden BB4 . . . . 1 B8
Sussex Pl SK14 . . . . . . 101 F5
Sussex Rd
Irlam M44 . . . . 105 C6
Partington M31 . . . . . . 105 E2
Stockport SK3 . . . . 123 B8
Sussex St
Leigh WN7 . . . . 76 E4
⬛ Manchester M2 . . . . 158 C1
Rochdale OL11 . . . . . . 139 C2
Salford M7 . . . . 158 A4
Sutch La WA13 . . . . 117 A3
Sutcliffe Ave M12 . . . . . 99 B2
Sutcliffes Pl ⬛ OL11 . . 31 A4
Sutcliffe St
Ashton-u-L OL7 . . . . 84 F1
Bolton BL1 . . . . 143 B2
Britannia OL13 . . . . 4 C8
Littleborough OL15 . . . . 16 B6
Middleton M24 . . . . 65 C8
Oldham OL8 . . . . 153 B1
Royton OL2 . . . . 49 A3

Sutherland Cl OL8 . . . . . 66 F1
Sutherland Gr BL4 . . . . . 60 C8
Sutherland Rd
Bolton BL1 . . . . 142 A1
Heywood OL10 . . . . 28 F1
Manchester M16 . . . . . . 97 A3
Wigan WN3 . . . . 55 A3
Sutherland St
Ashton-u-L OL6 . . . . 85 E3
Eccles M30 . . . . 79 B3
⬛ Farnworth BL4 . . . . . 60 C8
Hindley WN2 . . . . 56 C5
Swinton M27 . . . . 61 E1
⬛ Wigan WN5 . . . . 54 F6
Suthers St
Oldham OL9 . . . . 152 C2
Radcliffe M26 . . . . 44 C1
Sutton Ave WA3 . . . . 91 F4
Sutton Cl BL8 . . . . 44 B8
Sutton Dr M43 . . . . 83 E3
Sutton La PR6 . . . . 21 B8
Sutton Manor ⬛ M21 . . 97 A1
Sutton Rd
Alderley Edge SK9 . . . . 136 F2
Bolton BL3 . . . . 40 F4
Manchester M18 . . . . . . 99 C3
Poynton SK12 . . . . 134 A2
Stockport, Heaton Norris
SK4 . . . . 168 C3
Suttons La SK6 . . . . . . 126 A5
Sutton Way
Glossop SK13 . . . . 104 A5
⬛ Handforth SK9 . . . . . 131 E5
Salford M6 . . . . 154 C3
Swailes St ⬛ OL4 . . . . . 67 B6
Swaindrod La OL15 . . . . 16 F7
Swaine St SK3 . . . . 169 B1
Swain St OL12 . . . . 14 E1
Swainsthorpe Dr ⬛ M9 157 B4
Swale Cl SK9 . . . . 131 E2
Swalecliff Ave M23 . . . . 108 D1
Swaledale Cl OL2 . . . . . . 48 E5
Swale Dr WA14 . . . . 119 C6
Swallow Bank Dr OL11 . . 30 B3
Swallow Cl SK15 . . . . . . 86 F7
Swallow Ct
Handforth SK9 . . . . 131 B1
Stockport SK1 . . . . 169 B4
Swallow Dr
Bury BL9 . . . . 141 B4
Irlam M44 . . . . 94 A3
Rochdale OL11 . . . . 29 F7
Swallowfield WN7 . . . . . 76 A5
Swallow Fold SK13 . . . . 115 F8
Swallow La SK15 . . . . . . 86 F6
Swallow St
Manchester, Bradford
M11 . . . . 160 C1
⬛ Manchester M12 . . . . 99 A2
Oldham OL8 . . . . 66 D2
Stockport SK1 . . . . 170 C3
Swanage Ave
Sale M23 . . . . 108 D1
Stockport SK2 . . . . 124 D6
Swanage Cl BL8 . . . . 27 C6
Swanage Rd M30 . . . . . . 79 B3
Swanbourne Gdns SK3 . 123 C6
Swan Bsns Ctr BL3 . . . 147 A4
Swan Cl SK12 . . . . 133 B4
Swan Ct OL2 . . . . 149 B2
Swanfield Wlk WA3 . . . . 73 F2
Swanhill Cl ⬛ M18 . . . . . 99 F6
Swan La
Bolton BL3 . . . . 147 A4
Hindley WN2 . . . . 57 B4
Swanley Ave M40 . . . . . 157 B1
Swan Meadow Ind Est
WN3 . . . . 150 B3
Swan Meadow Rd WN3 . 150 B3
Swann Gr SK8 . . . . 123 B1
Swann La SK8 . . . . 123 B1
Swann St WN3 . . . . 150 B3
Swan Rd
Ramsbottom BL8 . . . . . . 10 F2
Sale WA15 . . . . 108 A1
Swansea St OL8 . . . . 67 B4
Swan St
Ashton-u-L OL6 . . . . . . 166 C3
Manchester M4 . . . . . . 159 B2
Wilmslow SK9 . . . . 137 B7
Swanton Wlk ⬛ M8 . . . 155 C2
Swarbrick Dr M25 . . . . . 62 F2
Swayfield Ave M13 . . . . 98 F3
Swaylands Dr M33 . . . . 108 B1
Sweetbriar Cl OL2 . . . . . 48 F4
Sweet Briar Cl OL12 . . . 14 E2
Sweetloves Gr BL1 . . . . 24 E5
Sweetloves La BL1 . . . . 24 E5
Sweetnam Dr M11 . . . . . 83 B2
Swettenham Rd SK9 . . 131 D5
Swift Bank SK13 . . . . . 115 F8
Swift Cl SK6 . . . . 113 C5
Swift Rd
Oldham OL1 . . . . 49 E5
Rochdale OL11 . . . . 29 F7
Swift St
Ashton-u-L OL6 . . . . 85 D5
Wigan WN5 . . . . 150 A3
Swiftsure Ave M3 . . . . . 158 A1
Swift Wlk ⬛ M40 . . . . . . 83 C5
Swinbourne Gr M20 . . . 110 C7
Swinburne Ave M43 . . . 84 A3
Swinburne Gn SK5 . . . . 99 D1
Swinburne Way ⬛ M34 . 113 A7
Swinburn Gr WN5 . . . . . 53 D1
Swinburn St ⬛ M9 . . . . 64 F1
Swindells St SK14 . . . . 101 E5
Swindell's St ⬛ M11 . . . 99 E7

Swindon Cl M18 . . . . 99 D5
Swinfield Ave M21 . . . . 108 F8
Swinford Gr OL2 . . . . . . 149 A1
Swinford Wlk ⬛ M9 . . . . 64 E3
Swinhoe Pl WA3 . . . . 91 D3
Swinley Chase SK9 . . . 131 F1
Swinley La WN1 . . . . 37 C2
Swinley Rd WN1 . . . . 37 C2
Swinley St WN1 . . . . 37 C2
Swinside WN1 . . . . 37 F1
Swinside Cl M24 . . . . . . 46 C2
Swinside Rd BL2 . . . . . . 42 F8
Swinstead Ave M40 . . . 157 B1
SWINTON 79 F8
Swinton Cres BL9 . . . . . 45 A1
Swinton Cty High Sch The
M27 . . . . 61 F1
Swinton Gr M13 . . . . . . 163 C1
Swinton Hall Rd M27 . . . 80 A8
Swinton Ind Est ⬛ M27 . 80 A8
SWINTON PARK 80 B6
Swinton Park Rd M6 . . . 80 B5
Swinton St
Bolton BL2 . . . . 42 E7
Oldham OL4 . . . . 67 C5
Swinton Sta M27 . . . . . . 61 F1
Swiss Cott SK9 . . . . . . 137 C1
Swiss Hill SK9 . . . . 137 B1
Swithemby St M38 . . . . . 22 A4
Swithin Rd M22 . . . . . . 130 E8
Swithland Rd ⬛ WA14 . 107 C1
Swithun Wells Ct M38 . . 60 A5
Swythamley Cl SK3 . . . 123 A8
Swythamley Rd SK3 . . . 123 A8
Sybil St OL15 . . . . 16 A6
Sycamore Ave
Altrincham WA14 . . . . . 119 A5
⬛ Denton M34 . . . . . . 100 F2
Golborne WA3 . . . . 74 A1
Heywood OL10 . . . . 46 E8
Hindley WN2 . . . . 56 F3
Newhey OL16 . . . . 32 A3
Newton-le-W WA12 . . . . 89 C3
Oldham, Greenacres OL4 . 67 D8
Oldham, White Gate OL9 . 65 F3
Radcliffe M26 . . . . 61 F8
Tyldesley M29 . . . . 59 D1
Wigan WN6 . . . . 36 F3
Sycamore Cl
Ashton-u-L OL6 . . . . 85 C5
Handforth SK9 . . . . 131 B2
Littleborough OL15 . . . . 15 F5
Manchester M20 . . . . . 110 C7
New Mills SK22 . . . . . . 127 E1
Stalybridge SK16 . . . . . 101 F8
Sycamore Cotts OL3 . . . 50 F1
Sycamore Cres
Ashton-u-L OL6 . . . . 85 C5
Hollinfare WA3 . . . . 105 A3
Sycamore Ct
⬛ Manchester M16 . . . . 97 D3
Manchester, Miles Platting
M40 . . . . 160 C1
⬛ Sale M33 . . . . 107 C6
⬛ Salford M6 . . . . 81 A3
Sycamore Dr
⬛ Bury BL9 . . . . 27 F7
Radcliffe M26 . . . . 44 A5
Wigan WN2 . . . . 54 C2
Sycamore Gr M35 . . . . . 84 B7
Sycamore Lo SK7 . . . . . 132 F7
Sycamore Pl M45 . . . . . . 62 F6
Sycamore Rd
Atherton M46 . . . . 58 E3
Bury BL8 . . . . 26 F5
Eccles M30 . . . . 79 A4
Hayfield SK22 . . . . 127 F2
Paddockhill WA16 . . . . . 136 B5
Partington M31 . . . . . . 105 E3
Romiley SK6 . . . . 113 A4
Sycamore St
Sale M33 . . . . 108 E4
Stockport SK3 . . . . 123 B8
Sycamores The
Glossop SK13 . . . . 171 C3
Kearsley M26 . . . . 61 B6
Mossley OL5 . . . . 68 C1
Oldham OL4 . . . . 67 E8
Stalybridge SK15 . . . . . 102 B8
Sycamore Wlk
Cheadle SK8 . . . . 122 D6
⬛ Horwich BL6 . . . . 22 E1
Sydall St SK7 . . . . 100 F3
Sydall Cl SK7 . . . . 132 D5
Syddal Cres SK7 . . . . . 132 D4
Syddal Gn SK7 . . . . . . 132 D5
Syddall Ave SK8 . . . . . 122 D6
Syddall St SK14 . . . . . . 167 A2
Syddal Rd SK7 . . . . . . 132 D5
Sydenham St ⬛ OL1 . . . 49 B1
Sydenham Terr OL12 . . . 14 D1
Syderstone Cl WN2 . . . . 56 E4
Sydney Ave
Eccles M30 . . . . 79 D2
Leigh WN7 . . . . 75 D7
Wythenshawe M90 . . . . 130 A8
Sydney Barnes Cl OL11 . 30 B2
Sydney Gdns OL15 . . . . . 6 C1
Sydney Jones Ct M40 . . 65 C1
Sydney Rd SK7 . . . . . . 132 F5
Sydney St
Failsworth M35 . . . . 83 E7
⬛ Mossley OL5 . . . . 68 C1
Platt Bridge WN2 . . . . . . 56 A3
Salford M6 . . . . 154 E2
Stockport SK2 . . . . 124 C7
Stretford M32 . . . . 96 D2

Sydney St continued
Swinton M27 . . . . 79 D7
SYKE 14 F4
Syke Croft SK6 . . . . 113 D3
Sykefield Cl WN2 . . . . . . 57 C3
Syke La OL12 . . . . 14 F4
Syke Rd OL15 . . . . 16 C2
Sykes Ave BL9 . . . . 45 B4
Sykes Cl OL3 . . . . 69 B5
Sykes Mdw SK3 . . . . . . 170 A2
Sykes Rd OL12 . . . . 15 A3
Sykes St
Hyde SK14 . . . . 167 C1
Newhey OL16 . . . . 32 A4
Reddish SK5 . . . . 111 F8
⬛ Rochdale OL16 . . . . . . 31 B6
Sykes Wlk ⬛ SK5 . . . . 111 F8
Sylvan Ave
Altrincham WA15 . . . . . 119 F8
Failsworth M35 . . . . 83 E5
Manchester M16 . . . . . . 97 D3
⬛ Sale M33 . . . . 108 C3
Urmston M41 . . . . 95 D3
Wilmslow SK9 . . . . 136 F5
Sylvan Cl M24 . . . . 46 D2
Sylvandale Ave M19 . . . . 99 A1
Sylvan Gr WA14 . . . . . . 119 D5
Sylvan St OL9 . . . . 153 D8
Sylvester Ave SK1, SK2 . 124 B7
Sylvester Cl SK14 . . . . . 102 E2
Sylvester Way
⬛ Denton M34 . . . . 113 A7
⬛ Hattersley SK14 . . . . 102 E2
Sylvia Gr ⬛ SK5 . . . . . 111 E7
Symond Rd M9 . . . . 64 E5
Symons Rd M33 . . . . . . 108 B5
Symons St M7 . . . . 155 B3
Syndall Ave M12 . . . . . . 164 A2
Syndall St M12 . . . . 164 A2
Synergy Ho M15 . . . . . 163 A1
Syresham St ⬛ WN2 . . . 56 B2

T

Taberner Cl WN6 . . . . . . 19 F1
Taberner St ⬛ WN2 . . . . 56 B2
Tabley Ave M14 . . . . 98 B2
Tabley Gdns
⬛ Droylsden M43 . . . . . 84 B1
Marple SK6 . . . . 126 A4
Tabley Gr
Manchester M13 . . . . . . 98 F2
Reddish SK5 . . . . 111 E7
Sale WA15 . . . . 120 A8
Tabley Mere Gdns SK8 . 122 F3
Tabley Mews ⬛ WA14 . . 119 D5
Tabley Rd
Bolton BL3 . . . . 146 B4
Handforth SK9 . . . . 131 D5
Sale M33 . . . . 108 C2
Tabley St
Dukinfield SK16 . . . . . . 101 E8
Mossley OL5 . . . . 86 D8
Salford M6 . . . . 81 B5
Tabor St M24 . . . . 46 F2
Tackler Cl M27 . . . . 79 F7
Tadcaster Dr M40 . . . . . 157 A2
Tadcaster Wlk OL1 . . . . 153 C2
Taddington Pl ⬛ SK13 . . 171 B1
Tadman Gr WA14 . . . . . 119 A6
Tadmor Cl M38 . . . . 59 F4
TAGG WOOD 138 A1
Tagg Wood View M13 . . 138 A1
Tahir Cl M8 . . . . 156 B3
Tahir Cl M8 . . . . 156 B3
Tait Mews SK4 . . . . 110 F2
Talavera St M7 . . . . 155 A1
Talbenny Cl BL1 . . . . 40 F8
Talbot Ave BL3 . . . . 43 A4
Talbot Cl
Oldham OL4 . . . . 67 C8
Rawtenstall BB4 . . . . 1 E8
Talbot Ct
Bolton BL1 . . . . 143 C4
⬛ Stretford M32 . . . . . . 96 E3
Talbot Gr BL9 . . . . 28 A6
Talbot Pl M16 . . . . 161 B1
Talbot Rd
Alderley Edge SK9 . . . . 137 B1
Altrincham WA14 . . . . . 119 B2
Dukinfield SK14 . . . . . . 101 F5
Glossop SK13 . . . . 116 C2
Manchester M14 . . . . . . 110 E7
Sale M33 . . . . 108 E4
Stretford M16, M32, M15 . 96 F3
Talbot St
Ashton-u-L OL6 . . . . . . 166 A3
Eccles M30 . . . . 79 E1
Glossop SK13 . . . . 104 C1
Golborne WA3 . . . . 90 A8
Manchester, Goose Green
M40 . . . . 47 A2
Rochdale OL11 . . . . . . 139 C2
Stockport SK1, SK4 . . . 169 B1
Talford Gr M20 . . . . 110 A5
Talgarth Rd M40 . . . . . . 159 C4
Talkin Dr M24 . . . . 46 E3
Tallarn Cl M20 . . . . 122 B1
Tallis St M12 . . . . 99 A3
Tallow Way M44 . . . . . . 106 A8
Tall Trees M7 . . . . 63 D1
Tall Trees Cl OL2 . . . . . . 48 C4
Tall Trees Pl SK2 . . . . . 124 C6
Tallyman Way M27 . . . . . 80 E7
Talman Gr WN4 . . . . 73 D3
Talmud Torah Chinuch
Norim Sch ⬛ M7 . . . . . 155 A3

Talmud Torah Yetev Lev ⬛
M7 . . . . 155 A3
Tamar Cl
Kearsley BL4 . . . . 61 B5
Whitefield M45 . . . . 63 A8
Tamar Ct ⬛ M15 . . . . . . 162 A2
Tamar Dr M23 . . . . 121 A4
Tamarin Cl M27 . . . . 61 C1
Tamar Way OL10 . . . . . . 29 A3
Tamebank OL5 . . . . 68 D3
Tame Barn Cl OL16 . . . . 32 A6
Tame Cl SK15 . . . . 86 C3
Tame Ct ⬛ SK15 . . . . . . 86 B2
Tame La OL3 . . . . 50 D7
Tamer Gr WN7 . . . . 75 C8
TAMER LANE END 57 C8
Tamerton Dr M8 . . . . . . 156 A2
Tameside Bsns Development
Ctr M34 . . . . 100 D3
Tameside Coll OL6 . . . . . 85 D3
Tameside Coll (Droylesden
Ctr) M43 . . . . 84 A1
Tameside Coll (Hyde
Clarendon Sixth Form Coll)
SK14 . . . . 167 B4
Tameside Coll (The Hyde
Ctr) SK14 . . . . 113 D7
Tameside Ct
Dukinfield SK16 . . . . . . 101 B8
⬛ Hattersley SK14 . . . . 102 E2
Tameside General Hospl
OL6 . . . . 85 E4
Tameside Gymnastics Ctr
SK14 . . . . 102 F3
Tameside Hippodrome
(Theatre)* OL6 . . . . . . 166 B3
Tameside Work Ctr ⬛
OL7 . . . . 84 F1
Tame St
Denton, Guide Bridge
M34 . . . . 100 F7
Denton M34 . . . . 160 A1
Manchester M4 . . . . . . 159 B2
Mossley OL5 . . . . 68 E3
Stalybridge SK15, SK16 . 85 E1
Uppermill OL3 . . . . 69 B8
Tame Valley Cl OL5 . . . . 68 E3
Tame View OL5 . . . . 68 C2
TAME WATER 50 F1
Tame Water Villas OL3 . . 50 F1
Tame Wlk ⬛ SK9 . . . . . 131 D2
Tamworth Ave WA5 . . . . 63 B7
Tamworth Cl
Hazel Grove SK7 . . . . . 133 D8
Manchester M15 . . . . . 162 B1
Tamworth Dr
Bury BL8 . . . . 27 C5
Wigan WN2 . . . . 37 F2
Tamworth Gn SK1 . . . . . 112 B2
Tamworth St
Manchester M15 . . . . . . 97 E4
Newton-le-W WA12 . . . . 89 A3
Oldham OL9 . . . . 152 C1
Stockport SK1 . . . . 112 B2
Tandis Ct M6 . . . . 80 A4
Tandle Hill Ctry Pk ⬛ OL2 48 A6
Tandle Hill Rd OL2 . . . . . 48 B6
Tandlewood Mews ⬛
M40 . . . . 83 C5
Tandlewood Pk OL2 . . . . 48 B6
Tanfield Dr M26 . . . . 61 B7
Tanfield Rd M20 . . . . . . 122 B8
TANG 113 B2
Tangmere Ave OL10 . . . . 46 E7
Tangmere Cl M40 . . . . . . 65 C3
Tangmere Ct M16 . . . . . . 97 D3
Tang The SK6 . . . . 113 B1
Tanhill Cl SK2 . . . . 124 E6
Tanhill La OL8 . . . . 67 A2
Tanhouse Ave M29 . . . . . 77 D7
Tan House Dr WN3 . . . . . 54 C2
Tan House La M41 . . . . . 94 D3
Tanner Brook Cl BL3 . . . 147 B4
TANNERS 138 B2
Tanners Croft BL0 . . . . . 138 B2
Tanners Fold OL8 . . . . . . 67 A2
Tanners Gn ⬛ M6 . . . . . 154 F3
Tanner's La WA3 . . . . . . 90 B8
Tanners St
Droylsden M43 . . . . 99 E5
Ramsbottom BL0 . . . . . 138 B2
Tanner St SK14 . . . . 167 A3
Tannery Way
Altrincham WA14 . . . . . 119 E2
Manchester M18 . . . . . . 99 E5
Tannock Ct SK7 . . . . . . 124 F1
Tannock Rd SK7 . . . . . . 124 F1
Tan Pit Cotts WN8 . . . . . 35 C4
Tan Pits Cl M29 . . . . 77 C7
Tanpits Rd BL9 . . . . 140 F3
Tanpit Wlk ⬛ M22 . . . . . 121 C2
Tansey Gr M7 . . . . 155 C3
Tansley Ave PR7 . . . . . . 19 D8
Tansley Cl BL6 . . . . 22 C2
Tansley Rd M8 . . . . 64 B2
Tansley Sq WN5 . . . . 54 D5
Tanworth Wlk ⬛ BL1 . . 143 B2
Tan Yard Brow M18 . . . . 99 E5
Tanyard Gr WN5 . . . . . . 129 C6
Tanyard La WA15 . . . . . 129 A5
Taper St BL0 . . . . 138 B2
Tape St BL0 . . . . 138 B2
Tapley Ave SK12 . . . . . . 133 E2
Taplin Dr M18 . . . . 165 C1
Taplow Gr SK8 . . . . 122 F2

Taplow Wlk M14 98 E3
Tarbet Dr BL2 42 F7
Tarbet Rd SK16 101 C7
Tarbet Wlk M8 155 C2
Tarbolton Cres WA15 120 C3
Target Life Cheadle Hulme SK8 132 B7
Tariff St M1 159 B1
Tarland Wlk 17 M11 83 C1
Tarleton Ave M46 58 B5
Tarleton Cl BL8 26 F1
Tarleton Ho 5 M6 80 C4
Tarleton Pl BL3 146 A3
Tarleton St M13 164 A2
Tarnbrook Cl M45 63 C8
Tarnbrook Dr WN2 38 B5
Tarnbrook Wlk M15 163 A1
Tarn Cl WN4 73 B5
Tarn Dr BL9 44 E6
Tarn Gr M28 60 F1
Tarnrigg Cl WN3 54 E3
Tarnside Cl
 Hazel Grove SK2 124 F6
 Rochdale OL16 15 C3
Tarnside Fold SK13 116 A7
Tarnside Rd WN5 53 E6
Tarns The SK8 122 B3
Tarnway WA3 90 F7
Tarporley Ave M14 110 A8
Tarporley Cl SK3 170 A1
Tarporley Wlk SK9 131 E2
Tarran Gr M34 101 B1
Tarran Pl WA14 119 E6
Tarrant Cl WN3 54 D2
Tarrington Cl M12 165 A1
Tartan St M11 83 B2
Tarves Wlk M11 83 B1
Tarvin Ave
 Manchester M20 110 A7
 Reddish SK4 111 D7
Tarvin Cl WA3 90 E7
Tarvin Dr SK6 112 E4
Tarvington Cl M40 156 C2
Tarvin Rd SK8 123 A4
Tarvin Way 1 SK9 131 D5
Tarvin Wlk BL1 143 B2
Tashbar Sch M7 63 E1
Tasle Alley M2 158 C1
Tatchbury Rd M35 84 A7
Tate St OL8 67 B5
Tatham Cl 3 M13 98 F3
Tatham Gr WN3 54 D1
Tatham St OL16 31 A7
Tatland Dr M22 121 F3
Tatlock Cl WN5 71 E5
Tattenhall Wlk 15 M14 110 D8
Tattersall Ave BL1 23 E2
Tattersall St OL9 153 A2
Tatton Cl
 Cheadle SK8 123 A4
 Hazel Grove SK7 124 F4
Tatton Ct
 4 Handforth SK9 131 E5
 8 Manchester M14 110 D8
 Stockport SK4 168 C4
Tatton Dr WN4 72 F4
Tatton Gdns SK6 113 D5
Tatton Gr M20 110 B6
Tatton Ho BL1 144 C3
Tatton Mere Dr M43 84 B1
Tattonmere Gdns SK8 123 A4
Tatton Pl
 Manchester M13 98 E4
 Sale M33 108 B5
Tatton Rd
 Denton M34 101 A1
 Handforth SK9 131 E5
 Sale M33 108 B5
Tatton Road N SK4 111 C5
Tatton Road S SK4 168 C4
Tatton St
 Hyde SK14 113 E7
 Manchester M15 162 A3
 Salford M5 161 B4
 Stalybridge SK15 86 B1
 Stockport SK1 169 C1
Tatton Terr 5 SK16 166 B1
Tatton View 6 M20 110 B6
TAUNTON 84 E5
Taunton Ave
 Ashton-u-L OL7 166 A4
 Eccles M30 79 B3
 Hindley WN7 57 D2
 Rochdale OL11 30 B7
 Urmston M41 107 B8
Taunton Brook La OL7 84 E5
Taunton Cl
 Bolton BL1 142 C1
 Hazel Grove SK7 125 A2
Taunton Dr BL4 147 C1
Taunton Gn OL7 84 F5
Taunton Gr M25, M45 63 A6
Taunton Hall Cl OL7 84 F5
Taunton Lawns OL7 85 A5
Taunton Pl OL7 84 F5
Taunton Rd
 Ashton-u-L OL7 166 A4
 Chadderton OL9 48 A1
 Sale M33 107 D4
Taunton St M4 160 A1
Taunton Wlk 13 M34 101 A1
Taurus St OL4 67 C8
Tavern Court Ave M35 84 B7
Tavern Ct M35 84 B7
Tavern Rd SK13 171 B3
Tavery Cl 4 M4 159 C2
Tavistock Cl SK14 102 E2
Tavistock Dr OL9 47 F1
Tavistock Rd
 Bolton BL1 145 A2
 Hindley WN2 57 A4
 Rochdale OL11 30 F2
 Sale M33 107 D5
Tavistock Sq M9 157 A3
Tavistock St M46 58 B4
Tawton Ave SK14 102 E3
Taxi Rd M90 130 B7
Tay Cl OL8 153 B1
Tayfield Rd M22 121 C2
Tayleur Terr WA12 89 D2
Taylor Ave OL11 29 F8
Taylor Bldgs BL4 61 B6
Taylor Bsns Pk WA3 91 F1
Taylor Gdns SK14 167 C3
Taylor Gr WN2 57 C3
Taylor Green Way OL4 67 F7
Taylor Ho BL8 27 C5
Taylor Holme Ind Est OL13 3 B8
Taylor La M34 100 D4
Taylor Rd
 Altrincham WA14 119 A5
 Hindley WN2 57 C3
 Urmston M41 95 E7
Taylor's La
 Ainsworth BL2 43 B7
 Ince-in-M WN3 55 F3
Taylorson St M5 161 B3
Taylorson Street S M5 161 A2
Taylors Pl 18 OL12 14 F1
Taylor's Rd M32 96 E3
Taylor St
 9 Bolton BL3 145 C2
 Bury BL9 141 A3
 Chadderton OL9 152 A3
 Denton M34 100 F4
 Droylsden M43 84 A1
 Golborne WN3 74 C1
 Heywood OL10 29 C2
 Hollingworth SK14 171 A4
 Horwich BL6 22 B3
 Hyde SK14 167 C3
 Leigh WN7 75 D8
 Manchester, Belle Vue M18 165 C2
 Manchester, Rusholme M14 98 C2
 Middleton M24 65 A8
 1 Oldham, Lees OL4 67 E6
 Oldham OL1 67 C8
 Prestwich M25 63 C4
 Radcliffe M26 44 A3
 Rochdale OL12 14 F1
 Royton OL2 48 D5
 Stalybridge SK15 86 B1
 Whitworth OL12 14 D8
 Wigan WN3 150 B4
Taylor Terr 18 SK16 166 B1
Tayton Cl M29 59 C1
Taywood Rd BL3 40 D2
Teak Dr BL4 61 D4
Teak St BL9 141 B2
Teal Ave SK12 133 A4
Tealby Ave M16 97 C4
Tealby Ct M21 97 C1
Tealby Rd M18 99 B4
Teal Cl
 Altrincham WA14 119 B8
 Hazel Grove SK2 124 F5
 Wigan WN3 54 B4
Teal Ct OL11 29 F7
Teal St BL3 147 C4
Teasdale Cl OL9 65 E3
Tebbutt St M4 159 B3
Tebworth Dr WN2 56 E4
Tedburn Wlk 13 M40 65 D2
Tedder Cl BL9 45 B2
Tedder Dr M22 130 F7
Teddington Rd M40 65 C1
Ted Jackson Wlk M11 164 C4
Teer St M4 160 A2
Teesdale Ave M41 95 A4
Teesdale Cl SK2 124 E6
Teesdale Dr WN7 76 C5
Teesdale Wlk 20 M9 64 E3
Tees St OL16 31 B6
Tees Wlk OL8 153 B1
Teignmouth Ave M40 159 C4
Teignmouth St M40 159 C4
Telfer Ave M13 98 E2
Telfer Rd M13 98 E2
Telford Cl M34 100 E7
Telford Cres WN7 75 D8
Telford Mews OL3 69 B8
Telford Rd SK6 126 A4
Telford St
 Atherton M46 58 A2
 Horwich BL6 22 D2
Telford Way OL11 31 A2
Telford Wlk M16 97 D4
Telham Wlk M23 121 A5
Tellers Cl M46 58 D3
Tellson Cl M6 80 D6
Tellson Cres M6 80 D6
Tell St OL12 139 A3
Telryn Wlk M8 156 C4
Temperance Sq SK14 103 A4
Temperance St
 Bolton BL3 145 B1
 7 Broadbottom SK14 115 A8
 Manchester, Ardwick M12 164 A3
 Manchester M1, M12 163 C4
Tempest Chase BL6 40 C4
Tempest Rd
 Alderley Edge SK9 137 C1
 Bolton BL6 40 C4
Tempest St BL3 146 B4
Temple Ave SK13 104 C5
Temple Cl OL4 67 E8
Templecombe Dr BL1 24 E7
Temple Dr
 Bolton BL1 142 C3
 Pendlebury M27 80 B7
Templegate Cl WN6 19 F2
Temple La OL15 6 D1
Temple Moor Inf Sch 2 M33 108 E4
Temple Prim Sch M8 156 B2
Temple Rd
 Bolton BL1 142 C3
 Sale M33 108 D4
Temple Sq M8 156 B2
Temple St
 Glossop SK13 104 C5
 Heywood OL10 29 D2
 Middleton M24 47 B1
 Oldham OL1 67 B7
Templeton Cl
 Altrincham WA14 119 B6
 Westhoughton BL5 57 E8
Templeton Rd WN2 56 B2
Ten Acre Ct M45 62 D7
Ten Acre Dr M45 62 D7
Ten Acres La M40 83 A4
Ten Acres L Ctr M40 83 A5
Tenax Circ M17 96 B8
Tenax Rd M17 96 B7
Tenbury Cl M6 154 C3
Tenbury Dr
 Ashton-in-M WN4 73 A4
 Middleton M24 65 A5
Tenby Ave
 Bolton BL1 142 A1
 Manchester M20 110 B6
 Stretford M32 96 E4
Tenby Ct M15 161 C2
Tenby Dr
 Cheadle SK8 123 B1
 Pendlebury M6 80 D5
Tenby Gr 6 OL12 14 C1
Tenby Rd
 Oldham OL8 66 B2
 Stockport SK3 123 B7
Tenby St OL12 14 C1
Tenement La SK7, SK8 123 C3
Tenement St WN2 56 B1
Teneriffe St M7 155 A1
Ten Foot Cl SK13 104 B2
Tenham Wlk 23 M9 64 E3
Ten Ho OL8 67 C2
Tennis St
 Bolton BL1 143 A3
 Manchester M16 97 B4
Tennyson Ave
 Bury BL9 44 F6
 Denton M34 113 A7
 Dukinfield SK16 102 A7
 Leigh WN7 75 C8
 Radcliffe M26 43 E4
Tennyson Cl SK4 168 B2
Tennyson Dr
 Longshaw WN5 53 D1
 Wigan WN1 37 C3
Tennyson Gdns M25 62 F3
Tennyson Rd
 Cheadle SK8 122 F6
 Droylsden M43 84 A2
 Farnworth BL4 60 B6
 Middleton M24 47 B2
 Reddish SK5 99 D1
 Swinton M27 79 D8
Tennyson St
 Bolton BL1 143 A1
 Manchester M13 163 C1
 Oldham OL1 49 C1
 1 Rochdale OL11 31 A5
Tennyson Wlk 3 BL1 143 B2
Tensing Ave
 Ashton-u-L OL7 85 B5
 Atherton M46 58 C5
Tensing Fold SK16 166 B1
Tensing St OL8 85 A8
Tentercroft
 Oldham OL1 153 B3
 Rochdale OL12 139 B3
Tenterden St BL9 140 A2
Tenterden Wlk M22 121 C3
Tenter Dr WN6 37 B7
Tenterfield St 6 BB4 2 F8
Tenterheads BB4 2 F7
Tenterhill La OL11 13 D2
TENTERSFIELD 140 A2
Tenters St BL9 140 A2
Tenth St M17 96 D6
Terence St M40 83 D5
Terminal Road E M90 130 C7
Terminal Road N M90 130 B7
Terminal Road S M90 130 B7
Tern Cl
 Altrincham WA14 119 B8
 Dukinfield SK16 101 E7
 Rochdale OL11 29 F7
Tern Dr SK12 133 B4
Ternhill Ct BL4 60 D8
Terrace St OL4 67 B7
Terrace The M25 63 B3
Terrington Cl M21 109 E7
Tetbury Cl WN5 36 D1
Tetbury Dr BL2 43 A8
Tetbury Rd M22 121 B1
Tetley Bye Rd OL3 51 E7
Tetlow Gr M30 79 C1
Tetlow La M7 155 B4
Tetlow St
 Dukinfield SK14 101 E5
 Failsworth M40 83 D5
Tetlow St *continued*
 Middleton M24 65 A8
 Oldham OL9 153 A2
Tetsworth Wlk 16 M40 65 D2
Teviot St 8 M13 98 E4
Tewkesbury Ave
 Altrincham WA15 120 C3
 Ashton-u-L OL6 85 C7
 Chadderton OL9 48 A2
 Droylsden M43 84 A3
 Middleton M24 46 F3
 Urmston M41 95 D4
Tewkesbury Cl
 Cheadle SK8 132 B6
 Poynton SK12 133 D4
Tewkesbury Dr M25 63 C2
Tewkesbury Rd
 Cheadle SK3 123 B6
 Golborne WA3 90 B8
 Manchester M40 160 A3
Texas St OL6 166 C2
Textile St M12 165 A3
Textilose Rd M17 96 B5
Teynham Wlk 5 M22 121 C1
Thackeray Cl M8 156 A2
Thackeray Gr M43 84 A2
Thackeray Pl WN3 150 A1
Thackeray Rd OL1 49 C1
Thames Ave WN7 75 F1
Thames Cl
 Bury BL9 27 F7
 Manchester M11 165 B4
Thames Ct 2 M15 162 A2
Thames Dr WN5 53 F7
Thames Ind Est M12 164 A3
Thames Rd
 Culcheth WA3 92 A2
 Milnrow OL16 32 B6
Thames St
 Oldham OL1 67 A8
 Rochdale OL16 31 B6
Thames Trad Ctr M44 105 F7
Thanet Cl M7 155 B1
Thanet Gr WN7 76 A5
Thankerton Ave M34 84 D1
Thatcher Cl WA14 119 C1
Thatcher St OL8 67 A4
THATCH LEACH 65 F5
Thatch Leach OL9 65 F5
Thatch Leach La M45 63 A7
Thaxmead Dr M40 83 D4
Thaxted Dr SK2 125 A5
Thaxted Pl BL1 144 C4
Thaxted Wlk M22 130 C8
Theatre St OL1 153 C3
Thekla St OL9 153 A4
Thelma St BL0 138 B2
Thelwall Ave
 Bolton BL2 42 D8
 Manchester M14 110 A8
Thelwall Cl
 2 Altrincham WA15 119 E6
 Leigh WN7 75 B4
Thelwall Ct M14 110 A8
Thelwall Rd M33 108 E3
Theobald Rd WA14 119 D1
Theta Cl M11 83 B2
Thetford 12 OL12 139 B4
Thetford Cl
 Bury BL8 27 D5
 Hindley WN2 56 E4
Thetford Dr M8 156 B3
THICKETFORD BROW 25 C1
Thicketford Brow BL2 25 D1
Thicketford Cl BL2 25 C2
Thicketford Rd BL2 25 C1
Thicknesse Ave WN6 36 F3
Thimble Cl OL12 15 D4
Thimbles The OL12 15 D4
Third Ave
 Bolton BL1 144 B3
 Bury BL9 28 D4
 Droylsden M11 83 C3
 Little Lever BL3 42 F4
 Mossley SK15 86 E6
 Oldham OL8 66 D1
 Poynton SK12 133 D1
 Stretford M17 96 D6
 Swinton M27 79 E5
 Tyldesley M29 77 B4
 Wigan WN6 37 A2
Third St BL1 23 F4
Thirkhill Pl 2 M30 79 F2
Thirlby Dr M22 121 D1
Thirlemere Rd SK1 124 B7
Thirlmere Ave
 Abram WN2 74 B8
 Ashton-in-M WN4 73 C4
 Ashton-u-L OL7 84 F4
 Haslingden BB4 1 C8
 Horwich BL6 22 C2
 Ince-in-M WN2 56 B7
 1 Orrell WN5 53 F7
 Pendlebury M27 80 A7
 Standish WN6 37 A7
 Stretford M32 96 C3
 Tyldesley M29 77 A7
 Up Holland WN8 53 B7
Thirlmere Cl
 Adlington PR6 21 B8
 Alderley Edge SK9 136 F1
 Stalybridge SK15 86 A4
Thirlmere Dr
 Bury BL9 44 E7
 Middleton M24 46 E2
 Walkden M38 60 A5
Thirlmere Gr
 Farnworth BL4 59 E8
Thirlmere Gr *continued*
 Royton OL2 48 D6
Thirlmere Mews M24 46 E2
Thirlmere Rd
 Blackrod BL6 21 C3
 Golborne WA3 74 C1
 Hindley WN2 56 E5
 Over Hulton BL5 58 F7
 Partington M31 105 E4
 Rochdale OL11 30 B4
 Urmston M41 94 E3
 Wigan WN5 54 C7
 Wythenshawe M22 121 B2
Thirlmere St WN7 75 E5
Thirlspot Cl BL1 24 E6
Thirlstone Ave OL4 49 F4
Thirsfield Dr 6 M11 83 C2
Thirsk Ave
 Chadderton OL9 47 F1
 Sale M33 107 C3
Thirsk Cl BL8 27 B5
Thirsk Mews M7 155 A2
Thirsk Rd BL3 43 A2
Thirsk St M12 163 C3
Thistle Bank Cl M9 64 C1
Thistle Cl SK15 102 E7
Thistledown Cl
 Eccles M30 95 D8
 Wigan WN6 37 A2
Thistle Gn OL16 31 E7
Thistle Sq M31 105 E2
Thistleton Rd BL3 40 F3
Thistle Way OL4 49 D2
Thistle Wlk 4 M31 105 E2
Thistlewood Dr SK9 137 D8
Thistley Fields SK14 113 C8
Thomas Chambers 3 SK13 116 C7
Thomas Cl M34 101 A4
Thomas Ct
 Bolton BL7 25 A7
 Manchester M15 162 A3
Thomas Dr BL3 145 A1
Thomas Garnet Ct 1 BL4 60 C8
Thomas Gibbon Cl 5 M32 96 C1
Thomas Henshaw Ct OL11 30 C4
Thomas Ho 1 OL2 48 E4
Thomas Holden St BL1 145 B4
Thomas Johnson Cl 4 M30 79 C1
Thomas More Cl BL4 60 F6
Thomason Fold BL7 9 D6
Thomas Regan Ct 4 M18 99 D6
Thomasson Cl 7 BL1 143 B1
Thomasson Ct BL1 144 B3
Thomasson Memorial Specl Sch 1 BL1 144 B4
Thomas St
 Altrincham WA15 119 E4
 Aspull WN2 38 B6
 Atherton M46 58 D3
 Bolton BL3 145 A1
 Compstall SK6 114 B2
 Farnworth BL4 60 E7
 Glossop SK13 104 E1
 Golborne WA3 90 A8
 Hindley WN2 57 B3
 Manchester M4 159 A2
 Oldham OL4 67 E5
 Radcliffe M26 44 B3
 Rochdale, Dearnley OL15 15 E4
 8 Rochdale OL16 31 A8
 Romiley SK6 113 A3
 Royton OL2 49 A3
 Salford M8 155 C4
 Shaw OL2 149 C2
 Stockport SK1 170 C3
 Stretford M32 96 D3
 Westhoughton BL5 39 E3
 Whitworth OL12 4 D2
Thomas Street W SK1, SK2 170 C3
Thomas Telford Basin M1 159 C1
Thompson Ave
 Ainsworth BL2 26 D1
 Culcheth WA3 91 E3
 Whitefield M45 63 A7
Thompson Cl
 Newton-le-W WA12 89 C1
 Reddish M34 100 B3
Thompson Court Apartments M27 80 E8
Thompson Ct
 Reddish M34 100 B3
 Stalybridge SK15 85 F2
Thompson Dr BL9 141 C3
Thompson Fold SK15 85 F2
Thompson Ho M46 58 C3
Thompson La OL9 66 A4
Thompson Rd
 Bolton BL1 142 B1
 Reddish M34 100 B3
 Urmston M17 95 E8
Thompson St
 Ashton-in-M WN4 73 D4
 Bolton BL3 145 C1
 Horwich BL6 22 A3
 Leigh WN7 75 B5
 Manchester M4 159 B2
 Manchester, Newton Heath M40 157 C1

Thompson St *continued*
Manchester, Strangeways
M3.......................... 158 C3
Wigan, Longshoot WN1... 37 E1
Wigan, Worsley Mesnes
WN3........................ 55 A4
Thomson Rd M18........ 99 C4
Thomson St
Manchester M18.......... 163 C2
Stockport SK3............ 170 B4
Thoralby Cl M12........ 165 A1
Thorburn Dr OL12...... 14 B7
Thorburn Ho WN5...... 54 C7
Thorburn La WN5...... 54 D8
Thorburn Rd WN5...... 54 D6
Thoresby Cl
Little Lever M26.......... 43 C5
Wigan WN3................ 54 E3
Thoresway Rd
Manchester M13.......... 98 E3
Wilmslow SK9............ 136 F5
Thorgill Wlk 10 M40... 83 A7
Thor Gr M5.............. 161 C4
Thoriby Rd WA3........ 91 F3
Thorley Cl OL9.......... 65 E2
Thorley Dr
Altrincham WA15......... 120 B5
Urmston M41.............. 95 D2
Thorley La
Altrincham WA15......... 120 B4
Wythenshawe M22, WA15 121 A1
Thorley Mews SK7..... 132 F7
Thorley St M35........ 83 F8
Thornaby Wlk M9...... 157 A2
Thornage Dr M40...... 159 C4
Thorn Ave M35........ 83 F6
Thornbank
Bolton BL3................ 144 C2
Eccles M30................ 79 E3
Thorn Bank SK15...... 86 F7
Thornbank Cl OL10.... 46 E7
Thornbeck Dr BL1...... 23 F1
Thornbeck Rd BL1...... 23 F1
Thornbridge Ave M21.. 109 B8
Thornbury 8 OL11..... 139 B2
Thornbury Ave
Golborne WA3............ 90 E7
Hattersley SK14.......... 102 E2
Thornbury Cl
8 Bolton BL1.............. 145 B4
Bramhall SK8............. 123 C1
Thornbury Rd M32..... 96 E4
Thornbury Way M18... 165 C1
Thornbush Cl WA3..... 74 E1
Thornbush Way OL16.. 31 C8
Thornby Wlk 8 M23... 121 A5
Thorn Cl OL10.......... 29 B3
Thorncliff Ave OL8..... 66 E3
Thorncliffe Ave
Dukinfield SK16.......... 101 C7
Royton OL2............... 48 C6
Thorncliffe Gr M19..... 99 C1
Thorncliffe Pk OL2..... 48 C6
Thorncliffe Rd
Bolton BL1................ 24 E5
Glossop SK13............. 171 C4
Thorncombe Rd 1 M16. 97 E3
Thorncroft Ave M29.... 77 A7
Thorncross Cl M15..... 161 C3
Thorn Ct
2 Salford M6............. 81 B2
18 Stalybridge SK15..... 86 A2
Thorndale Cl OL2....... 48 E5
Thorndale Ct M9........ 64 C2
Thorndale Gr WA15.... 120 A5
Thornden Rd M40...... 160 A4
Thorn Dr M22........... 131 A8
Thorndyke Gdns M25... 63 B3
Thorne Ave M41........ 95 A3
Thornecliffewood SK14 103 D5
Thorne Ho M14......... 98 D2
Thorneside M34........ 100 F5
Thorne St BL4.......... 42 C1
Thorneycroft WN7...... 76 C5
Thorneycroft Ave M41.. 109 C5
Thorneycroft Cl WA15. 120 B5
Thorneycroft Rd WA15. 120 B5
Thorney Dr SK8......... 132 C6
Thorney Hill Cl 9 OL4. 67 A6
Thorneyholme Cl BL6... 40 C6
Thorneylea OL12........ 4 C2
Thornfield SK9.......... 137 A4
Thornfield Ave 6 BB4.. 2 F8
Thornfield Cl WA3...... 90 C8
Thornfield Cres M38.... 59 F5
Thornfield Ct SK4...... 168 C3
Thornfield Dr 4 M27... 79 E7
Thornfield Gr
Cheadle SK8.............. 123 A2
Walkden M38............. 59 F5
Thornfield Hey SK9.... 137 E8
Thornfield Rd
Bury BL8.................. 26 E7
Manchester, Green End
M19....................... 110 E5
Stockport SK4............ 168 A3
Thornfield St M5....... 154 A1
Thornfield Terr OL6.... 166 C2
Thornford Wlk 14 M40. 65 D2
Thorngate Rd M8....... 156 A1
Thorn Gr
Altrincham WA15......... 119 E3
Cheadle SK8.............. 132 A7
Manchester M14.......... 110 D8
Sale M33.................. 108 A3

Thorngrove Ave 1 M23. 120 D7
Thorngrove Dr SK9..... 137 C6
Thorngrove Hill SK9.... 137 C6
Thorngrove Ho 4 M23. 120 D7
Thorn Grove Prim Sch
SK8....................... 132 A7
Thorngrove Rd SK9..... 137 C6
Thornham Cl BL8....... 27 C6
Thornham Ct OL16...... 48 C8
Thornham Dr BL1....... 25 A6
Thornham La
Royton OL6, OL2.......... 48 C8
Slattocks M24, OL11, OL2. 47 E6
Thornham New Rd OL11,
.... 47 E8
Thornham Old Rd M24,
OL2....................... 47 E8
Thornham Rd
Sale M33.................. 107 F3
Shaw OL2................. 48 E8
Thornham St James CE Prim
Sch OL2................ 48 C8
Thornhill Cl BL1........ 142 C3
Thornhill Dr M28....... 60 E1
Thornhill Rd
Droylsden M43............ 84 B2
Garswood WN4........... 72 C4
Manchester SK4.......... 168 C3
Ramsbottom BL0......... 11 A1
Thorn Ho 9 SK15....... 86 A2
Thornholme Cl M18.... 99 B3
Thornholme Rd SK6.... 125 F4
Thorniley Brow M4..... 159 A2
Thornlea
Altrincham WA15......... 119 F4
Droylsden M43............ 83 E1
Thorn Lea
Atherton M46............. 58 E2
Bolton BL2................ 25 D4
Thornlea Ave
Oldham OL1............... 66 C1
Swinton M27.............. 79 D6
Thorn Lea Cl BL1....... 40 F7
Thornlea Dr OL12...... 14 B2
Thornlee Ct OL4........ 68 B5
Thornleigh Rd M14..... 98 B1
Thornleigh Salesian Coll
BL1....................... 143 A4
Thornley Ave BL1...... 142 C2
Thornley Cl OL4........ 68 A5
Thornley Cres
Oldham OL4............... 68 A5
Romiley SK6.............. 113 A4
Thornley La 6 OL4..... 68 A5
Thornley Lane N M34, SK5. 99 F3
Thornley Lane S M34,
SK5....................... 100 A2
Thornley Mews BL1.... 142 C2
Thornley Park Rd OL4.. 68 A5
Thornley Rd
Denton M34............... 101 A4
Prestwich M25............ 63 C7
Thornley Rise M34..... 100 D7
Thornley St
Hyde SK14................ 167 B1
Middleton M24............ 47 B1
Radcliffe M26............. 44 B2
Thornmere Cl M27..... 61 C2
Thorn Rd
Bramhall SK7............. 132 E5
Oldham OL8............... 67 C3
Swinton M27.............. 79 E6
Thorns Ave BL1........ 143 A3
Thorns Cl BL1.......... 143 A3
Thorns Clough OL3..... 51 C5
Thorns The M21........ 109 B7
Thorns Villa Gdns M28. 78 A5
Thorn St
Bolton BL1................ 143 C2
13 Hindley WN2........... 56 D4
Ramsbottom BL0......... 11 C3
Thornsett M20.......... 110 B2
Thornton Ave
Ashton-in-M WN4........ 72 F4
Boothstown M28.......... 77 E7
Farnworth BL4............ 60 B7
Golborne WA3............ 75 A1
Leigh WN7................ 75 F1
Little Lever BL4.......... 43 A3
Thornton Cres M25..... 62 F5
Thornton Ct M16....... 161 C1
Thornton Dr SK9....... 131 D3
Thornton Gate SK8..... 122 A6
Thornton Pl SK4....... 168 B4
Thornton Rd
Boothstown M28.......... 77 E7
Gatley SK8................ 131 C8
Manchester M14.......... 98 A2
Thornton St 1 Bolton BL2. 148 A3
Manchester M40.......... 160 A4
Oldham OL4............... 153 C1
Rochdale OL16........... 31 A7
Thornton Street N M40. 157 A1
Thorntree Cl M9........ 157 B3
Thorntree Pl 2 OL12... 139 B4

Thornvale WN2......... 74 C7
Thorn View BL9........ 141 C3
Thornway
Bramhall SK8............. 132 C7
High Lane SK6............ 134 F7
Walkden M28.............. 78 A8
Thornway Dr OL7....... 84 F2
Thorn Well BL5......... 57 E7
Thorn Wlk M31......... 105 E2
Thornwood Ave M34.... 100 F2
Thornydyke Ave BL1.... 24 E5
Thorold Gr M33........ 108 E4
THORP.................. 48 C5
Thorpe Ave
Radcliffe M26............. 44 D5
Swinton M27.............. 61 E1
Thorpebrook Rd M40... 83 A6
Thorpe Cl
Altrincham WA15......... 120 C7
Denton M34............... 100 F4
Oldham OL4............... 68 A8
Thorpe Gr SK4......... 168 C3
Thorpe Hall Gr SK14... 101 F6
Thorpe La
Denton M34............... 100 F5
Oldham OL4............... 68 A8
Thorpeness Sq M18.... 99 D6
Thorpe St
Bolton BL1................ 143 A2
Glossop SK13............. 104 E2
Manchester M16.......... 97 C4
Middleton M24............ 64 C7
Ramsbottom BL0......... 138 B1
Walkden M28.............. 60 D4
Thorp Rd
Manchester M40.......... 83 A6
Royton OL2............... 48 D4
Thorp St
Eccles M30................ 95 B8
Whitefield M45........... 44 E1
Thorp View OL2........ 48 C6
Thorsby Ave SK14..... 167 C2
Thorsby Cl
Bolton BL7................ 24 F8
Droylsden M18............ 99 E5
Thorsby Rd WA15...... 119 E5
Thorsby Way 16 M34... 101 A1
Thorverton Sq M40..... 83 C8
Thrapston Ave M34.... 84 D1
Threadfold Way BL7.... 24 F7
Threadmill Pl M27...... 79 D8
Threaphurst La SK7.... 125 C1
Threapwood Rd M22.... 121 E1
Three Acre Ave OL2.... 49 A4
Three Acre La SK8..... 131 E7
Three Acres Dr SK5.... 111 E5
Three Counties Rd OL5. 68 D1
Three Lane Ends OL10. 45 F7
Three Sisters Rd WN4.. 73 B7
Three Sisters Recn Area ✱
WN4...................... 73 C7
Threlkeld Cl M24....... 46 C1
Threlkeld Rd
Bolton BL1................ 24 D6
Middleton M24............ 46 C1
Thresher Cl 3 M33..... 108 F3
Threshfield Cl BL9...... 27 F7
Threshfield Dr WA15... 120 C7
Threxton Pl BL3........ 40 F3
Throstle Bank St SK14. 101 C4
Throstle Ct 3 OL2...... 48 D4
Throstle Gr
Bury BL8.................. 27 C5
Marple SK6............... 125 E5
Throstle Hall Ct 1 M24. 46 F1
Throstle Nest Ave WN6. 37 A2
Throstles Cl M43....... 84 C3
Throstle St OL14....... 6 B6
Thrum Fold OL12....... 14 D3
Thrum Hall La OL12.... 14 D3
Thrush Ave BL4........ 59 F8
Thrush Dr BL9.......... 141 B4
Thrush Ho M6.......... 81 A5
Thrush St OL12........ 14 C1
Thruxton Cl M16....... 97 E3
Thurcaston Rd 3 WA14. 107 C1
Thurland Rd OL4....... 67 C6
Thurland St OL9....... 65 E8
Thurlby Ave M9........ 64 E5
Thurlby Cl WN4........ 73 D4
Thurlby St M13......... 98 D4
Thurleigh Rd M20...... 110 B3
Thurlestone Ave BL2... 26 D1
Thurlestone Dr
Stockport SK7............ 124 B2
3 Urmston M41........... 95 D3
Thurlestone Rd WA14.. 119 B6
Thurloe St M14......... 98 C3
Thurlow WA3............ 90 C7
Thurlow St M5.......... 154 C1
Thurlston Cres M8..... 156 B3
Thurlwood Ave M20.... 110 A7
Thurlwood Croft 17 BL5. 39 E1
Thurnham St BL3....... 146 C3
Thursby Ave M20....... 110 A6
Thursby Ho WN5....... 54 C7
Thursby Wlk M24....... 46 C2
Thursfield St M6....... 81 B5
Thursford St BL6....... 21 D1
Thurstan St WN3....... 55 E4
Thurstane St BL1....... 142 C2
**Thurston WN3.......... 55 B3
Thurston Ave WN3..... 55 B3
Thurston Cl BL9........ 45 A2
Thurston Clough Rd OL3,
OL4....................... 50 D2
Thurston Gn SK9....... 137 A1
Thurstons OL3.......... 51 D6

Thynne St
Bolton BL3................ 145 C1
Farnworth BL4............ 42 C2
Tiber Ave OL8.......... 66 C1
Tib La M2............... 158 C1
Tib St
Denton M34............... 101 A2
Manchester M1, M4...... 159 A2
Ramsbottom BL0......... 138 B1
Tideswell Ave
Manchester M40.......... 160 A3
Wigan WN5............... 36 A1
Tideswell Bank 18 SK13. 171 B1
Tideswell Cl SK8....... 131 D8
Tideswell Rd
Droylsden M43............ 83 E3
Hazel Grove SK7......... 133 E8
Tideswell Way M34..... 113 A8
Tideswell Wlk 18 SK13. 171 B1
Tideway Cl M7.......... 80 F8
Tidworth Ave M4....... 160 A2
Tiefield Wlk M21....... 109 E6
Tiernan Lo 14 WN6..... 37 A1
Tiflis St OL12........... 139 B4
Tig Fold Rd BL4........ 59 E8
Tilbury Gr WN6......... 35 D7
Tilbury St OL1.......... 153 B4
Tilby Cl M41............ 94 E2
Tildsley St BL3.......... 147 B4
Tile St BL3.............. 140 C3
Tilgate Wlk 17 M9..... 64 E3
Tillard Ave SK3........ 123 B8
Tillerman Cl M27....... 80 D8
Tillhey Rd M22.......... 121 D2
Tillington Cl 3 BL1..... 143 B3
Tilney Ave M32......... 96 E1
Tilshead Wlk M13...... 163 C2
Tilside Gr BL6.......... 40 B7
Tilson Rd M23........... 120 F5
Tilstock Wlk M23....... 120 E8
Tilston Wlk 18 SK9.... 131 E1
Tilton St OL1........... 49 C1
Timberbottom BL2...... 25 C4
Timbercliffe OL15...... 6 D1
Timberhurst BL9....... 28 D2
Timbersbrook Gr 5 SK9. 131 D2
Times Ret Pk OL10..... 29 C2
Times St M24........... 65 B8
Timothy Cl M6.......... 80 F6
TIMPERLEY............. 120 B7
Timperley Cl OL8....... 67 B2
Timperley Fold OL6.... 85 C6
Timperley La WN7...... 76 B2
Timperley Metro Sta
WA15..................... 119 F8
Timperley Rd OL6...... 85 C6
Timperley St M11...... 165 C4
Timpson Rd M23........ 120 E7
Timsbury Cl BL1........ 42 F5
Timson St 2 M35....... 83 F7
Tindall St
Eccles M30................ 95 B8
Reddish SK5.............. 99 F3
Tindle St M28.......... 60 F3
Tinkersfield WN7....... 75 D7
Tinline St BL9.......... 141 A2
Tinningham Cl 7 M11... 99 E7
Tinsdale Wlk M24...... 46 C1
Tinshill Cl M12......... 165 A1
Tinsley Cl M40......... 160 B2
Tinsley Gr BL2.......... 148 B4
Tin St BL3............... 145 B1
Tintagel Ct
Little Lever M26.......... 43 C5
Stalybridge SK15......... 85 F2
Tintagel Rd WN2....... 57 A4
Tintagel Wlk SK14..... 102 E3
Tintern Ave
Ashton-in-M WN4........ 73 D3
Bolton BL2................ 25 B2
Heywood OL10........... 29 C4
Littleborough OL15...... 16 A7
Manchester M20.......... 109 F5
Rochdale OL16........... 14 E2
Tyldesley M29............ 77 C7
Urmston M41.............. 107 A8
Whitefield M45........... 44 F1
Tintern Cl SK12........ 133 D5
Tintern Ct M20......... 109 F5
Tintern Dr WA15....... 120 C2
Tintern Gr SK1.......... 112 B1
Tintern Pl OL10........ 29 C4
Tintern Rd
Cheadle SK8.............. 132 B6
Middleton M24............ 47 A4
Tintern St M14........... 98 B2
TINTWISTLE........... 104 B8
Tintwistle CE Prim Sch
SK13..................... 103 F6
Tinwald Pl WN1........ 37 F1
Tipperary St SK15..... 86 E5
Tipping St
Altrincham WA14......... 119 D3
Wigan WN3............... 150 B2
Tipton Cl
Cheadle SK8.............. 123 B4
Radcliffe M26............. 43 D5
Tipton Dr M23.......... 109 B2
Tiptree Wlk 3 M9...... 157 B4
Tiree Cl SK7............ 124 F1
Tirza Ave M19.......... 110 F8
Tissington Bank 27 SK13. 171 A1
Tissington Gr 20 SK13. 171 A1
Tissington Terr 22 SK13. 171 A1
Titchfield Rd OL8...... 67 C4
Tithe Barn Cl OL12.... 15 D4
Tithe Barn Cres 1 BL1. 25 A4

Tithe Barn Ct SK4...... 110 F4
Tithe Barn Prim Sch
SK4....................... 168 A3
Tithebarn Rd
Altrincham WA15......... 129 C8
Garswood WN4........... 72 D2
Tithe Barn Rd SK4...... 110 F4
Tithebarn St
1 Bury BL9............... 140 C2
Radcliffe M26............. 44 D4
Up Holland WN8.......... 53 B7
Tithe Barn St 6 BL5.... 39 E1
Titian Rise OL1......... 49 D5
Titterington Ave M21.. 97 B2
Tiverton Ave
Hindley WN7.............. 57 D2
Sale M33.................. 107 F3
Tiverton Cl
Little Lever M26.......... 43 C5
Tyldesley M29............ 77 D7
Tiverton Dr
Handforth SK9............ 131 D1
Sale M33.................. 107 F3
Tiverton Ho M6......... 80 A3
Tiverton Pl OL7........ 85 A5
Tiverton Rd M41........ 95 E3
Tiverton Wlk BL1....... 142 C1
Tiviot Dale SK1......... 169 C2
Tiviot Way SK1, SK5... 169 C3
Tivoli St M3............. 158 B1
Tixall Wlk 3 M8......... 63 E2
**T'mimei Lev Sch M8...... 63 E1
Toad La OL12........... 139 C4
Toad Pond Cl M27...... 79 C6
Tobermory Cl M11...... 83 D1
Tobermory Rd SK8..... 122 C1
Toddington La WN2.... 38 B8
Todd's Pl M9........... 64 C1
Todd St
Bury BL9.................. 140 C4
Glossop SK13............. 116 D8
Heywood OL16........... 29 A2
Manchester M3.......... 159 A2
Rochdale OL16........... 31 A7
Salford M7................ 155 A2
Todmorden Rd
Calderbrook OL15........ 6 D2
Littleborough OL15...... 16 C7
Toft Wlk M18........... 99 C4
Toft Way SK9........... 131 E4
Toledo St M11.......... 83 D1
Tolland La WA15........ 128 F8
Tollard Ave M40....... 157 A1
Tollard Cl SK8.......... 132 B6
Toll Bar Bsns Pk 11 OL13. 3 D8
Tollbar St SK1.......... 170 C4
Toll Bar St M12........ 164 B2
Tollemache Ct SK14... 103 A5
Tollemache Rd SK14... 103 A5
Tollesbury Cl M40...... 160 A4
Toll Gate Cl M13....... 98 E4
Tollgate Way OL16..... 31 C8
Toll Green Cl WN2..... 56 A7
Toll St
Platt Bridge WN2......... 56 A1
Radcliffe M26............. 43 D4
Tolworth Dr M8........ 156 B3
Tomcroft La M34....... 100 D2
Tomlinson Cl OL8....... 153 B1
Tomlinson St
Horwich BL6.............. 22 B3
Manchester, Hulme M15. 162 B2
Manchester M40.......... 65 C3
Rochdale OL11........... 30 C4
Tomlin Sq 8 BL2....... 148 C3
Tom Lomas Wlk M11... 83 B2
Tommy Browell Cl 9
M14...................... 98 A3
Tommy Johnson Wlk 7
M14...................... 98 A3
Tommy La BL2.......... 26 C1
Tommy Taylor Cl 1 M40. 83 C5
Tom Shepley St SK14... 167 B2
Tomwood Rise SK13... 115 C6
TONACLIFFE........... 14 C6
Tonacliffe Prim Sch OL12 14 C6
Tonacliffe Rd OL12..... 14 C6
Tonacliffe Terr OL12... 14 C7
Tonacliffe Way OL12... 14 C6
Tonbridge Cl BL8....... 27 C7
Tonbridge Pl 3 BL2.... 25 B1
Tonbridge Rd
Manchester M19.......... 111 B8
Reddish SK5.............. 111 F8
Tonge Bridge Ind Est
BL2....................... 148 B4
Tonge Bridge Way BL2. 148 B4
Tonge Cl M45........... 45 B1
Tonge Clough BL2...... 24 F8
Tonge Ct M24........... 65 B8
Tonge Fold Rd BL2..... 148 C3
Tonge Gn SK15......... 102 E6
Tonge Hall Cl M24..... 65 B8
Tonge Mdw M24........ 65 B8
TONGE MOOR.......... 25 B1
Tonge Moor Prim Sch 32
BL2....................... 25 B1
Tonge Moor Rd BL2.... 25 B2
TONG END.............. 4 C2
Tong End OL12......... 4 C2
Tonge Old Rd BL2...... 148 C3
Tonge Park Ave BL2.... 25 C1
Tonge Roughs M24.... 65 D8
Tonge St
Heywood OL16........... 29 D2
Manchester M12.......... 164 A3
Rochdale OL16........... 31 A6

Tongfields BL7 .... 24 F8
Tong Head Ave BL1 ... 25 B4
Tong La
  Britannia OL13. ...... 4 C8
  Whitworth OL12. ..... 4 D1
Tongley Wlk 15 M40. .. 65 D2
Tong Rd BL3 .... 43 A5
Tong St BL4 .... 61 C5
Tonman St M3. .... 162 B4
TONTINE 53 D5
Tontine WN5 .... 53 C5
Tontine Rd WN5, WN8 . 53 C6
Toogood La WN6 ...... 18 D6
Tooley Ho M30 .... 95 D8
Toon Cres BL8 .... 80 C3
Tootal Dr M5, M6.. .... 80 C3
Tootal Drive Prim Sch 5
  M6 .... 80 C3
Tootal Gr M5 .... 80 C2
Tootal Rd M5. .... 154 A2
Toothill Cl WN4 ...... 73 B5
Topcliffe Rd M9 ...... 65 B3
Topcliffe St WN2. ..... 56 F6
Topcroft Cl M22 ...... 121 E8
Topfield Rd M22 ...... 121 C4
Topgate Brow M27. .... 80 D8
Topham St BL9 .... 45 A8
Topley St M40 .... 157 A2
TOP LOCK 38 B2
TOP OF HEAP 29 A1
Top of Heap OL10 ..... 28 F2
TOP OF HEBERS 46 F3
Top of Wallsuches BL6.. 22 F4
TOP O' TH' BROW 25 D2
Top o' th' Close Rd OL14. 6 C6
Top o' The Fields M45.. 62 F7
Top o' th' Gn OL9 ..... 66 C4
Top o' th' La BL2..... 42 D5
TOP O' TH' MEADOWS ... 50 A1
Top o' th' Meadows La
  OL4 .... 50 A1
Top Park Cl WA13. .... 105 E1
Topphome Ct BL4. ..... 60 E7
TOPPING FOLD 28 D3
Topping Fold Rd BL9.. . 141 C3
Topping Ho BL1 .... 143 B1
TOPPINGS 25 B8
Toppings Gdn BL7.. .... 25 A7
Topping St
  Bolton BL1 .... 143 B1
  Bury BL9 .... 141 A3
Toppings The SK6 ..... 113 A3
Topp St BL4 .... 60 E7
Topp Way BL1 .... 145 B4
Top Schwabe St M24. .. 64 C8
Topsham Wlk M40 .... 83 D5
Topside OL1. .... 48 E1
Top St
  Middleton M24. ..... 46 F1
  Oldham OL4 .... 67 D8
  Todmorden OL14. .... 5 F7
Torah St M8 .... 159 A4
Tor Ave BL8 .... 10 F2
Torbay Cl 1 BL3. ...... 144 C1
Torbay Dr SK2. .... 124 B7
Torbay Rd
  Manchester M21 ..... 109 C8
  Urmston M41. .... 95 C1
Torbrook Gr 1 SK9 .... 131 D2
Torcross Rd M9. ...... 64 B5
Tor End Rd BB4....... 1 A4
Tor Hey Mews BL8..... 10 F2
TORKINGTON 125 A2
Torkington Ave M27 ... 61 F1
Torkington Ho SK7.. ... 124 F2
Torkington La SK6, SK7. 125 B3
Torkington Manor SK7. . 125 B3
TORKINGTON PARK...... 125 A2
Torkington Prim Sch
  SK7................ 125 A2
Torkington Rd
  Gatley SK8.......... 122 B5
  Hazel Grove SK7 .... 125 B3
  Hazel Grove, Torkington Park
  SK7............... 124 F2
  Wilmslow SK9 ...... 137 D6
Torkington St SK3 .... 170 A4
Torksey Wlk M9 ...... 64 C5
Torness Wlk M11 ..... 83 B1
Toronto Ave M90 ..... 130 B7
Toronto Rd SK2. ...... 124 A6
Toronto St BL2 .... 42 E8
Torpoint Wlk 2 M40 .. 65 C1
Torquay Cl M13. ...... 164 A2
Torquay Dr WN5. ..... 71 E8
Torquay Gr SK2. ...... 124 B4
Torra Barn Cl BL7.... 8 E3
Torrax Cl M6. .... 80 B6
Torre Cl M24 .... 47 A3
Torrens St M6 .... 80 D5
Torridon Cl WN6.. .... 37 B7
Torridon Rd BL2. ..... 42 F7
Torridon Wlk 1 M22... 121 C1
Torrin Cl SK3. .... 170 C1
Torrington Ave
  Bolton BL1.......... 143 B3
  Manchester M9 ...... 65 A3
Torrington Dr SK14 ... 102 E2
Torrington Rd M27.. ... 80 B6
Torrington St OL10.. ... 46 E8
Torrisdale Cl BL3 ..... 144 B1
Torside Cl WN4 .... 73 A4
Torside Mews SK13 ... 104 A6
Torside Way
  Glossop SK13........ 104 A5
  Swinton M27 .... 61 F2
Torver Cl WN3 .... 55 A2

Torver Dr
  Bolton BL2.......... 42 F8
  Middleton M24....... 46 D2
Torver Wlk 1 SK2 .... 124 B7
Tor View Sch BB4 ..... 1 D8
Torwood Rd OL9 ...... 47 E1
Totland Cl M12 .... 99 B3
Totley Ave 42 SK13.. . 171 A1
Totley Cl 47 SK13 .... 171 A1
Totley Gdns 46 SK13.. 171 A1
Totley La 28 SK13..... 171 A1
Totley Lanes 43 SK13.. 171 A1
Totley Mews 20 SK13.. 171 A1
Totley Pl 45 SK13 .... 171 A1
Totnes Ave
  Chadderton OL9...... 47 F1
  Stockport SK7....... 124 A2
Totnes Rd
  Manchester M21 ..... 109 C8
  Sale M33 .... 107 D5
Totridge Cl SK2....... 124 D5
Tottenham Dr M23.. ... 120 E7
TOTTINGTON 26 E6
Tottington Ave OL4 ... 67 F7
Tottington High Sch BL8. 26 F6
Tottington La M25 .... 62 F5
Tottington Prim Sch BL8. 26 F5
Tottington Rd
  Bolton BL7, BL8...... 9 F2
  Bolton, Harwood Lee BL2.. 25 E6
  Bury BL8 .... 27 C4
Tottington St M11 .... 83 C2
Totton Rd M35........ 83 F7
Touch Hall Rd M24.. .. 47 D4
Touch Rd BL9 .... 27 E7
Touchstones* OL16... 139 B3
Toulston Rd WN6 ..... 36 F2
Tours Ave M23........ 109 A2
Towcester Cl M4...... 160 A1
Tower Ave BL0........ 138 A1
Tower Ct
  Bury BL8 .... 27 A8
  Chapeltown BL7..... 9 C4
Tower Gr WN7...... 76 D6
Tower Grange M7 .... 155 A4
Tower Hill Rd WN8.... 53 B6
Tower Nook WN8 ..... 53 A5
Towers Ave BL3....... 146 A4
Towers Bsns Pk M20.. 110 B1
Towers Cl SK12....... 133 F5
Tower Sq M13........ 163 C2
Towers Rd SK12 ...... 133 F5
Towers St 2 OL4 ..... 49 D1
Tower St
  Chapeltown BL7..... 9 C4
  Heywood OL10....... 29 C2
  Hyde SK14.......... 167 A1
  Radcliffe M26....... 44 D4
  Stalybridge SK16.... 86 B8
Towers Yard Barns SK12. 133 F5
Tower View BL6 ...... 21 C3
Towey Cl M18 .... 99 D6
Towncliffe Wlk 21 M15. 162 A2
Towncroft M34 .... 101 A4
Towncroft Ave M24.. .. 46 F2
Towncroft La BL1..... 40 E8
Townend St SK14 .... 167 A1
Townfield M41........ 95 B1
Townfield Ave WN4 .. 73 B2
Townfield Gdns WA14.. 119 D5
Townfield La WA13 ... 117 B7
Townfield Rd WA14 .. 119 D5
Townfields WN4 ..... 73 A3
Town Fields Cl BL9.... 140 C1
Townfield St 9 OL4... 67 B7
Townfield Wlk 15 M15.. 162 A2
Town Fold SK6....... 126 B2
Town Gate Bsns Ctr M38. 59 E5
Town Gate Dr M41..... 94 C2
TOWN GREEN 73 C4
Town Hall La 11 M2.. . 158 C1
Town Hall Sq OL16.... 139 C3
TOWN HEAD 139 C4
Town House Rd OL15... 16 B6
Town La
  Broadbottom SK13.... 115 D6
  Coppull PR7......... 19 B8
  Denton M34......... 100 E2
  Dukinfield SK16..... 101 C8
TOWN LANE 77 B4
Town Lane Ct M34 ... 100 E2
Townley Fold SK14.. ... 102 B6
Townley Rd OL16..... 32 A6
Townley St
  Manchester, Beswick
  M11............... 164 C4
  Middleton M24...... 65 A8
  Salford M8......... 155 C1
Town Mdws OL16 .... 139 B3
Town Mill Brow OL12.. 139 B3
TOWN OF LOWTON 90 B5
Townrow St OL10 .... 29 E2
Townscliffe La SK6.. ... 126 C6
TOWNSEND FOLD 1 E8
Townsend Rd M27 .... 61 F1
Townsend St M3...... 158 B4
Townsfield Rd BL5.... 57 B7
TOWNS GATE 94 C2
Townsgate Way M44.. 94 B1
Townside Row WN5.... 140 C1
Townsley Gr OL4..... 85 E5
Townson Dr WN7..... 75 F1
Town Sq M33........ 108 B4
Town Square Sh Ctr OL1 153 B2
Town St SK6......... 126 B7
Town's View SK15 .... 86 B1
Towton St M9 .... 157 B4
Towyn Ave M5........ 81 A2

Toxhead Cl BL6 ...... 22 A3
Toxteth St M11 ...... 99 F7
Tracey St 8 M8 ...... 64 A1
Tracks La WN5 ...... 53 D3
Tracy Dr WA12...... 89 E3
Traders Ave M41..... 95 E6
Trafalgar Ave
  Droylsden M34...... 100 C7
  Poynton SK12....... 134 A3
Trafalgar Bsns Pk M8. 158 B4
Trafalgar Cl SK12 .... 134 A3
Trafalgar Ct
  Bury BL9 .... 140 B1
  Manchester M16 ..... 97 E2
Trafalgar Gr M7 ..... 155 A1
Trafalgar Ho M40.... 100 C7
Trafalgar Pl M20 .... 110 A4
Trafalgar Rd
  Hindley WN2 .... 56 D5
  Sale M33 .... 108 C6
  Salford M6......... 80 A3
  Wigan WN1 .... 37 C1
Trafalgar Sq 9 OL7.. . 84 F1
Trafalgar St
  Ashton-u-L OL7 ..... 84 F1
  Oldham OL1........ 153 B4
  Rochdale OL16...... 31 A8
  Salford M7......... 155 B1
Trafalgar Wlk
  Manchester, Beswick
  M11............... 165 A4
  Manchester, Old Trafford
  M16............... 96 D5
Trafford Ave M41 .... 95 E3
Trafford Bank Rd M16.. 161 C1
Trafford Bar Metro Sta
  M16............... 161 B1
Trafford Coll (Altrincham)
  WA14 .... 119 D8
Trafford Coll (Manchester
  Music Base) M1 .... 159 B1
Trafford Coll (Talbot Rd)
  M32............... 96 F4
Trafford Coll (Technology
  Ctr) M32 .... 96 F4
Trafford Ct 7 M15.... 162 A2
Trafford Ctr The (Sh Ctr)
  M17............... 95 E6
Trafford Dr
  Sale WA15 .... 120 B8
  Walkden M38....... 59 D8
Trafford Ecology Park Nature
  Reserve* M17...... 96 C8
Trafford General Hospl
  M41............... 95 A3
Trafford Gr
  Farnworth BL4...... 42 E1
  Stretford M32 ...... 96 E1
Trafford Mans 2 M16.. 97 B2
TRAFFORD PARK 96 B6
Trafford Park Rd
  Manchester M17 .... 161 A1
  Stretford M17 ...... 96 D6
Trafford Park Sta M32.. 96 C3
Trafford Pl
  Manchester M15 .... 162 A2
  Wilmslow SK9 ...... 137 D6
Trafford Quays Leisure
  Village M17 .... 95 B6
Trafford Rd
  Alderley Edge SK9... 137 B1
  Eccles M30 .... 79 D1
  Handforth SK9...... 131 B1
  Hindley WN2....... 56 C5
  Salford M5, M16, M17... 161 A3
  Trafford Ret Pk M41.. 95 C5
Trafford St
  Farnworth BL4...... 42 D1
  Manchester M1, M3.. 162 C4
  Oldham OL8 .... 153 B1
  Rochdale OL11...... 139 B1
Trafford Wharf Est M17. 96 C4
Trafford Wharf Rd M17. 96 E6
Tragan Cl SK2 ...... 124 D6
Tragan Dr SK2....... 124 D6
Trail St M6......... 154 B2
Trail View SK13 ..... 104 B5
Trajan Ho OL1 ...... 153 C3
Tramore Wlk M22.... 121 E2
Tram St
  Manchester M11.... 165 C4
  Platt Bridge WN2.... 56 A1
Tramway Rd
  Ashton-u-L OL6 .... 166 C3
  Irlam M44 .... 105 F7
Tranby Cl M22...... 121 F4
Tranmere Cl M18 .... 165 B1
Tranmere Dr SK9 .... 131 E2
Tranmere Rd 1 SK3.. 123 B8
Trans Pennine Trad Est
  OL11.............. 30 D3
Transvaal St M11 .... 83 D1
Travers St BL6....... 22 D1
Travis Brow SK4 ..... 169 A1
Travis Ct OL2 .... 48 E4
Travis Ho OL14 ..... 6 A7
Travis St
  Hyde SK14......... 167 B2
  Manchester M1..... 163 C4
  Newhey OL16....... 32 B4
  Shaw OL2.......... 149 C3
Trawden Ave BL1 .... 142 C2
Trawden Dr BL9 ..... 27 E8
Trawden Gn SK2..... 124 D4
Traylen Way OL12 ... 14 A4
Traynor Cl M24 ..... 46 F1
Trecastell Cl WN1.. ... 37 F1
Tredcroft St SK13 ... 116 B8

Tredgold St BL6 ..... 22 C2
Tree Ave M43........ 84 A3
Tree Ct M14......... 98 C3
Tree House Ave 2 OL7.. 85 A6
Treelands Wlk M5 ... 161 B2
Treen Rd M29 .... 76 C8
Tree Tops BL7 .... 25 C6
Treetops Ave BL0 .... 11 A3
Treetops Cl
  Marple SK6 .... 125 E7
  Uppermill OL3 ..... 50 F1
Tree Wlk M32....... 96 C5
Trefoil Way OL5 ..... 15 F6
Tregaer Fold M24.... 65 C8
Tregaron Gr WN2.... 57 A3
Tremain Wlk 10 M9.. 157 A3
Trenam Pl M5 .... 81 B2
Trenant Rd M6 ...... 154 A4
Trenchard Ct M11, M43.. 83 D2
Trenchard Dr M22 ... 130 F7
Trencherbone M26.... 43 E5
Trencherfield Mill Steam
  Engine* WN3 ...... 150 B3
Trengrove St 7 OL12. 14 C1
Trent Ave
  Chadderton OL9..... 65 E8
  Heywood OL10...... 29 A3
  Milnrow OL16...... 32 A6
Trent Bridge Wlk M16.. 97 A3
Trent Cl
  Bramhall SK7...... 132 C6
  Brinnington SK5.... 112 C5
  Culcheth WA3 ...... 92 A2
Trent Ct
  Manchester M15 .... 162 A2
  Stockport SK3 ..... 170 A3
Trent Dr
  Bury BL9 .... 27 F8
  Hindley WN2....... 57 C3
  Walkden M28....... 60 B2
Trent Gr WN7....... 75 C4
Trentham Ave
  Farnworth BL4..... 42 C1
  Manchester SK4 .... 110 F4
Trentham Cl BL4 .... 42 C1
Trentham Gr M40 ... 65 A1
Trentham Lawns M6.. 81 B4
Trentham Rd M16.... 97 A3
Trentham St
  Farnworth BL4..... 42 C1
  Salford M15....... 161 C3
  Swinton M27 ...... 61 E1
Trent Ind Est Cl OL2.. 149 B4
Trent Rd
  Ashton-in-M WN4 .. 73 E5
  Billinge WN5 ...... 71 D3
  Shaw OL2.......... 149 A4
  Wigan WN5 .... 54 C7
Trent St OL16....... 31 B6
Trent Way M4....... 61 B5
Tresco Ave M20..... 110 C3
Trescott Mews WN6.. 36 F8
Treswell Ct WN2.... 56 E2
Trevarrick Ct
  Horwich BL6....... 22 E2
  2 Oldham OL4..... 67 C8
Trevelyan Dr WN5 .. 53 D1
Trevelyan St M30 ... 80 A2
Trevor Ave
  Bolton BL3........ 147 A3
  Sale M33 .... 107 F2
Trevor Gr SK1 ..... 124 A8
Trevor Rd
  Eccles M30 .... 79 B3
  Swinton M27 ..... 79 E6
  Urmston M41..... 95 A2
Trevor St
  Manchester M11.... 99 F7
  Rochdale OL11..... 30 C4
Triangle Sh Ctr The M4.. 158 C2
Triangle The WN1..... 150 B7
Tribune Ave WA14 ... 119 B7
Trident Rd M30 ...... 94 F7
Trillo Ave BL2 ...... 148 B2
Trimdon Cl M11 ..... 83 B2
Trimingham Dr BL8 .. 27 D5
Trimley Ave M40 .... 157 B1
Tring Wlk M9....... 64 B3
Trinity Ave M33 ..... 108 D4
Trinity Bridges OL5.. 56 A1
Trinity CE High Sch M15 163 A2
Trinity Cl SK16...... 101 E8
Trinity Cres M28 .... 60 E3
Trinity Ct
  Ashton-u-L OL6 .... 166 A3
  Salford M3........ 158 A2
Trinity Gdns
  Ashton-in-M WN4 ... 72 F4
  Salford M3........ 158 A2
  Stockport SK3 ..... 123 F3
Trinity Gn BL0 ...... 11 B2
Trinity Ho OL1 ...... 153 B4
Trinity Rd M33 ...... 108 D4
Trinity Ret Pk BL2.... 148 A2
Trinity Row Ind Est M3. 158 A1
Trinity Sch SK15 ..... 85 F1
Trinity St
  8 Bacup OL13...... 3 C8
  Bolton BL3......... 145 C2
  Bury BL9 .... 140 C1
  Marple SK6 .... 125 F6
  2 Middleton M24... 64 F8
  Oldham OL1........ 153 B4
  Rochdale OL11...... 13 E2
  Stalybridge SK15.... 86 A1
Trinity The BL3 ..... 145 B1

Trinity Way M3 ..... 158 B2
Trinity Wlk 13 M14.. . 98 B3
Trippier Rd M30 ..... 94 F8
Tripps Mews M20.... 109 F4
Triscombe Way M16.. 97 E3
Tristam Cl M13 ..... 163 C3
Trojan Gdns 7 M7.. . 81 C5
Trongate Wlk 18 M9.. 157 B3
Troon Cl
  Bolton BL3......... 40 F3
  Bramhall SK7....... 133 A7
Troon Dr SK8 .... 122 C1
Troon Rd M23 ...... 120 F6
TROUGH GATE 67 E1
Trough Gate OL8..... 66 D2
Troutbeck Ave M4 ... 160 A2
Troutbeck Cl BL8 .... 10 B2
Troutbeck Dr
  Ramsbottom BL0 ... 138 C3
  Tyldesley M29 ..... 77 A7
Troutbeck Gr WA11.. 71 B2
Troutbeck Rd
  Altrincham WA15.... 120 D5
  Ashton-in-M WN4 ... 73 C5
  Gatley SK8......... 122 B3
Troutbeck Rise WN5.. 54 B6
Troutbeck Way OL11.. 30 B4
Troutbeck Wlk 5 OL2.. 48 E4
Trowbridge Dr M40 .. 65 C1
Trowbridge Rd M34.. 101 A1
Trows La OL11...... 30 D1
Trowtree Ave M12 ... 164 B2
Troydale Dr M40..... 83 B6
Troy Wlk M5........ 161 B3
TRUB 47 D8
Trumpet St M1 ..... 162 C4
Truro Ave
  Ashton-u-L OL6 .... 85 D7
  Brinnington SK5.... 112 C5
  Stretford M32 ..... 96 E2
Truro Cl
  Bramhall SK7...... 132 F7
  Bury BL8 .... 140 A3
Truro Dr M33....... 107 D4
Truro Rd
  Chadderton OL9.... 48 A1
  Tyldesley M29 ..... 77 C8
Truro Wlk M34..... 100 F1
Trust Rd M18 ...... 99 C3
Tucana Ave M7 ..... 81 C3
Tucker's Hill Brow WN2. 21 B1
Tudbury Way M3.... 158 A2
Tudor Ave
  Bolton BL1........ 144 B3
  Failsworth OL9 .... 65 D3
  Farnworth BL4..... 60 B7
  Manchester M9 ... 64 E1
  Stalybridge SK15... 86 D3
Tudor Cl
  Mossley OL5 ...... 68 E1
  Reddish SK5....... 111 E7
Tudor Ct
  Bolton BL1........ 145 B4
  Leigh WN7 .... 76 C5
  Manchester, Old Trafford
  M16............. 161 C1
  Manchester, Sedgley Park
  M25............. 63 C3
  Rochdale OL12.... 15 B1
Tudor Gn SK9...... 131 E1
Tudor Gr
  Middleton M24.... 46 D3
  Wigan WN3 ...... 54 E2
Tudor Hall St OL11.. 30 C2
Tudor Ho M21 ..... 109 F8
Tudor Ind Est SK16.. 101 A7
Tudor Rd
  Altrincham WA15... 119 B7
  Handforth SK9..... 131 E1
Tudor St
  8 Bolton BL3..... 146 C4
  Middleton M24.... 65 B8
  Oldham OL8....... 153 A1
  Shaw OL2......... 149 B3
Tuffley Rd M23 ..... 121 A3
Tufton Wlk M9 ..... 157 A3
Tugford Cl 9 M16.... 97 E4
Tuley St M11 .... 164 C3
Tulip Ave
  Farnworth BL4..... 42 A1
  Kearsley BL4...... 60 F5
Tulip Cl
  Chadderton OL9.... 65 E7
  Sale M33 .... 107 C4
  Stockport SK3 ..... 170 A1
Tulip Dr
  Altrincham WA15... 119 F6
  Wigan WN6 ...... 36 F3
Tulip Gr OL12 ..... 14 E3
Tulip Rd M31 ...... 105 E2
Tulip Wlk M7....... 158 A4
Tulketh Ind Est M40.. 83 A8
Tulle Ct M25....... 63 A4
Tully St M7........ 155 B3
Tully Street S M7 ... 155 B2
Tulpen Sq OL9 ..... 152 B3
Tulworth Rd SK12.... 133 D4
Tumblewood Dr SK8.. 122 E4
Tumbling Bank M9.... 64 D3
Tumbling Bank Terr OL4. 67 F5
Tunbridge Sq M5 .... 81 A2
Tunicliffe's New Row
  WN7.............. 75 C5
Tunley La WN6 ..... 18 E5
Tunley Moss WN6.... 18 E4

TUNSHILL 32 D7
Tunshill Gr OL16 32 A6
Tunshill La OL16 32 C7
Tunshill Rd M23 108 E1
Tuns Rd OL8 67 B2
Tunstall Cl BL9 45 A7
Tunstall La WN5 54 D5
Tunstall Rd OL4 67 C6
Tunstall St
2 Manchester M11 99 E7
Stockport SK4 169 B2
TUNSTEAD 69 D5
Tunstead Ave M20 109 F6
Tunstead La OL3 69 D5
Tunstead Mill Terr 3 OL13 3 B8
Tunstead Rd OL13 3 C8
Tupelo St M13 164 A1
Turbary Wlk OL16 31 D6
Turf Cl OL2 48 E3
TURF HILL 31 C4
Turf Hill Rd OL16 31 C4
Turf House Cl OL15 15 F7
Turf La
Chadderton OL9 66 A3
Royton OL2 48 F3
Turfland Ave OL2 48 F3
Turf Lea Rd SK6 126 B1
Turf Park Rd OL2 48 F3
Turf Pit La OL4 49 F4
Turf St M26 43 F3
Turf Terr OL15 16 A6
Turfton Rd OL2 48 F3
Turks Rd M26 43 E5
Turk St 4 BL1 144 C4
Turley St M8 156 B2
TURN 2 A1
Turnberry BL3 40 F3
Turnberry Cl M29 77 C8
Turnberry Dr SK9 137 D8
Turnberry Rd SK8 122 C1
Turnberry Wlk M8 156 C4
Turnbull Ave M25 63 C7
Turnbull Rd
Altrincham WA14 119 C8
Manchester M13 98 F2
Reddish M18 99 F4
Turnbury Cl M33 108 B6
Turnbury Rd M22 121 E5
Turncliff Cres SK6 125 D7
Turncroft La SK1 112 B1
Turncroft Way M28 77 F7
Turnditch Cl WN6 37 A4
Turnell Way M28 79 A5
Turner Ave
Failsworth M35 83 E6
Irlam M44 94 A3
Leigh WN2 56 E1
Turner Bridge Rd BL2 148 C4
Turner Dr M41 95 F2
Turnerford Cl BL7 8 E1
Turner Gdns SK14 167 B4
Turner La
Ashton-u-L OL6 166 B4
Brinnington SK6 112 F6
Hyde SK14 167 C4
Turner Rd SK6 125 F5
Turner's Pl OL12 14 E3
Turner St
Ashton-u-L OL6 166 B4
1 Bacup OL13 3 C8
Bolton BL1 148 A4
Denton M34 100 E5
Droylsden M11 83 C1
Leigh WN7 76 A4
Manchester, Gorton M18 99 D5
Manchester M4 159 A2
Manchester, Old Trafford M16 161 C2
Oldham OL4 67 E8
Rochdale OL12 14 E1
Salford M7 155 B3
Stockport SK1 169 C2
Westhoughton BL5 57 E5
Wigan WN1 37 D1
Turnfield Cl 9 OL16 15 D3
Turnfield Ho SK8 122 D3
Turnfield Rd SK8 122 D3
Turnhill Rd OL16 31 B3
Turnill Dr WN4 73 B2
Turnlee Cl SK13 116 C7
Turnlee Dr SK13 116 C7
Turnlee Rd SK13 116 C7
Turn Moss Rd M21, M32 96 F1
Turnough Rd OL16 31 F7
Turnpike Cl
Diggle OL3 51 C5
5 Rochdale OL12 14 D2
Turnpike Gn 1 M6 154 C3
Turnpike The SK6 125 D7
Turnpike Wlk M11 160 C1
Turn Rd BL0 11 E8
Turn St OL6 85 D4
Turnstone Ave WA12 89 C4
Turnstone Cl WN7 76 A6
Turnstone Rd
2 Bolton BL2 148 A2
Hazel Grove SK2 125 A5
Turret Hall Dr 1 WA3 90 E8
Turriff Gr WN2 56 A8
Turton Ave BL3 43 A4
TURTON BOTTOMS 9 D4
Turton Cl
Bury BL8 44 A8
Heywood OL10 29 A2
Turton Com L Ctr BL7 25 B7
Turton Ct 1 BL1 148 A4
Turton & Edgworth CE Methodist Prim Sch BL7 9 D5
Turton High Sch Media Arts Coll BL7 25 B7
Turton Hts BL2 25 B6
Turton La M25 62 F5
Turton Rd
Bolton BL2, BL7 25 C5
Bury BL8 26 D8
Turton St
Bolton BL1 148 A4
Golborne WA3 90 A8
Manchester M11 99 D7
Turton Tower* BL7 9 C3
Turves Rd SK8 122 F1
Turville Ho SK9 131 D2
Turvin Rd OL15 7 D2
Tuscan Rd M20 122 B8
Tuscany Ho 2 M1 163 A4
Tuscany View M7 81 B8
Tutbury St M4 160 A1
Tutor Bank Dr WA12 89 D3
Tuxford Wlk M40 157 A1
Tweedale St OL11 139 B2
Tweedale Way M35, OL9 66 A1
Tweed Cl
Altrincham WA14 119 C6
Oldham OL8 153 B1
Tweedle Hill Rd M9 64 C4
Tweed St WN7 76 B4
Tweed Street Ind Est 6 WN7 76 B4
Tweenbrook Ave M23 121 A3
Tweesdale Cl M45 45 B1
Twelve Apostles RC Prim Sch WN7 75 D8
Twelve Yards Rd M44 93 D4
Twigworth Rd M22 121 C2
Twillbrook Dr M3 158 B3
Twinegate OL12 14 E3
Twine Valley Country Pk* BL0 12 A8
Twingates Cl OL2 149 B2
Twining Brook Rd SK8 123 B3
Twining Rd M17 95 E8
Twinnies Rd SK9 131 B1
Twin St OL10 29 E1
Twirl Hill Rd OL6 85 E8
Twisse Rd BL2 42 F7
TWISS GREEN 91 E4
Twiss Green Dr WA3 91 E4
Twiss Green La WA3 91 E4
Twiss Green Prim Sch WA3 91 E4
Twist Ave WA3 90 C8
Twist La WN7 75 E5
Two Acre Ave M22 121 C5
Two Acre Dr OL2 48 F7
Two Acre La OL4 50 B3
Two Bridges Rd OL16 32 C3
Two Brooks La BL8 10 B2
Two Trees La M34 101 A1
Two Trees Sports Coll M34 101 A1
Twyford Cl M20 109 F3
Tybyrne Cl M28 77 F7
Tydden St OL8 66 F3
Tydeman Wlk OL16 32 A5
Tyersall Cl M30 79 E4
TYLDESLEY 59 A1
Tyldesley Arc 11 WN1 150 C4
Tyldesley Old Rd M46 58 E2
Tyldesley Pas 5 M29 58 F1
Tyldesley Pool M29 58 F1
Tyldesley Prim Sch M29 77 B7
Tyldesley Rd M46 58 E2
Tyldesley St M14 98 A3
Tyler St SK9 137 A1
Tyler Wlk 2 WA3 90 F8
Tymm St M40 83 C8
Tyndall Ave M40 65 A1
Tyndall St OL4 67 C6
Tyne Ct M28 60 C3
Tynedale Cl SK5 111 F5
Tynesbank M28 60 C3
Tynesbank Cotts M28 60 C3
Tyne St 9 OL4 67 C7
Tyntesfield Prim Sch M33 107 E1
Tynwald St OL4 67 C7
Tynwell Wlk 2 M40 156 C1
Tyrer Ave WN3 54 F5
Tyrer Rd WA12 89 C1
Tyrol Wlk M11 164 C4
Tyrone Cl M23 120 D8
Tyrone Dr OL11 29 F5
Tyro St OL8 66 F3
Tyrrell Gr SK14 102 A1
Tyrrel Rd SK5 99 F1
Tysoe Gdns M3 158 A2
Tyson St M8 155 C4
Tytherington Dr M19 99 D1

U

Uganda St BL3 146 C2
Ukraine Rd M7 81 B6
Uldale Dr M24 46 E1
Ullesthorpe 13 OL12 139 B4
Ulleswater Cl BL3 42 F3
Ulleswater St BL1 143 C2
Ullock Wlk M24 46 D2
Ullswater Ave
Ashton-in-M WN4 73 B5
Ashton-u-L OL7 166 A4
Orrell WN5 53 F7
Ullswater Ave *continued*
Rochdale OL12 14 C1
Royton OL2 48 D7
Ullswater Ct WA3 74 C1
Ullswater Dr
Bury BL9 44 E7
Farnworth BL4 59 E7
Ince-in-M WN2 56 B7
Middleton M24 46 F2
Ullswater Gr OL10 46 D8
Ullswater Rd
Golborne WA3 74 C1
Handforth SK9 131 C4
Stockport SK1 124 B7
Tyldesley M29 77 B6
Urmston M41 94 E3
Wythenshawe M22 121 B2
Ullswater St WN7 75 E5
Ullswater Terr SK15 86 A4
Ullswater Wlk 26 M9 64 E3
Ulster Ave OL11 139 B1
Ulundi St M26 44 A3
Ulverston Ave
Chadderton OL9 152 A2
Manchester M20 109 F7
Ulverston Rd WN3 54 F3
Umberton Rd BL5 58 F7
Uncouth Rd OL16 31 E7
Underhill SK6 113 C2
Underhill Rd OL1 48 E1
Underhill Wlk M40 83 B4
Under La
Oldham, Factory Fold OL9 66 B3
Oldham OL4, OL5 68 B4
Underwood OL12 139 B3
Underwood Cl M18 99 F6
Underwood Court Apartments M27 80 E8
Underwood Rd
Alderley Edge SK9 137 C1
Hattersley SK14 102 D2
Underwood St SK16 101 B8
Underwood Terr 16 M29 59 A1
Underwood Villas OL15 15 E4
Underwood Way OL2 49 D8
Underwood Wlk 2 SK14 102 D2
Undsworth Ct 5 OL10 29 D2
Unicorn St M30 95 B8
Union Arc BL9 140 C2
Union Bldgs BL2 145 C2
Union Cl WN5 53 E5
Union Ct 13 OL13 3 C8
Union Rd
Ashton-u-L OL6 166 C4
Bolton BL2 25 A1
Marple SK6 125 F6
Rochdale OL12 15 E4
Union St
Ashton-u-L OL6 166 C3
Bacup OL13 3 C8
Bolton BL7 8 D2
Bury BL9 140 C2
Glossop SK13 116 C8
Hyde SK14 167 B2
Ince-in-M WN2 56 A8
Leigh WN7 75 F5
Manchester, Abbey Hey M18 99 E6
Manchester, Ardwick M12 163 C3
Manchester M4 159 A2
Manchester M14 98 B3
Middleton M24 47 A1
Oldham, County End OL4 67 E6
Oldham, Mumps OL1 67 A7
Oldham OL1 153 C2
Oldham, Werneth OL9 66 B4
Ramsbottom BL0 138 C2
Rochdale OL12, OL16 139 C4
Royton OL2 48 D3
Salford M6 81 A4
Stockport SK1 170 C4
Swinton M27 62 A1
Swinton M27 79 E8
Tyldesley M29 58 F1
Whitworth OL12 14 C8
Union Street W OL8 153 B2
Union Terr M7 155 C4
United Rd M17 96 F5
United Trad Est M17 96 F5
Unity Cl OL10 29 B1
Unity Cres OL10 29 B1
Unity Dr M7 155 C2
Unity St
Heywood OL10 29 B1
Walsden OL14 6 A8
Unity Way SK1 124 A8
Unity Wlk SK13 116 C7
University Rd M5, M6 81 B2
University Road W M5 81 B2
University Way BL3 145 B2
Univ of Bolton BL3 145 B2
Univ of Manchester M4 159 C2
Univ of Manchester The
Manchester M1 163 B4
Manchester M15 163 A1
Manchester, University M13 163 B2
Univ of Manchester The (Sch of Mechanical Aerospace & Civil Engineering) M30 94 D6
Univ of Salford
Salford M6 81 B4
Salford M6 81 C3
Univ of Salford (Adelphi Campus) M3 158 A2
UNSWORTH 45 C2
Unsworth Ave
Golborne WA3 74 E1
Unsworth Ave *continued*
Tyldesley M29 77 B8
Unsworth Prim Sch BL9 45 A2
Unsworth St
Bacup OL13 3 D7
Leigh WN7 75 E7
Radcliffe M26 43 F4
Tyldesley M29 59 B1
Unsworth Terr WN2 56 C5
Unsworth Way OL1 153 B4
Unwin Ave M18 99 D4
Unwin Ct M6 154 C2
Upavon Ct M7 155 C2
Upavon Rd M22 121 F3
Upcast La SK9 136 E3
UP HOLLAND 53 B6
Up Holland High Sch WN5 53 C4
Upholland Rd WN5 53 D2
Upland Dr
Ashton-in-M WN4 73 D4
Walkden M38 59 F6
Upland Rd OL8 66 E4
Uplands M24 65 A7
Uplands Ave M26 44 C2
Uplands Rd
Compstall SK14 114 A6
Flixton M41 106 E8
Glossop SK13 116 D8
Uplands The OL5 68 D1
Upper Brook St
Manchester M13 163 B2
Stockport SK1 112 A1
Upper Broom Way BL5 40 A2
Upper Campfield Mkt M3 162 B4
Upper Camp St M7 155 A1
Upper Chorlton Rd M16 97 C3
Upper Cliff Hill OL2 32 C1
Upper Conran St M9 157 B4
Upper Cyrus St M40 160 B2
Upper Dicconson St WN1 37 C1
Upper Downs WA14 119 C3
Upper George St
23 Rochdale OL12 14 F1
Tyldesley M29 77 A8
Upper Gloucester St M6 81 A3
Upper Hayes Cl OL16 31 C8
Upper Helena St M40 160 B2
Upper Hibbert La SK6 125 F4
Upper Kent Rd M14 98 E3
Upper Lees Dr BL5 40 A1
Upper Lloyd St M14 98 A3
Upper Mead BL7 8 F1
Upper Medlock St M15 162 C2
UPPERMILL 69 A8
Uppermill Dr M19 110 E3
Upper Monsall St M40 157 B2
Upper Moss La M15 162 B2
Upper Park Rd
Manchester, Broughton Park M7 63 E1
Manchester M14 98 C4
Upper Passmonds Gr OL11 30 B8
Upper St Stephen St WN6 150 B4
Upper Stone Dr OL16 31 D6
Upper West Gr M13 164 A1
Upper Wharf St M5 81 C1
Upper Wilton St M25 63 C4
Uppingham Dr BL0 138 B3
Upton OL11 139 B2
Upton Ave
Cheadle SK8 132 A8
Manchester SK4 110 E4
Upton Cl
Golborne WA3 90 D8
Middleton M24 65 A5
Upton Dr WA14 119 E8
Upton La M29 77 C8
Upton Rd M46 58 E4
Upton Way
Bury BL8 26 F5
12 Handforth SK9 131 D5
Upton Wlk 10 OL7 166 A1
Upwood Rd WA3 90 D7
Upwood Wlk 31 M9 64 E3
Urban Ave WA15 119 E4
Urban Dr WA15 119 E4
Urban Exchange Ret Pk M4 159 B1
Urban Rd
Altrincham WA15 119 E4
Sale M33 108 A4
Urmson St OL8 66 F3
URMSTON 95 D1
Urmston Ave WA12 89 B5
Urmston Gram Sch M41 95 C2
Urmston Inf Sch M41 95 C2
Urmston Jun Sch M41 95 C2
Urmston La M32, M41 96 B1
Urmston L Ctr M41 95 B2
Urmston Pk M41 95 E2
Urmston St WN7 75 D5
Urmston Sta M41 95 D2
Urwick Rd SK6 113 B2
Usk Cl M45 63 C7
Uttley St
Bolton BL1 143 A2
Rochdale OL11 30 C4
Uvedale Ho 11 M30 79 D1
Uxbridge Ave 16 M11 83 C2
Uxbridge St OL6 166 A3

V

Vaal St OL8 66 C3
Valance Cl M12 165 A2
Valdene Cl BL4 60 D7
Valdene Dr
Farnworth BL4 60 D7
Walkden M28 78 D8
Vale Ave
Bury BL9 44 D7
Horwich BL6 22 A3
Hyde SK14 102 A3
Kearsley M26 61 C7
Sale M33 108 E5
Swinton M27 62 A1
Urmston M41 94 E1
Vale Cl
Appley Bridge WN6 35 E8
Hazel Grove SK7 124 E4
Manchester SK4 110 F2
Romiley SK6 113 F2
Vale Coppice
Horwich BL6 22 A3
Ramsbottom BL0 11 C3
Vale Cotts
Dukinfield SK14 101 C4
Horwich BL6 21 F2
Littleborough OL15 16 A5
Vale Cres SK8 122 F2
Vale Croft WN8 53 A6
Vale Dr
Oldham OL9 153 A2
Prestwich M25 63 A2
Vale Edge M26 44 A5
Vale Head SK9 131 D2
Vale House Dr SK13 104 A5
Vale La M35 84 A4
Valemount SK13 104 A5
Valencia Rd M7 81 B6
Valentia Rd M9 64 D4
Valentines Rd M46 58 A1
Valentine St
Failsworth M35 83 E7
Oldham OL4 67 C6
Vale Park Ind Est M8 156 C3
Vale Park Way M8 156 C3
Vale Rd
Altrincham, Rosehill WA14 119 B1
Altrincham WA15 120 B5
Droylsden M43 84 B3
Manchester SK4 110 F1
Mossley SK15 86 E6
Romiley SK6 125 B8
Shaw OL2 49 D6
Wilmslow SK9 136 E8
Valerie Wlk 6 M15 162 C3
Vale Side OL5 86 C8
Vale St
Ashton-u-L OL7 85 A6
Bolton BL2 43 A7
Droylsden M11 83 C2
Heywood OL10 29 E2
Middleton M24 65 B8
Vale The
Appley Bridge WN6 35 D8
Mossley OL5 86 C8
Vale Top Ave M9 157 C3
Valetta Cl M14 110 B8
Vale View
3 Altrincham WA14 119 C1
Bolton BL7 24 F7
Valewood Ave SK4 168 A1
Vale Works M4 159 A3
Valiant Rd WN5 54 D8
Valiant Wlk 1 M40 65 E1
Valletts La BL1 142 C1
Valletts S BL1 142 C1
Valley Ave BL8 27 B4
Valley Cl
Cheadle SK8 122 E3
Mossley OL5 68 B2
Wigan WN6 36 E2
Valley Com Sch The BL1 143 C2
Valley Cotts OL3 69 C4
Valley Dr SK9 131 C3
Valley Gdns SK14 114 E8
Valley Gr M34 101 B2
Valley Mews OL3 69 C4
Valley Mill La BL9 141 A1
Valley New Rd OL2 48 E3
Valley Park Rd M25 62 F5
Valley Rd
Bramhall SK7 123 F1
Broadbottom SK14 114 E8
Cheadle SK8 122 E3
Glossop SK13 115 F8
Middleton M24 47 B2
Romiley SK6 112 D4
Royton OL2 48 E3
Stockport SK4 168 A1
Urmston M41 94 D4
Wigan WN5 54 D5
Wilmslow/Alderley Edge SK9 136 C7
Valley Rise OL2 32 A1
Valley Road S M41 94 C2
Valley Sch SK7 132 C5
Valley View
Bolton BL7 25 A7
Bury BL8 27 C4
Dukinfield SK14 102 A4
Newton-le-W WA12 89 B1
Whitworth OL12 4 D4
Valley Way SK15 86 C1
Valley Wlk M11 160 C1
Valpy Ave BL2 25 B3

Vanbrugh Gr WN5 . . . . 36 B1
Vancouver Quay M50 . . . . . 96 F7
Vandyke Ave M6 . . . . 80 B3
Vandyke St ⑬ OL12 . . . . 13 F1
Vane St M30 . . . . 79 D2
Vanguard Cl M30 . . . . 94 F7
Vannes Gr SK14 . . . . 102 F3
Vantage Quay M1 . . . . 159 B1
Vantomee St BL1 . . . . 143 B4
Vant St OL8 . . . . 67 C4
Varden Gr SK3 . . . . 170 A1
Varden Rd SK12 . . . . 133 E3
Vardon Dr SK9 . . . . 137 D6
Varey St M18 . . . . 99 D5
Varley Rd BL3 . . . . 146 A4
Varley St M40 . . . . 160 A3
Varna St M11 . . . . 99 D7
Varna Street Prim Sch
  M11 . . . . 99 D7
Vasser Rd M48 . . . . 165 B1
Vauban Dr M6 . . . . 80 B3
Vaudrey Dr
  Cheadle SK8 . . . . 123 A4
  Hazel Grove SK7 . . . . . . 124 E2
  Sale WA15 . . . . 120 A8
Vaudrey La M34 . . . . 101 A2
Vaudrey Rd SK6 . . . . 113 A5
Vaudrey St ⑮ SK15 . . . . 86 A1
Vaughan Ave M40 . . . . . . 83 A8
Vaughan Gr OL4 . . . . 67 E6
Vaughan Ind Est M12 . . . 164 C3
Vaughan Rd
  Altrincham WA14 . . . . . 119 C8
  Manchester, Chorlton-cum-Hardy
    M21 . . . . 109 D2
  ② Sale WA14 . . . . 107 C1
  Stockport SK4 . . . . 169 A3
Vaughan St
  Eccles M30 . . . . 79 B3
  Manchester M12 . . . . . 164 C3
  Royton OL2 . . . . 48 E3
Vauxhall Cl M40 . . . . 159 C4
Vauxhall Ind Est
  Reddish SK5 . . . . 111 E6
  Stockport SK5 . . . . 169 C4
Vauxhall Rd WN1 . . . . . . 151 A4
Vauxhall St M40 . . . . 159 B4
Vauze Ave BL6 . . . . 21 D1
Vauze House Cl BL6 . . . . 21 D2
Vavasour Ct ⑧ OL16 . . . 31 B6
Vawdrey Dr ⑥ M23 . . . . 108 F2
Vax Rd M13 . . . . 98 D4
Vaynor ⑮ OL12 . . . . 139 E4
Vega St M8 . . . . 158 B4
Vela Wlk M7 . . . . 81 C3
Velmere Ave M9 . . . . 64 A5
Velour Cl M3 . . . . 158 A3
Velvet Cl M1 . . . . 163 A4
Vendale Ave M27 . . . . 79 D6
Venesta Ave M6 . . . . 80 B4
Venetia St M40 . . . . 83 C5
Venice St
  Bolton BL1 . . . . 146 C4
  Manchester M1 . . . . . . 163 A4
  Yellow Gdns SK8 . . . . 123 B1
Ventnor Ave
  Bolton BL1 . . . . 143 C3
  Manchester M19 . . . . . 111 C8
  Sale M33 . . . . 108 B6
  Whitefield M45 . . . . 45 A3
Ventnor Cl M34 . . . . 113 B8
Ventnor Rd
  Manchester, Didsbury
    M20 . . . . 110 C3
  Stockport SK4 . . . . 168 A2
Ventnor St
  Manchester M9 . . . . . . 157 A4
  Rochdale OL11 . . . . . . 139 C1
  Salford M6 . . . . 81 B4
Ventura Ct M14 . . . . 98 A1
Ventura Ct SK22 . . . . . . 127 D1
Venture Scout Way M8 . 155 C2
Venture Way SK12 . . . . . 133 F3
Venwood Rd M25 . . . . 62 F2
Verbena Ave BL4 . . . . 42 A1
Verbena Cl M11 . . . . 105 F3
Verdant La M30 . . . . 94 F8
Verdant Way OL16 . . . . . . 31 C2
Verdun St WN2 . . . . 74 B8
Verdun Ave M6 . . . . 80 B3
Verdun Cres OL11 . . . . . . 30 C8
Verdun Rd M30 . . . . 79 B4
Verdure Ave
  Bolton BL1 . . . . 40 E8
  Sale M33 . . . . 108 C1
Verdure Cl M35 . . . . 84 B7
Vere St M50 . . . . 154 C1
Verity Cl
  Manchester M20 . . . . . 110 C6
  Royton OL2 . . . . 48 D3
Verity Wlk M9 . . . . 64 B3
Vermont Gdns SK7 . . . . . 132 E5
Vermont St BL1 . . . . 145 A4
Verna St BL0 . . . . 138 C2
Verne Ave M27 . . . . 79 E8
Verne Dr OL1 . . . . 49 E5
Verne Wlk WM4 . . . . 73 D3
Verney Rd OL2 . . . . 48 E2
Vernham Wlk BL3 . . . . . . 147 B4
Vernon Ave
  Eccles M30 . . . . 79 F2
  Stockport SK1 . . . . 112 B3
  Stretford M32 . . . . 96 D1
Vernon Cl
  Cheadle SK8 . . . . 122 E1
  Poynton SK12 . . . . 133 D2
Vernon Ct ⑧ M7 . . . . . . 63 C1

Vernon Dr
  Marple SK6 . . . . 125 D7
  Prestwich M25 . . . . 63 A2
Vernon Gr M33 . . . . 108 E4
Vernon Ind Est SK1 . . . . 112 A2
Vernon Park Mus* SK1 . 112 B2
Vernon Park Prim Sch ⑧
  SK1 . . . . 112 A1
Vernon Pk WA15 . . . . . . 120 A7
Vernon Prim Sch The ⑪
  SK12 . . . . 133 E3
Vernon Rd
  Droylsden M43 . . . . 83 E2
  Manchester M7 . . . . . . 63 C1
  Poynton SK12 . . . . 133 E2
  Ramsbottom BL8 . . . . . 11 A1
  Romiley SK6 . . . . 112 F3
Vernon St
  Ashton-u-L OL6 . . . . . . 166 C4
  Bolton BL1 . . . . 145 B4
  Bury BL9 . . . . 140 C4
  Farnworth BL4 . . . . 42 E1
  Hazel Grove SK7 . . . . . 124 D3
  Hyde SK14 . . . . 167 B2
  Leigh WN7 . . . . 75 F5
  Manchester, Harpurhey
    M9 . . . . 157 B3
  Manchester M16 . . . . . 162 A1
  Mossley OL5 . . . . 68 C2
  Salford M7 . . . . 155 A1
  Stockport SK1 . . . . 169 C2
Vernon View ⑤ SK6 . . . 112 F3
Vernon Wlk
  ⑤ Bolton BL1 . . . . . . 145 B4
  Stockport SK1 . . . . 169 B1
Verona Dr M40 . . . . 83 C4
Veronica Rd M20 . . . . . . 110 C3
Verrill Ave M23 . . . . 109 C1
Verwood Wlk ⑨ M21 . . 121 A5
Vesper St M35 . . . . 84 A8
Vesta St
  Manchester M4 . . . . . . 159 C1
  Ramsbottom BL0 . . . . . 138 B2
Vestris Dr M6 . . . . 80 B3
Vetch Cl WA3 . . . . 105 B5
Viaduct Rd WA14 . . . . . . 119 D7
Viaduct St
  Manchester, Ardwick
    M12 . . . . 164 B4
  Manchester M3 . . . . . . 158 C2
  Newton-le-W WA12 . . . . 89 A3
  Stockport SK3 . . . . 169 B1
Vicarage Ave SK8 . . . . . 132 B7
Vicarage Cl
  Adlington PR6 . . . . 21 A8
  Bury BL9 . . . . 27 E8
  Dukinfield SK16 . . . . . 101 E8
  Oldham OL4 . . . . 67 F7
  Platt Bridge WN2 . . . . . 56 A2
  Salford M6 . . . . 80 B3
Vicarage Cres OL6 . . . . . 85 D5
Vicarage Ct
  ⑧ Altrincham M23 . . 120 D6
  Hyde SK14 . . . . 167 A1
Vicarage Dr
  Dukinfield SK16 . . . . . 101 E8
  Rochdale OL12, OL16 . . 15 C3
Vicarage Gdns
  Hyde SK14 . . . . 167 C2
  Stockport SK3 . . . . 170 A4
Vicarage Gr M30 . . . . 79 F2
Vicarage La
  Altrincham WA14 . . . . . 119 C1
  Middleton M24 . . . . 65 D7
  Poynton SK12 . . . . 133 E5
  Shevington WN6 . . . . . . 36 A5
Vicarage Rd
  Abram WN2 . . . . 56 B1
  Ashton-in-M WN4 . . . . . 73 B2
  Ashton-u-L OL7 . . . . . . 85 B5
  Blackrod BL6 . . . . 21 D2
  Irlam M44 . . . . 94 A2
  Orrell WN5 . . . . 53 D4
  Stockport SK3 . . . . 170 B2
  Swinton M27 . . . . 79 E8
  Urmston M41 . . . . 95 B4
  Walkden M28 . . . . 60 C4
Vicarage Road N OL11 . . 30 D1
Vicarage Road S OL11 . . 30 C1
Vicarage Road W BL6 . . . 21 C2
Vicarage Sq WN7 . . . . . . 75 F5
Vicarage St
  Bolton BL3 . . . . 145 A1
  Oldham OL8 . . . . 66 C3
  ⑪ Radcliffe M26 . . . . 44 A3
  Shaw OL2 . . . . 149 B3
Vicarage View OL11 . . . . 30 D1
Vicarage Way OL12 . . . . . 14 D1
Vicar's Dr Or OL16 . . . . . 139 C2
Vicar's Gate OL16 . . . . . 139 C3
Vicars Hall Gdns M28 . . . 77 F5
Vicars Hall La M28 . . . . . 77 F4
Vicars Rd M21 . . . . 109 A8
Vicars St M30 . . . . 79 F2
Viceroy Ct M20 . . . . 110 B2
Vicker Cl M27 . . . . 61 F2
Vicker Gr M20 . . . . 109 F5
Vickerman St BL1 . . . . . 143 A2
Vickers Row BL4 . . . . 60 B8
Vickers St
  Bolton BL3 . . . . 145 B1
  Manchester M40 . . . . . 160 B4
Vickery Court Appts M27 . 80 D8
Victor Ave BL9 . . . . 140 E4
Victor Cl WN5 . . . . 54 D8
Victoria Ave
  Altrincham WA15 . . . . . 119 F7
  Cheadle SK8 . . . . 123 A2

Victoria Ave continued
  ⑪ Eccles M30 . . . . 79 F1
  Glossop SK13 . . . . 104 A5
  Hazel Grove SK7 . . . . . 124 E3
  Leigh WN2 . . . . 56 E1
  Manchester, Didsbury
    M20 . . . . 110 A3
  Manchester, Higher Blackley
    M9 . . . . 64 C5
  Manchester, Levenshulme
    M19 . . . . 111 A8
  Pendlebury M27 . . . . . . 80 A8
  ⑦ Romiley SK6 . . . . . 112 F3
  Whitefield M45 . . . . 63 A8
  Wigan WN6 . . . . 37 A1
Victoria Avenue E M24, M40,
Victoria Avenue Prim Sch
  M9 . . . . 64 D5
Victoria Baths* M13 . . . . 98 D4
Victoria Bridge St M3 . . 158 C2
Victoria Cl
  Aspull WN2 . . . . 38 B6
  Bramhall SK7 . . . . 132 D6
  Stockport SK3 . . . . 170 B3
  ⑧ Worsley M28 . . . . . 78 A6
Victoria Cres
  Eccles M30 . . . . 79 F3
  Standish WN6 . . . . 36 E8
Victoria Ct
  ⑤ Ashton-u-L OL7 . . . 166 A1
  Bury BL8 . . . . 26 F6
  ⑥ Farnworth BL4 . . . . 42 C2
  ⑤ Glossop SK13 . . . . 116 C8
  Horwich BL6 . . . . 22 C3
  ⑦ Manchester M20 . . 110 A3
  Manchester, Openshaw
    M11 . . . . 165 C4
  Platt Bridge WN2 . . . . . 56 A4
  Stretford M32 . . . . 96 C2
  Whitefield M45 . . . . 62 F7
Victoria Gdns
  Hyde SK14 . . . . 167 C4
  Shaw OL2 . . . . 149 B3
Victoria Gr
  Bolton BL1 . . . . 142 C1
  Manchester M14 . . . . . 110 C7
  Reddish SK4 . . . . 111 D5
Victoria Grange M20 . . . 110 A3
Victoria Ho
  Manchester M11 . . . . . 165 C4
  Salford M6 . . . . 80 A4
Victoria Ind Est WN7 . . . 75 E7
Victoria La
  Swinton M27 . . . . 79 D8
  Whitefield M45 . . . . 62 F7
Victoria Lo M7 . . . . 81 C5
Victoria Metro Sta M3 . 159 A3
Victoria Mews
  ⑪ Dukinfield SK16 . . 101 C6
  ② Glossop SK13 . . . . 116 C8
  Whitefield BL9 . . . . 45 B2
Victoria Mill M40 . . . . . . 160 A3
Victoria Par
  ⑦ Rawtenstall BB4 . . . 2 E8
  Urmston M41 . . . . 95 D2
Victoria Park Ind Est M35 83 D6
Victoria Park Inf Sch ⑥
  M32 . . . . 96 D2
Victoria Park Jun Sch
  M32 . . . . 96 D2
Victoria Pk SK1 . . . . 124 B8
Victoria Pl ⑪ M28 . . . . 60 D4
Victoria Rd
  Altrincham, Timperley
    WA15 . . . . 120 A6
  Altrincham WA15 . . . . 119 D3
  Bolton BL1 . . . . 40 D8
  Dukinfield SK16 . . . . . 101 C6
  Eccles M30 . . . . 79 E3
  Garswood WN4 . . . . 72 D4
  Horwich BL6 . . . . 22 C2
  Irlam M44 . . . . 93 F1
  Kearsley BL4 . . . . 61 A6
  Manchester, Fallowfield
    M14 . . . . 110 B8
  Manchester M16 . . . . . 97 D2
  Manchester, Whalley Range
    M16 . . . . 97 D2
  Newton-le-W WA12 . . . . 89 C3
  Platt Bridge WN2 . . . . . 56 A2
  Sale M33 . . . . 108 A4
  Salford M6 . . . . 80 A4
  Stockport SK1 . . . . 112 B1
  Stretford M32 . . . . 96 D2
  Urmston M41 . . . . 95 B2
  Wilmslow SK9 . . . . 137 A6
  Wythenshawe M22 . . . 121 D8
Victoria Sq
  ⑬ Handforth SK9 . . . 145 C3
  Manchester M4 . . . . . . 159 B2
  Walkden M28 . . . . 60 D3
  Whitefield M45 . . . . 62 F7
Victoria St
  Ainsworth BL2 . . . . 26 C1
  Altrincham WA14 . . . . . 119 D5
  Ashton-u-L OL7 . . . . . . 166 A1
  Bacup OL13 . . . . 3 D8
  Blackrod BL6 . . . . 21 D2
  Bury BL8 . . . . 140 A2
  Bury BL8 . . . . 140 A3
  Bury, Tottington BL8 . . . 26 E7
  Chadderton OL9 . . . . . 152 C4
  Denton M34 . . . . 100 F3
  Dukinfield, Newton SK14 . 102 A5
  Dukinfield SK16 . . . . . 101 D8
  Failsworth M35 . . . . 83 D6

Victoria St continued
  ④ Farnworth BL4 . . . . . 42 B2
  Glossop SK13 . . . . 116 C8
  Heywood OL10 . . . . 29 E1
  Leigh WN7 . . . . 75 E6
  Littleborough OL15 . . . 16 B5
  Manchester M3 . . . . . . 158 C2
  Manchester, Openshaw
    M11 . . . . 165 C4
  Middleton M24 . . . . 65 A8
  Oldham, Lees OL4 . . . . 67 E6
  Oldham, Mumps OL4 . . . 67 A6
  Oldham OL8 . . . . 84 F8
  Platt Bridge WN2 . . . . . 56 A2
  Radcliffe M26 . . . . 44 A3
  Ramsbottom BL0 . . . . 138 B2
  Rawtenstall BB4 . . . . . . 2 E8
  Rochdale OL12 . . . . . . 14 F1
  Shaw OL2 . . . . 149 B3
  Stalybridge, Millbrook SK15 86 D4
  ⑫ Stalybridge, Stamford Park
    SK15 . . . . 85 F2
  Westhoughton BL5 . . . . 57 F8
  Whitworth OL12 . . . . . . 14 C8
  Wigan WN5 . . . . 54 F6
  Worsley M28 . . . . 78 A6
Victoria Station App M3 . 159 A2
Victoria Street E OL7 . . 166 A2
Victoria Terr
  Bickershaw WN2 . . . . . . 74 F8
  Heywood OL10 . . . . 29 C4
  Manchester, Longsight M12 98 F4
  Manchester M13 . . . . . 98 C4
  Milnrow OL16 . . . . 32 A5
Victoria The M50 . . . . 96 F7
Victoria Trad Est
  Oldham OL1 . . . . 66 B3
  Wigan WN3 . . . . 150 B3
Victoria Way
  Bramhall SK7 . . . . 132 D6
  Leigh WN7 . . . . 75 E7
  Royton OL2 . . . . 48 C6
Victoria Wlk OL9 . . . . 48 C1
Victoria Works SK1 . . . . 124 B8
Victoria Works Ind Est
  M46 . . . . 58 B4
Victor Mann St M11 . . . 100 A7
Victor St
  ⑦ Heywood OL10 . . . . 46 E8
  Manchester M40 . . . . . 159 C4
  VICTORY 144 C4
  Victory Gr M34 . . . . . . 100 C7
Victory Rd
  Irlam M44 . . . . 105 C4
  Little Lever BL3 . . . . . . 43 B4
Victory St
  Bolton BL1 . . . . 144 C4
  Manchester M14 . . . . . 98 C3
  Victory Trad Est BL3 . . 148 A1
Vienna Rd SK3 . . . . 170 A2
Vienna Road E SK3 . . . . 170 B2
Viewfield Wlk ⑱ M9 . . 157 B3
Viewlands Dr SK9 . . . . . 131 D2
View St BL3 . . . . 145 A1
Vigo Ave BL3 . . . . 146 B3
Vigo St
  Heywood OL10 . . . . 29 E1
  Oldham OL4 . . . . 67 D5
  ⑪ Wigan WN2 . . . . . . 37 F2
Viking Cl M11 . . . . 160 C1
Viking St
  Bolton BL3 . . . . 42 A4
  Rochdale OL11 . . . . . . 30 C8
Villa Ave WN6 . . . . 37 A4
Village Circ M17 . . . . 96 D6
Village Cr
  ⑧ Handforth SK9 . . . 131 D1
  Stretford M17 . . . . 96 C6
  Whitworth OL12 . . . . . . 4 C1
Village Gn OL3 . . . . 69 B8
Village Manor OL3 . . . . . 51 B1
Village St M7 . . . . 81 C5
VILLAGE THE 94 F1
Village The M41 . . . . 106 F8
Village View WN5 . . . . . . 71 E5
Village Way
  ⑪ Handforth SK9 . . . 131 D1
  Manchester M4 . . . . . . 159 A2
Village Way (Ashburton Rd
  E) M17 . . . . 96 C6
Village Wlk ⑫ M11 . . . . 99 D1
Villa Rd OL8 . . . . 66 F4
Villa The SK14 . . . . 103 A5
Villdale Ave SK2 . . . . . . 124 C7
Villiers Ct M45 . . . . 63 A6
Villiers Dr OL8 . . . . 153 B1
Villiers Ind Est M46 . . . 154 C4
Villiers St
  Ashton-u-L OL6 . . . . . . 85 D2
  Bury BL9 . . . . 141 A3
  Hyde SK14 . . . . 167 C2
Vinca Gr M7 . . . . 155 A2
Vincent Ave
  Eccles M30 . . . . 79 D4
  Manchester M21 . . . . . 97 A1
  Oldham OL4 . . . . 67 C8
Vincent Ct BL3 . . . . 147 B3
Vincent St
  Bolton BL1 . . . . 145 A2
  Hyde SK14 . . . . 113 F8
  Littleborough OL15 . . . 16 A6
  Manchester M11 . . . . . 165 C4
  Middleton M24 . . . . 47 A2
  ⑦ Rochdale OL16 . . . 31 A5
  Salford M7 . . . . 155 B3
Vincent Way
  Bolton BL3 . . . . 42 B4
  Wigan WN5 . . . . 54 D8

Vine Ave M27 . . . . 80 B8
Vine Cl
  Sale M33 . . . . 107 C5
  Shaw OL2 . . . . 149 B3
Vine Ct
  Rochdale OL16 . . . . 31 B6
  Stretford M32 . . . . 96 D1
Vine Fold M40 . . . . 65 F1
Vine Gr
  Stockport SK2 . . . . 124 C6
  Wigan WN3 . . . . 150 C3
Vine Pl OL11 . . . . 139 C1
Vinery Gr M34 . . . . 100 E3
Vine St
  Eccles M30 . . . . 79 C1
  Hazel Grove SK7 . . . . . 124 E3
  Hindley WN2 . . . . 56 D6
  Manchester M11, M18 . . 99 E6
  Oldham OL9 . . . . 66 B3
  Prestwich M25 . . . . 63 C5
  Ramsbottom BL0 . . . . . 11 A4
  Salford M7 . . . . 81 C8
  Wigan WN1 . . . . 37 D1
Vineyard Cl OL12 . . . . . . 15 C7
Vineyard St OL4 . . . . 67 D7
Viola Cl WN6 . . . . 19 D2
Viola St
  Bolton BL1 . . . . 143 B3
  Droylsden M11 . . . . 83 D2
Violet Ave BL4 . . . . 42 A1
Violet Ct ⑪ M22 . . . . . 121 D3
Violet Hill Ct OL4 . . . . . . 67 E8
Violet St
  Ashton-in-M WN4 . . . . . 73 B2
  Droylsden M11, 8 . . . . . 99 F6
  Ince-in-M WN3 . . . . . . 151 B2
  Stockport SK2 . . . . 170 C2
Violet Way M24 . . . . 65 D7
Vip Centre Ind Est OL1 . 49 C1
Virgil St M15 . . . . 162 A2
Virginia Chase SK8 . . . . 131 F8
Virginia Cl M23 . . . . 120 D7
Virginia St
  Bolton BL3 . . . . 146 B4
  Rochdale OL11 . . . . . . 30 E4
Virginia Way WN5 . . . . . . 54 C8
Viscount Dr
  Gatley SK8 . . . . 131 D7
  Wythenshawe M90 . . . 129 F7
Viscount Rd WN5 . . . . . . 54 D8
Viscount St M14 . . . . 98 C3
Vista Ave WA12 . . . . 89 A4
Vista Rd M41, WA12 . . . . 89 A6
Vista The M44 . . . . 105 C4
Vista Way WA12 . . . . 89 A4
Vivian Pl ⑧ M14 . . . . . 98 C3
Vivian St OL11 . . . . 139 B1
Vixen Cl M21 . . . . 109 E7
Voewood Ho SK1 . . . . . . 124 B8
Voltaire Ave M6 . . . . 80 B3
Vorlich Dr OL9 . . . . 65 F8
Vulcan Cl WA12 . . . . 89 C1
Vulcan Dr WN1 . . . . 151 A3
Vulcan Ind Est WA12 . . . 89 C1
Vulcan Rd WN5 . . . . 54 D8
Vulcan St OL1 . . . . 49 B1
Vyner Gr M33 . . . . 107 F6

W

Wadcroft Wlk ⑱ M9 . . 157 B4
Waddicor Ave OL6 . . . . . . 85 E6
Waddington Cl
  Bury BL8 . . . . 26 E2
  Golborne WA3 . . . . 90 F8
Waddington Fold OL16 . . 31 C2
Waddington Rd BL1 . . . . 142 A1
Waddington St OL9 . . . . 152 C4
Wade Bank BL5 . . . . 57 F8
Wadebridge Ave M23 . . 120 D7
Wadebridge Cl ⑧ BL2 . 25 B1
Wadebrook Gr ④ SK9 . 131 D1
Wadeford Cl M4 . . . . 159 C3
Wade Hill La OL3 . . . . . . 68 E8
Wade Ho ⑧ M30 . . . . . . 79 D1
Wade Row OL3 . . . . 69 B8
Wadesmill Wlk M13 . . . 163 B3
Wadeson Rd M13 . . . . . 163 C3
Wade St
  ③ Bolton BL3 . . . . . . 147 B3
  Middleton M24 . . . . 65 D6
Wade Wlk M11 . . . . 165 A4
Wadham Gdns SK6 . . . . 113 C5
Wadham Way WA15 . . . 119 F1
Wadhurst Wlk ② M13 . 163 C1
Wadlow Cl M3 . . . . 158 B3
Wadsworth Cl SK9 . . . . 131 E3
Wadsworth Dr WN6 . . . . 36 F2
Wadsworth Ind Pk BL3 . 147 B4
Wadsworth Mews M43 . . 83 F1
Waggoners ② M27 . . . . 79 F7
Waggon Rd
  Bolton BL2 . . . . 42 D8
  Mossley OL5 . . . . 86 C8
Wagner St BL1 . . . . 143 A3
Wagstaffe Dr M35 . . . . . . 83 F7
Wagstaffe St M24 . . . . . . 47 A2
Wagtail Cl M28 . . . . 78 D8
Wain Cl M30 . . . . 79 B2
Waincliffe Ave M20, M21 109 D4
Wainfleet Cl WN3 . . . . . . 54 E2
Waingap Cres OL12 . . . . 14 D8
Waingap Rise OL12 . . . . 14 F4
Waingap View OL12 . . . . 14 D7

Wainman St M6 . . . . 81 B5
Wainscot Cl M29 . . . . 77 B7
Wain Stones Gn SK2 . . . . 124 E6
Wainwright Ave M34 . . . . . 99 F3
Wainwright Cl
  Oldham OL4 . . . . 68 A7
  Stockport SK2 . . . . 124 A7
Wainwright Rd WA14 . . . . 119 C5
Wainwright St
  Oldham OL8 . . . . 153 B1
  Urmston M41 . . . . 95 E3
Waithlands Rd OL16 . . . . . 31 B6
Wakefield Cres
  Romiley SK6 . . . . 113 A1
  Standish WN6 . . . . 37 A6
Wakefield Dr
  Chadderton OL9 . . . . 48 C1
  Swinton M27 . . . . 61 D4
Wakefield Mews BL2 . . . . 24 F7
Wakefield Rd SK15 . . . . . . 86 B3
Wakefield St
  Chadderton OL8 . . . . 48 C1
  Golborne WA3 . . . . 90 A7
  2 Manchester M1 . . . . . 163 A3
Wakefield Wlk M34 . . . . . 101 A1
Wakeling Rd M34 . . . . 112 E8
Wakes Dr M30 . . . . 79 D4
Walcot Pl WN3 . . . . 54 F2
Walcott Cl M13 . . . . 164 B1
Wald Ave M14 . . . . 110 E7
Waldeck St **1** BL1 . . . . . 145 A4
Waldeck Wlk 図 M9 . . . . . 64 E3
Walden 図 OL10 . . . . 29 C2
Walden Ave OL4 . . . . 49 D2
Walden Cl M14 . . . . 110 A8
Walden Cres SK7 . . . . 124 C3
Walderton Ave M40 . . . . . 83 A7
Waldon Ave SK8 . . . . 122 D5
Waldon Cl
  Bolton BL3 . . . . 146 C4
  Hindley WN2 . . . . 56 F4
Waldorf Cl WN3 . . . . 54 D2
Wales St OL1 . . . . 49 C1
Walford Rd WN4 . . . . 73 C3
Walgate Brow SK13 . . . . . 116 B7
WALKDEN 60 E4
Walkden Ave WN1 . . . . 37 B2
Walkden Avenue E WN1 . 37 C2
Walkden Ct M28 . . . . 60 C4
Walkden Dr M28 . . . . 60 A8
Walkden Gdns M33 . . . . . 108 C3
Walkden High Sch M28 . . 60 E1
Walkden Rd
  Walkden M28 . . . . 60 D1
  Worsley M28 . . . . 78 E7
Walkdens Ave M46 . . . . . . 58 A2
Walkden Sta M28 . . . . 60 D2
Walker Ave
  Bolton BL3 . . . . 147 C3
  Failsworth M35 . . . . 84 B6
  Prestwich M25, M45 . . . . . 63 A6
  Stalybridge SK15 . . . . 86 C2
Walker Cl
  Hyde SK14 . . . . 167 C2
  Kearsley BL4 . . . . 61 A6
Walker Fold SK14 . . . . . . 167 C2
Walker Fold Rd BL1 . . . . . 23 D4
Walker Gn M30 . . . . 79 D1
Walker Ho **9** M30 . . . . . 79 D1
Walker La SK14 . . . . 167 C2
Walker Rd
  Eccles M30 . . . . 79 A4
  Failsworth OL9 . . . . 65 F2
  Irlam M44 . . . . 93 F1
  Manchester M9 . . . . 64 E4
Walkers Cl OL3 . . . . 69 B8
Walker's Croft M3 . . . . . . 158 C2
Walkers St
  Farnworth BL4 . . . . 60 D8
  Oldham OL4 . . . . 68 A6
Walkers Dr WN7 . . . . 76 A5
Walker's La OL4 . . . . 68 A6
Walker's Rd OL8 . . . . 66 C2
Walker St
  Bolton BL1 . . . . 145 A2
  3 Bury BL9 . . . . 44 E8
  Denton M34 . . . . 100 E4
  Glossop SK13 . . . . 104 A4
  Heywood OL10 . . . . 29 C1
  Middleton M24 . . . . 64 C2
  Oldham OL8 . . . . 153 A2
  4 Radcliffe M26 . . . . . . 44 C1
  Rochdale OL16 . . . . 31 A7
  Stockport SK1 . . . . 169 B1
  Westhoughton BL5 . . . . . . 57 E8
Walkerwood Dr SK15 . . . 86 D2
Walkmill OL3 . . . . 50 F1
Walk Mill Cl OL12 . . . . . . 15 D4
Walk The
  Atherton M46 . . . . 58 D3
  5 Rochdale OL16 . . . . . 139 C3
Walkway The BL3 . . . . 40 F5
Wallace Ave M14 . . . . 98 D3
Wallace La WN1 . . . . 37 E1
Wallace St **2** OL8 . . . . . 66 F4
Wallasey Ave M14 . . . . . . 98 A1
WALLBANK 6 B7
Wallbank Dr OL12 . . . . . . 14 C7
Wallbank Rd SK7 . . . . . . 124 A1
Wallbrook Ave WN5 . . . . . 53 D1
Wallbrook Cres M38 . . . . 60 B6
Wallbrook Dr M9 . . . . 64 C1
Wallbrook Gr BL4 . . . . 42 B2

Walled Gdn The
  Manchester M16 . . . . 97 E2
  Swinton M27 . . . . 79 D6
Waller Ave M14 . . . . 110 C8
Walley St **3** BL1 . . . . . . 143 B3
Wallgarth Cl WN3 . . . . 54 E2
WALLGATE 150 A4
Wallgate WN3 . . . . 150 B3
Wallhead Rd OL16 . . . . . . 31 D7
WALL HILL 50 E1
Wall Hill Rd OL3 . . . . 50 E2
Wallingford Rd
  Handforth SK9 . . . . 131 C5
  Urmston M41 . . . . 95 E3
Wallis St
  Chadderton OL9 . . . . 66 A4
  Failsworth M40 . . . . 83 C5
WALLNESS 81 B3
Wallness La M6 . . . . 81 C3
Wallshaw Pl OL1 . . . . 67 A7
Wallshaw St OL1 . . . . 67 A7
Walls St WN2 . . . . 57 C2
Wall St
  Oldham OL8 . . . . 153 C1
  Salford M6 . . . . 154 C2
Wallsuches BL6 . . . . 22 F4
Wall Way M18 . . . . 99 E4
Wallwork Cl OL11 . . . . 13 E1
Wallwork Rd M29 . . . . 77 D6
Wallwork St
  Droylsden M11 . . . . 99 E8
  Radcliffe M26 . . . . 44 A4
  Reddish SK5 . . . . 99 F2
Wallworth Ave M18 . . . . . 99 D5
Wallworth Terr SK9 . . . . 136 E8
Wally Sq M7 . . . . 155 B2
Walmer Dr SK7 . . . . 124 A1
Walmer Rd WN2 . . . . 57 A5
Walmersley 27 E8
Walmersley Ct 図 SK6 . . 125 F6
Walmersley Old Rd BL9 . 27 F7
Walmersley Rd
  Bury BL9 . . . . 27 F6
  Failsworth M40 . . . . 65 E1
Walmer St
  Manchester, Abbey Hey
    M18 . . . . 99 E6
  Manchester M14 . . . . 98 C3
Walmer Street E M14 . . . 98 C3
Walmesley Dr WN2 . . . . . 56 B7
Walmesley Rd WN7 . . . . . 75 E5
Walmesley St WN1 . . . . . 151 A3
Walmley Gr BL3 . . . . 146 C3
Walmsley Ave OL15 . . . . . 15 F3
Walmsley CE Prim Sch BL7 . 8 E1
Walmsley St M41 . . . . 95 D2
Walmsley St
  1 Bury BL8 . . . . 27 B4
  Newton-le-W WA12 . . . . . 89 D4
  Reddish SK5 . . . . 169 C3
  Stalybridge SK15 . . . . . . 102 A8
Walney Rd
  Wigan WN3 . . . . 54 D2
  Wythenshawe M22 . . . . . 121 D4
Walnut Ave
  Bury BL9 . . . . 141 C3
  Oldham OL4 . . . . 67 D8
  Wigan WN1 . . . . 37 D2
Walnut Cl
  Hyde SK14 . . . . 102 A2
  Swinton M27 . . . . 61 A2
  Wilmslow SK9 . . . . 137 E8
Walnut Gr
  Leigh WN7 . . . . 75 F8
  Sale M33 . . . . 108 A4
Walnut Rd
  Eccles M30 . . . . 79 A4
  Partington M31 . . . . 105 D3
Walnut St
  Bolton BL1 . . . . 143 A4
  2 Manchester M18 . . . . 99 D5
  Salford M5 . . . . 161 B2
Walnut Tree Rd SK3 . . . . 123 A8
Walpole Ave WN3 . . . . 37 B5
Walpole St OL16 . . . . 31 A7
Walsall St WN3 . . . . 81 A5
Walsden 6 B7
Walsden Est OL14 . . . . 6 B7
Walsden St M11 . . . . 83 C2
Walsh Ave **4** M9 . . . . . . 64 C2
WALSHAW 26 E4
Walshaw Brook Cl BL8 . . 26 F4
Walshaw Dr M27 . . . . 79 F7
Walshaw La BL8 . . . . 26 F4
Walshaw Rd BL8 . . . . 27 B4
Walshaw Wlk BL8 . . . . 26 F5
Walsh Cl WA12 . . . . 89 C5
Walshe St **1** BL1 . . . . . 140 A2
Walsh Fold BL7 . . . . 9 D2
Walsh Ho M46 . . . . 58 D4
Walsh St
  Chadderton OL9 . . . . 152 B2
  Horwich BL6 . . . . 22 B4
Walsingham Ave
  Manchester M20 . . . . 109 F4
  Middleton M24 . . . . 65 A5
Walter Leigh Way WN7 . . 75 B1
Walter Scott Ave WN1 . . 37 B5
Walter Scott St **3** OL1 . 67 B8
Walters Dr OL8 . . . . 67 A3
Walters Green Cres WA3 . 74 A2
Walter St
  Ashton-in-M WN4 . . . . 73 D4
  Droylsden M18 . . . . 99 E6
  Leigh WN7 . . . . 75 B5
  Manchester, Harpurhey
    M9 . . . . 157 A4

Walter St continued
  Manchester, Old Trafford
    M16 . . . . 97 C4
  3 Oldham OL1 . . . . . . 153 C2
  Prestwich M25 . . . . 62 F4
  Radcliffe M26 . . . . 43 F6
  Walkden M28 . . . . 60 D2
  Wigan WN5 . . . . 54 D6
Waltham Ave
  Glazebury WA3 . . . . 92 C7
  Wigan WN6 . . . . 36 F2
Waltham Dr SK8 . . . . 132 B6
Waltham Gdns
  Leigh WN7 . . . . 76 C3
  Radcliffe M26 . . . . 43 E5
Waltham Rd M16 . . . . 97 E1
Waltham St OL4 . . . . 67 C4
WALTHEW GREEN 35 C3
Walthew House La
  Wigan, Marsh Green WN5 . 36 D2
  Wigan WN5 . . . . 36 B1
Walthew La
  Platt Bridge WN2 . . . . 56 A2
  Wigan WN5 . . . . 36 D2
Walton Cl
  Heywood OL10 . . . . 46 D8
  Middleton M24 . . . . 46 C1
  Stockport CL BL3 . . . . . . 147 C4
Walton Dr
  Bury BL9 . . . . 27 E8
  Marple SK6 . . . . 125 D7
Walton Hall Dr M19 . . . . . 99 D1
Walton Ho M35 . . . . 83 F8
Walton Park L Ctr M33 . 108 A2
Walton Pl BL4 . . . . 60 E7
Walton Rd
  Altrincham WA14 . . . . 119 B5
  Culcheth WA3 . . . . 91 F3
  Manchester M9 . . . . 64 D5
  Sale M33 . . . . 107 F2
Walton St
  Adlington PR7 . . . . 21 A6
  Ashton-u-L OL7 . . . . 84 F5
  Atherton M46 . . . . 58 E4
  Heywood OL10 . . . . 29 D1
  1 Middleton M24 . . . . . 47 A2
  Stockport SK1 . . . . 170 C3
Walton Way M34 . . . . 101 B1
Walworth Cl M26 . . . . 61 C7
Walwyn Cl M32 . . . . 96 E1
Wanborough Cl WN7 . . . . 75 F7
Wandsworth Ave M11 . . . 83 D2
Wanley Wlk 図 M9 . . . . . . 64 E3
Wansbeck Cl M32 . . . . 96 E1
Wansbeck Lo M32 . . . . . . 96 E1
Wansfell Wlk M4 . . . . 160 A2
Wansford St M14 . . . . 98 A3
Wanstead Ave M9 . . . . 65 B3
Wapping St BL1 . . . . 143 A2
Warbeck Cl
  Hindley WN2 . . . . 56 E3
  Reddish SK5 . . . . 100 A2
Warbeck Rd M40 . . . . 65 D2
Warbreck Cl BL2 . . . . 42 F7
Warbreck Gr M33 . . . . . . 108 D3
WARBURTON 117 C8
Warburton Bridge Rd WA13,
  WA3 . . . . 105 A1
Warburton Cl
  Altrincham WA15 . . . . 129 C8
  Lymm WA13 . . . . 117 A4
  Romiley SK6 . . . . 113 A1
Warburton Dr WA15 . . . . 129 D6
WARBURTON GREEN . . . 129 D6
Warburton La M31, WA15 105 C2
Warburton Pl **図** M46 . . 58 D3
Warburton Rd SK9 . . . . . 131 D4
Warburton St
  Eccles M30 . . . . 79 E1
  3 Manchester M20 . . . 110 B3
  Salford M5 . . . . 161 B2
Warburton View WA3 . . . 105 A2
Warburton Way WA15 . . 120 C7
Warcock Rd OL4 . . . . 67 C7
Wardend Cl M38 . . . . 60 A6
Warden La M40 . . . . 83 B6
Wardens Bank BL5 . . . . . . 57 E5
Warden St M40 . . . . 83 B6
Warde St M15 . . . . 162 B2
Wardham Cl BL5 . . . . 57 F5
Ward La
  Diggle SK12 . . . . 51 D3
  Disley SK12 . . . . 135 F4
WARDLE 15 C5
Wardle Brook Ave SK14 . 102 D3
Wardle Brook Wlk SK14 . 102 D3
Wardle Cl
  Radcliffe M26 . . . . 43 E5
  Stretford M32 . . . . 96 F4
WARDLE FOLD 15 C7
Wardle Fold OL12 . . . . 15 C7
Wardle Gdns OL12 . . . . . . 15 C3
Wardle High Sch OL12 . . 15 D5
Wardle Rd
  Rochdale OL12 . . . . 15 C4
  Sale M33 . . . . 108 C4
Wardle St
  Bacup OL13 . . . . 3 D8
  Bolton BL2 . . . . 148 C1
  Littleborough OL15 . . . . . . 16 A6
  Manchester M40 . . . . 160 B3
WARDLEY 61 C2
Wardley Ave
  Manchester M16 . . . . 97 E1
  Walkden M28 . . . . 60 B3

Wardley CE Prim Sch
  M27 . . . . 61 E2
Wardley Gr BL1 . . . . 144 A3
Wardley Hall Ct M27 . . . . 61 C2
Wardley Hall La M28 . . . . 79 A8
Wardley Hall Rd M27, M28 61 B1
Wardley Ho **1** M6 . . . . . 80 C4
Wardley Ind Est M28 . . . . 61 C1
Wardley Rd M29 . . . . 77 D8
Wardley Sq M29 . . . . 77 D8
Wardley St
  Swinton M27 . . . . 79 F8
  Wigan WN5 . . . . 54 B6
Wardlow Ave
  図 Gamesley SK13 . . . . 171 A1
  Wigan WN5 . . . . 36 A1
Wardlow Fold **図** SK13 . 171 A1
Wardlow Gdns **図** SK13 . 171 A1
Wardlow Gr **図** SK13 . . . 171 A1
Wardlow Mews **図** SK13 . 171 A1
Wardlow St BL3 . . . . 146 B4
Wardlow Wlk **図** SK13 . . 171 A1
Wardour St M46 . . . . 58 C2
Ward Rd M43 . . . . 84 B1
WARDSEND 134 A1
Wardsend Wlk 図 M15 . . 162 A2
Ward St
  Chadderton OL9 . . . . 152 C3
  Failsworth M35 . . . . 83 E8
  Hindley WN2 . . . . 56 E7
  Hyde SK14 . . . . 167 B2
  1 Manchester, Didsbury
    M20 . . . . 110 B3
  Manchester, Lower Broughton
    M40 . . . . 157 C4
  Manchester M9 . . . . 64 C2
  Oldham OL1 . . . . 153 A4
  Romiley SK6 . . . . 112 F3
  Stockport SK1 . . . . 124 A7
Ware Cl WN4 . . . . 73 D4
Wareham Gr M30 . . . . 79 C3
Wareham St
  Manchester M8 . . . . 64 B1
  Wilmslow SK9 . . . . 137 B7
Wareing St M29 . . . . 76 F8
Wareings Yd **5** OL11 . . 31 A4
Wareing Way BL3 . . . . . . 145 B2
Warfield Wlk **図** M9 . . . . 64 E3
Warford Ave SK12 . . . . . . 134 A2
Warford La WA16 . . . . 136 B1
Warford St M4 . . . . 159 B4
Warford Terr WA16 . . . . . 136 B2
WARGRAVE 89 D3
Wargrave House Sch
  WA12 . . . . 89 C1
Wargrave Mews WA12 . . 89 C1
Wargrave Prim Sch WA12 89 C1
Wargrave Rd WA12 . . . . . 89 C2
WARHILL 103 A3
Warhurst Fold **2** SK13 . 104 A5
Warke The M28 . . . . 78 F6
WARLAND 6 D5
Warland End Gate OL14 . . 6 C5
Warley Cl SK8 . . . . 122 E6
Warley Gr SK16 . . . . 101 C8
Warley Rd M16 . . . . 97 A3
Warley St OL15 . . . . 16 B5
Warlingham Cl BL8 . . . . . 27 B1
Warlow Crest OL3 . . . . . . 69 A7
Warlow Dr
  Leigh WN7 . . . . 57 D1
  Uppermill OL3 . . . . 69 A4
Warmco Ind Pk OL5 . . . . . 68 D2
Warmington Dr M12 . . . . 164 B2
Warminster Gr WN3 . . . . . 54 D2
Warmley Rd M23 . . . . 120 D8
Warne Ave M43 . . . . 84 C2
Warner Wlk **9** M11 . . . . 160 C1
Warnford Cl M40 . . . . 83 D4
Warnford St **3** WN1 . . . . 37 C2
War Office Rd OL11 . . . . . 29 E6
Warren Ave
  Altrincham WA15 . . . . 129 D7
  Britannia OL13 . . . . 4 C8
  Newton-le-W WA12 . . . . . 89 F4
  Swinton M27 . . . . 79 D5
Warren Bank M9 . . . . 64 D3
Warren Bruce Rd M17 . . . 96 D6
Warren Cl
  Atherton M46 . . . . 58 E5
  Denton M34 . . . . 100 D2
  Middleton M24 . . . . 46 F1
  Poynton SK12 . . . . 133 B4
  Stockport SK7 . . . . 123 D2
Warren Dr
  Altrincham WA15 . . . . 129 D7
  Swinton M27 . . . . 79 D5
Warrener St M33 . . . . 108 D4
Warren Hey SK9 . . . . 137 E8
Warren La OL8 . . . . 67 B4
Warren Lea
  Compstall SK6 . . . . 114 B2
  Poynton SK12 . . . . 133 E5
Warren Rd
  Cheadle SK8 . . . . 123 B2
  Stockport SK3 . . . . 170 B2
  Stretford M17 . . . . 96 B6
  Walkden M28 . . . . 60 E3
Warren St
  2 Bury BL8 . . . . 27 B1
  Manchester M9 . . . . 64 C2
  Salford M7 . . . . 155 C4
  Stockport SK5 . . . . 169 C2
Warren The WA12 . . . . 89 A3
Warren Wood Prim Sch
  SK2 . . . . 125 A6
Warre St OL6 . . . . 166 B3
Warrington La
  Broomedge WA13 . . . . . . 117 E2

Warrington La continued
  Wigan WN1 . . . . 151 A3
Warrington Rd
  Abram Brow WN2 . . . . 74 B7
  Ashton-in-M WN4 . . . . 73 B2
  Fowley Common WA3 . . . 92 C5
  Golborne WA3, WA12 . . . 90 A6
  Ince-in-M WN3 . . . . 151 B2
  Leigh WN7 . . . . 76 B3
  Manchester M9 . . . . 64 C4
  Platt Bridge WN2 . . . . 56 A1
  Wigan WN5 . . . . 54 F3
Warrington Road Ind Est
  WN3 . . . . 54 F5
Warrington St
  Ashton-u-L OL6 . . . . 166 B3
  9 Oldham OL4 . . . . 67 C6
  Stalybridge SK15 . . . . 86 B1
Warsall Rd M22 . . . . 121 C7
Warslow Dr M33 . . . . 108 C1
Warsop Ave M22 . . . . 121 C5
Warth Fold Rd M26 . . . . . 44 C6
Warth Ind Pk BL9 . . . . 44 D7
Warth La BB4 . . . . 2 D8
Warth Rd BL9 . . . . 44 D7
Warton Cl
  Bramhall SK7 . . . . 133 A7
  Bury BL8 . . . . 26 F1
Warton Dr M23 . . . . 121 A5
Warwick Ave
  Ashton-in-M WN4 . . . . 73 D2
  Denton M34 . . . . 100 F1
  Manchester M20 . . . . 109 F4
  Newton-le-W WA12 . . . . . 89 E2
  Prestwich M45 . . . . 63 B7
  Swinton M27 . . . . 61 D2
Warwick Cl
  Bury BL8 . . . . 27 B4
  Cheadle SK8 . . . . 123 A4
  Dukinfield SK16 . . . . 101 C6
  Glossop SK13 . . . . 116 F8
  Middleton M24 . . . . 65 A5
  Prestwich M45 . . . . 63 A2
  Ramsbottom BL8 . . . . 11 A1
  Shaw OL2 . . . . 48 F7
  Stockport SK4 . . . . 169 A4
Warwick Ct
  図 Denton M34 . . . . . . 113 A8
  Manchester, Firswood M16 . 97 A3
  Stockport SK4 . . . . 169 A4
Warwick Dr
  Altrincham WA15 . . . . 119 F1
  Hazel Grove SK7 . . . . 124 D1
  Hindley WN2 . . . . 56 F6
  Sale M33 . . . . 108 D4
  Urmston M41 . . . . 95 B3
Warwickgate Ho M16 . . . 97 A4
Warwick Gdns BL3 . . . . . 146 B2
Warwick Gr M34 . . . . 100 C8
Warwick Ho
  2 Manchester M19 . . . . 99 A2
  3 Sale M33 . . . . 108 C4
Warwick Mall SK8 . . . . . . 122 D6
Warwick Rd
  Altrincham WA15 . . . . 119 F1
  Ashton-u-L OL6 . . . . 85 C5
  Aspull WN2 . . . . 38 C5
  Atherton M46 . . . . 58 C5
  Failsworth M35 . . . . 84 A5
  Irlam M44 . . . . 105 D5
  Manchester, Firswood M16,
    M17 . . . . 97 A4
  Manchester M21 . . . . 97 B1
  Middleton M24 . . . . 65 B6
  Radcliffe M26 . . . . 43 F6
  Romiley SK6 . . . . 113 A2
  Stockport, Heaton Norris
    SK4 . . . . 168 C3
  Tyldesley M29 . . . . 59 A2
  Walkden M28 . . . . 60 C1
Warwick Road S M16 . . . . 97 A3
Warwick St
  Adlington PR7 . . . . 20 F6
  Bolton BL1 . . . . 143 B4
  Leigh WN7 . . . . 76 E3
  Manchester, Hulme M15 . 162 C1
  Manchester M1, M4 . . . . 159 B2
  Oldham OL9 . . . . 152 C1
  3 Rochdale OL12 . . . . . 15 B2
  Swinton M27 . . . . 61 F1
Warwick Terr **15** SK16 . . 166 B1
Wasdale Ave
  Bolton BL2 . . . . 25 F1
  Urmston M41 . . . . 95 B3
Wasdale Dr
  Gatley SK8 . . . . 122 B3
  Middleton M24 . . . . 46 E2
Wasdale Rd WN4 . . . . 73 A8
Wasdale St OL11 . . . . 30 C1
Wasdale Terr SK15 . . . . . . 86 A3
Wasdale Wlk **3** OL8 . . . 67 A8
Washacre BL5 . . . . 57 F7
Washacre Cl BL5 . . . . 57 F7
Washacre Prim Sch BL5 . 57 F7
Washbrook OL9 . . . . 66 B4
Washbrook Ave BL8 . . . . . 60 B1
Washbrook Cl **3** OL9 . . . 66 B4
Washbrook Dr M32 . . . . . . 96 B2
Washburn Cl BL5 . . . . 39 F2
WASH END 91 C8
Wash Fold BL8 . . . . 27 B5
Washford Dr M23 . . . . . . 120 D8
Washington Cl SK8 . . . . . 131 F8
Washington Ct **3** BL9 . . 140 C3
Washington Ctr The M50 . 96 E8
Washington St
  2 Bolton BL3 . . . . 144 C2
  Oldham OL9 . . . . 152 C3

Wash La
Bury BL9 .... 141 B2
Leigh WN7 .... 76 C5
Wash Terr BL8 .... 27 B5
Washway Rd M33 .... 107 F2
Washwood Cl M38 ... 60 B6
Wasnidge Wlk ② M15 .. 162 C1
Wasp Ave OL11 ...... 31 A3
Wasp Mill Dr OL12 ... 15 C6
Wastdale Ave BL9 ... 45 A3
Wastdale Rd M13 .... 121 A4
Waste St ② OL1 ..... 67 A7
Wastwater St ⑤ OL1 .. 49 A1
Watburn Rd SK22 .... 127 D1
Watchgate SK7 ...... 124 C2
Watchgate Cl M24 ... 46 D3
WATERBARN 7 A8
Waterbarn La OL13 ... 3 B8
Waterbeck Cl WN1 ... 37 F1
Waterbridge M28 .... 79 A5
Watercroft ② OL11 .. 13 D1
Waterdale Cl M38 .... 78 B6
Waterdale Dr M45 ... 63 A8
Water Dr WN6 .... 37 B7
Wateredge Cl WN7 ... 75 D3
Waterfield Cl BL9 ... 27 F7
Waterfield Way M35 .. 84 A6
Waterfold Bsns Pk BL9 .. 141 B1
Waterfold La BL9 .... 141 C1
WATERFOOT 2 E8
Waterfoot Cotts SK14 .. 103 A4
Waterfoot Prim Sch ⑭
BB4 .... 2 F8
Waterford Ave
Manchester M20 ..... 109 D3
Romiley SK6 .... 113 F2
Waterford Cl WN2 .... 56 A3
Waterford Ct BL4 .... 42 E1
Waterford Pl SK8 .... 131 B8
Waterfront Quay M50 .. 161 A3
Waterfront The M11 .. 83 A2
Waterhead M34 ..... 100 C8
Water Gate OL3 ...... 69 B8
Watergate Dr BL5 .... 59 C7
Watergate La BL4, BL5 .. 59 C7
Watergate Milne Ct ⑥
OL4 .... 67 D8
Water Grove Rd SK16 .. 101 F7
WATER HEYES
Waterhouse Cl OL12 .. 15 C6
Waterhouse Nook BL6,
PR7 .... 21 A5
Waterhouse Rd M18 .. 99 E4
Waterhouse St OL12 .. 139 E4
Waterhouse Way ⑪ SK5 .. 111 E7
Water La
Droylsden M43 .... 83 E1
Edenfield BL0 .... 1 D2
Farnworth BL4 .... 60 E7
Hollingworth SK14 ... 103 D5
Milnrow OL16 .... 32 A5
Radcliffe M26 .... 43 F3
Wilmslow SK9 .... 137 A7
Water Lane St M26 .... 43 F3
WATERLOO 85 A5
Waterloo Ct
Bury BL9 .... 44 E8
② Manchester M20 .. 110 A5
④ Stalybridge SK15 .. 86 A2
Waterloo Gdns OL6 .. 85 E5
Waterloo Ind Pk BL1 .. 25 A1
Waterloo Pk ① SK1 .. 112 A1
Waterloo Prim Sch ①
OL7 .... 85 A5
Waterloo Rd
Ashton-u-L OL6 ...... 85 B5
Bramhall SK7 .... 132 F8
Poynton SK12 .... 134 A2
Romiley SK6 .... 113 E2
Salford M8 .... 155 C2
Stalybridge SK15 .... 86 A2
Stockport SK1 .... 169 C1
Waterloo St
Ashton-u-L OL6 ...... 85 D4
Bolton BL1 .... 143 C1
Bury BL8 .... 140 A2
Manchester, Blackley M8 .. 156 C4
Manchester M1 ...... 163 A4
③ Wigan WN6 .... 37 A1
Waterman Ave
Horwich BL6 .... 22 C4
Manchester M19 ..... 111 A6
Waterman View OL16 .. 31 C8
Watermead M31 ..... 108 A1
Watermead Cl SK3 ... 123 E4
Watermede WN5 ..... 53 E3
Watermeetings La SK6 .. 113 D1
Watermill Cl OL16 .... 31 D6
Water Mill Clough OL2 .. 48 C2
Watermill Ct OL7 .... 85 A5
Watermillock Gdns BL1 .. 143 C4
Waterpark Hall ⑪ M7 .. 63 E1
Waterpark Rd M7 .... 155 B4
Waters Edge
Ashton-u-L OL6 ...... 85 E5
Manchester M24 ..... 65 C6
Marple SK6 .... 126 A8
Uppermill OL3 .... 60 F2
Walkden M28 .... 60 F2
Water's Edge BL4 .... 42 A2
Water's Edge Bsns Pk
M5 .... 161 B2
Watersedge Cl SK8 .. 123 B3
Waters Edge Fold OL11 .. 49 C4
Watersfield Cl SK8 ... 131 F8
WATERSHEDDINGS ... 49 D1

Watersheddings Prim Sch
OL1 .... 49 C1
Watersheddings St ⑨
OL4 .... 49 D1
Watersheddings Way ⑪
OL4 .... 49 D1
Waterside
Disley SK12 .... 135 E7
Glossop SK13 .... 104 A6
Hattersley SK14 ...... 102 D2
Marple SK6 .... 125 F5
Sale M33 .... 108 C5
Stretford M17 .... 96 F6
Uppermill OL3 .... 69 C4
Waterside Arts Ctr★ ⑩
M33 .... 108 B5
Waterside Ave ⑤ SK6 .. 125 F5
Waterside Bsns Pk SK13 .. 103 F6
Waterside Cl
Hattersley SK14 ...... 102 D2
Manchester M21 ..... 109 D4
Oldham OL4 .... 49 C4
Radcliffe M26 .... 44 D4
Waterside Cotts OL3 .. 69 C4
Waterside Dr WN3 .. 150 B3
Waterside Gdns BL1 .. 25 A3
Waterside Ind Pk BL3 .. 42 D4
Waterside La OL16 ... 31 B8
Waterside Mews BL3 .. 25 A3
Waterside Plaza ⑥ M33 .. 108 B5
Waterside Rd
Disley SK12, SK22 ... 135 E7
Ramsbottom BL9 ..... 11 C3
Waterside Trad Est ⑧
WN7 .... 76 B4
Waterside View M43 .. 99 E8
Waterside Wlk ④ SK14 .. 102 D2
Waterslea M30 .... 79 C2
Waterslea Dr BL1 .... 40 F8
Watersmead Cl BL1 .. 143 C2
Watersmeet M32 .... 96 D4
Waters Meeting Rd BL1 .. 143 C1
Water's Nook Rd BL5 .. 58 A8
Waterson Ave M40 ... 83 A7
Waters Reach
High Lane SK6 .... 134 E7
Mossley OL5 .... 68 E4
Poynton SK12 .... 133 F5
Wigan WN1 .... 151 C4
Water's Reach M17 .. 96 F6
Water St
Adlington PR7 .... 21 A6
Ashton-u-L OL6 ...... 166 B3
Atherton M46 .... 58 D3
Bolton BL1 .... 145 C3
Bolton, Egerton BL7 ... 8 D2
Denton M34 .... 100 F7
Glossop SK13 .... 104 E2
Hyde SK14 .... 166 C2
Manchester, Ardwick M12 .. 163 C4
Manchester, Harpurhey
M9 .... 157 A4
Manchester M3 ...... 162 A4
④ Middleton M24 .... 46 F1
Newton-le-W WA12 .. 89 C4
Radcliffe M26 .... 44 A3
Ramsbottom BL0 ..... 11 B8
Rochdale OL16 .... 31 A7
Royton OL2 .... 49 A4
Stockport SK1 .... 169 C3
Whitworth OL12 ...... 14 C8
Wigan WN1 .... 150 C4
Waterton Ave OL5 ... 68 B2
Waterton La OL5 ..... 68 B2
Waterview Cl OL16 ... 32 B3
Waterview Pk WN7 ... 75 E4
Waterworks Rd
Delph OL3 .... 51 A6
Oldham OL4 .... 49 E1
Watfield Wlk ⑤ M9 .. 157 A3
Watford Ave M14 .... 98 B2
Watford Bridge Ind Est
SK22 .... 127 D1
Watford Bridge Rd SK22 .. 127 D1
Watford Cl ⑮ BL1 ... 143 B2
Watford La SK22 ..... 127 C2
Watford Lodge SK22 .. 127 C1
Watford Rd
Manchester M19 ..... 111 A6
New Mills SK22 ...... 127 C2
Watkin Ave BL3 ..... 171 B4
Watkin Cl M13 ...... 163 C2
Watkins Dr M25 ..... 63 F3
Watkin St
Dukinfield SK14 ...... 102 A5
Rochdale OL16 .... 31 B4
Salford M3 .... 158 A3
Watling St
Bolton BL8 .... 26 B7
Bury BL8 .... 26 F1
Littleborough OL15 .. 15 F5
Watlington Cl OL1 ... 49 D3
Watson Ave
Ashton-in-M WN4 .... 73 C3
Golborne WA3 .... 73 F1
Watson Gdns OL12 .. 14 D2
Watson Rd BL4 ...... 59 F8
Watson Sq SK1 ...... 169 C1
Watson St
Denton M34 .... 101 B3
Eccles M30 .... 79 C2
Manchester M2, M3 .. 162 C4
Oldham OL4 .... 67 C8
Radcliffe M26 .... 44 A4
Swinton M27 .... 79 F8
Watton Cl M27 .... 61 F2

Watts St
Chadderton OL9 ...... 152 B3
Horwich BL6 .... 22 C2
Manchester M19 ..... 111 B8
Oldham OL8 .... 66 D2
❶ Rochdale OL12 ... 31 A8
Waugh Ave M35 ..... 83 F7
Wavell Dr BL9 .... 45 A1
Wavell Rd M22 .... 121 D2
Waveney Dr
Altrincham WA14 .... 119 C6
Handforth SK9 .... 131 D2
Waveney Rd
Shaw OL2 .... 149 A4
Wythenshawe M22 .. 121 E4
Waverley Ave
Kearsley BL4 .... 60 F6
Stretford M32 .... 96 F3
Waverley Cres M43 .. 84 A2
Waverley Dr SK8 .... 132 B7
Waverley Gr WN7 ... 76 D6
Waverley Rd
Bolton BL1 .... 143 B3
Golborne WA3 .... 74 D1
Hindley WN2 .... 56 C5
Hyde SK14 .... 113 D8
Manchester M9 ...... 157 C3
Middleton M24 .... 47 A3
Pendlebury M27 ...... 80 C7
Sale M33 .... 108 B5
Stockport SK3 .... 123 C7
Walkden M28 .... 60 B1
Waverley Road W M9 .. 157 C3
Waverley Sq BL4 .... 60 C6
Waverley St
Oldham OL1 .... 49 C1
Rochdale OL11 .... 30 C1
Waverton Ave M34 .. 11 D7
Waverton Rd M14 ... 98 A1
Wavertree Ave M46 .. 58 C4
Wavertree Ct ⑥ BL1 .. 145 B4
Wavertree Rd M9 ... 64 C4
Waybridge Ind Pk M50 .. 96 C8
Wayfarers Dr
Newton-le-W WA12 .. 89 E2
Tyldesley M29 .... 77 A8
Wayfarers Way M27 .. 79 F7
Wayfaring BL5 .... 39 F2
Wayford Wlk M9 .... 156 C6
Wayland Rd M18 .... 99 D3
Wayland Road S M18 .. 99 D3
Wayne St M43 .... 44 C8
Wayne St M11 .... 99 E8
Wayoh Croft BL7 .... 9 D6
Wayside Cl M41 ..... 133 C4
Wayside Gdns SK7 .. 125 A2
Wayside Gr M28 ..... 60 E4
Weald Cl M13 .... 163 C2
Wealdstone Gr BL2 .. 25 B2
Weardale Rd M9 .... 64 B5
Wearhead Cl WA3 ... 89 F7
Wearhead Row M5 ... 154 C1
Wearish La BL5 ...... 57 C6
WEASTE 154 B1
Weaste Ave M38 .... 60 B4
Weaste Dr M5 .... 154 A3
Weaste La M5, M6 ... 154 A3
Weaste Metro Sta M5 .. 154 A1
Weaste Rd M5 .... 154 A2
Weaste Trad Est M6 .. 154 A2
Weatherall Street N M47 .. 155 C3
Weatherley Cl OL8 ... 67 A1
Weatherley Dr SK6 ... 125 D6
Weaver Ave M28 .... 60 A2
Weaver Chase M26 .. 61 B8
Weaver Cl M14 ...... 119 C1
Weaver Ct M15 ..... 162 A2
Weaver Dr BL9 .... 27 F8
Weaver Gr WN7 ..... 75 C4
Weaverham ❷ M13 .. 98 F3
Weaverham Way SK9 .. 131 E4
Weaverham Wlk M33 .. 108 E3
Weaver Ho ⑤ BL1 ... 81 C5
Weavermill Pk WN4 .. 73 C2
Weaver Rd M22 ..... 92 A2
Weavers Ct
Bolton BL3 .... 145 B1
❶ Middleton M24 .... 46 F1
Mottram in L SK14 ... 103 A4
Weavers Gn BL4 ..... 60 D8
Weavers La SK7 ...... 132 D6
Weavers Rd M24 .... 46 F1
Weaver Wlk ⑤ M11 .. 99 D7
Webb Gr SK14 .... 102 F1
Webb La SK1 .... 124 A8
Webb St
Bury BL8 .... 140 A3
Horwich BL6 .... 22 C3
Webb Wlk SK14 ...... 102 F1
Webdale Dr M40 .... 83 A7
Weber Dr BL3 .... 145 A1
Webster Gr M25 ..... 62 F2
Webster Prim Sch M15 .. 98 A4
Webster's St WN2 ... 56 A2
Webster St
Bolton BL3 .... 148 B1
❸ Mossley OL5 ..... 68 C2
Oldham OL8 .... 153 C1
Wedgewood Dr WN6 .. 36 D3
Wedgewood St M40 .. 160 C4
Wedgwood Rd M27 .. 62 B2
Wedhurst St OL4 ..... 67 C7
Wednesburgh SK14 .. 103 C5
Weedall Ave M5 ..... 161 A2

Weeder Sq OL2 ...... 49 E8
Weedon Ave WA12 ... 89 B5
Weedon St OL16 .... 31 B8
Weeton Ave BL2 ..... 42 F7
Weighbridge Ct M44 .. 94 C3
Weint The WA3 ..... 105 B3
Weir Rd OL16 .... 31 E7
Weir St
Failsworth M35 ...... 83 E7
Manchester M15 ..... 162 B1
Welbeck Ave
Failsworth OL9 ...... 65 D3
Littleborough OL15 .. 16 A6
Newton-le-W WA12 .. 89 D2
Urmston M41 .... 95 F3
Welbeck Cl
Milnrow OL16 .... 31 E6
Whitefield M45 ...... 44 F2
Welbeck Gr M7 ...... 155 B3
Welbeck Ho ④ OL6 .. 166 A2
Welbeck Rd
Ashton-in-M WN4 .... 73 C4
Bolton BL1 .... 144 A4
Eccles M30 .... 79 E4
Hyde SK14 .... 167 C2
❶ Reddish SK5 ...... 111 F8
Rochdale OL16 .... 31 B4
Swinton M28 .... 79 B6
Wigan WN3 .... 54 E3
Welbeck St M18 ..... 99 E6
Welbeck Street N OL6 .. 166 A2
Welbeck Street S OL6,
OL7 .... 166 A2
Welbeck Terr OL6 ... 166 A2
Welburn Ave M22 ... 121 E3
Welburn Cl WN5 .... 53 E5
Welburn St OL11 .... 139 C1
Welburn Rd M23 .... 108 F1
Welby St M13 .... 98 D4
Welch Hill St WN7 .. 75 E4
Welch Rd SK14 ..... 167 C4
Welcomb Cl SK6 .... 112 F4
Welcomb St M11 .... 165 B3
Welcomb Wlk M45 .. 62 F7
Welcome Par OL8 ... 67 D3
Welcroft St SK1 ..... 170 C4
Weldon Ave BL3 .... 146 A2
Weldon Cres SK3 ... 123 E4
Weldon Dr M9 .... 64 D5
Weldon Gr WN1 ..... 37 E2
Weldon Rd WA14 ... 119 D6
Weld Rd M20 .... 110 D7
Welfold Ho ❸ OL4 .. 67 B5
Welford Ave WA3 ... 90 C7
Welford Cl SK9 ..... 137 E8
Welford Gn SK5 ..... 111 F5
Welford Rd M9 ...... 63 F3
Welford St M6 .... 81 B4
Welkin Rd SK6 .... 112 C3
Welkin Road Ind Est
SK6 .... 112 C3
Wellacre Ave M41 .. 94 D2
Wellacre Tech Coll M41 .. 94 D2
Welland Ave OL10 ... 29 A3
Welland Cl M15 ...... 162 A2
Welland Ct ④ M15 .. 162 A2
Welland St
Droylsden M11 .... 99 D8
❶ Reddish SK5 ...... 99 F1
Welland The BL5 ..... 57 E8
Wellbank SK15 .... 102 D8
Wellbank Ave OL6 ... 85 E6
Wellbank Cl
Little Lever BL3 ...... 43 B3
Oldham OL8 .... 67 A4
Wellbank Ct BL8 .... 26 F6
Wellbank St BL8 .... 26 F6
Wellbank View OL12 .. 13 F2
Wellbrook Ct SK9 ... 137 D4
Wellbrow Terr OL12 .. 14 D2
Wellbrow Wlk ⑱ M9 .. 64 E3
Wellburn Cl BL3 ..... 40 F2
Wellcroft Gdns WA13 .. 117 A2
Wellcross Rd WN8 ... 53 B6
Welldale Mews M33 .. 108 E5
Wellens Way M24 ... 64 C7
Weller Ave
Manchester M21 ..... 109 D7
Poynton SK12 .... 133 D2
Weller Cl SK12 .... 133 D2
Weller Ct M16 .... 97 E2
Weller Gdns M21 ... 109 D7
Wellesbourne Dr M23 .. 120 F7
Wellesley Ave M18 .. 99 D6
Wellesley Cl
Newton-le-W WA12 .. 89 B5
Wigan WN5 .... 54 E8
Wellfield SK6 .... 113 C4
Wellfield Cl BL9 ..... 44 E6
Wellfield Gdns WA15 .. 120 C3
Wellfield Inf Sch M33 .. 107 F6
Wellfield Jun Sch M33 .. 107 F6
Wellfield La WA15 .. 120 C3
Wellfield Pl ⑤ OL15 .. 31 A5
Wellfield Rd
Bolton BL3 .... 144 C1
Culcheth WA3 .... 91 F4
Hindley WN2 .... 57 A4
Manchester M8 ...... 156 A4
Stockport SK2 .... 124 C6
Urmston M29 .... 37 A3
Wythenshawe M23 .. 121 A7
Wellfield St OL11 .... 31 A5

Well Gate SK13 ...... 104 E2
Wellgate Ave M19 ... 111 B8
Well Gr M45 .... 44 E2
WELL GREEN 120 C2
Wellgreen Cl WA15 .. 120 C3
Wellgreen Lo WA15 .. 120 C3
Well Green Prim Sch
WA15 .... 120 C2
Wellham Rd WN3 ... 55 B3
Wellhead Cl M15 .... 162 C1
Wellhouse Dr ❸ M40 .. 65 C3
Well-i-Hole Rd OL3 ... 68 F4
Welling Rd M40 ...... 83 E8
Welling St ⑳ BL2 ... 25 B1
Wellington Ave M16 .. 97 D2
Wellington Cl
Newton-le-W WA12 .. 89 A3
Sale M33 .... 108 C6
Wellington Clough ④
OL7 .... 85 A6
Wellington Cres M16 .. 97 C3
Wellington Ct
⑨ Ashton-u-L OL6 .. 166 C3
⑥ Bury BL8 .... 27 B1
Oldham OL8 .... 66 D4
Wellington Ctr OL6 .. 166 C2
Wellington Dr M29 ... 59 E1
Wellington Gdns
Bury BL8 .... 27 B1
Newton-le-W WA12 .. 89 A3
Wellington Gr
Ince-in-M WN3 ...... 151 A1
Manchester M15 ..... 162 A2
Stockport SK2 .... 170 C3
Wellington Ho
Altrincham WA14 .... 119 F5
Manchester M20 ..... 110 C7
Wellington Lo OL15 .. 16 B6
Wellington Mews BL7 .. 9 D4
Wellington Mill SK4 .. 169 B1
Wellington Par SK16 .. 166 B1
Wellington Pl
Altrincham WA14 .... 119 D4
Manchester M13 ..... 156 B4
⑬ Rochdale OL16 ... 31 A8
Wellington Rd
Altrincham WA14 .... 119 F6
Ashton-u-L OL6 ...... 166 B3
Bury BL9 .... 140 C1
Chapeltown BL7 ..... 9 D4
Eccles M30 .... 79 F2
Hazel Grove SK7 ..... 134 B8
Manchester, Fallowfield M14,
M20 .... 110 C8
Manchester M8 ...... 156 B4
Manchester, Whalley range
M16 .... 97 C2
Oldham OL8 .... 153 B1
Over Hulton M46 .... 58 F5
Swinton M27 .... 79 F8
Uppermill OL3 .... 69 B6
Wellington Road N M19, SK1,
SK4 .... 169 A3
Wellington Road S M19,
SK2 .... 170 C4
Wellington Sch WA15 .. 119 F6
Wellington Sq ❸ BL8 .. 27 B1
Wellington St
Ashton-u-L OL6 ...... 166 B2
Bolton BL3 .... 145 B2
Bury BL8 .... 140 A1
Chadderton OL9 ...... 152 B4
Denton M34 .... 100 F6
Dukinfield SK16 ...... 166 B1
❷ Failsworth M35 .. 66 A1
Farnworth BL4 .... 60 D8
Hazel Grove SK7 ..... 124 F3
❶ Littleborough OL15 .. 16 B6
Manchester M18 ..... 99 D5
Milnrow OL16 .... 32 A6
Newton-le-W WA12 .. 89 A3
⑯ Radcliffe M26 ..... 44 C4
⑲ Rochdale OL12 ... 14 F1
Salford M3 .... 158 A2
Stockport SK1 .... 169 C1
Stretford M32 .... 96 C1
Westhoughton BL5 .. 39 E2
Wigan WN1 .... 151 D8
Wellington Street E M7 .. 155 B3
Wellington Street W M7 .. 155 A2
Wellington Terr
⑬ Dukinfield SK16 .. 166 B1
Salford M5 .... 154 A2
Wellington Wlk BL3 .. 145 B2
Well i' th' La OL11 ... 31 A5
Well La
Wall La M45 .... 44 F2
Well Mdw SK14 ..... 167 A4
Well Mead SK6 ..... 112 E3
Wellmead Cl M8 .... 155 C1
Well Meadow La OL3 .. 167 A4
Wellpark Wlk ㉑ M40 .. 83 C5
Well Rd WN7 .... 57 D1
Well Row SK14 ...... 113 A8
Wells Ave
Billinge WN5 .... 71 D6
Chadderton OL9 ...... 48 A1
Manchester M25 ..... 63 C2
Wells Cl
Droylsden M43 .... 99 F8
Gatley SK8 .... 131 C7
Middleton M24 .... 64 C7
Tyldesley M29 .... 77 C8
Wells Ct SK16 .... 101 C6

Wells Dr
Dukinfield SK16.........101 C6
Manchester SK4.........110 E2
Wigan WN2...............37 F2
Wellside Wlk 7 M8....156 A2
Wells Pl WN1.........151 B4
Wells Rd OL1.........49 E5
Wells St BL9.........140 B1
Well St
Ainsworth BL2..........26 C1
Bolton BL1.............148 A3
Heywood OL10...........29 E1
Manchester M4.........159 A2
6 Rochdale OL11........31 A5
Tyldesley M29..........77 A8
Wellstock La M38......59 F6
Well Street N BL0......1 C2
Wellwood Dr M40......83 A7
Wellyhole St OL4......67 D6
Welman Way WA15....119 F4
Welney Rd M16.........97 B3
Welshpool Cl M23....109 B2
Welshpool Way 9 M34..101 A1
Welton Ave M20......110 C2
Welton Cl
Leigh WN7..............76 C5
Wilmslow SK9..........136 F4
Welton Dr SK9.......136 E4
Welton Gr SK9.......136 E4
Welwyn Cl M41........95 B5
Welwyn Dr M6.........80 A5
Welwyn Wlk M40......160 A2
Wembley Cl SK3......170 A1
Wembley Gr M14......110 C8
Wembley Rd M18.......99 C3
Wembury St M9......157 B4
Wembury Street N M9..157 B4
Wembury Wlk M12....102 E3
Wemsley Gr 20 BL2....25 B1
Wem St OL9...........66 A4
Wemyss Ave SK5.......99 F1
Wendlebury Cl WN7....75 E1
Wendlebury Gn OL2...149 A1
Wendon Rd M23......121 B5
Wendover Dr BL3......40 E5
Wendover Rd
Urmston M41............95 C2
Wythenshawe M23.....120 D8
Wenfield Dr M9.......65 B3
Wenlock Ave OL6......85 B5
Wenlock Cl
Hazel Grove SK2......125 A6
Horwich BL6............22 C6
Wenlock Ct M12......164 C2
Wenlock Gr 3 WN2....56 D4
Wenlock St
Hindley WN2............56 D5
Leigh WN7..............75 E2
Sale M33..............108 A2
Wenlock St
9 Hindley WN2.........56 D5
Swinton M27............79 D8
Wenlock Way M12.....164 C2
Wenning Cl M45.......45 C1
Wennington Rd WN3....54 F4
Wensley Ct M7........63 A1
Wensleydale Ave SK8..122 C6
Wensley Dr
Hazel Grove SK7......133 D7
Manchester M20.......110 B5
Wensley Rd
Cheadle SK8...........122 C6
Golborne WA3...........90 E7
Manchester M7..........63 A1
Reddish SK5...........169 C4
Wensley Way OL16.....31 C6
Wentbridge Rd BL1....145 A4
Wentworth Ave
Altrincham WA15.......120 A6
11 Bury BL8............27 B4
Farnworth BL4..........60 C7
Heywood OL10...........46 D8
Irlam M44..............94 A3
8 Manchester M18......99 E6
Salford M6.............80 B2
Urmston M41............95 B1
Whitefield M45.........62 D7
Wentworth Cl
Marple SK6............125 F8
Middleton M24..........64 E8
Radcliffe M26..........43 D4
Wentworth Ct
Failsworth M35.........83 F6
Whitefield M45.........62 E8
Wentworth Dr
Bramhall SK7.........133 A7
Sale M33..............107 F5
Wentworth High Sch M30 79 F4
Wentworth Rd
Reddish SK5............99 F1
Salford M30............80 A4
Swinton M27............79 D6
Wentworth Wlk 2 SK14 101 F5
Werburgh Cl WA13....117 C8
WERNETH.............152 C1
Werneth Ave
Hyde SK14.............113 F8
Manchester M14.........98 B2
Werneth Cl
Denton M34............100 F2

Werneth Cl continued
Hazel Grove SK7.......124 E4
Werneth Cres OL6......66 C4
Werneth Ct SK14......167 B1
Werneth Hall Rd OL8...153 A1
Werneth Ho SK1.......167 B1
Werneth Hollow SK6....113 B6
Werneth Low Ctry Pk*
SK14.................114 A7
Werneth Low Rd
Compstall SK14........114 B6
Hyde SK14, SK6.......113 C5
Werneth Prim Sch OL8..153 B1
Werneth Rd
Glossop SK13..........116 A7
Hyde SK14.............167 C2
Romiley SK6...........113 C5
Werneth Rise SK14.....113 F7
Werneth Sch OL6......113 A2
Werneth Sta OL9......153 A2
Werneth Wlk M34......100 F2
Wescoe Cl WN5.........53 E5
Wesham Rd M11.........83 A2
Wesley Cl
Rochdale OL12..........15 C3
Westhoughton BL5......39 E2
Wesley Ct
Bury BL8...............26 E7
Manchester SK4........110 F2
Walkden M28............60 D4
Westhoughton BL5......39 E2
Wesley Dr
Ashton-u-L OL6.........85 D6
Worsley M28............78 F8
Wesley Methodist Prim Sch
M26....................43 F5
Wesley Mews 8 BL2....148 B3
Wesley Sq M41.........95 A2
Wesley St
Atherton M46...........58 E3
Bolton BL3............145 B1
3 Bolton, Toppings BL7..25 A8
Bury BL8...............26 E7
Eccles M30.............79 C2
Failsworth M35.........66 A1
Farnworth BL4..........60 E7
Glossop SK13..........104 E2
Hadfield SK13.........104 A5
Hazel Grove SK7.......124 E3
Heywood OL10...........29 C2
Milnrow OL16...........31 E6
1 Rochdale OL12........15 B3
Royton OL2.............48 E3
Stockport SK1.........169 C1
Stretford M32...........96 E3
Swinton M27............79 F8
Westhoughton BL5......39 E2
Wigan WN5..............54 D5
Wesleys The 4 BL4.....59 F8
Wessenden Bank E SK2.124 D5
Wessenden Bank W SK2.124 D5
Wessex Cl WN1.........20 B1
Wessex Dr 1 WN3......55 F4
Wessex Park Cl OL2...149 B4
Wessex Rd WN5........36 D1
Wessington Bank 7
SK13.................171 B2
Wessington Fold 12
SK13.................171 B2
Wessington Gn 11 SK13..171 B2
Wessington Mews SK13..171 B2
Westage Gdns M23.....121 A7
West Ashton St M50...154 C1
West Ave
Altrincham WA14.......119 A5
Droylsden M18.........99 E5
Failsworth M40.........65 D1
Farnworth BL4..........60 B8
Gatley SK8............122 C1
Golborne WA3...........74 B1
Leigh WN7..............76 C3
Manchester M19.......110 F7
Rochdale OL12..........15 C3
Stalybridge SK15.......86 A3
Walkden M28............60 D4
Whitefield M45.........44 E2
West Bank M11........100 A7
Westbank Rd
Bolton BL6.............40 D6
Manchester M20.......110 D5
West Bank St
Salford M5............161 C4
Tyldesley M46..........58 E1
Westbourne BB4........1 A8
Westbourne Ave
Bolton BL3............145 B1
Leigh WN7..............75 E7
Swinton M27............61 D5
Whitefield M45.........44 D1
Westbourne Cl WN3....55 E4
Westbourne Dr
Ashton-u-L OL7.......166 A4
16 Handforth SK9.....131 D1
Westbourne Gr
Manchester M9........157 A4
Manchester, Withington
M20...................110 A6
Reddish SK5...........111 F8
Sale M33..............108 A4
Westbourne Pk M41.....95 D2
Westbourne Range M18..99 F4
Westbourne Rd
Denton M34............100 E2
Eccles M30.............79 B4
Manchester M14.......110 D8

Westbourne Rd continued
Urmston M41............95 D2
Westbourne St OL9....153 A3
Westbridge Mews WN1..153 C6
West Bridgewater St WN7 75 F4
Westbrook Cl OL11.....47 D8
Westbrook Ct BL2.....148 A2
Westbrook Rd
Stretford M17..........96 D7
Swinton M27............79 F7
Westbrook Sq M12.....165 A2
Westbrook St BL9.....140 B1
Westbrook Trad Est M13 110 A8
Westbury Ave
Sale M33..............107 C1
Wigan WN3..............54 D2
Westbury Cl
Bury BL8...............27 A1
Westhoughton BL5......40 A1
Westbury Dr SK6......125 E6
Westbury Rd M8........64 B1
Westbury St
Ashton-u-L OL6........166 C3
Dukinfield SK14.......101 C5
Westbury Street Ind Est
SK14.................101 C5
Westbury Way OL1, OL2..48 D2
Westby Gr SK7........133 A7
Westby Gr BL2........148 C4
West Central Dr M27...89 B7
Westchapel Mews BL5...39 E3
West Charles St M5.....81 A1
West Church St 9 OL10..29 C2
West Cl
Bury BL9...............45 B4
Tyldesley M46..........58 E1
Westcliffe Ho 3 OL12...15 D4
Westcliffe Rd BL1......24 F6
Westcombe Dr BL8......27 C5
Westcott Ave M20.....110 A6
Westcott Cl BL2........25 E5
Westcott Dr WN5......162 A3
Westcott Dr WN3.......54 E4
Westcott Gr OL2......149 A1
West Cotts OL3.........68 F5
Westcourt Rd
Bolton BL3............147 A3
Sale M33..............108 A6
Westcraig Ave M40.....65 C3
West Craven St M5.....161 B3
West Cres M24..........64 F7
West Croft Ind Est M24..64 C7
Westcroft Rd M19, M20.110 D4
West Crown Ave M5....161 B4
Westdale Gdns M19.....111 A5
Westdean Cres M19.....110 F5
West Dean St M5.......81 C1
WEST DIDSBURY.......109 E4
Westdown Gdns 1 OL2..48 F8
West Downs Rd SK8....122 F3
West Dr
Bury BL9...............27 E5
Droylsden M43.........83 F1
Gatley SK8............122 A4
Glossop SK13..........103 F7
Pendlebury, Irlams o' th' Height
M6....................80 E6
Pendlebury, Swinton Park
M27...................80 B7
West Egerton St M5.....81 B1
West End M5..........114 F8
Westend Ave PR7.......19 D8
West End Ave SK8......122 A6
West End Prim Sch OL7..84 F2
Westend St BL4........60 D9
West End St OL9......153 A3
West End Trad Est 4
M27...................61 F1
Westerdale 1 OL4......67 C6
Westerdale SK14........79 B8
Westerdale Dr
Bolton BL3............144 A1
Bolton BL3............144 A1
Westerham Ave M5......81 A1
Westerham Cl BL8......27 C7
Wester Hill OL7........85 B8
Wester Hill Rd OL8.....67 A1
Westerling Way M16....97 E3
Western Ave M27.......62 D2
Western Circ M19.....110 F6
Western Ct OL13........3 B8
Western Rd
Bacup OL13.............3 C8
Urmston M41............94 E1
Western St
Manchester M18.........99 E6
Salford M6............154 B3
Westerton Ct BL3......145 A1
Westfield
Altrincham WA14.......119 C3
Salford M6............154 B4
Westfield Ave
Ashton-in-M WN4........73 A4
Middleton M24..........65 A7
Westfield Cl OL11.....113 C5
Westfield Com Sch WN5..54 D7
Westfield Dr
Romiley SK6...........113 C5
Uppermill OL4..........68 E5
Westfield Gr
Denton M34............100 E5
Wigan WN1..............37 B3
Westfield Rd
Bolton BL3............146 B2
Cheadle SK8...........131 F8
Droylsden M43.........83 E2
Manchester M21.........97 B1

Westfield Rd continued
Tyldesley M46..........58 E1
Westfields WA15......128 F8
Westfield St
Chadderton OL9.......152 C4
Manchester M7..........63 D1
Westgate
Altrincham WA15.......119 E2
Sale M33..............108 A4
Urmston M41............95 B1
Whitworth OL12.........14 B7
Wilmslow SK9..........137 A3
Westgate Ave
Bolton BL3............144 C3
Bury BL9..............140 B1
2 Manchester M9........64 C2
Ramsbottom BL0.........11 A2
Westgate Cl OL12......14 B7
Westgate Dr
Orrell WN5.............53 D5
Swinton M27............79 F6
Tyldesley M29..........77 C6
Westgate Ho 4 OL8.....66 D2
Westgate Rd M6........80 C4
Westgate St OL7......166 A1
West Gdns 1 OL13......3 B8
West Gn M24...........64 B7
WEST GORTON........164 C3
West Gr
Manchester M13.......164 A1
1 Mossley OL5..........68 C1
Sale M33..............108 B3
Westhoughton BL5......57 E6
Westgrove Ave BL1.....24 E6
West Hall M5..........74 E1
Westhide Wlk 6 M9.....64 F1
West High St M5.......81 A2
West Hill OL11........139 B2
West Hill Cl SK15......85 F2
West Hill Sch SK15.....85 F2
Westholm Ave SK4.....111 B7
Westholme Rd
Manchester M20.......110 B5
Prestwich M25.........63 C7
West Hope St M5.......81 B1
Westhorne Fold 1 M8...63 E2
WESTHOUGHTON........57 C8
Westhoughton Com L Ctr
BL5....................57 F8
Westhoughton High Sch &
Specialist Tech Coll 4
BL5....................57 E8
Westhoughton Parochial CE
Prim Sch BL5..........57 E8
Westhoughton Rd PR6,
PR7....................20 F8
Westhoughton Sta BL5..39 E2
WEST HULME..........48 D1
Westhulme Ave OL1.....48 D1
Westhulme St OL1......48 D1
Westhulme Way OL1.....48 C1
Westinghouse Ind Est
M17....................96 C5
Westinghouse Rd M17..96 B5
West King St M3.......158 B2
Westlake Gr WN2.......57 B4
Westlake St M11......165 C3
Westland Ave
Bolton BL1............142 A1
Farnworth BL4..........60 C6
Stockport SK1.........112 B1
Westland Dr M9........64 D4
Westlands M45.........62 F6
Westlands The M27.....80 C6
West Lea M34.........101 A2
Westlea Dr M18........99 D3
WESTLEIGH...........75 E7
Westleigh Ave M5.....100 A1
Westleigh Dr M25......63 D3
Westleigh High Sch WN7.57 D1
Westleigh La WN7......57 D1
Westleigh St Paul's CE Prim
Sch WN7...............75 E8
Westlerigh Cl M9......75 F8
Westleigh View WN7....75 E8
Westlock WN3.........150 C2
West Malling Cl OL10...46 F7
Westmarsh Cl 4 BL1...143 B1
West Marwood St M7...155 B2
West Mdw SK5.........100 A1
Westmead WN6.........36 E8
Westmeade Dr WA15...120 B7
West Meade
Bolton BL3............147 A2
Manchester, Chorlton-cum-Hardy
M21...................109 A7
Manchester, Sedgley Park
M25...................79 E6
Swinton M27............79 E6
Westmeade Rd M28.....60 C5
Westmere Dr M9......156 C2
Westminster Ave
Ashton-u-L OL6.........85 D7
Farnworth BL4..........60 C8
Manchester M16.........97 C2
Radcliffe M26..........43 D4
Reddish SK5...........111 F7
Royton OL2.............48 C6
Whitefield M45.........62 E8
Westminster Cl
Marple SK6............125 D7
Sale M33..............107 D3
Shaw OL2..............149 B4
Westminster Dr
Cheadle SK8...........132 B6
Leigh WN7..............76 E7
Wilmslow SK9..........137 A4
Westminster Ho M3....158 B3

Westminster Rd
Altrincham WA15.......120 A2
Bolton BL1.............24 E5
Eccles M30.............79 F3
Failsworth M35.........84 B8
Urmston M41............95 E4
Walkden M28............60 D2
Westminster St
Bury BL9..............140 B1
Farnworth BL4..........60 C8
1 Manchester M19.......99 B1
Oldham OL1.............67 B8
Rochdale OL11.........139 A1
Salford M15...........161 C3
Swinton M27............61 E1
Wigan WN5..............54 F6
Westminster Way SK16..101 D6
Westminster Wlk 8 BL4..60 C8
Westmoor Gables SK4..168 A4
Westmorland Cl 3 WN1..37 E1
Westmorland Cl
Altrincham WA14.......128 B8
Bury BL9...............44 E6
Westmorland Ave
Ashton-u-L OL7........166 B4
Dukinfield SK14.......101 E8
Westmorland Cl SK5....112 C6
Westmorland Dr
Brinnington SK5.......112 C6
Wardle OL12............15 D1
Westmorland Prim Sch 1
SK5...................112 C6
Westmorland Rd
Manchester M20.......110 A2
Partington M31........105 E2
Sale M33..............108 C2
Salford M30............80 A4
Tyldesley M29..........59 A2
Urmston M41............95 C1
Westmorland Wlk 2 OL2..48 E4
West Mosley St M2.....159 A1
West Mount
Orrell WN5.............53 F6
Wigan WN1..............37 D2
Westmount Cl M40.....156 C2
West Oak Pl SK8......122 F1
Weston Ave
Failsworth M40.........65 E1
Rochdale OL16..........31 B4
Swinton M27............61 F4
Wigan WN3..............55 B1
Westonby Ct WN4......73 D3
Weston Ct M14........98 D2
Weston Dr
Denton M34............101 A3
Stockport SK8.........123 D4
West One Ret Pk M50...80 A1
Weston Gr
Reddish SK4...........111 C6
Wythenshawe M22......121 E8
Weston Pk WN6........36 D3
Weston Rd
4 Irlam M44...........94 A2
Wilmslow SK9..........137 E6
Weston St
Atherton M46...........58 E4
Bolton BL3............42 A4
Manchester M4........160 A2
Milnrow OL16..........31 E6
Oldham OL8............67 C4
Reddish SK5...........169 B4
Westover St M27.......61 F1
Westover Rd M41......95 C3
Westover St M27.......61 F1
West Par M33.........107 C3
Westpark BL1.........144 C3
West Park Ave
Denton M34............101 B2
Poynton SK12.........133 A4
West Park Rd
Stockport, Bramhall Park
SK7...................123 D2
Stockport, Portwood SK1.112 B2
West Park St M5.......161 B3
West Pk SK14.........113 E6
West Pl M19..........111 B2
Westpoint Ent Pk M17..95 F7
West Point Lodge 1
M19...................110 F8
Westray Cres M5......154 B1
Westray Rd M13........98 E2
West Rd
Altrincham WA14.......119 C2
Manchester M41.........95 E7
Prestwich M25.........62 F5
Urmston M41............95 F7
Westrees WN7.........90 B6
Westridge Chase 4 OL2..48 D5
West St
Alderley Edge SK9.....137 A1
Ashton-u-L OL6.......166 B3
Bolton BL1............144 C3
Droylsden M11.........83 B2
Dukinfield SK14.......101 D5
Dukinfield SK16......166 B1
Failsworth M35.........83 F7
Farnworth BL4..........42 E1
Glossop SK13..........103 F7
Heywood OL10...........29 D2
Hindley WN2............57 B3
Ince-in-M WN2.........56 A8
Littleborough OL15....16 C5
Middleton M24..........47 A2
Oldham OL1............31 D7
Oldham, Nether Lees OL4..67 E5
Oldham OL9...........153 A3
Oldham OL9...........153 A2

West St — Whalley Ave

West St continued
2 Radcliffe M26. . . . . . 44 A3
Rawtenstall BB4 . . . . . . 2 E8
Rochdale OL16. . . . . . 31 A8
Stalybridge SK15. . . . . . 85 F2
Stockport SK3 . . . . . . 169 A1
Tyldesley M46 . . . . . . 58 E1
Wigan WN6 . . . . . . 37 B1
West Starkey St OL10 . . . . 29 C3
West Thorpe WA14. . . . . 119 B2
West Towers Mews SK6 . 126 A4
West Towers St M6 . . . . 154 C1
West Vale M26. . . . . . 44 A3
West Vale Rd WA15 . . . . 119 F6
West View
Bacup OL13 . . . . . . 3 B8
Denton M34. . . . . . 100 E7
Haslingden BB4 . . . . . . 1 A7
Littleborough OL15 . . . . 16 C5
Ramsbottom BL0 . . . . . . 1 C2
Shaw OL3. . . . . . 50 C6
West View Ct M22 . . . . 121 F8
West View Gr M45 . . . . 44 D1
West View Rd M22 . . . . 121 E8
Westville Gdns M19 . . . . 110 E5
Westward Ho OL16 . . . . 31 F6
Westward Rd SK9. . . . . 136 F6
Westway
Droylsden M43. . . . . . 100 A8
Manchester M9 . . . . . . 64 B6
Oldham OL4 . . . . . . 67 E5
Shaw OL2. . . . . . 149 B2
West Way
Bolton BL1. . . . . . 25 B3
Walkden M38. . . . . . 60 A5
Westwell Gdns 4 BL1. . 143 C1
Westwell Gr 3 WN7 . . . . 75 E8
Westwell St WN7 . . . . 75 E8
Westwick Terr 16 BL1. . 143 B2
West Wlk BL7. . . . . . 8 D2
WESTWOOD 152 C3
Westwood WA14. . . . . 119 B4
Westwood Ave
Altrincham WA15. . . . . 119 F7
Failsworth M40 . . . . . . 65 E1
Hyde SK14. . . . . . 102 B3
Salford M7. . . . . . 155 B4
Urmston M41. . . . . . 95 F1
Walkden M38. . . . . . 60 A3
Westwood Bsns Ctr OL9 153 A2
Westwood Bsns Pk WN3 150 C2
Westwood Cl BL4. . . . . . 60 D8
Westwood Cotts 6 M16. . 97 F4
Westwood Cres M30 . . . . 79 B4
Westwood Dr
Oldham OL9. . . . . . 153 A3
Pendlebury M27. . . . . . 80 C6
Sale M33 . . . . . . 108 B2
Westwood Ho 8 BL4. . 60 D8
Westwood Ind Est OL9 . . 152 C3
Westwood La WN3. . . . . 151 A1
Westwood Lo WA15. . . . . 119 F2
WESTWOOD PARK. 79 B4
Westwood Park Prim Sch
M30. . . . . . 79 B3
Westwood Pk WN3. . . . . 150 C2
Westwood Prim Sch
OL9 . . . . . . 153 A3
Westwood Rd
Bolton BL1. . . . . . 144 C4
Gatley SK8. . . . . . 131 B8
Stockport SK2 . . . . . . 124 B4
Stretford M32 . . . . . . 96 B2
Wigan WN3 . . . . . . 150 C2
Westwood St M14. . . . . . 97 F4
Westwood Terr WN3 . . . . 151 B1
Westwood Trad Est SK6 . 125 E5
Westwood Way OL1. . . . . 48 D1
West Works Rd M17, M22 . 96 C5
Westworth Cl 11 BL1. . 145 A4
Wet Earth Gn M27 . . . . 79 E7
Wetgate La WA13 . . . . 117 E4
Wetheral Cl WN2 . . . . . . 57 C3
Wetheral Dr BL3 . . . . 147 B3
Wetherall St M19 . . . . . . 99 B1
Wetherby Cl WA12 . . . . 89 C5
Wetherby Dr
Hazel Grove SK7 . . . . 125 A2
Royton OL2. . . . . . 48 D5
Wetherby St M11 . . . . . . 99 E7
Wexford Wlk M22. . . . . 121 E2
Wexham Gdns WN2 . . . . 56 A3
Weybourne Ave M9 . . . . 65 A2
Weybourne Dr
Romiley SK6. . . . . . 112 F4
Wigan WN3 . . . . . . 54 E3
Weybourne Gr 3 BL2 . . 25 B4
Weybridge Cl 4 BL1. . 145 B4
Weybridge Rd M4. . . . . 159 C2
Weybrook Rd M19 . . . . 111 C7
Weycroft Cl BL2 . . . . . . 43 A6
Weydale Gr WN3. . . . . . 56 E4
Weygates Dr WA15. . . . . 129 C7
Weyhill Rd M23. . . . . 121 A5
Weylands Gr M6 . . . . . . 80 B5
Weymouth Dr WN2 . . . . 57 A4
Weymouth Ho 6 OL9 . . 48 A1
Weymouth Rd
Ashton-u-L OL6 . . . . . . 85 F6
Eccles M30 . . . . . . 79 B3
Weymouth St BL1. . . . . 143 B2
Weythorne Dr
Bolton BL1. . . . . . 143 C4
Bury BL9 . . . . . . 28 F4
Whalley Ave
Bolton BL1. . . . . . 23 F3
Glazebury WA3 . . . . . . 92 C3
Littleborough OL15 . . . . 16 A6

Whalley Ave continued
Manchester, Chorlton-cum-Hardy
M21. . . . . . 109 C7
Manchester, Levenshulme
M19. . . . . . 99 B2
Manchester, Whalley Range
M16. . . . . . 97 D3
Sale M33 . . . . . . 108 C5
Urmston M41. . . . . . 95 E3
Whalley Cl
Altrincham WA15. . . . . 119 F8
Milnrow OL16 . . . . . . 31 E6
Whitefield M45 . . . . . . 44 F1
Wigan WN3 . . . . . . 55 A2
Whalley Dr BL8 . . . . . . 26 F2
Whalley Gdns OL12 . . . . 14 B1
Whalley Gr
Ashton-u-L OL6 . . . . . . 85 C7
Leigh WN7 . . . . . . 57 D1
Manchester M16. . . . . . 97 D2
WHALLEY RANGE. 97 E2
Whalley Range High Sch
M16. . . . . . 109 F8
Whalley Rd
Altrincham WA15. . . . . 120 A2
Heywood OL10. . . . . . 29 A2
Manchester M16. . . . . . 97 D3
Middleton M24. . . . . . 46 F3
Ramsbottom BL0 . . . . . . 11 E7
Rochdale OL12. . . . . . 14 B1
Stockport SK2 . . . . . . 124 C7
Whitefield M45 . . . . . . 44 F1
Wham Bar Dr OL10 . . . . 29 B3
Wham Bottom La OL12 . 14 D4
Wham La OL3. . . . . . 33 D1
Wham St OL10. . . . . . 29 B2
Wharf Bsns Ctr The OL6 . 166 B2
Wharf Cl
Altrincham WA14. . . . . 119 D7
Manchester M1. . . . . . 159 B1
Wharf Cotts OL5 . . . . . . 68 D1
Wharfdale 2 WN7 . . . . 76 A4
Wharfedale BL5 . . . . . . 39 F2
Wharfedale Ave M40 . . 65 A1
Wharfedale Rd SK5 . . . . 111 E8
Wharf End M17 . . . . . . 161 A2
Wharf Par OL6. . . . . . 166 C2
Wharf Rd
Altrincham WA14. . . . . 119 D7
Sale M33 . . . . . . 108 C5
WHARFSIDE 96 E6
Wharfside Ave 11 M30 . 79 B3
Wharfside Bsns Ctr M17. . 96 F6
Wharfside Bsns Pk M44 106 A7
Wharfside Way (Trafford
Park Rd) M17 . . . . . . 96 E6
Wharmton Rise OL4. . . . . 68 E6
Wharmton School Cotts
OL3 . . . . . . 50 F1
Wharmton View
Mossley OL5. . . . . . 68 E3
Uppermill OL3 . . . . . . 69 A6
Wharncliffe Cl SK13. . 171 B4
Wharncliffe St 5 WN2 . . 56 D5
Wharton Ave M21. . . . . 109 D7
Wharton Hall Cl M29. . 59 B1
Wharton La M38. . . . . . 59 D4
Wharton Lo M30. . . . . . 79 E3
Wharton Prim Sch M38 . 59 E4
Wheat Cl M13. . . . . . 163 C1
Wheatcroft SK13. . . . . 171 B4
Wheat Croft SK3. . . . . 170 C1
Wheater's St M7. . . . . 158 A4
Wheater's Terr M7. . . . 158 A4
Wheatfield SK15 . . . . 102 E7
Wheatfield Cl
Bury BL9 . . . . . . 27 F7
Romiley SK6. . . . . . 113 A4
Wheatfield Cres OL2 . . 48 C3
Wheatfield Ho OL2. . . . . 48 D3
Wheatfield St BL2. . . . 148 C1
Wheathill St 4 OL16 . . 31 A4
Wheatlea Ind Est WN3 . 54 F1
Wheatlea Rd WN3 . . . . 54 F2
Wheatley Ave WA12 . . 89 C4
Wheatley Rd M27 . . . . . . 61 D2
Wheatley Wlk M12 . . . . 165 A2
Wheatsheaf Ctr OL16. . 139 C4
Wheatsheaf Ind Est M27 . 62 B1
Wheatsheaf Wlk WN6 . . 19 C1
Wheeldale OL4 . . . . . . 67 D6
Wheeldale Cl BL1 . . . . . . 24 E5
Wheel Forge Way M17 . . 95 F4
Wheelock Cl SK9 . . . . 131 D1
Wheel of Manchester The *
M3. . . . . . 158 C2
Wheelton Cl BL8 . . . . . . 27 A1
Wheelwright Cl
Marple SK6 . . . . . . 125 F8
Rochdale OL16. . . . . . 30 B4
Wheelwright Dr OL16 . . 15 C3
Whelan Ave BL9 . . . . . . 44 E7
Whelan Cl BL9. . . . . . 44 E7
Wheler St M11, M43 . . . . 99 E8
Whelley WN1, WN2 . . . . 37 E2
Whernside Ave
Ashton-u-L OL6 . . . . . . 85 C7
Whernside Cl SK4. . . . . 169 B3
Whetmorhurst La SK6 . . 126 E4
Whetstone Hill Cl OL1 . . 49 B2
Whetstone Hill La 6 OL1. 49 C1

Whetstone Hill Rd OL1 . . 49 B1
Whewell Ave M26. . . . . . 44 C5
Whewell St 14 M29. . . . . 59 A1
Whickham Cl M14 . . . . . . 98 B3
Whiley St M13 . . . . . . 98 F4
Whimberry Cl M5 . . . . 161 C4
Whimberry Way M20. . 110 D6
Whimbrel Ave WA12 . . 89 C3
Whimbrel Rd
Hazel Grove SK2 . . . . 125 A5
Tyldesley M29 . . . . . . 77 C7
Whimbury Dr SK15. . . . . 86 E5
Whinberry Rd WA14. . 119 B7
Whinberry Way OL4 . . 49 F4
Whinchat Ave WA12. . . . . 89 C4
Whinchat Cl
Droylsden 3 . . . . . . 90 E7
Hazel Grove SK2 . . . . 125 A4
Whinfell Dr M24 . . . . . . 46 C1
Whingroves Wlk M40. 83 A6
Whinmoor Wlk M40. . . . . 83 B7
Whins Ave BL4. . . . . . 59 E8
Whins Crest BL6. . . . . . 40 C7
Whinslee Cl BL6. . . . . . 40 C7
Whinslee Dr BL6. . . . . . 40 C7
Whinstone Way OL1, OL9 . 47 E1
Whipney La BL8 . . . . . . 10 E1
Whipp St OL10. . . . . . 29 B3
Whirley Cl SK4. . . . . . 168 A4
Whistlecroft Ct WN3 . . 151 C2
Whistley St WN2 . . . . . . 56 B3
Whiston Dr BL2. . . . . . 148 C2
Whiston Rd M8 . . . . . . 64 A1
Whitaker St M24. . . . . . 64 F8
Whitbeam Gr WN2 . . . . 56 E2
Whitbrook Way M24. . . . . 47 C5
Whitburn Ave M13 . . . . . . 98 E2
Whitburn Cl
Bolton BL3. . . . . . 40 E4
Garswood WN4 . . . . . . 72 D4
Whitburn Dr BL8. . . . . . 27 C5
Whitburn Rd M23. . . . . 121 A4
Whitby Ave
Heywood OL10. . . . . . 29 C3
Manchester M14 . . . . . . 110 B8
Manchester, Whalley Range
M16. . . . . . 97 D3
Salford M6. . . . . . 80 C3
Urmston M41. . . . . . 95 C2
Whitby Cl
Bury BL8. . . . . . 26 F2
Cheadle SK8. . . . . . 122 C6
Poynton SK12. . . . . . 133 D4
Whitby Rd
Manchester M14 . . . . . . 110 B8
Oldham OL8. . . . . . 67 A3
Whitby St
Middleton M24. . . . . . 47 C1
Rochdale OL11. . . . . . 31 A5
Whitchurch Dr M16. . . . 162 A1
Whitchurch Rd M20. . . . 110 A7
Whiteacre WN6. . . . . . 19 A2
Whiteacre Rd OL6 . . . . . . 85 D4
Whiteacre Rd WN4. . . . 162 B1
White Bank Ave SK5 . . 112 C4
White Bank Rd OL8 . . . . . . 66 E1
Whiteacre Ave M8 . . . . 156 B3
Whitebeam Cl
Altrincham WA15. . . . . 120 E5
Newhey OL16. . . . . . 32 A3
Salford M6. . . . . . 81 A3
Whitebeam Ct M6 . . . . . . 81 A3
Whitebeam Wlk
M4 Sale M33 . . . . . . 107 D5
Westhoughton BL5 . . 39 F2
Whitebeck Ct M9 . . . . . . 65 A4
White Birk Cl M8 . . . . 10 F2
White Brook La
Uppermill OL3 . . . . . . 69 C8
Uppermill, Tunstead OL3 . . 69 D6
Whitebrook Rd M14. . 98 B1
White Broom WA13 . . 117 B4
Whitecar Ave M40 . . . . . . 65 C1
Whitecarr La M23, WA15 . 120 E3
White Carr La BL9 . . . . 12 A1
Whitechapel Cl BL2. . 42 E7
Whitechapel St M20 . 110 B3
White City Ret Pk M16 . 161 A1
White City Way M16. . . . 161 A1
Whitecliff Cl M14. . . . . . 98 C3
White Clover Sq WA13 . 117 A2
Whitecroft Ave
Golborne WA3. . . . . . 74 E1
Shaw OL2. . . . . . 49 D7
Whitecroft Dr BL8. . . . . . 26 F2
Whitecroft Gdns 3 M19 . 110 E4
Whitecroft Mdw 2 M24. 65 A8
Whitecroft Rd
Bolton BL1. . . . . . 142 A1
Marple SK6. . . . . . 126 C1
Wigan WN3 . . . . . . 55 B2
Whitecroft St 11 OL1 . . 49 C1
Whitecroft Villas M31. . 105 E2
WHITEFIELD 62 E7
Whitefield
Lymm WA13. . . . . . 117 A4
Pendlebury M6 . . . . . . 80 D6
Stockport SK4 . . . . . . 169 A3
Whitefield Ave
Newton-le-W WA12 . . 89 A7
Rochdale OL11. . . . . . 29 F8
Whitefield Cl
Golborne WA3. . . . . . 90 A8
Lymm WA13. . . . . . 117 A5
Whitefield Com Prim Sch
M45. . . . . . 63 A8
Whitefield Ct WA3 . . . . . . 91 F2

Whitefield Gr WA13 . . 117 A4
Whitefield Metro Sta M45 44 F1
Whitefield Rd
Bury BL9 . . . . . . 44 D7
Romiley SK6. . . . . . 112 E4
Sale M33 . . . . . . 108 A5
Whitefriar Ct M3. . . . . 158 B3
Whitefriars Wlk 2 M22 . 130 D8
WHITE GATE. 65 F4
Whitegate
Bolton BL3. . . . . . 40 C2
Rochdale OL15. . . . . . 15 E4
Whitegate Ave
Culcheth WA3 . . . . . . 91 F2
Oldham OL9. . . . . . 65 F5
Whitegate Bsns Ctr OL9 . 65 F5
Whitegate Dr
Bolton, Astley Bridge BL1 . 24 F5
Bolton BL1. . . . . . 143 C4
Salford M5. . . . . . 154 A2
Swinton M27 . . . . . . 62 B2
WHITE GATE END. 65 E3
Whitegate End Prim Sch
OL9. . . . . . 65 E3
Whitegate La OL9 . . . . . . 66 A4
Whitegate Pk M41. . . . . 94 E2
Whitegate Rd OL9 . . . . . . 65 E3
Whitegates
Cheadle SK8. . . . . . 122 D5
Mottram in L SK14. . 103 A1
Whitegates Cl WA15 . . 120 B5
Whitegates La OL4 . . . . . . 50 B2
Whitegates Rd
Cheadle SK8. . . . . . 122 D5
Middleton M24. . . . . . 47 C4
Whitehall Ave WN6 . . 35 E8
Whitehall Cl SK9. . . . . 137 A5
Whitehall La
Blackrod BL6. . . . . . 21 D3
Bolton BL1. . . . . . 24 D6
Oldham OL4. . . . . . 49 F4
Whitehall Rd
Manchester M20. . . . . 110 C3
Sale M33 . . . . . . 108 B3
Whitehall St
Ince-in-M WN3 . . . . . 151 B2
Oldham OL1. . . . . . 153 C4
Rochdale OL12. . . . . . 14 F1
White Hart Mdw 2 M24. 47 A2
White Hart St SK14. . . . 167 A4
Whitehaven Gdns M20 . 110 A2
Whitehaven Pl SK14. . 101 C5
Whitehaven Rd SK7 . . 132 C5
Whitehead Cl OL3. . . . . 68 E5
Whitehead Cres
Bury BL8. . . . . . 27 C5
Radcliffe M29. . . . . . 61 C7
Whitehead La M29. . . . . 77 C5
Whitehead Rd
Stretford M21. . . . . . 108 F8
Swinton M27 . . . . . . 62 B2
Whiteheads Pl OL4. . . . . 67 F7
Whitehead St
Denton M34. . . . . . 100 F7
Middleton M24. . . . . . 47 C1
Oldham OL16. . . . . . 31 E6
Newhey OL16. . . . . . 32 D4
Shaw OL2. . . . . . 48 F8
Whitehill Cl OL12 . . . . . . 14 D4
Whitehill Cotts BL1 . . 24 D6
Whitehill Dr M40 . . . . . . 83 A7
Whitehill Ind Est SK4,
SK5. . . . . . 111 E5
Whitehill Prim Sch SK4 . 169 B4
Whitehill St SK4, SK5 . . 111 F5
Whitehill Street W SK4. 169 B4
Whiteholme Ave M21 . 109 D4
White Horse Cl BL6 . . 22 C5
White Horse Gr BL5. . . . . 40 A3
White Horse Mdws OL16 . 31 C2
White House Ave M9 . 64 C6
White House Ave M8. . 63 F3
White House Cl OL16. . 30 D7
Whitehouse Dr
Altrincham WA15. . . . . 129 B8
Wythenshawe M23 . . 121 A5
Whitehouse La WA14. . 118 D8
Whitehurst Rd SK4. . . . . 110 F4
Whitekirk Cl M13. . . . . 163 B2
White Lady Cl 8 M28 . 59 F3
Whitelake Ave M41 . . . . 94 F2
Whitelake View M41. . . . . 94 F3
Whiteland Ave BL3. . 144 C1
Whitelands Ind Est OL6,
SK15. . . . . . 85 D2
Whitelands Rd OL6, SK15. 85 D2
Whitelands Terr OL6 . . 166 C2
Whitelea Dr SK3 . . . . . . 170 A1
White Lee Croft M46. . 58 A3
Whitelees Rd OL15. . . . . 16 A5
Whitelegge St BL8 . . . . . . 27 B4
Whiteley Dr M24 . . . . . . 65 C7
Whiteley Pl WA14. . . . . 119 D6
Whiteley's Pl 6 OL12 . . 139 B4
White Lion Brow BL1. . 145 B3
White Lodge Dr WN4. . 73 D4
Whitelow Rd
Manchester M21 . . . . . 109 A8
Ramsbottom BL0 . . . . . . 11 E5
Whitemoss SK13. . . . . . 14 B2
White Moss Ave M21. . 109 D8

White Moss Gdns M9 . . 65 A2
White Moss Rd M9. . . . . 64 E3
Whiteoak Cl SK6. . . . . 125 E7
Whiteoak Ct 7 M14. . 110 C8
Whiteoak Rd M14. . . . . 110 C8
Whiteoak View BL3 . . . . . . 42 D5
White Rd SK22. . . . . . 127 C2
Whites Croft M27 . . . . . . 79 F8
Whiteside Ave
Hindley WN2 . . . . . . 56 E7
2 Wigan WN6. . . . . . 37 A1
Whiteside Cl M5. . . . . 154 A2
Whiteside Fold OL12 . . 14 A1
White Slack Gate OL14 . 6 A6
Whitesmead Cl SK12. . 135 D5
White St
Bury BL8. . . . . . 27 C1
Leigh WN7 . . . . . . 76 C4
Manchester M15 . . . . . 162 A2
Salford M6. . . . . . 154 B1
5 Wigan WN5. . . . . . 54 B6
Whitestar St 3 M44 . . 94 A2
Whitestone Cl BL6 . . . . . . 40 D6
Whitestone Ho 10 OL1. . 153 B4
White Swallows Rd M27. . 80 B6
White Swan Ind Est 5
OL1. . . . . . 67 C8
Whitethorn Ave
3 Manchester M19 . . 110 F7
1 Manchester, Whalley Range
M16. . . . . . 97 D3
Whitethorn Cl SK6 . . 112 E7
Whitewater Dr M7 . . . . . . 80 F8
Whiteway St M7 . . . . . . 157 B3
Whitewell Cl
Bury BL9 . . . . . . 44 C1
Rochdale OL16. . . . . . 31 C8
Whitewillow Cl M35. . 84 A6
Whitewood Cl WN4 . . . . . . 73 A6
WHITFIELD. 171 B2
Whitfield Ave SK13. . . . . 116 C7
Whitfield Brows OL15. . 16 C7
Whitfield Cres OL16. . 32 B3
Whitfield Cross SK13. . 116 D7
Whitfield Ho OL16. . . . . 31 E5
Whitfield Pk SK13. . . . . 116 C7
Whitfield Rise OL2. . . . . 32 A1
Whitfield St
Leigh WN7 . . . . . . 76 C4
Manchester M3 . . . . . . 159 A4
Whitfield Wells SK13 . 116 D7
Whitford Wlk M40 . . . . 160 A3
Whiting Gr BL3. . . . . . 40 E6
Whitington Cl BL3 . . . . . . 43 B4
Whitinlea Cl WN2 . . . . . . 57 C3
Whit La
Manchester M6. . . . . . 80 F6
Salford M6. . . . . . 81 A5
Whitland Ave BL1. . . . . . 40 F8
Whitland Dr OL8. . . . . . 66 B2
Whitle Bank Rd SK22. . 127 B2
Whitledge Gn WN4. . . . . 73 A5
Whitledge Rd WN4. . . . . 73 A5
Whitle Rd SK22. . . . . . 127 C1
WHITLEY 37 C3
Whitley Cres
Abram Brow WN2 . . 74 B7
Wigan WN1 . . . . . . 37 C4
Whitley Gdns WA15 . . 120 C7
Whitley Pl WA15 . . . . 120 C7
Whitley Rd
Manchester M40 . . . . . 159 C4
Stockport, Heaton Moor
SK4. . . . . . 168 B3
Up Holland WN8 . . . . . . 35 D3
Whitley St BL4. . . . . . 42 D2
Whitley Wlk SK13 . . . . 115 F8
Whitlow Ave
Altrincham WA14. . . . . 119 B8
Golborne WA3 . . . . . . 73 F1
Whitman St M40, M9 . . 157 C4
Whitmore Rd M14 . . . . . . 98 B1
Whitnall St
Dukinfield SK14. . . . . 101 C3
Manchester M16. . . . . . 97 E4
Whitsand Rd M22 . . . . 121 C5
Whitsbury Ave
Hindley WN2 . . . . . . 56 D4
Manchester M18 . . . . . 99 D3
Whitstable Cl OL9 . . . . 152 B2
Whitstable Rd M40. . . . . 65 C1
Whitsters Hollow BL1 . 142 B3
Whitsundale BL5. . . . . . 39 F2
Whitswood Cl 2 M16 . 97 E3
Whittaker Dr OL15. . . . . 15 F2
Whittaker La
Littleborough OL15 . . 16 E4
Prestwich M25. . . . . . 63 C4
Rochdale OL11. . . . . . 13 B1
Whittaker St
Ashton-u-L OL6 . . . . . . 85 D5
Manchester M40 . . . . . . 83 A8
4 Radcliffe M26 . . . . 44 B4
Royton OL2. . . . . . 48 D4
Whittingham Dr BL0 . . 11 C3
Whittingham Gr OL1 . . 153 A4
Whittington St OL7 . . 166 A1
WHITTLE BROOK 60 E2
Whittlebrook Gr OL10. . 46 F7
Whittle Dr
Shaw OL2. . . . . . 49 D8

Whittle Dr *continued*
Walkden M28 . . . . 60 D5
Whittle Gr
Bolton BL1 . . . . 142 B1
Walkden M28 . . . . 60 E3
Whittle Hill BL7 . . . . .8 E3
Whittle La OL10 . . . . 46 B4
Whittles Ave M34 . . . . 101 A2
Whittle's Croft M1 . . . . 159 B1
Whittle's Croft Wharf
M1 . . . . 159 B1
Whittles St OL13 . . . . .4 B8
Whittle St
Bury BL8 . . . . 27 C3
Littleborough OL15 . . . . 15 F5
Manchester M4 . . . . 159 B2
Swinton M27 . . . . 79 E7
Westhoughton BL5 . . . . 60 E3
Whittles Terr OL16 . . . . 32 C4
Whittle's Terr ◼ BL5 . . . . . . 39 E1
Whittles Wlk M34 . . . . 101 A2
Whitton Mews ◾ BL6 . . . . . 22 B4
Whitwell Bank ◾ SK13 . . . 171 A2
Whitwell Cl
◾ Gamesley SK13 . . . . . . 171 A2
Standish WN6 . . . . 19 D2
Whitwell Fold ◼ SK13 . . . 171 A2
Whitwell Gdns BL6 . . . . 22 B5
Whitwell Gn ◾ SK13 . . . . . 171 A2
Whitwell Lea ◾ SK13 . . . . 171 A2
Whitwell Way M18 . . . . 165 C1
Whitwell Wlk ◼ M11 . . . . . 98 E4
WHITWORTH 14 D8
Whitworth Art Gall★ M15 . . 98 B4
Whitworth Cl OL6 . . . . 166 C4
Whitworth Com High Sch
OL12 . . . . .14 C8
Whitworth Heritage Mus★
OL12 . . . . 4 C1
Whitworth La M14 . . . . 98 D1
Whitworth Park Mans
M14 . . . . 98 D2
Whitworth Rake OL12 . . . . . 14 D8
Whitworth Rd OL12 . . . . 14 F2
Whitworth Sq OL12 . . . . 14 D8
Whitworth St
Horwich BL6 . . . . 22 C2
Manchester, City Centre
M1 . . . . 163 A4
Manchester, Openshaw
M11 . . . . 165 B3
Milnrow OL16 . . . . 31 F6
Rochdale OL16 . . . . 15 C2
Whitworth Street E M11, 165 C3
Whitworth Street W M1,
M3 . . . . 162 C4
Whitworth Water Ski &
Recreation Ctr★ OL12 . . . 4 C2
Whitworth Way WN6 . . . . . . 36 E2
Whixhall Ave M12 . . . . 164 B2
Whoolden St BL4 . . . . 42 C1
Whowell Fold BL1 . . . . 142 C3
Whowell St BL3 . . . . 145 B2
Wibbersley Pk M41 . . . . 94 F2
Wibsey Cotts OL3 . . . . 33 D2
Wichbrook Rd ◼ M28 . . . . 59 F3
Wicheaves Cres M28 . . . . . . 60 A3
Wicheries The M28 . . . . 59 F3
Wicken Bank OL10 . . . . 46 E7
Wickenby Dr M33 . . . . 108 A4
Wicken St SK2 . . . . 124 C7
Wickentree Holt OL12 . . . . . 14 A1
Wickentree La M35 . . . . 66 A1
Wicker La WA15 . . . . 129 C8
Wicket Gr M27 . . . . 61 E4
Wickham Terr M14 . . . . 47 A2
Wickliffe St ◼ BL1 . . . . . . 145 B4
Wicklow Ave SK3 . . . . 123 B7
Wicklow Dr M22 . . . . 121 E2
Wicklow Gr ◾ OL8 . . . . 66 E3
Wickmere Wlk M8 . . . . 155 C2
Widcombe Dr BL2 . . . . 42 F5
Widdop St OL9 . . . . 153 A3
Widdow's St WN7 . . . . 76 B4
Widdrington Rd WN1 . . . . . . 37 D2
Widecombe Cl M41 . . . . 95 B4
Widford Wlk BL6 . . . . 21 E1
Widgeon Cl
Manchester M14 . . . . 110 B8
Poynton SK12 . . . . 133 B4
Widgeon Rd WA14 . . . . 119 B8
Widnes St M11 . . . . 165 C3
Wiend WN1 . . . . 150 C4
WIGAN 150 B4
Wigan Ent Pk WN2 . . . . 56 A6
Wigan Flashes Nature
Reserve The★ WN3 . . . . 55 C2
Wigan Gallery ◼ WN1 . . . 150 C4
Wigan Investment Ctr
WN3 . . . . 150 C3
Wigan La
Adlington PR7, WN1 . . . . . 20 D7
Wigan WN1 . . . . 37 C4
Wigan & Leigh Coll WN7 . 76 A3
Wigan & Leigh Coll (Leigh
Sixth Form Coll) WN7 . . 75 D3
Wigan & Leigh Coll (Linacre
Bldg) WN1 . . . . 37 B1
Wigan & Leigh Coll
(Pagefield Bldg) WN1 . . 37 A2
Wigan & Leigh Coll (Parsons
Wlk) WN1 . . . . 150 B4
Wigan & Leigh Coll (Railway
Road Bldg) ◼ WN7 . . . . 75 E5

Wigan & Leigh Coll (The
Image Ctr) WN7 . . . . 75 E5
Wigan Little Theatre★
WN1 . . . . 151 A4
Wigan Lower Rd WN6 . . . . . 36 C3
Wigan North Western Sta
WN1 . . . . 150 C3
Wigan Pier★ WN3 . . . . 150 B3
Wigan Rd
Ashton-in-M WN4 . . . . 73 A5
Aspull WN2 . . . . 38 B4
Atherton M46 . . . . 58 B3
Billinge WN5 . . . . 71 F7
Bolton, Knutshaw Bridge
BL3 . . . . 40 E3
Bolton, Willows BL3 . . . . . 144 B1
Golborne WA3 . . . . 74 B3
Leigh WN7 . . . . 75 D7
Shevington WN6 . . . . 36 B5
Standish WN6 . . . . 37 A6
Westhoughton BL5 . . . . 57 C7
Wigan Sq WN1 . . . . 150 C4
Wigan St WN2 . . . . 56 A1
Wigan Wallgate Sta
WN1 . . . . 150 C4
Wiggins Wlk ◼ M11 . . . . . 98 C3
Wightman Ave WA12 . . . . . . 89 C5
Wighurst Wlk ◾ M22 . . . . 121 D1
Wigley St M12 . . . . 164 B3
Wigmore Rd M8 . . . . 156 B3
Wigmore St ◼ OL6 . . . . . . 85 D4
Wigsby Ave M40 . . . . 65 C2
Wigsey La WA13 . . . . 117 A7
WIGSHAW 91 D2
Wigshaw Cl WN7 . . . . 75 F1
Wigshaw La WA3 . . . . 91 D2
Wigwam Cl SK12 . . . . 133 C4
Wilberforce St BL3 . . . . . . 140 A3
Wilberforce Cl M15 . . . . . . 162 C1
Wilbraham Prim Sch M14 98 A1
Wilbraham Rd
Manchester M14, M16,
M21 . . . . 97 C1
Walkden M28 . . . . 60 E3
Wilbraham St
Leigh WN7 . . . . 75 C5
Westhoughton BL5 . . . . 57 E8
Wilburn St M5 . . . . 162 A4
Wilby Ave BL3 . . . . 43 B5
Wilby Cl BL8 . . . . 27 D5
Wilby St M8 . . . . 156 B2
Wilcock Rd WA11 . . . . 89 B8
Wilcockson Ho ◾ BL4 . . . . 60 D8
Wilcock St
Manchester M16 . . . . 97 C4
Wigan WN3 . . . . 150 A3
Wilcott Dr
Sale M33 . . . . 107 E5
Wilmslow SK9 . . . . 136 F4
Wilcott Rd SK8 . . . . 122 A5
Wild Arum Cl ◾ M22 . . . . 121 D1
Wildbank Chase SK15 . . . . 102 E7
Wild Bank Com Sch SK15. 86 D2
Wildbrook Cl OL8 . . . . 67 A2
Wildbrook Cres OL8 . . . . . . 67 A2
Wildbrook Gr M38 . . . . 59 E3
Wildbrook Rd M38 . . . . 59 E3
Wildbrook Terr OL8 . . . . . . 67 A2
Wild Clough SK14 . . . . 167 C1
Wildcroft Ave M40 . . . . 65 A1
Wilders Moor Cl ◼ M28 . . 78 C8
Wilderswood Ave BL6 . . . . . 22 C4
Wilderswood Cl M20 . . . . . 110 C5
Wilderswood Ct BL6 . . . . . . 22 C4
Wilde St M34 . . . . 100 F3
Wild Ho OL8 . . . . 153 C1
Wildhouse La OL16 . . . . 31 F8
Widing St WN3 . . . . 151 B2
Wildman La BL4 . . . . 59 F8
Wildmoor Ave OL4 . . . . 67 E4
Wild Moor Wood Cl SK15. 86 D5
Wild's Pas WN7 . . . . 75 F4
Wilds Pl BL0 . . . . 138 B1
Wild's Sq ◼ OL5 . . . . 68 C2
Wild St
Dukinfield SK16 . . . . 101 D8
Hazel Grove SK7 . . . . 124 D2
Heywood OL10 . . . . 29 E2
Oldham, Mumps OL1 . . . . . 67 A7
Oldham OL4 . . . . 67 E6
Radcliffe M26 . . . . 44 D4
Romiley SK6 . . . . 112 F3
Shaw OL2 . . . . 149 C2
Stockport SK2 . . . . 124 A6
Wildwood Cl
Ramsbottom BL0 . . . . 11 A4
Stockport SK2 . . . . 124 A5
Wilford Ave M33 . . . . 108 A2
Wilfred Dr BL9 . . . . 141 B4
Wilfred Rd
Eccles M30 . . . . 95 A8
Walkden M28 . . . . 60 D2
Wilfred St
Bolton BL7 . . . . 25 A7
Manchester M40 . . . . 83 A8
Oldham OL4 . . . . 67 B6
Wigan WN5 . . . . 54 F7
Wilfrid's Pl WN6 . . . . 19 F1
Wilfrid St M27 . . . . 61 F1
Wilham Ave ◼ M30 . . . . . . 79 D1
Wilkesley Ave WN6 . . . . 36 D8
Wilkes St OL11 . . . . 49 D3
Wilkin Croft SK8 . . . . 122 E1
Wilkins La SK9 . . . . 130 E5
Wilkinson Ave BL3 . . . . 43 A5
Wilkinson Rd
Bolton BL1 . . . . 24 D5
Stockport SK4 . . . . 169 B2

Wilkinson St
Ashton-u-L OL6 . . . . 166 A2
Leigh WN7 . . . . 75 E5
◼ Sale M33 . . . . 108 D4
Wilks Ave M22 . . . . 121 F3
Willand Cl BL2 . . . . 43 A6
Willand Dr BL2 . . . . 43 A6
Willan Ent Ctr
Chadderton OL9 . . . . 152 B3
Stretford M17 . . . . 96 C6
Willan Ind Est M50 . . . . . . 154 C1
Willan Rd
Eccles M30 . . . . 79 E2
Manchester M9 . . . . 64 C4
Willard Ave WN5 . . . . 53 D3
Willard St SK7 . . . . 124 D3
Willaston Cl M21 . . . . 109 A7
Willaston Way ◼ SK9 . . . . 131 D5
Willbutts La OL11 . . . . 30 C8
Willdale Cl M11 . . . . 83 A2
Willdor Gr SK3 . . . . 123 B6
Willenhall Rd M23 . . . . 109 C2
Willerby Rd M7 . . . . 155 B1
Willesden Ave M13 . . . . 98 E4
Will Griffith Wlk M11 . . . . 164 B4
William Chadwick Cl ◼
M40 . . . . 141 A1
William Cl M41 . . . . 95 C2
William Coates Ct ◼ M16. 97 D3
William Fairburn Way ◼
M4 . . . . 159 A2
William Greenwood Cl
OL10 . . . . 29 C2
William Henry St ◼ OL11. 31 A4
William Hulme's Gram Sch
M16 . . . . 97 F1
William Jessop Ct M1 . . . 159 C1
William Kay Cl M16 . . . . . . 97 E4
William Lister Cl M40 . . . . 83 D4
Williams Ave WA12 . . . . . . 89 C5
Williams Cres OL9 . . . . 65 F3
Williams Ct ◼ M14 . . . . . . 98 D4
Williamson Ave
Radcliffe M26 . . . . 43 F6
Romiley SK6 . . . . 113 A4
Williamson La M43. . . . . . 100 B8
Williamson St
Ashton-u-L OL6 . . . . 166 B3
Manchester M4 . . . . 159 B3
Reddish SK5 . . . . 111 F7
Williamson's Yd ◼ OL1 . . 67 B7
Williams Rd
Failsworth M40 . . . . 83 C7
Manchester M18 . . . . 165 C1
Williams St
Little Lever BL3 . . . . 43 B3
Manchester M18 . . . . 165 C1
William St
Ashton-u-L OL7 . . . . 166 A1
Britannia OL13 . . . . 4 C8
Failsworth M35 . . . . 66 A1
Hindley WN2 . . . . 56 E5
Horwich BL6 . . . . 22 A3
Hyde SK14 . . . . 167 A2
Ince-in-M WN3 . . . . 151 A2
◼ Leigh WN7 . . . . 76 A5
Leigh WN7 . . . . 76 A5
Littleborough OL15 . . . . . . 16 A5
Manchester, Ardwick M12 164 A4
Manchester, Didsbury M20 110 B3
Middleton M24 . . . . 65 B8
Radcliffe M26 . . . . 44 B4
Ramsbottom BL0 . . . . 1 C1
Rochdale OL11 . . . . 139 C2
Rochdale, Wuerdle OL16 . . 15 D4
Salford M3 . . . . 158 B2
Whitworth OL12 . . . . 4 C1
William Way WN7 . . . . 75 B1
William Wlk ◾ WA14 . . . . 119 D3
Willingdon Cl BL8 . . . . 27 C7
Willingdon Dr M25 . . . . 63 B5
Willis Rd SK3 . . . . 170 B2
Willis St BL3 . . . . 146 C4
Williton Wlk ◼ M22 . . . . . 121 E3
Willock St M7 . . . . 155 C2
Willoughby Ave M20 . . . . . 110 C4
Willoughby Cl M33 . . . . . . 108 A5
Willow Ave
Cheadle SK8 . . . . 122 F2
Middleton M24 . . . . 65 C8
Newton-le-W WA12 . . . . . . 89 E4
Reddish SK5 . . . . 169 C4
Tyldesley M29 . . . . 77 A4
Urmston M41 . . . . 95 C2
Willowbank M26 . . . . 61 F8
Willow Bank
Altrincham WA15 . . . . 120 A6
Cheadle SK8 . . . . 132 A6
Manchester, Fallowfield
M14 . . . . 110 C8
◼ Manchester, Harpurhey
M9 . . . . 157 E8
Oldham OL4 . . . . 67 E8
Willowbank Rd BL2 . . . . . . 148 B2
Willow Bank Cl SK2 . . . . . 124 D7
Willow Bank Ct M20 . . . . . 122 B2
Willow Bank Est WA12 . . . 89 F4
Willowbrook Ave M40. . . . . 83 A7
Willowbrook Dr WN6 . . . . . 36 B7
Willowbrook Gdns M22 . . 121 C4
Willow Cl
Adlington PR6 . . . . 21 B8
Bolton BL3 . . . . 146 B4
Dukinfield SK16 . . . . 101 F7
Paddockhill WA16 . . . . . . 136 B5
Poynton SK12 . . . . 133 C3
Whitefield BL9 . . . . 45 B3
Willow Cres WN7 . . . . 75 E8

Willowcroft Ave WN2 . . . . 38 F3
Willow Ct
Gatley SK8 . . . . 122 A6
Manchester, Fallowfield
M14 . . . . 110 C8
Manchester M14 . . . . 98 D1
Marple SK6 . . . . 125 F5
Sale M33 . . . . 108 E5
Standish WN6 . . . . 19 E2
Willowdale WA12 . . . . 89 E3
Willowdale Ave SK8. . . . . . 122 B2
Willowdene Cl
Bolton BL7 . . . . 24 F8
◼ Manchester M40 . . . . . 156 C1
Willow Dr
Handforth SK9 . . . . 131 D3
Hindley WN2 . . . . 56 F3
Sale M33 . . . . 107 E2
Whitefield BL9 . . . . 45 B2
Willowfield Gr WN4 . . . . . . 73 A2
Willowfield Rd OL4 . . . . . . 49 D2
Willow Fold M43 . . . . 100 B8
Willow Gr
Ashton-in-M WN4 . . . . 73 E5
Chadderton OL9 . . . . 152 B4
Denton M34 . . . . 100 E3
Golborne WA3 . . . . 74 A1
Manchester M18 . . . . 165 C5
Marple SK6 . . . . 125 F5
Willow Green Sch WN4. . . . 73 E5
Willow Hey BL7 . . . . 25 C6
Willow Hill Rd M8 . . . . 64 A1
Willow Lawn ◼ SK8. . . . . 123 A2
Willow Lo ◼ WN2 . . . . 56 B1
Willow Mead SK6 . . . . 113 D3
Willowmead Way OL12 . . . 14 A2
Willowmoss Cl M28 . . . . . . 60 E1
Willow Pk
Manchester M14 . . . . 110 C8
Stockport SK2 . . . . 124 C7
Willow Rd
Eccles M30 . . . . 79 A4
High Lane SK6 . . . . 134 F7
Newton-le-W WA12 . . . . . . 89 E4
Partington M31 . . . . 105 E2
Prestwich M25, M45 . . . . . 63 A6
Uppermill OL3 . . . . 69 C7
Wigan WN6 . . . . 37 A3
Willow Rise OL15 . . . . 15 F3
WILLOWS 144 C1
Willows St OL9 . . . . 136 F6
Willows Cotts OL16 . . . . . . 31 E6
Willows Dr M35 . . . . 83 F5
Willows End SK15 . . . . 86 D3
Willows La
Bolton BL3 . . . . 146 C4
Milnrow OL16 . . . . 31 E6
Willows Prim Sch WA15 120 A6
Willows Prim Sch The
M22 . . . . 121 C2
Willows Rd M5 . . . . 154 A2
Willow St
◼ Abram WN2 . . . . 56 B1
Atherton M46 . . . . 58 C4
Bury BL9 . . . . 141 B3
Droylsden M11 . . . . 83 A1
Heywood OL10 . . . . 29 D2
Manchester M8 . . . . 156 A4
Oldham OL1 . . . . 67 A7
Rawtenstall BB4 . . . . 2 E8
Swinton, Chorlton Fold M27 79 D5
Swinton, Hazelhurst M28 . . 79 C7
Willows The
◼ Atherton M46 . . . . 58 D3
Coppull PR7 . . . . 19 E8
Little Lever BL3 . . . . 43 A5
Manchester, Barlow Moor
M21 . . . . 109 A7
Mossley OL5 . . . . 68 C1
Partington M31 . . . . 105 F3
Stockport SK4 . . . . 168 A3
Whitworth OL12 . . . . 14 C5
Willow Tree Cl WN1 . . . . . . 37 B4
Willow Tree Ct
◼ Eccles M30 . . . . 79 C1
Sale M33 . . . . 108 B3
Willow Tree Mews SK8 . . . 122 B1
Willow Tree Rd WA14 . . . . 119 D3
Willow Way
Bramhall SK7 . . . . 132 D7
Manchester M20 . . . . 110 C3
Willow Wood Cl OL6 . . . . . . 85 E3
Wilma Ave M9 . . . . 64 C4
Wilmans Wlk SK13 . . . . . . 104 A6
Wilmcote Cl M16 . . . . 40 D6
Wilmcote Gdns ◼ SK6 . . 112 F3
Wilmington Rd M32 . . . . . . 96 B2
Wilmot Dr WA3 . . . . 89 F7
Wilmot St M11 . . . . 142 C3
Wilmott St
Manchester M15 . . . . 162 C3
Manchester M15 . . . . 163 A2
WILMSLOW 137 C5
Wilmslow Ave BL1 . . . . 24 E5
Wilmslow Ct SK9 . . . . 131 D3
Wilmslow Grange Prim Sch
SK9 . . . . 131 C4
Wilmslow High Sch SK9 . 137 B6
Wilmslow L Ctr SK9 . . . . . 137 B7
Wilmslow Old Rd M90. . . . 130 A6
Wilmslow Park N SK9 . . . . 137 D7
Wilmslow Park S SK9 . . . . 137 C7
Wilmslow Prep Sch SK9 . . 137 B7
Wilmslow Rd
Alderley Edge SK9 . . . . . . 137 A2
Cheadle SK8 . . . . 122 D3

Wilmslow Rd *continued*
Gatley SK8, SK9 . . . . 131 C6
Handforth SK9 . . . . 131 D4
Manchester, Didsbury M20 110 B1
Manchester, East Didsbury
M20 . . . . 110 C1
Manchester M20 . . . . 110 C7
Manchester, Rusholme M14 98 C2
Manchester, Withington M14,
M20 . . . . 110 B5
Woodford SK7 . . . . 132 C1
Wilmslow Sta SK9 . . . . . . 137 C7
Wilmur Ave
Salford M7 . . . . 155 B2
Whitefield M45 . . . . 63 A7
Wilpshire Ave ◼ M12 . . . . 99 B3
Wilsford Cl WA3 . . . . 74 B1
Wilsham Rd WN5 . . . . 53 E5
Wilshaw Gr OL7 . . . . 85 B6
Wilshaw La OL7 . . . . 85 A5
Wilson Ave
Heywood OL10 . . . . 29 A2
Swinton M27 . . . . 62 B2
Wigan WN6 . . . . 37 B2
Wilson Cres OL6 . . . . 85 E4
Wilson Fold Ave BL6 . . . . . . 39 F8
Wilson Rd
Manchester, Blackley M9. . . 64 D1
Stockport, Heaton Moor
SK4 . . . . 168 B3
Wilsons Pk M40 . . . . 157 B1
Wilson St
◼ Bolton BL3 . . . . 145 C2
Bury BL9 . . . . 141 A1
Farnworth BL4 . . . . 60 E8
Horwich BL6 . . . . 22 A4
Hyde SK14 . . . . 167 B2
Manchester, Brunswick M12,
M13 . . . . 163 C4
Manchester M11 . . . . 165 A4
Oldham OL8 . . . . 66 E4
Radcliffe M26 . . . . 43 F4
Rochdale OL12 . . . . 139 C4
◼ Sale M33 . . . . 108 B5
Stretford M32 . . . . 96 E4
Uppermill OL3 . . . . 69 A6
Wilson's Terr SK13. . . . . . 116 B8
Wilson Way OL1 . . . . 153 C4
Wilsthorpe Cl M19 . . . . . . 111 C7
Wilton Ave
Gatley SK8 . . . . 131 C7
Manchester, Firswood M16. 97 A3
Manchester, Sedgley Park
M25 . . . . 63 D2
Pendlebury M27 . . . . 80 C7
Wigan WN2 . . . . 37 F2
Wilton Cotts WA3 . . . . 75 A2
Wilton Cres SK9 . . . . 136 F2
Wilton Ct
Middleton M25. . . . . 63 E8
Reddish M34 . . . . 100 A4
Wilton Dr
Altrincham WA15. . . . . . . 129 C8
Whitefield BL9 . . . . 45 A5
Wilton Gdns M26 . . . . 44 C5
Wilton Gr
Heywood OL10 . . . . 29 C1
Reddish M34 . . . . 100 A4
Wilton La WA3 . . . . 91 B5
Wilton Paddock M34 . . . . 100 A4
Wilton Pl M3 . . . . 158 A2
Wilton Rd
Bolton BL1 . . . . 24 E5
Manchester, Crumpsall M8 . 64 A2
Manchester M21 . . . . 109 B8
Salford M6 . . . . 80 B4
Shevington WN6 . . . . 36 A6
Wilton St
Bolton BL1 . . . . 143 C3
Heywood OL10 . . . . 29 C2
Middleton M24 . . . . 64 B7
Oldham OL4 . . . . 66 B3
Prestwich M25 . . . . 63 C4
Reddish SK5 . . . . 99 F2
Whitefield M45 . . . . 62 F7
Wigan WN1 . . . . 151 A3
Wilton Terr OL12 . . . . 139 B4
Wiltshire Ave SK5 . . . . . . 112 C4
Wiltshire Cl BL9 . . . . 45 A8
Wiltshire Dr
Glossop SK13 . . . . 116 F8
Haslingden BB4 . . . . 1 B8
Wiltshire Pl WN5 . . . . 54 C6
Wiltshire Rd
Chadderton OL9 . . . . 152 B1
Failsworth M35 . . . . 84 A6
Partington M31 . . . . 105 E2
Wiltshire St ◼ M7 . . . . 155 C5
Wimberly Cl ◼ OL3 . . . . . . 69 B5
Wimberry Hill Rd BL5 . . . . 39 D3
Wimbledon Dr
Rochdale OL11 . . . . 139 A1
Stockport SK3 . . . . 123 C7
Wimbledon Rd M35 . . . . . . 84 B8
Wimborne Ave
Chadderton OL9 . . . . 48 A1
Urmston M41 . . . . 95 D3
Wimborne Cl
Cheadle SK8 . . . . 123 C4
Horwich BL6 . . . . 22 F1
Wimborne Rd WN5 . . . . 54 A8
Wimpenny Ho OL8 . . . . . . 153 B1
Wimpole St
Ashton-u-L OL6 . . . . 166 C3
◼ Oldham OL1 . . . . 49 A1
Wimpory St M11 . . . . 99 D7
Winbolt St SK2 . . . . 124 C4

Win–WOO 275

Winby St 1 OL11 31 A4
Wincanton Ave M23 120 D8
Wincanton Dr BL1 24 D7
Wincanton Pk OL4 67 D6
Wince Cl M24 65 C6
Wincham Cl 24 M15 162 A2
Wincham Rd M33 107 E2
Winchcombe Cl WN7 75 E1
Winchester Ave
Ashton-in-M WN4 73 A3
Ashton-u-L OL6 85 D8
Chadderton OL9 47 F1
Denton M34 100 F1
Heywood OL10 46 C8
Manchester M25 63 C2
Tyldesley M29 77 C7
Winchester Cl
Bury BL8 27 C7
4 Orrell WN5 53 F7
Rochdale OL11 30 A7
Wilmslow SK9 136 E5
Winchester Dr
Sale M33 107 D4
Stockport SK4 168 B2
Winchester Gr WN3 151 A2
Winchester Pk M20 109 F3
Winchester Rd
Altrincham WA15 120 C1
Ashton-in-M WA11 72 E1
Dukinfield SK16 102 A7
Longshaw WN5 53 D2
Radcliffe M26 43 D5
Salford M6 80 C4
Salford M30 80 A4
Urmston M41 95 E3
Winchester Way BL2 25 D1
Wincle Ave SK12 133 F2
Wincombe St M14 98 B2
Windale M28 60 B3
Windcroft Cl M11 165 A4
Winder Dr M4 159 C2
Windermere Ave
Atherton M46 58 D5
Little Lever BL3 43 A4
Pendlebury M27 80 A7
Reddish M34 100 B2
Sale M33 108 D2
Windermere Cl
Manchester M11 165 A4
Prestwich M25 62 F5
Stretford M32 96 C3
Windermere Cres OL7 84 F4
Windermere Ct WN7 75 E5
Windermere Dr
Adlington PR6 21 B8
Alderley Edge SK9 136 F1
Bury BL9 44 E7
Ramsbottom BL0 138 C3
Windermere Gr WN7 75 E6
Windermere Ho 3 M28 60 E2
Windermere Mews M24 46 E3
Windermere Rd
Abram WN2 74 B8
Dukinfield SK14 101 C5
Farnworth BL4 59 E7
Handforth SK9 131 C4
High Lane SK6 134 E8
Hindley WN2 56 E5
Ince-in-M WN2 56 B7
Leigh WN7 75 E5
Middleton M24 46 D3
Orrell WN5 53 F8
Royton OL2 48 D6
Stalybridge SK15 86 A4
Stockport SK1 124 B7
Urmston M41 95 C1
Windermere St
Bolton BL1 143 C2
4 Rochdale OL12 14 F2
5 Wigan WN1 37 E1
Windermere Wlk 5 OL4 67 C7
Winder St BL1 145 C4
Winders Way M6 81 B4
Windfields Cl SK8 123 B3
Windgate Rise SK15 86 D5
Windham St OL16 15 C3
Windle Ave M9 63 F3
Windle Ct SK2 124 E5
WINDLEHURST 125 E1
Windlehurst Ct SK6 134 D7
Windlehurst Dr M28 78 B7
Windlehurst Hall SK6 125 F1
Windlehurst Old Rd SK6 125 F2
Windlehurst Rd SK6 125 E2
Windlehurst Sch SK6 125 F2
Windleshaw St WN3 151 B2
Windley St BL2 148 A4
Windmill Ave M5 161 B3
Windmill Cl
Reddish M34 100 B2
Walkden M28 60 C5
Wigan WN1 151 A4
Windmill Ct 21 OL16 31 B6
Windmill Hts WN8 53 A8
Windmill La
Denton M34 100 C2
Reddish SK5 100 A1
Tyldesley M29 76 F4
Windmill Lane Ind Est
M34 100 C2
Windmill Rd
Sale M33 108 F3
Walkden M28 60 C5
Windmill St
Manchester M2 162 C4
20 Rochdale OL16 31 B6
Windmill Trad Est M34 100 D3
Windover Cl BL5 59 A7
Windover St 1 BL3 146 A4
Windrush Ave BL0 11 A2
Windrush Dr
Manchester M9 157 A3
Westhoughton BL5 39 F1
Windrush Millennium Ctr 12
M16 97 E4
Windrush The OL12 14 C4
Windsor Ave
Adlington PR7 20 F6
Chadderton OL9 66 A4
Failsworth M35 84 B8
Gatley SK8 122 A5
Heywood OL10 29 B2
Irlam M44 94 B3
Little Lever BL3 43 A3
Newton-le-W WA12 89 D2
Sale M33 108 B6
Stockport SK4 168 A3
Swinton M27 62 A2
Tyldesley M29 77 A6
Urmston M41 94 F2
Walkden M38 60 B5
Whitefield M45 63 A7
Wilmslow SK9 136 F7
Windsor Cl
Poynton SK12 133 D4
Ramsbottom BL8 11 A1
Windsor Cres
Aspull WN2 38 D5
Manchester M25 63 E3
Windsor Ct
Bolton BL3 147 A2
13 Denton M34 113 A8
2 Sale M33 107 F5
Windsor Dr
Altrincham, Bowdon
WA14 118 F1
Altrincham, Timperley
WA14 119 F8
Ashton-u-L OL7 84 F4
Bury BL8 44 B8
Droylsden M34 84 D1
Dukinfield SK16 101 F7
Haydock WA11 89 A7
Horwich BL6 22 E2
Marple SK6 125 E5
Romiley SK6 112 C3
Stalybridge SK15 86 A3
Windsor Gr
Ashton-u-L OL6 85 C7
Bolton BL1 142 C1
Cheadle SK8 131 F8
Hindley WN2 57 B3
Kearsley M26 61 B7
Romiley SK6 113 E2
Windsor Ho M21 109 F8
Windsor Rd
Ashton-in-M WN4 73 C1
Billinge WN5 71 F5
Bolton BL7 25 A7
Droylsden M43 83 E1
Failsworth M40 83 E4
Golborne WA3 90 C8
Hazel Grove SK7 124 F2
Hyde SK14 113 E7
Leigh WN7 76 E6
Manchester, Harpurhey
M9 157 B3
Manchester, Levenshulme
M19 99 A1
Manchester M25 63 E3
Oldham OL8 66 D4
Reddish M34 100 A3
Up Holland WN8 53 A8
Windsor St
Failsworth, Holt Lane End
M35 84 A8
Failsworth M40 83 E4
Manchester M18 99 C4
Oldham OL1 49 A1
Rochdale OL11 31 A5
Salford M5 81 B1
Stockport SK2 124 A6
Tyldesley M46 58 E2
Wigan WN1 37 D1
Windsor Terr
Milnrow OL16 31 E6
Rochdale OL16 31 C7
Stockport SK2 124 A6
Windsor Wlk SK2 170 C2
WINDY ARBOUR 72 B8
Windybank M9 64 C5
Windy Bank Ave WA3 90 E8
Windy Harbour La BL7 25 B8
Windyhill Dr BL3 146 A3
Winfell Dr M40 160 A3
Winfield Ave M20 110 D6
Winfield Dr M18 99 D6
Winfield Gr SK6 114 B1
Winfield St SK14 167 C2
Wingate Ave BL8 27 B2
Wingate Dr
Altrincham WA15 120 B5
Manchester M20 110 C2
Whitefield M45 44 E1
Wingate Rd
Stockport SK4 168 C4
Walkden M38 60 B4
WINGATES 39 E2
Wingates Gr BL5 39 D3
Wingates Ind Est BL5 39 D2
Wingates La BL5 39 E5
Wingates Rd WN1 37 C4
Wingates Sq BL5 39 E3
Wingate St OL11 13 E1
Wingfield Ave SK9 136 E6
Wingfield Cl WN6 37 A4
Wingfield Dr
Pendlebury M27 80 A6
Wilmslow SK9 136 E6
Wingfield Gr SK13 116 F7
Wingfield St M32 96 D4
Wingfield Villas OL15 16 C7
Wingrave Ho 3 M6 154 C2
Wings Gr OL10 46 D7
Winhill Rd SK22 127 C1
Winifred Ave BL9 28 F4
Winifred Rd
Failsworth M40 83 B7
Farnworth BL4 42 A1
Manchester M20 110 B3
Stockport SK2 124 A6
Urmston M41 95 D2
Winifred St
2 Eccles M30 79 B1
Hyde SK14 113 E7
Ince-in-M WN3 151 B2
Ramsbottom BL0 138 B1
Rochdale OL12 14 B1
Winmarith Dr WA15 129 D7
Winmarleigh Cl BL8 26 F1
Winmarleigh Gdns WN7 75 E3
Winnall Wlk 3 M40 83 C6
Winnard St WA3 74 B2
Winnats Cl SK13 116 F8
Winnie St M40 83 A8
Winning Hill Cl M18 99 D4
Winnington Gn SK2 124 D6
Winnington Rd SK6 125 F7
Winnipeg Quay M50 96 F7
Winnows The M34 100 D3
Winscar Rd WN2 56 D6
Winscombe Dr M40 159 C4
Winser St M1 163 A4
Winsfield Rd SK7 133 E8
Winsford Dr OL11 29 F5
Winsford Gr BL3 40 F5
Winsford Rd M14 98 A1
Winsford Wlk M33 108 E3
Winskill Rd M44 106 A8
Winslade Cl
Oldham OL4 49 D1
Stockport SK7 124 A2
Winslade Mews BL4 42 D1
Winsley Rd M23 108 F2
Winslow Ave SK14 103 A2
Winslow Pl M19 110 F6
Winslow Rd BL3 40 D3
Winslow St M11 165 A4
Winsmoor Dr WN2 56 E4
Winson Cl BL3 147 B4
WINSTANLEY 54 C3
Winstanley Cl 6 M6 80 D5
Winstanley Coll WN5 53 F3
WINSTANLEY PARK 54 B2
Winstanley Pl WN3 151 B2
Winstanley Prim Sch
WN3 54 C2
Winstanley Rd
Ashton-in-M WN2 73 F8
Garswood WN4, WN5 72 B6
Manchester M40 160 A3
Orrell WN5 53 F3
Sale M33 108 C5
Winstanley St WN5 54 F6
Winster Ave
Manchester M20 109 E4
Salford M7 81 B6
Stretford M32 96 A3
Winster Cl
Bolton BL2 25 F1
Whitefield M45 63 B8
Winster Dr
Bolton BL2 25 F1
6 Middleton M24 46 E2
Wigan WN2 55 F2
Winster Gn M30 95 B8
Winster Gr SK2 124 A6
Winster Mews SK13 171 B2
Winster Rd M30 95 B8
Winston Ave
Little Lever BL3 43 C3
Newton-le-W WA12 89 C3
Rochdale OL11 29 E6
Winston Cl
Marple SK6 125 D7
Radcliffe M26 43 E5
Sale M33 107 F5
Winston Rd M40, M9 157 C4
Winswell Cl M11 83 B2
Winterbottom Gr SK14 102 F2
Winterbottom St OL9 153 A3
Winterbottom Wlk 4
SK14 102 F2
Winterburn Ave
Bolton BL2 25 B6
Manchester M21 109 D4
Winterburn Gn SK2 124 E5
Winterbutlee Gr OL14 6 A8
Winterdyne St M9 157 B3
Winterfield Dr BL3 146 A3
Winterford Ave M13 164 A1
Winterford Rd
Mossley OL5 68 E1
Salford M7, M8 155 C3
Wintergreen Cl WN7 75 E4
Wintergreen Wlk 3
M31 105 F3
Winter Hey La BL6 22 B3
Winter Hill View BL7 8 D3
Wintermans Rd M21 109 E7
Winterslow Ave M23 108 D1
Winter St BL1 143 A3
Winterton Cl BL5 40 A1
Winterton Rd SK5 100 A1
Winthrop Ave M40 157 A1
WINTON 79 B3
Winton Ave
Denton M34 100 D7
Failsworth M40 65 D1
Wigan WN5 54 D5
Winton Cl SK7 123 D1
Winton Ct WA14 119 C2
Winton Gn BL6 22 F1
Winton Gr BL3 40 E4
Winton Rd
Altrincham WA14 119 C2
Golborne WA3 90 E6
Pendlebury M6 80 D5
Winton St
Ashton-u-L OL6 166 B3
Littleborough OL15 16 B5
3 Stalybridge SK15 86 B1
Winward St
Bolton BL3 146 A4
Leigh WN7 75 B5
13 Westhoughton BL5 39 E1
Winwick La WA3 90 E3
Winwick Rd WA12 89 F1
Winwood Dr M24 47 B1
Winwood Fold M24 46 F4
Winwood Rd M20 122 C8
Wirral Cl
Culcheth WA3 91 E4
Swinton M27 62 A2
Wirral Cres SK3 123 A8
Wirral Dr WN3 54 C2
Wisbech Dr M23 108 F1
Wisbeck Rd BL2 148 C4
Wiseman Terr M25 63 C4
Wishaw Sq M21 109 E7
Wisley Cl SK5 112 A8
Wistaria Rd M18 99 D5
Witham Ave M22 121 E5
Witham Cl
Heywood OL10 29 A3
Standish WN6 19 D1
Witham St OL6 85 E4
Withenfield Rd M23 120 F8
Withens Gn SK2 124 E6
Withern 16 OL10 29 C2
Withill Wlk 4 WN4 73 A5
WITHINGTON 110 B6
Withington Ave WA3 92 A3
Withington Cl 2 M46 58 B4
Withington Com Hospl
M20 109 F5
Withington Dr M29 77 C7
Withington Girls Sch
M14 110 C8
Withington Gn M24 47 A4
Withington Hospl M20 109 F5
Withington La WN2 38 C2
Withington Rd M16, M21 97 D2
Withington St OL10 46 E8
Withinlea Cl BL5 40 A2
Withins Ave M26 44 C5
Withins Cl BL2 42 E8
Withins Com L Ctr BL2 25 E2
Withins Dr BL2 42 E8
Withins Gr BL2 42 E8
Withins Hall Rd M35 84 B6
Withins La
Bolton BL2 42 E8
Radcliffe M26 44 C5
Withins Rd
Culcheth WA3 91 F3
Oldham OL8 66 B2
Withins St M26 44 C4
Withnell Cl WN6 37 A2
Withnell Dr BL8 27 A1
Withnell Rd M19 110 D3
Withycombe Pl M6 81 A5
Withy Gr M4 159 A2
Withypool Dr SK2 124 C5
Withy Tree Gr 1 M34 101 A2
Witley Dr M33 107 D6
Witley Rd OL16 31 B7
Witney Cl 14 BL1 143 B2
Wittenbury Rd SK4 168 B2
Wittenham Ho SK9 131 D2
Witterage Cl M12 164 C2
Witton Wlk M8 155 C2
Woburn Ave
Bolton BL2 25 C3
Leigh WN7 57 D1
Newton-le-W WA12 89 D2
Woburn Cl OL16 31 E6
Woburn Ct SK12 133 F4
Woburn Dr
Altrincham WA15 120 B2
Bury BL9 44 F5
Woburn Rd M16 97 A2
Woburn St 3 M16 97 F3
Woden's Ave M5 161 C3
Woden St M5 161 C3
Woking Rd SK8 132 A7
Woking Terr BL1 143 B1
Wolfenden Gn BB4 2 F8
Wolfenden St BL1 143 B2
Wolfenden Terr 25 BL1 143 B2
Wolf Grange WA15 119 E1
Wolford Dr M29 59 C1
Wolfreton Cres M27 62 A3
Wolfson Sq WN4 72 F4
Wollaton Wlk M34 100 E1
Wolmer St WN4 73 A4
Wolseley Ho M33 108 C6
Wolseley Pl M20 110 B5
Wolseley Rd M33 108 C6
Wolseley St
1 Bury BL8 27 B1
Newhey OL16 32 B4
Wolsey Cl
Ashton-in-M WN4 73 A5
Radcliffe M26 44 A3
Wolsey Dr WA14 119 A1
Wolsey St
Heywood OL10 29 C1
Radcliffe M26 44 A3
WOLSTENHOLME 13 C2
Wolstenholme Ave BL9 27 F6
Wolstenholme Coalpit La
OL11, OL12 13 B2
Wolstenholme La OL11,
OL12 13 C2
Wolstenvale Cl M24 47 B1
Wolver Cl M38 60 B6
Wolverton Ave OL8 66 D3
Wolverton Dr SK9 131 D1
Wolvesey OL11 139 B2
Wolveton St M11 164 C3
Woodacre M16 97 E1
Woodacre Cl M33 108 A2
Woodacres Ct SK9 136 F6
Woodall Cl M33 108 D4
Woodark Cl OL4 67 F5
Woodbank
2 Alderley Edge SK9 137 A2
Bolton BL2 25 D2
Stockport SK1 112 B1
Woodbank Ave
Romiley SK6 112 E3
Stockport SK1 124 C8
Woodbank Ct M41 95 B3
Woodbank Dr BL8 27 C4
Woodbank Park Nature
Reserve* SK1 112 C1
Woodbank Prim Sch
BL8 140 A4
Wood Bank Rd OL15 16 A3
Wood Bank Terr OL5 68 D2
Woodbank Works Ind Est
SK1 112 B1
Woodbine Ave M44 105 D4
Woodbine Cres SK2 170 C3
Woodbine Rd
Bolton BL3 146 C3
Lymm WA13 117 B4
Woodbine St
Manchester M14 98 A4
Rochdale OL16 31 A5
Woodbine Street E OL16 31 B5
Woodbine Terr 1 M44 94 A2
Woodbourne Ct M33 108 B2
Woodbourne Rd
Manchester SK4 111 C6
Sale M33 108 A2
Woodbray Ave M19 110 E5
Woodbridge Ave M34 100 E7
Woodbridge Dr BL2 25 B1
Woodbridge Gdns OL12 14 C2
Woodbridge Gr M23 109 A1
Woodbridge Rd M41 94 D3
WOOD BROOK 68 B8
Woodbrook Ave
Hyde SK14 167 C2
Oldham OL4 68 B7
Woodbrook Dr WN3 54 D4
Woodbrook La OL4 68 B7
Woodbrook Rd
Alderley Edge SK9 137 C1
Oldham OL4 68 B7
Woodburn Dr BL1 142 B3
Woodburn Rd M22 121 D8
Woodburn Row M29 77 C3
Woodbury Cres SK16 101 B7
Woodbury Rd SK3 123 B7
Woodchurch WN1 37 F1
Woodchurch Cl 3 BL1 143 B1
Woodchurch Wlk
Chadderton OL9 152 B2
7 Sale M33 108 F3
Woodcock Cl
Droylsden M43 84 C3
Rochdale OL11 29 F7
Woodcock Dr WN2 56 B2
Woodcock Gr SK13 104 E1
Woodcock Ho WN1 151 A4
Woodcock Sq 10 WN1 150 C4
Woodcote Ave SK7 123 C2
Woodcote Rd
Sale M14 & M31 107 A1
Sale WA14 107 D1
Woodcote View SK9 131 F1
Woodcote Wlk M8 156 C4
Wood Cottage Cl 4 M28 59 F3
Woodcott Bank BL1 143 B4
Woodcott Gr 3 SK9 131 E1
Wood Cotts SK6 113 A6
Woodcourt
Wigan WN3 150 B2
Wythenshawe M33 120 C8
Wood Cres OL4 67 E3
Woodcroft
Appley Bridge WN6 35 E6
Stockport SK2 124 D6
Woodcroft Ave M19 110 E4
Wooddagger Cl WN2 56 F5
Woodeaton Cl OL2 49 A4
Wooded Cl BL9 27 F5
Woodedge WN4 73 A3
Wood Edge Cl BL4 42 C2
WOODEND
Mossley 68 E2
New Mills 135 E8
WOOD END 149 B4

Woodend
Shaw OL2 149 C4
Stockport SK7 123 D2
Woodend Ct SK14 167 A1
Woodend Dr SK15 102 D6
Woodend La
Altrincham WA16 129 E1
Hyde SK14 167 A1
Stalybridge SK15 102 D6
Wardle OL12 15 D6
Woodend Mill OL5 68 D2
Woodend Mills OL4 67 F5
Woodend Mills Ind Est OL4 67 F5
Woodend Rd
Stockport SK3 123 F4
Wythenshawe M22 121 D4
Woodend St
Oldham, County End OL4 67 F5
Oldham, Oldham Edge OL1 48 E1
Oldham, West Hulme OL1 48 E1
Woodend View OL5 68 D2
Woodfield M22 121 D3
Woodfield Ave
Hyde SK14 113 D8
Rochdale OL12 14 E2
Romiley SK6 113 A4
Woodfield Cl
Glossop SK13 103 F5
Oldham OL8 66 C4
Woodfield Cres
Ashton-in-M WN4 73 A2
Romiley SK6 112 F2
Woodfield Ct SK2 124 A4
Woodfield Dr M28 78 B6
Woodfield Gr
Eccles M30 79 C1
Farnworth BL4 60 C6
Sale M33 108 A6
Woodfield Prim Sch WN1 37 C4
Woodfield Rd
Altrincham WA14 119 C6
Cheadle SK8 132 B7
2 Manchester, Crumpsall M8 64 A1
Manchester M24 64 E6
Salford M6 154 A4
WOODFIELDS 140 C3
Woodfields Ret Pk BL9 140 C3
Woodfield St
Bolton BL3 42 A3
Wigan WN2 38 A3
Woodfield Terr OL10 29 E3
Wood Fold BL7 25 C6
Woodfold Ave M19 99 A2
Wood Fold Prim Sch WN6 36 D8
WOODFORD 132 E2
Woodford Aerodrome SK7 133 A1
Woodford Ave
Denton M34 101 A4
Eccles M30 79 B2
Golborne WA3 90 D7
Shaw OL2 49 D7
Woodford Ct
Droylsden M43 100 B8
3 Hindley WN2 56 E6
Woodford Dr M27 61 E2
Woodford Gdns M20 110 A2
Woodford Gr BL3 146 C4
Woodford Lo SK12 133 C4
Woodford Mews SK9 131 D4
Woodford Rd
Bramhall SK7 132 E4
Failsworth M35 84 A7
Poynton SK12 133 B6
Woodford St
4 Hindley WN2 56 E6
7 Wigan WN5 54 B6
Woodgarth WN7 75 C5
Woodgarth Ave M40 83 D5
Woodgarth Dr M27 79 E6
Woodgarth La M28 78 F5
Woodgate Ave
Bury BL9 28 D4
Rochdale OL11 30 A6
Woodgate Cl SK6 112 F3
Woodgate Dr M25 63 C6
WOODGATE HILL 28 D4
Woodgate Hill Rd
Bury, Fern Grove BL9 141 C4
Bury, Woodgate Hill BL9 28 D4
Woodgate Rd M16 97 E1
Woodgate St BL3 42 A3
Wood Gdns SK9 137 B2
Wood Gove Gdns WN5 36 B1
Wood Gr
Denton M34 100 F4
Romiley SK6 113 A5
Whitefield M45 44 F3
Woodgrange Cl 2 M6 154 B2
Woodgreen Cl 5 WN2 56 D4
Woodgreen Dr M26 62 A8
Woodhall Ave
Manchester M20 110 A7
Whitefield M45 62 D6
Woodhall Cl
Bolton BL2 25 C3
Bramhall SK7 132 E3
Bury BL8 27 D5
Woodhall Cres SK5 112 A4
Woodhall Rd SK5 169 C4
Woodhall St M35 83 F8
Woodhalt Rd M8 156 A4
Woodham Rd M23 108 F1
Woodham Wlk BL3 145 A1
Woodhays St M6 154 C2
Woodhead Cl
Oldham OL4 67 E7
Ramsbottom BL0 11 C4
Woodhead Dr WA15 119 F1
Woodhead Gr WN3 55 B2
Woodhead Rd
Altrincham WA15 119 F1
Glossop SK13 104 D5
Tintwistle SK13 104 B8
Woodhead St 6 M16 97 E4
WOODHEY 11 B3
Wood Hey Cl M26 43 D3
Woodhey Ct M33 107 E1
Wood Hey Gr
2 Denton M34 101 A2
Rochdale OL12 14 F4
Woodhey High Sch BL0 11 A3
Woodhey Rd BL0 11 A3
Woodheys SK4 110 F3
Woodheys Dr M33 107 D1
Woodhey Sports Ctr BL0 11 A3
Woodheys Prim Sch M33 107 E2
Woodheys Rd OL15 16 A2
Woodheys St 1 M5 154 C1
WOODHILL 140 A4
Woodhill M24 46 F2
Woodhill Cl
Manchester M12 99 B4
Middleton M24 46 F2
Woodhill Dr M25 63 B3
WOODHILL FOLD 140 A3
Woodhill Fold BL8 140 A3
Woodhill Gr M25 63 B3
Woodhill Rd BL8 140 A4
Woodhill St BL8 140 A4
Woodhill Vale BL8 140 A3
Woodhouse Ct M41 95 A4
Woodhouse Dr WN6 36 E2
Woodhouse Farm Cotts OL12 13 D2
Woodhouse Knowl OL3 50 F4
Woodhouse La
Partington WA14 118 C4
Rochdale OL12 13 E3
Sale M33 107 C2
Wigan WN6 36 F2
Wigan WN6 37 A1
Wythenshawe, Benchill M22 121 D4
Wythenshawe M90 130 D7
Woodhouse Lane E WA15 108 A1
WOODHOUSE PARK 121 D1
Woodhouse Prim Sch M41 95 A4
Woodhouse Rd
Shaw OL2 32 C1
Urmston M41 94 F4
Wythenshawe M22 130 D8
WOODHOUSES 84 B6
Woodhouse St
Atherton M46 58 D2
Manchester M18 99 E5
Woodhouses VC Prim Sch M35 84 C6
Woodhurst Dr WN6 19 D1
Wooding Cl M31 106 A4
Wood La
Altrincham WA15 120 B5
Ashton-u-L OL6, OL7 85 B5
Edenfield BL0 1 D2
Marple SK6 125 E5
Middleton M24 65 B7
Partington M31 105 D3
Wilmslow WA16 129 D1
Wrightington Bar WN6, PR7 18 E8
Woodlake Ave M21 109 C4
Woodland Ave
Bolton BL3 42 B2
Hazel Grove SK7 124 E1
Hindley WN2 57 A3
Lymm WA13 117 A2
Newton-le-W WA12 89 F3
Reddish M18 99 E4
Woodland Cl BL2 25 E2
Woodland Com Prim Sch OL10 29 B1
Woodland Cres M25 63 B2
Woodland Ct M29 77 E8
Woodland Dr
Ashton-in-M WN4 73 B5
Lymm WA13 117 A2
Standish WN6 19 E2
Woodland Gr
Bolton BL7 8 D2
Wigan WN1 37 D2
Woodland Pk OL2 48 B6
Woodland Rd
Heywood OL10 29 E3
Manchester M19 111 A7
Reddish M18 99 E4
Rochdale OL12 14 C2
Tyldesley M29 77 B7
WOODLANDS
Stalybridge 102 D7
Urmston 94 D1
Woodlands
Failsworth M35 83 E4
5 Urmston M41 95 C3
Woodlands Ave
Cheadle SK8 123 A2
Eccles M30 95 A8
Ince-in-M WN3 151 C2
Irlam M44 94 A3
Woodlands Ave *continued*
Leigh WN7 75 F3
Rochdale OL11 30 A6
Romiley SK6 113 A5
1 Stretford M32 96 D2
Swinton M27 79 D6
Urmston M41 94 C2
Whitefield M45 44 E1
Woodlands Cl
Broadbottom SK14 102 F1
Cheadle SK8 132 A8
Glossop SK13 103 F6
Stalybridge SK15 102 D7
Worsley M28 78 E7
Woodlands Ct
Altrincham WA15 119 E5
Stockport SK2 124 D8
Woodlands Dr
Over Hulton M46 58 F5
Romiley SK6 113 A5
Sale M23, M33 108 C1
Shevington WN6 35 F4
Stockport SK2 124 D8
Woodlands Gr
Broadbottom SK14 102 F1
Bury BL8 27 B3
Woodlands Hospl M28 59 F4
Woodlands Ind Est WA12 89 C6
Woodlands La WA15 119 E5
Woodlands Park Cl WN1 37 C5
Woodlands Park Rd SK2 124 D8
Woodlands Parkway WA15 119 E6
Woodlands Pk WA12 89 C6
Woodlands Rd
Altrincham WA14, WA15 119 E5
Ashton-u-L OL6 85 E6
Edenfield BL0 1 D2
Handforth SK9 131 E3
High Lane SK12 135 A6
Manchester, Cheetham Hill M8 156 B3
Manchester, Heaton Mersey SK4 110 E2
Manchester, Whalley Range M21 97 E1
Milnrow OL16 31 E5
Sale M33 108 C4
Stalybridge SK15 102 D7
Wilmslow SK9 130 F1
Worsley M28 78 F7
Woodlands St M8 156 A4
Woodland St
Heywood OL10 29 D2
Manchester M12 165 B1
Rochdale OL12 15 A2
Woodlands The
Bolton BL6 40 C8
Bury BL8 140 A4
Droylsden M43 83 E3
Heywood OL10 46 E8
Pendlebury M27 80 B7
Prestwich M25 62 F1
Wigan WN1 37 D3
Woodlands View OL16 31 C8
Woodlands Way M24 64 F6
Woodland View
Bolton BL7 25 B8
Hyde SK14 167 C3
Wood Lane N SK10 134 B1
Wood Lane W SK10 133 F1
Woodlark Cl M3 158 A1
Woodlawn Ct M16 97 C3
Woodlea
Altrincham WA15 119 F4
Oldham OL9 65 D7
Worsley M28 78 E8
Woodlea Ave M19 110 E6
Wood Lea Bank 9 BB4 2 F8
Woodlea Chase M27 61 D5
Woodlea Rd SK13 116 B7
Wood Lea Rd BB4 2 F8
Woodleigh WA14 119 A5
Woodleigh Ct
1 Alderley Edge SK9 137 A2
Bury BL8 27 B5
Woodleigh Dr M43 84 C4
Woodleigh Rd OL4 68 A7
Woodleigh St M9 64 F1
Woodles M30 79 C4
WOODLEY 113 C6
Woodley Ave M26 44 B1
Woodley Cl SK2 124 D7
Woodley Gr WN7 75 D5
Woodley Prec SK6 113 A5
Woodley Prim Sch SK6 113 C5
Woodley St BL9 44 F8
Woodley Sta SK6 113 B6
Woodliffe St M16 161 C1
Woodlinn Wlk M9 157 A3
Woodman Dr BL9 27 E6
Woodman St SK1 169 B2
Woodmeadow Ct 11 OL5 68 C2
Woodmere Dr M9 64 E3
Wood Mount WA15 120 B5
Woodmount Cl SK6 113 F2
Woodnewton Cl M18 99 C4
Woodnook Rd WN6 35 E8
Woodpark Cl OL8 67 A3
Woodpecker Pl M28 78 D8
Wood Rd
Manchester M16 97 D3
Sale WA15 108 B1
Woodridings WA14 119 B3
WOOD ROAD 11 B1
Wood Road La
Bury BL8, BL9 27 B8
Ramsbottom BL9 11 C1
Wood Road N M16 97 C3
Woodrow Way M44 105 F8
Woodrow Wlk M12 164 C2
Woodroyd Cl SK7 123 D1
Woodroyd Dr BL9 141 C3
Woodruffe Gdns SK6 125 A8
Woodruff Wlk 7 M31 105 F3
Woodrush Rd WN6 36 D3
Woods Ct
Middleton M24 64 C7
Newton-le-W WA12 89 A3
Woodseats La SK13 115 B6
Woodseaves Cl 1 M44 94 B1
WOODS END 94 E4
Woods End M20 109 F4
Woodsend Circ M41 94 D3
Woodsend Crescent Rd M41 94 D2
Woodsend Gn M41 94 D3
Woodsend Rd M41 94 E3
Woodsend Rd S M41 94 E1
Woods Gr SK8 132 B7
Woodshaw Gr 2 M28 78 C8
Woodside
Manchester SK4 110 F1
Newhey OL16 32 C5
Poynton SK12 133 F4
Shaw OL2 49 D8
Wilmslow/Alderley Edge SK9 136 C7
Woodside Ave
Ashton-in-M WN4 73 A8
Manchester M19 110 F5
Walkden M28 60 F2
Woodside Cl
Oldham OL4 67 E6
Up Holland WN8 53 C8
Woodside Dr
High Lane SK6 134 F7
Hyde SK14 167 B1
Ramsbottom BL0 138 A1
2 Salford M6 80 C3
Woodside La
Lymm WA13 117 B1
Poynton SK12 133 E4
Woodside Mews SK7 123 C2
Woodside Pl BL2 148 C1
Woodside Rd M16 97 B2
Woodside Sq BL2 148 C1
Woodside St SK15 86 E6
Woods La
Cheadle SK8 132 B7
Uppermill OL3 51 A2
Wood's La WN4 73 C5
Woods Lea BL1 40 F7
Woodsleigh Coppice BL1 40 F7
Woodsley Rd BL1 23 F2
WOODS MOOR 124 B4
Woodsmoor La SK2 124 A4
Woodsmoor Rd 5 M27 79 D7
Woodsmoor Sta SK2 124 B4
Wood Sorrel Way WA3 90 E8
Wood Sq
Droylsden M43 100 A8
Uppermill OL3 69 B6
Woods Rd
Aspull WN2 38 C4
Irlam M44 105 F8
Wood's St WN3 150 C3
Wood St
Altrincham WA14 119 D4
Ashton-u-L OL6 166 B2
Atherton M46 58 B4
Bolton BL1 145 C3
Bury BL8 27 C3
Cheadle SK8 122 D6
Denton M34 100 F4
Dukinfield SK16 101 C6
Eccles M30 79 F1
Glossop SK13 116 C8
Golborne WA3 90 B8
Hindley WN2 57 B3
Hollingworth SK14 103 D5
Horwich BL6 22 C3
Hyde SK14 167 B2
Littleborough OL15 16 B5
Manchester, City Centre M3 158 C1
Manchester, Openshaw M11 165 B4
Middleton M24 64 F8
Newhey OL16 32 C4
Oldham OL1 67 B8
Radcliffe M26 61 E8
Ramsbottom BL0 138 B1
Rochdale OL16 31 A6
Shaw OL2 48 F8
7 Stalybridge SK15 85 F2
Stockport SK3 169 A1
Tyldesley M29 77 B8
Westhoughton BL5 57 E8
Wigan, Parson's Meadow WN5 54 F7
Wigan WN3 150 C3
Woods The
3 Altrincham WA14 119 E6
Oldham OL4 68 B6
Rochdale OL11 30 C3
Woodstock Ave
Cheadle SK8 132 A7
Newton-le-W WA12 89 D2
Reddish SK5 111 F5
Woodstock Cl
Heywood OL10 29 E2
Leigh WN7 75 E1
Woodstock Cres SK6 113 A5
Woodstock Dr
Bolton BL1 142 A1
Woodstock Dr *continued*
Bury BL8 26 D7
Pendlebury M27 80 B6
Worsley M28 79 A6
Woodstock Gn
Oldham OL8 67 A3
Reddish SK5 112 A5
Woodstock Rd
Altrincham WA14 119 C8
Failsworth M40 65 C1
Manchester M16 97 B3
Romiley SK6 113 A5
Woodstock St
Oldham OL4 153 C2
12 Rochdale OL12 14 C1
Wood Terr BL2 26 D1
Woodthorpe Ct M25 63 D2
Woodthorpe Dr SK8 123 A2
Woodthorpe Grange M25 63 D2
Woodtop Ave OL11 29 F5
Wood Top Cl SK2 124 E7
Woodvale
Altrincham WA14 119 C2
Middleton M24 47 A4
Woodvale Ave
Aspull WN2 38 F3
Atherton M46 58 B5
Bolton BL3 147 A2
Woodvale Dr
Bolton BL3 147 A2
Golborne WA3 74 E1
Woodvale Gdns BL3 147 A2
Woodvale Gr BL3 147 A2
Woodvale Rd M26 44 B2
Woodvale Wlk 18 M11 160 C1
Wood View
Heywood OL10 29 C4
Shevington WN6 36 B5
Wythenshawe M22 109 D1
Woodview Ave M19 110 F5
Woodville Ave SK9 136 C7
Woodville Dr
Marple SK6 125 E4
Sale M33 108 A5
Stalybridge SK15 86 D3
Woodville Gr SK5 111 F6
Woodville Rd
Altrincham WA14 119 C3
Ince-in-M WN3 55 F4
Sale M33 108 A5
Wilmslow/Alderley Edge SK9 136 C7
Woodville Terr 10 M40 64 F1
Woodward Cl BL9 27 F5
Woodward Ct M4 160 A2
Woodward Pl M4 159 C2
Woodward Rd M25 62 F2
Woodwards Rd BL5 57 F6
Woodward St M4 159 C2
Woodwise La M23 108 E1
Woodyates St WN5 54 F6
Woolden Rd M44, WA3 105 B8
Woolden St
Eccles M30 79 B3
8 Wigan WN5 54 F6
Wooler Gr WN2 56 D2
Woolfall Cl M12 164 C2
WOOLFOLD 27 B4
Woolfold Trad Est BL8 27 B4
WOOLFORD 27 B4
Woollacot St 2 OL1 153 C2
Woollam Pl M3 162 A4
Woolley Ave SK12 133 D2
Woolley Bridge Rd SK13 103 F5
Woolley Cl SK14 171 A4
Woolley La SK14 171 A4
Woolley Mill La SK13 103 E7
Woolley St M8 158 C4
Woolley Terr 3 SK16 166 B1
Woolmore Ave OL1 48 E1
Woolpack Gn 2 M6 154 C3
Wool Rd OL3 51 B2
Woolston Dr M29 77 C8
Woolston Ho 3 M6 80 C4
Woolton Cl
Ashton-in-M WN4 72 F5
3 Failsworth M40 65 C2
Wootton St SK14 167 A4
Worcester Ave
Brinnington SK5 112 C5
Denton M34 101 A1
3 Golborne WA3 90 B8
Hindley WN2 56 F6
Manchester M23 120 F8
Worcester Cl
Ashton-u-L OL6 85 D8
Bury BL9 45 A8
Romiley SK6 113 A1
Salford M6 80 C4
Worcester Gr SK13 116 F8
Worcester Rd
Cheadle SK8 123 A4
Little Lever BL3 42 F3
Middleton M24 64 F5
Sale M33 107 D3
Salford M6 80 C4
Swinton M27 61 D2
Worcester St
19 Bolton BL1 143 B1
Bury BL8 140 A4
Oldham OL9 152 B1
Rochdale OL11 30 E4
Salford M7 155 B2
Wordsworth Ave
Atherton M46 58 E5
Bury BL9 44 F6
Droylsden M43 84 A2
Farnworth BL4 60 B7

Wordsworth Ave continued
Leigh WN7 . . . . 75 D7
Longshaw WN5 . . . . 53 D1
Manchester M8 . . . . 156 A2
Orrell WN5 . . . . 53 F6
Radcliffe M26 . . . . 43 E4
Wigan WN1 . . . . 37 C3
Wordsworth Cl SK16 . . . 102 A7
Wordsworth Cres
Ashton-u-L OL7 . . . . 84 E5
Littleborough OL15 . . . . . 15 F7
Wordsworth Gdns M25 . . 62 F1
Wordsworth Ind Est ⓫
BL1 . . . . 143 A2
Wordsworth Rd
Denton M34 . . . . 113 A7
Manchester M16 . . . . 97 B3
Middleton M24 . . . . 47 B2
⑥ Oldham OL1 . . . . 49 B1
Reddish SK5 . . . . 61 E1
Swinton M27 . . . . 60 B5
Walkden M28 . . . . 60 B5
Wordsworth St BL1 . . . . 143 A2
Wordsworth Way OL11 . . 29 E6
Workesleigh St ⑨ M40 . . 83 C5
Works Bsns Ctr The
M12 . . . . 163 C3
World Freight Ctr M16 . . 96 E5
World Freight Terminal
M90 . . . . 129 F7
World Way M90 . . . . 130 B8
Worrall St
Failsworth M40 . . . . 83 A6
⓵ Rochdale OL12 . . . . . . 14 D2
Salford M3 . . . . 161 C3
Stockport SK3 . . . . 170 B3
Worrell Cl M26 . . . . 43 F4
Worsbrough Ave M40 . . . 60 C2
Worsefold St M40 . . . . . . 83 A8
Worsel St BL3 . . . . 146 C4
WORSLEY 78 E6
Worsley Ave
Manchester M40 . . . . 65 A1
Walkden M28 . . . . 60 A2
Worsley Brow M28 . . . . . 78 F7
Worsley Bsns Pk M28 . . 77 F8
Worsley Cl WN5 . . . . 54 C5
Worsley Cres SK2 . . . . . 124 B7
Worsley Ct
⓵ Manchester M14 . . . . 98 C2
Swinton M27 . . . . 79 F7
Walkden M28 . . . . 60 A2
Worsley Gdns M28 . . . . . 60 C4
Worsley Gn WN5 . . . . . . 54 B5
Worsley Gr
Manchester M19 . . . . 99 A1
Walkden M28 . . . . 60 A2
WORSLEY HALL 54 E7
Worsley Mesnes 55 A4
Worsley Mesnes Dr
WN3 . . . . 55 A4
Worsley Mesnes Prim Sch
WN3 . . . . 55 A4
Worsley Pl
Rochdale OL16 . . . . 31 B7
Shaw OL2 . . . . 149 A2
Worsley Rd
Bolton BL3 . . . . 146 A4
Eccles M30 . . . . 79 B3
Farnworth BL4 . . . . 60 D7
Swinton M27, M28 . . . . . . 79 C6
Worsley Road N M28 . . . . 60 D5
Worsley St
Bolton BL3 . . . . 145 B1
Bury BL8 . . . . 26 E7
Golborne WA3 . . . . 90 A8
Manchester, St George's
M15 . . . . 162 A3
Oldham OL8 . . . . 67 B5
Pendlebury M27 . . . . 80 A7
Rochdale OL16 . . . . 31 B7
Salford M3 . . . . 158 B2
Swinton M27 . . . . 61 F2
Wigan WN5 . . . . 54 B5
Worsley Terr WN1 . . . . . 37 C1
Worsley Trad Est M38 . . 59 E5
Worsley Woods Nature
Reserve* M28 . . . . 79 A7
Worston Ave BL1 . . . . . . 23 F3
Worth Ct SK12 . . . . 133 D2
Worthenbury Wlk M13 . . 98 E3
Worthing Cl SK2 . . . . . . 124 D6
Worthing Gr M46 . . . . . . 58 B3
Worthing St M14 . . . . . . 98 B2
Worthington Ave
Heywood OL10 . . . . 46 E7
⑨ Partington M31 . . . . 105 F3
Worthington Cl
Ashton-u-L OL7 . . . . 85 A5
⓶ Hattersley SK14 . . . 102 E2
Worthington Ct M33 . . . 108 E4
Worthington Dr M7 . . . . . 63 D1
Worthington Fold M46 . . 58 B3
Worthington Prim Sch
M33 . . . . 108 F4
Worthington Rd
Denton M34 . . . . 101 B1
Sale M33 . . . . 108 F4
Worthington St
Ashton-u-L OL7 . . . . 85 A5
⓶ Bolton BL3 . . . . 146 C3
Failsworth M40 . . . . 83 C8
Hindley WN2 . . . . 56 D6
Manchester M16 . . . . 97 C4
Stalybridge SK15 . . . . . . 85 F1
Worthington Way
Denton M34 . . . . 100 E4
Wigan WN3 . . . . 54 F2

Worth Prim Sch SK12 . . 133 F2
Worth's La M34 . . . . 113 A7
Wortley Ave M6 . . . . 80 C3
Wortley Gr M40 . . . . 65 B2
Wotton Dr WN4 . . . . 73 D3
Wragby Cl BL8 . . . . 27 D5
Wrath Cl BL2 . . . . 25 B5
Wraxhall Cres WN7 . . . . 75 D7
Wray Cl M22 . . . . 121 D4
Wray Gdns M19 . . . . . . 111 C8
Wray Pl OL16 . . . . 31 C6
Wraysbury Wlk ⓵⓸ M40 . 83 A7
Wray St WN1 . . . . 151 B4
Wrayton Lo M33 . . . . . . 108 B3
Wrekin Ave M23 . . . . . . 121 A3
Wren Ave M27 . . . . 62 B2
Wrenbury Ave M20 . . . . 109 F7
Wrenbury Cl ⑤ WN5 . . . 54 B5
Wrenbury Cres SK3 . . . 123 C8
Wrenbury Dr
⑥ Bolton BL7 . . . . 24 F6
Cheadle SK8 . . . . 122 E6
Rochdale OL16 . . . . 31 C4
Wrenbury Wlk M33 . . . . 108 E3
Wren Cl
Droylsden M34 . . . . 84 C1
Farnworth BL4 . . . . 59 F8
Hazel Grove SK2 . . . . . . 124 F5
Wigan WN3 . . . . 36 B1
Wren Dr
Bury BL9 . . . . 141 B4
Irlam M44 . . . . 94 A4
Wren Gdns M24 . . . . 46 F1
Wren Gn OL16 . . . . 31 B6
Wren Nest Cl SK13 . . . . 116 B8
Wren Nest Rd SK13 . . . 104 B1
Wren Nest Terr SK13 . . 104 C1
Wren's Nest Ave OL2 . . 149 F7
Wren St OL4 . . . . 67 C6
Wrenswood Dr M28 . . . . 78 C8
Wren Way M11 . . . . 164 B4
Wrexham Cl OL8 . . . . 66 B2
Wrigglesworth Dr BL8 . . 26 F3
WRIGHTINGTON 18 D4
WRIGHTINGTON BAR 19 D4
Wrightington Hospl WN6 . 18 D2
Wrightington Mossy Lea
Prim Sch WN6 . . . . 18 F6
Wrightington St WN1 . . . 37 C1
Wright Robinson Cl M11 . 164 B4
Wright Robinson Sports Coll
M18 . . . . 100 A6
Wrights Bank N SK2 . . . 124 E5
Wrights Bank S SK2 . . . 124 E5
Wright St
Abram Brow WN2 . . . . . . 74 B7
Ashton-in-M WN4 . . . . . . 73 A6
Ashton-u-L, Guide Bridge
M34 . . . . 100 E8
⓶ Ashton-u-L OL6 . . . . 85 D4
Chadderton OL9 . . . . 152 B1
Failsworth M35 . . . . 83 F8
Manchester M16 . . . . . . 161 C2
⓵⓶ Oldham OL1 . . . . . . 67 A7
Platt Bridge WN2 . . . . . . 56 A3
Radcliffe M26 . . . . 43 F3
Wright Street W ⓷ BL6 . . 22 B4
Wright Tree Villas M44 . 105 D5
Wrigley Cres M35 . . . . . 83 F7
Wrigley Fold M24 . . . . . . 46 D3
Wrigley Head M35 . . . . . 83 F8
Wrigley Head Cres M35 . 83 F8
Wrigley Pl OL15 . . . . 15 F3
Wrigley Sq ⓵ OL4 . . . . . 67 F6
Wrigley St
Ashton-u-L OL6 . . . . 166 B4
Oldham, County End OL4 . 67 F6
Oldham, Greenacres Moor
OL4 . . . . 67 B7
Oldham, Wood Brook OL4 . 68 B8
Wrington Cl WN7 . . . . . . 75 D8
Wroe St
⓵⓸ Oldham OL4 . . . . . . 67 F6
Salford M3 . . . . 158 A2
Swinton M27 . . . . 61 F3
Wroe Terr M27 . . . . 61 F3
Wrotham Cl ⓶ M5 . . . . . 81 A1
Wroxeter Wlk M12 . . . . . 164 C2
Wroxham Ave
Reddish M34 . . . . 100 A3
Urmston M41 . . . . 95 B3
Wroxham Cl BL8 . . . . 27 D5
Wroxham Rd M9 . . . . 64 B3
WUERDLE 15 E4
Wuerdle Cl OL16 . . . . . . 15 E4
Wuerdle Farm Way ⓷
OL16 . . . . 15 E4
Wuerdle Pl OL16 . . . . . . 15 E4
Wuerdle St ⓵ OL16 . . . 15 E4
Wyatt Ave M5 . . . . 161 C3
Wyatt Gr WN4 . . . . 73 D3
Wyatt St
⓸ Dukinfield SK16 . . . . 101 C8
Stockport SK4 . . . . 169 B2
Wybersley Rd SK6 . . . . . 135 A8
Wychbury St M6 . . . . . . 154 B2
Wychelm Rd M31 . . . . . 105 F3
Wycherley Rd OL12 . . . . 14 B2
Wych Fold SK14 . . . . . . 113 E7
Wych St OL6 . . . . 166 B2
Wychwood WA14 . . . . . 119 B1
Wychwood Cl M24 . . . . . 65 B7
Wycliffe Ave SK9 . . . . . 137 A7
Wycliffe Ct M41 . . . . 95 C2
Wycliffe Rd M41 . . . . 95 C2
Wycliffe St
Eccles M30 . . . . 79 C2

Wycliffe St continued
Stockport SK4 . . . . 169 A2
Wycombe Ave M18 . . . . . 99 E6
Wycombe Cl M41 . . . . . . 95 C5
Wycombe Dr M29 . . . . . . 77 B7
Wye Ave M35 . . . . 83 F7
Wyecroft Cl SK6 . . . . . . 113 B5
Wye St OL8 . . . . 153 A1
Wykeham Cl WN3 . . . . . 151 C2
Wykeham Gr OL12 . . . . . 14 B1
Wykeham Mews BL1 . . . 144 A3
Wykeham St M14 . . . . . . 98 A3
Wyke St M12 . . . . 67 D6
Wylam Wlk ⓸ M12 . . . . . 99 B3
Wylde The BL9 . . . . 140 B2
Wynard Ave WN1 . . . . . . 37 C2
Wychgate Rd SK7 . . . . . 125 A3
Wyndale Dr M35 . . . . 83 F5
Wyndale Rd OL8 . . . . 66 F3
Wyndcliff Dr M41 . . . . . . 94 E1
Wyndham Ave
Bolton BL3 . . . . 146 A3
Swinton M27 . . . . 61 F3
Wyne Cl SK7 . . . . 125 A3
Wynfield Ave M22 . . . . . 130 F7
Wynford Sq M50 . . . . . . 154 C1
Wyngate Rd
Altrincham WA15 . . . . . . 128 F8
Cheadle SK8 . . . . 122 F1
Wynne Ave M27 . . . . 62 A3
Wynne Cl
Denton M34 . . . . 100 F1
Manchester M11 . . . . . . 164 C4
Wynne Gr M34 . . . . 100 F1
Wynne St
Bolton BL1 . . . . 143 B2
Salford M6 . . . . 81 B3
Tyldesley M29 . . . . 58 F1
Walkden M38 . . . . 60 A4
Wynnstay Gr M14 . . . . . 110 C8
Wynnstay Rd M33 . . . . . 108 B5
Wynton Cl WN7 . . . . 75 E2
Wynnard Dr M33 . . . . . . 108 D2
Wynnard Rd M22 . . . . . . 121 C3
Wyre Ave WN2 . . . . 56 A2
Wyre Cl M45 . . . . 45 B1
Wyre Dr M28 . . . . 78 B7
Wyresdale Rd BL1 . . . . . 144 C4
Wyre St
Manchester M1 . . . . 163 B4
Mossley OL5 . . . . 68 B1
Wyrevale Gr WN4 . . . . . . 73 C3
Wythall Ave M38 . . . . . . 60 A6
Wythburn Ave
Bolton BL1 . . . . 142 A1
Manchester M8 . . . . 156 C2
Urmston M41 . . . . 95 B3
Wythburn Rd
Middleton M24 . . . . 46 E3
Stockport SK1 . . . . 124 B7
Wythburn St M6 . . . . . . 154 B2
WYTHENSHAWE 121 B6
Wythenshawe Ctr M22 . . 121 D2
Wythenshawe Rd
Sale M33 . . . . 108 F4
Wythenshawe M23 . . . . . 109 B1
Wythens Rd SK8 . . . . . . 131 B8
Wythop Gdns M5 . . . . . . 81 A1
Wyvern Ave SK5 . . . . . . 111 E5
Wyvern Rd M21 . . . . 109 D8
Wyverne Rd M21 . . . . . . 109 D1
Wyville Cl SK7 . . . . 125 A3
Wyville Dr
Manchester M9 . . . . 64 B6
Salford M6 . . . . 154 C3
Swinton M27 . . . . 79 E6
Wyvis Cl OL9 . . . . 48 A1

Xaverian Sixth Form Coll
M14 . . . . 98 C3

Yale Rd M18 . . . . 165 B1
Yale St BL7 . . . . 9 D4
Yarburgh St M16 . . . . . . 97 E3
Yardley Ave M32 . . . . . . 96 A2
Yardley Cl M32 . . . . 96 A2
Yard The ⓸ SK3 . . . . . . 104 C1
Yare St ⓻ BB4 . . . . 2 B8
Yarmouth Dr M23 . . . . . 109 B1
Yarn Croft M29 . . . . 77 A7
Yarnton Cl OL2 . . . . 149 A1
Yarn Wlk M4 . . . . 159 C1
Yarrow Cl OL11 . . . . 139 C1
Yarrow Gr BL6 . . . . 22 B4
Yarrow Pl BL1 . . . . 143 B1
Yarrow St WN2 . . . . 56 C4
Yarrow Wlk M45 . . . . 45 C1
Yarwell ⓶⓹ OL12 . . . . . 139 B4
Yarwood Ave M23 . . . . . 120 F7
Yarwood Cl OL10 . . . . . . 29 E3
Yarwood St
Altrincham WA14 . . . . . . 119 D3
Bury BL9 . . . . 141 A2
Yasmin Gdns OL1 . . . . . 48 D1
Yates Dr M28 . . . . 60 A3
Yates Gr WN6 . . . . 36 F4
Yates St
Bolton BL2 . . . . 25 A1
⓶ Leigh WN7 . . . . 75 E7
Manchester M46 . . . . 46 C1
Middleton M24 . . . . 64 C7
Oldham OL1 . . . . 49 B1

Yates St continued
Stockport SK1 . . . . 112 B3
Wigan WN3 . . . . 150 A3
Yattendon Ave M23 . . . . 120 D8
Yeadon Rd M18 . . . . 99 D3
Yea Fold OL15 . . . . 15 E3
Yealand Ave SK4 . . . . . . 169 A3
Yealand Cl OL11 . . . . 30 B6
Yealand Gr WN2 . . . . 57 A5
Yeardsley Cl SK7 . . . . . . 123 E3
Yeargate Ind Est BL9 . . . 28 D2
Yellow Brook Cl WN2 . . . 38 C6
Yellow Lodge Dr BL5 . . . 40 B1
Yelverton Wlk M13 . . . . 163 C2
Yeoford Dr WA14 . . . . . . 119 B6
Yeoman Cl SK7 . . . . 124 D3
Yeomanry Ct ⓸ M16 . . . 97 D3
Yeoman's Cl OL16 . . . . . . 31 F7
Yeoman Wlk M11 . . . . . 160 C1
Yeovil St M16 . . . . 97 F3
Yesoiday Hatorah Sch
M25 . . . . 63 B2
Yewbank Cl M13 . . . . 98 F3
Yewbarrow Cl M29 . . . . . 77 B7
Yewbarrow Rd ⓵ OL1 . . . 67 A8
Yew Cl BL3 . . . . 146 B4
Yew Cres OL4 . . . . 67 D8
Yew Ct ⓵ OL12 . . . . 15 B2
Yewdale
Shevington WN6 . . . . 36 B6
Swinton M27 . . . . 62 B1
Yewdale Ave
Billinge WA11 . . . . 71 B1
Bolton BL2 . . . . 25 F2
Yewdale Cres ⓷ WN1 . . . 37 B3
Yewdale Dr
Failsworth M35 . . . . 84 C8
Middleton M24 . . . . 46 E1
Yewdale Gdns BL2 . . . . . 25 F2
Yew Dale Gdns OL11 . . . 30 B4
Yewdale Rd
Ashton-in-M WN4 . . . . . . 73 A7
Stockport SK1 . . . . 124 B7
Yew Gr WN6 . . . . 36 A4
Yewlands Ave M9 . . . . . . 64 D5
Yew St
Bury BL9 . . . . 141 C3
Denton M34 . . . . 100 F5
Heywood OL10 . . . . 29 B2
Manchester M15 . . . . . . 162 B1
Salford M7 . . . . 81 C6
Stockport SK4 . . . . 168 C1
YEW TREE 101 E7
Yewtree Ave M46 . . . . . . 58 C4
Yew Tree Ave
Hazel Grove SK7 . . . . . . 124 F1
⓻ Manchester, Levenshulme
M19 . . . . 99 A1
Manchester M14 . . . . 98 A2
Newton-le-W WA12 . . . . . 89 A4
Wythenshawe M22 . . . . . 109 D1
Yew Tree Cl
Ashton-u-L OL7 . . . . 85 A6
Marple SK6 . . . . 125 E5
Wilmslow SK9 . . . . 137 D7
Yew Tree Com Prim Sch
SK16 . . . . 101 E6
Yew Tree Com Sch OL9 . . 66 A4
Yew Tree Cres M14 . . . . . 98 B1
Yew Tree Ct OL14 . . . . 6 A8
Yew Tree Dr
Bolton BL6 . . . . 40 B6
Chadderton OL9 . . . . 65 D7
Prestwich M25 . . . . 63 B4
Romiley SK6 . . . . 112 D3
Sale M33 . . . . 108 E4
Urmston M41 . . . . 94 F4
Wythenshawe M22 . . . . . 109 D1
Yew Tree Farm Trad Est
WA11 . . . . 89 A8
Yew Tree Gr
Gatley SK8 . . . . 122 A3
Rawtenstall BB4 . . . . 1 F8
Yew Tree La
Bolton BL1 . . . . 25 A4
Dukinfield SK16 . . . . 101 F3
Poynton SK12 . . . . 133 F3
Wythenshawe M23 . . . . . 109 B2
Yew Tree Park Rd SK8 . . 132 B6
Yew Tree Rd
Denton M34 . . . . 100 F1
Manchester M14 . . . . 98 B2
Stockport SK3 . . . . 123 F3
Wardsend SK10 . . . . 134 B1
Yew Tree Way WA3 . . . . . 90 B7
Yew Wlk ⓵ M31 . . . . . . 105 E2
York Cl
Cheadle SK8 . . . . 123 A5
Denton M34 . . . . 100 F4
York Cres SK9 . . . . 137 D8
Yorkdale Cl 67 D6
York Dr
Altrincham WA14 . . . . . . 119 D1
Hazel Grove SK7 . . . . . . 125 A2
Ramsbottom BL0 . . . . . . 11 A4
Wythenshawe M90 . . . . . 129 F7

York Pl
Adlington PR6 . . . . 21 A8
Ashton-u-L OL6 . . . . 166 A2
Manchester M13 . . . . 98 C4
York Rd
Altrincham WA14 . . . . . . 119 C1
Ashton-in-M WN4 . . . . . . 73 C3
Chadderton OL9 . . . . 65 F8
Denton M34 . . . . 100 F4
Droylsden M43 . . . . 83 F3
Hindley WN2 . . . . 56 F6
Hyde SK14 . . . . 113 C8
Irlam M44 . . . . 105 D5
Manchester, Heaton Moor
SK4 . . . . 111 B5
Manchester M21 . . . . . . 109 B8
Sale M33 . . . . 108 A5
York Road E W24 . . . . . . 65 C5
York Road S W24 . . . . . . 73 C2
York Road W M21 . . . . . . 65 C5
Yorkshire Cl M31 . . . . . . 105 E2
Yorkshire St
Ashton-u-L OL6 . . . . 166 B3
Oldham OL1 . . . . 153 C3
Rochdale OL12, OL16 . . . 31 A8
Rochdale OL16 . . . . 139 C4
Salford M3 . . . . 158 B2
Yorkshire Way SK13 . . . 116 F8
York Sq ⓺ OL2 . . . . 48 D4
York St
Altrincham WA15 . . . . . . 119 E3
⓵⓸ Manchester M34 . . 100 E8
Atherton M46 . . . . 58 D3
Bury BL9 . . . . 141 A2
Farnworth BL4 . . . . 60 E8
Glossop SK13 . . . . 104 E1
Golborne WA3 . . . . 74 A1
Heywood OL10 . . . . 29 D2
Leigh WN7 . . . . 76 D4
Manchester, Didsbury M20 110 B3
Manchester, Harpurhey
M9 . . . . 157 B4
Manchester, Hulme M15 . 162 B3
Manchester, Levenshulme
M19 . . . . 111 A8
Manchester M1 . . . . 163 A4
Manchester M1, M2 . . . . 159 A1
Manchester, University M1,
M13 . . . . 163 A3
Oldham OL9 . . . . 153 B2
Radcliffe M26 . . . . 44 D5
Rochdale OL16 . . . . 31 B6
Stockport SK3 . . . . 170 B4
Whitefield M45 . . . . 62 F8
Wigan WN3 . . . . 150 B4
York Terr
⓵⓼ Bolton BL1 . . . . . . 143 B2
Glossop SK13 . . . . 116 C8
Sale M33 . . . . 108 A4
Youd St WN7 . . . . 75 F5
Youlgreave Cres SK13 . . 171 A1
Young St
Farnworth BL4 . . . . 60 E7
Leigh WN7 . . . . 76 E4
Manchester M3 . . . . 158 B1
⓸ Radcliffe M26 . . . . . . 43 F5
Ramsbottom BL0 . . . . . . 138 B2
Yulan Dr M33 . . . . 107 C4
Yule St SK3 . . . . 170 A4
Yvonne Cl WN4 . . . . 73 D5

Zama St BL0 . . . . 11 A4
Zealand St OL4 . . . . 67 C8
Zedburgh ⓶⓶ OL12 . . . . 139 B4
Zeta St M9 . . . . 157 C3
Zetland Ave BL3 . . . . . . 146 B2
Zetland Avenue N BL3. . . 146 B2
Zetland Rd M21 . . . . 109 B8
Zetland St SK16 . . . . . . 166 B1
Zinda Dil OL8 . . . . 153 A4
Zinnia Dr M44 . . . . 105 E8
Zion Terr OL12 . . . . 13 E2
Zorbit Mews SK14 . . . . . 167 A4
Zulu St BL2 . . . . 148 B3
Zurich Gdns SK7 . . . . . . 123 E3
Zyburn Ct M6 . . . . 80 A3